CHURCH
HISTORY

VOLUME TWO

From Pre-Reformation to the Present Day

textbook*plus*⁺

Equipping Instructors and Students with
FREE RESOURCES for Core Zondervan Textbooks

Available Resources for Church History, Volume Two

Instructor Resources

- Instructor's manual
- Presentation slides
- Chapter quizzes
- Midterm and final exams
- Sample syllabus
- Image/map library

Student Resources

- Videos
- Quizzes
- Flashcards
- Exam study guides

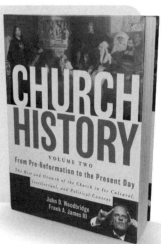

*How To Access Resources

- Go to www.TextbookPlus.Zondervan.com
- Click "Register Now" button and complete registration process
- Find books using search field or "Browse Our Textbooks" feature
- Click "Instructor Resources" or "Student Resources" tab once you get to book page to access resources

www.TextbookPlus.Zondervan.com

About the Authors

John D. Woodbridge (*Doctorat de Troisième Cycle*, University of Toulouse, France) is research professor of Church History and History of Christian Thought at Trinity Evangelical Divinity School in Deerfield, Illinois, where he has taught since 1970. He has also served as a visiting professor of History at Northwestern University, as a visiting professor of Religion at the Sorbonne, Paris, and as a senior editor of *Christianity Today*. He is the author of *Biblical Authority: A Critique of the Rogers/McKim Proposal* and coauthor of *Letters Along the Way*. He is the editor of *Great Leaders of the Christian Church* and coeditor of works including *The Mark of Jesus*. Woodbridge is the recipient of four Gold Medallion Awards.

Frank A. James III (PhD, Oxford University; PhD, Westminster Theological Seminary) is the president of Biblical Theological Seminary in Hatfield, Pennsylvania. He formerly served as provost and professor of Historical Theology at Gordon-Conwell Theological Seminary. He is the author of *Peter Martyr Vermigli and Predestination: The Augustinian Inheritance of an Italian Reformer*; editor of *Peter Martyr Vermigli and the European Reformations: Semper Reformanda*; coeditor with Heiko Oberman of *Via Augustini: Augustine in the Later Middle Ages, Renaissance and Reformation* and with Charles Hill of *The Glory of the Atonement*; and one of the founding members of the *Reformation Commentary on Scripture*. He has also been a consultant and scriptwriter for a historical documentary film series.

CHURCH
HISTORY

VOLUME TWO

From Pre-Reformation to the Present Day

*The Rise and Growth of the Church
in Its Cultural, Intellectual, and Political Context*

John D. Woodbridge
and
Frank A. James III

 ZONDERVAN®

ZONDERVAN

Church History Volume 2: From Pre-Reformation to the Present Day

Copyright © 2013 by John D. Woodbridge and Frank A. James III

This title is also available as a Zondervan ebook.
Visit www.zondervan.com/ebooks.

Requests for information should be addressed to:

Zondervan, 3900 *Sparks Dr., Grand Rapids, Michigan 49546*

Library of Congress Cataloging-in-Publication Data

Woodbridge, John D., 1941–
    Church history : the rise and growth of the church in its cultural, intellectual, and political
context / John D. Woodbridge and Frank A. James III.
        v. cm.
    Includes bibliographical references and index.
    Contents: — Volume 2. From Pre-Reformation to the Present Day.
    ISBN 978-0-310-25743-1 (v. 2)
    1. Church history. I. Title.
BR252.W66 2013
270 – dc23
2012051084

Cover design: Tobias' Outerwear for Books
Cover photos: The Bridgeman Art Library, © John Garrett/CORBIS
Interior design: Tracey Walker
Interior composition: Greg Johnson/Textbook Perfect

Printed in the United States of America

14 15 16 17 18 19 20 /DCI/ 22 21 20 19 18 17 16 15 14 13 12 11 10 9 8 7 6 5 4 3 2

To the readers who will use this book.
May they enter into the adventure of the life of the church
as they extend its history into the days ahead.

Contents in Brief

Contents

8. Christianity in an Age of Fear, Crisis, and Exploration (17th Century)

15. Adjusting to Modernization and Secularism: The Rise of Protestant Liberalism (1799–1919)

Maps, Charts, and Illustrations

Preface

As our esteemed colleague, Everett Ferguson, stated in his preface to the first volume, "Church history is the study of the history of God's people in Christ, a theological claim, or, speaking more neutrally, of those who have wanted to be God's people in Christ." It is, as he says, a "mixed story." He noted rather poignantly that "Just as the biblical record of the people of God is the story of a mixed people with great acts of faith and great failures in sin and unfaithfulness, so is the history of the people who made up the church through the ages." This is not to suggest a simplistic bifurcation between the instigators of iniquity who invariably are false brethren and the pious do-gooders who inevitably are the wellspring of orthodox theology.

Actually, church history is more complicated and nuanced than that. What Dr. Ferguson is getting at is that persecuted Christians can at another time become the persecutors. The history of the church reminds us that Christians can be culprits of foolishness as well as bold titans for truth. They can be egoistic and self-serving; they can be humble and generous. A single individual can embody conflicting traits. We may find it disconcerting to discover that our heroes are sometimes flawed. To alleviate in part this dissonance, may we suggest an aphorism to accompany your reading: *God works through sinners to accomplish his good purposes.* Such words remind us all that despite our frailties, we are yet serviceable to God.

This volume has sought to accomplish a number of goals. The first of these is to provide an academically responsible engagement with the facts of history as best we can determine them, whether or not these facts comport with personal convictions. We believe that such honesty, although at times painful, will ultimately serve the best interests of all, Christian or not. Second, this volume endeavors to provide a global perspective. We now inhabit a world where the center of Christianity has shifted from the West to the global South, which requires that due consideration be given to the theology and movements in Africa, Latin America, and Asia.

Third, we intend this volume to be contemporary and relevant to the church today. Change, whether cultural, technological, political, or social, is now happening at an ever-increasing pace. Although it is impossible to keep up with every new movement, we nevertheless endeavored to engage the most significant of those developments that are most likely to impact the Christian church. Fourth, we have not avoided controversial issues of the past or the present. But we do not presume to make final judgments. Rather, we seek to present the relevant dimensions of the debate in order to provide readers with enough information so that they can begin to reach their own conclusions.

Fifth, we are keenly aware that church history—like all history—is culturally conditioned. The social norms that governed an earlier era may not be the social norms today. For example, we do not execute heretics. However, even as we evaluate actions according to the cultural standards of the time, we are mindful that Christians affirm doctrinal beliefs and ethical standards that are culturally transcendent. Finally, we have embraced a broad ecumenical stance; that is to say, we have endeavored to be respectful of all Christian traditions and indeed, to give a thoughtful and faithful treatment to other religions.

We wish to express our deep appreciation to Jim Ruark for his patience and prudence in seeing this volume to completion. We would also like to express our sincere gratitude to Dr. Everett Ferguson for writing an exemplary first volume of this church history—a volume whose contents are assumed as the basis for the present one.

As the readers embark on their journey into church history, we commend these wise words of Martin Luther:

> God is no other than the one who loves the contrite, the tormented, the perplexed; [He is] the God of the humble. If I could understand this, I would be a [true] theologian.
>
> –Luther on Psalm 51

European Christianity in an Age of Adversity, Renaissance, and Discovery

(1300–1500)

I. INTRODUCTION

Should history be viewed as a succession of random events whose ultimate causes are irretrievably lost to us? Do history's days become years and its years become centuries, with no alpha or starting point to have launched them and no omega or final consummation to end them? Or did "history" begin? Is it heading toward a climactic ending? Put another way, do the events of days, years, and centuries, when contemplated through the eyes of faith, reveal not utter randomness but designs following a divine master plan?

Many Europeans during the Middle Ages thought they could discern divine patterns stitched into the warp and woof of their own personal experience and into the history of their respective societies. A few believed they knew how many years had passed since the creation of the world and between Christ's life and their own times.

More generally, Europeans assumed God was at work in their world accomplishing his purposes. Not only is the earth God's creation, but what happens in this ephemeral experience called life is somehow bound to the world of the spirit, that is, reality. This life with its toils and tears is but an antechamber for the next.

Medieval Europeans faced the serious problem of explaining the origin of evil within their world without making God its ultimate author. They worried about how to protect themselves from disasters caused by the seemingly whimsical forces of nature. Did God use disease, or the storms that ruined crops, or the accidents that overtook weary travelers, to display his anger regarding their sins? Or should they attribute any mishap or tragedy to other forces, to nature's untamed power, to Satan's malignancy, to the malevolent devices of witches and warlocks, to the potency of black and white magic, to certain conjunctures of the planets and stars, to fate, or to the wheel of fortune? Were their souls and nature joined in some kind of "chain of being"?

The clergy sometimes fretted and complained about the "ungodly" practices the laity relied on in attempting to fend off evil, whether sickness or death, bad weather, or accidents.

Complicating matters still further, the life cycle of millions of Europeans was dramatically interrupted by deadly perturbations. Indeed, if troubles encountered on earth count as evidence, large numbers of Europeans had every reason to conclude that God was angry with the children of Adam. Europeans experienced wrenching crises tearing roughly at their own personal lives and the fabric of their social, cultural, and religious institutions. The distinguished medievalist Robert Lerner has labeled the fourteenth century the "Age of Adversity."

The period 1300–1500 began ominously for the Western church with the so-called "Babylonian Captivity of the Church" (1309–77) that directly challenged its long-standing traditions and institutional identity because the papacy moved from Rome to Avignon (at the time on the French border). The period concluded on the eve of the "Protestant Reformation," which represented another momentous challenge to the Western church as an international institution. In the intervening years, the unity of the Western church was painstakingly pieced back together again, despite the "Great Schism," only to be shattered afresh by the Protestant Reformation. Powerful Protestant churches emerged outside of Italy. Protestant spokespersons claimed to preach the "pure gospel."

Whether the Babylonian Captivity of the Church combined with the Great Schism (1378–1417) served as a long-range cause of the Protestant Reformation remains a point of debate. Nevertheless, the disruptive nature of these two institutional dislocations leaves no doubt about at least one point: the late Middle Ages (c. 1300–1500) was a perilous period for the Western church's unity and for the survival of papal pretentions to dominate European political, social, and religious life. Moreover, during this same time frame the Eastern Byzantine Church suffered a devastating blow with the fall of Constantinople to the Turks in 1453.

II. A PIVOTAL TIME OF STRUGGLE WITHIN AND OUTSIDE OF THE CHURCH

A. The Epochal Tragedies of Massive Deaths

This period also witnessed epochal demographic dislocations for millions of Europeans. Sudden and unexpected death became even more prevalent as a fearsome specter, indiscriminately stalking kings and queens, popes and peasants. The ravages of the Hundred Years War (1337–1453) and other bloody conflicts devastated entire towns and regions. The introduction of gunpowder around 1400 changed long-standing patterns of warfare. Cannons could blow holes in fortified castle walls. A lowly peasant could fell a knight with musket-shot. Cannonballs and bullets could sometimes kill and wound from a greater distance than an arrow could be shot (though the arrow was often more accurate).

Perhaps even more sinister and unpredictable, waves of famines (1315–17; 1340–50; 1374–75) and plagues such as the Black Death (1347–50) swept like apocalyptic scourges through Europe, turning entire cities and countrysides into silent death zones. Scholars debate whether the Black Death was due to bubonic plague (with fleas and black cats the carriers) or whether it issued from an Ebola-like virus or even from anthrax.

On May 19, 1348, the great Italian writer Petrarch wrote to his brother about the almost unimaginable desolation caused by the Black Death:

> My brother! My brother! Alas what shall I say? Whither shall I turn? I would that I had never been born, or at least had died before these times. How will posterity believe that there has been a time, without lightnings of heaven or fires of earth, without wars or other visible slaughter, not this or that part of the earth, but well-nigh the whole globe has remained without inhabitants? When before has it been seen that houses are left vacant, cities deserted, fields are too small for the dead, and a fearful and universal solitude over the whole earth?

What was apparently the bubonic plague had arrived in Messina, Sicily, the year before, when twelve Genovese trading ships arrived, their crews already dying from the disease. So devastating were its effects in Messina that "Corpses were abandoned in empty houses and there was none to give them Christian burial."

At the inception of the plague, about 1348, the population of England numbered approximately 3,700,000. By 1377 it had plummeted to 2,000,000. As one contemporary observed, the plague reaped an especially plentiful and deadly harvest in overcrowded London: "So great a multitude eventually died there, that all the cemeteries of the aforesaid city were insufficient for the burial of the dead. For which reason very many were compelled to bury their dead in places unseemly and not hallowed or blessed; for some, it was said, cast the corpses into the river." On the Continent, a similar story was often repeated.

European demographic statistics for this period coldly reveal one of the greatest disasters humanity has ever experienced. Toward 1347 the population of Europe was approximately 75 million. By 1400, however, the population had fallen by 33–40 percent—more than 25 million people. Some historians grimly suggest that in 1450 the population of Europe may have actually been only one-third to one-half of what it was in 1300.

Seeking to explain these catastrophes, more than a few Europeans speculated that the calamities were related to God's judgment for their own sins and for the papacy's departure from Rome and the scandal of the Great Schism. These catastrophes were proof positive of God's anger for the church's sins. And if they were, what could Europeans do to assuage God's ire? Should groups of the faithful engage in forms of collective penance by going on new crusades or pilgrimages, or by forming confraternities whose members would beat their bodies in a penitential attempt to atone for their own sins and those of other Europeans?

After the Black Death a number of individuals practiced rigorous forms of hermit life, seclusion, asceticism, and mysticism in which they sometimes sought their own salvation (while not dissociating completely from the Catholic Church, even though they believed it stood in need of considerable reform). Women mystics like Birgitta of Sweden (1303–73) and Catherine of Siena (1347–80) boldly admonished and warned popes directly about the papacy's "sins." Devotions directed toward the Virgin Mary, the Mother of God and Queen of Heaven, became even more prominent. The faithful hoped that Mary might intercede with her Son in their behalf. The number of saints to whom the faithful could appeal for help and blessing increased.

Paradoxically enough, this same period (1300–1500), with its demographic and ecclesiastical tragedies, is simultaneously noteworthy for its innovative achievements in architecture, sculpture, and painting, its reforms in educational curricula, and its fascination with and recovery of Greek and Roman manuscripts—traits we often associate with the "Renaissance," or cultural "rebirth." The Renaissance in turn stimulated a number of the concerns dear to reforming Catholics as well as those who broke with the church and became Protestants. Likewise, European explorers ventured forth and discovered "new" lands, Constantinople fell to the Turks (1453), and Moscow emerged as a "Third Rome," the center of Russian Orthodoxy.

During the same centuries, western "schoolmen" engaged in sturdy theological reflection, often battling each other in hard-hitting controversies and disputations. Lay movements also assumed a larger role in the life of the church. Confraternities became especially widespread in Italy after the Black Death, and some 150 parish fraternities formed in London, a number of which were also created in response to the plague. These groups often engaged in exemplary acts of Christian charity and pursued rigorous forms of Roman Catholic asceticism and devotion especially directed toward the Virgin Mary, St. Catherine, and St. Anne. In the last decades of the fifteenth century, the number of priests grew significantly after a steep decline during the period of the Great Schism.

In a word, the religious, social, and political life of the period 1300–1500 defies facile characterizations. It was transfixed by conflicting and contradictory movements and events. The experiences of people living in one region of Europe might be relatively placid and calm, while contemporaneously in another area the local population was literally decimated by war, famine, or the plague.

B. The Papacy: Plunged into a State of Crisis

In the first decade of the fourteenth century, the Catholic Church encountered especially turbulent political seas. Individual popes and prelates found navigating these troubled waters all the more treacherous due to swirling crosscurrents set in motion by a number of monarchs. An international *Republica Christiana*, or "Christian republic," ostensibly bound together by Europeans' loyalty to the empire or to the papacy, did not appear capable of withstanding burgeoning aspirations of kings and princes for political independence. A unified Christendom seemed destined to founder and to yield to a more nebulous "commonwealth" of independent Christian nation-states. Indeed, in some regions primary loyalties to kings in nation-states or to princes in city-states had already superseded older loyalties of the laity to emperors or to Christ's Vicar on earth, the pope.

This development became painfully obvious to a number of observers when Pope Boniface VIII (1294–1303) came into conflict with Edward I of England (1272–1307) and Philip IV the Fair of France (1285–1314) because of their seeking to extract money from clerics to support their wars. Peace was initially restored between Boniface and Philip, the pope actually canonizing Louis XI, Philip's grandfather (1297).

Four years later, the conflict between pope and king renewed when Philip imprisoned a French bishop on accusations of treason. In April 1302, the Estates-General of France—consisting of representatives from the clergy, nobility, and the "Third Estate" (the people)—met and sided with their monarch against the pope. This stance left French bishops in a peculiarly awkward and vulnerable position.

In November, Boniface issued the papal bull *Unam Sanctam*, which reiterated very strong but certainly not new claims for the papacy's power over temporal rule at a time when the papacy's actual political influence was dramatically diminishing.

Philip spurned the pope's arguments and directives. He called for a council to depose Boniface for allegedly engaging in heresy, sodomy, and simony among other grievous charges.

The embattled pope replied by crafting the bull *Super Petri solio*, in which he excommunicated the king. However, on September 7, 1303, one day before this bull was scheduled to be published, Philip's supporters broke into the fortified papal summer palace in Anagni, thirty-seven miles from Rome, and for three days they incarcerated and physically brutalized Boniface. Townspeople rescued the pope, but he died a month later, on October 11, 1303.

C. The Political Order in Europe

In 1300, three years before Boniface's death, it was still not clear for some Europeans—at least at a superficial societal level—that the papacy's power and the unity of "Christendom" were tottering on the brink of disaster. Certainly, Catholic Jerusalem had fallen in 1187 to Saladin (c. 1138–93), and the last major stronghold of the Crusaders in the East had yielded in 1298. Moreover, Boniface VIII was facing especially vexing problems with the rambunctious French king, Philip IV, and the powerful Colonna family. But the city of Rome itself was teeming with the crush of thousands of pilgrims, many of whom were very anxious to buy a jubilee plenary indulgence, garnished as it was with a full absolution from the penalties of sin.

With sizable amounts of new monies brimming in the coffers of the pope and the cardinals, with enthused pilgrims pushing their way through the streets, and with the papacy's victory over the empire as represented by the Holy Roman Emperor Frederick II (1194–1250) of the Hohenstaufen family some fifty years earlier, Rome once again appeared poised to serve as the political and spiritual center of Europe.

How might we explain this dramatic loss of papal prestige and power as represented by Boniface VIII's humiliation at Anagni in 1303? The contexts for his predicament were both long-term and short-term in the making. In March 1075, Pope Gregory VII (1073–85) had boldly claimed in *Dictatus papae* that popes had the right to depose emperors. By implication this meant that papal powers were superior to the temporal power of kings. Popes Innocent III (1161–1216) and Innocent IV (1243–54) had believed themselves fortified with this theory when they confronted recalcitrant rulers, namely, John of England (1199–1216) and Emperor Frederick II.

At the same time, throughout Europe churches and even monasteries often belonged to nobles, bishops, and kings who viewed them as their personal property to sell or to inherit or to do with whatever they wanted. These "property owners" quite naturally esteemed churches and monasteries and the clergies associated with them as legitimate sources of income. This helps explain why Edward I of England and Philip IV of France believed it legitimate to take monies from their clergies, whereas Boniface VIII, armed with Gregory VII's dictum and a belief that kings and clergy owed him obedience, found the kings' acts indefensible and threatened them with strong sanctions.

Moreover, after Emperor Frederick II's death in 1250, the power of the Hohenstaufen, his family, did diminish substantially in Italy, only to be replaced by that of the Angevin family at Naples (the Kingdom of the Two Sicilies), whose members were cadet relatives of French royalty. In time this political circumstance made it easier for French monarchs such as Philip IV to believe that they had the right to interfere in the affairs of Italy, including those of the pope. Ironically, the papacy had facilitated the rise to power of the Angevin family to offset Hohenstaufen influence in Italy, a papal gambit that paid unforeseen and unwanted dividends.

Boniface VIII's immediate predecessor had complicated matters still further for the prideful pope. The elderly Celestine V (July–December 1294), who had been a spiritually minded recluse before his election, proved incapable of running the papacy and resigned the office, leaving its administration in shambles. Attempting to restore some kind of order, Boniface VIII felt obliged to take strong measures, which alienated disenfranchised cardinals from the Colonna family at Rome. Moreover, local clergies discontented by perceived encroachments of Rome in their own affairs and by the pope's own deeds and demands for money were on occasion willing to side with their monarchs rather than with the pope.

For diverse reasons, then, certain lay and clerical factions were quite prepared to join forces with Philip IV or other monarchs and princes to oppose Boniface VIII.

Nonetheless, the atrocities leading to Boniface's death in 1303 did provoke a sense of outrage even for several of the pope's strongest critics in life, including Dante Alighieri (1265–1321). This masterful poet, who blamed the pope for many of his own misfortunes, was aghast at Boniface's fate.

D. The "Babylonian Captivity of the Church"

Boniface VIII was succeeded by Benedict XI (1303–4), whose dismay over events at Anagni—that is, Boniface's ill treatment—was likewise deeply felt. After pardoning many of Boniface's opponents in an effort to appease the French king, Benedict more boldly condemned the assault at Anagni, reaffirming the excommunication of Philip IV's adviser and his Italian conspirators. But by July 7 the pope was dead, and one prevalent rumor was explicit: he had been poisoned. In all probability he had died of dysentery.

What Pope Benedict XI bravely refused to do—that is, comply fully with dictates of the French King Philip IV—his successor, Clement V (1305–14), the Cardinal of Bordeaux, did not shun. Elected pope with the help of French money, and himself a Gascon born at Villandrau, Gironde (France), not only did Clement exonerate Philip for his involvement in the events associated with the death of Boniface, but in the bull *Rex gloriae* (April 27, 1311) he asserted that Philip's actions had been motivated only by his love and respect for that church and her doctrines. Earlier, after wandering for several years in southern France, Clement had decided to establish the papacy in Avignon (March 1309), a town separated from France only by the width of the Rhone River and located in Angevin territory belonging to the kings of Naples and yet especially subject to French influence. Whereas Boniface VIII had been unwillingly humiliated by Philip IV, Clement V seemed quite ready to prostrate the papacy before the same monarch.

Petrarch (Francesco Petrarca).

The humanist poet Petrarch, along with English and German critics, adjudged the papacy's apparent dependence on the wishes of the French monarchy as nothing less than a form of servile bondage. Indeed, Petrarch labeled it "The Babylonian Captivity of the Church," an allusion to what became the seventy years during which the Israelites lived subjected to their Babylonian masters. This description has endured and now refers to the time frame dating from the establishment of the papacy in Avignon in 1309 to the year 1377, when Pope Gregory XI made his way back to Rome. Seven popes lived in Avignon during the "captivity," with Pope Benedict XII (1334–42) being the first to believe that the stay there might in fact be permanent and thus being the first to begin building a splendid papal palace in 1336.

Some historians have sought to offset contemporaries' somewhat negative laments about the transfer of the seat of the papacy from Rome to Avignon. Were not some of the popes undeniably orthodox and persons of upstanding moral character? Is it not true that a number of the Avignonese popes came from southern France (the province of Languedoc in particular), and thus their

THE POPES OF AVIGNON	
Clement V	(1305–14)
John XXII	(1316–34)
Benedict XII	(1334–42)
Clement VI	(1342–52)
Innocent VI	(1352–62)
Urban V	(1362–70)
Gregory XI	(1370–78)

political interests were focused more on local issues than those of bolstering the political fortunes of Philip IV and his successors? Is it not the case that the popes on occasion attempted to return to Rome, but political unrest there prevented them from doing so? During their stay in Avignon, did not the popes create administrative machinery admirably suited to extend the church's influence?

Contemporary critics, such as Dante, of the popes' residency in Avignon were much less forgiving. In regard to Clement V of Gascony and John XXII from Cahors, Dante complained, "In garb of pastors ravening wolves are seen from here above in all the pastures. Succor of God! Oh wherefore liest thou prone? Cahorsines and Gascons make ready to drink our blood. Oh fair beginning, to what vile ending must thou fall."

These critics saw in the popes at Avignon puppets of the French monarchy who not only enjoyed sumptuous lifestyles, but with a flair for nepotism arranged to staff key church administrative posts with their own relatives and other Frenchmen. In fact, 112 out of the 114 cardinals the seven popes created were French. Most of the curialists (members of the Curia or papal government) were not only French but from Languedoc.

It is difficult to know whether contemporaries were more disturbed by this blatant shifting of the church's leadership to Frenchmen—thereby wounding the pride and thwarting the ecclesiastical ambitions of Italians, English, Germans, and Spanish among others— or by the actual move of the papacy to a non-apostolic town such as Avignon, geographically removed from Rome, the eternal city and the traditional site of authority for the Western church. Or were they more disconcerted by rumors of papal opulence, rumors made all the more offensive by the living examples of Franciscan Spirituals who had espoused a lifestyle of poverty?

Petrarch called Avignon "the sewer of the world." In Montaillou (in very southern France), inquisitors harvested this contemporary complaint from locals about the wealth of the popes and other members of the clergy: "The Pope devours the blood and sweat of the poor. And the bishops and the priests, who are rich and honored and self-indulgent, behave in the same manner, whereas St. Peter abandoned his wife, his children, his fields, his vineyards and his possessions to follow Christ."

"The Pope devours the blood and sweat of the poor. And bishops and the priests, who are rich and honored and self-indulgent, behave in the same manner, whereas St. Peter abandoned his wife, his children, his fields, his vineyard and his possessions to follow Christ" (Criticism of the late medieval papacy).

Other Europeans such as the Dominican John of Paris (c. 1255–1306) and Marsilius of Padua (1275–1342), a theologian and a physician, attacked in differing ways the claim of the papacy to exercise authority over secular governments.

Europeans isolated by an oral culture may have known relatively little about the controversial happenings in Avignon. But the people of Flanders (in present-day Belgium), whether literate or not, were certainly cognizant of the popes' actions. Philip IV pressured the popes at Avignon to excommunicate the entire population of this region. Often the dead in Flanders were so numerous they could not even be buried.

Another fact engendering a spirit of independence from the papacy was the prototypic, intensely "nationalistic" aspirations of a number of European writers. The use of regional languages rather than Latin prose and poetry often gave expression to these longings. St. Francis of Assisi, founder of the Franciscans, had written the first poem in Italian, one devoted to the sun. In the early years of the fourteenth century, Dante Alighieri, who described himself as "a Florentine by birth but not in character," had penned *The Divine Comedy* in his native Tuscan rather than in Latin.

Although Dante's masterful poem reflected in part themes drawn directly from the theology of Thomas Aquinas and he remained with some exceptions an apologist for medieval Roman Catholic doctrine, his predilection to use Tuscan bespoke a fierce loyalty to and love for his home region in Italy. His criticisms of the Avignonese papacy often reiterated the complaint about its subservience to the French monarchy. A partisan of emperors, he also yearned for the day when a proper balance of powers could be restored between "the supreme pontiff, who would lead the human race to life eternal in accordance with revealed truth, and the emperor, who would direct mankind to temporal felicity in accordance with philosophic teachings." Conflicts between church and state would be reduced.

Also in the fourteenth century, Petrarch, a master of Latin, wrote extensively in Italian and claimed that "old Roman valor is not dead, Nor in the Italians' breast extinguished."

In *The Prince* (1513), chapter 13, Niccolò Machiavelli (1469–1527) cited this passage of Petrarch and called on the influential Medici family to rescue Italy from the foreign domination of French and Spanish armies:

> In order therefore that Italy, after so long a time, may behold its saviors, this opportunity must not be let slip. And I cannot express with what love he would be welcomed in all those provinces which have suffered from these foreign inundations, with what thirst for vengeance, with what resolute loyalty, with what devotion and tears.

What Italian would refuse him allegiance? This barbarous tyranny stinks in everyone's nostrils.

Machiavelli's contemporary, Martin Luther, evoked alleged German superiorities in his criticism of the "Roman" church that had "sucked Italy dry" of its revenues and was now turning to Germany. A spirit of loyalty to a "people" or a kingdom or city-states had entered into the prose and poetry of a number of writers and nurtured an attitude of independence toward the policies and decrees of the papacy.

E. The Social and Economic Order

The unity of a Christian Europe—loosely tiered in three divisions of the clergy, nobles, and the people, with the pope acting as universal spiritual and temporal shepherd—was increasingly put at risk by the conflicts of monarchs such as those between Philip IV and Edward I and the Hundred Years War. But the personal lives of large numbers of individual Europeans were also put dramatically at risk, due not only to the ravages of warfare but to the grim effects of famines and plagues. As observed, the fourteenth century witnessed a series of famines and plagues that devastated the populations of many areas of Europe.

Historians have attempted to explain the reasons the fourteenth century was susceptible to these demographic catastrophes. One interpretation suggests that by midcentury the levels of food production could no longer keep pace with the growth in Europe's population. A general scarcity of food in certain regions rendered various populations physically weakened and thereby more susceptible to the ravages of disease and the plague.

Whatever medical or economic explanations may account for the famines and plagues, scores of contemporaries saw behind them a divine cause: God's righteous anger at the sins of Europeans. They especially bemoaned the tragedy of the Avignonese papacy. Would not God withdraw his hand of judgment if in fact the papacy left Avignon and returned to Rome?

With repeated appeals from Petrarch and other anguished hearts such as the nuns Birgitta of Sweden and Catherine of Siena, several popes at Avignon sensed they must eventually move back to Rome. French cardinals and local officials in Avignon, worried about the loss of prestige and monies this would entail, attempted to countermand these rumored plans. But one Avignonese pope, Urban V (1362–70), brushing opposition aside, returned to Rome and actually resided there from 1367 to 1370 before concluding that he preferred to return to Avignon. Birgitta of Sweden, a mystic and sometimes hailed as Sweden's "Joan of Arc," warned him that if he took this course of action, he would die prematurely. On September 27, 1370, he arrived in Avignon, only to fall ill. Urban died in December, a few months after allegedly violating Birgitta's prophecy.

Another Avignonese pope, Gregory XI (1370–78), finally ended the papal displacement from Rome. Heavily engaged in Italian politics (the War of the Eight Saints with Florence), this pope yielded to the counsel of the mystic Catherine of Siena, author of *The Dialogue*. In 1376 she had arrived in Avignon, representing the cause of Florentines who wanted the pope to lift an interdict on their city. Gregory was much impressed by the spiritual bearing of this remarkable woman and her complaints about the "sins" of Avignon. The size of the prostitute population at Avignon, for example, had expanded with the arrival of the papacy in the city.

Catherine appealed to Gregory to return to Rome, optimistically claiming that Italy awaited him as a son awaits a father. On September 13, 1376, to the great consternation of many clerics in Avignon as well as his own father, Gregory XI set off for Rome. He entered the city on January 17, 1377, after an arduous journey.

On March 27, 1378, however, Gregory died. In his last days he had been disconcerted by the political and religious turmoil within the city of Rome and suspected it did not bode well for the papacy's own future. The French pope had also begun to second-guess himself and wished he had stayed in Avignon.

III. THE GREAT SCHISM (1378–1417)

Seldom have cardinals of the Roman Catholic Church faced a more perilous situation than the sixteen who entered the conclave at Rome to elect the successor to Gregory XI. The Roman populace was restive and gravely worried that the conclave might elect another Frenchman. Armed citizenry broke into the conclave and threatened to kill the cardinals.

The crowds were pacified and dispersed when they learned that Bartholomew, the archbishop of Bari, had been elected. If not a Roman, he was at least an Italian. Foiling the cardinals' stratagem, Bartholomew did not decline the election's results as it was assumed he would. On April 8, 1378, Bartholomew Prignano became the new pope as Urban VI, reigning until 1389.

Within a brief time Urban VI alienated many of the cardinals by his pride, impetuous speech, and harsh programs. Offended by the new pope's policies and believing he was actually quite deranged, French cardinals withdrew from Rome and moved to Anagni. They met together and concluded that the pope's election had been achieved under duress

POPES DURING THE GREAT SCHISM	
IN ROME	IN AVIGNON
Urban VI (1378–13)	Clement VII (1378–94)
Boniface IX (1389–1404)	Benedict XIII (1394–1417)*
Innocent VII (1404–6)	
Gregory XII (1406–July 4, 1415)	

*He was deposed on July 26, 1417, but continued to believe he was pope, until 1423.

and therefore was void, "as having been made, not freely, but under fear." They angrily demanded that Urban abdicate, and they verbally accosted him as an "apostate, anathema, Antichrist, and the mocker and destroyer of Christianity." In turn, on September 20, 1378, they elected Robert of Geneva to be pope. He took the name Clement VII.

Now there were two popes. The "Great Schism" had been born. After a series of mutual excommunications and military campaigns in which Urban's mercenaries gained the upper hand, Clement retreated via Naples and returned to Avignon. Urban remained in Rome. (The pope in Avignon is often referred to as the "antipope.")

Christian Europe was deeply troubled and embittered by these unsettling and unseemly developments. By what criteria could the faithful determine which of the two contenders, Clement VII or Urban VI, was the authentic Vicar of Christ on earth? The sorting-out process was made all the more bewildering for some because both popes could cite notable Christian leaders who accepted the legitimacy of their own respective claims.

The Great Schism lasted until 1417.

To complicate matters further, a third pope was elected at the Council of Pisa in 1409, thereby making the schism a three-chair affair. Christians from various corners of Europe bemoaned the schism, realizing it represented a genuine scandal of huge proportions. But what measures or who could remedy what contemporaries called a "sacrilegious schism"? Would unity ever be restored to the Catholic Church?

"[He is an] apostate, anathema, Antichrist, and the mocker and destroyer of Christianity" (College of Cardinals' denunciation of Pope Urban VI).

A. The Conciliar Movement

University professors, theologians, canon lawyers, and others devoted unstinting energies in proposing ways for Christendom to heal the schism. In 1381 Henry of Langenstein, a theologian and mathematician, suggested that after due penance by those involved in the schism, and after fasting, weeping, and prayer by other Christians, a general council should be held. In 1393 the University of Paris, which had served as one of the driving forces in the movement to end the schism, reiterated its earlier appeal (1381) for a general council, and it set forth three "ways" to end the schism: (1) Both sides should desist from claiming the papal office; (2) if these sides are unwilling to resign, then arbitration should determine who is the rightful pope or the arbiters could elect a pope; (3) if the two sides will not yield to either the first or second ways, then, a third "excellent" way could be pursued: a general council should be called of prelates and university doctors to remedy the schism.

The first two ways did actually fail, for neither pope would resign of his own accord or submit to the authority of arbitrators to adjudicate the rightfulness of his papal claims.

The "third way"—which as a proposal grew in popularity among European church leaders such as Pierre d'Ailly (1350–1420) and Jean Gerson (1363–1429)—had been prepared in part by canon lawyers of earlier generations. Its rationale was forged by claiming that the plentitude of power had resided in the *congregation fidelium*, the congregation of the faithful, since the days of the "primitive church." Ultimate authority did not belong exclusively to the office of the pope. Rather, it belonged to all the faithful in lesser or greater degrees, depending on their status within the church. These claims suggested the possibility that a general council of the church, encompassing cardinals and bishops and other clerics, had the right to determine who should be the pope. Even the laity could play a delimited role at a council.

During the first decade of the fifteenth century, the conciliar solution to the Great Schism triumphed over other proposals. In 1409 the Council of Pisa opened with the expressed goal of participants to end the scandal of the schism. A number of theologians met and proposed to the council that the two popes of the day, Benedict XIII and Gregory XII, "were, according to divine law, found to be pertinacious schismatics and fomenters of the ancient schism and also heretics, in the strict sense of the word. And, as such pertinacious schismatics and heretics, ought to be declared by the sacred general council to be *de jure* ejected from office."

The council did in fact depose both popes and, in 1409, elected a new pope, Alexander V. It appeared that the schism had been finally healed.

Such was unfortunately not the case. Neither Benedict XIII nor Gregory XII acquiesced before the negative judgments of the Council of Pisa on their respective claims to be pope. Ironically enough, the council's actions in electing a new pope had only expanded the scope of the schism. Now there were three popes in Christendom. Moreover, each had loyal followers in certain corners of Europe.

Troubled by the enormity of this travesty, European politicians and churchmen alike called for a new council to attempt to end the schism. After Pope Alexander V died under suspicious circumstances in 1410, he was replaced by a protégé of sorts, Pope John XXIII. Sigismund, the King of Hungary and Germany and later Holy Roman Emperor (1433–37), put pressure on Pope John (1410–15) to call a new council. This very ambitious pope, whose profligate lifestyle was publicly known, apparently hoped that if he did call the council, his own Italian entourage could help ensure a triumph over his two competitors.

B. The Council of Constance: Healing the Schism

In 1414 a colorful throng of Christendom's mighty and not so mighty descended on the German town of Constance, located on the Rhine River, bordering eastern Switzerland. According to the contemporary records of Ulrich von Richental, 38 cardinals and patriarchs (with 3,174 attendants), 285 bishops and archbishops (with 11,600 supporters), 1,978 doctors of theology and law, 530 "simple priests and scholars," and a king, two queens, and other members of the nobility attended the council. The presence of these clerics and nobility, the crush of large numbers of political leaders, merchants, craftsmen, physicians, and entertainers, and at least 700 prostitutes created a huge spike in population. Richental claimed 72,460 persons visited the town during the council.

On November 5, 1414, the Council of Constance opened its proceedings. The participants faced a daunting agenda: (1) to find a way to heal the schism; (2) to douse the flames of the Bohemian revolt led by John Hus; (3) to establish a means to reform the church of abuses.

In *Sacrosancta* (April 6, 1415), a benchmark decree for the conciliar movement, the council set forth the warrant for its right to sit in judgment of a pope and to reform the church:

> This sacred synod of Constance declares, in the first place, that it forms a general council, legitimately assembled in the Holy Spirit and representing the Catholic Church Militant, that it has its power immediately from Christ, and that all men, of every rank and position including even the pope himself, are bound to obey it in those matters that pertain to the faith, the extirpation of the said schism, and the reformation of the said Church in head and members.

This affirmation of conciliar authority countermanded the monarchical papal claim that the pope alone received his authority directly from Christ and that the bishops in turn received their authority from the pope. Because members of the council believed they represented the Catholic Church and received their authority directly from Christ, they concluded that even a pope must yield to their judgments. To their minds, they had every right to assess the claims of aspirants to the papal throne.

Much to his dismay, Pope John XXIII (an antipope) began to understand he could not get the council to do his bidding. Following the lead of the English, the council decided to vote by "nations." In consequence, the cardinals representing the English, the Germans, the French, the Spanish, and the Italians would cast only one vote per national party.

Pope John's Italian followers had less power than he had anticipated. Moreover, his enemies drew up a frightful list of charges related to his alleged moral and theological failures. Disguised as a groom, John opted to flee Constance the evening of March 20–21, 1415. In exile in the neighboring town of Freiburg, he urged his cardinals to join him. The council was thrown into a state of turmoil by John's sudden exit.

At this juncture, Sigismund—as King of the Romans, as Holy Roman Emperor, as King of Bohemia (Germany and Hungary)—stepped in to rally council participants discouraged by the recent turn of events. Moreover, on March 23, Jean Gerson preached a powerful sermon in which he argued that the council represented the supreme authority of the church, not the pope. An invigorated council then produced the decree *Sacrosancta*. A few weeks later, John XXIII was captured. The council put him on trial and found him guilty of perjury, simony, and other gross misconduct. The council deposed John on May 29, 1415, due to his scandalous behavior. He later received a position as a cardinal.

By June the other two aspiring popes knew what their respective fates would be. On July 4 the council accepted Gregory XII's resignation. Benedict XIII continued to assume a more recalcitrant posture. Sigismund persuaded the kings of Castile, Navarre, and Aragon to refrain from giving Benedict their full support. The council then deposed him on July 26, 1417, because he had allegedly engaged in acts of "perjury, heresy, and schism." Benedict and a number of his loyal Spanish followers refused to accept this verdict. In 1423 Benedict XIII died as an exile in Spain. To the very end, he apparently considered himself to be the true pope.

On November 11, 1417, the Council of Constance elected Cardinal Oddo de Colonna, a member of the powerful Colonna family, as the new pope. He took the name Martin V. With this pope's election the Great Schism had finally been healed. At last an element of unity was restored to Western Christendom.

The church Martin V began to rule had suffered enormous spiritual and material losses during the schism and during the Babylonian Captivity before that. In practical terms the absence of a papal presence in Rome for long periods of time during the fourteenth and early fifteenth centuries meant that numerous church buildings in the city had fallen into a state of disrepair.

Owing to Rome's occupation by different sets of foreign troops, Martin as a Roman pope did not return to the city until 1420. Nor could he forget that many churchmen believed that his authority as pope was circumscribed by conciliar decrees. In various ways Martin attempted to unloose conciliar restraints. Only with reluctance did he call the Council of Pavia (1423–24) and the Council of Basel (1431–37), thereby honoring the stipulation of the decree *Frequens* that councils should be held "frequently." Martin died in 1431.

C. The Trial and Execution of John Hus

The second issue on the Council of Constance's agenda was to find the means to bring to obedience Bohemians caught up in a spirit of full revolt against the council's authority. Many Bohemians had become the followers of Master John Hus (c. 1369–1415), the popular chancellor at the University of Prague. A brilliant theologian endowed with an attractive sense of humor, Hus preached reforming sermons in Czech and German at the Bethlehem Chapel (built in 1391). Hus had been influenced by earlier Czech reform-minded preachers such as Milic Kormeriz (c. 1325–75), sometimes hailed as the "father of Czech Reform," and Matthew of Janov (c. 1355–94). Hus had also read John Wycliffe's writings that entered Bohemia in the wake of the marriage in 1382 between Richard II of England and Anne of Bohemia.

John Hus.

In a generous gesture, in 1414 Sigismund, wanting to foster peace in his vast Christian kingdoms encompassing 20 million people, gave Hus a free-conduct pass to come to Constance to answer the Czechs' many critics in a public forum. Sigismund was worried that disputes between Christians could weaken them at the very time the Turkish threat was becoming even more ominous. Hus had already been excommunicated a couple years earlier (August 1412). Upon his arrival at Constance, Hus apparently believed he might successfully defend his own orthodoxy against charges of heresy. He was also concerned to salvage the reputation for Christian orthodoxy of his followers in the Kingdom of Bohemia.

Among a host of serious accusations, Hus faced the especially grievous charge that he was an overt disciple of John Wycliffe (1324–84). In Wycliffe's day the English government had attempted to curtail papal influence in the kingdom. The Statute of Provisors (1351) disallowed the pope from bestowing benefices in England, whereas the Statute of Praemunire (1353) rendered appeals to Rome illegal. Wycliffe had been master of Balliol at Oxford University. In *The Truth of Holy Scripture* (1372) he argued that Scripture is free from error and is the sole rule of faith. He urged that the Bible be translated into the vernacular for the benefit of the laity. Inspired by Wycliffe, five of his followers penned the "Lollard Bible."

In *The Power of the Papacy* (1379), Wycliffe indicated that a pope could be deposed for both heretical beliefs and immoral behavior. He also criticized sharply the doctrine of transubstantiation. For Wycliffe, a priest's words of consecration at the elevation of the host did not cause the miraculous transformation of the bread into the very body of Christ, but signified that God had brought about this miracle. In 1382 William Courtney, the archbishop of Canterbury, condemned twenty-four of Wycliffe's views and ordered that he no longer teach. After his death in 1382, Wycliffe's followers, known as Lollards—or "mumblers"—continued to spread his teachings, but due to persecution were forced to do so as an underground movement.

For his part, Hus declared that it was a calumny to say he had embraced all of Wycliffe's teachings; he approved only those that were supported by Holy Scripture. This qualification did not pacify the council. Nor did Hus's defense of his interpretation of transubstantiation satisfy its members.

On many doctrines Hus was as orthodox a Catholic as his contemporary accusers. He believed in purgatory and in a form of transubstantiation. But his accusers rebuffed his arguments. The council concluded that Hus was in reality a purveyor of the pestilent poison of heresy. Its members ordered Hus to accept their judgments, that is, "to stand by the decision of the Council" and to repent of his "heretical teachings." Hus professed a willingness to do so if these teachings were in fact heretical.

To Hus's mind, his accusers failed to demonstrate that what he had actually taught and written as distinct from what false witnesses alleged he had taught and written represented heresy. Here Hus took his stand, claiming the backing of the authority of Holy Scripture. On June 27, 1415, Hus wrote to his friends at the University of Prague:

> Moreover, dearly beloved in Christ Jesus, stand in the truth you
> have learned, for it conquers all and is mighty to eternity. You should

know that I have neither revoked nor abjured a single article. The Council desired that I declare that all and every article drawn from my books is false. I refused unless they should show its falsity by Scriptures.

On July 1, 1415, John Hus reiterated once again that he would not recant his beliefs:

> I, John Hus, in hope a priest of Jesus Christ, fearing to offend God and to fall into perjury, am not willing to recant all or any of the articles produced against me in the testimonies of false witnesses.... If it were possible that my voice could now be heard in the whole world, as at the Day of Judgment every lie and all my sins should be revealed, I would most gladly recant before all the world *every* falsehood and every error I ever have thought of saying or have said.

Four days later, on July 5, 1415, the council ruled that John Hus was not a disciple of Christ, but was actually a disciple of the arch-heretic Wycliffe. Hus was adjudged a "veritable and manifest heretic and that his errors and heresies have long ago been condemned by the Church of God." Because Hus remained "obstinate and incorrigible" and unwilling "to return into the bosom of the holy mother Church," he would be deposed from his priestly office and turned over to civil authorities.

What teachings in particular had provoked the council's indignation? Hus's doctrine of the church as presented in his book *De Ecclesia* (1413) had stoked the council's anger. In fact, thirty charges against Hus were based on the council's disputed understanding of this book. Hus attempted to prove that the council had in reality misread what he wrote. Moreover, he repeatedly appealed to the authority of Christ and to Holy Scripture as final arbiters of right doctrine. By these appeals Hus made it clear that he rejected the council's own assessment that what it stipulated as orthodoxy reflects true Catholic teachings based in Holy Scripture and the church fathers. Besides Scripture, Hus claimed that his position found warrant in the writings of St. Augustine and other church fathers.

Much like Wycliffe, Hus affirmed that Christ is the head of the church, not the pope. While by no means deprecating the institutional manifestations of Christ's church on earth, Hus also emphasized its spiritual dimensions. The church consists of a spiritual union of Christ's sheep, predestined from all times and joined in a spiritual union. By contrast, the council identified Christ's church in more earthly institutional terms. The council viewed itself as the prime ecclesiastical authority representing Christ's church militant on earth. It could decide the fate equally well of the likes of both a John XXIII and a John Hus.

"Dearly beloved in Christ Jesus, stand in the truth you have learned, for it conquers all and is mighty to eternity" (John Hus).

On July 6, 1415, executioners led John Hus outside Constance and through a meadow to his place of execution. He was heard to say, "You are now roasting a goose [the meaning of the Czech/Bohemian word *Hus*], but God will awaken a swan whom you will not burn or roast"—a statement cited years later by the minister officiating at Martin Luther's funeral. The Czech was stripped of his clothes. An eighteen-inch-high crown adorned with three devils and the words, "This is a heresiarch," was pushed onto his head. A witness described the last moment of Hus's life:

> When the executioners at once lit [the fire], the Master immediately began to sing in a loud voice, at first, "Christ, Thou son of the living God, have mercy upon us," and secondly, "Christ, Thou son of the living God, have mercy upon me," and in the third place, "Thou Who art born of Mary the Virgin." And when he began to sing the third time, the wind blew the flame into his face.

Hus died soon after.

Hus's executioners treated his remains in an inhumane fashion. Then they incinerated what was left of his body, clothing, and shoes, throwing the residue of ashes into the Rhine River. Authorities did not apparently want to risk giving Hus's followers any opportunity to acquire "relics" of their departed prisoner.

The council's actions against John Hus produced unintended results. The argument of Hus's accusers that his free-conduct pass had become void because he was deemed a heretic appeared less than persuasive to the Bohemians. The council had stolen from the Bohemians the life of their spiritual leader, but it returned to them memories of one whom they esteemed as a martyr whose example of resistance could only inspire fresh resolve.

On September 2, fifty-eight Hussite barons declared in a manifesto that Hus was by no means a heretic. Rather, any person who had the temerity to charge the Bohemians with heresy was really "a son of the Devil and the father of lies." When a bishop from the Council of Constance put Prague under an interdict, Bohemians became further enraged. "Utraquists"—Hussites who believed that laypeople should have access to both the bread and the wine—promptly countermanded the interdict by entering Prague churches and providing mass for the laity.

In 1416 the alienation of the Hussites intensified further when the incendiary news arrived that Jerome of Prague, a disciple of Hus, had been put to death at Constance. In 1419 civil disturbances and mob rule broke out. Bohemia was aflame with a spirit of revolt. Armed conflicts erupted between various parties: Roman Catholic, Utraquists, and Taborites (extreme Hussites named after Mount Tabor, their haven south of Prague).

IV. THE REFORM OF THE CHURCH

The third principal issue on the agenda of the Council of Constance was the reform of the church. For hundreds of years poignant voices could be heard urging reform. The Babylonian Captivity of the Church coupled with the Great Schism furnished ample illustrations why some Christians believed a thorough reform of the church was necessary. In 1363 Nicholas of Oresme put the matter bluntly: "From the sole of the foot to the crown of the head there is no health in it."

By the first decade of the fifteenth century, many churchmen agreed that the conciliar movement itself, besides helping to end the schism, might provide the best vehicle to bring about the needed reform for which so many longed. A number of the members of the lower clergy who gathered at Constance were especially hopeful that the reform of the church "from the sole of the foot to the crown of the head" could take place through the agency of the councils. Their hopes seemed to be rewarded when the Council of Constance set forth the decree *Frequens* (October 5, 1417), proposing that the "frequent" holding of councils was one of the most effective means of rooting out the briars and thistles of heresy and corruption from the church.

The decree stipulated that councils should be held regularly (every five years, or even more frequently) to help reform the church in its "head and members." The popes were specifically admonished not to avoid holding councils. It appeared that the continued existence of the conciliar movement as a major reforming force within the life the Western church would be assured by this stipulation of the decree *Frequens*.

A. The Papal Struggle against the Conciliar Movement

After the Council of Constance concluded in 1418, a number of fifteenth-century popes made a considered effort to regain what they believed had been taken from them: their rightful prerogatives as papal monarchs. In a certain measure, their century-long struggle (1417–1517) against the conciliar movement was a success.

In 1520, when Martin Luther called for the reform of the church, he looked to a general council as the means to do so. But he felt obligated to appeal to the German nobility to initiate such a council. Recent experience had convinced him that he could expect little serious help from the papacy in this regard. By Luther's day the popes had essentially reestablished their authority as papal monarchs. They initiated a few councils. They determined not to give conciliarists access to authority such as that which the Council of Constance claimed for itself.

The Fifth Lateran Council (1512–17), for example, took place in the years immediately adjacent to Luther's nailing of the *Ninety-five Theses* (1517). The reforms envisioned by the council reflected a curial top-down approach in which the papacy imposed its views of reform. Indeed, Pope Leo X, a Medici (1513–21), had the council's appeals for reform wrapped in the authority of his own papal bulls: *Pastoralis officii divina providencia* (1513) and *Supernae dispositionis arbitrio* (1514). The first bull attempted to restrict the amount of charges curial offices could levy; the second urged the clergy to forsake evil practices, whether blasphemy, concubinage, witchcraft, or other vices.

Earlier popes such as Pius II and Sixtus IV had proposed plans to reform the papacy by centralizing its operations, but their top-down efforts were not pursued in a thorough fashion. More generally, the popes invested their energies in a campaign for the restoration of papal authority in exchange for the benefits of serious church reform that the councils apparently could have afforded them. The popes could not have foreseen that the essential subjection of the conciliar movement made Luther's appeal for reform all the more acute and understandable to many Europeans in the first half of the sixteenth century.

By what means did the popes reestablish their dominance over the conciliar movement during the fifteenth century? The story of their efforts tracks an ebb and flow of papal power. Martin V, whom the Council of Constance made pope, was a gifted reorganizer of the papacy's administrative and financial institutions. He also engaged in minor reforms of the church hierarchy. He launched building projects to refurbish church properties in Rome. He urged Christians to treat Jews with more moderation and to eschew forced baptisms of their children under the age of twelve. Moreover, he made concordats with various kings that extended his influence throughout Europe.

Because of the decree *Frequens*, Martin V grudgingly called the Council of Pavia (1423–24) and the Council of Basel (1431–38, 1449). Members of this latter council still hoped to reform the church and to pacify the Bohemians caught up in revolt. When the Council of Basel opened in July 23, 1431, the authority of the conciliar movement appeared to possess substantial strength.

However, a number of months before the council was due to open, Martin V died. His successor, Eugenius IV (1431–47), attempted to crush the council's authority by ordering it dissolved in December 1431, only a few months after it had opened. Outraged by this preemptive papal strike, many cardinals and bishops at Basel refused to accept Eugenius's dictate. Under tremendous public pressure, Eugenius abjectly yielded to their counterattacks and recognized the Council of Basel's claims to legitimacy.

Soon after, Eugenius confronted another vexing and disruptive problem. In 1434 a revolt broke out against him at Rome, led by members of the Colonna family. Eugenius was forced to flee to Florence, where he lived until his return to Rome in 1443.

From Florence, Eugenius attempted to reassert his papal prerogatives. This was no paltry task. In 1438 the *Pragmatic Sanction of Bourges* afforded the French king the authority to rule in temporal affairs and to propose candidates for vacant benefices. Moreover, a reinvigorated Council of Basel was determined to bolster its own authority. In an attempt to end warfare in Bohemia, the council negotiated accords with more moderate Bohemians, according to which "Communion in both kinds" was permitted and the gospel could be preached without restriction. The council disallowed monies to be sent to the pope, and the papacy's income tumbled.

The conciliar movement looked robust, the papacy's authority muzzled, and its political policies in disarray.

In 1437–38, however, negotiations between Eugenius IV and the Byzantine Emperor John VIII (1392–1448) played a major role in redirecting the flow of political power within the Western church. Hard-pressed by the Turks, the Byzantines looked to the West for military and spiritual support. If a union with the Western church could be consummated, would not military aid be provided in consequence? Making a critically important decision, the Byzantines chose to deal with Eugenius rather than with the Baselites, who had also attempted to negotiate with them.

In 1437 Eugenius once again ordered that the Council of Basel be dissolved. He called for the council to meet in Ferrara, Italy, in 1437–38. (This council became known as the Council of Ferrara/Florence when it was moved to Florence in 1439 for financial reasons and the fear of plague in the city of Ferrara.) A number of the prelates at Basel obeyed Eugenius's command and attended the council, especially intrigued by the pope's efforts to bring about a union of churches with the Greeks.

B. A Union of the Western and Eastern Churches

Given the obvious weakness of Eugenius IV's political situation in the years immediately preceding the Council of Ferrara/Florence, the Byzantines' decision to submit to the pope's authority appears to have been a decisive factor in elevating his stature over that of the Baselites.

Pushed by desperation due to the severity of the Turkish threat, the Byzantine emperor, accompanied by members of his clergy and the great Greek scholars Bessarion and Plethro, made an epochal journey to Florence.

On July 6, 1439, the Greeks and Byzantines acquiesced to the decree *Laetentur coeli et exulta terra* ("Let the heavens rejoice and the earth be glad") and thereby accepted a union of churches with the Western church represented by Eugenius. The Byzantines acknowledged papal authority and endorsed the doctrine of purgatory and other disputed doctrines. Christendom had reason to rejoice. Unity among Christians East and West appeared to be restored.

Isidore, the Greek Metropolitan of the Russian Church, who had been appointed by the Patriarch of Constantinople, likewise attended the Council of Florence and heartily approved its decrees. Upon his return to Moscow (1441), he encountered opposition from Moscovites who opposed the Florentine accord. Isidore was imprisoned, but he escaped and fled Moscow. In 1448, Russian bishops began to choose their own metropolitan.

The accreditation from Eastern clergymen for Eugenius IV's authority bolstered the campaign to restore fully papal monarchy at the expense of conciliar authority. The Baselites found themselves immured in a deteriorating political situation. Many clerics had already abandoned them to join the council of Ferrara/Florence. Those who remained in Basel formed a "rump" council of prelates who would not accede to Eugenius's demands. In fact, they deposed him on June 25, 1439, and on November 5 elected Duke Amadeus of Savoy as Pope Felix V (1439–49).

These actions, though understandable from the Baselites' perspective, ultimately badly compromised their conciliar enterprise. Had not their conciliar theory been marshaled as a means to end the Great Schism? Now the Baselites, the purest of conciliar advocates, had created a new schism by their election of a second pope to compete with Eugenius IV. Their actions appeared to run at cross-purposes with the thrust of the earlier conciliar movement. During the next decade, whatever slight support had existed for Felix V's papal claims slipped away.

When Eugenius IV died, Nicholas V (1447–55) was elected the new pope. King Charles VII of France helped negotiate an arrangement that facilitated Felix V's abdication of his papal claims in 1449. Pope Nicholas made Felix a cardinal and gave him other benefices and honors. Felix, a pious man, died in 1455. With his death, the conciliar movement—already wounded—seemed to lapse into a state of irreality.

C. Pope Pius II and Blunting the Conciliar Movement

The irreality was such that within a decade Pope Pius II (1458–64) could claim in the bull *Execrabilis* (1460) that any appeal to a future council as an authority above that of a pope constituted an appeal to the nonexistent. In a decisive fashion the bull reasserted papal prerogatives. The bull's stipulations flatly countermanded the premises of the decrees *Sacrosancta* and *Frequens*, set forth by the Council of Constance. Pius perceived a spirit of rebellion as the animating force driving conciliarists. Ironically enough, earlier in his career Pius had been a defender of conciliar rights, had attended the Council of Basel, and had even worked as a secretary for the Baselite Pope Felix V. Pius then forsook his conciliarist perspectives and made his peace with Eugenius IV.

The bull *Execrabilis* appeared to signal a splendid victory for advocates of a restored papal monarchy and a crushing defeat for partisans of the conciliar movement. However, an awareness that councils could still serve as a means for the reform of the church lingered in certain quarters of the church's ranks during the period preceding Luther's posting of the *Ninety-five Theses* and beyond. While condemning the Council of Constance's execution of John Hus, Luther appreciated the restricted authority of councils.

In the seventeenth century the conciliarist theory found a new party of advocates in the Jansenist movement. Jansenists—that is, Augustinian Catholics—looked back with favor on the Council of Constance's conciliarism as faithfully representing the teaching of the primitive church before papal monarchs assumed authority within the Western church.

Since the days of the Council of Constance, various forms of conciliarism have resurfaced periodically above ground, contesting an ecclesiology of papal monarchy often in the name of collegial episcopacy, that is, the premise that all the bishops of the church in aggregate constitute an authority higher than that of the bishop of Rome, the pope.

V. THE RENAISSANCE POPES

In the decades following the Council of Constance, the papacy not only was preoccupied with blunting the conciliar movement, quenching the flames of the Bohemian revolt, and beseeching Christian rulers to launch crusades to beat back the Turks' advances, but also wanted to restore Rome's place as the center of Christendom. To accomplish the latter, the papacy attempted to establish a strong presence in the turbulent world of Italian city-state politics and culture.

Often dubbed the "Renaissance popes," a number of bishops of Rome were noteworthy for their patronage of the arts, support of humanistic studies, and efforts to return Rome to its former architectural glory. Some of them, however, pursued lives of remarkable sexual and materialistic indulgence, thereby tarnishing their own reputations and throwing disrepute on the papacy.

The invasion by the French in 1494 turned Italy into an even more contested region in which several great powers of Europe battled for control of city-states and principalities. In his *History of Italy*, Francesco Guicciardini (1483–1540), a contemporary historian, described his own day as marked by foreign ("barbarian") invasions leading to the sack of Rome in 1527 and the siege of Florence in 1529–30.

In 1494 Ludovico Sforza, the Duke of Milan, invited Charles VIII (1470–98), the young and impetuous French king, to make good a claim on the feudal Kingdom of Naples. The French launched an invasion and returned a second time in 1499. In 1500 the Spanish marched armies into Italy and eventually gained control of Naples (1503). Unruly mercenaries poured into Italy to be hired by the papacy, city-states like Florence, or foreign powers.

How to play off successfully the great powers, France and Spain, against each other and how to form shrewd alliances with other Italian city-states was an enterprise that demanded displays of political dexterity by the popes and their diplomats. On the eve of the first French invasion of 1494, the most important Italian entities included the Venetian Grand Council and Doge (principal magistrate), the King of Naples, the Duke of Milan, the Florentine Republic, and the papacy. By 1104 the Venetians, for example, had been at work building what became a huge maritime trading empire.

By 1500 the 3,300 ships of the Venetian Republic regularly visited ports around the Mediterranean and braved the Atlantic on their way to Bruges and London and Bristol. The Venetian overland trade routes penetrated the interior of the Middle East and wound north toward Augsburg, Germany, and the cities of the Hanseatic League. The republic's arsenal constituted the largest European shipbuilding enterprise. Its picturesque canals and splendid Basilica di St. Marco evoked admiration. Although Italian city-states like Venice sometimes made treaties with the French or Spanish, none wanted foreign governments to control all of Italy; nor did they want any other competing Italian state to gain dominance.

It was no easy task to reassert the papacy's spiritual and temporal claims in an Italy seething with political intrigue and trampled by foreign mercenaries and warring, powerful city-state armies. Bloody assassinations, bribery, and ripped-up treaties were not uncommon.

Into this political fray, the papacy plunged, attempting to secure its place among Italian powers.

Machiavelli was impressed by the success of the papal campaign: "Then came Alexander VI, who of all the pontiffs there have ever been was the first to show what a pope with money and troops could do." Owing to military exploits of Alexander (1492–1503) and Julius II (1503–13), the papal estates were expanded. By the advent of Pope Leo X's reign in 1513—21, the papacy had emerged as a state with which to reckon on the peninsula. Machiavelli commented, "His Holiness Pope Leo has found the papacy very strong, and therefore it may be hoped that, as his predecessors made it great through the use of arms, he will make it revered and still greater through his goodness and his other countless virtues."

One sign of Leo X's strength was the size of his papal *familia*. Whereas Pope Eugenius IV had 130 persons belonging to his papal *familia*—that is, those who worked for him directly and depended on him for support—Leo X had about 700.

In 1527, only fourteen years after Leo X had become pope, the troops of Charles V (1500–1558), the Holy Roman Emperor, entered the Rome of Pope Clement VII. As an undisciplined army including Lutheran mercenaries, they pillaged, murdered, and raped during their infamous "Sack of Rome." The horror the soldiers unleashed lasted more than a year and brought with it famine and plague. The Sack of Rome provided ample evidence that papal alliances and armies did not always provide the papacy with an effective buffer against its foes. Clement had to flee to the Castel Sant'Angelo for safety and pay a huge ransom to gain his release.

Thus the papacy did not always escape unscathed from the bloodletting and anguish of the Italian political scene. In the last chapter of *The Prince*, Machiavelli had called for a savior to rescue his beloved Italy (which he especially identified with Florence) from the barbarians.

A. Refurbishing Rome

Many of the popes calculated that as the fortunes of the city of Rome went, so went the fortunes of the papacy. For that matter, the papacy dominated the city government of Rome. These popes wanted to restore Rome's splendors by launching building programs and repairing standing structures. If Rome could vaunt stately architecture, resplendent paintings and statuary, and well-tended gardens and fountains, who would doubt that the popes and their cardinals were themselves deserving of honor as worthy political figures and spiritual leaders? The efforts to restore Rome as the center of Christendom were understandably linked to a less than subtle campaign of papal self-advertisement.

Indeed, a number of popes believed that respect for the Holy See would be greatly enhanced among the non-reading popular masses if these people could visually contemplate representations of papal authority portrayed in stone and canvas. Architecture, sculpture, and painting could be employed for their didactic capacities. In a death-bed speech explaining his hearty efforts to refurbish Rome with architectural splendor, Pope Nicholas V offered this strategy:

> Only the learned who have studied the origin and development of the authority of the Roman Church can really understand its greatness. Thus, to create solid and stable convictions in the minds of the uncultured masses, there must be something which appeals to the eye; a popular faith, sustained only on doctrines, will never be anything but feeble and vacillating. But if the authority of the Holy See were visibly displayed in majestic buildings, imperishable memorials and witnesses seemingly planted by the hand of God himself, belief would grow and strengthen from one generation to another, and all the world would accept and revere it. Noble edifices combining taste and beauty with imposing proportions would immensely conduce to the exaltation of the chair of St. Peter.

As ancient Rome could not be built in a day, so a thoroughly refurbished papal Rome could not be rebuilt in a few decades. The Rome to which Martin V returned in 1420 was a broken-down city. It had become encumbered by dilapidated buildings and gutted by streets in disrepair. The city was also overrun by large patches of wild forests. Even the best efforts of Martin V were not sufficient to return the city to its former architectural splendor. Nor was the political unrest that seized Rome in the 1430s, during the pontificate of Eugenius IV, conducive to urban renewal.

In the 1450s a Spanish visitor to Rome was struck by the paucity of the city's population and its stretches of wilderness within the city's walls. He observed, " [T]here are parts within the walls which look like thick woods, and wild beasts, hares, foxes, deer and even, so it is said, porcupines breed in the caves."

Yet, in 1450 Pope Nicholas V summoned multitudes of the faithful to Rome for Jubilee celebrations. Moreover, he enlisted Leon Battista Alberti, an innovative genius, to give him architectural advice regarding a significant building program. Churches were restored and new edifices constructed. Nicholas even contemplated razing old St. Peter's with the goal of replacing it with a new, grander edifice. The pope's successors ultimately followed through on this idea, with the first stone

Michelangelo's painting in the Sistine Chapel.

of the new building laid in April 1506. Fra Angelico, the painter, refurbished the Vatican chapel. Moreover, Nicholas spared no expense to have copies made of important manuscripts that were placed in what became the Vatican library. At his death, more than 1,200 books and manuscripts, both in Greek and Latin, were in his collection.

Other popes such as Sixtus IV (1471–84), Alexander VI, and Julius II lavishly financed painters, sculptors, and architects who graced Rome with new bridges, churches, tombs, fountains, gardens, and residential palaces, not to mention statuary and paintings. Michelangelo (1475–1564) sculpted the *Pieta* with Mary holding Jesus in her arms. Despite stormy relations with Julius, Michelangelo worked on the plans and the creation of Julius II's tomb with its *Moses* figure (1513–15) and painted the frescoes of Genesis stories on the ceiling of the Sistine Chapel (1508–12). Classical figures such as Sibyls also found their way into these frescoes.

Along with Baldassare Castiglione, the painter Raphael (1483–1520) urged Pope Leo X not to destroy pagan statuary but to treat classical ruins in general as "paragons of the ancients." Da Vinci, a mechanical and artistic genius, brushed the enigmatic *Mona Lisa*. Raphael painted the fresco *The School of Athens*, which depicts Aristotle and Plato in deep conversation as they walk in St. Peters (modeled after a Donato Bramante drawing). The patronage of the popes contributed to their reputation as significant supporters of the Italian Renaissance.

By the time of Julius II's death in 1513, Rome's splendors had become so noteworthy that a few reforming critics wondered whether the campaign to restore the city's former glory had in fact been too successful.

Papal power was enhanced not only by an extensive rebuilding program at Rome, but also by the propagation of a form of Roman humanism that embellished the glory of the city and the papacy, especially between the years 1475 and 1520. On occasion, humanist scholars such as Raffaele Maffei (1451–1522) argued that the papacy was a legitimate inheritor of the Roman Empire's culture, especially its Latin language, and that the popes were the heir of the temporal rights enjoyed by Roman emperors of antiquity. As a pope could be compared to the Roman emperor, so the church could be compared to the empire and the cardinals to Roman senators. These grandiose comparisons served the papacy well as it attempted to reassert monarchical prerogatives and privileges.

B. A Problem of Reputation

In the play *Julius Exclusis*, the great humanist Desiderius Erasmus flayed the reputation of the recently departed Pope Julius II (d. 1513). In it St. Peter interviews Julius to see if he is worthy of entering heaven's doors. Peter asks Julius if it is possible to reform the church by calling a council. Julius responds that it is not possible because he is not about to call one. Peter explodes:

> A novel prerogative for my successors, to be the wickedest of men, yet be safe from punishment. So much the unhappier the Church that cannot shake such a monster off its shoulders. The people ought to rise with paving stones and dash such a wretch's brains out. If Satan needed a vicar he would find none fitter than you.

Julius boasts that he had rebuilt Rome and was adored when he traveled through the streets of the city:

> Look now at our gorgeous churches, bishops like kings, cardinals gloriously attended, horses and mules checked with gold and jewels, and shod with gold and silver. Beyond all myself, Supreme Pontiff, borne on soldiers' shoulders in a golden chair, and waving my hand majestically to adoring crowds …

This is too much for St. Peter. He rebukes Julius by claiming that he, Peter, had brought pagan Rome to acknowledge Christ, whereas Julius has rendered Rome pagan once again.

Obviously, Erasmus's mischievous caricature of the papacy and Julius II's intentions were just that, a caricature. Nonetheless, this parody, even if slanted, helps us understand the reasons that a young German named Martin Luther found ostentatious displays of papal opulence in Rome so distasteful during his visit to that city.

Nevertheless, the Renaissance popes also included churchmen who earned more admirable reputations. Prior to Julius II, Pope Pius II (born Aeneas Sylvius) was well trained in the humanities. Early in his career

Aeneas wrote erotic poetry and a novel. He also fathered several illegitimate children. In 1445–46 Aeneas turned his back on a profligate lifestyle and became a priest. He rose steadily in the church's hierarchy, becoming the cardinal of Siena and finally, in 1458, the pope.

In his autobiographically styled *Commentaries*, Pius II rehearsed in sometimes meticulous detail the appeals to prototypic nationalism, the covenants made in the "privies," and the bargaining by certain members of the college of cardinals who had come to elect a new pope: "They begged, promised, threatened, and some shamelessly casting aside all decency, pleaded their own causes and claimed the papacy as their right." He continued:

> The Divine Mercy will not endure that this place, which has been the dwelling of so many Holy Fathers, shall become a den of thieves or a brothel of whores. The apostleship is bestowed by God not by men. Tomorrow will show that the Bishop of Rome is chosen by God not by men. As for you, if you are a Christian, you will not choose as Christ's Vicar him whom you know to be a limb of the devil.

Aeneas's own sincere concern for the sanctity of the papacy was revealed in these comments. He eventually received the twelve votes necessary to be elected pope. Rome, which had been on the brink of civil unrest, was pacified. Crowds poured into the city's streets to celebrate Pius II's election.

Aeneas as Pius II was an activist pope. As described earlier, he promulgated the decree *Execrabilis*, which boosted the authority of the papal office at the expense of councils. He also tried to improve relations with the Florentines, who disliked the fact that a Siennese cardinal had become pope. Then, like other Christians, the pope was greatly affected by the fall of Constantinople to the Turks in 1453. He feared for the very future of Christianity if the Turks were not fended off. He attempted to launch crusades (1461, 1463–64) against the Turks. Then death overtook a deeply worried Pius in Ancona.

Pius II serves as an example of various Renaissance popes prior to Julius II who became ardent defenders of the Catholic faith and maintained moral rectitude. Nonetheless, Julius also had predecessors whose reputations for questionable ethics and worldly ambition were even more notorious than his own. Indeed, Julius's near predecessor, Pope Alexander VI, engaged in personal, political, and military intrigues that won Machiavelli's admiration but did extensive damage to the papacy's reputation for Christian probity. Alexander, a Spaniard whose name became Borgia in Italian, was asked by the cardinals who had elected him what he wanted to be called. He replied, "By the name of the invincible Alexander," that is, Alexander the Great.

Alexander VI pursued a disreputable lifestyle, fathering a number of children on whom he doted. The historian Guicciardini, who worked for the papacy, observed, "Other popes, to conceal their infamy, were wont to term their offspring nephews; but Alexander took delight in letting all the world know that they were his children." The most famous of these children was Cesare Borgia (1476–1507). The epitome of a pragmatic politician, Borgia with his father entered into alliances and armed warfare in almost unending attempts to enhance familial and papal power during his father's pontificate. Between the years 1495–98 Alexander vigorously opposed Savonarola's reforming activities and preaching in Florence. Moreover, Alexander presided over the impressive Jubilee of 1500 that brought many pilgrims to Rome.

From Machiavelli's point of view, Alexander VI and Cesare Borgia were prime illustrations of politicians who did everything possible to guarantee their personal happiness and success. But both were overtaken by "fortune"—and fortune could be cruel. Rumor had it that when Alexander died in 1503, he may have been poisoned.

The lifestyles and actions of the likes of Alexander VI and Julius II did little to enhance the collective reputation of the Renaissance popes as faithful shepherds of Christ's flocks.

"Other popes, to conceal their infamy, were wont to term their offspring nephews; but Alexander [VI] took delight in letting all the world know that they were his children" (Francesco Guicciardini).

C. The Practice of Roman Catholicism in Italy

The portraits of the Renaissance popes by Erasmus, Luther, and Machiavelli may skew our perceptions of the religious life of Italian Roman Catholics on the eve of the Protestant Reformation. Despite the garish, opulent, and promiscuous side of Roman culture, many of the faithful lived by the teachings of the church daily. In the same way that many Italians did not manifest extraordinary devotion to their religion, relatively few were skeptical about its truthfulness.

In fifteenth-century Italy, the Catholic faithful fulfilled the duty of confessing their sins at least once a year and attending mass more regularly than that, if possible. They were often deprived of a sufficient number of priests to minister to their needs. Moreover, many bishops who held several benefices were frequently absent from one or the other. Italian priests were not especially well trained, some even quite ignorant of the meaning of the sign of the cross. Their bishops often neglected to attend the ordinations of priests as required by church teaching.

Despite these glaring weaknesses in the promotion of church life, the Catholic faithful of the Italian peninsula remained quite impervious to the teachings of the Protestant Reformers who called for a reform of the church, let alone to the Waldensians within their midst. There was, however, as historian Anthony Levi observes, an intellectual restlessness among "an educated elite of patrons, artists and scholars" and a thriving university life. In fact, Italy had more than 25 percent of the universities in all of Europe.

VI. THE "AGE OF DISCOVERY"

Several factors brought about the "Age of Discovery," an era when many European and Asian nations expanded their knowledge of the world because explorers were traveling into places they had never seen before. A leading cause was the scientific and technical advances of the Renaissance. Ships became more seaworthy and capable of surviving in the oceans. There was an increasing demand for unique goods, including spices such as cinnamon, nutmeg, and cloves. In addition, there was political and religious motivation for discovery of new routes because of Muslim dominance of trade from the East.

A. The Rise of the Ottoman Empire

From 1281 to 1923 the House of Osman dominated what became known as the Ottoman Empire. Following military victories at Bursa (1326) and Gallipoli (1353), the Ottomans subdued Bulgaria, Macedonia, and Serbia. Some Christians feared that the Ottoman advance was next to unstoppable.

The Turks kept their eyes focused on a particularly desirable prize—the capture of Constantinople. During the fourteenth century Byzantium fell into a weakened state, both economically and politically. For all practical purposes, it had no navy. Enervating civil wars (1341–71) sapped its strength. The Black Death of 1347–50 ruinously reduced Constantinople's population to approximately 100,000. Nonetheless, in 1422 Constantinople survived a siege prosecuted by Sultan Murat II. But on November 10, 1444, the sultan defeated a Christian Crusader army at Varna on the Black Sea.

This Ottoman victory quashed any realistic hopes that Crusader armies might relieve Constantinople by land. Hopes did remain that the papacy and Italian city-states such as Venice and Genoa might send fleets to rescue Constantinople by sea.

One of the earliest extant plans of Constantinople, by the Florentine traveler Cristoforo Buondelmonti. Although greatly simplified, it represents the city as it was in 1422, some thirty years before its fall to the Turks. On the right is the great domed Hagia Sophia.

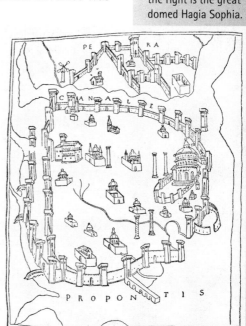

The capture of Constantinople by the Turks in 1453.

In February 1451 Sultan Murat II died. A Muslim chronicler wrote, "He left as a bequest to his illustrious successor the erection of the standards of the jihad for the capture of that city, by the addition of which … he might protect the prosperity of the people of Islam and break the back of the wretched misbelievers."

In March 1452 Pope Nicholas V sent three Genoese merchant ships to bring supplies to the hard-pressed Christian forces defending Constantinople. However, the expedition failed to accomplish its mission. Only a timely shift in the winds allowed the ships to elude what had appeared to be certain destruction, trapped as they were by the Ottoman navy. Christians viewed the ships' dramatic escape as an act of God. In April 1452 a Venetian expedition likewise tried to relieve embattled Constantinople. The Ottoman navy basically destroyed the fleet. Some Italian sailors were publicly impaled by their Ottoman captors. The perilous plight of Constantinople's citizens only worsened.

On May 29, 1453, the Ottoman forces of Mehmed II the Conqueror (1444–45, 1451–81), after a grueling siege, breached the walls of Constantinople and penetrated the city. The fall of Constantinople constituted an event of enormous historical import. Not only did this Turkish victory deal a rude blow to the Eastern Orthodox Church, but it created consternation and deep fear among many Western Catholic Christians. Mehmed II hoped to transform the Byzantine Empire into one of an Islamic orientation. He ordered that the chief Islamic leader, the Greek Orthodox patriarch, the Armenian patriarch, and the chief Jewish rabbi all reside in Constantinople.

Because the patriarch of Constantinople had escaped to Italy, in January 1454 Mehmed installed George Scholarios (1405?–72?), otherwise known as Gennadius, as the new Greek patriarch. The sultan treated Gennadius, a prominent Greek theologian and an archcritic of the papacy, with great honor. Viewing himself as Gennadius's protector, Mehmed declared, "Be Patriarch, with good fortune, and be assured of our friendship, keeping all the privileges that the Patriarchs before you enjoyed." Mehmed viewed Patriarch Gennadius as head of the Orthodox Church and as the leader of the dispersed "Greek nation." The sultan also expected the patriarch to obey his orders.

Mehmed II indicated that Christians would be tolerated under his rule, but he did place serious restrictions on them. Christians were not permitted to evangelize Muslims or marry Muslim women. Moreover, they were forced to pay onerous taxes.

The Turks divided the peoples whom they conquered into what came to be known as *millets*, or ethnic-religious communities. The "Rum" millet consisted of Greek Orthodox living in the Balkans and Asia Minor. A second millet was composed of other Christians (non-Chalcedonians) who were not otherwise subject to the Orthodox patriarch at Constantinople. A third millet was made up of Jews within the Ottoman Empire such as the Ashkenazi and Sephardic Jews. The Turks engaged Phanariots, or Greek merchants and clergy from the Phanar area of Constantinople, to help govern the millets. A certain measure of religious freedom and self-governance could exist in the millets. At the same time, the Turks enslaved many Christians and non-Christians whom their soldiers captured.

The Turks created a system (*devşirme*) in which they collected talented Christian children and Muslims from the Balkans and trained the brightest to be state officials, military commanders, and viziers (civil officers). Christian boys were sometimes converted into fierce Muslim fighters called Janissaries; their duty was to serve the sultans. Until the defeat of Ottoman forces at the gates of Vienna (1683), many European Christians believed the Ottoman Empire posed a singularly ominous threat.

As for the patriarchal throne of Constantinople, the sultans often sold it to those who offered the most money. From the mid-fifteenth

Cross section, plan, and elevation of the Byzantine basilica Hagia Sophia in Constantinople, 17th century.

Gianni Dagli Orti/The Art Archive at Art Resource, NY

to twentieth centuries, 159 patriarchs sat on the chair. Many (105) were forced out of their office by the sultans who profited from their departure by reselling the office to a new bidder. Thus, the fate of the patriarchs of Constantinople was often determined by the capricious, self-serving wishes of the Turkish sultans. Six patriarchs were apparently murdered.

B. The Russian Church

The conversion of Grand Prince Vladimir of Kiev (988) to the Byzantine Orthodox faith constituted an epochal event in Russian religious history. In time Orthodoxy became the religion of the Russians. Between 1237 and about 1450, the Mongol Golden Horde, after initial invasions (1223), placed Russia under the "Tartar Yoke." The armies of the Mongol Bau Khan devastated sections of Russia between the years 1237 and 1240.

Despite Mongol rule, the Grand Duchy of Muscovy (1283–1547) emerged as a significant commercial and religious center. In the Battle of Kulikovo (September 8, 1380), Grand Prince Dimitri II of Moscow won a heroic victory over a Mongolian army and helped establish Moscow's role as a leading power. Russian writers frequently presented Dimitri as a pious defender of the Orthodox faith.

In 1381 Cyprian, who had been designated by Byzantium as Metropolitan of Kiev and all Russia, returned to Moscow. He was determined to make Moscow the center of Russian Orthodoxy and to promote the Hesychast ideals of the monasticism of Mount Athos: the cultivation of quietness of spirit and the repetition of prayers preparing a person for mystical "deification," or union with God.

Until the fall of Constantinople to the Turks in 1453, the Russian Church had been a dependency of the patriarch of Constantinople and greatly benefitted from this relationship. The Russian Church generally demonstrated loyalty to the patriarchate of Constantinople until the Council of Florence (1438–39). But some Russian Orthodox believed the representatives of the Byzantine patriarchate and Isidore, the Metropolitan of Kiev and All Russia, who sought Western aid at that council, inexcusably capitulated to the demands of the papacy.

The conquest of Constantinople crippled the capacity of Byzantine emperors to protect Eastern Orthodox Christians. It also weakened further the patriarch of Constantinople's authority and standing among the Russian Orthodox. The patriarchs were coerced to obey the Turkish sultans.

A number of Russians began to think they should assume the role of protecting the Eastern Orthodox. In 1472 the marriage of Ivan III to the niece of a Byzantine emperor deepened this sense of responsibility. The Russians also appropriated the Byzantine title of "tsar" and applied it to their rulers.

It was not until 1589, however, that the patriarchate of Moscow (1589–1721) was established. That occurred when the patriarch of Constantinople, Jeremias II, designated Bishop Job as the city's first patriarch. The patriarchate of Moscow thereby joined the much older patriarchates of Rome, Alexandria, Antioch, and Constantinople.

C. Religious Persecution in the Age of Discovery

For centuries—since the days of the Roman Empire—Europeans had relied on what became known as "the Silk Road" to travel to the Far East and northern Africa. It reached its peak during the Byzantine era. But with the spread of Muslim territory and the Turkish Empire, land travel became more difficult and dangerous. The traders therefore turned to the seas.

Yet it was not only the Turkish intrusion that led to the passion to find new worlds. There were conflicts within "Christian" Europe that motivated the need for change.

The Roman Catholic kingdom of Portugal, founded by King Afonso Henriques (1139–85), took the initial lead in the competition for new lands. In 1415 the Portuguese defeated Muslim forces and seized Cueta near Gibraltar in North Africa. Prince Henry "the Navigator" (1394–1460) encouraged Portuguese explorations. An avid student of mapmaking and astronomy, he established a school for navigators, advocated the use of low-drafting caravel ships, and sought to plant Portuguese colonies along the Atlantic African coast. In 1487–88 Bartolomeu Dias, trying to find a water route to India, discovered the Cape of Good Hope on the southern tip of Africa. The explorer Vasco da Gama eventually reached India by sea in 1497–99.

In 1397 Christian authorities in Spain prosecuted frightful massacres against Jews, followed by "conversion" campaigns. In 1492 King Ferdinand and Queen Isabella ordered all Jews who had not converted to Christianity to be expelled from Spain. In 1497 Portugal did the same. Perhaps as many as 200,000 Jews were baptized in the Iberian Peninsula between 1470 and 1500. Those Jews who practiced their Jewish faith in secret were called "Marranos" or *conversos* or "New Christians." Some Marranos fled Spain and Portugal and sought refuge in the Papal States, England, Germany, Holland, and Latin America.

Also in 1492, Christian forces captured Muslim Granada, an event many contemporaries hailed as epochal. It signaled a capstone victory in the Catholic Church's campaign to reconquer Spain for the Christian faith. Muslims had been in Spain for eight hundred years and had created a sophisticated civilization. The seizure of Granada was much feted by Ferdinand and Isabella.

The ensuing Treaty of Grenada permitted religious toleration to Muslims. At the same time, Muslims also became choice targets for Christian conversion efforts. During 1499–1501 a Muslim revolt took place in Grenada and was harshly suppressed. In 1502 Muslims were ordered either to leave Castile or to convert to Christianity. Those who converted to Christianity were called "Moriscos." Still others attempted to remain in rural villages of Spain and hold on to their Muslim faith.

Another revolt took place during 1568–71. In the 1580s a Catholic churchman, Juan de Ribera in Valencia, unsuccessfully appealed to Philip II (1527–98) to drive Moriscos out of Spain. Finally, Philip III (1578–1621) stipulated that all Moriscos should leave Spain. By 1609 they were forced out of Castile; by 1614, out of the rest of Spain.

By that time, of course, the Age of Discovery was long under way.

D. The Glory of the Age of Discovery

European explorers often had mixed emotions for participating in the dangerous seafaring venture. Undoubtedly, some sought glory for their monarch and kingdom or city-state and for themselves. A number believed a "river of gold" existed in Senegal on the west coast of Africa. They came to understand that gold was in fact plentiful on the "Gold Coast" (present-day Ghana).

Others sought to make money off the slave trade. The papacy from Popes Eugenius IV to Nicholas V approved the Portuguese and Spanish involvement in slavery, whether of Muslims or Africans. In *Romanus Pontificus* (1455), Pope Nicholas gave to the Christian powers the right "to invade, search out, capture, vanquish, and subdue all Saracens, and other enemies of Christ wheresoever placed."

The traders set sail into the Atlantic Ocean and sometimes looked west and south, even if they ultimately hoped to reach "the East"—India and beyond—with its oriental luxury items such as spices and perfumes. On their ventures to search out new trade routes, they sometimes discovered "remote" and "unknown" regions. By heading west and south, they largely avoided interference from the Ottoman Turks (with whom Christian states eventually competed among themselves for trade).

Following a watery path around the south of Africa would eliminate the need for lengthy overland travel through inhospitable regions. Still others imagined they might be able to forge an anti-Muslim alli-

Christopher
Columbus.

ance with the Christian priest Prestor John (a legendary figure) or with a real, newly converted African such as King Nzinga Nkuwu of the Kongo Kingdom. Europeans hoped to outflank and in time thwart Muslim advances in Africa by these strategies.

Christopher Columbus (1451–1506), from the commercially vibrant city of Genoa, Italy, gained the patronage of the Spanish monarchs Ferdinand and Isabella to support an expedition to the East by counterintuitively going west. Upon his arrival in the Caribbean Islands in 1492, Columbus mistakenly thought he was in the Indies. He claimed an island for Spain and named it San Salvador ("Holy Savior").

Columbus, whose first name means "Christ Bearer," believed that God had ordained the explorer's four voyages to the New World. On his third voyage he thought he had discovered the site of the garden of Eden. On his fourth voyage he believed he had discovered the lost gold mines of Ophir, from which Hiram took gold destined for Solomon.

Viewing the capture of Jerusalem as a precondition for Christ's return, Columbus urged Ferdinand and Isabella to use gold or precious stones he brought back to Spain to help finance a crusade to reconquer Jerusalem from the Muslims. He wrote, "At the moment when I undertook to discover the Indies, it was with the intention of petitioning the king and the queen, our Sovereigns, that they might resolve to expend the potential revenues occurring to them from the Indies for the conquest of Jerusalem."

On May 4, 1493, Pope Alexander VI issued a bull that divided portions of the "non-Christian" world between the Spanish and the Portuguese monarchs. It projected a "Line of Demarcation" running north and south through the Atlantic Ocean. Spain received rights to most of the New World. Portugal obtained the rights to Africa, India, and a portion of the New World (the area of Brazil). The pope indicated that the monarchs of Portugal and Spain "for a long time had intended to seek out and discover certain islands and main-lands remote and unknown and not hitherto discovered by others, to the end that you might bring to the worship of our Redeemer and the profession of the Catholic faith their residents and inhabitants." In 1494 the Line of Demarcation was amended by the Treaty of Tordesillas. A new line was located 370 leagues west of the Cape Verde Islands.

In 1507 the humanist Martin Waldseemüller drew up a map that included the outline of an unknown land across the Atlantic. He named the land *America*, thereby honoring the explorer Amerigo Vespucci (1454–1512). In 1508 Pope Julius II gave the king of Spain authority over the Catholic Church in the New World. During the years 1519–22, Ferdinand Magellan's sailors completed a voyage around the world.

Sadly, the explorers who "discovered" and conquered new territories often treated the peoples of these lands with little dignity and respect, sometimes not viewing them even as fully human. European conquistadors such as Francisco Pizarro (c. 1475–1541), who conquered the Inca Empire and founded Lima (Peru), often seemed little interested in introducing natives to the "worship of our Redeemer." The natives, however, were sometimes introduced to new diseases from Europe and to the horrors of ruthless exploitation.

In *Sublimus Dei* (1537), Pope Paul II affirmed that Indians of the West and South are not "dumb brutes," but are truly people capable of understanding the Catholic faith. He also stipulated that Indians "may and should, freely and legitimately, enjoy their liberty and the possession of their property, nor should they be any way enslaved; should the contrary happen, it shall be null and have no effect."

VII. CONCLUSION

The Roman Catholic Church regained much spiritual authority in Western Christendom during the tumultuous century from the election of Pope Martin V (1417) to the posting of the *Ninety-five Theses* (1517) by another Martin, the German Reformer Martin Luther.

During the same century, however, the papacy was not able to acquire anything matching the temporal power it had enjoyed when a pope like Innocent III could bend monarchs and nobles to do his will through the threat of interdicts and excommunications. The kings of a greatly enlarged Spain and France would not tolerate such intervention in their affairs. They had for all practical purposes gained a position of supremacy over their respective churches.

In 1469 the marriage of Ferdinand and Isabella had brought together Castile and Aragon to create a greater Spain. Thereafter, Emperor Charles V founded the Hapsburg realm that would include Spain, the Low Countries, Naples, lands in Spanish America, and the Holy Roman Empire. The Spanish would exercise considerable influence over the life of Rome due to the financial resources and protection it provided the papacy. Likewise, the Kingdom of France had become even more formidable with the recent addition of Bretagne (today known as Brittany).

Moreover, the papacy (witness the reaction of Pius II) was genuinely shocked by the fall of Constantinople to the Ottoman Turks. Not only were the Ottoman Turks subjugating eastern Europe, but the sultans appeared to have designs on military incursions into central Europe.

Nonetheless, the popes could rejoice that they had largely beaten back the challenge of the conciliar movement. Papal "Renaissance" Rome was gloriously adorned with resplendent architecture, sculpture, and paintings. As historian James Hankins observes, by 1500 Rome had displaced "Renaissance" Florence as the "the undisputed queen of literary and intellectual life in Europe." Luther, then, was to face an invigorated papal monarchy in Rome.

FOR FURTHER STUDY

Davis, Natalie, and Arlette Farge, eds. *A History of Women in the West, Volume III: Renaissance and Enlightenment Paradoxes.* Cambridge: Harvard University Press, 1993.

Muir, Edward. *Ritual in Early Modern Europe.* New York: Cambridge University Press, 2005.

Ozment, Steven. *The Age of Reform, 1250–1500: An Intellectual and*

Religious History of Late Medieval and Reformation Europe. Farnham, UK: Ashgate, 2011.

Perry, J. H. *The Age of Reconnaissance, Discovery, Exploration and Settlement 1450–1650.* Berkeley: University of California Press, 1981.

Shinners, John, ed. *Medieval Popular Religion 1000–1500: A Reader.* Peterborough, Ontario: Broadview Press, 1997.

Spinka, Matthew. *John Hus at the Council of Constance.* New York: Columbia University Press, 1965.

The Renaissance and the Christian Faith

I. INTRODUCTION

A warm sun beating down from a high blue sky, a shimmering Arno River meandering through the town, the Palazzo Vecchio town hall looming fortress-like over the Piazza della Signoria square, hearty people bustling about their daily chores and business, wooden tables decked with drinks and savory delicacies, exquisite statuary and paintings gracing churches and palaces alike, students wending their way to a *rendezvous* with renowned teachers of the humanities, much talk in Latin concerning republican and civic virtues, women in colorful finery strolling through the streets: these were traits of Florence, Italy, in 1405, or so said a number of contemporaries.

For many of us, this description evokes pleasant reflections about life during a period of Western history called the Renaissance. What we may not recall, however, is the fact that the French expression *renaissance* is one of rather recent vintage. Moreover, the word is the subject of much spirited controversy about its meaning.

Since the second half of the nineteenth century, the contention that a European Renaissance took place between the years 1300 and 1600/1650/1700 has stirred considerable debate. Some historians flatly deny its existence. Others who say that a Renaissance did in fact occur have often struggled to agree on what its defining characteristics and temporal delimitations may have been and what factors brought about its inception and ending. Some scholars believe the Renaissance extended deep into the seventeenth century and are prepared to speak of an "English Renaissance" and "French Renaissance" in that century.

These historians have pondered a series of complex questions. What relationship did Renaissance "humanism" have, for example, with the Christian Scholasticism of the late Middle Ages? Is the dictum "without the Renaissance, no Reformation" really true? If a relatively small minority of Europeans could read as late as 1500, was the Renaissance experienced only by educated and economic elites? If so, did its literature exert any measurable influence on the lives of the mass of

Palazzo Vecchio.

296 *Firenze - Piazza Signoria*

Europeans who could neither read nor write? Was there a "Northern Renaissance" in France, the Low Countries, Germany, Hungary, Scandinavia, and England, distinct from a "Southern Renaissance"? Should the identification of historical periods be determined more by the ebb and flow of political and economic systems and by inventions such as gunpowder (beginning use in Europe about 1400) than by a set of innovations related to the arts, education, and religion?

II. THE RENAISSANCE: THE DISCOVERY OF THE WORLD AND THE DISCOVERY OF MAN?

"The Italian Renaissance must be called the mother of our modern age" (Jacob Burckhardt, *The Civilization of the Renaissance in Italy*).

Exorbitant claims about the impact of the Renaissance on the direction of Western civilization have fueled these discussions. In his multivolume *Histoire de France* (1833–67), the French historian Jules Michelet titled the seventh book *La Renaissance à la Révolution*. Michelet was apparently the first scholar to describe the period with the French word *Renaissance*, a derivative of the French verb *renaître*, meaning to be reborn. Michelet proposed the startling hypothesis that it was during the Renaissance that at least some Europeans made "the discovery of the world and the discovery of man."

A contemporary of Michelet, the Swiss historian Jacob Burckhardt (1818–97) reiterated these same themes in his own work, *The Civiliza-*

tion of the Renaissance in Italy (1860). In fact, Burckhardt quoted Michelet directly: "To the discovery of the outward world the civilization of the Renaissance added a still greater achievement, in that it was the first to discover and bring to light the full, whole nature of man." Burckhardt avowed that the Italian Renaissance broke with the Middle Ages and witnessed the beginnings of "modernity" by emphasizing a burgeoning individualism:

> In the Middle Ages ... Man was conscious of himself only as a member of a race, people, party, family or corporation—only through some general category. In Italy this veil first melted into air; an *objective* treatment and consideration of the state and of all the things of this world became possible. The *subjective* side at the same time asserted itself with corresponding emphasis; man became a spiritual *individual* and recognized himself as such.

According to Burckhardt, Renaissance Italians in particular shook off the collective dreamlike life of medieval Christianity to embrace a more secular individualism. Less committed to wistful, otherworldly Christian doctrine, talented writers, artists, and political figures viewed their interior beings and the world differently from those Europeans in other lands where religion still dominated.

A number of Italian writers such as Giovanni Boccaccio (1313–75; *The Decameron* and *On Famous Women*) and Baldassare Castiglione (1478–1529; *The Courtier*) began to promote the concept of a "perfect man" as an ideal for human existence rather than the ideal of a saint who seeks after holiness of life and a beatific vision. In *The Courtier*, Castiglione portrays the "universal man" as a person of worldly pursuits. He can as easily paint, sculpt, play a musical instrument, and with equal facility wield a sword or demonstrate remarkable dexterity in "noble sports." He studies the humanities, Greek and Latin, and literature. The courtier attempts to achieve excellence as a Christian gentleman and man-at-arms, whereas the lady at court is to manage her home life with wisdom and grace.

Burckhardt was a shrewd historian and a gifted essayist who had read extensively in primary sources. Indeed, many Italians made observations that seemed to justify his interpretation. Petrarch, often cited as the first "Renaissance man," had adopted the man-centered motto of Terence: "I am a man, and nothing human do I consider alien to myself." The Florentine leader Lorenzo de Medici indicated that "without Plato it would be hard to be a good Christian or a good citizen." Niccolò Machiavelli viewed the world of politics not through the prism of what rulers *ought* to do, based on Christian ethics, but on what rulers *actually* do in attempting to survive the vicissitudes of fortune.

Burckhardt knew that even if contemporaries did not use the word *Renaissance* to describe their era, a number such as Giorgio Vasari employed a parallel expression, the Italian *Rinascimento*, also signifying rebirth. Moreover, Matteo Palmieri announced that in his own day a new age had dawned, ushering in the rebirth of the arts and letters.

Palmieri's reading of his times was not an isolated one. The idea of a rebirth of letters and the arts after a long hiatus of cultural stagnation (eight hundred years according to Palmieri) can be discerned in the writings of Petrarch, Boccaccio, Bruni, and Coluccio Salutati. These thinkers believed that their age was recovering the beauty and wisdom of the arts, architecture, literature, moral philosophy, and languages of classical antiquity after a "Middle Ages" of cultural darkness. In the *Lives of Great Painters, Sculptors, and Architects* (1550), Georgio Vasari (1511–74) argued that some Christians had become so suspicious about pagan culture in the fourth and fifth centuries that they had smashed ancient sculptures.

This iconoclasm that destroyed much classical culture was stimulated by the Christians' association of the sculpture with the demonic worship of pagan gods. In one sense their hostile attitudes toward classical culture—or so thought Vasari—prepared the way for a period of alleged cultural stagnation. In the eighteenth century chronologists described this intervening era as "medieval."

According to Burckhardt, Italian scholars of the Renaissance became fascinated with classical antiquity. As they studied its literatures, arts, pagan ethics, and philosophies, they became anxious to shake off the hold of Christian medieval Scholasticism and distance themselves self-consciously from the Christian faith. Burckhardt observed, "And when, finally, classical antiquity with its men and institutions became an ideal of life, because it was the greatest Italian memory, ancient speculation and *skepticism* sometimes obtained a complete mastery over the minds of Italians."

In *Renaissance Thought: The Classic, Scholastic and Humanist Strains* (1955; 1961), Paul Oskar Kristeller (1905–99) revises Burckhardt on certain key points. He addresses the issue of whether the "humanism" of the Renaissance, recognized by historians as an essential defining component, had an inherently anti-Christian thrust. He argues that Renaissance humanism should not be related to any twentieth-century version of atheism or irreligion. Such would be an anachronistic interpretation. Instead, the concept of humanism should be linked to the word *humanista*, "coined at the height of the Renaissance period." This term was based on an older expression, *studia humanista*.

Because the curriculum that spread through a number of universities in the second half of the fifteenth century did not initially focus on theology, philosophy, or science, it did not assume either an inherent Christian or anti-Christian stance. Kristeller observes, "The view that the humanist movement was essentially pagan or anti-Christian cannot be sustained. It was successfully refuted by the humanists themselves when they defended their work and program against the charges of unfriendly theologians of their own time."

From the mid-twentieth century on, many scholars came to view Christianity in the Renaissance, not as a discredited faith, but as the dominant mode of thinking assumed by contemporaries from the fourteenth through sixteenth centuries. In 1990 art historian Timothy Verdon advanced the interpretation that Christianity's worldview so permeated the Renaissance that, if anything, humanism was superimposed on it.

The humanistic educational curriculum of the Renaissance, rather than being resolutely anti-Christian, was essentially religiously neutral, except for its emphasis on man's high moral character. It did provide, however, certain scholars with training in philology, the ancient languages Latin and Greek, and rhetoric in their quest to understand better the texts of Holy Scripture and to promote the Christian faith. These Christian humanists wanted to base their faith on the philological study of the texts of Scripture. Thus they began to do battle with other Christians, the "theologians" who used a "scholastic method." They accused "Scholastics" of founding their "school" theological systems on Aristotelian philosophy and rational deductions in syllogistic form. According to the Christian humanists, the Scholastics did not seem desirous of engaging in a philologically responsible exegesis of Holy Scripture.

The Renaissance—if we accept Kristeller's dating for it, 1300–1600—did not supersede the late Middle Ages in time. Instead, it overlapped both the late Middle Ages (dominated intellectually by schools of scholastic thought) and the Protestant Reformation. This helps explain why Luther believed a number of his contemporary foes were Scholastics, but understood simultaneously that some of his earliest partisans were humanists. Moreover, the Christian faith even in Italy continued to shape the thinking of many contemporaries, including the humanists of this period.

Those scholars and artists who demonstrated an enormous interest in and appreciation of pagan antiquity, whatever their personal beliefs and lifestyles, could not escape the pervasive influence of Christianity within European culture. Some humanists thought that a useful accommodation could be made between the study of classical pagan culture and the promotion of the Christian faith. Like Augustine, they believed that aspects of pagan culture such as the liberal arts, if used with circumspection, could be put to the service of the state and of

"The view that the humanist movement was essentially pagan or anti-Christian cannot be sustained" (P. O. Kristeller).

the church. These scholars included both Roman Catholics such as Petrarch, Salutati, and Erasmus, and later Protestants such as Ulrich Zwingli, John Calvin, and Philip Melancthon.

A. Petrarch: "The First Renaissance Man"?

Agreement concerning the precise dating of the inception of the Renaissance has been hard to come by. If a historian chooses the alleged appearance of "individualism" as a decisive marker, then the years surrounding 1300 might be selected. By contrast, if a historian designates as the Renaissance marker the emergence of city-state republicanism and "civic humanism" inspired by precedents from the Roman Republic, then the advent of a politically republican Florence in 1402 might be highlighted. Assuming civic responsibilities, citizens participated more fully in the governance of Florence. They were less inclined to accept the model of a "hierarchical" and "eternal" form of government such as existed in the Roman Empire in which one person, the emperor, ruled.

Then again, some historians might accept Vasari's judgment that Giotto (1267–1337) was the first painter to break away from medieval styles of painting. Giotto painted figures that appeared realistically life-like and rightly proportioned in his *Lamentation* (c. 1305), a fresco of the Arena Chapel of Padua. In the early fifteenth century in Florence a number of artists sharing a new understanding of perspective (putting a three-dimensional scene on a two-dimensional surface by using one or

Lorenzo Ghiberti's 3D artwork on the doors of the St. John Baptistery in Florence.

© David Parker/Alamy

The Tribute Money by Masaccio (Tommaso Guidi).

two "vanishing points") created breakthrough paintings, sculpture, and architecture: Masaccio's frescoes such as the *The Tribute Money* in the Church of Santa Maria del Carmine, Donatello's (1386–1466) *David* (the first freestanding bronze statue since antiquity), Filippo Brunelleschi's (1377–1446) geometrically based Dome of the Cathedral of Santa Maria del Fiore, and Lorenzo Ghiberti's (1378–1455) three-dimensional figures on the panels of the St. John Baptistery's doors. The use of linen paper and flaxseed oil in inks and paints enhanced printing and painting.

If the most notable trait of the Renaissance was the vogue of valorizing the authority of the Ancients, then Petrarch (Francesco Petrarca, 1304–74) merits the description "the first Renaissance man." Not only did Petrarch help create this vogue, but he devoted much time and effort in seeking to understand the ethics, views of history, and philosophy of one of the great Ancients, Cicero.

Even after finding Cicero's *Letters to Atticus* in Verona (1345)—through which he came to understand that the Roman rhetorician could be quite petty and a political schemer—Petrarch often championed Cicero's thought. Petrarch regarded Cicero, though a Stoic, as a worthy mentor for living. Moreover, in the *Invectives*, Petrarch argued against scholastic philosophy and medicine and for the thesis that Cicero's eloquent prose represented a sublime Latin style to imitate, in contrast to the medieval style of Latin. So-called "Ciceronian controversies" broke out between those scholars who esteemed Cicero's prose as *the* model for prose and those who preferred other styles of writing.

Petrarch often preferred to frequent the luminaries of antiquity rather than consort with his contemporaries. He penned *Letters to the Ancient Dead*, destined for Cicero, Horace, Virgil, and Livy. Like Machiavelli more than a century later, Petrarch on occasion dressed up in a Roman toga as he prepared to commune with the Ancients. He wanted to recover and extol the glories and nobility of spirit of these virtuous men who had lived in a civilization now lost.

Petrarch launched what became a major quest to find manuscripts of writers of antiquity, long forgotten in musty rooms of monasteries and churches throughout Europe. His prized personal library contained relatively few works from what he famously deemed the "Middle Ages," a time of "darkness and gloom." Instead, it consisted generally of copies of works by the church fathers and classical authors, made in the tenth through fourteenth centuries.

The huge tomes created by scholastic theologians did not greatly impress Petrarch. To him, many of their endless questions and their discussion of quibbles and quids appeared quite useless. History and philosophy should help people to live better. Indeed, philosophy should promote an art of living well. He was not convinced that scholastic tomes did this.

Petrarch's own earthly pilgrimage took many unexpected turns. His parents were Florentine and moved to a town near Avignon in 1312, toward the beginning of the Babylonian Captivity of the Church. For a time he studied law at the University of Montpellier and the University of Bologna. But in fact his great love was reading the Ancients.

Even as a young man, Petrarch pondered the fleeting character of life. As a cleric he struggled to justify his time-devouring study of the Ancients and his own prolific writing in Italian and Latin. His anguish of soul is revealed in a psychologically probing work, *The Secret* (1347–52), and in his correspondence with his brother about the horrific effects of the Black Death.

Several episodes in Petrarch's life demonstrate that despite his bouts of anguished self-reflection, he did not view this world simply as an antechamber to the next. He greatly appreciated this world's joys and its created order. He relates how at age twenty-three he attended a Good Friday service at Avignon's Sainte Claire church and caught a fleeting vision of a young woman named Laura. The vision of her loveliness would haunt him for the rest of his life. His naturalistic description of this woman distinguished Petrarch from many earlier commentators. He also commissioned the painter Simone Martini to make a portrait of Laura after she died—a painting that was perhaps the first secular portrait since antiquity. Yet Petrarch also owned a painting of the Madonna by Giotto.

In his notebook *The Secret*, Petrarch reveals the turmoil of his soul in an especially poignant fashion. He creates an engrossing dialogue between himself and Augustine, for whom he had great admiration and affection. He sees that Augustine's writing consistently defeats his best arguments and ploys. While Petrarch defends the innocence of his fascination for Laura, Augustine denies that his interest was so pure. Augustine adds, "... think how this woman has injured your soul, your body, and fortune." When Petrarch professes that his interest in classical scholarship is motivated by service to mankind, Augustine rebuffs this alibi: it is merely a ruse designed to cover Petrarch's pride in his scholarly attainments.

In one sense, if Petrarch experienced the "secularizing" tendencies of the Renaissance, they may have affected him far less through his study of the humanities per se than through his apparent reluctance to sift well pagan values, especially the Stoic teachings of Cicero and Seneca, to see if they countermanded Christian teachings. Instead, he apparently tried to hold contradictory beliefs in tension. This difficult task created within him a fractured mindset and led to much personal grief.

In 1374 Petrarch, a melancholic and troubled Christian scholar, the so-called "first Renaissance man," died at his desk with a pen in his hand. A distinguished Latinist and poet, he had apparently never fully reconciled his pursuit of the wisdom of the pagan Ancients with his desire to focus on the eternal state of his soul. His mind was troubled by the apparent competing counsel of his mentors Cicero and Augustine, although he felt "sure that Cicero himself would have been a Christian if he had been able to see Christ and to comprehend his doctrine." His passion for Laura made Petrarch wonder if he were a "good" Christian. Nor did he have full assurance that any scholar self-absorbed in his own literary career could serve God and neighbor in a faithful fashion.

Salutati, another of Petrarch's disciples, felt obliged to wrestle with a number of these same troubling issues.

B. Coluccio Salutati: Christianity and the Liberal Arts Conjoined

Later generations of humanists recognized Petrarch as their principal scholarly patron. Leonardo Bruni, a learned humanist of the fifteenth century, wrote, "... the honors of Petrarch were such that no man of his age was more highly esteemed than he, not only beyond the Alps, but in Italy itself." One indication of Petrarch's greatness was his noteworthy disciples, Coluccio Salutati and Giovanni Boccaccio.

The same year Petrarch died, Coluccio Salutati (1331–1406) arrived in the city of Florence, a center of the Italian Renaissance. The next year the urbane politician became the chancellor of Florence, a position he held until his death. A highly respected Latinist, Salutati built up a library of eight hundred manuscript books, a large collection by the standards of the day. The library included writings of the church fathers, a good sampling of medieval authors, and numerous copies of works by classical authors.

Undoubtedly, the writings of classical pagan authors such as Cicero, Horace, Ovid, Pliny the Younger, and Suetonius had been read during the Middle Ages. But by the mid-fourteenth century, Petrarch's enthusiasm for classical culture stimulated a genuine fascination in the writings of the Ancients. The burgeoning interest in pagan reading fare drew sharp criticism from a number of scholastic theologians. One cleric warned Boccaccio that his days were numbered if he continued to read the Ancients. With this in mind, Salutati decided to sell his library, only to have Petrarch dissuade him from taking this dramatic step.

Salutati, as chancellor, defended his deep interest in pagan literature by asserting that Christian rulers needed the insights of classical authors to be better statesmen. A Dominican, Giovanni Dominici (1356–1420), criticized Salutati's argument in a lengthy work titled *The Fire-Fly*. Dominici, a popular preacher, put in sharp relief the question of whether Christians should study pagan writings; he proposed that only those Christians who were well instructed in the faith could risk doing so. But as Salutati pointed out, many readers of Dominici's book thought the preacher had prohibited *any* reading of these works.

In his *Defense of the Liberal Arts*, Salutati responded to Dominici's criticisms. He indicated that his own appreciation for the Ancients had its limits. No matter how appealing and valuable the writings of an Aristotle or Plato might be, he would never forsake Christ to follow a pagan philosopher:

> Let the mob of philosophers run after Aristotle or Plato or the pestilent Averroes or any better man if there is one—never mind about their names! I am satisfied with Jesus Christ alone, who while learning flourished in Greece and Italy and while Italy was crushing everything at her pleasure by force of arms, "made foolish the wisdom of this world"—foolish, not through the wisdom of the wise nor the power of the strong, but through the foolishness of his preaching and his cross; through fisherman, not philosophers, through men of low estate, not those in worldly power.

At the same time, Salutati was determined to use pagan authors' writings selectively, given their many benefits. Those passages that helped reinforce the teachings of the church, he was prepared to exploit; those passages that subverted Christian doctrine, he was quick to eschew. Firm adherence to the Christian faith remained Salutati's chief objective.

Like Augustine, Salutati believed that the liberal arts—though invented by pagan thinkers—could well serve the interests of the church if used with care. Indeed, the study of the humanities was inextricably conjoined to the study of the Christian faith: "All studies in human affairs and in sacred subjects are bound together, and a knowledge of one subject is not possible without a sound and well-rounded education." Salutati's sturdy defense of the value of the liberal arts for the promotion of the Christian faith helped justify the enterprise of Christian humanism for some educators.

Salutati found another kind of serviceable justification for the study of antiquity during the agonizing siege of Florence by the tyrant Gian Galeazzo Visconti (1351–1402), the Duke of Milan. Toward 1390 Visconti decided to create an empire, but he first needed to subdue Florence. On May 1, 1390, he declared war on Florence and Bologna. As the war dragged on, a debate ensued over Visconti's claim that he was only attempting to restore the glories of the Roman Empire and that the Florentines were thwarting the realization of such a worthy project by their stubborn resistance.

Salutati defended the Florentines' recalcitrance in the name of something older than the Roman Empire—that is, the Roman Republic. In his Roman studies he discovered that Florence had been founded by some of Roman general Sulla's troops in the century before the Roman Empire began. He argued that Rome went into a period of declension during the empire, whereas it had reached its zenith during the days of the republic. The Florentines, encouraged by this rationale for resistance to those who favored an empire, took heart and called themselves the "New Romans." Salutati's study of the Ancients had provided rich propagandistic dividends, proving its definite political value. Visconti complained that Salutati's arguments did him more harm than a thousand cavalry.

The convergence of bad weather in 1399, a blockade of the city by Visconti, and a resurgence of the bubonic plague brought Florence to her knees in 1400. On some days as many as two hundred people died in misery. Yet Salutati continued to call upon the Florentines to muster their republican virtues and to refuse to give up. Rather dramatically, on August 13, 1402, Visconti fell ill. On September 3 he died. The siege was lifted. Dancing broke out in the streets of Florence. The psalm was sung, "Our bonds are broken and we are now free." A republican Florence was born, ushered into existence in part by Salutati's exploitation of pagan writings. Whereas interest in antiquity had been significant in the fourteenth century, now in the early fifteenth century it became something of a craze for certain manuscript hunters and collectors.

The city of Florence was refreshed with new cultural vitality after the disastrous years of 1399–1402. It was graced by painters like Massacio, the sculptor Donatello, and the architect Filippo Brunelleschi. In 1405 Bruni (1370–1444) wrote from the papal court at Viterbo about his longing to return to his native Florence. He was particularly impressed by the city's delights and devotion to humane letters:

> There flowed before my eyes the delights of Florence: the wealth of doctors, the exquisite and delicate foods.... There is no place in the world to compare with the splendor of Florence and the urbanity of the Florentines.

Salutati's efforts to demonstrate the value of studying the Ancients had triumphed. According to Bruni, who succeeded Salutati as the chancellor of Florence (1410–11; 1427–44), Florence had become the intellectual center for the study of the humane letters.

Later in the fifteenth century, members of the powerful Medici family, while curbing the participatory optimism of republican Florence through personal governing, nonetheless provided patronage to artists, architects, and humanists and helped to ensure Florence's role for a time as the epicenter of the Italian Renaissance. Cosimo de Medici the Elder (1389–1464) began to rule in 1434 and dominated the city's government until his death. When he died, he was honored as the "father of his country." Under his grandson, Lorenzo de Medici the Magnificent, Florence's reputation for literary studies, letters, and arts was enhanced even further. The correspondence of the poet Angelo Poliziano (1454–94) described the literary life of the city in considerable detail.

C. The Quest to Return to Original Manuscript Sources

Petrarch wanted to recover a purer Latin style in imitation of Cicero and other Ancients. Salutati shared a similar view, but emphasized the value of teaching drawn from both founts, Latin and Greek. The two scholars engaged in personal quests to recover lost manuscripts from antiquity. (In 1392 Salutati found a very important work of Cicero, *Letters to Familiar Ones*.) These scholars' quests helped foster a desire in humanists to return *ad fontes*, that is, to return to the manuscript sources of both pagan antiquity and Christianity. If scholars had in hand "lost originals" of pagan authors or of the New Testament in Greek, then they might come to a more adequate understanding of what Cicero or Paul had actually written. They would not be as dependent on faulty translations or corrupted copies of manuscripts. In fact, few "originals" from antiquity had survived the wearing effect of the passage of time. Nonetheless, the humanists were often recovering copies that more closely approximated the originals.

The quest to find "original manuscripts" (they were often copies) paid handsome literary dividends. It reached a new level when in 1394–95, Chrysoloras, an Eastern scholar from the court in Byzantium, came to the West seeking aid to fend off the Turks and Mongols. Two Florentines who had gone to study with him at Venice and later returned with him to Constantinople prompted Salutati to invite him to Florence. Chrysoloras accepted the offer, and between 1397 and 1400 he taught at the university in Florence and compiled a Greek grammar to help Italians learn Greek more easily.

Chrysoloras's promotion of Greek prompted the search for and restoration of many ancient Greek manuscripts in Byzantium. Chrysoloras eventually served in the court of Pope John XXIII from 1410 until his death in 1415.

Leonardo Bruni was one of Chrysoloras's students and later wrote not only a biography of Cicero but also the *History of the Florentine People*. Bruni has sometimes been hailed as the first modern historian.

Bracciolini Poggio (1380–1459) was perhaps the most successful manuscript hunter of the early fifteenth century. During the Council of Constance (1414–18), he traveled to various monasteries and churches on a quest to find lost manuscripts. His manuscript harvest was quite plentiful, including Cicero's orations at the monastery of Cluny in Burgundy, Asconius's *Commentaries on Five Speeches of Cicero* and various works of Quintilian in Saint Gall, and in France and Germany another eight speeches of Cicero.

Poggio's passion for classical culture prompted him to relate his discovery of manuscripts in dramatic terms. He described the location at Saint Gall where he found Quintilian's *The Training of an Orator* as "a most foul and dimly lighted dungeon at the bottom of a tower." Then he portrayed his discovery of the manuscript as if he had liberated Quintilian from a jail:

> I truly believe that, had we not come to the rescue, this man Quintilian must speedily have perished; for it cannot be imagined that a man magnificent, polished, elegant, urbane, and witty could much longer have endured the squalor of the prison-house in which I found him, the savagery of his gaoler, the forlorn filth of the place. He was indeed a sad sight: ragged, like a condemned criminal, with rough beard and matted hair, protesting by his expression and dress against the injustice of his sentence. He seemed to be stretching out his hands and calling upon the Romans, demanding to be saved from so undeserved a fate.

A "liberated Quintilian" (the manuscript) became the basis for even more emphasis on rhetoric in Renaissance schools.

Petrarch and Salutati had boosted Cicero's renown. Now Poggio's bounty of lost manuscripts allowed humanists to have an even more profound sense of Cicero's elegant prose, ideas about politics, education, and morality as well as Quintilian's masterful instruction regarding rhetoric. Cicero's and Quintilian's thought left a profound mark on Renaissance educational programs by proposing what curricula should be pursued if students were to emerge as worthy citizens or princes or rulers in a republican city-state.

On rare occasions, the manuscript hunters discovered writings of the Ancients copied as far back as the Carolingian Renaissance of the eighth and ninth centuries. More generally, their recovered manuscripts dated from the eleventh, twelfth, and thirteenth centuries. This accounts for the large number of manuscripts in the libraries of Petrarch and Salutati for those time periods. The goal of returning to the original sources stimulated an interest in philological and textual questions. Petrarch had engaged in philological studies. Guidelines for textual criticism remained quite rudimentary.

Whereas Christian Scholastics placed an emphasis on one segment of the trivium—dialectics, or the art of building an argument through citing authorities supporting it or drawing out a conclusion through syllogistic deductions—the humanists began to emphasize the two other elements of the trivium: grammar and rhetoric. Salutati recognized the importance of dialectics but also proposed that a student of divinity needed to understand grammar and the ancient languages of Scripture. In one sense, humanists began to part ways with Scholastics by accenting the latter two elements of the trivium at the expense of dialectics.

Tensions between scholastic theologians and humanists began to mount. By the time of the Protestant Reformation, they were often at each others' throats. Different appreciations of text criticism and the return to original sources, whether biblical or pagan, stoked the fires of these animosities.

D. Lorenzo Valla: Humanism and the Goodness of Man

These tensions were exacerbated by rationalistic humanists such as Lorenzo Valla (1407–57), who appeared to relish discrediting the authenticity of long-venerated documents of the Christian church. Quipped Valla, "I believe what Mother Church believes, even though she knows nothing." Indeed, Valla's controversial career provided a telling illustration to some scholastic theologians that critically minded humanists constituted a danger to the authority and orthodox teaching of the church.

To be sure, Boccacio's *Decameron*, written in the fourteenth century, had encompassed not only ribald tales but what could be reckoned as scurrilous attacks against the papacy. Yet Boccaccio was a complex personage who appreciated the spirituality of Dante more than had his mentor Petrarch. Boccaccio ended up his career as a monk. Valla, by contrast, early in his career published *On Pleasure* (1431; a later edition is titled *On the True God*), in which he lifted up pleasure as the goal of man's life, versus the teachings of Stoicism or certain views of Christianity. God had given man his appetites for pleasures, and they should be followed. For that matter, man is good and should enjoy what and who he is.

Valla's stance separated him from Christian teachers, who argued that certain instincts must be disciplined in order to achieve a virtuous life. Even though Valla believed in predestination and salvation by grace, his view of mankind (anthropology) represented a severe challenge to Augustinian perspectives regarding man's fallen moral state due to sin. Nonetheless, Valla's views were very much in line with the thinking of those Renaissance humanists who accented man's inherent goodness, worth, and dignity.

Valla portrayed himself as a sincere Christian and eventually worked as a papal secretary for Pope Nicholas V. His skills as a philologist and textual critic were impressive. He took a hefty swipe at "theologians" who did not pay sufficient attention to grammar or rhetoric:

> Some people deny that Theology is subject to the rules of grammar, but I say that theologians ought to obey the rules of a language, whether written or spoken. In fact, what is more stupid than to wish to corrupt the language you use and make yourself unintelligible to those whom you are addressing?

Valla was a gadfly who loved to pick a good literary fight. Whether vainglorious, brutally honest, or both, he irritated some contemporaries and won the praise of others. He was a superb Latinist and grammarian who believed reform of the educational curriculum of the liberal arts would come only if scholars knew well purer forms of Latin from antiquity rather than medieval Latin.

In *On the Falsely Believed and Lying Donation of Constantine*, Valla, deftly using his textual-critical skills, argued that the Donation of Constantine—which upheld the temporal authority of the papacy over the world—was in fact a "ridiculous forgery." The forger had given himself away by including a Byzantine expression like *satraps* or the anachronistic word *Huns* in the piece. Valla scoffed at the presence of

The Renaissance and the Christian Faith

the word *satraps* in the document: "Numbskull, blockhead! Do Caesars speak thus? Are Roman decrees usually drafted thus? Whoever heard of satraps being mentioned in the councils of the Romans?"

Valla even doubted that the Vulgate was edited by St. Jerome, given its allegedly poor quality as a translation into Latin. He contended that Jerome was too good a Greek scholar to have made such a flawed version. He proposed that the Vulgate's rendering of the Greek word *metanoia* for the Latin *poenitentia* (penance) was misleading. The word actually meant "repentance." Valla's observations challenged the biblical warrant for the Roman Catholic Church's sacrament of penance.

In a later generation, Erasmus looked back on Valla's writings with genuine but guarded admiration. He praised Valla's *On the Elegancies of the Latin Language* (1444) and cited his textual work of the New Testament as formative in his own thought. Erasmus observed, "Certainly I consider Valla deserving of the highest praise; he was a rhetorician more than a theologian, who had the diligence in treating of Sacred Scripture to compare the Greek with the Latin, although there are not many theologians who have read the Bible from cover to cover. Yet I disagree with him in a number of places, especially in those which have theological implications." Several Protestant Reformers also appreciated Valla's emphasis on the Greek text of the New Testament.

E. Marsilio Ficino: The Platonic Academy

A different kind of apology for man's dignity and worth was presented by the spiritualizing Florentine thinker Marsilio Ficino (1433–99). Cosimo de Medici had become enthralled by nightly lectures on Plato delivered by Gemisto Pletho, a Byzantine scholar who attended the Council of Florence (1439). In turn, Medici helped finance an effort by Ficino to found a Platonic academy.

In 1462 Ficino was given the Medici villa at Careggi as well as a collection of Greek manuscripts. The faithful gathered at the villa to do homage to Plato, especially on his birthday. They sang songs in the philosopher's honor and saluted each other with the phrase "Salvation in Plato." With a profound knowledge of Greek, Ficino translated the bulk of Plato's dialogues into Latin and thereby introduced many Western scholars to this major Greek philosopher. The completed works were published in Venice by the Aldine Press (1477).

Ficino's own reading of Plato was heavily indebted to the interpretations of Plotinus, a third-century thinker. Indeed, Ficino translated many of Plotinus's writings into Latin. Following Pletho's argument, Ficino argued that a *prisca sapientia*, or pagan wisdom, had been transmitted to Plato, whose teachings thereafter were later validated by the

Christian Scriptures. Hermes Trismegistus of Egypt was the ultimate originator of this pious philosophy.

Toward 1463 some of Hermes's writings had been found in Macedonia. Ficino translated these documents (*Corpus Hermeticum*) and became convinced that they represented a "single, internally consistent, primal theology" (*prisca theologica*) and that Hermes was the "father of all theology." Ficino and his disciples believed grandiosely that they stood in this same eclectic tradition that stretched back to Plato and Pythagoras and beyond and included strains of Byzantine and Arabic thought, magic, and the occult. As noted, Ficino claimed that a unity of thought (a primal theology) undergirds these otherwise disparate intellectual traditions.

Ficino became a Catholic priest in 1473. He thought that his admixture of Platonism with Christianity would create a bulwark against skepticism. In fact, he wrote a work titled *Platonic Theology* (1469–74), in which he argued that the backing of Platonic philosophy makes Christianity rational. Ficino proposed that man's spirit is the link between his body and soul. Through magic one can control nature; through astrology one can know the future. The goal of existence is for the soul through contemplation to ascend or return from the lowliness of human existence to the source of all being and ultimate good, namely, God.

Ficino also argued strongly for the immortality of the soul against the Averroists' arguments. Despite a mystic sense that man's soul needed to escape the confines of the physical body, Ficino's thought did reinforce the value of human existence. Professor Kristeller observed, "Assigning to the human soul the central place in the hierarchy of the universe, he [Ficino] gave a metaphysical expression to a notion dear to his humanist predecessors; whereas his doctrine of spiritual love in Plato's sense, for which he coined the term 'Platonic love,' became one of the popular concepts of later Renaissance literature."

F. Pico della Mirandola: On the Dignity of Man

Ambitious, prodigiously brilliant, with stunning good looks, Giovanni Pico della Mirandola (1463–94) rocked the academic world when at the young age of twenty-four he published nine hundred theses, inviting any scholar to debate them with him. At the time, according to his nephew's estimate, Pico was "full of pride and desirous of glory." In the theses he cited as authorities Plato, the Kabbalists (he collected Hebrew documents), Mohammed, Paul, Moses, Hermes Trismegistus, and Zoroaster among others.

Pope Innocent XIII condemned thirteen of the theses and remarked that Pico "wants someone to burn him some day." Pico responded by writing a defense of the theses, only to have the pope condemn all nine hundred of them. Pico felt forced to leave Italy. After a brief stay in prison in France, Pico came back to Florence. Like Boethius (480–c. 525) before him, among other tasks Pico attempted to reconcile the teachings of Aristotle and Plato. He renounced some of his froward ways under the influence of Savanarola and died in 1494, only thirty-one years of age.

Pico is best known for his work *On the Dignity of Man* (1486, the title appended posthumously). It constituted the introduction to his nine hundred theses. Owing to the contents of this work, Pico is often portrayed as having elevated man's dignity in this world to remarkable heights and therefore had secularist tendencies. He acknowledged that he had written in a daring fashion:

> There are those who do not indeed disapprove this kind of practice, but who in no wise approve it in me because I, born I admit but twenty-four years ago, should have dared at my age to offer a disputation concerning the lofty mysterys of Christian theology, the highest topics of philosophy and unfamiliar branches of knowledge, in so famous a city, before so great an assembly of very learned men, in the presence of the apostolic senate.

He argued strongly that human beings have free will. Taken in isolation, a number of his comments about man's dignity appear as harbingers of a "this-worldly" secularism.

A closer examination of Pico's thought, however, suggests that, despite remarkably syncretistic elements, it was more generally couched in a heterodox Christian and Neoplatonic framework. Pico belonged to the Platonic Academy in Florence. After celebrating natural philosophy's powers, Pico argued that "a true and unshaken peace" comes uniquely from her mistress, the "holiest theology." Harmony among peoples will emerge only as their minds "come into harmony in the one mind which is above all minds." He hoped that every soul would become

> the house of God, and to the end that as soon as she has cast out her uncleanness through moral philosophy and dialectic, adorned herself with manifold philosophy as with the splendor of a courtier, and crowned the pediments of her doors with the garlands of theology, the King of Glory may descend and, coming with his Father, make his stay with her.

In other works, including the *Disputations Against Astrology* and the *Heptaplus*, Pico argued that Christianity is superior to astrology, magic, and hermetic and cabalistic forms of religion. He advocated the pursuit of Christian disciplines: "Surely our zeal ought to be so turned toward higher things that we seek strength for our weakness through holy religion, through sacred rites, through vows, and through hymns, prayers, and supplications." Nonetheless, Pico's Christianity lacked a distinct view of the effects of the Fall and seemed to emphasize rational reflection and philosophy as a means to salvation rather than the uniqueness of Christ's redemptive work.

Undoubtedly, Valla, Ficino, and Mirandola did not give unqualified acceptance to certain teachings of the church. Their syncretistic perspectives differed not only from theologians of various stripes but in varying degrees from each other. At the same time, whatever their ultimate motivations and secret thoughts, it is clear they presented their scholarship as being concordant with the Christian religion. To convert their admittedly controversial thought into an atheistic humanism does not appear warranted. Their writings do help us to understand more fully the reasons Jacob Burckhardt could argue that the dignity of man constituted a major theme of the Renaissance.

G. Humanistic Studies

Besides Petrarch and Salutati, other writers and teachers contributed to the advance of humanism in various towns of Italy and eventually in northern Europe. Their writings were flavored with varying combinations of Christian and pagan elements.

As noted earlier, Petrarch's disciple, Boccaccio, authored *The Decameron*. This piece of a seemingly secular orientation was composed of a hundred tales, grouped in tens. A number of refugees were holed up in a villa outside Florence, attempting to escape the plague in the city. They often recounted racy stories to pass the time. Scandalous clerics and ladies of easy virtue peopled these tales. Little wonder that *The Decameron* did not find its way into the curriculum of pre-university schools. For that matter, neither did the writings of Petrarch.

The *studia humanitatis* did gain an entrance into a number of Italian schools as an alternative to medieval curricula. According to historian Craig Kallendorf, medieval scholastic schools stressed "practical, pre-professional, and scientific studies; it prepared men to be doctors, lawyers, or professional theologians and taught primarily from approved textbooks in logic, natural philosophy, medicine, law, and theology." By contrast, humanists argued that the study of the liberal arts was indispensable for a life of civic service. For example, how could one be a successful prince, politician, theologian, or citizen without having studied rhetoric?

In 1416 Bracciolini Poggio's discovery of a copy of Quintilian's *Institutio Oratoria* provided schoolmasters with insights regarding the nature of their instruction in rhetoric. Other works from antiquity became the basis for reshaping the liberal arts.

Historian Paul F. Grendler has observed,

> Renaissance schools sought to teach practical skills for different social roles. Latin schools taught the Latin that enabled students to go on to university studies and prepared them for careers in the civil service, the church, or the highest ranks of society, where a knowledge of Latin was expected. Vernacular schools taught the essential commercial skills of reading, writing, and bookkeeping.

According to Grendler, both kinds of schools "attempted to instill personal and social values based on classical and Christian sources and standards."

Nor did most Renaissance educators apparently sense that their interest in the writings of the Ancients compromised loyalty to the Christian faith. For example, in *The Education of Boys*, Aeneas Silvius Piccolomini (the future Pope Pius II) drew up a plan of education for boys heavily dependent on the thought of Ancients such as Quintilian, Plutarch, Plato, and Socrates.

In his *The Study of Literature*, Leonardo Bruni not only recommended to Lady Battista Malatesta of Montelfeltro the Christian writers Lactantius Firmianus, Augustine, Jerome, Ambrose, and Cyprian among others, but also proposed that if she enjoyed "secular literature," she should read the writings of Cicero, Vergil, Livy, Sallust, and other writers of antiquity. In advance, Bruni attempted to fend off opponents of his educational program: " 'I am a Christian,' my critic says. But are you suggesting that they [the Ancients] lived without morality? As though honor and moral seriousness were something different then from what they are now! As though the same and even worse cannot be found in the Holy Scriptures!"

Italian school curricula became models of education to emulate and modify in northern Europe, especially in the second half of the fifteenth century. Italian universities in Florence, Rome, Pavia, Arezzo, and Perugia had notable humanist scholars. As late as the eighteenth century many a young scholar from northern European believed that a trip to Italy was a prerequisite experience if one were to be truly educated. This was an intellectual pilgrimage not to miss. How could we be scholars if we have not tasted of the glories of Florence or Rome? Preceptors, or teachers, often accompanied their young charges on trips to see the ruins of antiquity in Rome and to bask in the cultural riches of other cities of the Italian peninsula.

"Humanists" served as teachers in Latin schools and as diplomats, civic leaders, secretaries of princes, printers, and clerics, among other professions. Numerous Benedictines and Cistercians pursued humanist studies in monasteries in Germany. The appeal of studying antiquity, whether Christian or pagan, remained powerful for centuries to come for educated Europeans.

H. The Renaissance: Critics and Partisans

The spread of the Renaissance did not take place without opposition. As we saw, a number of so-called Scholastics entered into pitched battles with "Christian" humanists. Historian Eugene Rice has aptly described the clashing approaches of the two parties:

> The scholastics sought to make theology a science, a *scientia* in the Aristotelian sense, that is, to establish a systematically ordered body of true and certain knowledge derived from the certain but undemonstrable principles of revelation. This effort, too, humanists typically attacked as misguided, arrogant, and dangerous because it produced only sophistry, arid intellectualism, emotional poverty and lack of charity. The learned and eloquent piety of the fathers, in contrast, was not a science but a positive wisdom, a holy rhetoric derived from the holy page of Scripture.

The struggle between the parties could be intense. At the same time, some humanist-leaning scholars such as Jacobus Faber appreciated Aristotelian thought, believing that in its proper expression the philosophy was fully compatible with Christianity.

A different kind of opposition to the Renaissance emerged in Florence itself. During the 1490s, Girolamo Savonarola (1452–98), a fiery preacher and reformer, temporarily gained political and spiritual ascendancy in Florence. Advocating a demanding set of ethics, the priest attempted to rid townspeople of their materialistic and sensual cravings. He urged young men to seek out and burn "vanities," provocative clothing, ornaments, and secular paintings—items that were apparently diverting local citizens from their devotion to God. Savonarola did not oppose all artistic creations, but he did enjoin patrons of the arts to withhold their support for the creation of any religious painting that failed to capture the interior spirituality of its subject, whether a biblical figure or a saint: " … the body is more beautiful that houses a beautiful soul."

The famous painter Sandro Botticelli (1445–1510) changed his painting style due to the priest's injunctions. Savonarola also criticized the classical authorities Plato and Aristotle: "For those who drag the

The burning of
Savonarola.

"For those
who drag the
ancient philo-
sophers into
our Academy
easily deceive
themselves or
cause others to
be deceived. For
Plato taught
insolence of
spirit, and
Aristotle,
impiety"
(Savonarola).

ancient philosophers into our Academy easily either deceive themselves or cause others to be deceived. For Plato taught insolence of
spirit, and Aristotle, impiety."

In 1498 the Florentines turned on Savonarola, and the pope
excommunicated him. Savonarola was executed by hanging, his body
consumed by fire on a pyre in the Piazza della Signoria.

With the return to Florence of Leonardo Da Vinci (1452–1519)
in 1500 and Michelangelo in 1501, sculpting and paintings that often
mingled Christian and classical themes slowly began to flourish again
(for example, Michelangelo's sculpture of *David* [1504]). In Rome,
Renaissance humanism prospered among certain members of the papal
court.

III. THE "NORTHERN RENAISSANCE"

Outside the borders of the Italian states, the Renaissance continued
to spread to northern Europe. Germany, France, England, the Netherlands, Hungary, and other countries began to experience their own
rebirths, often adding distinctive traits. Sometimes Italian ideas, motifs,

and styles were simply imported and left unmodified; sometimes they were reworked or in time rejected by northern scholars and artists.

Painters such as Jan van Eyck (*Giovanni Arnolfini and His Bride*, 1434), Albrecht Dürer (self-portrait, 1500), and Hans Holbein the Younger (*Portrait of Sir Thomas More*, 1527) achieved great renown. Johannes Gutenberg of Mainz, Germany, introduced moveable type printing (1439) and the printing press (1440). He published the Gutenberg Bible (1450–55).

The advent of printing, a change agent, made it difficult to stop the diffusion of Renaissance ideas. Publishers such as the Frobens in Basel, Aldus Manutius in Venice, and Christopher Plantin in Antwerp created a dazzling array of new editions of classical texts as well as vernacular versions of the Bible.

Many French, Germans, Dutch, and others traveled to Italy in the entourage of princes and kings, on business, as tourists, as soldiers, or as students. They brought back to their homelands knowledge of different aspects of Italian Renaissance culture, whether originating in Venice, Bologna, Naples, Florence, Padua, Rome, or elsewhere.

According to Erasmus, Rudolf Agricola (1444–95) was the first scholar to bring Italian humanism across the Alps to northern Europe. Agricola fostered interest in the humanities in Heidelberg, Germany. Whereas a number of German universities were founded for traditional scholastic purposes—such as Basel, Freiburg, Ingolstadt, Mainz, and Tübingen—the universities of Wittenberg (1502) and Frankfurt-on-the-Oder (1506) were

A Gutenberg Bible opened to the beginning of the gospel of Luke.

more hospitable to humanists, as was Marburg (1527), the first Lutheran university.

Guillaume Budé (1468–1540), serving as the librarian for King Francis I, helped introduce Christian humanism to France, a kingdom that appeared on the brink of political and economic greatness. In 1453 the French had driven the English from the kingdom. Over the next thirty-eight years the crown added the large provinces of Gascony, Provence, Burgundy, and Britanny. Budé, the leading Greek scholar of France, established the College of Royal Lecturers, where the study of classical texts and Scripture was encouraged. He also wrote *Commentaries on the Greek Language* (1529), a lexicographical thesaurus.

In the last decades of the fifteenth century, Italian traders complained that some customers were now looking north for their purchases, thinking the skills of German gold and silver artisans had surpassed those of Italians. By contrast, there were northerners who looked south and searched out the artistic production of Italian architects, painters, and sculptors. In the 1460s King Mattias Corvinas of Hungary constructed several residences in an Italian, Renaissance-style of architecture. The king had hired an Italian architect and imported Italian sculpture. In the 1470s the king of Poland likewise funded architectural work in a Renaissance style. Northern cities such as Bruges ("the Venice of the North"), Antwerp, and Augsburg also became renowned for their Renaissance art and architecture.

Northern "Christian humanism" often accented the Bible's authority and the imitation of Christ's life and ethical teachings in daily living. In the Netherlands, Master Geerte Grote (1340–84) initially came under the influence of the mysticism and sacramental teachings of John Ruysbroeck. For his part, Grote, with his colleague Forentius Radewijns, emphasized interior spirituality and devotion to Christ, but likewise the value of the use of logic and reason. Grote established the Brethren of the Common Life—a lay order (that is, no formal monastic vows) whose members provided education for many of the young in northwestern Europe. Grote also established Sisters of the Common Life—an order of women who lived in community but also participated in the outside day-to-day life of Deventer.

Thomas à Kempis, who lived in a monastery of the *Devotio Moderna* in Windesheim, published *The Imitation of Christ*, a classic of Christian devotion. It winsomely summarized much of the spiritual teaching of the Brethren movement. Historian Steven Ozment contends that the Brothers were like humanists in the sense that they sought to eliminate textual corruptions from their liturgies, the Vulgate, and the writings of the church fathers. Like later Protestants, they also gave Holy Scripture a prominent role in shaping their own spirituality. Their works of

Devotio Moderna (1380–1430) penetrated the Hapsburg Lowlands and Spain among other regions.

Many Catholic scholars continued to retain a great interest in classical culture while simultaneously studying the church fathers and Scripture, especially the Greek New Testament. In Spain, Francisco Jimenez (Ximenez) de Cisneros (1436–1517), a Franciscan, established the University of Alcala. Appreciative of evangelical spirituality, he helped create the Complutensian Polyglot Bible in six volumes (published by the University of Complutum, 1521). It included the Hebrew Bible (vols. 1–4) and the Greek New Testament (vol. 5) along with Jerome's Vulgate, the Greek Septuagint, and Latin and Aramaic translations.

In France, a number of scholars pursued or supported humanistic and biblical studies, including Guillaume Briçonnet, Marguerite of Navarre (sister of King Francis I), and most notably Jacobus Faber (Lefèvre d'Étaples or Stapulensis; 1455–1536). Although remaining Catholics, they arrived at "reforming" beliefs somewhat similar to those of early evangelical Protestants (although Faber became critical of evangelicals).

Faber's Bible study led the distinguished professor of philosophy to abandon a belief in purgatory and emphasize Christ's redemptive death on the cross as the basis for our salvation. We do not earn it through "good works," although "whoever performs good works, whether he has and knows the Law or not, will not lack for God's reward." An ardent proponent of a "humanist Aristotlelianism," then later a proponent of Neoplatonism, the professor argued against Scholastics who portrayed theology as a science. Rather, he believed theology constituted a form of wisdom based on Scripture.

In 1518 Faber's patron, Briçonnet, became the bishop of Meaux. In 1521 the bishop enlisted Faber, along with Guillaume (William) Farel, Girard Roussel, and others, to help him reform the diocese. They instituted the regular preaching of the Gospels and Paul's writings. Faber translated the New Testament into French so that "the simplest members of the body of Jesus Christ can be as certain of the Gospel's truth as those who have it in Latin."

By 1523 Franciscans, the Sorbonne, and the *Parlement* of Paris feared that the "Meaux circle" was affected by Luther's "heresy." In 1524 Matthieu Saulnier and Jacques Pauvant of Meaux were arrested for suspected anti-Catholic activities. In 1525 the *Parlement* of Paris requested Faber to appear before it; instead, he sought refuge in Strasbourg. In 1526 King Francis I asked the distinguished scholar to return to France to serve as a royal librarian at Blois and as the tutor for his children. Faber accepted the invitation. On August 26, 1526, the prisoner Pauvant was put to death.

"I long for the ploughboy to sing them [the words of Scripture] to himself as he follows the plough, the weaver to hum them to the tune of his shuttle, the traveler to beguile with them the dullness of the journey" (Desiderius Erasmus).

A. Erasmus and Paracelsus: On the Brink of the Reformation

The brilliant and witty Dutchman Desiderius Erasmus (1469–1536) demonstrated a dual interest in humanistic and biblical studies. Trained at the Latin School of Deventer (1478–83), he lived at a hostel of the Brethren of the Common Life in 1485–87. While in a monastery, he read deeply the writings of St. Jerome, classical authors, and Lorenzo Valla. In his *Adages* and *In Praise of Folly*, Erasmus displayed a breathtaking knowledge of classical sources. He called Christians to a "learned piety"—that is, "scriptural, practical, and theologically serious" (per historian Philip Benedict's description). In living out their faith, believers were to emulate the "philosophy of Jesus"—that is, Christ's ethical teachings and example of self-sacrifice.

John Colet (1467–1519), an English Catholic humanist, speculated that it was Erasmus's work in New Testament studies that would "make his name immortal." Erasmus carefully constructed a much-improved edition of the Greek New Testament—the *Novum Instrumentum* (March 1516). In the introduction to *Annotations* (1519), Erasmus explained his scholarly humanist approach:

> I have taken what they call the New Testament and revised it, with all the diligence I could muster and all the accuracy that was appropriate, checking it in the first instance against the true Greek text. For that is, as it were, the fountain-head to which we are not only encouraged to have recourse in any difficulty by the example of eminent divines, but frequently advised to do so by Jerome and Augustine, and so instructed by the actual decrees of the Roman pontiffs. Second, I checked it against the tradition of very ancient copies of the Latin version.

Erasmus hoped his text would become the basis for more accurate translations of the New Testament into vernacular languages. He believed that Scripture reveals "the living image of [Christ's] holy mind and of Christ himself speaking, healing, dying and rising...."

William Tyndale (c. 1494–1536), an admirer of Wycliffe, Erasmus, and Luther, created the first printed English translation of the New Testament (1525–26) and portions of the Old Testament. For his efforts, Tyndale was betrayed, imprisoned, strangled, and burned at the stake.

Luther used Erasmus's edition as the basis for his translation of the New Testament into German. Initially, Erasmus thought Luther's "reforming" concerns were quite similar to his own. Nonetheless, he could not ultimately countenance Luther's willingness to break with the Catholic Church. In the mid-1520s Erasmus debated the Protestant Reformer regarding the issue of the freedom or bondage of the will. The debate revealed rather clearly that the two men had

Desiderius Erasmus.

different perceptions of the Fall's effect on our wills. Luther defended the bondage of the will.

In England, the learned Catholic scholars Colet, the dean of St. Paul's Cathedral, and Sir Thomas More (1478–1535), author of *The Utopia*, also pursued humanistic and biblical studies. In fact, both men had helped stimulate Erasmus's growing interest in studying Scripture during his first trip to England (1499–1500). Erasmus was very appreciative of Colet's piety. He developed a long-standing friendship with More, who defended him against detractors.

A number of notable Christian humanists became Protestants. They included Melanchthon, Zwingli, Calvin, Martin Bucer, and Conrad Grebel, an early Anabaptist. The study of Scripture in the original languages contributed to their evangelical conversions to Protestantism. Yet they did not turn their back on humanistic studies after they became Protestants.

In 1518 Melanchthon, Luther's associate, gave an inaugural address at the University of Wittenberg, titled "On Improving the Studies of Youth," in which he extolled a revival of letters as a component

AN INVENTION "ORDAINED BY GOD"

Protestants often viewed the printing press as an invention God ordained for the greater propagation of the gospel and the Bible and as a useful weapon to be deployed for the defeat of Roman Catholicism. In his *Address to the Estates of the Empire* (1542), the German historian Johann Sleidan wrote, "As if to offer proof that God has chosen us to accomplish a special mission, there was invented in our land a marvelous new and subtle art, the art of printing." A segment of Foxe's *Book of Martyrs* reads:

"The Lord began to work for His Church not with sword and target to subdue His exalted adversary, but with printing, writing and reading.... How many presses there be in the world, so many block-houses there be against the high castle of St. Angelo, so that either the pope must abolish knowledge and printing or printing must at length root him out."

"A city's best and greatest welfare, safety, and strength consist rather in its having many able, learned, wise, honorable, and well-educated citizens" (Martin Luther).

of a humanist curriculum. In 1526 Zwingli of Zürich wrote, "For what else brings greater benefits to the whole human race than letters? No art, no work, not, by Hercules, the very fruits born of the earth, not, finally this sun, which many have believed is the author of life, is as necessary as the knowledge of letters."

Calvin, who was well trained in the classics, made extensive allusions to pagan sources in his *Institutes of the Christian Religion* (1536, first edition). He approved the import of a number of statements by classical authors while criticizing other assertions they made. He apparently based his assessments of a particular passage by whether or not it conformed to the teachings of Holy Scripture.

As for Luther, he regretted that he had received a scholastic education as a young person: "I was compelled to read the devil's rubbish, the scholastic philosophers and sophists with such cost, labor and detriment, from which I have had trouble enough to rid myself." Thereafter he became an advocate of a humanist education. He went so far as to claim that the recovery of Greek permitted scholars of the sixteenth century to understand Holy Scripture better than many church fathers did. Luther averred that certain Latin church fathers, for example, made errors in their theologies because they did not know Greek sufficiently well.

In *To the Councilmen of All Cities in Germany That They Establish and Maintain Christian Schools* (1524), Luther indicated that "a city's best and greatest welfare, safety, and strength consist rather in its having many able, learned, wise, honorable, and well-educated citizens." To train such citizens, he recommended they receive a classical liberal arts education and instruction in Hebrew and Greek so that they could study Holy Scripture with diligence. With this education in hand, students would be well prepared to assume their role as competent Christian citizens to serve the church and state.

In 1545 Conrad Gesner published *Bibliotheca Universalis*, which referenced 10,000 volumes and 3,000 authors. Gesner, the "father of bibliography," had harvested these titles and authors from the catalogues of publishers and booksellers. Many of these works were in Latin, Greek, and Hebrew and represented the continuing interest of scholars in classical and biblical culture. Gesner was also a distinguished botanist.

The Swiss Paracelsus (1493–1541)—Theophrastus Bombastus von Hohenheim—was much influenced by Ficino, Pico, and the Hermetic tradition. A proud man, Bombastus chose the name "Paracelsus"—"beyond Celsus"—to flaunt his supposed superiority over the famous ancient physician Celsus.

Paracelsus sometimes turned his back on the authority of antiquity in other ways. For example, he burned the medical works of Avicenna and Galen. An alchemist, physician, astronomer, and Catholic theologian, he argued that below the four elements of earth, fire, air, and water could be found the *tria prima*, more basic materials: salt, sulfur, and mercury. Whereas Christ provided healing for sins, Paracelsus thought he could use alchemy to help people find healing for their physical ailments. In *Nine Books of Archidoxus* he revealed secret remedies for various ailments. He urged that an alchemist needed to be a virtuous person.

After experiencing a spiritual conversion, Paracelsus sold his belongings. An enigmatic man, he could evidence considerable compassion for people. At the same time, he could verbally quarter his enemies, who deemed him a fraud or quack: "Let me tell you this: every little hair on my neck knows more than you and all your scribes." The influence of Paracelsus on the emergence of early modern science is not negligible.

B. Christian Hebraism

After 1450 a movement of Christian Hebraism emerged. Some Christians and Jews entertained amicable contacts despite the polemics, intolerance, and hatred that more generally poisoned relations between their respective communities.

The Christian Hebraists, who included both men and women, ranged from clerics to physicians to philosophers and scientists. They surmised that knowledge of Hebrew would permit them to read the original Hebrew of the Old Testament, the *Talmud*, the Kabbalah, and other Jewish literature. These Christians often learned Hebrew from Jewish acquaintances who were experts in grammar. For example, for ten years Elia Levita (1469–1549), a Jewish grammarian, lived in quarters of Cardinal Egidio da Viterbo, a humanist patron and reform-minded Catholic theologian. Levita instructed the cardinal in Hebrew. He also copied Hebrew manuscripts, especially those treating the Kabbalah. Viterbo was fascinated by the mysteries of the Kabbalah. He also became adept in reading the *Talmud*.

Johann Reuchlin (1455–1522) learned about Kabbalah from Pico della Mirandola and was intrigued. He recommended the philological study of Hebrew in the *Wonder Working Word* (1484) and created the first Hebrew grammar and lexicon, *De Rudimentis Hebraicis* (1506; built on the work of David Kimhi). He hoped to reform preaching.

Backed by the emperor's authority, Johann Pfefferkorn (1469–1523), a Jewish Christian convert, sought to confiscate and destroy the Hebrew books of Jews in Cologne and Frankfurt. By contrast, in 1510 Reuchlin counseled an imperial commission to limit the seizure to the few Jewish books that blasphemed Christ. Pfefferkorn accused Reuchlin of being pro-Jewish.

In 1511 a significant controversy erupted that pitted various academic faculties, the Dominicans, and writers like Ulrich von Hutten against each other. In 1513 Reuchlin was brought before the Inquisition and later appeared in various courts. He was finally exculpated of guilt in 1520. Pfefferkorn confessed a desire to win his own salvation and prove he was a faithful Catholic by attacking Jews and Reuchlin. Flagrant anti-Semitism and academic competition fueled the Reuchlin Affair.

In 1517–18 a chair in Greek and a chair in Hebrew were established at the University of Wittenberg. In 1518 Melanchthon, whose great-uncle was Reuchlin, became the professor of Greek. The chair in Hebrew was filled in 1523. The study of Hebrew in universities was becoming more widespread. In 1520 a chair in Hebrew had been instituted at the Sorbonne, Paris. Later, Christian Hebraists such as Johann Buxtorf (1564–1623) became noteworthy specialists in the *Targum* and the *Talmud* and the history of the Jews.

The movement dwindled greatly by the early nineteenth century but has seen some resurgence since the latter decades of that century.

IV. RENAISSANCE MEN AND WOMEN

"Don't be born a woman if you want your own way," shrewdly observed Nannina de Medici of Florence (1447–93) in a letter to

Lorenzo the Magnificent, her brother. During the Renaissance, men generally exercised extensive power over the lives of women; this made it difficult for women to control their own ways. The Roman Catholic clergy were male and administered the sacraments. Husbands demanded obedience and a humble spirit from their wives. The best educational opportunities were reserved for men. Nannina de Medici, a person of high social station and wealth, understood the difficulty women faced in attempting to live independently in Florence.

In certain high-society circles of Italian city-states, both men and women esteemed the ideal of a "Renaissance man," or *Uomo universale*. Such a person displayed remarkable intellectual, artistic, and physical gifts. In the service of his prince, he performed mighty deeds with non-chalance, poise, and grace. He was to be wellborn, physically strong, and good-looking. According to Baldassare Castiglione, he was not to be "womanish in his sayings or doings." He should not be a liar or flatterer. He should be wise and possess an upright conscience. He should speak and write well. He should know Italian, French, and Spanish. He should have the capacity to wield "all kinds of weapons." He should be able to swim and wrestle. He should know how to draw and paint and dance and play the lute and sing. This omnicompetent Renaissance man was indeed an accomplished person.

Ladies in European courts sometimes evidenced an admirable interest in the arts and letters. Some women exercised considerable influence over the affairs of state. More generally, however, women from the lower classes were excluded from the artistic endeavors and educational opportunities associated with the Renaissance and excluded from access to levers of political power. If married, they were to submit to their husbands' wishes. Law codes often gave husbands the right to beat their wives with impunity.

In France, if a woman committed adultery, she could be killed by her husband. If a woman had a child out of wedlock, she was often shunned by her community. One of the central tasks of women was to bear children and raise them. At serious risk to their health, women often had one child after another. Many children died at birth or in the first years of life. Wet nurses often cared for the children of wealthy women.

Families from the upper classes assumed the responsibilities of keeping their daughters chaste and providing a significant dowry for them. If daughters had no dowries, they were frequently constrained to enter convents and become nuns. Poor women, even if married, frequently had no choice but to be servants or work in the fields. They received much less pay than their male counterparts for equal work. In urban areas women did work in a variety of jobs.

During the Renaissance, a number of women attempted to challenge the patriarchal nature of their societies. Italian-born Christine de Pizan (c. 1364–c. 1430) earned her living as a writer in France, one of the first women to do so. Among other works, she penned *Letter to the God of Love* (1399), *The Tale of the Rose* (1402), and *The Book of the City of the Ladies* (1405). Laura Cereta (1469–99) from Italy, while appreciating the opportunities some women of the upper classes had to receive a good education, criticized men for thinking that women could not be as equally brilliant as they. "Nature has generously lavished its gifts upon all people, opening to all the doors of choice through which reason sends envoys to the will, from which they learn and convey its desires." Those women who challenged the male domination of Renaissance society encountered considerable opposition.

"Nature has generously lavished its gifts upon all people, opening to all the doors of choice" (Laura Cereta).

Even proponents of greater educational opportunities for women sometimes restricted what forms of education should be made available to them. For example, Juan Vives, a Spanish humanist and author of *Instruction of a Christian Woman* (1523), noted that the education of women was "a subject that [had] yet to be treated." Although he favored education for girls, wives, and widows, he wanted them to concentrate on domestic duties, not on basic skills such as reading and writing. Nor did he favor their receiving the same education as men: "Men must do many things in the world and must be broadly educated; but only a little learning is required of women."

Earlier, about 1362, Boccacio had penned *Famous Women* "for the ladies." The work consisted of 106 biographies, the first personage being Eve. *Famous Women* constituted the first "dictionary" in western Europe that focused solely on women.

V. CONCLUSION

During the period from 1300 into the seventeenth century, many Europeans were caught up in an oral culture. For them, neither the newly reformed "humanist" curricula of certain schools, nor the rich literatures of the various "renaissances," nor the private art collections of the wealthy were accessible. Their only contact with the Renaissance came as it was mediated to them through the words of traveling preachers, priests, civic leaders, or other readers or through what they happened to see in architecture and publicly displayed paintings and sculpture of the different locales they lived in or visited. Consequently, the Renaissance affected directly the thinking of a relatively small, albeit influential, segment of the European population.

The Renaissance was superimposed on a civilization imprinted by Christian thought, traditions, and customs. Even Machiavelli could not escape Christianity's long cultural reach. He claimed a personal attachment to that faith, despite the non-Christian entailments of the pragmatic ethics he articulated. Moreover, relatively few atheists dared to make known their unbelief publicly, especially in Spain, where Ferdinand and Isabella reinstituted the Inquisition in the late fifteenth century, nor after the 1540s when the papacy more generally launched the Inquisition as a means to counter proponents of Protestant "heresy," especially the followers of John Calvin.

Between the years 1300 and 1650, the Renaissance and the Christian faith became linked in numerous ways, despite the efforts by certain scholastic theologians to uncouple the relationship or to deny the possibility of its very existence. Often Christian humanists, whether Roman Catholic like Erasmus or Protestant like John Calvin, made clarion calls for the reform of the Roman Catholic Church faith based on Scripture. They believed their knowledge of Greek and Hebrew helped them to understand Scripture better than their scholastic opponents.

Some of the humanists identified the Christian faith principally with a life of interior Christian devotion and following the "philosophy" or simple moral teachings of Jesus. They criticized Scholastics for allegedly losing the essence of the Christian faith in penning ponderous theological systems. They thought Scholastics sometimes raised questions that were, after all, unanswerable and useless. Others, however, appreciated specific writings of the Scholastics and attempted to meld their own biblical studies with these works. Still other scholars broke away from the hold of the authority of ancient writers, whether pagan or Christian. Historian Theodore Rabb proposes that these latter scholars ushered in "the last days of Renaissance" (toward 1700) and the onset of an age of revolution (1700–1900).

FOR FURTHER STUDY

Bainton, Roland H. *Erasmus of Christendom*. New York: Scribner, 1969.

Bartlett, Kenneth. *The Civilization of the Italian Renaissance: A Sourcebook*. 2nd ed. Toronto: University of Toronto Press, 2011.

Burckhardt, Jacob. *The Civilization of the Renaissance in Italy*. Edited by Peter Murray. London: Penguin, 1990.

D'Amico, John F. *Renaissance Humanism in Papal Rome: Humanists and Churchmen on the Eve of the Reformation*. Baltimore: Johns Hopkins University Press, 1983.

Daniell, David. *William Tyndale: A Biography*. New Haven: Yale University Press, 1994.

Grendler, Paul F. *Schooling in Renaissance Italy: Literacy and Learning 1300–1600*. Baltimore: Johns Hopkins University Press, 1989.

Kristeller, Paul Oskar. *Renaissance Thought and Its Sources*. New York: Columbia University Press, 1979.

Rummel, Erika. *The Humanist-Scholastic Debate in the Renaissance and Reformation*. Boston: Harvard University Press, 1995.

Luther's Reformation

A Conscience Unbound

I. LUTHER'S THEOLOGICAL EVOLUTION

If there is anything moderns know about Martin Luther, it is that he nailed the *Ninety-five Theses on the Power and Efficacy of Indulgences* to a church door and with each blow of the hammer openly defied a moribund and even corrupt Catholic Church. The *Ninety-five Theses*, it was thought, were Luther's declaration of independence from Rome. Unfortunately, this popular view of the *Ninety-five Theses* is historically inaccurate. To be sure, October 31, 1517, would indeed turn out to be the first hint that the Western world was about to be turned upside down. But Luther's act on All Hallows Eve in 1517 was not an act of rebellion. It was, in fact, just the opposite—the act of a dutiful son of mother church.

Martin Luther posting his *Ninety-five Theses.*

Someone (scholars are unsure who it was) took the original Latin text of Luther's *Ninety-five Theses*, translated them into German, and distributed them all over Germany. When the German people realized that Luther was standing up against abuses in the church, he became a hero throughout Germany, and the Reformation was born.

Events did overtake the conscientious German monk late in October 1517, but what kind of man was he and where did he come from? Perhaps one of the more intriguing aspects of Luther's early life was his education. It was not every day that a peasant's son received a university education. Luther's father, Hans Luder, was a respectable and successful Thuringian miner who attained considerable although not enormous wealth. He was therefore able to ensure that his second son received a good education.

One of eight children, Martin was born on November 10, 1483, in Eisleben, but grew up in Mansfeld. When Martin turned fourteen, he was sent to a preparatory school in Magdeburg and later in Eisenach, where he seems to have come under the influence of the Brethren of the Common Life. He attended the University of Erfurt, where he received his baccalaureate in 1502 and a master's degree in January 1505, graduating second in his class. In an age when fathers ruled, the elder Luther decided his son was to become a lawyer, so Martin went off to law school in Erfurt. But circumstances soon would place young Luther on a different path.

Luther took unusual pride in his peasant roots. His ambitious and hardworking father seems to have been a strict parent who did not spare the rod in disciplining his children. While some scholars claim that Luther's rebellion against the pope was rooted in his hatred for his father, other evidence and other historians suggest the contrary. Philipp Melanchthon, for example, asserted that Luther's father was "beloved by all good men." As for Luther's mother, by all accounts she was a pious woman given to prayer and seen by her contemporaries as a model of virtue.

Martin Luther.

It would appear that several experiences turned Luther's attention from law to the monastery. Not long before his change of heart, the plague had swept through Erfurt and taken the life of a close friend. This loss seems to have shaken the young Martin and turned his attention to deeper spiritual concerns.

Soon after beginning law school, he was returning to Erfurt from Mansfeld when he was overtaken by a sudden thunderstorm. A lightning bolt struck a tree perilously close by, and the young Luther, in a fit of fear, called upon St. Anne, the patron saint of distressed travelers, vowing to become a monk if only she would spare his life. St. Anne did spare his life, and Luther, true to his promise, entered the monastery of the Augustinian Hermits.

While this event seems to have been the immediate cause for his entrance into the monastic life, we must recognize that the lightning bolt landed in a medieval world where the religious ideal was the life of a monk. Late medieval piety taught that the only way someone could be assured of salvation was to flee the temptations of the secular world and devote oneself to God. To this conventional wisdom, Luther bowed his head and entered the monastic life in July 1505.

A. The Monastic Life

In July 1505 Luther entered the black cloister, the observant congregation of the Augustinian Hermits in Erfurt and one of the more rigorous religious orders, convinced that the life of a monk was the surest path to salvation.

Luther had the good fortune to come under the tutelage of Johann Staupitz, who exercised a fatherly influence on the devout young monk. When his severe efforts at monastic piety proved spiritually unsatisfying, and he was plagued with doubt (*Anfechtungen*), Staupitz took young Luther under his pastoral wing, urging him to contemplate God's grace. In later years, Luther praised Staupitz for first opening his eyes to the gospel.

Despite his anxieties, Luther was a successful monk. He was ordained to the priesthood in 1507, and his academic abilities were quickly recognized by Staupitz, who then arranged to have his young protégé appointed as an instructor at the new University of Wittenberg. After receiving his doctorate in 1512, Luther succeeded Staupitz as Professor of Scripture at the new university. As a young professor, Luther lectured on books of the Bible, but he was no ivory-tower theologian. He was also a pastor and preacher in the parish church, regularly preaching three sermons a week.

"If anyone could have earned heaven by the life of a diligent monk, it was I" (Martin Luther).

B. The Evangelical Breakthrough

Scholars differ on the timing of Luther's discovery of the decisive doctrine with which he was so identified, justification by faith alone (*sola fide*). Rather than seeing his theological discovery as a single decisive event, we should view it more as a gradual process.

It is clear that as early as his lectures on the Psalms (1513–15) and Romans (1515–16) he was beginning to think differently about how the individual sinner finds forgiveness from a righteous God. In these years of intensive study he retained some of the older traditional concepts alongside his radical new ideas. Only after some years of biblical study under the inspiration of the theology of Augustine did Luther arrive at a more fully formed distinctive doctrine of justification by faith alone.

As Luther continued to lecture on the Bible, his conception of God's righteousness underwent a profound transformation. His early education had taught him to think of God's righteousness as an "active righteousness" that demands that humans in their own strength measure up to God's righteous standards. Luther, however, came to the conviction that human effort is utterly unable to achieve this standard of righteousness unless God grants it graciously without regard to merit.

It was in the words of Romans 1:17 ("For in it the righteousness of God is revealed from faith to faith") that Luther found solace for his own spiritual strivings. The "righteousness of God" in this text is not, as he had been taught, referring to a divine attribute, but to the divine activity of clothing sinners in the righteousness of Christ through the gift of faith. Luther's Romans lectures in particular contain most of the key concepts that would resound throughout history, such as the "alien righteousness" of Christ, "faith alone justifies," and we are "at the same time sinners, yet non-sinners." But like a pebble in a pond, it took some time for the early theological insights to ripple throughout his whole theological system.

Certainly, Luther had rejected the concept of meritorious works by 1513–15. Further, he discovered the gracious character of God's righteousness by the time he lectured on Romans in 1515. These insights were beginning to come into view for Luther at that time, but his own understanding of justification underwent considerable development. In the early years of the Reformation (that is, before 1535), Luther did not make a sharp distinction between justification and sanctification. Early on, he considered justification both an event and a process. For the German Reformer, both are gifts from God, and both come to the Christian via faith.

Geoffrey Bromiley observes that the relationship between justification and sanctification is so close in these early years that "Luther does not scruple to use the one word justification to cover the process of sanctification as well as justification in the narrower and stricter sense." Luther's understanding of justification underwent a shift after 1530, when he was much more inclined to stress the difference between justification and sanctification. This shift is first clearly manifested in his commentary on Galatians (1535).

There are a number of reasons why the doctrine developed in a distinctively forensic direction. First, it seems quite clear that Melanchthon was the main impetus behind this reorientation. In the early years of the Reformation, Luther did not necessarily characterize justification in forensic categories. His metaphors for justification tended to be of the marriage relationship or the medical process of healing. But Melanchthon seems to have inspired him to employ legal language. This was first done explicitly in Luther's *Apologia* of 1530, and thereafter the theological trend led to such an emphasis on forensic imputation that sanctification was distinguished from forensic justification. Within Lutheranism, the Formula of Concord of 1577 marks the final consolidation of this doctrinal development.

One of the important historiographical insights garnered from any historical analysis is that the development of the Protestant doctrine of justification came in a period of intensive theological transition. To be sure, Luther set the course that others would follow, but a proper understanding of this period must recognize that his initial insights provoked decades of Protestant refinement. In the midst of this intellectual transition period, it is probably more historically accurate to speak of the parameters of a Protestant doctrine of justification, and within those parameters are considerable differences among early Protestant theologians. However, despite the diversity, there seems to have been an irreducible core of a distinctive Protestant doctrine of justification, centering on the imputed righteousness of Christ for the forgiveness of sins.

Philipp Melanchthon.

(It is worth noting that in the sixteenth century, an "evangelical" was simply another word for "Protestant." The first Protestants appropriated the term because they believed they had recovered the *euangelium*, which they were convinced had been long obscured by the medieval church. Protestant theologians tended to define the gospel in doctrinal terms of justification by faith alone, priesthood of all believers, and the ultimate authority of the Bible.)

Even though Luther may have differed in some respects from other Protestant theologians of his day, on the core distinctives he was in full accord with the other members of his theological fraternity, such as Martin Bucer, John Calvin, Heinrich Bullinger, Pietro Martire Vermigli (Peter Martyr), John Oecolampadius, and Ulrich Zwingli. The crucial distinction between Roman Catholics and Protestants was that the latter saw the exclusive ground of justification as the imputed righteousness of Christ. This was the one thing all Protestants held in common and the thing that distinguished them from Rome. With this central

Luther's Reformation: A Conscience Unbound

idea in place, Reformers variously configured other accompanying aspects of justification.

C. The Indulgences Controversy

It may seem odd to moderns that a piece of paper with papal insignia became the straw that broke the proverbial camel's back in the sixteenth century. The selling of indulgences (remission of temporal punishment for sin) was the historical fulcrum around which the early events of the Reformation revolved. Pope Julius II permitted the sale of indulgences in 1507 to raise money to build St. Peter's Basilica in Rome, and Pope Leo X renewed approval in 1513. Pope Leo later made a deal with Albert of Brandenburg, archbishop of Mainz (Germany): If Archbishop Albert would agree to allow the sale of indulgences, Leo agreed to split the profits with him.

Luther had already criticized indulgences as early as 1514, so why did the *Ninety-five Theses* cause such uproar? The flashpoint centered around Johan Tetzel, a Dominican who had been hired to travel all over Germany selling indulgences. This was fully in keeping with the church and Pope Leo's agreement. But there was something especially crass about Tetzel, whose sales pitch was, "Once a coin into the coffer clings, a soul from purgatory springs."

Since Frederick the Wise, a prince in the electorate of Saxony, refused to let Tetzel into his territory, Tetzel set up shop just over the border in the duchy of Saxony. Frederick was concerned about the money leaving his territory, so he was very sympathetic when Luther expressed his outrage over this practice. Perhaps key to Frederick's support was George Burckhardt (known as Spalatin), Frederick's private secretary, a court preacher, and an advocate for Luther.

"Once a coin into the coffer clings, a soul from purgatory springs" (Johan Tetzel).

Prince Frederick the Wise of Saxony.

D. The Sacrament of Penance

At the heart of medieval Catholicism was the sacrament of penance, which sometimes is called the "second plank of salvation." Tetzel was obligated to sell indulgences within the proper theological and ecclesiastical confines of this sacrament. This was, after all, the very means by which a faithful believer would go to heaven. As such, it was central to the experience of laypeople. The medieval Roman Catholic Church believed that the first plank was baptism, which was commonly administered to infants. Baptism washed away the *culpa* (guilt) of original sin, but neither plank washed away the *poena* (punishment).

In late medieval theology, every sin deserved two kinds of punishment, eternal and temporal. Christ's atoning work on the cross took away the eternal punishment of sin, but the temporal punishment still required a payment. It was necessary for the sinner to provide some sort of penance to remove the temporal effects of sin.

The Fourth Lateran Council defined penance in 1215 as requiring three responsibilities of the sinner: contrition, confession, and satisfaction. Contrition can be defined as genuine sorrow over the commission of a sin. Confession in the Catholic Church, according to 1 John 1:9, required an oral admission of sins to a priest, who serves as the intermediary between God and man. Finally, satisfaction required that God be satisfied, or compensated somehow, for the dishonor incurred by the sin. Typically this came in the form of having to say special prayers, fasting, almsgiving, or taking a pilgrimage. This sacrament was not intended to be a purely mechanical or perfunctory exercise, but a means of relieving the sinners of their burden.

Having successfully completed these three things, absolution or forgiveness for sins could be granted by the priest, based on the condition that the sinner sincerely and successfully completed the acts of penance or satisfaction. If contrition was not genuine, the confession not entirely complete, or the acts of penance not fully carried out, the sinner was required to spend some time in purgatory in order to burn off temporal punishment for sin. Purgatory was pictured as a burning by fire or a cleansing of those sins that still remained outstanding at the end of life. Almost all people, in the eyes of the Catholic Church, would go to purgatory. This naturally gave the clergy a great deal of power over the lives of the laity, as they depended on the clerics to dispense certain blessings that had eternal benefits.

One such tool that the clergy used to dispense these blessings was the so-called "treasury of merit." The question could be asked, on what basis did a priest or pope claim to have the authority to produce satisfaction? The answer was the treasury of merit, a "spiritual reservoir" containing an infinite number of meritorious deeds. These merits were dispensed by the pope or his designated agents, but ultimately the pope had the only key. The merits were accumulated through Christ's death on the cross, which was infinitely meritorious.

The overflow and excess of these merits that were not required to deal with the sins of the world now filled the treasury of merit. Moreover, good deeds done by great saints of the past, especially the Virgin Mary, were also added to this infinite number of good deeds. Consequently, all of these merits were at the disposal of the pope.

In 1460 Pope Sixtus IV decided that the buying of indulgences not only was good for the sinner in this life, but could be applied to deceased family members in purgatory as well. This had a profoundly powerful emotional appeal. Sinners were given the opportunity to reduce or even end the suffering, pain, and punishment of beloved family members.

During Luther's generation these elaborations of the doctrine of indulgences were still relatively new. The spirituality of the late medieval church was in profound decline, and there was significant corruption with respect to the way the religious system functioned. The personal lives of many priests reflected this decay. It was common for priests, who could not marry, to have mistresses or concubines. In the words of one modern historian, "By the sixteenth century, there was not an intelligent man in Europe who did not know that a reformation was at hand."

II. FROM CONTROVERSY TO REFORMATION

A. The October Revolution of 1517 (*Ninety-five Theses*)

Luther was appalled that people were lured across the border into ducal Saxony to be relieved of their money and persuaded to purchase indulgences. To be sure, Luther was concerned with Tetzel's crass abuse of a papal indulgence. He was also concerned about the economic exploitation. He explicitly mentions "money" or "wealth" in nine of the theses, thereby suggesting that he was contemptuous of Tetzel's financial exploitation of Luther's fellow Wittenbergers.

There had been long-standing resentment in Germany that so much money was funneled to Italy to support the lavish lifestyles of cardinals and other clergy. A strong economic and social element existed in the Reformation, which made it more complex than a matter of people simply hearing and responding to the gospel.

Luther was troubled by Tetzel's actions and wrote up these ninety-five assertions to be debated with his theological colleagues at the University of Wittenberg. The church door functioned as an academic bulletin board, so it was the appropriate place to notify fellow faculty members of a faculty meeting.

Following proper ecclesiastical protocol, Luther sent a copy to Archbishop Albert. As said earlier, someone realized its significance and had it translated into German, printed, and distributed throughout Germany. Perhaps it was someone from Albert's court who, like so many Germans, was disturbed by Roman interference in German affairs.

In a relatively short period of time, Luther was perceived as a loyal German standing up to the Roman religious occupation of Germany, and Albert was seen as a collaborator with the enemy of the German people. A groundswell of support for Luther emerged in late 1517 and early 1518. When faced with ecclesiastical opposition, this new German Hercules (as early woodcuts make clear) would not back down.

Despite Luther's boldness, there was nothing in the *Ninety-five Theses* that rejected traditional Catholic doctrine. The posting of the theses was not an act of rebellion against the church, but the work of a responsible church theologian who was seeking to address what he perceived to be distortions of Catholic teaching. Luther's concerns were fundamentally no different from Erasmus's criticism of the church. He did not reject papal authority, the sacrament of penance, or the concept of indulgences. He did, however, stand firmly against exploitation of his congregants.

Even though the *Ninety-five Theses* were intended for discussion purposes of the theological faculty at Wittenberg, the papacy saw in them an implicit challenge to the authority of Rome. The official response to the theses by Sylvester Prieras (1518), as the title indicates (*Dialogue Concerning the Power of the Pope*), asserted that the deeper issue beneath Luther's criticism of Tetzel was papal authority.

The repercussions of the theses reverberated even in Luther's own cloister. Luther's colleague at Wittenberg, Dr. Jerome Schurff, professor of canon law, cautioned, "Do you wish to write against the pope?... It won't be tolerated." Emperor Maximilian in his letter to Pope Leo X (August 5, 1518) asserted that in the *Ninety-five Theses* "the authority of the Pope is disregarded" and added that they appear to be "injurious and heretical."

Tetzel himself (in 1518) characterized Luther's challenge as an overt denial of the authority of the pope. From Tetzel's perspective, the pope had authorized him to sell the indulgences, and therefore to challenge the sale of indulgences was in fact a challenge to papal authority.

What Luther intended to address as a matter of the abuse of indulgences quickly became a matter of the authority of the pope.

B. The Heidelberg Disputation (1518)

Among Augustinian Hermits (Luther's own order), tongues were wagging. In April 1518, Luther was sent as a delegate to the triennial meeting of the Augustinian Hermits in Heidelberg. Staupitz gave him the opportunity to articulate and defend his views in the customary disputation. Luther proposed forty theses, and his Wittenberg student Leonhard Beier defended them.

Heidelberg provides an early glimpse into what was important to Luther immediately after the indulgences controversy. Remarkably, the topic of indulgences was not addressed. Rather, Luther was much more concerned to address the larger theological doctrines that underlay his deepest convictions, such as original sin, free will, law-gospel distinction, and grace.

In general, two things were very clear. First, Luther had embraced an intensively Augustinian reading of the apostle Paul. Over and over again, Paul and Augustine are the twin sources of his theology. His understanding of original sin was so rigorous that he rejected out of hand the notion of free will. In thesis 13 he stated that "free will, after the fall, exists in name only, and as long as it does what it is able, it commits a mortal sin." This same Augustinian conviction became the focus of one of Luther's most important writings, *The Bondage of the Will* (1525). There can be no doubt that not only had he read Augustine's anti-Pelagian writings, but they had entered his spiritual bloodstream.

Second, the forty theses manifest Luther's white-hot anti-Scholastic and anti-Aristotelian sentiments. His antipathy toward his own Nominalistic education is evident in thesis 16 when he states, "The person who believes that he can obtain grace by doing what is in him (*facere quod in se est*) adds sin so that he becomes doubly guilty." Luther had reached the conclusion that Scholasticism and Aristotle could not coexist with Paul and Augustine. Many who read his Heidelberg theses decided they could not coexist with Luther. His old friend Jodocus Truttvetter placed a *Theta* (Greek abbreviation for *thanatos*, which means "death") by each thesis.

"I have just seen the next Erasmus" (Martin Bucer, speaking of Martin Luther).

But others embraced Luther with enthusiasm. Martin Bucer, a Dominican monk who attended the disputation, was captivated by Luther and paid him the highest compliment he could: "I have just seen the next Erasmus." At this point, no one realized where Luther would lead.

C. Encountering the Power of Rome

Pope Leo X got wind of Luther's theses and initially concluded that Luther was merely a "drunken monk" who would change his mind once he sobered up. But three months went by and the "drunken monk" was still at it, so the pope asked Prierias (Silvester Mazzolini), the Master of the Sacred Palace and Dominican professor of theology, to investigate.

Prierias concluded that Luther had crossed the line into heresy, and he wrote a dialogue against him, thinking this would put an end to the German problem. But Luther was bolder than anyone realized and wrote a reply in early August 1518 calling Prierias's dialogue "supercilious." The two theologians exchanged writings again with no resolution or repentance. The effect of this brief exchange was to fan the flame of suspicion.

Pope Leo lost patience and on August 7 ordered Luther to appear in Rome within sixty days to recant his heresies. Further, the pope demanded that Elector Frederick should arrest and deliver this "child of the devil" to the papal legate. Frederick did not arrest Luther, but he did arrange a meeting with the papal legate—another Dominican, Cardinal Cajetan (Thomas de Vio)—at the upcoming Diet of Augsburg in October.

Cajetan initially took an avuncular approach to Luther, calling him "my dear son." The monk and the cardinal met three times in Augsburg (October 12–14). The cardinal was courteous, but insisted on a retraction and submission to papal authority. However, Luther stubbornly refused to recant his opinions. He asserted that Scripture has ultimate authority, to which Cajetan thundered in response, "The pope is above the council and also above the Holy Scripture. Recant!"

Cajetan then pressed Staupitz to put pressure on Luther to recant. Instead, Staupitz secretly released Luther from his monastic obedience so that he no longer represented the Augustinian order. Frustrated and angry, Cajetan described Luther as a "deep-eyed German beast filled with strange speculations." Afraid of retaliation, Luther fled the city and soon afterward (in November) made a formal appeal to a general council to settle the dispute.

It is no accident that two Dominicans were the first into the fray with Luther. Dominicans viewed themselves as the self-appointed guardians of Catholic doctrine and papal primacy. It is helpful to understand that these Dominican preoccupations inevitably inclined them to frame the indulgences controversy principally as an attack on papal authority. For his part, Luther did not initially see the indulgences controversy that way, but merely as an academic dispute. It was only later that he concluded that indulgences were indeed symptomatic of the much deeper matter of papal authority.

There was one final papal attempt to persuade Luther to recant his views. Pope Leo sent his nuncio (ambassador) and chamberlain, Karl von Miltitz, to meet with Luther. Instead of confrontation, Miltitz employed a circuitous strategy. At their meeting on January 6, 1519, the papal nuncio expressed sympathy toward Luther and laid blame for the indulgences controversy at the feet of Tetzel, but he also implored Luther not to destroy the unity of the church. Miltitz agreed that the accusations against Luther should be settled in Germany by a German

Luther's Reformation: A Conscience Unbound

bishop and not in Rome. For his part, Luther agreed that he would seek the pardon of the pope and advocate unity.

In a letter of March 3, 1519, Luther humbly acknowledged the authority of the papacy and affirmed that he had never sought to undermine the Roman Church, although he still expressed concerns over the sale of indulgences.

D. The Leipzig Disputation (1519)

In response to the courtesy of Miltitz, Luther agreed to cease public hostilities. But as it turned out, this was the calm before the storm. Dr. Johann Eck (Johann Maier of Eck), one of the leading theologians at the University of Ingolstadt, sought a public debate with Luther and published twelve (later thirteen) theses against Luther in December 1518. Luther immediately replied with thirteen countertheses. Sparks flew, so it was agreed that a disputation should be held in Leipzig between Eck and Luther and his senior colleague at the University of Wittenberg, Karlstadt (Andreas Rudolph Bodenstein von Karlstadt).

When Luther arrived at Leipzig on July 27, Professor Peter Schade Mosellanus described him this way:

> Martin is of medium height. He is emaciated from care and study, so that anyone who observes him carefully can almost count every bone in his body. He is in the vigor of manhood and has a clear, penetrating voice. His learning and mastery of Scripture are astounding. In addition,... he is affable and friendly; in no sense is he dour or arrogant.

The exchange between Luther and Eck was explosive. On July 5 Eck accused Luther of being dangerously close to the "Bohemian heresy" (of Jan Hus). Initially Luther rejected the association, but later reversed himself, declaring, "Among the articles of Jan Hus, I find many that are plainly Christian and evangelical." In the eyes of Duke George of Saxony, this was tantamount to sympathy for the Devil. In the hearing of all, the duke shouted, "The plague is upon us!"

The more Luther was provoked, the more defiant he became. On July 7 he argued that church councils could err. Eck seized on this as undeniable heresy: "If you believe that a council, legitimately called, has erred and can err, be then to me as a Gentile and a publican. I do not have to explain further what a heretic is."

Eck was declared the victor by Duke George, and the theological faculties at Cologne and Louvain joined in condemning Luther as a heretic. However, not everyone gave the victory to Eck. Town councilman Lazarus Spengler of Nuremberg sided with Luther, as did the

humanists Willibald Pirckheimer and Johann Oecolampadius. As it
turned out, Leipzig was Luther's Rubicon.

E. The New Holy Roman Emperor

During the Leipzig disputation, the combatants received news
that a new emperor had been elected on June 28 for the Holy Roman
Empire (which covered generally what is modern-day Germany). It
was Charles V of Spain. Emperor Maximilian had died on January 12,
and much political haggling ensued. Charles was the front runner, in
large part because Maximilian was his grandfather and had been advocating for Charles in order to retain the Hapsburg hold on the empire.

Rome opposed the election of Charles because it would enhance
his already vast power. Charles was already the King of Spain, the
Netherlands, and Naples; the Duke of Burgundy; and with his brother,
Ferdinand, heir to Austria. Furthermore, the king's rule extended to
the new world of the Americas. The Catholic Church did not want such
a powerful rival.

Initially, the papacy found common cause with Francis I of France and supported his candidacy. Like the church, Francis did not want to see Charles's power grow, especially since it would mean that France was surrounded entirely by Hapsburg territories. However, as summer grew near and the political maneuvering escalated, it became clear that Francis did not have the clout or the finances to secure election. For a time, the papacy supported Frederick the Wise as the alternative imperial candidate. Although Frederick had little ambition for this title, the papal courting of the elector had an unexpected benefit for Luther. The papacy realized it would be imprudent to pursue actively the elector's favored theologian, and the movement that would soon emerge gained precious time to incubate.

F. Luther's Growing Defiance

It was fortuitous that the new Holy Roman Emperor was Charles and not Francis. As it happened, Francis was a poor loser and became a thorn in Charles's flesh, launching four wars against him during the remainder of Luther's life (Hapsburg-Valois Wars). To make matters worse, Suleiman the Magnificent and his Turkish armies posed a serious threat on the eastern border of the empire. The effect of this two-front war was to pull the emperor's attention away from the empire and distract him from dealing decisively with Luther.

In 1520 Luther boldly began to put his distinctive convictions to pen and paper. The result was the publication of several books, which marked Luther's break from Rome. One of the most significant works of Luther is *On the Papacy of Rome*, written in May 1520. In August he wrote *The Address to the German Nobility*. A third book was written in September and a fourth in November, titled *On the Babylonian Captivity of the Church* and *The Freedom of the Christian Man* respectively. All of these were either written or translated in the German vernacular, thus ensuring broad circulation.

1. *On the Papacy of Rome*

Luther became convinced that the true church was not necessarily identified with the Roman Catholic Church, and he said so in this provocative volume. According to Luther, the true church is the person who listens to God's Word.

In 1517 Ulrich von Hutten had published Lorenzo Valla's proof that the ancient ecclesiastical documents supporting papal supremacy—the *Isodorian Decretals* and the *Donation of Constantine*—were forgeries. This research fueled Luther's conclusion that the Antichrist was on Peter's throne in Rome. In Luther's mind, the Antichrist was not necessarily a particular person, but a devilish outlook that infected the Roman leadership. The most egregious manifestation of the Antichrist in Rome was the papal claim to infallibility. To Luther, this assertion was the epitome of anti-Christian behavior.

2. *The Address to the German Nobility*

In this address Luther argued that the church was corrupt and unable to reform itself and therefore it was the German nobles who must take up the task of reformation.

Luther maintained that the Roman Church had built three walls to preserve its power over people and nations. The first wall attacked by Luther was the idea that popes, bishops, monks, and priests are spiritually superior to laity. His view was that all Christians belong to the same spiritual estate by virtue of their baptism and faith. These alone grant entrance into the kingdom of God. This was an early version of what came to be known as the "priesthood of all believers."

Luther demolished the second wall when he rejected the Roman assertion that only the pope has the right to interpret Scriptures. Luther strongly emphasized that laypeople have the right to read and interpret the Scripture for themselves.

The third wall torn down was the claim that only the pope could summon church councils. Luther reminded his German readers that the emperor, not the pope, had called the famous Council of Nicea in 325. Thus the German nobility had every right to convene a church council if it so willed.

Luther added insult to injury in the remainder of the book by chastising the worldly pomp and greed of the pope and his cardinals. Kissing papal feet, said Luther, was "antichristian," for it usurped adoration that is due Christ alone. Rather, popes should renounce temporal power and dedicate themselves to prayer and the study of Scripture.

Further, Luther made a long list of practical reforms that needed to take place, such as each congregation should elect its own pastor, ministers should be free to marry, prostitution should be abolished, and the universities should be reformed. Luther was advocating nothing less than the complete abolition of papal authority over the state—and he found a receptive German audience.

3. *On the Babylonian Captivity of the Church*

In Luther's most defiant work, published in 1520, his attack penetrated to the very heart of the Roman Church, namely, its sacramental system. For Luther, the papacy was a lustful Babylon that had maliciously abused the sacraments as a means of holding the church captive. The sacraments, including baptism and the Lord's Supper, controlled

"The time for silence is gone, and the time for speaking has come" (Martin Luther in *The Address to the German Nobility*).

every key event in the lives of ordinary Christians from the cradle to the grave.

Luther reserved his most serious challenge for the sacrament of the Eucharist. He identified three errors of the sacrament by which the papacy held the church captive. The first eucharistic error was the practice of withholding the cup from the laity. Since the thirteenth century it was common practice not to give the common people Communion wine. Scripture, Luther argued, requires that both the bread and wine be offered to the faithful (called "Communion in both kinds"). "To deny reception of both kinds is an act of impiety and tyranny," he thundered.

Second, Luther believed that something profoundly mystical is present with the bread and wine, but he rejected the medieval theory of "transubstantiation" to explain this mystery. He held that there is no miraculous change from the bread and wine into the actual body and blood of Christ. Luther attacked this by rejecting the underlying Aristotelian distinction of "substance" (internal qualities) and "accidents" (external appearance). Luther had disparaged Aristotle as a "dead, blind, accursed, proud, knavish heathen teacher" and thus regarded any doctrine built on Aristotelian logic as foolish in the extreme.

One might affirm this theory without forfeiting salvation, but Luther much preferred another theory in which Christ is "really present" in, with, and under the elements yet without a miraculous change in the elements themselves. Some have called this view "consubstantiation," although Luther himself never used this term to describe his personal view. The elements do not themselves become the body of Christ, but for Luther, the sacrament is more than just a symbolic event or a memorial.

The third error for Luther was the church's teaching of the sacrifice of the mass. The Roman Catholic Church taught that every time the Lord's Supper is celebrated, Christ is actually resacrificed. For Luther, this was the most abominable bondage of all. The mass was a gift of God to man, not a gift of man to God. "They [the Roman Church] make God no longer the bestower of good gifts to us, but the receiver of ours. Such impiety!" So that everyone could better understand this gift of God, Luther stressed that the mass should be in the vernacular.

When it came to the sacrament of baptism, Luther had a much more agreeable attitude toward Rome. He even expressed gratitude that this sacrament had been largely untouched by the "monstrosities of avarice and superstition" of the Roman Catholic Church. Luther did think the church had overly relied on the second plank of penance rather than the first plank of baptism for bringing regeneration.

He affirmed infant baptism, but also ascribed faith to infants. It is not beyond the realm of possibility, he speculated, that infants themselves may exhibit a kind of seed faith. Luther has been widely criticized as holding a view of baptismal regeneration that was inconsistent with his view of justification by faith alone.

As for the remaining traditional sacraments (confirmation, marriage, penance, ordination, and extreme unction), Luther rejected all as without a divine promise or an external sign. In an interesting side comment he dismissed the sacrament of extreme unction partly because it was traditionally based on James 5:14–15, an epistle he judged unworthy of the apostolic spirit. He retained a measure of affection for the sacrament of penance, yet it too ultimately failed to measure up to the biblical qualification for a sacrament.

In the final analysis, Luther upheld only two of the traditional seven sacraments: baptism and the Lord's Supper. He concluded his most provocative book with a bold taunt to the Roman Church: "I hear a report that fresh bulls and papal curses are being prepared against me, by which I am urged to recant, or else be declared a heretic. If this is true, I wish this little book to be part of my future recantation."

4. The Freedom of the Christian Man

In a last-ditch effort at reconciliation, the papal nuncio Miltitz persuaded Luther to make a conciliatory gesture. Luther complied in what is considered one of his best writings (October 1520). *The Freedom of the Christian Man* is a popular and irenic summary of the Christian life. Contained in this work is the famous Lutheran paradox of the Christian life: The Christian is the lord of all, and subject to none, because of faith; he is the servant of all, and subject to everyone, because of love. Faith and love are, for Luther, the two governing principles for the Christian life. Faith expresses the Christian's relationship to God, love the relationship to humanity. These two Christian principles are interdependent, that is, where there is faith, there will also be love.

Luther brings this treatise to an end with this statement: "We conclude, therefore, that a Christian lives not in himself, but in Christ and in his neighbor. Otherwise he is not a Christian. He lives in Christ through faith, in his neighbor through love. By faith he is caught up beyond himself into God. By love he descends beneath himself into his neighbor."

Accompanying the treatise was Luther's third and final letter to Pope Leo X. Luther's first letter (1518) humbly submitted to the authority of the pope; in his second letter (1519) Luther portrayed himself as the pope's humble servant, but refused to recant; in this third letter (1520) he addressed the pope as an equal and pitied him as a "lamb in

"Good works do not make a person good, but a good person does good works" (Martin Luther, *The Freedom of the Christian Man*).

the midst of wolves." While sincere, the letter was remarkably direct. Luther absolved Leo personally, but characterized the church as a "lawless den of thieves, the most shameless of all brothels, the very kingdom of sin, death and hell." Whatever reconciliation was to be gained by the treatise was lost by the personal letter.

Johann Eck's work was not finished after the Leipzig debate in 1519. He soon went to Rome and assisted papal jurists in preparing the papal bull titled *Exsurge Domine*, issued on June 15, 1520. Quoting from the opening words of Psalm 74:22, the opening sentence of the papal bull read, "Rise up, Oh Lord, and judge Thy cause. A wild boar has invaded Thy vineyard." The boar, of course, was referring to Martin Luther. The papal bull cited forty-one alleged errors and gave Luther sixty days to recant or be excommunicated.

Luther defied the pope, and on December 10, 1520, in front of the people of Wittenberg he burned the papal bull at a bonfire on the bank of the Elbe River. The sixty days had already passed, and Luther had not recanted, so the pope issued the bull of excommunication (*Decet Romanum Pontificem*) on January 3, 1521.

Elector Frederick had been remarkably supportive of Luther, even in the face of papal threats. Why? Certainly Frederick was not eager to get into hot water with the pope, but German pride may have inclined him to support Luther against the greed of the papacy. Further, Luther was a major draw for the prince's pride and joy, the newly established University of Wittenberg. Frederick's support was all the more remarkable, since there is no clear evidence that he embraced Luther's theology or that the two men had ever had a personal conversation.

Frederick did solicit opinions of others, including the most respected scholar in Europe, Erasmus of Rotterdam. To the papal charge that Luther was a heretic, Erasmus replied to Frederick: "Luther has committed two sins. He has grasped the pope's crown and the monks' bellies." Even if his theology is unclear, what is clear is that Elector Frederick did support and defend Luther at great risk to his own crown.

G. The Diet of Worms (April 1521)

Rome had rendered its ecclesiastical decision about Luther. Now it was the emperor's turn to deal with Luther from the perspective of the state. Once the pope excommunicated Luther, it then became the judicial responsibility of the Holy Roman Emperor to bring Luther to trial. Ever since the Leipzig disputation, Frederick the Wise had pressed the young Charles V to allow Luther to appear at the next imperial diet (the formal assembly of all the princes of the Holy Roman Empire). Initially, the emperor hesitated, but the elector finally prevailed, and

Luther was summoned to a hearing at the imperial Diet at Worms in April 1521. The summons included a safe conduct (imperial protection) and spoke only of a hearing. Luther was fully aware of the danger, but was equally determined to take his case to the emperor.

It took Luther two full weeks to travel from Wittenberg to Worms, and every mile along the way revealed immense popular support. Word of this triumphant procession created enormous anxiety among the imperial dignitaries in Worms. As his wagon neared the city on April 16, a hundred nobles rode out to accompany Luther, which made for a rather grand entrance to Worms.

The imperial marshal informed Luther that he was scheduled to appear before the Diet the next day (April 17) at 4 pm. He arrived promptly at the Bishop's palace, but was not summoned until 6 pm. As he entered the great hall of the Bishop's palace, he found himself standing before more than two hundred of the most powerful men in Germany. Besides the young Emperor Charles V, there were six of the imperial electors, papal legates, archbishops, bishops, dukes, margraves, princes, counts, deputies, and various ambassadors from foreign courts. Several hundred Spanish soldiers ringed the hall, and thousands of spectators filled the streets. What would Luther do?

As his eyes scanned the hall, Luther heard his name. The imperial prosecutor, Dr. Johann von der Eck (not Johann Eck who debated Luther at Leipzig), called out to him with two questions. Pointing to a table with his writings, Dr. von der Eck asked Luther if they were his. Dr. Schurl, Luther's advocate, asked that the titles be read, and they were. Luther acknowledged authorship of the books. The imperial prosecutor then asked Luther to renounce them.

This second question caught Luther off guard, for he had expected a hearing and not a summary condemnation. No doubt fearful and awed by the august assembly, Luther appealed to the emperor for additional time to think before answering the question. After brief consultation, the young emperor gave Luther twenty-four hours.

Luther spent a sleepless night consulting with friends and regaining his composure. His resolve remained. In a letter he wrote that evening to a friend, he said, "I will not retract one iota, so Christ help me." After waiting two hours again the next day at the Bishop's palace, he was admitted to the diet. Because of the darkness, torches were lit and Luther could see the crowded room. Though somewhat timid the day before, on this day his voice was firm and resonant.

After apologizing for his unfamiliarity with courtly etiquette, Luther explained, first in German and then in Latin, that his writings belonged to different categories. First, some were devotional writings that were edifying for Christians, and even his opponents would not want him to renounce those. Second, there were some writings against the corruptions of the papacy. To renounce those would be tantamount to affirming wickedness, and that he could not do. Third, some of his works were directed against individuals who defended papal corruption. He confessed that he had at times used harsh words, but wickedness had to be dealt with, and therefore he would not retract them either. He then urged Charles V to begin his reign by upholding the Word of God.

The imperial princes felt Luther had evaded the question. They had asked for a simple yes or no, but he had offered qualifications and explanations. They again asked for an unequivocal statement. Luther then gave his famous reply in Latin:

> Unless I am convinced by the testimony of the Scriptures or by clear reason (for I do not trust either in the pope or in councils alone, since it is well known that they have often erred and contradicted themselves), I am bound by the Scriptures I have quoted and my conscience is captive to the Word of God. I cannot and will not recant anything, since it is neither safe nor wise to go against conscience.

Then he was reported to have concluded with these words in German: "Here I stand, I cannot do otherwise. God help me. Amen."

The immediate response was dramatic. Dr. von der Eck blasted Luther, saying, "Abandon your conscience, Martin, for your conscience errs." Luther began to reply, but the emperor quickly dismissed the proceedings amid shouting from the Spanish soldiers, who were chanting, "To the flames!" Charles V was only twenty-one, but he kept his word and permitted Luther to walk out of the Bishop's palace alive. When Luther reached his rooms, he threw up his arms and exclaimed, "I made it through! I made it through!"

The following day, Charles called the diet back into session to discuss its response. Frederick the Wise defended Luther. Complicating the decision was the fact that the German people were solidly behind Luther. Popular support became evident that evening when a placard appeared, declaring that four hundred nobles and eight thousand soldiers were prepared to defend Luther against the emperor. The placard carried the dreaded word *"Bundschuh"* (that is, a tied shoe of the German peasants) — which was the ominous sign of rebel peasants. The last thing the new emperor needed was civil war in Germany.

Fear of a peasants' revolt prompted the archbishop of Mainz to plead with the emperor to make another effort to persuade Luther to cooperate. In the immediate aftermath of the diet, a series of imperial and ecclesiastical emissaries met with Luther, desperately seeking some kind of compromise. Various concessions and modifications were offered if only Luther would recant. Luther steadfastly rejected every proposal.

On April 26 Luther was finally permitted to leave Worms with only the emperor's promise of protection for twenty-five days. The diet continued to discuss Luther's fate for nearly a month. Finally, Elector Frederick left on May 23 before any decision was rendered. Two days later, the emperor made the inevitable decision and issued an imperial edict declaring Luther an outlaw of the empire.

The Edict of Worms was severe. It not only proclaimed Luther a criminal, but also prohibited anyone from assisting him in any way on penalty of death. All his books were banned as well. For the rest of his life, Luther was declared a heretic of the church and an outlaw of the state.

Much to his surprise, Luther departed Worms alive. Jan Hus had been given the same imperial promise of safe conduct, yet was burned at the stake at the Council of Constance in 1415. Danger was still in the air as Luther departed on April 26. As his wagon neared the small town of Moehra, on the evening of May 4, five soldiers intercepted the wagon and kidnapped Luther. When news reached the artist and Lutheran sympathizer Albrecht Dürer, he lamented, "O God, Luther is dead. Now who will preach the holy gospel to us so clearly?"

As it turned out, this kidnapping was part of an elaborate plan to save Luther's life. Before Luther left Worms, a clandestine message from Elector Frederick was conveyed to Luther that his journey home would be interrupted and he would be taken to a secret location for his own safety. After running alongside the elector's soldiers for a short distance, Luther mounted a waiting horse, which took him to the Wartburg Castle in the Thuringian forest. Elector Frederick's bold act not only saved Luther's life; it also saved the Reformation movement.

H. The Wartburg Castle: Luther's Patmos

When he was seized by the elector's soldiers, Luther had managed to bring one of his most precious possessions: his Greek New Testament. This would turn out to be one of the most important actions of the Reformation period, because this text became the primary resource for his German translation. Luther's presence at the Diet of Worms was his last act of obedience to Rome. The first and perhaps most important act of reenvisioning a new church was his translation of the New Testament.

For nearly a year (May 1521 – March 1522) Luther submitted to the elector's enforced isolation at what he called his "Patmos." Luther grew his own disguise—a full beard and a full head of hair covering

Wartburg Castle in Germany.

his tonsure. He wore the garments of a knight and took the name "Junker George." But the residents of the Wartburg must have noticed that Junker George was rather unusual. This soldier seemed to have an unusual devotion to the Bible, for he spent endless hours reading and writing, even taking his meals in private.

Although in protective custody, Luther used his time to produce a barrage of writings. Besides many letters from the "land of the birds" to colleagues, he wrote a commentary on the Magnificat, a Latin exposition of the Psalms, a tract against Latomus (Jakob Masson) in which he provides one of his most articulate expositions of his doctrine of justification, the German "*postils*" (sermons) for Advent, and various polemical works. One of his most bitter barbs was against the secretary to Duke George of Saxony, Hieronymus Emser, whom Luther dubbed "the goat of Leipzig." But the most enduring literary legacy from the Wartburg was his brilliant translation of the New Testament.

In the remarkable period of three months, Luther produced a German translation unlike any previous translation. His translation was based on the original Greek text rather than the outdated Latin Vulgate, and it used a philosophy of translation that stressed clarity and sensitivity to the rhythms of everyday German. Luther later expressed his view that a good translation will look to "the mother in the home, the children on the street, the common man in the market place." He added, "We must be guided by their language, the way they speak, and do our translating accordingly."

Erasmus's 1519 critical Greek edition of the New Testament was never out of reach during the crucial months of translation. When Luther returned to Wittenberg, he brought his completed translation to his close friend, the Greek scholar Philipp Melanchthon, who offered refinements.

There is little doubt that Luther's theology informed and even determined his translation. When he translated Romans 3:38, he added the word "alone," so that it read, "... justified without works of the law, by faith *alone*." Critics accused him of distorting the teaching of the Bible, but he insisted that this was the apostle's true intent.

Luther's theological commitment also affected his view of the canonicity of the book of James. While he did include this epistle in his New Testament translation, he denigrated it in the preface as "an epistle of straw," because it appeared to teach justification by works. If it was canonical—and Luther was not entirely sure it was—it belonged to the lesser New Testament epistles. Although somewhat dubious about the canonicity of Jude, Hebrews, and Revelation (which he described as a "dumb prophecy"), he did not exclude them from his German translation.

Luther's German New Testament was an immediate success. It was first published in Wittenberg in September 1522 and was so popular that it had to be republished in December. Luther then turned his efforts to the Old Testament, and the complete German Bible was finally published in 1534.

I. Luther's Collaborators in Reformation

While translating the New Testament at Wartburg Castle, Luther's reformation continued without him. Leadership of the reform movement fell to two of Luther's university colleagues: Melanchthon (1497–1560), who was the first professor of Greek, and Karlstadt (1480–1541), the dean of the Wittenberg faculty. Of the two men, Melanchthon was closer to Luther.

Melanchthon had fallen under Luther's spell and became a favorite almost immediately upon his arrival in 1518. These two men had a profound spiritual connection that was so deep that it survived theological differences when Luther's other relationships did not. Melanchthon completed the first draft of the first Protestant systematic theology, *Loci Communes*, in April 1521 and sent it to Luther in the Wartburg. Luther was so enthusiastic about this book that he said it was worthy of inclusion within the canon of Scripture.

Melanchthon would have a significant impact on Lutheranism as a great educator—he was called the *"Praeceptor Germaniae"* (the teacher of Germany)—and as the author of one of the primary documents of Lutheranism, the Augsburg Confession (1530). Particularly after Luther's death, Melanchthon's own theology developed in a different direction, leading to decades of theological wrangling among Lutherans for Luther's "true" legacy, which finally reached resolution in the Formula of Concord (1577).

Luther's relationship with Karlstadt began well but ended badly. When the young Luther arrived at the University of Wittenberg in 1512, Karlstadt was dean of the faculty. The two colleagues collided in 1516 when Karlstadt rejected Luther's interpretation of Augustine. The junior professor challenged his dean to read Augustine for himself. Karlstadt did and humbly confessed that Luther was right.

The dean became a champion for Luther's new Augustinianism, although over time, subtle differences eventually caused division. Karlstadt tended to focus on the Christian's regeneration and internal moral renewal, in contrast to Luther's more external legal justification and the paradoxical notion of *simul justus et peccator* (simultaneously a sinner and righteous). Inevitably, these differences led to a breach in their relationship.

During Luther's Wartburg period, a struggle surfaced for the soul of the Reformation. Clearly, Luther had not thought through the full implications of his Reformation or what would happen in Wittenberg while he was in the Wartburg. How does one move from the old discredited ecclesiastical structures to new structures and new relationships? How does one distinguish between those who would join the Reformation movement for personal gain, and those whose consciences compel them to embrace the new religion with sincerity?

Moreover, who would lead the Reformation? There were other contenders besides the faculty members Melanchthon and Karlstadt. Certainly Prince Frederick had a vested interest in the progress of the Reformation, as did the city council of Wittenberg. The people of the community also were concerned about religious change, but who would lead the charge?

III. THE SOCIAL AND POLITICAL IMPACT OF THE REFORMATION

A. Wittenberg Chaos

With Luther in the Wartburg, Wittenberg lost its bearings for a time. With papal authority rejected in favor of biblical authority, Luther and his followers had to work out the practical and social implications of the new theology. In confronting the practical realities of establishing new ecclesiastical structures, Luther was, perhaps surprisingly, quite conservative and sought to bring gradual rather than radical change. Long-established practices and policies were now put to the biblical test.

From the Wartburg, Luther had sought to designate Melanchthon as interim leader of the reform movement in Wittenberg. He requested that Melanchthon replace him temporarily as the preacher in the city church, but the town council balked at the thought of a married layman leading the worship. Although he was a brilliant theologian, Melanchthon's natural timidity and youth did not prepare him for leadership at such a tumultuous time. Almost by default, leadership fell to Karlstadt, thus setting the stage for the first significant breach within the new reform movement. In his enthusiasm to establish a "New Order" for Wittenberg, Karlstadt unleashed a firestorm.

Without Luther's presence to qualify his bold assertions, Karlstadt took Luther's criticism of the Roman mass to heart and began to preach mandatory reforms. On Christmas Day in 1521, Karlstadt broke with tradition by celebrating mass without vestments, dressed as a layman, employing the German language, and most significantly, distributing the bread and the wine to the laity—something that had been prohibited since the twelfth century.

Although Karlstadt sought orderly reform, his break with tradition inspired outbreaks of iconoclasm: sermons were disrupted, and priests were pelted with stones and dung. Subsequent sermons denounced pictures and images as violations of the second commandment. Gabriel Zwilling led some of the Augustinian monks in smashing statues, burning pictures, and destroying other symbols of the old faith. Moreover, Karlstadt, who as a priest had taken a vow of celibacy, flaunted centuries of church law by openly marrying Anna von Mochau. In January 1522 he presented the Wittenberg city council with a proposal for social and religious reform.

Into this increasingly volatile situation in Wittenberg came the "Zwickau Prophets"—Nicholas Storch, Marcus Thomae (Stübner), and Thomas Dreschel. These "prophets" had come under the apocalyptic teaching of Thomas Müntzer in the south German city of Zwickau. Arriving soon after Christmas, they claimed divine authority through dreams and visions. Under the influence of the Spirit they rejected traditional teaching on infant baptism and the priesthood, and they were convinced the world would soon come to an end. Luther was not impressed with them and wisecracked, "They have swallowed the Holy Ghost, feathers and all."

The Zwickau Prophets eventually left Wittenberg, but things were clearly getting out of hand. Melanchthon was overwhelmed and made an appeal to Luther to return to Wittenberg and restore order. Elector Frederick, still fearing for Luther's life, wanted him to remain at the Wartburg, but Luther defied his elector, arguing, "Satan has entered my sheepfold and committed ravages which I cannot repair by writing, but only by my personal presence."

By February the city was in such an uproar that the city council begged Luther to return. He arrived back in Wittenberg on March 6, and the following Sunday began his famous "Invocavit sermons," in which he denounced violence and made a plea for patience and tolerance. "Do you know what the Devil thinks when he sees men use violence to propagate the gospel? He sits with folded arms behind the fire of hell and says with malignant looks and frightful grin: 'Ah, how wise these madmen are to play my game!'" Almost immediately, calm was restored to Wittenberg.

Luther retained many of the old forms of worship and for a time even resumed wearing the monk's hooded cowl. He did change the wording of the mass so that there was no hint of a repeated sacrifice or transubstantiation, and he continued distributing the bread and wine to the laity. Reforms would come in due course, but only through the persuasion of the gospel and not through violence.

Karlstadt quietly submitted to the slower pace of reform, but he was deeply disappointed. He renounced his academic achievements and his title while dressed in peasant garb, and he asked to be addressed as "Brother Andrew." He left Wittenberg in the summer of 1523 to become the parish priest in the small town of Orlamünde, where he implemented reforms as he saw fit.

The Wittenberg Reformers did not approve of Karlstadt's ideas, and a small treatise war ensued between Luther and Karlstadt. The Wittenbergers especially became concerned (unfairly as it turns out) that Karlstadt was in league with the violent revolutionary teaching of Thomas Müntzer and moved to have him expelled from the electorate of Saxony (September 1524). In the following years, Karlstadt came to identify most closely with the Zürich Reformers and their eucharistic theology. He served as a pastor in Zürich from 1530 to 1534 and later as a professor of Old Testament in Basel until he died in 1541. There is a measure of irony in the fact that one of Luther's earliest advocates died as a Zwinglian.

B. The Peasants Revolt (1524–25)

Luther's reformation movement, although he never intended it, opened the door for ideas much more radical than those of Karlstadt. The world of early sixteenth-century Germany was full of injustice and oppression. Not only did the Catholic Church spiritually exploit Christians, but landowners also exploited peasants for financial gain. When Luther published his book *The Freedom of the Christian Man*, it touched a nerve not just among Christians, but among the lower classes of German society. A reformation in doctrine was not worth its salt if it did not impact the people and their daily lives—or so they believed.

In such tumultuous times, all kinds of opportunists and fanatics crawled out of the woodwork. Thomas Müntzer (c. 1489–1525) was one of those strange persons who led the oppressed astray. Müntzer himself was probably from the artisan class, and this comports with the fact that he received a university education, first at Leipzig and then at Wittenberg (1517–19). There is little doubt that he sat under Luther's teaching, and at first Müntzer hailed Luther as a hero.

Drawing from the medieval mysticism of the Dominican monk John Tauler, Müntzer came to believe that the Word of God must be heard from God's own mouth and not from theology books or even the Bible. One apprehends the true Word of God internally through mystical experience. Müntzer replaced Luther's *sola scriptura* with a *sola experientia*. This message was not well received, and Müntzer was repeatedly dismissed from pulpits in Zwickau, Prague, and Allstedt.

Müntzer's *sola experientia* took a violent turn in Allstedt. He began referring to himself as the "hammer and sickle" of God against the ungodly. In his infamous "Prince sermon" (July 13, 1524), he pressed Duke John of Saxony to embrace violent revolution: "Do not therefore allow the evil-doers, who turn us away from God, to continue living … for a godless man has no right to live."

Müntzer fell in with the leadership among peasant rebels in Mühlhausen and added his violent apocalyptic vision to the deepening dissatisfaction among peasants. On May 12, 1525, he led seven thousand peasant soldiers into battle near Frankenhausen against the German nobles. It was a slaughter. Over six thousand peasants were killed, while the nobles lost only six soldiers. Müntzer fled to the nearby town, where he was discovered hiding in an attic. After being tortured, he was beheaded, and his head impaled on a pike as a warning to other peasants.

Even if Müntzer was beguiled by his apocalyptic vision, the peasants had legitimate economic and social grievances. This was not without precedent. For the previous two hundred years, peasants had periodically revolted throughout Europe (most notably Italy, France, England, and Bohemia). In southern Germany the *Bundschuh* revolt from previous decades, signified by the laced shoes of peasants in contrast to the buckled shoes of the upper classes, had been a subterranean threat fueling animosity among the peasants and fears among the German nobility.

> "Do not therefore allow the evil-doers, who turn us away from God, to continue living … for a godless man has no right to live" (Thomas Müntzer).

The revolts in southern Germany arose from a conjunction of causes. The power of territorial princes increased at the expense of the rights of the peasantry. Traditional freedoms and economic rights were regularly trampled underfoot by powerful lords who infringed on traditional peasant rights to forests, pastures, and rivers, thus increasing the misery index for many peasants. Add to this a series of bad harvests and increased taxes, and all the ingredients of rebellion were present.

In Upper Swabia, Sebastian Lotzer, a tanner, and Christoph Schappeler, a pastor, declared the peasant grievances in the *Twelve Articles of Memmingen* (March 1525), all justified by biblical proof texts. This rather modest document clearly manifested evangelical influence by linking the gospel and divine justice with the peasants' cause.

Marxist historians have long argued that the Peasants Revolt was driven primarily by socioeconomic causes. Yet, while there was widespread resentment against the very real social and economic exploitation of the peasants, it was not the exclusive cause. Reformation scholar Heiko Oberman has rightly argued that the reformational concepts of Christian freedom and the priesthood of all believers gave significant impetus to what he calls the "gospel of social unrest." With the rise of the Reformation as a popular movement, the common man linked socioeconomic justice with Christian salvation. As later became evident, the revolt included not only peasants, but also other disaffected persons, including miners and townsmen.

Luther was very sympathetic to the plight of the peasants. He responded to the *Twelve Articles* with his *Admonition to Peace* in May 1525. He placed the largest part of the blame for the trouble squarely on the shoulders of the secular and ecclesiastical landowners. Their greed, Luther argued, was pressing Germany to the precipice of civil war. "You [landowners] are the cause of this wrath of God [and] it will undoubtedly come upon you, unless you mend your ways in time." However, just as Luther had a word for the oppressors, he also had a word for the oppressed: No matter how just your cause, rebellion is never excusable for the Christian. He concluded by urging both groups to negotiate peacefully. Unfortunately, events overtook his admonition for a peaceful resolution.

Unrest spread to Thuringia (part of eastern Germany). The peasants destroyed castles and monasteries and seized several towns. Amid reports of peasant atrocities, Luther exploded with another book, *Against the Robbing and Murdering Hordes of Peasants*, in which he infamously exhorted the landowners to "smite, slay and stab, secretly or openly, remembering that nothing can be more poisonous, hurtful or devilish than a rebel."

Luther later admonished the landowners for their cruelty, and he

"… smite, slay and stab, secretly or openly, remembering that nothing can be more poisonous, hurtful or devilish than a rebel" (Martin Luther, *Against the Robbing and Murdering Hordes of Peasants*).

urged clemency, but it was too little too late. Estimates are that more than 100,000 peasants were killed in the war. The Reformation had uncovered deeper social unrest and had failed to curtail injustice for productive long-term change. For Luther, rebellion has no justification.

C. Reformation and Political Realignment

No matter how much Luther wanted the Reformation movement to focus on spiritual and theological matters, it necessarily involved him in politics. It must be remembered that there was no separation of church and state in the world of the sixteenth century. To challenge the church was to challenge the state. Luther's trial at the Diet of Worms was the classic expression of how the church and state worked hand in hand. It was the church that declared Luther a heretic, but it was the state that had the responsibility to put heretics on trial. Luther had the dubious distinction of living out his last twenty-five years as both a heretic of the church and an outlaw of the state.

The Holy Roman Empire (broadly, modern-day Germany) had a population of about 15 million, and they were ruled over by various territorial princes, prince-bishops, counts, dukes, and various lesser lords in more than 350 principalities. Ostensibly, this vast empire was ruled by the Holy Roman Emperor, who held a sacred duty to uphold and defend Christianity.

The title of "Emperor" carried with it responsibility for the medieval concept of the *Corpus Christianum*, by which the state and society are unified under the ultimate authority of the Roman Catholic Church. But this theory was not always a reality, and that was nowhere more true than in the empire. Charles V discovered to his dismay that the emperor had only limited power over the princes and, as it turned out, over the people.

There were compelling and competing forces that converged on Charles when he became emperor in 1519. Charles firmly believed that the Reformation movement should be crushed, Roman Catholicism upheld, and the unity of the empire restored. However, complex circumstances worked against the emperor's desires.

First, the German princes were committed to maintaining political power within their realms, regardless of the emperor's policy. This political self-aggrandizement served the Reformation well. Throughout the early period of the Reformation, political opportunities trumped support for traditional Catholic religion.

Second, the constantly challenging and shifting alliances between the empire, France, and the papacy kept Charles distracted from what appeared to be a minor squabble among monks in Saxony. The incessant Hapsburg-Valois wars between France and the emperor allowed the papacy to play one side against the other and always kept Charles off balance.

Third, the Turkish threat of Suleiman the Magnificent (1520–66) on the eastern borders of the empire sent chills down Charles's spine. Suleiman led an army of more than 200,000 soldiers and posed the first serious threat in six hundred years to the *Corpus Christianum* and the integrity of Europe. He destroyed the Hungarians at the battle of Mohacs in 1526 and laid siege to Vienna in 1529. Vienna, the gateway to the Holy Roman Empire, may very well have fallen if Turkish supply lines had not been overstretched.

These three political realities shadowed every major religious debate, colloquy, or treatise of the early Reformation period. They also explain why Charles V was largely absent from the empire for most of the turbulent years and was unable to deal decisively with the defiant German monk.

With an absentee emperor and an inherent sense of independence, the territorial princes saw an opportunity to advance their cause and in some cases to enhance their coffers. In his *Address to the German Nobility* in 1520, Luther had already called on the German princes to take the lead in bringing reform to Germany. Many responded in the affirmative. Some acted out of theological conviction; others were more opportunistic, viewing adherence to Luther as veritable entitlement to the wealth of the old church. To preserve their gains, various alliances were formed. The Catholic princes of northern Germany allied themselves in 1525. The following year, the leading evangelical princes, Philip of Hesse and Duke John of Saxony, formed a defensive alliance.

The one political mechanism that allowed for direct interaction between the emperor and the princes was the imperial diet (*Reichstag*). Two key imperial diets held at Speyer in 1526 and 1529 led to religious division in the empire. At both diets the Archduke Ferdinand (the brother and representative of the emperor), the territorial princes, the ecclesiastical nobility, and the representatives of the imperial cities met to discuss the important issues confronting Germany.

As fate would have it, the year 1526 was a bad year for the empire. Turkish armies had invaded Hungary, and Pope Clement VII had joined forces with Francis I of France to wage war against Charles V. When the issue of religion came to the fore, the participants realized the military maelstrom that threatened the empire made it impossible to enforce the Edict of Worms and bring Luther to justice. In the light of the practical realities of the situation, it was agreed by Catholics and evangelicals alike at the Diet of Speyer (1526) that each territorial prince would decide the religious issue on his own. This was music to the ears of the evangelicals, who seized on the compromise to move full speed ahead with religious reform in their territories.

The diet returned to Speyer in 1529, but the political landscape had changed yet again. Charles V had been victorious over Francis I, and his troops savagely sacked Rome, forcing Pope Clement VII to take refuge in the castle San Angelo. With the pope firmly under the control of the emperor, Archduke Ferdinand, again presiding over the diet, tried to regain the imperial upper hand on the religious issue and demanded that the 1526 agreement be nullified. The goal was the religious reunification of the empire as a Catholic nation.

The Lutheran princes were defiant and issued a *protestatio* (protestation) against this abrupt turn, arguing that they were bound by the agreement of 1526. The *protestatio* was signed by five imperial princes—John of the electorate of Saxony, Philip of Hesse, George of Brandenburg-Ansbach, Wolfgang of Anhalt, Ernst of Braunschweg-Lüneburg—and fourteen imperial cities. These "protests" by the Lutheran princes and the imperial cities at the Diet of Speyer mark the historical origins of the term "Protestant" as well as the religio-political division in Germany.

The defiant protestations of the Lutheran princes prompted Charles V to turn his personal attention to the religious question in Germany once again at the Diet of Augsburg in 1530. He returned to Germany for the first time since the Diet of Worms in 1521 to bring the full weight of his imperial majesty to this nagging matter. The emperor had reason for optimism: he was fresh from victory over France, the pope was in a subservient and therefore cooperative mood, and Suleiman and his Turkish armies had withdrawn from the siege of Vienna. Charles intended to settle the religious question at the Diet of Augsburg once and for all.

Charles had requested that the Protestants present a statement of their beliefs at the diet. Melanchthon, with Luther's consent and advice, produced the famous Augsburg Confession for the emperor. The confession was remarkable for its careful wording and conciliatory tone. Melanchthon skillfully avoided controversial doctrines such as purgatory or papal authority. Luther said, "I have read Master Philip's *Apologia* [Augsburg Confession] and it pleases me very much. I know of nothing to improve or change in it." It was a clear attempt at reconciliation without giving up the essentials of the Lutheran faith—all in an effort to maintain peace in the empire.

After hearing the Confession on June 25, 1530, Charles appointed Johann Eck of Ingolstadt and others to provide a *Confutatio*, which was presented on August 3. Charles then demanded that the Protestants acknowledge they had been refuted, without having had opportunity to interact with their detractors. Melanchthon hastily managed to compose an *Apology* (a defense of the Confession), but Charles refused to receive it.

Augsburg was a defining moment in the history of the Reformation, for now it was absolutely clear that the emperor was unwilling to engage serious religious debate. Moreover, the Protestant princes for their part were unwilling to capitulate to a foreign emperor. Augsburg signaled that the religious divide was now unbridgeable, and the parties began to prepare for a possible war.

Within months, the Protestant princes formed the Schmalkald League—a defensive alliance led by John Frederick of electoral Saxony and Philip of Hesse. The Protestant princes as well as Luther realized that the emperor was prepared to use force, and they had to be ready. This raised the thorny question of resistance. Luther had long been on the record opposing any active resistance to the authorities, as he had in the Peasants War; but when his movement was threatened, he reluctantly conceded that armed resistance to the emperor was justifiable in order to defend the gospel.

Just when a war seemed inevitable, the Turks renewed their attacks on the eastern border of the empire, and Charles judged that the time was not right for a military solution to the religious problem in Germany. Charles was forced to grant formal religious toleration for more than a decade in exchange for military and financial support from the Protestant princes in his war against the Turks. Throughout the decade the Schmalkald League played a dangerous game—on the one hand supporting the emperor against the Turks, while also promoting Lutheran expansion in Germany, Scandinavia, and England.

Despite his opposition to Lutheranism, Charles did sanction exploratory dialogues between select Protestant and Catholic theologians. Discussions in 1540 and 1541 culminated in the famous Colloquy of Regensburg. The Catholics led by Cardinal Contarini and the theological moderate Johann Gropper were able to reach surprising agreements on clerical celibacy and Communion in both kinds and even reached formal agreement on the doctrine of justification. But the Protestants, led by Melanchthon and Martin Bucer, could not accept transubstantiation or papal authority, so the colloquy eventually foundered.

It must have seemed to Charles that the longer he postponed military action, the more entrenched Lutheranism became. In 1543 the archbishop of Cologne embraced Protestantism, and in 1546 the elector of the Palatinate converted to the Reformed faith. This had clear political implications: Now the Protestants had a four-to-three majority among the imperial electors (Saxony, Brandenburg, Palatinate, and the archbishop of Cologne) over the Catholic electors (the king of Bohemia and the archbishops of Trier and Mainz). If Charles were to die, this majority of electors would determine the next emperor.

D. The Schmalkald War

Charles prepared for war. With France subdued for the moment, he secured financial support from Rome. Further, he was able to bribe Duke Moritz of Albertine Saxony with the promise of an elector's title if he would betray his prince (John Fredrick, elector of Saxony).

Philip of Hesse had entered into a bigamous marriage, putting his throne at risk and thus making him vulnerable to imperial pressure. Philip reluctantly agreed to remain neutral if the emperor attacked the Schmalkald League. Philip's complicity exposed the league militarily and was especially disheartening, in view of the fact that Philip was one of the primary leaders of the Schmalkald League. Above all, Luther's death in February 1546 left the Protestants in mourning and unprepared for war.

Charles launched the so-called "Schmalkald War" with his assault on the Protestant princes in July 1546. With the ruthless Duke of Alba directing imperial troops, the decisive coup de grâce was delivered to the Protestants at the battle of Mühlberg (April 24, 1547).

Mühlberg was a hollow victory. Neither the Protestants nor the papacy were any more cooperative than before. Charles imposed the Augsburg Interim as a temporary religious solution until the Council of Trent reconvened. He also sweetened the deal for the Protestant territories by permitting clerical marriage and Communion in both kinds. Protestant opposition was especially strong in Saxony, where the new elector Moritz granted even more concessions in what was known as the Leipzig Interim. But Protestant leaders in Magdeburg denounced the interim as the work of the Devil and produced the first Protestant justification for active resistance to ungodly state authority. In the final analysis, the interim failed.

Elector Moritz soon betrayed the emperor. Enlisting the secret support of Henry II of France, in 1552 Moritz rallied Protestant princes and launched a surprise attack on Catholics, forcing Charles to flee across the Alps. An uneasy stalemate between Protestants and Catholics held sway until the Diet of Augsburg in 1555. The political realities of the past decade had demonstrated that Germany was irrevocably divided.

Charles now accepted the realization that the religious settlement within any given territory would be decided, not by the emperor, but by the territorial prince. The principle of *cuius regio, eius religio* ("the ruler determines the religion") became political reality. The Peace of Augsburg now recognized two legal religions in the empire: Lutheran and Catholic. This legalization did not extend to the Reformed branch of Protestantism or Anabaptists. The settlement was not a triumph for toleration, but for political pragmatism.

E. The Reformation of Marriage

While Luther was living *incognito* in Wartburg Castle, Karlstadt implemented another of Luther's proposals from 1520, namely, marriage for clergy. Karlstadt not only advocated it, but led by example.

On Christmas Day 1521, Karlstadt caused a stir by celebrating the mass in German without his vestments, and then he distributed both elements to the parishioners—but he was not yet finished with his rejection of Catholic Tradition. The following day he announced his engagement to Anna von Mochau, daughter of a poor nobleman, and married her a few weeks later (January 19, 1522). The next month, on February 10, Justus Jonas, a fellow professor at Wittenberg and one of Luther's most intimate friends, followed suit and married.

Suddenly, married clergy were all the rage—for everyone except Luther. While approving these particular clerical marriages and generally upholding the right of clergy to marry, Luther was reticent to take the plunge himself. "I will never take a wife," Luther declared to his friend Spalatin on November 30, 1524. "Not that I am insensible to my flesh..., but my mind is adverse to wedlock, because I daily expect the death of a heretic." And then he met Katie von Bora.

Katharina von Bora (1499–1552) was born to a noble family near Leipzig. Following the customs of the time, the ten-year-old daughter was placed in the Cistercian convent of Nimbschen. Katie appears to have accepted her life until she and several nuns secretly read Luther's *On Monastic Vows* in 1522. The nuns embraced Luther's rejection of clerical celibacy and decided to abandon the cloistered life. When family members refused to assist the nuns, they turned to Luther himself, who was happy to help.

Luther enlisted as a coconspirator Leonhard Koppe, who smuggled twelve nuns from the Nimbshen nunnery in empty herring barrels in April 1523. Koppe delivered nine to Luther's doorstep in Wittenberg. (Three nuns had returned to relatives.) Remarkably, he found husbands for all except Katie von Bora. Luther found not one, but two prospective husbands for her. The first, Hieronymus Baumgartner, under pressure from his family, married a richer bride; the second prospect, Dr. Kaspar Glatz, was rejected by Katie as too old. Katie took matters into her own hands and specifically suggested two other prospects—Luther or his friend Nicolaus von Amsdorf.

Katie's timing was just right. Luther had begun to feel the loneliness of bachelorhood, and he expressed his willingness to "take pity" on poor Katie and marry her. The private ceremony took place on June 13, 1525, and a public celebration was held on June 27. It is clear that Luther married primarily as an act of theological defiance: "to spite the pope."

Frankly, Luther did not marry for love. On the wedding invitation to Amsdorf, Luther confessed, "I feel neither passionate love nor burning for my spouse." However, a remarkable thing happened after Luther married: he fell in love with his wife. Unlike other Reformers, Luther openly declared his love: "I love my Katie; yes, I love her more dearly than myself."

Luther and Katie enjoyed a feisty, vibrant, and deeply affectionate twenty-one-year marriage relationship that produced six children.

Luther's marriage was certainly significant for him personally and also as a theological statement about the viability of married clergy. But perhaps most significant is the fact that because it was such a public event, it became the paradigm for a new Protestant understanding of marriage. Indeed, many scholars contend that Luther inaugurated a cultural paradigm shift in the very concept of marriage.

For centuries marriage had been entangled with dowries and social status. In fact, the essential criteria for a good marriage match had centered on the amount of the dowry and the enhanced social status of marrying into a socially prominent family. Luther's marriage changed all that. He and Katie had no social status—he was a heretic and outlaw, and she was a runaway nun with no dowry at all. But Luther's outspoken affection for his wife became the new criteria for a good marriage. Luther's marriage reconfigured the reason for marriage from a consideration of dowry and social status to mutual affection. From that point on, social historians have noted that European cultures embrace love as the essential component for a happy marriage.

Luther and Katie changed the way the Western world thought about marriage. Luther's advocacy for married clergy and his own example inaugurated a social reformation every bit as momentous— perhaps more so—than the ecclesiastical reformation. For more than a millennium, celibacy had been the ideal of the Christian life. Augustine argued that sex, even in marriage, inevitably involved sin. Jerome ranked celibacy above widowhood, and to him, both existed on a higher spiritual plane than marriage. Luther and Katie changed that valuation for the modern world.

F. The Reformation of Poor Relief

By the sixteenth century poverty had become a persistent reality in more lives than ever before. Estimates are that 25 percent of the population of Europe was regularly underfed. Begging was rampant. There were deserving poor, such as widows, orphans, and the sick, as well as the undeserving poor, who chose to live a life of begging, not out of need, but for selfish reasons.

Part of Luther's genius was that he conceived of reformation broadly, not only in terms of theology, but also in terms of society. One's theology inevitably affects everything else. Luther became the first major reformer to address the theory and praxis of early modern poor relief and social welfare, and he did so from the standpoint of his theology.

It is too much to say that Protestantism caused the reform of poor relief, but it was certainly more thorough and widespread in Protestant communities. As principalities and territories became Protestant, they became independent from Catholic authority. In a very real sense, when city councils and territorial princes embraced Protestantism, they not only assumed authority for the practice of religion, but also acquired new jurisdiction over the wealth and property of the old church.

Before the Reformation, relief of the poor came from a plethora of loosely affiliated church agencies—local parishes, mendicant orders, and confraternities. With the Reformation came a sociopolitical reconfiguration whereby responsibility for poor relief was allocated to a centralized secular authority. This centralization gave Protestant regimes a more coherent and therefore more effective policy for the poor. Begging was prohibited in Protestant communities. Hospitals, schools, orphanages, soup kitchens, and shelters came under the authority of the government and were funded through a "common chest" that was replenished by the entire community.

This reconfiguration of poor relief was directly related to the central theological convictions that gave rise to Luther's reformation. For two hundred years the legacy of Francis of Assisi had linked begging with Christian piety. Francis and the Franciscans taught that begging most fully represented one's relationship with God. That is, begging powerfully illustrated a person's spiritual impoverishment and thus one's absolute dependence on the gifts of God.

Luther's theology disputed the implications drawn from this theological logic. He insisted that charity to the poor did not hold meritorious value. Luther, with his vigorous Augustinian anthropology, agreed that all humanity is spiritually impoverished and in need of God's grace, but he absolutely denied that any human good works, including giving to the poor, could merit God's grace in salvation. Salvation, said Luther, is based exclusively on God's grace, not on meritorious works. Salvation by grace alone does not preclude good works; it merely makes them a consequence of God's grace.

The true children of God would indeed practice *caritas* (charity), but it would be mediated through the Protestant governing authorities that were to dispense charity to the poor based on the Christian ethic of brotherly love. In keeping with the Protestant view of unmerited grace, Christians were not to view the poor as beggars, but as poor brothers and sisters who, through divine providence, had been deprived of the means of subsistence through no fault of their own.

Protestants could not eradicate poverty or even begging, but they did reconfigure the practical and theological significance of *caritas*. Charity was no longer meritorious, but was rather an act of worship.

IV. THE DARK SIDE OF LUTHER

Protestants have been inclined to cast Luther into the role of religious hero. Calvin himself called Luther an "Apostle." It is true that Luther was heroic in risking his life at the Diet of Worms for what he believed is the heart of the gospel. But heroism became more difficult when struggling to preserve the Reformation movement and his legacy. The early Luther lived and taught as if he had nothing to lose. Yet success was a powerful intoxicant, especially when truth was at stake. Over time, with the expansion of Lutheranism, the founder had much to lose, and Luther the risk-taker became Luther the defender of the movement at any cost.

A. Philip's Bigamy

Philip, landgrave of Hesse, not only was one of the first princes to ally with the Lutheran cause, but was also the architect of the Schmalkald League, a defensive alliance of princes who supported the Protestant movement. Only the electors of Saxony were more strategically important than Philip of Hesse. So it was a very delicate matter when Philip sought Luther's support for a bigamous marriage.

Like most princes, Philip had married for political purposes—in his case, Christina, daughter of Duke George of Saxony. Because of the political nature of the marriage, no one raised an eyebrow when he continued to enjoy a long string of mistresses. This was considered acceptable (even by Christina) as long as Philip remained discreet. His newfound evangelical faith seems to have troubled his conscience somewhat, and while he continued the affairs, he declined to partake of Communion for fifteen years. Then he met and fell deeply in love with a beautiful young noblewoman from his court, Margaret van der Saal. At first he sought to make her his mistress, but her mother refused and insisted on marriage or nothing. Divorce was out of the question, and that left only bigamy.

Interestingly, Philip did not pursue this course of action without consulting with his wife, who actually agreed to the bigamous marriage as long as her offspring were designated rightful heirs. Strange as this may seem to moderns, it needs to be remembered that Christina too was a victim of the politics of princely marriage. Philip was not unaware that some of the Old Testament patriarchs had more than one wife and, in keeping with the Protestant stress on the authority of Scripture, convinced himself that his case for bigamy had biblical precedent.

Philip sought out Luther, as well as Melanchthon and Martin Bucer, as to the permissibility of a bigamous marriage. Luther had argued years earlier, regarding Henry VIII and Queen Catherine of Aragon, that bigamy was preferable to divorce. Luther fatefully approved the bigamous marriage, partly out of concern for Philip's troubled conscience and partly out of political expediency. It was a decision that would cost many lives and nearly destroy Lutheranism itself.

Luther urged Philip to keep the second marriage secret, but such things rarely succeed. Biblical and moral considerations aside, there were serious legal issues as well. Bigamy, it turns out, was against imperial law, which meant that Philip was vulnerable to his archnemesis—Emperor Charles V. In order to keep his title and domain, Philip was compelled to sign a nonaggression pact with Charles V. Six years later, when the time was right, Charles would launch a surprise attack against the Lutheran princes and the Schmalkald League while Philip, the most powerful member, remained neutral. The results were catastrophic.

Luther's actions regarding bigamy can be understood, even if they do not exhibit the highest Christian morality. Some have argued that his support for Philip's bigamy reflects the antinomian tendency in Luther's theology. Whatever the judgment on this matter, Luther failed both as a moral leader and as a political strategist. By supporting Philip, Luther jeopardized the very movement he sought to preserve.

B. Anti-Semitism

Toward the end of his life, Luther's dark side manifested itself in one of the most hostile and belligerent writings of the sixteenth century. In 1543 he wrote *On the Jews and Their Lies*, urging Germans to burn Jewish synagogues, schools, and homes; destroy all Jewish religious writings; and prevent rabbis from teaching on penalty of death. In a decision that would reverberate in the Nazi era of the mid-twentieth century, Luther advocated that Jews be enslaved to the German people.

Luther's rage against the Jews in 1543 marks a dramatic *volte face* from his pro-Jewish stance in earlier years. In 1523 he had written a tract with the intentionally provocative title *Jesus Was Born a Jew*. Against the prevailing anti-Semitism of his day, Luther urged the German people to see Jews as God's chosen people, whom Christians should view in a cordial, even brotherly manner. In a world that blamed the Jews for everything from the plague to ritual murder of Christian youths and profanation of the eucharistic host, Luther was remarkably tolerant. Instead of advocating pogroms against the Jews as was done in the Crusades (where Jews were slaughtered in Germany), or expulsion as was done in England (1290), France (1306), Spain (1492), and Portugal (1497), Luther sought to evangelize the Jews.

How does one explain Luther's change of heart toward the Jews? Luther was gravely disappointed when his personal attempts to evangelize Jewish rabbis in the 1530s were without success. A few years later, he heard a rumor that rabbis actually managed to convert some Lutherans to Judaism, which sent Luther into a rage. Against the advice of friends, Luther unleashed a furious assault on the Jews in the 1540s.

But was Luther really anti-Semitic? This is a more complex question than is generally realized. Certainly, Luther shared many of the cultural biases of his century and his countrymen. In this general sense, Luther exhibits a racially motivated anti-Semitism. However, this was not the primary motive behind his virulent attacks of the 1540s. Rather, there is a growing scholarly awareness that Luther was animated primarily by a *theological* anti-Semitism. In other words, he was angry because the Jews, as he perceived them, had consistently rejected the gospel and for that reason should be utterly condemned.

Luther's zealousness for the gospel seems to have clouded his better judgment. Whatever his primary motivations were for his belligerence toward the Jews, in the final analysis no excuse is adequate.

C. Luther's Death

The older Luther got, the more temperamental he became. This animus shows itself in more broken personal relationships, more virulent attacks against the Zwinglians, and hostility toward the Jews. Exacerbating the cantankerousness of his later years was a growing number of physical ailments. He was plagued with all sorts of medical problems: kidney stones, constipation, hemorrhoids, and headaches — to name the illnesses he mentions most often. There may well have been a connection between his ailments and his repeated attacks of *Anfechtungen* (anxiety).

Perhaps the most storied episode of kidney stones occurred during a trip to Schmalkald in February 1537. Urination became impossible, he could not keep food down, and his entire body became swollen. So severe was this medical condition that Luther commended himself to God and prepared to die. On the way back to Wittenberg, he passed the kidney stone and wrote joyously to his wife, "I feel as if I were born again."

Luther's life ended in 1546 where it had begun, in Eisleben. He had traveled there with his three sons (Hans, Martin, and Paul) to mediate a dispute between two brothers, both counts of Mansfeld. He seems to have suffered a mild heart attack upon arrival, but recovered sufficiently to bring the negotiations to a successful end. Once the affair was settled, Luther was exhausted and retired to his room on February 17. A series of further heart attacks followed, causing him to drift in and out of consciousness throughout the night.

In the early morning hours of February 18, his close friend Justus Jonas leaned over the barely conscious Luther and asked: "Reverend Father, are you ready to die trusting in your Lord Jesus Christ and to confess the doctrine you have taught in his name?" Luther weakly but audibly replied "yes," which was the last word he ever spoke. Word quickly reached Wittenberg the next day. Melanchthon announced to his students, "Alas, the charioteer and the chariot of Israel, who ruled the church in this time-worn world, has passed away." Luther was gone, but his legacy survived.

V. LUTHERANISM AFTER LUTHER

After the debacle of the Schmalkald War, Lutheranism regained its balance at the Diet of Augsburg (1555). With legal status in the empire, Lutheranism continued to expand, principally in the Scandinavian countries. Denmark, under the reign of Christian III and with the assistance of Luther's colleague Johannes Bugenhagen, became Lutheran. The Lutheran movement was introduced in Sweden by King Gustavus Vasa and in Finland by the theologian Michael Agricola (1510–57).

Adherents to Lutheranism could be found even in the remote region of Russia known as Muscovy, when Czar Ivan IV (1553–84) expressed curiosity about Lutheran writings that had been imported from Denmark. The marriage of Ivan's niece to his Danish vassal, Duke Magnus of Oesel, increased the flow of Lutheran ideas into Russia. For a time, a small German church was established in Moscow, until Orthodox bishops complained and had it shut down.

Lutheran expansion was, however, hindered significantly by doctrinal divisions. Luther's death in 1546 and the defeat of the Protestant princes in the Schmalkald War precipitated internal strife between competing factions. Even before Luther's death there were theological quarrels, but they were held in check because Luther was the final arbiter in all disputes. With Luther gone, the competition for Luther's true legacy nearly destroyed Lutheranism.

Two warring factions emerged: the "Gnesio-Lutherans" (genuine Lutherans) led by Nicolaus von Amsdorf (1483–1565) and Mattias Flacius Illyricus (1520–75), whose stronghold was the University of Jena; and the "Philippists," who looked to the leadership of Philipp Melanchthon and the University of Wittenberg.

The Gnesio-Lutherans believed themselves to be the true inheritors of Luther's reformation, while the Philippists were more moderate and revisionist in theology. In the wake of the Augsburg Interim, the first major quarrel emerged between the two Lutheran factions—the *adiaphora* controversy. Duke Moritz had negotiated a more lenient version of the interim for Saxony, called the Leipzig Interim. Melanchthon judged it the better part of wisdom to accept the restoration of some of the traditional Catholic ceremonies on the grounds that these were "matters indifferent" (*adiaphora* in Greek) or peripheral to the essence of the gospel. Flacius took exception, arguing that "nothing is an *adiaphoron* in the case of confession."

This was the beginning of a series of controversies (Majorist, Synergist, Crypto-Calvinist, and others) that would engulf Lutheranism for the next twenty years.

The Philippist Georg Major, a professor in Wittenberg, argued that salvation must be attended by good works, hence "good works are necessary for salvation." This infuriated Amsdorf, who replied infamously that "good works are harmful for salvation." Although it was primarily a difference concerning theological emphasis, tempers continued to flare in the Majorist controversy over the proper relation of good works and salvation.

Another version of this dispute flared in what came to be known as the Synergist controversy. In 1555 the Philippist Johann Pfeffinger (1493–1573) inquired as to the role of the human will in conversion. The Gnesio-Lutherans Amsdorf and Flacius charged Pfeffinger with the heresy of "synergism," the assertion that the human will cooperates (*synergein* in Greek) with divine grace in salvation.

Yet another controversy materialized, centering on the presence of Christ in the Lord's Supper. Gnesio-Lutherans accused Melanchthon and the Philippists of reconfiguring Luther's understanding of the Eucharist in favor of a more Calvinistic view, hence the Crypto-Calvinist controversy. Luther had taught that Christ's body is ubiquitous and thus able to be present in heaven and also really present "in, with and under" the elements in the Eucharist. Melanchthon inclined toward

"Good works are harmful for salvation" (Nicolaus von Amsdorf).

a more Calvinistic view, which stressed the bodily presence of Christ in heaven, but that the believer who rightly partakes of the elements is spiritually lifted by the Holy Spirit into the real spiritual presence of Christ. And so it was, Lutheranism was plagued by incessant controversy for decades.

It was not until the 1570s that efforts at reconciliation began to make headway. Jacob Andreae (1528–90), chancellor of the University of Tübingen, became a credible mediator and led the way to unity between the Gnesio-Lutherans and the Philippists. Andreae, ably seconded by Martin Chemnitz and others, produced the Formula of Concord in 1577. The Formula managed to satisfy most Lutherans by creatively combining the thought of Luther and Melanchthon so that it was endorsed by two-thirds of all German Lutheran princes. Theological unity was finally achieved and Luther's legacy preserved.

FOR FURTHER STUDY

Althaus, Paul. *The Theology of Martin Luther*. Minneapolis: Fortress, 1966.

Brecht, Martin. *Martin Luther*. 3 vols. Minneapolis: Fortress, 1985–1992.

Edwards, Mark U. *Luther and the False Brethren*. Stanford, CA: Stanford University Press, 1975.

Edwards, Mark U. *Luther's Last Battles*. Minneapolis: Augsburg-Fortress, 2004.

Lohse, Bernhard. *Martin Luther: An Introduction to His Life and Work*. Minneapolis: Fortress, 1986.

Oberman, Heiko. *Luther: A Man between God and the Devil*. New Haven: Yale University Press, 1989.

The Swiss Reformations

The Maturation of International Calvinism (16th Century)

I. THE SWISS CONFEDERATION

The Switzerland of today is nothing like the Switzerland of the sixteenth century. Reformation Switzerland was not a single political unity, but rather a confederation of thirteen political entities called "cantons." Closely intertwined with these Swiss cantons were the allied regions of Saint Gall, Valais, Neuchâtel, Vaud, and the Grisons.

The wealthier, more urban cantons included Zürich, Berne, Basel, Schaffhausen, Lucerne, Fribourg, and Solothurn. The largest cites were Basel and Zürich, the former with a population of about 10,000 and the latter about 8,000. The poorer, more rural cantons comprised Uri, Schwyz, Unterwalden, Zug, Appenzell, and Glarus. These thirteen cantons made up the Swiss Confederation, which began to band together in 1291, primarily for mutual economic support.

Taken as a whole, Switzerland was a relatively poor region, with 25 percent of its land unable to be farmed. There was a weak political assembly called the *Tagsatzung*, but no real federal government, no head of state, no unifying language, and no overarching legal code. Although nominally a part of the Holy Roman Empire, the Swiss Confederation fiercely maintained its independence.

In 1525 Zürich was the first of the Swiss cantons to reject Roman Catholic authority and thus became the leading advocate of Protestantism within the Swiss Confederation. By 1529 Berne, Basel, and Schaffhausen had followed Zürich in adopting the Reformation, and major progress had been made in the cantons of Appenzell and Glarus and also in the associated Swiss region of Saint Gall.

The history of Geneva is somewhat different. For several centuries a series of prince-bishops ruled Geneva in close alliance with the neighboring duchy of Savoy. However, over the centuries the city acquired a significant measure of local autonomy, including the right to elect the four magistrates, called Syndics, who governed the city. Although not a member of the Swiss Confederation until 1815, Geneva developed a growing affinity with the Swiss while maintaining its sense of autonomy. By 1527 Geneva formed a political alliance with the Swiss cantons of Bern and Fribourg, thereby declaring its independence from Savoy. By 1533 Geneva expelled the prince-bishop.

Despite repeated attempts by the prince-bishop and Savoy to reassert authority, the new republic of Geneva was able to maintain its independence, largely because of the strong military support of the canton of Bern. When Charles III, Duke of Savoy, laid siege to Geneva in 1536, the Bernese army came to the rescue. The increasingly close relationship between Bern and Geneva had profound religious implications. When Bern embraced the Reformation in 1528, its people felt a duty to share the good news with Geneva.

II. ULRICH ZWINGLI AND ZÜRICH

The reformation of Zürich finds its primary inspiration in the charismatic Swiss patriot Ulrich Zwingli (1484–1531). He was a rather complex figure in whom a variety of theological, social, and political currents converged. He is a vivid reminder that defining a Protestant is more difficult than one might expect.

Ulrich Zwingli.

Zwingli was born on New Year's Day 1484 in the small alpine village of Wildhaus in Saint Gall. He was the third child among nine siblings in a family of farmers. His father, also named Ulrich, served as the *Amtmann*, or chief local magistrate. Saint Gall was associated with the Swiss Confederation, and it fostered in Zwingli a strong sense of political independence and a deep-seated patriotism.

A. Zwingli and Humanism

Zwingli himself seems to have undergone several reformations. Initially, he was heavily indebted to Erasmian humanism, which he first encountered during a two-year stint in Bern (1496–98) studying under the humanist Henry Wölfflin and then nurtured further at the universities of Vienna and Basel. Upon completing his M.A. from Basel in 1506, he took a parish church in the Swiss town of Glarus, where he remained for ten years. In typical Erasmian fashion, he devoted himself to the study of New Testament Greek and the early church fathers. He even corresponded with Erasmus himself. What is perhaps most significant about the Glarus years was his growing conviction of the primacy of Scripture.

By 1516 Zwingli had gone beyond Erasmus in one respect. Erasmian humanists tended to be more subtle in their call for reform, disinclined to make a frontal assault on the church or the state. Zwingli's humanism was a more active civic humanism that was openly critical of certain policies. Having served as chaplain to the Swiss mercenaries and witnessing firsthand their brutal defeat at the Battle of Marignano in 1515, Zwingli began publicly to criticize the Swiss mercenary trade. His political opposition to the mercenary trade led to his departure from Glarus to the parish of Einsiedeln in 1516.

In Einsiedeln, Zwingli's growing facility with the Greek and Hebrew of the biblical text led him to begin preaching in a different way. Instead of preaching from appointed texts as directed by the lectionary, he expounded the biblical text, verse by verse, chapter by chapter (*lectio continua*), and quickly gained a reputation for his expositional preaching. Moreover, his activist brand of Erasmian humanism compelled him to denounce publicly the exploitive Franciscan indulgence-seller Bernard Sampson and run him out of town.

Zwingli's biblical fervor and reputation for excellent preaching prompted his selection as *leutpriester* (people's priest) in December 1518 at the Grossmünster (Great Minster) in Zürich on the banks of the Limmat River. His appointment was nearly undone by his confession of a sexual dalliance with a local girl while serving in Einsiedeln. But for the fact that his main competitor for the post was a priest with six illegitimate children, Zwingli may have never preached a single sermon in Zürich. Yet he did preach his first sermon on January 1, 1519, and it created quite a sensation among the Zürichers. Although his expository preaching in the vernacular was highly unusual, it was still an echo of Erasmus, who had long espoused the same idea.

B. Zwingli and Swiss Mercenaries

While in Glarus, Zwingli served as a chaplain for Swiss mercenaries from his canton. After a series of notable victories in the Burgundian wars in the latter part of the fifteenth century, the Swiss mercenaries had developed a fearsome reputation throughout Europe as skilled warriors. With their distinctive military abilities with the long pike, their refusal to take prisoners, and their consistent record of victory, they were greatly feared and admired. The Valois kings of France were loathe to take to the field of battle without Swiss pikemen at the core of their armies. In recognition of their military prowess, Pope Julius II in 1506 made the Swiss guards his personal body guards at the Vatican (a policy that continues today).

During this period, Swiss mercenaries were embroiled in various military campaigns in Europe. Zwingli served as a chaplain alongside Swiss soldiers when they defeated the French on behalf of the papacy at the Battle of Novara in 1513. His support for the pope garnered for him an annual pension from Pope Julius II (which he renounced in 1520). However, the brutal defeat of the Swiss in the Battle of Marignano (1515) turned Zwingli into a vocal opponent of Swiss nationals serving as mercenaries. Shortly thereafter, he decided to accept an invitation to serve as priest in Einsiedeln (in the canton of Schwyz), whose famous Benedictine Abbey, dedicated to the Virgin Mary, was one of the most popular pilgrimage sites in Switzerland.

Zwingli had become convinced that mercenary service was immoral and that the Swiss were mere fodder for the political ambitions of foreigners. Two of his earliest writings, *The Ox* (1510) and *The Labyrinth* (1516), used satire to denounce the mercenary system. He portrayed his Swiss countrymen as virtuous people exploited by the political maneuverings of France, the empire, and the papacy.

C. Zwingli and the Plague

Between August 1519 and February 1520 more than a quarter of the population of Zürich became victims of the plague. Zwingli did not retreat from his pastoral responsibilities as he sought to console the sick and dying. By autumn, he too contracted the disease. Bedridden and with his own death before him, Zwingli rather poignantly surrendered himself to the will of God.

In his famous prayer-poem, titled the *Pestlied* (Plague Song), Zwingli solemnly declared to God, "Do as you will for I lack nothing. I am your vessel to be restored or destroyed." This sense of absolute resignation to the divine will, which some see as a Stoic influence, finds fuller expression in his important work *On Providence*. Against the odds, Zwingli did recover from the plague and pursued reform with even more vigor.

"Do as you will for I lack nothing. I am your vessel to be restored or destroyed" (Zwingli's *Plague Song*).

D. The Politics of Reform

The reformation in Zürich was political as well as theological. Zwingli displayed extraordinary political skill, persuading the city councilors that the political goals of the city were intertwined with the doctrinal teaching of Protestantism. Zwingli was convinced that the success of Zürich depended on a mutually beneficial relationship between the church and the city council. His reformation was in a very real sense a reformation in collaboration with the city magistrates—a magisterial reformation.

Up to 1522, Zwingli's criticism of the church was confined to matters of moral corruption. But after 1522 his criticisms became more trenchant and reached beyond the moral to the doctrinal realm. In this regard he bypassed Erasmus and entered the domain of Protestantism.

The decisive point of departure occurred during Lent of 1522, when Zwingli defended the right of several of his parishioners to reject the church's prohibition against eating meat during Lent. In the famous "Sausage Affair," Zwingli mounted the pulpit in the Grossmünster and argued that Scripture nowhere requires such a rule. The magistrates were persuaded and released the parishioners from jail.

Zwingli seized the moment. A few months later, he and ten other Swiss priests petitioned the presiding bishop of Constance to allow them to marry. At the time, Zwingli was already living with the widow Anna Reinhart, so he had a vested interest in this petition. The bishop, of course, denied their request, but in defiance of the bishop, Zwingli secretly continued his living arrangement with Anna. He subsequently married Anna in a public ceremony in 1524, shortly before the birth of their first child.

After 1522 the pace of reform in Zürich picked up significantly. Through a series of three disputations in 1523 and 1524, under the auspices of the city council, Zwingli took a distinctively Protestant stance on clerical celibacy, salvation by grace alone, and the ultimate authority of Scripture over the traditions of the church, while rejecting papal authority, the mass, good works for salvation, intercession of the saints, penance, and purgatory. The fundamental principle guiding Zwingli was that every doctrine and practice must be judged according to Scripture. The final rejection of Catholic authority came in April 1525, when the city council abolished the mass in Zürich. From that point on, Zürich was a Protestant city.

Zwingli famously claimed that he had embraced the Protestant gospel independently of Luther as early as 1516. Scholars continue to debate the accuracy of this assertion. Like most of the early Reformers, Zwingli gradually developed his theology under several influences. Certainly, Erasmus had a constitutive impact, but Luther was also significant, perhaps even determinative. Zwingli admits to having read Luther, although he claimed it was a cursory reading. What is clear is that Zwingli was familiar enough with Luther's defiant remarks at Leipzig in 1519 to describe Luther as a "new Elijah."

Historians are left with a perplexing dilemma: If Zwingli had discovered salvation by grace alone independently of Luther in 1516, why is there no clear record of this, and how was it that he continued to minister with the approbation of the hierarchical church until the early 1520s? Did Zwingli discover *sola fide* but fail to realize its seismic significance? If Zwingli discovered the Protestant theological distinctives independently of Luther, it would have been, as one scholar noted, "the most breathtaking coincidence of the sixteenth century."

E. Zwingli and the Radicals

Once Luther's reformation got under way, one of the pressing questions facing every Reformer was the extent of reform: how much reformation is enough? Some of Zwingli's closest supporters judged that he was inconsistent with his own pronouncement: "I came at length to trust in no words so much as those which proceeded from the Bible. If I saw a teaching could bear the test, I accepted it; if not, I rejected it."

Zwingli's friend Conrad Grebel (1448–1526) took Zwingli's words to heart, searched the Scriptures, but could not find any examples of infant baptism. He reached the conclusion that therefore only those professing faith should be baptized. A circle of supporters grew up around Grebel, calling themselves the Swiss Brethren.

Zwingli actually debated the issue with Grebel before the city council on January 17, 1525, and was officially declared the victor. Grebel and the Swiss Brethren were admonished and told to cease pressing the matter. Grebel responded in defiance on January 21, 1525, when he baptized Georg Blaurock in the home of Felix Manz. This event is generally considered the beginning of Anabaptism.

The Zürich city council became frustrated when it could not silence the three Anabaptists, and it finally jailed them on March 7, 1526, "until they die and decay." Shortly after their imprisonment, the three escaped and fled the city with the certain knowledge that if they set foot back in Zürich, they would face death.

There is some suggestion that Zwingli himself had at one time contemplated abandoning infant baptism. The Anabaptist theologian Balthasar Hubmaier claimed that in May 1523 he and Zwingli had discussed the matter and agreed that "children should not be baptized before they were of age." Whatever hesitations Zwingli may have once entertained, he had firmly resolved those doubts by 1524. A year later, Zwingli had Hubmaier arrested and tortured, forcing him to recant his Baptist views and expelling him from Zürich.

It must be remembered that in this period, politics and religion were two sides of the same coin. Zwingli understood that his reform movement depended on the political support of the Zürich city council. It may very well have been the case that the political realities played a significant role in his debates with Grebel and the Swiss Brethren.

As important as one's understanding of the Bible was to Zwingli, the perception that Grebel and company were social revolutionaries also informed his judgment. It could not be denied that there were some connections between Anabaptist leaders and the Peasants Revolt of 1524–25. Indeed, Grebel had been in communication in 1524 with one of the leaders of the Peasants Revolt in Thuringia, Thomas Müntzer, whose vision of reform entailed societal disruption. Social upheaval would never do for Zwingli or the Zürich magistrates.

In December 1526, Felix Manz was rearrested and the Zürich officials were true to their word. On January 5, 1527, Manz was pushed, hands and feet bound, from a boat into the Limmat River, thereby becoming Zürich's first Anabaptist martyr. Upon hearing the sentence, Manz is reported to have declared, "That is real baptism."

How does one explain such a harsh response to these Anabaptists? Part of the explanation lies in the fact that infant baptism not only was a religious rite of entrance into the church, but also was viewed as a civic rite of entrance into citizenship of the canton. There was no separation of church and state, as evinced by Zwingli's famous assertion: "A Christian city is nothing other than a Christian church."

Hence, rejection of infant baptism was not just religious heresy, but a political act of treason, for which death was seen as the only appropriate punishment. This helps to explain why the Catholics and the Holy Roman Emperor, Charles V, made Anabaptism a capital offense. In this milieu of intense patriotism, the Swiss response to Manz is not really surprising. Both the Catholics and the emperor said that Zürichers saw the suppression of the Anabaptist movement as a matter of societal survival, not just a doctrinal dispute. Scholars estimate that in the century from 1525 to 1625 between one thousand and five thousand Anabaptist radicals were executed.

F. The Marburg Colloquy

The interaction of theology and politics was much in evidence at the famous Colloquy of Marburg, when Zwingli and Luther met face-to-face. Zwinglian theology had considerable success and had spread among other Swiss cantons of Basel, Berne, Schaffhausen, Appenzell, and Glarus. Beyond Switzerland, Zwingli found support in southern Germany in Augsburg, Ulm, Strasbourg, Memmingenn, Frankfurt, and Constance.

Philip of Hesse wanted to capitalize politically on the expansion of Protestantism to form a defensive alliance between the Lutherans and the Zwinglians. Philip understood that there could be no political alliance without theological agreement, so he proposed that Zwingli and Luther meet face-to-face at his castle in Marburg (October 1529) to resolve theological differences and thus establish the basis for a political alliance.

Philipp Melanchthon, on the other hand, feared that a political alliance with Zürich and the southern Germans might provoke the emperor, so his political sensibilities predisposed him against any formal theological agreement. With these political concerns suffusing the theological discussion, it is little wonder that the talks failed.

Luther had only reluctantly agreed to participate in the Colloquy of Marburg, but Zwingli was especially eager to secure a political alliance if at all possible. At the very outset, Luther was determined to stand his ground, which was symbolized by his writing the words of institution on the table in chalk: *Hoc est corpus meum* ("This is my body"). This was Luther's shot across the Zwinglian bow—that any agreement would acknowledge that Christ is really present in the sacramental elements.

Luther proposed fifteen articles to be discussed and was rather astonished that he and Zwingli quickly came to agreement on fourteen of the articles (dealing with topics such as the Trinity, infant baptism, and governmental authority) and even found common ground on much of the fifteenth. This final article concerned the Eucharist, and both men agreed in rejecting transubstantiation and Christ's sacrifice in the mass. But neither Reformer would budge on the matter of Christ's presence in the Eucharist. Luther insisted that Christ is really substantially present "in, with and under" the elements, while Zwingli stressed that Christ's body is in heaven at the right hand of the Father and therefore could not be really present in the Eucharist.

The success of the colloquy hinged on this one point, and when no theological compromise could be found, the hoped-for political alliance could not materialize. Luther summed up the colloquy by saying, "It is obvious that we do not have the same spirit." Efforts to end this historic meeting with a joint celebration of the Lord's Supper also failed. The two parties did agree to refrain from further denunciations—an agreement that also failed.

> "It is obvious that we do not have the same spirit" (Luther to Zwingli at the Colloquy of Marburg, 1529).

G. Death in Battle

By 1529 religious hostilities between Swiss cantons heated up. The Protestant preacher Jacob Kaiser was executed as a heretic in the Catholic canton of Schwyz. War was narrowly averted in June 1529 with the First Peace of Kappel. But Zwingli's activism got the best of him, and he persuaded the Zürich city council to mount an economic blockade against the Catholic cantons that prohibited Protestant preachers in their territories. The Catholic cantons refused to accept passively the blockade and launched a surprise attack on an unsuspecting and unprepared Zürich in October 1531.

This so-called Second Battle of Kappel ended with a decisive defeat of the Zürichers. Discovered among the wounded in the battle, Zwingli was dealt a deathblow. Then, befitting a heretic, his body was quartered and burned, his ashes mingled with dung. The Second Peace of Kappel was signed shortly thereafter, firmly establishing the principle that religious affiliation was determined by the authority of the cantons.

H. Zwingli and Heinrich Bullinger

Upon Zwingli's death, the city council invited Heinrich Bullinger (1504–75) to succeed the fallen Zwingli. Bullinger had been well known in the Zürich Church since 1523, when he became the head of the cloister school at Kappel just outside Zürich. In 1527 he spent several months in Zürich studying ancient languages and regularly attending the *Prophezei* (small group Bible studies). In 1528, at the urging of the Zürich synod, Bullinger left the Kappel cloister to reform the town of Bremgarten, where he replaced his father as parish minister until called to succeed Zwingli in December 1531.

Bullinger proved to be a remarkable leader. In Zürich he supported and maintained the existing dynamic where the Zürich Council had ultimate authority over the church. As the *Antistes* (chief pastor) of Zürich, he earned the respect of the city council and thus had significant influence. He preached regularly in the Grossmünster and wrote commentaries on all of the New Testament books except the Revelation of John. A hundred of his sermons were collected into his famous *Decades*, which provided a general summary of his theology.

Heinrich Bullinger.

Perhaps his crowning achievement is the *Second Helvetic Confession*, which he composed in 1561. Believing he was on his deathbed, he wrote a theological last will and testament, which was vetted by his trusted colleague Peter Martyr Vermigli. Bullinger recovered, and his last will and testament became the most influential of all

Reformed confessions in the sixteenth century. It was accepted by the Protestant cantons of Switzerland as well as the Reformed churches in the Palatinate, France, Hungary, Poland, and Scotland.

Like the *Consensus Tigurinus* (1549), with which Bullinger worked out an agreement with Calvin on the Eucharist, the *Second Helvetic Confession* represented a further consolidation of the Zwinglian and Calvinist branches of the Reformed church. In the end, Bullinger proved to be a great theological unifier, succeeding where Zwingli failed.

III. JOHN CALVIN AND GENEVA

A. An Accidental Reformer

Protestantism arrived in Geneva a couple of months before John Calvin. By 1536 Geneva had managed to gain independence from its prince-bishop and the Duke of Savoy. Two Swiss cantons — Catholic Fribourg and Protestant Bern — were in competition for both political and religious influence on the newly independent city-state.

In the early 1530s, Bern sent Guillaume Farel (1489–1565) to win Geneva to the Reformation. Through public disputations and fiery sermons, in August 1535 Farel persuaded the magistrates to abolish the mass, and in December all Catholic clergy were given the option of conversion to Protestantism or exile. On May 21, 1536, the General Council of Geneva formally ratified the new Protestantism and pledged to "live according to the Gospel and the Word of God."

In a remarkable providence, a young twenty-seven-year-old John Calvin was passing through Geneva on his way to Strasbourg in July 1536 when his world was turned upside down. Calvin had fled from Paris in the aftermath of the *Affaire des Placards* (*Affair of the Placards*) amid accusations that he was partly responsible for the overtly Protestant address by the newly appointed rector of the University of Paris, Nicolas Cop.

Calvin made his way to the safe-house of Louis du Tillet in Angoulême, where he began to write what would become known as the *Institutes of the Christian Religion*. This small book of six chapters gained notoriety and quickly earned him a reputation as a Protestant theologian of marked ability. This taste of success persuaded the young Calvin that he could best serve the cause of Christ as a writer — and that all he needed was a quiet hideaway to write his books.

The free imperial city of Strasbourg, now fully in the Protestant camp, was just such a safe haven for an aspiring theologian, so he set off in the summer of 1536, with his brother Antoine and sister Marie, to settle there in the quiet life of a Christian scholar.

John Calvin.

As it happened, the route to Strasbourg was cut off by the third of the Hapsburg-Valois Wars. The small entourage detoured through Geneva, intending to stay a single night. Someone—whom Calvin describes only as one who later "apostatized and returned to the Papacy" (almost certainly a reference to Louis du Tillet)—reported to Farel that the author of the *Institutes* was passing through Geneva. The fiery redheaded preacher immediately confronted the young Calvin and passionately appealed to him to remain in Geneva to help consolidate the reformation of the city. Calvin politely declined the invitation, which only fueled Farel to a more dramatic appeal.

Calvin recounts the story in the preface to his *Commentary on the Psalms* (1557): "I had resolved to pass quickly by Geneva, without staying longer than a single night." Initially, Calvin explained to Farel that his "heart was set upon devoting himself to private studies, for which I wished to keep myself free from other pursuits." But Farel would not be denied, and Calvin, fearing the worst, gave up the journey. So began Calvin's lifelong association with Geneva.

B. Calvin's Early Life

Calvin's journey to Geneva began years earlier in the French cathedral city of Noyon, where he was born in 1509. The city was about sixty miles northeast of Paris, and John grew up in the shadow of the Noyon cathedral. His father, Gerard Calvin, was an attorney for the cathedral and secretary to the bishop. Little is known of John's mother, Jeanne, who died when he was five or six years old. Due to the patronage of the bishop, Gerard was able to secure a modest church benefice (scholarship) to provide for John's education.

At fourteen, John began studies at the University of Paris, first with general studies at the College de la Marche and then theological studies at the College de Montaigu. He graduated with an M.A. in 1528, intending a career in the church. But his plans went awry. In the preface of his *Commentary on the Psalms* (1557) Calvin offers a brief if incomplete explanation: "the study of law commonly enriched those who followed it," and therefore Calvin "was withdrawn from the study of philosophy and put to the study of law."

But this was not the full story. Gerard had fallen foul of the Noyon church authorities and had been excommunicated in 1528. The specific reasons for the excommunication are unclear except that they had nothing to do with Protestantism. Gerard must have concluded that all prospects of a high-church appointment were lost for any son of an excommunicated father, hence the redirection of young Calvin's career. Ever the obedient son, John then pursued legal studies at the universities of Orleans (c. 1528–29) and Bourges (c. 1529–31), gaining his law degree in 1532.

After the death of his father (May 1531), Calvin went to Paris, where he fell in with a group of French humanists influenced by Erasmus and Faber Stapulensis. During his Paris period (1531–33), Calvin published his first book—a commentary on Seneca's *De Clementia* (*On Clemency*)—combining his expertise in law with his affinity for French humanism. There is nothing in this work to suggest he had embraced Protestantism. While in Paris, Calvin became friends with a physician from Basel, Nicolas Cop, who subsequently was appointed rector of the University of Paris.

C. Calvin's Conversion

Calvin's first significant encounter with Lutheranism may have come in the person of Melchior Wolmar, a German Hellenist in Orleans who taught Greek. Wolmar, as it turned out, was a secret Lutheran at the time. While it impossible to know with certainty, Wolmar may have introduced Lutheran ideas to his young Greek student. When

Calvin migrated to the University of Bourges, he again found Wolmar there in a new post. There is little doubt that a close personal relationship existed between the closet Lutheran and the young law student. It is notable that in 1546 Calvin dedicated his commentary on 2 Corinthians to Wolmar—his "most distinguished teacher."

Orleans also proved hospitable to one of Calvin's kinsmen, Pierre Robert (c. 1506–38), also known as Olivetanus ("Midnight Oil"), so-called because of his proclivity to work late nights. Little is known of Olivetanus except that he was the translator of the French Bible (1535), for which Calvin wrote a preface. Olivetanus was at Orleans at the same time as Calvin (1528), and it is believed he too may have been a conduit for Protestant ideas.

Whether through the evangelistic efforts of Wolmar or Olivetanus or not, the young Calvin had undergone a life-changing experience and embraced the Protestant cause sometime during 1533 and 1534. Before this period, there is simply no evidence of his having crossed the Rubicon. He may very well have engaged in discussions with Protestant friends, but he was not persuaded. However, by 1535 he was in Basel putting the finishing touches on the first edition of the *Institutes*.

Unlike Calvin's first book (his commentary on Seneca's *De Clementia*), this one was an immediate success. First published in May 1536, the *Institutes* was Calvin's effort to present a summary of the main points of the Christian faith. Initially only six chapters, he continued to expand it over the course of his life until it grew to eighty chapters in the final definitive 1559 edition.

In one of the rare moments of self-revelation, Calvin speaks passionately of his conversion to Protestantism. In the preface to his commentary on the Psalms (1557), he describes his "unexpected conversion":

> What happened first was that by an unexpected conversion, God tamed and made teachable a mind too stubborn for its years. For I was obstinately addicted to the superstitions of the papacy and nothing less could draw me out of so deep a quagmire. And so this mere taste of true godliness that I received set me on fire....

Although Calvin seems to refer to a particular conversion experience, most scholars believe there was some kind of process. It is likely that he encountered Protestantism during his studies, perhaps through Wolmar or Robert, but resisted because he was "obstinately addicted" to Rome. Then over time, certainly by 1533 or 1534, he fully committed to the Protestant faith. It was "unexpected" in that he had been a devout Catholic who never contemplated leaving the mother church.

There may have been no Damascus-road experience, but Calvin's conversion was no less profound.

D. Calvin and Geneva

When Calvin inadvertently ventured into the new republic of Geneva in the summer of 1536, he found himself in a bustling city in transition. Geneva had established its own governing structure: the Council of Two Hundred assumed judicial and legislative functions, while the Little Council took over the executive role of governance. Within the Little Council, the real power lay with four syndics, who were elected annually by the male citizens of Geneva. If Geneva was to be reformed, Calvin and Farel had to work through these existing political structures.

Then there were the Genevan citizens themselves. Not all Genevans were enthused about the decision to become a Protestant city or with the new foreigners who were given pastoral oversight. Indeed, most Genevans still retained loyalty to Rome. To make matters even more complicated, both pastors soon became objects of animosity for one Pierre Caroli, a Sorbonne-educated theologian, who publically accused them of denying the divinity of Christ. The early years of 1536–38 were arduous for Calvin and Farel, who discovered just how difficult it was to navigate the political and religious minefield that was Geneva.

For the next two years Calvin worked side by side with Farel to make Geneva a Protestant city, not only in name, but in reality. The two Reformers made new proposals for greater discipline and drafted a new *Confession of Faith* (1537), both of which had the support of the city council but were strongly resisted by the people as too burdensome. In February 1538 four new syndics were elected with a mandate to restrain the new Protestant pastors.

Tensions mounted between the city council and the Reformers, and matters finally came to a head on Easter Sunday in 1538, when Calvin and Farel defied the newly elected syndics. They refused to administer the Lord's Supper according to Bernese prescriptions, which required unleavened bread. Irate city magistrates banished both Calvin and Farel, ordering them to leave Geneva within three days.

E. Calvin and Strasbourg

Farel accepted a pastoral call to Neuchâtel, and Calvin finally made it to Strasbourg when he was invited by Martin Bucer to pastor the French congregation and serve as a professor of theology at the Strasbourg *Gym-*

nasium. Over the next three years Calvin was remarkably active. He revised the *Institutes*, wrote his commentary on Romans, and participated in important theological conferences with Catholics at Frankfort (1539) and Worms (1540) and then at the Colloquy of Regensburg (1541), where Protestants and moderate Catholics, under Cardinal Contarini, actually reached agreement on the doctrine of justification.

The Strasbourg years were significant for many reasons, but particularly important was the influence of Bucer, whom Calvin addressed as "my much honored father in the Lord." Certainly Calvin's theology began to mature under Bucer's influence. From the prominence given to the role of the Holy Spirit, to the conception of theology as piety, church polity, the Eucharist, and the doctrine of predestination, all were derived in significant measure from Bucer's influence. This is not to deny Calvin's own theological genius, but in the words of historian Willem Van 't Spijker, one may rightly conclude that "Calvin became himself because of his friendship with Bucer." In short, one cannot overestimate the profound impact of Bucer on Calvin.

Strasbourg brought changes to Calvin's personal life as well. While there, Calvin married Idelette de Bure, the widow of a prominent Anabaptist, Jean Stordeur of Liège. Calvin's friends worried about his propensity to overwork and thought a wife would be good for his health. In a letter to Farel, he gives some insight into his outlook on the prospect of marriage: "I am none of those insane lovers who when once smitten with the fine figure of a woman, embrace also her faults. This is the only beauty which allures me, if she is modest, decent, plain, thrifty, patient and able to look after my health." Several candidates were presented, but Calvin demurred each time. One was too wealthy, and another did not speak French.

> "I am none of those insane lovers who, when once smitten with the fine figure of a woman, embrace also her faults. This is the only beauty which allures me, if she is modest, decent, plain, thrifty, patient and able to look after my health" (Calvin on what he wanted in a wife).

Although there is no record of courtship (probably because there was none), Calvin married Idelette in August 1540, and along with her came her two children. It is quite clear that Calvin's ministry responsibilities took precedence over his marriage. This is not to suggest that he did not appreciate and honor his wife, only that marriage was not his first calling. This ministry priority is reflected in the fact that Calvin spent thirty-two of the first forty-five weeks of his marriage away from home on church business. Calvin, as he himself confesses, was no "insane lover."

Martin Bucer.

Unlike Luther, Calvin was not prone to public displays of affections for his wife and only rarely mentions her in his correspondence, so it is difficult to know if it was a successful marriage. A son, Jacques, was born in July 1542, but did not survive. Idelette never completely regained her health and finally succumbed in late March 1549.

In the immediate aftermath of Idelette's death, Calvin informed Farel that he had restrained his sorrow "so that my duties may not be hindered." While this remark seems rather emotionally detached, there are a few letters that reveal something of his depth of feeling at his loss. To his friend Pierre Viret he wrote on April 7, "Truly mine is no common grief. I have been bereaved of the best companion of my life, of one who ... would not only have been the willing sharer of my exile and poverty, but even of my death ... she was the faithful helper of my ministry." Even in his most tender reflections, Idelette's primary virtue was that she supported his ministry.

F. Calvin Returns to Geneva

In what is one of the most surprising developments in early Reformation history, the Genevan city council did an about-face and invited Calvin to return. After Calvin and Farel were banished, the Erasmian Cardinal Jacopo Sadoleto seized the opportunity to reel Geneva back into the Roman fold. Sadoleto wrote a powerful and eloquent appeal to the city fathers, pleading with them to return to the mother church. Finding no one in Geneva able to respond to Sadoleto's challenge, the magistrates sought the wisdom of the leaders in Bern, who in turn asked Calvin to reply.

Although banished, Calvin reveals that he still felt a "paternal affection" and a spiritual responsibility toward Geneva: "God, when he gave it [Geneva] to me in charge, ... bound me to be faithful forever." Composed in six days, Calvin's reply (August 1539) was a *tour de force*. Step by step, Calvin bested Sadoleto both in eloquence and argument. Calvin confesses:

> We [Protestants] abound indeed in numerous faults; too often do we sin and fall. Still ... modesty will not permit me to boast how far we exceed you [Catholics] in every respect.... Rome, that famous abode of sanctity ... has so overflowed with all kinds of iniquity, that scarcely anything so abominable has been seen before.

The letter is masterful in its dignity and power. Having read it, Luther rejoiced.

Calvin's reply bolstered the Protestant party in Geneva and led to the surprising invitation to return. He was still recovering from his earlier wounds and had no desire to return to Geneva. Writing a letter on behalf of Geneva and the Protestant cause was one thing. Returning was another. He wrote to Farel, "I would rather submit to death a hundred times than to go to that cross [Geneva].... Who will not excuse me if I am unwilling to plunge again into the whirlpool I know to be so dangerous?" Farel again threatened divine curses if he should fail to heed the call. Remarkably, Calvin submitted once again and returned to Geneva on September 13, 1541.

In a gesture meant to stress his devotion to the Bible, Calvin's first sermon in Geneva picked up the text exactly where he left off on Easter Sunday in 1538. It also expressed his determination to establish the Genevan church on the firm foundation of Scripture. The main condition for his return was that he be permitted to structure the Geneva church "such as is prescribed in the Word of God and as was in use in the early Church." The *Ecclesiastical Ordinances* were made law in Geneva in November 1541.

The *Ecclesiastical Ordinances* organized the Genevan church under four offices: pastor, teacher, elder, and deacon. Pastors were principally charged with preaching the Scriptures, administering the sacraments, and exercising discipline jointly with the elders. Teachers were to serve the church through education of clergy as well as maintaining doctrinal purity. Elders were duly appointed laymen focused on discipline within the community, especially ensuring church attendance and moral behavior. Deacons were responsible for poor relief and overseeing the hospitals. The deacons especially concentrated on ministry to the poor, the orphans, and the sick. As refugees began to flood into Geneva, these offices took on greater significance.

Beyond the four offices, two ecclesiastical organizations were established to facilitate their responsibilities. The Venerable Company of Pastors was composed of pastors and teachers and met weekly (Fridays) for the study of Scripture and quarterly to oversee ecclesiastical affairs, especially education, ordination, and mutual discipline. More significant was the consistory, a mixed body of clergy and laymen (five pastors, twelve elders, and ten magistrates) whose main concern was enforcement of morality. According to the *Ecclesiastical Ordinances*, every home was to be visited annually by a pastor and elder to ensure moral conformity. To facilitate the visitations, the city was divided into three parishes: St. Pierre, St. Gervais, and la Madeleine.

While one of the syndics presided officially, Calvin exercised considerable influence over the decisions of the consistory. Any citizen found to be in violation of the moral code appeared before the consistory on Thursdays. Recent research has shown that the consistory spent the vast majority of its time issuing admonishments for such things as

"God raises up men who will give the last blow to popery, and finish the war against Antichrist which I began" (Martin Luther, after reading John Calvin's letter).

failure to attend church, dancing, laughing during the sermon, gambling, retaining Catholic customs, and public disrespect for Calvin.

Even leading officials such as Pierre Ameaux, a member of the Little Council, were not immune from reprimand. When he publicly criticized Calvin in 1546, Ameaux was sentenced to walk around Geneva dressed only in a penitential shirt, begging for mercy on his knees in each of the public squares.

It was emphasized that all admonitions should be moderate, and the goal was restoration to the church. There were harsher punishments for more serious offenses. The death penalty was prescribed for heresy, blasphemy, adultery after a second offense, and following sixteenth-century norms, torture was used in the most serious offenses. Jacques Gruet, for instance, was tortured before being executed for sedition. As intrusive as the consistory could be, according to historian Robert Kingdon it was designed "to see to it that every resident of Geneva was integrated into a caring community."

IV. CALVIN AND DOCTRINAL DISPUTATION

A. Calvin the Pastor

One of the ironies is that Calvin, as far as we know, was never officially ordained as a pastor. When he was first employed in Geneva, he was a "reader"—that is, a teacher—but after some months, he was also referred to as "pastor" or "preacher." It may be that he was made a "pastor" by the city council of Geneva rather than the church. In any case, there is little doubt that he was de facto the senior pastor of Geneva.

The moral tone of the city was reinforced by the frequency of church services established in Geneva. On Sunday mornings there were multiple sermons in each of the three parish churches at dawn, midmorning, and midafternoon as well a children's catechism class at noon. Also, on Mondays, Wednesdays, and Fridays, sermons were preached in each of the three churches.

A typical Genevan Sunday service followed this general pattern and lasted about an hour and a half: corporate confession of sin, absolution, singing the first four commandments, pastoral prayer, singing the remaining commandments, pastoral prayer leading to the Lord's Prayer, singing of a psalm, pastoral prayer, the sermon, pastoral prayer, short explanation of the Lord's Prayer, singing another psalm, and then the Aaronic blessing.

Calvin followed the *lectio continua* approach and usually expounded two to five Scripture verses in an hour. It was his practice ordinarily to preach five times a week—the Old Testament on weekdays, the New Testament on Sunday morning, and the Psalms on Sunday evening.

Calvin scholar T. H. L. Parker maintained that Calvin "is not fully seen unless he is seen in the pulpit." For Calvin, the pulpit was a sacred place. By nature diffident, Calvin came alive in the pulpit and poured out his heart in preaching. He often speaks of the "hidden energy" that takes the words of the preacher beyond his own preparation to penetrate the hearts in the pew. For Calvin, preaching had a kind of sacramental quality in which the Holy Spirit—the hidden energy—is actively present and communicating grace to the people.

Calvin practiced what he preached. Something of the level of his pastoral activity is seen in a letter by another preacher, Nicholas Calladon, who wrote, "I do not believe there can be found his like. I don't believe there is any man in our time who has more to listen to, respond to, write, or do.... [he] never ceased working day and night in service to the Lord."

Pastoral ministry brought out the best in Calvin. In a letter from April 1549 he mentioned his daily visits to a dying woman in his congregation. When she began to express her fear of death, he told her, "God is able to help you. He has indeed shown you how He is a present aid to His own." He then proceeded to reflect on the pastor's responsibility: "We ought to weep with those who weep. That is to say, if we are Christians, we ought to have such compassion and sorrow for our neighbors that we should willingly take part in their tears, and thus comfort them." This is a side of John Calvin seldom noted in modern scholarship.

B. Calvin against the Libertines

Not everyone in Geneva appreciated Calvin's pastoral gifts or the moral rigor of the *Ecclesiastical Ordinances*. Some of the older, more established families resented the church's intrusion into their lives as well as the influx of refugees into the city. Between the years 1550 and 1562, more than seven thousand immigrants flowed into Geneva, nearly doubling its population. Leaders feared that these refugees, who were overwhelmingly supportive of Calvin, gave his regime too much power. This fear increasingly turned to resistance to Calvin and the consistory.

Calvin did not endear himself to opponents when he censured the wife of a prominent citizen from an old Genevan family for lewd dancing at a wedding. The husband, François Favre, and his son-in-law, Ami Perrin, challenged the consistory. Both were briefly imprisoned, which served only to enflame their opposition to Calvin.

"If I should dare to climb the pulpit ... without carefully pondering how I must apply the Holy Scripture to the edification of the people, then I should be a charlatan" (John Calvin).

Perrin, a syndic and early advocate for Calvin, now became Calvin's chief opponent. Calvin labeled Perrin and his supporters "libertines"—that is, freethinkers—alleging that they preferred loose living. The libertines were a constant challenge to Calvin's leadership, especially from 1548 to 1555. In 1553, at the height of the tensions with the libertines, Calvin was so weary of the battle that he actually submitted his resignation to the city council, but it was refused.

The very existence of the libertines is evidence that Calvin was not the "dictator of Geneva," as some allege. For the greater part of his career, he battled the Genevan authorities to achieve his goals. Although he had the pulpits of Geneva under his influence, his authority was, in fact, very fragile. Indeed, he was not granted full citizenship until 1559, five years before he died.

C. Calvin and Servetus

If Calvin is known for nothing else, he is often identified with the execution of the Spaniard heretic Michael Servetus (1511–53). Servetus was infamous in his time for challenging the traditional doctrines of the deity of Christ, the Trinity, original sin, and infant baptism. Theology, however, was an avocation for Servetus. His primary occupation was as a physician, who gained some notoriety as the first person to discover the pulmonary circulation of the blood.

In 1531 Servetus published his infamous *De Trinitatis Erroribus* (*On the Errors of the Trinity*), requiring him to conceal his identity. He eventually settled in Vienne, France, where he became personal physician to the archbishop. As early as 1545, he began corresponding with Calvin, whose *Institutes* Servetus later contemptuously mocked with his 1553 publication titled *Christianismi Restituto* (*Restitution of Christianity*).

Calvin passed on the correspondence to the Catholic authorities in France, who arrested Servetus. He was convicted of heresy and sentenced to death by fire, only to escape just before the sentence was to be carried out.

Curiosity ultimately may have killed Servetus. On his escape in 1553, planning to go to Italy, the Spaniard made the disastrous decision to stop in Geneva and attend services in Calvin's church. It was a fatal attraction. Servetus cannot have been unaware of the hostile reception he would receive if discovered. Calvin had made his feelings absolutely clear in a letter to Farel that if Servetus were ever to come to Geneva, "I will never let him depart alive, if I have any authority."

Perhaps Servetus wanted to be able to taunt Calvin by later gloating over his clandestine venture into the church of St. Pierre. Whatever his intent, it failed when Servetus was recognized by French refugees.

He was immediately arrested and soon put on trial—this time by Genevan Protestants.

The trial of Servetus has become to many an example of the harsh reign of Calvin. To others it has been viewed as merely a political venue by the libertines to silence Calvin's voice in Genevan affairs. What is clear is that Calvin did not act as judge, jury, or executioner in the trial; he never possessed that kind of power.

Whether the libertines sought to exploit the trial of Servetus as a means to remove Calvin cannot be determined with certainty. What is clear is that his enemies were gunning for him. In reality, Calvin served as the prosecution's expert witness in the trial. Calvin was, after all, the leading theologian and one who had direct knowledge of Servetus's views. After consultations with other Protestant cities (Basel, Bern, Schaffhausen, Zürich, and Wittenberg), there was a unanimous agreement that Servetus's views were heretical and he should be burned to death according to the standards of sixteenth-century justice. Historian Roland Bainton wryly remarked that Servetus "had the singular distinction of being burned by the Catholics in effigy and by the Protestants in actuality."

It is not well known that Calvin, some years earlier (in the 1530s), risked his life in an effort to win Servetus to orthodoxy. In the dangerous days after the Affair of the Placards when Calvin was on the run, the two men had agreed to a face-to-face meeting in Paris, and a date and time were established. Despite the peril, Calvin appeared at the appointed time, but Servetus was a no-show. After the sentence was passed, Calvin made a final visit to Servetus and provides the following account: "Sixteen years ago, I spared no pains at Paris to win you to our Lord. You then shunned the light. I did not cease to exhort you by letter, but all in vain. You have heaped on me I know not how much fury.... But ... I pass by what concerns me. Think rather of crying out for mercy to God, whom you have blasphemed."

Both Farel and Calvin made last-ditch efforts to persuade Servetus to recant, but again it was in vain. Calvin even appealed for a more humane form of death, but his request was denied. Servetus was burned to death on October 27, 1553, with this prayer on his lips: "Jesus, Son of the Eternal God, have mercy on me." Even with his last breath, Servetus was unwilling to speak of the "eternal" Son.

The Servetus affair marked a turning point for Calvin. Adversaries had dogged his every step almost from the beginning of his arrival in Geneva. But his opponents' failure to exploit Servetus's execution to their advantage led to greater influence for Calvin. With the increasing influx of persecuted refugees, especially French, he was able to build a strong, supportive constituency in Geneva. As a sign of his newfound stature, he was finally granted citizenship in Geneva in 1559.

Servetus "had the singular distinction of being burned by the Catholics in effigy and by the Protestants in actuality" (Roland Bainton).

D. Calvin and Luther

It must be remembered that Calvin was a second-generation Reformer. By the time he emerged onto the historical stage in 1536, Luther had only another ten years to live. Zwingli had already been dead for five years. While Calvin appreciated both Zwingli and Luther, he acknowledged only Luther as an "Apostle" of God in the last days. Moreover, as much as he admired the "Lion of Wittenberg," Calvin was not blind to Luther's shortcomings.

Calvin's assessment of Luther is this: "I have often said that even if he [Luther] were to call me a devil, I would still regard him as an outstanding servant of God. But with all his rare and excellent virtues he has also serious faults. Would that he had studied to curb his restless uneasy temper which is so ready to boil over everywhere."

Luther and Calvin never actually met, but there were a few exchanges toward the end of Luther's life. After reading Calvin's treatise on the Eucharist (1540), Luther was reported to have said that Calvin was "a learned and godly man, and I might well have entrusted this controversy to him from the beginning. If my opponents had done the same we should soon have been reconciled." Luther also had a favorable impression of the 1539 edition of the *Institutes* and, through Bucer, passed on his congratulations to Calvin.

Amid all the fireworks over the Eucharist in the 1540s, Calvin wrote a personal letter to Luther in hopes of healing the Protestant breach. He deferentially addressed the letter to "my much revered father." However, Melanchthon, who was to deliver the letter, decided at the last moment not to give it to Luther, fearing that it would provoke further wrath. It seems Luther's stormy temperament prevented what could have been a profitable alliance.

E. Calvin the Ecclesiastical Politician

Calvin was no Protestant hermit, disconnected from the world and surfacing only to deliver the Sunday sermon. He was actively engaged in the church as well as the politics of the Reformation. By 1550 Geneva had become one of the main centers of Protestant Europe, rivaling both Zürich and Wittenberg. As the leading churchman of Geneva, he found himself involved in the great issues of the day, both political and ecclesiastical. He wrote long, detailed letters offering advice to kings and queens as well as key church leaders throughout Europe and England.

Perhaps the grandest dream of the early Reformation period was Archbishop Thomas Cranmer's proposal for a Protestant General Council that would speak with one voice in response to the Council of Trent. A panoply of the leading Protestants, Lutherans, Reformed,

> "... even if he [Luther] were to call me a devil, I would still regard him as an outstanding servant of God" (Calvin).

and Anglicans would assemble in England to address the critical theological issues arising from the first sessions of Trent. Included among those actually invited to this Protestant summit was John Calvin, who responded enthusiastically, "If I could be of any service I would not grudge to cross ten seas if it were necessary."

With dynastic upheaval in England and the transfer of power from Protestant Edward VI to Catholic Mary I, the dream was never realized. It does, however, suggest Calvin's international stature as well as his willingness to act on the larger stage.

One of the most historically significant ecclesio-political achievements of Calvin's life was the crafting and signing of the *Consensus Tigurinus* with Heinrich Bullinger, Zwingli's successor in Zürich. If Cranmer's dream of a Protestant General Council was illusory, Calvin managed to achieve theological unity on one of the most contentious issues of the entire Reformation—the Eucharist. As the Colloquy of Marburg demonstrated, political unity depended on theological agreement. Calvin had long bewailed the hardening of eucharistic positions and the resultant discord among those who agreed on so much else. His own view owed a great debt to the insights of Zwinglians as well as Lutherans.

Between 1546 and 1549, Bullinger and Calvin exchanged letters on the matter. While acknowledging there were differences, Calvin insisted that "we shall not on that account cease to hold the same Christ and to be one in him." By May 1549 the two Reformers were ready to bring the negotiations to a close. Calvin went to Zürich, and within two hours, agreement was reached.

Both Calvin and Bullinger understood that this document, the *Consensus Tigurinus* (Zürich Agreement), was in fact a compromise document. Its genius is that it focuses on points of agreement and ignores differences. It was flexible enough to allow each side to interpret it in accord with their own views. The implications of the agreement were profound. It not only contributed to the unity between Zürich and Geneva, but also removed the last major obstacle in the establishment of the Reformed branch of Protestantism. Calvin learned a great deal of theology from Martin Bucer, but he also learned from him the virtue of theological flexibility in the name of unity.

F. Calvin the Theologian

Philipp Melanchthon once described Calvin as *"ille theologus,"* (the theologian). This is high praise indeed, coming from the man Luther hailed as the "greatest theologian that ever lived." Calvin wrote commentaries on nearly every book of the New Testament and much in the Old Testament as well as treatises on various theological topics. But

"True and sound wisdom consists in two parts: the knowledge of God and of ourselves" (The opening words of John Calvin's *Institutes*).

there is little doubt that his *Institutes of the Christian Religion* (1536–59) represents his monumental theological achievement. It is widely regarded as one of the greatest theological writings in the history of the Western church.

Over the course of his adult life, Calvin devoted enormous energy to revising and expanding the *Institutes*, which he did five times. The final definitive edition of 1559 represents his most mature theological conclusions. He intended that the *Institutes* have a symbiotic relationship with his commentaries, which provided the exegetical basis for the theological conclusions in the *Institutes*. He also intended that one's theology should never be divorced from one's heart. In the *Institutes* he asserts, "Christianity is a doctrine not of the tongue, but of the life, and is not apprehended merely by the intellect and memory like other sciences, but it is revealed only when it possesses the whole soul and finds its seat and habitation in the innermost recesses of the heart" (III.6.4).

The first edition of the *Institutes* originally had much more specific and modest goals, namely, as a brief catechism for the instruction of the laity and as an apology defending the orthodoxy of the French Protestants. It was modeled on Luther's *Little Catechism* of 1529. The first three chapters expound the three traditional religious authorities: the Ten Commandments, the Apostles' Creed, and the Lord's Prayer. The remaining three chapters are devoted to the sacraments, Christian liberty, and church-state relations.

The primary audience was his fellow Frenchmen who were being persecuted in the wake of the *Affaire des Placards* in 1534, as he makes clear in his prefatory letter to King Francis I. "… all I had in mind was to hand on some rudiments by which anyone who was touched with an interest in religion might be formed to true godliness. I labored at the task for our own Frenchmen in particular, for I saw that many were hungering and thirsting after Christ, and yet that only a few had even the slightest knowledge of him."

The 1539 edition of the *Institutes* represents a significant enhancement (it is three times the size of the 1536 edition) with a vastly broader scope. In contrast to the first edition, which was aimed at laymen, the purpose of the new edition was "to prepare and train students in theology."

All editions follow the basic structure of the Apostle's Creed by dividing the *Institutes* into four books:

1. Book I, *The Knowledge of God* corresponds to "I believe in God the Father almighty...."

2. Book II, *The Knowledge of God the Redeemer in Christ* corresponds to "And in Jesus Christ his only Son our Lord...."

3. Book III, *The Way we receive the Grace of Christ* corresponds to "And I believe in the Holy Ghost...."

4. Book IV, *The External Means or Aids by which God Invites us into the Society of Christ and Holds us therein* corresponds to "The Holy Catholic Church...."

By the time of the 1559 edition, the *Institutes* had grown from six to eighty chapters.

There can be no doubt that Luther's spirit hovers over much of Calvin's theology. The great German historian Karl Holl called Calvin "Luther's true follower," and indeed he was. Calvin writes of Luther, "We regard him as a remarkable Apostle of Christ, through whose work and ministry most of all, the purity of the gospel has been restored in our time."

In a general sense, Calvin takes Luther's ideas and expands them. Like Luther, Calvin was a man of the Bible, which held ultimate authority in the church and in the lives of Christians. With Luther, he held to the absolute sovereignty of God in all things. With Luther, he affirmed that all humans are born sinners unable to perform meritorious works before God. With Luther, he wholeheartedly believed that salvation is possible through grace alone. With Luther, he embraced Augustine as the most reliable theological guide and was utterly convinced that the sixteenth-century Roman Church fundamentally had betrayed Augustine's legacy. With Luther, he acknowledged only two sacraments: baptism and the Eucharist.

Despite his conviction that Luther was "a distinguished Apostle of Christ," Calvin bowed only before the ultimate authority of Scripture and so, inevitably, there were points where he differed in emphasis or in substance with Luther. In some respects he favored Luther over Zwingli on the matter of the Eucharist, but in the final analysis, he carved out a new position. While he could not agree with Zwingli that the elements are mere symbols of Christ's sacrifice, neither could he embrace Luther's insistence on the physical presence of Christ "in, with and under" the elements. For Calvin, Christ is indeed seated at the right hand of the Father and therefore cannot be physically present in the bread and wine. The key for Calvin's understanding of the Eucharist is the role of the Holy Spirit, who spiritually lifts the believer into the real but spiritual presence of Christ. In this way, grace is communicated to the believer.

The biographer Bernard Cottret describes the doctrine of predestination as "the werewolf of Reformed theology, which [cannot] be approached without terror." It may surprise moderns, but Calvin and Luther were in basic agreement on predestination, although Calvin

Predestination is "the werewolf of Reformed theology, which [cannot] be approached without terror" (Bernard Cottret).

gave it more emphasis, largely because he was called on to defend it. Consequently, the doctrine has particularly come to be associated with him, even though it certainly is not the epicenter of his theological system. There is no developed doctrine of predestination in the 1536 edition of the *Institutes*, although it is gradually developed in subsequent editions. François Wendel points out that Calvin "very rarely speaks of predestination except in the four chapters that are devoted to it in the edition of 1559."

Contemporary scholars generally agree that predestination was not the wellspring of Calvin's theology. It does garner more of his attention toward the end of his Protestant career, primarily because of controversies inspired by such detractors as the ex-Carmelite Jerome Bolsec. In October 1551 he accused Calvin of heresy, specifically that his doctrine of predestination makes God the author of sin. Calvin was vindicated, and Bolsec was banished from the city in December, but it was a hollow victory, for it revealed a theological divide among Swiss Protestants. Calvin had many advocates (Farel, Viret, and Theodore Beza), but received only tepid support from Basel, Bern, and Zürich. This mixed review seems to have prompted Calvin to give greater attention to articulating this doctrine in later editions of the *Institutes*.

In considering Calvin's controversial doctrine of predestination, it is important to recognize that he approached the topic not from the perspective of a speculative theologian, but as a pastor in the pulpit. In the *Institutes* (III.21.1) he begins his exposition by observing the plain fact that when the gospel is preached to a congregation, "it does not gain the same acceptance" by all. Why some fervently embrace the gospel while others reject it can only be explained, he argues, by the "decision of God's eternal election."

Calvin defends predestination as a biblical doctrine supported by ample biblical texts and, furthermore, states that it was affirmed by no less a theologian than Augustine. Precisely because he believed that predestination is a biblical doctrine, Calvin did not soft-pedal his definition: "We call predestination God's eternal decree, by which he compacted with himself what he willed to become of each man. For all are not created in equal condition; rather, eternal life is foreordained for some, eternal damnation for others" (III.21. 5). As a pastor, Calvin was not unmindful of the emotional difficulty inherent in such a doctrine. Even though he firmly draws the implication that Adam's fall was ordained by God, Calvin paused to say: "The decree is dreadful indeed, I confess" (III.23.7).

Calvin brings his exposition to a close, resting in the shade of his twin oaks of orthodoxy, Paul and Augustine. "Let this be our conclusion: to tremble with Paul at so deep a mystery, but if froward tongues

"We call predestination God's eternal decree, by which he compacted with himself what he will to become of each man. For all are not created in equal condition; rather, eternal life is foreordained for some, eternal damnation for others" (Calvin).

clamor, not to be ashamed of this exclamation of his: 'Who are you, O man, to argue with God?' For as Augustine truly contends, they who measure divine justice by the standard of human justice are acting perversely" (III.25.17).

As important as Calvin was to the Reformed tradition, it is an exaggeration to view him as the "father of the Reformed faith" in the same way that Luther is the "father of Lutheranism." Calvin himself strongly repudiated the very idea of a movement named after him. The Reformed tradition rightly is seen as arising from the cross-fertilization of a number of Protestant divines, among whom the four most important were Calvin at Geneva, Bucer at Strasbourg, Bullinger at Zürich, and Peter Martyr, the peripatetic Protestant who labored at Oxford, Strasbourg, and Zürich. These four theologians in particular are properly viewed as the principal "codifiers" of Reformed theology. To be sure, Zwingli has a place in this constellation, but more as a precursor than a founder.

G. Calvin and Evangelism

Many have noted that the *Institutes* do not have a specific section devoted to evangelism. Detractors argue that this is exactly what one would expect for someone who espouses such a rigorous doctrine of predestination, which they believe necessarily undermines all evangelistic endeavor. Interestingly, Calvin addresses this age-old accusation in the *Institutes* (III.23.24) by citing his ancient theological mentor, Augustine: "For as we do not know who belongs to the number of the predestined or who does not belong, we ought to be so minded as to wish that all men be saved." Calvin then adds his own admonition: "So shall it come about that we try to make every one we meet a sharer of our peace."

For Calvin, evangelism fundamentally belongs to the church, which always has the responsibility of extending the kingdom of Christ. As a practical matter, Calvin was rather consistent at pressing his congregation to share the gospel. Like many modern pastors, he tended to conclude his sermons with a formulaic prayer. Although the particular words may vary somewhat with each sermon, the prayers hit on common themes that Pastor Calvin wanted to emphasize. One of the common themes to which he returned again and again was the need to share the gospel with others.

> Seeing that God has given us such a treasure and so inestimable a thing as His Word, we must employ ourselves as much as we can, that it may be kept safe and sound and not perish. And let every man

be sure to lock it up securely in his own heart. But it is not enough to have an eye to his own salvation, but the knowledge of God must shine generally throughout the whole world.

Faith produces its legitimate fruit only when zeal is kindled to increase the kingdom of God and to gather the straying, so that the Church may be filled. For if anyone is concerned only with his own private benefit and has not compassion for others, he betrays his own inhumanity. And where there is no love, the spirit of God does not rule.

God has deposited the teaching of His salvation with us not for the purpose of our keeping it to ourselves, but of our pointing out the way of salvation to all mankind. "This," he says, "is the common duty of the children of God."

For Calvin, it was axiomatic that the salvation of our souls necessarily carried with it an inevitable duty to share the gospel with others. This conviction, to the surprise of many, involved Calvin in evangelistic activities extending well beyond the perimeter of Geneva.

H. Calvin and Missions

The pioneering Protestant missiologist Gustave Warnack categorically denied that the Reformers, including Calvin, had any interest in missions. "We miss in the Reformers," he writes, "not only missionary action, but even the idea of missions." Warnack believed that the Protestant doctrine of predestination necessarily undermined the missionary impulse.

The influx of refugees into Geneva, prompted by widespread persecution, now turned it into a pan-European city and created an unusual dynamic within the Genevan church. Englishman John Bale, one of those refugees, recorded his astonishment at the variety of nationalities thriving in the city:

Geneva seems to me to be the wonderful miracle of the whole world. For so many from all countries come here, as it were, to a sanctuary. Is it not wonderful that Spaniards, Italians, Scots, Englishmen, Frenchmen, Germans disagreeing in manners, speech, and apparel, should live so lovingly and friendly, and dwell together like a spiritual and Christian congregation?

The great majority of those refugees who descended on Geneva came from France. Stirred by a deep desire to return to their homeland to spread the gospel, French refugees approached Calvin for direction, and he set about preparing them for their mission. He believed that a good missionary is a good theologian, so he trained them theologically, tested their preaching ability, and examined their moral character. Having passed muster, the Genevan consistory then sent them back to France as missionaries.

Nicolas Calladon records that 151 missionaries were sent from Geneva in 1561. Calvin remained intimately involved with these missionaries, offering counsel even after they had returned to France.

Then, as now, missionaries often faced terrible danger. When Calvin learned that one of the missionaries sent from Geneva had been arrested by Catholic authorities and was awaiting execution, he with tenderness wrote to this young missionary, "My dear and beloved brother,... this letter, which is a living image of my heart, and shows all its inward emotions, will speak to you no less clearly than I could, were I present and a partaker of your troubles. And certainly, if the worst should happen, it would be my wish to be united with you in death rather than survive you."

Obviously, from this letter we see just how personally engaged Calvin was with the Genevan missionaries. Indeed, one historical researcher concludes that in the last decade of Calvin's life his overriding preoccupation was his missionary project.

Although it is not well known, the Genevan missions enterprise was an extraordinary success. The historical data indicate that in 1555 five Protestant churches were established in France. By 1559 that number jumped to more than one hundred churches. And by 1562, scholars estimate that more than 2,150 churches were planted in France with the support of the Genevan consistory. It is estimated that there were some 3,000,000 Protestants in France by the time of Calvin's death in 1564. Ironically, Calvin's success led to greater repression and eventually to the infamous Wars of Religion.

Reports of amazing church growth made their way back to Geneva. One missionary in Bergerac boasted, "There is, by the grace of God, such a movement in our district, that ... we are able to provide ministers for ourselves. From day to day, we are growing, and God has caused His Word to bear such fruit that at sermons on Sundays, there are about four to five thousand people." Another letter from Montpellier in southern France declared, "Our church, thanks to the Lord, has so grown and so continues to grow every day that we are obliged to preach three sermons on Sundays to a total of five to six thousand people." A missionary in Toulouse informed Calvin that "Our church has grown to the astonishing number of about eight to nine thousand souls." Apparently Gustav Warnack was unaware of these letters.

As a French-speaking city, Geneva naturally was involved in France, but the consistory also sent missionaries to Italy, the Netherlands,

Hungary, Poland, and the free imperial city-states in the Rhineland. In what was one of the most ambitious Protestant missionary efforts of the sixteenth century, Geneva even sent missionaries to what is now Brazil. Because persecution of Protestants had intensified in France, Admiral Gaspard de Coligny, a wealthy Protestant nobleman, hatched a plan to establish a French Protestant colony in South America as a place of refuge. Geneva partnered with Coligny and sent two missionaries to Brazil, Pierre Richier and William Chartier, who were tasked to be chaplains to the colonists and missionaries to the natives. They landed on March 10, 1557, in what is now Rio de Janeiro.

The story of the expedition to Brazil took a dark turn. The leader of the expedition, Nicholas Durand de Villagagnon, suddenly betrayed the Protestants, who fled into the Brazilian jungle, where they found refuge with the Tupi, a tribe of cannibals. Over time, these Protestant colonists and missionaries eventually made their way back to France, where one of them, Jean de Léry, actually wrote an account of his harrowing adventure: *History of a Voyage to the Land of Brazil*, published in 1578. In the midst of their terrifying ordeal, de Léry describes how the missionaries remained faithful to their calling by attempting to share the gospel with the Tupi cannibals. He confessed that these attempts were ultimately unsuccessful, but not for a lack of effort.

The Brazilian missionary expedition provides compelling confirmation of Philip Hughes's assertion: "Calvin's Geneva was nothing less than a school of missions and a dynamic center of missionary concern and activity."

V. CALVIN'S LEGACY

A. Calvin's Death

Calvin's fellow Reformer, Wolfgang Musculus, once described Calvin as a "bow always strung." Calvin's extraordinary work ethic eventually took its toll. After years of sleep deprivation (he slept only four or five hours a night), often one meal a day, and overwork, his body finally gave way. Moreover, his last years were complicated with a variety of physical ailments, including intestinal parasites, hemorrhoids, kidney stones, arthritis, tuberculosis, and headaches. He died at the age of fifty-five on May 27, 1564.

Yet, even on his deathbed Calvin continued to work. When friends begged him to stop, he replied, "What? Would you have the Lord find me idle when he comes for me?"

Upon Calvin's death, his colleague and successor in Geneva, Theodore Beza, eulogized, "I have been a witness of him [Calvin] for more than sixteen years, and I think I am fully titled to say that in this man there was exhibited to all an example of the life and death of the Christian, such as will not be easy to depreciate, and it will be difficult to imitate." Calvin would not have viewed himself as a victorious Christian, but merely as a weak servant. For all of his intensity and conviction, he retained a real humility even at the end of his life. He requested and was granted burial in an unmarked grave.

B. Calvin's Endowment

One measure of Calvin's impact was the reaction of his opponents. It was a backhanded compliment when Pope Pius IV, upon hearing of Calvin's death, is reported to have murmured under his breath, "The strength of that heretic was that money never had any charm for him." Pius rightly recognized something of Calvin's (and hence Calvinism's) steely determination to expand the kingdom of God, which of course meant extending Calvinist churches throughout Europe. In the latter half of the sixteenth century, Calvinism surpassed Lutheranism as the most vibrant and far-reaching expression of the Protestant faith.

Calvin was fortunate to be succeeded by Beza (1516–1605), a man remarkable in his own right. Calvin invited him to Geneva in 1557, and in 1559 Beza was appointed as the first rector of the newly established Geneva Academy, where he served until 1599. Under Beza, the academy quickly became one of the leading Protestant schools in Europe. He was no innovator, but a faithful epigone of Calvin's theology, ably defending the Calvinist view of double predestination, baptism, and the Lord's Supper.

If anything, Beza was more logically rigorous than Calvin, frequently utilizing Aristotelian methodology in his theological articulations, which led to his being widely regarded as the father of Reformed Scholasticism. During the Wars of Religion in France, it was Beza who continued Calvin's role as chief counselor to the French Huguenots. He was a significant adviser to Henry of Navarre, and the relationship continued even after Henry's formal conversion to Catholicism in order to succeed to the French throne as Henry IV. Out of having an international network, Beza became the chief articulator of what came to be known as Calvinism.

By the mid-1550s a legion of Genevan missionaries, armed with a French translation of Calvin's *Institutes*, launched a Protestant assault on the Catholic Church in France. In what came to be known as the Huguenot movement, Protestantism made substantial inroads to such an extent that reformation was seen as a real possibility. Initially, the first Protestant churches were little more than clandestine house churches (*églises plantées*), but by 1562 they had evolved into more formally structured churches (*églises dressées*).

The first national synod of Reformed churches was held secretly in Paris in May 1559. By 1562 it was reported that there were 2,150 Huguenot churches scattered throughout France, and nearly three million Protestants located largely in the "Huguenot crescent" from La Rochelle on the west coast, to the Midi-Pyrénées of the south, to the Dauphiné in southeastern France.

C. Wars of Religion

After years of mounting tensions, passions exploded on March 1, 1562, when the Catholic Duke of Guise massacred Calvinist worshipers at a church service at Vassy-sur-Blaise. The Huguenot Jean de la Fontaine described the massacre:

> The Protestants were engaged in prayer outside the walls, in conformity with the king's edict, when the Duke of Guise approached. Some of his suite insulted the worshippers, and from insults they proceeded to blows, and the Duke himself was accidentally wounded in the cheek. The sight of his blood enraged his followers, and a general massacre of the inhabitants of Vassy ensued.

The massacre set off a series of religious civil wars that engulfed France for the rest of the sixteenth century, with only brief interludes of peace. This conflict, known as the Wars of Religion (1562–98), pitted the Protestant house of Bourbon against the Catholic house of Guise.

On the international front, the battles in France became a war by proxy between the Catholic King Philip II of Spain and the Protestant Queen Elizabeth I of England. Perhaps the most egregious event of these wars was the notorious Saint Bartholomew's Day Massacre in August 1572, when enraged Catholics virtually wiped out much of the Huguenot leadership, including the famous Admiral Coligny. The mayhem spread to more than a dozen cities across France. Some 2,000 Huguenots were slaughtered by Paris mobs, and in the days that followed, thousands more were killed in the provinces. Scholars estimate that perhaps as many as 10,000 Huguenots were killed over all.

France descended further into chaos when Jacques Clément, a Dominican priest, assassinated King Henry III by driving a knife into his spleen (1589). Before he died, Henry III pleaded with his heir, Henry of Navarre, to convert to Catholicism. It was, the dying king contended, the only path to peace. Henry of Navarre was reticent, but after more years of bloodshed, he was finally convinced and agreed to convert, reputedly stating *"Paris vaut bien une messe"* ("Paris is well worth a mass"). He was formally received into the Catholic Church in 1593 and crowned Henry IV at Chartres in 1594.

Henry IV issued the Edict of Nantes in 1598, granting Protestants a measure of toleration and finally ending the Wars of Religion. In the final analysis, Catholicism won out when Louis XIV issued the Edict of Fontainebleau in October 1685, formally revoking the Edict of Nantes and making Protestantism illegal in France. Calvin's big dream of a Protestant France was never realized.

Calvin's dream had more success in other regions of Europe, however. Calvinism had its greatest impact in such areas as the Netherlands, the Palatinate, Scotland, and England. In the Netherlands, under the leadership of William of Orange, the Reformed Church took root amid a revolt against Catholic Spain. The Palatinate became the only German territory to embrace the Reformed Church when Elector Fredrick III introduced Calvinism in 1561 and the University of Heidelberg became a leading center of Calvinist thought. The *Heidelberg Catechism* is one of the lasting theological legacies of Elector Fredrick's decision.

Certainly Calvin's thought impacted Scotland through the efforts of the thundering Scot John Knox, who actually lived in Geneva for some years. He exuberantly described Geneva as "the most perfect school of Christ that ever was in the earth since the days of the apostles." After his return to Scotland, Knox led the way in establishing Presbyterianism in that nation.

England too was significantly impacted by Reformed theology through the efforts of Peter Martyr Vermigli and Martin Bucer, Regius Professors at Oxford and Cambridge respectively. In collaboration with these two theologians, Archbishop Thomas Cranmer was able to shape significantly the theology of the Church of England during the short reign of the Protestant boy king, Edward VI.

With Edward's death in 1553, Protestant bishops suddenly found themselves under the ecclesial authority of the avenging Catholic Queen Mary I and fled to Calvinist strongholds in Geneva, Zürich, and Frankfort. Having been nurtured on Reformed theology, these Marian exiles returned during the reign of Elizabeth I with a desire to inculcate a more distinctive Reformed theology and introduce a more Reformed liturgy. Elizabeth resisted these changes, but this group remained firm in its Calvinist convictions and thus formed the base for the emergence of the Puritan movement.

Surprising to many is the fact that Calvin's theology even impacted the Orthodox patriarch of Constantinople, Cyril Lucaris, whose *Confessio Fidei* of 1629 manifests a Calvinistic soteriology.

Despite his often negative reputation, Calvin is properly judged the great theological heir of Augustine and the theological refiner of

"... the most perfect school of Christ that ever was in the earth since the days of the apostles" (John Knox's description of Calvin's Geneva).

Luther's theological insights. He belongs in the pantheon of the greatest theologians in all of church history. He has had many detractors, who were convinced, in the words of Will Durant, that he was a dangerous "neurotic" who "darkened the human soul with the most absurd and blasphemous conception of God in all the long and honored history of nonsense." Yet Karl Barth beautifully captures the irresistible enigma that is John Calvin: "Calvin is a cataract, a primeval forest, a demonic power ... strange [and] mythological. I ... could gladly and profitably spend the rest of my life with nothing but Calvin."

FOR FURTHER STUDY

Niesel, Wilhelm. *The Theology of Calvin*. Reprint, Grand Rapids: Baker, 1980.

Olson, Jeannine E. F. *Calvin and Social Welfare: Deacons and the Bourse Francaise*. Selinsgrove, PA: Susquehanna University Press, 1989.

Parker, Thomas L. *Calvin's Preaching*. Edinburgh: Edinburgh University Press, 1992.

Potter, G. R. *Zwingli*. Cambridge: Cambridge University Press, 1984.

Selderhuis, Herman J. *John Calvin: A Pilgrim's Life*. Downers Grove, IL: InterVarsity Press, 2009.

Stephens, W. P. *The Theology of Huldrych Zwingli*. Oxford: Oxford University Press, 1986.

Walton, Robert C. *Zwingli's Theocracy*. Toronto: University of Toronto Press, 1967.

Radicals and Rome

Responses to the Magisterial Reformation (16th Century)

I. PROLOGUE

In his justly famous work *Mathematical Principles of Natural Philosophy* (1687), Sir Isaac Newton first articulated his third law of reciprocal actions, which states that for every action there is an equal and opposite reaction. Newton's law not only describes a physical law of motion, but also is an apt explanation for the various responses to the magisterial reformation.

Martin Luther's defiance was like a spring rain that became a thunderstorm. On the one hand, the Reformation revealed long-standing social discontent and pent-up frustration with the abuses of the church. Peasants began protesting, and lay theologians emerged overnight: suddenly the local baker by trade became a self-appointed prophet of God. If Luther could defy the emperor and the church and live to talk about it, then anything was possible. On the other hand, if Luther thought the Catholic Church would not respond to ascendant Protestantism with an "equal and opposite reaction," he was gravely mistaken.

A. Social Upheaval

As it inevitably turned out, some of Luther's original allies, such as Andreas von Karlstadt, became his fiercest critics, who judged him not revolutionary enough. By February 1522 the city was in such an uproar that the city council begged Luther to return. He returned to Wittenberg in March, and calm was restored. Luther reasserted his leadership of the reform movement and inevitably marginalized Karlstadt.

Upheaval in Germany continued to escalate in other ways. Franz von Sickingen took up the cause of Luther and led what came to be known as the "Knights Revolt." As a German knight, Sickingen belonged to a warrior class of soldiers who served various royal patrons, but mostly offered their military prowess for personal gain. In 1519 Sickingen befriended the humanist knight and supporter of Luther, Ulrich von Hutten, who called for a reformation by military force.

The two German knights decided to lead a popular revolt against the Roman Catholic Church in support of Luther. Sickingen convened a "Brotherly Convention" of knights and was able to assemble an army from the upper Rhineland. Then in August 1522, Sickingen declared war on his old enemy, the archbishop of Trier, and marched against the city. Trier managed to hold off the assault until reinforcements arrived on the scene, and Sickingen was forced to retreat to his fortified castle, Burg Nanstein at Landstuhl.

The Knights Revolt came to an ignoble end when the combined forces of the archbishop of Trier, Philip of Hesse, Elector Palatine Louis V, and knights of the Swabian League marched on Burg Nanstein. Sickingen refused to negotiate and was seriously wounded during the bombardment of his castle. On May 6, 1523, Sickingen surrendered, but died the following day.

B. Disappointment with Luther

Luther's reformation, as he envisioned it, was fundamentally about right doctrine. He was absolutely clear:

> Life is as bad among us [Lutherans] as it is among the papists. Hence we do not fight and damn them because of their bad lives.... But when it comes to whether one teaches correctly the Word of God, there I take my stand and fight.... To contest doctrine has never happened until now. Others have fought over life; but to take on doctrine—that is to grab the goose by the neck!

Luther was not unmindful of the existence of social injustices in Germany, but that was not his battle. Little did he anticipate that his gospel message would capture the imagination of many thousands of economically oppressed peasants who linked his message of doctrinal reform with a demand for social reform, thus contributing to the largest mass uprising in Europe before the French Revolution.

When Luther's book *Freedom of the Christian Man* was published in 1520, he intended it to be read by theologians and the German intelligentsia, but he had no idea that it would touch a raw nerve among the peasant classes of German society. The notion that Christians were "free" proved intensively inspirational to peasants, who had a history of rebellion when faced with economic and social inequities. Professor

Peter Blickle calculates that Germany had experienced sixty peasant uprisings from 1336 to 1525.

Recent research confirms that landowners were indeed taking advantage of the traditional rights of peasants. Feudal lords were excluding peasants from common lands that traditionally had been open to all, restricting access to fish and game, raising rents, adding taxes, and overriding local laws and customs in the name of higher laws. Burghers, artisans, and miners from the cities and villages also found common cause with peasant complaints. Add to this the severe crop failures in 1523 and 1524, and all the ingredients for a popular revolt were in place. Luther's title said it all—or at least that was all the peasants needed. By 1524 peasant revolts broke out in the Black Forest and spread to Swabia in February 1525.

In March, Swabian peasants met in the city of Memmingen and summarized their grievances in the so-called *Twelve Articles*. The prime authors were Sebastian Lotzer, a local furrier, and Christoph Schappeler, a Lutheran pastor in Memmingen, whose very occupations represent the convergence of economic concerns with religious conviction. These articles clearly reveal that the peasants understood the Lutheran gospel vision to include socioeconomic justice.

The Memmingen manifesto begins and ends with religious statements of conviction. The first article asserts the right of each community to choose its own pastor. This was no doubt engendered by Luther's 1523 pamphlet titled *Proof of Holy Scripture that a Christian Congregation or Community has the Right and Power to Judge All Doctrine and to Call, Install and Depose its Teachers*. Article 3 explicitly conjoined the gospel with a revolutionary call for the abolition of serfdom. It was argued that since Christ gave himself to death on the cross, Christians are liberated from the dominion of sin and are therefore liberated from feudal servitude.

The remaining articles center on the social and economic injustices inflicted on the peasants by the feudal lords. The final article returns to a Lutheran fundamental of the faith, namely, that if anything in the *Twelve Articles* is found to be in violation of the clear teaching of Scripture, then it will be retracted. For the peasants, Luther's reformation not only was about doctrine, but also incorporated their social and economic well-being.

Luther responded to the *Twelve Articles* in his *Admonition to Peace*, in an effort to avert a full-scale rebellion. Reviewing each of the articles, Luther plainly informed the peasants that their concerns had nothing to do with the gospel, but rather were centered on "worldly matters." Despite acknowledging the injustice of their economic plight, he appealed to the Sermon on the Mount: "No matter how right you are,

"Christians fight
for themselves
not with sword
and gun, but
with the cross
and suffering,
just as Christ,
our leader,
does not bear
a sword, but
hangs upon
the cross"
(Martin Luther,
*Admonition to
Peace*).

it is not for a Christian to appeal to law or to fight, but rather to suffer wrong and endure evil; there is no other way."

This admonition left the peasants deeply disappointed with Luther. His advice was rejected, and within a month, massive revolts broke out in Swabia, Franconia, and Thuringia. Angered at their rejection, Luther took the side of the feudal lords, even as they slaughtered thousands of peasant rebels. His harsh treatise *Against the Robbing and Murdering Peasants* only served to deepen the sense of betrayal peasants felt toward Luther. Catholic apologists seized the opportunity to ridicule Luther with tracts such as the one by Johannes Findling, titled *Luther Speaks with Forked Tongue, or How Luther on the One Hand Led the Peasants Astray, While on the Other, He Condemned Them* (1525). Such writings had a distressful impact on the peasants.

Feeling betrayed by the Catholic Church's abuse of power and then betrayed by Luther's message of Christian freedom, the surviving peasants often found refuge among the emerging Swiss Anabaptists. If they could not return to the bosom of Rome and if they were unwilling to join with a Luther who encouraged killing peasants, where else could they turn but to Anabaptism?

Sickingen's revolt, Karlstadt's radical reforms, the iconoclasm in Wittenberg, the Zwickau Prophets, and the peasant revolts were signs of the turbulent times. These volatile events of 1521–25 immediately following Luther's defiance at Worms reveal that his message was a spark that fell into a German tinderbox of pent-up spiritual, social, and political frustrations.

Although unanticipated, Luther's reformation benefited enormously from the social anxieties of his day. These early events illustrate the fact that at the very outset of Luther's reform movement there were already those who wanted more radical reforms. These episodes were a mere foretaste of the troubles that would plague the new movement and thus validate one of the fundamental fears of Rome: rebels beget rebels.

II. THE REVOLUTIONARY ROAD

A. Reformers and Revolutionaries

Although it was not his intention, Luther's reform movement opened the floodgates of long-standing, deep-seated social and ecclesiastical discontent. In the words of historian George Huntston Williams, the Reformation impulse "drained the brackish pools and opened the sluices for innumerable religious currents long impounded in the interstices of late medieval Christendom."

At the outset, the modern student must distinguish between a "reformer" and a "revolutionary." The magisterial reformers emphatically denied they were revolutionaries. They sought orderly reform through the city magistrates and princes—thus the term "magisterial." The reformers sought to return and rebuild the true historic church, which they were convinced had been corrupted by centuries of greed and idolatry sanctioned by Rome.

In his famous reply to Cardinal Jacopo Sadoleto (1539), Calvin speaks for all the Reformers: "all we have attempted has been to renew that ancient form of the Church, which ... was afterward flagitiously mangled and almost destroyed by the Roman Pontiff and his faction." The magisterial reformers ardently sought to distance themselves from the revolutionaries, who were viewed as anarchists, charlatans, or demon-possessed lunatics stirring up violent mobs of illiterate and uninformed peasantry. This pejorative assessment was shared by magisterial reformers and Catholic conservatives alike. Indeed, the greatest threat to a civil society was neither a Protestant nor a Catholic, but a radical.

B. Radicals and Anabaptists

Historian Lewis Spitz likened the Reformation to a banyan tree "sprouting a maze of roots and branches." Among the maze that emerged from Luther's revolt were disparate clusters of disgruntlement that have generally come to be known as Anabaptism or simply as "the Radicals."

Because of the complexity of this "other" movement (in contrast to the Lutheran and Reformed movements), it has resisted easy categorization and remains difficult to define, in part because it was not a single movement with a primary leader or a coherent set of doctrines. Rather, it was a series of reactions and ripostes, which were out of sync not only with the mainstream Reformers and Rome, but often with other so-called radicals. The most one can accomplish is to overview the general trends and distinctive themes of these multivalent reactions that quickly emerged in the wake of the main Protestant break with Rome.

A good deal of scholarly debate has centered on the question of the proper terminology to describe this series of movements. Were they radicals or Anabaptists? To be sure, these various groups were indeed "radical" according to the accepted norms of the sixteenth century. Some claimed to have experienced or observed miracle healings, *glossolalia*, and even resurrections. Some declared they were prophets in direct communication with the Holy Spirit; many were convinced the end of the world was imminent; some in imitation of the early church turned to Christian communism; others embraced pacifism.

Many believed they should separate from the ungodly, and in a few rare instances, some even advocated violence against the ungodly. Many affirmed the authority of the Bible (and its literal interpretation) over the authority of the medieval church. In the main, they took a memorialist view of the Lord's Supper. Whether it was the affirmation of pacifism or violent apocalypticism, they were radical departures from the social, political, and religious norms of the day.

This designation certainly reflects the Protestant and Catholic perception of these radicals, who were variously described as "enthusiasts," "fanatics," and *"Schwärmer"* (Luther's pejorative term for a swarm of wild-eyed extremists). In all these ways, these groups were radical in relation to the civil and cultural standards of the sixteenth century.

From the outset, however, it was the sacrament of baptism that came to be the primary signifier of this diverse conglomerate of individuals and ideas. All, or nearly all, rejected infant baptism and affirmed the need for "rebaptism"—hence the term "Anabaptist," from the Greek words *ana* (again) and *baptizō* (baptism). It was the one theologically distinctive conviction that was common amid all the diversity.

Adult baptism signified much more than rejection of infant baptism. It also was the touchstone for the foundational commitment to biblical authority, which was inevitably accompanied by a literalistic and individualistic interpretation of the Bible. To embrace adult baptism was in effect a public declaration of independence from the authority of the medieval church and its traditional interpretation of the Bible. Therefore "Anabaptist" became the signature designation for a host of other theological convictions, all of which depended on an individual interpretation of the Bible.

It is noteworthy that baptism also had significant political overtones. In Zürich, for example, infant baptism not only signified church membership, but also was identified with citizenship. To reject infant baptism was tantamount to treason.

For our general purposes, we will use the term "Anabaptist" broadly to refer to the more typical groups and reserve the term "Radical" in a more restrictive sense of those who went beyond even the Anabaptist mainstream in their advocacy for violence or rejection of cardinal and historic Christian teachings.

It is worth noting that Anabaptists did not aspire to be identified as Protestants. Instead, they actually repudiated the Protestantism of the Lutherans and Reformed. Anabaptists acknowledged that Protestants were right to break away from the Roman Church, but they judged that the Protestants fell well short of the more extensive social, moral, ecclesiastical, and theological reforms that were needed and had succeeded only in creating another institutional church, to which the Anabaptists were equally opposed.

C. Monogenesis and Polygenesis

The traditional view holds that the Anabaptist movement arose from the Swiss Brethren. The origins are dated quite specifically to January 21, 1525, when Conrad Grebel baptized Felix Manz in the home of George Blaurock in the Swiss canton of Zürich. This view generally argues that Swiss Anabaptism was transmitted to southern Germany, Austria, the Netherlands, and northern Germany, where it developed into its various branches. This remains the dominant view for the historical origins and diffusion of Anabaptism.

Thomas Müntzer also had asserted the connection between faith and baptism, but he was more concerned about reinstituting the apostolic church in preparation for the return of Christ. It was the Swiss Brethren who made rebaptism a hallmark of their movement.

However, in a seminal 1975 essay titled "From Monogenesis to Polygenesis," leading Reformation scholars James Stayer, Werner Packull, and Klaus Deppermann dispute the traditional idea of a single origin (monogenesis) of Anabaptism in favor of a multiple-origins (polygenesis) theory. According to the latter, the Anabaptist movement had three points of origin: (1) Zürich in 1525, when the biblical literalism of Zwingli inspired Grebel to baptize Manz; (2) Augsburg in 1526, when Hans Denck baptized Hans Hut, inaugurating a Spiritualist brand of Anabaptism drawn partly from Rhineland mysticism; and (3) Emden in 1536, when Melchior Hoffman ignited an apocalyptic-millennialist version of Anabaptism in northern Germany.

Although the debate continues, the best evidence seems to favor the traditional view—namely, that a movement with a distinctive stress on rebaptism of adults began in Zürich but mutated somewhat as it spread to Germany, Austria, and the Netherlands. Local conditions determined the particular strain of Anabaptism.

III. THE MANY FACES OF REVOLT

Anabaptists were composed of such diversity that modern scholars have struggled to find appropriate categorizations. George Williams, in his famous work *The Radical Reformation*, has provided what is perhaps the most helpful analysis by subdividing Anabaptists into three groupings according to their primary authority.

First, there were the "mainstream" Anabaptists who, like the mainstream Reformers, looked to the Bible as their final authority. They also tended to idealize the early church and sought to return to its doctrines and practices. This grouping is generally identified with the Swiss Brethren; Grebel and Michael Sattler were key representatives, and adult baptism was a leading theological distinctive. In general, these Anabaptists were evangelical in orientation.

Williams has labeled a second grouping the "Spiritualists." This Anabaptist subgroup tended to rely heavily on the subjective experience of the Spirit of God, in some cases asserting direct communication with God. The German laymen Hans Hut and Hans Denck are typical representative Spiritualist Anabaptists. In the case of Hut, the Spiritualist inclinations were further excited by an intense apocalypticism, which in turn could lead to violence. Hut actually participated in the Peasants Revolt of 1525 led by Müntzer, but managed to escape the vengeance of the feudal lords. For our purposes, we have distinguished the nonviolent Spirituals from those with a proclivity for violence; these we have categorized as "Revolutionaries."

Michael Servetus.

The final category identified by Williams is the "Rationalists," who, as the name suggests, placed ultimate confidence in their reason. Although those belonging to this category judged that the mainstream Reformers had not gone far enough, they were in fact far removed from the mainstream Anabaptist movement.

While such rationalists generally rejected infant baptism, it was not central to their outlook. They were truly "radical" in that they were willing to reject traditional doctrines if they did not measure up to rational scrutiny. Representatives of this group include Michael Servetus, Johann Faust (Faustus), and Lelio Sozzini, all of whom rejected the traditional doctrine of the Trinity as well as the eternal deity of Christ (that is, Jesus was divine in the same sense as God the Father). These historic Christian doctrines were judged false because they violated reason. Since respectable mainstream Anabaptists would not have wished to be identified with these anti-Trinitarians, they are best viewed as marginal to the broader Anabaptist movement.

A. Archetypal Anabaptists

1. Swiss Brethren

As the Peasants Revolt was being crushed in Germany, a sacramental revolt was taking place in Zürich. Zwingli's reformation was successful because he was able to persuade the Zürich magistrates that his vision of the church was fully in accord with biblical authority and a straightforward interpretation of the Bible. His colleague, the patrician Conrad Grebel, took Zwingli's teaching seriously. As they studied the Scriptures, they could find no explicit warrant for infant baptism in the New Testament, so they rejected it as unbiblical and adopted adult baptism.

Thus a movement developed in Zürich whose highest ideal was a literal hermeneutic of the Bible, and the conspicuous doctrinal manifestation of that hermeneutic was a stress on adult baptism upon a profession of faith. These Anabaptists were concerned that the mainstream Reformers were still under the influence of the medieval church and had failed to do justice to the teaching of the New Testament.

Perhaps the most representative brand of mainstream Anabaptism came from the former Benedictine monk Michael Sattler. Sattler had been the prior of the Black Forest monastery of St. Peter at Freiburg im Breisgau, but some scholars believe the peasant revolts in Germany triggered his transition to Anabaptism. After the Peasants Revolt, he turned up in Zürich, where he seems to have embraced the Anabaptist ideas of the Swiss Brethren. Forced to flee Zürich, he made his way to Strasbourg, where he had cordial relations with Martin Bucer. By early 1527 he had returned to the Black Forest, where his destiny was tragically forged.

By most accounts, Sattler was the primary author of the *Schleitheim Articles*, which resulted from a secret meeting of Swiss and southern German Anabaptists on February 24, 1527. The seven articles assert that (1) baptism is contingent on repentance and a moral life; (2) brethren who fail to live according to the Christian code of ethics are to be banned from the community; (3) a memorialist or Zwinglian view of the Lord's Supper is the correct one; (4) there should be a radical separation of Christians from secular society; (5) the pastor must maintain high moral standards in his life and ministry; (6) true Christians must not serve the civil government; and (7) all oaths to the state are to be prohibited.

Beneath the specific articles one can easily discern two main currents: separation from the world, and maintenance of moral purity within the Christian community. The Anabaptist vision is to restore the church of their day to the pristine purity of the first-century

Christian church with a radical moral purity that distinguishes and separates them from the surrounding world. Sattler and Swiss Anabaptists were unsettled by what appeared to be antinomian implications from Luther's doctrine of justification. Sattler certainly opposed Catholics who stress works while neglecting faith, but he also rejected the notion of faith without works. For him, true faith must be accompanied by good deeds.

Perhaps surprising to moderns, mainstream Protestants and Catholics alike perceived in Sattler's articles a sinister challenge to the stability of society. The late medieval feudal worldview understood society to be locked in a delicate equilibrium between church and state (*Corpus Christianum*). If the equilibrium were upset, then all of society would crumble into chaos. Thus, to separate church from the state was tantamount to sedition.

In the minds of Catholics and mainstream Reformers alike, there was no substantial difference between the violent apocalypticism of Thomas Müntzer and Sattler's *Schleitheim Articles*. Many perceived in the *Schleitheim Articles* an effort to continue the Peasants Revolt under a different guise. If its fundamental principles were followed, social upheaval would inevitably result. Neither Catholics nor mainstream Protestants were willing to tolerate such ideas.

Sattler sought to live in the light of the *Schleitheim Articles* and soon became a "shepherd in the church of God," in the little town of Horb in Württemberg. Soon after taking up his new pastorate, he was arrested by Catholic authorities along with his wife, Margartha, in March 1527, less than a month after composing the *Schleitheim Articles*. He was given a trial, but the outcome was a foregone conclusion. The official sentence read:

> In the case of the attorney of His imperial majesty vs. Michael Sattler, judgment is passed that Michael Sattler shall be delivered to the executioner, who shall lead him to the place of execution and cut out his tongue, then forge him fast to a wagon and there with red-hot tongs twice tear pieces from his body; and after he has been brought outside the gate, he shall be plied five times more in the same manner. . . .

After gruesome torture, Sattler was burned at the stake on May 20, 1527, at Rottenberg am Neckar. But the authorities were not yet finished. They turned next to his wife, a former Beguine sister. When Margartha repeatedly refused to renounce the views of her husband, she too was put to death by drowning in the Neckar River. Even in death, the Anabaptists were mocked.

At least one magisterial reformer, Martin Bucer, opposed the execution of Sattler. Bucer said of him, "[I] do not doubt that Michael Sattler, who was burned at Rottenburg, was a dear friend of God, although he was a leader of the Anabaptists...."

2. Pacifism

The Swiss Brethren, harkening back to the ancient Christian centuries, early on embraced absolute pacifism as a Christian virtue. To be sure, Christian pacifism was nothing new, but it had received a renewed emphasis in the writings of Erasmus, who in turn exercised an important influence on the Swiss Brethren.

Based on his reading of the New Testament, Conrad Grebel's letter to Thomas Müntzer in September 1524 clearly asserted that "killing has been done away with altogether." Grebel advocated an absolute pacifism in which the Christian should not take up the sword for any reason, and his vision of pacifism became normative for the Swiss Brethren. Sattler also had affirmed the same pacifism in the *Schleitheim Articles*, although he acknowledged that the state has biblical authority to employ the sword in defense of the good and punishment of evil.

Balthasar Hubmaier was in broad sympathy with Grebel's pacifism except in the case of self-defense. He argued that Christians could serve in the military and that the Christian magistrate could take up the sword for defense or justice. Hence, Hubmaier's followers became known as the *"Schwertler"* (sword carriers). But the prevailing view was that of Grebel, whose advocates were called the *"Stäbler"* (staff carriers). Although there is no clear connection with the Swiss Brethren, Menno Simons was in basic alignment with the pacifism of the Swiss Anabaptists.

3. Anabaptism and Communalism

Early on, both Erasmus and Zwingli recognized the sharing of wealth and goods as a Christian ideal. It was, after all, characteristic of the early Christians in Acts 2 and 4. In Zürich, Zwingli did not require the sharing of goods, but neither was it disparaged. As the Swiss Brethren rose up, they tended to embrace more fully the notion of Christian communalism. In the first Anabaptist congregation in Zollikon (a village church within the canton of Zürich pastored by Johannes Brötli), all goods were held in common. Felix Manz made it clear that alongside adult baptism, he also advocated "the community of all things, as in Acts 2."

Balthasar Hubmaier.

The Swiss Anabaptists increasingly came under attack from established churches that accused them of being unwilling to pay their debts and even desiring the property of others. As a consequence, some Swiss Anabaptists began to retreat from the New Testament ideal.

The Bavarian Anabaptist theologian Hubmaier, who sought refuge in Zürich in the wake of the Peasants Revolt, was tortured by the authorities and forced to renounce his Anabaptist views. Later he bitterly remarked that Zwingli advocated theological education by torture. Hubmaier fled to the south Moravian community of Nikolsburg in 1526, where he garnered the support of Count Leonhard von Liechtenstein, who was himself rebaptized as an adult.

The Anabaptist church in Nikolsburg became a beacon for many alienated Anabaptists throughout the region, especially from Tyrol in Austria. Disenfranchised Anabaptists flocked to Nikolsburg in droves and brought with them their cultural and religious diversity. These differences led to controversy in 1527. One group, the *Gemainschaffter* ("community people"), under the leadership of Jacob Wiedmann, insisted that it was a Christian duty to share all things with immigrants. The controversy reached a boiling point in March 1528, when Wiedmann and the *Gemainschaffter* were expelled from Nikolsburg. Dispirited and in disarray, they eventually settled in the Moravian town of Auspitz, and that is where Jacob Hutter first encountered them in August 1533.

Hutter had become a disciple of the Swiss Anabaptists under the influence of George Blaurock in Tyrol. After Blaurock's execution in September 1529, Hutter assumed the leading role among the Tyrol Anabaptists. When persecution intensified, Hutter made his first contact with the remnants of the *Gemainschaffte* community in Moravia and formed a strong bond with Wilhelm Reublin, one of the early Swiss Brethren in the canton of Zürich. By 1533 the Tyrol persecution compelled Hutter to resettle in Moravia among the Anabaptists at Auspitz. Once there, he found the church in desperate need of leadership. He was able to restore order and reestablished the haphazard communalism into a well-ordered community with complete sharing of wealth.

For two years Hutter and his Anabaptist community were able to live in relative peace. However, in the wake of the Münster Debacle (1534–35), the fires of persecution heated up, and Archduke Ferdinand of Austria pressured the lords of Liechtenstein to expel the Hutterites, leaving them vulnerable to greater misery. Hutter was arrested in late 1535 and executed on February 25, 1536. Archduke Ferdinand had declared, "Even if Hutter should renounce his error, we will not pardon him, ... but we will let the penalty which he has so abundantly merited take its course."

In spite of the intense harassment, the Hutterites persevered, and when the persecution abated, they again found refuge in Moravia. Their distinctive Christian communalism has remained intact to the present day.

B. Spiritualists

A second distinct form of Anabaptism arose in southern Germany and Austria that was especially indebted to Hans Denck. He was educated at the University of Engolstadt, but his earliest influence was German humanism. Like good humanists, he became trilingual—mastering Greek, Hebrew, and Latin. In 1523 he made his way to Basel to bask in the glow of Erasmus and German Reformer John Oecolampadius, the latter assisting Denck in securing the post of principal at the prestigious St. Sebald's School in Nuremberg. During his brief tenure in Nuremburg, Denck's humanist inclinations fused with the mystical piety of Johann Tauler and the Spiritualism of Thomas Müntzer, which alarmed some of his fellow Reformists there.

Although his theology at this point is somewhat ambiguous, Denck too came under suspicion because of his association with some Anabaptists, and he was expelled in January 1525. He made his way to Augsburg, where he had a fateful encounter with Hubmaier, who persuaded him to be rebaptized. Thus Denck entered the ranks of the Anabaptists.

At least two key influences shaped Denck's distinctive brand of Anabaptism. First was his humanist background, which put him at odds with Luther's doctrine of *sola fide*. Denck opposed any teaching that seemed to obfuscate the moral imperatives of the gospel. Original sin, predestination, bondage of the will, the stress on the external rites of preaching, and the administration of the sacraments seemed to him to undermine the need for sinners to yield to God. Denck stressed the need for discipleship (*Nachfolge*), that is, the living of a godly life.

Second, the influence of the German mystics led Denck to question any outward religious forms that might be construed as mediating God's grace. True religious authority, he believed, is found in the inner dimension of the soul. External forms function only as witnesses to the inward truth revealed by the Spirit. For Denck, this meant that even the Scriptures and the sacraments serve as secondary witnesses to the truth first grasped inwardly, and in the final analysis, those external witnesses are ultimately dispensable. Christ is the great exemplar who demonstrates how Christians are to live.

These two features established the basic contours of the southern German and Austrian brand of Anabaptism.

Denck found himself repeatedly expelled from Protestant cities—Nuremburg in 1525 and Strasbourg in 1526. Exhausted by the violent persecutions of the Catholics and magisterial reformers and disillusioned with some of the excesses of the early Anabaptist movement, he sought refuge again in Basel with Oecolampadius. Denck was allowed to return, but he was required to submit an acceptable doctrinal statement of his views. In his personal statement of faith, he still regarded infant baptism as unbiblical, but he no longer insisted on rebaptism. In general, this statement represents perhaps a shift away from Anabaptism toward a more distinctive Spiritualism.

Shortly after submitting his doctrinal statement, Denck contracted the plague and died in 1527, but not before inaugurating a distinctive Spiritualist form of Anabaptism.

IV. REVOLUTIONARIES

A. Melchiorites

Although a center of magisterial reform, Strasbourg was rather tolerant of religious dissenters and therefore, inevitably, collected a wide variety of marginal religious sectarians. A third distinctive brand of Anabaptism arose in tolerant Strasbourg that was associated with the furrier and lay preacher Melchior Hoffman (c. 1495–1543). Before coming to Strasbourg, Hoffman had been an early advocate of Luther's ideas in Scandinavian lands from 1522 to 1529, but ran afoul of the Lutherans and was banished to southern Germany.

It was not until he arrived in Strasbourg in 1529 that Hoffman embraced the Anabaptist movement. There he fell in with the so-called Strasbourg prophets—Barbara Restock and Leinhard and Ursula Jost—who persuaded Hoffman that he was Elijah of the last days (as prophesied in Revelation 11:3). In Strasbourg Hoffman progressively absorbed various radical strains, especially the Spiritualism of Hans Denck and the divinization Christology of Kaspar von Schwenckfeld.

However, Hoffman's most distinctive teaching was his apocalypticism. He declared that Strasbourg was the "New Jerusalem," where Christ would establish his millennial kingdom upon his return. Borrowing from the medieval Calabrian Joachim of Fiore, Hoffman believed that the third stage of history was imminent (the Old Testament being the age of the Father, and the New Testament being the age of Christ). In this final stage God would pour out his Holy Spirit upon 144,000 apostolic messengers (Rev. 14:1–5), who would spread the gospel throughout the world, and the false religious leaders would be destroyed (although Hoffman did not advocate violence). All of this would take place before Christ's return, which Hoffman predicted would be in 1533.

Hoffman traveled throughout the upper Rhineland and Holland, where he gained a following for his millennial ideas. One of his Dutch converts was Jan Mathys. Hoffman returned to Strasbourg in 1533, where he was arrested and imprisoned. Reformers Bucer and Wolfgang Capito attempted to persuade Hoffman to moderate his views, and he did in fact yield on the issue of requiring adult baptism (although he still rejected infant baptism).

Hoffman languished in prison until his death in 1543. His theology was an unstable mixture of late medieval mysticism, Joachimite apocalypticism, quasi-Lutheranism, Zwinglian sacramentarianism, Spiritualism, and Anabaptism. The Melchiorite movement continued to gain adherents until his ideas were disastrously linked with the justification of violence in the Münster tragedy.

B. The Radical Kingdom of Münster

It did nothing to reassure Catholic or Protestant concerns when radicals seized control of the Westphalia city of Münster in 1532. Their worst fears were realized and even surpassed. Bedeviled by a series of tribulations—friction with the Catholic bishop, the plague, and crop failure—this city of 15,000 near the Dutch border in northwest Germany found itself in crisis. Bernard Rothmann, a dissident Catholic priest, capitalized on these tensions in 1532, pressing for religious reform and eventually persuading the city council to reject Catholic authority in favor of the new religion (March 1533).

Rothmann's early theological influences were varied. In most respects, he was a follower of Luther, but he tended toward a Zwinglian view of the Eucharist. Melchior Hoffman's prophecy that Christ would return by the end of 1533, bringing an end to world history, apparently affected Rothmann dramatically, and he adopted the radical apocalyptic vision for the imminent end of the world. Soon other Melchiorites found their way to Münster, and then leadership shifted to the charismatic Dutch radical Jan Matthys.

When the second coming failed to materialize, Matthys prophesied a new date (Easter/April 5, 1534) and amid the frenzy sent his proxy John of Leiden (Jan Bockelson) to prepare the way in January 1534. Unusual astral phenomena appeared in the sky in mid-February, and Matthys himself arrived shortly thereafter to take personal control of the city he now declared was the New Jerusalem. Following the example of the early Christians, he pronounced Münster to be a communist state with all property held in common.

This new way of life was mandatory, not voluntary. When a blacksmith resisted the new order, he was killed immediately by Matthys himself. Many people fled the city, but many more radicals arrived. At the same time, the bishop, Count Franz of Waldek, began to lay siege to the city. Matthys advocated the Melchiorite apocalypticism that the elect should wield the sword against all ungodly persons in preparation of the millennial reign of Christ. He announced plans to slay all the "godless"—that is, those who refused to be rebaptized—but he was persuaded to banish the ungodly instead of executing them.

Easter arrived, but the Messiah did not. In a vain attempt to enhance his dwindling credibility, Matthys claimed to have received a divine vision in which he was told he was invulnerable to the weapons of the godless. So he launched a suicidal attack on the much larger besieging army outside the city wall and was immediately struck down. It is difficult to imagine more harrowing circumstances, but Matthys's death led to madness in Münster.

Upon hearing that Matthys was dead, his lieutenant, John of Leiden, assumed the prophetic mantle. In early May, Leiden ran naked through the streets and fell into a trance for three days, after which he insisted on absolute obedience upon penalty of death. He soon introduced polygamy, arguing an Old Testament precedent and asserting that the resultant population growth in the New Jerusalem would hasten the second coming. In reality, he seems to have hankered after Matthys's beautiful young widow, Divara. In short order, he accumulated a harem of sixteen wives. When one of his new wives resisted his authority, Leiden himself publicly beheaded her in the marketplace.

After successfully resisting attacks from the Catholic army (May and August 1534), Leiden, full of messianic pretension, declared himself the "king of righteousness" and absolute ruler of the New Jerusalem. He controlled the city through his twelve "elders of Israel" and identified himself as the new King David, who would rule the world as a warrior king in preparation for the return of the "peaceful Solomon."

In one of the oddest alliances in the sixteenth century, the specter of a radical Münster persuaded Philip of Hesse to send his Protestant troops to join the Catholics besieging the city. As the siege tightened its grip, famine ravaged the city and reports of cannibalism seeped out. Finally in June 1535, two hungry Münster deserters revealed the vulnerable points in the city's defenses.

After a furious battle, the city was taken on June 25. "King John" was captured and held up to public display for several months before his execution (January 22, 1536). It was a slow and painful execution with red-hot irons. Because he was in shock or perhaps a catatonic state, Leiden did not make a sound during the gruesome torture. His body (along with those of two fellow radicals) was thrown into an iron cage and hung from the tower of St. Lambert's Church in Münster as a visual reminder to all of the end result for radicals.

C. Menno Simons the Anti-Revolutionary

There is perhaps no greater indication of the dramatic differences among Anabaptists than the disparity between Menno Simons (1496–1561) and the radical kingdom of Münster. Although Menno's own theological heritage arises out of the same Melchiorite wing as the Münster radicals, he absolutely rejected the use of violence. It must be remembered that the original Melchiorites were nonviolent, and it was that branch that inspired Menno Simons. In most respects, his theological and ecclesiological ethos resembles the Swiss Brethren.

The rise of Anabaptism predates Menno's enlistment in the movement by a decade, but his role among the Dutch Anabaptists was so significant that it has taken his name, "Mennonites." Around 1525 he was serving as a village priest in Pingjum, East Frisia, when he came into contact with Protestant writings and seems to have acquired doubts about the doctrine of transubstantiation, but harbored his doubts in secret.

In 1531 Menno began to question infant baptism, but again said nothing publicly and continued his ministry as a Catholic priest. Three years later, followers of Melchior Hoffman visited Menno's new parish of Witmarsum and began promulgating Anabaptist ideas. By this time Menno was seriously studying the Bible and grappling with the implications. His brother, Pieter Simons, cast his lot with followers of the revolutionary Münsterites and stormed the Cloister at Bolsward in Friesland, only to lose his life in the retaliation of the authorities. His brother's death marked a turning point for Menno.

Deeply angry, Menno wrote (but did not publish) a tract condemning the leadership of the Münster revolt titled *The Blasphemy of Jan van Leyden*. By January 1536, Menno fully embraced Anabaptism and dedicated himself to rescuing the scattered remnant from Münster and giving it a nonviolent focus.

Menno's basic beliefs are summarized in his magnum opus, *The Fundamentals of Christianity*. In this many see an Erasmian soteriological orientation in which repentance must precede divine

Menno Simons.

grace. Like other Anabaptists, Menno's literal biblical hermeneutic led him to reject infant baptism. His primary pastoral emphasis was on discipline. He organized his irenic Anabaptism around the apostolic model in which the Christian community mutually supports one another on the path of sanctification. Although the Mennonites faced internal divisions, they were able to retain their distinctive communal and pacifistic ethos down to the current day.

D. Rationalists

One other intriguing vector materialized in the Reformation period that transcended the theological and ecclesiological norms of sixteenth-century Christianity and, indeed, went beyond the pale of the Swiss Brethren, the Spiritualists, and the Radicals. This very loosely affiliated group was designated the "Rationalists" by George Williams, because they typically elevated reason above the traditional doctrines of historic Christianity.

Although some of the rationalists rejected infant baptism, they bore little resemblance to the Anabaptists and Spiritualists. They tended to be well educated, and most had a clerical background or even aristocratic heritage. Generally, they shared with the other renegade groups a preference for pacifism and the imminent return of Christ, but exhibited a tendency to minimize or dismiss entirely the sacraments. Perhaps the most distinctive feature of this third grouping is their rejection of the historic doctrine of the Trinity.

One of the most prolific of the rationalists was the Spaniard Michael Servetus. He published at least four works on the Trinity. His earliest composition, *On the Errors of the Trinity*, was published in 1531. That was followed by two treatises in 1532, his *Dialogue on the Trinity* and *The Reign of Christ*. In each of these volumes Servetus defended a modalist understanding of the Trinity, that is, the one God revealed himself under three names or modes. His magnum opus, *The Restitution of Christianity*, was published in 1553.

It appears that Servetus drew inspiration from two early hesiarchs, Paul of Samosata and Sabellius, both of whom were condemned by the early church. Although Servetus never established a church, Italian anti-Trinitarians Valentino Gentile and Giorgio Biandrata carried Servetus's books to Poland, Lithuania, and Transylvania. Others such as Francis David and Jacob Paleologus translated sections of Servetus's writings into Polish and Hungarian and helped lay the foundation for Unitarianism.

Servetus also may have inspired the founders of Socinianism, Lelio and Fausto Sozzini. In 1552 Lelio Sozzini came into contact with the writings of Servetus in Padua through his friend Matteo Gribaldi. Although Lelio never went public with his views, he did leave behind a manuscript titled *A Brief Explanation of the First Chapter of John*, composed in 1561. When his nephew, Fausto Sozzini, discovered the manuscript in 1562, it exercised profound influence on his theology.

Both uncle and nephew felt compelled to measure traditional doctrines according to the ultimate standard of reason, which led them to a strict adoptionist view of Christ. They explicitly denied the preexistence of Christ, arguing that he was a mere mortal to whom God gave divine qualities. While Socinian anti-Trinitarianism is not the same as the modalism of Servetus, these two strains together contributed to the development of Unitarianism in eastern Europe. In many respects, these sixteenth-century rationalists were precursors to the Enlightenment.

E. The Triumph of Anabaptism

Not everyone who fled the ecclesiastical boundaries of Rome in the early sixteenth century was a follower of Luther. As Luther and Zwingli discovered, a consequence of *sola scriptura* was a myriad of interpretations. There was, in fact, considerable disenchantment with the pace and substance of Luther's reform movement.

This disillusionment took varied forms. Some, like Thomas Müntzer, linked spiritual disaffection with social unrest and thus joined the Peasants Revolt of 1524–25. Some, such as Melchior Hoffman, concluded that the world was on the precipice of the millennial kingdom and embraced an apocalyptic vision; others such as Hans Denck, inspired by medieval mysticism, turned inward to the voice of the Spirit. Still others, including Servetus, turned to the rational capacities of the mind and judged that the traditional doctrine of the Trinity is both irrational and unbiblical.

These variations on the Reformation theme tended to be disjointed, erratic, and localized movements. Still, the modern historian can discern the broad outlines of a movement characterized by a vision of a restored New Testament Christianity with a pronounced emphasis on discipleship (*Nachfolge*), biblical literalism, the power of the Holy Spirit, a conception of church as pure and independent of state control, as well as a commitment to nonviolence and the sharing of goods.

These were radical ideas for sixteenth-century Catholics and Protestants and seemed to hold the prospect of social upheaval. This fear was realized in the Peasants Revolt and the Münster Debacle, which led to the wholesale rejection of Anabaptists as revolutionaries. For this, Anabaptists were persecuted to death. Estimates vary, but as many as

5,000 of them were executed in the sixteenth century, by both Protestants and Catholics. Only three groups survive in our day: the Mennonites, the Hutterites, and the Unitarians.

The Anabaptist movement has been described as an "abortive counter revolt within the Reformation." Yet, ironically enough, the values and principles of the Anabaptists have become part and parcel of American evangelicalism. The separation of church and state, advocacy of religious toleration, the proliferation of independent churches as voluntary associations, and the Spirit-led Pentecostalism are all fundamental, not only to the American evangelical landscape, but to the emerging global Christianity. Perhaps the Anabaptist movement was not abortive after all.

V. CATHOLIC RIPOSTE

By its very nature, Protestantism was an aggressive movement. Almost like dominoes, Catholic principalities fell to the promise of Protestantism. Significant inroads were made in Germany, France, England, and Scandinavia, and Protestantism seemed to be sweeping over what remained of Catholic Europe. The popularity of Luther's protest caught the papacy and Catholic monarchs off guard.

Initially, the papacy did not take seriously the protests of the German monk. Besides, much of Europe was mired in kingly feuds between Francis I of France and Charles V, who was King of Spain and the Holy Roman Emperor (and called himself "God's standard bearer"). Even more ominous was the threat of Suleiman the Magnificent and his Ottoman Turks. The papacy and the Catholic monarchs had more to worry about than the grumblings of a "drunken German monk," as Pope Leo X salaciously described Luther.

By the mid-1560s, however, the progress of the Protestant movement had slowed to a crawl, gaining only one new principality to its cause in the Netherlands. Indeed, there were some reversals: Poland and Lithuania, which were predominantly Protestant for some time, were won back to the mother church. The reason for the slowdown was that a reenergized Roman Catholicism was fighting back with renewed vigor, and the Counter-Reformation was born.

There has been some scholarly debate about the proper designation for this revitalized Catholicism, so a brief word of explanation is in order. Recent trends among scholars have tended toward the descriptor "Catholic Reformation" rather than the older term "Counter-Reformation."

The preference for the new terminology is to stress the historical fact that efforts were under way to reform the church before Luther, and therefore the Catholic aspiration for reform was not merely a reaction to Protestantism. While it is important to acknowledge these pre-Luther reform efforts, it must also be noted that these concerns avoided doctrinal reform and for the most part were unsuccessful. In the final analysis, it remains true that in its most fundamental aspects, the Catholic Reformation was primarily a reaction to the rise of Protestantism.

Not all Catholics were hostile to Protestant ideas. Two competing factions existed within the Catholic Church itself, each with quite different attitudes toward Protestants. The *spirituali* led by Cardinal Gaspar Contarini sought reconciliation. These Catholic progressives were painfully aware of the need for ecclesial reform. Some even harbored a certain affinity for Luther's understanding of justification. The other faction was equally convinced of the need for reform, but by retrenchment into traditional doctrines rather than reconciliation with heretics.

Led by the severe Neapolitan Pope Paul IV (Gian Pietro Caraffa), these *zelanti* (zealots) advocated suppression of Protestantism by force if necessary. By 1542 the *zelanti* triumphed over the *spirituali* and launched an aggressive counterattack against the Protestants. This counteroffensive took place on several different fronts: prohibiting heretical books, a reinstituted inquisition, a new brigade of Jesuits, and a general church council.

A. Prohibition and Inquisition

The invention of the printing press by the goldsmith from Mainz, Johannes Gutenberg, around 1440 has been hailed as one of the greatest achievements of the early modern world, comparable to the creation of the Internet. When Luther posted his *Ninety-five Theses* on the north door of the Wittenberg Church on October 31, 1517, he had no idea that the printing press would play so crucial a role in sparking the Reformation movement. Unbeknownst to him, copies of his *Ninety-five Theses* were translated, printed, and circulated throughout Germany. He had discovered the power of the printing press.

1. Index of Prohibited Books

The Catholic hierarchy discovered that the proliferation of books could also be a problem. By 1521 theological faculties at Paris and Louvain became alarmed at the growing mountain of Protestant writings. Pope Paul IV was concerned to protect the faith and morals of the faithful, so in 1559 he issued the first authorized list of prohibited books (*Index Librorum Prohibitorum*).

Catholic authorities reasoned that only by controlling what came off the printing press could they prevent the spread of heresy. A revised

"The printing press made it possible for a little mouse like Wittenberg to roar like a lion across ... Europe" (Historian Steven E. Ozment).

A Gutenberg printing press in 1568. In the left foreground, a "puller" removes a printed sheet from the press. The "beater" to his right is inking the form. In the background, compositors are setting type.

form (the *Tridentine Index*) was authorized at the Council of Trent. The index was aimed primarily at Protestants, but also encompassed dubious Catholics such as Erasmus. Perhaps the most startling prohibitions were the many editions of the Bible, as well as editions of the church fathers, unless granted special permission by bishops and Inquisitors.

2. Inquisition

Inquisitional courts have a long history in the medieval church. The most notable was the Spanish Inquisition, which first arose in the fifteenth century (1478) to combat Judaism and *Moriscos* (secret Muslims). With the emergence of Protestantism, the Spanish Inquisition turned its attention to ferreting out suspected Protestants and their sympathizers, which included Erasmian humanists. The particular harshness of the Spanish Inquisition was evidenced in the fact that Erasmian Reformers such as Juan de Valdés were forced to flee their homeland. The Spanish Inquisition acted with impunity, largely because of its close ties with the Spanish monarchy.

Impressed with the effectiveness of the Spanish Inquisition, Italian Cardinal Gian Pietro Caraffa pressured Pope Paul III to introduce the inquisition to Italy as a necessary measure to suppress the advance of Protestantism. The Roman Inquisition was thus inaugurated in July 1542 with the bull *Licet ab initio*, and its authority extended over all of Christendom. Caraffa was appointed one of six General Inquisitors. He was so eager to activate his newly acquired inquisitional powers that he actually set up interrogation rooms in his own home. He once proclaimed, "If our own father were a heretic, we would carry the faggots to burn him!"

With Caraffa's elevation to Peter's chair as Pope Paul IV in 1555, the Roman Inquisition shifted into high gear. One recent scholar has noted that during Caraffa's pontificate, the church fell "into the grip of a witch-hunting mentality."

> "If our own father were a heretic, we would carry the faggots to burn him!" (Cardinal Gian Caraffa, later Pope Paul IV).

B. The Jesuits

Especially since the Fifth Lateran Council (1512–17), many within the Roman Catholic Church were fully aware that reform was an urgent matter. This reform impulse was manifested in the emergence of new religious orders dedicated to personal piety. Matteo de Bascio (d. 1552) sought to return the Franciscans to the primitive simplicity of St. Francis. The Capuchins were established and quickly became one of the most influential orders of their day. The Theatines were inspired by the ideals of the *Oratory of Divine Love* (a confraternity of laymen and priests dedicated to charitable works and spiritual renewal) and sought to reform the church by imposing an austere spirituality on the clergy. It was, however, another religious order that was to have the greatest impact in the Reformation period: the Society of Jesus, more popularly known as Jesuits.

1. Ignatius of Loyola

If the Roman Inquisition was a defensive measure against the rise of Protestantism, then the Jesuits represented the offensive weapon of the Counter-Reformation. There was no person who embodied the Counter-Reformation more than the founder of the Jesuits, Ignatius Loyola. Born into a noble family in the Basque region of northern Spain around 1491, Loyola was baptized Ignacio López de Loyola. He later adopted "Ignatius" as his name because he thought it was more acceptable among foreigners.

In 1509 Ignatius became a career soldier, serving the Duke of Nájera. On May 20, 1521, while defending the city of Pamplona against the army of Francis I, his life was changed forever when a French cannonball shattered his right leg and injured the other leg. He endured several surgical operations, all without the benefit of anesthesia. While convalescing in his hometown of Loyola, Spain, he underwent a profound conversion experience. During this time he read *De Vita Christi* (*The Life of Christ*) by Ludolph of Saxony.

Particularly notable was Ludolph's proposal that the reader place himself in the gospel story—that is, one ought to imagine being in attendance at the Sermon on the Mount or a witness of the crucifixion. This visualization technique or contemplation became a distinctive feature of Loyola's famous book, *Spiritual Exercises*.

Loyola resolved that he would henceforth be a soldier for Christ. After his physical recovery, he visited the Benedictine monastery of

Ignatius of Loyola.

Santa Maria de Montserrat (March 25, 1522), where he placed his sword before an image of the Virgin Mary and walked away from his military career. He then spent a year in seclusion outside of Manresa, near Barcelona. After a year of rigorous asceticism and mystical experiences, he emerged with a clearer vision of how he would serve God, now as a soldier for Christ. He began writing down his insights, which became the basis for his *Spiritual Exercises*, although this work did not reach final form until 1541.

After a pilgrimage to the Holy Land in 1523, Loyola returned to Spain and pursued education at the famous University of Alcalá de Henares. Ironically, he was briefly imprisoned by the Spanish Inquisition, which suspected him of heresy. Exonerated, he continued his education at the University of Paris, where he remained seven years (1528–35) and received his M.A. at the age of forty-three.

By 1534 Loyola had gathered a group of six like-minded students who also dedicated themselves to becoming "a soldier of God." These six became the nucleus of what would become the Society of Jesus and included Francis Xavier, a missionary to Japan and India, and Diego Laínez, an influential theologian at the Council of Trent and Loyola's successor. Initially, they called themselves the "Company of Jesus," which had military overtones as in an infantry company, but later settled on the name "Society of Jesus."

2. The Society of Jesus

Ignatius and his six comrades intended to go to Jerusalem as missionaries to the Muslims, but war between the Venetian Republic and the Turks interrupted those plans. Instead, they offered themselves in service to Pope Paul III, and on September 27, 1540, the Society of Jesus was approved as a new order with the bull *Regimini militantis ecclesiae* (*To the Government of the Church Militant*). Membership was initially limited to sixty, but this restriction was removed through the bull *Injunctum nobis* on March 14, 1543.

Loyola was elected the first Superior General of the Society of Jesus. In the opening words of the "Formula of the Institute," Ignatius describes each member of the new order as "a soldier of God under the banner of the cross," whose mission was "to serve the Lord alone and the Church his Spouse, under the Roman pontiff, the vicar of Christ on earth."

The new order was not without detractors. The very term "Jesuit" originally was a derogatory term referring to one who employs the name of Jesus too quickly and too often. Ignatius himself never used the term, but over time, members of the society rehabilitated the term, and it became the normative designation.

As Loyola envisioned the new society, it was to be an elite order organized along military lines and distinguished by its iron discipline and obedience to the papacy. They recruited only the most dedicated and gifted candidates. Ignatius insisted on an extremely high level of academic preparation. After two trial years as novices, the candidates took the traditional vows of poverty, chastity, and obedience. This was followed by ten years of rigorous academic study of philosophy and theology, and training in practical aspects of ministry. Only then were they allowed to take the special oath of obedience to the pope and thus were formally incorporated into the Society of Jesus.

In the Jesuit *Constitutions*, Ignatius stressed that obedience to the pope must be *perinde ac cadaver* ("in the manner of a corpse"), which was Ignatius's way of demanding absolute obedience. Even more striking was Rule 13 of the *Spiritual Exercises*: "If we wish to proceed securely in all things, we must hold fast to the following principle: What seems to me white, I will believe black, if the hierarchal church so defines."

"If we wish to proceed securely in all things, we must hold fast to the following principle: What seems to me white, I will believe black, if the hierarchical church so defines" (Ignatius Loyola).

This is a soldier's survival creed. In the midst of battle there is little time to ponder complexities; a good soldier must obey superiors without thinking. Failure to obey without question may very well be a life-and-death matter in the heat of battle.

The Jesuits were often viewed as willing to do anything to further their goals. The unofficial Jesuit motto *Ad Maiorem Dei Gloriam* ("For the greater glory of God") reflected the conviction that no act is evil if performed with the intention of bringing greater glory to God. Indeed, such actions are meritorious, even though outwardly they appear evil. The conviction that the ends justify the means was a hallmark of Jesuits and a key to their success.

As the Jesuits developed, they concentrated on three primary activities. First, they established schools and universities throughout Europe. Second, they were committed to missionary activity abroad. Their third objective, which became preeminent, was to stop the advance of Protestantism. To a remarkable degree, the Jesuits were successful. By the time of Ignatius's death, the Jesuits were already operating a network of seventy-four colleges on three continents. Perhaps one of the most significant accomplishments is that Jesuits were largely responsible for stopping the progress of Protestantism and even managed to reverse Protestant gains in Poland, Lithuania, and southern Germany.

Ignatius died in Rome on July 31, 1556, as a result of the "Roman fever," a severe strain of malaria. Many of the details of his life and philosophy were dictated to his secretary, Gonçalves da Câmara, in his waning days. He was beatified by Pope Paul V on July 27, 1609, and canonized by Pope Gregory XV on March 13, 1622. Not surprisingly, Ignatius is venerated as the patron saint of Catholic soldiers.

VI. THE COUNCIL OF TRENT

Pope Leo X issued the papal bull *Exsurge Domine* in 1520, demanding that Luther repent of his sins. In a bold act of defiance, Luther replied by publicly burning the papal bull before a crowd of cheering Wittenberg students. He felt he had done nothing for which he should repent, and he called for a general council to decide the matter. By 1522 Emperor Charles V also concluded that the only means of unifying the church and settling the Reformation controversies was a church council.

On the other hand, Pope Clement VII (1523–34) vehemently opposed the idea of a council, fearing the specter of a revived conciliarism. Once the Great Schism (1378–1417) was resolved, Pope Pius II officially renounced any lingering conciliarism in his bull *Execrabilis* (1460), which asserted papal supremacy over general councils. Pope

Clement was loath to do anything that might renew conciliar ideas. Luther did live to see a general church council convene in Trent, but by that time the religious differences had hardened into religious bulwarks.

When the Protestant Reformation would not go away, Pope Paul III (1534–49) had to face the awkward reality that a general church council was necessary despite his fear of conciliarism. When he proposed the idea to his cardinals, it was unanimously rejected. Nonetheless, he pressed forward and issued a decree for a general council in Mantua, Italy, to begin on May 23, 1537.

Luther responded by preparing the *Schmalkald Articles* for discussion at the general council, but the council failed to convene after yet another war broke out between Francis I and Charles V. An effort to move the council to Vicenza found little enthusiasm, and it was postponed indefinitely on May 21, 1539.

A. The Nineteenth General Church Council

It was not until December 13, 1545, just two months before Luther's death, that the long-awaited council held its first session at Trent (Trento) in Italy. Amid the constant jockeying for control, the pope and the emperor had finally settled on a location at Trent. This imperial free city (ruled by a prince-bishop) satisfied the pope because it was in Italy, and it pleased the emperor because it was within the empire. The pope had the last laugh, because the voting structure was amended so that individual votes would be cast rather than voting by nation, as was the case with previous church councils. This gave the papacy an advantage, since Italian representatives far outnumbered those from other nations.

The nineteenth general church council at Trent extended over nearly twenty years and under three popes during three distinct phases: 1545–47 (under Paul III) included sessions one through eight; 1551–52 (under Julius III) encompassed sessions nine through fourteen; and 1561–63 (under Pius IV) incorporated sessions fifteen through twenty-five. The tenuousness of the council was evidenced by the fact that during the intervals its continuation was often in doubt.

Trent began inauspiciously with only about thirty prelates in attendance, most of whom had little firsthand knowledge of the writings of the Reformers. The Italian and Spanish prelates were vastly preponderant in power and numbers. At the passage of the most important decrees, no more than sixty clerics were present. Of particular significance was the presence of Jesuits, who were viewed as papal theologians and thus invested with special authority.

The council found its focus by the third session (1546), when the council goal was clarified as the "rooting out of heresy and the reform of conduct [of the clergy]." It was decided that the council would weave together both goals so that reform and doctrine would be considered concurrently.

B. Politics and Prelates

As mentioned earlier, there was bad blood between the two most powerful Catholic monarchs of the Reformation period—Francis I of France and Charles V of Spain. For there to be a general church council, the political desires of these two titans had to be considered.

The emperor welcomed a council, because it seemed to be his only hope for resolving religious tensions in Germany. For the sake of unity, he was willing to make concessions to the Protestants, such as Communion in both kinds and the marriage of priests. On the other hand, Francis feared that such a council might threaten the prerogatives of the French church and, if successful, would favor the interests of his old nemesis.

The matter of a general church council was further complicated by the fact that the popes were caught in the middle between these two Catholic combatants. Therefore, the calling of a church council depended on a condition of peace, or at least a truce, between the warring monarchs.

The council itself was repeatedly interrupted by papal and imperial maneuverings. In March 1547, Pope Paul attempted to transfer the council to Bologna on the pretext of avoiding the plague, but the emperor saw through the gambit and resolutely opposed any move that would bring the council into the papal orbit of influence. This confrontation paralyzed the council until it was officially suspended in September 1549. The council reconvened at Trent on May 1, 1551, under the auspices of Pope Julius III (1550–55), but it too was interrupted when Maurice, the Lutheran Elector of Saxony, launched a surprise attack and nearly captured Emperor Charles V in April 1552.

The council was delayed for more than a decade during the pontificate of the virulent anti-Protestant Paul IV. It was finally reconvened at Trent by Pope Pius IV (1559–65) for the last time, meeting from January 18, 1562, until its final adjournment on December 4, 1563. It closed with a series of ritual acclamations honoring the reigning pope, the popes who had convoked the council, and the emperor and the kings who had supported it. The great council concluded with further acclamations of acceptance of the decrees of the council and of anathema for all heretics.

Trent was important for a myriad of reasons, but perhaps most significant is that it gave formal affirmation to doctrines that had not received formal clarification in previous centuries. Historically, the medieval church was ponderously slow in making formal declarations on some of its more time-honored doctrines. For the most part, it offered its affirmation of doctrines and practices only after they had achieved normative status in the church. Transubstantiation, for example, had been in play for centuries before the church formally endorsed and made it binding at the Fourth Lateran Council in 1215. Surprisingly, the church had not yet pronounced on the matter of justification by the sixteenth century, nor had it addressed precisely the matter of the dual authority of Scripture and Tradition. This explains in part why Luther called for a church council: the official understanding was yet undefined.

C. Scripture and Tradition

The first phase of Trent was particularly significant, since it was during those sessions that the more important work was done. One of the most disputed issues between Protestants and Catholics centered on authority. Luther famously coined the phrase *sola scriptura* to indicate that the Bible is the final authority, not the church or its councils. Trent responded by affirming two sources of authority — Scripture and Tradition:

> The council ... accepts and venerates all the books of both the Old and New Testament..., it also accepts and venerates traditions concerned with faith and morals as has having been received orally from Christ or inspired by the Holy Spirit and continuously preserved in the Catholic church.

Along with its affirmation of the authority of Scripture and Tradition, Trent declared the Latin Vulgate (along with the Apocrypha) as the only authorized version of the Bible.

D. Justification

It was also in the first phase, during 1546–47, that Trent devoted its sixth session to the issue so close to Luther's heart, the doctrine of justification. It is generally conceded that Trent's decree on justification represents the most significant achievement of this council. Clearly, the Tridentine (Trent) theologians had ample reason to allot so much effort to this particular matter (16 chapters and 33 canons condemning errors), since Luther's forensic conception of justification represented "a complete break with the teaching of the church...." Neither the Catholic Church nor Trent was inclined to accept doctrinal innovation of any kind.

Perhaps one of the most surprising aspects of Trent was the presence of high-ranking theologians who were somewhat open to Luther's new doctrine. The general of the Augustinian friars, Girolamo Seripando, took up the mantle of these moderates and pressed for a doctrine of "double justification" (meaning that there are two causes of justification: God's gracious forgiveness of human sin, and the obedient human response to the moral demands of the gospel). The Augustinian general was passionately opposed by the Jesuit Diego Laínez, who in a three-hour harangue challenged Seripando's orthodoxy.

In one of the remarkable moments of the council, Cardinal Pole, who was a presiding papal legate, excused himself at a crucial moment of the debate on justification and did not vote. Pole, whose own views were sympathetic to Luther, had seen the writing on the wall and realized that the conservatives would not allow any concessions on this matter, so he feigned illness so that he did not have to register a vote.

> "If anyone says that a sinful man is justified by faith alone ... let him be anathema" (Canon 9 of the Council of Trent).

Trent defined justification somewhat negatively as "not only the remission of sins, but sanctification and renovation of the interior man through the voluntary reception of grace and gifts, whereby a man becomes just instead of unjust and a friend instead of an enemy...." The canons that follow extrapolate further. Canon 9 states rather unequivocally, "If anyone says that a sinful man is justified by faith alone ... let him be anathema." Canon 11 adds, "If anyone says that men are justified either through the imputation of Christ's justice [righteousness] alone, or through the remission of sins alone ... let him be anathema." With Luther clearly in view, canon 32 declares: "If anyone says that the good works of a justified man are gifts of God to such an extent that they are not also the good merits of the justified man himself ... let him be anathema."

One contemporary historian summed up the spirit of Tridentine Catholicism as "the religion of that portion of Christendom which anathematized the rest."

In general terms, Catholics and Protestants used the term "justification" to mean different things. It is clear that both Trent and Protestants affirm legal justification and moral sanctification—that is, the sinner is saved by grace through faith in Christ (justification), and sinners must live godly lives (sanctification) through the internal power of the Holy Spirit. However, the fundamental difference lies in the fact that Trent understands this term to include both legal justification and moral sanctification, while Protestants restrict the term to legal justification only.

To Catholics, the Protestant doctrine of justification seemed to be a legal fiction, undermining human responsibility. To Protestants, the Tridentine understanding seemed to suggest that justification, because it includes sanctification, is based on human effort, thus demeaning God's grace. To be sure, the differences are more substantial than this general overview suggests, but this does underscore the main issues at stake.

E. Sacraments

It was during the second phase that Trent fully addressed the crucial matter of the sacraments. It had earlier affirmed the traditional seven sacraments rather than two (baptism and Eucharist) as Protestants claimed with regard to canon 1 of the seventh session, stating, "If anyone says that … there are more or less than seven [sacraments] … let them be anathema."

It was not until the thirteenth session (1551) that Trent turned its full attention to the heart of sacraments, namely, the doctrine of transubstantiation. Trent would brook no modification on this point and firmly reasserted that when the bread and wine are consecrated, "a change is brought about of the whole substance of the bread into the substance of the body of Christ and of the whole substance of the wine into the blood of Christ. This change the Holy Catholic Church properly … calls transubstantiation." Trent defiantly reaffirmed a central doctrine that had been the practice of the church for a millennium.

In a last-ditch effort, the emperor insisted that Protestants be invited to Trent. The council fathers actually received a Protestant delegation during this second phase in January 1552, but it turned out to be futile. The Protestants demanded that discussions on decrees already approved be revisited, but the Tridentine fathers were not about to concede to the Protestant petition. With the resumption of hostilities in 1552 between the emperor and France, the council disbanded and did not meet again for ten years.

F. Ecclesial Reform

The third and final phase of Trent was attended by some two hundred bishops from nearly every corner of Christendom. But all was not well. Its last sessions (1562–63) were marred by bitter clashes between the Italian faction of the pope and the Spanish, who were suspicious of papal power. Tensions were so high that riots engulfed the city and blood was shed. The council itself ground to a halt for ten months (September 1562 to June 1563).

In spite of the fracas, the council managed to get back on track and issued decrees affirming traditional doctrines of purgatory, intercession of saints, and indulgences. Up to this point, no reform decrees of real substance had yet been passed, but the council well understood that they could not conclude their work without addressing the vital matter of ecclesial reform. In the final sessions, the Tridentine theologians forbade nonresident bishops, the holding of multiple benefices, simony, the granting of abbeys in commendam as favors to wealthy laymen, and clerical sexual immorality, while at the same time stressing the need for more education for clergy and renewing devotional practices.

The council ended by submitting its decrees to the pope for approval—an act that recognized his supremacy in the church and marked the defeat of any lingering conciliarism. When the Council of Trent had finished its work on December 4, 1563, all hope of reconciliation with the Protestants was gone and Christendom was now divided yet again.

VII. THE SPIRIT OF THE CATHOLIC COUNTER-REFORMATION

Not all the decrees of Trent were adopted enthusiastically or unanimously by European rulers. They were approved in the Italian states, Portugal, Poland, Savoy, the Holy Roman Empire, and Spain. The French, however, never officially accepted them. The old abuses did not immediately vanish. Resistance could be found among local clergy, who had vested interests in perpetuating old habits, and at times the papacy itself would prove reticent to reform. Nevertheless, Trent did eventually succeed in infusing a new spirit into the church.

A. The Persistence of Pius V

Much of the new reforming energy derived its impetus from Pius V (1566–72). Instead of living in papal luxury, he remained an ascetic, living in a monastic cell, and was even known to walk barefoot through the streets of Rome. Pius V lost no time in carrying out the disciplinary decrees of the Council of Trent, particularly in Rome. The Curia was reorganized, and serious measures were taken to eradicate simony and nepotism. The streets of Rome were cleared of prostitutes. And in a decision that would have a lasting theological effect, Pius V elevated Thomas Aquinas to a Doctor of the Church in 1567, republished his *Summa Theologiae*, and required Catholic universities to teach Thomism exclusively. Aquinas was to become the heavy artillery in the theological warfare of the centuries that followed.

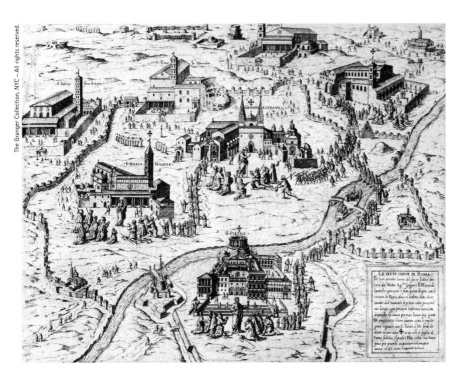

The churches of Rome in 1575.

Pius was relentless in resisting Catholic reticence and Protestant opposition. When Emperor Maximilian II contemplated concessions to Protestants in Germany, Pius threatened excommunication. When the Queen of Sweden partook of Communion in both kinds, she was excommunicated. When Queen Elizabeth I did not return England to the Roman fold, she too was excommunicated. When Huguenots were gaining ground in France, Pius sent troops to aid the king.

Perhaps more than any other pope, Pius V embodied the vigor and the spirit of the Counter-Reformation. Subsequent Popes Gregory XIII (1572–85) and Sixtus V (1585–90) followed in his footsteps.

B. Tridentine Piety

In the wake of Trent, there was a genuine revival of Catholic piety led by a number of men and women of outstanding devotion and sanctity. Charles Borromeo, nephew of Pius IV, epitomized the reforming ideal. As archbishop of Milan (1565–84) he vigorously carried out the Tridentine reforms and raised the standards of the clergy. Seminaries were founded, and discipline was enforced in religious orders. Borromeo also established schools and hospitals for the poor. His personal piety was demonstrated during a plague in Milan when he endeavored to visit the sick despite the danger to himself.

In Spain, two outstanding Carmelites did much to instill the spirit of revival: St. Teresa of Avila and St. John of the Cross.

St. Teresa, a daughter of the Spanish nobility, had joined the Carmelite order as a young girl. After undergoing a severe religious crisis and experiencing mystical visions in 1562, she went on to establish a convent in Avila, Spain, where she modeled piety and strict obedience. Her mystical writings did much to further her reputation.

St. John of the Cross, as he had come to be known, was also a member of the Carmelites and an ascetic who longed to see a renewed spiritual awakening. Like Teresa, he was a mystic. He collaborated with Teresa in bringing reform to Carmelite men. His reform efforts resulted in suffering and indignity, which gave rise to his famous phrase "dark night of the soul."

After their deaths, the reformed Carmelites received permanent papal recognition, and their mystical piety continues today among modern Carmelites.

By the dawn of the seventeenth century, the Catholic Church had restored in large measure its moral authority and spiritual prestige. It had weathered the storm of sixteenth-century Protestantism, but the challenge of the modern world would prove even more formidable.

VIII. PONDERING THE REFORMATION AFTERMATH

When Luther threw down his theological gauntlet in 1521, little did he know that his anguished study of the Bible with his theological insights would lead to a century of bloodshed. He knew, of course, that he was likely to lose his own life and, indeed, was fully prepared to meet his Maker. But he never envisioned his ideas leading to hundreds of thousands of souls dying from religious wars and their offspring dying inevitably from famine and disease.

The fact that church and state were so intimately intermingled meant that theological convictions inevitably fell prey to political maneuverings. This state of affairs proved highly combustive, and Europe fell into a century of brutal and nasty repression and warfare. Abraham Lincoln's poignant words about the American Civil War capture well the complexity of the Reformation period: All combatants "read the same Bible and pray to the same God, and each invokes His aid against the other."

The religious wars finally staggered to a resolution with the Peace of Westphalia (1648). All parties agreed to a formula that was supposed to ensure religious peace: *Cuius regio, eius religio* ("Whose Reign, His Religion"). This formula gave the ruler the right to establish the religion of his principality, and any citizens who did not share that conviction were allowed to move to another principality whose religion was more congenial.

No sooner was the formula adopted than rulers found it unenforceable. Although not its original purpose, the Westphalian peace formula inadvertently hastened the European trajectory toward secularization. Religious identities remained intact even if they were not willing to go to war to defend them.

Tensions between Catholics and its "unholy" offspring of Protestants and Anabaptists continued for centuries. Hostilities began to thaw between magisterial Protestants and Anabaptists by the eighteenth century. Ironically, in the modern era, Anabaptists are generally embraced as Protestants.

As for the discord between Catholics and Protestants, it was not until the second half of the twentieth century with the Second Vatican Council (1962–65) that relations became more cordial and tolerant. There Catholics referred to Protestants as "separated brethren"—misguided perhaps, but "brethren" nevertheless. Protestant groups such as the Presbyterians revised their confessional standard (Westminster Confession) so that the pope was no longer identified as the "Antichrist."

Few of the protagonists of the sixteenth century could have foreseen Protestants and Catholics arm in arm, addressing the pressing social issues of twenty-first-century America. The religious "iron curtain" that had befallen Western Christianity has lifted ever so slightly.

The bloody aftermath of the Reformation led to a kind of religious exhaustion, which is another way of saying that few were willing to die for an abstract theological idea anymore. In a strange turn of historical events—one Luther could never have imagined—theological debates prepared the way for the rationalism of the Enlightenment and its accompanying secularism.

FOR FURTHER STUDY

Estep, William R. *The Anabaptist Story*. Grand Rapids: Eerdmans, 1995.

Gleason, Elisabeth G. *Gasparo Contarini: Venice, Rome and Reform*. Berkeley: University of California Press, 1993.

Klaassen, Walter. *Anabaptists: Neither Catholic nor Protestant?* Kitchener, ON: Pandora, 2001.

Olin, John C. *Catholic Reform: From Cardinal Ximenes to the Council of Trent, 1495–1563*. New York: Fordham University Press, 1990.

Williams, G. R. *The Radical Reformation*. Reprint, Kirksville, MO: Truman State University, 2000.

Reformations in England

The Politics of Reform (16th Century)

I. INTRODUCTION

The sight of German merchant ships docked in English port cities, buoyed on the ebb and flow of the tide, virtually guaranteed that Reformation ideas would infiltrate the English Church. It was the inevitable by-product of international trade.

German merchants brought more than goods to sell in the English market; they brought books and enthusiasm for the bold Augustinian Martin Luther. These new ideas found receptivity among the early reform-minded humanists, clandestine Lollards, and a long-standing lay mistrust for a corrupt clergy and church. These new ideas became a perfect storm when the winds that brought the German merchants combined with the winds of political change. Like the tide, the English Reformation would ebb and flow.

Historians have long debated the true origins of the English Reformation: was it a native development or a continuation of the continental Reformation? Or does it lie somewhere in between? It is significant that King Henry's dalliance with Protestants was an unequivocal political maneuver and, in fact, he never for a moment embraced even a little of Luther's reformation. Henry was interested only in what served his dynastic purposes.

The English had endured the bloody War of the Roses (1455–1485) between the Houses of York (whose emblem was the white rose) and Lancaster (whose emblem was the red rose), with the final victory going to the Lancastrian King Henry VII (1457–1509) at the famous battle at Bosworth Field. Henry defeated and killed the Yorkist King Richard III in August 1485, thus creating the Tudor dynasty.

In an effort to quell further conflict, Henry married Elizabeth, the daughter of the previous Yorkist king, Edward IV, thus uniting the red and white roses. To strengthen international ties, he used strategic matrimonial diplomacy, marrying his oldest son, Arthur, to Catherine, daughter of Ferdinand and Isabella of Spain; his daughter Margaret to James IV of Scotland; and his daughter Mary to Louis XII of France.

The dynastic conflict of the War of Roses was set against the complex background of economic depression, financial woes of the government, and the decline of the feudal system. But with the Tudor victory came economic growth, driven significantly by the wool trade. In the course of Henry's reign, England doubled its revenues from the cloth trade. Economic prosperity was the best dynastic insurance.

Throughout Europe the Catholic Church was under a cloud of anticlericalism, that is, a jaded cynicism that it was populated by men of low character. This was true also in England. Some scholars hold that there was a relative degree of popular appreciation of the church. However, the evidence strongly suggests that all was not well. In their striving for advancement, bishops were all too often absent from their dioceses, leaving poor uneducated curates to care for parish souls. English clergy were, on the whole, royal servants chosen for their usefulness to the crown. Wealth and power became strong intoxicants to higher clergy.

The most infamous example of clerical opportunism is the career of Thomas Wolsey (c.1474–1530). Born the son of a Suffolk butcher, Wolsey, through natural intelligence, hard work, and careful plotting, managed to secure an Oxford education and ingratiate himself to the young King Henry VIII, for which he was richly rewarded by church and state. Henry made him a privy counselor in 1509, archbishop of York in 1514, and lord chancellor in 1515—the same year he was made cardinal by Pope Leo X. In 1518 Wolsey also was made a papal legate or special representative of the pope in England. Popular resentment of Wolsey's wealth, power, and ambition exacerbated the anticlericalism toward all clergy.

The river of anticlericalism was fed by the tributary of the indigenous reform movement known as Lollardy, deriving from the Oxford theologian John Wycliffe. Lollardy was further stimulated by corruption and aggrandizement by the clergy. After Wycliffe died, the Lollards became a shadowy underground church that had a special affinity for the vernacular Bible, especially in London, Kent, and York. They held unorthodox views: denying or questioning veneration of saints,

John Wycliffe.

transubstantiation, pilgrimages, and confession to a priest. This underground movement managed to survive more than a century of persecution and seems to have been on the rise in the reign of Henry VIII.

The infamous case of Richard Hunne illustrates the heavy-handed ways of the clergy and the resultant anticlericalism among the people. Hunne was a London tailor who refused to pay what he considered the excessive mortuary fees charged by the clergy for the death of his infant son. He was arrested and charged with heresy for being a secret Lollard. While he was in prison awaiting trial, his body was found hanging from a beam in his prison cell. Investigation led to a charge of murder against associates of the bishop of London. The bishop invoked the traditional clerical privilege of a trial by a special ecclesiastical court rather than by the government authorities. The ecclesiastical court promptly found the bishop's men not guilty.

News of the Hunne affair spread like wildfire and fed the flames of anticlerical sentiment throughout England. Such clerical entitlements and judicial exemptions reinforced a growing alienation toward the church and its tonsured toadies.

English laypeople were scandalized by the heavy hand of the church, but there was also a contingent of scholars within the church who sought reform. This intrachurch reform movement was especially associated with the English humanists. Erasmus had sparked renewed interest in classical thought with his first visit to England in 1499. His Christian humanism—with its stress on the Scriptures, the wisdom of the church fathers, moral lives, and especially toleration—had a significant impact on English intellectuals.

The fusion of Erasmian humanism and Pauline theology in a single person can be seen in the work of the Oxford theologian John Colet. He lectured on Paul's epistles at Oxford (1496–97) and then became dean of St. Paul's London in 1504. He was an earnest church reformer; he even challenged Erasmus to engage more seriously the Bible.

In his famous sermon to the Convocation of Clergy on the appointment of Archbishop of Canterbury William Warham in 1512, Colet issued a public call for church reform, citing St. Bernard's dictum that wicked clergy damage the church more than heresy. Colet's call for reform went unheeded, but it did reflect a simmering discontent, especially among the church leaders, that later proved a breeding ground for the reforming ideas of Luther.

Through the good auspices of German merchants, the religious pamphlets of Luther began to infiltrate English universities, especially Oxford and Cambridge, as early as 1519. Archbishop Warham warned Cardinal Wolsey of Lutheran heresy at Oxford. The White Horse Inn in Cambridge was the first meeting place of the first English Protestants:

Robert Barnes, Thomas Bilney, Hugh Latimer (c. 1485–1555), John Frith, Miles Coverdale (1488–1568), Thomas Cranmer (1489–1556), Nicholas Ridley (c. 1500–1555), and Matthew Parker (1504–75). Some scholars believe William Tyndale (1495?–1536) may have participated as well.

Five of these early Protestant sympathizers became bishops, and all but Coverdale and Parker suffered martyrdom for their faith.

Perhaps Tyndale was the most significant of these early Protestants. After studies at Oxford and then Cambridge, young Tyndale served as a tutor to Sir John Welsh. It was during this time that Tyndale became convinced of the necessity of translating the Bible into the vernacular. In 1522 he proposed an English translation to the bishop of London, Cuthbart Tunstall, who declined, saying, "We must root out printing or printing will root out us."

In 1524 Tyndale went to Wittenberg, where he began his translation of the New Testament, with Luther's German translation as his model. Beginning in March 1526, copies of Tyndale's English New Testament as well as the Pentateuch and other parts of the Old Testament began to flood into England. Bishop Tunstall was greatly alarmed and decided the best way to stem the flow was to purchase as many copies of the translation as possible, but this strategy was flawed, since Tunstall's money unwittingly financed Tyndale's second edition.

William Tyndale.

Tyndale's translations were very influential for the next century. Indeed, even though his translations were banned, others clandestinely incorporated much of his translation into subsequent editions such as the Matthew Bible and the Coverdale Bible.

In his later years Tyndale found refuge in the community of English merchants in Antwerp, where he enjoyed legal immunity from King Henry VIII, from Tunstall, and from the emperor Charles V. But in May 1535 he was betrayed by a friend, Henry Phillips, and was arrested and imprisoned in the Castle of Vilvorde near Brussels, where he languished for sixteenth months before being brought to trial. He was found guilty, and on October 6, 1536, he was strangled to death, and his body was burned at the stake. His last words were, "Lord, open the King of England's eyes."

II. HENRY VIII'S REFORMATION

With Lutheran subcurrents pulsating through English universities and villages, Henry VIII inadvertently found allies in his effort to restructure church and state. Although he remained convinced of the verity of Catholic theology, he decided to throw off the shackles of Rome in order to establish his own supreme ecclesiastical authority. One gets a sense of Henry's theological commitments in his published rebuttal to Luther's defiant *On the Babylonian Captivity of the Church* (1520), titled *Assertion of the Seven Sacraments* in 1521, which won for him from Pope Leo X the title *fidei defensor* ("Defender of the Faith").

The journey that led Henry to break from Rome began when his brother Arthur married Catherine of Aragon, daughter of Ferdinand and Isabella of Spain in 1502. Arthur, always sickly, died five months later, leaving his young bride a widow. Henry became the heir apparent, taking the crown in 1509, and almost immediately thereafter he took his brother's widow as his wife. According to church law, such a marriage was forbidden, but Pope Julius II granted a special dispensation permitting the marriage.

Catherine always maintained that the brief marriage had never been consummated and therefore she was free to marry Henry. Although Catherine was nearly seven years older than Henry, the marriage began well. Six children were born to the couple, but only their daughter Mary survived.

A. A Male Heir

By 1526, when Catherine was forty-one, it dawned on Henry that a male heir was probably no longer a realistic possibility. This was an important dynastic issue, because never before in its history did England have an undisputed queen. Matilda claimed the title of queen in the thirteenth century, but royal legitimacy was successfully challenged by Stephen, thus plunging England into a nasty civil war. With the War of the Roses still a recent memory, there was a nagging fear that should Henry die without a male heir, it could incite another bloody civil war.

Besides the driving force of dynastic succession, two other factors seemed to have propelled Henry. First, he seems to have developed some theological scruples about the validity of his marriage. After all, Leviticus 20:21 explicitly forbade marriage to a brother's widow with the promise that if such a marriage took place, they would be childless. Henry began to wonder if God was punishing him by not giving him a son. To complicate matters even more, Henry had developed a royal passion for one of Catherine's ladies-in-waiting, the dark-eyed Anne Boleyn. The young and fertile Anne made a now-barren Catherine seem expendable.

Henry tasked his well-connected Cardinal Wolsey to approach Pope Clement VII for an annulment. Normally, popes were willing to accommodate powerful kings in overcoming such inconveniences. Henry VIII had already earned kudos for defending the papacy and traditional Catholicism against Luther. But this was no ordinary situation.

In a remarkable turn of events, the troops of the King of Spain and Holy Roman Emperor Charles V, fresh from victory over Francis I of France, mutinied and rampaged through Rome in 1527, leaving Pope Clement little more than a captive. It just so happened that Charles V was the nephew of Catherine of Aragon, and he was none too pleased with Henry's plans for annulling marriage to his aunt. To complicate matters further, granting Henry's request would pit one pope against another, thus undermining the notion of infallibility. In the final analysis, Cardinal Wolsey's protracted backroom maneuverings failed, and the pope was unwilling or unable to grant the annulment.

Henry's disappointment turned to wrath. He signaled his rejection of papal authority by vindictively charging Cardinal Wolsey—papal legate and one of the church's most powerful figures—with treason. Wolsey was spared a humiliating trial and horrible death by conveniently dying on his way to his trial on November 29, 1529.

By this time Henry was absolutely determined to have his marriage annulled one way or another so that he could find a queen who would produce the male heir he so desperately desired. By the early 1530s Henry had concluded that he must break free of Rome if he was to secure a male heir.

Outraged by papal refusal to grant an annulment, Henry initiated a series of defiant ecclesio-legal gestures in England that led inevitably to the break from Rome. Returning to the good graces of the king would come at great cost. In May 1532 a convocation (leading clergy representing the two provinces of the English Church: York and Canterbury) reluctantly agreed to make an exorbitant financial contribution to the king's coffers and to the so-called Submission of the Clergy by which they accepted Henry as "Protector and Supreme Head of the English Church and Clergy." The clergy did manage a modicum of dignity by adding the phrase "as far as Christ's law allows."

This piece of legislation proved too much for Sir Thomas More, who had succeeded Wolsey as Henry's Lord Chancellor. More resigned his office, was imprisoned for resisting the king, and was beheaded three years later, in 1535.

"Had I but serv'd my God with the half the zeal I serv'd my King, he would not in mine age Have left me naked to mine enemies" (William Shakespeare, capturing Cardinal Wolsey's secret thoughts in *Henry VIII*).

From this political maelstrom Thomas Cromwell emerged as the most prominent of those who suggested to Henry VIII that the king should be the head of the English Church. By 1532 he had shaken off his association with Wolsey and had become a trusted member of Henry's inner circle. In 1535 Henry appointed Cromwell as his Vice-gerent in Spirituals, giving him enormous power over all ecclesiastical affairs. As Henry VIII's vicar-general, he presided over the dissolution of the monasteries. As reward, he was created Baron Cromwell in 1536 and Earl of Essex in 1540.

Besides his determination to secure a male heir, it is clear that Henry's break from Roman authority had another motivation: wealth. Cromwell enticed Henry with an opportunity he could not refuse — bilking the wealth of the church. By severing the link to Rome, Henry acquired an enormous amount of property and assets. His dissolution of the monasteries dramatically increased the royal coffers; the crown more than tripled its landholdings.

By the end of 1532 Anne Boleyn was pregnant with the king's heir, and the die was cast. All of Henry's energies were galvanized to secure the legitimacy of the child in Anne's womb. His first step was secretly to marry Anne Boleyn in January 1533. The second step was to pass the Act in Restraint of Appeals in February 1533, which forbade all appeals to Rome in temporal or spiritual matters. This act effectively ended papal authority in England.

The third step was to ensure that the new archbishop of Canterbury (Archbishop Warham having died in August 1532) was sympathetic to the king's desire for a marriage annulment. Henry's man was the Cambridge theologian Thomas Cranmer — who just happened to be closely associated with the Boleyn family, who had recommended him to the king. With Cranmer consecrated in March 1533, Henry was now in position to deal once and for all with the so-called "King's Great Matter" — the annulment of his marriage to Catherine of Aragon.

Archbishop Cranmer presided over a church commission that officially declared the marriage to Catherine annulled on May 23, 1533, based on the Act in Restraint of Appeals. Five days later, Cranmer declared Henry's marriage to Anne Boleyn lawful, albeit *ex post facto*.

Finally, the break with Rome was formalized with the passage of the Act of Supremacy in November 1534, declaring the king to be the "only supreme head in earth of the Church of England" without any qualifiers, as had been the case in the Convocation of 1532. Now all that remained was to crown Anne Boleyn queen in June 1533 and await the birth of a male heir. As it turned out, Henry was sorely disappointed at the birth of Princess Elizabeth in September 1533.

The acrimony between pope and king led to Henry's excommunication in 1538. He had crossed the ecclesiological Rubicon, and there was no turning back.

B. Reform Triumvirate in the King's Court

The Act of Supremacy represented a decisive break from papal authority, but it was not a conscious effort to introduce Protestantism to the English Church. Even so, it inevitably opened the door. Ironically, the price Henry paid for breaking away from Rome was the infiltration of a host of Protestant sympathizers. Those most willing to risk supporting Henry's defiance of Rome were, as it turns out, all too often inclined toward Luther's new teaching.

Cromwell, the first great executive of the state reformation, "displayed a cool but unmistakable affinity with the Lutherans." He gained the favor of King Henry, not only because of his competence but also because he was as committed to the break with Rome as was Henry, although for different reasons. Cromwell, as it turns out, was sympathetic to Protestantism; he was especially interested in seeing the Bible in the vernacular. Whether by conviction or compliance, it was Cromwell who seems to have promoted policies congenial to Protestants. He rose quickly in Henry's esteem, first entering the king's council, then being appointed the king's principal secretary, then being appointed vice-regent and vicar-general for ecclesiastical affairs.

Cromwell proved a brilliant parliamentary strategist working through the House of Commons to achieve his aims. He urged a view of church-state relations in which the king would be head of both the state and the church.

Most importantly, Cromwell was the "mastermind" who spearheaded the passage of the so-called "reformation statutes" in Parliament from 1532 to 1536. The effect of this multiple legislation was to exclude the authority of the pope from the realm and grant full authority over the church and state to the king.

Archbishop Cranmer also did his fair share to promote the cause of Protestantism in England. Although taciturn and cautious by nature, the archbishop was supportive of Henry's willingness to break from Rome. Cranmer may very well have embraced Lutheranism even before his appointment as archbishop, since he already had secretly married the niece of Andreas Osiander, the Lutheran Reformer of Nuremberg, in 1532.

Cranmer had first come to Henry's attention when he suggested that the king should solicit the opinions of the great European universities on the validity of his marriage to Catherine of Aragon—convinced the scholars would uphold traditional canon law. Henry liked the idea and prevailed on Cranmer himself to travel to the universities on the Continent. It was during his diplomatic travels that Cranmer met and married (despite his vow of celibacy) Margaret Osiander in Nuremburg, at least a year before he was made archbishop. As an ordained priest, Cranmer discreetly kept his wife hidden from view. Some of Cranmer's contemporaries smugly sponsored the rumor that he kept his wife in a box.

The political climate allowed Cromwell and Cranmer to promote vernacular translations of the Bible. Remarkably, they persuaded Henry to allow an official English translation of the Bible—this after Henry relentlessly pursued and finally orchestrated the execution of William Tyndale because of his translation of the Bible. Cromwell used his own funds to support translation work and presided over a series of official translations of the Bible into English. Tyndale's translation covered only the New Testament, but his colleague Coverdale produced the first complete English Bible in 1535, and another colleague, John Rogers, produced the second complete English Bible, known as the Matthew Bible (Rogers's pseudonym).

With political winds blowing in a Protestant direction, Cranmer and Cromwell secured Henry's permission to publish the Matthew Bible in 1537. Soon thereafter the Coverdale Bible was licensed for publication and, with the authority of the king, all parish churches were required to have an English Bible. Not satisfied with these translations, Cromwell commissioned yet another new translation and entrusted the task to Coverdale. The result was the publication in April 1539 of the Great Bible, to which Cranmer contributed his famous preface in the 1540 edition.

All these translations drew heavily from Tyndale's work. Tyndale's dream had come true amid the remarkable confluence of political pressure on the king and strategically placed Protestant opportunists.

The efforts of Cromwell and Cranmer to make the Bible available in English found support from the new queen, Anne Boleyn. Scholars have speculated that Anne Boleyn may have acquired a taste for reform ideas while in France at the Court of Margaret of Navarre—sister to King Francis I of France. It is well known that despite a royal prohibition, she kept an English translation of the Bible in her royal apartments—always open so that sympathetic servants could read. There is a general consensus that she favored distribution of the Bible in the vernacular and that she strongly supported the break from Rome. According to her chaplain, William Latimer, she "debated the Scriptures: with the King."

The queen not only read the dangerous books of Simon Fish (*A Supplication for the Beggars*) and William Tyndale (*Obedience of a Christian*

Man), but also gave them to King Henry. Further, she supported the appointment of several reform clerics, including Thomas Cranmer as Archbishop of Canterbury and Huge Latimer as Bishop of Worcester. For these reasons, Anne is believed to have belonged to a secret triumvirate with Cromwell and Cranmer that conspired to promote church reform, if not outright Protestantism, in the realm. She and the Boleyn family had a long-standing relationship with Cranmer.

C. The Rise and Fall of Anne Boleyn

For her continued refusal to acknowledge the new queen, Henry banished Catherine of Aragon to the decaying and remote Kimbolton Castle in 1535 and forbade her to see or communicate with her daughter, Mary. In late December 1535, sensing death was near, Catherine made her will and wrote a final letter to Henry. It said in part, "For my part, I pardon you everything, and I wish to devoutly pray God that He will pardon you also." Catherine died in January, and Henry not only failed to attend her funeral but, in an act of consummate cruelty, also refused to allow his daughter Mary to attend.

Had Catherine lived longer, it would have been some small consolation to her that Henry's marriage to Anne Boleyn, whom Catherine considered the "king's whore," turned sour. Anne had birthed three children, but only Elizabeth survived. Some scholars believe Anne miscarried a deformed male child in January 1536 and that Henry fell prey to the common superstition that a deformed fetus was an indication of sorcery. Even before she recovered from her miscarriage, Henry declared that he had been seduced into the marriage by means of *"sortilege"*—a French term connoting a magical spell. This superstition coupled with her failure to produce a son left Anne vulnerable to the political crossfire from the rival factions at court.

Cranmer, upon hearing the charges against Anne, wrote in her defense to Henry, but when pressed by the king, Cranmer presided over the annulment of the marriage. On May 16 he heard Anne's confession, and the next day he pronounced the marriage null and void. Three days later, Anne was beheaded at the Tower of London.

With surprising speed even for the king, Henry married his pregnant mistress Jane Seymour eleven days after Anne was executed. Jane had the privilege of producing the male heir (Edward VI) Henry longed for, but she did not get to enjoy the celebration. She died twelve days later, on October 12, 1537, from complications of the birth.

Where there are progressives, there inevitably are conservatives, and Henry's court was divided into two main factions. Initially the progressives gained the upper hand, largely because they were sincere supporters of Henry's break with Rome. The progressives played a dangerous game with a king who believed it was possible to dissolve ties to Rome without changing the doctrine and worship of the church.

Henry always retained his conservative theology, but from 1532 to 1540, he was caught between these two rival factions: progressives headed by Cromwell and Cranmer, and the conservatives led by Stephen Gardiner, Bishop of Winchester, and Thomas Howard, Duke of Norfolk. The progressives supported Henry's annulment and thus held sway, and even after Anne's execution, Cromwell and Cranmer managed to keep the conservative faction at bay for the time being.

D. Dalliance with Lutherans

International politics of the period played into the hands of Cromwell and Cranmer. Henry was officially excommunicated in 1538, and when Francis I and Charles V agreed to a peace treaty in June 1538, the pope seized the opportunity to urge these two most powerful Catholic monarchs to mount a joint crusade against Henry. Fearful of an invasion, Henry felt compelled to seek new alliances among the German Protestants, which made it politically necessary to make some gestures indicating he was moving in a Protestant direction.

Cromwell and Cranmer could not have been more delighted with this turn of events. Cromwell sent emissaries to Wittenberg for doctrinal discussions to explore the possibility of joining the German defensive alliance, the Schmalkald League.

The Lutherans insisted that membership depended on subscription to the Augsburg Confession. Henry's own Catholic convictions could not abide such an overt affirmation, but he did make an important gesture by passing the *Ten Articles*. These articles mentioned only three of the seven sacraments—Henry neither affirmed nor denied the other four—and actually rejected the notion that the pope could deliver a soul from purgatory. The document did contain some ambiguous statements about justification by faith in Christ and softened, but did not renounce, the physical presence of Christ in the Eucharist, confession, images, or masses for the dead.

Cromwell continued to push Henry toward the German Protestants. Knowing that Henry was on the prowl for another queen, Cromwell thought he could strengthen his position by securing a German bride for his king. He arranged Henry's fourth marriage, to Anne of Cleves, the second daughter of John III, Duke of Cleves, and Maria, Duchess of Julich-Berg. Her father followed a moderate path within the Reformation.

Hans Holbein was commissioned to paint a portrait of Anne that later proved overly flattering. Based on the portrait and the political benefits, Henry formally agreed to the marriage, but Cromwell did not anticipate Henry's physical repulsion upon meeting Anne. Henry confided to Cromwell that he had been unable to consummate the marriage, saying, "I liked her before not well, but now I like her much worse." The marriage was quickly annulled, and Anne was given a generous settlement, including Richmond Palace and Hever Castle. Ironically, Henry and Anne became good friends, and she was referred to as "the King's Beloved Sister." She died in 1557.

"I liked her before not well, but now I like her much worse" (Henry VIII's response to his fourth wife, Anne of Cleves).

E. Conservative Retaliation

Cromwell's failure became an opportunity for his political and religious enemies. Duke Howard realigned the religious orientation of the crown toward traditional theology by putting forward his niece, Catherine Howard, and orchestrated events to capture the king's passions. Cromwell was, for the first time, seriously out of step with the king. Secretly the conservatives persuaded Henry that Cromwell was a traitor and heretic as evidenced by his advocacy for an alliance with the German Protestants.

Cromwell's fall was sudden. In June 1540 he was condemned without trial for treason and heresy and was beheaded on July 28 at the Tower of London. Henry married Catherine Howard the same day. After his execution, Cromwell's head was boiled and then set on a spike on London Bridge. Within months of Cromwell's execution, Henry regretted his decision, saying that Cromwell was "the most faithful servant he ever had." Cranmer remained in the shadows and somehow managed to survive plots against him.

Negotiations with the German Lutherans dragged on, but eventually the threat of a joint invasion of France and the Holy Roman Empire diminished, and Henry defaulted to his own theological proclivities. In June 1539, under royal pressure, Parliament passed the Six Articles Act, or as Protestants called them, "the bloody whip with six strings." These articles unequivocally affirmed transubstantiation, clerical celibacy, Communion of one kind, sanctity of priestly vows, private masses, and auricular confession with the added threat that denial of any of these was heresy and justly warranted death. The *Six Articles* signaled that the tide had turned yet again, this time in favor of the Catholic conservatives.

Then there came another turn. Henry's nineteen-year-old queen was repulsed by his obesity; he weighed about three hundred pounds and had a foul-smelling, festering ulcer on his thigh. Catherine Howard proved to be a reckless young lady, and soon after her marriage, she began a romance with one of Henry's courtiers. Her indiscretions rapidly became known. She was charged with adultery and beheaded in February 1542.

F. Progressives Regaining the King's Favor

Henry was growing too old for all the palace intrigue, and he decided to settle down with a more mature sixth wife, Catherine Parr, whom he married on July 12, 1543, at Hampton Court Palace. Catherine had been widowed twice before. After her second marriage, she was courted by Thomas Seymour, the brother of the late Queen Jane Seymour. Although she was in love with Seymour, she was obliged to accept the king's marriage proposal.

As queen, Catherine was less an object of sexual passion and more nursemaid to the ailing king and mother to his children. She was largely responsible for reconciling Henry with his daughters Mary and Elizabeth. She also developed a warm relationship with Henry's son Edward. When King Henry set out in 1544 to undertake the invasion of France, he named his wife as regent during his absence, a sign of his great respect for her, as well as of implicit trust.

Perhaps emboldened by her successful regency on behalf of Henry, she felt free to discuss theology with him, and, as with Anne Boleyn, the king eventually became irritated. Sometime later, after a particularly intense discussion, Henry complained to his conservative Bishop Gardiner, of the unseemliness of being lectured by his wife. Gardiner seized the opportunity and was granted permission to investigate the queen.

Catherine had reason to fear such an investigation into her religious views. Of all Henry's queens, Catherine Parr was the most inclined to Protestant ideas. The newly appointed Lord Chancellor Thomas Wriothesley accused the queen of having some association with the Yorkshire noblewoman and outspoken Protestant Anne Askew.

It is doubtful that the two women had ever met, but on May 24, 1546, the Reformist was arrested and horribly tortured, yet she refused to implicate the queen despite repeated questioning. When the constable of the Tower of London was ordered to put Anne on the rack, he balked: it was not the custom to torture women and especially one from a noble family. But she was tortured nonetheless, and actually managed to smuggle to Protestant friends an account of the torture, which was later published. On July 16 Anne Askew was burnt at the stake for heresy. The queen was to be next in line.

The conservative faction led by Wriothesley had persuaded the king to sign an arrest warrant for Catherine. The conspiracy was in full swing when a copy of the signed warrant was mysteriously brought to Catherine's attention, perhaps by the king's own doctor, Thomas Wendy.

Fearing for her life, Catherine immediately went to the king and made it abundantly clear that she humbly submitted to his religious authority. She apologized for her assertiveness in their theological discussions and explained that she had done so only to distract him from the pain of his ulcerous leg. Henry relented and said, "Then Kate, we are friends again." The following day, Wriothesley arrived to arrest the queen, only to find her strolling with the king, who unleashed a royal dressing-down to his lord chancellor. From that point on, the conservative faction lost favor.

Henry did not have much longer to rule his realm and died on January 28, 1547, holding Archbishop Cranmer's hand. There was no extreme unction, no last rights, only a whispered affirmation of faith in Christ. And so it was that in the religious ebb and flow of the Henrician reign, the progressives had regained the upper hand at the final months and thus were positioned to guide the new king and direct religious change in England.

III. EDWARD VI'S REFORMATION

A. Protestantism Restored

When his son Edward was born in 1537, Henry finally had the male heir he so longed for. Edward's birth triggered a reconfigured order of succession: Henry's only son, followed by Elizabeth and then Mary. Despite the fact that he was only nine years old, he was crowned king immediately upon his father's death. Henry intended that a sixteen-member council constitute the regency, but there is little doubt that as Henry lay dying, his advisers were clandestinely plotting their way to wealth and power. Most prominent was Edward Seymour, Earl of Hertford, who dispensed significant titles and landholdings confiscated from the disgraced Duke of Norfolk, Thomas Howard. Seymour managed to secure for himself the title Duke of Somerset.

One of the more intriguing developments of Henry's reign was the decision to entrust the education of his young son to humanist-inspired Cambridge dons, who as it turned out, were largely sympathetic to Protestantism and all of whom later became noted Protestant leaders, among them Richard Cox, John Cheke, and Roger Ascham. Edward proved to be a gifted student. By the age of thirteen, he was able to read Aristotle's *Ethics* in Greek, translate Cicero's Latin treatise *De philosophia* into Greek, and interact theologically with Peter Martyr Vermigli's *De sacramento eucharistiae*. It is noteworthy that after he became king, Edward wrote an essay in which he described the pope as the "Antichrist." One can only assume this was a deeply held conviction from early on.

B. The Ascent of Edward Seymour

Recent research has revealed that Seymour was rather dictatorial, more politically ambitious, and less devoted to the principles of Protestantism than tradition would have us believe. Nevertheless, Protestantism advanced considerably during his two-year protectorate (1547–49). Henry's Catholic *Six Articles* were revoked, all restrictions on the publishing and reading of Scripture were repealed, the Eucharist was administered in both kinds, and marriages of priests were made legal. Perhaps Seymour was simply bending to Protestant winds, but the theological and ecclesiastical trajectory was unmistakable. For such an autocratic leader, he at least passively supported these changes.

Seymour's status was undone by revolts in 1549, growing French presence in Scotland, government corruption, and betrayal by his own brother, Thomas Seymour. His brother attempted to usurp power by kidnapping the young king. Whether there was a real kidnapping plot or not, in January 1549 the protector signed the death warrant for his own brother, and Thomas Seymour was executed on March 17.

All of this upheaval surrounding the protector prompted a coup d'etat by the regency council in October 1549, from which John Dudley, the Earl of Warwick, emerged as the new regent with the title "Lord President" of the council from 1549 to 1553 (and was named Duke of Northumberland in 1551). He is often portrayed as a *politico* and convenient Protestant, but whatever Dudley's personal religious convictions were, Protestantism continued to grow during his regency. His three years of rule witnessed the transformation of the English Church into a more distinctively Reformed Protestantism.

C. Thomas Cranmer's Reformation

As important as Seymour and Dudley were to furthering the cause of Protestantism, the true architect of the Protestantization of England was Thomas Cranmer, Archbishop of Canterbury. Cranmer, almost miraculously, was the lone survivor of the bloody reign of Henry VIII and brought all his survival skills to the reign of Edward VI. It was as if, having survived the political carnage of Henry's reign, Cranmer was doubly determined to see his religious agenda succeed in the Edward's reign.

Edward's Protestant-inspired education led to a natural affinity with Cranmer; it was a good match for bringing decisive religious change to the English Church. With Cranmer as his religious guide, Edward strongly supported the efforts to redefine Anglicanism as a Protestant church. Edward wanted Cranmer to start bringing the Reformed view into the English faith. Cranmer laid out a careful, cautious, yet deliberate plan for bringing the Church of England fully into the Protestant fold. The three benchmarks of this plan included revisions of the *Book of Common Prayer*, a new doctrinal statement, and a reworking of English canon law.

Cranmer's revision of the prayer book was incremental. The first revision in 1549 was a cautious and somewhat ambiguous move toward Protestantism. Generally, it was a significant simplification of the Catholic forms of worship: it was written in English; ceremonies, feasts, and festivals were severely reduced; and the elevation of the Host was forbidden. The central element in the Catholic mass was missing; nothing was mentioned about the sacrifice of the mass, and reference to the corporeal presence of Christ was ambiguous.

Despite this ambiguity and simplification, Bishop Gardiner, the leader of the opposition, ironically declared he found the revision acceptable. There was some clamor among the Protestants that it did not go far enough, but they were soon to learn that this edition was merely the first phase of Cranmer's plan and that another revision was already in view before the first was published.

The 1552 prayer book was distinctively Protestant. It removed all prayers for the dead, all praise for Mary and the saints, and moreover embraced a Reformed view of the Eucharist. It is important to note that the Protestant words of the liturgy were now mouthed by every priest, bishop, and parishioner in England in a language everyone understood.

Cranmer did not stop with the double revision of the prayer book. He reworked the (at the time) Forty-two Articles. Additionally, he produced the *Reformatio legum ecclesiasticarum* (1552), which was designed to replace the medieval Catholic basis of society with a Reformed view.

Furthermore, Cranmer's plan would have been meaningless without trained clergy to implement the new forms. So he reinforced his reformation by securing leading Reformed theologians from the Continent to prepare clergy for the English Church. To this end, he appointed the Italian Reformer Peter Martyr Vermigli as the Regius Professor of Divinity at Oxford (1547–53) and the Alsatian Reformer Martin Bucer as Regius Professor of Divinity at Cambridge (1549–52). These two Reformers were charged with training up an army of Protestant priests to bring the Reformation to the people.

To consolidate further English reforms with continental reform, Cranmer sought to hold an international council to produce a united response to Trent. Calvin agreed to attend, and Melanchthon was invited, although he declined. The council never took place because the young king became ill. But it does suggest that Cranmer wanted English Protestantism to take its place at the forefront of the movement.

D. Death of the Boy King

Young Edward succumbed to pneumonia at sixteen, and the reformation of Anglicanism was cut short. As Edward lay dying in July 1553, and the prospect of Mary's succession to the throne loomed large, Dudley made a desperate and risky attempt to circumvent the Succession Act of 1544. According to this document, the throne was to descend to Mary if Edward died childless, and if Mary died childless, Elizabeth was to succeed to the throne. In the months before his death, Edward, under the influence of Dudley, excluded both of his half sisters and vested the succession on Lady Jane Grey, the granddaughter of Henry VIII's sister Mary.

It is worth noting that in May 1553 Lady Jane became the new wife of John Dudley's son, Lord Guildford Dudley. John pressed hard to secure approval for the new succession by the Privy Council, many of whom received titles and significant gifts of land. Alas, his gambit failed.

IV. MARY I'S RESTORATION

A. John Dudley's Folly

It is difficult to know whether John Dudley's plan ever had any real chance of success. But his fatal mistake was his failure to arrest Mary before Edward's death on July 6, 1553. Somehow Mary learned that Edward was near death on July 4 and fled to the protection of Catholic nobles in East Anglia. Although Lady Jane Grey was officially proclaimed queen on July 1, the next day a letter was delivered to the Privy Council from Mary claiming the throne as her rightful inheritance. Realizing his blunder, Dudley left London shortly thereafter with an army to arrest Mary—to no avail. By July 19 everything had changed, and Mary was acknowledged as the rightful heir by the Privy Council.

The hapless Lady Jane was queen for all of nine days before she and her consort, Lord Guildford, were taken to the Tower along with John Dudley. Even Protestant London supported Mary. The English people had linked lawful succession to peace and security. Dudley's attempt to circumvent the established succession plan was doomed to failure. Despite his abjuration of Protestantism, he was convicted of treason and executed shortly thereafter, on August 22. Lady Jane and Guildford Dudley faced their own execution six months later, in February 1554. Like a house of cards, the plot to have Lady Jane succeed Edward collapsed.

B. The Return of Catholicism

When Queen Mary I (also known as Mary Tudor) came to the throne, one thing was absolutely clear: she was a devout Catholic and determined to restore England to the Roman fold. Immediately, Bishop Gardiner, Catholic leader of the opposition, was released from the Tower and soon became lord chancellor. Parliament declared her mother's marriage to Henry VIII valid; and public worship was restored to the forms established in the last year of Henry's reign. But one of the most important decisions Mary made early in her reign was to marry Philip II, the son of Emperor Charles V.

This marriage on July 1554 failed on at least two counts. Not only was it against the advice of her closest Catholic advisers, who feared the foreign influence of the emperor, but Mary failed to realize it was a political marriage intended to recall England from the Protestants. Mary had fallen head over heels for Philip, but he was merely doing his dynastic duty. This marriage made Mary deeply unhappy, and it profoundly discouraged her advisers. Above all, it cast a dark shadow over the English people.

Those Protestant leaders who thrived in the reign of Edward VI expressed their reaction to Mary with their feet. Eight hundred bishops and other leaders fled to the Continent—mainly to centers of Protestantism such as Geneva, Zürich, Basel, Strasbourg, Emden, and Frankfurt. The English Protestants kept the fires burning by producing in April 1560 one of the most enduring translations in the history of the English language: the Geneva Bible.

C. Marian Persecution

While the English Reformation preserved itself by flight, the Marian restoration of Catholicism became official with the return of Cardinal Reginald Pole (1500–1558). As papal legate, Pole formally absolved the nation of heresy and restored England to Roman obedience in November 1554. A year later, Pole himself was made archbishop of Canterbury, thus consolidating the restoration.

With the official restoration came official persecution. The first victim was the Bible translator John Rogers, who was burned at London on February 4, 1555. As he was led to execution, the people cheered

"Play the man, Master Ridley. For this day we shall light a candle which shall never fail in England" (Hugh Latimer to Nicholas Ridley at their execution).

him. Mary could change the laws of England, but she could not change the hearts of the people. Hugh Latimer, Bishop of Worcester, and Nicholas Ridley, Bishop of London, bravely faced the fire when they were burned to death in Oxford on October 16.

But the primary object of persecution was Thomas Cranmer. He was, after all, the man who declared her mother's marriage invalid, thus making Mary a bastard child. To add insult to injury, it was Cranmer who legitimized her father's marriage to Anne Bolyen. It was payback time.

D. Cranmer's Last Stand

Cranmer refused to flee with the other bishops and boldly offered to debate Mary's Catholic theologians: "I with Peter Martyr ..." will defend the prayer book as "more pure and more agreeable to the Word of God than what has been in England for the past thousand years." Mary responded by banishing Peter Martyr and putting Cranmer on trial.

The trial took place at St. Mary the Virgin, the university church of the University of Oxford. Cranmer was found guilty of heresy, stripped of his insignia of ecclesial office in a humiliating ceremony, and officially condemned to death. He was remanded to the Oxford gaol, where he waited for nearly a year. Repeated efforts were made to get him to recant, to which he finally succumbed. He was a broken man who eventually signed six recantations, each more incriminating than the previous one. Historically, such recantations resulted in a stay of execution, but Mary would not have it. Cranmer had to die.

On March 21, 1556, Cranmer was placed on a platform opposite the pulpit of St. Mary's, where he was supposed to make a final recantation before his death. With tears streaming down his face Cranmer surprised everyone by recanting his recantations.

In a rage, Cranmer's detractors pulled the old man (nearly seventy years old) from the platform, and he was dragged to the ditch outside the city wall, where his friends Latimer and Ridley had been burned the previous year.

Mary and Pole gravely miscalculated. Cranmer's death did more for the cause of Protestantism than if they had let him die in prison. Word spread of Cranmer's heroic death, and John Foxe immortalized his death in his *Book of Martyrs*, thus ensuring the ultimate victory of Protestantism in England.

The celebrations that greeted Mary on her ascension to the throne turned sour. Mary's restoration of Catholicism had a backward, almost medieval cast to it. Her marriage to the son of the Spanish king was a marriage with England's historic enemy and resulted in a disastrous alliance with Spain that entangled England in a war with France for which it was not prepared. This political failure resulted in England's loss of Calais, its last stronghold on the Continent. At nearly every point, whether politically or spiritually, Mary was deemed a failure by her people.

When Mary Tudor—now known as "Bloody Mary"—died the morning of November 17, 1558, the succession of the new young Queen Elizabeth was greeted with celebration throughout the realm.

V. ELIZABETH I'S REFORMATION

Winston Churchill once mused that "history is written by the victors" and that truth is borne out by Protestant sobriquets assigned to King Henry's offspring: Edward was the "young Josiah," Mary was "Bloody Mary," and Elizabeth, the last in the Tudor line, was hailed as the "new Deborah." Like Deborah of old, the new Deborah came to her throne facing harsh realities. The majority of England's citizens were Catholic, but with the return of the Marian exiles, most of the church leaders were dedicated Protestants; many were Calvinistic. The challenge, put bluntly: could Elizabeth prevent a religious civil war in her realm?

Having spent her teenage years in the warm and genial household of Queen Catherine Parr, Elizabeth soaked up Protestant piety. During Mary's reign Elizabeth wisely worshiped as a Catholic and reassured her sister of her intention to remain obedient to Rome. However, in the wake of Thomas Wyatt's Rebellion in 1554, led largely by Protestants, the Spanish ambassador pressed Queen Mary to execute Elizabeth, fearing she was and would continue to be a rallying point for rebel Protestants. Remarkably, Elizabeth survived. Early on, it seems the young Elizabeth innately sensed Churchill's future adage, namely, that if she could stay alive, she would be the victor and determine the history of England.

A. The Elizabethan Settlement

One modern historian describes the twenty-five-year-old Elizabeth as a woman who could "speak French, Latin and Italian ... [and] was also skilled at double talk." This ability at "double-talk" served Elizabeth well in both religion and politics. It was expected that she would follow the cultural protocol of making a swift and suitable marriage. But she understood that her virginity could be a political tool in support of English interests, so she coyly entertained marriage proposals from Catholic and Protestant princes alike.

Elizabeth's Catholic brother-in-law, Philip II of Spain, offered to marry her, as did the Lutheran Eric XIV of Sweden. Her dalliances with prospective marriage partners effectively kept papal condemnation at bay and Protestant hopes alive. She shrewdly kept everyone guessing. All the while she and her chief adviser, Sir William Cecil, ushered a religious settlement through Parliament.

The Elizabethan Religious Settlement was set forth in two acts of Parliament. The first was the Act of Supremacy of 1559, which reestablished independence from Rome and conferred on Elizabeth the title "Supreme Governor" of the Church of England. The second was the Act of Uniformity of 1559, which set out the form the English Church would now take, including a return to the 1552 *Book of Common Prayer*.

As Elizabeth anticipated, virtually all the sitting Catholic bishops refused to abide by the Act of Supremacy, and they were thus removed. The queen then turned to Protestants who had been forced to flee from Mary's reign. The former exiles now appointed to the bishops' bench included such Protestant notables as Edmund Grindal (Bishop of London), Richard Cox (Bishop of Ely), John Jewel (Bishop of Salisbury), and Edwin Sandys (Archbishop of York).

The Royal Injunctions (1559) directed the implementation of the Act of Uniformity, opting for a blended worship. On the one hand, all clerics were required to affirm royal supremacy and renounce papal claims to rule over the Church of England. Clergy were permitted to marry upon approval of their bishop. On the other hand, kneeling at prayer, bowing at the name of Jesus, and clerical vestments were retained.

It has become commonplace to characterize Elizabeth's religious settlement as a *via media* (a middle way) between a Catholic liturgy and Protestant doctrine. Some have seen the settlement largely in political terms as a pragmatic compromise driven by political exigency. While political calculations certainly were made, these should not obscure the Reformed theological influences that shaped this religious resolution.

For all the talk of a *via media*, it must be remembered that the religious settlement was at its core a Protestant movement. Continental Reformed theologians such as Peter Martyr Vermigli and Heinrich Bullinger supported Elizabeth's efforts. Key elements of the liturgy were directly in opposition to Catholicism. It is a historical fact that at the beginning of Elizabeth's reign, Catholics were a majority of the population, but by the end, they were a small minority. (It has been said that while they were a majority of the population, most Catholics were religiously indifferent.)

What the average English person wanted was political and religious stability, and more than anything else, that is what Elizabeth gave them. Her chief advisers throughout her long reign, William Cecil and Francis Walsingham, were Protestants, as were her archbishops of Canterbury: Matthew Parker, Edmund Grindal, and John Whitgift. Her Privy Council was composed of Protestants. It was at her direction that Cranmer's Protestant 1552 *Book of Common Prayer*, with minor modifications, was made normative in the church, and the Protestant Forty-two Articles were slightly modified as the *Thirty-nine Articles*, with its express rejection of transubstantiation.

To be sure, Elizabeth did not wish to antagonize Rome or Catholic Spain, so she and her advisers made some practical decisions, such as retaining clerical vestments and removing from the prayer book the insulting remarks about the papacy. It is perhaps suggestive that it was John Jewel, the devoted disciple of Peter Martyr Vermigli and a committed Calvinist, who composed the Apology for the Anglican Church in 1562.

Peter Martyr Vermigli.

B. English Catholicism

With the anger of a jilted lover, the papacy also became active in trying to bring Elizabeth down. After twelve years, Elizabeth's Protestantism was too obvious to ignore. Pope Pius V issued the papal bull of excommunication *Regnans in excelsis* ("ruling from on high") on February 25, 1570, which declared "Elizabeth, the pretended Queen of England ... [who] monstrously usurped the place of the supreme head of the Church of England ... to be a heretic ... and to have incurred the sentence of excommunication."

Furthermore, Pius released all the queen's subjects from any loyalty to her and threatened excommunication to any who obeyed her orders. This amounted to an ecclesiastical declaration of war. (Rumors abounded that later popes sanctioned assassination plots against Elizabeth. In 1580 a kind of papal fatwa was issued, stating that anyone who assassinated Elizabeth with the "pious intention of doing God service not only does not sin, but gains merit." The assassination of William of Orange in 1584 was rather compelling evidence that Protestant monarchs were in real danger of Catholic assassins.)

Elizabeth responded to her excommunication in two ways. First, she made a statesmanlike proclamation to her subjects that "as long as they shall openly continue in the observation of her laws" no one will be "molested" by any inquisition or examination of their consciences in causes of religion. Second, she made it clear that she would not tolerate dissent, and in 1571 the Treason Act was published, making it a capital offense to deny she was the lawful queen.

Queen Elizabeth I of England.

From the outset of her reign Elizabeth desired good relations with her Catholic subjects, but the favor was not always returned. Many Catholics supported her as queen but opposed her Protestantism. Other Catholics took a more radical approach.

There were several plots against Elizabeth, but only one actual Catholic rebellion. The so-called "Revolt of the Northern Earls" in 1569 was led by Charles Neville, Earl of Westmorland, and Thomas Percy, Earl of Northumberland. Its ostensible aim was to depose Elizabeth and place Mary I of Scotland (Mary Queen of Scots) on the English throne, thus reestablishing Catholicism in England. The rebel earls raised a small army and occupied Durham, but hearing of a large force being raised by the Earl of Essex and finding little popular support, the rebels retreated and eventually dispersed. The Earl of Westmorland managed to escape to Flanders and died impoverished in Spain. The Earl of Northumberland fled into Scotland, but was repatriated to the English and was summarily beheaded in York.

There were a number of assassination plots against Elizabeth that sought to replace her with her cousin, Mary Queen of Scots. While under the protective custody of Elizabeth in England, Mary became embroiled in a conspiracy with the Italian merchant Roberti di Ridolfi to overthrow Elizabeth. The plot was discovered, and the participating Duke of Northumberland was executed in June 1572.

Another infamous scheme to overthrow Elizabeth was the so-called "Throckmorton Plot." A devout Catholic, Sir Francis Throckmorton had developed a network of recusant Catholics in England as well as various continental Catholics, Mary Stuart, and the Spanish ambassador Bernardino de Mendoza. The conspiracy was uncovered by Sir Francis Walsingham, Elizabeth's spymaster, and Throckmorton was apprehended and tortured on the rack. Convicted of high treason, Throckmorton was executed in 1584.

The papacy also fostered a new corps of militant missionaries who were sent to England clandestinely to foster a renewal of Catholicism, if not outright insurgency. William Allen became the prime inspiration for this incentive. After refusing the Oath of Supremacy, he was eventually forced out of the University of Oxford in 1561. He was convinced that the majority of the English would happily return to Roman Catholicism if given the opportunity.

In 1567 Allen went to Rome, where he first developed his plan for establishing a missionary college, or seminary, to supply priests to England as long as the country remained separated from Rome. His missionary college was established in 1568 in the Spanish Netherlands as the English College of Douai. The first missionary priests began to arrive in England in 1574. Eventually Allen moved the college to Rheims in northeast France under the protection of the Duke of Guise. Allen's success prompted Pope Gregory XIII to invite him to establish a similar college in Rome in 1575.

One of the chief accomplishments in the early years of the Douai College was the preparation of the Douai Bible. The Douay-Rheims Bible, as it was known, was a translation of the Bible from the Latin Vulgate into English. The New Testament was published in 1582, and the Old Testament followed in 1609–10, both with extensive polemical commentary upholding the Catholic faith.

By 1577 Allen had come under Jesuit influence, the most militant of the Catholic orders. He formed a close association with one of the more zealous Jesuits, Robert Parsons. Together they inaugurated a scheme to send Jesuits to England. Parsons and Edmund Campion in 1580 were the first Jesuits to infiltrate England. Both Jesuits traveled around England, staying with Roman Catholic families, preaching sermons, and publishing attacks on Protestant ideas on a secret press.

In 1581 Campion was captured, tortured, and executed. Parsons fled to Spain, where he sought to persuade Philip II to invade England and restore Catholicism. Campion's capture and execution was portrayed as martyrdom, which only inspired more Jesuits to dedicate themselves to the Catholic cause in England. Alarmed by so many missionary priests, Elizabeth banned the Jesuits from England in 1585.

Allen's desire to see England return to the bosom of Rome led to involvement with the Spanish Armada. Angered by the execution of Mary Queen of Scots, Allen wrote to King Philip II, encouraging him to undertake an invasion of England, stating that the Roman Catholics there were clamoring for the king to come and punish "this woman, hated by God and man." He was so deeply involved with the invasion that he was to have been made the archbishop of Canterbury and lord chancellor if it met with success. His adamant support to the planned invasion led to his elevation as cardinal by Pope Sixtus V in August 1587.

The mighty display of the Spanish Armada in 1588.

In concert with the planned invasion of England, Cardinal Allen attempted to rally English Catholics with his pamphlet *An Admonition to the Nobility and People of England*. "Elizabeth," he wrote, was as "an incestuous bastard, begotten and born in sin ... an infamous, depraved, accursed, excommunicate heretic, the very shame of her sex." Allen then strongly discouraged English Catholics from defending England against the invasion: "fight not, in that quarrel, in which if you die, you are sure to be damned."

In the final analysis, Allen misjudged English loyalty to the queen. As it turned out, the large majority of English Roman Catholics sided with their own nation against the Spanish, and the defeat of the Armada, in 1588, was a subject of rejoicing to them no less than to their Anglican countrymen.

Allen was deeply disappointed at the defeat of the Armada, but to the end of his life he remained fully convinced that England would be Roman Catholic again. He died at the English College in Rome in October 1594.

C. The Puritans

While the Elizabethan Settlement proved acceptable to the vast majority of the English nation, there remained small minorities at either extreme who were dissatisfied with the state of the Church of England. On one end were the deeply committed Catholics who complained that the Church of England had strayed too far from the Church of Rome. On the other end were the deeply committed Protestants who grumbled that the church retained too many remnants of Roman Catholicism and was therefore in need of "purification." A "Puritan," therefore, was one who wanted to "purify" the Elizabethan settlement of all Catholic resemblance.

During Elizabeth's reign, Puritan ministers outwardly conformed, although there were telltale signs that Puritans had not gone away, just underground. Puritan clergy, for example, tended to shorten the prayer book service to allow more time for preaching and were more likely to offer an extemporaneous prayer instead of simply reading the set prayer out of the prayer book. While the majority of Puritans remained "nonseparating Puritans," they nevertheless came to constitute a distinct social group within the Church of England by the turn of the seventeenth century.

Since the Church of England under Elizabeth was broadly Reformed, theology was not the primary difference between mainstream Anglicans and Puritan Anglicans. It was only well into the seventeenth century that doctrinal Calvinism came to be particularly associated with Puritanism.

At the first Convocation of the English Clergy of Elizabeth's reign, held in 1563, some Puritan clergy set forth their desires for further reforms, including the elimination of vestments—which they associated with Catholicism (even though the Reformers Vermigli and Calvin did not feel that way). The queen's Archbishop Parker reasserted that vestments were the required clerical dress. The Puritan faction appealed to the continental Reformers for support, but were disappointed to be turned down on the grounds that they were "overreacting." Heinrich Bullinger, the Zürich theologian, accused the Puritans of "a contentious spirit under the name of conscience." This, of course, took the wind out of the Puritan sails.

In the early 1570s Rome began to take a much more aggressive stance and sought to undermine Elizabeth—through excommunication, the Northern Earls Revolt, and the Ridolfi plot. She responded in kind and began to clamp down on Catholicism. Indeed, 164 Catholic missionary priests were executed from 1580 to 1588. The queen would brook no disobedience from Catholics or Protestants.

When Archbishop of Canterbury Edmund Grindal had the audacity to defy the queen in 1575, she trampled him underfoot. Elizabeth became aware of Puritan conventicles, modeled on the Zürich *Prophezei*, where ministers met weekly to discuss "profitable questions." The queen objected to these conventicles or "prophesyings," fearing they

The English Puritans were of "contentious spirit under the name of conscience" (Heinrich Bullinger).

could stir up opposition, and she ordered the archbishop to suppress the movement. He refused and consequently was disgraced, thus undermining the rest of his tenure.

Some of the notable Puritans, however, saw an opportunity to exploit anti-Catholic sentiment. At Cambridge, Thomas Cartwright, a longtime opponent of vestments, called for the abolition of episcopacy and the creation of a presbyterian system in England. Two London clergymen, Thomas Wilcox and John Field, followed in Cartwright's footsteps by advocating that the English Church should be remodeled according to the Presbyterian Church of Scotland. Elizabeth moved decisively, and Wilcox and Field were imprisoned for a year, while Cartwright fled to exile on the Continent.

Presbyterianism reared up again in the so-called "Marprelate tracts," which circulated illegally in 1588 and 1589. Under the pseudonym of Martin Marprelate, the tracts unleashed virulent attacks on episcopacy, describing bishops as "vile servile dunghill ministers of damnation." Archbishop of Canterbury John Whitgift swiftly and successfully suppressed the Puritan faction.

VI. FOREIGN AFFAIRS

William Paget, 1st Baron Paget of Beaudesert, managed to survive the Tudor storms and served as a counselor to Henry VIII, Edward VI, and Mary I. When Elizabeth came to the throne, Lord Paget retired from public service, but left the new queen with some parting advice on foreign affairs. Paget asserted that one of the guiding principles was that there was a "natural enmity" between England and France. The other basic tenet, with which Elizabeth was already familiar, was the need to maintain good relations with Spain, the most powerful nation in Europe.

The Tudors had cultivated the Spanish connection since 1501 when Henry's older brother, Prince Arthur, married Catherine of Aragon, the daughter of Ferdinand and Isabella of Spain. When Arthur died prematurely, it only made sense to the English to offer Prince Henry as a replacement groom. Over the course of Elizabeth's long reign, she discovered the same practical truth observed by the weeping philosopher Heraclitus that "nothing endures but change."

In the early years of her reign, Elizabeth shrewdly used the possibility of marriage as a tool of foreign policy. As a young queen, Elizabeth was expected to marry, and accordingly the offers rolled in. King Philip II of Spain—even though he was her brother-in-law, having been married to Mary Tudor—proffered a marriage proposal soon after her coronation. She negotiated for several years to marry Archduke

Charles of Austria. Elizabeth then considered marriage to two French Valois princes: Henri, Duke of Anjou, and later, his brother François, Duke of Anjou.

Whether she ever intended to marry or not is unknown, but the mere prospect of marriage to the queen of England inclined Catholic foes to proceed with caution with regard to the Protestant queen.

A. France

Lord Paget's missive about the natural enmity between England and France had much to do with England's northern neighbor, Scotland. There had been a long-standing alliance between the French and the Scots, which was an ongoing source of English concern. It did not make matters easier when Mary of Guise became Regent of Scotland on behalf of her daughter Mary, Queen of Scots.

Matters came to a head in 1560 when a Protestant rebellion broke out in Scotland. Fearing the French would send an occupying army to subdue the rebels and thus extend their influence in the aftermath, her adviser William Cecil persuaded a reluctant Elizabeth to send troops in support of the Protestant revolt. The resultant standoff produced the Treaty of Edinburgh, which ensured the withdrawal of both English and French troops from Scotland. The French threat on England's northern border was thus removed.

In 1562 the English again found themselves drawn into a confrontation with France. On March 1, the Duke of Guise attacked Huguenot worshipers at Vassy and slaughtered them. The massacre of Vassy provoked the so-called French Wars of Religion between the Protestant Bourbons and the Catholic Guise. From a political perspective, it appeared the Huguenots would likely fail without outside help.

Elizabeth decided to intervene on the side of the Huguenot rebels, and English troops landed at the French port city of Le Havre in 1562 (in part to try to recover Calais, the last English possession on the Continent, which had been lost under Mary I). But all came to naught when Huguenot and Catholic factions temporarily resolved their differences and turned unilaterally against the English. By 1563 the English forces withdrew, leaving Le Havre and Calais to the French. Elizabeth had succeeded in Scotland but failed in France.

Elizabeth made one last venture into France to support the Protestant Henry IV when he inherited the French throne in 1589. Elizabeth sent 20,000 troops and £300,000 when Henry's succession was contested by the Catholic League and Philip II of Spain. More importantly, Elizabeth feared that Spanish involvement in France could lead to control of the English Channel, thus posing a real threat to English sea power. Elizabeth continued to support Henry IV in various military campaigns, but all were very disorganized and militarily ineffective.

To secure the French crown, Henry IV famously converted to Catholicism in 1593 and quipped, *"Paris vaut bien une messe"* ("Paris is well worth a mass"). Although Henry's conversion was disappointing to Elizabeth, the Franco-English alliance survived, because the new French king would provide a check on Spanish power. In particular, France's war with Spain was a boon for England because it drew Philip's resources away from the Netherlands, where a Protestant revolt was under way.

B. Spain

Elizabeth was quite fortunate that Philip II of Spain, the most powerful monarch in Europe, had expressed interest in marriage. Although Elizabeth declined Philip's marriage proposal, a positive atmosphere remained. Indeed, following the Elizabethan Settlement, it was Philip's influence over the pope that delayed Elizabeth from being excommunicated from the Catholic Church. But Philip's good favor diminished after Elizabeth provided military support for Protestant rebels in Scotland, France, and the Spanish Netherlands.

The Netherlands came into the Spanish orbit in 1516 when Charles V became the King of Spain. Charles, raised in the Netherlands, was already the Lord of the Burgundian States (since 1506), which included the Netherlands. As was the case in much of Europe, Protestantism already had gained a foothold in the Netherlands by the time the crown passed to Philip II.

Tensions flared in the Netherlands over heavy taxation and suppression of Protestantism. By 1566 Protestant frustrations boiled over in widespread iconoclastic upheaval—churches were stormed, statues destroyed, and images of Catholic saints desecrated. Philip saw no other option but to suppress the rebellion. In August 1567 the "Iron Duke," Fernando Álvarez de Toledo, Duke of Alba, marched into Brussels at the head of 10,000 Spanish troops. With backing from Philip, the Iron Duke used an iron fist to bring order in the Netherlands. Prominent leaders were charged with high treason, condemned, and decapitated at the Grand Place in Brussels. Alba went on to execute more than a thousand people in the so-called "Blood Court." Rather than pacifying the Dutch, Alva only fueled more unrest.

It was under these harsh circumstances that William of Orange led a revolt in 1568. Initially the revolt centered on reduced taxation and freedom of worship rather than rejection of Spanish authority, but by 1581 the rebels produced the Act of Abjuration, in which they renounced loyalty to Spain. The abjuration riled Philip II, and he redoubled his efforts to subdue the Protestant rebels.

Early on, Elizabeth showed her sympathies for the Dutch Protestants in an episode known as the "Affair of the Spanish Bullion." Sir Francis Drake, with the apparent compliance of Elizabeth, seized five Spanish ships that were sailing to the Netherlands with £85,000 in gold bullion to pay the Spanish Army. This act of piracy so enraged Philip that all English merchants in the Netherlands were arrested, and trade between England and Spain/Netherlands broke down completely for five years. After the embargo was lifted in 1573, an uneasy peace followed that saw Elizabeth flirt more with France as England prepared for an increasingly inevitable clash with Spain.

The assassination of William of Orange on July 10, 1584, was a decisive reality check and marked a pivotal change of perspective for English policy regarding Spain. While Elizabeth had unofficially supported the Dutch for years, she now decided to intervene directly. In 1585 she signed the Treaty of Nonsuch, which obliged her to send an army to assist the Protestant rebels. As it turned out, the English army was led by the Earl of Leicester, who was a poor military commander who failed to win the confidence of the Dutch leaders. When Leicester returned to England, the Dutch governing body, the States General, turned to William's son Maurice of Orange to lead the Dutch rebels in 1587.

When Spain found itself distracted by a more challenging conflict with France, Spain signed a truce with the Dutch that lasted for twelve years (1609–21). The seven northern Dutch provinces were securely under Protestant control, while the ten southern provinces remained under Spanish rule. The Dutch had achieved independence *de facto* from Spain even though the final resolution did not come until 1648 with the Peace of Westphalia.

C. The Armada

In the thirty years since ascending the English throne in 1558, Elizabeth's relationship with Spain had steadily deteriorated from Philip's marriage proposal to an attempted invasion of England. The Treaty of Nonsuch was the final straw for Philip, and he decided to invade England. On July 12, 1588, the Spanish Armada set sail for the Netherlands. The English were outnumbered and outgunned.

However, fortune smiled on the English when they caught the Armada anchored in close formation near Calais. At midnight on July 28, the English sent fireships loaded with pitch, brimstone, and gunpowder directly into the heart of the Armada. The English defeated the

Armada, which suffered even more destruction due to fierce storms occurring on its way back home. When Philip learned of the defeat, he was reported to have lamented: "I sent the Armada against men, not God's winds and waves."

The war with Spain did not end immediately. In 1596 and 1597 Spain sent more ships, but these were wrecked in storms before they even reached England. The defeat of the Armada was a potent propaganda victory, both for Elizabeth and for Protestant England. The English saw themselves as the object of God's special favor and of the divine blessing on the Virgin Queen. This victory signaled that England had come of age and was a force to be reckoned with.

D. Ireland

Although Elizabeth was the titular ruler of Ireland, the Gaelic chieftains proved to be very independent-minded. While these chieftains had long been an irritant to the English crown, it was a much weightier matter when the Gaelic chieftains negotiated with the Spanish to provide a staging ground for an invasion of England. Between 1594 and 1603, Elizabeth faced her most severe challenge in Ireland.

There had been Irish revolts against the English before. But when Hugh O'Neill, Earl of Tyrone, began a revolt in 1595, known as "Tyrone's Rebellion," it grabbed Elizabeth's attention because it had Spanish sponsorship. She knew that to avoid a Spanish invasion, she had to nip this in the bud. It took several years to quash the rebellion, in part because the Spanish did in fact send troops, and they had to be defeated as well. O'Neill finally surrendered in 1603, a few days after Elizabeth's death.

E. Mary Queen of Scots

Mary Stuart was born on December 8, 1542, to King James V of Scotland and his French wife, Mary of Guise. Six days later she became the "infant queen" of Scotland after her father died suddenly from cholera. The French king, Henry II, proposed to unite France and Scotland by arranging the marriage of the little queen to his three-year old son, Francis. With her marriage agreement in place, at age five Mary was sent to France, where she spent the next thirteen years at the French court of Henry II.

On April 24, 1558, Mary was married to Francis at the cathedral of Notre Dame. When Mary Tudor died later that year, Henry II immediately proclaimed Francis and Mary to be the rightful king and queen of England. But those proved to be words only.

When Henry II died in July 1559, Mary's young husband became Francis II, and she became queen of France. Mary's reign was short-lived, however, when Francis II died on December 5, 1560, of an ear infection that led to an abscess in his brain.

Mary returned to Scotland soon after her husband's death, but there was no rejoicing in England. Mary not only was a devout Catholic, but also believed she had a legitimate claim to Elizabeth's crown. Under the English laws of succession, Mary Stuart was next in line to the English throne if Elizabeth remained childless. Yet, in the eyes of many Catholics, Elizabeth was illegitimate and therefore not a viable successor to the English throne anyway, thus making Mary the true queen of England.

Mary clearly shared this conviction, as evidenced by her repeated refusal to ratify the Treaty of Edinburgh of 1560 between England and Scotland, which acknowledged Elizabeth as the rightful heir to the English throne. This claim to the English throne was the source of bad blood between Mary and Elizabeth.

Marriage to Henry Stuart, Lord Darnley, in July 1565 proved to be Mary's undoing. Elizabeth felt threatened because both Mary and Darnley were claimants to the English throne, being direct descendants of Margaret Tudor, the elder sister of Henry VIII. The marriage soured because Darnley was jealous of Mary's friendship with her private secretary, David Rizzio. In a bloody scene Darnley murdered Rizzio in front of the pregnant Mary on March 9, 1566. Darnley fled to Glasgow, and a few months later their son, James, was born.

At this point the facts become murky. Early in the new year, Mary persuaded Darnley to return to Edinburgh. Darnley had become ill and was recuperating at the former abbey of Kirk O'Field. In February 1567 there was a violent explosion at the abbey, and Darnley was found dead in the garden. The odd thing was that Darnley was found to have died of strangulation. Suspicion immediately turned to Mary and James Hepburn, Earl of Bothwell. Suspicions grew after Bothwell was quickly acquitted of Darnley's murder, and a month later he and Mary were married—twelve days after Bothwell divorced his wife.

The Protestant nobility turned against Mary and Bothwell. He fled to Denmark, and she was imprisoned in Loch Leven Castle. There she miscarried twins in July 1567. That same month she was also forced to abdicate the Scottish throne in favor of her one-year-old son, James.

In May 1568 Mary escaped and fled to England, where she expected Elizabeth to help her regain her throne. Instead, Elizabeth put her in prison and ordered an inquiry into Darnley's murder. The inquiry ended with no finding of guilt, but she remained in Elizabeth's protective custody—for the next eighteen years.

Elizabeth considered Mary's designs on the English throne to be a serious threat, so she instructed her adviser Walsingham to keep a vigilant eye on her Scottish cousin. Several plots swirled around Mary, but when Walsingham intercepted Mary's own letters, it was clear that Mary had sanctioned the attempted assassination of Elizabeth. Mary vehemently denied the accusation, but was ultimately convicted of treason and sentenced to death.

Although Mary had been found guilty, Elizabeth hesitated to order her execution. She was fearful that Mary's son, James of Scotland, might seek his revenge by forming an alliance with one of the Catholic powers and invading England. Seeking to avoid direct responsibility, Elizabeth asked the jailer to contrive some accident to remove Mary. He refused on the grounds that he would not allow such "a stain on his posterity."

Elizabeth did eventually sign Mary's death warrant, and after that, the Privy Council met secretly and decided to carry out the sentence at once before the queen could change her mind.

At Fotheringhay Castle, Northamptonshire, Mary ascended the scaffold on February 8, 1587. According to a contemporary account, Mary granted forgiveness to her executioner and told him, "You are about to end my troubles!" She then slowly removed her outer garments, revealing a deep red chemise—the liturgical color of martyrdom in the Catholic Church. Eyewitnesses said it took two strikes to decapitate Mary. Afterward, the executioner held up her head and shouted, "God save the Queen." Mary was forty-four years old.

When the news of the execution reached Elizabeth, she was indignant, claiming she had not authorized it to proceed. Not long after Mary's death, the Spanish Armada sailed for England with the intention of dethroning Elizabeth, but alas, Mary would not have her revenge.

F. The Final Days of the Virgin Queen

In 1603, after forty-four years on the English throne, Queen Elizabeth was very ill, indeed dying. Her closest adviser and secretary of state, Sir Robert Cecil, gently told her that she must get her rest. Elizabeth shot back: "Little man, little man! The word 'must' is not to be used with princes." She was a royal tigress to the end.

In her later years she endured personal disappointments, none more painful than her tragic affair with the charming but petulant young Robert Devereux, Earl of Essex. She unwisely appointed him to military posts despite his record of irresponsibility. His misconduct at one point put him under house arrest, and later on the queen had to send him to the chopping block. Devastated by this turn of events, it was reported that the queen would "sit in the dark, and sometimes with shedding tears to bewail Essex."

The queen's health steadily declined, accompanied by severe depression. She died on the morning of March 24, 1603. A few hours later, Robert Cecil and the Privy Council proclaimed James VI of Scotland as King of England. At her funeral on April 28, the coffin was taken to Westminster Abbey on a hearse drawn by four horses hung with black velvet.

The Virgin Queen was no more.

VII. REFLECTIONS ON THE ENGLISH REFORMATION

Pope Sixtus V gave Elizabeth a backhanded compliment, but a compliment nevertheless. He declared, "She is only a woman, the mistress of half an island, and yet she makes herself feared by Spain, by France, by the Empire, by all!"

By the standards of her day, it was counterintuitive for a queen to remain unmarried. As her father, Henry VIII, demonstrated, producing an heir was all-important and a primary duty of a monarch. Yet Queen Elizabeth not only forged her own royal path, but also turned her virginity and childlessness to her advantage. She kept Rome and Catholic adversaries at bay by coyly entertaining marriage proposals from European royals—stringing them along as it served her political purposes. And when her marriage eligibility declined with age, she managed to create the myth of the Virgin Queen who was married only to the English people.

In the popular imagination, the Virgin Queen became fused with the Blessed Virgin Mary. Elizabeth, it was believed, was divinely appointed to rule a chosen people who had a divine mandate to extend the kingdom of God via the kingdom of England. The poet Edmund Spenser made her the Faerie Queene; for others she was Gloriana. The extraordinary longevity of her reign, surviving the myriad of assassination plots and revolts, and especially the victory over the Spanish Armada gave wings to the Elizabethan myth.

> "She is only a woman, the mistress of half an island, and yet she makes herself feared by Spain, by France, by the Empire, by all!" (Pope Sixtus V referring to Elizabeth I).

FOR FURTHER STUDY

Collinson, Patrick. *The Elizabethan Puritan Movement*. Oxford: Oxford University Press, 1990.

Dickens, A. G. *The English Reformation*. Reprint, University Park: Pennsylvania State University, 1989.

Elton, G. R. *Reform and Reformation: England 1509–1558*. Cambridge: Harvard University Press, 1977.

Haigh, Christopher. *English Reformations: Religion, Politics and Society under the Tudors*. Oxford: Oxford University Press, 1993.

MacCulloch, Diarmaid. *Thomas Cranmer*. New Haven: Yale University Press, 1996.

Refining the Reformation

Theological Currents in the Seventeenth Century

I. HISTORICAL ARC

A. Religious Wars

Although it would have grieved him, Luther's immediate legacy was more than a century of religious wars, not only between Catholics and Protestants, but also among various Protestant factions. Religious conviction and political designs became indistinguishable. Some of the more devastating wars included the French wars of religion (1562–98), the Dutch revolt against Philip II of Spain (1572–1609), the attempted invasion of England by the Spanish Armada in 1588, the Thirty Years War in Germany (1618–48), and the Puritan revolution in England (1640–60).

The century following the Reformation became a century of theological and political entrenchment. With Western Christendom now divided among three communions—Roman Catholic, Lutheran, and Reformed—each developed impenetrable confessional bulwarks against each other.

B. Catholic Orthodoxy

Catholic orthodoxy achieved its definitive theological shape with the Council of Trent (1545–63). Jesuit theologians played determinative roles at Trent, especially in the formulation of the council's decrees on justification and grace, the sacraments, and the Eucharist. Significantly, the Society of Jesus was theologically indebted to Thomas Aquinas as evidenced by Ignatius of Loyola's stipulation that the theology in the society should look to Thomas for guidance.

The Council of Trent.

Pope Paul III sent two Jesuits to Trent to represent papal theological concerns, and it was largely through their influence that Thomism prevailed at Trent. Trent concluded in 1563, and by 1567 Pope Pius V recognized Aquinas as one of four Doctors of the Church. It was the triumph of Thomism at Trent that set the future trajectory of Catholic theology.

C. Protestant Orthodoxy

There has been a good deal of confusion regarding the terminology of Protestant orthodoxy and Protestant Scholasticism to describe the post-Reformation developments in the Lutheran and Reformed branches. "Orthodoxy" differs from "Scholasticism" in that the former concerns correct theological content, while the latter had to do with an academic method.

Over the course of a century and a half, Protestant orthodoxy defended, clarified, and codified the insights of the first Reformers. After the deaths of the second-generation Reformers, one may generally identify three successive periods of Protestant orthodoxy. (Both Lutheran and Reformed orthodoxy developed at roughly the same pace.) "Early orthodoxy" extended from the mid-sixteenth to mid-seventeenth century and is characterized as the period of confessional solidification. "High orthodoxy" spans from mid-seventeenth to late seventeenth century and rests on the earlier confessional foundation, but engages in somewhat sharper polemics. "Late orthodoxy" is a period of decline and loss of dominance in the eighteenth century.

In the aftermath of the Reformation, Lutherans, Calvinists, and Roman Catholics felt the need to differentiate their communions theologically. All theologians inevitably resorted to the academic tools at their disposal, hence Aristotelian logic assumed a major role in the defense and articulation of Christian theology. In the highly polemical atmosphere of the seventeenth century, theological formulation could veer toward metaphysical speculation, especially concerning the nature of God and, above all, the doctrine of predestination.

II. THEOLOGICAL POLEMICS

After the Council of Trent the opportunity for theological dialogue was lost, and each camp dug in for the long haul—each defining itself over against the other. Emil Brunner described seventeenth-century theology as "a frozen waterfall" that devolved into *theologismus*, that is, ever greater theological precision regarding the mysteries of the faith. Increasing theological precision eventually produced intra-confessional polemics.

A. Arminianism

1. Mixing Theology and Politics

It was during the twelve-year peace between Spain and the Dutch Protestants that the religious tensions surfaced in the Northern Provinces. The two main Protestant factions were those who preferred a more theologically tolerant church and the more narrow Reformed Protestants who insisted on religious conformity. When Spain was the common enemy, the differences among Protestants managed to coexist peacefully, but with the truce, the theological differences intensified.

The controversy centered on a rather well-regarded Reformed theologian, Jacobus Arminius (Jakob Harmenszoon). Arminius endured a difficult upbringing. His father died when he was an infant, and his mother was slain during the Spanish massacre of Oudewater in 1575. He was taken under the wing of a Dutch minister and was one of the first students to enroll in the new Protestant University of Leiden. He took advanced studies in Geneva and studied with Calvin's successor, Theodore Beza.

In 1588 Arminius became a pastor in Amsterdam and eventually began to criticize some of the harsher aspects of the doctrine of predestination. Detractors were none too pleased when he was appointed professor of theology at Leiden in 1603. Almost immediately upon his arrival in Leiden, one of his colleagues on the faculty, Franciscus Gomarus, began to challenge his orthodoxy.

The specific theological issues at the center of the debate were supralapsarianism, unconditional predestination, and irresistible grace. Arminius's theology put him in conflict with the Belgic Confession, which had become the confessional standard of the Dutch Protestants. Supralapsarianism (*supra* [before] + *lapse* [the Fall] = before the Fall) was concerned with the logical order of God's decrees in eternity before the creation of the world. Supralapsarianism argues that in eternity God's decree to predestine preceded his decree to permit the fall of humanity. In its crudest form, supralapsarianism uses the Fall as the means of realizing the prior decision to send some individuals to hell and others to heaven, thus providing the grounds of condemnation in the reprobate and the need for redemption in the elect.

As for his understanding of divine grace, Arminius posits God's prevenient (*going before*) grace granted to all of fallen humanity. This is necessary because the Fall had rendered the human stubborn and disobedient. So in his mercy God grants to all a grace that "goes before" to assist the fallen will. But this prevenient grace is resistible. Those who do not resist but allow this grace to work efficaciously will be saved. Those who resist this prevenient grace will be punished for their sins.

Arminius believed that his order of divine decrees was within the bounds of the Reformed faith. Gomarus believed otherwise.

2. The Synod of Dort

Gomarus began mixing politics and religion when he accused Arminius not only of heresy, but of having sympathy for the Spanish devil. The controversy raged until Arminius's death in 1609. The following year, supporters of Arminius, led by Jan Uytenbogaert and Simon Episcopius, presented a Remonstrance treatise in five articles formulating their points of disagreement with Gomarus: (1) election was conditioned on foreseen faith; (2) Christ's atonement was unlimited in scope; (3) fallen humanity is unable to exercise a saving faith; (4) grace was resistible; and (5) falling from grace is possible.

The Synod of Dort.

In reply, the Gomarists drew up a Counter-Remonstrance.

This theological debate turned political when Johan van Olden-barnevelt upheld the Remonstrant view and Maurice of Orange declared himself on the side of the Contra-Remonstrants. Tensions mounted and the United Provinces (also known as the Dutch Republic) were on the brink of civil war. Maurice prevailed, and in August 1618 Oldenbarnevelt was arrested pending the outcome of a national synod.

The Synod of Dort met from November 1618 until January 1619 and was attended by more than a hundred delegates, including those from England, Scotland, France, and Switzerland. Representatives to the synod were exclusively Calvinist. Three Arminian delegates from Utrecht managed to gain entrance, but were forcibly ejected. Simon

Episcopius was summoned before the synod, but was prohibited from making his case. When he protested, he was dismissed.

The synod ultimately ruled that Arminius's teachings were heretical, and it rejected the five articles of Remonstrance. In response the synod affirmed: total depravity, unconditional election, limited atonement, irresistible grace, and the perseverance of the saints. These are referred to as the "Five Points of Calvinism" and remembered by many using the mnemonic "TULIP."

When Arminius's theology is measured by Dort, it is clear that he rejected three of the five points: U, L, and I. It is not clear that he rejected total depravity. He specifically affirms that "man himself is dead in sins." Arminius was undecided about the perseverance of the saints. He did not deny the doctrine, only that one must be careful about offering false assurance. Followers of Arminius were more definitive in rejecting both perseverance of the saints and total depravity.

During the synod Oldenbarnevelt was arraigned before a special court comprised primarily of personal enemies, and he received a death sentence. On May 13, 1619, at the age of seventy-one, the old statesman was beheaded in The Hague. More than two hundred pastors were deposed from their pulpits, and another eighty were exiled or imprisoned. The famous jurist Hugo Grotius was given a life sentence in prison, but escaped with the help of his wife.

After the death of Maurice in 1625, Arminianism was gradually allowed back in the Netherlands. By 1634 a Remonstrant Brotherhood was established and later became the Remonstrant Reformed Church.

B. Amyraldism

Within two decades after the Synod of Dort, another theological controversy was brewing in Reformed circles, this time in France. The controversy swirled around the brilliant French theologian Moses Amyraut, professor at the famous School of Samur. Amyraut famously took issue with one of the articles of the Canons of Dort, the doctrine of limited atonement. He argued instead for unlimited atonement, believing that Christ's atonement was sufficient for all humanity, but efficient only for the elect. His view is sometimes known as "Hypothetical Universalism" or four-point Calvinism.

In *A Short Treatise on Predestination* (1634), Amyraut proposed that God foreordained a universal salvation through the universal sacrifice of Christ for all. However, that universal salvation would not be effectual unless appropriated by personal faith. In so far as it concerns God's will, his grace is universal. But in so far as it concerns individuals, it is conditioned on faith.

Amyraut's modification of Calvinist theology sparked repeated charges of heresy, first at the national synod held at Alençon in 1637, then at the national synod of Charenton in 1644, and a third time at the synod of Loudun in 1659. Amyraut was exonerated, yet opposition to him persisted in the Reformed churches of France, Holland, and Switzerland. Especially in Geneva, Francis Turretin (1623–87) opposed Amyraldism as a departure from the orthodox faith and a compromise between Calvinism and Arminianism. But in the final analysis, most Reformed churches accepted or tolerated Amyraut's views.

C. Jansenism

The success of the Council of Trent did not quash the theological enterprise among Catholics. In what was one of the more remarkable theological developments of the seventeenth century, the specter of Calvinism emerged within the bosom of Rome itself. While studying theology at the Catholic University of Leuven, Cornelius Jansen and his lifelong friend, Jean Du Vergier, developed a deep interest in the thought of Augustine of Hippo. Later Du Vergier became the abbot of Saint-Cyran, and Jansen was consecrated as bishop of Ypres.

Jansen died suddenly during an epidemic in 1638, but before his death, he committed a manuscript to his chaplain, which was his magnum opus on Augustine's theology. Published in 1640 under the title *Augustinus*, Jansen took a strict Augustinian stance on such doctrines as original sin, human depravity, and the necessity of divine grace. Fully embracing Augustine's strict notion of predestination, he argued that God predestined only a certain portion of humanity for salvation, leaving the rest to their just desserts.

Jesuits especially were indignant and claimed that Jansen was a clandestine Calvinist. Du Vergier took up the cause of his deceased friend. In 1634 he became the spiritual adviser of the Cistercian convent at Port Royal and managed to persuade Abbess Marie Angélique Arnauld of Jansen's view, along with her brother, Antoine Arnauld. Thereafter the Port Royal convents became major strongholds of what was termed "Jansenism." Du Vergier's advocacy landed him in prison in May 1638, where he remained until 1642. He died the next year. Following Du Vergier's death, Antoine Arnauld became the chief proponent of Jansenism.

In 1653, at the prompting of the Sorbonne, Pope Innocent X issued the bull *Cum Occasione* condemning *Augustinus*. The papal condemnation centered on three basic Jansenist assertions: (1) that without God's prevenient enabling grace, fallen humans cannot obey divine commands, exercise faith, or merit divine favor; (2) that God's grace cannot be resisted; and (3) that Christ died only for the elect. Antoine Arnauld defended *Augustinus*, and Blaise Pascal took up the pen in defense of Arnauld in his famous *Provincial Letters*. Neither was able to turn the tide, and Jansenism was systematically dismantled.

The convent of Port Royal was prohibited from receiving the sacraments and forbidden to accept new novices. Finally, in 1708 the pope issued a bull dissolving Port-Royal-des-Champs. The remaining nuns were forcibly removed in 1709, and most of the buildings were razed in 1710.

III. THEOLOGICAL RENEWAL IN GERMAN PIETISM

After Luther's death, the movement that bore his name fell into disarray and infighting. Gensio-Lutherans decried the Philippists and remained at loggerheads until they concluded a theological peace treaty with the Formula of Concord in 1577, which became the definitive statement of Lutheran orthodoxy. Most of the massive destruction of the Thirty Years War (1618–48), which convulsed Europe, took place on German soil. Agriculture collapsed, famine ravaged the land, and universities closed. By the end the war, there were at least eight million fewer souls in Germany.

The Peace of Westphalia made room for Catholicism, Lutheranism, and Calvinism, depending on the religious sensibilities of the prince. Weary of bloodshed, the three communions withdrew behind polemical firewalls and, instead of firing cannonballs, lobbed theological bombs at the other.

Pietism was a war-weary reaction to the perceived scholastic theology of Lutheranism that seemed to the Pietists more a "dead orthodoxy" than a vibrant faith. Pietism did not set out to change the Lutheran doctrine or seek to form a new church. It was an intrachurch renewal movement that sought a "living orthodoxy." Pietism saw itself as an *Ecclesiola in Ecclesia*, that is, "a little church within the [larger] church," which was to be the vehicle for renewed attention to Christian piety.

To see things in a clear perspective, we must note that acknowledging German Pietism as a reaction to the dead orthodoxy of confessional, state Lutheranism of the early seventeenth century is not necessarily to suggest that Lutheran orthodoxy was inherently opposed to personal piety. The same scholastic theologians who composed the erudite and abstract theological systems could also produce stirring hymns and deeply personal devotional writings. Johann Gerhard, author of one of the definitive scholastic expositions of Lutheran theology, the *Loci communes theologici*, was also deeply concerned with piety, as witnessed by his popular devotion titled *Sacred Meditations for the Stirring of True Piety*.

This proved to be a popular devotional work surpassed only by another work of devotion, titled *True Christianity* (1606) by the Lutheran pastor Johann Arndt.

A. Philipp Jakob Spener

Philipp Jakob Spener (1635–1705) is generally acknowledged as the "father of German Pietism." Born at Rappoltsweiler in 1635, Spener was nurtured by a devout godmother, Agatha von Rappoltstein, and her chaplain, Joachim Stoll (1615–78), who became his spiritual mentor, introducing him to devotional writings such as Arndt's *True Christianity*. Stoll also introduced the young Spener to writings of English Puritans that, along with Arndt, generated "the first spark of true Christianity."

Spener studied theology at Strasbourg, where his primary theological professor was Johann Konrad Dannhauer, one of the leading orthodox theologians of seventeenth-century Lutheranism. Not only Dannhauer's theology, but also his personal piety deeply inspired the young Spener.

Philipp Jakob Spener.

When Spener entered his first pastoral charge at Frankfurt am Main in 1666, he was convinced of the necessity of a moral and religious reformation within German Lutheranism. His sermons emphasized the necessity of a lively faith and the sanctification of daily life. Perhaps his most significant innovation was his establishment in 1670 of the *collegia pietatis* ("pious gathering"). These were smaller gatherings (also called "conventicles") of congregants in his home that focused on discussions of sermons, devotional reading, and mutual edification.

In 1675 Spener was asked to write a preface for a collection of sermons by Johann Arndt. The result was his famous *Pia Desideria* (*Pious Wishes*), which became a short précis of German Pietism: He called for (1) "a more extensive use of the Word of God"; to this end, he advocated small group meetings (*Ecclesiola in ecclesia*) to encourage greater knowledge of the Bible among the congregants; (2) a renewed focus on the role of the laity in Christian ministry; (3) an emphasis on the connection between Christian doctrine and Christian life; (4) restraint and charity in theological disputes; (5) reform in the education of ministers—they must be trained in piety and devotion as well as in academic subjects; (6) the preaching of edifying sermons, understandable by the people, rather than technical discourses, which few were interested in or could understand.

Spener's *Pia Desideria* won him many adherents, but also aroused strong opposition among Lutheran theologians and pastors. Despite such criticism, the movement rapidly increased.

B. August Hermann Francke

Spener had the good fortune to be succeeded by August Hermann Francke (1663–1727), who was born in Lübeck and raised by his devout mother. He graduated from the University of Leipzig, where he excelled in biblical languages. In1687, while a student at Leipzig, he experienced a dramatic and angst-ridden conversion, which he described as the *grosse Wende* ("great change").

Francke's conversion experience became paradigmatic for Pietism: genuine conversion is inevitably preceded by an agonizing conviction of sin that is a datable event to which one can point for confirmation.

Returning to Leipzig, he led a collegiate revival that spilled over to the town. The revival provoked conflict with the university, and Francke was expelled from the city. It was at this point that the term "Pietist" was first coined by a detractor, Joachim Feller, professor of rhetoric at the university. A Pietist, Feller asserted, was "someone who studies God's Word and, in his own opinion, also leads a holy life."

> "… someone who studies God's Word and, in his own opinion, also leads a holy life" (Joachim Feller's definition of a Pietist).

By this time, Francke had become closely associated with Spener. It was due to Spener's influence that Francke was appointed to the chair of Greek and Oriental languages at the new University of Halle (founded in 1694). Francke emerged as the natural successor to Spener. From his position at Halle he exercised enormous influence in preparing a generation of Pietist pastors and missionaries all over the world, but his impact was not only as an educator. Under his guidance the university showed what Pietism could mean when put into practice. In rapid succession Francke opened a school for poor children, a renowned orphanage, a home for indigent widows, an institute for the training of teachers, a medical clinic, a home for street beggars, a publishing house for printing and distributing Bibles, and the famous Paedagogium, a preparatory school for upper-class students.

For thirty-six years his energetic endeavors established Halle as the center of German Pietism and its diffusion. Together Spener and Francke had created a true *Ecclesiola in ecclesia*.

C. Theology of the Pious

Spener and Francke were adamant in their affirmation of Lutheran orthodoxy, but insisted that "orthodoxy" goes hand in hand with "orthopraxis"—that is, correct belief goes hand in hand with ethical and liturgical conduct. Indeed, they would argue that orthodoxy is not orthodoxy if it does not lead to pious living. Although Pietism is essentially a practical theology, one can identify the basic theological strains that undergird its practice.

1. Conversion

The starting point for Pietist theology is the necessity of the "new birth." While Pietists affirmed the Lutheran doctrine of justification, their theological emphasis shifted from justification to regeneration of the individual. Following the pattern of Francke's dramatic conversion experience, many Pietists tended to maintain that genuine conversion is always preceded by agonizing repentance.

2. Centrality of Scripture

The Bible stands at the center of Pietist theology. Franke's students frequently heard his mantra: *"Theologus nascitur in scripturis"* ("A theologian is born from the Scriptures"). Pietists viewed Scripture as their supreme authority, but studied it devotionally for the purpose of spiritual edification rather than academic theology. The Scriptures were so central for Spener that he encouraged laity to learn the biblical languages. Also, Pietists saw an intimate and essential connection between the Holy Spirit and Scripture because it is the Spirit who transforms the dead letter of the text into living power in a person's life.

3. Sanctification

For Pietists, theology was never about abstract speculation but always had as its goal personal piety and sanctification. Thus, preaching was mostly aimed against moral laxity rather than Luther's doctrine of justification by faith alone. With the emphasis on a godly life came a tendency toward moralism and legalism. Spener expended noticeable energy denouncing drunkenness in the *Pia Desidera*, and Francke's advice in his *Scriptural Rules for Living* warned against "trifling jests and anecdotes." Worldly amusements, such as dancing, the theater, and public games were condemned as sin.

4. Church Renewal

From the outset Pietists eagerly sought church renewal, and one of the keys to renewal was an enhanced role for laity. Luther's doctrine of "the priesthood of all believers" became a rallying call for Christian laity to engage in the work of ministry. Church renewal included clergy as well as laity. Pietists insisted that pulpits must be manned only by the regenerate, whose primary concern was the edification of parishioners. The formation of small groups was yet another vehicle for spiritual nurture of the laity and thus church renewal.

"Each one should modestly and in love share for the edification of the others what God has enabled him to understand in the Scriptures" (Philipp Jakob Spener).

D. The Pietist Legacy

Spener and Francke inspired other varieties of German Pietism. Count Nikolas von Zinzendorf, head of the renewed Moravian Church, was Spener's godson and Francke's pupil. Zinzendorf organized refugees from Moravia into a kind of *collegia pietatis* on his estate and later shepherded this group in reviving the Bohemian Unity of the Brethren.

These Moravians, as they came to be known, carried the Pietistic concern for personal spirituality almost literally around the world. This was of momentous significance for the history of English-speaking Christianity when John Wesley found himself in the company of Moravians during his voyage to Georgia in 1735. What he saw of their behavior then and what he heard of their faith after returning to England led to his own evangelical awakening. The fruit of these Pietist influences can still be seen among modern American Methodists and members of the Holiness movement.

IV. THEOLOGICAL RENEWAL IN ENGLISH PURITANISM

Defining Puritanism has long been a matter of academic debate. This is due in part to the fact that Puritanism was not only identified with a spiritual and theological orientation, but also has been allied with political and social viewpoints at various stages of its historical evolution.

Part of the difficulty of definition is compounded by the many caricatures that began in the sixteenth century. The word "Puritan" was originally a term of abuse devised in the 1560s by antagonists and had the connotation of "peevishness, censoriousness, conceit, and a measure of hypocrisy." This same meaning carried into modern times as evidenced in the scornful depiction by the American journalist H. L. Mencken, who defined Puritanism as "the haunting fear that someone, somewhere, may be happy."

Puritanism is "the haunting fear that someone, somewhere, may be happy" (H. L. Mencken).

The problem of definition is further complicated by the surprising diversity among Puritans. Although all shared a common theological referent, some Puritans approved of the existing church hierarchy with bishops, while others sought to restructure the Anglican Church according to a Presbyterian model. Some Puritans were Presbyterian, but most embraced congregational polity. Some advocated separation from the established church, but others remained. Some were royalist and others were revolutionary, even to the point of regicide. Puritans could differ in church polity, in worship style, even in their expressions of piety, but all wanted the English Church to resemble more closely the Reformed churches on the Continent.

Whatever difficulties and ambiguities attend the term "Puritan," scholars are nevertheless obliged to employ it. For general purposes "Puritanism" refers to an identifiable group of English Protestants from the period of Elizabeth I to the interregnum who embraced Reformed theology to a substantial degree and sought in various ways further to reform the Church of England. When these reform efforts were met with increasing persecution, what had begun as an ecclesiastical reform movement within the Anglican Church morphed into a political revolution. Thus any definition of Puritanism must include not only its theology, piety, and ecclesiology, but also its political dimension.

A. From Tudor to Stuart

When Sir John Harrington went to see his ailing royal Tudor godmother at Richmond, he was overcome with grief. He remarked in a letter to his wife that the queen was displaying "human infirmity too fast for that evil we shall get by her death and too slow for that good which we shall get by her releasement from her pains and misery." After forty-four years on the throne, Queen Elizabeth I died in her sleep in the early morning hours of March 24, 1603. It was not only the end of a life, but the end of an age.

With Elizabeth's departure, the Puritan faction saw a new opportunity to purify the English Church. Her successor, James I, had ruled Presbyterian Scotland as a Stuart monarch since 1567, and the English Puritans had high hopes that he would be more receptive to their reform aspirations. So in 1603, even before he arrived in London, a group of Puritans intercepted the royal entourage and presented him with the famous "Millenary Petition," so-called because it purported to have a thousand signatures of support.

Although "loyal subjects," the group exhorted the new king to abolish such popish ceremonies as the sign of the cross in baptism, the wearing of the surplice, the exchange of rings in marriage, and bowing at the name of Jesus. They also pleaded for shorter services with less music, more rigid observance of the Sabbath, and better preaching. James listened patiently to the demands, but referred the matter to a conference to be held at Hampton Court in January 1604.

At the Hampton Court conference James revealed his true colors, declaring, "I shall make them conform themselves, or I will harry them out of the land." The new king was no closeted Roman Catholic, but he was determined to enforce episcopacy because it was far more aligned with his royal authority than Puritan presbyters. Hence, James declared, "No bishop, no King." Although it was not specifically mentioned in the Millenary Petition, James did approve a new "Authorized

"I shall make them conform themselves, or I will harry them out of the land" (King James I on the Puritans).

The spread of religion in 16th-century Europe.

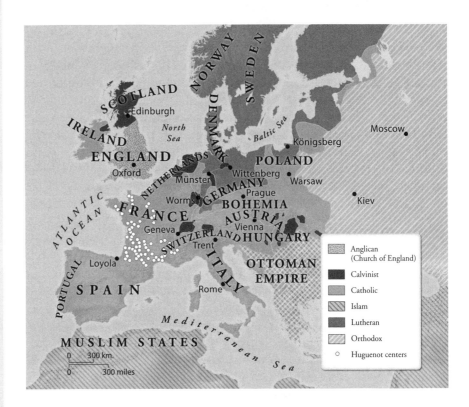

Version" of the Bible, which appeared in 1611, known popularly as the "King James Version."

B. Stumbling toward Civil War

When James I died in 1625, he was succeed by his son, Charles I. English Puritans greeted the new king with less enthusiasm than they had his father. Charles's belief that kings are "little Gods on Earth" did not bode well for future relations. Neither did it help matters that the new king almost immediately married a Roman Catholic princess, Henrietta-Marie de Bourbon, which raised the specter of a Roman Catholic heir to the English throne.

The relationship between the Crown and the predominantly Puritan Parliament went from bad to worse. Charles aroused more Puritan antagonism when in 1633 he appointed William Laud as archbishop of Canterbury, who embarked on a religious policy of High Anglicanism with its sacramental emphasis on ceremonies and a theological inclination toward Arminianism. One gets a sense of the growing hostility reflected in the encounter between the Puritan minister Thomas Shepherd and Archbishop Laud in 1618:

[Laud] looked as though blood would have gushed out of his face … by reason of his extreme malice and secret venom. I desired him to excuse me. He fell then to threaten me and withal to bitter railing, calling me all to naught, saying, "You prating coxcomb."

C. Revolt in Scotland

In what proved to be his undoing, Charles sought to impose on the Scottish Church a new Anglican version of the prayer book in the summer of 1637. One Scottish wag called it the "vomit of Romish superstition." When Jenny Geddes, a vegetable seller, heard the dean of St. Giles Cathedral in Edinburgh read from the new prayer book, she stood up and threw her "creepie-stool" (a folding stool) directly at his head. As she hurled the stool, she is reported to have yelled: "Devil cause you colic in your stomach, false thief: dare you say the Mass in my ear?"

Jenny Geddes's reaction was a harbinger of a national rebellion. Riots soon broke out in Edinburgh, and in February 1638, the Scots formulated their opposition in a National Covenant. Many Scots signed the document with their own blood, signifying they would die before submitting to Anglicanism. Charles led two futile military campaigns, known as the Bishops' Wars (1639–40), in an effort to quell the Scottish rebellion.

D. Revolt in Parliament

When the Scottish army occupied northern England and threatened to march south, Charles finally bowed to pressure and in November 1640 summoned a Parliament that had never been more hostile to the king. Immediately Parliament passed a law forbidding the king to dissolve it without its consent; it came to be known as the "Long Parliament," since it remained in session until 1660. Then Archbishop Laud was charged with high treason. One MP, Harbottle Grimston, famously declared Laud "the roote and ground of all our miseries and calamities … the sty of all pestilential filth that hath infected the State and Government"—and so the archnemesis of the Puritans was imprisoned in the Tower of London in February 1641.

Inevitably, the conflict between king and Parliament reached a flash point. Charles became convinced that a number of Puritan MPs had committed treason by conspiring with the Scots to invade England. The traitors were identified, and Charles, accompanied by four hundred soldiers, dramatically burst into the House of Commons in January 1642, only to find the five had fled. A few days later, fearing for his own personal safety and for that of his family, Charles fled London.

E. The English Civil War

Civil war had dawned, and it was played out in three phases from 1642 to 1653. The first phase (1642–46) commenced with the battle at Edgehill in October 1642. Although this first skirmish was inconclusive, royalist armies proved victorious in most of the other early battles. Unable to defeat the king on the battlefield, the Long Parliament entered into a military alliance with the Scots, which led to its first important success at Marston Moor in July 1644. Oliver Cromwell, a leader of the parliamentary forces, famously attributed this victory to "God [who] made them as stubble to our swords."

With extraordinary skillfulness, Cromwell restructured his forces into the more effective New Model Army, and in two decisive engagements in 1645—the Battle of Naseby on June 14 and the Battle of Langport on July 10—they effectively defeated Charles. With his resources exhausted, Charles surrendered in May 1646 to the Scottish army but was handed over to the English.

The second phase of the civil war (1648–49) was prompted by Charles's secret negotiations with the Scots. Under the terms of the agreement, the Scots would join royalists to defeat parliamentary forces and restore Charles to the throne on condition of the establishment of Presbyterianism for three years in both England and Scotland, after which a permanent solution would be worked out. After a number of skirmishes, Cromwell decisively routed Scottish and royalist forces at the Battle of Preston in August 1648.

F. Pride's Purge

Despite military success, Parliament could not avoid the growing tensions among the various Puritan factions. Parliament was dominated by Presbyterians, but the New Model Army (including Cromwell) was largely composed of Independents (Congregationalists). The Presbyterians and Anglicans were willing to restore the king to power, but with limited authority.

Infuriated that Parliament would even consider restoring Charles to the throne, Cromwell's army marched on Parliament. On December 6, 1648, Colonel Thomas Pride's regiment took up positions on the stairs leading to Parliament. As MPs arrived, only Independents who were viewed as supporters of the army were permitted entrance. Most of the Presbyterians and Anglicans were turned away, and forty-five were imprisoned. It is estimated that of the 470 members of Parliament, approximately 100 members were allowed to take their seats. This came to be known as "Pride's Purge."

After the purge, the remaining members of Parliament were allied with the Independents and the army. This "Rump Parliament," as it came to be known, proceeded to put Charles on trial. On January 27, 1649, Charles I was judged guilty of high treason. The execution took place in front of the Banqueting House of the Palace of Whitehall three days later.

The king was dead, but the war was not. The last phase of the English civil war (1649–53) concentrated on new revolts in Ireland and Scotland. In 1648 Irish confederates formed an alliance with English royalists in opposition to Parliament. Cromwell responded by invading Ireland in August 1649 and harshly suppressing the royalist alliance. He notoriously laid siege to the town of Drogheda and then massacred nearly 3,500 people, including 700 civilians, prisoners, and Catholic priests. The Drogheda massacre still enflames Irish Catholic–English Protestant strife to the present day.

The English conquest of Ireland continued until 1653, when the last Irish confederate and royalist troops surrendered. Historians have estimated that around 30 percent of Ireland's population either died or had gone into exile by the end of the war.

In Scotland, the execution of Charles I decisively altered the dynamics of the civil war. The Scottish Covenanters not only opposed the execution of Charles, but also feared for the future of Presbyterianism and Scottish independence under the new commonwealth. The Scots turned to Charles II, the son of the late king, and bestowed the throne of Scotland upon him. He was crowned on June 23, 1650, and immediately signed the Solemn League and Covenant, guaranteeing Scottish Presbyterianism.

In response to the Scottish threat, Cromwell left his lieutenants in Ireland to finish the pacification of the Irish and invaded Scotland. He took Edinburgh in the summer of 1650, and in July 1651 his forces defeated the Scots at the Battle of Inverkeithing, forcing Charles II to head south into England. Cromwell followed Charles II and defeated him at Worcester on September 3, thus ending the civil war. Charles eluded capture by hiding in the Royal Oak at Boscobel House and managed to escape to France.

G. From Commonwealth to Restoration

After the execution of King Charles I, the monarchy was abolished, and a commonwealth was declared on May 19, 1649. The Commonwealth of Great Britain (England, Ireland, and Scotland) was a republic from 1649 to 1660. A body of representatives from the Rump, called the "Council of State," took over the executive functions of the government. However, on closer examination it was clear that the Rump depended on the support of Cromwell's army, and that was a very uneasy relationship.

Frustrated with the bickering among the various factions, Cromwell forcibly dismissed the Rump in April 1653, declaring, "You have sat here too long for the good you do." He replaced it with what has been known as the "Barebone's Parliament," a derogatory reference to one of its members, Praise-God Barebone.

The Barebone's Parliament was short-lived and was soon replaced by the Protectorate. Cromwell was offered the crown by Parliament, but refused it, declaring, "I would not seek to set up that which Providence hath destroyed and laid in the dust." Instead, he became the first Lord Protector ruling under England's first written constitution, which mandated that the Lord Protector summon triennial parliaments. The motto of the Protectorate reflects Cromwell's outlook: *"Pax quaeritur bello"* ("Peace is sought through war"). Cromwell ruled Great Britain until his death in 1658.

Cromwell's strong rule brought new stability to England. One of the characteristic features of his Protectorate is the principle of religious freedom. He established a broad policy of tolerance for most religious groups, of which there were many.

Conventional Presbyterian and Congregational churches multiplied, but so did unconventional sects. Levellers sought a more democratic society, although the rights for women were excluded. The Diggers wanted an even more egalitarian society, advocating communal ownership of land and absolute equality for males and females. Ranters were antinomians who denied most traditional Christian doctrine, including the existence of sin. Baptists formed congregations based on adult rebaptism, and Fifth Monarchy Men wanted to establish a "government of saints" in preparation for the imminent return of Christ. Only Catholics were excluded.

Cromwell's toleration even extended to the Jews. King Edward I had expelled Jews from England in 1290, but Cromwell gave informal permission for Jews to return. While Jews could not openly practice their faith, they were no longer prosecuted if caught worshiping.

When Oliver Cromwell died, his son, Richard Cromwell, inherited the title Lord Protector, but the lack of support from the army and internal divisions led to his resignation and thus the collapse of the Protectorate in May 1659. Amid the chaos that ensued, General George Monck, who commanded English forces in Scotland, marched south to London to restore order. Monck organized the Convention Parliament, which met initially on April 25.

By May 8 Parliament proclaimed that King Charles II had been the lawful monarch since the execution of Charles I in January 1649.

When Charles II was crowned king at Westminster Abbey on April 23, 1661, it was not only a public demonstration that the monarchy was restored, but also a demonstration that the English Puritan experiment had failed.

V. PURITANISM IN NEW ENGLAND

During the reign of James I some Puritans grew discouraged at the pace of reform and separated entirely from the Church of England. After a short sojourn in the Netherlands, one group of "separating Puritans," better known historically as the "Pilgrims," eventually established the Plymouth Colony in 1620 in what is now southeastern Massachusetts.

In the meantime, England was witnessing the crown's increasing intolerance of the Puritan faction in Parliament. When Archbishop Laud began systematically to suppress Puritans, emigration to the New World increased. As the Puritans' relationship with the new king soured, John Winthrop, a Puritan lawyer, began to pursue seriously the prospect of a Puritan colony in New England. In March 1629 Winthrop obtained a royal charter to establish the Massachusetts Bay Colony, and in 1630 he was joined by 700 colonists on eleven ships to set sail for New England.

While on board the *Arbella*, Winthrop preached a sermon in which he declared to his fellow travelers, "We shall be as a city upon a hill [and] the eyes of all people are upon us." Others were captivated by this Puritan vision of a Christian commonwealth, and from 1630 to the beginning of the English Civil War, nearly 21,000 Puritans emigrated to New England. Winthrop's expedition of English Puritans was but the first in what came to be known as the "Great Migration."

These later Puritans were different from the Separatists of Plymouth Colony. Massachusetts Bay Colony settlers believed in reform, but not separation. Indeed, on the eve of their departure from England, they publically declared that we "esteeme it our honour, to call the Church of England, from when wee rise, our dear Mother." Winthrop's colonists were nonseparating Puritans who wished to reform the established church by embracing a quasi-congregational church structure. Even though the Puritans in Massachusetts erected their church along congregational lines, they remained in full communion with the Church of England.

A. From Tolerance to Intolerance

Winthrop and his fellow English expatriates embraced a vision of a "purified" society committed to biblical principles every bit as much as

> "We shall be as a city upon a hill [and] the eyes of all people are upon us" (John Winthrop).

they desired a "purified" church. The idea of the "covenant" between God and his people lay at the nucleus of their New England enterprise. Winthrop believed it is the "essence of every society to be knit together by some covenant." In this covenant they promised to obey God's commands on the grounds that he in turn promised to bless them. This meant strict observance of the Sabbath. Families were also covenantally structured as "little churches," with the father bestowing blessings for obedience and punishments for disobedience.

The covenantal social structure included a public piety. It prohibited secular entertainments, such as games of chance, maypoles, horse racing, bear baiting, and the theater. Christmas celebrations were viewed and outlawed as pagan rituals. The Puritan vision also included a rich and sometimes odd personal piety.

One of the more important ecclesiastical distinctives of the New England Puritans was the emphasis on a credible public declaration of conversion as a condition for admission to church membership. Problems arose in subsequent generations, however, when children failed to describe a vivid conversion experience and were thus excluded from church membership. Bitter divisions erupted, and Puritan ministers, led by Richard Mather, developed the so-called "halfway covenant" as a way to address the problem. This granted quasi-membership (including baptism but not participation in the Lord's Supper) to the children of church members. Puritan preachers hoped to expose these "halfway members" to teaching and piety that would lead to the "born again" experience and thus full church membership.

Some have asserted that the Puritans envisioned a theocracy. Winthrop had been declared the governor of the colony, and although he sought to base the colony's laws on biblical principles, he disallowed the clergy any formal role in governing. Church officials had no authority over the magistrates except insofar as they were members of a congregation. Winthrop and government officials did not hesitate to seek the advice of ministers, which was immensely valued, but political authority rested firmly in the hands of laypeople. Theocratic tendencies existed, but the colony's congregationalist orientation necessarily restrained such tendencies. In the final analysis, New England never presented sufficient unity to be a theocracy.

English Puritanism was always a minority movement, even when it held the reins of political power. New England Puritanism was more thoroughly dominant in colonial society. Puritans had come to New England in pursuit of religious freedom — yet once they were established, they proved intolerant of others with the same dream. Among the more notable recipients of this intolerance were Roger Williams, Anne Hutchinson, and Mary Dyer.

B. Roger Williams

The historian Edmund S. Morgan described Roger Williams as a "charming, sweet-tempered, winning man, courageous, selfless, God-intoxicated—and stubborn." That stubbornness was bound up with his deeply held separatist convictions. Arriving in Boston in 1631, he was almost immediately invited to become the pastor of the local congregation. Williams refused the invitation on the grounds that the congregation had not publically repented for having failed to separate from the Church of England. This and other actions so infuriated the Puritan leaders of the Massachusetts Bay Colony that they expelled him.

In 1636 Williams settled at the tip of Narragansett Bay on land purchased from the Narragansett Indians. He named his settlement "Providence" in thanks to God and declared religious freedom—the first colony in the world in which religious liberty was genuinely obtained for all. With newfound religious freedom, Williams became convinced that baptism should be granted upon a profession of faith, and thus infants were to be excluded. He established the first Baptist Church in America in 1638.

C. The Hutchinson Controversy

William and Anne Hutchinson arrived at the Massachusetts Bay Colony in 1634, following their Puritan minister John Cotton, who had become pastor of a Boston congregation. Like many English Puritans, the Hutchinsons set up a conventicle in their home—a group meeting to discuss John Cotton's sermon from the previous Sunday. Anne Hutchinson excelled at propounding on Cotton's ideas, and eventually her conventicle swelled to nearly eighty men and women.

Controversy arose when she began expounding an unusual theology that combined the covenant with double predestination. Hutchinson argued that all are under either a covenant of works or a covenant of grace. Those under the first are relying on good works for their salvation, while those under the other are depending on God's grace alone for salvation. The former, she said, are lost while the latter are truly saved.

Anne crossed the line in 1637 when she began denouncing various Puritan ministers in the colony as preaching a "covenant of works." Detractors were alarmed and accused her of antinomianism—the view that the elect (under the covenant of grace) did not have to follow the laws of God. It did not help her case that she was a woman teaching the Bible to men and women.

Anne was called before the Massachusetts General Court to give an account. Much to the dismay of the magistrates, she was anything but contrite. Sparks flew when she proved more adept at citing Scripture

> "…charming, sweet-tempered, winning man, courageous, selfless, God-intoxicated—and stubborn" (Edmund S. Morgan's description of Roger Williams).

than her adjudicators. But the tide turned against her when she made an unguarded comment that her knowledge came "by an immediate revelation." The magistrates, who were already suspicious of her orthodoxy, seized on her claim that God was speaking directly to her and voted to banish her from the colony.

D. Mary Dyer

On another front, the Puritan vision of the Massachusetts Bay Colony did not include toleration of Quakers. In 1660 one of the most notable victims of the religious intolerance was English Quaker Mary Dyer. Like many English Puritans, William and Mary Dyer emigrated to New England in search of religious freedom. She first aroused misgivings by her association with Anne Hutchinson. So devoted was she that when Hutchinson was excommunicated, a pregnant Mary Dyer dramatically stood by her side, and after Hutchinson was banished, Mary followed her to Rhode Island.

Suspicion of Mary was greatly increased when it was learned that before departing Massachusetts, she had given birth to a deformed stillborn baby. Governor Winthrop had the baby exhumed in March 1638 and described it in gruesome detail, including "a face, but no head,... four horns,... two mouths," and claws instead of toes. For many New England Puritans, such a birth was a signal of divine disapproval.

While visiting England in 1652, Mary joined the Religious Society of Friends (Quakers) after hearing the preaching of its founder, George Fox. She became not only a devoted Quaker, but an activist. She returned to Rhode Island in 1657, and the following year she was in Boston protesting a new law banning Quakers. She was arrested and expelled repeatedly from the colony. She escaped hanging in 1658 through a last-minute appeal by her son. She was banished with the solemn warning that there would be no further mercy.

But Mary Dyer was not to be denied her martyrdom. She again returned to Boston in 1660 to defy the anti-Quaker law and was again sentenced to death on May 31. This time the sentence was carried out.

E. The Salem Witch Trials

Religious intolerance and superstition were all too often two sides of the same coin in the seventeenth century. Witch hunts first emerged during the fifteenth century in southeastern France and western Switzerland. The European witch craze was further fueled by the publication of such works as *The Hammer of the Witches* in 1486, written by the inquisitors Heinrich Kramer and Jacob Sprenger.

This manic superstition reached its height between 1581 and 1675 and included victims from both sexes, all ages, and all classes. The best estimates are that from the late fifteenth to the early eighteenth centuries an estimated total of 40,000 to 60,000 people were executed as witches, the vast majority of whom were women.

The same witch craze found its way to New England, although somewhat belatedly. The first signs of trouble occurred in Salem Village (Danvers) during the winter of 1692, when the daughter of the village pastor, Betty Parris, age nine, and her cousin Abigail Williams, age eleven, began to display strange behavior. The girls screamed uncontrollably, threw things, uttered strange groans, and contorted themselves into peculiar positions. Witchcraft immediately surfaced as a possible explanation.

Suspicion centered on three local women who lived on the margins of the village. Sarah Good was a homeless beggar. Sarah Osborne was considered an unsavory character who rarely attended church meetings. Tituba was an Indian slave who was accused of fortune-telling. These three women were interrogated in March 1692 and then sent to jail.

Accusations poured in, and more arrests made. With tensions mounting, Governor William Phips established a special court to adjudicate the cases. The first person brought to trial was Bridget Bishop, who was accused of being a witch because of her immoral lifestyle and her tendency for wearing black clothing. She was found guilty and was executed by hanging in June 1692. Five more women were executed in July, and then four men and one woman were executed in August. The last executions took place in September, when six women and three men were hung.

Giles Corey, an eighty-year-old farmer and husband of one of the accused, was also arrested in September. Corey refused to cooperate with the authorities and was subjected to *peine forte et dure*, a form of torture in which the subject is placed beneath an increasingly heavy load of stones in an attempt to compel him to enter a plea. After two days of *peine fort et dure*, Corey died without entering a plea.

The last trial occurred at the end of April, and all five accused were found not guilty, thus bringing an end to the episode. In the final count, twenty had been hung, one crushed to death, and at least four others died in prison.

In the aftermath of the witch trials, some of the principals expressed regret. Samuel Sewall, who had served as clerk in the first trial, asked Reverend Samuel Willard to read aloud his apology to the congregation of Boston's South Church, "to take the Blame & Shame" of what had happened.

F. The New England Legacy

Within a generation, the original Puritan vision was lost. A new cosmopolitan worldview from Europe transformed cities like Boston. By the early eighteenth century, American Puritanism had split into three factions.

First were the Congregational churches, which de-emphasized the Calvinist doctrines and looked to the Enlightenment for guidance. These were the "Old Lights." Then there were those who continued to practice the rigid Calvinism of their forebears, hence "Old Calvinists." The third group emerged in the wake of the "Great Awakening" and its focus on the "new birth." Adherents of the new revivalism were called "New Lights." Like its English counterpart, New England Puritanism ultimately failed. Winthrop's city on a hill crumbled under its own moral weight.

VI. PURITAN THEOLOGICAL TRAJECTORIES

In general, the Puritans of England and New England shared the same basic theological convictions. Of course, Puritanism was not static on either side of the Atlantic, nor was the political context precisely the same. English Puritans found themselves engulfed in a civil war, while their brethren in New England were carving out of the frontier a new colonial existence. As noted earlier, there were some theological innovations in New England, such as the halfway covenant, but for the most part, the theological core remained the same. Whether in England or New England, the work of the Westminster Assembly is a reliable guide in identifying the prime theological tenets of Puritanism.

A. The Westminster Assembly

At the outset, it is important to acknowledge two important facts about the Westminster Assembly (1643–49). First, without denying their theological sincerity, the calling of the assembly was at its core a political-military decision. With a civil war raging and parliamentary forces on the defensive, Parliament forged a religious-military alliance with Scotland. As a condition for entering into the alliance with the Scots, the English Parliament signed the *Solemn League and Covenant* in 1643, which required the Church of England to abandon Episcopal polity and establish Presbyterian standards of doctrine and worship.

Second, it was not an ecclesiastical assembly, but rather a subcommittee appointed by the authority of Parliament. The assembly was charged with drawing up a new liturgy to replace the *Book of Common*

Prayer and implementing a new church polity. In both cases, the role of the Westminster Assembly was advisory—that is, it could only make recommendations to Parliament, which had the final word on all theological matters.

In 1643 the English Parliament called on "learned, godly and judicious Divines" to provide advice on issues of worship, doctrine, and church government for the Church of England. The Westminster Assembly, so-called because it met in the Henry VII Lady Chapel of Westminster Abbey, met for the first time on July 1, 1643. The Long Parliament appointed 121 divines and 30 laypeople to the assembly.

Initially, Episcopalians were probably in the majority, but they often failed to attend the critical evening meetings, thus allowing the Presbyterians and Independents to dominate the assembly's debates. In a famous *bon mot*, Lord Falkland observed that "those that hated the bishops hated them worse than the devil and those that loved them loved them not so well as their dinner."

The arrival of the Scottish commissioners, with their strong commitment to Presbyterianism, triggered serious debate. In February 1644 five members of the assembly—known as the "Five Dissenting Brethren" (Thomas Goodwin, Philip Nye, Sidrach Simpson, Jeremiah

The Westminster Assembly of Divines.

Burroughs, and William Bridge)—published a pamphlet strongly advocating congregational authority.

The primary undertaking of the assembly centered on worship and doctrine. The *Book of Common Prayer* was supplanted by the *Directory of Public Worship* in 1645, and the doctrinal standards (*Thirty-nine Articles of Religion*) were replaced by the Westminster Confession in 1646. Initially the House of Commons returned the Confession with instructions to add biblical proof texts. The revisions were made, and the Confession was ratified by Parliament. Two catechisms were added. The Larger Catechism (designed to be comprehensive for adults) and the Shorter Catechism (designed to be easier for children to memorize) were both approved in 1648.

The Church of Scotland also adopted the document without amendment, thus satisfying compliance with the *Solemn League and Covenant*. Its work being completed, the Westminster Assembly was dissolved in 1649.

B. Purified Theology

Modern scholars have variously identified the theological core of Puritanism. William Haller concluded that the central dogma of Puritanism was its doctrine of predestination. Perry Miller found the "marrow of Puritan divinity" in the idea of the covenant. Alan Simpson locates the animating center of Puritanism in the conversion experience. The Marxist historian Christopher Hill tends to view Puritanism in terms of its social and political ideology.

Generally speaking, Puritan theology was practical theology whose ultimate aim was spiritual renewal for the individual as well as society. This is not to suggest that they avoided the more technical theology. They did not, as the many Puritan theological treatises demonstrate. Any modern reader of William Perkins's *Golden Chaine* will be quickly disabused of any lack of theological density. However, the goal of the Puritan theological enterprise was always to connect the theology of the head to a devotional heart and a transformed life.

C. Reformed Theology

Whatever differences in polity, all Puritans shared the same fundamental theological commitment to Reformed theology (Calvinism). Patrick Collinson has argued that "the theological achievement of the Puritans, from William Perkins onwards, can be roughly interpreted as the adaptation and domestication of Calvinism to fit the condition of voluntary Christians...." Indeed, Puritans were active participants at the Synod of Dort and fully endorsed the Dortian "TULIP."

This Reformed theological orientation explains much of the suspicion and hostility toward Archbishop Laud's reputed Arminianism. Reformed theology also explains the anti-Catholicism of the Westminster Confession, which openly declares the pope to be the "Antichrist, that man of sin and son of perdition, that exalteth himself in the Church against Christ, and all that is called God" (XXV.vi).

Like their Reformed forebears, Puritans held the Bible in the highest esteem. Indeed, the Westminster Confession begins not with God, but with "Holy Scripture," which is "the Word of God written." It is the "rule of faith and life" and "the supreme judge, by which all controversies of religion are to be determined." The God of the Bible is absolutely sovereign over all and works "all things according to the counsel of his own immutably and most righteous will for his own glory." The sovereignty of God logically led the Puritans to a robust doctrine of double predestination. The Westminster Confession boldly states, "By the decree of God ... some men and angels are predestined unto everlasting life, and others foreordained to everlasting death."

D. Covenantal Theology

One of the distinctive Puritan theological emphases is its covenant theology. The sixteenth-century Reformers had already noted the significance of the covenant. Calvin, Zwingli, and especially Heinrich Bullinger saw the covenant as an interpretive framework for understanding the overall flow of the Bible and as an organizing principle for Christian theology.

Although the fundamental ideas of a covenantal theology had been developing in Reformed circles since the mid-sixteenth century, it was the Westminster divines who were the first to give the concept of the covenant confessional status. The divines recognized two covenants: one of works and one of grace.

The covenant of works was an agreement in which God promised Adam and his progeny eternal life if they obeyed him. The Westminster Confession states, "The first covenant made with man was a covenant of works, wherein life was promised to Adam; and in him to his posterity, upon the condition of perfect and personal obedience" (VII.ii). Having violated the terms of the agreement, Adam and all his posterity were thus subject to the penalty. But God in his mercy established another covenant—one of grace. The Westminster Confession describes it this way:

> Man, by his fall, having made himself incapable of life by [the first covenant], the Lord was pleased to make a second, commonly called the covenant of grace; wherein he freely offereth unto sinners life and salvation by Jesus Christ; requiring of them faith in Him, that they may be saved, and promised to give unto all those that are ordained unto eternal life his Holy Spirit, to make them willing and able to believe (VII.iii).

In this covenantal scheme, Christ is the substitutionary covenantal representative fulfilling the covenant of works on their behalf, in both the positive requirements of righteousness and its negative penal consequences. The covenant of grace became the basis for all future covenants that God made with mankind such as with Noah, Abraham, Moses, David, and finally for the New Covenant founded and fulfilled in Christ.

Some covenant theologians posited a third covenant, the covenant of redemption. This is not mentioned at Westminster, but was accepted by most. This refers to a covenantal agreement, not between God and humanity, but between the members of the Trinity before creation. God the Father agreed to send the Son as a sacrifice on behalf of the elect. As the mediator of the covenant, the Son agreed to pay the penalty for Adam's disobedience by dying on the cross. The Holy Spirit agreed to empower Christ for his mission and apply the benefits of Christ to the elect.

E. Sabbatarianism

Another theological distinctive is the Puritans' view of the Sabbath (Sunday), which set them apart from other Reformed groups on the Continent. Like continental Reformers, the confession affirms that the Sabbath is a "perpetual commandment binding all men in all ages." But unlike continental Reformers, the Puritans defined adherence to the Sabbath much more narrowly. The day is to be given wholly to the Lord whereby they not only "rest all the day from their own works, words and thoughts about their worldly employments and recreations; but also are taken up the whole time in the public and private exercises of his worship and in the duties of necessity and mercy" (XXI.viii).

Sabbatarianism became an acute theological issue during the reign of James I when he issued his *Declaration of Sports* (1618), allowing personal freedom on how people spend their Sunday afternoons. Although the king's declaration required everyone to attend church, the Puritans insisted that everyone should adhere to their more restrictive view of the Sabbath. Once they attained political power, the Westminster divines made the Puritan conception of the Sabbath mandatory on all of England.

F. Conversional Piety

Puritan theology has been described as "a theology of regeneration," and indeed, the whole of Puritanism is grounded in the conversion experience. It is this signal spiritual event that gave meaning and purpose to the whole of their lives. For Puritans, conversion and piety formed a seamless garment. The regenerate life is an integrated life where prayer unites with action, worship with work, and labor with rest, and the love of God necessarily requires love of neighbor.

For the Puritans, conversion entails not only a lifelong pursuit of external godliness, but the purification of one's internal conscience as well. Their Reformed theology told them they were fallen creatures prone to sin, and so they practiced methodical self-examination to identify spiritual blind spots for improvement. While at St. John's College, Cambridge, the Puritan Samuel Ward recorded in his college diary a catalogue of his failings, such as falling asleep without his last thought being about God, not preparing adequately for Sunday worship, "immoderate laughter in the hall at nine o'clock," and talking on Sunday of "matters that are not meet to be talked of on the Sabbath." Such self-examination could be extreme, but sin, after all, was a very serious matter.

G. Political Theology

Puritanism progressively became more militant. The first Puritans in the reign of Elizabeth I pressed for moderate reforms such as the removing of vestments. Jacobean Puritanism pushed a bit harder. They sought to rid the English Church of "Popish relics" such as Christmas, exchange of rings in marriage, and bowing at the name of Jesus. Some Puritans such as Thomas Cartwright pressed for Presbyterian polity.

But there was a marked change during the reign of Charles I. As royal suppression turned into full-fledged persecution, Puritans became political and eventually rebelled against the crown and executed the king. Affecting each of these reform efforts were deep theological convictions traceable to Calvin and the Reformed tradition. Puritan activism derived in large measure from the same theological tradition that inspired political revolt in the Netherlands, the German Palatinate, and France. Calvinism, as history demonstrates, was predisposed to a more active view of political resistance.

VII. THEOLOGICAL CONFLUENCES: PURITANISM, PIETISM, AND *NADERE REFORMATIE*

Seventeenth-century theology does not lend itself easily to simple cause-and-effect explanations. It is much more complex and seemingly paradoxical than it appears at first sight. It was a century in which theological currents ran on two circuits simultaneously. On the one hand, it was a century of theological polemics and rigid ecclesial entrenchment amid brutal religious warfare. On the other hand, it was a century that longed for spiritual renewal. This was not a rejection of the Reformation theological heritage, but a refocusing on its theological connection to a transformed life. As it turned out, this spiritual longing was European-wide and transcended confessional lines.

A. Puritanism

The historical genesis of these renewal movements initially arose among the English Puritans during the reign of Elizabeth I. Many of the Marian exiles came under the tutelage of leading Protestant theologians in Zürich and Geneva, and when they returned to their homeland, they began agitating for a more distinctive Protestant worship.

Christianity "is not apprehended merely by the intellect ... but it is revealed only when it possesses the whole soul" (John Calvin).

It is sometimes forgotten that the leading Reformers well understood the intimate connection of theology and piety as well. Calvin, for example, reminded followers that Christianity "is not apprehended merely by the intellect ... but it is revealed only when it possesses the whole soul and finds its seat and habitation in the innermost recesses of the heart." The Marian exiles took this admonition to heart, and thus their initial focus was largely on practical matters of worship. The desire for a purified worship naturally invited a renewed interest in a purified piety.

B. Pietism

It is generally recognized that German Pietism was deeply indebted to English Puritanism. A great deal of Puritan devotional literature was translated into German and had a significant impact on the development of German Pietism. The leaders of the German movement read and promoted the writings of English Puritans such as Lewis Bayly, Edmund Bunny, Joseph Hall, Daniel Dyke, Richard Baxter, and John Bunyan. For example, the young Spener was spiritually shaped by reading Bayly's *Practice of Piety* and Emanuel Sonthomb's *Golden Jewel*.

Furthermore, historical research has demonstrated that characteristic language of German Pietism draws directly from English Puritanism. The German words *Gnadenerfahrung* ("experience of grace") and *Wiedergeburt* ("born again") are traceable to Puritan literature.

C. Quietism

Quietism was a mystical philosophy that spread through France, Italy, and Spain. It was stimulated by the meditation and contemplation of Catholics such as Teresa of Avila and John of the Cross and over time took different forms and was influential in the founding of the Quaker movement. But in the seventeenth century, when it was first called "quietism," it developed into a form of perfectionism that rejected prayers and hymns and rites because the soul can be swallowed up and laid in the arms of God. Quietism was declared heretical in a papal bull in 1687.

D. *Nadere Reformatie*

Although the Low Countries experienced a variety of Reformation influences from Lutherans, Zwinglians, and Anabaptists, it was the penetration of Calvinism that had the most enduring legacy. By the mid-seventeenth century Dutch Calvinism grew restless with a dead orthodoxy and insisted on a *praxis pietatis* (the "practice of piety").

The Dutch version of this renewal movement was called the *Nadere Reformatie*, most often rendered "the Dutch Second Reformation" or the "Continuing Reformation." Building on the sixteenth-century Reformation, the *Nadere Reformatie* sought to integrate the theology of the Synod of Dort with a zealous urgency for personal conversion, church renewal, and societal reform.

As was true with German Pietism, English Puritanism exercised significant influence on the *Nadere Reformatie* through the many Puritan writings translated into Dutch. Research reveals that more Puritan books were printed in seventeenth-century Netherlands than in all other countries combined. William Ames, an English Puritan expelled from Cambridge who found refuge in the Netherlands, was another Puritan influence through his magnum opus, *The Marrow of Theology*.

Willem Teelinck, the most influential early representative of the movement, was converted by Puritans in England and married an English Puritan. He became a significant conduit of Puritanism through his Dutch translation of the Cambridge Puritan William Perkins.

Recent scholarship has documented that during the seventeenth century there were tens of thousands of English (and Scottish) Puritans in the Netherlands, including more than 350 ministers. Through these various avenues of influence the *Nadere Reformatie* came to embody many Puritan theological values: the central importance of practical piety, covenantal theology, observance of the Sabbath, a purified church, and the final authority of the Scriptures. The Dutch also embraced some of the more rigid Puritan taboos, which forbade "playing with dice, the wearing of luxurious clothes, dancing, drunkenness, revelry, smoking and the wearing of wigs."

VIII. CONCLUSION

In the century following the Reformation there seems to have been a deep-seated European-wide desire for spiritual renewal that crossed Protestant confessional lines and penetrated French Catholicism as well.

It is intriguing that the Catholic renewal movements parallel the Protestant renewal movements at roughly the same time. While there do not seem to be any direct influences, Catholics too were weary of the theological and military conflagration, and thus they turned their attention to nourishing the soul. Like Protestants, Jansenists and Quietists realized that in the midst of a struggle for ecclesial survival, the spirit may be damaged and piety ignored.

The seventeenth century is a testimony that the story does not end in entrenchment. The longing for a theology that renews, not a new theology, may be suppressed for a time, but in the final analysis cannot be destroyed. This is the story of church history.

FOR FURTHER STUDY

Bangs, Carl. *Arminius: A Study in the Dutch Reformation*. Nashville: Abingdon, 1971.

Bremer, Francis J. *The Puritan Experiment: New England Society from Bradford to Edwards*. Lebanon, NH: University Press of New England, 1995.

Lindberg, Carter. *The Pietist Theologians: An Introduction to Theology in the Seventeenth and Eighteenth Centuries*. Malden, MA: Blackwell, 2011.

Olson, Roger E. *Arminian Theology: Myths and Realities*. Downers Grove, IL: InterVarsity Press, 2006.

Ryken, Leland. *Worldly Saints: The Puritans As They Really Were*. Grand Rapids: Zondervan, 1986.

Stoeffler, F. Ernest. *Continental Pietism and Early American Christianity*. Grand Rapids: Eerdmans, 1976.

Stoeffler, F. Ernest. *The Rise of Evangelical Pietism*. Leiden: Brill, 1995.

Christianity in an Age of Fear, Crisis, and Exploration

(17th Century)

I. INTRODUCTION

Fear, dread, and despair occasionally engulfed portions of the European populace in the seventeenth century. These feelings of anguish did not appear groundless. Life in Europe could seem very precarious. It was often played out in harsh and unforgiving conditions. Warfare, famine, and poverty frequently prowled as unwelcome visitors in corners of Europe.

The true causes of communicable diseases were often unknown. In 1495 syphilis began infecting occupying French troops in Naples, Italy. Conquistadors and others brought syphilis and smallpox with them as deadly exports to the New World. In 1518 the first reported outbreak of smallpox occurred in the Americas.

Even a small sampling of the dire conditions and circumstances some Europeans faced reads like a dark litany of untrammeled evil. By contrast, certain Europeans did enjoy economic prosperity and explored new ways of viewing and enjoying the world. They made advances in commerce, the sciences, and the arts that were nothing less than breathtaking. In the main, however, the characterization of the seventeenth century as generally an age of fear and crisis remains quite apt.

A. The Scourge of Massive Deaths

Death on occasion relentlessly stalked Europeans, cutting them down at very early ages as judged by modern mortality rates for developed nations. In the province of Anjou, France, infant mortality rates ranged from 300 to 350 per 1,000 for the first year of life. In early seventeenth-century England, the average person lived to age thirty to thirty-five. (Half the population died before age thirty.) Worse yet, the average age for life expectancy at birth, with all European populations considered, settled at a dismal twenty-three to twenty-six years of age.

During the Thirty Years War (1618–48), brutal warfare created killing fields within central Europe and left cities like Magdeburg in ruins and desolation. The population of Germany fell from about 21 million to 13 million, with regions such as Swabia, Pomerania, the Palatinate, and Bohemia especially hard hit by fighting. Between the years 1598 and 1602, a bubonic plague killed 600,000 in Castile. In 1603 a virulent plague broke out in England.

On the Italian peninsula, the horrific plague of 1630 decimated populations, in cities such as Mantua (where 25,000 out of 32,000 died or fled), and killed up to 40 percent of the inhabitants in Lombardy and Tuscany, the Venetian Republic, and the Este states.

In France, two million people died of the plague between 1600 and 1670. Fires on occasion charred homes in villages and burned sections of cities to the ground. In 1665 an overcrowded and dirty London was struck by a horrendous plague, with nearly 70,000 people losing their lives; then London was set ablaze in 1666 with 100,000 people deprived of their places of shelter.

Nor were famines uncommon in Europe. A fear of hunger is referenced in the popular literature of the day. Bad weather, especially bitter cold, ruined growing seasons and thereby reduced harvests in the 1590s, 1620s, 1640s, 1650s, and 1690s. The year 1601–2 was apparently the coldest to grip portions of Europe in six hundred years. Due to crop failures, two million Russians died of starvation during the year 1602–3.

B. Revolts and Revolutions

Antagonism between various Christian churches and factions stoked fierce theological disputes, intemperate rhetoric, rude personal attacks, and even violence. Economic, political, and religious competition precipitated a series of wars in Europe and elsewhere in the world. In the late 1640s Robert Mentet de Salmonet, a Scot in exile in France, complained that Europeans lived in an age "famous for the great and strange revolutions that have happen'd in it.... Revolts have been frequent in both the East and the West."

In 1643 Spanish authors of a political tract lamented worldwide political disruptions:

> All the north in commotion ... England, Ireland and Scotland aflame with Civil War ... The Ottomans tearing each other to pieces

... China invaded by the Tartars, Ethiopia by the Turks, and the Indian kings who live scattered through the region between the Ganges and the Indus all at each other's throats.

During the 1640s England was wracked by a painful civil war, which culminated in the execution of Charles I (1649), a "divine right monarch." Spain faced revolts in Catalonia and Portugal, whereas Poland–Lithuania was ravaged by Cossacks. The *Fronde* (civil wars, 1648–53), inspired in part by nobles caught up in revolt, violently shook political life in France. In 1649–50 the troops of Oliver Cromwell meted out very harsh reprisals on rebels in Ireland.

In the 1680s Louis XIV's *dragonnades*—known as "booted missionaries"—resorted to any means of intimidation short of murder while billeting in the homes of the king's Huguenot subjects in France. They forced thousands to abjure the Reformed faith and convert to Roman Catholicism, at least formally.

Sizing up the political unrest of the mid-seventeenth century, the French philosopher-author Voltaire asserted that a "general crisis" had overwhelmed the age:

> This unfortunate time for Ibrahim [deposed as Sultan in 1648] was unfortunate for all monarchs. The crown of the Holy Roman Empire was unsettled by the famous Thirty Years War. Civil War devastated France and forced the mother of Louis XIV to flee with her children from her capital. In London Charles I was condemned to death by his own subjects. Philip IV, king of Spain, having lost almost all his possessions in Asia, also lost Portugal.

A number of modern historians have concurred with Voltaire's analysis. They propose that the seventeenth century in western Europe was indeed characterized by disparate crises, although they have differed strongly in identifying the essential traits of the age.

II. NEW WAYS OF THINKING, THE "SHOCK OF DISCOVERY," AND THE "NEW WORLD"

In eastern Europe things were not much more politically stable. The much-feared Ottoman Turks—despite a sultan's earlier peace agreement with the Hapsburg family (the Peace of Zsitvatorok, 1606) bringing a respite in warfare, and despite occasional military defeats—continued to advance westward. Already controlling vast swathes of eastern Europe including Greece and much of the Balkans, the Turks invaded Hungary in 1664, captured Crete from Venice in 1669 after a twenty-year siege, and were menacingly poised at Vienna's gates in 1683.

The success of the Turks provoked enormous anxiety and dread. Since the fall of Constantinople in 1453, various popes had called for new crusades. Christian thinkers attempted to explain the reasons the Turks were continuing to advance successfully again in Christian states. A number of western Europeans speculated that God was punishing the Eastern Orthodox for their sins. Earlier in the sixteenth century, no less than Martin Luther thought that Western Christians were likewise being punished for their sins. The Reformer attempted to explain the reasons the empire was having such difficulties in defeating the Turks in his own day:

> Our sins have stirred up the wrath of God against us. Since He, therefore, wished to lay a punishment on us, He armed our enemies, the Turks, with anger and cruelty against us. But to us He sent fear, so that it is rightly thrown up to us that we have forgotten our valor and have degenerated from our ancestors.

Printing presses turned out a wave of anti-Turkish books, thereby pursuing one of the first ideological campaigns carried on in print.

Other kinds of worries could traumatize Europeans. Alarming reports circulated that witches and warlocks were preying on souls and bodies. Interest in apocalyptic biblical passages concerning the Antichrist surged. Contemporary events seemed to confirm that this malevolent being was roaming abroad in the land.

A number of writings on biblical prophecy focused on such themes as the expected conversion of Jews to Christianity in 1655 or 1656 and the soon return of the Messiah. In 1655 Menassah ben Israel proposed that Jews should be permitted to return to England because they needed to be "dispersed into all places and countries of the world" before "the Messiah would come and restore our nation." The Quaker Margaret Fell (later married to George Fox) likewise favored the resettlement of Jews in England. She was persuaded that Jews would convert to Christianity in 1655. Jean de Labadie, a founder of a Dutch Quietist sect, taught that the millennial rule of Christ would begin in 1666. His prediction coincided with the announcement in that year by Sabbatai Zevi of Smyrna that the messianic age had begun. More than 90 percent of Jewish communities worldwide believed that Sabbatai Zevi (1626–76) was the "promised" Messiah. Many were rudely disappointed when he later converted to Islam.

A. Commerce, Culture, and Christianity

By no means were all Europeans beset by despair of one kind or another on a regular basis in the seventeenth century. Certain regions of Europe escaped relatively unscathed from the bane of disease, famine, or grinding poverty. The Dutch, despite decades of fighting, enjoyed remarkable economic prosperity, especially after 1648 during their "Golden Age."

According to historian Simon Schama, the Dutch experienced an "embarrassment of riches." Calvinist burghers or wealthy citizens in Amsterdam sometimes felt guilty about having too much wealth. They were torn between the lure of material abundance and the demands of their Calvinist ethics to care for the poor and indigent widows and children in their midst.

The dining tables of the rich in Amsterdam were piled high with food, the wharfs of their ports stacked with goods and crowded with ships from around the world. As great maritime traders, the Dutch profited from investments in joint-stock companies such as the Dutch East India Company (1602–1798) and the Dutch West India Company (1621–1791). They controlled Europe's Baltic trade. Dutch citizens needed the permission of the Dutch West India Company to trade along the African and American coasts. In North America the company founded Fort Orange (1624), Fort Nassau (1624), and Fort Good Hope and Fort Amsterdam (in New York City, 1625). The French minister Jean-Baptiste Colbert once complained that three Dutch ships plied the high seas for every single French vessel.

Ships filling the harbor of Amsterdam.

Other Europeans received large sums of money or landholdings from the patronage of a noble or a king or a tsar, or through other forms of feudal obligations, or through more capitalistic ways of earning noticeable wealth.

Some Europeans experienced the satisfaction of making and learning about scientific discoveries and inventions. Natural philosophers ("scientists" of a sort) worked less in singular isolation. They shared their findings with others and joined newly formed societies of scholars such as the *Académie française* in Paris (1635), the Royal Society for the Improvement of Natural Knowledge in London (1660), or the Academy of Sciences in Moscow (1681). They did not view natural philosophy (the study of "science") and philosophy as necessarily distinct disciplines. The Italian astronomer Galileo Galilei was much influenced by Plato, and the French mathematician and philosopher René Descartes was much influenced by Galileo and the Polish astronomer Nicholas Copernicus.

Talented musicians and composers—whether in Germany, Italy, France, Poland, or elsewhere in Europe—produced a remarkable array of musical offerings for royal festivals, worship services, and concerts. Among the foremost were the Italian Claudio Monteverdi (1567–1643), the English Henry Purcell (1659–95), the French Jean-Baptiste Lully (1632–87), and the German Paul Gerhardt (1607–76). They sometimes complained, however, about the paltry pay they received for their efforts.

Court painters, sculptors, and architects demonstrated remarkable talents in creating and adorning splendid churches, palaces, government buildings, and stately residences.

In 1662 Louis XIV's Chateau de Versailles began to rise majestically over a French countryside outside of Paris. Enhanced by stunning statuary, its beautifully coiffed gardens stretched into the far distance. Prompted by jealously of the French court, foreign kings and nobles attempted to replicate the buildings at Versailles. The Austrian Schönbrun Palace outside Vienna, the English Boughton House in Northamptonshire, and the royal palace in Stockholm represent samples of the extensive phenomenon of imitation. In Paris, the Louvre was built between the years 1667 and 1678.

The French sometimes honored the seventeenth century as the *Grand Siècle* ("Great Century") and *l'Age Classique* ("Classical Era"), in which literature and the arts reached a certain "perfection of form" characterized by rationality and clarity. This was thought to be particularly the case during the reign of Louis XIV (1661–1715). The French influenced European culture in other areas as well. In 1648 the Pole Lacasz Opalinski complained, "France seems to be the only country, excluding Spain, that sets the tone for all European peoples in decorations and clothes. And whatever she invents or introduces is considered beautiful and fashionable. She arbitrarily demands others observe her and condemns those who oppose her."

Outside of France, painters and men and women of letters also made significant artistic contributions to their national artistic heritages. The Council of Trent had proposed that paintings, statues, and frescoes should extol the lives and deaths of the martyrs and thereby teach Christian virtues. The laity was to identify more fully with the suffering of Christ by seeing statues of him as an emaciated, bleeding, and agonizing Savior.

Turning from "Mannerism," this didactic approach to the arts prepared the way for the "Age of Baroque," associated with the arrival of Lodovico Carracci (1555–1619) and Michelangelo Caravaggio (c.1571–1610) in Counter-Reformation Rome.

The Age of Baroque was an especially auspicious period for the arts, architecture, and music. Its painters and sculptors sometimes emphasized the emotional, the turbulent, and the grandiose. Baroque painters often used flowing lines, much pigment, and the techniques of illusion and *chiaroscuro* (contrast between light and dark).

Painters of genius flourished in Flanders with Peter Paul Rubens, in Spain with Diego Velázquez, in France with Nicolas Poussin, and in the Protestant United Provinces with Rembrandt Harmenszoon van Rijn (1606–69). Sculptors and architects such as Gian Lorenzo Bernini, who took over the task of completing St. Peter's along with Francesco Borromini (1599–1677), created grandiose architecture and sculpture for the papacy in Rome—a material testament of sorts of a more confident Roman Catholic Church on the Counter-Reformation offensive. Examples include Bernini's High Altar of St. Peter's, *Cathedra Petri*, and the tombs of Urban VIII and Alexander VII. Baroque architecture evidenced rhythmic or wave-like patterns in facades and offered sweeping staircases.

In literature, Mateo Alemán's *Guzmán de Alfarache* (1599/1604) and Miguel de Cervantes's *Don Quixote* (1605–15), some of the earliest European novels, appeared. William Shakespeare's *Macbeth*, apparently written in 1606, was staged in 1611. Later in the century Jean-Baptiste Poquelin Molière entertained audiences with clever verse and mordant satire in plays such as *Le Misanthrope* (1666). From John Bunyan's *Pilgrim's Progress* (1678) and Richard Baxter's *The Saints' Everlasting Rest* (1650) to Pascal's *Pensées* and Madame Guyon's *Short and Easy Method of Prayer*, Protestants and Catholics penned classics of Christian spirituality.

The century provided reasons to hope, if not at least wonder, about the possibilities of beneficent changes due to increased understanding of

The Night Watch
by Rembrandt.

the natural sciences, medicine, and commerce. In an epochal moment of 1609, Galileo became the first person to study the skies with an improved telescope. He also contributed to the creation of an experimental method in science based on mathematical calculations.

In 1628 William Harvey published *An Anatomical Study of the Motion of the Heart and the Blood in Animals*, in which he described the key role of the heart in the circulation of the blood. Significant inventions were made from a barometer (Evangelista Torricelli, 1644) to a more accurate pendulum clock (Salomon Coster, 1657). On May 30, 1631, Théophraste Renaudot published *La Gazette*, which became France's first newspaper. It imitated Dutch and Venetian gazettes. In the 1650s the English began to sip tea, a drink that began to compete with ale as the national beverage.

The century also witnessed the daring exploration of "old" territories with innovative new approaches. The territory of the way the mind functions was explored most notably by Descartes, Blaise Pascal, Antoine Arnaud, Nicholas Malebranche (all from France), John Locke (England), and Gottfried Leibnitz (Germany). The territory of land masses beyond Europe was explored by Christian missionaries, conquistadors, and merchants. The territory of vast expanses in the heavens was penetrated with greater power, owing to the newly created telescope. A few religious leaders such as Leibnitz, Jacques Bénigne Bossuet, and Christopher Royas de Spinola, the bishop of Thina, even dared to investigate controversial religious territory by proposing ecumenical plans to unite Christians across confessional borders.

Due to the "shock of discovery," Europeans sometimes questioned time-honored ideas taught by ancient authorities such as Aristotle and Ptolemy. Geographical exploration and scientific experiments on earth and renewed observation of the heavens proved these authorities less than trustworthy guides.

By contrast, some Europeans embraced old ideas of the Hermetic tradition with renewed fervor. Forms of Aristotelian "scholastic" thought gained greater prominence in a number of theological faculties throughout Europe. For example, Francisco Suárez's massive commentary on Thomas Aquinas promoted a "Second Scholasticism." Extolling the virtues of a "golden age" in antiquity, many scholars cited rather eclectically the authority not only of Aristotle and Plato but of other ancient writers. Still others incorporated philosophical concepts from more contemporary philosophers—Pierre Gassendi, Pierre Ramus, and Descartes—in constructing their theologies, philosophies, and cosmologies.

B. The Americas

The exploration of the non-European world seemed to indicate that greatly enhanced political and economic power in Europe might reside with the nation that laid claim to or acquired vast lands in the Americas, Africa, and Asia. A number of explorers sincerely professed a desire to see the peoples of these areas "converted" to the Christian faith. Indeed, explorers and missionaries were on occasion one and the same persons. Their missionary efforts sometimes cost them their lives.

Upon Columbus's arrival in the Americas (1492), many diverse indigenous political, social, and linguistic groups existed in sedentary communities. But within the previous century two civilizations had emerged as dominant powers in Mesoamerica: the Aztecs in Mexico and the Incas in South America (in territory stretching south from present-day Ecuador to Argentina). Both the Aztecs and Incas possessed advanced cultures and evidenced architectural, engineering, agricultural, and communication skills. However, they did engage in ruthless and cruel tactics in conquering and subduing other native groups.

In 1496 the Spanish founded Santo Domingo in Hispaniola (present-day Haiti and the Dominican Republic). In 1518 Cuba became the launching site for the conquest of other lands. The Conquistador Hernán Cortés (1485–1547) defeated the Aztecs and set up a colony of "New Spain," the capital of which was Mexico. Spanish Franciscans arrived in Mexico in 1524. They published the first book in the Americas, a catechism for Indians, in Mexico City in 1539. In the 1530s large amounts of silver were discovered in Mexico; enslaved natives worked the silver mines. Whereas there were 25 million native peoples in Mexico when Cortés arrived, a century later there was apparently only a small fraction of that number there.

In 1510 the explorers Vasco de Balboa and Francisco Pizarro discovered the Pacific Ocean. Pizarro later conquered the Incas in Ecuador and Peru.

Toward 1544, Indians on the plains of Kansas put to death Spanish Friar Minor Juan de Padilla, who had previously ministered in Mexico. Between the years 1581 and 1598, Spanish Franciscan friars entered what is now New Mexico and then settled at San Juan de los Caballeros. By the 1620s, between 20,000 and 25,000 Indians had been converted to the Catholic faith in New Mexico. Mexico City and Lima became governmental centers. The Spanish built large cathedrals, hospitals, orphanages, and shelters for women in these cities.

In 1500 the explorer Pedro Alvares Cabral claimed Brazil for the Portuguese. The Portuguese discovered much gold and silver in Brazil.

Francisco Pizarro, conqueror of the Incas.

African slaves became essential workers in mining gold and silver as well as in harvesting sugar cane. Brazil became a dominant producer of sugar.

In 1649 Jean de Brébeuf, a Jesuit missionary, was killed by Iroquois Indians near the Georgian Bay in Canada. French missionaries Jacques Marquette, René-Robert Cavelier, Sieur de La Salle, and Louis Joliet explored regions around the Great Lakes, paddled on waterways such as the newly discovered Mississippi River and the Illinois River, built settlements, and taught the Catholic faith to natives.

Nonetheless, as noted, the exploration of newly acquired lands sometimes tragically included the enslaving of their peoples. Exploitation of slaves, warfare, and diseases like smallpox took a deadly toll. Europeans on occasion justified their exploitation by saying they were Christianizing the natives. But their motivation for exploration was often fueled by an unquenchable desire to find gold and silver to stash in the coffers of European governments. According to contemporary mercantilistic theory (a form of economic nationalism), a fixed amount of bullion existed in the world. The nation procuring and holding the greatest amount of this gold would be the most powerful.

The discovery of gold and silver in the New World and gold in Africa provided an even more acquisitive thrust for European conquest. Colonies should be planted whose inhabitants could help search out raw materials to send to the mother nation. In turn, the colonies could become potential markets for her finished goods carried on her ships. The English Navigation Acts (1661–1849), for example, converted a number of these principles into law. The acts were initially intended to thwart the Dutch maritime trade. The English were to use English ships in maritime trade.

To facilitate exploration and land acquisition, a greater knowledge of the world was needed. As explorers, missionaries, adventuresome merchants, and other travelers who had crossed the high seas brought back more credible reports of non-European lands, it became clear that older maps of the world were simply not accurate. By the 1680s "travel" accounts regarding Africa, Asia, India, and the "New World" possessed less of the fabulous and exotic and more of the factual in their contents. For some Europeans it was no longer satisfactory to relate the origins of certain inhabitants of the New World to the offspring of Noah.

After the Treaty of Westphalia (1648) ended the Thirty Years War, Europeans needed maps that could take account of the new political boundaries in Europe, some of which paradoxically enough reiterated several older borders and religious strictures of 1624. In 1654 Nicholas Sanson, a distinguished mapmaker, became the first Frenchman to publish a world atlas.

As natural philosophers peered into the starry heavens with the telescope, they began to realize that new charts would be useful to track more accurately the path of planets through the skies. In 1627 Johannes Kepler published the Rudolphine Tables that calculate the location of planets in the future and in the past. In a word, knowledge of this world and the heavens surrounding it expanded in a significant fashion during the seventeenth century.

III. THE POLITICAL AND RELIGIOUS SITUATION IN 1598

A. The Politics of the Time

In 1598 Europe remained a loosely defined geographical entity. A number of contemporaries believed its shifting boundaries stretched from Edinburgh to Moscow and even to Constantinople. Others considered

England, Russia, and Turkey not to be part of Europe. A well-informed diplomat would have probably designated Spain (7.6 million) and Sweden under the leadership of Gustavus Adolphus (1594–1632) as the most powerful nations, with France (20 million in 1600 and 19.3 million in 1700) as the most populous. The most densely populated area was the Italian peninsula with its various principalities and republics (13 million in 1600 and 19.3 million in 1700) and boasting Naples, the largest city in Europe other than Constantinople.

Also in 1598, European wars continued to ebb and flow in intensity, depending on the region. Several great European powers, spent by the religious and dynastic wars of the sixteenth century, felt obliged to regroup their political and economic forces. This regrouping effort was difficult, given oppressive features of seventeenth-century life. As noted, a number of European nations were struck repeatedly by wars, disease, and famine. By the 1620s a general economic depression gripped much of Europe. Nonetheless, despite very real demographic reversals and setbacks, the overall population of Europe managed at least some growth during the century (85 million in 1600 and 100–110 million in 1700).

From a religious point of view, in 1598 the dominant issue troubling European Christians remained what it had been since the Reformation: the painful divisions of Christendom. These divisions now extended beyond those separating the Roman Catholic Church from the Greek Orthodox Church and the Russian Orthodox Church to new sets of divisions within Protestant churches. Did not Holy Scripture teach that only one true faith exists?

Now the Christian world could no longer identify the word *religion* solely with Roman Catholicism, as Roman Catholics were prone to do. Some thought there were now "religions" that claimed to be Christian but in fact were not. Did not many Roman Catholics believe Protestants were outright heretics and the followers of another religion? In France, for example, governmental officials often referred to the Huguenot Reformed faith as "*la Religion Prétendue réformée,*" the "so-called reformed religion." And did not many Protestants bluntly identify the papacy with the Antichrist and deem the statues of saints in Roman Catholic churches and shrines as lingering manifestations of pagan idolatry?

Although amiable relations existed between Protestants and Roman Catholics in various local settings of Europe, sometimes both parties evinced bitter hostility toward the others. Protestant leaders feared that Spain, a citadel for Roman Catholic orthodoxy, was determined with the emperor's help to establish a universal Roman Catholic monarchy. Likewise, animosities festered within the Roman Catholic Church itself, especially between the Jansenists and Jesuits. Then again, Protestants sometimes battled with each other over doctrinal issues. In the sixteenth century, a "Confessional Age" (Wolfgang Reinhard's term) set in. Doctrinal distinctions between Protestant churches were refined and spelled out in binding confessions. The Lutheran Formula of Concord (1577–78) made cooperation between Calvinists and Lutherans within the empire more difficult, given the anti-Calvinist thrust of the confession. The Council of Trent (1545–63) provided authoritative doctrinal and moral teaching for Roman Catholics.

Divisions and tensions between Protestants and Roman Catholics and between Protestants and Protestants raised yet another fear. Would a politically and religiously divided Christian Europe possess enough resolve and military strength to mount a successful defense against the feared intruders, the Ottoman Turks advancing westward from eastern Europe?

At the Sublime Porte, the Sultan's Court in Turkey, ambassadors from Western Christian nations commonly believed that Eastern Christians in general had not fared especially well under the millet (a kind of judicial) system of Turkish rule, despite the fact that the Turks allowed the various Christian millets a certain amount of autonomy.

Paradoxically, while both fearing and condemning the Turks' advances, a number of Western powers vied with each other to acquire favorable trade agreements with the Turks. Would the pope's appeal for a crusade be heeded? Would Louis XIV or Emperor Leopold I, themselves competing with each other to dominate Europe in the early 1680s, lend support for a common military effort? Or were the Turks destined to seize not only Vienna but other cities in their ongoing military incursion into western Europe?

In many regards, it was not surprising that powers such as the Holy Roman Empire and the Polish-Lithuanian Commonwealth, due to their considerable strength and proximity to Turkish controlled lands, contributed the most militarily to stop the advance of the Turks.

B. The Papacy: Stability Regained

By the papal reign of Clement VIII (1592–1605), the city of Rome was adorned with a new array of grandiose architecture and sculpture of a baroque flavor. The papacy's emphasis on liturgical and ethical reform had helped restore Rome's reputation for piety and virtue, a worthy host city for the huge crowds of pilgrims bustling through its streets in the Jubilee Year, 1600.

The Roman Catholic Church in aggregate was once again on the political, educational, and evangelistic offensive. Roman Catholic missionaries and explorers, educators (some of whom belonged to religious orders such as the Society of Jesus), parish clergy, the papacy and hierarchy, kings and queens, governmental officials, men and women of commerce, soldiers, and others on occasion energetically sought to spread the message of the Counter-Reformation. Even if certain areas of Europe such as the United Provinces (the Dutch Republic) were lost to Protestantism, the influence of the Roman Catholic Church continued to grow in portions of Europe intermittently, from the middle of the sixteenth century through the seventeenth and into the eighteenth. Catholic missionaries were also engaged in attempts to win Orthodox Christians to the Roman Catholic Church.

Bolstering the confidence of the Roman Catholic clergy in their struggle against Protestant "heretics," Caesar Baronius, Clement VIII's confessor, published the *Annales Ecclesiastici* (1588–1607), a series of twelve apologetic historical volumes. These books were intended to demonstrate the antiquity of the sacred traditions and the power of the Roman Catholic Church and prove that a genuine continuity existed between the doctrines and practices of the Tridentine Roman Catholic Church of the day and those of the early Christian churches.

King Henry IV of France.

Baronius was attempting to answer charges of doctrinal innovation as articulated in the massive study the *Magdeburg Centuries*, written by Lutheran theologians under the guidance of Matthias Flacius Illyricus (1520–75). Flacius and his colleagues had claimed that the beliefs and practices of the Roman Catholic Church were departures ("corruptions") from the beliefs and practices of the church fathers and early churches. *Centuries* had appeared formidable and its arguments persuasive. Many Roman Catholics were relieved to read Barionius's *Annales*. They concluded that this work successfully refuted the Protestants' central charge. Baronius received numerous letters of thanks and commendation for his painstaking historical efforts.

In addition, Clement VIII called on the Jesuit Robert Bellarmine (1542–1621)—destined to become one of Rome's most admired disputants (challenging Protestants such as William Whitaker)—to correct the errors in the recent edition of the Vulgate sponsored by Pope Sixtus V. The resulting text of the Vulgate became the official edition for the Roman Catholic Church for centuries to come.

In a controversial move that irritated the Spanish, Clement VIII removed the excommunication from the newly converted Henry IV (who renounced the Reformed faith on July 25, 1593) in an attempt to assure the role of the Kingdom of France as a great Roman Catholic power. The pope also tried to calm passions among Roman Catholic theologians who were caught up in acrid debates regarding the nature of grace.

Upon his death in 1605, Clement VIII left a much more self-confident Roman Catholic Church. The faithful believed that the good reputation of Rome had been largely restored. Poland—thought lost to the Protestant cause in 1555—as well as other lands had been won back to the church. Following Francis Xavier's example, Roman Catholic missionaries were fanning out to various corners of the world. The popes were prepared to use "necessary" means to thwart the efforts of anyone who opposed the church's truths, whether Protestant "heretics" or freethinkers such as Leonardo Bruni (put to death in 1600).

The popes believed that reforms stipulated by the Council of Trent were in the process of being carried out. By the 1570s preachers had begun to claim that Rome's moral life was exemplary, by the 1580s that the city had few vices. The Jesuit Francesco Benci declared, "So I decree, new Rome seems not only better and more outstanding than the old Rome but even greater and more illustrious." In eulogizing the recently departed Pope Clement VIII, the Jesuit Cesare Recupito recalled that in the Holy Year 1600, pilgrims had come "not so much to Rome that wonder of antiquity, but to Christian Rome, motivated as they were by admiration for such new displays of virtue." Celebrating the canonization of Francesca Romana, Cardinal Domenico Pinelli declared on April 28, 1608, "There is in the whole world no well-instructed people or republic established with law and customs that does not admire Rome, that does not imitate Rome insofar as it can be done. Whenever people anywhere in this world are incited to embrace virtue, Roman examples are proposed."

IV. EUROPEAN PROTESTANTISM IN JEOPARDY?

As the seventeenth century dawned, the political and religious gains of an expansive Roman Catholicism greatly troubled many Protestants. To some, it appeared that the very future of Protestantism on the Continent was in question. Even in the 1680s, the English philosopher John Locke still fretted about Roman Catholic expansion—not only in England, where King James II actively promoted it, but also on the Continent, where France's Louis XIV had aspirations of creating a unified Roman Catholic Europe. Locke identified "popery" with the suppression of liberties.

In several countries such as Poland, France, and Bohemia the spread of Protestantism was all but halted. In certain regions, Protestants converted to Roman Catholicism in large numbers or emigrated to other lands.

Given this overall pattern of widespread Roman Catholic expansion, it may appear paradoxical that in 1689 Bossuet, a leading French Catholic cleric, complained that never had the challenge of Protestantism been "more menacing." Bossuet was apparently worried about the accession of the Protestants William and Mary to the throne of England in the wake of the "Glorious Revolution" of 1688.

As the century wore on, religious issues seemed to fade somewhat into the background as the principal causes of warfare. Instead, "reasons of state"—that is, what benefits the state—became more determinative of the foreign policy of a nation. Consequently, pragmatic alliances were made between powers. These alliances crossed confessional divides. During the Thirty Years War, Cardinal Richelieu (Armand Jean du Plessis) helped France enter an alliance with Protestant Sweden. On occasion during the century, Protestant powers fought Protestant powers and Roman Catholic powers fought Roman Catholic powers.

During the century France, England (4 million in 1600 and 5.8 million in 1700), and the United Provinces emerged as major players on the European economic and political stage. They fought Spain in Europe or overseas—as in the lengthy revolt of the Dutch against Spain (1555–1648); France versus Spain (1648–59); and the War of the Spanish Succession (1701–14). Moreover, France and England battled against each other, as in the War of the League of Augsburg (1689–97).

The overseas trade of the Dutch, so worrisome to the French, the English, the Spanish, and the Portuguese, did diminish later in the century, owing in large measure to enervating warfare that overtook the Dutch (Anglo-Dutch Wars, 1652–54, 1664–67, 1672–79), including Louis XIV's invasion of the United Provinces (1672), during which he entered more than forty cities).

In addition, Muscovy (Russia, with 11 million in 1600 and 16 million in 1700) became a political entity with which Western diplomats began to reckon more seriously. Between 1614 and 1617, Sweden fought against Muscovy. Even though Michael (1596–1645) became tsar in 1613, the first of the Romanov family that would rule the nation until 1917, Muscovy remained in a weakened state for decades. By the end of the century, however, Muscovy was making serious territorial encroachments into Poland.

THE FRENCH SCHOOL OF SPIRITUALITY

Spanish mystics such as the Carmelite Teresa of Avila (1515–82) and St. John of the Cross (1542–91), the founder of the Discalced ("barefoot") Carmelites, influenced several members of the French school. For example, the French mystic Madame Acarie (1566–1618), the founder of the Reformed Carmelites, received spiritual inspiration from contemplating the life story of Teresa of Avila.

Other major figures of the French School of Spirituality included François de Sales (1567-1622); Cardinal Pierre de Berulle, founder of the Oratorian Order (1611); Jeanne Chezard de Matel, founder of the Sisters of the Incarnate Word (1639); Jacques Olier, founder of the Society of St. Sulpice (1642); and Jean Eudes, founder of the Eudists (The Congregation of Jesus and Mary, 1643). For François de Sales, "to speak to God and to hear God speak in the depths of the heart" constituted the essence of mystical theology—the union of our hearts with God's heart.

A. France

In 1598 France was just extricating herself from decades of bloody fighting between Protestants and Catholics. In that year Henry IV (1553–1610) granted the Edict of Nantes to his former Reformed coreligionists, the Huguenots, permitting them certain liberties to worship God more freely. Nonetheless, the fact remained that in 1593 Henry IV, the great Huguenot leader, had converted to the Roman Catholic faith.

The Huguenots' hopes of the early 1560s that France would become a land in which the majority of the French embraced the Reformed faith had been largely dashed. The intervening nine politico-religious wars between 1552 and 1598, compounded tragically by the horrendous bloodletting of the Saint Bartholomew's Day Massacre of 1572, had diminished the Huguenots' military power, reduced the number of their nobles, largely sapped their missionary zeal, and transformed their overall spirit into one of a suffering minority, "under the Cross." Then again, Henry IV, their notable benefactor, was assassinated in 1610, a knife driven deep into his chest by François Ravaillac.

Toward 1598 a French Roman Catholic "mystic" tradition that had emanated from the Middle Ages and passed through the "Golden Age" of French mysticism (Jean Gerson, 1363–1429, to Jacques Lefèvre d'Étaples, 1450–1537) continued to flourish. Indeed, a "French School of Spirituality" emerged in the seventeenth century. It highlighted in various ways the adoration of Christ, Mary, the Eucharist, the Cross, and the pursuit of a rigorous life of self-renunciation and self-abnegation.

B. The Hapsburgs

From 1516 to 1659, beginning with Charles V, the Hapsburg family was the dominant force in European politics. The German and Spanish branches of the Hapsburg family maintained four different courts. They continued to project varying degrees of influence over the Holy Roman Empire, Austria, Spain, Burgundia, Tyrol, the Netherlands, Franche-Comté, Sicily, Sardinia, and southern Italy as well as over Spain's colonies in the Philippines and in the New World—Peru, Mexico, and the Caribbean Islands. All told, about a thousand territories belonged to the empire. In Germany, the large electorates of Saxony and Brandenberg were Protestant, and the duchy of Bavaria was Roman Catholic.

Charles V, King of Spain (1516–56) and Holy Roman Emperor (1519–58), in 1556 abdicated in favor of his son, Philip II, King of Spain (1556–98). Both father and son diligently attempted to advance the cause of Roman Catholicism, although Philip received the Council of Trent in July 1565 on condition that his "royal rights" be protected. Philip's Roman Catholic convictions reinforced (1) his desire to marry Queen Elizabeth and thereafter bring England back to the "mother church," (2) his fateful decision to invade England with an armada (1588), and (3) his attempt, only partially successful, to put down the Protestants' revolt in the Spanish Netherlands.

The fact that Philip II had to contend with the challenge of Islam in the east diminished his effectiveness in fighting the Dutch. The various Hapsburg families competed with the Bourbon family of France for political and economic preeminence among the Roman Catholic powers. This competition was also carried on outside of Europe. As late as 1652, with the addition of Portugal and her colonies Brazil, Angola, Mozambique, and outposts around the Indian Ocean, Philip III of Spain laid claim to a vast empire upon which "the *Sunne* can neither rise nor set," as one contemporary put it.

By 1598, troubling signs were surfacing that the fragile peace within the Holy Roman Empire that had existed since the Religious Peace of Augsburg (1555) might be shattered. The peace agreement had served as a fundamental law of the empire. It stipulated that two religions were legal in Germany: Roman Catholicism and Lutheranism as represented in the Augsburg Confession (1530). German Calvinists and Anabaptists were essentially ignored. According to the Peace of Augsburg, princes were permitted to choose the faith for their lands: *Cuius regio, eius religio* ("Whose realm, whose religion"). They had the right to "reform" their church according to their consciences.

But triangular tensions mounted between Roman Catholic and Protestant princes and between Reformed and Lutheran princes in the various judicial courts of the empire. Often local conflicts erupted when a prince confiscated the buildings and other possessions of a displaced religious community. Moreover, Emperor Rudolf II (1552–1612), the King of Bohemia and Archduke of Austria, defended Roman Catholicism in a heavy-handed fashion.

Given to outbursts of anger, Rudolf seemed intent on depriving his Protestant subjects of their rights. In 1607, for example, the emperor asked Duke Maximillian I of Bavaria to enter the free city of Donauwörth in order to protect the Catholic minority. The duke did this and then drove the Protestant majority out of the city. Contemporaries believed that the outbreak of the Thirty Years War (1618–48) was in part provoked by incidents of this kind. Many Protestants feared that the Hapsburgs were determined to force them out of the empire in an attempt to fulfill an old dream of Charles V (Charles I of Spain)—the creation of an exclusively Roman Catholic Holy Roman Empire.

C. Poland, Lithuania, and Ukraine

On July 4, 1569, "The Commonwealth of Two Nations, the Polish and the Lithuanian" was born. Four years later (May 16, 1573), Henri, the French Duke of Anjou, became the King of Poland. Upon the death of his brother (1574), Charles IX, the King of France, Henri abruptly returned to France and assumed the kingship as Henri III. In Poland and Lithuania, magnate families owned vast territories and attempted to protect their "liberties."

In 1596 four bishops and the Metropolitan of Kiev, Ukraine, created what became known as the Uniate Church. They submitted to the authority of the pope and embraced Catholic doctrine. At the same time, they continued to observe the Eastern liturgical rite and allowed their priests to marry. For three centuries, Uniate Christians became the subjects of fierce persecution. Cossacks in Ukraine and in Poland proved to be determined enemies. During the Cossack-Polish Wars (1648–57), many Uniates were killed. The Orthodox often disdained the Uniates. Nor were Uniate bishops especially well received by the papacy.

In 1598 hostilities broke out between Poland and Sweden. Fighting lasted until 1611, but resumed from 1617 to 1629 and once again from 1655 to 1660, thereby overlapping in part and constituting for a time one theater of the Thirty Years War outside of Germany. The secession of Ukraine from Poland in 1648, coupled with the devastation caused during the war with Sweden (1655–60), signaled the apparent end of the Polish-Lithuanian state as a first-class European power.

V. THE THIRTY YEARS WAR: A RELIGIOUS-SECULAR CONFLICT?

On May 23, 1618, an acrimonious verbal exchange inflamed the emotions of some two hundred Protestant members of the estates of the Kingdom of Bohemia who were crowded into the lower quarters of Hradcany Castle in Prague. The Protestants had come to complain to four members of the kingdom's council of regency about Archduke Ferdinand's persecution of Protestants, his disputed assumption of the Bohemian throne, and other alleged infractions of their rights. As tensions continued to mount, a number of Protestant Czech nobles made their way to upper rooms of the castle and then proceeded unceremoniously to throw two councillors, Jaroslav von Martinitz and Wilhelm von Savata, along with a secretary through open windows.

Why the Roman Catholic councilors survived the fall of sixty feet into a moat far below became a subject of hot debate. Catholics proposed that angels had caught the councilors in midair and saved their lives. Did not this divine intervention demonstrate the rightness of the Roman Catholic cause? Protestants retorted that the legates had been preserved from almost certain death by the cushioning effect of falling into a dung heap in the moat.

This curious episode, known as the "defenestration of Prague," constituted one of the most well-known events of the seventeenth century. In some regards, the window incident appeared as a calculated reprise or repeat of a similar episode that had taken place two hundred years earlier and had touched off the Hussite Wars. However intriguing the incident is in retrospect, it did help to precipitate armed hostilities of what became known as the Thirty Years War (1618–48).

As contemporary accounts by writer Hans Jakob von Grimmelshausen and others make clear, this war with its looting and savagery did untold damage to people and material in central Europe. The war was a disaster for parts of Germany, with a loss in population from 21 million in 1618 to 13 million by the war's end in 1648.

The religious stakes in the early years of the warfare seemed only too obvious to contemporaries. Protestants throughout Europe believed their forces were fighting for the defense of Protestant liberties. Roman Catholics often thought that if the Bohemians were able to overthrow their Hapsburg governmental officials, their example could inspire other Protestants to revolt. Better to put down with force this demonstration of Protestant temerity. Better to return formerly Roman Catholic territories to the mother church. Whatever sincerity was wrapped around their religious concerns, the participants in the Thirty Years War soon manifested other concerns having nothing to do with religion but having much to do with raw contests for economic and dynastic power.

The Bohemian phase of the war (1618–21) ended with advantages accrued to the Roman Catholic cause. In 1620 the Catholic League forces defeated decisively the rebel Bohemians, their Hungarian allies, and the troops of the elector prince of the Palatinate at the Battle of White Mountain. Archduke Ferdinand, the contested king of Bohemia, essentially eliminated the Protestant nobility from Bohemia and forced many other Protestants, including pastors, into exile.

In 1629 the Holy Roman Emperor stipulated in the Edict of Restitution that Roman Catholics throughout the empire could reclaim the ecclesiastical goods that had been taken from them by Protestants. Given the disasters that befell Protestants after the defeat at White Mountain, this battle has sometimes been described as a turning point, marking the end of Protestant advances in central Europe. Without the intervention of the Protestant Swedes and the Roman Catholic French in the next decade, the Protestant forces in central Europe might have been completely routed by Roman Catholic armies.

Indeed, after the defeat at White Mountain, the future of Protestantism in central Europe appeared bleak. But thereafter, Roman Catholic forces did not encounter easy and uninterrupted victories in their struggle with Protestant "heretics." In 1629, after victories against Poland and Russia, the Lutheran King of Sweden, Gustavus Adolphus, landed with twelve thousand troops at the Odor River. He portrayed himself as the savior of German Protestantism and won a number of impressive victories over the Spanish troops and the empire's Imperialist troops. In 1631 Gustavus Adolphus received a promise of aid from France. However, the great Protestant military leader was killed at the battle of Lutzen in 1632. Two year later, the Imperialist-Spanish forces won a decisive victory at Nordlingen.

As early as 1620, France's Louis XIII, a sincere Roman Catholic, indicated that when matters of his own monarchy's welfare were at issue, he would do what was best for his kingdom and not what confessional loyalties would otherwise dictate. He declared that "interests of state must not be mixed in any way with religious ones...." Fearful that the Spanish Hapsburgs might garner too much power, Louis XIII, working in tandem with Cardinal Richelieu, entered into alliances with the Dutch Protestants (1635) and the Swedish Protestants against the Roman Catholic Spanish and the Imperialists.

These alliances were designed to provide relief for beleaguered Protestants with the goal of thwarting Hapsburg political designs. The alliances provided striking evidence that religious loyalties no longer necessarily represented a decisive factor for some European diplomats in determining foreign policy. Rather, "reasons of state"—in this instance, the concern of the Roman Catholic Bourbons to counter the formidable growth of power of their Roman Catholic competitors, the Spanish and the Hapsburg Imperialists—trumped loyalties to international Catholicism. On occasion, "indifferentism" also characterized mercenary armies with soldiers switching sides according to who would give them the best pay.

In a word, the Roman Catholic Church's ability to advance its cause was blunted by those Roman Catholic monarchs, leaders, and soldiers for whom loyalty to the faith was sometimes supplanted by more secular ambitions.

The fact that Pope Innocent X, in his brief *Zelo domus dei*, harshly criticized the Treaty of Westphalia that had brought an end to the Thirty Years War, is yet another indication that the papacy was not always having its way in international politics. Not only were the pope's wishes basically ignored by Ferdinand III of Bohemia and Elector Maximilian I of Bavaria, who influenced the treaty's contents, but Innocent X was convinced, whether rightfully or wrongfully, that Protestants had emerged as the principal beneficiaries of its stipulations.

On the face of it, the pope's assessment appeared accurate. The political independence of the Protestant United Provinces was acknowledged; France, the Roman Catholic supporter of the Protestant cause, received the bishoprics of Metz, Toul, and Verdun; and Protestant Sweden acquired western Pomerania and the bishopric of Bremen.

Owing to Innocent X's restricted ability to influence the international politics of his day, a number of historians have proposed that the Thirty Years War and the Treaty of Westphalia contributed to the "secularization" of diplomacy in Europe. Several governments appeared less concerned to weigh religious factors in determining foreign policy, although certainly religion's influence on governments' policies did not completely recede. Whereas Richelieu (ministry, 1624–42), a key strategist for Louis XIII, was ready to support selectively the cause of foreign Protestants, Louis XIV (1661–1715) was much less inclined to do so. Deep into the eighteenth century and beyond, matters of religion often affected the internal and external policies of many European nations.

VI. THE SEVENTEENTH CENTURY: A CULTURALLY "CHRISTIAN AGE"?

Was the seventeenth century a culturally "Christian age" in Europe? If the standard for making an affirmative judgment is that all Europeans had to embrace Christianity in a serious fashion, then it was no such age. Non-Christians existed in significant numbers. Members of Jewish communities in Amsterdam, Venice, and other cities and in regions such as Poland were generally unresponsive toward Christian efforts to convert them.

A number of Jewish authors such as Elijah de Montalto wrote apologetic pieces for "Marranos"—that is, Jews forced to convert to Christianity. He tried to encourage them to remain Jews in their hearts. In 1687 Isaac Orobio de Castro, a Jewish physician, theologian, and philosopher, debated the Remonstrant Philip van Limborch regarding the veracity of the Christian faith.

Hostility toward Jews remained a virulent force in seventeenth-century Europe. Muslims living in Europe on occasion also had to pretend they were Christians. They were called "Moriscos." By 1614 Castile had forced 275,000 Moriscos out of their homes; many went to France or North Africa. Then again, Turks controlled sections of Europe in which Christians lived.

Sizeable numbers of witches and warlocks also plied their fearsome wares in Europe. During the so-called European "witch craze," up to 100,000 persons were accused of witchcraft, some of whom were suspected followers of Satanism. Between the years 1675 and 1690, a series of witchcraft trials took place in Catholic Salzburg, with some two hundred boys and men, mostly beggars, executed in consequence.

In France, *libertines érudits* ("erudite libertines") such as Pierre Charron, Guy Patin, Gabriel Naudé, and Samuel Sorbière wrote in such ambiguous ways that Christian critics suspected these authors were covert skeptics, possibly even atheists. In 1625 Marin Mersenne, a prominent Roman Catholic cleric and scientist, made the shocking claim that 50,000 atheists resided in Paris.

Cities such as Amsterdam, Naples, Paris, and London had well-organized underworlds of criminals and quarters where prostitution, thievery, drunkenness, and other unsavory practices thrived. Prostitutes especially haunted fairs, theaters, parks, church entrances, and other public places. Robbers and thieves sometimes rendered travel between villages and cities dangerous.

Executions of criminals were often public and as festive as they were gruesome. They could attract huge, raucous crowds. The corpses of the executed were sometimes left exposed to public view for a lengthy period of time—graphic object lessons of what awaited captured criminals.

The fact remains, however, that whatever the exact number of witches and warlocks, skeptics and atheists, members of other religions, and the unchurched, seventeenth-century Europe was in general "culturally" Christian. By this affirmation, it is simply meant that the culture of an overwhelming majority of Europeans, or the way they viewed the world and lived out daily life ("the assumptions underlying everyday life"—Peter Burke), was heavily affected by "Christian" values and symbols whether they resided in Spain or England or Italy or Poland or Russia.

Christopher Hill, for example, writes about Christianity's pervasive influence in mid-seventeenth-century England: "Moreover, Christianity was the real (if conventional) belief of almost everyone. The Bible was almost universally esteemed as an inspired text that offered guidance on life's problems and matters of salvation."

This is not to say that all English and other Europeans necessarily had well-formed views of the Christian faith or considered themselves disciples of Christ or displayed virtuous lifestyles. Many contemporaries were often mortified by the dubious activities they witnessed or heard about that occurred at carnivals, festivals, and other celebrations in which "Christian" peasants and townspeople joined in raucous revelry.

The licentious character of life at a number of Europe's "Christian" courts fed the gossip mills. Nobles and even members of the clergy were not above engaging in unseemly behavior. Mistresses for kings and nobles were commonplace. In addition, in certain regions of Europe barely any Christian presence was evident or none at all. In 1628 a speaker in the English House of Commons lamented that there were places in northern England and Wales "where God was little better known than amongst the Indians."

In Catholic countries more than one hundred holy days dotted a calendar year. In regions in which Reformed churches were dominant, the Sabbath was often observed with meticulous care. Although living under the millet system of the Ottoman Turks, the clergy of the Orthodox Church were on occasion able to superintend the customs and practices of their faithful in a rigorous fashion. Whether noble, city dweller, or peasant, most Europeans other than Jews and Muslims were generally baptized in a church (as infant or adult, depending on the church connection), attended its services at least minimally—that is, once a year—and in dying sought a Christian burial. Quite simply, the church with its graveyard was frequently at the center of community relations in a village.

The Bible was deemed an infallible authority, and its teachings gave comfort regarding how a person might have a right standing with God. A number of European kings believed that the Bible confirmed that they were divinely appointed by God to their royal office and that they were accountable to God alone.

In England, before the advent of the novel, the Bible's stories about Jesus Christ's life, miracles, death, and resurrection and about Adam and Eve, Moses, David, Ruth, Mary, Peter, John, and Paul were etched in the minds of the young and the old. From the lyrics of songs to the drawings on wall coverings, from the preached word to the printed page, the English people were surrounded by a culture greatly impacted by Holy Scripture. In France, the Iberian Peninsula, Italy, Poland, and southern Germany, the impact of the Catholic Church on daily life was widespread and deep.

In countries where Lutheran and Reformed churches predominated, church and state relations were often very close. The clergy of the Reformed churches greatly affected the cultural life of Scotland and the United Provinces, whereas Lutheran clergy did the same in northern Germany and Scandinavia. Despite the rule of the Turks, in Greece and portions of the Balkans the worship practices and authority of Orthodox churches held sway over the minds and hearts of millions. In Muscovy, the same was also true despite periodic controversies such as the battle between the Orthodox Russian Patriarch Nikon (1652–67) and Tsar Alexis (1645–76) and disputes between "Old Believers" and the Russian Orthodox.

A. "Popular Religion" (The Religion of the People)

What did these Europeans believe about Christianity? For some, their beliefs were conventionally summarized in the Roman Catholic, Protestant, and Orthodox catechisms, creeds, confessions, and traditions. For the theologically sophisticated, the books of contemporary theologians and Christian writers from earlier centuries added elements to their beliefs. This literature explained Scripture or expounded on creeds and confessions and other church doctrines and traditions and instruction regarding Christian living. Popular religious publications such as Bibles, broadsheets, missals, and catechisms also nourished readers.

But for about one-half of the population of Europe who could not read, what the local parish priest or pastor or member of a religious order taught them orally or what they had learned about religion through word of mouth from their families, local townspeople, and community storytellers was the true faith. The use of Latin in the celebration of the mass disallowed many of the laity from gaining a full understanding of its significance for their lives. At the same time, they could acquire certain impressions of the Christian faith from what they saw in the architecture, paintings, stained-glass windows, and statuary of the churches or what they witnessed and experienced in the ceremonies and religious services of the various churches.

In these circumstances, the forms and deformations of the Christian faith that European and non-European people practiced could vary in significant ways. Distinctions were sometimes only too obvious between what clerical guardians of right doctrine and practice for the various churches viewed or stipulated as orthodox and spiritually uplifting and what the people actually believed and did.

These distinctions resulted from many factors, including (1) the level and quality of the Christian instruction the people received; (2) the social and economic estates and groups to which people belonged that determined what level of access they had to Christian teachers; (3) the capacity of the clergy to exercise church discipline and of rulers and other officers of the state to enforce religious conformity within churches or a region; and (4) the willingness of individuals to follow the teachings of Christ and the Bible and the doctrines of their churches, if exposed to them.

As attractive as it is to speak about "popular religion," restricting its contents to the beliefs and actions of the Third Estate in kingdoms (the "people"), we should recall that the so-called "elites" in kingdoms (the members of the clergy and the nobility) often shared with peasants and townspeople similar views both of the visible and invisible worlds — worlds that in their minds were very much melded together. Belief in the reality of vampires, witches and warlocks, sorcerers, practitioners of black and white magic, fortune-telling, the predictive capacity of wheels of fortune, the benefits of judicial astrology (divination), and alchemy was not restricted to the "people." Scientists, theologians, philosophers, and members of the nobility and kings' households sometimes upheld these same beliefs with as much fervor as any peasant or worker.

Jean Bodin, for example, a distinguished humanist and man of letters and proponent of absolute monarchy, published *Of the Demon Mania of the Sorcerers* (1580), which described witchcraft in frightening detail. This very popular volume went through nineteen French editions by 1608 as well as numerous editions in other languages. Similar books giving directions on how to identify and search out witches appeared, such as, in Germany, Bishop Peter Binsfeld's treatise *Of the Confessions of Warlocks and Witches*; in Spain, the Jesuit Martin del Rio's *Six Volumes on Magical Controversies* (1599 – 1600); in Scotland, King James VI's *Demonology* (1597); and in Italy, Francesco Maria Guazzo's *Book of Witches* (1608).

From James VI, the future king of England, to peasants in Germany, to the townspeople of Salem, Massachusetts, the existence of witches was a widely held belief. Passages of the Bible could lend significant credence to this view. The upper classes often celebrated the same religious customs and festivals as members of the Third Estate. In consequence, the expression "popular religion" should not be restricted too sharply to the beliefs and practices of a certain social group of non-European and European Christians, the ill-defined "people."

At the same time, it is true that members of the First and Second Estates, generally speaking, had more sustained exposure to instruction or education in the Christian faith than did peasants and craftsmen. Less-educated Europeans often incorporated into their festivities and celebrations such as Carnival and May Day elements that horrified better-instructed Christians, who condemned these practices as pagan and sometimes as licentious. The list of offensive practices of the "people" was quite long: charivaris (mock raucous serenading for just-married couples), bullfights, bearbaiting, dicing, certain forms of dancing, drunkenness, the haunting of taverns, and the playing of cards.

B. Reforming Popular Culture

So concerned were "reforming" Christians, whether Protestant or Catholic, about the deficient practices and beliefs of less-educated Christians that they attempted to reform these practices. Historian Peter Burke writes, "I would like to launch the phrase, 'the reform of popular culture,' to describe the systematic attempt by some of the educated (henceforth described as 'the reformers,' or 'the godly'), to change the attitudes and values of the rest of the population."

Their reforming program, sometimes a part of post-Tridentine initiatives, was no small undertaking, given the embedded character and pervasive presence of many of these festivals, celebrations, and practices in the culture of peasants and townspeople. Moreover, the beliefs of many of these people were frequently embroidered with folktales, legends, and superstition. The historian Emanuel Le Roy Ladurie observes, "In the case of peasant societies in western Europe, rural religion essentially means a form of Christianity interpreted according to the ways of local folklore."

Until the 1650s, belief in sorcerers who could cast spells and change a person into a toad or another being or object, if they so chose, was widespread. After 1648 some Roman Catholics, feeling oppressed by their minority status in the United Provinces, espoused prophecies that foretold the return of Catholicism as the dominant religion and gave reports of miracles, apparitions, and exorcisms that confirmed God actually favored them and not the Protestants.

In the cities, Christian governmental officials sometimes attempted to reform the lives of vagrants, prostitutes, petty thieves, and hardened criminals. In Amsterdam's houses of correction, inmates were to listen to Bible readings and hear a sermon on Sunday. One of the most

"In the case of the peasant societies in [17th-century] western Europe, rural religion essentially means a form of Christianity interpreted according to the ways of local folklore" (Emanuel Le Roy Ladurie).

notorious "reforming" techniques was associated with the "water house" in Amsterdam. Rumor had it that a person who refused to work was placed in a room that would fill with water unless the person pumped the water out. The lesson was as simple as it was ominous: work or drown.

Whether or not such a "water house" actually existed, a number of prisoners were drowned to death for punishment, or strangled before their bodies were put into barrels of water. The reform programs of the seventeenth century could be torturous indeed. Many criminals received arbitrary punishments, including hanging, being broken on a wheel, physical mutilations, or imprisonment in dank cells. Petty theft could earn a hanging, as could the writing of derogatory lines about Madame de Maintenon, "wife" of the "Most Christian King," Louis XIV. A number of hack writers were put to death for the infraction of having insulted her honor.

The goals of the "reformers" of "religious practice" could vary. Aware of the lax observance of the sacraments, Roman Catholic priests and members of religious orders called on peasants and townspeople to a more faithful obedience to the sacramental teachings of the church.

Greatly concerned about the public morality of France in the 1630s, King Louis XIII wrote to Chancellor Pierre Seguier, "You will give me an unspeakable pleasure by seeing to the punishment of swearing and blasphemy that are current, not just in Paris but through France — not to mention thefts, murders and duels." A eulogist praised Louis XIII for his efforts: "He reformed abuses, regulated all the orders of the realm, policed the towns, eliminated embezzlement, repressed violence, drove out dissoluteness, punished blasphemy."

After claiming that a number of Lutheran theological schools harbored students who drank too much and fought too much and professors who vaunted themselves too much about their weighty theological tomes, Jakob Spener, in his *Pia Desideria,* called for the transformation of the schools into "workshops of the Holy Spirit."

Lutheran and Reformed theologians attempted to tamp down movements of religious "enthusiasm" whose members claimed special extrabiblical revelations. These theologians feared that the "enthusiasts" might overthrow the social order and even foster atheism. The "reformers" of religious practice found that the list of problems to be rectified not only in the popular religion of the "people" but among the "social elites" was lengthy.

That the culture of the seventeenth century was generally "Christian" is indeed true. That adherence to even basic doctrinal teachings and ethics of the Christian churches was universally evident is not.

VII. CONCLUSION

Life in seventeenth-century Europe was often precarious. Recurring crises including food riots characterized the age. Wrenching political upheaval was in abundance. War, famine, and disease were not unfamiliar strangers; they wandered through both the countryside and the towns. Death struck people down in ways that seemed arbitrary and incomprehensible. Europeans were often beset by fears. Historian Jacques Le Brun writes, "Fear was omnipresent for believers: fear of natural phenomena, fear of diseases, fear of wars."

It is little wonder that many Europeans, including some Christians, were tempted to seek relief, understanding, and protection from these fearsome foes by repairing to divination, astrology, black magic, and the wheel of fortune. Roman Catholics more generally prayed for protection, help, and care from Mary and the saints. Both Roman Catholics and Protestants sought succor in various forms of Christian mysticism.

Still others sought consolation in the teachings of the Christian churches about God's providential love and care for his children. As in previous centuries, the belief that God knows when the smallest sparrow falls and that things do not simply happen without God knowing about them provided genuine comfort. People also sought solace in turning to Christ, the only Savior, the only hope for their salvation.

In 1642 the English Puritan Arthur Hildersam gave this counsel:

> That God's people, when they are in any distress must fly to God by prayer and seek comfort that way; That pardon of sin is more to be desired than deliverance from the greatest judgments that can befall us; That the best of God's servants have no other ground of hope to find favor with God, for the pardon of their sins, but only in the mercy of the Lord.

In an age of fear and crisis that witnessed much personal distress and agony, many Christians believed counsel of this type was wise indeed.

FOR FURTHER STUDY

Benedict, Philip. *The Faith and Fortunes of France's Huguenots, 1600–85*. Farnham, UK: Ashgate, 2001.

Burke, Peter. *Popular Culture in Early Modern Europe*. Hants, UK: Scolar Press, 1994.

Dandelet, Thomas James. *Spanish Rome 1500–1700*. New Haven: Yale University Press, 2001.

Eisenstein, Elizabeth. *The Printing Press as an Agent of Change*. Cambridge: Cambridge University Press, 1980.

> "Fear was omnipresent for believers: fear of natural phenomena, fear of diseases, fear of wars" (Jacques Le Brun on seventeenth-century life).

Games, Alison. *The Web of Empire: English Cosmopolitans in an Age of Exploration 1560–1660*. Oxford: Oxford University Press, 2008.

Grafton, Anthony. *New Worlds, Ancient Texts: The Power of Tradition and the Shock of Discovery*. Cambridge: Harvard University Press, 1995.

McGuiness, Frederick J. *Right Thinking and Sacred Oratory in Counter-Reformation Rome*. Princeton: Princeton University Press, 1995.

Parker, Geoffrey. *Europe in Crisis 1598–1648*. Ithaca, NY: Cornell University Press, 1979.

Rapley, Elizabeth. *The Dévotes: Women and Church in Seventeenth-Century France*. Montreal: McGill-Queen's University Press, 1990.

Roustang, Francis. *Jesuit Missionaries in North America*. San Francisco: Ignatius Press, 2006.

Christianity and the Question of Authority

(17th Century)

I. INTRODUCTION

From the late sixteenth century until deep into the eighteenth century, a number of scholars periodically picked up intellectual cudgels and sparred with each other over a key question: What constitutes the authority or warrant for establishing the "truth" of a matter? Some scholars such as earlier humanists justified their intellectual views by appealing to the authority of writers from classical antiquity. For them, an accord between intellectual or religious traditions from antiquity could serve as a potentially decisive guarantee of the truthfulness of their own beliefs. If Homer, Aristotle, Ptolemy, or Augustine said something was true, then it was most likely true.

In the 1690s a specific literary "Quarrel of the Ancients and Moderns" broke out in the *Académie française* in Paris. Nicolas Boileau and Jean Racine, partisans of the authority and writing styles of the "Ancients," disputed with Bernard Le Bovier de Fontenelle, a proponent of "modern" (Cartesian) scholarship. In *Digression on the Ancients and Moderns* (1688), Fontenelle claimed "moderns" had superior knowledge over that of Ancients.

Francis Bacon (1561–1626), an earlier "modern" and "utopian" of sorts, advocated an inductive, "experimental philosophy." He wrote, "Our only hope ... lies in a true induction." He launched a full-scale attack on the prevalent use of deductive, syllogistic logic by contemporary Scholastics:

> There are and can be only two ways of searching into and discovering truth. The one flies from the senses and particulars to the most general axioms, and from these principles, the truth of which it takes for settled and immovable, proceeds to judgment and to the discovery

315

of middle axioms. And this way is now in fashion. The other derives axioms from the senses and particulars, rising by a gradual and unbroken ascent, so that it arrives at the most general axioms last of all. This is the true way, but as yet untried.

Moreover, he called for the removal of so-called "Idols of the Mind"—bad habits in the way we customarily think. These habits distort and hinder our understanding of the world as it is.

Bacon downplayed the authority of classical authors by claiming that the Greeks, for example, had speculated too much in philosophy and had only a "narrow and meager knowledge" of history and geography. A true philosopher should not be held captive to the writings of antiquity that could "break and corrupt" the study of a more important subject: nature. Bacon claimed that empirical research could often reveal the truth of a matter, even if this truth were discovered by a "modern," and even if this truth contradicted what a writer from antiquity had taught. He urged his contemporaries to "commence a total reconstruction of sciences, arts, and all human knowledge, raised upon proper foundation." The acquisition of "true" knowledge would promote "the glory of God and the relief of man's estate." It should permit humankind to have greater power or control over nature.

Likewise, René Descartes (1596–1650), a pioneer in modern philosophy, was especially blunt in his criticism of the Ancients. In *The Passions of the Soul* (1649) he rejected the value of their teachings: "What the ancients have taught is so scanty and for the most part so lacking in credibility that I may not hope for any kind of approach toward truth except by rejecting all the paths which they have followed." By contrast, Descartes had argued in his *Principles of Philosophy* (1644) that we "must believe everything which God has revealed, even though it may be beyond our grasp."

"Moderns" often claimed that their various approaches to acquiring knowledge would improve society and promote progress. They were convinced that their writing styles surpassed those of writers of antiquity. Both Moderns and Ancients generally professed respect for the Bible, an ancient authority, or they acknowledged that Europeans customarily esteemed scriptural authority.

II. DOING SOMEONE ELSE'S WILL

In classical culture the Latin word for authority, *auctoritas*, had as one of its definitions "will, pleasure, decision, bidding, command, precept, decree." Many seventeenth-century scholars would have understood this classical definition as reflective of a major characteristic of their own times. People lived in hierarchical, usually nonegalitarian societies in which they were obliged to yield obedience to the authority of "superiors," that is, to their "will, decision, bidding, command, precept, and decree." Historian Paul Hazard observed (1935): "An hierarchical system ensured by authority; life firmly based on dogmatic principle, such were the things held dear by the people of the seventeenth century." Even in the United Provinces, where citizens enjoyed significant liberties, an oligarchy of wealthy burghers nonetheless expected to receive due respect and honor for their high station in society.

Like the fish that does not reflect about the water in which it swims, many Europeans apparently never reflected much on the authoritarian character of the society in which they lived. By contrast, other Europeans openly challenged authorities and sought freedom from various forms of oppression. The seventeenth century could sometimes seethe with revolts.

In general, the personal liberties of Europeans were often restricted except in republics, in free cities, in high society and libertine circles, in the criminal underworld, among illicit book printers and sellers, and in corners of Europe where the policing abilities of authorities were limited or nonexistent. In *The Prince* (X, 1513), Machiavelli, for example, had earlier claimed that "the cities of Germany enjoy unrestricted freedom, they control only limited territory, and obey the emperor only when they want to." In the United Provinces a measure of toleration created breathing space for Mennonites and other Anabaptists, various Christian dissenters and heterodox thinkers, Unitarians, and Jewish refugees from Spain, Portugal, and other countries.

In kingdoms, however, speaking or writing too critically about the king, a noble, or a religious leader or saying something detrimental to the Christian religion could sometimes trigger a duel, an arbitrary arrest, prison time, or even an execution. Politics and religion were often organically united. If a person appeared to dissent from accepted religious beliefs, authorities might suspect that the individual was politically seditious and prone to disturb societal peace. Someone who did not believe in the Trinity or infant baptism or the eternality of the Son could be politically dangerous. The codes of Justinian and Theodosius as well as the Imperial Constitutions appeared to support this kind of argument.

A. The Web of Hierarchical Relations

In certain lands the "people" were frequently enmeshed in a complex web of hierarchical relations in which they were legally bound subjects to "superior" powers. They were subject to the sovereign authority of the king or tsar; subject to the teaching and demands of the clergy; subject to the orders of the king's or tsar's officers, lawyers, tax collectors, and soldiers; and subject to the commands of a feudal lord, a noble, a corporation, a guild, or the owner of a business. A king or queen or tsar was to be obeyed, the orders of royal officers and book censors heeded, a noble's wishes honored, a pope's declaration believed, a professor's words given credence, a husband's commands obeyed by wife and children, a feudal lord's dictates carried out by a peasant or serf, the admonishments of a priest or pastor accepted.

In the late seventeenth century, an obscenity sworn against Louis XIV was punishable by death. Deep into the eighteenth century, if a drunken reveler in a Parisian tavern infelicitously muttered a *mauvais mot* (a bad word or expression) about the king, he or she could be incarcerated in the Bastille. Authorities feared the power of words. Words could be dangerous, they could inflame riots and revolts. It is difficult for those who enjoy personal liberties such as freedom of speech to imagine fully what life was like for many Europeans who had serious restraints placed on their actions and words by repressive, authoritarian governments of the "Old Order," or the *Ancien régime*, that essentially ended in 1789 (with the outbreak of the French Revolution).

B. The Three Estates

Especially in certain kingdoms, the European populace continued to remain divided not so much by class distinctions as by orders or estates. In France, for example, the First Estate consisted of the clergy, ranging from prestigious prelates like the archbishop of Paris to an impoverished country *curé* in Ardèche. The Second Estate consisted of the nobility, ranging from wealthy princes of blood (*princes du sang*) to poor nobles with little land. The Third Estate consisted of those who were left, what we might call "the people" (or more negatively, the "mob," or "rabble") — that is, townspeople ranging from a wealthy "bourgeois" man or woman in Paris to a peasant in Provence. These divisions provided a structural framework for a hierarchical society. The dividing lines between the estates were sometimes quite hardened; sometimes they could be porous. Wealthy people from the Third Estate, for example, could be ennobled if they paid enough money for an office of a noble, or nobles could likewise become members of the clergy by taking holy orders.

The overwhelming majority of Europeans lived in rural areas and were frequently quite poor. Likewise, many city dwellers experienced grinding poverty. Conditions among "the poor" could vary, however. A peasant in France might possess a relatively higher standard of living than did a serf in poverty-ridden areas of eastern Europe.

C. The Authority of Divine Right Kings

In the hierarchical world of kingdoms, a king or queen enjoyed an unequaled privileged position, claiming as they often did a "supreme" authority over nobles, the people, and sometimes the clergy. In various regions of Europe the monarch's religion constituted the established faith of a particular kingdom. Although monarchies by no means represented the only form of government, they were sufficiently noteworthy that the seventeenth century has been labeled the "Age of Kings." (See also chapter 12.)

Even the emperor of the Holy Roman Empire often viewed himself as a divine right monarch who overlooked a *monarchia* and answered to God alone. On occasion, the princes and kings of the empire yielded unquestioned obedience to him as if he were a divine right monarch. On other occasions they claimed their autonomous rights to make their own laws and policies. The officials of governments of the Free Cities of the Empire, attempting to protect their liberties, also had equivocal political relations with the emperor.

In 1562 John Jewel, the bishop of Salisbury, published *An Apology of the Church of England*, a landmark book in the history of the English monarchy. Citing the Bible's authority, Jewel defended the legitimacy of the Elizabethan church's break from Rome. For Jewel, teachings of the Old Testament in particular provided a warrant for the theory of divine right monarchy. This theory in various versions enjoyed an especially prominent role in the political life of such realms as England, France, Denmark, and Sweden and in smaller principalities. It was no idle chatter for notable lawyers and theologians in Paris to say, "What the king wills, so wills the law."

James I (1566–1625), the future king of England, fashioned a sturdy defense of the divine right of kings in two books, *Trew Law of Free Monarchies* (1598) and *Basilikon Doron* (1599). He boldly wrote, "Kings are called Gods by the prophetical David because they sit upon God's throne in the earth and have the count of their administration to give unto him." James criticized what he thought were the anti-monarchical notes of one version of the Geneva Bible. He claimed that these notes were "partial, untrue, seditious, and favouring too much of dangerous and trayterous conceits."

Other advocates of divine right monarchy were somewhat less presumptuous in their claims, but often they made a similar point: the

"It is possible the church may err, but it is not possible the Scriptures may err. And the Scriptures of God have authority to reform the church, but I never heard that the church hath authority to reform the Scriptures" (John Jewel).

authority of kings comes directly from God. It is not mediated to them through the people. Does not St. Paul teach this in Romans 13:1–2? "Every person is to be in subjection to the governing authorities. For there is no authority except from God, and those which exist are established by God. Therefore, he who resists authority has opposed the ordinance of God; and they who have opposed will receive condemnation upon themselves" (NASB). Should not they rather count on God's judgments and retribution to punish a king's evil deeds?

In an earlier era, Thomas Aquinas (1225–74) had said as much:

> Finally, when there is no hope of human aid against tyranny, recourse must be made to God the King of all, and the helper of all who call upon Him in time of tribulation. For it is in His power to turn the cruel heart of a tyrant to gentleness.... As for those tyrants whom He considers unworthy of conversion, He can take them from among us or reduce them to impotency.

The Spaniard Francisco Suárez, a learned Jesuit theologian, argued that if a people have formed a political society and have chosen a king to lead them, they also have the right to revolt against and kill the king if he acts in a tyrannical manner. Suárez defended this position in his *Defense of the Catholic Faith against the Errors of the Anglican Sect* (1613). England's James I, a staunch defender of a conservative divine right theory, ordered the hangman to burn the book, established the "severest penalties" for anyone who dared read it, and denounced Suárez as "a declared enemy of the throne and majesty of kings."

Several more restrained versions of divine right theory—for example, the influential exposition of the doctrine by Claude de Seyssel in his *The Monarchy of France* (1515)—stipulated that a Christian monarchy was to be tempered, paternal, and limited by the "fundamental laws" and the rights of the *Parlement*. The Christian king had a responsibility to take care of his people the way a loving father cares for his own children. The king was to respect their rights and not take advantage of them. In his *The Six Books of the Republic* (1576), Jean Bodin asked if he had not been courageous when he wrote "that not even to kings is it lawful to levy taxes without the fullest consent of the citizens."

In 1579 the Reformed theologian Theodore Beza of Geneva published *Psalmorum sacrorum libri quinque* (*Sacred Psalms, Book 5*), a book intended to give guidance to French princes on how to rule righteously. Beza proffered the example of King David as a "mirror" of a godly king who did just that. According to the Reformer, David's authority was "limited by specific laws and conditions." In his *History of the Turks* (1650), François Eudes de Mézeray compared "the Monarchies of the

Orient which have almost always been despotic, and properly speaking more tyrannies than sovereignties" with those of the "West, where the kings remain within the limits of law and are content to regulate the liberty of their subjects, without wanting to suppress it."

Robert Bellarmine (1542–1621), a staunch defender of the papacy, proposed that the pope, superior to kings, should mediate their relationships with God. In 1675 Jacques Bénigne Bossuet counseled the "Sun King" Louis XIV: "You should consider, Sire, that the throne which you occupy is from God, that you are taking his place and that you ought to govern according to his laws."

In emulation of King David, the Christian king was anointed with holy oil at his coronation. Through this ceremony he became priestly and semidivine. The Christian king, in serving God, had specific functions to fulfill. As a Christian warrior, he was to lead his soldiers in battle for the Christian religion. In fulfilling his priestly function, a Christian king had the responsibility periodically to "touch" his subjects afflicted with scrofula, a glandular disease ("the king's evil"). As he touched the afflicted, he would utter the liturgical phrase, "The king touches you, God heals you."

An oil canvas, *Louis the Miracle Worker* by Jean Jouvenet (1690), shows Louis XIV "curing scrofula" by laying his hand on the sick. In 1775 Louis XVI as a *Roi thaumaturge*—"king of miracles"—did so as well, much to the disgust of several nobles present at the "healing" ceremony.

The practice continued in France unto the 1820s. As late as 1714, English kings participated in these "healing" ceremonies. In principle, then, a Christian king was not to act as a despot or a tyrant in the manner of a Turkish sultan or an autocratic Russian tsar. He was to act as a caring Christian father. In grateful appreciation, the king's subjects were to love and venerate His Majesty. A common expression fell from their lips when they honored him: "It's for the king."

Another pillar buttressing the king's authority consisted of venerable traditions about the history and origins of the royal family. These traditions stretched deep into the past to Clovis (466–511), the "first Christian king" for the French, or Cerdic (c. 464–534), ancestor to kings of Wessex for the English. According to a general theme of these historical/mythological reconstructions, a number of tribal leaders yielded obedience to one of their more powerful warrior competitors in exchange for his protection. This latter interpretation held within it the subtle but powerful proviso that French "nobles," for example, might withdraw their loyalty from the king if he did not honor the "fundamental laws" of his kingdom or did not demonstrate sufficient respect for the honors and rights of the nobles themselves.

D. Louis XIV and "Absolute Monarchy"

French King Louis XIV (reign, 1661–1715) is often singled out as an example, par excellence, of an "absolute monarch." Ironically enough, as the English kings were losing some of their divine right powers, Louis was consolidating his own power. During the *Fronde*, rebellious *Parlements* agitated by ambitious nobles had challenged the monarchy's authority. The story goes that a young Louis, fearing for his life as an heir to the throne, went into hiding. He was obliged to bed in straw in Saint Germain, so desperate and uncertain was his personal safety. He witnessed with trepidation the political chaos accompanying the failed *Fronde*.

With the inception of his personal rule, Louis XIV proceeded to tame the rebellious nobles by wooing, cajoling, and threatening them. He was also very skillful in self-advertisement. Using poets such as the tragedian Pierre Corneille, baroque painters such as Charles Le Brun, architects such as Jules Hardouin-Mansart, and finance ministers such as Jean-Baptiste Colbert, and seconded by renowned clerics such as Bossuet, the Sun King glorified his own person and deeds and spelled out his divine right "absolutist" designs to both his own people and foreign governments. Lustrous medals were struck that rehearsed his mighty deeds in battle. Resplendent paintings portrayed the king as the new Apollo, the handsome god who had driven his horses through the skies. Louis XIV grandiosely claimed, *"L'état, c'est moi"* ("The state, it is I").

Not to be outdone, a number of Austrians compared their Emperor Leopold I (reign, 1658–1705), Louis XIV's principal European competitor, to Emperor Constantine and the god Apollo. Moreover, Leopold's eldest son, Joseph I (reign, 1705–11), upon his election as King of the Romans in 1690, was extolled as a "new sun," an apparent slap at Louis XIV's notorious vanity.

From the pretensions of King James I to the pronouncements of Louis XIV, from Sir Robert Filmer's *Patriarcha or the Natural Power of Kings* (1680; the target of John Locke's criticisms) to Bossuet's *Politics Drawn from the Very Words of Holy Scripture* (1697, 1709), various versions of divine right theory circulated through the seventeenth century.

Declarations by monarchs could give the impression they perceived their rule as "absolute." In point of fact, these same monarchs often realized that their actual exercise of power was constrained by certain realities: (1) the ideology of divine right kingship often placed on them a responsibility to care for their people; (2) the kings sometimes did not have sufficient funds and policing capabilities to enforce royal laws; (3) the kings had to deal with warring factions among their nobles (including princes), fractious parliaments, treacherous intrigues at their courts, and recalcitrant provincial assemblies, in addition to the challenges of foreign powers; (4) the kings could not ignore the fact that if they pursued economic or social policies deemed harsh, urban and peasant revolts might ignite; and (5) members of the Roman Catholic clergy on occasion appealed to be tried by their church's ecclesiastical court systems rather than submit to trial in the kings' courts.

Sometimes the clergy claimed ecclesiastical exemptions from royal decrees or local governmental orders. A number of factors could hobble the kings' capacity to act in an arbitrary or "absolutist" fashion.

III. FORMS OF GOVERNMENT: MONARCHY, ARISTOCRACY, AND DEMOCRACY

Samuel Rutherford (1600–1661), who attended the Westminster Assembly as a representative of the Scottish Church, described three principal varieties of government: by one person—monarchy; by some chief leading men—aristocracy; by the people—democracy.

Within the same century, a country such as England experienced different types of governments: divine right monarchies with absolutist pretensions, namely, the reigns of James I (1603–25) and Charles I (1625–49); a republican "commonwealth" (1649–60) with Oliver Cromwell (d. 1658) as Lord Protector and with chiliastic Fifth Monarchy men, Levelers and Diggers, calling for radical reforms; the Restoration monarchies with renewed absolutist pretensions, the reigns of Charles II (1660–85) and James II (1685–89). Ultimately, the Glorious Revolution (1689) thwarted James II's attempt to establish Roman Catholicism as *the* religion of the land and to harness Parliament's ability to make laws. Eventually a constitutional monarchy was reinstituted that invested Parliament with important powers. A mixed form of government, this constitutionalism was part monarchy, part representative democracy.

Likewise, the cantons and dominions of Switzerland manifested diverse forms of government. Neuchâtel was governed by autocratic rulers; Berne, Fribourg, Solothurn, and Lucerne by an aristocracy of nobles; the forest cantons of Schwyz and Uri by democratic elements.

Much farther east in Muscovy, tsarist autocracy emerged. On January 16, 1547, the first "Tsar of all Russians," Ivan IV "the Terrible" (1530–84) was crowned. The autocracy associated with the tsars had different traits from those of a number of monarchies in the West. All subjects owed absolute obedience to the tsar, a sacrosanct figure.

Whereas in the Western kingdoms, subjects often retained at least certain rights, such was not generally the case in Russia. The tsars attempted to grasp absolute personal power for themselves. After a major contest of wills between the Patriarch Nikon and Tsar Alexis III in 1667, the tsars gained even greater sway over the church. They were bound by few if any legal checks on the exercise of their power. Their own personalities and governing abilities and concern for the Orthodox faith did on occasion restrain some tsars from acting as ruthless tyrants, while other tsars personified just such individuals. The relatively little information that Western diplomats possessed about the Russian government in the first half of the seventeenth century often led them to associate the tsars with unbridled despotism.

Thus politicians and rulers advocated or upheld different types of government across the wide expanse of Europe in the 1600s. These governments ranged from "free cities" to princedoms and kingdoms to city-states and the Papal States in Italy, to the federated republic of the United Provinces, to various forms of "absolute monarchies" such as in France, to magnate noble families exercising extensive control over lands in Poland, to a monarchical Holy Roman Empire in Germany, to a tsarist autocracy in Russia.

A. Republics: Nurseries of Revolt?

Republics (or kingless states) and republican-like monarchies with parliamentary constitutions, which assured some personal freedoms, stood out as particularly troublesome foils for absolute monarchies in the seventeenth century. From Plato to Machiavelli, from the Roman Republic to the republican government of Renaissance Florence, partisans for diverse forms of republicanism made their case and sometimes sought to implement their theories. In the first lines of *The Prince*, Machiavelli had written, "All the states, all the dominions under whose authority men have lived in the past and live now have been and are either republics or principalities. Principalities are hereditary, with their prince's family long established as rulers, or they are new."

Proponents of divine right monarchy often feared that those who extolled the virtues of republics sheltered potentially seditious and traitorous sentiments and were prone to foment revolt. Could advocates of a "republic" (from Latin, *res publica*), run by citizens elected in a democratic fashion and united by citizens' civic virtue, look favorably on divine right monarchies?

If need be, proponents of republican forms of government could cite notable Christians who had advocated such. Was not one of the Florentine republic's greatest apologists, Coluccio Salutati (see chapter 1), a humanist and a Roman Catholic? In the political crisis of 1402, had he not strengthened the resolve of his fellow citizens to withstand the siege of a tyrant by arguing that Rome had reached its heights of glory while it was a republic and had begun to slide into mediocrity after it became an empire? Were there not other successful republics in Venice, Genoa, and Lucca as well as in several Protestant Swiss cantons? Was divine right monarchy the only form of government a faithful Christian could espouse?

For certain defenders of the divine right theory of kingship, these questions had little merit. They believed that Holy Scripture stipulates divine right kingship; it does not approve of republics. It disallows subjects from dissenting from and rebelling against their monarchs. For anyone to justify the legitimacy of a republic or a limited monarchy, they would have to furnish persuasive scriptural warrants.

A number of John Calvin's followers believed that the Reformer and others offered robust arguments that did this. In the *Institutes of the Christian Religion* (Book IV), Calvin wrote, "We know from Holy Scripture that the Lord wished this perverse and cruel tyrant [Nebuchadnezzar] to be honored and obeyed and implicitly for no other reason than he ruled over the kingdom.... It is clear beyond a doubt that we owe obedience to the person set in authority over us." But then Calvin cited a major exception to his general rule. If kings ordered something "contrary to God's will, it should be disregarded. The dignity of their high office must not be taken into account in such cases." That is, Christians have no obligation to obey a ruler if he asks them to worship God in a manner contrary to their consciences informed by Holy Scripture.

French Huguenots and other Calvinists living under Roman Catholic monarchies on occasion took a stance similar to Calvin's. They claimed that the king had no more loyal subjects than they. But for conscience' sake, they would not accept the king's dictates if he attempted to force them to worship God in accord with his Roman Catholic religion.

After the Saint Bartholomew's Day Massacre decimated especially the class of nobles among Huguenots in the fall of 1572, Theodore Beza apparently penned *Response to an Address Presented Recently at the Helvetian Council* (1573, under the name Wolfgang Prisbach) as an opening volley in a "resistance literature" aimed at Roman Catholic accounts justifying the massacre. François Hotman wrote a similar work, *Discours simple & véritable* (1573). Hotman's *Francogallia* (1573) and Beza's *The Right of Magistrates* (1574) especially stirred the hot coals of controversy. Hotman and Beza indicated that if a king were truly tyrannical, he could be resisted. As historian Scott Manetsch points out, Beza even set forth the stunning idea that it was the people who furnished "lesser magistrates" their authority; it did not come from the king.

Roman Catholic apologists vehemently denounced the "resistance literature." They often charged Calvinism with a republican spirit and a spirit of revolt. If Calvinists happened to gain political control, would they then proceed to overthrow divine right monarchs? This kind of gnawing fear also contributed to James I's decision to back his Anglican bishops rather than a Puritan party at the beginning of his reign. To royalists, this fear seemed amply justified as Puritans and Independents of various stripes took up arms against Charles I in the English Civil War. Moreover, in his book *Lex Rex* (1644), Samuel Rutherford challenged the idea that "destructive" kings received their authority directly from God. He warned that "no law, in its letter, has force.... If the law, or King, be destructive to the people, they are to be abolished."

The publication of John Milton's *Areopagitica* (1644), a defense of writers' freedom, and later his *A Treatise of Civil Power in Ecclesiastical Causes: Shewing That It Is Not Lawful for any Power on Earth to Compell in Matters of Religion* (1659) likewise appeared to have "seditious" implications.

Thomas Hobbes (1588–1679) argued that individuals, to escape societal anarchy caused by a "war of every man against every man ... [in which] the notions of right and wrong, justice and injustice, have no place, should confer all their power and strength upon one man, or upon one assembly of men, that may reduce all their wills, by plurality of voices, unto one will...." This person, preferably a monarch, or a political assembly in a commonwealth should be fully sovereign and enjoy sufficient power to ensure societal peace and safety. Hobbes did acknowledge there were legitimate reasons subjects could withdraw from their covenant with a sovereign. For example, he observed, "The obligation of subjects to the sovereign is understood to last as long as, and no longer than, the power lasts by which he is able to protect them."

To some Roman Catholic critics, Protestants of whatever stripe were not only heretics but politically subversive. The execution of Charles I (1649) allegedly by "Calvinists" reinforced the dark suspicions of Roman Catholic monarchs that Calvinists in particular were dangerous covert republicans. This worry haunted the thinking of Louis XIV. It apparently contributed to his decision to revoke the Edict of Nantes in 1685. After all, were his Huguenot subjects, despite their professions of fidelity, actually loyal? Did they not share the same Calvinist beliefs as the English Puritans, some of whom had seized power and apparently approved the execution of Charles I?

B. The Jansenists and Authority

Potential opposition to divine right theory also issued from quite a different religious quarter: the Jansenists. These Augustinian Catholics constituted a distinct minority group within the Roman Catholic Church. They firmly believed they represented the true Catholic Church. They portrayed themselves as loyal monarchists. Nonetheless, their insistence on the right to worship God as they saw fit, not in the way the king or the Jesuits—their fierce opponents—stipulated, rendered them suspect. They too appeared to endorse an ecclesiology with subversive entailments for absolute monarchs. Some embraced conciliarism and forms of Gallicanism (see chapter 12) that ostensibly challenged especially the authority of the pope. During the "Peace of the Church" (1668–69), the Jansenists enjoyed a brief respite of toleration. Thereafter, Louis XIV's government sought to weaken and eventually crush the movement.

IV. SCRIPTURE AND TRADITION AS AUTHORITIES

The Latin word *auctoritas* could also mean, besides authority, "the things that serve for the verification or establishing of a fact." As the seventeenth century began, the Bible remained the most authoritative book in Western civilization. The authority of Scripture stemmed from the authority of its ultimate author, God himself. The Protestant theologian Amandus Polan observed, "The authority of Holy Scripture is the dignity and excellence pertaining to Holy Scripture alone, above all other writings, by which it is and is held to be *authentic*, i.e., infallibly certain, so that by absolute necessity it must be believed and obeyed by all because of God its Author." The Roman Catholic cleric François de Sales (1567–1622) indicated much the same thing:

> The Christian faith is founded on the word which God himself has revealed; and it is that which puts it in the supreme rank of infallibility. The faith that does not have its foundation and support upon the word of God is not the Christian faith; thus it follows that the word of God is the true rule and a foundation of faith for Christians, because to be the foundation and to be the rule is the same thing in this case.

Whether Roman Catholic, Protestant, or Orthodox, Europeans generally revered the Bible as the inspired written revelation from God. It tells the gospel story of humankind's redemption from sin through Christ's death on the cross and resurrection. Christians meditated on Holy Scripture in personal and household devotions and recited it in liturgies. One English writer commented, "Thou hast ... (in) the holie Bible, the most necessary, the most profitable booke, even the Booke of Life, and that dispersed in infinit numbers, easi to be gotten."

Proponents of divine right kingship cited Holy Scripture to justify their political theory. By contrast, so-called Fifth Monarchist writers such as William Aspinwall likewise appealed to Scripture to justify the removal of Charles I, a divine right monarch. In 1653 Aspinwall castigated Charles I, who had been executed in 1649, as "a fierce & arrogant Tyrant and persecutor of the Saints, whose dominion continued until the judgment was set, to wit the Parliament, and High Court of Justice, who slew the Beast, and utterly overthrew his dominions."

Fifth Monarchists believed they were playing a role in ushering in a "Faith Monarchy" in which King Jesus would rule. At the beginning of the century many natural philosophers ("scientists") believed that the validity of their investigations could be rendered suspect if their findings did not accord with biblical teaching. Biblical chronologists such as Thomas Burnet (1635–1715) drew up "sacred theories of the earth" that charted the history of the world since creation. Some mapmakers continued to place Jerusalem at the center of the world.

Preachers and priests warned and comforted their parishioners with the teachings of the Bible. Christian polemicists attempted to clinch arguments by citing scriptural passages. In his *Triumphus Biblicus* (1625) the Reformed theologian Johann Heinrich Alsted, a professor at Herborn, sought to demonstrate the unity of knowledge in accord with Holy Scripture.

In sum, the Bible represented one of the central authorities of the West that Europeans claimed to justify their own ways of viewing the world. As God's Word, it was truthful in all that it affirms regarding matters of faith and practice as well as details of history, the natural world, and other areas of human concern.

A. Roman Catholic Tradition

Leading representatives for the various Christian communions, however, did not necessarily weigh or appropriate the authority of Scripture in quite the same way. Historian Scott Manetsch observes, "... for Catholics, the primary role of the clergy remained sacramental and liturgical; for the Protestant reformers, it was to preach the Word of God."

Roman Catholic theologians asked a number of pertinent questions. Although the Bible is authoritative, they said, does it tell us all we need to know about our salvation? Did not the Council of Trent declare that from divine revelation flow two authoritative sources: Holy Scripture and apostolic Tradition? Are not some elements about how we are saved absent in Holy Scripture but supplied in "apostolic" Catholic Tradition? Have not Protestants downplayed or denied the indispensable role of the mass in obtaining our salvation?

The Jesuit Robert Bellarmine summarized succinctly a major distinction between Protestants and Roman Catholics on this point:

> The controversy between the heretics [Protestants] and ourselves focuses here on two points: first, when we affirm that the Scriptures do not contain the totality of necessary doctrine, for faith as well as for morals; then when we say that apart from the Word of God written, it is necessary to have his non-written Word, that is to say, divine and apostolic traditions.

Echoing Bellarmine, the Roman Catholic Guillaume Baile provided this question and answer in a 1609 catechism: "Are all things necessary for our salvation found expressly in Scripture? No. It is for this reason that Scripture sends us back to Tradition, some of which being divine have as much authority as if they were written."

By contrast, Protestants claimed that the Bible itself is a "sufficient rule for faith and practice," that is, it tells us all we need to know about our salvation and more. In his influential book *Disputations on Holy Scripture* (1588), William Whitaker, a Cambridge professor admired as one of Protestantism's most astute apologists, wrote, "We say that the scriptures are a rule, because they contain all things necessary to faith and salvation, and more things may be found in them than absolute necessity requires. We do not attach so strict and precise a notion to the term 'rule' as to make it contain nothing but what is necessary." The Bible should serve as the final judge in theological controversies, Whitaker declared, even though the Catholics said that "the church never errs; the pope never errs."

The Bible, therefore, was considered a judge or rule of traditions, whether Protestant or Catholic. These traditions, helpful as some of them were, remained man-made and fallible. In consequence, they could be reformed. Even conciliar statements of the early church could be reformed. Regarding councils, Luther had written, "I assert that a council cannot make divine right out of that which by nature is not divine right. Councils have contradicted each other, for the recent Lateran Council has reversed the claims of the councils of Constance and Basel that a council is above a pope."

> "We say that scripture never errs, and therefore judge that interpretation to be the truest which agrees with scripture" (William Whitaker in *Disputations on Holy Scripture*).

B. Protestant Confessions and Scripture's Authority

Protestant confessions reiterated these same perspectives. The Belgic Confession drawn up in 1561, for example, was revised and accepted at the National Synod of Dort in 1619. Article VII reads, "We believe that these Holy Scriptures fully contain the will of God, and that whatsoever man ought to believe unto salvation, is sufficiently taught therein."

Many Protestants, however, did evidence great respect for the creeds of the early church and the beliefs of the early church fathers. In his influential *Examination of the Council of Trent*, the Lutheran Martin Chemnitz (1522–86) wrote, "We examine with considerable diligence the consensus of the true, learned, and purer antiquity, and we love and praise the testimonies of the fathers which agree with the Scripture. For it is the opinion of the men on our side that in religious controversies the Word of God itself is the judge and the confession of the true church is added later" (Sect. VI, 2). Thus, Chemnitz argued that Protestants accepted certain traditions of the early church as having significant authority—if they agreed with Scripture.

A number of the Protestant confessions acknowledge the great value of the creeds of the early church. For example, the "Epitome of the Article" of the Formula of Concord (adopted in 1577) reads,

> And inasmuch as immediately after the times of the Apostles, nay, even while they were yet alive, false teachers and heretics arose, against whom in the primitive Church symbols were composed, that is to say, brief and explicit confessions, which contained the unanimous consent of the Catholic Christian faith, and the confession of the orthodox and true Church (such as the Apostles', the Nicene, and the Athanasian Creeds): we publicly profess that we embrace them, and reject all heresies and all dogmas which have ever been brought into the Church of God contrary to their decision.

Protestants believed that these particular creeds, reformable though they were, reflected the teachings of Holy Scripture and thus served as rules by which heresies could be judged. Moreover, the Protestant confessions often took on great authority for them, and for the same reason: these confessions were thought to mirror directly the teachings of Holy Scripture.

C. The Authority of Editions of Scripture

Roman Catholics and Protestants differed regarding which edition of the Bible constituted the infallible Word of God. The Council of Trent (fourth session, April 8, 1546) stipulated that Jerome's Latin Vulgate was the "authentic" text.

Protestants generally replied that the Hebrew and Greek texts of the Bible were the Word of God. William Whitaker wrote, "We, on the contrary side, say that the authentic and divinely-inspired scripture is not this Latin, but the Hebrew edition of the Old Testament and the

VERNACULAR VERSIONS OF THE BIBLE	
Tyndale New Testament	1526
Coverdale Bible	1535
Geneva Bible	140 editions published between 1560 and 1640
Matthew Bible	1549, pieced together from Tyndale's and Coverdale's
The Bishops' Bible	1568
Authorized Version	1611, later known as the King James Bible

Greek of the New." He continued, "… we do not say that one should stand by these translations as of themselves authentic, but appeal to the originals alone as truly authentic." Furthermore, Whitaker believed that "authentic" Scripture comes directly from the Holy Spirit: "For authentic scripture must proceed immediately from the Holy Ghost himself (2 Tim. 3:16); now Jerome's translation is not divinely inspired; therefore it is not authentic scripture."

Historian Richard Muller observes that orthodox Protestant theologians, whether Reformed or Lutheran, sometimes did distinguish between the infallible *autographs* of Scripture, the original manuscripts that had perished, and the *apographa*, "original and authentic" extant texts in Greek and Hebrew. These latter texts were also deemed as "infallible," any errors being those of copyists. Thus, unlike Whitaker, some Protestants believed that the *apographa* of Scripture had as much authority as the *autographa*.

In the wake of Erasmus's appeal for vernacular versions and the influential example of very successful translations of the Bible by William Tyndale, Miles Coverdale, and Luther, Protestant scholars continued to create new editions of the Bible in vernacular languages. (It is thought that perhaps as much as 90 percent of Tyndale's New Testament made its way into the King James Version.)

A number of Protestant scholars such as Matthias Flacius Illyricus, Niels Hemmingsen at the University of Copenhagen, and the renowned

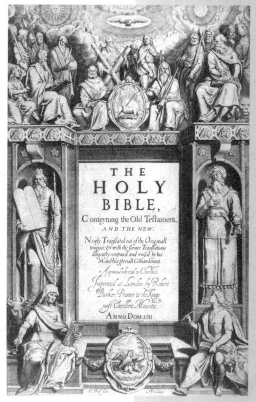

Title page of the King James Bible, 1611.

Josephus Justus Scaliger at the University of Leiden, along with scholars at Cambridge University and other schools, pursued biblical studies regarding exegetical methods and forms of lower textual criticism, or what became known as *Critica sacra.* Some Roman Catholic biblical scholars engaged in lower textual criticism as well. Periodically, they found themselves in an uncomfortable quandary. Their own studies in Hebrew and Greek texts suggested that the Vulgate itself could be profitably revised, a project the papacy eventually approved.

In 1582 English Roman Catholics in exile published the Rheims New Testament based on the Vulgate. In 1590 the Vulgate of Sixtus V (1521–90) was published. This proved to be a flawed edition. It was corrected by the so-called Clementine Vulgate of Clement VIII in 1592. In 1609–10 the English Rheims New Testament (1582) was joined to the just completed Douay Version of the Old Testament. The combined two testaments became the basis for the widely accepted Rheims-Douay Roman Catholic version of the Bible.

Front page of the Vulgate Bible, 1590.

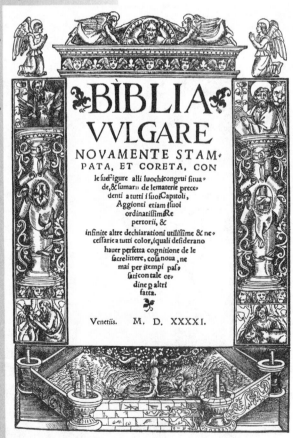

D. The Struggle over the Interpretation of Scripture

Yet another issue divided Protestants and Roman Catholics concerning the Bible's authority. What real authority, Roman Catholics asked, could the Bible possess if it were not interpreted properly? This kind of question became a cornerstone for Roman Catholic apologists. In the 1560s Juan Maldonat (1533–85), a Jesuit teaching in Paris, raised skeptical arguments about the ability of Protestants to determine and interpret their own rule of faith, Holy Scripture, without the help of the Roman Catholic Church and its Tradition. In 1595 St. François de Sales put the matter bluntly:

If then the Church can err, O Calvin, O Luther, to whom will I have recourse in my difficulties? To Scripture, they say; but what will I do, poor man that I am? For it is with regard to Scripture itself that I have trouble. I do not doubt whether or not I should adjust faith to Scripture, for who does not know that it is the word of truth? What bothers me is the understanding of Scripture.

Another Jesuit, François Veron (1575–1649), developed a veritable "war machine" of skeptical arguments with which to try to overwhelm Protestants. In debates with French Reformed pastors, he claimed that Protestants, owing to the fact they did not accept Catholic Tradition, were bound to fall into skepticism due to their private interpretations of the Bible. Was not every Protestant free to interpret Scripture as he or she saw fit?

According to Veron, the results of this interpretative license were disastrous. Protestants simply could not agree on the interpretation of many biblical passages. This explains why so many Protestant groups existed, each claiming that its particular beliefs and distinctives had scriptural grounding. And if there are so many different interpretations, will not a person fall into skepticism if he or she cannot discern which one represents true biblical teaching? The Congregation of the Propagation of the Faith claimed that Veron "converted more heretics to the Catholic faith than a thousand others."

For many Roman Catholic apologists, the proper approach to biblical interpretation was to accept by faith what the papal magisterium relying on church Tradition taught is the correct interpretation of a biblical text. After all, the church is infallible. François de Sales wrote, "Here then are the two ordinary and infallible rules of your belief: the Word of God which is the fundamental and the formal measure, and the Church of God which is the rule of application." Under "Word of God" François included Holy Scripture and Tradition; under "Church" he included the church as a body, general councils, the church fathers, and the pope. For him, "Scripture is nothing except the tradition reduced to writing." This fideistic-leaning approach of Roman Catholic apologists did not exclude, however, their use of rational arguments to defend their approach to biblical interpretation.

Protestants were quick to offer a rejoinder to these lines of arguments. Were not a number of interpretations proposed by the popes and bishops patently in error? Was not the papacy's own presumed authority, for example, based among other things on a faulty reading of Matthew 16:18? Until the Council of Trent's decrees, had not Roman Catholic exegetes indicated the verse's reference to a rock could be an allusion to Peter, the confession of Peter, Christ, or all of the apostles? No consensus of interpretation here. And did not divisions between Jansenists and Jesuits offer proof positive that the Roman Catholics themselves lacked a uniform understanding of Scripture?

Protestants proposed that they followed more sound principles of interpretation: Let infallible Scripture interpret infallible Scripture; let doctrine interpret doctrine (the "analogy of faith"); let the more clear passages of Scripture clarify the meaning of the more obscure passages. For that matter, the Bible is self-authenticating. The Holy Spirit persuades believers of its authority. A person does not need to resort to the authority of the Roman Catholic Church to authenticate the Bible's authority. In addition, the Bible is sufficiently clear in its presentation of salvation truths that believers do not need to have recourse to any tradition or to the magisterium to understand how we might be saved and how we should live.

These kinds of arguments and counterarguments stamped polemical debates over Scripture and Tradition. In these debates, the nature of the church's authority emerged as a key consideration in weighing the authority of both Scripture and Tradition. Both Roman Catholics and Protestants believed that the teachings of the true church had authority. Nonetheless, they disagreed thoroughly regarding which was the true church, what were the marks *(notae)* of the true church, and what was the weight of the true church's authority vis-à-vis Holy Scripture.

E. The Authority of the Church

For Roman Catholics of that time, unity constituted one of the most decisive marks identifying the true church. According to Scripture, there is one true faith and one true church. Roman Catholic apologists believed the visible Roman Catholic Church exhibited unity; therefore it possessed the prerequisite mark identifying it as the true church. This Roman Catholic claim echoed through polemical discussions of the seventeenth century. With stunning success, Bossuet, for example, used the "variations" among Protestant churches—that is, their different denominations based on varying doctrines and practices—as proof that none was the true church.

The argument helped persuade a number of Protestant notables such as the Marshal Turenne in France to convert to Roman Catholicism. Moreover, some Catholic apologists also claimed that the Bishop of Rome, the pope, was infallible when he spoke about faith and morals. In his teaching office he could pronounce which interpretation of Scripture is the correct one and which tradition represents apostolic orthodox doctrine. Some apologists added the further claim that the Roman Catholic Church determines and authenticates what is true Scripture. Did not the early church establish or authenticate which books of the Bible are canonical? Could one properly speak of the Bible's authority without immediately relating it to the authority of the church?

Protestants also believed there are marks identifying the true church as the body of Christ. They too valued unity, but many believed this true unity is found in the catholic, or universal, invisible church of Christ, not in the visible Roman Catholic Church. Those who belong to the true church of Jesus Christ are the sheep who hear their Master's voice. Chapter 25:1 of the Westminster Confession of Faith reads, "The catholic or universal Church, which is invisible, consists of the whole number of the elect, that have been, are, or shall be gathered into one, under Christ the head thereof; and is the spouse the body, the fullness of him that filleth all in all."

For many Protestants, the marks of the true church include the faithful preaching of the gospel and the faithful administration of the ordinances. In this regard, individual churches are "more or less pure, according as the doctrine of the gospel is taught and embraced, ordinances administered, and public worship performed more or less purely in them" (Westminster Confession 25:4). Because Christ is the head of the church, the pope cannot possibly be such.

For Protestants in Geneva, it was the Reformed pastor who had the responsibility and authority to offer Christian consolation, instruction, and discipline through regular home visitations and the preaching ministry to the laity. Theodore Beza had earlier described the pastor's role in this fashion:

> It is not only necessary that [a pastor] have a general knowledge of his flock, but he must also know and call each of his sheep by name, both in public and in their homes, both night and day. Pastors must run after lost sheep, bandaging up the one with a broken leg, strengthening the one that is sick.... In sum, the pastor must consider his sheep more dear to him than his own life, following the example of the Good Shepherd.

V. THE INCREASED AUTHORITY OF "SCIENCE"

Even though many seventeenth-century "natural philosophers" were eclectic and dabbled in the occult and alchemy, they participated in a modern "scientific revolution." Historians often present this revolution as one of the most important developments in world history.

A. The Scientific Revolution

The general duration of the revolution ostensibly ran from Copernicus (1473–1543) through Isaac Newton (1642–1727), although scientists such as Pierre-Simon Laplace (1749–1827), author of *Celestial Mechanics*, believed they were contributors to the same revolution.

This revolution sometimes overthrew existing cosmologies, especially traditional views of astronomy based on Aristotle, Ptolemy, and a certain reading of the Old Testament. It challenged the premise that the earth, an inert and immobile body, is at the center of the universe and is circled by a series of planets.

In his *Harmony of the Worlds* (1619), Johannes Kepler (1571–1630), a brilliant mathematician and scientist, described the revolt against ancient authorities in astronomy:

> In the beginning let my readers understand this: that the old astronomical hypotheses of Ptolemy, as they are set forth in the Theoriae of Puerbach and the writings of the other epitomisers, are to be kept far from the present enquiry and banished wholly from the minds; for they fail to give a true account either of the arrangement of the heavenly bodies or of the laws governing their motions. In their place I cannot do otherwise than substitute simply Copernicus' theory of the universe, and (were it possible) convince all men of its truth....

A number of traits characterized this "scientific revolution":

1. From Isolation to Community

In the days of Copernicus, natural philosophers (or scientists) generally worked in relative isolation from other scholars. In the second half of the sixteenth century, however, naturalists impacted by Renaissance humanism and caught up in the "science of describing" species developed a greater sense of working in community across religious and national divides. The number of known species jumped from 500 in 1550 to 4,000 by the 1620s. By the time of Newton, scientists could avail themselves of the benefits of collective associations made up of like-minded scholars. The meetings, publications, and correspondence between members of learned societies such as the Royal Society (1660 to the present) or the Paris Academy of Sciences (1663–1803) promoted an expansive exchange of ideas.

2. From Organism to Machine

In earlier centuries, it was commonplace for scholars to view the world as a divine, living organism sometimes described as possessing feminine traits ("mother nature," for example). The world was not easily susceptible to description in mathematical terms. Some believed in a "Great Chain of Being" linking all things. Many reputable thinkers thought astrology provided them with a profound understanding of this world. Pico della Mirandola described astrology as an art, not as a science. By contrast, as historian Claudia Brosseder observes, "Lutheran scholars from Wittenburg like Philipp Melanchthon, Caspar

Peucer and Erasmus Reinhold believed that astrology was a science with hermeneutic potential in multiple spheres of life.... Together with theology, it was *the* science because it made it possible to spell out Divine Providence."

With the scientific revolution, a number of scientists, referring to the world, changed the metaphor from a living organism to a machine. Kepler wrote,

> My aim is to show that the heavenly machine is not a kind of divine, live being, but a kind of clockwork (and he who believes that a clock has a soul attributes the maker's glory to the work), insofar as nearly all the manifold motions are caused by a most simple, magnetic and material force, just as all motions of the clock are caused by a simple weight. And I also show how these physical causes are to be given numerical and geometrical expression.

As a machine, Kepler said, the world is susceptible to mathematical description and follows fixed laws.

3. From Natural Law to Divine Revelation

As the emerging parlance of natural "laws" became more common, so eventually did the definition of a miracle as a contravention or violation of a natural law. Natural philosophers thought they gave the truth claims of the Christian religion a boost when they indicated "impartially" that the evidences for God's existence are utterly convincing.

Robert Boyle, for example, declared that "the *New Philosophy* may furnish us with some new Weapons for the defence of our ancientest *Creed."* Boyle, a determined foe of Aristotle's influence in science, claimed that atheists in an idolatrous and superstitious fashion exalted nature inordinately (1686): "... many atheists ascribe so much to nature that they think it needless to have recourse to a deity for giving an account of the phenomena of the universe." For his part, Isaac Newton indicated that it is impossible "to pretend that it [the universe] might arise out of a chaos by the mere laws of Nature."

Boyle, author of *The Christian Virtuoso* (1690), believed that Christian scientists who possess "right reason" seasoned by Christian revelation have a superior capacity to study and understand nature than do atheists, "infidels and libertines" who use reason alone: "For the reason of man ... is capable of receiving a higher and more excellent information, by supernatural discoveries and revelations." According to Boyle, Christian scientists access this "excellent information" through their study of Scripture, a revelation.

"Lutheran scholars ... believed that astrology was a science with hermeneutic potential in multiple spheres of life.... Together with theology, it was *the* science because it made it possible to spell out Divine Providence" (Claudia Brosseder).

A number of Christian apologists became enamored with writing "impartial" and evidence-based, rational defenses of Christ's resurrection. Thomas Sherlock's *Tryal of the Witnesses of the Resurrection* (1729), set in a juridical context, constituted an especially popular apologetic piece. It ran through seventeen editions.

4. From Paradigms to the Unity of Knowledge

The scientific advances accompanying the revolution did not follow a predetermined linear path. Many roads of investigation were tried and abandoned; sudden insights could sometimes change the paradigms in which research was pursued. "Scientists" varied considerably in their approaches to their work. Practitioners of "Mosaic" science (based on Moses' writings) sometimes challenged defenders of Aristotle's scientific views, whereas Baconians and Cartesians, though generally dismissive of the authority of the "Ancients," might retain great respect for scriptural authority.

Antiquarians and alchemists (often one and the same person) such as Elias Ashmole (1617–92) and the polymath Athanasius Kircher (1602–80) collected alchemical, astrological, and heraldic manuscripts as well as remnants of birds, animals, fruits, and flora. They studied esoteric traditions and comparative languages and interpreted and illustrated biblical texts (Kircher's *Noah's Ark* and *The Tower of Babel*). Kircher threw himself into a search for "lost knowledge." Ashmole not only was interested in turning a base metal into gold, but also thought that an "Angelical Stone" possessed by Hermes, Moses, and Solomon "no Devill can stay or abide."

Whereas many seventeenth-century historians concentrated on writing the history of kings and dynasties, these antiquarians attempted to do precise studies that would reveal the unity of all knowledge (whether historical, "scientific," or biblical and theological).

5. From Ancient Authority to Inductive Knowledge

For certain scholars, Francis Bacon's empirically based "inductive" method for acquiring knowledge began to regulate research in the natural sciences, overthrowing the authority of ancient writers, including Aristotle and Ptolemy.

6. From a Closed System to an Infinite System

A number of scientists such as Thomas Digges (1576) began to envision the universe not as a closed system but as one that stretches into infinity.

7. From Absolute Certitude to Probable Certitude

Protestant cleric and scientist John Wilkins (1614–72), who was a founder of the Royal Society and presided over its first meeting, developed a category of probable certitude as helpful in scientific investigations. He rejected both the skeptical idea that we can know nothing with certainty and the theory that a premise must possess absolute certitude before it possesses scientific worth.

8. Physics and Metaphysics

By Newton's day, some scholars such as Nicholas Malebranche (1638–1715) of France appeared to separate metaphysics from physics (the study of the workings of the natural world).

B. Copernicus and Kepler and the Bible

In his posthumously published *On the Revolutions of the Heavenly Spheres* (1542–43) Copernicus provided convincing evidence that the sun rather than the earth is at the center of this universe. He proposed that the earth rotates in an orbit around the sun. Historian Maurice Finocchiaro points out that strong criticism greeted Copernicus's work: "The Copernican theory immediately came under attack for reasons stemming from astronomical observation, Aristotelian physics, traditional epistemology, and scriptural interpretation."

Nicolas Copernicus.

Many Christians believed that the Bible teaches a geocentric theory (earth-centered) rather than heliocentric (sun-centered). In 1571 Cardinal Bellarmine, a major figure in the Roman Catholic Church's condemnation of the Copernican theory (1616), gave lectures at Louvain defending the fluidity of the heavens. He used a literal interpretation of Scripture to back his contention.

According to Johannes Kepler, who provided striking mathematical corroboration of the heliocentric theory, opponents of the Copernican perspective believed in the Bible's infallibility but thought anyone who defended the heliocentric viewpoint did not.

For Kepler, the issue at stake was not in fact the infallibility of the Bible. He affirmed his belief in that doctrine just as Galileo would do after him. The matter at hand was otherwise:

How should readers interpret statements of Holy Scripture regarding the natural world? Kepler, as did Galileo and Newton, argued that the Bible was written in accommodated language. That is, God accommodated the language of Scripture to the weaknesses of our understanding. The Bible is written in the language of appearance; it describes things as they appear to us. The Bible, then, is not in strict terms a "scientific" textbook. Nonetheless, what it relates about the natural world is "true": it describes things truthfully as they appear. The Bible, therefore, is infallible.

In many regards, what Kepler and Galileo proposed echoed the thinking of earlier Christian advocates of an Augustinian definition of "accommodation." This view of accommodation indicates that God did in fact accommodate Holy Scripture to the capacities of weak humans to understand. John Calvin could even speak about the Holy Spirit lisping when inspiring Scripture.

C. The Trial of Galileo

With this understanding of the conflict over the heliocentric theory in mind, we should probably look beyond the trial of Galileo, despite its notoriety, to locate a militant contest that pitted "science" against Christianity. Using an improved telescope, Galileo had gathered startling evidence that indicated the Copernican theory was probable. He

Galileo Galilei.

published his provocative findings and discoveries in *The Starry Messenger* (1610) and the *Sunspot Letters* (1613).

Galileo felt compelled to explain how his advocacy of the heliocentric view of the universe comported with his beliefs about the Bible's authority. He seemed to indicate in some correspondence that passages of Scripture are true inasmuch as they correspond with what scientists have discovered: "... it is the office of wise expositors to work to find the true senses of passages in the Bible that accord with those physical conclusions of which we have first become sure and certain by manifest sense or necessary demonstrations." But in other instances, Galileo seemed to make Scripture the standard of truth with which scientific investigations must accord.

In 1616 the Catholic Congregation of the Index ruled in a decree that the thesis of the earth's motion was contrary to Scripture and was not in fact physically the case. Also in 1616, the Inquisition outrightly condemned the heliocentric theory of the universe as "foolish and absurd, philosophically absurd, and formally heretical." Copernicus's book was put on the Index ("suspended until corrected"). On August 26, 1623, Cardinal Barberini, an admirer of Galileo, assumed the chair of St. Peter as Pope Urban VIII.

In this new ecclesiastical environment Galileo felt greater freedom to present his views more openly. Eventually, in 1632, he published *Dialogue on the Two Chief World Systems, Ptolemaic and Copernican*, in which he tried to weigh fairly the strengths and weaknesses of the two systems. The work appeared to shelter an implicit defense of the Copernican perspective. A 1632 injunction had forbidden any discussion of the earth's motion. The appearance of Galileo's book violated this ruling, and in 1633 he was put on trial. Members of the Inquisition adjudged him "vehemently suspected of heresy" for maintaining heliocentric views and the belief "that one may hold and defend as probable an opinion after it has been declared and defined contrary to the Holy Scripture."

The fact that Galileo was put on trial and forced to recant his views about the movement of the earth reinforces the perspective that Christians upholding the geocentric view of world had won the day and that the first major battle between "science" and religion had been fought. But it should be recalled that Galileo, a petulant person, viewed himself as a faithful Christian. Moreover, his punishment was relatively mild. And no early modern scientist was put to death for innovative scientific beliefs.

Some Christians such as John Wilkens (1614–72) continued to argue that the infallible Bible was written in accommodated language, that the Bible is not a scientific textbook, and that clashes do not need to ensue between "religion" and science. Later, distinguished Christian scientists such as Robert Boyle indicated that scientific investigation is valuable because it enhances our knowledge of how God is at work in nature. Therefore the study of science is a doxological enterprise—that is, it renders glory to God. The Christian belief that God, the Creator, is orderly indicates that the world is orderly and runs according to "laws"; the fact that God made matter suggests that studying his creation is a worthy enterprise for the Christian; the Christian responsibility to care for one's neighbor might be fulfilled by making scientific advances that benefit humankind.

D. Isaac de la Peyrère, Science, and Biblical Authority

Historian Richard Popkin contends that Isaac de la Peyrère (1596–1676) was the first scholar to precipitate a genuine clash between science and Christianity. In his work *Men before Adam* (1655), La Peyrère argued that the Bible recounts the history of the Jews but not of other people who lived before the Jews, the so-called "Pre-adamites." He believed that this theory would account for the apparent existence of men and women before 4004 BC, a date that allegedly correlated with the way creation is described in the book of Genesis.

According to La Peyrère, everyone would be saved when the second Messiah for the Jews arrives. He eventually recanted his beliefs in Rome, blaming his Protestant background for leading him astray. His influence on the thinking of biblical critics such as Baruch Spinoza and Richard Simon was significant. Moreover, his theories suggested that scientists need not confirm their research with Holy Scripture because it does not necessarily give a full account of how things came into being. In addition, La Peyrère claimed that the Bible is errant.

By the end of the seventeenth century, a number of scientists no longer felt obliged to correlate their research with the teachings of the Bible. They thought that through works of biblical criticism Spinoza and Simon had allegedly demonstrated La Peyrère's point that it is a fallible book. In a remarkable reversal of roles, the Bible seemed to receive accreditation if its teachings were confirmed by "scientific" research. In a not-too-subtle fashion, "science" became a major authority in the worldview of a number of leading Europeans thinkers.

Whereas for some European scientists, including Isaac Newton, the findings of science demonstrate wonderfully the glory of God as seen through his creation, for others "science," while confirming that God exists, challenged the Bible's teachings that miracles take place, including even those of Jesus Christ.

Francis Bacon's methodology for doing research included careful research, the collection of facts, and good record keeping. From this "inductive" research would emerge axioms on which experiments could be based and more general axioms revealed. Thus, this approach moved from the gathering of particulars to the establishment of general covering principles that could account for them, thereby describing nature as it is. Bacon, unlike Galileo, had little use for mathematics in his methodology. Nor did he rely on hypotheses to guide his research. For example, in criticizing the "Idol of the Marketplace," he proposed that "all theories should be steadily rejected and dismissed."

Bacon appeared to identify the "school of experience" as the source of scientific truth. Bacon anticipated that his own research would bring about a great synthesis of scientific knowledge within several decades. Although neither Bacon nor Galileo sought to overthrow the authority of the Bible (an ancient source), their research and methods seemed to suggest that the "truth" of science captured the world more precisely than did the accommodated language of Holy Scripture, which treats the natural world only in passing.

VI. THE AUTHORITY OF PHILOSOPHY

During the Middle Ages, Christian scholars often portrayed "philosophy" as the handmaiden to theology. Scholastic theology became very prominent at the University of Paris. Aristotle's influence on Thomas Aquinas was significant.

In *On the Babylonian Captivity of the Church* (1520), Martin Luther severely criticized this influence as a cause contributing to the departure of the Roman Catholic Church's doctrine of the Eucharist from biblical teaching: "What shall we say when Aristotle and the doctrines of men are seen to be the arbiters of these lofty and divine matters?" Luther went so far as to label the Catholic Church the "Thomist, i.e. the Aristotelian, Church." Luther claimed that his own views were based on the "word of Christ." A number of scholars, however, have countered that Luther's theology was allegedly greatly influenced by philosophical thought, especially the nominalism of William of Occam and Gabriel Biel.

In the seventeenth century, theology and philosophy often remained intertwined. Indeed, the writings of Descartes, Malebranche, Leibnitz, Locke, and others become less understandable if they are not placed against the backdrop of the heated religious controversies agitating intellectual life. For example, various philosophers and theologians attempted to answer the skeptical arguments proposed in *Essays* (1580, 1588, 1595 editions) by Michel de Montaigne (1533–92) and the writings of libertine erudites such as Pierre Charron, the author of *La Sagesse*, a disciple of Montaigne and a reputed leader of "free spirits." An "academic" form of skepticism proposed that truth exists, but we cannot access it and our opinions are only probable. A "Pyrrhonian" form of skepticism raised more radical questions about the nature of truth.

Montaigne sought to make philosophy less theoretical and less scholastic and more practical as the "molder of judgment and conduct." A reading of the skeptical writings of *Sextus Empiricus* (new editions, 1562, 1569), the relativizing import of travel literature, and doubts about the capacity of reason and experience to arrive at absolute certitude led Montaigne to espouse a moderate form of skepticism. (That is, he did not deny the reality of objects.)

Montaigne was especially aware of the role of customs in shaping our thinking: "The laws of conscience, which we pretend to be derived from nature, proceed from custom; everyone having an inward veneration for the opinions and manners approved and received among his own people, cannot without very great reluctance, depart from them...." He also observed, "Miracles appear to be so, according to our ignorance of nature, not according to the essence of nature...."

Whereas Gisbertus Voetius had proposed in *Disputations concerning Atheism* (1648) that Cartesian philosophy could subvert the Christian faith, a number of Dutch Cartesians such as Johannes Clauberg and Christopher Wittich countered that Cartesian philosophy as they envisioned it had no negative entailments for theology or science or law.

Although Descartes is sometimes portrayed as a thinker who opened the door to subjectivity with his famous and disputed dictum *"Cogito ergo sum"* ("I think, therefore I am"), the brilliant philosopher and mathematician viewed himself otherwise. He was attempting to counter the menace of various forms of skepticism for Christianity and for knowledge in general by establishing an indubitable starting point upon which reliable knowledge could be based.

Descartes's epistemology (a kind of hard foundationalism) as expressed in his *Discourse on Method* and *Meditations* could be viewed as establishing reason as *the* criterion for establishing truth and thereby overthrowing the authority of the Bible and the Roman Catholic Church. But Descartes denied that his work had any bearing on the validity of the Christian religion. Malebranche, theologians of the Jansenist movement, and some Dutch Reformed theologians did appropriate aspects of Cartesian thinking in developing their own theologies.

Besides Cartesian thought, several other philosophical schools significantly influenced discussions of Christian doctrine and apologetics in the seventeenth century. A resurgent neo-Aristotelianism impacted the thinking of both Roman Catholic and Protestant theologians. The Spanish Jesuit Francisco Suárez (1548–1617), a moderate Thomist, was the Roman Catholic Church's premier Scholastic authority regarding metaphysics—the study of the nature of real essences, first principles and "being." In his *Disputationes metaphysicae* (1597), Suárez made distinctions between general metaphysics, general ontology, and special metaphysics. In his attempt to create a synthesis of Christian metaphysics, he interacted with the thinking of Thomas Aquinas, Occam, and Duns Scotus—sometimes with approval, sometimes with disapproval. The influence of his thought on Descartes was profound.

Many English Puritans turned to the philosophical work of the French Protestant Pierre Ramus (1515–72), a logician and humanist, as a counterweight to scholastic Aristotelian thought. John Locke, likewise a Protestant and a student of the Puritan John Owen, esteemed the writings of Pierre Gassendi.

Richard Baxter worried about any philosophy exercising decisive authority over theology. In *The Reformed Pastor* he counseled, "Our evidence and illustrations of divine truth must also be spiritual, being drawn from the Holy Scriptures, rather than from the writings of men. The wisdom of the world must not be magnified against the wisdom of God; philosophy must be taught to stoop and serve, while faith doth bear the chief sway."

A. "All Truth Is God's Truth": The Quest for an Authoritative Christian Worldview

In the seventeenth century, a confessional age, many Protestant thinkers had a settled conviction that they knew what truth is. They were quite willing to defend their beliefs in polemical disputes, if need be. God had revealed truth in two books: the Bible, a divine "special" revelation; and the book of nature, a "general" revelation. Because Truth (*Veritas*) is one, no contradiction exists between the teachings of the two books.

A number of Christian thinkers (Scholastics as well as humanists) did believe that, due to common grace, non-Christians possess insights about truth and have designed valuable logical methods or procedures to acquire it. Students at Cambridge University, for example, commonly heard lectures on rhetoric that extolled the writings of Quintilian, Cicero, and other Ancients; lectures on logic that honored Aristotle and Cicero as authorities; and lectures on philosophy that embraced aspects of the thinking of Aristotle, Pliny, and Plato. In 1619 a statute establishing the Savilian Professor of Astronomy at Oxford University stipulated that a nominated professor had the duty "to explain the whole of the mathematical economy of Ptolemy."

Nonetheless, the conjunction of the increased authority of natural philosophy ("science"); the stiff contests between schools of philosophy and natural philosophy (including Bacon, Paracelsus, William Burnet); the "shocking" challenge to long-standing beliefs provoked by the exploration of the heavens with the telescope and by mariners' reports about formerly "unknown" oceans, lands, and peoples; the battles between "Ancients" and "moderns"; and the growing mountain of published materials on disparate topics did raise an unsettling question: Is it possible to construct a unified Christian view of the world that takes into account the surge of new data and sort out responsibly claims between competing authorities? After all, adherence to the premise "All truth is God's truth" appears to call for some kind of engagement with the "New Learning." Might not the fragmentation and division of disciplines subvert the possibility of a unified Christian "worldview"? In 1643 a European scholar fretted, "How is it possible to understand the whole universe?"

A small army of scholars stepped up to organize scholarly data and arrange the disciplines into what they thought were logical relationships. They constructed "encyclopedias," "marrows," compendia, textbooks, and other volumes. Some were convinced that various fields of human knowledge could be unified in a harmonious and synthetic whole. Prominent among these were the English Alexander Richardson and William Ames, the German Johann Alsted, and his student, the Czech Jan Amos Comenius.

The Puritans Richardson and Ames proposed that the disciplines are integrated by *Technologia*, a circle of knowledge, or "Encyclopedia." The circle begins with the mind of God, proceeding to the material things God created, then proceeding to the human beings made by God, and finally proceeding to the arts humans use to honor and glorify God (praxis and piety). In his dialectical manual called the *Logician's School Master* (1629; a commentary on Pierre Ramus's *Dialectica*), Richardson defined art as "the wisdome of God, but yet as it is energetick in the thing ... the Law of God, whereunto he created things whereby he gouverneth them, and whereunto they yeeld obedience."

Ames, the author of *Technometry* and *Marrow of Divinity*, greatly appreciated Richardson's perspectives. Ames defined *Technologia* as "the precognition of all the arts which adequately circumscribes the boundaries and ends of all the arts and of every art." He indicated that art is "the idea of eupraxia or good action, methodically delineated by universal rules." Ames noted, "The comprehension of all those arts by which things emanate from the Ens Primum [God] and return again to him is called *Encyclopedia*, whose first link of the circular chain is logic and the last theology." The discipline of logic could help reveal divine principles, whereas grammar and rhetoric could enhance the communication of these principles. This explains in part why a preacher should gain rhetorical skills in order to communicate biblical teaching in an effective manner. Some words and emotive feelings serve better than others in assuring the faithful delivery of biblical teaching.

Alsted also stood out as a brilliant exponent of the essential unity of divine and secular knowledge. A Calvinist and a professor of theology, Alsted attended the Synod of Dort (1618–19) and subscribed to its Reformed doctrinal canons. He penned works such as *Cursus philosophici encyclopaedia* (1620). In his *Triumph of the Sacred Books, or, the Biblical Encyclopedia* (1625), he argued that there "is no book but Sacred Scripture." The disciplines of learning—whether physics, geography, economics, politics, jurisprudence, or others—find their grounding in the Bible. The Bible even includes subject matter such as *theriologia sacra*, the "special physics of the nature of terrestrial beasts."

In his multivolume work *Encyclopaedia Scientiarum Omniium* (1630),

Alsted attempted to provide a summary of human thought until his day. He sought to demonstrate that the divine is reflected in the unity and the logical order of all human knowledge. He reviewed the thinking of five hundred writers, from the Greek philosopher Aristotle to the English King James I. Alsted rejected Copernicus's heliocentric views as not being in line with Scripture. At the same time, he enjoyed the study of alchemy.

Alsted also had a passionate interest in biblical prophecy (especially the interpretation of Revelation 20) and the idea of the return of Christ as the Jewish Messiah. In his *Diatribe de Mille Annis Apocalypticis* (1627), Alsted penned one of the first defenses of a future millennium written by a Reformed theologian. (Joseph Mede wrote another in his *Clavis apocalyptica* in 1627.) Alsted concluded that the millennium would begin in 1694.

Often hailed as one of Europe's greatest educators, Jan Amos Komensky, otherwise known as Comenius (1592–1670), studied with Alsted. Comenius drew up a remarkable program called "Pansophy." Its purpose was to bring about the harmonious integration of all knowledge with the Christian faith. Such a perspective would hopefully foster a better life for all peoples.

Comenius's appeal for the "welfare of humanity" in an age of religious, economic, and political warfare was nothing less than breathtaking:

> We are all citizens of one world, we are all of one blood. To hate a man because he was born in another country, because he speaks a different language, or because he takes a different view on this subject or that, is a great folly. Desist, I implore you, for we are all equally human.... Let us have but one end in view, the welfare of humanity; and let us put aside all selfishness in considerations of language, nationality, or religion.

Born in Moravia in the Czech Kingdom, Comenius belonged to the *Unitas Fratrum*, the "Unity of the Brethren Church," whose heritage reached back to the teachings of another Czech, Jan Hus. Comenius studied at Herborn and Heidelberg. He taught and served as a pastor in Fulneck (1618). During the Thirty Years War (1618–48), he became especially disconsolate after the defeat of Protestant Czech forces at White Mountain in 1620. In 1628, with other Bohemian Protestants, he thought it necessary to leave his beloved Czech Kingdom. He sought refuge in Leszno, Poland. In 1632 he became a bishop of his church of exiles.

In 1633 Comenius published *The Gate of Languages Unlocked*. He urged students to learn Latin so that they might better understand the whole world "that is Nature, Man and God." A number of Puritan divines considered asking Comenius to become the first president of Harvard College (founded 1636) in the Massachusetts Bay Colony.

In *The Way of Light* (1641, 1668) Comenius set forth a universal, if not utopian program for education and peace and plans for a Universal College. Students at the Universal College would be instructed in "new schemes for the better cultivation of all languages, and for rendering a polyglot speech more accessible and finally for establishing a language absolutely new, absolutely easy, absolutely rational, in brief a Pansophic language, the universal carrier of Light." Comenius believed that the speaking of a universal tongue could help foster peace among peoples.

Comenius thought that education is for all: "Not the children of the rich or of the powerful only, but of all alike, boys and girls, both noble and ignoble, rich and poor, in all cities and towns, villages and hamlets, should be sent to school." He advocated pedagogical methods designed to engage students more fully in the learning process than did the common practice of rote memorization. He recommended the use of illustrated textbooks and the playing of games.

The goal of gaining a unified Christian "worldview" captured the imagination of teachers at Harvard and later at Yale. Students studied the textbooks of Richardson, Ames, Alsted, and Comenius among others. During Harvard's first decades, the writings of the Puritans Richardson and Ames in particular greatly influenced the intellectual life of the school. On Saturdays students studied theology and biblical exposition as articulated in Ames's *Marrow of Divinity*. A college law of 1646 expressed the overarching goal of a Harvard education: "Everyone shall consider the main End of his life and studies, to know God and Jesus Christ which is Eternal life. John 17:13." Students were urged to engage in secret prayer every day and the reading of Scripture twice a day.

B. The Dreaded Authority of the Ottoman Turks

Enervating fear of the Ottoman Turks advancing farther into western Europe continued to haunt the minds of many Christians in Europe during the seventeenth century. Western images of the Ottomans portrayed them as hypocritical, merciless, murderous, and licentious. Ottoman leaders—sultans and grand viziers, their prime ministers—were known to execute anyone, of whatever rank, who disobeyed or crossed them.

To Westerners, these sultans represented the very epitome of evil despotism and tyranny. In *The Prince* (IV, 1513), Machiavelli wrote,

"The Turkish Empire is ruled by one man; all the others are his ser-vants." These others are "all slaves bound in loyalty to their master." Unsavory stories about the sultans' seraglio—their palatial harem of enslaved Christian women, eunuchs, and dwarfs—fascinated as well as disgusted Christian readers and writers. Nonetheless, with the accord of the sultans, the French government had assumed the responsibility to protect the Christian holy places and all Christian peoples in Turkish-controlled lands.

An epochal military struggle between Christian forces and the navies and armies of the Turkish Empire eventually repulsed the Otto-mans' advance into central Europe. On October 7, 1571, Don Juan's Spanish galley fleet along with the papal and Venetian squadrons roundly defeated the Turkish navy of Ali Pasha at the Battle of Lep-anto—a turning point in the struggle between Christian forces and the Turkish Muslim Empire. In his novel *Don Quixote*, Miguel de Cervantes underscored the critical importance of the victory on "that day so for-tunate to Christendom when all nations were undeceived of their error in believing that the Turks were invincible."

In the rest of the sixteenth century, negotiators and diplomats from England and France competed for favorable trading treaties (capitula-tions) at the port in Constantinople. In the next century Dutch traders entered the competition for lucrative trade with the Turks.

The Treaty of Zsitvatörök (1606) engaged the Sultan and the Haps-burgs in a significant accord. It appeared to set borders on any further land advances of the Ottomans into Europe. The treaty was to hold sway for approximately a half century; it provided a temporary respite from conflicts. But by the 1660s the Ottoman armies were on the move again toward the West. Eventually, in 1683, the armies of the Grand Vizier reached Belgrade. Thereafter, under the leadership of Kara Mus-tafa, they encamped menacingly at the walls of Vienna and laid siege to the city. Mustafa indicated that his goal was that "all the Christians would obey the Ottomans."

In defense of his beleaguered capital, Leopold I, the Holy Roman Emperor, received help from the armies of the German electors of Bavaria and Saxony and timely reinforcements from King John Sobieski of Poland. The Christian forces prevailed in battle. The Ottomans were routed. Christians throughout Europe rejoiced and heaved a sigh of relief. Austrians, Venetians, and Poles united in a Holy League in an attempt to pursue the Muslims toward the East. The Austrians recap-tured Buda in Hungary from Turkish control, the Venetians advanced into Dalmatia and Greece, but the Poles had little success in taking Moldavia. In 1687 the armies of Charles Lorraine defeated a large force of Ottomans at Mohacs Fields. By the end of the seventeenth century, the threat of renewed incursions by Ottomans into central Europe had been substantially reduced.

In eastern Europe, Christians and Jews under Turkish rule continued to live in "millets" run by Phanariots (Greeks) for the Turkish sultans. These Eastern Christians enjoyed a semblance of autonomy and generally attempted to uphold their Orthodox beliefs. In the 1670s the Roman Catholic Richard Simon—more widely known for his biblical scholarship—drafted a wide-ranging survey of the beliefs, church life, and status of Eastern Christians, many of whom were living under Turkish rule.

C. Patriarchal Authority in Family Life

Fathers often continued to "rule" family life in the seventeenth century. Wives and children were generally expected to obey and honor them. Both Christian and classical teaching appeared to provide warrants for this male-dominated, hierarchical structure. In *A bridebush: or, A direction for married persons* (1617), English Puritan William Whately urged a woman to be submissive to her husband: "If ever thou purpose to be a good wife, and to live comfortably, set down this with thyself; mine husband is my superior, my better; he hath authority and rule over me; nature has given it to him.... God hath given it to him." After marriage, a wife's property often became the property of her husband.

At the same time, there were women who wrote popular manuals about domestic life. Dorothy Leigh in *The Mother's Blessing* (1616) and Elizabeth Jocelin in *The Mother's Legacie to her unborne Childe* (1624) gave maternal spiritual and domestic advice to children. Between 1475 and 1640, some 163 books appeared in English intended for a female reading public. The most comprehensive volume (1,500 pages) was Thomas Bentley's *The Monument of Matrones* (1582).

Historian Steven Ozment has proposed that some fathers "ruled" their families with kindness and love. They showed genuine affection toward their wife and children. The Protestant Reformers had encouraged the clergy of their respective churches to maintain homes that could serve as models of Christian piety and tranquility.

In pre-industrial Europe, many women bore onerous workloads. They labored in the fields or in a shop while simultaneously raising children and performing household chores. Some women ran successful businesses. Generally speaking, most women did not have the same educational opportunities as men. Daughters of the nobility and middle classes on occasion received a measure of education. For example, daughters of poor French nobility for whom dowries had not been provided might enter the academy at St. Cyr, established by Madame de Maintenon, Louis XIV's "wife." There they received instruction in reading, domestic work, marital home duties, and religion. François de Salignac de la Mothe-Fénelon also argued in his *Treatise on the Education of Girls* (1687) that girls should learn skills that would help them be good wives and mothers (reading, writing, elementary math, and religion).

In the wake of the Revocation of the Edict of Nantes (1685), Louis XIV stipulated that teachers should be designated in all parishes (especially those where there were "former" Protestants) to instruct children "in catechism and the necessary prayers, and to take them to Mass on working days and give them appropriate instruction on the subject ...; they will teach reading and even writing to those who need to learn." In the rural areas of France, boys and girls went to primary schools (*petites écoles*) together.

In 1684 George Hickes delivered a sermon before the Lord Mayor of London in which he called for greater educational opportunities for women:

> I will also put you to mind of establishing a Found[ation] for Endowing of poor Maids, who have lived so many years in Service, and of building Schools, or Colleges for the Education of young women much like unto those in the Universities, for the Education of young Men, but with some alternation of the Discipline, and Oeconomy, as the nature of such an Institution would require.

Likewise, Mary Astell, often described as the first "English feminist," published *A Serious Proposal to the Ladies for the Advancement of their True and Greatest Interest* (1694) and *A Serious Proposal Part II* (1697), in which she called for the creation of an educational institution where women might study and teach. In *Some Reflections upon Marriage* (1700), she pondered the complex issues women faced in trying to find a suitable husband. She also shrewdly criticized the inequalities women often encountered in their marriages.

Astell remained single. She was a firm Christian believer and wrote *Letters Concerning the Lord of God* (1695). As a staunch royalist Anglican, she also defended the divine right of kings.

Thus, both Hickes and Astell advocated greater educational opportunities for women. But Hickes did challenge Astell's contention that wives are under no obligation to submit to the political judgments of their husbands if such would compromise their consciences before God. (Interestingly enough, in 1702 Susannah Wesley, the mother of John and Charles Wesley, refused to endorse the family prayers of her husband, Samuel, for King William III. Samuel was greatly offended by Susannah's refusal.)

More English than French women kept diaries and wrote more intimately about family matters and general household duties. But for candor, few diaries surpassed Samuel Pepys's daring recitation for the years 1660–69. In great detail he described his turbulent relations with his wife, Elisabeth Marchand. On one occasion she was so disgusted with his infidelities that she "did fall to revile me in the bitterest manner in the world, and could not refrain to strike me and pull my hair."

Some prominent American colonialists kept diaries about family matters as well. In his diaries (1673–1729), the American Puritan Samuel Sewall, judge at the Salem Witch Trials, reflected on his wives (three), family members, friends, and enemies in an unusually frank fashion. His diaries provide a remarkable gaze into the everyday social life of colonial Boston.

In New England, when a husband died, his wife generally inherited his property and belongings. In his *Ornaments of the Daughters of Zion* (1697), the Puritan Cotton Mather counseled women on how they could gain the respect of men.

Interestingly, colonial women such as Sara Edwards, Jonathan Edwards's wife, often played a critical role in family and church life. Although they could not vote on church matters, they with their children appeared to attend services in greater numbers than men.

At the turn of the eighteenth century, a number of women forthrightly criticized the patriarchal society in which they lived. If the concept of an absolute monarchy in a state could be questioned (as it was per John Locke's criticisms), could not the authority of men in a family be questioned as well? Mary Astell put the seeming parallelism this way: "If absolute sovereignty be not necessary in a state, how comes it to be so in a family? . . . Is it not then partial in men to the last degree to contend for and practice that arbitrary dominion in their families which they abhor and exclaim against in the state? If all men are born free, how is it that all women are born slaves?"

VII. CONCLUSION

The "top-down" hierarchical structure of many societies in seventeenth-century Europe made it almost inevitable that Christians were obliged to interact with "superior" authorities of diverse kinds. The impact these authorities exercised on them could vary greatly. Many Christians yielded to certain authorities without questioning them. Others wrestled with the perplexing issue of determining which among competing authorities should have precedence.

Some Europeans attempted to extricate themselves from the constraints of "superior" authorities. In 1591, for example, students from the University of Padua initiated a revolt against the authority of Jesuits in the city. The Venetian Senate expelled the Jesuits from the Venetian Dominion. For a time, the students and faculty members from the University of Padua, including Galileo, enjoyed greater freedom to pursue their scientific and philosophical endeavors. Other Europeans, especially in Free Cities, attempted to protect their liberties.

The challenge to and competition between "authorities" could take different forms. The "shock of discovery"—regarding what voyagers to the New World and elsewhere reported they actually encountered versus what writers from antiquity had indicated they should experience or witness—led to questioning of the ancient authorities.

Indeed, by the 1620s some scholars believed they and their colleagues could make discoveries that invalidated the claims of authors from antiquity. More than in previous centuries, natural philosophers (early modern scientists) felt obliged to ponder the relationship between the authority of Holy Scripture and the validity of their scientific investigations. Could an apparent finding of "science" countermand a common interpretation of Genesis that suggested creation took place in 4004 BC? Or was it possible that James Ussher had not properly determined the date 4004 BC in his interpretation of Scripture?

French Huguenots had to explain the reasons they felt obliged to violate the authoritative commands of Louis XIV, a divine right king, when he ordered them to espouse Roman Catholicism. Had John Calvin furnished a legitimate escape clause from the principle that subjects should always submit to the commands of their rulers? English Puritans and Independents had to create a rationale for their risky decision to revolt against another divine right king, Charles I. Jansenist apologists had to provide evidence from the Bible and Tradition to justify their unwillingness to submit to every demand of the papacy in Rome. Particular Baptists had to explain the reasons they affirmed the Westminster Confession but rejected its teaching about infant baptism. Did not both they and the Westminster Divines whom they admired read the same Bible? Christians who embraced aspects of Descartes's epistemology had to explain this acceptance to other Christians who believed the philosopher's thought sowed the seeds of atheism, or at least fostered skepticism.

In 1680 Sir George Mackenzie of Rosehaugh sought to underscore in an edition of *The Declaration of Arbroath* (1320; a declaration of Scotland's independence) the reason Scots could refrain from giving allegiance to a Scottish king if the monarch in question yielded to English authority.

A sense of proportion, however, should restrain us from portraying the seventeenth century as a cauldron always boiling over with dissent.

Certainly, it witnessed well-known wars and tens and twenties of peasant revolts. But many Europeans were not inclined to challenge the authorities with which they interacted in a quest to establish a more "just" hierarchical order. The weight of traditional ways of doing things, customs, and thought patterns remained heavily on many Europeans. Numerous scientists continued to seek ways to demonstrate that their research was thoroughly compatible with the authority of Scripture. Moreover, the common people often had enough to do in simply trying to survive the troubles and travails associated with daily living. They spent their time in backbreaking labor in the fields, attempting to put bread on the table for their families, working in a shop, burying the dead, grieving the loss of a newborn, seeking consolation in Christ the Good Shepherd, who they believed cared for even the smallest lamb.

In the rural households of Europe the names of Descartes, Galileo, Cervantes, Blaise Pascal, or John Milton were scarcely known. It was much more likely the common people knew the names of the local priest or pastor, the names of their kings and queens, the name of a local baker who was hoarding bread or selling it at exorbitant prices, the name of a ruthless tax collector, the name of a roving brigand, or the name of a firebrand leader of a peasant revolt. Even if the common people often did not have a sophisticated understanding of the Christian faith, most continued to uphold the tradition of identifying themselves as "Christians," whatever the actual level of their personal devotion might have been.

FOR FURTHER STUDY

Atwood, Craig. *The Theology of the Czech Brethren from Hus to Comenius.* University Park: Pennsylvania State University Press, 2009.

Funkenstein, Amos. *Theology and the Scientific Imagination from the Middle Ages to the Seventeenth Century.* Princeton: Princeton University Press, 1986.

Heyd, Michael. *"Be Sober and Reasonable": The Critique of Enthusiasm in the Seventeenth and Early Eighteenth Centuries.* Leiden: Brill, 1995.

Hill, Christopher. *The English Bible and the Seventeenth-Century Revolution.* New York: Penguin, 1993.

Manetsch, Scott. *Calvin's Company of Pastors: Pastoral Care and the Emerging Reformed Churches (1536–1609).* New York: Oxford University Press, 2013.

Muller, Richard A. *Post-Reformation Reformed Dogmatics: The Rise and Development of Reformed Orthodoxy ca. 1520 to ca. 1725.* 4 vols. Grand Rapids: Baker, 2003.

Oslar, Margaret, ed. *Rethinking the Scientific Revolution.* Cambridge: Cambridge University Press, 2000.

Popkin, Richard. *The History of Scepticism from Savonarola to Bayle.* New York: Oxford University Press, 2003.

Preus, Robert. *The Inspiration of Scripture: A Study of the 17th-Century Dogmaticians.* Edinburgh: Oliver and Boyd, 1957.

10

Christianity under Duress: The Age of Lights

(1680–1789)

I. INTRODUCTION

They were very good at self-advertisement, this small band of passionate social activists, battling propagandists, and clever wordsmiths: the *philosophes* (French for philosophers). So effective was their campaign to promote their own day as an "Age of Lights" or an "Age of Reason" that many of their contemporaries and later generations of historians identified the eighteenth century by those very terms. An expression coined in the nineteenth century calls it the "Age of Enlightenment."

One common perception of eighteenth-century Europe suggests that *philosophes* such as Voltaire, Jean-Jacques Rousseau, Denis Diderot, Edward Gibbon, and David Hume—all of whom were antagonistic to orthodox Christianity—came to dominate high intellectual culture. In consequence, the Christian faith in its various historic expressions was thrown on the defensive. Many Europeans would no longer accept the teachings of the Christian churches. Moreover, some Christians would only accept these teachings on condition that they were conformable to the imperial dictates of reason.

According to this interpretation, reason at long last had gotten the upper hand on Christian revelation, judged it, and found it wanting. Moreover, reason could give practical direction on how a philosopher should live. The article "Philosophe" (*Encyclopédie*, ed. Diderot), states, "The true *philosophe* is thus an honest man [*honnête homme*] who does everything in accord with reason, and who joins to a spirit of reflection and of justice, morals and sociable qualities." Therefore ethics, political theories, and views of the natural world need not be shaped or constrained by what the Bible teaches, let alone by what the Christian churches stipulate. For the *philosophe*, reason should shape them all: Reason is immutable, having remained the same through all ages; it is a faculty shared by all humankind.

The *philosophes* announced that an exciting new day of the *"Siècle des lumières"* ("Age or Century of Lights") was dawning. They used the word light in several different ways, and the potential sources for their light metaphor were many. But the *philosophes* were united in countering one of the specific ways Christians spoke about light. Whereas Christians contended that Jesus Christ is the light of the world dispelling the darkness of sin, the *philosophes* retorted that the actual light illuminating the world was reason. This light was accompanying the advance of *la philosophie*. Reason would dispel the oppressive darkness of superstition, ignorance, metaphysical speculation, fanaticism, and intolerance allegedly engendered by the Christian faith.

In this particular context *la philosophie* was not defined as a technical discipline or field of study in philosophy but rather as an attitude or a habit of critical thinking. Humankind would benefit enormously from this new era of "reason," no longer encumbered by the doctrines of sin and redemption through Christ's sacrificial death on the cross. Religious wars would cease; toleration and respect for the rights of others would grace personal relations; and civility, reasonableness, and urbanity would characterize polite society at large. Happiness and material well-being would also increase due to advances in science, medicine, and technology.

The *philosophes* hoped their liberating program of "enlightened" thinking would spread throughout the world. Voltaire (pseudonym for François-Marie Arouet) intimated that the principles could be universally applied and therefore had export value. In 1762 he recommended to another *philosophe*, Claude Adrien Helvétius, that despite their eclectic and disparate views on numerous issues and their personal grievances with each other, and despite persecution, the *philosophes* only needed to remain basically united to triumph in the war against the "foolish" (*les sots*), that is, orthodox Christians and other foes of their attractive program: "Intelligent people will be their disciples, the light will spread in France as in England, in Prussia, in Holland, in Switzerland, in Italy."

What did it matter if the "little flock" of leading *philosophes* bickered rudely among themselves about many things—some like Diderot and Baron d'Holbach embracing atheism, for example, while others extolled deism or even an eviscerated theism? They all shared a burning passion for societal and religious reform in the name of reason.

However, a close look at the religious and intellectual culture of the eighteenth century and a close reading of the *philosophes'* own perceptions of their times reveals a complex picture. That a singular

"Reason is to the *philosophe* what grace is to the Christian. Grace determines the Christian to act; reason determines the *philosophe*" (Diderot's *Encyclopédie*).

"Enlightenment" exercised a predominant, unitary, or paradigmatic influence on Western culture is not certain. Historian Jonathan Israel, for example, argues that a number of thinkers were outright partisans of an atheistic "Radical Enlightenment" inspired in part by a reworking of aspects of Descartes's thought and a refashioning by Spinoza and Pierre Bayle. They included John Toland, Anthony Collins, Diderot, Jean le Rond d'Alembert, Baron d'Holbach, Julien Offray de La Mettrie, Jean Meslier, Nicolas de Condorcet, Thomas Paine, and Franciscus van den Enden (Spinoza's teacher) among others who as "Radicals" sharply criticized "all forms of authoritarianism, orthodoxy, intolerance, xenophobia and group chauvinism."

More "conservative" *philosophes* such as Voltaire agreed with much of this program of criticism but strongly opposed atheism. Also, the teachings of the *philosophes* did not suffuse French society but were often restricted to higher classes such as the middle and upper bourgeoisie and the nobility.

The fact that the expression *Enlightened* bore different connotations in various European countries also reveals that not all contemporaries experienced or defined the "Enlightenment" in the same way. The English word *Enlightenment* (coined by the British in 1860) and the term "Age of Enlightenment" (philosopher Edward Caird, 1889) are often assumed to mean the same things as the expressions *Siècle des lumières* (for France), *Aufklärung* (for Germany), *Illuminismo* (for Italy), and *Verlichting* (for the United Provinces), due to a common allusion to light. However, even the English expression did not carry exactly the same cultural connotations. Various "enlightenments" (using the term conventionally and masking internal intellectual battles) existed in eighteenth-century Europe with different intellectual shadings.

Their prime years of intellectual dominance did not always overlap: England, 1680–1750–1789; United Provinces, 1680–1789; France, 1680–1715–1789; Italy, 1740–1789; Poland, 1740–1820; Portugal, 1750–1777; Northern Germany, 1680–1748–1794.

Certain Enlightenments such as the one in France were more recognizably known for promoting hostility to the Christian faith, while others such as in Scotland offered intellectual components that Christians assimilated rather easily into their religious beliefs.

Even "national enlightenments" did not always shelter uniformity of belief among their partisans. Acrid battles sometimes broke out between various enlightened parties. Several streams of Enlightenment thought might course through one city or province and leave another region relatively untouched. The Roman Catholic "Enlightenment" in Bavaria had different traits from the *Aufklärung* in towns of northern Protestant Germany such as Halle or Berlin. Moreover, atheistic radicals inspired by Spinoza or Bayle might sharply pan Christians and deists alike in clandestine, illicit literature (underground newspapers, pamphlets, books, often passed hand to hand).

Were there any core components that the various Enlightenments shared besides the common reference to light? Immanuel Kant's famous definition of *Aufklärung* in his essay *"Was ist Aufklärung?"* (1784, "What Is Enlightenment?") seemed to serve up such a definition. But it supposed a more radical elevation of human autonomy in the name of reason than most of his German compatriots were prepared to embrace:

> Enlightenment is man's release from his self-incurred tutelage. Tutelage is man's inability to make use of his understanding without direction from another. Self-incurred is this tutelage when its cause lies not in lack of reason but in lack of resolution and courage to use it without direction from another. Sapere aude! Have courage to use your own reason! that is the motto of enlightenment.

Most Germans could not countenance such an admonition. A good number of northern German Protestant theologians, schoolteachers, publishers, and scientists appreciated many aspects of a more moderate *Aufklärung* that advocated the advantages or utility of toleration, technology, and education in the name of reason without apparently jeopardizing their Christian faith commitments.

What elements or themes, then, could be encompassed by most of the Enlightenments? The Dutch historians Hans Bots and Jan De Vet suggest that representatives of the *Lumières* throughout Europe commonly sought to struggle against prejudices (intolerance), authorities (allegedly "intolerant church and state officials"), and institutions (colonialism, slavery) when the latter were supported by arguments that clashed with reason. "Enlightened" individuals were those "who used reason as a means to combat the vices of society and for whom reason was an instrument of emancipation for neglected and oppressed human groups."

With this definition in mind, Bots and De Vet can speak of Dutch intellectuals who were both Christian and "enlightened," but who opposed vigorously the atheism or materialism of some of the French *philosophes*. This approach to the definition problem is helpful. It can account for the diversity of Enlightenments throughout Europe and North America, and it does not necessarily identify the Enlightenment with the stark materialism and atheism touted by a number of French *philosophes*. As noted, Voltaire and also Rousseau, leading figures of the Enlightenment, were by no means atheists or materialists.

The definition also captures the social reforming zeal of a number of enlightened Europeans in the name of reason. Yet, even this approach to the definition problem is not totally satisfactory. A number of atheistic partisans of an "enlightened" age never conceded that believing Christians could be "enlightened."

The bitter conflicts between Catholic Jesuits and Jansenists in France, the successful preaching missions of John Wesley (1703–91) and George Whitefield (1714–70) in England, the ministries of Jonathan Edwards (1703–58) and Whitefield in the "Great Awakening" of the American British colonies, and the Moravian influence of Herrnhut in Germany also attest to a residual and powerful Christian presence in the eighteenth century, the existence of which is incomprehensible if either an atheistic or deistic form of enlightenment had in fact secured a total victory over the Christian churches in that century.

In the 1760s Voltaire himself acknowledged that the *Siècle des lumières* might not ultimately triumph over and replace another age, what he disdainfully called the "Age of Superstition." He said that this other age, characterized in part by the continued commitment of many Europeans to Christian beliefs, customs, and institutions, existed and sometimes thrived side by side with and in opposition to the *Siècle des lumières.*

Other *philosophes* concurred with Voltaire's assessment. In 1769 Denis Diderot complained to David Hume, "Ah, my dear philosopher! Let us weep and wail over the lot of philosophy. We preach wisdom to the deaf, and we are still far indeed from the age of reason." Edward Gibbon, the famous historian of Rome's rise and fall, was rudely disappointed when he discerned that the "majority of English readers were so fondly attached even to the name and shadow of Christianity." By the 1770s Voltaire began to despair that French society was in retreat culturally. A serious "Counter-Enlightenment" movement existed.

Given the *philosophes'* own perceptions of a persistent if not significant Christian presence in the eighteenth century, it would appear that a more sustained analysis of what the Age of Lights represented for both Christians and non-Christians alike and how Christians lived out their faith is appropriate.

II. THE "AGE OF LIGHTS" OR "AGE OF REASON": ORIGINS

Intellectual historians have offered a number of instructive interpretations concerning the origins of the so-called Enlightenment, including the general revolt against Christianity by several of its celebrated representatives. According to Paul Hazard, Western culture, especially in France, essentially severed its intellectual ties to Christianity in 1715 with the death of Louis XV. Hazard described this momentous cultural shift as nothing less than a revolution: "One day, the

French people, almost to a man, were thinking like [Jacques Bénigne] Bossuet. The day after, they were thinking like Voltaire. No ordinary swing of the pendulum, that. It was a revolution."

A. An "Enlightenment" Prelude: 1680–1715

Hazard overstated his case by claiming that on one day in 1715 all Frenchmen were Christians and on the next the followers of Voltaire. Nonetheless, it remains true that a series of critical challenges to orthodox Christian beliefs did emerge in the period 1680–1715, but not in quite the way Hazard proposed. A number of the scholars whom Hazard targets as subverting the Christian faith viewed themselves as Christians, even if they were less dogmatic about certain orthodox doctrines than their contemporaries. They never envisioned that their scholarship would be ransacked by the *philosophes* for anti-Christian purposes.

In fact, Voltaire, a leading *philosophe* along with the encyclopedists d'Alembert and Diderot, claimed that their own "philosophic" perspectives were based directly on the thought of Bacon, Newton, and Locke, the latter two doing much of their publishing in the period from 1680 to 1715. Voltaire, for example, heaped praise on these thinkers and generally identified his thinking with their own, save for their Christianity. Voltaire claimed that Bacon was a Moses who led humanity from the captivity of ignorance to knowledge of nature as it really is.

For his part, Voltaire extolled Newton and Locke to the "philosophic" heavens. About Newton, he wrote, "... if true greatness consists in having received from heaven a mighty genius, and having employed it to enlighten our own minds and that of others; a man like Sir Isaac Newton, whose equal is hardly found in a thousand years, is the truly great man." Voltaire observed that Locke's approach to studying the soul was related to natural philosophy as well: "Mr. Locke has displayed the human soul, in the same manner as an excellent anatomist explains the springs of the human body. He everywhere takes the light of physics for his guide."

Many other scholars, whether Christian or non-Christian, appreciated Bacon's "experimental philosophy" with its inductive approach to gathering knowledge. In the 1660s the English poet and critic John Dryden praised the forceful blow that Bacon and other natural philosophers had delivered against the Stagirite Aristotle's reigning influence among many scholars and natural philosophers:

> The longest tyranny that ever sway'd
> Was that wherein our ancestors betray'd
> Their free-born reason to the Stagirite
> And made his torch their universal light.

"Nature, and Nature's laws lay hid in night. God said, 'Let Newton be!' and all was light" (Alexander Pope, in epitaph to Isaac Newton).

Had not Bacon been direct in his attack when he wrote, "The logic now in use serves rather to fix and give stability to the errors which have their foundation in commonly received notions than to help the search after truth. So it does more harm than good"?

Newton and Locke followed in Bacon's wake and allegedly finished the task of vanquishing the rationalistic systems builders Aristotle and Descartes. Indeed, some contemporaries thought that Newton and Locke, with their inductive approach, had ushered in genuinely new ways of viewing the world. Who could not be thrilled at the possibilities offered by the new insights and knowledge? Was it not now possible to map nature with simple laws, whereas before nature's ways had seemed so inscrutable and complex? Could not nature be charted with mathematics? Was not God himself a marvelous mathematician whose glory is only more greatly magnified when his laws of nature are quantified and confirmed by experiments?

A new age of intellectual discovery seemed to be dawning. And what an age it was! It witnessed a stunning advance in the global information available to scholars. Between 1630 and 1680 this information was multiplied by a great factor of five, but from 1680 to 1780 it was multiplied by another staggering factor of ten. This flood of information daunted scholars who had dared hope they could retain a total grasp of all there was to know. In one sense the so-called Enlightenment was an age of adjustment to an information revolution.

Isaac Newton.

LOC: LC-USZ62-95738

B. Isaac Newton: Christianity Compatible with Nature's "Laws"

Interestingly enough, Christian apologists sometimes turned to Newton's thought as supportive of their own beliefs. Isaac Newton (1642–1727) was an assiduous student of the Bible, particularly fascinated by biblical prophecy (especially the books of Daniel and Revelation) and biblical chronology. Newton also wrote about one million words devoted to alchemy. He secretly tried to discover the "philosopher's stone."

Henry More, a Cambridge Platonist, warned Newton about the potential dangers of Descartes's mechanistic philosophy. More appreciated the wisdom of the Ancients. Newton became fascinated by this "wisdom" as well. He apparently viewed his research as an attempt to revive and amplify the "ancient wisdom" (*prisca sapientia*) of the pre-Socratic Ionian Greeks, Pythagoreans, and Egyptian thinkers (the Hermetic tradition). He believed that certain Ancients had a pure understanding of philosophy, theology, and cosmology that in time had been corrupted.

Like many Christian *virtuosi*, the Cambridge professor believed that natural philosophy (science) and biblical revelation did not contradict each other, especially if one used a hermeneutical principle of accommodation in interpreting Scripture. In fact, Newton announced explicitly in the *Mathematical Principles of Natural Philosophy* (1687), in which the "law of gravity" or attraction is described, that one of his purposes was to defend the existence of God. To this great scientist, God must exist because Nature reveals such signs of a regular order that only a divine Architect could have created it.

A number of scientists and theologians such as Cambridge professor Richard Bentley used Newton's thought to defend God's existence in the Boyle Lectures series (1692–1732), named after the distinguished Christian natural philosopher Robert Boyle. The express purpose of the series was to "portray the Christian Religion, against notorious Infidels, viz. Atheists, Theists, Pagans, Jews and Mahomedans, not descending lower to any controversies, that are among Christians themselves." Newton's thought informed many of the lecturers as they defended natural theology and special revelation against the likes of Hobbes and other materialists and deists.

Moreover, in England as well as in the United Provinces and Germany, Christian apologists wrote *theologico-physico* books. They argued that nature not only reveals in its largest configuration God's design, but that the very intricacy of plants and the bodies of the smallest animals and insects display his designing craftsmanship as well. God's existence can be inferred from the "Frame of the Universe." John Ray's *The Wisdom of God manifested in the Works of Creation* (1691) represents well this kind of book. Therefore, Newton's work boosted the value of the "design argument" for God's existence in the thinking of many Christian apologists.

Striking a contrary note, English deists—with Voltaire soon to follow suit—claimed that Newton's thought bolstered their own anti-Christian and rational beliefs. They acknowledged that God does exist, the design argument seemingly providing irrefutable evidence to that effect. But their God was not the God of theism who providentially intervenes in this world. Rather, he was like a master watchmaker who made the world like a watch only to leave it to run on its own, following the laws of nature. And if nature's laws are inviolable, then the miracles that Christians cite in arguing for Christ's deity did not take place.

The meaning of Newton's legacy became something over which to battle. Scientists debated his sophisticated theories with various "Newtonianisms," or admixtures of Newton's thought, emerging in consequence.

These Newtonianisms penetrated European intellectual circles at different time frames and in different formats.

By contrast, a number of Christians and the *philosophes* disputed the meaning of Newton's scientific thought as it pertains to matters religious. Voltaire, for example, knew that Newton was a Christian, albeit with Arian proclivities, but enlisted the renowned scientist as a predecessor whose findings made his own Enlightenment opposition to the Christian faith credible.

Voltaire played a pivotal role in introducing Newton's thought to France. He published *Eléments de la philosophie de Newton* (1738), a work that challenged Cartesianism, the reigning scientific worldview in France as late as the 1730s. A Jesuit journal reflected on the remarkable impact of Voltaire's book in disseminating Newton's thought: "Newton, the great Newton was, it is said, buried in the abyss in the shop of the first publisher who dared to print him.... M. de Voltaire finally appeared, and at once Newton is understood or in the process of being understood; all Paris resounds with Newton, all Paris stammers Newton, all Paris studies and learns Newton."

Newton's empirical method, in which he described the natural world through inductive investigation backed by mathematical calculations, became a normative approach for many scientists, some of whom argued that no true knowledge of the world had existed until the great Newton began to describe the law of attraction.

Colin MacClaurin (1698–1746), an evangelical scientist-mathematician from Scotland, had a personal acquaintance with Newton. He may not have known of Newton's privately held anti-Trinitarian beliefs, for he argued that the greatest mathematicians of his day were, like Newton, Christians. For MacClaurin, one purpose of the Bible as a special revelation of God is to fill in the gaps in our understanding that natural revelation unpacked by experimental philosophy and mathematics simply cannot explain. Like Newton, MacClaurin did not separate special revelation (the Bible) from natural revelation.

C. Richard Simon and Biblical Criticism

But what if the Bible, a form of special revelation from God, were discovered to be fallible? Why should a "natural philosopher" or scientist feel constrained any longer to determine whether his scientific findings are in line with biblical teaching? The Oratorian priest Richard Simon's biblical criticism seemed to place into jeopardy this very doctrine, the infallibility of Holy Scripture.

Born in Dieppe, France, Simon (1638–1712) was trained by the Jesuits at Rouen before he became the librarian at the house of the Oratorian order in Paris on Rue Saint Honoré. The young Simon quickly became one of the leading biblical scholars in Paris. He proposed that students of the New Testament could understand it better if they were familiar with the institutions, ceremonies, and customs of the Jews. After all, the first Christians were Jews, and their customs and ceremonies constituted one of the essential backgrounds for the New Testament. In a number of writings the priest also revealed his vast knowledge of the beliefs and liturgies of the Eastern Christians.

In the mid-1670s Simon had secretly become involved with Jean Claude and Pierre Allix, the Huguenot pastors of Charenton (outside Paris), who had wanted him to help them create a new version of the Bible with notes to replace the Geneva Bible commonly used by the Reformed churches of France. The Protestant pastors also hoped that the new version would compete with a very popular Catholic Bible in the making by the Jansenist Le Maître de Sacy. Heartily disliking the Jansenists, Simon agreed to help the Protestants, but for an appropriate fee.

The Charenton Bible project, as it became known, fell apart when Swiss theologians who were cooperating with their French Huguenot colleagues in its funding and creation discovered that the French pastors had covertly enlisted Simon, a "Papist," to do their translating and commenting work for them and that they were going to buy his translation with notes outright.

In 1678 Simon published what became his most controversial study, *Histoire critique du Vieux Testament* (*A Critical History of the Old Testament*), in which he developed the famous "public scribes" hypothesis. In part he was responding to an earlier assertion made by Baruch Spinoza in *Tractatus Theologico-politicus* (1670) that Moses could not have written all the Pentateuch, given the account of Moses' own death, references to Moses in the third-person singular, and the like (issues that had been raised by the Jewish author Aben Ezra centuries earlier).

Spinoza's denial of Mosaic authorship provoked consternation among Christians in Europe who believed that Christ had indicated that Moses was the author of the Pentateuch. Spinoza was thus accused of attacking Christ's authority. Spinoza's *Tractatus* — smuggled into France under the cover of front pages disguised with false titles (such as "The Key to the Sanctuary"), false authors' names, and other misleading publishing information — made him a pariah for many orthodox Christians and Jews.

For his part, Simon proposed that so-called "public scribes" kept the archives of the republic of Israel. Guided by the Holy Spirit, these public scribes emended the writings of Moses, adding references in which the great leader was spoken of as "he," the third-person singular pronoun.

In this way Simon indicated that Moses was indeed the principal author of the Pentateuch, but that unknown public scribes had also contributed segments to its creation.

After reading a small portion of Simon's *Histoire critique*, Bossuet, the bishop of Meaux and tutor for the king's son, urged the government of Louis XIV to condemn the volume. In 1678 the licking flames of a governmental bonfire destroyed nearly all of the 1,300 books in the first edition. Members of the Oratorian house in Paris expelled Simon from the order the same year.

Simon has sometimes been hailed as the "father of biblical criticism." He claimed that he was the first scholar to apply the French word *critique* to the study of the Bible. He also indicated, quite immodestly, that he was the first scholar to understand how the Bible should be translated and commented on. Earlier commentators had attempted to justify the doctrinal stances of their own churches in their works. Simon indicated that he was going to take another approach, assuming the stance of "perfect neutrality"—that is, he would translate and comment with no partisanship for a particular Christian theology. The Hebrew and Greek words of Scripture alone would determine how he would translate. In the *Histoire critique*, the priest provided guidelines for this enterprise.

Simon acknowledged that St. Augustine had pursued a program of lower criticism—that is, the attempt to correct scribal errors in the copies of Scripture with the goal of restoring as much as possible the "lost originals," or the infallible original text of Scripture. He wrote,

> Is there then any person, whether Jew or Christian, who does not recognize that this Scripture, being the pure Word of God, is at the same time the first principle and foundation of Religion? But in that men were the depositories of the Sacred Books, as well as of all the other books, and that the first Originals have been lost, that it was in some regards impossible that several changes occurred, due as much to the length of the passage of time as to the negligence of copyists. It is for this reason Augustine recommends before all things to those who wish to study Scripture, to apply themselves to the Criticism of the Bible and to correct the errors in their copies.

In the *Histoire critique* Simon moved quickly beyond Augustine's position and defined criticism in another fashion. By arguing that unknown writers—the public scribes—wrote portions of the Old Testament, Simon helped shift the study of the Bible from what we often call "lower criticism" to "higher criticism."

Moreover, Simon claimed that the scribes only chose certain sample histories from the many that existed in Israel's archives to put in

Holy Scripture. These histories, packaged in abbreviated renditions, and sometimes not placed in correct chronological order, were selected due to their didactic value in instructing the people. Given the way the Bible was put together, Simon concluded that Scripture should not be viewed as presenting an infallible chronological history, setting forth the full history of Israel.

Protestants and Roman Catholics who had assumed that the Bible offered an infallible historical chronology were outraged by a number of Simon's claims. According to Simon, Roman Catholics need not draw skeptical implications from his approach to Scripture, because they could look to the Roman Catholic Church and to her Tradition to guarantee a proper understanding of "unclear" Scriptural passages created by the equivocal meanings of certain Hebrew or Greek words. Protestants, by contrast, did not have any sure means with which to restore the "lost originals" of Scripture or to know which translations or interpretations most closely approximated the Bible's "original" texts.

Simon also spelled out his proposals in a number of other huge tomes. From 1678 until his death in 1712, the priest fought numerous battles attempting to defend his own orthodoxy. Among his most prominent critics were the Catholic bishop Bossuet and the Protestants Bentley and Edward Stillingfleet.

Then again, between the years 1685 and 1687, the Arminian man of letters Jean Leclerc dueled with Simon in one of the most closely watched struggles of the age over the Bible's authority. The back-and-forth exchange ran through five books (two volumes by Leclerc and three by Simon). Leclerc charged that little or no evidence supported the existence of public scribes in Israel's history in the way Simon described them.

But Leclerc in turn took more radical positions than Simon, denying the Mosaic authorship of the Pentateuch outright. He claimed that an unknown person after the return of the Jews from the Babylonian captivity had been the ultimate compiler of portions of the Old Testament. Moreover, he claimed that the only inspired portions of the Bible were Jesus' own words and a few other statements made by prophets, and that the Bible only had to be historically accurate for it to serve as a worthy basis for the Christian faith. It did not need to be inspired by the Holy Spirit in all its parts.

Simon was enraged by Leclerc's attack.

Both Simon and Leclerc denied the infallibility of the Bible, and they did so in French, whereas Latin had traditionally been employed for theological debate in order to shelter laypeople from theological controversies. Following their battle closely, Locke, Newton, Bayle, and a host of other leading intellectuals throughout Europe were challenged to rethink their commitment to this doctrine. Voltaire and the encyclopedists Diderot and d'Alembert looked back on this bitter exchange as a decisive encounter in which the traditional doctrine of the Bible's infallibility and authority lost much of its credibility for many intellectuals.

For their part, many orthodox English, French, German, and Dutch theologians of the late seventeenth and early eighteenth centuries portrayed Simon and Leclerc as dangerous heretics, placing them in the ranks of the feared arch-heretics Hobbes and Spinoza. But by the mid-eighteenth century, German theologians such as Johann S. Semler and Johann David Michaelis no longer excoriated Simon and Leclerc. Instead, they hailed Simon as the "father of biblical criticism" and a precursor to the kinds of biblical critical studies ("higher criticism") they themselves were beginning to pursue, especially after 1750.

D. John Locke and a "New" View of Human Nature

The much admired John Locke (1632–1704) did not lack for talent. He did serious work as a physician, an educator, an economist, a politician, a theologian, and of course as a philosopher. Locke was born into a Puritan home at Somerset village, England. He was schooled at Christ Church College, Oxford, where he heard John Owen, the school's dean, preach regularly. Although a Puritan, Owen was a defender of religious toleration. Locke studied theology, philosophy, and medicine.

Although praising Descartes for having delivered him "from the unintelligible way of talking of the philosophy in use in the schools in his time," Locke reacted strongly to his concept of innate ideas and the assumption that a rationalistic deductive approach based in mathematics is the best way to gain knowledge. He became particularly appreciative of the writings of the philosopher Pierre Gassendi (1592–1655), who had criticized Descartes and affirmed that "every idea which exists in the mind originates in the senses."

After a teaching stint at Oxford, in 1666 Locke met Lord Ashley, who the next year asked Locke to become his personal physician. In 1668 Locke performed an operation on Lord Ashley which probably saved his life. Ashley became the First Earl of Shaftesbury and a very powerful personage in the court of Charles II. When Shaftesbury (in the so-called "Exclusion Controversy") became embroiled in efforts to persuade Charles II to deny the throne to James II, his Roman Catholic brother, and earned several rounds of exile, his close associate Locke became a suspect, a co-conspirator of sorts.

During a stay in France from 1675 to 1679, Locke apparently worked on his *Two Treatises on Government*. He returned to England, only to flee again to the United Provinces in 1683, where he lived while hiding his identity under the false name "Dr. van der Linden." He became well acquainted with Leclerc, who years later published the first segment of Locke's *Essay on Human Understanding* in his French journal. Locke also appreciated the work of Newton, Boyle, and Huygenius (Dutch physicist Christiaan Huygens) in science and of Richard Simon in biblical criticism. Boyle's *The Origins of Forms and Qualities* (1666) informed much of his thinking about primary and secondary qualities.

After the Glorious Revolution of 1689, in which James II was replaced by the Protestant William of Orange, Locke returned to England. In 1690 he published his *Second Treatise on Government*, in which he continued his attack on Sir Robert Filmer's divine right views of kingship. This work laid down reasons why it is legitimate for people to overthrow a divine right monarch if that monarch violates his covenant to care for his people as a loving father. The king was in this instance the guilty party who broke a covenantal relationship, not the people who attempted to overthrow him. The book appeared to justify the Glorious Revolution, even if portions of the volume had been written before the revolution took place. It had significant influence on the thinking of American revolutionaries regarding a doctrine of limited government, the right of revolution, and property as a natural right.

In the same year, Locke also set forth his own "sensationalist" approach to epistemology in *The Essay on Human Understanding*, a work highly esteemed and meditated on by the *philosophes*. As Bacon and Newton created an experimental philosophy (science) for the study of nature, Locke attempted to create an experimental science for the study of the mind.

In that work Locke proposed that his goals were (1) "To inquire into the original, certainty, and extent of *human understanding*"; and (2) to determine "the grounds and degrees of *belief, opinion and assent.*" He attacked Descartes's principle of innate ideas and the distinction between *a priori* knowledge and empirical belief. Indeed, Descartes had written that an infant in its mother's womb "has in itself the ideas of God, itself, and all truths which are said to be self-evident."

For his part, Locke tried to demonstrate the weaknesses of this position, alleging that children do not suddenly lose the innate knowledge with which they were born, nor do idiots possess innate ideas, nor is there a consensual set of moral standards shared by people throughout the world. He proposed, therefore, that all our ideas, whether simple or compound, come from experience. In turn, our knowledge comes from our ideas, direct products of the external world, or from our reflection on the ideas we have received from the external world. God guarantees that our ideas of the external world correspond to the world as it is. The mind itself is a blank slate, or *tabula rasa*, on which ideas of the external world are impressed.

Despite beguilingly lucid prose, Locke's presentation of his understanding of epistemology is not always easy to follow. For one thing, he uses the pivotal word *idea*, the "object of our understanding," in a number of different ways. Moreover, his thought resembled that of Descartes more than contemporaries sometimes recognized.

In fact, Voltaire viewed Locke as an anti-Cartesian for "demolishing the notion of innate ideas." Voltaire thought Locke especially bold in indicating that "We shall never be able to determine, whether a being, purely material, is capable of thought or not." This statement of Locke appeared to open the door to materialistic perspectives.

Locke's epistemology, in which the premise of innate ideas was denied, seemed to imply not only that Descartes was in error but that the orthodox Christian view of man was deeply flawed as well. Did not Christians affirm that man has a sinful nature at birth? Locke's stance appeared to suggest by contrast that we are morally neutral at birth and that our natures are shaped ultimately by our experience and environment. We are not bound to sin due to a sinful nature inherited from Adam.

Those who read Locke in this fashion believed that the English philosopher had overthrown the Christian doctrine of original sin with its needlessly pessimistic teachings about our sinful nature. By contrast, for many partisans of the Enlightenment, Locke had rehabilitated human nature and given hope that we humans can progress morally and be more successful in our pursuit of happiness. It was not much of a jump to propose that if you can change a person's environment, you can change the very core of the personality of the individual. For the *philosophes*, Locke had opened up the possibilities of genuine "enlightenment."

How the *philosophes* read Locke and how Locke wanted to be read were not necessarily one and the same. Locke viewed himself as a Protestant Christian, and like many of his English Protestant contemporaries, he was worried about the advances of Roman Catholicism in England and on the Continent.

In writing to his friend Philipp van Limborch, a Dutch Arminian theologian, in 1695, Locke made it clear that he wanted Scripture to be the basis of his theology.

Locke's view that Christianity is reasonable contradicted one of the standard assumptions of deists and later *philosophes* that the Christian faith could not withstand reason's scrutiny. At the same time, the actual content of his reasonable Christianity included relatively few fundamental beliefs when compared to the principal creeds of Christendom. To be saved, we only need to believe that Christ is the Messiah and obey his teachings. In his paraphrases of St. Paul's epistles, Locke indicated that God will punish those who do not obey Christ's law.

Locke's commitment to a rational Christianity appears sincere. On one occasion he mused that he should have worked in biblical studies rather than write about philosophy. He did not believe that his teachings regarding epistemology, substance, and human nature impugned the truth claims of the Christian faith. Has not God given us reason by which we can determine what is good and what is evil? Is it not proper to accept the authority of the Bible because there is reasonable evidence that it is a revelation from God? As a revelation from God, does not the Bible tell us humans about our duties to obey God's law? Did not the Messianic prophecies in the Old Testament fulfilled in Christ's life and the miracles he performed prove in a reasonable fashion that he is the Messiah?

In 1695 Locke summed up his religious convictions in *The Reasonableness of Christianity as delivered in the Scriptures*, the title of the book underscoring the central role reason played in his formulation of Christianity. Several orthodox critics complained that Locke had denied basic doctrines of the Christian faith, including the substitutionary atonement of Christ and orthodox anthropology. It was especially troubling that Locke would not affirm in a categorical way that he believed in the Trinity. Nor was his reputation for orthodoxy enhanced by his friendship with the deists John Toland and Anthony Collins, who sometimes referred to his thought as stimulating their own. Was it simply a coincidence that a new surge of deistic writings appeared after 1695, as if prompted by the publication of Locke's book?

Whatever might have been the apparent incongruities and contradictions in Locke's religious beliefs, the great philosopher gave a boost to a reasonable, tolerant form of Protestant Christianity—one especially well-suited to an Age of Reason. Locke appeared short on a list of doctrinal essentials Christians needed to affirm. He appeared long in confidence in reason's capacity to guide us in our moral lives, on the grounds that it was unaffected by the Fall. We need Christian Scripture to give us a more thorough and divine perspective. And he indicated that some of the teachings of Scripture are "above reason" but not "contrary to reason."

In approaching death, Locke wondered if a book he had written on miracles "may be of use to the Christian religion" and affirmed his belief in the resurrection of the just. On October 28, 1704, the great John Locke passed away.

"I have lived long enough, and I thank God I have enjoyed a happy life; but after all this life is nothing but vanity" (John Locke).

E. Pierre Bayle: Christianity and Skepticism

The Huguenot Pierre Bayle (1647–1706), a prodigious intellect, was another writer whose works the *philosophes* ransacked for arguments.

Born into the home of a Reformed pastor in southern France, Bayle studied for the ministry at the Reformed Academy of Sedan. By the early 1680s it was clear to many Huguenots that Louis XIV was determined to extirpate the Reformed faith from France. In 1681 Bayle left France, seeking exile in Rotterdam, the United Provinces.

During 1684–87 Bayle served as the influential editor of the journal *News of the Republic of Letters*. As far back as the fifteenth century, scholars had spoken about a *respublica litteraria*, a community of scholars in Europe who shared similar humanist aspirations. Bayle's book reviews in the journal provided him with an arbiter's role in assessing the literary, historical, and theological works that circulated in this international and non-confessional community of scholars.

In *Pensées sur la Comète de 1680*, Bayle seemed to separate morality from religion by attacking the authority of tradition and indicating atheists could create a moral society. In *Commentaire philosophique* (1686), he argued for freedom of conscience in matters religious.

When in 1685 his Huguenot brother died in a prison in France, Bayle apparently experienced a spiritual crisis. He wrestled with the problem of evil and became an even more ardent apologist for religious toleration.

Bayle's most important work is the *Historical and Critical Dictionary* (1697). Four thick volumes in folio, it contains hundreds of articles, a number of which, if read a certain way, seem to subvert the Christian faith. In one article Bayle argued against the widely held belief that atheists are incapable of forming a moral society. Bayle proposed that they in fact can. Not only did Pastor Pierre Jurieu, an old foe, excoriate Bayle, but other Reformed pastors also pressed charges against him.

The *Dictionary* represents a work of incredible brilliance. Its author had the mental acumen to cross-reference articles in volumes not yet written. It became one of the most popular sets of the eighteenth century, found in numerous personal libraries throughout Europe. Bayle's admirers included not only Voltaire and other *philosophes*, but a good number of Christians such as the German Moravian Count von Zinzendorf and the French Protestant Antoine Court. The *Dictionary* also became a model of sorts for the *Encyclopédie* edited by Diderot and d'Alembert.

Bayle's *Dictionary*, with its labyrinth of cross-referenced notes tightly packed under various article headings, afforded the *philosophes* an arsenal of arguments to use against the Christian faith and especially against the Roman Catholic Church. The *philosophes* thought that Bayle had provided them with a marvelous strategy for sowing skeptical thought without risk: State a thesis that on its own is orthodox but whose import becomes heterodox when cross-referenced to and juxtaposed beside another thesis.

Historian Elisabeth Labrousse argues that Bayle's position regarding the grounds for establishing the truth claims of the Christian religion stems from his Reformed theology, not from doubts that he entertained about Christianity's basic veracity. She portrays Bayle as a sincere Calvinist—admittedly of a more liberal stripe—who thought that Christians obtain the conviction that their religion is true through the work of the Holy Spirit, not through rational deductions demonstrating its validity. Labrousse's interpretation of Bayle appears persuasive. It counters decisively Paul Hazard's portrait of the exiled Huguenot as an archskeptic.

Other scholars such as Jonathan Israel argue that Bayle was an agnostic or an atheist. Whatever the case, the *philosophes* borrowed from this great thinker of the late seventeenth century, reworked his ideas, and used them for anti-Christian purposes apparently not anticipated by the author.

The *philosophes* acknowledged that Newton, Simon, Locke, and Bayle portrayed themselves as Christians. But this awareness did not hinder the *philosophes* from drawing out anti-Christian entailments from the thought of each scholar. The *philosophes*, after all, were propagandists and pamphleteers. Whatever argument would advance the *Siècle des lumières*, the Age of Lights, they were prepared to commandeer.

III. THE "ENLIGHTENMENT": THE FRENCH *PHILOSOPHES*

A number of the most celebrated *philosophes* of the eighteenth century were raised in a French culture, residing either in the Kingdom of France or the Republic of Geneva. They ranged from deists such as Voltaire and Rousseau to atheists such as Diderot, Baron d'Holbach, and La Mettrie. They included both monarchists such as Voltaire and Baron de Montesquieu and republicans such as Rousseau. Until the publication of Montesquieu's *Spirit of the Laws* (1748), so fearful were the *philosophes* of doing jail time that they often disseminated their writings of a seditious character in the form of handwritten manuscripts passed hand to hand. Or they published pieces such as Montesquieu's *Persian Letters* (1721), allegedly written by Usbek and Rica, Persian visitors to Paris—a book in which the political, religious, and social institutions of France were satirized. Readers had to infer from their utopian stories and exotic tales what the hidden criticism of these institutions might have been.

But in the second half of the eighteenth century, the *philosophes* came out from the shadows and strutted across center stage in French society. They published their works openly. By this time, they had friends in high places, such as Guillaume-Chrétien de Lamoignon de Malesherbes, who would protect their interests and could sometimes even help them to obtain privileges for their books from the king's Bureau of the Library.

A. Baron de Montesquieu

Whereas Newton had attempted to discover the laws of nature, Charles-Louis de Secondat, Baron de Montesquieu (1689–1755), a powerful politician and *noble de robe* from Bordeaux, tried to discern the "laws" that govern human relations. In one sense, *De l'esprit des lois* (*The Spirit of Laws*) is a sophisticated early work of sociology. In the huge volume, Montesquieu musters factors such as "climate, religion, laws, maxims of government, the example of things past, habits, manners" to explain what the "general spirit" of a society is and how the society functions. He wrote, "In this sense all beings have their laws, the material world its laws, the intelligences superior to man their laws, the beasts their laws, man his laws" (Book I.1.1).

The work is studded with many fascinating correlations. Montesquieu, for example, asserted that monarchies thrived better in Catholic lands, whereas republics generally fared better in Protestant lands. He proffered compelling reasons that the separation of powers is necessary in a government. If the executive branch of government also controls the legislative and judicial branches, then the people will have no protection against an executive who makes tyrannical laws and enforces them with his own police. Montesquieu himself was no revolutionary; he favored a constitutional monarchy. He did not think that his calm and rational explanation of the "laws" governing human relations needed Christian warrant to give them persuasive force.

Montesquieu was well aware of the fact that he could not identify all the factors that drive human relations. Nor could he explain satisfactorily how personal freedom can survive, faced by the overwhelming influence of blind "laws." His approach possessed a materialistic and secular orientation, and his God appeared somewhat impersonal.

B. Voltaire and Jean-Jacques Rousseau: Civilization versus Nature

The witty, irrepressible, and often sacrilegious Voltaire was the most famous of the *philosophes.* A remarkable letter writer, poet, dramatist, historian, and social commentator, Voltaire stood out as one of most prolific writers of his age. Fifteen million words are credited to his literary output. If there were a shepherd of the "little flock" of *philosophes*, it was the virulent, wily, and anti-Christian Voltaire.

Voltaire (François-Marie Arouet).

Born in November 1694, François-Marie Arouet attended the Jesuit college Louis-Le Grand (1704–10), where he encountered teachers with deistic leanings. As an adolescent, he became troubled by the problem of evil. By 1716 he was already engaged in doing biblical criticism. The next year he was incarcerated in the Bastille for one of his writings. In 1718, in full reaction against his father, young Arouet changed his name to Voltaire. He also revolted against the God of his Jansenist brother Armand.

After a second stay in the Bastille, Voltaire traveled to England in 1725. He was quite taken by England, where "the people think freely and nobly" and "Reason is free." The English even practiced religious tolerance, something unknown in France. The stay in England, plus a growing familiarity with the writings of the great English scholars Newton and Locke, gave Voltaire ample ammunition for writing a book that is sometimes described as the first bomb thrown at the institutions of the *Ancien régime* ("Old Order"). It was published in England as *The English Letters* in 1733 and in France as the *Lettres philosophiques* the next year.

In this work Voltaire elevated English society before the French people as an attractive alternative model of what a society could be. He extolled the likes of the Englishmen Locke and Newton and attacked the metaphysics of his fellow countrymen Nicholas Malebranche and Descartes.

In addition, Voltaire dared criticize Blaise Pascal, the "sublime misanthrope," whose view of man the *philosophe* believed had to be overthrown. In *Pensées* (*Thoughts*) Pascal had written that man "is nothing but a subject full of natural error that cannot be eradicated except through grace. Nothing shows him the truth, everything deceives him. The two principles of truth, reason and the senses, are not only both not genuine, but both are engaged in mutual deception." Voltaire also attacked Pascal's wager argument. He viewed Pascal as a formidable Christian opponent. One of the very last books Voltaire published was titled *Remarks on Pascal*.

Man "is nothing but a subject full of natural error that cannot be eradicated except through grace" (Blaise Pascal, *Pensées*).

From 1744 to 1747 Voltaire resided at the court of Louis XV at Versailles, where he happened to irritate the king's mistress, Madame de Pompadour. Fleeing the court, Voltaire traveled throughout Europe and spent time with his mistress, Madame du Chatelet, a brilliant coworker and mathematician (d. 1749) and at the court of Frederick II, a visit (1750–53) that ended unhappily when the king favored another *philosophe*, Pierre Louis Maupertuis, over Voltaire.

By late 1754, as a fatigued European traveler, Voltaire arrived in Geneva, where he hoped to woo the Reformed Christians to his form of deism. Residing in a stately manor, he entertained the leading Calvinists of Geneva, including members of the clergy and seminary students, with sumptuous feasts, music, and plays. He believed he had found potential disciples in Jacob Vernes and Jacob Vernet, two of Geneva's principal pastors, but he was to be sorely disappointed, not only by the actions of these Reformed pastors, but also by the arguments of another of Geneva's own, the remarkably gifted and troubled writer Jean-Jacques Rousseau.

Rousseau was born in 1712 into a Protestant home in Geneva. His mother was the daughter of a pastor. Rousseau recounts his life in graphic detail in *Confessions*, an autobiography that reads like a well-crafted, tell-all novel. He believed misfortune had stalked him from his very birth: "I was born, a poor, sickly child, and cost my mother her life. So my birth was the first of my misfortunes."

Jean-Jacques Rousseau.

As an adolescent of sixteen, Rousseau was locked out of Geneva's city walls one late afternoon when the city gates closed. Fearing a beating from his employer, he fled south first to Confignan in Savoy, where a priest told him to go to Annecy to meet a woman named Madame de Warens, a convert to Catholicism. After meeting the young Rousseau, Madame de Warens sent him on his way even farther south to Turin, Italy, where on April 12, 1728, he too converted to Roman Catholicism. Thereafter Rousseau lived off and on with Madame de Warens, whom he affectionately called "Maman." He also worked as a preceptor, or personal teacher, in Lyon.

In 1742 Rousseau made his way to Paris, thinking that he could win fame through a new system of notations for music. Prone to exploit women sexually, such as Thérèse Le Vasseur, who became the mother of his children, Rousseau also counted on contacts with influential women to help insinuate himself into high society. In Paris he met a number of the *philosophes*. On occasion, he played checkers with Diderot in the parks. In 1743 Rousseau served as an assistant for the French ambassador to Venice. After a falling out with the ambassador, a petulant Rousseau returned to Paris. He was also fearful that he had contracted a disease from one of his encounters with women of ill-repute in Venice.

In 1749 Rousseau had an experience that would change the direction of his life and in one sense redirect the intellectual history of France in the eighteenth century. He decided to visit his friend Diderot, one of the editors of the *Encyclopédie*, who was jailed in Vincennes, a prison not far from Paris. Diderot had written a piece that earned for him this brief prison stay.

At the prison Diderot encouraged Rousseau to give his "ideas wings and compete for the prize." As Rousseau put it, "I did so and from that moment I was lost. All the rest of my life and of my misfortunes followed inevitably as a result of that moment's madness." In a prize-winning essay, "Discourse on the Sciences and the Arts," in 1750, Rousseau argued that humans are born good since they come from the hands of God; it is their encounter with civilization that corrupts them and steals away their primitive happiness. In consequence, the closer we can emulate the state of nature, the happier we will be.

In attempting to return to nature, Rousseau took definite and dramatic steps: "I began my reformation with my dress; I gave up gold lace and white stockings, and wore a round wig. I gave up my sword and sold my watch, saying to myself with unbelievable delight: 'Heaven be praised, I shall not need to know the time anymore.'"

Rousseau's advocacy of a return to nature won him a rather large following in Paris, but it also provoked a series of refutations and alienated him from the encyclopedists and Voltaire. Earlier in his writing career, Voltaire had written *Le mondain* (*The Man of the World*, 1736), in which he reveled in the joys of luxury and identified the progress of humankind with the advance of civilization. Now Rousseau seemed to be working directly at cross-purposes, raising suspicions about the value of the arts and sciences. When Rousseau asked Voltaire for an assessment of his essay, the *philosophe* responded with more than a touch of sarcasm. Voltaire indicated that, due to his age, he could no longer return to nature by getting down on all fours like an animal. Nor would he be able to return to nature by embarking on a trip to Canada in order to live with the savages there.

Rousseau was grievously wounded by Voltaire's jocular but hurtful reply. Mindful of certain criticisms, Rousseau let his readers know that he had no intention of torching libraries.

In a second essay, "On the Origins of Inequality" (1755), Rousseau once again argued that primitive humans had originally been innocent and happy in a state of nature. Then along came the person, the true founder of society, who ruined everything: "The first man who, having enclosed a piece of land, thought of saying 'This is mine' and found people simple enough to believe him was the true founder of civil society. How many crimes, wars, murder; how much misery and horror the human race would have been spared if someone had pulled up the stakes and filled in the ditch...."

Rousseau explained the origins of evil within society through imaginative historical reconstructions of this kind. Despite professing great respect for the Bible, Rousseau was quite ready to neglect what the book of Genesis taught about the creation of Adam and Eve and the Fall.

In 1754 Rousseau successfully applied for citizenship in Geneva, converting to Protestantism in the process. He wrote,

> My association with the Encyclopaedists, far from shaking my faith, had strengthened it because of my natural aversion for quarreling and for parties. My study of man and the Universe had shown me everywhere final causes and the intelligence which directed them. My reading of the Bible, particularly of the Gospels, to which I had applied myself for some years, had led me to despise the base and foolish interpretations given to the words of Jesus Christ.

During a stay in Paris, Rousseau learned that Geneva was soon to have a new neighbor, living just outside the city—none other than Voltaire. In despair, Rousseau decided not to return to the city. Eventually he would write to Voltaire, "Sir, I hate you."

In one sense Rousseau became the arch-heretic of the "philosophic" movement and a herald of Romanticism. Whereas Voltaire had great confidence in reason's powers, Rousseau proposed that besides reason we should rely on our "interior sentiments," or conscience. Our conscience will guide us infallibly in our moral decision. Whereas Voltaire believed that plays and the theater were valuable, Rousseau argued in his letter to d'Alembert on the spectacles that they corrupted audiences who were drawn into an artificial immoral world, far removed from what is natural and good. He described acting as "the art of assuming a personality which is not one's own, of simulating passions one does not feel, saying things ones does not believe."

Whereas Voltaire denied that God intervenes providentially in the world, Rousseau argued that in fact God does intervene. Rousseau claimed that Voltaire did not really believe in God: "Though Voltaire has always appeared to believe in God, he only believed in the Devil, because his so-called God is nothing but a malicious being who, according to his belief, only takes pleasure in doing harm" (*Confessions*, Book Nine).

As for providence, Rousseau exclaimed to Voltaire, "I have suffered too much in this life not to look forward to another. Not all the subtleties of metaphysics can shake for one moment my belief in the immortality of the soul and a beneficent Providence. I sense the existence of Providence. I believe in it, I insist on it, I hope for it, I shall defend it to my last breath."

In 1757 Diderot and d'Alembert published volume 7 of their *Encylopédie*, which contained entries for the letter "G." D'Alembert had written the article on "Genève" (Geneva). Relying on information that he had apparently received from Voltaire, he described the Reformed pastors of Geneva as "perfect Socinians," the followers of the natural religion of John Locke. Pastors Vernes and Vernet reacted in horror at this characterization of their beliefs. They turned in anger on Voltaire, whom they assumed had furnished d'Alembert with this perspective on the Genevan clergy.

In genuine disgust, Voltaire decided to leave Geneva and moved across the border to Ferney in France. The *philosophe* now believed that even the more liberal followers of the Christian religion would not forsake their faith commitments when pressed, and he regarded them as hypocrites.

As for d'Alembert, so concerned was he about the negative fallout from the article "Genève" that he resigned the editorship of the *Encyclopédie* in January 1758. In resigning, however, he protested lamely that the article had nothing to do with his decision. In any case, Diderot had to carry on by himself as the sole editor.

The vexing relations with Vernes and Vernet apparently contributed to Voltaire's mounting hostility toward Christianity, particularly as represented by the Roman Catholic Church. In 1759 Voltaire launched his most virulent war cry: *"Ecrasez l'Infâme"* ("Crush the infamous thing"—that is, Christianity). His anti-Christian writings were voluminous, ranging from *An Important Study by Lord Bolingbroke, or The Fall of Fanaticism* (1736) to *The Philosophical Dictionary* (614 articles; 1764). Voltaire mocked the orthodox understanding of the incarnation, that Christ was God in the flesh. He professed being offended by the claim that Christ had to shed his blood to bring about the redemption of sinners. He railed at the Roman Catholic Church for its intolerance, particularly toward French Protestants; he scoffed at the Doctors of the Church for their battles over theological inanities. While professing respect for Jesus Christ and "our holy Christian faith," he let it be known in satirical and jocular prose and poetry that he was no Christian.

At the same time, Voltaire was no great optimist about the human condition. In his masterpiece *Candide*, the *philosophe* struck out at Gottfried Leibnitz's proposition that this is the best of all possible worlds and at Rousseau's naïvete that nature is beneficent. Troubled by the great tragedy of the Lisbon earthquake in 1755, in which some 20,000 people perished, Voltaire argued that given nature's blindness to our welfare and the general vicissitudes of life as represented in the horrendous experiences of the naïve but good-hearted Candide, we would be wise to cultivate our own gardens, that is, do the best we can do with matters at hand.

Realizing that all might not end well whatever one did, Voltaire nonetheless opted for action when confronted by injustice. In 1762 the Calas case grabbed his attention and provided him with an opportunity to act. Jean Calas, a Huguenot from Toulouse, France, was put to death on the wheel for having allegedly murdered his son Marc-Antoine the year before. The motive for the crime was purportedly this: Marc-Antoine had wanted to convert to Roman Catholicism. He needed to do so in order to gain a certificate that would permit him to become a lawyer. To avoid this abjuration, the father and family members conspired to murder the errant son by hanging him.

When Voltaire first learned about the case, he did not know whether to feel more incensed by the intemperate zeal of the Huguenots or by the judicial injustice of the *Parlement* of Toulouse, inflamed by Roman Catholic prejudice. Once convinced that Jean Calas and other family members were innocent of the crime, Voltaire launched a three-year campaign to exculpate the Calas family name. In 1765 his efforts were finally rewarded when a higher court reversed the decision of the *Parlement* of Toulouse. Voltaire's reputation as a righter of wrongs grew dramatically throughout Europe. Here was a fearless battler, a reformer who was an anti-Christian, but who did the right thing in seeking justice and promoting toleration.

"One good deed is worth a hundred doctrines" (Voltaire).

In 1763 Voltaire published the *Traité sur la tolerance* (*Treaty on Toleration*). His generous actions on behalf of the Calas family and other Protestants seemed to demonstrate that *la philosophie*, anti-Christian though it was, had practical value.

When Voltaire came to Paris in 1778 to see his play *Irène* mounted on the stage of the *Comédie française*, he was cheered by crowds in the streets as the "Calas-man," the person who had saved the Calas family's good name.

Though not a Christian, Voltaire did profess to believe in God. In fact, his professions of worship of this God were on occasion quite lyrical. But the nature of his exact beliefs have been much debated, some scholars arguing that he was a deist, others a theist, and some even a mystic. The confusion is caused in part by the fact that Voltaire on occasion used the words *deist* and *theist* interchangeably. Then again, thinking that a belief in "God" helped keep the "people" in line, Voltaire wrote in 1770, "For the rest, I think that it is always a very good thing to maintain the doctrine of the existence of a god. Society needs this opinion." He then repeated an earlier remark that still retains a certain shock value: "If God did not exist, he would have to be invented."

When the *philosophe* was approaching death, he seemed to moderate his attitude toward Christianity. Voltaire declared on February 28, 1778, "I die worshiping God, loving my friends, not hating my enemies, detesting superstition." He hoped to receive a proper burial as only Christians could receive, others having their bodies thrown into a refuse heap with vagrants. Perhaps this desire explains Voltaire's confession to a priest two days later: "I die in the holy Catholic religion in which I was born, hoping from the divine mercy that it will deign to pardon all my faults, and that if I have ever caused scandal to the church I ask pardon for that from God and the Church." There was no mention of Christ in this confession.

On May 30 Voltaire, the most famous *philosophe* and long-standing enemy of the Christian faith, died. During the French Revolution, his bodily remains were taken to Paris and placed in the Pantheon.

As for Jean-Jacques Rousseau, after his break with Voltaire he proceeded to have a falling out with a number of other *philosophes*, including Diderot and later David Hume. In the 1760s Rousseau's own fame or notoriety continued to mount due to a series of remarkable publications, even as he seemed personally to retreat into a state of mental unbalance.

In 1761 Rousseau published *La Nouvelle Héloïse*, a heartrending novel in which Julie the heroine and St. Preux discuss religious sentiments at length. In a touching scene, Julie declares, "I have lived and I die in the Protestant communion, which draws its unique rule in Holy Scripture and in reason."

The next year Rousseau published *Emile*, an educational guide indicating how a young boy, Emile, and a young girl, Sophie, should be raised. Rousseau wanted them to be nurtured according to the principles of nature and to be sheltered from the nefarious effects of civilization. Little matter that Rousseau himself had abandoned his own children to an orphanage; he could still write, "The family is the first and most holy institution of nature."

Rousseau professed great respect for Jesus Christ: "If the life and death of Socrates are those of a philosopher, the life and death of Christ are those of a God." Yet, in many regards his ultimate authority was not Christ, but himself, Jean-Jacques Rousseau. Theologically, Rousseau was an outright Pelagian. In the first lines of *Confessions*, Rousseau let it be known that he, despite his painful moral failures, was the best person who had ever lived.

In 1762 Rousseau published *The Social Contract*, a work in which he unpacked a compact theory of government and described his concept of a "general will." According to Rousseau, people cannot really be free unless they are free to make their own laws within the context of the general will. Rousseau's writings exercised a profound influence on the thinking of a number of radical leaders of the French Revolution, including Maximilien Robespierre.

Rousseau also argued that any society should have a "civil religion" to help bind its populace together. The tenets of this civil religion were fourfold: (1) God exists and rewards good deeds; (2) God punishes evil deeds; (3) there should be tolerance for all religions; and (4) a natural religion underlies all religions. Like Voltaire and a number of other *philosophes*, Rousseau had a difficult time envisaging a society in which the "people" are not restrained by the fear that God would punish their evil deeds. Apparently Bayle's thesis that atheists could create a moral society had not convinced Rousseau.

The publication of *The Social Contract* and *Emile* caused an uproar and provoked warrants for Rousseau's arrest and orders for the public burning of these books. Rousseau believed his list of enemies had dramatically expanded. In 1768 he named his enemies, including among others the *philosophes* and especially Voltaire: "The *philosophes*, whom I have unmasked, seek at all costs to ruin me, and will succeed in so doing; writers plagiarize me and accuse me; scoundrels chase me; the rabble boo me . . .; Voltaire, who is jealous of me, will parody these lines. His coarse insults are the tribute he is obliged to pay me against his will."

In general, Rousseau's last years were unhappy ones. He felt alone, betrayed by his former *philosophic* friends. He sensed that he was being tracked by foes both imaginary and real. Upon hearing of Voltaire's death on May 30, 1778, he commented, "My existence was linked to his; now that he is dead, I shall not be long in following him." Rousseau was right. On July 2 he died, with Thérèse Le Vasseur at his side. Like Voltaire, his earthly remains were transferred to the Pantheon during the French Revolution.

Rousseau's views of conscience greatly influenced Immanuel Kant's conception of a "categorical imperative" and Robespierre's view of the nature of society's "general will." In the nineteenth century, thinkers from diverse political persuasions, including Marxists, cited him as an authority.

C. Denis Diderot and the Philosophic Atheists

Denis Diderot (1713–84), erstwhile friend of Rousseau, was quite simply an intellectual genius. His fields of expertise ranged from art criticism to philosophy of science, chemistry, and various forms of technology.

Born in Langres, France, Diderot was trained by the Jesuits. On August 22, 1726, he was tonsured and became an *abbé*. He may have experienced a falling out with the Jesuits before he left Langres for Paris in 1728 or 1729 to gain further education. Whatever the reason, Diderot as a young man turned against the Christian faith. His view of God was very negative. In his *Pensées philosophiques* (*Philosophical Thoughts*, 1746), Diderot wrote, "The thought that there is not a god has never frightened anyone, but rather the thought that there is one, such as the one that has been described to me" (Thought 10).

In 1747 he was denounced to the police in Paris as "a very dangerous man who speaks of the holy mysteries of our religion with contempt." In that same year he began work in serious fashion on the *Encyclopédie*.

As editor of the *Encyclopédie*, Diderot kept at his Herculean task despite huge obstacles. They included energy-sapping troubles with his publisher, Le Bréton; the departure of his coeditor, d'Alembert; the suppression of the privilege (1759) to print the *Encylopédie* due to ecclesiastical pressure exercised on the government; and the rigors of preparing tomes in an "underground" shop without knowing if they would ever see the light of day. Finally Diderot was able to resume publication of the *Encyclopédie* in 1765, with the release of the remaining volumes occurring in 1772.

In sum, the seventeen volumes of text and eleven volumes of drawings and millions of words represent one of the great publishing achievements of the eighteenth century. More than 220 writers—including priests, pastors, theologians, *philosophes*, and scientists, ranging from obscure hacks to noted luminaries such as Voltaire and Rousseau—contributed thousands of articles to this massive set of volumes. Diderot wrote scores of articles himself, but his associate, the Protestant Chevalier de Jaucourt (1704–80), actually penned 4,700,000 words in 17,050 articles, or 28 percent of the articles of the *Encyclopédie*.

In the *Discours Preliminaire* (*Preliminary Discourse*), d'Alembert set forth the two principal goals of the *Encyclopédie:* (1) To show the order and relationships that exist in fields of human knowledge; (2) to propose the general principles upon which each science and each art, liberal or mechanical, are based. The *Encyclopédie* provided readers with information on the latest technology and scientific advances. Scores of drawings illustrated technological advances and illuminated the social life and shops of workers.

Diderot was also quite explicit about another one of his intentions for the *Encyclopédie:* to change the way people think. He wanted readers to adopt the major premises of *la philosophie.* Following Bayle's lead, Diderot adopted the tactic of having things written in cross-reference notes that were compatible with orthodox Christian teaching but became heterodox or subversive by their entailments or when placed side by side with other statements. In the article "Encyclopédie," Diderot described the stratagem: "It is the art of tacitly deducing the most radical conclusions. If these cross references of confirmation or refutation are foreseen ahead of time and prepared with skill, they will give to an encyclopedia the character that a good dictionary ought to have, namely the character of changing the general way of thinking." Diderot hoped that this strategy would keep governmental censors at bay.

There were other ruses Diderot orchestrated. For example, Polier de Bottens, a friend of Voltaire and a very prominent pastor of Lausanne, wrote the article "Messie" ("Messiah") for the *Encyclopédie.* The pastor listed Christ as one among many messiahs, not as the Messiah. In one sense this approach presented factual information. At the same time, Christ's placement in a list as simply one of many messiahs robbed him of his status as the Savior of the world. Another ruse is that the author of an article on "Noah's Ark" gave the impression that Noah's vessel would have possibly sunk if it had been constructed according to the specification outlined in the Bible.

Diderot did in fact advocate atheism, thinking deism an untenable halfway house between theism and atheism. In *D'Alembert's Dream* (three related dialogues written in 1769), he wrestled with the question many an atheist has tried to answer: How can matter or something inanimate become a living being? Diderot used a spider's web analogy to provide a framework for a prototypic form of evolution. An advocate of personal freedom, he also struggled to explain how this prized value could exist in a world made up only of matter. If our actions are determined by materialistic forces, in what meaningful sense do we enjoy personal freedom?

Diderot was not alone in espousing atheism. Underground "radical" authors such as the priest Jean Meslier had made the case for atheism in subversive pieces passed from hand to hand. La Mettrie, a physician, proposed in *Man, a Machine* (1747) that empirical research reveals we are machines made of matter without an immortal soul. La Mettrie wrote, "It is demonstrated that the human body is nothing more in its origin than *a worm,* whose metamorphoses have nothing more surprising about them than those of an insect." While claiming that he did not call into question the existence of a divine being, La Mettrie nonetheless wrote, "We know nothing about nature: causes hidden within nature itself may have produced everything."

When La Mettrie died in 1751, apparently due to eating contaminated pâté, some Christian critics speculated that God had judged him for his atheistic effrontery. Diderot also repudiated him: "Dissolute, impudent, a buffoon, a flatterer; made for life at court and the favor of nobles. He died as he should have, victim of his own intemperance and his folly." Other *philosophes* wanted to have nothing to do with him owing to his radical materialism and atheism.

For his part, Paul Heinrich Dietrich, the Baron d'Holbach, attacked religion in his *Common Sense or Natural Ideas Opposed to Supernatural* (1772) and in his more famous *System of Nature* (1770). In *Common Sense* he drove home many of the themes of the *Siécle des lumiéres*, placing them into an atheistic context: "Ignorance and servitude are calculated to make men wicked and unhappy. Knowledge, reason and liberty can alone reform them, and make them happier, but everything conspires to blind them, and confirm their errors. Priests cheat them, tyrants corrupt, the better to enslave them."

Few contemporaries surpassed d'Holbach in his disdain for so-called "priestly religion." In 1783 the Marquis de Sade (1740–1814), known for his sexual promiscuity, wrote to his wife from prison: "The System of Holbach is verily and indubitably the basis of my philosophy, and I am and shall remain a faithful disciple of that philosophy even at the cost of my life, if it came to that."

De l'Esprit (1758), an atheistic book by Helvétius, caused a serious stir and contributed directly to the temporary interruption of the publication of the *Encyclopédie*. Voltaire had little appreciation for atheistic books, although he came to the defense of Helvétius. More commonly, like a number of other *philosophes*, Voltaire was concerned about what evil acts the "people" might commit if they lost their belief in a God who would punish them for bad deeds. This utilitarian concern to advocate God's existence as a means to foster social control also militates against the simple identification of the *Siècle des lumières* with atheism. Voltaire and Rousseau, bitter enemies on so many points, professed a desire to distance their own thinking from atheism, even though some materialists claimed Voltaire's "Letter on Locke" was in fact a principal source for materialist thinking.

All in all, members of the "little flock" of *philosophes* often had difficulty getting along with each other, given their personal animosities, egoisms, and different perspectives on certain topics. They had abandoned the Christian Good Shepherd. They also sometimes abandoned each other. Nonetheless, the *philosophes* were very successful in selling the premise to some of their contemporaries and later historians that the eighteenth century was "enlightened," or the Age of Reason.

D. The *Siècle des Lumières* and the French Revolution

Before his death in 1778, Voltaire despaired that the *philosophic* movement in France was becoming obsolete. In 1776 Jakob Heinrich Meister, a *philosophe*, concurred. He attributed the retreat of the "philosophic" influence to a renewal of Roman Catholic devotion in Paris. "Could this religious effervescence prove that *philosophie* had not made all the progress so much touted about it? Perhaps."

Years later, others thought that the deaths of Voltaire, Rousseau, and Diderot signaled the onset of the *philosophic* demise. On the eve of the French Revolution (1788), the Reformed pastor Jean-Paul Rabaut Saint-Etienne declared, "Nothing is left of the *philosophic* school to the writings of which we [the Protestants] owe the little toleration that exists in France. Reason has not advanced. She has even been receding during the last ten years. A class of anti-*philosophic* people is gaining control and bringing in the old opinions."

Rabaut Saint-Etienne was a shrewd political observer. He later became a key player in the political life of France, serving for a time as the president of the National Assembly. His assessment cautions us that at least one major observer did not think that the French *philosophes* had ushered in an Age of Lights (*Siècle des lumières*) that could long endure beyond their own deaths.

There were other signs, however, that the lumières had not been totally extinguished in France. A coterie of governmental officials known as the *"Magistrats-Philosophes"* continued to work with Rabaut Saint-Etienne for Protestant toleration, a prime *philosophic* cause. They faced strong opposition from many Roman Catholic clergymen, a principal exception being the Jansenists, who lent support to the Protestant cause. Eventually Louis XVI approved the Edict of Toleration (1787), thereby granting the Huguenots of France at least a number of civil rights.

Then again, the *philosophe* Jean Antoine-Nicolas Caritat, Marquis de Condorcet, born fifty years after Voltaire, was still at work in 1789 promoting an "enlightened" agenda, extolling reason's rights, and arguing for the "perfectibility" of man. In one sense, Condorcet, an atheist, was more than Montesquieu the founder of the "social sciences." Influenced by Hume's reservations about the difficulty of establishing empirical truths, Condorcet acknowledged that the "laws" of the social sciences are not certain and only probable. Nonetheless, he believed that "the probability of all statements of experience can be expressed and evaluated mathematically within probability theory."

In his posthumously published *Sketch for an Historical Picture of the Progress of the Human Mind* (1795), Condorcet projected into a final epoch of human history the eventual triumph of reason over the forces of darkness (including Christianity). The irony of Condorcet's "optimistic" proposal was that its author wrote the work in very dire personal circumstances.

During the Terror of 1793–94 the French Revolution turned especially bloody. Condorcet was imprisoned and then executed. The double irony surrounding his tragic death is the fact that many of the more radical revolutionaries like Robespierre prosecuted the Terror as a "rational" program to preserve the internal security of the nation and did so in the names of *philosophie* and reason. They looked back especially to Rousseau's concept of the general will as providing a warrant for their attempt to exterminate opponents of the revolution. In addition, Robespierre, the leader of the Convention, attempted to establish the "Cult of Reason" and later the "Cult of the Supreme Being" to replace Roman Catholicism in France. Now reason, so extolled by the *philosophes*, had taken on "salvific" value; the revolutionaries ordered that "reason" should be worshiped in "Temples of Reason"—former Christian churches.

By late 1793–94, however, Frenchmen in a majority of the departments of France were restive or in revolt against the revolutionaries in Paris. These partisans of the "Counter-Revolution" were often Catholics loyal to Rome. They had been especially consternated by the "Civil Constitution of the Clergy," which mandated that the clergy of France be elected. They were also deeply offended that the revolutionaries of the Convention ordered "reason" worshiped and justified the Terror in the name of "public salvation," "philosophy," and "reason."

Debate still ensues regarding the ways the ideologies associated with the *Siècle des lumières* may have contributed to both the origins and unfolding of the French Revolution. Moreover, an emerging consensus suggests that the role of "religion" must likewise be considered alongside philosophic or economic or social factors in any explanation of the revolution's origins. Historian Dale Van Kley carefully unpacks the ways Jansenist-influenced clerics, legislators, judges, and propagandists affected developments leading up to the French Revolution. Elsewhere, he proposed that on the eve of the revolution, contemporaries perceived "… quadruple divisions between Jansenism, devout Catholicism, and Rousseauian and Voltairean 'lights'" as the dominant schools of thought prevalent in their tumultuous society.

As for Pastor Rabaut Saint-Etienne, who in 1788 had prematurely declared that the *philosophic* movement no longer existed, he likewise succumbed to the Terror and ironically was put to death by those who claimed that his execution was in accord with "reason." Voltaire and Rousseau, who had defended doctrines of tolerance, would have been appalled that some of their ideas were exploited to justify bloody and heinous acts during the French Revolution. In a similar fashion, intellectuals such as Newton, Simon, Bayle, and Locke, who were major actors in Paul Hazard's "Crisis of the European Mind," would have been appalled by the way the French *philosophes* Voltaire, Rousseau, and others had exploited their own writings.

Ideas are often reworked and exploited in ways not envisioned by their originators. This phenomenon was especially noticeable during the Age of Lights and the French Revolution, a time when the Christian faith was under considerable duress.

FOR FURTHER STUDY

Aston, Nigel. *Art and Religion in Eighteenth-Century Europe*. London: Reaktion Books, 2009.

Barnett, S. J. *The Enlightenment and Religion: The Myths of Modernity*. Manchester, UK: Manchester University Press, 2003.

Black, Jeremy. *Eighteenth Century Europe 1700–1789*. London: Macmillan, 1990.

Hazard, Paul. *The Crisis of the European Mind: 1680–1715*. 1935; New York: New York Review of Books Classics, 2013.

Hempton, David. *The Church in the Long Eighteenth Century*. London: I. B. Tauris, 2011.

Hyland, Paul, ed. *The Enlightenment: A Source Book and Reader*. New York: Routledge, 2003.

Mason, Haydn. *Voltaire: A Biography*. Baltimore: Johns Hopkins University Press, 1981.

McInelly, Brett C., ed. *Religion in the Age of Enlightenment*. 3 vols. New York: AMS Press, 2009, 2010, 2012.

Sorkin, David. *The Religious Enlightenment: Protestants, Jews and Catholics from London to Vienna*. Princeton: Princeton University Press, 2008.

Christianity in the Age of Lights (1)

The British Isles (1680–1789)

I. INTRODUCTION

Although the *philosophe* Voltaire claimed he lived in both an "Age of Lights" and an "Age of Superstition," many historical accounts do not take into account his idea that the latter existed in the eighteenth century. Instead, they focus on what came to be called conventionally the "Enlightenment." They assume it fostered an all-pervasive secularism. Did not some Christian thinkers fear that the deists' attacks on miracles, scriptural authority, and Christ's divinity had subverted the confidence of many Europeans in the truth of the Christian religion? Did they not notice among their contemporaries a "this-worldly" orientation and satisfaction, evidenced by a quest for wealth? Had not concern for the afterlife—the reward of heaven and the punishment of hell—apparently diminished?

A number of historians in turn have challenged this well-respected interpretation of European history, 1680–1789. They propose that the Christian faith retained a dominant role in the thinking of the vast majority of Europeans, at least until 1750. Nigel Aston writes, "From Ireland to Russia and from Sweden to Sicily, the peoples and states of Europe in the mid-eighteenth century predominantly professed Christianity. Even Europeans living within the Ottoman Turkish Empire—in the Balkans, Greece, and the eastern Mediterranean littoral—had largely held on to the faith and not adopted the rival Islamic monotheism of their overlords."

These historians contend that Christianity by no means withered away during the *Siècle des lumières*. Jeremy Black observes, "The concept of a de-christianized and enlightened Europe is increasingly questioned. It is not simply that the Enlightenment can be seen to have had a dark side, such as the preoccupation with the occult, but rather that the culture of the elite was still generally Christian." Yvon Belaval and

Dominique Bourel add that the eighteenth century was in fact an "Age of the Bible": "Whereas the production of religious books crumbled during the eighteenth century, never were more Bibles printed; it was the most read, the most edited, the most sought after [book]. Never since Luther were there so many translations and commentaries."

Voltaire provided a backhanded confirmation of the Bible's widespread presence in Europe: "Christians are divided into an infinity of sects; however all of them recognize the divinity of Scripture, all make use of it" (1756).

For his part, Jean-Jacques Rousseau claimed that Christianity was the glue of whatever union Europeans enjoyed: "Europe, even now, is indebted more to Christianity than to any other influence of the union which survives among her members" (1761).

In some instances, the Christian religion more than held its own in the Age of Lights. Such was the case in the British Isles.

II. BRITISH SOCIETY: "POLITE" AND AFFLUENT— HARSH AND POOR

In 1700 many Irish, Welsh, Scots, and English still generally viewed themselves as living in separate, independent countries. Through threats, cajoling, and the use of military arms, the English government sought to bring about a "union" of these peoples. According to the Act of Union (1707), for example, England and Scotland would be ruled by a joint Parliament. Despite bitter opposition to unification efforts (the Jacobite rebellion), a British "nationality" including the English, the Scots, the Irish, and the Welsh was in the making—a process that lasted deep into the nineteenth century.

Interestingly enough, the monarchy that ruled during the formative years of the "United Kingdom of Great Britain" and the creation of a British nationality came not from Scotland or England but from Germany. On August 1, 1714, Queen Anne, a Protestant daughter of James II and thus a Stuart, had died. She had no male descendants who lived long enough to succeed her. Therefore, George Louis (1660–1727), the Elector of the Holy Roman Empire from Hanover, Germany, became George I, the King of England. His father, Ernest Augustus, had married Princess Sophia of the Palatinate, the only Protestant surviving in the line of James I of England, thereby affording him rights to the throne of England and Scotland and excluding any Roman Catholic aspirant.

George knew little English and liked to speak in French. On October 20, 1714, his coronation service was held in Latin.

Upon George I's accession to the throne, England remained basically an agricultural country. It was dotted with small towns and hamlets. Economically privileged families, the Crown, and the Anglican Church owned sizeable swathes of land. London was the largest city, followed by Norwich and Bristol. The overall population of the country was between 4 and 5 million. (By 1801 it reached 8.7 million.)

During the eighteenth century England witnessed a stunning commercial revolution that brought about great economic and social changes. The population of London surged rapidly: in 1600, it numbered about 200,000; in 1750, 575,000; in 1801, 900,000 to 1,000,000. In the early eighteenth century, London was known for its dirt and grime; by the last decades of the century, it had attained a reputation as a commercially vibrant city.

By midcentury, affluence and prosperity created conditions in which the architecture and interior decorations of numerous English homes and public buildings were definitely improved. A consumer revolution was in full swing. The possibility for people to free themselves from the ranks of the "miserable poor" was more within reach. They could advance to become the "laboring poor" or even the "middle sort."

Men and women of gentility and wealth fancied calling themselves more frequently "Mr.," "Mrs.," and "Esquire" and calculated how they might counter the rampant factionalism of the day by fostering a "polite" society. They appreciated Anthony Ashley Cooper, the Lord of Shaftesbury, for his advocacy of "common sense" and objective judgment and ethics as expounded in his *Sensus Communis: An Essay on the Freedom of Wit and Humour* (1708). They placed a premium on the cultivation of good taste, the avoidance of nontempered zeal, imagination, religious enthusiasm, and a divisive spirit. Many enjoyed the "reasonable" presentation of the Christian faith in the sermons of the Latitudinarian Anglican clergy. Thomas Gainsborough's famous paintings such as *A Lady in Blue, The Morning Walk,* and *River Landscape* capture well their idealized serene and "polite" eighteenth-century England.

These paintings, however, must be put side by side with the horrific images of the inhumane slave trade that enriched the pockets of English business entrepreneurs and their counterparts on the European continent, in the New World (including the British Thirteen Colonies), and in Africa itself. Historian David B. Davis observes that, whereas in the seventeenth century many English associated the word *slavery* with the seizure of white Englishmen by pirates and Muslims, in the eighteenth century the English more commonly identified the word with the capture and selling of black Africans. He points out that by the 1820s, "nearly 8.7 million slaves had departed from Africa for the New World, as opposed to 2.6 million whites, many of them convicts or indentured servants, who had left Europe." African slaves, he adds,

The slave deck of the bark *Wildfire*, brought into Key West, Florida, on April 30, 1860.

"provided the basic power that drove the interconnected economies of the entire New World."

In the eighteenth century, the "African Trade" also contributed significantly to the English economy. In England, between the years 1700 and 1807, four thousand ships with slaves cruelly stashed below and on their decks set sail from the ports of Liverpool, Plymouth, and Bristol.

These images must be also juxtaposed to William Hogarth's paintings such as *A Harlot's Progress, Gin Lane,* and *Beer Street.* Even if they are caricatures, these paintings of seedy life and slums relay a sense of the very real pain and suffering many city dwellers experienced. As for serenity, it was on occasion rudely shattered by factionalism and social unrest. Fierce riots—the pro-Jacobite riot of 1715, the riot of 1736, the Gin Riots of 1743 and 1757, and the Gordon Riots of 1780—broke out repeatedly and made the monarchy, or the Parliament, or the town of London sense only too well that, even if temporarily, they had lost control of the "people." Mob rule could easily overwhelm a town or city, even London. During the Gordon Riots, Horace Walpole recalled on June 10, 1780, that he remembered well earlier riots of the century "but I never till last night saw London and Southwark in flames!"

Throughout the century, the Jacobite threat persisted in the form of riots, in alarming hearsay, in the underground world of espionage, and in the plots of those who never accepted the legitimacy of James II's forced "abdication" during the Glorious Revolution and who wanted to restore the heirs of the Catholic Stuarts. Despite Jacobite riots, England remained staunchly a Protestant nation with Roman Catholic contenders excluded from access to the English throne. Queen Anne (1702–14), an Anglican Stuart, and the Hanoverian kings George I (1714–27), George II (1727–60), and George III (1760–1820) all viewed themselves as the defenders of the Protestant cause. As noted, on the eve of the Seven Years War (1756–63) George II joined forces with another "Protestant" monarch, Frederick II of Prussia, in an alliance against the Catholic powers France, Spain, and Austria.

The emerging, so-called "polite" society of England left behind vast numbers of the population locked in abject poverty and despair. Young children by the scores succumbed to the measles epidemics of 1705–6, 1716, and 1718–19. A gin epidemic (1720–51) blighted the lives of many Englishmen. By 1735, more than seven thousand shops sold "Mother Gin" or "the Ladies Delight." According to one contemporary, ladies "even of the first quality" used it "to administer Relief under the many Disappointments and Affections" they experienced as women. Some members of the poor and working classes attempted to drown their sorrows in gin. Many descended into drunken stupors.

Advocates of the Gin Act of 1736 tried to curtail the drink's accessibility by boosting its cost. In time, a riot ensued (1743) of those who resented this tactic. Others rioted because they felt betrayed by their bosses, who had replaced them with cheap, Irish Catholic labor. The Gin Act of 1751 contributed to beating back the epidemic of gin addiction.

In London, prostitution, violence, and crime flourished. Pickpockets relieved the unsuspecting of their money. Bawdy houses relieved them of their virtue. Ravaging epidemics of disease relieved them of their lives. Unhygienic housing conditions for the poor contributed to the easy spread of smallpox and other horrific diseases. J. H. Plumb's description of London and its slums in the early eighteenth century is graphic: "In the reign of George I, and for the early part of that of

George II, London was a stinking, muddy, filth-bespattered metropolis, polluted with slums.... St. Giles, Drury Lane, Shoreditch, Alsatia, were full of crowded tenements, the cellars as stuffed with human beings as the attics." The advent of smallpox inoculations later in the century helped curb that much-feared disease of the eighteenth century.

Wealthy members of high society had an additional concern: how to ease boredom. Many nobles fell headlong into lives of license, giving themselves over to unfettered sensuality, yielding to a gambling craze, to "masquerading" at dances, to brutal games, and engaging in rough horseplay. Coarse and vulgar speech could pepper family and political life. Adultery was commonplace.

Nor did King George I or George II make significant efforts to cover up their avaricious sexual appetites and relations with multiple mistresses. On her deathbed, Queen Caroline, George II's wife, urged him to remarry upon her passing. Disconsolate, the king replied in French, "Never, never. I shall only have mistresses."

In 1734 Joseph Trapp, an Anglican churchman from Oxford, lamented what he believed was the pervasive corruption within English society: "I presume it will be allowed by everybody that all manner of wickedness, both in principles and in practice, abound among us to a degree unheard of since Christianity was in being.... I have lived in six reigns; but for about twenty years past, the English nation has been ... so prodigiously debauched that I am almost a foreigner in my own country." For Trapp, the ideals of England's "polite" society had by no means been reached.

III. THE ANGLICANS

Earlier, the Anglican Church had once again become the established church of England. In 1660, with great fanfare the Stuart king, Charles II (1630–85), returned to England after exile on the Continent. On April 23, 1661, William Juxon, the archbishop of Canterbury, crowned him king. Ironically enough, in 1649 the same cleric Juxton had been present at the execution of Charles II's royal father (Charles I).

Charles II began to preside over a court famous for its notorious, licentious morals. His realm was beset by enormous tragedies. In 1665–66 the Great Plague of London took the lives of 70,000 people. Richard Baxter (1615–91), the renowned Non-Conformist minister of Kidderminster, wrote, "The plague which began at Acton, July 29, 1665, being ceased on March 1 following, I returned home, and found the churchyard like a ploughed field with graves, and many of my neighbors dead." Not many months later, London was swept by the Great Fire of 1666. Baxter continued,

On September 2, after midnight, London was set on fire; and on September 3 the Exchange was burnt; and in three days almost all the city within the walls, and much without them. The season had been exceeding dry.... The people having none to conduct them aright could do nothing to resist it, but stand and see their houses burn without remedy.... The streets were crowded with people and carts, to carry away what goods they could get out.

At the beginning of the Stuart Restoration, many Englishmen had hoped that the days of turmoil and bloodshed associated with the English civil war and the Commonwealth under Cromwell would be relegated to the past. Despite Charles II's Roman Catholic proclivities, the *Ecclesia Anglicana* regained its prerogatives as the established church of the land. And none too soon, according to its clergy. In 1661 Jeremy Taylor, bishop of Down and Connor, explained why Englishmen should be Anglicans: "What can be supposed wanting [in the Church of England] in order to salvation? We have the Word of God, the Faith of the Apostles, the Creeds of the Primitive Church, the Articles of the four first General Councils, a holy liturgy, excellent prayers, perfect Sacraments, faith and repentance, the Ten Commandments, and the sermons of Christ and all the precepts and counsels of the Gospel."

Baxter, who was also author of *The Reformed Pastor* (1656), believed that godly pastors were needed to catechize families in their homes, to fend off antinomianism, to calm political chaos, to bring an end to an era of religious divisions, and to foster a "mere [meaning 'nothing less than'] Christianity" among the English people. He asked, "Do not your hearts bleed to look upon the state of England?" He observed that "few towns or cities there be (where is any forwardness in religion) that are not cut into shreds and crumbled as to dust by separations and divisions." He also provided wise counsel regarding how unity among Christians might be achieved: "In things necessary, there must be unity; in things less than necessary, there must be liberty; and in all things, there must be charity."

From the Restoration on, the archbishops and bishops of the Church of England, whether High Church Laudians or Latitudinarians, sought to protect their church's privileged position. In 1662 the government stipulated that all ministers should have an Episcopal ordination and subscribe to the *Book of Common Prayer* or forfeit their rights as ministers. Refusing to submit to this ruling, over two thousand ministers lost their posts, whereas others such as the Presbyterian John Tillotson became Anglicans, risking censure for what critics castigated as expedient conversions.

Unsuccessful in excluding the Roman Catholic James II (1633–1701) from accession to the throne in 1685, Anglican bishops and other Protestants became very alarmed that the king might try to reestablish Roman Catholicism as the religion of the realm. After putting down the Monmouth rebellion (spurred by James, Duke of Monmouth, an illegitimate son of Charles II), James II did in fact attempt to restore Roman Catholicism and end the Anglican Church's status as the privileged state church. He promulgated the Declaration of Indulgence (1687) that permitted all Christians (including Roman Catholics) equal religious rights. When seven bishops protested, including William Sancroft, the archbishop of Canterbury, they were imprisoned in the Tower of London. The birth of James II's son on June 10, 1688, consternated many Protestants; they knew a Roman Catholic successor was in the wings.

James II's plans for a Roman Catholic monarchy, however, were thwarted by the Glorious Revolution. The protesting bishops were released from prison. Then the English Protestants invited William III, the Dutch son of William II, Prince of Orange and Stadthouder of the United Provinces, to invade England to confront James II. It is no coincidence that William III was married to Mary, a Protestant daughter of James II. On November 5, 1688, at the invitation of English Protestants, William III landed with 15,000 troops at Torbay, England. William III dispersed James II's troops, and James II fled to France, where he received the support of Louis XIV. But James II's troops were defeated in Scotland (1688) and in Ireland (1690).

On January 22, 1689, Parliament approved the Declaration of Rights, or the English Bill of Rights, which redefined the authority of monarchs and also barred any Catholic from becoming a monarch in the future. The Anglican clergy rejoiced that their church could enjoy a renewed privileged status. On January 31 they praised God's providence in delivering England. A much relieved Bishop John Tillotson declared that the English were "next to the Jewish nation … a people highly favored by God above all the nations of the earth."

On February 13 "William and Mary"—as they are commonly referred to—were proclaimed king and queen of England. Nonetheless, divisions about whether or not James II had actually "abdicated" the throne wracked the Anglican clergy. Archbishop Sancroft, eight bishops, and four hundred other clergy refused to take an oath of allegiance to William and Mary. These "nonjurors" were in turn deprived of their posts. Intense worries about alleged plots of Jacobites (individuals who wanted to see the Stuart family return to the throne) stirred passions.

The English Revolution of 1688 and the 1689 Settlement subordinated the church to the state, essentially subverted the doctrine of divine right kingship, and gave a measure of toleration to dissenting groups. In time, the Anglican Church witnessed a reconciliation with breakaway nonjurors (clergy), and the hierarchy negotiated closer working ties with the state.

A. The Archbishops of Canterbury

The king nominated and Parliament approved candidates to be the archbishop of Canterbury. Samuel Johnson, a shrewd man of letters, would write, "No man can be made bishop for his piety or learning; his only chance for promotion is his being connected with somebody who has parliamentary interest." Even if overwrought, this verdict has a ring of truth about it. Otherwise, excellent candidates were sometimes bypassed if they had demonstrated an apparent spirit of independence.

This is not to say that all archbishops (and other bishops) were timeservers who had no interest in reforming the Anglican Church. A good number encouraged their clergy to implement the 59th canon of the Canons and Constitutions of their church: "... every parson, vicar, or curate, upon every Sunday and Holy-day ... shall, for half an hour or more, examine and instruct the youth and ignorant persons of his parish in the Ten Commandments, the Articles of the Belief, and in the Lord's Prayer, and shall diligently hear, instruct, and teach them the Catechism, set forth in the book of Common Prayer." It does suggest that performing responsibly an archbishop's duties of confirmation, of the ordination of priests and consecration, acting with moderation as the royal family's chief cleric, demonstrating a tolerant spirit in parliamentary duties, offering hospitality at Lambeth—in a word, not shaking up the status quo—were desirable and honored traits for many eighteenth-century prelates.

Archbishop Thomas Herring, for example, indicated that he was delighted to have his post "at a time [1747–57] when spite, and rancor, and narrowness of spirit are out of countenance; when we breathe the benign and comfortable air of liberty and toleration."

The archbishops tried to foster peace and secure stability within the church. They recalled only too well the traumatic events the Anglican Church had traversed leading up to the Glorious Revolution of 1688.

B. "Enthusiasm"

The archbishops' sense of toleration, however, did have its limits. They felt a responsibility to protect their church's prerogatives and rights from the rising power of Dissenters and other Non-Conformists and to evidence little tolerance to Roman Catholics. They were very cautious about any form of religious "enthusiasm," defined later in Samuel Johnson's *Dictionary of the English Language* as "a vain belief of private revelation, a vain confidence of divine favor." They criticized religious leaders who claimed personal revelations through visions or prophetic words or who indicated the Holy Spirit was giving them specific directives. They were suspicious of French Camisard "prophets," some of whom had sought refuge in England in the first decade of the eighteenth century.

They were especially hostile toward the followers of George Fox (1624–91), who after a mystical conversion (1647) indicated that Christ, the "Inner Light," through "immediate revelations" directly leads believers. Fox, the founder of the Religious Society of Friends (the Quakers), was arrested eight times. In 1681 William Penn, who had also spent time in prison, was allowed to emigrate to America and there established a refuge for Quakers in what got called "Penn's Woods"—that is, Pennsylvania.

A few years earlier (1676), Robert Barclay (1648–90) had published *An Apology for the True Christian Divinity: Being an Explanation and Vindication of the Principles and Doctrines of the People Called Quakers*, a classic theological exposition and defense of the Quaker faith. In an introductory letter to King Charles II, Barclay indicated that Quakers affirmed "beliefs agreeable to scripture, reason and true learning." They were a peaceful people, open in their dealings, and they had never entered into any conspiracies against the monarchy. They felt they should not be hassled but rather enjoy liberty of conscience.

C. Archbishop William Blake

Scandalized by the open license of contemporaries, a number of bishops preached sermons in which they emphasized the value of Christian morality. They sometimes linked moral decline to the nefarious influence of Arianism, atheism, and deism within English society. They believed that the real goal of atheistic and deistic authors was to justify licentious lifestyles. In 1721 William Blake, who served as archbishop of Canterbury from 1716 to 1737, cosponsored a bill with Lord Nottingham "for suppressing blasphemy and profaneness." A person could be imprisoned for three months if he or she criticized the Thirty-nine Articles, the inspiration of Scripture, or the Being of God. Parliament failed to approve the law.

Interestingly enough, the same Archbishop Blake engaged in extended correspondence with Reformed Protestants on the Continent about church unity. He believed that many Christians, including Gallican Catholics, shared far more agreement on "fundamental" beliefs than they realized. In response to Archbishop Blake's openness, Ellis Du Pin, a leading theologian in Paris, responded in 1718 that he earnestly desired "that some way might be found of initiating a union between the Anglican and Gallican churches. We are not so very far separated from one another in most things as to preclude the possibility of our being mutually reconciled. Would that all Christians were one fold." Du Pin was willing to call for a General Council if the pope rejected the idea of launching negotiations regarding the creation of this union.

The bold ecumenism of Du Pin and Blake came to naught when Du Pin died and it became clear that Blake had no intention of sacrificing any of the privileges of the Anglican Church. But an ecumenical initiative continued after his death.

D. Latitudinarians

Critics often scorned the Anglican clergy for currying the favor of the wealthy and their alleged doctrinal laxity and for the rational and moralizing tendencies of their preaching. In fact, many of these clergy viewed their theology as emphasizing the essential teachings of their Latitudinarian predecessors in the Restoration Church: John Tillotson, Gilbert Burnet, Edward Stillingfleet, Joseph Glanwell, and others. These men had affirmed traditional Christian creeds, the Thirty-nine Articles of the Anglican Church, and the *Book of Common Prayer*, yet they thought reason, carefully employed, could support revelation's truth claims.

Archbishop Tillotson (1691–95), for example, had gained a notable reputation as one of the finest preachers of his day. In his sermons he often emphasized the value of virtue: "I speak now to a great many Persons, the eminence of whose rank and quality renders their examples so powerful, as to be able to give authority to either Virtue or Vice. People take their fashions from you, as to the habits of their minds as well as their bodies."

An Arminian in theology, Tillotson thought that a rational Christianity could defeat the claims of deists, religious "Enthusiasts," and Roman Catholics, his major opponents. He sought to make Christianity intellectually acceptable to England's upper classes and to the monarchy. Eschewing Pelagianism, he believed the use of reason could bolster the claims of Christian revelation without overthrowing them. A firm believer in the Trinity and in other fundamental doctrines, he demonstrated "latitude" in de-emphasizing "secondary" doctrines. He argued that the truths of Christianity could not be proven with absolute certitude, but high probabilities made belief in their veracity a far more reasonable religious choice than atheism or deism.

Other Anglicans seemed to embrace a form of Arianism, however. One was Samuel Clarke, the rector of St. James, Westminster, who served as a chaplain for Queen Anne. In his book *Scripture Doctrine of the Trinity* (1712), Clarke argued that the doctrine of the Trinity has no biblical warrant. Daniel Waterland, a well-respected master of Magdalene College, Cambridge, criticized Clarke sharply for his anti-Trinitarianism. Even Clarke's efforts to fend off atheism were found wanting. The freethinker Anthony Collins wryly observed that "nobody doubted the existence of God until Dr. Clarke strove to prove it."

Still other Anglican clerics such as Bishop George Bull made good works and faith the basis for God's election of the believer. They seemed to neglect if not deny the doctrine of justification by faith alone, a doctrine clearly taught by their own *Thirty-nine Articles*. Article XI reads, "We are accounted righteous before God, only for the merit of our Lord and Savior Jesus Christ by Faith, and not for our own works or deservings. Wherefore, that we are justified by Faith only, is a most wholesome Doctrine, and very full of comfort."

During various rounds of the so-called "Subscription Controversy," Anglican prelates debated sharply what theological leeway they would allow their colleagues to entertain in interpreting the *Thirty-nine Articles* and still minister with a good conscience. Some critics wondered if the very idea of a creed was countermanded by the doctrine of *sola scriptura*.

John Wesley and George Whitefield, both Anglicans, faulted certain members of the Anglican clergy for not teaching justification by faith alone, a doctrine "full of comfort." Whitefield was especially critical of a number of Tillotson's sermons, arguing that the Latitudinarian archbishop did not in fact preach the gospel.

IV. THE DISSENTERS

The word *Dissenters* refers broadly to religious groups, ranging theologically from orthodox Protestants to members of heterodox sects, all of whom dissented or did not conform to the teachings of the Church of England from the seventeenth to the nineteenth centuries. They included, among others, Puritans, Quakers, General Baptists, Particular Baptists, Fifth Monarchy Men, Ranters, and Socinians.

In 1652 Richard Baxter indicated that English Protestants were divided into four parties: the Episcopalians, the Presbyterians, the Independents, and Erastians (advocates of the supremacy of the state over the church in church affairs). In 1658 the Independents, who advocated a congregational form of church government, drew up *The Savoy Declaration of Faith and Order*, a document that retained many elements of the Westminster Confession while adding chapters affirming principles of Congregationalism such as the autonomy of the local church.

With the "restoration" of the Stuarts in 1660, the Anglican Church with High Church Laudians and Latitudinarian clergy in top leadership positions soon became again the established church of the land. The failure of the Savoy Conference (1661) to create a prayer book acceptable to both Anglicans and Presbyterians suggests that Anglican bishops who dominated the discussions were not disposed to share ecclesiastical power with Non-Conformists. The Clarendon Code (the Corporation Act of 1661; the Act of Uniformity, 1662; the Conventicle Act, 1664–70; the Five Mile Act, 1665) along with the Test Act of 1673 placed punitive strictures on anyone who was not an Anglican. Non-Conforming government officials, members of the military, and the clergy were subject to dismissal from their employments. As noted, in 1662 some 2,000 Non-Conforming ministers, lecturers, and fellows at colleges were "ejected" from their posts.

For his refusal to submit, John Bunyan (1628–88), a Reformed Baptist who emphasized open church membership, spent years in jail two times. In prison he ministered to other inmates, studied Scripture, and made laces to support his family. Bunyan penned the spiritual classics *Grace Abounding* (1666) and *Pilgrim's Progress* (1678). In very dire circumstances, his personal faith remained steadfast: "I found myself a man encompassed with infirmities: the parting with my wife and poor children hath often been to me in this place as the pulling of the flesh from my bones.... But yet, recalling myself, thought I, I must venture yon all with God, though it goeth to the quick to leave you." He hoped his imprisonment might be an "awakening to the saints in the Country."

A. Baptists: General and Particular

General Baptists (Arminians) rejected infant baptism and double predestination. They dated their origins to the year 1611, when their church in exile in Holland (1608–11) led by Thomas Helwys moved back to England. The year before (1610), this church had separated from John Smyth's congregation. In 1609 Smyth had founded what many Baptist historians identify as the first Baptist church of modern times. After Smyth's death in 1612, one of his congregations joined the Mennonites. Thomas Grantham (1634–92) stood out as a major theological writer for the General Baptists later in the seventeenth century. The General Baptists believed that Christ died for the sins of all ("general atonement"), not that all would believe. In the eighteenth century a number of them espoused anti-Trinitarian views.

The origins of the Particular Baptists (Calvinists) date from the 1630s. In 1644 Particular Baptists of seven churches drafted the First London Confession (1644–46). In 1677 they adopted the Second London Confession, which incorporated much of the Westminster Confession but differed regarding the ordinances, ecclesiology, and relations between church and state. The Particular Baptists affirmed that Christ died only for the elect; his substitutionary atonement was efficient only for the elect ("particular atonement"), even though sufficient for all. They argued that the Bible teaches believers' baptism and not infant baptism, and Congregational not Presbyterian church governance. Each of their churches viewed Christ as its head. At the same time, their churches enjoyed "associational" relations with like-minded churches.

In 1689 the Act of Toleration gave Dissenters relief but not the same rights as Anglicans. Those English subjects who would swear allegiance to William and Mary, accept the basic doctrines of the *Thirty-nine Articles*, and renounce the teachings of the Roman Catholic Church gained the rights of freedom of worship. As the threat of repression subsided in part, some dissenting churches, especially those with a Congregational polity, grew in numbers in the last decades of the seventeenth century. In 1720 about 230 Congregational (independent) churches existed in England and Wales.

In the eighteenth century, Dissenters often made formal professions of loyalty to the government. Yet some Dissenters chafed under continued restrictions placed upon them. They could not attend Cambridge or Oxford. Consequently, Philip Doddridge (1702–51) established one of the dissenting academies at Northampton. In *The Rise and Progress of Religion in the Soul* (1745), Doddridge explained why he thought the gospel "is the best news that ever was heard":

> MY DEAR READER, it is the great design of the Gospel and, wherever it is cordially received, the glorious effect of it, to fill the heart with feelings of love; to teach us to abhor all unnecessary rigor and severity, and to delight not in grief but in the happiness of our fellow creatures.

The Dissenters like Doddridge viewed the Anglican Church as an institution blocking their full acceptance as equal religious partners within Protestantism. In 1750 Michaiah Towgood indicated that the key issue of disagreement between Anglicans and certain Dissenters "depends absolutely and entirely upon the single point;... Is there any *other* Lawgiver or King in the Church of God besides *Jesus Christ; or*, is there not?" Evangelical Dissenters believed their first loyalties should belong to Christ and not to an institution such as the Anglican Church.

B. The Evangelicals

The "Evangelical Revival" of the eighteenth century took place against a harsh societal backdrop for segments of the English population. Disastrous social, economic, and health conditions ravaged the poor. A number of offensive theater offerings seemed to condone immorality. National gin addiction and gambling (176 state lotteries took place between the years 1694 and 1826) tore at the fabric of family life. Riots were a common occurrence. Many leading scientists, clerics, and members of the upper classes embraced varieties of heterodox theology or the teachings of the deists. "Atheists" and "freethinkers" haunted taverns, coffeehouses, and "bawdy houses," where they injected ridicule, jest, and blasphemies into conversations about things holy.

In 1717 four lodges of Masons in London united to form a Grand Lodge. In its secret teachings, rites, and lore, this particular lodge emphasized not orthodox Christianity, but a belief in God as the master architect of the universe, adherence to the moral law, and "natural religion" with pantheistic overtones.

The leaders of the Evangelical Revival—John and Charles Wesley, George Whitefield, and others (sometimes viewed as Dissenters)—believed that "Christian" England was desperately in need of gospel preaching. Wesley wrote, "What is the present characteristic of the English nation? ... It is ungodliness." Many evangelicals saw themselves as recovering a core doctrine of the gospel, justification by faith alone—a doctrine they thought the clergy of the Anglican Church had largely neglected. With a concern for the gospel of Christ, they embraced the word *evangelical* to describe themselves, just as Lutherans of the sixteenth century and Puritans of the seventeenth had done before them. Like their forebears, these evangelicals stressed conversion to Christ, a commitment to the Bible's final authority, and the living out of the faith as evidenced in good works.

Some other members of the Anglican Church also called themselves "Evangelicals." The center of this movement was Cornwall in southwest England, its leader Samuel Walker of Truro. Although sharing many of the same beliefs as the "evangelical" Methodists, they criticized those who did not attend local Anglican parishes and thereby were cut off from Anglican Holy Communion. The fact that Methodist laypeople preached also irritated Anglican bishops.

V. THE EVANGELICAL REVIVAL OF THE METHODISTS

Wesley's Methodists are known for having played a pivotal role in the English Evangelical Revival. Nonetheless, Wesley believed the revival represented a movement of the Spirit of God that was transatlantic and included major leaders such as Jonathan Edwards and George Whitefield, who were Calvinists.

Jonathan Edwards.

Wesley was inspired by reading Edwards's *A Narrative of the Surprising Work of the Spirit of God* (1737). In it Edwards proposed that in 1734–35 Northampton, Massachusetts, and neighboring towns in the Connecticut Valley had been blessed by a "special dispensation of God's providence." Edwards observed, "When God in so remarkable a manner took the work into His own hands there was as much done in a day or two, as at ordinary times, with all the endeavors that men can use, and with such a blessing as we commonly have, is done in a year." In 1743 James Robe of Scotland, the author of *Faithful Narrative of the Extraordinary Work of the Spirit of God at Kilsyth*, indicated that thirty of the thirty-six publications sent from the American colonies favored the revival.

In 1749 Edwards published *An Account of the Life of the Late Reverend David Brainerd.* Later evangelical missionaries such as William Carey extolled this book as "almost a second Bible." Brainerd's sincere devotion and love for Christ became an inspiring example for many Christians. In his journal Brainerd had also described what he perceived to be the powerful work of the Holy Spirit abetting his missionary efforts with the Delaware Indians in New Jersey: "The power of God seemed to descend upon the assembly 'like a rushing mighty wind,' and with an astonishing energy bore down all before it. I stood amazed at the influence that seized the audience universally." Brainerd noted that his convicting work among the Indians had occurred "independent of means." Cut down by a disease after only four years of missionary service, Brainerd died in Edwards's home. He was only twenty-nine years old.

In Wales, the young lay evangelist Howell Harris of Trevecka, Wales, admired greatly Griffith Jones, who for years had preached the "new birth" in the open fields and had founded "circulating schools" in which students learned about the faith through reading the Welsh Bible. On June 18, 1735, Harris came to the conviction that Christ had saved him:

> … being in secret prayer, I felt suddenly my heart melting within me, like wax before the fire, with love to God my Savior. I felt not only love and peace, but longing to be dissolved and to be with

Christ. Then was a cry in my inmost soul, which I was totally unacquainted with before. "Abba Father!" I could not help calling God, "my Father." I knew that I was his child, and that he loved me, and heard me.

In December 1735 Harris began to preach home-to-home and in the open air. Through his enthused and fiery preaching, many Welsh came under deep conviction for sin and turned to Christ for forgiveness. In 1737 Harris, like Wesley, was encouraged in his ministry by reading Edwards's *A Narrative of the Surprising Work of the Spirit of God.*

"Circuits" for lay preachers (Harris), "small groups" (the "conventicles" of German Pietist Jakob Spener), field preaching (Jones, Harris), and an emphasis on heartfelt religion (German Pietists, Moravians, and Puritans) and the "new birth" (John 3:1–8) existed before the Wesleys made them familiar traits of the Methodist movement.

A. John and Charles Wesley

John Wesley, a relatively slight man at five-and-a-half feet tall and just over 120 pounds, was known for being exact, punctual, and never hurried. Samuel Johnson wrote to James Boswell, "I hate to meet John Wesley. The dog enchants me with his conversation and then breaks away to go and see some old woman." Wesley observed, "I bear the rich and love the poor; therefore I spend almost all of my time with them." Wesley appreciated in many of the poor a "pure, genuine grace, unmixed with paint, folly, and affectation."

LOC, LC-USZC2-2716

John Wesley preaching at his father's grave in the churchyard at Epworth, England, on Sunday, June 6, 1742.

In fifty years of preaching, Wesley traveled approximately 250,000 miles in his itinerant ministry and preached at least 40,000 times. On his eighty-first birthday he attributed his incredible stamina and strength to (1) the power of God, (2) traveling 4,000 to 5,000 miles yearly, (3) the ability to sleep whenever and wherever he wanted, (4) getting up at a set hour between 4 a.m. and 5 a.m., and (5) constant preaching, particularly in the morning.

John (1703–91) and Charles (1707–88) were born into the home of Samuel and Susannah Wesley in Epworth, Lincolnshire. Their father was a High Church Anglican priest, but their grandparents had been Dissenters. Susannah raised the eight children in the family in the fear and admonition of the Lord. She would say later, "Never were children in better order. Never were children better disposed to piety or in more subjection to their parents." John himself said, "... from a child I was taught to love and reverence the Scripture, the oracles of God."

When John was five years old, both he and his brother Charles were trapped in the Epworth rectory of their parents by a raging fire. A neighbor engineered a last-minute rescue. John would view himself as a "branch snatched from the burning" (see Zech. 3:2), someone set aside for God's work. When Wesley sat for a portrait later in life, he asked that the backdrop of the painting include the scene of his rescue from the burning parsonage.

A brilliant student, John Wesley pursued his education at Oxford University from 1720 until 1724. He was adept in a number of languages and appreciated classical culture. He became very interested in the writings of the church fathers (especially St. Chrysostom, Gregory of Nyssa, and later Macarius). He meditated on Bishop Taylor's *Rules and Exercises of Holy Living* and *Rules and Exercises of Holy Dying* and also read German mystics. In 1728 he was ordained a priest in the Anglican Church.

After returning to Oxford in 1729, John joined his brother Charles, who had formed a group at Oxford that became known as the "Holy Club" and later included George Whitefield. Much impressed by William Law's *Christian Perfection*, John and other members "methodically" sought to follow a life of Christian self-denial and devotion through fasting and good deeds, ministering to the poor and visiting prisoners, attending to the Eucharist, and engaging in regular prayer and Bible reading. Critics derisively called members of the Holy Club "Bible Moths" or "Methodists." Later, John defined a "Methodist" as "one that lives according to the method laid down in the Bible."

In 1737 John went to Savannah, Georgia, as a missionary for the Society for the Propagation of the Gospel in Foreign Parts (founded in 1701) to work with Chickasaw Indians. Charles, recently ordained, accompanied him as the secretary for Indian affairs. When a series of storms overtook their ship, John and Charles were impressed that German Moravian passengers did not apparently share the same fear of death that particularly gripped John. The Wesleys also admired the unfeigned humility of the Moravians.

John had relatively little success in his missionary work with the Indians and with English parishioners in Savannah. His problems were greatly compounded by a failed courtship with a woman named Sophie Hopkey. When she married William Williamson and came to a service with her new husband, John refused to admit the couple to the Eucharist. Faced with legal action, in December 1737 John left Savannah precipitously for South Carolina on his way back to England. Much dismayed in spirit, he wrote, "In vain have I fled from myself to America. I still groan under the intolerable weight of inherent misery.... Go where I will, I carry my hell about me, nor have I the least ease in anything."

Upon his return to England, a despairing John Wesley came under the influence of Peter Boehler, a Moravian, who told him that the two signs of conversion were "Dominion over sin, and constant Peace from a sense of forgiveness." After studying Scripture, Wesley came to the conviction that Boehler was correct. On May 24, 1738, he attended quite unwillingly a meeting largely made up of Moravians in Aldersgate Street, London. Upon hearing the reading of Martin Luther's *Preface to the Epistle to the Romans*, Wesley felt his "heart strangely warmed": "I felt I did trust in Christ, Christ alone for salvation and an assurance was given to me, that he had taken away my sins, even mine, and saved me from the law of sin and death."

Remarkably enough, three days earlier, Charles Wesley had experienced a similar heartfelt sense of forgiveness of sins: "I felt a strange palpitation of heart." Experiential religion, or the "religion of the heart," constituted an essential emphasis of the Methodists.

B. The Methodist Revival

In the summer of 1736 George Whitefield, a Methodist, preached to large crowds in the open air near Bristol, the pulpits of many Anglican churches having been closed to him. A revival spread quickly throughout England. Welsh evangelists had earlier practiced field preaching before Whitefield appropriated it and later invited an Oxford don, John Wesley, to do the same. In February 1738 Whitefield asked miners emerging from the deep coal pits, "What think ye of Christ?" At Moorsfields in September, John Wesley enjoined a large crowd: "Believe in the Lord Jesus Christ, and thou shalt be saved."

In the wake of strong gospel preaching, numbers of the poor and even some members of the aristocracy were converted to Christ. The

"Evangelical Revival" was born in England, eliciting the approval of segments of the public and engendering hearty denunciations and hostility in others. Wesley's *Journal* and Whitefield's *Journals* recount in remarkable detail the evangelists' sometimes harrowing experiences as they preached the gospel in the prisons, fish markets, town squares, and fields of England and Scotland (and also for Whitefield, Wales and the British American colonies). Wesley, a fearless preacher, was at the center of more than fifty riots, on occasion barely escaping with his life. His confidence in God's providential care gave him this boldness.

The revival served as a major spiritual impulse for the Methodist movement. On New Year's Day 1739, Wesley, Whitefield, their associates, and sixty brethren were praying at a love feast at Fetters Lane when at 3:00 a.m. "the power of God came mightily upon us, insomuch that many cried out for exceeding joy, and many fell to the ground."

Wesley's theology was thoroughly Arminian. He defined prevenient grace as "the first wish to please God." He urged believers to seek Christian perfection — living life in pure love and not knowingly sinning. Nonetheless, he indicated that he affirmed the doctrine of justification by faith alone in the way John Calvin did. He was very appreciative of Christian tradition, Christian experience, and the proper use of reason in doing theology. At the same time, he portrayed himself as "a man of one book." Holy Scripture remained his final authority:

> The Scripture, therefore, of the Old and New Testament is a most solid and precious system of divine truth. Every part thereof is worthy of God; and all together are one entire body, wherein is no defect, no excess. It is the fountain of heavenly wisdom, which they who are able to taste prefer to all writings of men, however wise or learned or holy.

Wesley believed Scripture was "infallibly true." When Soame Jenyns argued that "all Scripture is given by inspiration of God; but the writers of it were sometimes left to themselves, and consequently made some mistakes," Wesley replied, "Nay, if there be any mistakes in the Bible, there may as well be a thousand. If there be one falsehood in that book, it did not come from the God of truth."

John Wesley wanted his followers to be a people of prayer. Like Charles Spurgeon after him, Wesley greatly appreciated insights about prayer found in *A Short and Easy Method of Prayer* (1665), a classic of Christian mysticism, penned by the Quietist Catholic Madame Guyon.

An emphasis on persevering and believing prayer, attentive obedience to the moral commands of Scripture, reliance on the empowering work of the Holy Spirit, faithful gospel preaching, the pursuit of Christian perfection evidenced in love toward God and neighbor—these became characteristics of the Methodist movement.

Although John Wesley was a fine preacher, a prolific author of many books, and editor of *The Christian Library*, he also excelled as a tireless organizer. Because John and Charles wanted to remain within the Anglican Church, they established "societies," not churches, for new believers. John defined a society as "a company of men having the form and seeking the power of godliness, united in order to pray together, to receive the word of exhortation, and to watch over one another in love, that they may help each other work out their salvation."

A society was subdivided into classes of twelve people, one of whom was the leader. Classes were in turn divided into smaller bands. In 1742 the first Methodist class meeting took place in Bristol. Class members were to give a penny a week. In 1743 John Wesley drafted *Nature, Design and General Rules of the United Societies*. He indicated that Methodists would evidence three marks: "Avoiding all known sin, doing good after his power, and attending all the ordinances of God." They would seek after perfection, doing everything in love, even if they remained "liable to ... involuntary transgressions" due to ignorance. They would do good to others by "giving food to the hungry, by clothing the naked, by visiting or helping them that are sick, or in prison," and by "instructing, reproving, or exhorting ..." In 1744 the first Conference of Methodists was held.

Lacking enough pastors to minister to the societies, John Wesley created the itinerant or circuit system in which his assistants would care for several societies. Unlike Charles, John was firmly convinced that lay preachers could minister even if they had little if any theological training. He gave his preachers a solemn charge: "It is not your business to preach so many times and to take care of this or that society; but to save as many souls as you can; to bring as many sinners as you possibly can to repentance, and with all your power to build them up in that holiness without which they cannot see the Lord."

In this light Wesley insisted that his pastors and leaders of classes apply church discipline. Each week members of classes were to enumerate sins they had committed and temptations they had confronted. If they violated Methodist rules for holy living and evidenced no signs of repentance, they were removed from their class's list. As Wesley said, this person "hath no place among us." In 1759–60 Wesley published *Thoughts on Christian Perfection*, in which he argued that it is possible for Christians to die to sin completely.

In a letter of July 7, 1765, Sarah Crosby, a heartfelt Methodist, continued to press John Wesley concerning whether he would permit women to preach. Her own convictions about the matter were forthright:

"I do not think it wrong for women to speak in public provided they speak by the spirit of God." In 1769 Wesley indicated to Crosby that she could give "short exhortations" in a Methodist service, but in 1771 he seemed to suggest that Crosby might preach in "extraordinary cases." The Methodist Conference of 1787 went further and indicated that women could indeed preach.

Women played a significant role in the spread of the Methodist faith. They were notable for their hospitality and loving care for their families. A number served as class leaders, preachers, and evangelists.

The Methodists often suffered persecution and internal divisions. Critics portrayed itinerant preachers (nearly two hundred in the 1790s) as a "ragged legion of preaching barbers, cobblers, tinkers, scavengers, draymen and chimney sweepers." Satirical attacks were especially virulent in the years 1739, 1760, 1772, and 1778. In 1742 William Seward, a Methodist preacher, was killed when hit by a stone. More than once, ruffians assaulted Wesley. Some Anglican clerics denounced Methodist preachers as "enthusiasts." These attacks were not totally unexpected for Methodists. After all, even in their hymnbooks (1780) Methodists warned about "Christians" who did not really believe:

> O wouldst thou, Lord, reveal the sins,
> And turn their joy to grief:
> The world, the CHRISTIAN world convince
> of damning unbelief.

The Methodists thus constituted a "reforming" movement in a "Christian state."

John Wesley pursued his ministry while on occasion undergoing deep personal grief. He was dismayed when (like his earlier experience with Sophie Hopkey) Grace Murray, whom he loved, married another; he in turn entered an unhappy marriage with Mary Vaizelle. Then again, Wesley broke fellowship with other Christians whom he had greatly appreciated: with the Moravians over their teaching that unbelievers should remain "still" and not "seek the Lord" (1740), with Howell Harris over the extent of the atonement (1742), and several times with George Whitefield over unconditional election, imputation, irresistible grace, and final perseverance.

Despite Wesley's personal hurts, the Methodist movement continued to grow. Between 1771 and 1791, for example, its numbers increased from 26,000 to nearly 57,000 in England and Wales, 14,000 in Ireland, and 1,000 in Scotland. Many came from England's poorest classes. Methodists expanded even more rapidly in the next century.

In 1771 Wesley spoke to the Methodist Conference in Bristol: "Our brethren in America call aloud for help. Who are willing to go over and help them?" A young man, Francis Asbury (1745–1816), stepped forward and answered the call. In 1784 Wesley ordained Thomas Coke (1747–1814) as a "superintendent," who in turn ordained Asbury. Both men played key roles in establishing the Methodist movement in the United States.

In December 1784 the Methodist Church was founded at the Christmas Conference in Baltimore. In time, Asbury alone ordained four thousand pastors. Methodist circuit riders such as Peter Cartwright took the gospel into sparsely settled regions of the "West" (Kentucky, Tennessee, and elsewhere) as well as in the "East." Despite the ordinations of Coke and Asbury, John Wesley continued to maintain that he had not separated from the Anglican Church. In 1795, however, with the Plan of Pacification, the Methodists did make the break. By the 1830s there were more than 500,000 Methodists in the United States.

Charles and John Wesley were both talented poets and hymn writers. Charles penned more than 9,000 hymns and poems, including "And Can It Be That I Should Gain," "Christ the Lord Is Risen Today," and "Hark the Herald Angels Sing." The Wesleys published hymnbooks ranging from *Hymns and Sacred Poems* (1739) to a *Collection of Hymns for the Use of the People Called Methodists* (1780). They believed hymns serve as a marvelous medium to communicate the Christian faith as a religion of the heart.

C. George Whitefield and the Calvinist Methodists

George Whitefield came from a home of modest means. He wrote, "I was born in Gloucester, in the month of December 1714. My mother and father kept the Bell inn." As a young boy he enjoyed reading plays and had a flair for acting. He indicated that he was "addicted to lying, filthy talking, and foolish jesting." Due to his mother's persistence, he gained entrance into Oxford University, where he joined the Holy Club. After much turmoil of soul, he experienced a life-changing conversion in 1735. In his words, he had cried out from his bed, " 'I thirst! I thirst!' Soon after this, I found and felt in myself that I was delivered from the Burden that had so heavily oppressed me! The Spirit of Mourning was taken away from me, and I knew what it was truly to rejoice in God my Savior."

In June 1736 Whitefield was ordained as an Anglican priest. Within a week, he began preaching sometimes in very crowded churches, his reputation as a persuasive evangelist having grown quickly, his sermons selling briskly. In 1737 he traveled to Georgia as a missionary. In Savannah he spent time working on plans for an orphanage modeled after the one founded by the German Pietist Hermann Francke.

George Whitefield.

Upon his return to England in 1738, Whitefield discovered that many Anglican bishops viewed him as a gospel "enthusiast" and closed their pulpits to him.

Consequently, in February 1739 Whitefield attempted field preaching for the first time. His audience consisted of coal miners emerging from the coal pits at Kingswood, near Bristol. He wrote, "Having no righteousness of their own to renounce, they were glad to hear of a Jesus who was a friend to publicans, and came not to call the righteous but sinners to repentance. The first discovery of their being affected was the sight of the white gutters made by their tears, which plentifully fell down their black cheeks as they came out of their coal pits." Two months later, he was field preaching to large crowds in London. By the end of the year, John Wesley had joined him in field preaching. Wesley admired Whitefield's preaching ability, once claiming that Whitefield could say the word "Mesopotamia" and people would weep.

Whitefield made seven trips to the British American colonies as an evangelist and organizer of the Savannah orphanage. In the fall of 1740 Whitefield's field preaching tour through New England (45 days, 175 sermons) before large crowds became a major component of the "First Great Awakening." In New England Whitefield preached for and spoke with Jonathan Edwards, who reinforced the Calvinist orientation of his theology. Edwards was deeply moved by Whitefield's preaching. So was Nathan Cole, a layperson, who heard Whitefield preach in the open air:

When I saw Mr. Whitefield come upon the scaffold he looked almost angelic, a young slim, slender youth, before some thousands of people and with a bold, undaunted countenance; it solemnized my mind and put me in a trembling fear before he began to preach for he looked as if he was clothed with the authority from the great God. Hearing him preach gave me a heart wound [so that] by God's blessing, my old foundation was broken up and I saw that my righteousness would not save me, then I was convinced of the doctrine of election and went right to quarreling with God about it because all that I could do would not save me.

In a letter to Charles Wesley in 1740, Elizabeth Hinson, a barely lettered woman, gave an account of how the preaching of George Whitefield and John Wesley affected her:

I was a Pharisee but god was pleast to convince me by heareing mr Witfeald sermon.... I know my self a damd sinner.... Satan raged within and I have reson to bles my god for he iustifyd the ungodly in me. Your brother [John Wesley] expounded the 12 chap of sant John and the lord work mytelly in me and I felt a strong conviction ... I am lost in wonder when I see what god has done for my soul I have now peace with god and I know that my redemer liveeth to make intersection for me.

Not everyone evidenced a favorable impression of Whitefield. A number mocked the evangelist without mercy, calling him "Dr. Squin-tum" due to an eye infirmity. On one occasion as he was preaching, unruly members of the crowd pelted him with "stones, rotten eggs and pieces of dead cat." He thought "persecution" was "every Christian's lot."

On the whole, however, Whitefield was greatly admired—even by a number of non-Christians. In his *Autobiography* Benjamin Franklin, who printed some of Whitefield's sermons and journals, noted the beneficent effects of the evangelist's ministry in Philadelphia:

It was wonderful to see the change soon made by his preaching in the manners of the inhabitants. From being thoughtless or indifferent about religion, it seemed as if all the world were growing religious, so that one could not walk through the town in an evening without hearing psalms sung in different families of every street.

Franklin indicated that Whitefield "was in all his conduct a perfectly *honest* man." He "computed" that the evangelist might be able to preach to a crowd of more than 30,000. Whitefield's speaking abilities quite charmed Franklin.

In England, Lord Bolingbrook—by no means an evangelical Christian—was likewise impressed by Whitefield's rhetorical skills: He observed, "He [Whitefield] is the most extraordinary man in our times. He has the most commanding eloquence I ever heard in any person."

After Wesley gave a sermon at Bristol on "Free Grace" in 1739, Whitefield became alarmed by the Arminian theology underlying Wesley's preaching. Whitefield felt more at ease with fellow Calvinists such as Jonathan Edwards and Howell Harris. Nonetheless, he apologized to Wesley: "I find I love you as much as ever and pray God, if it be his blessed will, that we may be all united together.... May God remove all obstacles that now prevent our union."

In 1741 Whitefield ministered in Scotland and Wales, accompanied by Harris. In 1742 he returned to Scotland to preach outdoors to large crowds gathered during the "Cambuslang Awakening" (February–August). At "Holy Fairs" ("Sacramental Occasions") organized by Pastor William McCulloch, Whitefield witnessed Scots (and some English and Irish) by the scores awed by what they believed was God the Holy Spirit's presence, confessing their sins before they took Holy Communion. Deep into the night, thousands of Scots prayed, confessed, and worshiped the Lord.

In the following years, Whitefield made repeated trips back to Scotland and the British American colonies besides his preaching ministries in England.

D. The Reformed Methodists

On January 5, 1743, Whitefield and a number of other Calvinist Methodists, including Howell Harris, Daniel Rowlands and John Cennick, met together in Waterford, South Wales. They established the organizational principles for a Reformed Methodist association. The Reformed Methodist movement was about one-tenth the size of Wesley's Methodists. It received significant backing from the Countess of Huntingdon and a talented pastor, William Romaine.

In 1739 Selina Shirley Hastings, the Countess of Huntingdon, came to saving faith in Christ. She gave Christian witness of her faith to aristocratic friends, some of whom did not always welcome her solicitation. The Duchess of Buckingham, for example, responded, "I thank your ladyship for the information concerning the Methodist Preachers. Their doctrines are most repulsive and strongly tinctured with impertinence and disrespect towards their superiors, in perpetually endeavoring to level all ranks and do away with all distinctions. It is monstrous to be told that you have a heart as sinful as the common wretches that crawl the earth."

In 1742 Lady Huntingdon met Harris and then in 1748 Whitefield. She became Reformed in her theology and created the "Countess of Huntingdon Connection" of itinerant Reformed evangelists, some of whom ministered to her aristocratic friends. In 1768 she lent her financial support to the Trevecka House in Wales, which Harris, who had broken fellowship with Rowland over Christology, had founded as a training center for Reformed Methodist pastors. Lady Huntingdon also funded the construction of buildings for some of the churches in which these pastors would serve. In addition, she urged evangelical women of means to use their "Drawing-Rooms" to reach out with the gospel to other wealthy women.

Thomas Wills, a contemporary Methodist minister, thankfully extolled Lady Huntingdon's witness for the gospel: "Thousands, I say tens of thousands, in various parts of the kingdom have heard the gospel through her instrumentality that in all probability that never would have heard it at all; and I believe through eternity will have cause to bless God that she ever existed. She was truly and emphatically a Mother of Israel."

After 1766, William Romaine served as the rector of St. Ann's, Blackfriars. Besides Whitefield, he was one of the most popular Reformed Methodist preachers of England. He sometimes traveled with Lady Huntingdon as an itinerant evangelist. In 1756 he commented that in Derby he "had there a most refreshing time." He noted that fifteen pulpits were open and "Showers of grace came down. Sinners in great numbers awakened, and believers comforted...."

Romaine had serious misgivings about aspects of Wesleyan Arminian theology. He criticized them as "very flattering to nature, exceedingly pleasing to self-righteousness, very exalting, yea, it is crowning *free will* and debasing King Jesus." Elsewhere he wrote, "In my present view of things, I would not be an Arminian for the world; because I am not only willing, but happy in getting more into Christ's debt.... Although I have learned but little, yet I would not be saved in any other way than by sovereign grace."

The disputes between John Wesley and George Whitefield from 1739 to 1770, the year Whitefield died, hindered their evangelistic cooperation: 1739–40, disagreement over Wesley's Bristol sermon on "Free Grace"; 1752, Whitefield's *A Letter to Rev. Mr. John Wesley* regarding the latter's alleged belief in universal redemption; 1769–70, the Predestinarian Controversy. Initially, Whitefield claimed that the two "preached two different Gospels." He worried that Wesley's Arminianism, with its view of prevenient grace given to all rather than only to the elect, did not take into account sufficiently the impact of sin on humankind. Wesley in turn feared that Whitefield's views of particular election and predestination and imputed righteousness opened the door to antinomianism and overthrew free grace.

Wesley's follower John Fletcher stoked bad feelings even further by publishing *Checks to Antinomianism.* For his part, Augustus Montague Toplady, a defender of Calvinism within the Anglican Church, offered bruising criticisms of the "reigning Heterodoxy of Arminius" and Wesley's theology.

On several occasions Wesley and Whitefield sought reconciliation. They recognized that some of their disagreements had been fanned by their partisans and were based on misunderstandings. In 1770, upon hearing that Whitefield had died in Newburyport, Massachusetts, Wesley was deeply saddened. In a moving funeral sermon, Wesley paid homage to the remarkable ministry of his fellow evangelist: "Have we read or heard of any person who called so many thousands, so many myriads of sinners to repentance? Above all, have we read or heard of anyone who has been the blessed instrument of bringing so many sinners from darkness to light, and from the power of Satan unto God?" One of the greatest English preachers of all time (over 7,500 sermons), Whitefield, the "Grand Itinerant," in sincere humility had remarked years earlier, "Let the name of George Whitefield perish, so long as Christ is exalted."

VI. ROMAN CATHOLICS

Well known for his advocacy of religious toleration, John Locke made it clear that toleration stopped at the doorstep of Roman Catholics. The fear of Jacobite conspiracies made Locke and the Anglican clergy wary of any campaign to give Roman Catholics full civil rights. Instead, a 1699 statute made the saying of the Latin mass a crime.

Roman Catholic apologists were often talented writers. They were quite prepared to challenge the legitimacy of Anglican teachings. For example, Bishop Tillotson felt obliged to answer John Sergeant's *Sure Footing in Christianity, or Rational Discourses on the Rule of Faith* (1665). He worried that leading Protestants might convert to Roman Catholicism. His anxieties were heightened in 1685 when the Duke of York, James II, a Roman Catholic, became king. It will be recalled that James II's Declaration of Indulgences (1688) removed restrictions blocking Roman Catholics from serving in governmental posts.

The arrival of William III from the United Provinces and the ensuing Glorious Revolution cut short James II's efforts to return England to the Roman Catholic fold. James II was allowed to leave England for France in December 1688. In an agreement of the Peace of Utrecht (1714) ending the War of the Spanish Succession, Louis XIV, the king of France, indicated that he would no longer back the Stuart claim to the throne of England.

During the eighteenth century Roman Catholics in England constituted a very small minority. For example, in 1703 only two convents existed in England, with a total of twenty-five nuns. The overall Catholic population numbered only 80,000 as late as 1770. Catholics did not possess many civil and political rights and generally remained religious outsiders. The Marriage Act of 1753 disallowed any marriage other than one following Anglican rites (with exceptions for Quakers and Jews). Fears that Roman Catholics might be covert supporters of a Jacobite rebellion sometimes unfairly trailed them.

Nonetheless, Roman Catholics sometimes lived without experiencing outright persecution. In fact, some members of the English Protestant upper classes gloried in their tolerant spirit. They appreciated aspects of Roman Catholic culture. They frequently owned and displayed in their spacious homes engravings and paintings crafted by Roman Catholic Italian and French artists. They thought it important to make the "Grand Tour" to Rome as a capstone for their cultural understanding. They respected works of artistic genius, even if classical pagan instead of Roman Catholic in origin.

The ugliness of the anti-Catholicism demonstrated by unruly mobs in the Gordon Riots (1780) surprised those English people. In 1778 a Catholic Relief Act had removed the penalties of the 1699 statute that had criminalized the Latin mass. In response, a furious "bigoted multitude" (statesman Edmund Burke's expression) then burned down Roman Catholic homes, chapels, and churches. Despite the Catholic Relief Acts (1778, 1791), Roman Catholics did not receive full civil liberties until the Emancipation Act of 1829.

VII. CHRISTIAN RESPONSES TO DEISM

If Anglicans, Dissenters, Evangelicals, and Roman Catholics sometimes sharply criticized each other, they generally agreed that deism represented a serious threat to the Christian faith as a revealed religion. Moreover, England constituted one of the earliest and most formidable strongholds of deism. Pierre Viret (1511–77) had first used the word *deist* in French, whereas Robert Burton in his *Anatomy of Melancholy* (1621) employed the expression for the first time in English.

In 1645 Lord Herbert of Cherbury, commonly considered the "father of English deism," proposed five articles generally associated with its principal beliefs: (1) God exists; (2) we are obliged to give reverence to God; (3) worship consists of pursuing practical morality;

(4) we should repent of our sin; (5) we will receive divine recompense in the world to come according to how we lived.

The public deist attack against revealed religion in the name of "natural religion" affected various regions of Europe in different time frames.

Charles Blount published several works, including *Anima Mundi* (1679), that furthered the deist cause in England. The appearance of John Toland's *Christianity not Mysterious* (1696) seemed to open up the floodgates of deistic literature in England. Some contemporaries viewed John Locke's *The Reasonableness of Christianity* (1695) as preparing the way for Toland's explicitly deist work. Locke attempted to parry the accusation that the controversial views of Toland, his friend, were based on his own writings.

In his *Demonstration of the Being and Attributes of God* (1704–6), Samuel Clarke identified four types of deists:

> 1. those who pretend to believe the existence of an eternal, infinite, independent, intelligent Being; and teach also that this Supreme Being made the world, though at the same time, they fancy God does not at all concern himself in the government of the world, nor has any regard to, or care of, what is done therein; 2. those who also believe in divine providence; 3. those who also believe in the divine perfections of God; 4. those who believe we have duties to God who rewards or punishes us in a world to come.

In the first half of the eighteenth century the onslaught of deistic literature and "unbelief" was powerful and provocative. In 1722 Daniel Defoe complained that "no age, since the founding and forming the Christian Church was ever like, in open avowed atheism, blasphemies, and heresies, to the age we now live in." Whereas in his *English Letters* (1728), Voltaire had praised the piety of the Anglican clergy, Montesquieu claimed during a visit to England in 1729 that "[here] there is no religion, and the subject if mentioned in society, excites nothing but laughter."

Major deistic works included Anthony Collins's *Discourse on Free Thinking* (1713) and *Discourse on the Grounds and Reasons of the Christian Religion* (1724); Thomas Whiston's *The True Text of the Old Testament* (1722); Matthew Tindal's *Christianity as Old as the Creation; or the Gospel, a Republication of the Religion of Nature* (1730); Thomas Chubb's *True Gospel of Jesus Christ Asserted* (1738); and Thomas Morgan's *The Moral Philosopher* (1737–1740). The arguments of a number of these books could not be easily dismissed.

In response to this wave of literature, Christian apologists undertook a massive effort to defeat not only deism, but atheism, Arianism,

Socinianism, and Unitarianism. The task of the Christian apologists was complicated by the fact that many of their deistic opponents assumed the guise of defending the "true" teachings of the Christian faith. Tindal, Toland, and Collins claimed to be Christians.

In the 1730s, Nathaniel Lardner, a dissenting pastor, observed: "I truly think that the Christians of this nation are at present under a great trial." In *A View of the Principal Deistical Writers*, John Leland wrote, "No man that is not utterly unacquainted with the state of things among us can be ignorant, that in the last and especially in the present age, there have been many books published that manifest design of which was, to set aside revealed religion."

Deism highlighted reason's right to judge "special revelation." In his very influential book Tindal wrote, "If nothing but Reasoning can improve Reason, and no Book can improve my Reason in any Point, but as it gives me convincing Proofs of its Reasonableness; a Revelation, that will not suffer us to judge of its Dictates by our Reason, is so far from improving Reason, that it forbids the Use of it." Tindal not only attempted to subvert Christian revelation, but also offered a substitute "natural" religion that was allegedly "reasonable," that upheld truths and morals as "old as creation."

Philologist Richard Bentley observed that the claims of deistic "evangelists" attacked the very heart of the Christian faith: "That the soul is material, Christianity a cheat, Scripture a falsehood, hell a fable, heaven a dream, our life without providence, and our death without hope, such are the items of the glorious gospel of these evangelists."

A number of deists argued that God, the Architect and Creator of the universe, does not providentially involve himself in his creation. Rather, he established fixed laws to govern the way the world runs. Since the laws are fixed, no biblical miracles could have taken place. The Bible is replete with errors, a premise that deists such as Anthony Collins claimed was confirmed by the biblical criticism of Spinoza, Richard Simon, and others. Prophetic references to a Messiah in the Old Testament are not fulfilled in the life of Jesus Christ, as Christians claim. The Christian faith condemns unfairly to perdition people who have never heard the gospel in other parts of the world. In reality God requires all peoples to follow his rationally construed moral laws regarding what is right and wrong. Owing to the fact that reason is given equally to everyone throughout the world, God is fair in holding everyone accountable to the same rational, moral standards.

Deists believed that their "natural religion" underlies all other religions. We learn about it, not from the Christian special revelation, but from (as Immanuel Kant puts it) "the starry heavens above us, and the moral law within us."

The Christian apologists unleashed an anti-deist counterattack that numbered in the scores of books. Jacques Abbadie's *Treatise on the Truth of the Christian Religion* (1684) represented one of the earliest and most widely circulated apologetics for the truthfulness of the Christian faith based on "facts." A Protestant pastor who ended his ministry in London, Abbadie attempted to answer deists' arguments against the resurrection of Jesus Christ and against alleged discrepancies in the gospel records. He pointed out the public nature of Christ's appearances after the resurrection, that is, eyewitnesses including a number of the disciples had seen Christ at different places and times. The change in the disciples' attitudes—from a spirit of loss and defeat due to Christ's crucifixion to a confidence in the truthfulness and power of Christ's gospel as evidenced in their preaching and willingness to die for the faith—would not make any sense unless they were convinced that Christ had been indeed resurrected. In the eighteenth century, Abbadie's work was found in the libraries of more French nobles than the writings of even Bossuet or Pascal.

In his *Vindication of the Divine Authority of the Old and New Testament* (1692), William Lowth, a fellow at St. John's College, Oxford, while acknowledging the danger of deism and the "atheism" of Thomas Hobbes and Spinoza, devoted his major effort to refuting challenges of Jean Leclerc and Richard Simon to the authority of Holy Scripture.

Other apologists attacked arguments of atheism and deism head on. John Ray penned *The Wisdom of God Manifested in the Works of the Creation* (1691). Richard Bentley added *A Confutation of Atheism from the Origin and Frame of the World* (1691). Peter Browne's *Letter* answered Toland's *Christianity not Mysterious*. Charles Leslie's *A Short and Easy Method with the Deists* (1698) convinced a number of deists to reconsider the truth claims of the Christian faith. Bentley answered Collins in *Remarks upon a late Discourse of Free-Thinking*. Thomas Sherlock's *Trial of the Witnesses of the Resurrection of Jesus* (1729) responded to Thomas Woolston. William Law addressed the arguments of Matthew Tindal, whereas John Wesley interacted with those of Henry Dodwell and Conyers Middleton.

English apologists who believed in natural revelation themselves often moved onto the same ground as the deists in assuming that reason rightly employed could serve as a valued tool to use in defeating their arguments. John Leland observed, "They [the deists] have appealed to the bar of reason; the advocates for Christianity have followed them to that bar, and have fairly shown that the evidences of revealed religion, are such as approve themselves to impartial reason, and if taken together they are fully sufficient to satisfy an honest and unprejudiced mind."

A number of contemporaries deemed Joseph Butler's *The Analogy of Religion, Natural and Revealed* (1736) a superb example of a Christian's measured arguments in the deployment of reason to vanquish deists' arguments. Butler wrote, "It is come, I know not how, to be taken for granted, by many persons, that Christianity is not so much a subject for enquiry but that it is now at length, discovered to be fictitious." He observed that the same defects Christians face in defending special revelation are analogous to those encountered by deists who find defects in nature. If the deists accept nature as divine, why should they not accept the divinity of revelation?

Success generally greeted the efforts of Christian apologists. By 1756, when William Warburton, a "polemic divine," published a rejoinder to Bolingbroke's "infidelity and naturalism," deism was largely contained. The Evangelical Revival of the 1730s and 1740s helped undermine the deist movement. In English colonial America, however, Jonathan Edwards believed deism continued to remain a serious threat.

The skeptical entailments of David Hume's *Enquiry Concerning Human Understanding* (1748), with its essays targeting miracles, providence, and revealed religion, likewise remained troubling. Hume attacked the basic concept of "cause and effect," claiming that without custom, we could have no knowledge of fact "beyond what is immediately present to the memory and senses." John Wesley described Hume as "the most insolent despiser of truth and virtue that ever appeared in the world, an avowed enemy to God and man, and to all that is sacred and valuable upon earth."

In Scotland, philosopher Thomas Reid (1710–96) developed a well-honed, sophisticated response to Hume's skepticism. In his *An Essay on Inquiry into the Human Mind on the Principles of Common Sense* (1764), Reid sharply criticized Hume's theory of ideas: "The theory of ideas, like the Trojan horse, had a specious appearance both of innocence and beauty; but if those philosophers had known, that it carried in its belly death and destruction to all science and common sense, they would not have broken down their walls to give it admittance." Hume's principles, if followed carefully, led to absurd conclusions.

Influenced in part by Lord Shaftesbury's earlier defense of "common sense," Reid proposed that the "learned and the Unlearned, the Philosopher and the day laborer" share a common understanding of the world as it is. Our "external senses" give us direct knowledge of the world: "The constancy of nature's law connects the sign with the thing signified." According to philosopher William Alston, Reid proposed that "there is no rationally attractive alternative to accepting the testimony of our basic cognitive faculties as (prima facie) correct, and that only if we do this will we ever have any chance to acquire any knowledge whatever."

A number of contemporary authors attacked Hume's *Of Miracles*, including Philip Skelton (1749), William Adams (1752), and John Leland (1755). Hume knew of twenty-two such rejoinders opposing this provocative work.

Many authors continued to provide an evidentialist apologetic to support the truth claims of Christianity. Toward the end of the century, William Paley's *A View of the Evidences of Christianity* (1794) became a classic evidentialist defense of miracles and prophecies recorded in the Bible. English Christians often highly esteemed the works of Butler and Paley deep into the nineteenth century. Others were less convinced about the wisdom of the evidentialist strategy of these apologists.

In 1790 Edmund Burke rejoiced that Christian apologists had largely carried the day against English deists: "Who, born within the last forty years has read one word of Collins, and Toland, and Tindal, and Chubb, and Morgan, and that whole race who called themselves Free Thinkers? Who now reads Bolingbroke? Who ever read him through?" Even though a potential exaggeration, Burke's claim rightfully suggests that the deistic movement had lost much of its appeal in certain quarters of English society. At the same time, in the 1790s some Christians cautioned about the possibility of a resurgent atheism.

VIII. SCOTLAND

As the eighteenth century dawned, the Scottish clans with their rough-hewn lifestyles and fierce warlike traditions continued to reign over wide expanses of the Highlands (one third of Scotland). By contrast, Edinburgh, the capital in the Lowlands (two thirds of Scotland), was a small, spatially constricted town with 35,000 inhabitants crowded into dirty tenements, stacked one story above another. Even though in 1695 the Scottish Parliament in Edinburgh had founded the Bank of Scotland, economic stagnation characterized the country's commercial life during the first half of the eighteenth century.

By the Act of Union of 1707, Scotland and England became one again. The Scottish Parliament was dissolved and merged into the English Parliament. The Scots were given forty-five members in the House of Commons. Large numbers of Scottish Highlanders were angered by this development. They were partisans of the Stuart claim to the monarchy. The Stuart dynasty (James I, Charles I, Charles II, James II, Anne) had deep family roots in Scotland. In 1603 James VI of Scotland had gone south to become King James I of England. In this context, a number of Highlanders participated in Jacobite revolts against the English government in 1708, 1715, and 1745. In the failed revolt of 1715 they backed James VIII, the son of James II.

In the more serious insurrection of 1745, the Highlanders supported "Bonnie Prince Charlie" (James VIII's son, the Young Pretender, Charles Edward). After winning a number of victories and taking Edinburgh, Bonnie Prince Charlie's army was defeated at Culloden in 1746, thereby ending the Jacobite threat to the Hanoverian monarchy. The English passed laws that stipulated that the Catholic clans be broken up and that kilts, viewed as a symbol of Highlander rebellion, be forbidden. Many Highlanders were forced to leave their lands, which reverted to large wildernesses where grazing sheep largely outnumbered people. Influenced by Gaelic poets and lay exhorters, after 1746 a large number of Highlanders began to embrace the Reformed faith.

The Patronage Act of 1712 also served as another major irritant in Scottish-English relations. The Crown assumed the right to choose Scottish pastors, a privilege that could allow the government to extend its authority into the religious and social life of Presbyterian Scotland. Refusing to acquiesce to this claim, "Seceder" Presbyterians led by brothers Ebenezer and Ralph Erskine separated and created their own churches.

In 1742 the remarkable Cambuslang Revival moved upon many people of Scotland. From February through May, Pastor William McCulloch of the Church of Scotland's Cambuslang parish, located four miles from Glasgow, noted a growing number of people who were coming to prayer meetings and had a "deep concern about their salvation." In June, George Whitefield came to Cambuslang and preached numerous times. In August, meetings celebrating the Lord's Supper attracted crowds ranging from 30,000 to 40,000 people. McCulloch wrote, "People sat unwearied till two in the morning to hear sermons, disregarding the weather. You could scarce walk a yard, but you must tread upon some, either rejoicing in God for mercies received, or crying out for more. Thousands and thousands have I seen ... melted down under the word and power of God. At the celebration of the holy communion, their joy was so great."

Whitefield also preached to large crowds in Edinburgh and other cities. Another center for the revival was in Kilsyth under the ministry of James Robe.

In the second half of the eighteenth century, Scotland gained a reputation as a center for the Enlightenment. Its luminaries included David Hume, Thomas Reid, Adam Smith, and Francis Hutchison. With a flair for exaggeration, Voltaire wrote that "today it is from Scotland that we get rules of taste in all the arts, from epic poetry to gardening."

In 1747 Scottish feudalism was put to rest with the abolition of the Baron Courts. As in England, some members of the wealthy classes wanted to establish a polite, literate, and tolerant society in which Presbyterians, Anglicans, and even a skeptic like philosopher Hume could feel at home. "Literati" in Edinburgh participated in various clubs such as the Society of Improvers and the Select Society, in which they discussed among other things the natural philosophy associated with Newton, the empiricism associated with Locke, and the utilitarian moral philosophy associated with Hutchison. They sought "enlightened" ways to reform and improve Scottish society, especially its agriculture. In the inaugural edition of the *Edinburgh Review* (1755), the editor encouraged Scots "to a more eager pursuit of learning themselves, and to do honor to their country."

In the Church of Scotland an Evangelical party battled with members of a so-called Moderate party. Moderates such as William Robertson, a clergyman and president of the University of Edinburgh, along with the editors of the *Edinburgh Review*, eagerly embraced a vision of knowledge and improvement of society they thought could reform Scottish institutions. They proposed that God would bless Scotland if the Scottish were enterprising and prosperous.

Evangelical spokespersons such as Edinburgh pastors John Erskine and Robert Walker also wanted to reform society and use new learning to do so. Moreover, they sought to promote civil liberties. Unlike some of the Moderates, however, they believed personal conversion to Christ was a prerequisite for any reform of Scottish life. Erskine appreciated George Whitefield and edited and published a number of Jonathan Edwards's writings. Perhaps unfairly, the Evangelicals sometimes suspected that the Moderates did not fully uphold orthodox Calvinist doctrines. Hume's friendship with a number of the Moderates added depth to their suspicions.

The struggles between the Evangelicals and Moderates influenced the thinking of John Witherspoon, a leader of the Evangelicals in Glasgow. Before he left Scotland in 1768 to become the president of the College of New Jersey (later Princeton University), he had come to appreciate selective aspects of Thomas Reid's response to David Hume's skepticism. Years earlier (1740), as noted, other conservative Calvinists, the "Seceders," who were much disturbed by the teaching of the Moderates, felt obliged to leave the Church of Scotland and formed an independent presbytery.

IX. IRELAND

The Glorious Revolution of 1689 looked not at all "glorious" for many Irish Catholics. On July 1, 1690, the armies of the Protestant William III defeated the forces of the Catholic James II at the Battle of the Boyne and seized Dublin. In 1691 many Jacobites in Ireland surrendered or fled. The Banishment Act of 1697 ordered members of the

Catholic clergy to leave Ireland or run the risk of execution. The Protestant minority began to control more of the countryside, as land ownership by Catholics dropped from 22 percent in 1688 to 10 percent in 1714 to 5 percent in 1778. Abject poverty and illiteracy made life miserable for large numbers of Irish Catholics. One foreign visitor observed, "The Irish peasant is poorer than the lowest serfs in Poland and Germany."

In 1718 the archbishop of Dublin lamented that "the misery of the people here is very great, the beggars innumerable and increasing every day. One half of the people in Ireland eat neither bread nor flesh for one half of the year, nor wear Shoes or Stockings; your Hoggs in England and Essex Calves live better than they." Many Irish went to England, where they were exploited as cheap labor.

English mercantilistic legislation had contributed to ruining Irish trade in livestock and wool. The Woolen Act of 1699, for example, disallowed the Irish from exporting woolen goods to *any* country; it allowed only the exportation of unworked wool to specific English ports.

Much power lay in the hands of a small group of wealthy Anglican elite who belonged to the established Church of Ireland. Even Scottish Presbyterians who had settled in Ulster were excluded from certain civil and military roles, although they could serve in the Irish Parliament.

The Irish Parliament, subservient to the desires of the English king and Privy Council, was forced to pay the cost for the stationing of English troops in Ireland to keep the peace. The English were fearful that Irish Catholics might support future Jacobite revolts. Through secretive means, some members of the Catholic clergy in secular clothes attempted to minister to the Catholic faithful.

In the last decades of the eighteenth century the Irish population grew rapidly. Irish Methodists, numbering 14,000 in 1790 and closely allied with English Protestants, clustered more and more in the north of the country. Protestants in Ireland, whether Anglican, Scottish Presbyterian, Methodist, or Huguenot, often evidenced anti-Catholic sentiments, just as Catholics were often ill disposed toward Protestants.

In 1778 the Catholic Relief Act allowed Catholics to buy and inherit land. In 1782 the Irish Parliament gained independence, and penal laws against Catholics were challenged. The English monarchy, however, managed to maintain its authority, putting down the Irish Rebellion of 1798.

X. THE ENDURING PRESENCE OF CHRISTIANITY IN THE BRITISH ISLES

Between the years 1680 and 1800, Christianity in the British Isles (England, Scotland, Ireland, and Wales) by no means withered away.

If anything, on occasion it seemed to flourish. From an evangelical perspective, the birth of the Methodist movement; the spiritual awakening in England, Scotland, and Wales; and the weakening of the deist challenge abetted the advance of the Christian faith.

In 1795 John Newton commented on the growing numbers of evangelical clergy in the Anglican Church: "I am not sure that in the year 1740, there was a single parochial minister, who was publicly known as a gospel preacher, in the whole kingdom: now we have, I know not how many, but I think not fewer than four hundred."

The theologically moderate Richard Watson, who had penned apologies against historian Edward Gibbon and political theorist Thomas Paine, reminded his readers that many eminent writers had been Christians:

> It is proper that young men should be furnished with a ready answer to arguments in favor of Infidelity, which are taken from the high literary character of those who profess it; let them remember then, that Bacon, Boyle, Newton, Grotius, Locke, Euler, that Addison, Harley, Haller, West, Jenyns, that Lord Nottingham, King, Barrington, Lyttleton with an hundred other *laymen*, who were surely as eminent for their literary attainments in every kind of science as either Bolingbroke or Voltaire, were professed *believers* in Christianity.

So-called "Blue Light" Evangelicals such as Admiral Charles Middleton were beginning to gain flag-rank stature in the Royal Navy. They called themselves "Blue Lights" to designate they could serve as signals in distress circumstances. Along with a growing number of Methodist below-deck hands, they hoped to see their fellow navy men come to Christ. They organized prayer meetings aboard ships.

From an Anglican perspective, the Church of England, even if subordinated to the state, had regained its central place in the religious life of the realm. The Anglican Church recruited potentially talented clergy from its schools. Its clergy produced scores of popular devotional materials and preached an abundance of well-received sermons. Moreover, members of the Anglican hierarchy believed they had largely held in check the campaigns of Dissenters and Roman Catholics for greater rights and recognition.

From a Catholic perspective, a faithful witness for the Roman Catholic Church in Ireland and England had at least survived the century, even if barely so on some occasions. Anti-Catholicism, however, remained a virulent force in English social, religious, and political life toward the end of the century.

Many Christians, especially the "middle sort" between the landed aristocracy and the "miserable poor" and "working poor," did find the new wealth associated with the commercial revolution in England and Scotland, and the gaining of new territories and markets, not without temptations in fostering an acquisitive, materialist mind-set. For their part, wealthy aristocratic landholders devoted a considerable amount of time to diversions such as gambling, fox hunting, and trips to Paris. The evangelical Newton wrote, "How fat we were when the war [Seven Years War] terminated in the year 1763 and how we have kicked and forsaken the Rock of our salvation of late years." In 1778 Samuel Johnson complained that his contemporaries were not showing proper respect for their superiors:

> Subordination is sadly broken down in this age. No man now has the same authority which his father had, except a gaoler. No man now has it over his servants; it is diminished in our colleges, nay in our grammar schools.... There are many causes the chief of which is, I think, the great increase of money; Gold and silver destroy feudal subordination.

The slave trade constituted a scandalous underside of British Christian "polite" society. It had received a significant boost due to the Treaty of Utrecht. In 1712 Queen Anne reported that the British had acquired a monopoly through the *Asiento* Agreement, according to which they were to buy, send, and sell 4,800 "Negroes" a year for thirty years to Spanish America.

A number of European powers (including Britain) benefited handsomely from a triangular trade in which they transported slaves to plantations in the Americas, received back products from the American plantations, and sent weapons and other products to Africa. Numerous European businessmen became wealthy due to their participation in the heinous slave trade.

In 1754 Anthony Benezet read a paper, *An Epistle of Caution and Advice, Concerning the Buying and Keeping of Slaves*, to a Quaker Meeting in Philadelphia. John Woolman, another Quaker, was apparently the principal author of this text. Convinced abolitionists, both men attempted to bring about a halt to slavery and the transatlantic slavery trade. Benezet corresponded with Benjamin Franklin and John Wesley. Franklin decided no longer to own slaves.

Between 1787 and 1792 the antislavery movement gathered momentum. It received especially effective leadership from tireless organizers such as the Quakers Thomas Clarkson and Elizabeth Heyrick. In 1788 Prime Minister William Pitt created a committee to report on the slave trade and called John Newton, a former slaver, to testify as a knowledgeable witness. Then in 1791, William Wilberforce made a powerful speech in the House of Commons urging his colleagues to abolish the slave trade. In 1792, 30,000 British boycotted West Indian sugar. Between 1791 and 1803, Haitian slaves revolted. The publication of Olaudah Equiano's gripping account of his life as a slave also stirred antislavery sentiments. Other African writers numbered in their midst Quobna Ottobah Cugoano and Ignatius Sancho.

The power of slavers often remained entrenched. John Wesley worried that the forces arraigned against abolition were so virulent they might completely dishearten Wilberforce. In one of his last letters, dated February 24, 1791, Wesley reminded Wilberforce that God was yet stronger than the opponents of abolition:

William Wilberforce.

Unless the divine power has raised you up to be as "Athanasius against the world," I see not how you can go through your glorious enterprise in opposing that execrable villainy, which is the scandal of religion, of England, and of human nature. Unless God has raised you up for this very thing, you will be worn out by the opposition of God and devils. But if God be for you, who can be against you? Are all of them stronger than God? O be not weary of well doing!

Not until 1807 would slavery be abolished throughout the British Empire by law.

The concerns of well-to-do English people in particular about constructing a "polite" society, about extending Britain's economic and political reach through empire building in overseas colonies, and about making intellectual adaptations to the "enlightenment" (using the term conventionally) sometimes paid unexpected dividends. These concerns could make traditional Christian teachings regarding humankind as a sinful people in need of a Savior seem not necessarily untruthful but simply mundane and less relevant than more pressing, this-worldly wants and aspirations. The Earl of Chesterfield went so far as to tell his godson that "religion is by no means a proper subject of conversation in a mixed company."

This tendency toward religious indifference is by no means the full story, however. Christians of vital faith made their presence felt. In 1784 Pastor John Sutcliff of Olney called for Christians to "earnestly implore a revival of our churches and the general cause of our Redeemer."

In an age of growing national self-confidence, John Newton, the repentant former slaver, preached the gospel in his parish of Olney;

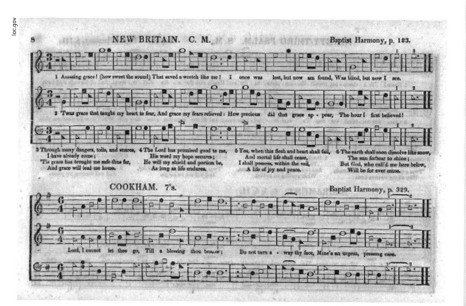

The Southern Harmony and Musical Companion (1831), containing the earliest pairing of the words to "Amazing Grace" with the tune now associated with the hymn.

created the Eclectic Society, whose members asked questions like "What is the best way of propagating the Gospel in the East Indies?"; and penned the famous lyrics of "Amazing Grace": "Amazing grace, how sweet the sound, That saved a wretch like me. I once was lost, but now am found, was blind but now I see."

In an age of growing ostentatious wealth, Isaac Watts (1674–1748) had earlier written "When I Survey the Wondrous Cross," which included a reference to riches: "When I survey the wondrous cross On which the prince of glory died, My richest gain I count but loss And pour contempt on all my pride."

During the French Revolution, interest in biblical prophecy soared among the English people. Many Christians sought to understand that revolution in the context of biblical prophecy.

Then, in 1797, as the Age of Lights dimmed, the evangelical Wilberforce was emboldened to claim that England still remained resolutely a "Christian Nation," having only a fringe of "skeptics and Unitarians." On April 17, 1774, Theophilus Lindsey had established the Essex Street Church, the first openly Unitarian church in England. The Unitarian Joseph Priestly, who corresponded with Lindsey, was a prominent English scientist and political observer. Quite possibly Wilberforce substantially underestimated the influence of unbelief and radical thought in certain corners of English society. Nonetheless, it is clearly evident that Christianity (in its various expressions) exercised a pervasive influence on English culture as the eighteenth century drew to a close.

FOR FURTHER STUDY

Clark, J. C. D. *English Society 1660–1832: Religion, Ideology and Politics during the Ancient Regime.* Cambridge: Cambridge University Press, 2003.

Dallimore, Arnold. *George Whitefield: God's Anointed Servant in the Great Revival of the Eighteenth Century.* Wheaton, IL: Crossway, 1990.

Fea, John. *Was America Founded as a Christian Nation? A Historical Introduction.* Louisville: Westminster John Knox, 2011.

Harrison, Peter. *"Religion" and Religions in the English Enlightenment.* Cambridge: Cambridge University Press, 2002.

Marsden, George: *A Life of Jonathan Edwards.* New Haven: Yale University Press, 2003.

Metaxas, Eric. *Amazing Grace: William Wilberforce and the Heroic Campaign to End Slavery.* New York: HarperSanFrancisco, 2007.

Noll, Mark. *The Rise of Evangelicalism: The Age of Edwards, Whitefield and the Wesleys.* Downers Grove, IL: InterVarsity Press, 2001.

Rack, Henry. *Reasonable Enthusiast: John Wesley and the Rise of Methodism.* London: Epworth Press, 1989.

Sher, Richard B. *Church and University in the Scottish Enlightenment: The Moderate Literati of Edinburgh.* Edinburgh: Edinburgh University Press, 1985.

Ward, W. R. *The Protestant Evangelical Awakening.* Cambridge: Cambridge University Press, 1992.

Christianity in the Age of Lights (2)

The Kingdom of France (1680–1789)

I. INTRODUCTION

During the Age of Lights, the struggle of the French monarchy to enforce its royal will on two outsider groups, Jansenists (Augustinian Catholics) and Huguenots (Reformed Protestants), frequently dominated the religious-political history of the Kingdom of France. In play was the monarchy's critically important claim that it alone possessed the right to determine the religion of the French people.

The Kingdom of France was the most populous and wealthy country of Europe. It was also probably the most feared, hated, admired, and imitated realm on the Continent. In the *Encyclopédie*, the Chevalier de Jaucourt, Diderot's prolific editorial associate, gave this definition of the kingdom's borders: "France (Geography), great kingdom of Europe, bounded to the north by the Netherlands [the Austrian Netherlands]; to the east by Germany, Switzerland, and Savoy; to the south by the Mediterranean Sea and the Pyrenees; and to the west by the Atlantic." The kingdom was divided into regions or provinces such as Languedoc and Provence in the south, Bretagne in the west, Picardie in the north, and Franche-Comté in the east. Lorraine became part of France in 1766, as did Corsica in 1769.

At the time of the French Revolution (1789), the population approached a hefty 28 million. An overwhelmingly Catholic realm, France was divided into 36,000 parishes. In 1790 the revolutionary Abbé Henri Grégoire indicated that between 6 and 8 million people could not speak French but used one of the thirty dialects of the country. Not all Frenchmen could sing Claude-Joseph Rouget de Lisle's *"Marseillaise,"* the French revolutionary song, even if they had wanted to do so.

II. THE FRENCH KINGS

From 1680 to 1789 the Court at Versailles, the principal residence of the Bourbon kings, generally constituted the epicenter of French political life. Nonetheless, the formal and informal discussions of the *philosophes* in the Parisian *salons* (drawing rooms of homes) of worldly minded hostesses such as Madame Geoffrin, Madame de Tencin, and Madame Necker; the power of the *Parlement* of Paris (a law court) and other *Parlements* of France; the free exchange of ideas at various Masonic lodges; the illegal books and broadsides of a clandestine press—all these began to challenge seriously Versailles's political dominance in the second half of the eighteenth century. A powerful "court of public opinion" was continuing to emerge.

France's Bourbon kings sought to protect the inheritance rights of members of their own dynastic family and to expand the kingdom's economic and political power on the Continent and overseas. They were obsessed with burnishing the luster of their own glory and that of France. They fought wars on the Continent that often had counterparts in colonial regions. Louis XIV (1661–1715) on occasion spoke of "French Europe" and France's "permanent enmity" with Spain.

France was often the aggressor in Louis XIV's wars. These wars included the War of Devolution (1667–68), the Dutch War (1672–78), the War of the League of Augsburg (1688–97), and the War of the Spanish Succession (1701–14). After initial military successes, Louis XIV later prosecuted wars that failed and nearly bankrupted the royal treasury. The wars of Louis XV (1715–74), the *Bien-Aimé* ("Beloved"), included the War of the Polish Succession (1733–35), the War of the Austrian Succession (1740–48), the Seven Years War (1756–63)—which was a "world war" of sorts—and military theaters spread from India to North America. In the Seven Years War, England and Prussia eventually defeated France and her allies Austria and Spain. The Treaty of Paris (1763) recognized the stunning loss of French Canada to the English.

After the American victory at the Battle of Saratoga (1778), Louis XVI, in part to spite the English, supported republican American colonists (via the Franco-American Alliance, 1778) in their quest to gain independence from the British during the American Revolution. This aid had an ironic underside: the monarch was abetting the cause of republicans, and the aid exacerbated France's ballooning financial debt. In May–June 1789, Louis XVI was ultimately forced to call for the meetings of the Estates-General to deal with the severe fiscal crisis.

After histrionic debates, delegates of the Third Estate (the people) declared they represented the "nation" and invited members of the First Estate (clergy) and Second Estate (nobles) to join them. In time, a good number did just that. On June 17, 1789, the Third Estate (the *Communes*) changed its name to the *Assemblée Nationale*, claiming that it, rather than the monarchy, represented the nation. A century earlier, during the reign of Louis XIV, the French people would have thought such an action outrageous—an egregious affront to their "monarch appointed by God."

A. Divine Right Monarchs

In 1680 the Kingdom of France constituted a divine right monarchy. In his *Politics Drawn from the Very Words of Holy Scripture*, Jacques Bénigne Bossuet, an apologist for divine right monarchy, an advisor and confessor for Louis XIV, and an instructor for the dauphin (heir apparent), justified this form of government by citing principally scriptural warrant. He argued that the king received his authority directly from God: "God is the King of kings: it is for him to instruct them and to rule them as his ministers. Listen then, Monseigneur, to the lessons which he gives them in his Scripture, and learn from the examples on which they must base their conduct."

Bossuet continued, "Rulers then act as the ministers of God and as his lieutenants on earth. It is through them that God exercises his empire." Bossuet claimed that the king's royal power was "absolute" because the "prince need render account of his acts to no one." The king, however, was not to act like a Turkish despot who made arbitrary decrees. Rather, the king had a covenant with his subjects to care for them the way a loving father cares for his children.

According to divine right theory, the French king was a sacred personage who resided at the center of a religious world. Without him there would be chaos. His lineage stretched back to Adam through Pharamond (a mythical figure), Clovis, Pepin, and Charlemagne. From the Middle Ages on, writings called *Mirrors of Princes* charged him to be "pious," "just," and "good," and to avoid luxury, cruelty, weakness, and incontinence.

At the coronation, the archbishop of Reims anointed him with sacred oil and blessed his gloves, scepter, and ring, and the new king swore an oath to uphold the Catholic faith. Elements of the ceremony accented both the divine and civil nature of his union with the kingdom. If his subjects should rebel against or attack his sacred person, they deserved the most severe punishment. An assassination attempt warranted a gruesome public execution, an example for any other would-be assassins. In 1757 Robert François Damiens, who had made an attempt on the life of Louis XV, was literally pulled apart before a crowd of thousands of raucous Parisian onlookers. A subversive word

> "God is the King of kings: it is for him to instruct them and to rule them as his ministers" (Jacques Bénigne Bossuet).

written or uttered against His Majesty could earn its author time in the king's dank and dark prisons.

Until the 1750s, *the* center of French life was wherever the king's court was. To be away from the Court at Versailles or other royal residences such as Fontainebleau—even in nearby Paris with its rich cultural world, its *Parlement*, and homes of some nobles; with its Champs-Elysées (1667) and other Grands Boulevards—was to distance oneself from the seat of the government and the real source of power and privilege—namely, the king. To be outside of Versailles and Paris was to be "provincial."

Many of the nobles spent their days in this hierarchical world scheming how to advance their own interests, trying to escape boredom through amusements and sensuality, engaging in prattling gossip, ridicule, and court intrigue. They scurried about trying to gain entrance into Louis XIV's presence so as to win from him a reassuring glance, a word of commendation, and a favor. Prized opportunities included the right to attend the king's *Lever* when he arose in the morning or the ceremonial *Coucher* when he went to bed, or an invitation to a royal audience, a sumptuous diner party, or a robust hunt.

Between the years 1669 and 1688 Louis XIV had expanded the Chateau de Versailles (originally a hunting lodge) with monumental architecture, sweeping gardens, and fountains as a tribute to France and to himself as Apollo, the "Sun King." Some 10,000 people lived at the chateau and in the surrounding area. They ranged over time from members of the royal family—Maria Theresa of Spain, his cousin and queen (d. 1683); Françoise d'Aubigné Scarron (Madame de Maintenon), whom he married secretly in 1683; his council of governmental ministers; his mistresses, including Madame Louise de La Vallière and Françoise-Athénaïs (Marquise de Montespan); the great nobles (*les grands*); and his royal chaplains—to soldiers, gardeners, cooks, and stable stewards who attended to his every royal need and whim.

In the 1690s Louis XIV also attempted to turn Paris into a "New Rome."

In a word, Louis XIV adroitly promoted the royalist argument for the cult of the king. He summed up his viewpoint with the famous phrase, *"L'état, c'est moi"* ("The state, it is I").

B. Louis XIV and the Gallican Catholic Church

Louis XIV (1638–1715) became king at age five but, given his youth, did not assume full authority until 1661, at age twenty-two. In the intervening time, his mother, Anne of Austria (who was in fact Spanish), and Cardinal Mazarin attempted to govern a realm beset by great civil unrest and armed conflicts associated with the various *Frondes*. Nobles of France (the Gondi faction and the Condé/Conti faction) revolted against Mazarin, using the *Parlements* as venues where their opposition was expressed. They attempted to gain power for themselves and thwart the plans of other factions. In 1649 Paris was placed under a state of siege; the next year civil war broke out. Forced to go into hiding, Louis XIV witnessed firsthand the anarchy and bloodshed of the *Fronde*.

Traumatized by what he experienced, Louis XIV determined to countermand any future revolts by nobles through the establishment of an absolute monarchy. He learned well the trade of a king (*métier de roi*) under the watchful eye of Cardinal Mazarin (1602–61), a shrewd politician. Louis XIV's actual control of France, however, extended just as far as his agents were successfully able to enforce or project his will. He sought to oblige the "people of quality" (the princes of the blood, cardinals and bishops, dukes and peers and other nobles) to do his bidding by making them depend on him for advancement in offices and the reception of gratifications from the royal treasury. He tried to gain control of the royal courts (*Parlements*), the military, and the tax collection system.

The "very Christian" king, Louis XIV, tried to impose a Gallican form of Catholicism upon his people—whether they were Jansenist, Jesuit, Quietist, Protestant, or other—as a basis of the kingdom's unity. After his secret marriage to Madame de Maintenon, he apparently became more concerned about his soul's eternal welfare.

Since 1516, French kings had exercised the right to select the bishops of the French church. The kings usually filled the positions with nobles who were loyal to them. When Pope Innocent XI rejected Louis XIV's naming of bishops and his appropriation of monies from vacant bishoprics, the king, with the backing of the Assembly of the Clergy, encouraged Bossuet to draw up the Declaration of Gallican Liberties of 1682. This important document stipulated that the kings of France "were not subject to any ecclesiastical power in temporal affairs" (Article 1). Other articles of these "Gallican

Louis XIV of France, the "Sun King."

Liberties" reiterated the themes of the Council of Constance such as how the "plentitude of power in spiritual matters" resided in all the church. Even if the pope "has the chief voice in questions of faith, his decision is unalterable unless the consent of the Church is given" (Article 4).

Thus the bishops of the Gallican church had great authority to rule both in temporal and spiritual matters. Besides their episcopal visits, ordinations, and baptisms, until 1702 they mandated that religious books could be published only with their permission. Thereafter they regularly called on governmental censors of the *Librairie* (the institution that assessed books) to condemn "wicked books." The bishops' own privileges were exorbitant. They ruled over a church that owned approximately 10 percent of French land. In exchange for immunities from taxation, they were to give a "free gift" of money to their defender, the monarch, at their Assemblies of the Clergy.

In 1690 Pope Alexander VIII condemned the Declaration of Gallican Liberties. In 1693 Louis XIV had the declaration rescinded. In 1695 he gave his bishops greater authority over priests. He was worried about the spread of Jansenism among them. Nonetheless, the French church continued to exhibit the spirit of "Gallicanism," a willingness of the king and bishops of France to defy the papacy in temporal and even sometimes spiritual matters. On occasion, however, Louis XIV and his royal successors did seek the support of the papacy in dealing with one of their most vexing religious and political problems: the heated rivalry between the Jansenists and the Jesuits.

III. THE STRUGGLE BETWEEN THE JANSENISTS AND JESUITS

The bitter controversy between Jansenists and Jesuits and their respective allies in the *Parlements* and among the nobles often held center stage in the political life of France, not only during the reign of Louis XIV, but during the regency of Phillippe d'Orléans (1715–23) and the reign of Louis XV. Contests between Jansenists and Jesuits also flared up in Spain, Austria, Austrian Netherlands, the city-states of Italy, and Utrecht.

Jansenists were the followers of Cornelius Jansen (1585–1638), a professor of theology at the University of Louvain who for a time was a bishop of Ypres. Jansen had proposed an interpretation of St. Augustine in his posthumous work *Augustinus* (1640) that—in extolling God's majesty, awesome power, justice, and righteousness—challenged any role we humans might have in winning our salvation through free will. Instead, the elect are saved by God's grace alone. As their lives are transformed, the elect want to do the will of God by performing acts of love for God and their neighbors. The elect, in anxiously seeking assurance of salvation, attempt to overcome temptations of the world, the flesh, and the Devil by following an austere life of sincere contrition, by doing acts of rigorous penance, by celebrating frequent Communion, and by demonstrating true love for God.

The Jansenists employed a distinctive "Figurist" form of scriptural exegesis in discerning a warrant for "the witness to truth" of a religious minority. They argued for the inviolability of the Christian conscience even to the extent of refusing to accept a church teaching they deemed in error.

Jansenists were especially critical of the Jesuits, whom they believed had succumbed to the teachings of Molinism, an anti-Augustinian theology based on Luis Molina's *A Reconciliation of Free Choice with the Gifts of Grace, Divine Foreknowledge, Providence, Predestination and Reprobation* (1588). Molina, a Spanish Jesuit, had argued that "sufficient grace" provides us with the strength to do good using our free will. God elects us according to his foreknowledge of what he knows we will do using our free choice. Jansenists also did not accept the Jesuits' defense of

Cornelius Jansen.

papal monarchy. Rather, like Gallicans, they held a conciliarist position: the authority of the church was vested in all the members of the body of Christ, including themselves as a Catholic minority. They pitted their Jansenist Gallican constitutionalism against Jesuit Ultramontane absolutism (loyalty "beyond the mountains" to the papacy).

The Jansenists thought the casuistry of the Jesuits in ethics, their overbearing appreciation of classical pagan culture, and their supposed worldliness were reprehensible. In the *Provincial Letters* (1660), Pascal (1623–62), an associate of the Jansenists Antoine Arnauld and Pierre Nicole, cleverly parodied the Jesuits much to the delight of many Parisians. Louis XIV was not amused; he ordered the book burned.

For their part, Jesuits accused the Jansenists of being crypto-Protestants and republicans. Having sworn an oath to serve the papacy, Jesuits were particularly suspicious of any proclivities among Jansenists to favor Conciliarism and Gallicanism. Moreover, they proposed that the natural man does have a capacity to live "morally" if he follows reason. A work of moral theology titled *Medulla theologiae moralis* declared, "Although all knowledge of God were absent, yet a man could act morally for good or for bad, if only he chose of his own free will to act in keeping with, or in contradiction to, the first principles of right reason placed in us by nature." (*Medulla* was written by the Jesuit Hermann Busenbaum [1645], but did not get a lot of attention until it was revised by Pierre LaCroix [1733], who added to it considerably, including offensive sections on murder and regicide. The book was publicly burned in 1757.)

Given this long-standing perspective on moral theology, Jesuit missionaries were thus inclined to make major adaptations of the Christian faith to the beliefs of peoples of other religions. In the so-called Chinese Rites Controversy, for example, the Italian Jesuit missionary Matteo Ricci (1552–1610), in his *The True Meaning of the Lord of Heaven*, made a controversial claim: "He who is called the Lord of Heaven in my humble country is He who is called Shang-ti (Sovereign on High) in Chinese." Ricci allowed new Chinese converts to continue ancestor worship and the making of offerings to the emperor, a practice Pope Innocent X (1644–55) condemned, only to have Pope Alexander VII (1655–67) and Pope Clement X (1670–76) approve it, with the practice once again condemned by Popes Clement XI in 1715 and Benedict XIV in 1742.

Responding to Clement XI's decrees, in 1721 Chinese Emperor K'ang-hsi ordered: "From now on Westerners should not be allowed to preach in China to avoid further trouble." Serious persecution of Christians ensued under Emperor Yung Chen (1723–36) and Emperor Chung Lung (1736–96).

As if to clear themselves of the serious charge of sympathy for Protestantism, the leading Jansenists of the mid-seventeenth century, Pierre Nicole (1625–95) and Antoine Arnauld (the "Great Arnauld," 1612–94), became major protagonists in the eucharistic controversy of the 1660s and 1670s. They attacked the works of Jean Claude, the well-respected Reformed pastor of Charenton (near Paris), who had argued that the Roman Catholic doctrine of transubstantiation was a doctrinal innovation of the eleventh and twelfth centuries. Pierre Bayle characterized the controversy as "the most famous dispute one had ever seen in France between Catholics and Protestants."

In response, Nicole and Arnauld wrote *The Perpetuity of the Faith of the Catholic Church concerning the Eucharist* in a "small" version (1664) and a multivolume "large" version (1669, 1672, 1674). They defended the thesis that the doctrine had been "perpetually" upheld by the church throughout Christian history. To add weight to their thesis, they added "attestations" gathered from Eastern Orthodox Christians that allegedly indicated that these believers also believed in transubstantiation. Claude disputed the authenticity of these attestations, gaining covert help from an unexpected quarter, the Catholic biblical critic Richard

Simon. In the *Brerewood Additions*, Simon, posing as an Anglican priest, scorned the quality of the Jansenists' linguistic skills and argued that the eucharistic beliefs of Eastern Christians were in fact closer to those of Reformed Christians than to those of the Jansenists.

Despite their best anti-Protestant efforts, the Jansenists Nicole and Arnauld did not ultimately win the favor of Louis XIV. In 1678 they were forced to leave France. Arnauld lived in exile in Brussels.

Under the influence of Madame de Maintenon and Jesuit confessors, Louis XIV's hostility toward Jansenists only intensified. In 1704 his grandson, the Bourbon King Philip V of Spain (1683–1746), stoked this animus by calling for the destruction of Jansenism as a "sect so pernicious to the state and church." Louis XIV apparently associated Jansenism with a spirit of rebellion and with Protestant tendencies. In 1709 he ordered that twenty Jansenist sisters (*religieuses*) be removed from Port-Royal-des-Champs southwest of Paris because they would not sign a formulary that indicated certain doctrines of Jansen were heretical. Two years later he commanded the buildings at the site to be destroyed.

In 1712 Louis urged Pope Clement XI to issue *Unigenitus Dei Filius*. The pope promulgated the bull in 1713. It condemned 101 propositions allegedly found in Pasquier Quesnel's *Moral Reflections on the New Testament* (1699). These propositions were supposedly Jansenist, but a number were clearly Augustinian more than Jansenist. After delaying actions by Cardinal Noailles, the archbishop of Paris, the *Parlement* of Paris only reluctantly and in silence registered the bull on February 15, 1714.

A. Jansenism and Religious and Political Conflicts

On September 1, 1715, Louis XIV died, leaving a divided French church. In learning about the "Sun King's" death, Jean Soanen, a Jansenist bishop from Senez, wrote to Cardinal Noailles and rejoiced: "God has arisen to defend his cause, and all his enemies are overthrown."

Historian Dale Van Kley has argued that "the whole eighteenth century might just as appropriately have been christened the century of *Unigenitus* as that of 'lights.'" The bull's reception within French society was very divisive and disruptive. In 1717 four bishops called for a council to reconsider the validity of the bull. They were joined by 3,000 other "appellants" (those calling for a council), who were quickly excommunicated by Pope Clement XI. Between the years 1717 and 1728 the number of "appellants" reached 7,000, or 5 percent of the French clergy.

In 1730 the *Parlement* of Paris, with the support of influential bishops, delivered a further blow to the Jansenist movement by making the bull *Unigenitus* a state law. A series of healing miracles, however, took place, first in Paris in 1725, then in 1727 at the tomb of the Jansenist Gerard Rousse in Reims, and then at the tomb of Deacon François de Pâris, located in the cemetery of St. Médard in Paris. These happenings accredited the Jansenist cause, as if it were blessed of God, and brought throngs of Parisians to the cemetery in search of healing or moved by curiosity.

In 1732 the government closed the cemetery of St. Médard to curb its propaganda value for Jansenism and to stem the commotions and physical excesses associated with its "convulsionary" miracles. Either a lieutenant of police or a jokester posted a sign on the cemetery's entrance: "By order of the king: It is prohibited to God to do miracles in this place."

While the Jansenists lost the support of many bishops, their movement with its "miracles" and egalitarian emphasis (that is, priests could object to bishops' orders if deemed in error) gained followers in the lower classes of French society. Edmond Richer (1559–1631) had proposed that priests were the successors of Christ's disciples, thereby undercutting the grounds for the bishops' authority over them. Jansenism's ecclesiology, with its warrant for the lower clergy to challenge the authority of bishops, also found favor among certain magistrates in various *Parlements* of France who believed in a somewhat parallel fashion that they could challenge the king's legislation by failing to register it. Such, they said, was a "fundamental" law of France. These magistrates disliked the bishops' allegedly heavy-handed interference in matters of civic importance.

Thus Jansenism, originally very much a theological movement, took on political dimensions in its diverse permutations as an oppositional force. Its partisans were found in various walks of life. They very effectively used the printed page, especially the underground journal *Nouvelles Ecclésiastiques* (1728–1803), to keep a large public current regarding Jansenists' struggles flowing throughout Europe.

From 1749 to 1754 Paris once again became the site of another dramatic dispute related to the bull *Unigenitus*, the Refusal of Sacraments Controversy. In 1749 Christophe de Beaumont, the archbishop of Paris, required that before Catholics could receive the last rites, they had to produce an attestation of confession (*billet de confession*) indicating they accepted the bull *Unigenitus*. A number of Jansenists refused to sign such an attestation and died without receiving last rites. News of priests refusing to offer the last rites provoked an enormous scandal, greatly agitating large numbers of Parisians. On April 18, 1754, the *Parlement* of Paris delivered an order placarded throughout Paris: "The Court forbids all ecclesiastics to perform acts which lead to schism, notably to make any public refusal of the sacraments, under the pretext of failure to present a *billet de confession*, or to give the name of the confessor, or to accept the bull *Unigenitus."*

Louis XV, whose views vacillated on the bull's merits, supported the *Parlement* and ordered that silence should be maintained regarding the validity of the bull. When Christophe de Beaumont broke the silence, he was promptly exiled. In 1755, Jean Victor Marie Moreau, a royal historiographer, described the fallout of this controversy for the king's own authority: "In 1714, it was a matter of knowing whether Father Quesnel had explained the nature and effects of grace well in a very devout and rather boring book. In 1753 it was a matter of knowing whether the king was master in his realm. All authority was compromised, all order was disturbed."

B. The Damiens Affair

Rumors of revolt swirled through Paris in December 1756 and January 1757 after Louis XV promulgated a *lit de justice* quashing the *Parlement* of Paris's failure to register his "compromise" edict to resolve the religious crisis. The rumors mentioned the subversive activities of the Prince de Conti (Louis François I de Bourbon). Perhaps three-fourths of the people of Paris backed the Jansenists against the Jesuits, or so said one contemporary. One rumor suggested that Jesuits would soon be slaughtered.

King Louis XV
of France.

In the late afternoon of January 5, 1757, a bitterly cold day, a servant named Robert-François Damiens broke through the ranks of the king's guards and drove a knife into the side of Louis XV. Damiens was immediately arrested. The king initially thought he was going to die, but the wound proved only superficial. His thick coat and the assassin's choice of a small knife saved the king's life. Many Parisians were shocked and saddened and feared what might happen next.

On January 22 Frederick II ("the Great") of Prussia discounted the truth of news coming from Paris as "having to do with an alleged insurrection by the people led by the Prince de Conti." Through his Jansenist lawyer, Adrien Le Paige, the Prince de Conti had been an advisor of sorts to the magistrates in the *Parlement* of Paris who were partisan to the Jansenist cause, and he had engaged in secret negotiations with outlawed Protestants regarding how they might gain toleration. He also knew the assassin Damiens.

Despite torture, Damiens remained resolute in denying the existence of coconspirators. After a trial in which judges assumed his guilt, Damiens's body was literally pulled apart at a public execution witnessed by a large, boisterous Parisian crowd, simultaneously fascinated and horrified.

Louis XV was badly shaken by these events and his unnerving suspicions that his rebellious first cousin and former confidant, the Prince de Conti, was plotting against him. In an unconfirmed report, a spy indicated to the British government that the French king, so overwhelmed by melancholy, was contemplating resigning from the throne of France. By September, Louis XV had apparently lost the will to enforce strictly the religious restrictions against Jansenists (as well as against Protestants).

A major crack appeared in the monarchy's ideology that the sacraments of the Catholic Church bound all French subjects into a unified people. Now religious outsiders, such as the Jansenists and Protestants, could worship God in their own ways, generally without fear of being sought out and arrested.

The Jansenists also gained a sense of revenge against the Jesuits (some 3,300 members) when the *Parlements* of France, reluctantly seconded by Louis XV on November 26, 1764, expelled the Society of Jesus from the kingdom and the French colonies. The Jesuits' reputation had been badly tarnished in the Chinese Rites Controversy, the "Paraguay Reductions" case, and a lawsuit (1761) in which Jansenist lawyers Adrien Le Paige and Charlemagne Lalource furnished damaging evidence against the order.

In 1767 Charles III of Spain, the King of Naples and Duke of Parma, expelled the Jesuits from their lands. Eventually, in 1773, the papacy dissolved the order with its 26,000 members worldwide and its nearly 1,000 colleges and seminaries. Only in 1814 was the Society of Jesus reestablished.

Despite complaints that Protestants were brazenly touting their new toleration, the Assembly of the Clergy continued to affirm the standard premise that Catholicism was the only legitimate religion in France. In 1765 the Assembly of Clergy declared, "There is, Sire, in your Kingdom, only one master, one single monarch whom we obey: there is only one single cult and one single faith." The assembly called upon the king to uphold his anti-Protestant legislation. Louis XV indicated he would do this, but in fact he apparently did not have the will to enforce his sacramental policy toward the Jansenists and Protestants with rigor.

In 1774 Louis XV, the *Bien-Aimé*, died in a gruesome manner from smallpox. Louis XVI was crowned king in the cathedral of Reims. During a magnificent coronation service, Louis XVI affirmed his desire to uphold the Catholic religion and tried to reinvigorate the sacred character of his union with the people of France. In 1776 a resurgence of Roman Catholic devotion did take place in Paris. But in 1787 Louis XVI yielded to a well-orchestrated campaign by "Magistrate *Philosophes*," Jansenists, and the Protestant Pastor Rabaut Saint-Etienne, and he issued the Edict of Toleration for Protestants. The king's sacramental ideology of "one religion" now was shredded. It lay in tatters.

Other ideologies including social contract theories with a Rousseauist orientation, already much discussed in ongoing pamphlet wars and in other courts of public opinion, rushed to fill the widening political void by providing warrants for other types of government to replace a divine right monarchy.

IV. GALLICAN CATHOLICISM AND THE *SIÈCLE DES LUMIÈRES*

The Gallican church constituted a significant institutional presence in the life of the French people during the *Siècle des lumières*. Historian John McManners writes, "Because the Church was such an integral and dominating factor in social life, it exercised great power, but the price it paid was that its most sacred mysteries were treated as commonplace and routine."

Madame Guyon.

Many church bishops were very wealthy nobles, well connected with the monarchy. Its Assemblies of Clergy attempted to influence governmental policy and public morality. Debates between its clerics— such as between Jansenists and "devout Catholics" associated with the Jesuits—stirred popular unrest. The church's teachers had access to the kingdom's young in the classrooms of the Sorbonne and other universities and in city and village schools. Its missionary-minded clerics attempted to catechize the young and "evangelize" rural France.

The church's writers—ranging from Bossuet, François Fénelon, and the Quietest Madame Guyon (Jeanne-Marie Bouvier de la Motte-Guyon, 1648–1717), to Jesuit directors of conscience—provided various guidelines for Catholic spirituality. Between 1694 and 1699, a major theological contest ensued between Bossuet and Fénelon over Madame

Guyon's contention (later seconded by Fénelon in his *Maxims of the Saints* [1697]) that Christians should aspire to "pure love." This is a state of perfection in which "the desire of recompense and the fear of punishments do not occur." In 1699 Pope Innocent XII condemned twenty-three propositions ostensibly found in Fénelon's book.

The church's great cathedrals and smaller churches, schools, hospitals, convents, and monasteries were dispersed throughout the land. Its clerics often engaged in sacrificial efforts to care for the physical and spiritual needs of the Catholic faithful. The *bon curé* (good priest) of the countryside, often poorly paid and overworked, became a model of the good Catholic cleric when resentments arose sharply against wealthy bishops who controlled what were perceived to be excessive landholdings on the eve of the French Revolution.

Catholic mothers instructed daughters about feminine virtues and motherhood. Catholics were expected to confess and take Communion each Easter. The penalties for not doing so could be severe, including excommunication and refusal for Christian burial. Catholics were also expected to attend mass on one out of every three Sundays. Compliance with these rules and others was great in the countryside but less prevalent in the large cities like Paris, especially in the decades preceding the French Revolution. Going to church was generally viewed as an activity that wedded community, spiritual, and social functions.

Michelle Vovelle's study of the "last testaments" of Catholics in Provence does suggest that especially after 1760, the Gallicans' piety and loyalty to the Catholic Church may have flagged somewhat. The phenomenon of a potential nascent "secularism" (a noticeable attachment to the things of this world at the expense of a concern for the things of God) was also apparent in Paris and in larger urban areas.

Be that as it may, as late as 1787 one visitor to Paris pointed out that the chief tourist attraction in the capital was to watch the huge religious processions that coursed through the streets on a regular basis. The most celebrated parade was the *Fête Dieu, Corpus Christi*, in which the Eucharist was carried on high in such a way that it could be easily venerated and adored by the crowds of onlookers. On occasion the faithful could earn plenary indulgences if they became a participant in the parades. The faithful also "honored" the relics of St. Geneviève and other revered saints. They did not "worship" them, as Gallican Catholic apologists were quick to point out in an effort to head off potential Protestant criticisms.

Yet the Gallican church did not lack critics. Pornographic books allegedly recounting the sexual life of monks and nuns behind monastic walls often sold well. In the *Encyclopédie*, Jaucourt, Diderot's assistant, likewise criticized the monasteries: "The prodigious number of monasteries, which has continued to subsist in the Catholic Church, has become a charge on the public, oppressive, and manifestly promoting depopulation; it is enough to look at Protestant and Catholic countries to be convinced of it. Commerce enlivens one, and monasteries bring death to the other."

Indeed, French Catholic apologists stepped forward to write defenses of their faith against all comers, whether Protestant, deist, or atheist. Some 950 apologetic pieces appeared between the years 1670 and 1802. One of the best-known authors was Nicolas-Sylvester Bergier (1718–90), who penned *Deism Refuted by Itself* (1765), in which he attacked the views of Jean-Jacques Rousseau expressed in the *Vicar Savoyard*.

Catholic contemporaries believed Bergier's work *Examination of Materialism* (1771) constituted a most persuasive refutation of Baron d'Holbach's materialistic *Système de la nature* (*System of Nature*). Bergier wrote:

> We do not hesitate to repeat the observation, that the *Système de la nature*, far from favoring the progress of unbelief, is perhaps the decisive blow to disconcert its projects; and that the monstrous errors brought together in this work are the fairest trophies that philosophy could have raised to the glory of religion.

Bergier also pulled no punches in criticizing fellow Catholics, the Jansenists, for claiming that the miracles of St. Médard accredited their cause: "Prejudiced persons obstinate in certain opinions wanted miracles in order to give themselves authority; they were resolved to have them at any price, and it is not surprising that they should boast of having succeeded." He also warned about the dangers of superstition and the veneration of fraudulent relics. Likewise, the Benedictine Louis-Mayeul Chaudon, a notable physicist, penned a penetrating critique of materialism in his *Anti-dictionnaire philosophique* (1775).

Other Catholic writers such as Antoine Guénée, who in a Pascalian fashion cleverly spoofed Voltaire's arguments, participated in a potent anti-*philosophe* campaign. They disseminated their views through books and conservative journals such as the *Année littéraire, Journal historique et littéraire*, and *Affiches*. Anti-Enlightenment clerics in the Austrian Netherlands, Spain, and Italy translated these writings into their own languages.

At the same time, a number of French Catholic clerics, including *abbé-philosophes* and even some Jansenists, appropriated aspects of "philosophic" thought in surprising ways that indicate that the "walls" between the Gallican Catholic Church and the *Siècle des lumières* could (in McManners's assessment) be more porous than the hostile rhetoric of the *philosophes* and their Catholic opponents might intimate.

V. PROTESTANTS

In the 1560s, evangelistically inclined French Huguenots (Calvinists) representing 10 percent of the French population envisioned the day that France might become Reformed. Instead, their hopes were dashed, owing to their resounding defeat in a series of nine politico-religious wars during which they were relegated definitively into a minority status of a suffering church ("under the Cross").

Henri IV, who had formerly been a Protestant, did afford the Huguenots some rights in the Edict of Nantes (1598). Article 6 permitted Reformed subjects "to live and dwell in all the Cities and places of this our Kingdom and Countries under our obedience, without being inquired after, vexed, molested, or compelled to do anything in Religion, contrary to their Conscience." In 1629 the Peace of Alais took away a number of the Protestants' civil and military rights after they had engaged in failed rebellions in the 1620s. The siege and capitulation of La Rochelle, a Protestant stronghold (1627–28), represented the end of any realistic hope Protestants had of retaining areas of the kingdom as a fortified "state within a state."

Between 1661 and 1685 Louis XIV launched a serious anti-Protestant campaign. Between 650 and 700 Reformed churches were demolished. The government promulgated more than 400 pieces of legislation curtailing the Protestants' remaining rights. Finally, in 1685 Louis XIV, encouraged by Madame de Maintenon (ironically, the granddaughter of the Protestant poet Agrippa d'Aubigné), revoked Henri IV's Edict of Nantes.

Louis XIV propagated the fiction that all of his subjects were Catholics bound together by the sacraments of the Catholic Church. Many Protestants had "converted" to Catholicism. In 1681, *dragonnades* made up of "booted missionaries") moved into Poitou, Béarn, Languedoc, and Dauphiné, where Huguenots sometimes constituted the majority of the population. Feared dragoons forcibly lodged in the houses of Huguenots. The soldiers terrorized the Protestants until they abjured their faith—what the government called *"Religion Prétendue Réformée"* (self-styled Reformed religion). The dragoons were allowed to use any means possible (except murder and rape) in their "converting" campaign.

The revocation of the Edict of Nantes (via the Edict of Fontainebleau) denied to French Protestants their very right to exist in France. The king attempted to fulfill his goal of realizing the "one religion" component of the "one king, one law, one religion" dictum.

About 200,000 Huguenots fled the kingdom before and after the revocation. They undertook their sometimes perilous escapes as they sought refuge in the United Provinces, Geneva, Prussia, England, North

America, and elsewhere. The refugees contributed greatly to the intellectual and economic life of their newly adopted countries. Later critics would fault Louis XIV for not facilitating the emigration of Protestants to his underpopulated colony of New France. This failure was cited as another indication of the king's apparent lack of sufficient attention devoted to France's colonial empire.

Thousands of Huguenots remained in France, many of whom converted to Roman Catholicism, some in name only. The government called them *"Nouveaux convertis"* ("newly converted"). A smaller number of Protestants formed an underground church, the "Church of the Desert," consisting of those Huguenots who refused to yield to pressures to convert to Gallican Catholicism. Between the years 1684 and 1698 twenty outlawed pastors who tried to minister to the Huguenots were hunted down and executed.

Louis XIV feared that Huguenots harbored antimonarchical republican sentiments and thus could act as agents of political subversion. Had not Puritans (Calvinist "regicides") put King Charles I of England to death in 1649? Moreover, Louis XIV was competing with the Holy Roman Emperor, Leopold I, for political hegemony in Europe. How could he present himself as a dominant Catholic leader if he had a restive Protestant population troubling the social and religious life of his realm? Was he not already suspect in some quarters for having failed in 1683 to send French troops to defend Christian Europe when 200,000 Turks approached Vienna? By contrast, had not his competitor, Leopold I, dispatched forces? Had not the troops of Count von Starhemberg of Germany, Duke Charles of Lorraine, and John Sobieski of Poland defeated the Turks and thus countered Louis XIV's cynically construed tactic of becoming a hero by defeating the Turks after they overran Vienna? After all, Louis XIV was a warrior king who set Europe on edge with his acquisitive foreign policy and penchant for unfettered warfare against England, the United Provinces, Germany, and the Hapsburg territories.

The king's suspicions about the seditious proclivities of Huguenots appeared justified. A number of them known as Camisards engaged in the Cévenol or Camisard Wars (1702–4) against his government. They called for "freedom of conscience" and "no taxes." Cévenol prophets, ranging from boys and girls to men and women, predicted a future liberation of the Protestants from their oppressors. The prophets were mistaken. The troops of Louis XIV put down the revolt. Abraham Mazal, a major Camisard prophet, however, was not killed until 1710, when he was still attempting to stir a revolt in the Vivarais. In 1711 a number of "Inspired" prophets went to England, the United Provinces, and Germany.

In 1715 Antoine Court held the first synodal meeting of pastors whose purpose was to restore an organizational framework for the outlawed Church of the Desert. Court described the "spirit of the Desert" as "a spirit of reflection, of great wisdom and especially of a martyr that prepares us and disposes us to forsake our lives courageously, if Providence calls us to this." Court urged his colleagues to profess sincere loyalty to the monarchy and shun the "infection" of fanaticism that had led the Camisards to pick up arms, a plan of action culminating in disastrous results.

About 1726, Court and others founded a clandestine seminary for young French men in Lausanne, Switzerland. It secretly received financial support from Protestants in Switzerland, England, and the United Provinces. After their studies from six months to three years in Lausanne, the young pastors returned to face the rigors and risks of ministering to outlawed churches in France. If captured, they were executed. The pastors preached in services held in the secluded ravines of the Cévennes Mountains or on windswept beaches along the Atlantic Ocean or anywhere else that might escape the attention of governmental spies and soldiers.

Antoine Court.

Mary Evans Picture Library

In the second half of the century, Paul Rabaut of Nîmes gave leadership to the Reformed churches of France, assisting Court, who died in 1760. Rabaut, too, called on the Huguenots to submit to the monarchy's laws, except for those forbidding Protestant worship.

During the Seven Years War (1756–63), the Protestants became the beneficiaries of a de facto toleration (1758), much to the dismay of some Roman Catholic clergy. Between 1762 and 1765, Voltaire also abetted the cause of Huguenot toleration by successfully gaining the exculpation of the name of Jean Calas (see chapter 10). Voltaire defended other Huguenots and wrote a book defending toleration for Protestants. Finally, in the Edict of Toleration (1787), Louis XVI granted Huguenots the right to worship but did not accord them full civil rights.

Between 1685 and 1787, the French government's persecution of Huguenots extracted a heavy human toll: 219 men and 32 women were executed, 635 killed by gunfire or other means, 3,484 men and 3,493 women incarcerated, 1,940 forced to serve on the king's galleys—this out of a population growing to 593,000 in 1760. Approximately 40 pastors were executed. Some Huguenot women such as Marie Durand spent years imprisoned in the infamous Tower of Aiguesmorte. Durand resisted efforts to persuade her to renounce the Reformed faith.

After 1760 a number of Reformed pastors were greatly influenced by the thought of the *philosophe* Voltaire, who had defended the Protestant cause. Court de Gébelin, Antoine Court's son, and Rabaut Saint-Etienne, Paul Rabaut's son, abandoned distinctive Reformed convictions and advocated beliefs quite compatible with those of certain *philosophes*. A number of other Protestant pastors from provinces such as Languedoc did the same.

VI. CONCLUSION

Despite Voltaire's virulent war cry, "Crush the infamous thing [the Christian faith]," the Christian churches—whether Gallican Catholic, Ultramontane, Jansenist, or Protestant—generally weathered the *philosophes'* attacks during the Age of Lights. Toward the end of his life, Voltaire himself began to realize that his "philosophic" message (*la philosophie*) might not carry the day in France. Likewise, in other continental European countries and city-states the Christian churches sometimes proved less receptive to diverse teachings of the Age of Lights than the *philosophes* had apparently anticipated.

Moreover, by the time the Bastille fell on July 14, 1789, the Gallican monarchy's claim that it alone could determine the religion of the French people no longer possessed much persuasive force in the court of public opinion.

FOR FURTHER STUDY

Darnton, Robert. *The Literary Underground of the Old Regime*. Cambridge: Harvard University Press, 1982.

Diefendorf, Barbara. *Beneath the Cross: Catholics and Huguenots in Sixteenth-Century Paris*. New York: Oxford University Press, 1991.

Hardman, John. *Louis XVI*. New Haven: Yale University Press, 1993.

Kors, Alan. *Atheism in France, 1650–1729, Volume 1: The Orthodox Sources of Disbelief*. Princeton: Princeton University Press, 1990.

Roche, Daniel. *France in the Enlightenment*. Cambridge: Harvard University Press, 1998.

Van Kley, Dale. *The Jansenists and the Expulsion of the Jesuits from France*. New Haven: Yale University Press, 1975.

Van Kley, Dale. *The Religious Origins of the French Revolution: From Calvin to the Civil Constitution, 1560–1791*. New Haven: Yale University Press, 1996.

Woodbridge, John. *Revolt in Prerevolutionary France: The Prince de Conti's Conspiracy against Louis XV, 1755–1757*. Baltimore: Johns Hopkins University Press, 1995.

Christianity in the Age of Lights (3)

The Continent of Europe (1680–1789)

I. INTRODUCTION

During the Age of Lights, the Bourbon kings of France starred as marquee actors with top billing. Bejeweled and cloaked in finery, they strutted pompously across the European political stage. Their France was much admired and imitated. Their France was also much feared and hated.

Until his death in 1715, the "Sun King" Louis XIV could keep Europe on razor edge by threatening and launching repeated wars against his neighbors. This bellicose king spoke presumptuously about a "French Europe." Later, Voltaire, Diderot, d'Alembert—all significant French writers in the Republic of Letters—preached forms of "enlightened" thought and decried the Christian religion.

The French, of course, were not the only actors on the European scene during the Age of Lights. We now turn to these other Europeans and their religious beliefs.

II. "GERMANY" AND THE HOLY ROMAN EMPIRE

During the years 1680–1789, "Germany" did not formally exist as a unified state. Rather, it represented a patchwork quilt of 343 kingdoms, electorates, principalities, duchies, bishoprics, archbishoprics, free cities, and other political entities. "Germany" made up a sizable part of a larger realm known as the Holy Roman Empire that consisted of a welter of 1,800 territories including Poland, the Hapsburg Empire–Austrian Netherlands (1714–97), Bohemia, Moravia, Austria, the Kingdom of Hungary, Serbia (1718–39), Transylvania, Italy (Tuscany, 1737–1801; Naples, 1714–34; Parma, 1737–48), and other areas.

A Council of Electors, ranging from seven to nine members depending on the time frame, chose the Holy Roman Emperor. The king of

Bohemia; the archbishops of Mainz, Trier, and Cologne; the duke of Saxony; the margrave of Brandenburg; the duke of Bavaria; the duke of Brunswick-Hanover (1692); and the count palatine of the Rhine served as electors. They selected Austrians as emperors for this period: Leopold I (1658–1705), Joseph I (1705–11), Charles VI (1711–40), Charles VII (1742–45), Francis I (1745–65), and Joseph II (1765–90).

The Holy Roman Emperor's actual ability to raise armies and collect imperial taxes through the Imperial Diet and to make laws through Imperial Courts was sometimes hobbled by the fact that many of the political bodies belonging to the empire enjoyed "sovereignty," that is, sets of liberties and rights. Voltaire, in exaggerating the weakness of the Holy Roman Empire in his day, quipped that it was neither "Holy," nor "Roman," nor an "Empire." During the years 1803–6, the Holy Roman Empire finally expired under Napoleon.

With the accession of the unstable Bourbon king Philip V to the throne of Spain in 1700, the power of the Spanish Hapsburgs was greatly diminished. By contrast, the Austrian branch of the Hapsburg family, Roman Catholic and promoters of a baroque culture, dominated the political life of the Holy Roman Empire.

In the 1740s, however, Frederick the Great, the King of Brandenburg-Prussia from the Hohenzollern family (Calvinist since 1613), effectively challenged Austrian Hapsburg power. At the beginning of the War of the Austrian Succession, Frederick's well-trained troops successfully attacked the armies of the Austrian Hapsburgs and seized Silesia (1740–42). Thereafter many politicians looked to Brandenburg-Prussia as a more dominant continental European power than the Hapsburg court in Austria. They admired the efficiency of the Prussian governmental administration and the military prowess of Frederick II and his armies.

In German lands the leading kingdoms were Brandenburg-Prussia, Saxony, the Rhineland Palatinate, Hanover, and Bavaria. The predominant religion of these kingdoms often mirrored the beliefs of their prince or king. Bavaria remained staunchly Roman Catholic, the church controlling 56 percent of the land. A distinctive "Catholic *Aufklärung*" did emerge among those clerics who wanted to reform educational institutions and the worship practices of their parishioners. A few Catholic writers portrayed witchcraft as irrational superstition.

After 1773 Benedikt Stattler led the Catholic *Aufklärung* movement at the University of Ingolstadt. In 1776 Adam Weishaupt, a fierce opponent of the Jesuits and also associated with the University of Ingolstadt, founded a shadowy Masonic-like group, the Bavarian Order of Illuminati. Perhaps as many as two thousand people, including Johann Wolfgang von Goethe, Johann Gottfried von Herder, and

Friedrich Nicolai belonged to this secretive, radical society throughout Europe. Suspected of harboring anti-Christian sentiments, the order was banned by the elector of Bavaria in 1784. In the territory of the elector of the archbishop of Mainz, the theological faculties of Würzburg and Bamberg also supported a Catholic *Aufklärung*.

A. Brandenburg-Prussia

In northern Germany the kings of Brandenburg-Prussia were in principle Calvinists with pietistic leanings. During the first half of the eighteenth century, the population remained largely orthodox Lutheran or Pietist. The future king of England, George I, came from the electorate of Hanover, a realm of 600,000–700,000. Its established church was Lutheran, with Reformed Christians and Jews in distinct minorities. A unified "Germany" as a nation would not emerge until the days of the "Iron Chancellor" Otto von Bismarck in the second half of the nineteenth century.

The emergence of Brandenburg-Prussia as a great military power in the eighteenth century impressed contemporaries. The kingdom's army (83,000 by the 1730s) ranked fourth in size among European powers, even though its landmass ranked tenth and its population thirteenth. Its kings promoted disciplined lifestyles like those of the Pietists as a model for Prussian nobles (the *Junkers*), bureaucrats, and military leaders. Frederick III with a very militaristic mind-set ruled Brandenburg from 1688 to 1713. In 1701 he made himself King of Prussia. Reformed in theology, he encouraged French Huguenots who had escaped from Louis XIV's persecution to settle in his kingdom. In 1694 he founded the University of Halle as a Lutheran university. He welcomed Pietists like Jakob Spener and Hermann Francke. In 1698 Francke began teaching theology at the University of Halle. Frederick III also made the University of Konigsberg another Pietist center.

B. The Pietists: Bible Study, Reform, and World Missions

In *Pious Desires* (1675), Jakob Spener, the founder of German Pietism (see chapter 7 for Spener and Pietism), anchored his program for the reform of the church in the faithful appropriation of Scripture:

> This much is certain: the diligent use of the Word of God, which consists not only of listening to sermons but also of reading, meditating, and discussing (Ps. 1:2) must be the chief means for reforming something.... The Word of God remains the seed from which all that is good in us must grow. If we succeed in getting the people to seek

eagerly and diligently in the Book of Life for their joy, their spiritual life will be wonderfully strengthened and they become altogether different people.

Spener continued: "It is not enough that we hear the Word with our outward ear, but we must let it penetrate to our heart." He advocated daily private Bible reading and meditation and the reading of Scripture in small groups.

Spener urged that pastoral training schools should not be sites for students brawling and tippling but be known as "workshops of the Holy Spirit." Nor should seminary professors seek glory by writing books of showy erudition, but rather provide students examples of Christian humility. Spener also emphasized the priesthood of believers. Ministers should seek help from laypersons to ease their own pastoral burdens.

At the University of Halle, Hermann Francke (1663–1727) insisted that divinity school students study Scripture in the Hebrew and Greek. His own thinking about hermeneutics was influenced by Johann Conrad Dennhauer (1603–66) as mediated through Spener. Francke observed: "The exegetical reading of Holy Scripture is that which concerns finding and explaining the literal sense intended by the Holy Spirit himself." Francke indicated that the exegete needed to have experienced true conversion and daily spiritual renewal.

In 1702 Francke founded the *Collegium Orientale Theologicum.* Advanced students could learn Aramaic, Arabic, Ethiopian, Chaldean, Syriac and "Rabbinisch." Professor and hymnist Johann Jacob Rambach (1693–1735) from Giessen provided one of the standard "Pietist" studies of hermeneutics in his *Institutiones hermeneuticae sacrae* (1724; eight editions).

Like Spener, the Pietist scholar Johann Albrecht Bengel (1687–1752) of the duchy of Württemberg, believed the church's reliance upon Scripture determined its spiritual well-being. He offered a careful analysis of the New Testament's textual variants in his *Gnomen novi testamentum.* John Mill had claimed there were some 30,000 variants for the New Testament. By establishing the textual genealogical traditions of many variants, Bengel was able to reduce this number by four-fifths. He also employed the textual critical principle, "the harder reading is better than the easy."

Bengel emphasized the authority of the original autographs: "Most important of all, ancient witnesses are to be preferred to modern ones. For since the original autographs (and they were written in Greek), can alone claim to be the well-spring, the amount of authority due to codices drawn from primitive sources, Latin, Greek, etc., depends upon their nearness to the fountainhead."

"Scripture is the life of the church: The church is the guardian of Scripture. When the church is strong, Scripture shines abroad; when the church is sick, Scripture is imprisoned" (Johann Albrecht Bengel).

Much like Francke, Bengel believed the interpreter of Scripture should be a Christian: "... [p]ray, place the Holy Scripture before you on the desk of your heart and acquaint yourself with the matter before you come to a decision."

According to J. G. Eichorn (1752–1827), the professors at Halle in the 1720s "pertinaciously held to the infallibility of the vulgar text" and some to the "absolute infallibility" of the Masoretic pointing. In the 1730s, an "awakening" stirred the religious life of Württemberg and Tübingen. After 1743 Pietism's influence among orthodox Lutherans in Württemberg expanded further.

With the financial support of Baron von Canstein, Francke established an orphanage in Halle (1695). He created schools and businesses including a printing house where orphans and others could learn a trade. By 1700, Francke's various institutions had garnered the support of Frederick III (I), who valued their contribution in fostering Christian discipline among his students, the Prussian populace, and his soldiers. For his part, Francke intended to make Halle a center for Christian reform and world missions. In *Of the Visible and Wonderful Providence of God Attending These Endeavors to Establish the Orphanage and Charity-Schools from Their First Rise to This Present Time* [1707], Francke presented examples of how he prayed for specific needs and then monies with which to feed the poor and keep the charity schools open sometimes arrived at the last conceivable moment. He wrote: "These instances I was willing here to set down so that I might give the reader some idea both of the pressing trials and happy deliverances we have met with; though I am sufficiently convinced that narratives of this kind will seem over-simple and fanciful to the great minds of our age."

Cotton Mather, a British American, rejoiced that the "world begins to feel a warmth from the fire of God, which ... flames in the heart of Germany." He greatly admired Francke's ministry: "Dr. Francke is a person truly wonderful for his vast erudition, but much more so for his ... shining piety; and yet more so for his ... peerless industry; and most of all for the astonishing blessings of God upon his undertakings to advance His Kingdom in the world."

On one occasion, Frederick IV (1671–1730), the King of Denmark, gave a direct order to his chaplain: "Find me missionaries." In turn, the chaplain asked Francke for help. Francke proposed two students from the University of Halle to be the missionaries. The famous Danish-Halle Mission was launched. On November 29, 1705, Bartholomew Ziegenbalg and Heinrich Plütschau set sail for Tranquebar, India, a city whose residents numbered 250 Europeans and 25,000 Tamils.

Not until July 1706 did the two missionaries arrive at their destination. To their dismay they discovered that the "abominably wicked

Life of Christians here" constituted a large barrier to their evangelistic efforts. Many Hindus believed that Christians were "the vilest and most Corrupted people under the sun." Ziegenbalg translated the Bible into the Tamil language. He also set up a "charity school" and a "College of Missionaries" before he died in 1719 at age thirty-six.

Christian Friedrich Schwartz (1726–98) also served with distinction as a missionary in India. Johann Steinmetz (1680–1762) ministered in Teschen, Silesia, Moravia, and Bohemia. Others took the gospel to the Russia of Peter the Great, who wanted his governmental officials to benefit from their linguistic skills. The missionaries also addressed the physical and spiritual needs of captured Swedish troops who, when they were allowed to return to Sweden, facilitated Pietist missions in their homeland. All told, some sixty students went forth from the University of Halle as missionaries.

From the press of the Canstein Bible Institute (founded in 1710) in Halle came more than 80,000 copies of the entire Bible and more than 100,000 New Testaments and a repertory of Christian literature in the first years of its existence.

In 1713 Frederick William I (1688–1740) became king. He was devoted to the building up of his military. At the same time, he was greatly influenced by Pietism. He subsidized the distribution of thousands of Bibles in Prussian schools "so that the Word of God will be made known to all my subjects." He designated Francke as the rector of the University of Halle. In "Most Significant Aspects of the Work of Reformation, Carried on in the Lutheran Church in Germany Since the Year 1688" (an appendix to brochures published in 1707), Francke and others summarized their perceptions of the remarkable advances Pietism had made in reforming the religious life of Germany. At the time of Francke's death (1727), 2,000 students attended his schools in Halle that had 175 teachers. Francke's orphanage served as a model for Griffith Jones's schools in Wales and George Whitefield's orphanage in Savannah, Georgia.

In 1723 King Frederick William I supported the campaign of Pietist Johann Joachim Lange and other faculty members at the University of Halle to have Christian Wolff, a rationalist philosopher, removed from his teaching post at the university. Wolff had been a friend and partisan of the brilliant mathematician-philosopher Gottfried Wilhelm Leibniz (1646–1716), the author of *Theodicy* (1710). Leibniz had posited an ontology in which "monads," supposedly immaterial and simple entities, make up matter. Critics claimed that Leibniz ruled out God's intervention in the world and human freedom by proposing the apparently "deterministic" thesis that "this is the best of all possible worlds."

For his part, Wolff, in his *On the Practical Philosophy of the Chinese*

(1721), had raised theological suspicions about himself by arguing that belief in God is not a prerequisite for moral reasoning. Wolff underscored the value of natural religion in an attempt to demonstrate a harmony between reason and revelation. At the same time, he believed in the divine inspiration of Scripture, cited it frequently as an authority in his works, and professed his belief that Christian truths could not be ultimately overthrown by reason.

In 1729 Frederick William I mandated that all students who hoped to teach theology in Brandenburg-Prussia should attend the University of Halle for two years, thereby affording Pietists with a measure of leverage over the careers of the clergy of Prussia. In 1736 the king also banned the sale of the *Wertheimer Bibel* of Johann Lorenz Schmidt, claiming that it "disputes the chief foundations of the Christian religion." In 1737, on the behest of Frederick William I and others, the Holy Roman Emperor ordered Schmidt's arrest and condemned the sale of the *Wertheimer Bibel* throughout the empire under penalty of fines.

1. Radical Pietists

The mystical theology of Jakob Böhme (1575–1624) as well as the Quietism of Miguel de Molinos (1628–97), Antoinette Bourignon (1616–80), and Madame Guyon helped shape the thinking of a number of "radical Pietists" (and John Wesley). A cobbler by trade, Böhme was not satisfied with having simply an "opinion" about who God is. Rather, he personally sought to encounter "the living Word, through which the heart experiences certainty" and gains "insight into the great mystery." The Christian is a "new being in Christ in whom love has found its home."

In accounts of his powerful mystical experiences, Böhme observed, "When thou are gone forth wholly from the creature [human], and art become nothing to all that is nature and creature, then thou are in that Eternal One, which is God himself, and then thou shalt perceive and feel the highest virtue of love." For Böhme, the person who experiences the mystery of God's being has a much more intimate understanding of the Christian life than does the "school" or scholastic theologian. Böhme's reflections promoted universalism.

Gottfried Arnold (1666–1714), a student of Jakob Spener, emphasized the transformative power of the Christian's "new birth." He indicated that a "perfect servant of Christ possesses nothing but Christ, and if he does possess anything other than Christ, he is not perfect." In his work *The First Love: That is, a True Portrait of the Earliest Christians according to Their Living Faith and Holy Life*, Arnold presented the early Christians as models of holiness and sacrificial faith that believers should attempt to emulate.

In his *Impartial History of the Church and Heretics* (1699–1700), Arnold observed, "Those who make heretics are the heretics proper, and those who are called heretics are the real God-fearing people." In that book he treated members of some medieval sects and "free churches," Anabaptists, and Mennonites in a more favorable manner than the orthodox did. A number of orthodox Lutherans were infuriated by Arnold's stinging criticism.

When Arnold died, someone suggested the following epitaph: "Here lies Gottfried Arnold, not so much a theologian, as the bitterest enemy of orthodox theologians; the persistent defender of heretics, the stupid representative of mystical theology, perhaps the first of all distorters of church history."

A radical Pietist such as Johann Christian Edelmann eventually became a partisan of the German *Aufklärung*. By contrast, in the last years of his life, Arnold became more appreciative of confessional Lutheran theology.

Johann Lorenz Mosheim (1694–1755) attempted to write church history in a more objective fashion than his predecessors, including Arnold. Mosheim's well-respected *Institutes of Ecclesiastical History* (four volumes) earned for him the title the "father of church history." He wrote, "My principal care has been to relate events with fidelity and authority."

2. The Moravians

Jakob Spener served as a sponsor at the baptism of Nicolaus Ludwig von Zinzendorf (1700–1760). The young Zinzendorf read widely, including works from Catholic writers such as Fénelon and Madame Guyon and Huguenots such as Pierre Bayle. He embraced Pietist convictions during his studies at Francke's school in Halle. He became especially committed to the value of prayer. Thereafter he gained an appreciation of "orthodox" Lutheran theology. In 1722, when members of the *Unitas Fratrum* (Unity of the Brethren), a movement from Moravia and Bohemia, needed a place of refuge from persecution, Zinzendorf graciously allowed them to settle on his estate at Berthelsdorf.

The Unity of the Brethren traced their spiritual lineage back to the followers of John Hus. They built a village called *Herrnhut*, "the Lord's watch," on Zinzendorf's property. In the summer of 1727, Zinzendorf and a number of others covenanted to pray for the community. At a Communion service on August 13, a powerful work of the Holy Spirit surged through the congregation. Sometimes called the "Moravian Pentecost," this occurrence greatly strengthened the commitment of the Moravians to heartfelt religion, prayer, disciplined lifestyles, and ultimately, world missions.

In the same year Zinzendorf, who wanted to keep the Moravians within the Lutheran church, became their leader. He viewed them as soldiers of Christ and encouraged some to become missionaries. Indeed, Leonhard Dober and David Nitschmann went to the West Indies in 1732, Christian David to Greenland in 1733, and August Spangenberg to Georgia.

In 1736 a Moravian missionary named Friedrich Martin arrived on the Dutch island of Saint George in the Caribbean Islands with a desire to minister to blacks. He wrote in his diary, "I spoke with a mulatto woman who is very accomplished in the teachings of God. Her name is Rebecca." Martin married Rebecca (Protten), a former slave. She helped establish the first African Protestant church in the New World. Despite determined opposition from sugar planters, she brought the gospel to hundreds of slaves as she faithfully pursued an itinerant evangelistic ministry. Rebecca's "revival" contributed to the creation of "Black Christianity in the Atlantic World" (according to historian Jon Sensbach).

During fierce storms, John Wesley was very impressed by the resolute calm of Moravians on board the ship he and brother Charles took to Georgia. He talked with Spangenberg in Georgia. Peter Boehler, a Moravian missionary, helped John Wesley to reflect on the nature of Christian assurance before his conversion on May 24, 1738. He told Wesley, "Preach faith till you have it; and then, because you have it, you will preach faith."

In June 1738 John Wesley traveled to Germany, where he met Count Zinzendorf and visited *Herrnhut* and spoke with the Moravian leader Christian David, a carpenter. They discussed whether justification and the "new birth" were one and the same. In 1740 Wesley broke with the Moravians but continued to admire their Christian witness, charity, humility, and evangelistic zeal.

Earlier, in 1727, Zinzendorf had urged Herrnhutters to exhibit "brotherly union" and "to remain in a constant bond of love with all children of God." In 1732 he claimed religion "must be a matter which is able to be grasped through experience alone without any concepts. If this were not so, a deaf or a blind or a mentally deficient man or a child could not have the religion necessary for salvation." At the same time, he argued that "Revelation is indispensably necessary in human experience."

A number of Moravians got caught up in less than wholesome lifestyles. Zinzendorf for a time became overly fascinated with the blood and wounds of Christ and recommended actual childlike behavior as a precondition for entering the kingdom of Christ. His particular presentation of the marital relationship as a description of the believer's relationship with Christ gave some critics pause. The Pietist Johan Bengel criticized Zinzendorf's biblical translation work. Friedrich Christoph Oetinger accused him of completely giving up on the "Halle method of reasoning."

Nonetheless, evangelicals of the eighteenth century such as Wesley generally appreciated the Moravians. William Carey, often considered the "father of modern missions," pointed to the Moravians as an example of a Christian people with a passion for missions: "See what the Moravians have done! Cannot we follow their example and in obedience to our Heavenly Master go out into the world, and preach the Gospel to the heathen?"

C. German Christians and the *Aufklärung*

Scholars have found agreement elusive regarding the date of the inception of the German *Aufklärung*. In the late 1680s, Christian Thomasius (1655–1728), sometimes hailed as the "father of the German Enlightenment," reiterated themes often considered "enlightened." A jurist and educator, he argued that the state should guarantee individual rights and sought to separate natural law from theology. He repudiated the use of torture and fought against religious persecution.

A Christian believer, Thomasius helped found the University of Halle and taught there. He appreciated the theology of the Pietist Spener. He did not believe the use of reason for the social good necessitated the abandonment of revealed religion. By contrast, some of his contemporaries, writers of a subversive underground radical literature, called for intellectual liberties and attacked the Christian faith. Still other contemporaries of the 1690s became noted for their "literary sociability" and writing of poems and novels. By the 1730s, reading rates among German women improved significantly.

A German such as Karl F. Bahrdt (1741–92) claimed to be "enlightened" and linked *Aufklärung* with militant unbelief. Other "enlightened" Germans generally self-identified as one kind of Christian or another. They believed that to be "enlightened" signaled a willingness to exploit the new knowledge gained from science to improve societal life in various realms—whether medicine, education, technology, or farming.

During the 1740s, "Germany" did witness an increase in published attacks on the Christian faith. In 1741 a German translation of Matthew Tindal's *Christianity as Old as the Creation* appeared and provided a number of German intellectuals with their first access to deistic thought. Moreover, the ideas of heterodox thinkers such as Johann Christian Edelmann (1698–1767), author of *Unschuldige Wahrheiten*, were gaining a following.

But more than anything, the crowning of Frederick the Great as the King of Prussia appeared to signal a new era of openness to "enlightened" views. As a young man Frederick disdained military life and became enamored with the literature of the French *Siècle des lumières*. He had a very serious falling out with his father, who on one occasion began to strangle him. After Frederick attempted to flee to England, his father had him imprisoned. Frederick was court-martialed and sentenced to death.

Eventually Frederick emerged from his father's disgrace. He fought with distinction in the War of the Polish Succession. Upon becoming king in 1740, he turned his resplendent court of *Sans Souci* into a haven for French *philosophes* like Voltaire and Maupertuis who competed for his favor. In time his capital, Berlin (population 55,000 in 1700 and 150,000 in 1800) became a center of the *Aufklärung*, boasting leading publishers such as Freidrich Nicolai, distinguished journals such as *Berlinishe Monatsschrift*, and discussion groups (some secret such as the *Mittwochsgesellschaft*). In 1740 Frederick lifted the ban on the controversial philosopher Christian Wolff, who returned to teach at the University of Halle.

In this new intellectual environment, a coterie of German theologians, while critical of deism, attempted to adapt Christianity to new currents of thought. Siegmund Jakob Baumgarten (1706–57), professor of theology at Halle, constructed a "transitional" theology (*Theologie des Ubergänges*) that joined elements of historic Protestant orthodoxy with Wolff's concerns about the harmony between reason and revelation and with a circumspect use of the "new" biblical criticism. Likewise, a number of professors, school teachers, scientists, pastors, and book dealers appreciated an "enlightened" use of the sciences and advances in technology for their utilitarian value in improving society.

These *Aufklärers* saw no incompatibility between this kind of enlightenment and their Christian beliefs. At the same time, they were worried about other forms of Enlightenment thought that might subvert the Christian faith and the loyalties of the people to the state. In the 1780s, the question "What is enlightenment?" provoked considerable debate among learned scholars who saw themselves as "enlightened." Immanuel Kant's famous essay *Was ist Aufklärung?* (*What Is Enlightenment?*) represented only one of the more important essay responses to this question, albeit a marked departure from the more "moderate" views of *Aufklärung* advocated by certain Neologians.

D. The Neologians

A group of theologians known as the *Neologians* (1740–90) specifically attempted to accommodate Christian theology to Wolff's emphasis on reason's rights and the findings of the new science and biblical criticism. They included Johann Joachim Spalding (1714–1804), Wilhelm Abraham Teller (1734–1804), and Johann Gottfried Eichhorn (1752–1827), who became open critics of the doctrine of the verbal inspiration and infallibility of the Bible. For them, the truths of reason were supported by revelation. They viewed personal "edification" as the goal of the Christian's life. They thought that an "edified" believer would be a tolerant and moral person and a useful member of society.

In 1737 the University of Göttingen was founded with the goal of preparing students for professions supported by the state. By the 1770s, the university's distinguished faculty had become notable advocates of Neologian theology and defenders of the state.

The thought of Johann David Michaelis (1717–91) captures well the shifting contours of German theology during the middle decades of the eighteenth century.

In 1739 Michaelis, a Pietist student at the University of Halle, had defended the inspiration of the Masoretic pointing of the Hebrew text. By contrast, in 1765 the same Michaelis, now a prominent philologist at the University of Göttingen, hailed the controversial priest Richard Simon as the "father of newer criticism" of the Bible he himself practiced. Michaelis pinpointed the year 1750 as the date the new biblical criticism began to take hold among certain academics: "Since 1750 the world of scholarship has received new and important contributions to the Criticism of the New Testament which have given to this discipline a new *gestalt*."

E. Johann Salomo Semler: The Founder of German Higher Criticism

In 1751 Johann Salomo Semler (1725–91) began teaching at the University of Halle and contributed to these developments. Semler was a prized student of Baumgarten and his successor. In his diary he noted his great appreciation for the writings of Richard Simon, Jean Leclerc, and a number of English and Dutch biblical scholars. From Baumgarten's death in 1757 until 1779, Semler was probably the most influential German theologian. He called for the "free" investigation of the Bible, an inquiry not tethered by the presuppositions of "scholastic" orthodoxy about Scripture's canon and infallibility. He claimed he had no sympathy for Socinians or Naturalists.

Semler proposed important distinctions between "religion" and "theology" and between the "Word of God" (the great moral instruction for all peoples as well as aspects of the gospel) and "Holy Scripture." About this latter distinction, Semler wrote, "*Holy Scripture and*

Word of God must certainly be differentiated because we know the difference. To the *Holy Scripture*, as this historical, relative term came to be used among the Jews, belong, *Ruth, Esther, [Ezra,] Song of Songs* etc., but to the *Word of God*, which makes all men in all times wise unto salvation, [to the divine *instruction* for all men,] not all of these *books* called *holy* belong."

Semler thought biblical criticism revealed that parts of Holy Scripture are not the Word of God. He wrestled with the canonicity of 1 John 5:7. He realized that most of his contemporaries—whether Reformed, Pietist, or orthodox Lutheran—did not share his perspective: "It is also astonishing that scarcely a few scholars of our time have perceived and taught this and that so many on the contrary want that all parts of the same are the pure and simple Word of God."

He resorted to a doctrine of accommodation (a non-Augustinian version) to explain further his distinction between Scripture and the Word of God. The biblical authors accommodated their writings to the faulty views of their contemporaries (especially the Jews) about the world. Sifting out the authentic Word of God from the mythological, local, fallible, and noninspired dross in Scripture (a belief in demons, heaven, and hell, for example), caused by this accommodation, is the task of the wise Bible student. Once elements of an authentic canon within a canon have been identified, then a number of "orthodox" doctrines based on Scripture and not on the Word of God will stand in need of reformulation.

Semler claimed that his work was faithful to the teachings of Martin Luther. In fact, it appeared deeply indebted to Wolff and earlier English (William Whiston), Dutch, and French biblical scholars. Semler translated a few of Richard Simon's works into German.

The reception of Semler's writings was quite mixed. Some scholars believed he had constructed a valuable theological position that upheld essential Christian beliefs while presenting a more accurate account of the way the Bible is related to the Word of God. A number wrote works in which they promoted the Socinian definition of accommodation to justify their own forms of biblical criticism.

At the same time, several critics pounced on Semler's writings. The orthodox Lutheran Johann Melchior Goeze (1717–86), the "head" (*Haupt*) pastor of the Lutheran Church of St. Catherine in Hamburg and sharp critic of Carl F. Bahrdt's New Testament translation, attacked Semler's views of canon and abandonment of the infallibility of Scripture. Semler complained about a "violent and utterly unfounded condemnation" of his writings.

From another perspective, Gottfried Ephraim Lessing (1729–81), famous author of *Nathan the Wise* and bitter opponent of Goeze, scored

Semler for upholding an inconsistent theological stance. Lessing believed that "the accidental truths of history can never become the proof of necessary truths of reason." This gap constituted his famous "ugly, broad ditch" across which he thought there was no bridge. The ditch possessed temporal, metaphysical, and existential dimensions. For Lessing, historical apologetics for the Christian religion retained little value. He turned to Spinoza and Eastern thought and identified God as the soul of the universe, which was itself eternal. In the "Pantheism Controversy," Friedrich Heinrich Jacobi (1743–1819) and Moses Mendelssohn (1729–86) debated the extent of Spinoza's influence on Lessing.

In 1779 Semler had sharply criticized Lessing's publication of the *Fragments of an Unnamed (Author)* (1774, 1777) without naming the author, Hermann Samuel Reimarus (1694–1768). Lessing, at the time a librarian, had claimed he found these documents, portions of Reimarus's *Apology or Defense of the Rational Worshippers of God*, in the Herzog August Bibliothek of Wolfenbüttel. In fact, Lessing had come into possession of Reimarus's work in Hamburg.

Reimarus had been a teacher of oriental languages at the Hamburg Gymnasium Johaneum, attended a Lutheran church, and was not publicly known for entertaining heretical beliefs. In the published fragments, Reimarus attacked the truthfulness of Scripture and had advocated that reason and not revelation is the source of our religious knowledge (natural religion). He proposed that Christ did not view himself as the Messiah but that the apostles had invented the idea of a "suffering spiritual redeemer of the human race." Moreover, the disciples had stolen Christ's body to give their story more credibility.

Lessing did not see how Semler, who affirmed the resurrection of Jesus Christ, could do so, given premises of the professor's biblical criticism. In fact, Semler thought a belief in the resurrection of Christ was something a Christian upholds in faith; the belief need not be backed by historical arguments to sustain its legitimacy.

Just before he died in 1791, Semler indicated that he had felt obliged in the name of truth to propose his contested views of Scripture and the Christian religion. At the same time, he lamented his perception that so few young Germans seemed to want to study theology.

F. Johann Philipp Gabler and Biblical Theology

Johann Philipp Gabler (1753–1826) taught at the University of Altdorf. He helped initiate the study of biblical theology in his 1787 inaugural lecture, "An Oration on the Proper Distinction between Biblical and Dogmatic Theology and the Specific Objectives of Each." He took note of the "fatal discords of the various sects" of his day. Gabler hoped to provide a methodology that would guide those who "aspired to a solid understanding of divine matters" and "to obtain a firm and certain hope of salvation."

Gabler's methodology seemed to reiterate aspects of Semler's program. He proposed that

> we distinguish carefully the divine from the human, that we establish some distinction between biblical and dogmatic theology, and after we have separated those things which in the sacred books refer most immediately to their own times and to the men of those times from those pure notions which divine providence wished to be characteristic of all times and places, let us then construct the foundation of philosophy upon religion and let us designate with some care the objectives of divine and human wisdom.

Gabler believed that by relying on practical reason he could identify the universal "pure" truths of biblical theology that were "historical in origin." By contrast, dogmatic theology had "a didactic character, teaching what each theologian philosophizes rationally about divine things" according to his "ability or of the time, age, place, sect, school, and other factors."

In agreement with his professor at Göttingen University, Christian Gottlob Heyne (1729–1812), Gabler believed that Scripture could contain "myths" that stemmed from primitive cultures. An expert in ancient classics, Heyne proposed that *mythus* (myth) was a common characteristic of primitive cultures during the childhood of mankind. These primitive people created "myths" about the gods' interventions in nature and human affairs to account for unexplainable happenings. The Hebrews allegedly included myths within the Old Testament.

For Gabler, these myths might encompass valuable truths their writers wished to communicate. Through the careful use of reason, the biblical scholar could allegedly sift out what constitutes the flawed, error-pocked human knowledge in Scripture from its pure universal truths and end up with the stuff of biblical theology.

Gabler contended that the exegete needs to understand how "myths" functioned in Scripture. The "myths" were not purposeful deceits. Instead, like other Ancients, the biblical writers and other figures really believed them and took ordinary events and converted them into miracles. But these miracles recorded in certain "mythic" portions of Scripture should be explained by natural causes. The biblical exegete had an obligation to separate these "myths" of human derivation from revealed materials in Scripture.

It is possible that the Socinian doctrine of accommodation informed

Gabler's proposal. Interestingly enough, between the years 1763 and 1817, at least thirty-one studies appeared in German that emphasized a doctrine of biblical accommodation (often with a Socinian orientation).

G. Frederick William II and the Censorship Edict

Upon the death of Frederick the Great in 1786, his nephew Frederick William II became the King of Prussia. Given counsel by Johann Christoph von Wöllner, the new king tried to rein in a growing body of heterodox literature. These writings varied in their theological orientations from those of the Neologians, of Reimarus, and of the hack-writer Karl Friedrich Bahrdt (1741–92). Bahrdt, author of *The Story and Diary of My Imprisonment*, castigated biblical miracles and claimed that Moses was an expert in fireworks.

The Renewed Censorship Edict of December 1788 obligated authors who wrote books about God, morality, and the state to submit them to a government commission of censors for approval. Von Wöllner indicated that many Protestant clergy had given new life to "the miserable, long-refuted errors of the Socinians, deists, naturalists, and other sectarians." A number of Lutheran pastors resigned their posts in protest, and Nicolai, the publisher, moved his operations out of Berlin. The government feared that radical expressions of the *Aufklärung* simultaneously subverted the Christian faith and loyalties to the state.

In March 1758, Johann Georg Hamann (1730–88), an intriguing and brilliant "counter Enlightenment" intellectual, was converted to Christ after engaging in a dissolute lifestyle in England. In 1784 he condemned both Kant's definition of *Aufklärung* and emphasis upon reason as a "cold, unfruitful moonlight without enlightenment for the lazy understanding and without warmth for the cowardly will." Hamann claimed that Kant had a "Gnostic hatred of the material and a mystical love for form." Hamann believed that faith and reason are compatible and that nature itself is a kind of revelation alongside that of Scripture.

III. SCANDINAVIA

Famine, disease, and warfare took a dreadful toll on the Swedish provinces of Estonia and Livonia at the turn of the eighteenth century. Apparently 60 percent of the population died in the famine of 1695–97. The brutal hardships associated with the Great Northern War (1700–1721) followed thereafter. The times were desperate. Little wonder that the Lutheran clergy in Scandinavia created a devotional literature with the purpose of giving Christian hope and comfort. The pastors also called upon their people to pray and to repent.

Besides northern Germany, the regions of Denmark-Norway and Sweden-Finland constituted strongholds for Lutheranism. Citizens were obliged to take oaths to the Lutheran state church. In 1687 the Dane Hector Masius, a divine right kingship advocate, claimed that Lutheranism alone could bolster public order. In 1693 the Swedish monarch proposed that he gave account to God alone. Sweden controlled Finland, areas around Saint Petersburg, Russia, Estonia and Livonia, Pomerania, Wismar, and Bremen Verden.

On June 28, 1709, during the Great Northern War, Swedish King Charles XII (1682–1718) suffered a devastating military defeat at Poltava by the armies of Peter the Great. In consequence, not only did Sweden lose its Baltic territories except for Finland, but also the monarchy lost its absolutist pretentions. The so-called "Age of Liberty" (1719–72) followed. Four Estates of the Diet gained power, displacing the authority of the absolute monarchy. Educational reformers attempted to give a utilitarian and "rational" thrust to Swedish education. They sometimes battled with the Lutheran clergy, who wanted to retain a significant theological component in the educational curriculum of Sweden's youth.

Captured Swedish soldiers confined in Russian prisons after their country's defeat in the Great Northern War returned home in 1722–24. Many had experienced a spiritual conversion under the influence of Pietist missionaries sent from Halle by Francke to minister to them. Peter the Great wanted to take advantage of the missionaries' linguistic skills. Newly converted soldiers sometimes became advocates of Pietism in Sweden. Moravians also attempted to promote revivals. In the Conventicle Act of 1726 the government tried to frustrate the advance of Pietists and any advocates of heterodoxy.

After a power grab of 1772, Gustavus III (1746–92) nullified an earlier Constitution of 1720 that had restrained the reach of royal power. He imposed a new Constitution of 1772 designed to reinforce Lutheranism as the basis of government: "Unanimity in religion, and the true divine worship, is the surest basis of a lawful, concordant, and stable government." Nonetheless, in 1781 a measure of toleration came to Sweden, although Catholicism remained an outlawed faith. Some Lutheran clergy viewed Pietists as theologically suspect. Others such as Henrik Schartau (1757–1825), known as the "Awakener of Southern Sweden," appreciated their emphasis on repentance and personal holiness.

Emanuel Swedenborg (1688–1772) emerged as one of Sweden's more controversial religious thinkers. From 1743 to 1745, Swedenborg, who had established a reputation as a brilliant engineer and metallurgist, became convinced that through dreams (in which he retained consciousness of this world) and conversations with angels, God had given

"Unanimity in religion, and the true divine worship, is the surest basis of a lawful, concordant, and stable government" (King Gustavus III of Sweden).

him understanding of the world of the spirit as it really is. With this knowledge, he sought to explain the "internal sense" of the Bible, or its true meaning. He wrote volume after volume to do so. He believed members of the "New Church," made up of his disciples scattered throughout various Christian churches, would spread his doctrines. In 1787 some of his followers established the New Jerusalem Church in London.

Pietism's influence also extended to Lutheran Denmark-Norway and Finland. As noted earlier, in 1706 the Danish king Frederick IV (1671–1730) solicited the Pietist Francke to provide German missionaries for the Danish mission in India. At the same time, orthodox Lutheranism in Denmark grew stronger, owing in part to the emigration of more Germans into the kingdom. In 1715 the Danish government backed a mission to the Sami, the Laplanders of northern Norway. Paavo Ruotsalainen (1777–1852) encouraged the "awakened" in Finland.

IV. THE UNITED PROVINCES

From 1609, the year the northern Dutch provinces won a de facto liberation from Spain, until the invasion of Louis XIV's armies during the Dutch War (1672–78), the United Provinces experienced its "Golden Age" and enjoyed an "embarrassment of riches" (Simon Schama's expression), due in part to its lucrative international trade. The seven United Provinces constituted the Dutch Republic, with authority residing in the Estates-General, to which each province sent representatives.

Amsterdam thrived as a commercial and cultural center. It boasted a remarkable semi-concentric system of canals, dating from the mid-seventeenth century. Its population grew from 100,000 in 1600 to 221,000 in 1795. As painted in 1686 by Willem van de Velde, Amsterdam's busy port remained crowded with ships. Its docks were the site of a cavernous warehouse of the Dutch East India Company (founded in 1602). From its earliest days, this trading company supported Reformed missionary work at posts in the Malay Archipelago, Sri Lanka, and South Africa. In July 1625, Dutch traders established New Amsterdam (later known as New York City).

The United Provinces constituted an intellectual and religious crossroads for Europe through its universities, publishing houses and journals, and churches. Young Protestant students from lands such as Germany, Finland, and France flocked to the United Provinces to study at the University of Leiden (1575) and other notable schools such as the University of Franeker.

The initial central task of the theology faculty at the University of Leiden was "the unfolding of the Holy Scriptures." Among Leiden's professors was "the glory of the university," Joseph Scaliger (1540–1609). His expertise in the classics and biblical textual criticism made him one of the premier scholars of Europe. Other scholars included Jacob Arminius (1550–1609), Francis Gomarus (1563–1641), Simon Episcopius (1583–1643), and Johannes Coccejus (1603–69).

The seventeenth century constituted the Dutch "Golden Age" of art. Thousands of Dutch painters created literally millions of paintings with themes ranging from battles and landscapes to churches, everyday life scenes, and portraits. Among the more famous master painters were Rembrandt (1606–69; "The Night Watch"; "Isaac and Rebecca"), Frans Hal (1582/1583–1666; "The Merry Drinker"), Johannes Vermeer (1632–73; "The Kitchen Maid"), and Jacob van Ruisdael (1628/1629–82; "View of Haarlem with Bleaching Fields"). By the eighteenth century, contemporaries sensed that the quality of Dutch art was diminishing.

The Dutch Reformed Church affirmed the Belgic Confession of Faith of 1561. This statement addressed topics ranging from the Trinity, the work of Christ, and the sacraments to church and state relations. Although the Reformed Church was the "public" one permitted, the United Provinces became known for the coexistence (if not toleration) of diverse religious communities. Nonetheless, intense theological controversies were not foreign to ecclesiastical life. Two parties emerged in the Reformed Church: the *preciezen* ("precise") Calvinists who wanted the churches to possess binding doctrinal authority, and the *rekkelijken* ("looser or moderate") Calvinists who desired greater freedom of religious thought.

Jakob Hermanszoon, later known as Arminius (1560–1609), attempted to refute the charges of Dirck Coornhert (1522–90) against the Calvinist doctrine of predestination. After studying Romans 7 and 9, Hermanszoon modified his beliefs and affirmed that God predestined all who believe in Christ.

As a professor of divinity at the University of Leiden (after 1603), Arminius engaged in a harsh dispute with fellow professor Francis Gomarus, a committed supralapsarian Calvinist and admirer of Calvin and Beza. Both Arminius and Gomarus affirmed a belief in justification by faith alone, but Gomarus suspected that Arminius had been influenced by the Roman Catholic Scholastic thought of Suarez and Molina and was in fact a "papist." It was decided to consider their controversy at a synodal conference, but Arminius died in 1609. (For a discussion of Arminianism and Calvinism, see chapter 7.)

The United Provinces often served as a haven for people seeking relief from persecution. Amsterdam was the home of a Sephardic

Jewish community. French Huguenots of the *Réfuge* (50,000 to 70,000) intermarried with members of the Dutch populace. An Anabaptist community flourished. Religious dissidents such as Baruch Spinoza and the freethinker Anthony Collins, an exile from England, were not unduly hassled. Masons such as Charles Le Vier, a member of the Knights of the Jubilee, could ply controversial ideas with relative impunity.

Many Europeans admired the Dutch Republic for its successful war of liberation from the Spanish, its government (which, even if oligarchical, was not despotic), its promotion of freedom and toleration, and its vital economy (slowed down in the eighteenth century). Already by 1675, fifty-five printing presses were operational and over two hundred booksellers in Amsterdam helped prime the rich intellectual life of the Republic of Letters with a diverse reading fare. In Rotterdam, a city of 53,000, Pierre Bayle established and served as editor of the journal *News of the Republic of Letters* (1684–87), one of the leading reviews of books. Renier Leers, an influential printer of Rotterdam, published not only Bayle's journal but also the works of Protestants and Catholics (Richard Simon, Malebranche).

During the eighteenth century the Dutch people generally continued to uphold their religious beliefs. The Dutch Republic was a confessional Reformed state, with Roman Catholics, Dissenters, and Jews generally considered religious outsiders. Revivals periodically coursed through villages. In the 1730s a report reached Scotland "that in several places up and down Holland, the Lord is following the Gospel and the endeavors of Ministers with visible success and remarkable conversions; not so much in their great towns, as up and down the country villages." In 1749–50, emotion-laced revival meetings took place in Nijkerk under the ministry of Pastor Gerardus Kuypers. Other villages in the Netherlands and in neighboring Germany experienced similar revivals.

Missionary-minded Reformed scholars completed the translation of the New Testament into the Malay language (1734; the Old Testament having been completed in 1688). A number of theologian-scientists wrote works of "physico-theology" in which they sought to demonstrate that the intricacy of designs in nature proves God's existence. Until the 1770s, the Reformed Church played a dominant role in public life. Approximately 55–60 percent of the population was Reformed, 35 percent Roman Catholic, and 5–10 percent Dissenters and Jews.

A Dutch form of "enlightenment" did exist. Most of its partisans did not espouse a militant atheism, but rather sought to accommodate their Christian beliefs with a desire for educational reforms and religious toleration. They appreciated the new science and advances in technology. Others such as Jean Frederic Bernard and Bernard Picart downplayed Christianity as *the* faith. In *Ceremonies and Religious Customs of All the People of the World* (Amsterdam, 1723 – 37), they proposed that all men, except for views of revelation, "agree on several things and have the same foundations." These common beliefs included the teachings of Jesus before the "church" added its theological strictures and a general belief in the divine.

Bernard and Picart apparently hoped to further the cause of a toleration of religious differences. The Dutch did debate what should be the extent of toleration's reach. Some orthodox Calvinists, for example, attempted to ban books such as La Mettrie's *L'Homme machine* (1747). Between 1760 and 1796, a large number of publications (1,130) of German origin became reading fare for the Dutch.

Earlier, in 1713, the Dutch Republic began to proclaim solemn, national days of prayer accompanied by fasting. Since the founding of the Republic, the Dutch, especially providentially minded ministers, had often linked their military or economic setbacks to their own sins and God's judgment. In 1765 the Dutch people were called on to pray for "the welfare of all Protestant churches in the whole world, and especially for those of these United Provinces, to the end that the labors of their ministers may bear more and more fruit, affirming Christian belief and spreading piety and justice, love and concord."

During the Dutch Patriot Revolution (1786 – 87), Dutch "Patriots" challenged the authority of William V (1748 – 1806), the *Stadtholder* from the House of Orange who sought to make his position hereditary. In 1795, faced by the forces of the Patriots and the French, William V left the United Provinces for England. In 1798 the Patriots established the Batavian Republic.

V. THE REPUBLIC OF GENEVA

In the early 1750s the Republic of Geneva became simultaneously the home of Voltaire and Rousseau (who was born in Calvin's Geneva in 1712). Both men had a falling out with Jacob Vernes and Jacob Vernet, two prominent ministers of Geneva.

These two pastors pursued a "moderate" approach to theology. They proposed a reasonable and tolerant form of Christianity. Nonetheless, they claimed that d'Alembert's article "Genève" (1757) in the *Encyclopédie* misrepresented them badly when it characterized them and other pastors of Geneva as "perfect Socinians" and the followers of the "natural religion of John Locke." The article engendered animosities between Voltaire and the pastors, whom he knew very well. Some suspected that Voltaire had been the source for d'Alembert's controversial treatment of the two pastors. Even if the judgment in the article was possibly off the mark, the fact remains that Polier de Bottens, the first pastor of Geneva and a friend of Vernes and Vernet, was a notable ally of the *philosophe* Voltaire. Bottens wrote the article *Messie* (Messiah) in the *Encyclopédie*. It portrayed Christ as just one Messiah among other messiahs in world history.

Undoubtedly many Genevans remained faithful Christians despite these disputes. The temptations of wealth, however, stayed seductive. Vernet warned Genevans about their materialistic predilections. He supported the Reformed consistory's ban (1739) against the theater. Much like Rousseau, Vernet identified the theater and actors with vice and immorality. He also worried that the *philosophes* would use the theaters "as a school of totally pagan philosophy."

That Voltaire and Rousseau believed Vernes and Vernet were susceptible to their ideas suggests that the pastors' theology reflected tendencies far removed from Francis Turretin (1623–87) and other Reformed conservative theologians of Geneva who had earlier dominated the religious life of the city in the late seventeenth century.

Turretin, a professor of theology at the Academy of Geneva, had proposed that the city was a "theocracy, having God always for its ruler." He recommended that the Geneva government should always defend "the culture of pure religion and the pious care of nurturing the church." Historian Timothy Philipps, in attempting to moderate negative assessments of Turretin's "Scholasticism," proposed that the Genevan viewed theology "as an infused *habitus* of principles that provides a qualitatively new cognizance and volition for reality." In his *Institutio*, Turretin argued that the Word of God "lays the foundation for a full assurance of faith ... which suffices for expelling doubt and tranquilizing the conscience and generating the hope of salvation."

Along with other Genevan theologians, Turretin also defended the Masoretic pointing of the Hebrew text, making this belief binding in the Helvetic Consensus Formula (1675). These pastors feared that if Hebrew vowels were left unpointed, the Hebrew words of the Old Testament would become even more susceptible to multiple interpretations. The professors also attempted to obligate pastoral students to repudiate the doctrine of "universal grace" championed by theologians in Saumur, France, and by the Genevan professor Louis Tronchin. Tronchin, a Cartesian, approved reason's rights to inform correct theology.

In 1706 Turretin's son, Jean Alphonse Turretin (1671–1737), led a movement in the Genevan Company of Pastors to repudiate the Helvetic Consensus Formula. He espoused a form of natural theology and emphasized reason's right to determine religious truth. He denied the supralapsarianism of his father, Francis. He eschewed other doctrines such as the limited atonement. By the 1720s, a number of contemporaries fretted about their perception that an openness to Arminianism and forms of heterodoxy existed in Geneva.

Jean Frédéric Ostervald (1663–1747) believed that both "incredulity" and "atheism" were beginning to spread, not just among the learned, but in "towns, among the vulgar and even among country clowns." In 1702 he published a *Catechism or Instruction in the Christian Religion*. He hoped his catechism would help remedy the ignorance of laypeople regarding the Christian faith and answer its detractors' objections. The theological orientation of Ostervald's catechism was essentially Reformed. At the same time, it highlighted the role of reason in defending the faith. Moreover, it did not reference Calvin's teaching about the pivotal role of the Holy Spirit in persuading Christians regarding Holy Scripture's authority. Ostervald's catechism circulated widely among French-speaking Reformed Christians.

Due to French urging, a theater opened in Geneva in 1766. By the 1780s, Genevans permitted dancing and attended the theater in large numbers—practices the pastors of Calvin's Geneva would not have countenanced. Already in 1764, after noting Genevans engaged in card-playing on a Sunday with a minister "rampaging amongst them," James Boswell wrote in his journal, "O John Calvin, where art thou now?" In 1782 the French intervened in the patrician-bourgeoisie struggle of 1781–82. The French took the side of the patricians. The patricians then reduced the number of clergy in the city, reduced the number of sermons preached, and took greater control of appointments at the Genevan Academy.

VI. THE AUSTRIAN HAPSBURGS

On February 28, 1670, Leopold I, the Holy Roman Emperor and a devout Roman Catholic, ordered all Jews to leave Austrian lands. By 1683, when the Turks were defeated at the city's walls by Leopold I and others, Vienna was largely Catholic. Its population grew thereafter from 100,000 in 1700 to 175,000 in 1754 to 200,000 in 1783. Its stately character was enhanced by the construction of the Schwarzenberg Palace and the Schönberg Palace, its culture enlivened by the music of Franz Joseph Haydn and Wolfgang Amadeus Mozart.

The Holy Roman Emperors Joseph I and Charles VI continued to support the missionary efforts of Jesuits to convert Protestants. The Jesuits helped create a baroque Catholic culture in Austria and Bohemia with the construction of magnificent churches both in cities and in the countryside. The architecture of these lavishly decorated churches evidenced few straight lines and was designed to focus attention on the eucharistic host placed on a central high altar so that parishioners might adore and venerate it.

Protestants near Salzburg attempted to hold onto their faith. In 1722 a report from Carinthia noted that

> just about every inhabitant here can read and many can write, but they never learned or allowed [their children] to learn reading and writing in the towns and markets, for fear of the religious instruction and catechizing that would go with it there, but rather from a local schoolmaster or very often from a peasant, where in wintertime especially even the farmhands and maidservants come together for this, and take such instruction with no other purpose, than to read and to understand the old or newly arrived Lutheran books.

In 1731–32 these same Protestants were forced to emigrate from Salzburg, some 20,000 receiving help from Protestant East Prussia to move to its more hospitable lands.

The Austrian Hapsburg emperors, though Catholic, did not accept the papacy's right to intervene in Austria's religious or political life. They believed that their empire was universal and that they had defended Catholicism well. Had not Leopold I saved Christendom in 1683? Was not Austria in one sense the "rock" upon which the Catholic Church was built?

Upon the death of her father, Charles VI, on October 20, 1740, Maria Theresa took the titles of Archduchess of Austria, Queen of Bohemia, and Queen of Hungary. In 1745 her husband, Francis Stephen, became the Holy Roman Emperor under the name Francis I (1745–65). Disturbed by Frederick II's seizure of Silesia, Maria Theresa attempted to reform the military and governmental structures of Austria in a rational fashion. She became the proponent of what some have called "Enlightened Absolutism." At the same time, she was quite ready to apply repressive measures against minorities. On one occasion she warned that he is "no friend to humanity who allows everyone his own thoughts."

Maria Theresa was a devout Catholic influenced by counselors favorable to Jansenism. With the advice of her chancellor, Wenzel Anton von Kaunitz-Rietberg, she tried to establish a national Catholic Church in which the pope had authority only in spiritual matters. Along with her son, Joseph II (1741–90), Maria Theresa was also influenced by the thinking of Joseph Eybel, who argued that church authority does not ultimately belong to the pope but to "a general council, consisting of bishops from all of Christendom, [that] represents the complete Church of God." Owing to the fact that a general council receives authority directly from God, it could even depose a pope. In 1764 Pope Clement XIII condemned this German variant of Gallicanism known as Febronianism.

Joseph II, a less devout Catholic believer than his mother, ruled with her as coregent after 1765 until her death in 1780. Maria Theresa did not allow Protestants to sell their property or leave her lands. She required those who refused to convert to Catholicism to emigrate to Transylvania, where Protestantism was permitted. Nor did Maria Theresa intercede to save the Jesuits when their society was on the brink of dissolution. She did allow some two thousand Protestants to live in Vienna, but she forced the city's Jews to live in a ghetto.

Upon the death of Maria Theresa, Joseph II promulgated Edicts of Toleration in 1781 that allowed greater freedoms for non-Catholics (Protestants and Jews). He promulgated hundreds of edicts at a very rapid clip in promoting "Josephism," a "reform" program of church and state. It emphasized the cure of souls as opposed to baroque forms of spirituality. It reinforced the state's authority at the expense of the papacy's right to intervene in spiritual affairs. Bishops were obliged to make an oath of loyalty to the state. The government had to give its approval before papal bulls could be published.

Joseph II also proceeded to confiscate properties of 738 monasteries (out of 2,047), displacing 27,000 monks and nuns (out of 65,000) and using the monies from the properties to build new Catholic churches. Nevertheless, the warm reception a crowd of 100,000 gave to Pope Pius VI in 1782—when he came to Vienna to entreat Joseph II as emperor to change policies toward the papacy—suggests that a good number of the Austrian laity retained a first loyalty to the pope despite their government's policies.

VII. "ITALY" AND THE PAPACY

In the eighteenth century "Italy" did not yet exist as a unified nation. Rather, "Italy" consisted in the north of the Duchy of Savoy, Duchy of Milan, Republic of Venice, Duchy of Parma, Duchy of Modena, Republic of Genoa, Republic of Lucca, and Grand Duchy of Tuscany; in the center as the Papal States; and in the south the Kingdom of Naples and the islands of the Kingdom of Sardinia, Corsica (until it became part of France), and the Kingdom of Sicily among other political entities. Nor did complete linguistic unity exist. Not all "Italians" spoke Tuscan. In Naples, for example, elites on occasion wrote plays and other literary pieces in Neapolitan, a dialect. The population of the Italian peninsula grew from 11.5 to 15.5 million in the first half of the century. In 1763–64 a particularly severe famine struck Florence, Rome, and Naples.

Austria constituted a dominant outsider power, especially for a number of the northern Italian states. Tuscany evidenced a kind of Austrian "Josephism" and a flourishing Jansenist party. Jansenists were also influential in Genoa and Milan. By contrast, the Bourbon family ruled Naples, and Savoy ruled Sardinia. Sometimes city-states changed hands. (The Kingdom of Sicily went to Austria in 1720 and to Charles of Bourbon in 1735.)

Historian Anne Schutte has described Italian Catholic religion of the eighteenth century as "normalized, routinized and conformist." Yet some Italians attempted to promote "enlightened" views and to eliminate what they perceived as repressive features of the general culture. They included Giambattista Vico (1668–1744), professor of rhetoric at the University of Naples, who proposed in his *New Science* (1725) to study "the common nature of nations in the light of divine providence" with a view to discovering "the origins of divine and human institutions"; Anna Morandi Manzolini (1714–74), a "pious wife" and anatomist from Bologna who gained a more accurate knowledge of male and female anatomy; Cesare Beccaria (1738–94), author of *On Crimes and Punishments*, who called for the end of torture and the substitution of long imprisonments for the death penalty; Girolamo Tartarotti (1706–61), who defended impoverished women falsely accused of witchcraft; and Lodovico Antonio Muratori (1672–1750), librarian at Modena, who published sources of Italian history (AD 500 to 1500) and early Christian sources including the "Muratorian Canon" of the New Testament. Others called for more rigorous, traditional forms of Christian devotion. In 1720 St. Paul of the Cross founded the order of Passionists, and in 1732 Alphonsus Liguori created the order of the Most Holy Redeemer.

The absolutist powers of the eighteenth century had uneasy if not outright hostile relations with the papacy. The French church vaunted its Gallicanism. The Austrian church presented itself as Catholic, autonomous, and national. England had an Anglican state-church. Prussia was ruled by Calvinist kings; even Frederick II claimed that he fought for the Protestant cause. The French kings, the Austrian emperors, the English kings, and the Prussian kings often showed little respect for the papacy's claims to universal religious authority, let alone temporal authority. The popes of the eighteenth century faced steep challenges in dealing with these powerful rulers, who sometimes treated the Papal States as just one more political entity among other Italian city-states.

The Papal States were periodically invaded by foreign powers that departed only after they had extorted handsome ransoms to do so. The popes were repeatedly forced to make concessions that exposed the papacy's overall weakness in temporal affairs during the eighteenth century. Nonetheless, Italy and the city of Rome attracted and beckoned large numbers of pilgrims, students, and artists from all over Europe. Some pilgrims hoped to receive a blessing from the pope or to experience a miraculous healing while venerating the appropriate saint or shrine.

By contrast, young graduates of Cambridge and Oxford universities on a "Grand Tour" of Europe (the vogue, 1660–1840) headed to Italy in part to gain knowledge of classical culture. In 1776 Samuel Johnson underscored the importance of Italy as an essential destination for those making the Grand Tour: "A man who has not been in Italy, is always conscious of an inferiority.... The grand object of traveling is to see the shores of the Mediterranean.... On those shores were the four great Empires of the world; the Assyrian, the Persian, the Grecian, and the Roman."

Earlier, in 1740, the English poet Thomas Gray extolled Rome's beauty: "As high as my expectation was raised, I confess, the magnificence of this city infinitely surpasses it. You cannot pass along a street but you have views of some palace or church, or square, or fountain, the most picturesque and noble one can imagine."

Several popes supported educational institutions and encouraged the general advance of scholarship. The generous patronage of the papacy added to Rome's artistic riches in painting, sculpture, music, and monuments. For example, Clement XI (1700–1721) initiated architectural plans for the Trevi Fountain and the Spanish Steps. Artists perched their studios beside the descending Spanish Steps, near the French (top), German (near the top), and English (bottom) steps.

This same Clement XI, however, faced a set of serious challenges. In 1709 Emperor Joseph I invaded the Papal States and forced the pope to withdraw his support for Philip V, the French candidate for the throne of Spain. Pressured by Louis XIV, in 1713 the pope issued the bull *Unigenitus dei Filius*, which profusely fueled antagonisms in the Jesuit-Jansenist controversy. Moreover, he took a stand against the Jesuits in the Chinese Rites Controversy.

During the reigns of Pope Innocent XIII (1721–24), Benedict XIII (1724–30), and Clement XII (1730–40), the papacy continued to have relatively little success in thwarting the aggressive foreign policies and blandishments of the absolutist states. Benedict XIV (1740–58), a gifted and urbane scholar, made concessions to the leading powers. At the same time, he condemned Freemasonry and the works of several *philosophes*. He also defended the authority of the bull *Unigenitus*. Clement XIII (1758–69) found himself beset by the Marquis de Pombal, the Minister of Portugal, and other absolutist ministers who tried to pressure him to dissolve the Society of Jesus. He refused. When Clement

"I am more attached to churches than to the palaces of dukes" (Gilles Caillotin, a Catholic pilgrim to Italy).

excommunicated the Duke of Parma, who had attempted to take over the ecclesiastical affairs of his city-state, French troops retaliated by seizing a number of papal lands. In 1773 Clement XIII's successor, Clement XIV (1769–74), finally yielded to the threats of the Catholic powers and dissolved the Society of Jesus, the Jesuits.

Nor did the well-being of the papacy improve during the French Revolution. Pius VI (1775–99) felt obliged to condemn the "Declaration of the Rights of Man" (1789) and the "Civil Constitution of the Clergy" (1790). The pope's actions reinforced significant divisions in the French populace between some "counter-revolutionaries" who wanted to remain faithful to Catholicism and radical revolutionaries like Robespierre who sought to rid France of vestiges of the Christian religion. The Age of Lights, therefore, witnessed serious challenges to the papacy's temporal and spiritual authority.

VIII. THE IBERIAN PENINSULA: SPAIN AND PORTUGAL

A. Spain

From 1640 to 1713, the decline of the Spanish Empire continued generally unabated. Through warfare or revolt, Spain lost Portugal (1640), the United Provinces, various city-states in Italy, Artois, Franche-Comté, and other areas. However, the economic and social prospects of Roman Catholic Spain generally turned around in the eighteenth century, despite the loss of her silver fleets struck by hurricanes as they sailed back from Mexico and South America (1715; 1733) and despite setbacks during the Seven Years War (1756–63). Its population, largely peasant, increased from 6 million in 1700 to 11 million in 1800 and the amount of land under Spanish control in the Americas doubled between the years 1740 and 1790.

In 1700 Philip V (1683–1746), a Bourbon grandson of Louis XIV, became king of Spain. A bitter dispute ensued as various powers contested the legitimacy of his claims to the Spanish throne. The dispute helped precipitate the War of the Spanish Succession (1701–14). This "world war," with military theaters outside of Europe, pitted France and Spain against Britain, Austria, Holland, Portugal, and Savoy. With a Bourbon king in power, elements of French culture spread in Spain, French classicism replacing baroque culture by the 1720s. Philip V was followed by Fernando VI (1746–58) and Carlos III (1759–88).

Foreign travelers to Spain frequently commented about the intense Catholic devotion of the Spanish populace. In 1705 a British naval officer observed that "at the Corner of every Street, and, indeed, in almost

Façade of the
Cathedral of Guadix
(Granada, Spain).

every Stable, there's a Statue of our Blessed Virgin, with a pair of Beads in her hand. Dressed after the Country Fashion, with a Wax-Candle or Lamp burning before her, for these people are most abominably Superstitious, or rather Abominably Religious." Other British were appalled by horrific tales of torture by Spanish Inquisitors and by the report of an *Auto de fe*, the alleged public burning of a Jewish mother, father, and daughter. Most Cambridge and Oxford graduates excluded Spain from the itinerary of their Grand Tour.

In 1753 the Spanish government approved a concordat that set forth the doctrine of *regalism* with its central premise that the state's authority is superior to that of the church. Buttressed by this regalist premise, the orthodox Catholic Carlos III attempted to initiate supposed "enlightened reforms" of Spain's religious life: (1) the expulsion of the Jesuits who professed a first loyalty to the pope and not to the king; (2) the selective use of the Inquisition's authority; (3) the control over an abusive church tax, the *excusado*; (4) the creation of new seminaries.

The impact of these "enlightened reforms" on Spain remained quite "moderate," however, owing in part to a fairly common Spanish trait, *misoneismo*, a strong dislike of new things. Moreover, the church's clergy (2.5 percent of the population in 1768) continued to direct many educational institutions and works of charity. The church retained great power, and its landed wealth was very substantial.

"New Spain," or Mexico, possessed a population ranging between 4 and 4.5 million people. The Royal and Pontifical University of Mexico City tended to be theologically conservative. Until their expulsion, Jesuits controlled the education in "New Spain" and greatly influenced the privileged classes of *Peninsulares* (Spanish-born people) and *Criollas* (persons of Spanish blood born in New Spain).

Religious art flourished in the eighteenth century in Spain. Among her great painters were Jacinto-Miguel Meléndez (1679–1734), Domingo Martinez (1689–1750), and Bernardo German Llorente (1680–1759), who produced significant works focused on religious themes.

B. Portugal

The first half of the eighteenth century constituted a "golden" cultural age for Catholic Portugal. The country's well-being depended in large measure on successful trade in sugar and slaves with its colonies and on receiving military protection from England—a long-standing ally. The Portuguese had signed the Treaty of 1654 with the English, linking the two nations in commercial relations. The Portuguese had also gained the upper hand against the Dutch in Brazil. In the 1690s, mines in Brazil belonging to the Portuguese began to produce large quantities of gold. The monarchy of King John V (1689–1750) and a small group of elites profited handsomely from this gold. They in turn fostered an arts and building program. The royal palace boasted a world-class music library and collection of paintings.

Vast regions of Portugal remained economically undeveloped and backward. Likewise, an unfavorable trade imbalance emerged with the English. England exported woolens to Portugal and imported wine from Portugal. Portuguese gold sometimes ended up in English coffers. Between the years 1728 and 1732 John V broke off diplomatic relations with the papacy when it refused to grant a patriarchate to Portugal.

On November 1, 1755, All Saints' Day, the horrific Lisbon earthquake struck, followed by flooding and an outbreak of fire. The earthquake constituted one of the great natural catastrophes of the eighteenth century. Between 10,000 and 20,000 people (some estimates ranged up to 100,000) lost their lives out of a population of 275,000. Many buildings were completely destroyed. Huge waves from the Tagus River rushed into parts of the city.

An English nun recalled the terror provoked by the earthquake's sudden onslaught: "I was washing the tea things when the Dreadfull affair hapned. itt began like the rattleing of Coaches, and the things befor me danst up and downe upon the table, I look about me and see the Walls a shaking and a falling down then I up and took to my heels, with Jesus in my mouth." From Voltaire to John Wesley, European commentators weighed in, attempting to make sense of the catastrophe. Were divine providence or divine punishment involved in it, or was the earthquake's cause solely due to "natural" causes?

Sebastian Carvalho e Melo, the Marquis de Pombal, a tough-minded minister of King Joseph I, supported the latter explanation. He gave direction to the remarkable reconstruction of Lisbon. He viewed Jesuits and certain members of the nobility as resolute opponents to his economic and social reform measures. He accused the Jesuits of complicity in a failed assassination attempt against Joseph I (September 3, 1758). On September 1, 1759, he put Jesuits on ships bound for Italy, thereby expelling them from Portugal. He also confiscated their huge landholdings in Brazil.

Pombal curtailed the use of the Inquisition as a tool of religious oppression and gave both Jews and blacks certain freedoms. Ironically enough, Portugal continued to engage in the slave trade and to exploit Brazil and Angola, its colonies. Upon the accession of Queen Maria I in 1777, conservative religious forces sought to undo aspects of Pombal's work.

IX. CHRISTIANS IN OTTOMAN TURKISH LANDS

After the fall of Constantinople in 1453, the Turks conquered the Balkans except for Dalmatia and Montenegro. They controlled what was formerly the Byzantine Empire and Armenia. They forced the patriarchs of Constantinople to obey their dictates. In Ottoman-controlled lands, young Christian boys were often required to convert to the Muslim faith and to serve in the military and in government posts. Christians and Jews were allowed considerable autonomy in running their own communities, or *millets.*

Nonetheless, in his *Additions to Curious Research concerning the Diversity of Languages and Religions of Edward Brerewood* (manuscript c. 1676), the Catholic priest Richard Simon described the Greek Orthodox dependent on the patriarchate of Constantinople as living under "pitiful" conditions. He listed among contemporary "Oriental Christians" the following people groups: Greeks, Melchites (Syrian Arabs), Chaldeans, Nestorians, Jacobites, Maronites, Copts, Armenians, Iberians, Georgians, Mingrelians, Albanians, Moscovites, and Circassians. He indicated that the liturgies of these "Oriental Christians" were quite similar in basic substance and in prayers invoking the Holy Spirit.

"Orthodox" Slavs living under Ottoman rule especially resented Phanariots, or privileged Greeks, who worked for the Turkish sultans.

Phanariots often enjoyed access to key governmental positions. They frequently tried to force Greek culture upon Slavic peoples. For a time (1557–1766), the Serbian Orthodox Church did gain independence from the patriarchate of Constantinople.

The governments of France, England, United Provinces, and other Western countries sometimes seemed unmoved by the sorry plight of Eastern Christians. Instead, these governments were anxious to maintain diplomats and chaplains at the Porte, or Constantinople, and vied with each other for favorable trade treaties with the Turks.

X. THE PATRIARCHATE OF MOSCOW, THE UNIATE CHURCH, AND CYRIL LUCARIS

In 1589 the patriarchate of Moscow and All Russia (1589–1721) was established when the patriarch of Constantinople, Jeremias II, designated Bishop Job (d. 1607) as the first patriarch of Moscow. The patriarchate of Moscow thereby joined the much older patriarchates of Rome, Alexandria, Antioch, Jerusalem, and Constantinople.

In 1595, four bishops and the metropolitan in Kiev, Ukraine, created what became known as the Uniate Church (eastern Catholic churches). They submitted to the authority of the pope and embraced Catholic doctrine. At the same time, they continued to observe the Byzantine liturgy and reserved the right of their priests to marry. For three centuries, Uniate Christians became the subjects of fierce persecution. Cossacks in Ukraine and Poland proved to be determined enemies. For example, during the Cossack-Polish War (1648–57), many Uniates were slaughtered. In Austria, the Uniate Church did prosper.

Orthodox theologians rejected the Protestant Reformation's emphasis on the doctrine of justification by faith alone. When Cyril Lucaris, (1572–1637), a Greek Orthodox patriarch of Constantinople, published a confession (1629) with eighteen chapters that appeared Calvinist in orientation, he provoked a firestorm of theological controversy and elicited fierce opposition from Orthodox theologians. Chapter 2 taught that Holy Scripture was infallible and could not err. It possessed authority above the church. Chapter 13 indicated that sinners are justified by faith and not by works and that Christ's righteousness applied to repentant sinners alone justifies.

The Ottoman Sultan Murad IV arranged for Cyril Lucaris, whom he viewed as a political and theological troublemaker, to be murdered by his elite guards, the *Janissaries* (June 27, 1638). Cyril's body was unceremoniously dumped off a ship into the waters below. Still later, the Orthodox Synod of Jerusalem (1672) specifically repudiated each point of Cyril's confession. A number of Orthodox apologists argued the confession was a forgery. They claimed the patriarch's other writings did not comport with its contents.

XI. THE EMERGENCE OF RUSSIA AS A EUROPEAN POWER

After a so-called "Time of Troubles" (1598–1613), the tsars of the Romanov family dynasty began a lengthy rule of Muscovy-Russia from 1613 until 1917. During the period from Peter the Great (1672–1725) through Empress Catherine II the Great (1729–96) Russia emerged as a worthy military competitor for the traditional Western powers—the French, the Spanish, the English, the Prussians, and the Austrian Hapsburgs. Russia's armies grew from 170,000 in 1690 to 330,000 in 1756. Her navy more than doubled in size from the 1730s to the 1780s. She gained vast lands at the expense of Sweden (the Great Northern War, 1700–1721), of Poland (the War of the Polish Succession, 1733–38; the First Partition of Poland, 1772; the Second Partition of Poland, 1793; the Third Partition of Poland, 1795), and of Turkey (the Russo-Turkish Wars of 1768–74 and 1787–92).

Tsar Peter the Great of Russia.

LOC, LC-USZ62-121999

Russia's conquests brought many non-Orthodox under her control, including Roman Catholics from Poland and Jews. Monarchs and diplomats became increasingly wary of Russia as an aggressor state that could overthrow carefully calibrated alliances designed to balance power in western Europe. In 1763 Louis XV declared, "Everything that may plunge Russia into chaos and make her return to obscurity is favorable to our interests."

The impact of the reign of Peter the Great (1694–1725) on Russian society was profound. Fascinated by things military even as a child, Peter as ruler could be as ruthless with his enemies as he was charming with those he was trying to woo. He took upon himself the daunting task of transforming the religious, political, and economic life of his essentially backward and rural country. During a fifteen-month trip to Germany, the United Provinces, England, and Austria in 1697–98, he gained greater knowledge about economics, farming, munitions, and shipbuilding. He visited diverse educational institutions, hospitals, and factories. He was received by monarchs as well as the members of the Royal Society in England. The English Bishop Burnet described him as a "man of very hot temper, soon inflamed and very brutal in his passion," who, when he had to return suddenly to Moscow to put down a takeover attempt by his sister, reportedly proceeded to "cut off many heads with his own hand."

Using forced labor, Peter the Great began to build the port city of Petersburg (1703) as a "window on the West." In 1713 it became the capital of Russia. He ultimately defeated the armies of the Swedes, thereafter gaining more territory. His trip to western European countries had provided him new insights regarding how he might streamline his military, governmental, and educational institutions.

Opponents of Peter the Great were often impassioned. They included clerics from the Russian Orthodox Church as well as "Old Believers" or "Old Ritualists" who had a notable following in Little Russia and among Cossacks. Some Orthodox clerics believed that Peter engaged in blasphemous temerity by moving the imperial capital of Russia from Moscow—the "Third Rome" and center of Russian Orthodoxy—to Petersburg.

Old Believers were also enraged by what they thought were his irreligious, pragmatic actions. They had earlier entered into schism (*Raskol*) from the Russian Orthodox Church in the 1650s due to their opposition to the anti-Slavic, Byzantine nature of Metropolitan Nikon's revisions of the church's liturgy. Nikon had specifically stipulated that believers should henceforth cross themselves, not using two fingers, but rather with "the three first fingers of the right hand. Any Orthodox Christian who does not make the sign of the cross according to this Eastern church tradition ... is a

St. Basil's Cathedral and Red Square in Moscow, 1634.

heretic and imitator of the Armenian. He will be damned." In 1682 Archpriest Avvakum Petrov, the leader of the Old Believers, was burned at the stake. Some of his followers who lived apart in their own religious communities engaged in tragic mass suicides.

Peter's clerical opponents were especially agitated that he required both men and women to wear Western dress and forced *boyars* (Russian nobles) to shave (a Western custom) unless they paid a tax. Some Russian men believed they would not be permitted to enter heaven beardless. This policy, one contemporary noted, "the Russians regarded as an enormous sin on the part of the tsar and as a thing which tended to the abolition of their religion." They were also offended by Peter the Great's promotion of secular education (1714).

Peter professed to believe in the Christian faith. He venerated icons, could quote Scripture at length, could cite the Liturgy by heart, and sang on occasion in a church choir. Nonetheless, he evidenced little patience toward Patriarch Adrian of Moscow, who opposed his "Western" innovations.

Historian Isabel de Madariaga has indicated that Peter the Great's actions toward the Church of Muscovy "led to a cultural shock from which Russia never perhaps recovered." When Patriarch Adrian died in 1700, Peter postponed the election of a new patriarch of Moscow and put Stefan Iasvorski into the role of protecting the vacant chair. This gambit dealt a staggering blow to the traditions and the hierarchical structure of the Russian Orthodox Church. In 1716 Peter declared that he alone ruled Russia, thereby setting himself over the church.

In 1721 Peter approved Bishop Theophan Prokopovich's "Ecclesiastical Regulation" for the Orthodox Church. This constitution established the "Spiritual College," later called the Holy Governing Synod. The emperor was to choose its members, who were to swear the following oath: "I acknowledge the Monarch of all-Russia, our Gracious Lord, to be the final Judge of this College." This body, led by the Procurator, a layman, was granted authority over the clergy and worked with the government on religious matters. It essentially served as a replacement institution for the patriarchy and gave Peter the Great authority over the Orthodox Church. When Peter died the next year, he left behind the Russian Empire.

The reigns of the Romanovs Catherine I (1725–27), Peter II (1727–30), Anna Ivanona (1730–40), Ivan VI (1740–41), Elizabeth I (1741–61), and Peter III (1762) were marked by intrigue and palace coups, by nobles gaining greater control over serfs, and by the founding of the University of Moscow (under Elizabeth).

Peter III, for example, had a very brief reign. He had married the German-born and Lutheran-raised Catherine II, who had recently converted to Orthodoxy. He disbanded the secret police and seemed to favor religious toleration. In 1762 he ruled that the gentry no longer had to serve the state. He disdained the Orthodox Church and was accused of favoring "Lutheranism." A party headed by Grigori Orlov, a lover of Peter's wife (then known as "Catherine the Great"), forced Peter to resign the throne and murdered him.

Catherine II then became the sole ruler. She continued to build on the expansionist policies of Peter the Great, adding 200,000 square miles to Russia. Her armies put down the rebellion of Emelian Pugachev's Cossacks in 1773–75 and helped extend the borders of Russia, especially in the Crimea and in Poland-Lithuania, Belorussia, and western Ukraine. She centralized the government, which was run by civilian elites who had skills much like those of their counterparts in France and England. Indeed, for a time, Russia, with its Orthodox and deep mystical traditions and tendency to look inwardly and venerate its own culture, seemed to display a greater openness to intellectual currents of western Europe.

Sometimes portrayed as an "Enlightened Despot" (a disputed characterization), Catherine the Great was steeped in the literature of the French *philosophes*. Diderot and Friedrich Melchior Grimm (Franco-German diplomat and author of *Correspondence littéraire*) spent time at her court, as did other Western thinkers. She generally refrained from the use of terror in attempting to bring about reforms.

In 1773 Catherine promoted a measure of religious toleration, promulgating a directive: "As Almighty God tolerated on earth all faiths tongues and creeds, so her Majesty, starting from the same principles, and in accordance with His Holy Will, proposed to follow in the same path." She defended the rights of Jesuits to exist in Russia, despite the papacy's dissolution of the Society of Jesus. Roman Catholics and Protestants enjoyed certain religious rights.

Catherine's openness to "enlightened ideas" had definite limits, however. She took over the lands of monasteries, turning them into state property. She became hostile to the Masonic movement and feared the spread of subversive republican ideas propagated by partisans of the French Revolution. She castigated these ideas, labeling them "poison." She promulgated three decrees (1783, 1791, 1794) that forced Jews to settle within an area called "the Pale." This region stretched from the Black Sea to the Baltic Sea. It encompassed present-day Poland, Latvia, Lithuania, Ukraine, and Belorussia. Jewish settlers lived in the Pale under harsh conditions. Many were poverty-stricken.

Along with Prussian armies, Catherine the Great's troops brutally put down the allegedly "Jacobin" Polish revolt of 1794, led by Tadeusz Kosciuszko. The Russian General Alexander Suvorov described the ensuing carnage: "The whole of Praga was strewn with dead bodies, blood was flowing in streams." Moreover, Catherine did little to improve the plight of serfs during her reign.

As for the tsarina's personal lifestyle, it was on occasion dissolute. Her lovers were many, including Prince Grigori Potemkin. For a time the politically astute Potemkin acted like her co-tsar. Catherine's own religious beliefs were probably agnostic.

XII. CONCLUSION

Eighteenth-century religious life on the Continent defies facile descriptions, so variegated were its diverse manifestations. Despite the anti-Christian campaign of the *philosophes*, in 1789 the peoples of most European countries remained broadly self-identified as "Christian." During the century, a number of Christian monarchs attempted to retain one church as *the* only legitimate one in their kingdom; others, whatever their motivations, tried to establish rights for Christian Dissenters, Jews, and "nonbelievers"—that is, anyone outside the state churches.

At the same time, what was probably a sizeable minority of Europeans remained aloof from the Christian churches. The Christian faith played relatively little role in the everyday decision making of these Europeans. Some indulged or believed in occult practices—witchcraft, black magic, the satanic, and sorcery. Vampire attacks supposedly took place in East Prussia in 1721. Voltaire noted skeptically that reports of vampires had surfaced in Poland, Hungary, Silesia, Moravia, Austria, and Lorraine. In an investigative treatise (1746), Dom Augustine Calmet, a distinguished Roman Catholic theologian and biblical scholar, judiciously sought to weigh evidence regarding the existence and practices of vampires. He concluded that vampires might possibly exist.

During the Age of Lights, the capacity of the Christian religion to shape the general culture and customs of Europeans probably diminished, but certainly did not disappear. The Bible was the most frequently published and most read book of the century. Even some of those Europeans who viewed themselves as "enlightened" professed a desire to "purify" the Christian religion, not to overthrow the faith itself. They sought to halt renewed religious warfare, promote religious toleration, and eradicate "superstition" and credulity.

As in the British Isles, many continental Christians believed they were acting as faithful stewards of the traditional teachings of their Christian churches. Even the sometimes haughty and bejeweled kings of France viewed themselves as "Most Christian" rulers.

FOR FURTHER STUDY

Ahnert, Thomas. *Religion and the Origins of the German Enlightenment: Faith and Reform in the Thought of Christian Thomasius*. Rochester: Rochester University Press, 2006.

Craig, William Lane. *The Historical Argument for the Resurrection of Jesus during the Deist Controversy*. Lewiston, NY: Edwin Mellen Press, 1985.

Jacob, Margaret C. *Living the Enlightenment: Freemasonry and Politics in Eighteenth-Century Europe*. New York: Oxford University Press, 1991.

Le Brun, Jacques, and John Woodbridge, eds. *Simon (Richard): Recherches curieuses sur la diversité des langues et religions d'Edward Brerewood*. Paris: Presses Universitaires de France, 1983.

Lindberg, Carter, ed. *The Pietist Theologians: An Introduction to Theology in the Seventeenth and Eighteenth Centuries*. Malden, MA: Blackwell, 2005.

Mulsow, Martin. *Moderne aus dem Untergrund: Frühaufklärung in Deutschland 1680–1720*. Hamburg: Fritz Meiner Verlag, 2002.

Pospielovsky, Mitry. *The Orthodox Church in the History of Europe*. Yonkers, NY: St. Vladimir's Seminary, 1990.

Schmidt, James, ed. *What Is Enlightenment? Eighteenth-Century Answers and Twentieth-Century Questions*. Berkeley: University of California Press, 1996.

14

Christianity in an Age of Revolutions

(1770–1848)

I. INTRODUCTION

The French Revolution (1789–99) often stunned onlookers who watched the unimaginable happen before their eyes. Accounts of untamed riots and pitiless massacres, of contorted, lifeless heads on pikes, and of creaking carts hauling "traitors" to their deaths by guillotine provoked feelings of consternation and disgust as well as outright fear and horror among many people both inside and outside of France. Other contemporaries rejoiced because the alleged aristocratic "traitors" to the French Republic were receiving their "just" punishments.

Edmund Burke, the famous Irish author of *Reflections on the Revolution in France* (1790), wrote, "All circumstances taken together, the French Revolution is the most astonishing thing that has hitherto happened in the world." He observed, "What a play, what actors." What contradictory passions unleashed: a "strange chaos of levity and ferocity, and of all sorts of crimes jumbled together with all sorts of follies."

A stupefied Wilhelm von Schirach, editor of Hamburg's *Politisches Journal*, lamented, "The pen quivers in the hand of the historian who takes hold of it in order to try to portray the scenes of a year [1793] which seem to have surpassed human powers of description and feeling and which future generations will hardly believe actually took place."

A. The Fall of the Bastille: July 14, 1789

On July 17, 1789, a boisterous crowd of working people (including chimney sweeps, beggars, and fishwives) accompanied French king Louis XVI (1754–93) from the Chateau of Versailles to the Hôtel de Ville in Paris, where he met Sylvain Bailley, the mayor of the city. Bailley wrote, "The way was lined on both sides by national guards armed with guns, swords, pikes, lances, scythes, sticks, etc. There were

The taking of the Bastille on July 14, 1789.

women, monks and friars all carrying guns." From the vast crowd, relatively few cries arose of "Vive le Roi" but there came the repeated cry, "Vive la Nation, Vive Messieurs Bailly, La Fayette!"

After observing the scene, a Russian minister gave this ominous assessment: "The Revolution has taken place in France, and the royal power no longer exists." Louis XVI was no longer *the* father of his people; if anything, he had become an ordinary father trying to protect his own children from an uncertain fate.

A few days earlier, on July 14, 1789, members of the *gardes françaises* had joined Parisians (the 954 "conquerors of the Bastille") in the taking of the Bastille prison, thought to hold munitions the government could use in a preemptive strike against the "people" of Paris. In the assault, ninety-one people were killed. A contemporary described the scene: "Never have more courageous actions been witnessed in an unruly crowd. It was not only the soldiers, the *gardes françaises*, but townspeople of all classes, simple working men of every description, who, with inadequate weapons or none at all, defied the gunfire from the ramparts and seemed to mock at it."

Seven prisoners were released. Governor de Launay, the commander of the Bastille, was taken prisoner, paraded in the streets, and decapitated, and then his head was triumphantly held aloft on a pike.

The Bastille was demolished, pieces of it sold as souvenirs. No longer would the Chateau of Versailles be the center of French life. Paris with its revolutionary governments had assumed that role.

Like the Bastille itself, the *Ancien régime* ("Old Order"), collapsed in a near heap in 1789. The already weakened authority of Louis XVI, France's divine right monarch, crumbled. Revolutionaries declared that the sovereignty of the nation resided not with the king, but with "the people" who were "citizens" and only secondarily "subjects" of the king. This was indeed a revolution.

B. Interpreting the French Revolution

For more than two centuries historians of various ideological stripes and nationalities have attempted to identify the long-term and proximate "origins" of the French Revolution, to explain the forces that impacted its unfolding, and to weigh its influence not only on European political, social, and economic institutions but also on Christianity's role and status in nineteenth-century Europe.

Of particular note, Marxist and socialist-leaning historians such as Jean Jaurès (1859–1914), Albert Mathiez (1874–1932), and Georges Lefebvre (1874–1959) viewed the revolution as a major step on the path of world history toward socialism, if not communism. The revolution under the banner of capitalism represented the victory of the bourgeoisie over the Bourbon monarchy, the nobility, and feudalism. Albert Soboul (1914–82), a leading Marxist historian, wrote, "The essential cause of the Revolution was the power of a bourgeoisie arrived at its maturity and confronted by a decadent aristocracy holding tenaciously to its privileges." Karl Marx, Vladimir Lenin, and Leon Trotsky viewed the French Revolution as a guide for their own revolutionary activities.

C. The Contested Role of the "Bourgeoisie"

Did the "bourgeoisie" orchestrate the French Revolution? Many historians believe such is the case. They argue that in the 1780s elite nobles continued to block wealthy members of the bourgeoisie from having access to social and political offices and privileges commensurate with the bourgeoisie's increasing wealth.

Between February 22 and May 25, 1787, the Assembly of Notables, consisting of leading nobles caught up in an "aristocratic reaction," claimed they were the "only authentic representatives of that nation." They refused to approve the levying of new taxes to remedy the ominous debt problem caused in part by France's earlier support of the American Revolution. They forced the king's hand. Louis XVI was obliged to call the Estates-General (First Estate—the clergy, Second Estate—nobles, Third Estate—"the people") to meet in May–June 1789 to address the issue of the worsening fiscal crisis. In 1787 France was tottering on the brink of a financial collapse. For that year alone, her imports equaled 611 million *livres*, whereas her exports were 542 million. This created a significant trade imbalance. A precipitating cause of the French Revolution, therefore, was fiscal insolvency.

The Estates-General had not met since 1614. In *What Is the Third Estate?*, Abbé Sieyès argued that the nation consisted of 200,000 privileged people (the First and Second Estates) and 25 to 26 million underprivileged people (the Third Estate).

In the eighteenth century the bourgeoisie along with peasants nursed a common hatred of aristocratic nobles. The bourgeoisie were agitated in part by the publication of Jacques Necker's flawed but significant report (1781) on the nation's finances. It revealed that even though France was encumbered by a massive and growing debt, the king continued to dispense huge pensions to his favorite nobles.

Peasants were disturbed by the continued oppression perpetrated by their noble lords. Many were suffering badly from the effects of a drought and a disastrous harvest (1788) that created the context for flour and bread shortages and higher prices. Famine became a haunting specter, for bread was the essential staple of peasants' diets. They traditionally ate two pounds of bread a day, but now a loaf of bread could cost one month's wages. Between March and May 1788, peasants in certain provinces engaged in revolts against their lords. Louis XVI gathered troops in Paris.

After the fall of the Bastille on July 14, 1789, large numbers of peasants were also seized by feelings of panic (the "Great Fear" during the last third of July). The Great Fear was stimulated in part by false rumors that the armies of nobles were prowling the countryside, trampling crops, and seeking revenge on those sympathetic to the revolution.

During the week of August 4–11, the National Constituent Assembly (June 1789–September 1791) with a sizeable bourgeois contingent dramatically subverted the power of the nobles. On the night of August 4 it stripped nobles of the feudal privileges and fealty rights with which they had oppressed peasants. The National Constituent Assembly indicated that henceforth society would have one law applying equally to all citizens who enjoyed liberty: "All citizens, without distinction as to birth, may be admitted to all ecclesiastical, civilian, and military employments and dignities, and no useful profession shall constitute derogation."

On August 26, 1789, the National Constituent Assembly spelled out these rights further in the "Declaration of the Rights of Man and of the Citizen." The Marquis de Lafayette, with the assistance of Thomas

Jefferson, the American envoy to France, served as the principal author of the declaration.

The National Constituent Assembly also delivered rude blows to the Gallican church. On August 11 it struck down the *dîme*, a hated tax that peasants and others were obliged to pay to the church. In November the assembly made the Gallican church responsible for paying the national debt. Following the proposal of Charles-Maurice Tallyrand-Périgord, bishop of Autun, it placed the lands of the church "at the disposal of the nation."

The National Constituent Assembly also set up property requirements for people to vote, thereby allegedly revealing its intention of keeping power for propertied members of the bourgeoisie.

In 1789 the majority of French people remained monarchists. The cult of the king, however, was giving way to the patriotic cult of the nation among more radical revolutionaries, especially after Louis XVI's attempt to escape from France (the flight to Varennes, June 20–21, 1791). Marie Antoinette, disguised as a Russian baroness, and the king, disguised as her business agent, were recognized, apprehended, and escorted back to Paris. Louis XVI was now deemed a traitor, one who should be put on trial. Many of France's people no longer wanted to be Louis XVI's subjects; they wanted to be *citoyens* (citizens).

Many aspects of this "standard" interpretation were doubtless accurate; however, several issues related to the bourgeoisie begged for serious revision. In 1955 the English historian Alfred Cobban delivered a lecture, "The Myth of the French Revolution." He contested a key Marxist thesis that the revolution represented "the substitution of a capitalist bourgeois order for feudalism." He argued that very few capitalists in fact made up the bourgeoisie. In 1967 the American historian George Taylor proposed that the French Revolution was "not a social revolution with political consequences, but a political revolution with social consequences."

For their part, in 1965 the French historians François Furet and Denis Richet began their own assault on the orthodox Marxist historiography. In *Interpreting the French Revolution* (1978), Furet challenged Marxist claims that the revolution of 1789 was essentially orchestrated by a class-conscious French bourgeoisie. With others he reiterated the point that partisans of the revolution did not act in a necessary lock-step fashion according to the supposed dictates of class consciousness and that propertied bourgeoisie often shared many of the same values and aspirations as the nobility. Actually, some nobles revolted against the king.

In *The Myth of the French Bourgeoisie* (2003), Sarah Maza proposed the endgame thesis that "no group calling itself bourgeois ever emerged in France to make claims to cultural and political centrality and power." In *From Deficit to Deluge: The Origins of the French Revolution* (2011), editors Thomas Kaiser and Dale Van Kley, after taking into account the various "origins" of the revolution, argued "that the French revolution is best conceived of as a political event with diverse and other than political origins." They emphasized a political indeterminacy factor against any reductionistic, all-encompassing economic explanation: "Despite the sheer accumulation and seeming intractability of some of the Old Regime's structural problems, the growing limits placed on decision-making at the top by the role of public opinion, and the decline in the prestige of the monarchy itself, the French political elite was not without some room for maneuver in the face of the crisis of 1787–1789."

II. REVOLUTIONS: "WESTERN DEMOCRATIC," "SOCIALIST," AND "MARXIST"

Some historians place the French Revolution in a context of a series of revolutions that shook and transformed European society. These revolutions were very important for the histories of their respective countries. Before the French Revolution, revolutions took place in North America and Europe; after the French Revolution, they erupted in Europe and Latin America.

R. R. Palmer called this time frame (1770–1848) the "Age of Democratic Revolutions": conflicts united by the "democratic" ideologies of their partisans, by their "Western" or "Atlantic" geographical settings, and by specific individuals such as the Marquis de Lafayette who participated in both the American and French revolutions.

The rise of socialist and Marxist ideologies provided additional rationales to justify a revolution. Radical revolutionaries appealed to the authority of socialists such as Henri Comte de Saint-Simon, Pierre Joseph Proudhon, and Marx (after a revolution in 1848) to justify their attacks on capitalists of industrial societies who "exploited" the "people," members of the lower economic classes. Marx indicated that "religion is the opiate of the people." That is, religion dulls the sensitivities of the people to the ways capitalists exploit them. By contrast, a number of revolutionaries and social activists, in the name of Christ and the gospel, sought to ameliorate the plight of the people and to overthrow or reform repressive social, political, and religious institutions.

A. Democratic Revolutions

For the European Christians living in that "democratic" revolutionary age, the French Revolution, albeit very important, constituted only one of many revolutions. From 1783 to 1787, revolutionaries in the United Provinces attempted to thwart the *stadtholder* from converting his position into a hereditary kingship. In Switzerland, democratic revolts (1768, 1782) in Geneva were put down. France experienced the revolutions of 1789, of the Napoleonic era, of 1830, and of 1848. Germany witnessed revolutions in 1830 and 1848. In 1849, Vienna, Austria, faced three revolts. Italian states experienced revolutions in 1798–99 and 1848. After an initial revolt in 1821, Greece gained independence from Turkey in 1827–28. Poles engaged in unsuccessful revolts against the Russians in 1794 and 1831. In North America, the American Revolution took place between 1775 and 1783. In South America, the countries Bolivia, Peru, Chile, and Uruguay declared their independence from Spain, with Brazil declaring independence from Portugal in 1822. In Central America, Costa Rica, Guatemala, and Mexico declared independence from Spain in 1821. Other countries were convulsed by revolutions, Britain constituting a notable exception.

B. Defining a Revolution

During the period 1770–1848 the turmoil, fears, and hopes of "revolutions" created an important backdrop for understanding the beliefs, attitudes, and actions of both professed Christians and non-Christians. The stance of the nineteenth-century papacy toward "democracy," for example, was in part influenced by its essentially negative perceptions of the French Revolution.

The word *revolution* did not bear the same connotations for all Europeans. Until the late eighteenth century the meaning of *revolution* was often derived from astronomy and signified "the return of previous forms of existence." Or it could refer to "vicissitudes in human life, extraordinary changes in public affairs, reversals in the fortunes of nations." Relying on the first definition, a number of observers viewed the Glorious Revolution of 1688 in England and the American Revolution as "a return to a previous form of existence"—the restoration of English rights that had been lost.

French revolutionaries generally abandoned the identification of the word *revolution* with the concepts of return or restoration. Rather, they indicated that a revolution signified the initiation of a new order, a totally new beginning. They were prone to speak of the French Revolution as *The* Revolution. They dared to imagine that the society they were inaugurating would totally replace and constitute a clean break with the Old Order of Europe. On September 21, 1792, the era of the monarchy ended. The era of the republic began the next day. On November 23, 1793, revolutionaries of the Convention abandoned the Gregorian calendar; they established a revolutionary calendar that began on September 22, 1792, as 22 Vendémiaire, Year I.

Louis de Saint-Just (better known as St. Just), a radical revolutionary, thought that the French Revolution had indeed given birth to a new era of happiness for humanity. He claimed, "Happiness is a new idea in Europe." Because the Christian faith constituted one of the principal molds in which the Old Order of Europe had been cast, revolutionaries often singled out its defenders for especially bitter criticism.

III. THE FRENCH REVOLUTION: RELIGIOUS ORIGINS?

Jacobin revolutionaries believed they should excise Christianity's influence from French culture. Their campaign had only limited success. They themselves used words such as *regeneration* (a Christian expression) to describe what they hoped France would experience politically and socially. Their "dechristianization" campaign of 1793–94 did not eradicate the Christian faith. Due to a popular backlash of opinion, the fastidious lawyer Maximillian Robespierre (1758–94) from Arras felt constrained to exchange his advocacy of a "Cult of Reason" for a "Cult of the Supreme Being."

Maximillian Robespierre.

After the outbreak of the French Revolution in 1789, the lingering influence of the Christian religion remained evident in France—even if only to provide motifs that revolutionaries secularized. But this influence had more heft than that. A considerable percentage of counterrevolutionary forces both in the Vendée (western France below the Loire River) and on France's borders were Catholics alienated not only by the Terror but by the ostensibly anti-Christian agenda of Robespierre and his Jacobin colleagues in the Convention.

In *The Religious Origins of the French Revolution: From Calvin to the Civil Constitution, 1560–1791* (1996) Professor Dale Van Kley adds the further intriguing point that the French Revolution itself issued in part from Jansenist and Jesuit debates over the nature of grace and the Eucharist. As we saw, these disputes transfixed and roiled French political and social life during much of the eighteenth century. Van Kley by no means discounts the importance of economic and political causative factors in explaining the revolution's origins. Nor does he dispute the roles Voltaire, Rousseau, and other *philosophes* played in "secularizing" some Europeans' thinking. But he does demonstrate that developments in Catholic theology gave many Frenchmen a needed vocabulary and political examplars with which to justify opposition to the monarchy of Louis XVI.

Professor David Bell concurs with the basic thrust of Van Kley's arguments and notes that the French nation "arose simultaneously out of, and in opposition to, Christian systems of belief." Indeed, some French people began to express their loyalty to the nation-state in language they may have earlier reserved for describing their sacrificial loyalty to and adoration for God. They sometimes did so in a surging wave of pamphlets published before the revolution that contested repressive aspects of French life. These pamphlets also included political discourses influenced by Rousseau and a host of other writers, whether famous or hack.

A. French Christians and the Revolution

Initially, many French Protestants and Catholics supported the French Revolution. They thought that the revolution was compatible not only with patriotism and liberty but with the gospel. They initially assumed that the revolutionaries and Louis XVI would reach an accord from which a constitutional, Christian monarchy similar to that of the English monarchy would emerge. French Protestants also believed that the revolutionaries might remove remaining restrictions on their civil rights. Their hopes were rewarded. The National Constituent Assembly gave Protestants the right to access public office. On September 27, 1791, the later Republican Convention afforded Jews citizenship. Slave-owning planters from the Caribbean initially were able to thwart efforts in the National Assembly to free slaves, but the Republican Convention abolished slavery.

As the French Revolution veered toward its more radical phases, a number of professing Christians became distraught about a perceived "anti-Christian" orientation of the revolutionary governments. Influential revolutionaries had quickly turned away from any form of divine right monarchy. Instead, they wanted to build a new social order on the basis of a social contract between free individuals.

As mentioned earlier, the National Constituent Assembly completed a first draft of "Declaration of the Rights of Man and of the Citizen" that was "accepted by the King." Under "the auspices of the Supreme Being," the assembly gave as its goal to set forth the "natural, inalienable rights of man." Article 1 indicated that all men are born and remain free and equal in their rights. The declaration also noted that "all sovereignty resides essentially in the nation" (Article 3). Rejecting efforts of the Catholic clergy to make Gallican Catholicism *the* religion of France, the writers of the declaration affirmed, "No one shall be disturbed for his opinions, even in religion provided that their manifestation does not trouble the public order established by law" (Article 10).

The action of the National Constituent Assembly that turned many Catholics decisively against the revolution was its issuance of the "Civil Constitution of the Clergy" (July 12, 1790). François Furet underscored the constitution's importance: "The vote finalized the divorce between the Revolution and the Catholic tradition, a divorce that polarized public opinion and provided the counter-revolution with its first troops."

The constitution stipulated that bishops and priests should be elected by electors. This provision overthrew Catholic teaching that priests' authority issued from their ordinations. Priests now became servants of the state. The constitution also outlawed any subservience of the Gallican church to foreign churchmen, including the pope. It cut back the number of bishoprics from 130 to 83. It ordered that the clergy of France should swear an oath of allegiance to uphold the constitution. This last measure placed members of the clergy in a difficult quandary: if they became jurors, they could be perceived as supportive of the revolution; if they became nonjurors, they could be deemed hostile to the same revolution and loyal to the papacy. Approximately 55 percent of the clergy took the oath.

In February 1791 Pope Pius VI condemned both the "Declaration of the Rights of Man and of the Citizen" and the "Civil Constitution of the Clergy." France responded by annexing the papal territories of Avignon and Comtat Venaissin (where inhabitants voted to join France).

The ever shrewd Tallyrand, the bishop of Autun, indicated that the "Civil Constitution of the Clergy" represented a capital mistake of the National Constituent Assembly. It generated great fissures in French public opinion. Emigrant nobles including the Comte d'Artois (later Charles X) and the Prince de Condé had earlier left France and formed counterrevolutionary movements in towns such as Coblenz and Mainz, Germany, and Turin, Italy. These nobles attempted to raise armies with which to invade France.

Refractory priests in France refused to take the oath of allegiance to the "Civil Constitution of the Clergy" and appeared to further the cause of the counterrevolutionaries. During the revolution some 25,000 Catholic clergy (one sixth of the total) went into exile or were deported from France. As was noted, on June 20, 1791, Louis XVI attempted to flee but was recognized and apprehended in Varennes and then returned against his will to Paris.

The Legislative Assembly (October 1791 – September 1792) replaced the National Constituent Assembly. On April 20, 1792, it declared war on Austria, which had earlier made a defensive alliance with Prussia. Members of the Legislative Assembly worried that many Catholics would not accept the sacraments from those juristic priests who had sworn allegiance to the "Civil Constitution of the Clergy." On August 26, 1792, the assembly ordered all nonjuring clergy to leave the country. Between September 2 and 7, anticlerical mobs in Paris slaughtered 230 priests and 3 prelates and possibly 1,500 or more lay prisoners (the "September Massacres"). On September 20 the Legislative Assembly took away record keeping of births, marriages, and deaths from Catholic priests and legalized divorce. It also began to send out "Representatives on Mission" to destroy "external signs" of the Christian faith.

These actions only intensified antagonism between revolutionaries and Catholics who wanted to remain true to the king and the papacy. In time, angry Catholic peasants fought the Vendée War (1793 – 96) against the revolutionary armies of the Convention, the political assembly that had in turn replaced the Legislative Assembly. As members of the "Catholic and Royal Army," these peasants proudly put the words *God* and *King* on their flags. At one time, the majority of the Departments of France raised the standard of revolt against the Convention with centers of hostility evident in the Vendée, Provence, and Normandy and in sections of Paris. Royalists temporarily controlled the cities of Lyon, Marseilles, and Toulon. A young Napoleon Bonaparte eventually suppressed the revolt at Toulon.

B. The Terror

Interpreting revolts—especially the one in the Vendée—as an extension of an "aristocratic plot," Jacobin revolutionaries in the Convention took even more draconian measures to defeat the revolution's external and internal foes. Gripped by a "siege mentality," on August 23, 1793, they attempted to draft larger armies (*levée en masse*) of citizen soldiers to protect the republic from foreign foes: "From this moment until that in which the enemy shall have been driven from the soil of the Republic, all Frenchmen are in permanent requisition for the service of the armies."

On September 20, 1792, the Legislative Assembly also tried to eliminate France's internal foes by the use of terror. Some historians view the execution of Louis XVI as its opening bloody act. After putting Louis

XVI (*Citoyen Louis Capet*) on trial for the alleged treachery in plotting with France's enemies, the members of the Convention on a fourth vote decided the king's fate: 380 votes in favor of the death penalty, 310 against.

Just before his execution on January 21, 1793—a cold and foggy morning—Louis XVI declared, "I die innocent of all the crimes laid to my charge; I pardon those who occasioned my death, and I pray to God that the blood you are going to shed may never be visited on France." Then his head was placed below a guillotine's sharp blade.

A Dutch painter, an eyewitness to the event, captured on canvas the king's death. Another observer reported that several onlookers dipped their handkerchiefs in the king's blood, tasted it, and noted that it was "good" or "too salty" in taste. On October 16, 1793, the Austrian-born queen of France, Marie Antoinette, was also executed. During her trial an accuser declared that she "from the beginning of her sojourn in France, has been the scourge and bloodsucker of the French people." At her execution, she inadvertently stepped on the foot of her executioner and was heard to say, "Monsieur, I ask your pardon, I did not do it on purpose." On October 31, twenty-one Girondins (moderate republicans) were put to death.

The revolutionaries, especially the Jacobins with 2,000 clubs having 100,000 members, terrorized "suspects" by hauling them before revolutionary tribunals. "Suspects" included anyone who "either by their conduct, their contacts, their words or their writings, showed themselves to be supporters of tyranny, of federalism, or to be enemies of liberty." If a suspect were found guilty, he or she could be guillotined, deported, or imprisoned. Between March 1793 and July 1794 a half million people were arrested and some 16,600 executed. The bloodiest months for the Terror from revolutionary trials ran from December 1793 to July 1794, when Robespierre ruled as a dictator of France. But it should be recalled that revolutionary army troops who suppressed the Vendée rebellion resorted to mass deaths by drowning suspects and the burning of homes. Priests were drowned in the Loire River and nuns murdered.

A German described the terrorist atrocities he witnessed in Lyon:

> The churches, convents, and all the dwellings of the former patricians were in ruins. When I came to the guillotine, the blood of those who had been executed a few hours beforehand was still running in the street.... I said to a group of sansculottes ... that it would be decent to clear away all this human blood. Why should it be cleared? One of them said to me. It's the blood of aristocrats and rebels. The dogs should lick it up.

C. The Dechristianization Campaign

In 1793 the Jacobins, radical activists in the Convention led by Robespierre, thwarted the Federalist Revolt. So-called "Federalists," who ostensibly appreciated the Constitution of the United States, called for a more decentralized form of government and restrictions on voting rights. After a trial, Girondins suspected of federalism were purged from the Convention. The "Committee of Public Safety," made up of hardened Jacobins, wanted to establish a centralized dictatorship thought necessary to defend the revolution. For them the use of terror was "rational"; it was a means to eliminate counterrevolutionaries who threatened the revolution.

Robespierre assumed the role of central dictator, the "absolute master of France." Even as he prosecuted the Terror without mercy against France's alleged foes, he portrayed himself in Rousseauist terms as a defender of liberty and equality:

> What is the end towards which we are striving? The peaceful enjoyment of liberty and equality: the reign of that eternal justice whose laws are engraved, not on marble and on stone, but in the hearts of all men.... What sort of government can realize these prodigies? Only democratic or republican government; these two words are synonyms.

Under Robespierre's malevolent direction, the Convention in Paris abetted not only the Terror but a movement of "dechristianization," a campaign designed to thwart the activities of suspected Christian opponents of the revolution. "Dechristianizers" rejoiced when on November 6, 1793, Jean-Baptiste-Joseph Gobel, the elected constitutional archbishop of Paris, abdicated his ministry. Gobel's act of renunciation provided a model for other clerics to follow. The same day the Convention ordered the Departments of France to suppress parishes. On November 10, 1793, some anti-Christian revolutionaries, inspired by journalist Jacques Hébert, participated in a great festival dedicated to the Cult of Reason at Notre Dame Cathedral. An actress was "worshiped" as the Goddess of Reason.

On November 13 the Convention ruled, "All constituted authorities are authorized to receive from ecclesiastics and ministers of every cult, the declaration that they abdicate their function." Cloaked in the Convention's authority, a number of representatives on mission sought to oblige Catholic priests and Protestant pastors to abdicate their functions as clerics, assure the closing of Christian churches, and confiscate the churches' gold and silver utensils of worship and clocks for the coffers of the revolution. Those clerics who refused to comply with the dictates of the representatives on mission risked arrest and even execution.

Out of the 114,500 Catholic clergy (in 1790), 20,000 to 25,000 emigrated or were deported; 3,000 to 5,000 were executed; 20,000 abdicated; and 25,000 had discontinued their ministries for diverse reasons.

The success of certain representatives on mission was quite spectacular. Convention deputy Jean Borie, for example, sent enthused reports back to the Convention regarding the Departments of the Gard and Lozère in the Languedoc, a former province with a sizable Protestant population. Borie claimed that the Departments of Gard and Lozère had "spontaneously" accepted his demands: 268 priests and pastors abdicated, and 233 "Temples of Reason" were erected. From various sources we know that nearly all of the 103 Protestant pastors of Languedoc in 1794 ceased their ministries. For all practical purposes, formal worship services of the Reformed churches ceased. Whatever gatherings did occur, whether Protestant or Roman Catholic, were sometimes held in secret. Catholic women were often in the vanguard in attempting to reopen Roman Catholic churches in their villages or towns.

Robespierre believed that religion could serve as an essential bond to unite the French people. Because the Cult of Reason was largely rejected by the general population, he ordered (decree of 18 *Floréal*) that it be replaced by the Cult of the Supreme Being. Robespierre oversaw a grandiose festival celebrating the Supreme Being in Paris.

A number of members of the Convention suspected that Robespierre planned to guillotine them. They preemptively turned on the "tyrant." On July 28, 1794, Robespierre, who had tried to commit suicide, was guillotined. Two days later, sixty of his supporting colleagues met the same fate. The revolution was adept at devouring its own.

"The French people recognize the existence of the Supreme Being and the immortality of the soul" (Maximillian Robespierre).

D. The Thermidorian Reaction and the Directory (1794–99)

Robespierre's Reign of Terror ended on 9 Thermidor, Year II. On that day the cry "Down with the tyrant" echoed through the Convention. By 4 *Brumaire* (October), Year IV (1796), the Convention collapsed and was eventually replaced by the Directory. The intervening time between the two dates of the revolutionary calendar represented an era in which the people of France engaged in a full-scale reaction against the "tyrant" (Robespierre), against those who prosecuted the Terror ("drinkers of blood," "cannibals"), and against the mayhem of the Terror. For some historians, the French Revolution concluded with Robespierre's death. For others, the "Thermidorian Reaction" and the activities of the Directory together (1795–99) constitute a second phase of the revolution.

The Convention attempted to dismantle the Terror. It ordered the selective release of prisoners and arranged for the trials of terrorists like Jean-Baptiste Carrier and members of the revolutionary committee of Nantes who had drowned so many peasants in the Vendée. On November 16, 1794, Carrier was guillotined. Revelations of Jacobin atrocities stoked further hatred and sentiments of revenge. Jacobin prisoners were massacred in various parts of southern France. In 1794–95, fears, suspicions, and retributions haunted French life. With worries about both anarchy and despotism, "bourgeois" elites formed a new government, the Directory (1795–99). Its leaders often promoted republican cults such as the deistic-oriented Theo-philanthropy.

During the revolution, French armies occupied numerous countries and regions in an effort to set up sister republics. Sometimes the French were greeted as liberators by factions that supported their "democratic and republican" ideology. On other occasions, they were scorned as invading oppressors. The French attempted to support revolutionaries in a failed revolt in Ireland (1798); they helped create the Batavian Republic (1795–99); in Holland they annexed what would later become Belgium, where many resented their presence (1795); they overran territories on the west bank of the Rhine (1798); they annexed cantons of Switzerland (1798). Napoleon Bonaparte seized Milan (1796) and invaded the Papal States.

On February 15, 1798, the French troops entered Rome. They deposed Pope Pius VI and brought him back to France as a prisoner. On August 29, 1799, the pope died in Valence. With his demise, the future of the papacy appeared very bleak indeed. In Rome, revolutionaries attempted to win the populace to a form of republican patriotism.

Given the suffering, the humiliation, and the loss of lands the Roman Catholic Church experienced during the French Revolution, the popes of the nineteenth century understandably had to think long and hard regarding what stance they should take toward any self-proclaimed, "democratic" revolutionary movement.

IV. CONTEMPORARY ASSESSMENTS OF THE FRENCH REVOLUTION

Traumatized by the shock of the French Revolution, writers from Copenhagen to Rome launched a barrage of critiques. Speculative conspiracy theories abounded about the origins of the "godless" revolution that had culminated in the Terror. Obviously, it was the "fault of Voltaire and Rousseau." No, Protestants along with Masons had conspired to overthrow the monarchy. No, it was really the work of Jansenists. Multiple jumbled versions of these theories surfaced in pamphlets, books, and gossip throughout Europe. Among well-known critiques were writings from the Irish Edmund Burke, the English John Wesley and Hannah More, the French Joseph de Maître and Louis de Bonald, and the Swiss Jacques Mallet du Pan.

England eventually joined Austria and Prussia in a coalition designed to hold back the advance of France's revolutionary armies. But during 1789, English radicals often viewed the revolution favorably and in millennial terms. The Dissenter Richard Price (1723–91) declared, "I have lived to see THIRTY MILLIONS of people, indignant and resolute, spurning at slavery, and demanding liberty with an irresistible voice."

In his *Reflections on the Revolution in France* (1790) Edmund Burke rejected Price's positive assessment: "The French have completely pulled down to the ground their monarchy, their church, their nobility, their law, their revenue, their army, their navy, their commerce, their arts and their manufactures." Whereas Burke believed the English Revolution of 1688 and the American Revolution were legitimate because they restored lost rights, he viewed the French Revolution as illegitimate because it promoted a theoretical form of so-called natural rights that subverted worthy past traditions and institutions and lacked a prerequisite grounding in Trinitarian Christianity, "the basis of civil society."

"We know, and, what is better, we feel inwardly, that religion is the basis of civil society, and the source of all good, and of all comfort" (Edmund Burke).

For Burke, so-called natural rights can lead to tyranny unless recognized as God-given. Burke declared that English people considered the Anglican Church "as the foundation of their whole constitution, with which, and with every part of which, it holds an indissoluble union. Church and State are ideas inseparable in their minds, and scarcely is the one ever mentioned without mentioning the other."

Thirty-one responses greeted Burke's work, including an important stiff rejoinder, Mary Wollstonecraft's *A Vindication of the Rights of Men* (1790). In a later work, *A Vindication of the Rights of Woman* (1792), Wollstonecraft complained that women were not receiving adequate opportunities of education and were "kept in ignorance under the specious name of innocence." Wollstonecraft noted that "if a woman be allowed to have an immortal soul, she must have, as the employment of life, an understanding to improve." Arguing against Rousseau, she continued, "I here throw down my gauntlet, and deny the existence of sexual virtues. For man and woman, truth must be the same."

Radical Unitarians were also unhappy with Burke. They viewed him as a former liberal, now a turncoat, who upheld the Test Acts and the authority of the Anglican Church when they, along with some Dissenters, had hopes of disestablishing the church. Burke in time blamed the "atheism" of the revolutionaries for the revolution's excesses.

For his part, John Wesley also stood out as a defender of the English monarchy, worried about civil unrest at home and disturbing news coming from France. During the time of the American Revolution, Wesley had pointed out that he was a "High Churchman" who supported the British monarchy, whatever sympathies he may have had for the cause of the American revolutionaries. In the poem "Written on the Peace of 1783," Charles Wesley hoisted his royalist colors by roundly criticizing the British politicians who had signed a treaty of peace with the upstart Americans:

> They force their country to receive
> A peace which only Hell could give,
> Which deadly feuds creates,
> Murders and massacres and wars;
> A peace which loyalty abhors
> And each true Briton hates.

The Methodist Conferences of the 1790s called on their faithful to submit to the king's authority. A number of Methodist pastors claimed that it was their preaching of submission to the king that helped prevent a violent revolution similar to the one in France from erupting in England.

In fact, numerous High Anglican churchmen had also preached loyalty to throne and altar. The Anglican William Agutter (1758–85) declared, "Therefore, my beloved Brethren, whether as loyal Subjects to the best of Kings, or as Christian Soldiers to the King of Kings, be ye ready, be ye true to every engagement." Moreover, in 1793 Hannah More (1745–1833), a very popular Christian author of the "Cheap Repository Tracts," published *Village Politics* "to counter the pernicious doctrines, which owing to the French Revolution, were then becoming seriously alarming." This work was directed to readers from the working classes in England and reiterated in a more popular rhetoric a number of Edmund Burke's themes.

In the United States, many Christians roundly criticized "Republican" Thomas Paine and Thomas Jefferson, both of whom were deists and both of whom had spent time in revolutionary Paris and had spoken well of the revolution. The French government had declared Paine (1737–1809), who was a tireless pamphleteer, an honorary citizen. Paine's radical ideas circulated widely in England and in the United States. His *The Rights of Man: Being an Answer to Mr. Burke's Attack on the French Revolution* (1791–92) sold possibly 200,000 copies, more than seven times Burke's *Reflections on the French Revolution*. In his immensely popular *The Age of Reason* (1794–96) Paine roundly criticized the truthfulness of Holy Scripture: "It is a book of lies, wickedness and blasphemy; What is it the Bible teaches us? rapine, cruelty, and murder." Paine wrote, "My own mind is my own church." Many Christians both in England and in the United States vilified Paine as a "filthy" atheist.

Some French writers had little patience for the talk of any counter-revolutionary Catholic writers such as Joseph De Maître, Bonald, and Du Pan about the horrors of the revolution, restoration, and the glories of the *Ancien régime*. In 1814 Benjamin Constant declared, "The authority that would attempt today to reestablish feudalism, serfdom, religious intolerance, the Inquisitions, and torture, that authority would claim in vain to wish for nothing more than to reinstate ancient institutions. Those ancient institutions would only be absurd and somber novelties." Whatever complaints Constant had about the excesses of the French Revolution, he did not want to see the restoration of an Old Order with a monarchy or a papacy enjoying absolute authority. Neither did Napoleon Bonaparte.

Napoleon Bonaparte.

V. NAPOLEON, REVOLUTION, AND EMPIRE (1799–1815)

Born in Ajaccio, Corsica, Napoleon Bonaparte (1769–1821) received an excellent military education at the *École Militaire* in Paris. He gained fame by deftly using artillery in defeating royalists with their English allies during the siege of Toulon and by putting down summarily a rebellion in Paris (1795) with "a whiff of grapeshot." After military campaigns in Italy and Egypt, Napoleon, with the help of Tallyrand and Sieyès, engineered the coup d'état of 18 *Brumaire* (November 9–10, 1799), overthrowing the Directory. An advocate of a centralized form of government that had been in favor with Robespierre, the Jacobins, and the Committee of Public Safety, Napoleon took action to thwart a rumored possible restoration of the Bourbon monarchy.

In the new government of the Consulate, Napoleon served as First Consul. Initially, he attempted to project an accommodating attitude toward the Roman Catholic Church in France. After lengthy negotiations, on July 15, 1801, he signed the concordat with

---

> ## THE ROSETTA STONE
>
> On July 15, 1799, during the French incursion into Egypt, a French soldier, Pierre François Bouchard, discovered the Rosetta Stone, a black basalt stone bearing texts in three forms: hieroglyphics, Egyptian (Demotic), and Greek. The French were forced to relinquish the Rosetta Stone to the victorious English. However, it gave Jean-François Champollion (in 1822) and other scholars the key to translating hieroglyphics and provided significant insights into ancient Egyptian history.

Pope Pius VII that recognized Roman Catholicism's dominant role in France without establishing it as the state church. The Concordat of 1801 simultaneously allowed Jews and Protestants to practice their religion and enjoy civil rights. But then, without the pope's approval, Napoleon added the *Organic Articles* (April 1802) to the concordat that limited further the papacy's ability to intervene in France's religious affairs. In the *Napoleonic Code* he reduced more than a thousand disparate French laws into one rational code.

On May 18, 1804, Napoleon was declared the emperor of France. On December 2, at Notre Dame Cathedral in Paris, with his wife Josephine looking on and Pope Pius VII presiding, Napoleon crowned himself Emperor of the French. In 1806 Napoleon indicated to Pius VII that he would permit freedom for the Papal States but stipulated that "Your Holiness is Sovereign of Rome, but I am Emperor. All my enemies must be his."

Napoleon invaded Rome in 1808. Pius VII refused to abdicate, and the next year he was arrested and imprisoned in France and Italy. He was not released until 1814. The pope's resolve and endurance during these trying circumstances increased his political stature in Europe.

The Austrian Klemens von Metternich (1773–1859) believed that Napoleon's stance toward Christianity was quite utilitarian:

> Napoleon was not irreligious in the ordinary sense of the word. He would not admit that there had ever existed a genuine atheist; he condemned Deism as the result of rash speculation. A Christian and a Catholic, he recognized in religion alone the right to govern human societies. He looked on Christianity as the basis of all real civilization; and considered Catholicism as the form of worship most favorable to the maintenance of order and true tranquility of the moral world; Protestantism as a source of trouble and disagreements.

Napoleon won notable military victories against the Austrians at Marengo (June 14, 1800) and Austerlitz (December 2, 1805). In time,

Napoleon's military exploits allowed him to control much of western Europe. Napoleon set up his relatives as kings in newly created occupied states: Jerome Bonaparte, King of Westphalia (1807–13); Joseph Bonaparte, King of Naples (1806–8) and King of Spain (1808–12), and Louis Bonaparte, King of Holland (1806–10). He declared himself the Protector of the Rhenish Confederation in Germany.

By 1806, Napoleon's control of the Confederation and other German regions and his decisive defeat of the Prussian armies at Jena sped up the demise of the Holy Roman Empire. On August 6 Holy Roman Emperor Francis abandoned his claims to the crown of Germany. On October 27 Napoleon himself entered Berlin.

For a time England remained one of the few major powers in a position to thwart French expansionary policy. After the defeat of a Spanish-French fleet on October 21, 1805, at Trafalgar by the English Admiral Horatio Nelson, Napoleon basically abandoned plans to invade England. Instead, from Berlin in 1806 he promulgated the "Continental" system that forbade countries under his control from trading with England. He hoped to ruin England economically by cutting off her trade. This policy became doomed by its frequent violation.

Tsar Alexander I of Russia.

On July 7, 1807, Napoleon made peace with the Russian Tsar Alexander I at Tilsit. But angered that the tsar was permitting violations of the Continental system, Napoleon in 1812 decided to invade Russia. On June 24, 1812, portions of his "Great Army" (*Grande Armée*) of 500,000 French and other European troops (another 250,000 left in reserve) crossed the Neman River into Russian territory. The army had to fight a number of costly battles on its way to Moscow. At the Battle of Borodino (September 7, 1812), for example, 44,000 Russians and 30,000 French were killed in a single day. On September 14 Napoleon did indeed capture Moscow, portions of which were ablaze. The Russians, however, would not surrender.

Retreating to the west, the French army experienced staggering losses of troops, owing to early snowstorms, bitterly cold weather (on occasion 38 degrees below zero), lack of food, and Cossack attacks. The ranks of the Great Army were decimated. Only 20,000 troops survived the punishing ordeal and straggled back to their homelands.

A number of factors spelled Napoleon's complete ruin: his ill-advised invasion of Russia; the resistance of Spanish rebels (1808–14); the capture of Paris by the Allies on March 31, 1814; his abdication on April 4 and exile on the island of Elba; his brief return to power in Paris as emperor on March 21, 1815 ("The 100 Days"); and the defeat of his forces at Waterloo by British and Prussian forces under the leadership of the Duke of Wellington and Gebhard von Blecher respectively (June 12–18, 1815). On May 5, 1821, Napoleon died of cancer in exile on Saint Helena Island in the South Atlantic.

Voraciously ambitious and unquestionably a military genius, Napoleon, the "Little Corporal" with hand in vest, asserted that his chief motive was to "purify" the French Revolution: "I closed the gulf of anarchy and brought order out of chaos. I rewarded merit regardless of birth or wealth, wherever I found it. I abolished feudalism and restored equality to all regardless of religion and before the law. I fought the decrepit monarchies of the Old Regime because the alternative was the destruction of all this. I purified the Revolution."

A number of observers have accepted Napoleon's assessment that he staved off at least temporarily a Bourbon restoration. François Furet wrote, "Revolutionary France was indeed under the spell of the new sovereign, who was its son and had saved it from the danger of a restoration. France had finally found the republican monarchy toward which it had been groping since 1789."

VI. RESTORATION AND THE CONGRESS OF VIENNA

By no means did all Europeans subjected to French rule think that Napoleon's intentions were generous and altruistic, that he sought their good. The existence of seven different coalitions of allies attempting to defeat his armies underscores this point. The seventh coalition (1815) included Great Britain, Russia, Sweden, Prussia, Austria, the Netherlands, and various German states. By the First Treaty of Paris, Louis XVIII accepted the directive that France should return to her 1792 borders. At the Congress of Vienna (beginning in September 1814), Robert Castlereagh (Britain), Tsar Alexander I (Russia), Metternich (Austria), and Tallyrand (France) along with many princes, kings, and diplomats pursued a number of goals: (1) to achieve a balance of power in Europe; (2) to have France respect her 1792 boundaries; (3) to set up means whereby any future French expansion could be checked; and (4) to restore "legitimate" monarchies to power.

Splicing and pasting together pieces of the map of Europe, the major powers negotiated with an eye to furthering their own interests in the larger context of these goals. Tallyrand, with catlike ability to land on his political feet, often played one European power off against another in seeking advantages for France. The diplomats of lesser states, excluded from the behind-the-door wheeling and dealing, spent their time dancing at balls, some learning the "Viennese Waltz."

The accomplishments of the Congress of Vienna, given its agenda, were noteworthy. Genuine steps took place toward the restoration of lands and thrones. By the Second Treaty of Paris, France was obliged to stay within her 1790 borders and pay reparations of 700 million francs. The buffer states of the Kingdom of Sardinia and the Kingdom of the Netherlands were constituted to block French expansion. Austria received the independent states of Italy, whereas the Kingdom of Poland came under the control of Russia. Due to the brilliant diplomacy of Cardinal Ercole Consalvi, a close associate of Pope Pius VII, the papacy received back the Papal States, and its overall prestige was enhanced.

The "Quadruple Alliance" of Austria, Prussia, Russia, and Great Britain was created. It was followed in 1818 by the "Quintuple Alliance" (France added). Participants agreed to submit international disputes to a group of nations for adjudication, the so-called "Congress System." Even though the Congress System fell apart rather rapidly, no European war engaging the governments of the entire continent would take place until World War I (1914–18).

In addition, on September 25, 1815, Tsar Alexander I, allured by the mystical thought of Baroness von Krudener, initiated a "Holy Alliance" with Emperor Francis I of Austria and King Frederick William III of Prussia. These rulers pledged to follow the principles of the Christian religion (justice, love, and peace) in their interactions with each other and in their own lands. Privately, a number of foreign ministers scoffed at this alliance, deeming its goals impractical. Nonetheless, the Holy Alliance received the lip-service backing of most crowns and diplomats of Europe (except the English king and the pope). Indeed, for many Europeans, restoration meant reinvigorating Christianity's role in their particular countries after the political trauma and bloodshed of the last quarter century. Moreover, on August 14, 1814, the papacy restored the Society of Jesus, some 600 strong.

Earlier, in 1802, François-René de Chateaubriand (1768–1848), having recently returned from rationalistic unbelief to the Christian faith of his pious mother ("I wept and I believed"), had published *The Genius of Christianity*. This apologetic buttressed the faith of many Roman Catholics and spurred them on in their restoration efforts. Turning away from rationalistic argumentation, Chateaubriand emphasized the beauties of the Christian faith. He wrote, "Though we have not employed the arguments usually advanced by the apologists of Christianity, we have arrived by a different chain of reasoning at the same conclusion: Christianity is perfect; men are imperfect. Now, a perfect consequence cannot spring from an imperfect principle. Christianity, therefore, is not the work of men."

In 1814 Abbé Dominque-Dufour de Pradt took the measure of the remarkable impact of Chateaubriand's work on certain European Roman Catholics: "He reinstated religion in the world, establishing it on a better footing than it had occupied, for until then it had followed, so to speak, in the wake of society, and since then it has marched visibly at the head."

Political and religious conservatives who sought to reinvigorate the Christian faith's influence and restore certain European institutions of the Old Order to a pre-1789 status often underestimated how powerful the messages of "republicanism" and "Bonapartism" had been. Nor did some of those politicians and diplomats who spoke the language of restoration and legitimacy intend to destroy the "advances" (improved legal codes, for example) associated with the revolution and Napoleon. Alexis de Tocqueville noted that "what was really substantial in his work lasted; his government died, but his administration continued to live." Moreover, Lord Castlereagh, the Foreign Secretary for England, called Tsar Alexander I's creation of a Holy Alliance to support the Christian religion a "piece of sublime mysticism and nonsense."

Many Europeans resented the way the Great Powers had cavalierly manipulated the map of Europe with little concern about the welfare of the peoples affected. They despised imposed elites, some of whom ruled as foreigners over nations and ethnic groups to which they did not belong. They abhorred the obvious widespread social, political, and economic inequities of post-1815 Europe.

As the productivity of industry increased, the "bourgeoisie's" interest in making money appeared insatiable. Critics found this development deplorable because the bourgeoisie were often profiting at the expense of workers but cared little for their welfare. In *An Essay on the Duties of Man Addressed to Workingmen* (1844), Giuseppe Mazzini, an Italian revolutionary, summarized the complaint of workingmen against the "upper classes": "We are the slaves of labor, poor and unhappy; speak to us of material improvement, of liberty, of happiness. Tell us if we are doomed to suffer forever; if we are never to enjoy in our turn. Preach duty to our employers; to the classes above us, who treat us like machines, and monopolize the sources of well-being, which, in justice belong to all men." Mazzini asserted that workingmen needed to turn to God for help and forsake the leadership of godless revolutionaries.

Other critics protested the prevalence of crime, venereal disease, prostitution, and poverty among vast segments of city dwellers. Overcrowding in the cities had become an immense problem. The population of Paris, for example, grew from 634,000 in 1816 to 1,360,000 in 1846. Critics rued the fact that so many Europeans even up to 1831 were excluded from voting because they failed to meet property, money, religious, or gender qualifications: having the right to vote were 620,000 English from a population of 16.5 million; 167,000 French from 33 million; 40,000 Belgians from 4 million. The critics deeply resented "foreign" powers occupying their lands. Some "nationalists" in particular were prepared to rebel. Political "liberals" who advocated the freedom of individuals and the creation of constitutions often opted for attempts at reform rather than recourse to revolution.

In 1834 an overly enthused Chateaubriand rejoiced that "Europe is racing towards democracy" and that France and England were tearing down "the crumbling ramparts" of the Old Order. In fact, conservative forces defending the Old Order often ruthlessly repressed democratic movements between 1815 and 1850. Historian Eugen Weber has written, "Reaction triumphed in Germany, in Italy, in Hungary, wherever Russia and Austria held sway. Hangings, whippings, stifling repression, marked the restoration of legitimate order." The Restoration's watchdogs of eastern Europe—Metternich of Austria and Tsars Alexander I and Nicholas I of Russia—not only barked but bit.

VII. REVOLUTIONS FROM 1815 TO 1832

A. The Greek Struggle for Independence

Not every revolution that ensued was directed against a "Christian" European state. From 1821 to 1832, Greeks fought a costly bloody war for independence from the Ottoman Empire. As a people they had been subjected to Turkish rule since the fall of Constantinople in 1453. Resisting conversion to the Muslim faith, Greeks generally remained true to Orthodox beliefs.

A number of Greeks had earlier attempted to gain their liberties in the failed Orlov Rebellion (1778–79). The Orlov brothers had anticipated substantial help from the Russians, who had indicated they wanted to free Christians from Ottoman rule. In 1805 Adamantios Korais, a learned Greek exile who appreciated democratic and republican ideals, published *What Graecans Must Do against the Current Conditions*. In it he provided counsel concerning how the Greeks might win independence. He was quite critical of the Orthodox Church.

During the Greek war, tens of thousands of civilians perished when

Greeks and Ottomans massacred each other and Jews. The Greeks who sought liberation from the Turks benefitted from an ideology calling for the preservation of Hellenic culture; from the negative effects of a weakened economy on the Turkish military; from the assistance of secret revolutionary societies such as the *Filiki Eteria* ("Friendly Society," that is, Society of Friends) in Odessa, Russia (which apparently wanted to create an Orthodox Balkan state using Greek as its language); from the daring exploits of leaders such as the pro-Russian commander Theodor Kolokotronis; and from the military support of the French, English, and Russian governments whose ships trapped and then set on fire the Turkish-Egyptian navies on October 20, 1827.

With the Treaty of Adrianople (1829), the independence of Greece and Serbia was assured, and Romanian principalities came under Russia control. On April 24, 1830, the Ottoman government under military pressure from the Russians recognized the independence of Greece. Briefly, a president ruled over the newly established Greek democracy, but he was assassinated. Otto of Bavaria (1815–67), who had supported the struggle for independence, in turn became the Greek king.

The Greek revolution stirred the imagination of Europeans and Americans. In 1824 the Scottish poet Lord Byron (1788–1824), author of "Isles of Greece"—a poem celebrating the country's heroic past—died of a fever in Greece while engaged in its struggle for independence. Greece was the first modern European state to emerge in the post-Napoleon era.

B. The French Revolution of 1830

The Charter of 1814 established a constitutional monarchy in France with Louis XVIII, a Bourbon, as king (1814–24). The new monarch faced rising dissension between *émigrés* nobles who sought the restoration of their properties and political liberals in the Chamber of Deputies (the legislature) who wanted to preserve the "gains" of the revolution and the Napoleonic era.

Charles X (1824–30) attempted to turn back the royal clock to pre-1789 days, if judged by his coronation (May 29, 1825). The archbishop of Reims anointed him (*sacre*) in the cathedral of Reims. Charles participated in a healing service for those afflicted with the "King's disease" (scrofula). Prime Minister Joseph, the Comte de Villèle, and other conservative Catholics known as Ultras pushed through a bill restoring the Roman Catholic Church as *the* church of France. A contemporary observed that "one talks of nothing but bishops, priests, monks, Jesuits, convents and seminaries."

The Ultras gained control over the educational system of France and passed the "Law of Sacrilege," which stipulated that anyone who defaced the sacraments could be put to death. The agenda of the Ultras deepened anticlerical sentiments in various corners of the French public. In 1830 Charles X further antagonized many Frenchmen by promulgating the "Four Ordinances," which limited freedom of the press, and by dismissing the Chamber of Deputies.

In the elections of 1830, political liberals won a majority of seats in the Chamber of Deputies. Charles X tried to stymie them by ordering that the chamber be dissolved and new elections held. Likening their actions to the revolutionaries of the English Revolution of 1688, liberals and bourgeois revolutionaries joined workers in the streets of Paris in a revolt of three "Glorious Days." Charles X abdicated, thereby ending the rule of the Bourbon family.

The victors of the Revolution of 1830 created the "July Monarchy" and installed Louis Philippe (1773–1850) of the Orléans family as the King of France (1830–48). François Guizot, Louis Philippe's very influential Protestant minister of instruction (1832–37) and premier (1847–48), indicated that the "promise" of the July Monarchy was "order and liberty" reunited under a constitutional monarchy. Guizot firmly opposed universal suffrage because it allegedly brought about "the ruin of democracy and liberty." He once stated, "Not to be a republican at 20 is proof of want of heart; to be one at 30 is proof of want of head."

Victor Hugo, the famous author, noted that Louis Philippe carried his own umbrella as he walked to work in Paris and bore "in his own person the contradiction of the Restoration and the Revolution." The king and his ministers defended well the interests of wealthy members of the bourgeoisie, who with flair and bombast now took center stage in the social and political life of France. The upper middle class with the right to vote and with great money displaced royalists and the old nobility in the process.

The wealthy built multistoried, luxurious homes in Paris, the very top floors of which were reserved for servants, who lived in squalid, unhealthy conditions. The wealthy sometimes feared the common people and viewed them as depraved and "barbarians."

Hugo described the bourgeois king as "one of the best princes who ever sat on the throne." Some of the poor people of Paris thought otherwise. In June 1832, at the time of the funeral of General Lamarque, a republican hero, they took to the streets and erected barricades in a failed insurrection. Hugo captured the story of their struggle for freedom in his poignant novel *Les Misérables* (1862). Their economic plight had not improved under the "liberal bourgeois" government of Louis Philippe. He was the target of numerous assassination attempts.

Hugues-Félicité Robert de Lamennais, perhaps the foremost advocate of the restoration of Roman Catholicism in France, became convinced that his church should enjoy independence from the monarchy. Initially he approved the July Monarchy of Louis Philippe. On October 16, 1830, with Charles de Montalembert and Henri Dominique Lacordaire, Lamennais published the first edition of *L'Avenir* (*The Future*), a journal devoted to the message of "God and Freedom"—that is, religious belief and political liberty are compatible concepts. Lamennais advocated "the total separation of church" (from the state), freedom of education, freedom of the press, and other measures. On August 15, 1832, Pope Gregory XVI, in the encyclical *Miravi Vos* ("On Liberalism and Religious Indifferentism"), condemned appeals of this kind. On March 12, 1833, Lamennais observed, "Now our old Europe is divided into two parties, one of which wants liberty without religion, and the other religion without liberty; that is to say, both alike are striving to realize the impossible. The only remedy, then, is to attach the Catholics to the cause of liberty, in order to win back the friends of liberty to Catholicism. That is what we tried to do in the *Avenir*."

Lamennais also penned *Words of a Believer*, in which he attacked the rich for their exploitation of the poor and extolled the brotherhood of mankind. Published in 1834, the provocative book became a huge bestseller. The papacy condemned the book as "immense in perversity." By 1836 Lamennais had decided to give up his Roman Catholic beliefs. His experience reflected the difficulty some liberal Catholics encountered in promoting political liberty and the welfare of workers without incurring the papacy's wrath and sanctions.

C. The Belgium Revolt (1830)

Like revolutionaries in Paris, other Europeans dreamt of political liberty and freedom. They remembered earlier successful revolutions such as the 1820 insurrection in Spain in which two cavalry units forced Ferdinand VII, a Bourbon divine right monarch, to accept a constitutional monarchy.

On August 25, 1830, rioting broke out in Brussels. Spectators who had been attending Daniel Auber's opera *La Muette de Portici* about earlier Spanish revolutionaries became agitated and took to the streets. A successful revolt led by political liberals and Catholics ensued in the southern region of the Netherlands. The revolutionaries formed the second modern European state, Belgium. Its liberal constitution (1831) sanctioned freedom of religion, freedom of the press, and freedom of education.

Benefitting from the political turmoil in Spain and Portugal, revolutionaries in South America had earlier mounted independence movements that resulted in the creation of a number of nations such as Columbia between 1810 and 1825 (led by General Simon Bolivar, 1783–1830) and Argentina in 1816 (led by soldier-statesman José de San Martin, 1778–1850), Chile between 1810 and 1818 (San Martin), and Peru in 1821 (San Martin).

D. Poland and Russia: The Suppression of Revolutions

By no means were all revolutions successful. Poland's nationalistic revolutionaries often suffered grievously. In 1764 Catherine the Great of Russia imposed Stanislaw Poniatowski on the country. Prussia and Russia eventually partitioned Poland three times (1772, 1793, 1795). These same powers put down several efforts by Poles in 1794 and 1830 to gain their liberation from foreign domination. In 1794 Thaddeus Kosciusco, a veteran of the American Revolution, attempted to establish a republic in Poland only to have the Russians and Prussians crush the rebellion. Thousands of Poles lost their lives in the conflict.

In Russia, when Tsar Alexander I died in 1825 (the rumor existing that he had faked his death), reforming aristocrats and members of a Moscow regiment of the military staged a revolt in Saint Petersburg in an attempt to block the succession of Nicholas I. They intended to establish Constantine Nicholas I's brother as a constitutional monarch. Caught off guard by the rebellion, Nicholas I dramatically wrote in December 1825, "In the early hours of the day after tomorrow, I shall either be a sovereign or a corpse." He survived. Troops loyal to him put down the "Decembrist Revolt."

Not only did Tsar Nicholas I (1825–55) seek to expand Russia at the expense of the Ottoman Turks (1828–29), but he also supported efforts to suppress revolutionaries in Europe, thereby earning the title of the "gendarme of Europe." In 1830–31, his forces brutally suppressed Polish revolutionaries. In his *Imperial Manifesto on Poland* (March 25, 1832), the tsar explained his plans for Poland's union with Russia:

> Now that an end has been put by force of arms to the rebellion in Poland, and that nation, led away by agitators, has returned to its duty, and is restored to tranquility, We deem it right to carry into execution our plan with regard to the introduction of the new order of things, whereby the tranquility and union of the two nations, which Providence has entrusted to Our care, may be forever guarded against new attempts.

Nicholas professed a desire that the Poles might enjoy "security of persons and property, liberty of conscience, and all the laws and privileges of towns and communes." In fact, Polish nationalists attempted to launch another revolution in 1863–64.

In Russia, Nicholas ruled what was tantamount to a police state. His government attempted to propagate the theory of "Official Nationality"—"Orthodoxy, Autocracy and Nationality." In 1833 the Minister of Education, Count Sergey Uvarov, explained the theory's rationale:

> Amid the rapid decline of religious and civilian institutions in Europe and the universal dissemination of destructive concepts, and in view of the sad occurrences surrounding us on every side, it became necessary to strengthen the fatherland on the firm foundations which are the basis of the prosperity, strength, and life of the people. It has become necessary to discover the principles that are the distinguishing marks of the Russian character and that belong to it exclusively. It has become necessary to assemble the sacred remnants of its nationality into one whole, and on it to anchor our salvation.

For Uvarov, the upholding of Orthodoxy was linked to Russia's very existence: "Without love for the faith of their ancestors, peoples as well as individuals must perish. The Russian devoted to the fatherland, is no more likely to consent to the loss of one of the dogmas of our orthodoxy than to the theft of even one pearl from the Crown of Monomakh."

This program struck a national and deeply spiritual chord with some Russians. So-called "Slavophiles" promoted a return to the rural and monastic values of Russia that supposedly existed before Peter the Great had "westernized" it. The lay theologian Alexis Khomiakov (1804–60), a leader of the Slavophiles, urged the recovery of true "Orthodox" Christianity.

Although Khomiakov's influence on instruction at Russian seminaries was restricted, it meshed well with the Russian government's view that "Orthodoxy" should constitute the religious basis for Russian society. Government spies and the secret police of the "Third Section" kept a watchful eye for anyone who appeared to oppose the regime's autocratic policies.

Russian intellectuals, so-called "Westernizers," were often atheists. They loved Russia, but also appreciated various western European cultures. They sometimes reacted strongly against what they perceived to be the folding back of Russian culture into itself. Pyotr Chaadaev wrote eight "Philosophical Letters" (1826–31), which could not be published in Russia because of their highly critical nature. They bemoaned Russia's increasing isolation from the West: "Cut off from European cultural growth by the adoption of Byzantine Christianity, Russia had contented herself with the wholesale appropriation of the superficial

"In fact, the unity of the Church is not imaginary or allegorical, but a true and substantial unity, such as the unity of many members in a living body" (Alexis Khomiakov in *The Church Is One*).

products of other cultures." He indicated that "if Russia was to play a positive role in the history of the world, she must rejoin the European cultural organism and repeat, if need be, the whole history of that world." In the 1830s, sharp debates broke out between Slavophiles and Westernizers.

People suspected of holding revolutionary sentiments were sometimes arrested and sent to Siberia. In 1839 a Frenchman in Russia described well the suffocating atmosphere created by the loss of personal liberties: "One does not die here or breathe, except by permission of Imperial *authority*."

VIII. LABOR UNREST AND REVOLUTIONS (1832–48)

Even though many western European countries remained essentially agrarian deep into the nineteenth century, the "Industrial Revolution" continued to transform daily life for millions of workers. Labor unrest, whether in England, France, Germany, Italy, or elsewhere, became a prominent feature of urban life. Sometimes workers joined secret societies and labor unions seeking to redress grievances inflicted by members of the upper classes who owned factories and businesses and thereby dictated their living standards.

While some labor leaders openly disdained the Christian religion, others consistently referenced Christian values in their appeals for justice for workers. They often railed at "Democratic Liberals." The utopian socialist Henri Comte de Saint-Simon (1760–1825) believed that Europe was like a body and could only become "healthy" when all of its members, including the "poorest and most numerous class," enjoyed more of the fruits of their labor. He offered a strong critique of liberalism: "All who played a role in the Revolution, first as *patriots*, then as *Bonapartists*, today claim to be *liberals*."

Unfortunately, the self-serving goal of some liberals was to "overthrow every possible government so that they can take over themselves." The followers of Saint-Simon urged the upper classes to forsake egoism and for workers and others to show Christian love to each other. The Italian revolutionary Giuseppe Mazzini, who had called workers to a spiritual revolution, also strongly criticized liberals for not changing the lot of workers: "Has the condition of the people improved? Have the millions who live by the daily labor of their hands acquired any, the smallest amount, of the promised and desired well-being? No; the condition of the people has not improved." Other liberals such as Pierre Leroux (1797–1871) attempted to give their forms of Christian socialism intellectual heft.

A. The Revolutions of 1848

From 1848 to 1850, like delayed timing of bursts in a spectacular fireworks display, rounds of revolutions went off, lighting up the European countryside at different moments. The initial burst came from the French in February 1848. Soon, news of their revolution spurred peoples such as Germans, Magyars, Czechs, and Italians to revolt. Some revolutionaries cried out in a utopian spirit, "All change!" Regimes were overthrown, and intoxicating talk of national unity and of new eras of freedom of speech, press, and religion wafted through the air.

In the end, however, the forces of restoration generally succeeded in extinguishing most of the revolts. For example, the Russians put down the Hungarian revolt of Louis Kossuth in 1848–49. Interestingly enough, Marx and Friedrich Engels published their *Communist Manifesto* in 1848.

B. France

In France, dissatisfaction with the liberal government of Louis Philippe simmered. Based on guidelines from the Napoleonic era, public education no longer specifically supported the Catholic faith. Some members of a Catholic party, including Catholic liberals and Ultramontanes, demanded the right for the Catholic Church to institute its own schools open to people of all faiths. Social critics complained that the governments of Louis Philippe continued to ignore the grinding poverty of workers and seemed only too intent in protecting the economic interests of the upper classes. This attitude appeared substantiated in 1847, when the government refused to extend voting rights to a greater number of the populace.

As members of the "petty bourgeoisie," students and workers began holding banquets where they discussed in an animated fashion the need for "reform." When in 1848 the government outlawed these banquets, they took to the streets and confronted the French military. A contemporary observer wrote, "When the harassed military moved against the insurrection, they found that the auxiliary force had interposed itself; and the National Guard, which should have been the last police force of the monarchy, melted into a vaguely cheering mass of middle-class politicians." Elsewhere in the streets of Paris, barricades were hastily erected, fierce fighting broke out, and blood was shed.

After republican and socialist rebels seized the Hôtel de Ville, Louis Philippe abdicated and went to England. Alphonse de Lamartine (1790–1869) established the Provisional Second Republic. Property requirements for voting were abolished, but the demands of workers were not met to their satisfaction by Lamartine's government. Once again, they revolted. This time the French army put down the rebellion. In December 1848, Louis Napoleon Bonaparte was elected the president of the French Republic. In a coup of 1852 he took the title Emperor Napoleon III and was in fact the dictatorial head of the Second Empire.

C. Germany

After the Congress of Vienna, thirty-five monarchs and four independent Free Cities formed the German Federation as a replacement of sorts for the German Empire that had collapsed in 1806. This loose federation, the results of Metternich's efforts to restore the old order, did not satisfy the desires for German unity evident particularly among students. At the Wartbergfest in October 1817, students celebrating Martin Luther's nailing of the *Ninety-five Theses* and a victory over Napoleon at Leipzig called for "Honor, Freedom and Fatherland" and chose for their flag the colors black, red, and gold and the emblem of a black eagle.

On various occasions (1830, 1832, 1833, 1837), nationalistic rebellions occurred in portions of Germany with revolutionaries calling for the freedom of the press, the right of assembly, elective representation of the people, and other liberties. None of these stirrings led to great change, however.

In 1848 many students and professors, enthused by news of the fall of Louis Philippe's regime in France, anticipated that finally the moment of German unity had arrived and that repressive German regimes would be overthrown. Carl Schurz (1829–1906) described his own excitement as a student in Bonn upon learning about the toppling of the French government: "... since the French had driven away Louis Philippe and proclaimed the republic, something of course must be done here. Now had arrived in Germany the day of the establishment of 'German Unity,' and the founding of a great powerful, national German empire."

Schurz added, "Great news came from Vienna! There the students of the university were the first to assail the Emperor of Austria with the cry for liberty and citizens' rights. Blood flowed in the streets, and the downfall of Prince Metternich was the result." Schurz was referring to a popular uprising in Austria involving Magyar, German, and Czech nationalists that forced Metternich to seek exile on March 13, 1848. In the same month a number of German states had adopted liberal constitutions. After bloodshed occurred in a crowd demanding reform, Friedrich Wilhelm IV of Prussia initially appeared ready to accept a liberal constitution.

At a meeting at St. Paul's Church in Frankfurt, learned delegates of a national assembly gathered on May 18, 1848, with the goal of establishing a liberal constitution for Germany. Disputes ensued, however, over whether Germany should be large or small (with Austria or without). The restoration of conservative aristocrats (Otto von Bismarck) to power in Berlin by the fall of 1848, the Austrian emperor's decision to create an Austrian Hapsburg state including Hungary and portions of Italy and the Balkans (March 1849), and Friedrich Wilhelm IV's refusal to accept the national assembly's offer of the crown of Germany (April 3, 1849) contributed to the collapse of efforts to establish a politically liberal Germany.

Friedrich William IV, a divine right monarch, had declared, "I am not able to return a favorable reply to the offer of a crown on the part of the German National Assembly, because the Assembly has not the right, without the consent of the German governments, to bestow the crown." A good number of German intellectuals, very disappointed by these developments, emigrated from Prussia in consequence, some like Schurz pursuing distinguished careers in the United States. Schurz served as a U.S. Senator, as the Secretary of the Interior (1877–81), and as the editor of a number of influential newspapers.

St. Paul's Church in Frankfurt.

D. The Papacy and Revolutions in Italy (1848)

The French Revolution and the Age of Napoleon constituted traumatic eras for the papacy: papal condemnations flaunted, popes imprisoned, papal lands seized. It is understandable that after 1815 the restored papacy often viewed with suspicion revolutionary movements that heralded the virtues of nationalism and republicanism. Gregory XVI (1831–46), a beneficiary of archconservative Metternich's support, criticized freedom of conscience and spoke out against Italian nationalism, only to have a revolt break out in the Papal States. Austrian troops were needed to quell the unrest and eventually occupied the Papal States for seven years.

By contrast, Pope Pius IX (1846–78) initially attempted to accommodate the democratic republican aspirations of certain Italians with Roman Catholic Church teachings. Upon learning in early 1848 that Ferdinand II of Naples had permitted a constitution, the pope followed suit by creating a constitution for the Papal States. Then news reached Rome that the Austrian Metternich had fallen and various Italian cities had erupted in revolutions seeking to throw off the yoke of Austrian rule. Pope Pius IX decided not to give full support to Italian revolutionaries in their campaign for liberation. After all, the Austrians were likewise Roman Catholics.

A revolution broke out in Rome, and Pius IX felt forced to flee. Giuseppe Mazzini and other revolutionaries who sought the unification of Italy established the "Roman Republic," only to have their regime overthrown in turn by French troops. In 1850 a chastened Pope Pius IX returned to Rome from exile, disabused of pro-democratic or republican sympathies. Moreover, he understood very well that his own rule in Rome depended on the presence of French bayonettes. It is little surprise, then, that Pius IX generally demonstrated overt hostility toward "liberal" political movements in the remaining years of his pontificate.

IX. CONCLUSION

The "Age of Democratic Revolutions" (1770–1848) witnessed waves of revolutions that swept through portions of Europe and the Americas at different times. For many revolutionaries the "gospel of republican democracy" was antagonistic to the gospel of Jesus Christ. For other revolutionaries, the gospel of Jesus Christ and republican democracy were mutually supportive. For many nonrevolutionaries, defending the "Old Regime" was tantamount to defending the Christian religion.

After the publication of *The Communist Manifesto* by Marx and Engels in 1848, revolutionaries arose as "evangelists" for the Marxist gospel that challenged not only the Christian gospel but the "gospel" of Western political liberalism. Then again, Luddites, the followers of the mythical figure Ned Ludd, espoused a form of destructive anarchism that gave no quarter to institutions whether political or commercial.

Although the forces of restoration emerged as apparent victors from the revolutions of 1848, they could not block the unification of Italy and Germany later in the century. Moreover, after 1848 they could not ultimately shelter the Christian religion itself from the impact of another kind of revolution, one of changing worldviews. Historian A. P. J. Taylor observes,

The year 1848 was of great moment in European history both as an end and as a beginning. It was the year of revolutions, the culmination of the political upheaval that had started with the French Revolution of 1789.... Yet 1848 marked much more a beginning than an end. This new revolution was less specific than the political turmoil that had preceded it. It was a change in men's beliefs, in their view of the universe and more prosaically in their way of life.

This "change in men's beliefs" contributed to derailing efforts, especially among many intellectuals, to restore Christianity to the central role it had enjoyed in European culture before the French Revolution of 1789.

FOR FURTHER STUDY

Aston, Nigel. *Religion and Revolution in France, 1780–1804*. Washington: Catholic University Press of America, 2000.

Aston, Nigel. *Christianity and Revolution, 1750–1830*. Cambridge: Cambridge University Press, 2003.

Chadwick, Owen. *The Popes and European Revolution*. Oxford: Oxford University Press, 1981.

Englund, Steven. *Napoleon: A Political Life*. New York: Scribner, 2004.

Furet, François. *Interpreting the French Revolution*. Cambridge: Cambridge University Press, 1977.

Godechot, Jacques. *1789: The Taking of the Bastille*. London: Faber and Faber, 1970.

Kaiser, Thomas, and Dale Van Kley. *From Deficit to Deluge: The Origins of the French Revolution*. Stanford, CA: Stanford University Press, 2011.

Adjusting to Modernization and Secularism

The Rise of Protestant Liberalism (1799–1919)

I. INTRODUCTION

On a sunny spring day, Paris, France, offers up a sensory bouquet of sights, sounds, and smells. At the heart of the French capital is the picturesque Île de la Cité (Island of the City), bordered on all sides by the Seine River. Historic bridges link the island to the "Left" and "Right" banks of Paris and to the Île de Saint Louis. From the tourist boats (*bateaux mouches*) that ply the waters around the island, Parisians and visitors alike can shoot breathtaking pictures of the magnificent Notre Dame Cathedral on the Île de la Cité. This Gothic cathedral looms majestically overhead, flanked as it is with flying buttresses. Its north and south towers thrust upward toward the heavens.

Elsewhere, Paris puts on public display her spacious avenues and boulevards (Avenue des Champs Elysées); well-tended parks, squares, and gardens (Jardin des Tuileries); famous monuments (Tour Eiffel and Arc de Triomphe); museums and stately buildings (Palais-Royal); and bustling neighborhoods. Few visitors dispute that Paris ranks among the most beautiful cities in the world.

As late as the 1830s, however, the city was sometimes known more for its ugliness than its stately elegance. In 1838 the Vicomte de Launay wrote, "How ugly Paris seems after a year's absence. How one chokes in these dark, narrow and dank corridors that we like to call the streets of Paris! One would think that one was in a subterranean city, that's how heavy is the atmosphere, how profound is the darkness."

In 1853 Emperor Napoleon III (1852–70), asked Georges-Eugène, Baron Haussmann, Prefect of the Seine, to modernize Paris. Over a period of seventeen years (1853–70), Haussmann tore down and

Notre Dame Cathedral in Paris.

rebuilt 60 percent of Paris. He leveled many medieval buildings on the Île de la Cité. He disrupted the lives of Parisians, especially the poor, forcing 350,000 people from their dwellings.

In 1859 Haussmann stipulated precise dimensions for many of the new buildings. These edifices often served as residences and businesses for members of a powerful middle class. He constructed straight avenues and twelve boulevards to improve travel speed and facilitate trade. He gave thoroughfares sufficient width to discourage any Parisians daring to revolt from erecting barricades to block the advance of the emperor's troops.

Haussmann wanted Paris filled with light and open-air parks. One of his engineers, Jean-Charles Alphand, created parks bedecked with woods, waterfalls, and walkways (Le Parc des Buttes-Chaumont, Le Parc Monsouris). Haussmann enhanced water and sewage systems and increased public lighting by adding 20,000 gas outlets. But the monetary undergirding for his renovation plans created huge debts and fueled rampant speculation. In 1870 Napoleon III, alarmed by social unrest, fired the innovative "modernizer."

During the Restoration (after 1815), a number of Europeans, whether in France or elsewhere, wanted to reinstitute aspects of "Christian" Europe that had existed before the French Revolution and

Napoleonic era. They understood that between the years 1789 and 1814, numerous long-standing institutions, traditions, customs, and beliefs had been rudely assailed. Nonetheless, they sought to restore the Old Order.

In their efforts to turn back the cultural clock, some "restorers" may have underestimated the durability of a number of changes that took place during the French Revolution and Napoleon's rule. (An example is the attraction and commitment of many Europeans to democratic ideals and disdain for monarchies.) Moreover, they apparently did not foresee the extent to which the powerful forces of "modernization" would transform the physical, economic, political, social, and intellectual traits of Europe, making it difficult to reinstitute fully prerevolutionary institutions, values, and sensibilities.

II. "MODERNIZATION": A CONTROVERSIAL CONCEPT

Sociologists and historians often define "modernization" as a society's complex and multiphased movement from an agricultural and rural or traditional condition to a "modern" industrial, technological society that is urbanized, democratic, and pluralistic. The origin of the concept is frequently sought in a liberal political philosophy that emphasizes the value of personal individual rights (John Locke), a liberal theory of economics promoting free enterprise (Adam Smith), and deregulated commerce. This was a social evolutionary theory of a society's inevitable development and "progress" from a "traditional" to a "modern" condition and in the social and economic entailments of the Industrial Revolution that first appeared in England in the eighteenth century and then on the Continent, first in Belgium, in the nineteenth century.

Some critics of the modernization concept do not deny the existence of the phenomenon. Rather, they decry the "abuses" that can follow in its wake. They point out that not all of its effects are necessarily good. "Modernization" can weaken a person's sense of corporate belonging to and identity with a family, a neighborhood, a church, or the local town. It can wear down loyalties to worthy older customs, habits, and traditions. It can afford a tool such as modernized weaponry with which allegedly "superior" (modern) peoples can subjugate allegedly "inferior" (traditional) peoples whose lands are coveted for their natural resources.

Modernization is also often linked to a disputed "secularization" premise that the evolution of a society inevitably results in progress and a turning away from religion. Historian Christopher Clark, for example, writes, "The days are long past when historians conceived of modernization in terms of a linear decline in religion, but there is still a tendency to view the phenomenon of religious revival as a detour, a distraction, from the 'norm' of an irreversible process of secularization."

Other critics complain that "modernity," a concept closely associated with modernization, is frequently portrayed as a "Western," European-centric phenomenon. They claim that at least its economic origins were Asian and that there were powerful non-Western economies before the nineteenth century. For these critics, history should be written, not from a European perspective, but from a world perspective that acknowledges the worth of other cultures.

This would suggest that the history of European colonization should be told with appreciation and respect for the perspectives of colonial peoples. The colonialists should not be treated solely as passive subjects but as agents who reacted to and in some instances determined their own destinies. For example, historian John Thompson, while by no means minimizing the Europeans' essential role in the slave trade, proposes the provocative thesis that his "examination of the military and political relations between Africans and Europeans concludes that Africans controlled the nature of their interactions with Europe. Europeans did not possess the military power to force Africans to participate in any type of trade in which their leaders did not wish to engage."

Ideally, then, the historian should attempt to distinguish the ofttimes competing perceptions some Europeans had of their colonization efforts (beneficial) as compared with the perceptions (exploitative) of those peoples colonized by Europeans.

Notwithstanding all these reservations, a consideration of the impact of modernization on European societies can offer significant insights into the origins of many of the religious and social conflicts that took place during the nineteenth century between Protestant and Roman Catholic "liberals" and Protestant and Roman Catholic "conservatives" as well as the disputes between secularists and agnostics and people of faith.

A. The Impact of Modernization on Nineteenth-Century Europe

What was Europe like before the changes due to nineteenth-century modernization took place? Historians John Belchem and Richard Price provide us with a verbal snapshot of life in Europe in 1800:

> The ways people thought, dressed, lived would be strange and
> alien [to us]; they moved on foot or in horse-drawn carriages; they

dwelt, in the main, in small settlements and were closer to the land; their loyalties were to families, tribes, local communities. Monarchs and central-governments, when they existed, were distant bodies, playing little role in the day-to-day lives of ordinary people.

Then the forces of modernization began to set in, including the emergence of the "modern state." These forces often disrupted rhythms of daily life and modified or transformed values, particularly of inhabitants of European cities.

Haussmann's renovation of Paris may serve as an illustration of the beneficial and less worthwhile changes one kind of modernization—regulated city planning—could elicit. Portions of Paris substantially took on a new look, quite different from what Paris resembled in the mid-eighteenth century. This earlier, smaller Paris, still had the feel of a walled, medieval town.

Although graced with many magnificent churches such as Notre Dame on the Île de la Cité, the Palais Royal, monuments, and gardens, this Paris also encompassed unhygienic and dangerous neighborhoods where disease and crime flourished. Few streets had sidewalks. They were poorly lit and were strewn with garbage and human waste. The streets twisted through the poverty-stricken central and eastern districts of the city that had dilapidated housing.

By the 1860s Paris, like a number of other French cities, was alarmingly overcrowded. Newcomers from the countryside often poured into impoverished, cramped neighborhoods. But Paris was now larger, boasting new and renovated sections. Eight *arrondissements* (districts) were added to Paris in 1860. Upper-middle and aristocratic elites lived in Haussmann's apartment buildings that lined amply illuminated avenues or boulevards such as were found in the seventeenth *arrondissement*. (The elite generally lived on the first floors, while servants lived in the small top-floor garrets.)

The upper classes of Parisian society enjoyed a greater sense of economic and political power. Nonetheless, they continued to fear potential revolts erupting among the "barbarians," or the "people." They were also scandalized by the "Bohemian" (a term first used in 1834) lifestyles of poets such as Paul Verlaine and Jean Rimbaud.

Poor artists and writers barely eking out a living had thronged into the Latin Quarter of Paris. They often championed the pursuit of a non-conformist, "free" lifestyle, unfettered from conventional, Christian, bourgeois restraints. The Bohemian painter Gustave Courbet (1819–77), for example, put the matter bluntly: "I am fifty years old and I have always lived in freedom; let me end my life free; when I am dead let this be said of me. 'He belonged to no school, to no church, to no institutions, to no academy, least of all to any regime except the regime of liberty.'"

B. The Industrial Revolution, Modernization, and the Projection of European Power

The "Industrial Revolution" (a term thought to have originated in the 1830s) first took hold in England (1780–1840). Coal was a principal fuel along with water and steam as sources of power. Modernization in the form of improved machinery (the steam engine) and technical innovations brought significant change to the lives of workers. The surge of patents issued in England charts but one indicator of a powerful technological revolution: 82 (1740–69); 924 (1800–1809); 2,453 (1830–40); 4,581 (1840–49).

For many factory owners, time was no longer viewed in terms of what could be accomplished manually during daylight hours, but in terms of how much time it took to produce an item by a machine. Work often took place at a factory away from home. The craftsmanship of a single piece or item was often not as important as standardized, mass-produced exchangeable parts. A technological society could tend to make life impersonal.

Travel times for people and heavy freight diminished within countries due to improved road systems, the building of canals, and the use of trains, horse-buses, and trams. In 1836 London had its first railway. In 1840 Friedrich Harkort, a German businessman, even ventured the idea that "The locomotive is the hearse which will carry absolutism and feudalism to the graveyard." Europeans took advantage of new train services. By 1860 there were 300 million passenger trips by train in Europe; by 1880 there were 1,355 million.

Steamboats shortened travel time from months to weeks along rivers and across oceans. The Scot Henry Bell built the Comet, an innovative steamboat in 1812. The time it took to communicate across distances shortened dramatically. The American Samuel Morse made a telegraph machine in 1835; Alexander Graham Bell, a Scottish immigrant to America, received a patent for an electric telephone in 1876.

Europe in general became a greater economic and political powerhouse. Historian Norman Davies

Nineteenth-century steam engine.

© World History Archive/Alamy

observes, "There is a dynamism about nineteenth-century Europe that far exceeds anything previously known. Europe vibrated with power as never before: with technical power, economic power, cultural power, intercontinental power. Its prime symbols were its engines, the locomotives, the gasworks, the electric dynamos. Raw power appeared to be made a virtue in itself."

During the nineteenth century the population of Europe more than doubled, from 187 million to 401 million.

England, France, Belgium, Portugal, and Germany continued to undertake major colonization ventures from Africa to Asia. During the last third of the century they sometimes scrambled and competed as "empire builders" to acquire overseas territories. Toward 1870 the word *imperialism* was first used to describe the control of European nations over colonial lands and peoples (see chapter 16).

C. Modernization and Democratic Revolutions

After 1815, efforts at restoring or reinforcing institutions from pre-revolutionary Europe (1789) on occasion did meet with some success. A number of "Christian" monarchies were reestablished. The papacy, while greatly weakened during the French Revolution and the Napoleonic era, regained its footing and considerable respect. In 1815 the Russian tsar Alexander I proposed the creation of a European "Holy Alliance" that had as its goal "the application of the principles of Christianity to politics" (Prince Metternich's assessment).

Nonetheless, nineteenth-century monarchs and popes faced serious political and intellectual challenges. As we saw, between 1770 and 1848 periodic waves of democratic and nationalistic revolutions swept across Europe (see chapter 14). French revolutionaries were often blamed for sparking political and social unrest in other countries by providing examples of revolt. Metternich, the conservative Austrian leader, lamented, "When Paris sneezes, Europe catches cold." In the last half of the nineteenth century, conservative political forces could not halt movements toward state unification in Italy and Germany. Nor could they always thwart campaigns to extend personal liberties and voting rights to non-propertied people.

D. Modernity and the Rise of "Natural Knowledge" and "Secularism"

Especially after 1848, intellectual revolutions in the name of "modernity" and "evolution" gained further momentum. In some uses the word *modernity* simply alludes to the most up-to-date and progressive school of thought in a field of knowledge. More particularly, it often refers to the most recent scientific and technological advances.

The word *evolution* could reference the assumed "natural" development of numerous entities from a simple to a more complex form, including an idea, society, institution, philosophy, religion, or living beings. Scientist Richard Lowentin proposes that its original meaning was "an unrolling or unfolding, the emergence from an enveloped form, of a final result that is immanent in the original state."

A variety of thinkers became genuinely enthralled by and promoted modern, new ways of looking at the world. They extolled the authority of "natural knowledge" as opposed to "revealed knowledge" and metaphysics. They hailed "modern science" for producing multiple benefits for humanity. They wanted to pursue "objective," empirical scientific research untethered from religious strictures. They cited "reason" as a final authority in assessing what is "truthful," what is "right," and what is "useful." They frequently touted utilitarian values, especially the value that what brings happiness to the greatest number should be sought and esteemed. They rather naïvely believed that the mastery of nature through scientific research would bring happiness and well-being to humankind.

New academic disciplines emerged, such as sociology, to give natural, scientific explanations of the origins of societies and the general history or evolution of human relations. In the tradition of Montesquieu and Condorcet, these practitioners often looked for natural "laws" governing the ways societies and peoples functioned. In 1834 Auguste Comte used the French term *sociologie* for the first time. Older disciplines such as history were "professionalized."

Leopold von Ranke (1795–1886) of the University of Berlin advocated intensive archival research and the quest to write a "total history." He established an important goal for historians: after a rigorous assessment of primary documents, they should recount history "as it really happened." A believer in God, he nonetheless refrained from attributing specific events to God's providence. The seminar system he inaugurated became a centerpiece for learning historical methodology. New professional societies for historians were founded in Europe and the United States. University professors attempted to apply the rules of "modern historical scholarship" to their work. As practitioners of "objective" history, many of these scholars tried to exclude their own religious beliefs from influencing the way they did history. They bracketed out any reference to God and divine providence as causative agents in history.

In his *Data for Ethics* (1879), Herbert Spencer, the originator of the expression "the survival of the fittest," attempted to build the case for the existence of "natural ethics." He said these ethics should be grounded in a scientific study of humanity's evolution, and he claimed that they are not necessarily incompatible with "theological ethics."

In an essay of 1880, "Science and Culture," Thomas Huxley, the author of *Man's Place in Nature* (1863), argued that the emergence of "natural knowledge" was *the* defining trait of the age. Known as Darwin's "bulldog" defender, Huxley observed,

> The distinctive character of our own times lies in the vast and constantly increasing part which is played by natural knowledge. Not only is our daily life shaped by it, not only does the prosperity of millions of men depend upon it, but our whole theory of life has long been influenced, consciously or unconsciously, by the general conceptions of the universe, which have been forced upon us by physical sciences.

Huxley criticized contemporary British academic culture when it closely identified scholarship with the humanities and classical studies while neglecting the importance of science.

In 1923 Clement Webb, Oriel Professor of the Philosophy of the Christian Religion at Oxford, seconded Huxley's perception regarding the import of natural knowledge. In a lecture with a retrospective orientation, "A Century of Anglican Theology in Relation to the General Movement of European Thought," Webb declared that "the increase of natural knowledge during the last fifty years has been the outstanding fact of the intellectual life of Europe."

E. Charles Darwin's *Origin of Species*

The appearance of Charles Darwin's *Origin of Species* (1859) created a turning point in the scientific, intellectual, and religious history of nineteenth-century Europe. (The original title was *On the Origin of Species by Means of Natural Selection, or the Preservation of Favoured Races in the Struggle for Life*; the first printing of 1,250 copies sold out the day book came off press.) The book advocated a theory of organic evolution, even though the specific word *evolution* appears only once in its pages. The volume seemed to represent the best of natural knowledge and modern science. Darwin's arguments appeared based on scrupulous empirical and impartial research.

Darwin (1809–82) attended the University of Edinburgh and Cambridge University and in student days viewed himself as a Christian. He did not "doubt the strict and literal truth of the word in the Bible." At first, he thought he would be a physician. Then he considered a career as a Christian cleric. But in 1831 he signed on as a naturalist for voyages of the *Beagle* (1831–36). Along the coasts of South America, Tahiti,

New Zealand, and Australia, he made "observations in Natural History and Geology" later published in his *Journal of Researches*. He studied Sir Charles Lyell's important work *Principles of Geology* (1830–33).

In 1838 Darwin pondered Thomas Malthus's *An Essay on the Principle of Population* (1798). Malthus had proposed that, if population grows exponentially while food production grows only arithmetically, a struggle for survival would ensue among peoples. Darwin indicated that while reading Malthus, "... it at once struck me that under these circumstances favorable variations would tend to be preserved, and unfavorable ones to be destroyed. The result of this would be the formation of new species." Darwin became convinced that the hostile environment of nature set the stage of the struggle for survival of the fittest within and between species.

Despite Darwin's own respectful review of the contributions of his predecessors, the theory of evolution had a rather potted history. His grandfather, Erasmus Darwin—along with the French zoologist Jean-Baptiste Lamarck in his *Philosophie Zoologique* (1801, 1809) and Robert Chambers in *Vestiges of the Natural History of Creation* (1844) among others—had proposed significant evolutionary schemes. Darwin credited Lamarck for upholding "the doctrine that all species including man, are descended from other species. He first did the eminent service of arousing attention to the probability of all change in the organic, as well as in the inorganic world, being the result of law and not of miraculous interposition."

Many naturalists, however, opposed Lamarckian "Vestigianism." They included Lyell, who challenged the validity of biblical chronologies. Darwin praised Chambers's work, despite its flaws, for its "excellent service in this country in calling attention to the subject, in removing prejudices, and in this preparing the ground for the reception of analogous views." But at the time of the book's anonymous publication (1844), Darwin told a friend that advocating evolution was tantamount to "confessing murder."

In 1858 Darwin was stunned when he read an article by Alfred Russell Wallace (1823–1913), who proposed views about evolution that were nearly identical with his own. It is probably fair to say that Wallace and Darwin were the cofounders of the modern evolutionary theory. Nonetheless, it was Darwin's *Origin of Species*, based on careful research dating back to the 1830s, that elevated the theory of evolution to a new status of respectability within the wider scientific community.

In *Origin of Species* Darwin, who had earlier abandoned the Christian faith and had apparently experienced "no distress" in doing so, challenged a central belief of contemporary naturalists: the independent creation of each species (that is, by God).

Darwin defined "natural selection," the mechanism for modification (besides sexual selection), in this fashion: "I have called this principle, by which each slight variation, if useful, is preserved, by the term natural selection, in order to mark its relation to man's power of selection. But the expression often used by Mr. Herbert Spencer of the Survival of the Fittest is more accurate, and is sometimes equally convenient." Darwin's specific theory of natural selection would not be generally accepted by scientists for another fifty years.

Darwin indicated that *Origin of Species* should not trouble religious people: "I see no good reason why the views in this volume should shock the religious views of anyone." But shock many Christians the book did, even though Darwin had included only one line about man: "Much light will be thrown on the origin of man and his history." The book more generally spelled out a theory, yet it appeared to countermand the biblical creation accounts of plants and animals recorded in Genesis 1 and 2. A number of Darwin's Christian critics charged the scientist with subverting the Christian faith by bringing discredit on the Bible. Other believers sought to demonstrate that Darwin's theories could be aligned with Scripture and Christian theology.

The naturalist forthrightly acknowledged that his second major work, *The Descent of Man* (1871), addressing more specifically the origins of "man," would be widely castigated: "I am aware that the conclusions arrived at in this work will be denounced by some as highly irreligious." His research ostensibly declared that humans evolved from lower forms of being, that could include an "ape-like creature": "In a series of forms graduating insensibly from some ape-like creature to man as he now exists, it would be impossible to fix any definite point when the term 'man' ought to be used."

Darwin did not profess to deny God's existence. In fact, he struck out against anyone who would argue that creation was due to blind chance: "The birth of the species and of the individual are equally parts of that grand sequence of events which our minds refuse to accept as the result of blind chance. The understanding revolts at such a conclusion." Controversy still exists regarding whether or not Darwin was in fact a theist, an agnostic, or covertly an atheist. In his two principal books he indicated there was a "creator."

In the 1880s Edward Peace reflected on the jolting revolution in thinking that Darwin's writings precipitated in the minds of numerous young scholars:

> It is nowadays not easy to recollect how wide was the intellectual gulf which separated the young generation of that period from their parents. The *Origin of Species*, published in 1859, inaugurated an

intellectual revolution such as the world had not known since Luther nailed his thesis to the door of All Saints Church at Wittenberg.... The young men of the time grew up with the new ideas and accepted them as a matter of course.... Our parents, who read neither Spencer nor Huxley, lived in an intellectual world which bore no relation to our own; and cut adrift as we were from the intellectual moorings of our upbringings, recognizing, as we did that the older men were useless as guides in religion, in science, in philosophy, because they knew no evolution, we also felt instinctively that ... we had to discover somewhere for ourselves what were the true principles of the then recently invented science of sociology.

Even as Peace was writing, a full-scale reaction against the worth of "science," "reason," and "modernity" had already begun to emerge. In *The Crisis of Reason: European Thought, 1848–1914*, J. W. Burrow describes the multiple and complex forms this reaction took, including a movement in the arts ironically called "Modernism."

F. Atheistic Attacks on the Christian Faith

In the nineteenth century Christians sometimes found themselves swept up in a world of bewildering changes. They witnessed their cherished traditional religious beliefs assailed by unbelieving philosophers and social critics. Authors ranging from Karl Marx to Friedrich Nietzsche launched spirited attacks on the Christian religion.

Ludwig Feuerbach, a "loner," provocative philosopher, and author of *The Essence of Christianity* (1841), in many ways reduced God to man. He argued that "God" is, after all, the projection of certain qualities of humans: "God, as the quintessence of all realities and perfections, is nothing else than the quintessence, comprehensively summarized for the assistance of the limited individual, of the qualities of the human species, scattered among men, and manifesting themselves in the course of world history." With this premise in mind, Feuerbach indicated that when we pray, we do not actually pray to a "god" exterior to ourselves, but instead are engaged in "self-catharsis." He also argued for the materialist menu: we are what we eat.

In 1855 Ludwig Büchner (1824–99) claimed that advances in natural knowledge by science had discredited supernaturalism. He argued the "scientific" case for materialism: "That which appeared inexplicable, miraculous, and the work of a supernatural power, has, by the torch of science, proved to be the effect of hitherto unknown natural forces. The power of spirits and gods dissolved in the hands of science." He continued, "The theologians, with their articles of faith, must be left to themselves: so the naturalists with their science: they both proceed by different routes. The province of faith rests in human dispositions, which are not accessible to science." Büchner claimed that warrants for belief in God are not "scientific," that is, "objective," open to public scrutiny and subject to confirmation or falsification based on empirical research.

Alfred Grotjahn (1869–1931), a professor from the University of Berlin and well known as a prominent Social Darwinist and advocate of eugenics, recalled the significant impact that Büchner's book *Force and Nature* had in shaping his own materialist worldview: "Like hundreds of thousands of other young people it swept my brain clear of metaphysical conceptions at an age decisive in the development of my world view and freed me up to receive positivist views and this-worldly ethical values."

Nietzsche (1844–1900), another loner German philosopher, also made the case for atheism. However, he did so not as a "modernist," but as an "unmodern." The son of a Lutheran pastor, Nietzsche received a solid education in theology and philology at the University of Bonn and the University of Leipzig. A reading of Arthur Schopenhauer's *The World as Will and Representation* (1818) and Michel de Montaigne's skeptical arguments reinforced a growing disdain for traditional Christian values.

A musician, Nietzsche became close friends with Richard Wagner, the great composer, who also appreciated Schopenhauer. Later in life, Nietzsche became an archcritic of Wagner's music. He claimed that Wagner had been corrupted by his lingering interest in Christianity.

Nietzsche taught philology at the University of Basel from 1869 to 1879, except for a brief period of military service during the Franco-Prussian War, 1870–71. Afflicted by ill health (1879–89), he traveled from place to place in Europe. His notable works included *Human, All Too Human; Thus Spake Zarathustra: A Book for All and None* (1883–85); *The Anti-Christ: Curse on Christianity* (1888); *Twilight of the Idols; Ecco Homo: How One Becomes What One Is* (1888); and *The Will to Power*. In 1889 he experienced a mental collapse from which he did not recover. He died in 1900.

Nietzsche emphasized nonrational forces as the source for creativity, true living, and art. He identified himself as a follower of Dionysus, the god of wine and fertility. He indicted Christianity with its emphasis on humility and its alleged creation of false guilt as a "religion of the weak." In reality, he said, people are driven to release their strength, thereby exercising a "will for power." The *Übermensch* (superman) is the person who lives with the most vitality and creativity and does so liberated from useless, unprovable Christian morals. Nietzsche argued

"Without music, life would be a mistake.... I would only believe in a God who knew how to dance" (Friedrich Nietzsche in *Twilight of the Idols*).

that "one cannot *believe* [the] dogmas of religion and metaphysics if one has in one's heart and head the rigorous methods of acquiring truth."

Despite urging caution in making definitive judgments, Nietzsche claimed that "God is dead," no absolutes exist, "there are no facts, only interpretations," and man should be "translated back" into nature. Many authors, painters, and scientists looked to Nietzsche's provocative writings as a source of inspiration for their own thought.

Proponents of "comparative religions" argued that Christianity should be studied, not from a confessional perspective, nor as *the* religion, but scientifically analyzed and described as one of a number of religions. They often assumed that religions "evolve" from a primitive to a more complex stage of development.

G. The Coining of the Words *Secularization, Secularism, Agnostic, Eugenics,* and *Anti-Semitic*

By the second half of the nineteenth century, words such as *secularization, secularism, agnostic, eugenics,* and *anti-Semitic* began to penetrate the vocabulary of Europeans. According to historian Owen Chadwick, "In England of the 1860s the word *secularization* began its metaphorical phase in phrases like the *secularization of art* or the *secularization of politics.* In Germany the word *Säkularisation* only began its metaphorical career some twenty years later." The word became identified with an emerging "modern" separation of morality from a traditional grounding in religion.

In the journal *Reasoner,* which he founded, George Holyoake coined another term, "secularism" (1851) as "the improvement of life by material means." In 1883 Professor W. G. Blaike of New College, Edinburgh, observed that Holyoake's form of secularism, now deemed a utilitarian movement, while not necessarily atheistic, took little note of religion:

> It maintains ... that it is not by religion that the social welfare of humanity is to be advanced. The welfare of man in this world is a thing by itself, and is to be promoted solely by secular means. The main attention of all men should be given to the things of the present life. The aim of men in this world should be to seek their own highest good, and the highest good of their family, their country and their race.

Thomas Huxley introduced the word *agnostic* to distinguish skeptics from atheists. In 1883 he indicated what he had meant by the term he had coined years earlier: "Some twenty years ago, or thereabouts, I invented the word 'Agnostic' to denote people who, like myself, confess themselves to be hopelessly ignorant concerning a variety of matters about which metaphysicians and theologians, both orthodox and heterodox, dogmatise with utmost confidence." In the last decades of the nineteenth century, agnosticism became an attractive alternative stance for English students and members of the upper classes in Victorian England who had gnawing doubts about the truth of the Christian religion.

In 1883 Francis Galton introduced the word *eugenics* to designate efforts to make the human race better by "improved" breeding. Galton, a scientist and evolutionist, indicated that eugenics would favor the fittest human beings and suppress the birth of the unfit.

In the 1880s the word *anti-Semitic* entered German vocabulary.

III. INTERACTING WITH MODERNIZATION AND MODERNITY

A number of Christians became more than a little suspicious that "modernity" and "secularization" apparently went hand in hand. Certain materialists had made this specific claim. In 1874 John W. Draper published *History of the Conflict between Science and Religion*, in which he claimed that religion is an implacable enemy of reason and scientific advances. Historian T. C. W. Blanning has argued that some traditional elites, including Christians, actually experienced a "crisis of modernization" that raised doubts about their status in society. He noted that European society witnessed the "decline or collapse of its old political, religious, or social masters" and the emergence of intellectuals who sought to find "a secular substitute for or supplement to 'revealed religion.'"

At the same time, few Europeans could deny that aspects of modernization and modernity—advances in science and technology, for example—had brought genuine benefits to humankind. For many Christians who desired to uphold "the faith once delivered," discerning what stance to take toward modernity, especially as represented by science, constituted a perplexing challenge. Was it possible to be both an "orthodox Christian" and "modern"?

The problem was intensified due to the work of Charles Darwin. In 1859 an evangelical writer observed, "We do not see how to reconcile with our Christian faith the hypothesis ... that our moral sense is no better than an instinct like that which rules the beaver or the bee." Believers encountered scientists—some of whom were Christians of good standing—who told them Charles Darwin was correct: human beings had not descended from Adam and Eve but evolved from "ape-like" creatures.

How could Darwin's views be meshed with the teachings of Genesis 1 and 2? In *Darwin and the General Reader: The Reception of Darwin's Theory of Evolution in the British Periodical Press, 1859–1872*, Alvar Ellegard describes in detail the various kinds of reactions Darwin's books elicited in the British press. He points out that most of the British public assumed that the Bible is the Word of God and should be interpreted quite literally: "... the general accuracy of the Biblical story of the early history of the world, and especially of our race, was not allowed to be called in question." As judged by articles in the press, Darwin's arguments, therefore, genuinely consternated and angered some segments of public opinion while fascinating others.

A. Bishop Samuel Wilberforce: God the Author of the Book of Nature and Scripture

Christians such as Bishop Samuel Wilberforce (1805–73) were quick to claim that Darwin's teachings were incompatible with Christian revelation. In 1860 Wilberforce published in the *Quarterly Review* a well-crafted and lengthy response to the *Origin of Species*. He praised Darwin's remarkable research and engaging writing style, and he even indicated that "Mr. Darwin writes as a Christian, and we doubt not that he is one." Nonetheless, Wilberforce did not hesitate to criticize specific claims of Darwin as erroneous and examples of the scientist indulging his "fancy."

Wilberforce believed that God is the ultimate author of both the Book of Nature and the Book of Scripture: "He who is as sure as he is of his own existence that the God of Truth is at once the God of Nature and the God of Revelation, cannot believe it to be possible that His voice in either, rightly understood, can differ, or deceive His creatures." Thus the two should not contradict each other. In this light, Wilberforce argued that Darwin's application of the principle of natural selection to man, given its apparent conflict with scriptural teaching, must be rejected:

> ... such a notion is absolutely incompatible not only with single expressions in the word of God on that subject of natural science with which it is not immediately concerned, but, which in our judgment is of far more importance, with the whole representation of that moral and spiritual condition of man which is its proper subject-matter. Man's derived supremacy over the earth; man's power of articulate speech; man's gift of reason, man's free-will and responsibility; man's fall and man's redemption; the incarnation of the Eternal Son, the indwelling of the Eternal Spirit, all are equally and utterly irreconcilable with the degrading notion of the brute origin of him who

was created in the image of God, and redeemed by the Eternal Son assuming to himself his nature.

In October 1860 Wilberforce and Huxley engaged in a famous debate at a meeting of the British Association in Oxford regarding the merits of Darwin's theories. Huxley shrewdly portrayed Wilberforce, the cleric, as meddling in "scientific" matters beyond his training and competency. When Wilberforce asked Huxley whether he traced his ancestry from a grandfather or through a grandmother to an ape, Huxley coyly replied that he would prefer to have that kind of ancestry than from a man [by inference Wilberforce] "highly endowed by nature and possessing great means and influence, and yet who employs those faculties and that influence for the mere purpose of introducing ridicule into a grave scientific discussion."

B. Darwinism and the Search for Truth

The debate over Darwin's work took many turns. Some critics wondered if he was right in affirming that evolutionary processes moved toward perfection. Darwin had written, "And as natural selection works solely by and for the good of each being, all corporeal and mental endowments will tend to progress towards perfection." Why, they asked, did not "natural selection" sometimes provoke "devolution"? Other critics were dismayed by the fact that a number of its partisans claimed that Darwin's teaching demonstrated the truth of naturalism or provided a rationale for various forms of racism (Social Darwinism) and even eugenics (the elimination of inferior offspring).

For example, Ernst Heinrich Haeckel, author of *General Morphology of Organisms* (1866), introduced Darwinism to Germany. In 1899 Haeckel, a brilliant zoologist, published *The Riddle of the Universe*, in which he argued a case for monism, a basic unity between organic and inorganic nature. He denied the immortality of the soul and the existence of a personal God. He promoted infanticide, suicide, and the elimination of the unfit. Using a hundred lithographs drawn from nature (1904), Haeckel campaigned for the teaching of evolutionary biology in Germany as an established fact.

By contrast, many scientists proposed that Darwin's thought was not fixed but was evolving and a "theory." Nor did it mandate atheism or monism. In the *Ascent of Man* (1894), the American Henry Drummond wrote,

> The attacks on the Darwinian theory from the outside were never so keen as are the controversies now raging in scientific circles, over the fundamental principles of Darwinism itself. On at least two main

points, sexual selection and the origin of the higher mental characteristics of man, Mr. Alfred Russell Wallace, co-discoverer with Darwin
of the principle of Natural Selection though he be, directly opposes his
colleague. The powerful attack of [evolutionary biologist August] Weis-
mann on the Darwinian assumption of the inheritability of acquired
characters has opened one of the liveliest controversies of recent years,
and the whole field of science is hot with controversies and discussions.

Drummond was referencing a raging debate regarding the thesis that
traits acquired through contact with the environment could be inherited.

Drummond thought belief in God and belief in evolution are compatible. He criticized naturalists for claiming otherwise.

As the twentieth century dawned, the debate over Darwinism continued, with various parties claiming victory. Authors of two articles devoted
to evolution in *The Fundamentals: A Testimony to the Truth* (1910–15), an
American publication, claimed that Darwinism was "dead" and cited
European scholars to that effect. Many other commentators heartily disagreed. Some preferred Drummond's earlier perspective.

Under mounting cultural and intellectual pressures, those Europeans who wanted to be "modern" and "scholarly" and remain "Christian" sometimes attempted to make accommodations in the way they
expressed their faith. Early in the century, Protestant "liberal" theologians in particular recommended new ways of describing the Christian
faith. Friedrich Schleiermacher, for example, proposed that Christianity's warrant for "truthfulness" is found in personal religious experience
and not solely in arguments based on "reason." He criticized "Scholastic" Protestant orthodoxy that allegedly emphasized assent to verbal
propositions about God and not what he thought more pertinent, our
direct experience and consciousness of and encounter with the divine.

Later in the century, so-called Catholic "modernists" argued that
the Roman Catholic Church needed to accommodate its teaching to the
"advances" in knowledge made by biblical critics and evolutionists and
partisans of democracy. In 1910 Pope Pius X condemned modernism
as the "synthesis of all heresies."

Faced by dramatic changes—whether political, social, or intellectual—some nineteenth-century European Christians often felt the
need to define and defend their faith in new ways. These were not
always easy tasks. Those Christians who attempted to align the Christian faith with the "rules of modern scholarship" discovered that those
rules on occasion sheltered strong naturalist presuppositions. Roman
Catholic neo-Thomists and others who continued to emphasize eviden-
tial apologetics and theistic proofs were on occasion accused of promoting reason's rights as if they had not been affected by the Fall.

Anglo-Catholics and participants in the Oxford Movement felt no such need to adjust their beliefs. They sought to reaffirm the authority of their respective churches. They emphasized the critical importance of confessions, creeds, and Scripture. On July 14, 1833, the Anglican divine John Keble preached a famous sermon, "National Apostasy," that triggered the beginning of the Oxford Movement. Keble warned the British about the dire repercussions of forsaking the Anglican Church: "I do not see how any person can devote himself too entirely to the cause of the Apostolical Church in these realms."

Another leader of the Oxford Movement, Vicar John Henry Newman, who later converted to Roman Catholicism (1845), was concerned about subjecting Christian doctrine to human judgment as liberalism apparently did: "Liberalism is the mistake of subjecting to human judgment those revealed doctrines which are in their nature beyond and independent of it, and of claiming to determine on intrinsic grounds the truth and value of propositions which rest for their reception simply on the external authority of the Divine Word." Ultramontane Roman Catholics such as Joseph de Maistre and Louis Veuillot called on the Catholic faithful to submit more fully to the authority of a restored papacy.

IV. THE RISE OF PROTESTANT LIBERALISM

From the publication of Friedrich Schleiermacher's *Speeches to Religion's Cultured Despisers* (1799) to Adolf von Harnack's *What Is Christianity?* (1899–1900) and Auguste Sabatier's *Religions of Authority and the Religion of the Spirit* (1901) and beyond, "Protestant Liberalism," an international theological movement with distinguished representatives exercised a significant influence on many Protestant professors, pastors, students, and laypeople—especially in Germany, but also in Switzerland, England, France, the United States, and other countries and on the "Western" mission fields.

Protestant liberals by no means concurred with each other on every point. Students often disagreed with their teachers on specific issues, and various schools of thought and opinions emerged. Nonetheless, Protestant liberals believed in common that they offered to Europeans intellectually viable alternatives to (1) what some thought were the discredited theologies of "orthodox" ("Scholastic") Protestant Christians, and (2) what some thought were the subversive proposals of radical biblical critics.

A number of Protestant liberal scholars boldly announced that their theology captured the essence of religion—that is, our feeling (intuition) of total dependence on God. It allowed for the acceptance of responsible modern scholarship, including biblical criticism (and after 1859, Darwinian evolution), while it simultaneously remained faithful to essential evangelical beliefs. Some argued that they were recovering the true teachings of the historical Jesus as distinct from the religion about Jesus that Paul and the early church had created and that orthodox Christians mistakenly identified with true Christianity.

Orthodox theologians offered cogent criticisms of the various schools of Protestant liberalism. Adolf Schlatter (1852–1938), for example, not only called in question views of liberal colleagues, but argued that an inappropriate use of the historical critical method in biblical studies could foster atheism. Nonetheless, not until the publication of Karl Barth's *Commentary on Romans* (1919) did Protestant liberalism's grip on certain Protestant faculties of theology in Europe seriously begin to loosen. Barth specifically criticized the theology of Schleiermacher, whom he perceived to be the chief architect of liberal theology. At the same time, Barth honored Schleiermacher's greatness as a theologian: "The first place in a history of theology of the most recent times belongs and will always belong to Schleiermacher, and he has no rival."

A. Friedrich Schleiermacher: The Emergence of "Modern Theology"

Friedrich Schleiermacher.

Often hailed as the "father of modern theology," Friedrich Daniel Ernst Schleiermacher (1768–1834) was born into the home of a Moravian pastor in Breslau, Silesia. His father served as a Reformed chaplain at the Prussian court. Schleiermacher received a "Pietistic" education before attending the University of Halle (1787). There he followed intently debates between advocates of Immanuel Kant and Christian Wolff and became acquainted with the biblical criticism of Johann Salomo Semler, who was still teaching at the university. His reading fare was extensive, ranging from Plato to Spinoza. Schleiermacher in the main turned his back on his Moravian upbringing.

In 1796 Schleiermacher assumed the position of chaplain at the Charity Hospital in Berlin. He frequented the heady intellectual centers of Berlin, where his closest associates included Friedrich von Schlegel, Moses Mendelssohn, Henriette Herz, and other partisans of German Romanticism.

Schleiermacher was a brilliant theologian, a Greek scholar, a churchman, an eloquent preacher, and a German patriot critical of Napoleon's imperialistic aggressions. He attempted to create an innovative theology, set of ethics, and method of hermeneutics that took into consideration many of the issues raised by German Romantics such as Johann Gottffied Herder, by Kant, by Neologian biblical critics, and by unbelieving contemporaries. Beginning in 1804, he served brief terms as a professor at the University of Halle and the new University of Berlin, then ministered at the Holy Trinity Church of Berlin before returning to teach as a professor and dean at the University of Berlin in 1810. He also lent support to Frederick William III's efforts to create the Prussian Union (1817), which brought together Lutheran and Reformed Christians.

Schleiermacher was particularly impressed by the writings of Herder (1744–1803), who had rejected the claim of rationalists that reason is the chief criterion by which religion should be judged. Herder proposed that religion is primarily based in feeling, not reason. Schlegel panned partisans of the *Aufklärung* as "harmonious dullards."

In the early 1790s the state of German Protestant theology was far from auspicious, despite the fact that Germany boasted seventeen Faculties of Theology. The Neologian Semler said as much. One commentator complained bitterly that in the hands of Semler's disciples the doctrine of accommodation had become "the most formidable weapon ever devised for the destruction of Christianity." Until 1815, Neologian theology exercised a considerable appeal for German students.

Many young scholars opted for the study of philosophy. Kant's critique of "pure" reason had ostensibly undercut the value of metaphysics in general and deductive theistic proofs and the historical arguments for Christ's resurrection in particular. Kant had argued that we cannot know the *noumena*, "things in themselves" (what they actually are) but only their appearances, or the "phenomena." If Kant's views were accepted, the quest for knowledge of God in himself through the use of theoretical reason was likely doomed. Moreover, arguments from design for God's existence became much less compelling. How would we know that the design we think we discern in nature corresponds with any actual design in the "things in themselves"? After all, our mind possesses categories of thought that may be responsible for giving us the illusion that design exists when it in fact does not.

Schleiermacher, for one, was impressed by Kant's assessment of reason's limitations. By contrast, he was not persuaded by the German philosopher's attempt to rebuild theology on the basis of "morality," including our sense of "oughtness" (the so-called "categorical imperative"). In *Religion within the Limits of Reason Alone*, Kant had explained how we should live out our sense of oughtness: (1) "Act only on that maxim whereby thou canst at the same time will that it should become a universal law"; and (2) "Act as if the maxim of thy action were to become by thy will a universal law of nature."

Nor was Schleiermacher convinced by the arguments of orthodox Christians that the Bible is infallible. His study of the works of German biblical critics helped elicit this judgment.

At the same time, Schleiermacher worried about Johann Gottlieb Fichte's *Theory of Knowledge* (1794) and the "Atheism Controversy" it apparently fostered. Schleiermacher thought his unbelieving contemporaries had been so impacted by aspects of contemporary German culture that they evidenced little interest in religion.

In *On Religion: Speeches to Its Cultured Despisers* (1799), Schleiermacher as an apologist for religion tried to woo educated moderns of his day to reconsider its worth. He complained that they did not bother to consider religion's merit because they thought it lacked any persuasive rational warrant. He called on these unbelieving contemporaries to reflect on another kind of warrant for "religion": the feeling or intuition of utter dependency on the "One," or the "World All," a feeling that preceded any rational construction of dogma. The impact of Spinoza's pantheism on this proposal was possible, though Schleiermacher firmly denied any such influence.

In a later edition of his book, Schleiermacher identified the "World All" more closely with the God of Christianity. Theologian Jack Forstman indicates that *Speeches* "marks the beginning of the era of Protestant Liberal Theology."

Schleiermacher's greatest achievement, however, was the production of many well-written works in which he set forth his theology. He believed theology should be practical, that is, useful for the Reformed Church. He criticized the reduction of religion to simply knowing and assenting to a body of rationally deduced doctrines. Rather, religion embraces immediate feelings of the infinite. In *On Religion* he offered an important definition of religion:

> Religion is to seek this and find it in all that lives and moves, in all growth and change, in all doing and suffering. It is to have life and know life in immediate feeling, only as such an existence in the Infinite and Eternal.... Wherefore it is a life in the infinite nature of the whole, in the One and in the All, in God, having and possessing all things in God, and God in all.

In *The Christian Faith* (1821–22), he provided the most sustained

"Christianity is a monotheistic faith ... and is essentially distinguished from other such faiths by the fact that in it everything is related to the redemption accomplished by Jesus of Nazareth" (Friedrich Schleiermacher in *The Christian Faith*).

presentation of his theology. In this book he hoped to demonstrate that "every dogma truly representing an element of our Christian awareness can also be formulated in such a way that it leaves us uninvolved with science." Schleiermacher wanted to preserve Christian dogma from falsification by the contemporary scholarship of any age. He indicated that the essence of piety is "the consciousness of being absolutely dependent or, which is the same thing, of being in relation with God." *The Christian Faith* is generally recognized as one of the most important theology texts of the nineteenth century.

Schleiermacher's theology was Christocentric. He declared that "Christ alone is our Savior and we have to await no other." Christ is like us through an "identity of human nature," except that in him was "the constant potency of His God-consciousness, which was a veritable existence of God in Him." Sin is anything such as our sensuous nature that prompts us to forget about or hinders us from experiencing God-consciousness. Christ's role as redeemer is intimately associated with his perfect knowledge of God-consciousness. By grace he saves us. We have our "communion" with him as "the fully God-conscious man Jesus Christ." We are to partake in the life of Christ's church and have faith the way Christ did.

The historian Otto Heick observes, "For Schleiermacher, to believe is not to believe *in* Christ but to believe as Christ."

In time, Schleiermacher thought that his emphasis on religious consciousness meshed with the pietistic background he had earlier rejected. In 1802 he claimed that he had become a "Herrnhütter [Moravian Brethren] again, only of a higher order." His appeal to both his orthodox and nonbelieving contemporaries to reconsider religion as experiencing a "consciousness" of God was a helpful reminder. For the orthodox, it could help them remember that faith is more than assent to right doctrine. For unbelieving contemporaries, it could lead them to consider grounds for belief that exist other than those of rational argumentation.

At the same time, Schleiermacher's teachings launched a trajectory for liberal theology that departed from the beliefs of orthodox Christian churches. For all his "Christocentrism," Schleiermacher did not teach that Christ is perfect God and perfect man as the Christian creeds affirm. Moreover, Schleiermacher redefined the Fall, the nature of sin (lack of God-consciousness), and the nature of Christ's redemption (communication of God-consciousness to believers). He denied traditional definitions of miracles: "Every event, even the most natural and usual, becomes a miracle; or as soon as the religious view of it can be dominant. To me all is miracle." He discounted Christ's miracles as recorded in Scripture and dismissed any historical investigation of the resurrection as fruitless and thus of "no importance." He appeared to deny the personal nature of God.

Some contemporary critics were convinced that Schleiermacher's teaching regarding "God-consciousness" and "religious" experience was tinctured with pantheistic elements. Nonetheless, it gained a remarkable following among clerics in Germany. Friedrich Tholuck claimed that by 1817 the "pantheistic systems" of Schleiermacher and philosopher Georg Hegel had spurred a number of pastors to recognize "the insufficiency of the neological systems" (for example, the theology of Semler). They were attracted to Schleiermacher's writings and especially appreciated his portrayal of Christ.

After 1815, Schleiermacher and Hegel, gifted and creative thinkers both, competed with each other to dominate German intellectual life. Their deep antipathy for each other was well known. Schleiermacher blocked Hegel from gaining entrance into the Berlin Academy, and Hegel portrayed Schleiermacher as a hypocrite for defending Schlegel's controversial novel *Lucinde* (1799) with its ambivalent presentation of the sexual roles of men and women.

B. German Biblical Critics and Liberal Theology

Spokespeople for various schools of Hegelianism were particularly generous in their praise of reason. Georg Wilhelm Friedrich Hegel (1770–1831), who was philosophically an Absolute Idealist (a proponent of a monistic view joining being and thought), disdained Schleiermacher's emphasis on religious experience. In *The Philosophy of History*, Hegel proposed a grand dialectical scheme to explain all of history through the working out of "reason."

According to Hegel, the world Spirit or Absolute Idea passes through stages in history—that is, a thesis stage, an antithesis stage, and a synthesis stage that in turn becomes a new thesis stage. Hegel believed he could make rational sense of history's evolution. Moreover, he thought the end of this historical process would take place when Spirit/reality reached its final state of freedom or self-realization: "Universal history ... shows the development of the consciousness of Freedom on the part of Spirit, and of the consequent realization of that Freedom." Then Spirit attained "the highest unity with itself. This development implies a gradation, a series of increasingly adequate expressions of manifestations of Freedom, which result from its Idea."

The impact of Hegel's writings was enormous. Karl Marx was greatly influenced by Hegel's dialectical approach to understanding history, whereas a number of radical biblical critics believed his thesis/

antithesis/synthesis approach afforded an especially helpful framework for understanding the New Testament.

For his part, Schleiermacher did not uphold traditional views of the Bible's authority: "The holy books have become the Bible in virtue of their own power, but they do not forbid any other book from being or becoming a Bible in its turn." At the same time, he proposed that a truthful theology must comport with the "evangelical confessions, and, in the absence of such, partly by the New Testament writings and partly by the connection of a doctrine with other recognized doctrines." By contrast, he had little appreciation for the value of the Old Testament in constructing Christian theology.

Many biblical scholars did not appreciate Schleiermacher's supposed substitution of religious consciousness for Scripture as the authoritative source for doing theology. They preferred the approach of biblical criticism that Semler had advocated, calling for "free inquiry" to search out a canon within a canon (the Word of God from the Bible) by the use of historical criticism.

This approach received a boost due to the fact that between the years 1763 and 1817, at least thirty-one volumes devoted to the subject of biblical accommodation were published in Germany. Many advocated a Socinian form of accommodation (as distinct from an Augustinian version), which means that the biblical writers had "accommodated" their writings to the primitive cosmologies and myths believed by their contemporaries. The task of the biblical critic, then, was to separate out from the Bible what was properly the "authentic" Word of God from what was cultural dross owing to its origins in primitive worldviews.

As stated earlier (see chapter 13), this approach was further enhanced by Göttingen Professor Christian Gottlob Heyne and Heyne's student, Johann Philipp Gabler.

Likewise, Johann Gottfried Eichorn (1752–1827)—who admired Semler, calling him the "greatest theologian of the century"—distinguished between "higher criticism" and "textual criticism." Eichorn declared that some accounts in Scripture have mythical origins. For example, he alleged that biblical writers and other figures of the Bible had imported myths from Judaism regarding angels and miracles. He thought the texts of Scripture should be studied without referencing any doctrine of biblical inspiration.

Eichorn and Gabler realized that conservative Christians would not appreciate their approach to Scripture. Eichorn wrote,

> To strict supernaturalists and believers in revelation it is true that the use of this term [*myth*] will be offensive, but so also will the whole way of treating the Bible as mythological.... If, however,

you have already reflected without prejudice on the conditions of a divine revelation and have learned to distinguish between revelation and the documents of revelation, then neither the name New Testament myth, nor the thing itself causes any shock.

The scholars who followed this program of biblical criticism believed that their reliance on reason would permit them to identify more accurately the actual teachings of Christ unencumbered from "myths." In this sense they were "rationalists."

In *Contributions to the Introduction to the Old Testament* (1806–7), Wilhelm M. L. De Wette called for the study of Scripture using the same historical critical methods that are used in the study of secular documents. With his emphasis on discrete authors contributing to the Pentateuch's composition, De Wette is often credited with initiating new insights in Old Testament criticism that prepared the way for what later became known as the Graf-Wellhausen "documentary hypothesis."

C. The Tübingen School: D. F. Strauss and F. C. Baur

A number of those biblical critics who assumed that the Gospels include "myths" believed that the reader of Scripture cannot create a scholarly life of Christ simply by taking each story in the Gospels at face value. Instead, the critic should construct a life of Christ that discounts supposed myths about him found in the Gospels.

European scholars ranging from Schleiermacher to the French Catholic Ernest Renan (*The Life of Jesus*) attempted to write lives of the real Jesus. A cottage industry of "lives" written by liberals was jolted when Albert Schweitzer (1875–1965), author of *The Quest of the Historical Jesus* (1910), famously argued that many of these "lives" did not do justice to the first-century historical Jesus with his apocalyptic vision. Rather, they constructed a "half historical, half modern Jesus," reflecting the authors' own theological predilections and times.

In 1835–36 David Frederick Strauss (1808–74) of Tübingen University published early editions of *The Life of Christ Critically Examined.* Earlier he noted he had been "repelled" by reading Schleiermacher's lectures on the life of Christ. Strauss's own work devoted to the same topic was highly controversial. He assumed a Hegelian framework in piecing together who Christ was. Christ could not be perfect God in the flesh because he did not fully represent the movement in history of the Universal Idea to its final perfection or realization. What we often have in Scripture are myths that grew up about Christ—myths that are untrue and often block the reader from grasping the more beautiful real meaning of the text.

Orthodox Christians such as Ernst Wilhelm Hengstenberg, an influential theologian from Berlin, reacted strongly against Strauss's writings. Strauss was forced out of his teaching position at Tübingen for making such radical proposals. He also lost a possible teaching position at the University of Zürich in 1839 due to pressures from orthodox Protestants. In 1846 the famous poet George Eliot (Mary Anne Evans) translated Strauss's life of Jesus into English. In his later works Strauss eventually concluded that Christ's resurrection was "humbug."

Strauss's teacher, Ferdinand Christian Baur (1792–1860), had opted for views rooted in those of Hegel as a set of presuppositions to inform his study of the New Testament. He proposed that, whereas Peter viewed the gospel as especially a message for the Jewish and Judaizing Christian community, Paul thought the gospel should be presented to the Gentiles in a format free from the dictates of the law. Paul's approach had a universalistic, Hellenistic, and Greek emphasis. A clash ensued between Peter and Paul over their disagreement. By the middle of the second century, the early church arrived at a compromise ("early Catholicism") between the Judaizing Christian community and Gentile Christianity.

According to Baur, writings of the New Testament such as the Pastorals and John dated from the second century.

Whereas Baur attacked orthodox understandings of the New Testament, a number of other scholars launched criticisms of orthodox views of the Old Testament. For example, in 1875 Julius Wellhausen (1844–1918), a German Semitic specialist, published *Prolegomena to the History of Ancient Israel*, an influential work. He once candidly declared, "It strikes me as a lie ... that I should be educating ministers of an Evangelical Church to which in my heart I do not belong." Wellhausen denied that Moses wrote the Torah (Pentateuch). Instead, he purported that a clever forger had dispersed four documents through it, what is called the JEDP Theory: the J Document (Jahvistic or Jehovistic), the E Document (Elohistic), the D Document (the book of Deuteronomy), and the P Document (the Priestly Code). He also argued that the Jewish religion had evolved from a primitive idolatry (Yahweh viewed as a tribal deity) to a pristine monotheism (Yahweh viewed as a God demanding universal obedience).

Rudolf Kittel and other scholars believed they demonstrated the serious deficiencies of Wellhausen's forger hypothesis.

D. Albrecht Ritschl and the Kingdom of God

Albrecht Ritschl (1822–89), a professor of New Testament and systematic theology at Bonn and Göttingen, famously pointed out the weaknesses of Baur's approach to Scripture. Author of *Justification and Reconciliation* (1870–74) and *The History of Pietism* (1860–86) and, perhaps not insignificantly, Baur's son-in-law, Ritschl starred among a constellation of prominent liberal theologians at northern German universities.

In *The Origin of the Old Catholic Church* (1856), Ritschl broke ranks with Baur. He contended that Baur had not only skewed his presentation by basing it on a philosophical presupposition, but also exaggerated the depth of the divisions in perspective between Peter and Paul. Ritschl wrote, "In light of these indications, we are far from presupposing a fundamental conflict between Paul and the original apostles. If such a conflict had existed, they could not have had the common history which, according to the documents that no one questions, was theirs." Ritschl indicated that Baur had engaged in an "incomplete use of the sources for the historical period" he was studying. In addition, Baur had pushed forward the dating of some New Testament books too far, that is, to the second century. However, Ritschl did think a conflict existed between apostolic Christianity and Judaistic Christianity.

Ritschl's corrections of Baur helped to steer some German theologians away from embracing a particular philosophy or metaphysic as a standard with which their research and doctrines necessarily had to conform. Paradoxically enough, Ritschl himself was a "neo-Kantian" who, in following Kant's claim that we cannot have direct access to the *noumena* (the world of the spirit), concluded that we are thus excluded from a theoretical knowledge of God. Nonetheless, Ritschl believed that we can know God by the way he reveals his "saving influence" upon us: "We know God only by revelation, and therefore also must understand the God head of Christ, if it is to be understood at all, as an attribute revealed to us in his saving influence upon ourselves."

Ritschl urged learning about the Christian faith through the study of Scripture in the context of the Christian community, the church. He recommended serious reflection on the historical accounts of Christ's life. This does not mean, however, that a person's faith should be solely identified with the results of this historical research. An individual makes "value judgments" about who Christ is. Ritschl wrote, "If by trust for my salvation to the power of what he has done for me, I honor him as my God, then that is a value-judgment of a direct kind. It is not a judgment which belongs to the sphere of disinterested scientific knowledge."

According to Ritschl, there are two focal points to the Christian faith: redemption (divine grace at work) and the kingdom of God (the ethical work that Christians do). The Christian, reconciled to God by faith, is called to a life of perfection, including the pursuit of Christian ethical actions as a participant in the kingdom of God. This participation is especially accomplished by loving one's neighbor as oneself. This kind of ethical living contributes to the spread of God's kingdom. Ethics—particularly social ethics—are at the heart of the Christian message.

Among Ritschl's partisans were the American Walter Rauschenbusch, Wilhelm Herrmann of the University of Marburg, and Professor Adolf von Harnack of the University of Berlin. Like Ritschl, a number of Protestant liberals appeared to embrace a philosophical framework of neo-Kantian thought.

E. Adolf von Harnack and *What Is Christianity?*

Adolf von Harnack (1851–1930) was one of Ritschl's students and became professor of church history at the University of Berlin. Harnack valued Ritschl's admonition that any history of Jesus Christ should not be based on *a priori* philosophical or metaphysical presuppositions but on careful historical research.

In Harnack's day, interest in antiquities, Near Eastern geography, and archaeology remained high. Heinrich Schliemann's excavations at Troy (1871–73) intimated that Homer's "mythological" epics actually had some historical grounding. Sir William Flinders Petrie, a renowned specialist in Egyptian antiquities (excavating from 1880 to 1906), helped regularize the methodological guidelines for doing responsible archaeological research. Sir William Ramsay, the first professor of classical archaeology at Oxford University, after much research in Asia Minor published *St. Paul the Traveler and the Roman Citizen* (1895). This study provided valuable historical insights regarding Paul's missionary journeys.

Adolf von Harnack.

Harnack was born in Dorpat (now Tartu), Estonia. He benefitted academically from the learning of his father, Theodosius Harnack, an orthodox Lutheran church historian and professor of homiletics. The younger Harnack threw himself into the study of the historical origins of doctrine. He developed a special interest in Marcion and wrote a doctoral dissertation, "Source Criticism and the History of Gnosticism." He became convinced that Gnosticism represented the "acute secularization or *Hellenization* of Christianity" and had impacted the contents of the New Testament writings. From this premise he concluded that the Christian faith as presented in the New Testament is not identical with Christ's own teachings.

To recover the true teachings of Jesus, according to Harnack, a scholar must engage in the historical critical study of the New Testament and separate out extraneous elements added by the apostle Paul, Gnostics, and others. The scholar must also assess the history of "dogma," the beliefs within the Christian churches that emerged in the first four centuries and possessed authority.

Harnack came to the conviction that many of these dogmas do not necessarily reflect the teachings of Jesus. He argued that church dogma represents "the product of the Greek spirit rooted in the Gospels." For Harnack, then, the study of history provided a privileged means to ferret out the "essence" of the Christian faith.

After teaching stints (beginning in 1874) at the University of Leipzig, the University of Giessen, and the University of Marburg, Harnack was nominated in 1888 for an appointment as a professor at the University of Berlin. The Supreme Council of the Evangelical Church of Prussia contested his nomination. Otto von Bismarck, the Chancellor of Prussia, intervened and helped assure his appointment. In 1892 Harnack became embroiled in further controversy. He had offended the theological sensitivities of certain Lutherans such as Professor Adolf Schlatter by suggesting that the Apostles' Creed should not be used in the liturgies of the state church.

Harnack's massive works, including *The History of Dogma* (1886–89) and *The Mission and Expansion of Christianity in the First Three Centuries* (1902), won for him great renown. He served as the historian of the Prussian Academy of Sciences and as the director of the Royal Library of Berlin (1906). A prodigious worker, he produced a bibliography of 1,611 assorted titles. In 1914 many contemporary Germans viewed Harnack as one of their nation's premier intellectuals. He also acted as a confidant for Kaiser Wilhelm II and various chancellors.

The Swiss Karl Barth studied with Professor Harnack at the University of Berlin. Barth recalled that even though Berlin was a beautiful city, he found himself so enthralled by Harnack's teaching that he was largely oblivious to the city's charms: "I was so enthusiastic about him that I missed going to concerts and museums. In the midst of Berlin, I saw little of the city, doing only my work." Harnack's classes could draw up to four hundred students, so enthused were many attendees for his instruction. Barth became attracted to Protestant liberalism, as did many students from other lands, including the United States.

In 1900 Harnack's university lectures for the year 1899–1900 were published under the title *What Is Christianity?* (15 editions). Harnack intended that this book might elicit the interest of German students who thought "the Christian religion had outlived itself" or that contemporary German Protestantism was "a miserable spectacle." In this regard Harnack's goal resembled that of Schleiermacher, who, a century earlier, had published *On Religion: Speeches to Its Cultured Despisers* in an attempt to woo unbelievers to reconsider the worth of religion.

In *What Is Christianity?* Harnack provided in a popular format a synopsis of what he thought was an impartial presentation of the essence of Christianity. He cautioned that in history "absolute judgments are impossible." Nonetheless, he thought that by employing the science of history he could discover the essence of the faith: "... we shall employ the methods of historical science and the experience of life gained by witnessing the actual course of history." He indicated that "there can be no such things as 'miracles.'" He removed what he thought were the accretions the early church and Gnostics, later dogmaticians, and church institutions had added to the faith over the years.

Harnack proposed that Christ was a human being just as we are and was not God in the flesh as orthodox Christians proposed. Christ's very life was his message. The description of Christ as the Son of God simply refers to Christ's "consciousness" of God the Father: "The consciousness which he possessed of being *the Son of God* is, therefore, nothing but the practical consequence of knowing God as the Father and as his Father. Rightly understood, the name of Son means nothing but the knowledge of God." The gospel focuses on the Father and not on the Son: "Not the Son, but only the Father belongs in the gospel as Jesus proclaimed it. But the way he knows the Father, no one else has ever known Him, and he brings this knowledge to others." How Christ gained this special knowledge was "his secret," and psychology will never reveal the secret's contents.

Therefore the message of the gospel, according to Harnack, is the fatherhood of God, the brotherhood of man, and the infinite value of each individual soul. The Christian knows about the Father's caring love. The Christian is to pursue a life of caring for others, and in so doing, the Christian participates in Christ's kingdom. Harnack wrote, "Ultimately the kingdom is nothing but the treasure which the soul should possess in the eternal and merciful God."

Harnack defined the Christian religion as "simple" and "sublime." He claimed that "... it means one thing and one thing only: Eternal life in the midst of time, by the strength and under the eyes of God."

Not all who read Harnack's writings welcomed his perspectives on the nature of the Christian faith. His critics ranged from the Catholic modernist Alfred Loisy to his former student Karl Barth to his own father, Theodosius Harnack. The elder Harnack had once warned his son that he had departed not only from evangelical Lutheran orthodoxy but from the Christian faith itself: "Our difference is not theological, but rather one which is profoundly and directly Christian. Thus if I would ignore it, I would deny Christ as He who views the resurrection as you do, is in my view no longer a Christian theologian." By contrast, other Protestant liberal scholars, such as Otto Harnack, Adolf's brother, praised his work as facilitating a true understanding of the Christian faith, stripped of miraculous and dogmatic accretions.

F. Louis Auguste Sabatier: The Christian Faith Adjusted to Modernity

Protestant liberalism flourished elsewhere besides Prussia. For example, Louis Auguste Sabatier (1839–1901), one of Protestant liberalism's leading luminaries, taught in Haussmann's renovated Paris, France. Sabatier, a prolific writer, helped establish the Protestant Faculty of Theology in Paris and served as the school's dean. He also taught as a professor at the newly founded *École des Hautes Etudes* of the Sorbonne, where it was stipulated that religion was to be taught without confessional bias. He was particularly concerned about how the Christian faith might adjust to "modernity."

In his last book, *Religions of Authority and the Religion of the Spirit* (published posthumously in 1901), Sabatier argued that "traditional theology" (whether Protestant or Catholic) was based on the "method of authority." In his own day this method was rapidly being supplanted by the method of "modernity," one based on autonomous reason and "the modern experimental method" that "puts us in immediate contact with reality." Sabatier proposed that Christian theology must change its method from authority to that of "the modern experimental method" in order to remain intellectually viable:

> Yet this infantile method [authority] was vanquished on the day when Galileo and Bacon opposed to it the realm of physics, the method of observation and experiment, and when Descartes, in philosophy, subjecting all traditional ideas to a provisional doubt, resolved to accept as true only those which appeared to him to be evidently such.... If theology persists in subjecting itself to an ancient method from which all other disciplines have freed themselves, it will not only find itself in sterile isolation, but it will expose itself to the irrefutable denials and unchallengeable judgments of a reason always more and more independent and certain of itself.

Sabatier proposed that a central question confronting theology is whether or not "it may achieve a place in the consecrated choir of modern science, or whether it will be shut out for want of any common interest with them."

"The question is no longer of theology being the queen of the other sciences, but whether they will accept her as their sister" (Louis Sabatier).

Sabatier viewed his own form of Protestant liberalism as having fully adjusted to modernity's "empirical method." He rejected efforts to try and save Christianity by placing it in a separate compartment of "pure sentiment ... beyond the jurisdiction of science." Instead, he proposed that a proper "scientific" theology could withstand "reason's judgments" and be "modern." It could be accepting of Darwinism or any form of biblical criticism that is intellectually responsible.

Moreover, Sabatier was straightforward in his criticism of orthodox Christianity, which he claimed was based on the vanquished "method of authority." He proposed that the "orthodox doctrine of the divinity of Christ distorts the true character of the gospel of salvation not less than the rational doctrine, and is no less outside the authentic preaching of the Master." He went so far as to postulate that the doctrine of the Trinity contains a "root of paganism." He was critical of what he labeled the commonly accepted "Protestant" doctrines of biblical infallibility and justification by faith alone.

Sabatier claimed that the "Protestant" doctrine of biblical infallibility had been created by Protestant Scholastics of the seventeenth century. It had been challenged later, he said, by the likes of "Richard Simon, Jean Leclerc, Lessing, Semler, and the German theologians of the nineteenth century." He postulated that the "final crisis" for the doctrine in the French Protestant world took place between the years 1848 and 1860, during which period Edmond Scherer of the Oratoire Theological School of Geneva resigned his position in 1849.

Scherer was no longer able to uphold the doctrine in good faith. In his own day, Sabatier noted there were theologians who, unable to maintain the absolute character of the infallibility of the Bible—without which infallibility does not exist—were attempting to defend "a sort of indefinite and limited infallibility, a fallible infallibility which it is simply impossible to define."

Much like Schleiermacher and Harnack, Sabatier did not view Christ as God in the flesh. Rather, he emphasized Christ's humanity and experience of God-consciousness: "How could Jesus modify and renew the religious consciousness of his disciples, otherwise than by imparting to them the purely religious and moral content of his own consciousness, by making them experience what he himself experienced, in other words, by transforming them into his image and resemblance by the insistent influence of his whole being?" Christ invited his disciples "into the mystery of his own inward life, the sacred place where the Father and the Son hold communion, and reveal to one another their mutual love and faith. If he did not do this, Jesus did nothing and could do nothing, since he taught us no new religious doctrine."

Sabatier was convinced that his views of the Christian faith reflected not only Christ's own preaching but were commendable to modern contemporaries of the late nineteenth century. Only in the 1920s did Protestant liberalism lose its hold on the Protestant Faculty of Paris. In that decade, proponents of Barth's theology gained considerable influence among the faculty.

V. CONCLUSION: THE WANING OF EUROPEAN PROTESTANT LIBERALISM

Schleiermacher had professed a desire to shield Christian doctrine from external criticism ("uninvolved with science"). By contrast, many Protestant liberals later in the nineteenth century believed that adjustments of Christian theology to the canons of "modern" scholarship were needed if Christianity were to remain a viable and attractive faith for Europeans. Some embraced full stop the application of "modernity's" standards of autonomous reason and the use of the empirical method as worthy tools for making judgments about religion. They sought to foster "liberty" and "free inquiry" in theological reflection. This approach would allow them to proclaim that their writings were "scientific" and that theology is an academic discipline worthy of esteem by academics from other university disciplines. Some assumed that their studies in biblical and historical criticism had been successful in recovering the "essence" of the Christian gospel and in identifying the "historical Jesus."

The renowned Protestant liberal Wilhelm Herrmann (1846–1922), a teacher of Karl Barth and Rudolph Bultmann at the University of Marburg, believed the Christian faith could not be anchored in historical research due to that method's inability to provide assured results. Nor did Herrmann think it should be based on a belief in the infallibility of Scripture, a doctrine he attributed to Martin Luther: "Luther lived in an age when the authority of Holy Scripture as the Infallible Word of God and the authority of the dogma of the ancient Church enjoyed unquestioning recognition."

Herrmann continued, "It is true that the same reverence for dogmas is still among Protestants bound up in many ways with the mistaken conception of the Scriptures as an infallible law; but it is no longer a sure, unassailable assumption as it was for Luther." Instead, for Herrmann, Christianity's warrant should be found in the person and inner life of Jesus Christ spoken of in Scripture and in the life of Christ's church. Influenced by Ritschl, Herrmann indicated that "communion with God" through Christ constitutes the heart of a person's encounter with revelation.

Historians of religions had another quest. They sought to compare accounts of the Old and New Testaments with the histories of various ancient cultures. The Parliament of World Religions in Chicago (1893) gave a significant boost to the study of comparative religions.

A number of scholars went so far as to abandon completely the Christian faith. The skeptically oriented Franz Overbeck (1837–1905), a New Testament scholar at Basel and close friend of Nietzsche, dismissed Scripture as a revelation of God. He proposed that "every theology which … restrains the scientific freedom of its teachers abandons its scientific character." Wilhelm Wrede (1859–1906), a student of Ritschl and Harnack, fostered a kind of biblical criticism that assumed nothing divine existed behind the writings of the New Testament.

Between 1890 and 1914, liberal Protestant theologians enjoyed considerable prominence and prestige at German universities but a diminished influence among the German public. Sometimes their own personal spirituality and devotion commended their theology to students. For example, during his studies in Germany, the American J. Gresham Machen, who later became a New Testament professor and theologian at Princeton Theological Seminary, wrote to his father a glowing commendation about the theological acumen, beliefs, and Christian devotion of Professor Herrmann: "He [Herrmann] speaks right to the heart; and I have been thrown all into confusion by what he says, so much deeper is his devotion to Christ than anything I have known myself during the past few years." Given the attractiveness of Herrmann's teaching, Machen felt obliged to weigh liberalism's claims in a serious and systematic fashion, especially its various attempts through historical research to reconstruct the life and teachings of Christ.

Critics of Protestant liberalism included members of the laity who sometimes deemed its message inadequate to meet their practical, spiritual needs. Johann Christian Konrad von Hofmann (1810–77), associated with the Erlangen School of Theology, upheld baptismal regeneration, the Lutheran Confessions, and a "salvation-history" approach to Christian history. Appreciating some aspects of Schleiermacher's theology and contemporary views of historical consciousness, he wrote, "Theology is a free science only when what makes the Christian a Christian, his independent relationship to God, makes the theologian a theologian with a scientific knowledge and account of himself, when I, the Christian, am the innermost material for the discipline that I, the theologian, pursue."

But Hofmann was no radical spiritual subjectivist, nor a Protestant liberal. Resolutely Christocentric and Trinitarian in focus, he observed, "Where things go right, Scripture and the Church must present us with precisely what we discover from ourselves."

Conservative theologians such as Theodosius Harnack viewed Protestant liberalism's program as ultimately a serious departure from Protestant orthodoxy. In 1895 Adolf Schlatter sided with those German Protestants who criticized liberal theologians in Berlin for their condemnation of confessional Christianity. He observed, "If colleagues force the decision between faith in Christ and their 'science,' between the faculty and the church, the church being those who do not deny Christ, then in my view the apostolic word still applies today: 'I regard it all as refuse.'"

A number of other thinkers were likewise critical of Harnack. The Catholic modernist George Tyrell criticized Harnack's depiction of who Christ was: "The Christ that Harnack sees, looking back through nineteen centuries of Catholic darkness, is only the reflection of a liberal Protestant face, seen at the bottom of a deep well." Albert Schweitzer added, "Harnack, in his 'What is Christianity?' almost entirely ignores the contemporary limitations of Jesus' teaching, and starts out with a Gospel which carries him down without difficulty to the year 1899."

Professor Ernst Troeltsch (1865–1923), though a proponent of a neo-Kantian rationalism in higher criticism, argued that Harnack had miscalculated in thinking that the essence of the Christian faith could be established on the basis of impartial historical research in the biblical documents. The American Richard Niebuhr (1894–1962) scored Protestant liberalism with these telling words: "The romantic conception of the Kingdom of God involved no discontinuities, no crises, no tragedies, or sacrifices, no loss of all things, no cross, and resurrection.... A God without wrath brought men without sin into a kingdom without judgment through the ministrations of a Christ without a cross."

Machen concluded that the quest for the historical Jesus had ended in failure.

In 1923 Machen published *Christianity and Liberalism*, in which he characterized Protestant liberalism not as a variant form of Christianity but as an entirely different religion stemming from naturalism.

The outbreak of World War I in 1914 spelled the end of the "long" nineteenth-century old order of democratic, optimistic Christian Europe. The savagery of the fighting during the war appeared to falsify liberals' claims about civilization's inevitable progress and the inherent goodness of humankind. During his ministry in Safenwil, Switzerland, Pastor Karl Barth (who called himself a "country parson"), for example, found it genuinely difficult to preach Protestant liberalism's key themes from the pulpit.

In time, Barth launched an incisive attack against Protestant liberalism. He faulted the "ethical" and theological failure of Protestant liberal theologians in Germany to stand up against German militarism on

"I know scarcely any more brilliant chapter in the history of the human spirit than this 'quest of the historical Jesus.' The modern world has put its very life and soul into this task. It has been a splendid effort. But it has also been 'a failure'" (J. Gresham Machen).

the eve of World War I. In October 1914, ninety-six leading scholars, including Harnack and other liberal theologians, had signed a manifesto of German intellectuals backing the kaiser's military plans. Earlier, Harnack had helped draft the kaiser's speech declaring a state of war between Germany, France, and Russia.

Influenced by John Calvin and Søren Kierkegaard among others, Barth lamented the fact that Protestant liberalism with its focus on God's immanence and on personal religious experience was resolutely anthropocentric. Its focus was quite alien to the view of God's transcendence in biblical Christianity. For his part, Barth preferred to speak of an "infinite qualitative difference between God and man" and to recognize that God is "wholly other" — "the infinite aggregate of all merely relative others." Barth's theological method, therefore, had a vertically "from above" orientation. It highlighted God's transcendence, emphasized Christ, the living Word, as the self-disclosure of God, and proposed that Scripture becomes the revealed, written Word of God through the agency of the Holy Spirit.

In *The Word of God and the Word of Man*, Barth wrote,

> The Bible tells us not how we should talk with God but what he says to us; not how we find the way to him, but how he has sought and found the way to us; not the right relation in which we must place ourselves to him, but the covenant which he has made with all who are Abraham's spiritual children and which he has sealed once and for all in Jesus Christ. It is this which is within the Bible. The word of God is within the Bible.

Barth also took direct aim at the theology of Schleiermacher, the "father of Protestant liberalism": "With all due respect to his genius, I consider Schleiermacher a poor teacher of theology, because he seems dangerously unaware of the fact that man as man is in need, in desperate need; unaware further of the fact that the whole fabric of religion, and not least of the Christian religion, shares in this need; unaware finally, that to speak of God is a totally different thing from speaking of man in somewhat lofty language."

Later in his career, Barth acknowledged that Schleiermacher's influence was "incomparably stronger in 1910 than in 1830" and that the liberal theologian owned the "theological field" in the nineteenth century. Barth continued, "Nobody can say today whether we have really overcome his influence, or whether we are still at heart children of his age."

Barth also offered a negative judgment of Ritschl's accommodation to "modernity." "Nobody either before or since Ritschl ... has expressed the view as clearly as he, that modern man wishes above all to live in the best sense according to reason, and that the significance of Christianity for him can only be a great confirmation and strengthening of this very endeavor."

In 1919 the publication of Barth's own *Commentary on Romans* (*Römerbrief*) offered to European professors, pastors, and students the makings of an alternative ("Theology of Crisis") to Protestant liberalism. Barth did not completely turn his back on modernity. He accepted a chastened use of biblical criticism and believed that Scripture could contain "errors." At the same time, he opposed "natural theology." He refused to grant autonomous reason and the empirical method full sway in doing theology.

From Barth's point of view, some Protestant liberals had tended to do just that and sometimes fell prey to distorting Christian revelation and denying its intrinsic authority. He objected to Protestant liberals' attempts to understand the incarnation of Christ by relying essentially on the use of historical criticism. The project of Protestant liberalism was desperately flawed despite the genius of its eloquent defenders, including the great Schleiermacher, Ritschl, Herrmann, Harnack, and others. Barth did not think their attempts to adjust creedal Christianity (any of their denials notwithstanding) to the canons of modernity had necessarily well served the Christian churches.

On April 17, 1920, Harnack and Barth spoke at the same student conference in Switzerland and defended their respective positions. In correspondence with Barth (1923), Harnack, not at all welcoming of Barth's criticisms, accused him of being the leader of "despisers of scientific theology." In response to Harnack's criticisms, Barth drew up a piece titled *Fifteen Answers to Professor Adolf von Harnack.* He did not take Harnack's accusation lightly.

FOR FURTHER STUDY

Barth, Karl. *Protestant Theology in the Nineteenth Century: Its Background and History.* Translated by Brian Cozens and John Bowden. 1942. New ed. Grand Rapids: Eerdmans, 2002.

Blanning, T. C. W., ed. *A Short Oxford History of Europe: The Nineteenth Century: Europe, 1785–1914.* Oxford. Oxford University Press, 2000.

Helmstadter, Richard, ed. *Freedom and Religion in the Nineteenth Century.* Stanford, CA: Stanford University Press, 1997.

Reardon, B. M. G. *Religious Thought in the Nineteenth Century.* Cambridge: Cambridge University Press, 1966.

Smart, Ninian, et al., eds. *Nineteenth-Century Religious Thought in the West.* 3 vols. Cambridge: Cambridge University Press, 1985.

Smend, Rudolph. *From Astruc to Zimmerli: Old Testament Criticism in Three Centuries.* Tübingen: Mohr Siebeck, 2007.

Welch, Claude. *Protestant Thought in the Nineteenth Century.* 2 vols. New Haven: Yale University Press, 1985.

Yarbrough, Robert W. *The Salvation Historical Fallacy: Reassessing the History of New Testament Theology.* Leiden: Deo Publishing, 2004.

Nineteenth-Century Christianity in the British Isles

Renewal, Missions, and the Crisis of Faith

I. INTRODUCTION

During the storied, long reign of Queen Victoria (1837–1901), many British sang with gusto, "'Rule, Britannia!' Britannia, rule the waves! Britons never shall be slaves." After all, the reach of the British Empire was expanding rapidly.

By the 1850s the British economy was thriving. Britain was the leading industrial power and trading nation, controlling 25 percent of the world's commerce. British soldiers, governmental officers, and merchants were hoisting the Union Jack flag in new territories. Britain's Royal Navy was second to none on the high seas. British missionaries were taking the gospel to "heathen peoples" and promoting the values of "Christian" civilized Europe.

The English and Irish population grew from 20.9 million in 1821 to 27.4 million in 1851, despite the tragic loss of life during the Irish Potato Famine (about 1 million) and massive Irish emigrations (2.5 million). The Welsh population numbered about 700,000 in 1821. The Scottish population expanded from 1.6 million in 1801 to 3.2 million in 1861.

The English monarchy and Parliament constituted key institutions at the hub of political life of the "four nations" in the British Isles (England, Scotland, Wales, and Ireland). The governance of the four nations from London, however, sometimes proved to be a difficult and onerous task. The peoples did not all share identical "national" (or "regional") histories, nor have access to equal economic opportunities, nor enjoy a common religious, ethnic, and linguistic heritage. Even within the "nations," local ethnic groups and dialects existed. Appeals to disestablish the Church of England could inflame religious and political discourse.

The largest Christian bodies in England were the Anglicans (established Church of England), Dissenters, and Roman Catholics; in Scotland, the Church of Scotland, other Presbyterians, and Roman Catholics; in Wales, Anglicans and Non-Conformist Methodists, Presbyterians, and Baptists; in Ireland, Roman Catholics, Anglicans, and Presbyterians. English was increasingly used as the common linguistic coin of the realm, but Irish, Gaelic, and Welsh survived.

This social and religious diversity characterized in part the "nineteenth century"—a term remarkably made popular by the poet laureate Alfred Lord Tennyson. In 1846 he had read a reflection on the Bible he characterized as "very clever and full of a noble 19th century-ism (if you will admit such a word)." The expression "nineteenth century" was "admitted" as a derivative of a "19th century-ism."

Later generations of historians have sometimes preferred to use the expression a "long nineteenth century," dating the period from 1789 to 1914 or even from 1750 to 1950. Writing from a world history perspective, Edmund Burke III proposed that the "long" version was characterized by diverse "crises" such as (1) a long-term global crisis that ran through the late eighteenth century and permitted the rise of Britain as an empire builder; (2) a crisis of the years 1848–63, marked by the revolutions of 1848; (3) the Irish Potato Famine (1845–52); (4) the Taiping Rebellion in China (1850–64), in which 20 million people

---

MEMORABLE SIDE EFFECTS OF THE CRIMEAN WAR

As tragic as the Crimean War was, it bore two positive side effects in England that have long been remembered.

First, in his 1855 patriotic poem "The Charge of the Light Brigade," Lord Tennyson (who had been installed as the Poet Laureate in 1850) accented the Victorian ideals of duty and honor, recounting the bridge of British cavalry that had bravely stormed a Russian fortress in Balaclava in October 1854, with sizeable losses. The poem deeply moved the British public.

Second, in January 1856 Queen Victoria wrote a warm letter of commendation to Florence Nightingale, a nurse caring for British troops in the Crimean War: "You are, I know, well aware of the high sense I entertain of the Christian devotion which you have displayed during this great and bloody war, and I ... repeat to you how warm my admiration is for your services, which are fully equal to those of my dear and brave soldiers, whose sufferings you have had the privilege of alleviating in so merciful a manner."

Nightingale was the founder of modern nursing and began a nurses' school in 1860. In 1907 she became the first woman to be given the British Order of Merit.

died; (5) the Crimean War (1853–56), with Russia fighting against Turkey, England, France, and Sardinia; and (6) the American Civil War (1861–65)—the bloodiest war in U.S. history, measured by the percentage of deaths to total population.

In the late nineteenth century, competition for empire building heated up among the European powers. Commentators sometimes labeled these acquisitive efforts as *imperialism* or *colonization*. The word *imperialism* (1870) could mean the extension of a state's control by the acquisition (often forced) and political and economic subjugation of lands outside a nation's borders. *Colonization* could mean the settling and establishment of governance of those same acquired areas. Later on, the Russian revolutionary Vladimir Ilyich Lenin argued that capitalistic countries dependent on manufacturing were forced to pursue imperialism to assure access to natural resources and new markets.

II. BRITAIN'S DOMINANCE AS AN EMPIRE BUILDER

The defeat of Emperor Napoleon in 1815 signaled the end of the first French Empire. Despite the worrisome loss of the thirteen American colonies during the American Revolution (1775–83), Britain had replaced France as the dominant overseas empire builder and colonizer by the last third of the eighteenth century.

Three kings and one queen ruled over the United Kingdom of Great Britain and Hanover during its greatest empire years: George III (1760–1820), George IV (1820–30), William IV (1830–37), and Queen Victoria (1837–1901). The kings were not especially auspicious monarchs. George III, the grandson of George II, is often remembered for two things: presiding over the loss of the American British colonies, and eventually going "mad" due to porphyria, a hereditary disease. He was at times mentally confused and at one point adjudged insane, and by 1810 he was incapable of ruling. This led to his son's presiding as "regent" until George III died in 1820.

During the regency, George IV, the Prince of Wales and a convinced Protestant, was reluctant to allow Roman Catholics greater liberties. He was pleased that the English people customarily read Bibles in their cottages. Despite his religiousness and being initially a favorite in high society, however, George IV, nicknamed "Prinny," became a royal embarrassment. Many contemporaries viewed him as an incorrigible spendthrift and sexual profligate. His notorious lifestyle attracted scathing critical commentary.

In 1785 George IV had secretly married a Catholic widow, a union that would in principle disqualify him from ever becoming king due to the Royal Marriage Act of 1772. The marriage was later judged invalid. In 1795 he acceded to pressure and married Caroline of Brunswick, whom he later tried to divorce.

George IV's successor, King William IV, served in the navy. He lived with an actress, Dorothea Bland (stage name, Mrs. Jordan), who bore ten of his children out of wedlock. Then he married Adelaide of Saxe-Meiningen. In 1830 he became king. He helped force the Reform Act of 1832 through Parliament. The act doubled the number of voters to one million (often landowners).

Queen Alexandrina Victoria (1819–1901), nicknamed "Drinny," was small in physical stature, but large in heart. More than her three male predecessors, she witnessed the extraordinary expansion of the British Empire. Only eighteen years old when she became queen in 1837, she resolved to serve England well. She wrote in her diary, "Since it has pleased Providence to place me in this station, I shall do my utmost to fulfill my duty towards my country."

In 1840 Victoria married Prince Albert of Saxe-Coburg-Gotha (1819–61), a man of great culture. The couple had nine children. When Albert, her consort, died in 1861, Victoria was overcome by grief. For ten years she went into mourning and became known as "the Widow of Windsor."

Toward the last third of her reign, Prime Minister Benjamin Disraeli helped arrange for her to acquire the title Empress of India (1877–1901). In the years 1887 and 1897 (her fiftieth Golden Jubilee and sixtieth Diamond Jubilee), the British celebrated Victoria's remarkably long reign. They feted both their queen and their great empire. A few commentators compared the British Empire favorably to the vastness and power of the Roman Empire. Some claimed the sun never set on the British Empire, so widely scattered were its territories.

In the preceding eighteenth century, England's future as an aggressive empire builder had appeared much less likely. By 1763 England had wrested "New France" in North America (in eastern Canada) and portions of India from the French during the Seven Years War (1756–63; in North America, the French Indian War, 1754–63). She also governed the West Indies, the thirteen British colonies in North America, other portions of Canada, and South Africa and supported additional outposts throughout the world.

Nonetheless, critics questioned whether England, despite her formidable navy, could rule her colonies effectively from a distance of thousands of miles. The ensuing loss of the thirteen British colonies during the American Revolutionary War (1775–83) confirmed this premonition. As late as 1852, Disraeli (at that time already a prominent politican) lamented, "These wretched colonies will all be independent in a few years and are millstones around our necks." Ruling the colonies did appear too costly.

Worries about colonial rule did not hinder William Carey, however, who in 1792 boldly set sail for Calcutta, India, as a Protestant missionary. Nor did they keep the Scottish Protestant missionary Robert Morrison from heading to China via New York in 1807.

Some observers thought the early nineteenth-century missionary movement with its intention of bringing the gospel of Christ to the "heathen" might simultaneously project the political power of England. Others heartily disagreed. In the *Edinburgh Review* (1808), Sydney Smith argued that missionaries like Carey were "insane" and "ungovernable" and might thwart English empire building in India. He scoldingly added that missionaries were like "little detachments of maniacs benefitting us much more by their absence, than the [heathen] by their beliefs." He indicated that the "wise and rational part of Christians" understood they had "enough to do at home."

Historian Duncan Bell points out that the advent of steamship technology (perfected by Robert Fulton in the *Clermont* in 1807) and the telegraph system (perfected by Samuel Morse in 1844) began to "dissolve distance" and make missionary undertakings and renewed empire building more manageable.

These technological advances cut down the time needed to travel to and communicate with missionaries and government agents and to transport troops and provisions to far-flung corners of the world. In 1838, I. K. Brunel's SS *Great Western*, a paddle-driven ship, departed from Bristol and crossed the Atlantic Ocean, docking in New York City in fifteen days and nearly cutting in half the normal time by sail. Steamships had the added advantage of being able to travel upstream against the currents of rivers and thereby penetrate the interior of countries.

Especially after 1870, a second wave of European colonization gathered momentum. Europeans—with the English, French, and Italians leading the way—continued to acquire colonies throughout the world, especially in Africa and Asia. In the 1880s Germany belatedly entered the "scramble" for empire in Africa. For their part, the Russian government continued to expand its rule in the steppe regions and elsewhere, but it did sell Alaska to the United States in 1867.

By contrast, the Ottoman (Turkish) Empire suffered substantial territorial losses.

In 1900 contemporaries estimated that England's extensive empire encompassed a quarter of the world's landmass and nearly 400 million people. Yet the statisticians apparently did not include women in this figure. England's "colonies," "protectorates," and "dominions" and other territories stretched around the world. They included among others, the West Indies, Gibraltar, Australia, New Zealand, Burma, British India, Egypt, Canada, and vast portions of eastern, western, and southern Africa.

A. Western "Christian" Civilization

Along with other countries, the British entertained a conviction that western Europe's Christian nations were in fact the most powerful in military might, economics, and political institutions and that a Christian civilization is intellectually, morally, and religiously superior to non-Christian cultures. Professor W. G. Blaikie of New College, Edinburgh, promoted this perspective. In *Christianity and Secularism Compared in Their Influence and Effects* (1883), he attempted to fend off charges of secularists against Christianity:

> In our own time we have had some beautiful illustrations of the power of Christianity to civilize and elevate the most barbarous communities.... We fear no challenge when we affirm that in its purest form Christianity has fostered the ideas and encouraged the habits out of which all true civilization springs.

Many British appeared to believe sincerely that the essential goal of empire building was an altruistic one. As Christians they had the obligation to spread the gospel and Christian civilization, to evidence the love of Christ in compassionate deeds, and to "reform" the morals of the "heathen." Hundreds of missionaries mainly from artisan economic classes departed for "heathen" lands. Some were willing to sacrifice their lives, not thinking this cost too exorbitant for a disciple of Christ. At a meeting with students at Cambridge University, Scotsman David Livingstone (1813–63), in describing his own danger-laden missionary efforts in Africa, declared, "I never made a sacrifice. Of this we ought never to talk, when we remember the great sacrifice which He made Who left His Father's throne on high to give Himself for us."

In the early nineteenth century a debate ensued in both Scotland and England regarding the priority issue: Does "civilizing" come before "evangelizing," or should the reverse be the case? In 1829 James Montgomery of Scotland observed, "The wisdom of man says, 'First *civilize*, and then *Christianize* barbarians,' but the wisdom of man has proved itself foolishness in every experiment of the kind.... The counsel of God is the reverse; 'Go and preach the gospel to the Gentiles ... 'you will *civilize them by Christianizing them.*'"

As their armies and navies, businesspeople, and missionaries crisscrossed the world reinforcing colonial expansion, some British and Europeans on the Continent believed it was "the white man's burden" to bring Christian civilization to non-Christian peoples throughout the world.

In 1899 the British poet Rudyard Kipling captured these sentiments in his poem "The White Man's Burden." He was referring in particular to the seizure of the Philippines by the United States. Both Europeans and Americans sometimes viewed with condescension and disdain the race, customs, and civilizations of the peoples they encountered or forced to submit to their colonial control. Moreover, some began to turn away from describing Europe in the older tripartite manner of north, middle, and south. Rather they spoke of "western Europe" as a whole.

By the 1820s, several cartographers began to distinguish the "civilized peoples" of "western Europe" from the peoples of "eastern Europe" (the Slavs and the Russians), stereotyping them as barbarous and despotic. In *The Philosophy of History*, G. W. F. Hegel exalted Europe's allegedly preeminent place in world history: "The History of the World travels from East to West, for Europe is absolutely the end of History, Asia the beginning."

B. The Perilous Lives of the Poor

With notable increases in industrial productivity and scientific innovations and the perception of enhanced quality of university academic life after the 1850s, empire-building countries such as England, France, and Germany became the envy of many throughout the world. Yet

The poor and industrial area of Sheffield, England, in 1884.

large numbers of Europeans did not benefit from these advances. Surviving the challenges of daily life constituted their chief preoccupation.

This was particularly the experience of the politically voiceless masses—the urban and country poor and destitute, who remained generally neglected and sometimes despised by members of the middle and upper classes. In the nineteenth century the poor of the English countryside in large numbers poured into the cities in search of work. It has been estimated that in 1800, 20 percent of the population resided in cities; by 1900, 75–80 percent. In 1800 London had a population of nearly 1 million; in 1900, it was 6.5 to 6.7 million.

Often owners of workshops, factories, and mines paid paltry sums, thereby forcing workers to live in "row houses," bleak tenements, attics, and cellars. Suffering from grinding poverty, these people were sometimes called "white wage slaves."

Friedrich Engels, author of *The Conditions of the Working Class in England* (1844), characterized the working districts of Manchester, England's most notable industrial city, as subject to "filth, ruination and uninhabitableness." A large percentage of Manchester's workers died by the age of twenty. In 1840 the English average age of death was 39.5 years for men and 42.7 years for women. Mortality rates were high in other parts of Europe.

> "I wished to show in little Oliver the principle of Good surviving through every adverse circumstance, and triumphs at last" (Charles Dickens in a preface to *Oliver Twist*).

The poor were referenced in political tracts of Karl Marx and Engels as the "dangerous" poor. The poor also appeared in the writings of social reformers seeking to alert a "Christian" public to their agony, exploitation, and spiritual needs. Charles Dickens (1812–70) in *Oliver Twist* (first installments, 1838) and other novels and Victor Hugo (1802–85) in *Les Misérables* gave the poor a voice. The Poor Law Amendment Act of 1834 had forced indigent paupers (the infirm, older people, and children) to live and work for menial wages in regimented "poorhouses," where most died and exited unmourned in plain wooden coffins. In "A Walk in a Workhouse," Dickens described in graphic detail the pitiful struggle for survival he had witnessed within the somber walls of a poorhouse.

A number of novelists focused their principal story lines on the vicissitudes of members of the upper classes. Some commentators, however, did lament the huge discrepancies that existed between the living standards of the poor and the middle and upper classes. Evangelizing, educating, and caring for the physical needs of these people, especially the very poor, were daunting tasks for the churches. In 1835 David Nasmith (1799–1839) founded the London City Mission, intended to extend "the knowledge of the Gospel among the poor." Anglicans and Dissenters supported the mission. "Bible Women" distributed Bibles among the very poor for a shilling a piece. By contrast, on occasion members of the upper classes frequented slums for another reason: to seek out the services of prostitutes.

The causes for the social agitation and suffering of Europeans were multiple: dramatic inequalities of income between social classes; the turmoil associated with riots, revolts, and revolutions; the struggles to win universal suffrage; the difficulties of organizing labor unions; labor strikes; the exploitation of workers including women and children; the displacement of families from the countryside to harsh tenement life in overcrowded cities; sparse or deficient diets; and the outbreak of virulent diseases, such as cholera, typhus, and influenza. Rounds of violence occurred in Manchester at the so-called Peterloo Massacre in 1819, the Captain Swing riots in 1830–31, and more riots in 1842.

In Britain, gender bias was flagrant as women workers generally received a quarter of what men earned for similar work. Women sometimes turned to prostitution to earn money for the care of their children. Alternatively, women and children, sometimes half naked, worked long hours for pittances in dank and dangerous coal mines. In 1842 Anthony Cooper, Seventh Earl of Shaftesbury (1801–1885), a dedicated Christian, helped pass the Mines Act in Parliament that largely stopped this form of exploitation. Earlier, in 1833, the government had issued the British Factory Act, which stipulated that children aged thirteen to eighteen should not work more than twelve hours a day and children nine to thirteen no more than nine hours a day.

In 1848 the Queen's College for Women was established in London.

The Brickyards of England – Children Carrying the Clay, 1871.

C. The Emergence of the "Modern State"

Whatever their circumstances, many citizens in the wake of the French Revolution found their lives affected by a new political and desacralized entity, sometimes called the "modern state." Its sanction was often a democratic constitution and not a religious warrant such as divine right. This "state" began to keep civil records of births (instead of baptisms), marriages, and deaths, often taking over that function from the clergy. This was promoted in England and Wales with the Registration Act and the Marriage Act of 1836. Ministers could register non-Anglican Christian marriages with the government. State bureaucracies strengthened social infrastructures by providing postmen, police, and eventually schoolteachers. The state could levy taxes.

In some states, national unity was anchored, not in religious or dynastic loyalties to a prince, but in the use of a common language or in ethnic identity. In other states, nationhood was constructed from a "democratic" base of those who possessed the prerequisite qualifications to vote (male gender, wealth including property). During the Napoleonic era, however, some revolutionaries were spurred on by the vision of reestablishing a Catholic monarchy in Spain. Other revolutionaries of the nineteenth century—such as the Italian Guiseppe Garibaldi, a fierce anticlerical foe of the Papal States—sought to "liberate" their peoples from foreign powers and unify them on the basis of a democratic constitution.

D. Religious Currents in British Life 1789–1837

England was not unaffected by political developments and intellectual and religious movements taking place on the Continent between the years 1789 and 1837, that is, an era beginning with the French Revolution and culminating with the last year of the British "Hanoverian Age." The campaign to "restore" and bring stability to the life of the Christian churches during and after the French Revolution, the enormous energies devoted to Christian missions, and the spiritual revivals that affected France, Germany, Switzerland, and Scandinavia seemed to suggest that Christianity would remain the principal religion on the Continent into the foreseeable future. The Christian faith appeared firmly rooted in the British Isles as well.

Neither the anti-Christian writings of the *philosophes* nor the "dechristianization" campaign of the French Revolution had completely subverted the Christian religion's pivotal role in defining European culture. In the 1790s, most Europeans still thought in categories informed in part by the Christian faith. Historian Nigel Aston writes,

Mobilising a people in the 1790s required politicians to have recourse to religious commonplaces and slogans. It was, quite literally, the only language that many people understood and, irrespective of how much or how little they grasped the finer points of their Christian faith and the economy of salvation it offered them, it defined their culture as nothing else yet did.

In the 1790s the British public generally revered the Bible as authoritative and "infallible," that is, truthful and reliable given its divine origin. Some theologians did debate whether Scripture was "dictated" and "verbally inspired." Many British believed that salvation comes through Christ and that morality and religion cannot be separated. The Genesis account of God's creation of the world, animal and plant life, and Adam and Eve informed them of the earth's origin and their own. They generally believed God rules the universe providentially and was its creator.

Numerous Christians, whether Anglican, Dissenter, or Unitarian, read their Bibles with a goal of understanding current events. Even Joseph Priestly (1733–1804), the famous chemist and Unitarian minister, delivered a sermon, "The Present State of Europe Compared with the Ancient Prophecies" (1794), in which he explained how the French Revolution was foretold in biblical prophecy. It was commonly thought that particular biblical passages, if properly understood, predicted the emergence of a Millennium, a period of a thousand years that would take place in the "end days." Historian Tim Fulford observes, for example, that in the 1790s, as the French Revolution raged on the Continent, many Englishmen "expected the millennium to come in their own lifetime, preceded by apocalyptic destruction."

Revivals also marked the last decade of the eighteenth century. From 1792 to 1796 the Methodist preacher William Bramwell (1759–1818) and Anne Cutler (1759–94), a woman known for her prayer life, were much involved in the significant Yorkshire Revival. In 1797 James Alexander Haldane (1768–1851), a lay Presbyterian preacher, effectively ministered in sparsely settled back regions of Scotland. Likewise, a revival took place in Ontario, Canada, during the years 1797–98.

In the 1790s, revivals (led by Reformed pastors) also broke out in the Connecticut Valley in the United States. They became early manifestations of the so-called "Second Great Awakening" (late 1780s–early 1840s). This awakening encompassed multiple disparate elements: the widespread distribution of Christian literature; Reformed preaching in Connecticut by theological descendants of Jonathan Edwards; the faithful gospel witness of Methodist circuit riders; the occurrence of emotionally high-octane camp meetings in Kentucky and Tennessee (the "West"); stunning conversions and changed lives; waves of college revivals (as at Yale and Princeton); urban church revivals; and the physical phenomena called the "exercises" (running, singing, "the jerks") that overtook believers and unbelievers. There was also the revivalist preaching of Charles Finney (1792–1875), author of *Lectures on Revival* and a critic of the view that God alone determines when revivals occur.

Some contemporary observers attributed the awakening to the spread of a "heavenly fire." Others dismissed it as the purveyor of overheated religious enthusiasm. Still others viewed the awakening as a mixed spiritual blessing. In the United States the number of Methodists and Baptists multiplied dramatically during the first half of the nineteenth century.

E. Religion and Romanticism

During the French Revolution (1789–1799), a number of Europeans began efforts at "restoration." Restoration could mean different things to them: a quest to reopen churches closed by "dechristianizers," an effort to return the pope to a position of greater authority and respect in Europe, an initiative to reestablish a divine right monarchy, and a court battle to recover lost properties. For some it could also signify a heartfelt quest for meaningful values in an agitated world turned upside down by revolutions.

Various writers and artists embraced a movement called "Romanticism." As the French Revolution careened toward the Terror, these intellectuals, including poets William Wordsworth (1770–1850) and Samuel Taylor Coleridge (1772–1834), often experienced sickening feelings of betrayal and revulsion. The revolution's early promises of freedom and liberty had evaporated before the tyranny of mob rule and unwarranted death sentences mercilessly meted out by Jacobin revolutionary tribunals. "Romantic" critics of the revolution sometimes held the *philosophes* of the Age of Reason accountable for the revolution's "infidelity" and its murderous, bloody excesses.

A group of German philosophers, including Friedrich Schlegel (1772–1829), became convinced that rationalistic *philosophes* ignored the "true" object of philosophy, the study of the "inner mental life." The *philosophes* had allegedly downplayed the reality that humans experience deep feeling, and passions. Men and women cannot be reduced to matter or rational machines wrapped in human flesh.

A desire to explore the inner spiritual life and emotions of human beings became an essential aspiration of Romantic writers, painters, musicians, and theologians.

In 1801 Louis-Sebastien Mercier (1740–1814) observed that when you attempt to give meaning to the word *romanticism*, "you can feel it but cannot define it." Because of the disparity of beliefs among so-called Romantics, many students of the movement have been reluctant to establish a fixed body of traits that any particular writer, musician, or painter had to exhibit to qualify for the term. Instead, they propose "tendencies" that Romantics seemed to share in thinking about the human condition and their world.

The historian Bernard Reardon, however, does designate one trait as characteristic of the Romantic movement: "… [the] feeling that the finite is not self-explanatory and self-justifying, but that behind it and within it—shining, as it were, through it—there is always an infinite 'beyond.'" He cites the Romantic poet William Blake to sustain his point, namely, that an infinite reality lies behind what we can taste, touch, see, or hear. Blake (1757–1827) exalted art as the "Tree of Life" and castigated science as the "Tree of Death."

> To see a world in a grain of sand,
> And a heaven in a wild flower,
> Hold Infinity in the palm of your hand
> And Eternity in an hour.
>
>   (William Blake, from "Auguries of Innocence")

Many Romantics self-identified as one kind of Christian or another. While criticizing the supposed rationalistic excesses of the Age of Reason, Romantics often appropriated selectively the conclusions of thinkers of that same age. Thus the religious reflections of the Romantics about the Christian faith on occasion jarred more conservative believers who upheld traditional doctrines of the Bible's authority or other orthodox doctrines.

On other occasions, the religious reflections of Romantics soothed Christians, giving them comfort and reassurance. In 1827 the prominent Anglican divine John Keble (1792–1866) published *The Christian Year*, a popular book of devotional poetry. In a dedication to another book, Keble credited Wordsworth, the Romantic poet who emphasized "feelings," with inspiring people to consider "holy things": "To William Wordsworth, True philosopher and inspired poet, who by the special gift and calling of Almighty God, whether he sang of man or of nature, failed not to lift up men's hearts to holy things."

The poems and essays of Coleridge and William Cowper (1731–1800) also affected the religious "feelings" of their contemporaries in a deep fashion. Cowper, an agonized soul, struggled with depression and doubts about his own salvation. He worked closely with John Newton in creating a number of evangelical hymns.

Besides the Christian faith, Romantic intellectuals and artists drew their inspiration from many other sources: the "cult of sensibility" of the eighteenth century, the *Stürm und Drang* movement of the 1770s in Germany; the fairy tales of the Grimm brothers; the folklore of particular "primitive" peoples that supposedly revealed genuine truths about life; and medieval stories and tales of chivalry, love, and heroism at King Arthur's Court.

Romantics often looked to the writings of Jean-Jacques Rousseau (1712–78) and Immanuel Kant (1724–1804) for guidance. They often agreed with Rousseau that primitive nature is "good" and appreciated his rejection of "artificial" aspects of contemporary civilization. They often affirmed Rousseau's elevation of "interior sentiments" and conscience (besides reason) as a guide for our moral choices. They likewise thought that a linkage existed between human autonomy and the enjoyment of true freedom.

Often accepting Kant's criticism of reason's limits, Romantics thus saw the acquisition of knowledge as a more subjective enterprise than partisans of the Age of Reason had presumed. Influenced by Rousseau's concept of "interior sentiments," Kant had also proposed that we possess within us a "categorical imperative" that should direct our attitudes and actions toward our neighbors: we are to act as if what we do would become a universal law or maxim to be followed by others.

Romantics explored deep feelings not only of pathos but of paranoia. They associated their personal experiences not only with other living creatures but with nature in general. Not only did they revel in idyllic pastoral scenes and descriptions of exotic far-off places, but some, such as Mary Shelley, culled their fertile imaginations in crafting riveting tales of horror.

Mary Shelley (1797–1851), the daughter of the feminist Mary Wollestonecraft and William Goodwin, was the wife of the Romantic poet Percy Bysshe Shelley. The Romantic poet Lord George Byron urged Mary to write a good ghost story for a competition. Familiar with gothic novels, Mary indicated that she wanted her story to speak to "the mysterious fears of our nature and awaken thrilling horror—one to make the reader dread to look around, to curdle the blood, and quicken the beatings of the heart." The novel *Frankenstein* (1818) more than fit the billing. Frankenstein, a frightening character, has aroused sentiments of "thrilling horror" in generations of readers.

Other Romantics included German writers Johann Wolfgang von Goethe, Friedrich Wilhelm Joseph von Schelling, and George Wilhelm Friedrich Hegel; the Scottish writers Robert Burns and Sir Walter Scott; the English landscape painters John Constable and Joseph M. W. Turner; the French writers François-René de Chateaubriand and Victor

Hugo; the Swiss Madame Germaine de Staël; and musicians such as the Frenchman Louis-Hector Berlioz.

A number of Protestant theologians, including Friedrich Schleiermacher, emphasized themes that had affinities with those of the Romantic movement.

F. Societal Unrest

Despite societal unrest and the presence of radical political groups, England did not experience the equivalent of a French Revolution. Talk of revolt was fairly common, however. Bread prices soared between 1790 and 1801 and stoked anxieties. Threats surfaced in handbills: "Peace and a Large Bread or a King without a Head." In 1792 a worried George III laid down a "Proclamation against Seditious Writings." Some members of the government were fearful that English radical partisans of the French Revolution and advocates of certain forms of millennialism might incite the lower classes to revolt.

In 1792 Richard Brothers prophesied that England's war with France would precede the collapse of monarchy in Europe. In 1795 Brothers's millennial assertions struck even closer to home: King George III was going to surrender his crown to Brothers; London was Babylon and would be destroyed; only those who followed Brothers to Jerusalem, where the millennium would ensue, could be saved.

The English government arrested Brothers and ultimately placed him in an asylum. But one such arrest could not dampen a desire of the English people to understand Scripture's teaching about the "last things." As historian W. H. Olivier notes, in the 1790s interest in millennial thinking affected every social group in England "from landed proprietors to out-of-work factory hands."

Worries about conspiracies by the likes of Brothers were compounded by fears that those Dissenters (especially Methodists) and Roman Catholics who remained without full civil rights might be lured into rebellious activity against the English government. In 1797 radical United Irishmen who sought to establish an Irish independent republic were pursuing conspiratorial contact with Irish immigrants in England and Scotland. The English put down an Irish rebellion (1797–98). Ireland dutifully joined England as part of the United Kingdom of Great Britain and Ireland in 1800.

Many English adjudged that their constitution, in backing the established Anglican Church, served as a bulwark against the spread of revolutionary fervor. In 1828 Reverend Stephen Cassan condemned the Dissenters' appeals for disestablishment and their criticism of "constituted authorities" as "schismatic," "sin," "rebellion," and "spiritual republicanism." Other pastors suspected that "Unitarians, deists and Infidels" were behind the drive to get rid of the Corporation and Test Acts.

In 1838 William Gladstone (1809–98), a future prime minister, published *The State in Its Relations to the Church*, in which he articulated a fairly common opinion of Anglicans regarding their church's foundational position in English society: "The Established Church was the conscience of the English state, and that State was bound to give an active, informed, consistent, and exclusive financial and general support to the Anglican religion which was of the purest and most Apostolic descent." Gladstone, an evangelical, in time became a Broad Church Anglican.

III. ANGLICAN RENEWAL AND DEBATE

In the late eighteenth century some 13,500 priests ministered as vicars or rectors in local Anglican parishes. Clusters of local parishes were organized into "deaneries." A bishop presided over a diocese made up of parishes. Suffragan bishops served as assistants to certain bishops. Above the bishops in rank were the archbishop of York and the archbishop of Canterbury. The archbishop of Canterbury ruled as the primate of all England. Above him in authority were the king or queen, the supreme governor of the Church of England, the established church of the land.

The Anglican clergy and laity of the nineteenth century included various groups, ranging from members of the Oxford Movement to Evangelicals to "Broad Churchmen" (discussed later), associated with an openness to biblical criticism. Many Anglicans agreed that to give Dissenters or Non-Conformists, Roman Catholics, and Jews full civil and religious rights could ultimately displace the Anglican Church from its central role in society and could be politically destabilizing. They also realized that not to afford members of these groups their civic liberties might tempt them to participate in subversive activity in order to gain these rights through force of arms.

Some Anglican clergy candidly acknowledged that their church did not enjoy popular favor due to the glaring disparity between the wealthy and the poor and the common practice of upper clergy to absent themselves from their parishes. In the 1820s a number of members of Parliament believed the Anglican Church needed serious reform. An Ecclesiastical Commission of 1835–1836 that included Archbishop of Canterbury William Howley helped initiate a set of significant reforms for the church.

Earlier, a concern about a potential revolt of Catholics in Ireland created the backdrop for the passage of the Roman Catholic Relief Act in 1829. This act allowed Roman Catholics to sit as members of Parliament. At the same time, it frightened Anglican Ultramontanes—

"Ultras"—and even writers like Coleridge, who believed the dominant role of the established church had now been undermined. Some wondered why King George IV had not more forcefully criticized this measure. After all, his coronation vow included these words: "I will, to the utmost of my power, maintain the laws of God, the true profession of the gospel, and the Protestant reformed religion established by law ..." Fears were further deepened by news of the revolution in France in 1830. The Anglican vicar John Henry Newman wrote, "The effect of this miserable French affair will be great in England."

High Church Anglicans called for a renewed commitment of the English people to the Anglican Church. John Keble's attention-grabbing sermon, "National Apostasy," in 1833 chastised Parliament's decision to eliminate ten of the twenty-two Anglican parishes in Ireland. He thought the state had overstepped its prerogatives in interfering in the life of the church. Things soon went from bad to worse from Keble's point of view.

Vicar Newman deemed Keble's sermon the launch point of the Oxford Movement: "I have ever considered, and kept the day, as the start of the religious movement of 1833."

A. The Oxford (Tractarian) Movement

Members of the Oxford Movement, or "Tractarians," urged the English people to recommit themselves to the "apostolic" Anglican Church. The group's leaders included John Keble, John Henry Newman (1801–90), and Oxford scholars Richard Froude (1803–36) and Edward B. Pusey (1800–1882). They published a series of ninety tracts in which they reiterated their contention that the Anglican Church was historically linked ("Our Apostolical Descent") to the one holy, apostolic church founded by Jesus Christ. Anglican bishops were the "Successors of the Apostles." Froude introduced "High Church" liturgies and worship practices into the Anglican Church.

By the 1840s, a number of High Church Anglicans warmly endorsed an Anglo-Catholic ritualism and emphasis on Christ's real presence in the Eucharist. Indeed, Pusey's sermon "The Holy Eucharist, a Comfort to the Penitent" (1843) promoted support for "high" sacramental theology. At the same time, Pusey esteemed the evangelicals' emphasis on vital Christian piety. The Tractarians often agreed with evangelicals in their criticism of Protestant liberals.

Some evangelical critics thought the Oxford Movement fostered a belief in baptismal regeneration, a teaching they said did not comport with the doctrine of justification by faith alone affirmed in the Thirty-nine Articles. They claimed that the "High Church" Anglo-

Catholicism of the Oxford Movement constituted a stepping-stone to Roman Catholicism. In *Tract 90* (1841), Newman tried to answer this criticism by claiming that Roman Catholic doctrine was compatible with the *Thirty-nine Articles*.

Four years later, Newman converted to the Roman Catholic faith. A number of other High Church Anglicans, including Henry Manning and two sons of William Wilberforce, did so as well. With Newman's conversion, the Tractarian Movement weakened substantially.

B. The Evangelical Anglicans

Members of the "Evangelical Party" within the Anglican Church were often known for their "experimental piety," their belief in the final authority of Scripture, their moral seriousness (a desire to be like Christ), and their view of conversion ("the great change") linked to the doctrine of justification by faith alone. They promoted hymn singing within the Anglican Church. Their zeal for missions and social reform was noteworthy. In many regards they resembled their evangelical predecessors of the eighteenth century, John and Charles Wesley and George Whitefield.

John Venn (1759–1813) and his son, Henry Venn (1796–1873), gave significant leadership to the Evangelical Anglicans. John Venn served as the pastor in Clapham, a village near London. His evangelical parishioners included some members of the "Clapham Sect" (or "Clapham Circle"), who were generally quite affluent. In the 1790s they began to meet at the well-appointed home of Henry Thorton, a banker. The group of twelve included, among others, William Wilberforce, the renowned social reformer; Zachary Macaulay, a convinced foe of slavery; Charles Grant, a director of the East India Company; James Stephen; and Hannah More. Not all were Anglicans.

This group energetically organized and helped finance religious societies and missions and educational initiatives. They engaged in social reform such as the antislavery campaign in Parliament. At age forty-five Henry Venn began to serve as the secretary of the Church Missionary Society. Henry Thorton's book on prayer was widely distributed among Christians. Critics of the evangelicals sometimes accused them of religious "enthusiasm" and claimed they lacked loyalty to the Anglican Church.

C. Evangelical Identity

Faced by the challenge of the Tractarian Movement and the rise of Anglo-Catholicism, a number of evangelicals such as John James

(English) and Robert Baird (American) sought to forge a "great Protestant union" of evangelical Christians worldwide. In 1845 they initiated steps leading to the formation of the Evangelical Alliance. On August 19, 1846, more than 900 delegates from fifty countries met in London for the alliance's first major gathering. Many hoped to dispel "sectarianism."

The delegates agreed that the purpose of their alliance was "to enable Christians to realize in themselves and to exhibit to others that a living and everlasting union binds all true believers together in the fellowship of the Church." The "allies" accepted a broad Protestant creed of nine "cardinal principles," including the divine inspiration, authority, and sufficiency of the Bible and justification by faith alone. They did not want to create, however, an international ecclesiastical body with juridical, funded power to enforce compliance on "subsidiary" doctrines. Rather, members were "free to hold [their] own views in regard to subsidiary principles."

Disputes between American and English delegates over the legitimacy of slavery hobbled the ecumenical enterprise as an international entity. The Americans resented the pointed scolding they received from the British regarding slavery. Over time, various countries did establish their own "evangelical alliances."

Evangelicals gained further strength in the Anglican Church. In 1848 John Sumner became the first evangelical archbishop of Canterbury. Two years later, a ruling permitted Reverend George Gorham to serve as an Anglican cleric even though he did not affirm a belief in baptismal regeneration; many High Church Anglicans were perturbed by this decision. In 1853 W. J. Conybeare claimed that nearly 32 percent of the Anglican clergy had evangelical convictions.

In 1877 Bishop J. C. Ryle (1816–1900), a popular Anglican writer and an evangelical, provided a more detailed doctrinal definition of the evangelical faith, explaining five doctrines: (1) "The absolute supremacy of Holy Scripture," (2) "the doctrine of human sinfulness and corruption," (3) "the work and office of Jesus Christ," (4) "the inward work of the Holy Spirit in the heart of man," and (5) "the outward and visible work of the Holy Ghost in the life of man." Ryle claimed these beliefs conformed to the *Thirty-nine Articles* of the Anglican Church and the teachings of the Protestant Reformers.

> "A divided, alienated church cannot convert the world to Christ.... It is Satan's object to keep us separated at home, that he may reign unmolested abroad" (Vicar John James).

D. Anglican Social Reformers

Societal reform stood out as a particular concern of evangelical Anglicans such as William Wilberforce (1759–1833), who had become a member of Parliament at age twenty. During two "Grand Tours" in

"Surely the principles as well as the practice of Christianity are simple, and lead not to meditation only but to action" (William Pitt the Younger).

Europe (1784–85), Wilberforce's traveling companion, Isaac Milner, introduced him to the evangelical faith. They discussed books such as Philip Doddridge's *The Rise and Progress of Religion* (1745). Wilberforce came to saving faith in Christ.

In 1787, at the urging of his political associate and Christian friend, William Pitt the Younger (1759–1806), Wilberforce began a lengthy struggle as a member of Parliament to end the international slave trade. He was encouraged to persevere in this struggle by John Wesley and a number of Quakers. In *Thoughts on Slavery* (1774), Wesley had written, "I absolutely deny all slaveholding to be consistent with any degree of natural justice." For his part, Wilberforce, despite suffering bouts of physical pain, wrote in his diary (1787), "God has put before me two great objects: the Abolition of the Slave Trade and the reformation of manners."

On May 12, 1789, in the House of Commons, Wilberforce launched an opening, verbal broadside against the slave trade, what he condemned as the "foulest blot that ever stained our national character." Eventually, on February 23, 1807, Parliament ruled the slave trade illegal. In 1833, just before Wilberforce's death, Parliament passed the Abolition of Slavery Act forbidding the slave trade in the British Empire. In the United States and elsewhere, however, it persisted. Historian David Davis goes so far as to claim that slavery was "the central fact of American history."

Wilberforce sought vigorously to reform the morals of the upper classes. In 1787 he formed the Proclamation Society against Vice and Immorality and ten years later published *A Practical View of the Prevailing Religious System of Professed Christians in the Higher and Middle Classes in This Country Contrasted with Real Christianity*. In this book he called on "nominal" Christians in the upper classes of England to match their everyday morals with their outward religious profession.

Between 1782 and 1832 at least one hundred evangelicals served as members of the House of Commons and another one hundred in the House of Lords. Like Wilberforce, many believed they could help change the nation's morality by applying their religious principles to the world of politics. Wilberforce's own virtuous example inspired them. Evangelicals also organized groups designed to address England's social and economic ills.

Wilberforce supported financially the efforts of Hannah More (sometimes called the "Queen of Methodists") and her sister Martha to minister to the physical, spiritual, and educational needs of England's poor in the rural countryside. Hannah, an evangelical poet and social reformer, came from a home of considerable wealth. She criticized the lax morals of her contemporaries in *Thoughts on the Importance of the*

Manners of the Great to General Society (1788). She also fought against the slave trade. She established a home for poor children. Her *Cheap Repository Tracts*, with a circulation in the millions, encouraged members of the lower classes to embrace the evangelical faith and its morals. She supported local Sunday schools. Much like Edmund Burke, she attempted to counter any appeals of radicals to entice the English people to engage in seditious political activity.

E. Cambridge University: The Ministry of Charles Simeon

Whereas Oxford University was linked to the Tractarian Movement, Cambridge University became associated with evangelical students much influenced by the life and ministry of the Anglican Charles Simeon (1759–1836). In 1779, as a student at Cambridge, Simeon came to an evangelical understanding of salvation: "What! May I transfer my guilt to another? Has God provided an offering for me, that I may lay my sins on another? Then I will not bear them any longer."

Soon after his Anglican ordination, Simeon became a priest at Holy Trinity Church in Cambridge, where he ministered for fifty-four years. On one occasion Simeon declared, "He is no Christian who does not see the hand of Christ constantly."

Simeon also served as a Fellow at King's College, where his teaching, his godly example of a man of prayer, and his desire for evangelical unity affected many students—who adopted the name "Sims" or "Simeonites." They founded a branch of the British and Foreign Bible Society at Cambridge and the Jesus Lane Sunday School for young boys. In 1848 evangelical students formed a group that in 1854 became the Cambridge University Prayer Union. Years after Simeon's death in 1836, many still cherished and appreciated his Christian example.

F. Dissenters (Non-Conformists)

In the 1790s, Dissenters continued to object strenuously to the privileged status that the Anglican Church enjoyed as England's established state church. In that decade, Methodists, who by 1795 had more distinctly separated from the Anglican Church, added their strong voice to the complaints of other Non-Conformist Presbyterians, Quakers, Baptists, Congregationalists, and Unitarians. Some evangelical Dissenters based their calls for disestablishment on their congregational ecclesiology.

The most vocal Dissenters were probably the Unitarians Richard Price and Joseph Priestley. They opposed Edmund Burke's apology for the Anglican Church's position as the established church. Because Dissenters were not permitted entrance to attend Cambridge or Oxford, many attended dissenting academies, some of which had allegedly become nurseries for "subversive doctrines and arguments" (Burke's judgment) due to Joseph Priestley's influence on their curriculum.

Methodists emerged as one of the fastest-growing dissenting groups. Between the 1780s and the 1820s their numbers climbed rapidly from 80,000 to nearly 220,000. Thomas Coke founded Methodist missions in the British West Indies after 1786 and in Sierra Leone in 1811. Methodists split into various denominations (the Methodist New Connection, 1797; the Primitive Methodists, 1811) due to internal debates. Sometimes upper-class Anglicans accused Methodists of seditious activity, of purveying religious "enthusiasm," and of heeding unauthorized (non-Anglican) preachers. On occasion, the Anglican Wilberforce attempted to defend the Methodists from their accusers.

Despite serious opposition, many Methodist men and women continued to attend cottage prayer meetings and encourage gospel preaching, demonstrate love for the poor, and perform good deeds in a sacrificial fashion. John Wesley had provided a model in this regard. He gave to the poor large sums of money that he had earned from his publications. Moreover, he had not been shy in providing strong counsel about the use of wealth. To a rich Methodist woman he wrote, "Go and see the sick in their own poor little hovels. Take up your cross, woman, remember the faith.... Put off the gentlewoman."

Methodists collected funds for the poor in their chapels. They founded orphanages and Sunday schools, visited the prisons, and began medical programs. Not surprisingly, many laboring poor turned to the Methodists for spiritual solace, community fellowship, material aid, and a heightened sense of respect for women.

By the 1820s Dissenters constituted close to 20 percent of the British population. Some of their leaders urged the suppression of the Test and Corporation Acts that restricted Dissenters' access to certain employments and narrowed their educational choices. In 1828 these laws were finally repealed. The Reform Act of 1832 also indirectly permitted a number of Dissenters of means to enjoy greater political participation. Dissenters often supported efforts to extend greater rights to Jews.

G. Roman Catholics: An Expansion of Influence

Not only were Protestant Dissenters anxious to see the end of the privileged status of the Anglican Church, Roman Catholics sought this as well. They lived under onerous restrictions until the Roman Catholic Relief Act of 1829. Then their overall situation improved. In 1845 John Henry Newman, a master wordsmith and theologian, converted from

High Church Anglicanism to Roman Catholicism. He commented, "I would not have left the English Church had I thought it possible for me to remain in God's favor and remain a member of it." He urged others like the Marquise de Salvo to convert: "I earnestly exhort you to join the Catholic Church. It is necessary for your salvation."

In the same year, Newman published a seminally important work, *An Essay on the Development of Christian Doctrine.* He argued that the church's doctrine could evolve from the purity of the deposit of faith without taking on corruptions: "A living idea becomes many but remains one." Newman believed this approach to tradition and Christian truth could explain why aspects of Catholic theology might have a different doctrinal presentation from the teachings of the early church and yet constitute innovative theological clarifications, not heretical "corruptions."

In 1851 Newman began serving as the Rector of the Catholic University of Ireland. In the *The Idea of a University*, he argued that if the study of special revelation is excluded from the curriculum of a university, "you will break up into fragments the whole circle of secular knowledge." In 1864 he defended himself against cleric and novelist Charles Kingsley in *Apologia pro Vita sua.* In 1879 Newman became a cardinal. While open to a circumspect use of new critical methods in scholarship, Newman criticized "Liberalism" — "the doctrine that there is no truth in religion, but that one creed is as good as another." At the same time, he was hesitant to affirm the inerrancy of Scripture. Rather, he argued "that the issue of inspiration is for doctrine and morals."

The second half of the nineteenth century witnessed an expansion of the influence of the Roman Catholic Church in British society. In 1850 the so-called "Papal Aggression" of Pope Pius IX occurred. He divided England into Catholic dioceses, and members of the Catholic hierarchy returned. Nicholas Wiseman (1802–65), a cardinal, became the Catholic archbishop of Westminster (London). The number of convents increased, with 77 of the 114 convents in England founded in the last quarter of the century. The nuns devoted themselves sacrificially to spiritual contemplation, education, the care of orphans, and "fallen women," among other concerns.

In the wake of the catastrophic Potato Famine, many Irish emigrated to England, thereby adding to the overall population of Roman Catholics. Virulent anti-Catholicism ensued, however, as some worried Protestants attempted to turn back the growing strength of the Roman Catholic Church. In 1851 the *Bulwark or Reformation Journal* of the Scottish Reformation Society published a hard-hitting article with the telling title "The Blight of Popery." Most English believed their nation's religious identity remained indelibly Protestant.

IV. PROTESTANT CHRISTIAN MISSIONS

In *An Abridgement of Mr. David Brainerd's Journal Among the Indians* (1748), Philip Doddridge (1702–55), a Non-Conformist, indicated that reading about Brainerd's life should "awaken my Brethren in the ministry to bear their Testimony with greater zeal and Affection." He also called for regular prayer meetings devoted to foreign missions. In 1784 John Ryland Jr. of Northampton extended an invitation to various Christian societies to join a common effort in "the spread of the gospel to the most distant parts of the habitable globe."

Debate ensued among Particular Baptists (Reformed Baptists) regarding the role of human agency in missions and the practicality and the biblical warrant for foreign missions. In his *The Gospel Worthy of All Acceptation* (1785), Andrew Fuller (1754–1815), a Baptist minister, reiterated Jonathan Edwards's distinction between the "natural and moral inability" of the sinner. Elsewhere, Fuller argued that pastors had the duty to preach the gospel to "all who will hear it."

William Carey.

A. The Pioneering Role of William Carey

William Carey (1761–1834), the "father of modern missions," also played an important part in persuading his Baptist colleagues that they had an obligation to engage in foreign missions because the Great Commission applied to them and not solely to the apostles.

Having converted from Anglicanism, Carey became a Particular or Calvinistic Baptist Non-Conformist in 1779. A shoemaker by trade, Carey served as a Baptist layminister in 1786 and later as a pastor of the Baptist church at Moulton in Northamptonshire, England. One person who had significant influence on Carey was Andrew Fuller of Kettering, who argued that Calvinism does not preclude evangelistic responsibility.

Cobbling by day, running a Christian day school, and serving as a pastor, Carey added to an already busy bivocational life the study of languages. He soon discovered he was a natural linguist and taught himself Hebrew, Greek, Latin, French, and Dutch.

Inspired by the Polynesian adventures of Captain James Cook as well as the missionary exploits of the Moravians and Puritans, Carey became convinced that the Great Commission required implementation. He articulated his philosophy in 1791 to the Northampton Baptist Association in a pamphlet titled "An Enquiry into the Obligations of Christians to Use Means for the Conversion of the Heathens." Avoiding its being a dry work of theological discourse, in it Carey made his case by using the best available geographic and ethnographic data to map and count the number of people who had never heard the gospel.

On May 31, 1792, he delivered a sermon at the Northamptonshire Baptist Association in which he issued a "missionary" call and articulated a famous injunction: "Expect great things from God. Attempt great things for God." Carey's appeal led four months later to the creation of the Particular Baptist Society for Propagating the Gospel among the Heathen, later renamed the Baptist Missionary Society. It was the first missionary society of its kind and the model for hundreds of future societies. Influenced by Carey's arguments, its leaders rejected the notion that the Calvinist doctrine of election relieved Reformed Christians of their obligation to pursue foreign missionary activity.

Not only did Carey urge his Christian brethren to "expect great things" and "attempt great things," but the next year he and his wife, Dorothy, and his children and John Thomas, a medical doctor, set out for India (see chapter 18).

Although historians often propose that these happenings signaled the birth of the "modern era of Protestant missions," it should be recalled that Carey recognized and appreciated the contributions of earlier missionaries throughout church history, including John Wesley and the Moravians. Moreover, in the *History of the Propagation of Christianity and the Overthrow of Paganism* (1723), Reverend Robert Miller had earlier called for missionary efforts to reach the "heathen" for Christ.

The Society for the Propagation of the Gospel in New England, the earliest English Protestant missionary society, had also supported the fourteen-year effort of John Eliot (1604–90), an "Apostle to the Indians," to translate the Bible into Algonquian (which was completed in 1663). Toward the end of his life, some Algonquians, who were Native Americans of New England, thanked Eliot for his forty years of faithful ministry in "making known to us the Glad Tidings of Salvation of Jesus Christ."

Toward the year 1800, from a Protestant perspective the task of world evangelism remained daunting. More than 90 percent of the

> "Expect great things from God. Attempt great things for God" (William Carey).

world's Protestants lived in England, Europe, and North America. In 1900 Eugene Stock, Editorial Secretary of the Church Missionary Society, London, observed retrospectively that in 1800 Asia was nearly "wholly heathen or Mohammedan"; Islam was dominant in the "lands of the Bible"; China was "closed"; Japan was "hermetically sealed"; William Carey had just entered Bengel, India; and Africa was a "coastline" with an interior "utterly unknown."

Australia did have a small Protestant settlement around Sydney. After exploring portions of the coastline, in 1770 Captain James Cook claimed for King George III the eastern region of Australia, what he called New South Wales. On January 18, 1788, the first fleet of eleven ships with 1,350 settlers aboard—many of whom were convicts accused of minor crimes—arrived at Botany Bay. Richard Johnson, an evangelical chaplain, and his wife, Mary, accompanied them. Johnson had been recommended for the post by the evangelicals Wilberforce and Newton. On January 26, 1788, the fleet sailed into Sydney Cove. Johnson celebrated the first Anglican service a few days later. In 1814 Samuel Marsden (1765–1838), an evangelical chaplain who had ministered in New South Wales, began a gospel mission to New Zealand.

In 1800, Protestants generally viewed Roman Catholics, Jews, the followers of other world religions, and the "heathen" as needing the evangelical "gospel of Jesus Christ." Joseph Frey, the founder of the London Society for the Promotion of Christianity Amongst the Jews (1809), claimed that Christ would return after a massive conversion of Jews. Between 1780 and 1830, postmillennial eschatology would serve as a major stimulus for Christian missions. Premillennial eschatology did so as well, especially in the second half of the nineteenth century.

Because many potential converts lived in "unknown" territories, Western missionaries were obliged to trek into totally unfamiliar areas. They sometimes reported witnessing "primitive" and "savage" practices by inhabitants that reinforced a sense of racial superiority and the widespread view that Western civilization was in general superior to other cultures. By contrast, a missionary like William Carey developed a genuine respect for aspects of the culture of the Indian people he was trying to reach with the gospel.

British mission organizations included the well-known Society of Promoting Christian Knowledge (1698) and its partner, the Society for the Propagation of the Gospel in Foreign Parts (1701); the Methodist Missionary Society (1786); the Baptist Missionary Society for Propagating the Gospel among the Heathen (1793); the London Missionary Society (1795); the Church Missionary Society (1799; initially known as the Society for Missions to Africa and the East); the Religious Tract Society (1799); the British and Foreign Bible Society (1804); the Wesleyan Missionary Society (1813); and the English Presbyterian Society (1847).

Although the Church Missionary Society, which was Anglican, had a member of the royalty as a stipulated "patron" and the archbishop of Canterbury as vice patron, it should not be assumed that all mission societies were pawns of the English government or commercial interests. Until the 1840s, missionary initiatives were sometimes charged with complicating the task of British diplomats, businessmen, and military leaders. Moreover, a number of missionaries (especially Dissenters) condemned the exploitation of natives by commercial companies and governmental agents.

Several mission strategists became worried that Western missionaries were creating native churches whose members were becoming too dependent upon the missionaries themselves for their spiritual and material well-being, As a remedy they urged that mission churches should become "self-propagating." For example, Rufus Anderson (1796–1880), foreign secretary for the American Board of Commissioners for Foreign Missions, enjoined that "missions are instituted for the spread of Scriptural self-propagating Christianity." Henry Venn, honorary clerical secretary of the Church Missionary Society (1841–72), along with Anderson advocated the "indigenous church mission theory"—that is, a scripturally formed indigenous church should be: "1. Self-supporting; 2. Self-governing; 3. Self-propagating."

In 1886 John L. Nevius (1829–93), an American Presbyterian missionary to China and Korea, drew up a "New System" (the "Nevius Method") to replace an "Old System" of missions. Native churches should follow "the principles of independence and self-reliance from the beginning" and not rely on a "paid native agency." That is, members of native churches should financially support their leaders chosen from their own ranks and have a sense of responsibility for the life of the church.

Toward the end of the century, Eugene Stock observed that "native Christians [were] the best evangelists to their heathen fellow-countrymen." This was partially due to the fact that the ranks of European and American missionaries were frequently thinned by disease. Sometimes missionaries were victims of murder. For example, just before he was speared to death in 1885 at age thirty-eight, James Hannington, an Anglican missionary committed to gospel witness, declared, "Tell your king that I have purchased the road to [Uganda] with my death."

"Native Christians," or "native workers," played critical roles as missionaries, preachers, teachers, deacons, and catechists in the evangelization of their countries. Indeed, most Africans were won to Christ by the witness of other Africans. Philip Quaque, an ordained Anglican (from 1765 to 1816); Samuel Ajayi Crowther, the first Anglican bishop in West Africa (1864); and Apolo Kivebulaya (c. 1864–1933) in the Congo stood out as "native" leaders.

Crowther declared, "About the third year of my liberation from the slavery of man, I was convinced of another worse state of slavery, namely, that of sin and Satan." He emphasized the strategic contribution of Africans—in this instance, teachers—in spreading the gospel. "In like manner native teachers can do [things], having the facility of the language in their favor, to induce their heathen countrymen to come within reach of the means of Grace and hear the word of God."

Several thousand African Americans from Nova Scotia, the majority of whom were freed slaves, migrated to Sierra Leone as "recaptives" and "resettlers," starting in 1787, and they were especially effective in evangelistic witness.

James Africanus Beale Horton (1835–83) from Sierra Leone, the first African graduate from the University of Edinburgh, served as a surgeon, soldier, and politician. While he appreciated British political and Christian educational institutions, in his *Western African Countries and Peoples* (1868), he attempted to parry racism: "... and dare you tell me that the African is not susceptible of improvement of the highest order, that he does not possess in himself a principle of progression and a desire of perfection far surpassing many existing nations—since it can not be shown in the world's history that any people with so limited advantages has shown such results within fifty years." Horton advocated the creation of African states with an English "Dominion" status.

Dwight L. Moody.

In the second half of the nineteenth century, the number of African missionaries began to swell. In 1841 the Church Missionary Society (CMA, Anglean) had only nine African and Asian missionaries. By 1873 its ranks had expanded to include 148 African and Asian missionaries.

The number of CMA women missionaries also grew. Between 1820 and 1885, 99 women (not including wives) and 1,018 men served as missionaries, but between the years 1885 and 1900 there were 485 women and 581 men. After 1860, the number of single women in various other missionary societies also increased substantially.

In the last decades of the nineteenth century, missionary endeavors gained more momentum. In July 1886, at Dwight L. Moody's "College

Students' Summer School" located in Mount Hermon, Massachusetts, one hundred students signed a statement indicating their intention to serve as missionaries. On December 6, 1888, one of the students, John R. Mott, helped organize the Student Volunteer Movement. A British Student Volunteer Movement was also established. The *Missionary Review* (July 1888) reported, "The wonderful wave of missionary zeal which has swept through our American colleges during the last eighteen months has moved about 1800 young men and 600 young women to offer their lives in service to Christ as foreign missionaries."

Contemporaries attributed the greater interest in missions in the United States and England to various factors: the launch of a prayer movement (1872); Dwight L. Moody's British evangelistic campaigns of 1872–73 and 1882–84; the example of the "Cambridge Seven"; the "Higher Life" sanctification teaching of the English Keswick Movement (1873), "Let go and let God," with victory over all known sin; and the inspirational story that the missionary David Livingstone had died praying on his knees. Improved means of travel and communication also made missionary work more logistically feasible.

David Livingstone.

B. David Livingstone: Missionary Explorer

The Scot David Livingstone (1813–75) of the London Missionary Society was trained in theology and medicine. A hard-driving man, he gained great fame as a discoverer. After 1841, Livingstone took the gospel into the Lake District of Central Africa and labored among the Tswana people from 1843 to 1853. He thought that Christianity could play a helpful role in "civilizing" the peoples he encountered. He also encouraged the establishment of commerce as a substitute for the slave trade in which some Africans participated.

By 1856 Livingstone had emerged as a national hero. He was famous for his evangelical missionary efforts, geographical discoveries, and attack on the slave trade. In 1857 he sought the government's backing, as he hoped to "make an open path for commerce and Christianity." Livingstone's concern for commerce did not escape criticism, nor did the fact that his wife, Mary, and his children had suffered from his long absences.

In 1870 the rumor circulated that Livingstone had been killed somewhere in Africa. Then Henry M. Stanley (1841–1901), a journalist and explorer, "found" him and famously asked, "Dr. Livingstone, I presume?" Despite arguments to the contrary, Livingstone's primary desire was to penetrate "darkest Africa" with the gospel of Jesus Christ.

C. Mary Slessor: "Mother of All Peoples"

Toward the end of his life, Livingstone made a strong appeal that someone should step forward to continue the work he had begun in Africa. A young Scottish woman, Mary Slessor (1848–1915), responded. Overcoming deep-seated fears, she volunteered to serve as a single woman with a Presbyterian mission in the Calabar in West Africa (now Nigeria), a region known for animist beliefs and poisonous snakes.

Often alone in perilous circumstances, Slessor wrote from Africa, "Heaven is now nearer to me than Britain, and no one will be anxious about me if I go up country." In a land of headhunters, witch doctors, and sudden death, she taught that Jesus is the "Great Physician and Savior, the Son of the Father God who made all things." In the name of Christ she defied the threats of hostile chiefs and warriors engaged in evil acts. She ministered to abandoned children, especially sets of twins. In Calabar she became deeply loved and known as the "White Ma," the mother of the people. She recalled, like the apostle Paul, that nothing, including death itself, can separate us "from the love of God which is in Christ Jesus our Lord."

Single women such as Mary Slessor sometimes enjoyed more leadership opportunities on the mission field than they did back in their home churches.

D. Hudson Taylor: "Faith Missions"

As a young man, James Hudson Taylor (1832–1905) turned away from the Christian faith of his father, who was a druggist and a lay Methodist preacher. But in 1849 Taylor picked up a tract in which he read the words, "It is finished." He was converted after he realized that Christ's death on the cross was totally sufficient to pay for his sins. In 1854 Taylor arrived in China as a missionary and eventually founded the China Inland Mission (CIM; 1865). He also inspired the Cambridge Seven, a group of university athletic students who decided in 1885 to accompany him to China and were applauded for this by Queen Victoria. One of the Cambridge Seven was the cricketer C(harles) T(homas) Studd (1860–1931).

Taylor promoted "faith missions." He declared, "Depend upon it. God's work, done in God's way, will never lack God's supplies." He also advocated the "secret" of Christian living: "I have striven in vain to abide in Him. I'll strive no more. For has not He promised to abide with me—never to leave me, never to fail me?"

In 1900 Taylor spoke on "The Source of Power" at the Ecumenical Missionary Conference in New York City. Despite great advances, he cautioned the delegates about the "great weakness" of the missionary movement: "We have given too much attention to methods, and to machinery and to resources, and too little to the Source of Power; the filling with the Holy Ghost." He reminded the delegates that "the gospel itself is the power of God unto salvation to everyone that believeth."

When Taylor died in 1905, many of CIM's 849 missionaries had moved out from missionary stations along China's coast and penetrated the interior of China, and this despite enormous hardships.

Lottie Moon (1840–1912), an American Southern Baptist, also sacrificially ministered to the Chinese people from 1873 until her death (except for furloughs). She too emphasized faith missions, calling on her fellow Baptists in 1888 to give a Christmas faith offering for foreign missions. Over the years, Southern Baptists have given between one and two billion dollars to the Lottie Moon Christmas offering.

E. "The Evangelization of the World in This Generation" (1900)

Like Hudson Taylor, John R. Mott (1865–1955; see also chapter 18), the General Secretary of the World's Student Christian Federation, addressed the Ecumenical Missionary Conference in New York City in 1900. He declared, "It is the obligation of the church to evangelize the world in this generation. It is our duty because all men need Christ." He gave reasons: "... it is possible to evangelize the world in this generation," highlighting "the recent missionary achievement of the Church" and the "remarkable resources" of the present day.

Among these resources he cited the 135 million members of the Protestant churches worldwide, the enormous "money power of the Church," the 500 missionary societies, the Scriptures translated in whole or in part into 421 languages, the 1,500 Christian associations for students, the 20 million Sunday school "scholars," the 2,000 students from the World's Student Christian Federation already on the mission fields, and the "Native Church" with its 1.3 million communicants and more than 4 million adherents.

Mott rejoiced that for the first time in the history of the church "practically the whole world is open." He pointed out that "improved means of communication constitutes one of the chief facilities of which the Church of this generation can avail itself." They included extensive "railway lines in non-Christian lands," the reduced amount of time for missionaries to reach foreign fields, "submarine cables," the "universal Postal Union," and the improved productivity of printing presses. According to Mott, God had made "the whole world known and accessible to our generation" so that the kingdom of Jesus Christ could be extended and built up throughout the earth.

Nonetheless, the task of world evangelism remained daunting, especially in non-Western lands. In 1900 approximately 80 percent of Christians in the world were white.

V. RELIGION IN THE VICTORIAN AGE (1837–1901)

The Protestant faith exercised a pervasive influence in England, especially among the middle class, during the reign of Queen Victoria. Some historians refer to a prevalent form of Protestantism as "Victorian religion." William Gladstone, the queen's Liberal Party Prime Minister four different times, was an eminent Christian statesman.

Between the years 1837 and 1847 the publishing output of English Bibles and Testaments was enormous: from the Queen's Printer, 2,284,540 Bibles and 1,971,877 Testaments; from Oxford, 2,612,750 Bibles and 2,062,250 Testaments; from Cambridge, 895,500 Bibles and 1,111,600 Testaments. The British and Foreign Bible Society (founded in 1804) also sold millions of Bibles and Testaments.

In 1851 a Religious Census provided data on church attendance in England and Wales: 400,000 Dissenters; 100,000 Established Church. On a particular Sunday, something like 7.26 million people out of 18 million attended churches and chapels. The American educator and politician Horace Mann reported two sets of statistics in 1854 based on the census: the percentage of church attendees belonging to a religious group; the same percentage with an addition of one-third of the totals to account for those people with legitimate reasons for nonattendance (such as the elderly and the sick). The first set of statistics reads: Anglicans, 17.6 percent; Methodists, 14.9 percent; Independents, 6.6 percent; Baptists, 5.1 percent; Roman Catholics, 2.0 percent.

British evangelical Protestants were heartened by the Revival of 1859 in England, Ireland, and Wales. Reports about Jeremiah Lanphier's Fulton Street prayer meetings (1857–58) and other noonday prayer meetings in New York City, Boston, Philadelphia, Chicago, and other cities, towns, and villages throughout the United States, and accounts of the thousands of conversions reached Britain, Ireland, and Wales. News from the "Business Men's Awakening" prompted some pastors to call on their people to pray for a similar outpouring of the Holy Spirit. According to Reverend Adam Magill, even before the awakening in the United States, in 1856 four young men had begun to pray for a special work of the Holy Spirit in Boveva, Ireland. Returning from a fact-gathering mission to the United States, Dr. William Gibson, the moderator of the General Assembly of the Presbyterian Church of Ireland, and Reverend William McClure reported on the spiritual awakening they had witnessed across the sea.

In the village of Kells, Ireland, a powerful revival broke out, followed by awakenings in other towns. Pastor James Morgan described the Ulster Revival: "In the town of Belfast there has been a very marked outpouring of the Spirit. There is an extraordinary change on many of its congregations. Some churches that were well nigh empty are now filled." On March 14, 1859, a crowd of three thousand gathered outside the First Presbyterian Church of Ahoghil. Listening to the preaching of a layperson, hundreds came under deep conviction for their sins. During the Ulster Revival of 1859, possibly as many as 100,000 people confessed Christ as Savior. Dr. William Gibson described this spiritual awakening in his book *The Year of Grace: A History of the Ulster Revival of 1859.*

Likewise, in Wales, a land well-known for its revivals, another 100,000 were converted. In England, much "open-air and theater preaching" took place.

Evangelical Christians were also heartened by George Williams's creation of the Young Men's Christian Association (YMCA) in 1844. Young men gathered together to study Scripture, pray, and enjoy interacting with each other. In 1851 the first YMCA in the United States was founded in Boston. In 1855 the Young Women's Christian Association (YWCA) was formed.

A. Church Divisions and Spiritual Renewal in Scotland

In 1843 the established Church of Scotland (the Auld Kirk) which upheld the Westminster Confession of Faith, suffered a "disruption," or major split. Some 450 ministers withdrew to Tanfield Hall and created the "Free Church of Scotland." They claimed that they were the true defenders of Calvinism, the Westminster Confession of Faith, and the Bible's infallibility. They denied that they were "Voluntarists," or creators of a secession. They viewed their church as the "pure" established church. They successfully created a competitive church similar in organizational structure to the Church of Scotland (with its approximately 750 pastors).

After the "Disruption of 1843," yet another denomination was formed, the United Free Presbyterian Church (1847). Members of this church believed in the separation of church and state. Their church joined together with the United Succession Church and the Relief Church. Toward 1875, the Church of Scotland had about 460,000 members, the Free Church of Scotland 256,000, and the United Free Presbyterian Church 187,000.

In 1872 and 1873 Dwight L. Moody (1837–99) and Ira Sankey (1840–1908), a gospel composer and singer, pursued evangelistic campaigns in England and Scotland. Many pastors of the Free Church of Scotland supported the evangelists. Other clerics argued that the evangelists' message did not accord with the Westminister Confession. Large numbers of people attended the meetings. According to a contemporary account, Moody's evangelistic efforts in Scotland were especially effective: "In thousands of Christian households the deepest interest was felt by parents for their children, and by masters and mistresses for their servants; and so universal was this that Dr. Horatius Bonar declares his belief that there were scarcely a Christian household in all Edinburgh in which there were not one or more persons converted during this revival."

In a different manner, the prolific Scottish author and pastor George MacDonald (1824–1905) called on his Scottish readers and others to remember that we "must love him [God] or be desolate." His imaginative works of fantasy and faith exerted a profound influence on later writers such as J. R. R. Tolkien, C. S. Lewis, and G. K. Chesterton.

The much publicized trial (1877–81) of Professor William Robertson Smith (1846–94) shocked conservative members of the Free Church of Scotland. Smith, an Old Testament scholar, had defended and taught higher critical views of the Bible at the University of Aberdeen. Removed from his teaching chair, Smith nonetheless received strong support from three hundred friends who interpreted the verdict of the trial as allowing "all Free-Church ministers and office-bearers free to pursue the critical questions raised by Professor W. R. Smith."

As the nineteenth century drew to an end, troubled relations continued between certain members of the Free Church of Scotland and the United Church of Scotland regarding the latter church's alleged acceptance of higher criticism, departure from Reformed doctrines, and openness to Arminianism.

B. Wales: "Land of Revivals"

John Wesley once commented that Wales was "ripe for the Gospel." Beginning in the mid-1730s, Wesleyan and Calvinist Methodist preachers such as Howell Harris established reading groups and churches as they spread their gospel message in Wales (see chapter 11). In 1811 Thomas Charles (1755–1814) helped orchestrate the departure of Welsh Calvinists from the Church of England. For his part, Christmas Evans (1766–1838), the "Bunyan of Wales," preached with fervor and founded Baptist churches. Multiple spiritual revivals helped propel the Non-Conformist advance, despite opposition and civil disturbances. Non-Conformist chapels were built at a rapid clip. These chapels joined Anglican churches as fixtures of one town after another in the Welsh countryside.

In the 1840s, many Non-Conformists feared what they thought was an increased influence of the Roman Catholic Church over the Church of England. This perception fueled the desire of Welsh Non-Conformists to see the disestablishment of the Anglican Church. Thomas Gee published a newspaper that specifically called for disestablishment. The Welsh sensitivities of some Non-Conformists were wounded when the government published *Blue Books* (1847), which criticized the quality of Welsh education. For them, religious non-conformity and Welsh patriotism had become inextricably bound together.

The Religious Census of 1851 revealed that the number of Non-Conformists in Wales had surpassed the membership of the Church of England. Non-Conformists were especially galled by the fact that the Church of England in Wales received a tithe—one-tenth of their income—even though they were not members of the established church. Eventually, so-called "Tithe Wars" broke out between the years 1886 and 1890. These conflicts pitted government troops against farm workers attempting to thwart the efforts of tithe collectors.

In 1904–5 another great revival swept through Wales. Evan Roberts (1878–1951), a young coal miner, had prayed for eleven years that he might be used in a great revival. In 1904 Roberts attended a meeting in which Seth Joshua, a leading Calvinist Methodist evangelist, spoke. Joshua's closing words, "Lord ... bend us" (in Welsh meaning "shape us"), greatly impacted Roberts: "It was the Spirit that put the emphasis for me on 'bend us.' That's what you need, said the Spirit to me. And as I went out I prayed, O Lord, Bend me." Elsewhere, Roberts declared, "I felt ablaze with a desire to go through the length and breadth of Wales to tell of the Savior."

Roberts urged his listeners to observe what became known as the "Four Points" if they desired an "outpouring of the Holy Spirit" in their own lives: confess any sin from the past, give up anything that is "doubtful," obey what the Spirit prompts you to do, and confess publicly your faith in Christ as your Savior. Other preachers felt a similar passion to preach and call the Welsh people to repentance.

"My mission is first to the churches. When the churches are aroused in their duty, men of the world will be swept into the Kingdom. A whole church on its knees is irresistible" (Evan Roberts, a leader in the Welsh Revival).

Hundreds upon hundreds of meetings consisting of prayer, singing, preaching, soul searching, and confession enveloped Wales. *The Times*, a newspaper, provided this stunning account of the revival: "The whole population had been suddenly stirred by a common impulse. Religion had become the absorbing interest of their lives. They had gathered at crowded services for six and eight hours at a time. Political meetings and even football matches were postponed . . . quarrels between trade-union workmen and non-unionists had been made up."

Some 100,000 people, ranging from college students to coal miners, confessed Christ. One witness to the revival wrote, "Former blasphemers were the most eloquent, both in prayer and praise. . . . Drunkards forgot the way to saloons . . . they were busy worshiping. . . . It was the young people who responded with the greatest alacrity to the challenge of absolute surrender and consecrated to the service of the Lord."

Interestingly, a mine manager believed that the conversion of coal miners had indirectly brought confusion to the mines. Why? Newly converted coal haulers no longer swore at their horses, and this lack of cursing confused the animals. Said the mine manager: "They have driven their horses by obscenity and kicks. Now they can hardly persuade their horses to start working, because they have no obscenity and kicks."

Many judges no longer had cases to judge in court, so steeply did crime rates decline.

The Welsh Revival constituted but one of a cluster of revivals at the dawn of the new century. News of revival in one country often encouraged laity and missionaries alike to pray for an outpouring of the Holy Spirit on their own lands. In 1905 revivals were reported in Norway, Denmark, Sweden, Germany, and elsewhere in Europe. Between 1906 and 1909, revivals broke out in Kassia Hills and Assam, India; in Los Angeles, California, in the Azusa Street prayer meetings under the leadership of the African-American William Seymour; in Wonsan, Pyongyang, Makpo, and Seoul, Korea; in Zimbabwe, Africa; in Manchuria, China; and in Valparaiso, Chile.

R. A. Hardie, a medical doctor and Methodist missionary, played a key role in the beginning stage of the epochal Korean revivals. In 1903 he was convicted by Jesus' teaching that his disciples should ask for the Holy Spirit (Luke 11:1–13). Hardie confessed to other missionaries he had been prideful and depended too much on his own efforts in ministry and not enough on the work of the Holy Spirit. Deeply moved by Hardie's confession, a number of missionaries and Koreans began to confess their own sins and sought the power of the Holy Spirit to sanctify their own lives. Revival fires began to spread through Korea.

Jonathan Goforth (1859–1936), a Canadian Presbyterian missionary serving in China, was thrilled to learn about the "Pentecost" great revival of 1907 in Korea. He traveled to Korea so that he could witness firsthand the spiritual awakening there. He indicated that thousands of Koreans were caught up in deep remorse, repentance, reconciliation with those they had offended, incessant prayer, listening to the words of Scripture, craving to experience more of Christ, and sensing the powerful presence of the Holy Spirit in their meetings.

When Goforth returned to Manchuria, he related to expectant Chinese audiences what he had witnessed in Korea. The "Manchurian Revival" broke out—one if the first major revivals in China.

C. Ireland: Religious Tensions over "Home Rule" and "Union" with England

Sharp antagonisms festered between Protestants (Episcopalians and Presbyterians) and Catholics in Ireland. Said one Protestant, "Sir, I hate a Papist as I do a toad and none of my neighbors has gone further in their extirpation than I have." In 1791 the association "United Irishmen" was formed. It brought together Ulster Presbyterians, Free Thinkers, and Catholics alike. Their common goal: to drive out the English.

In 1798 British soldiers roundly defeated the United Irishmen's attempt to establish an Irish Republic with French support. Atrocities were perpetrated by the warring parties. Up to 30,000 people perished in the conflict. Thereafter the Act of Union (1800) forged a United Kingdom of Great Britain and Ireland. It engendered resentment among some Irish because they no longer had their own Parliament, but instead sent 100 Irish members to the House of Commons and 25 peers to the House of Lords. In fact, Protestants generally favored the union with England, whereas the 4 million Irish Roman Catholics spurned it.

Protestants sought to foster evangelistic outreach by forming the Hibernian Bible Society (1806) and the Religious Tract and Book Society (1810). In Ulster, Henry Cooke (1788–1868) gave leadership to conservative Presbyterians. Between the years 1815 and 1845 many Irish (probably 1,500,000) left to settle in other lands. By the 1840s, England's Irish population had soared to more than 400,000. Many were impoverished workers.

In 1823 the Catholic Association was founded with the goal of winning Catholic emancipation. Irish members of Parliament often lent their support to the Liberal party. This party worked for both Catholic emancipation (1829) and the winning of rights for Non-Conformist Protestants. Led by Daniel O'Connell (1775–1847), some Catholic nationalists championed "Home Rule" for Ireland through peaceful political means.

By contrast, radical republicans envisioned the creation of a secular Irish state. They were prepared to resort to force of arms if such were deemed necessary. They opposed those Protestants in Northern Ireland who, with certain notable exceptions (Charles Parnell, 1846–91, an influential Home Rule advocate), insisted on a continued "union" with England. These latter Protestants included militants prepared to fight for their religion.

In 1834 the vast majority of the Irish remained Roman Catholic. Only 10.7 percent of the populace were members of the Church of Ireland (Anglican), and only 8.1 percent were Presbyterians.

The Irish people depended on potatoes as the basic staple of their diet. Between the years 1816 and 1842 various potato famines rendered life miserable for the Irish. Then in 1845, a "blight of unusual character" (a new fungus) devastated the potato crop. Famine and food riots ensued. Approximately 775,000 died (some estimates ranging up to one million), and two million Irish emigrated to England, Canada, and the United States.

An article from *The Illustrated London News* (May 10, 1851) painted a grim picture of the tragedy and the resultant "depopulation" of Ireland. The article indicated there were not enough ships "to transport to the States the increasing swarms of Irish who have resolved to try in the New World to gain the independence which has been denied them in the old." Approximately 800,000–900,000 Catholic Irish emigrated to the United States, whereas Irish Protestants in smaller numbers often chose to settle in Canada.

The Irish frequently blamed British colonial policies as creating the conditions conducive to the famine's onslaught. They also criticized British relief efforts. Many Irish had no choice but to live in woeful workhouses. At least 200,000 perished.

In the last third of the nineteenth century the "Irish Question"—that is, the status of Ireland's contentious relations with England—often grabbed the rapt attention of British politicians. In 1869 the Anglican Church was disestablished in Ireland. Irish members of Parliament promoted the case for Home Rule, whereas republican revolutionaries such as the Fenians loomed menacingly in the shadows. In 1879 the Irish Land League entered the fight to protect the land rights of Irish tenants. A republican armed revolt erupted and was rudely suppressed.

William Gladstone, the Liberal Party Prime Minister of England, argued in favor of Home Rule. In 1886 the First Irish Home Rule Bill was proposed and defeated in the House of Commons. The Second Irish Home Rule Bill was offered in 1893 and suffered the same fate in the House of Lords. Thereafter, the economic status and familial and religious commitments of the Irish often determined whether they favored Home Rule or a continued Union with England.

D. Charles Spurgeon: The "Prince of Preachers"

During the 1857–58 "Businessmen's Awakening" in the United States, perhaps as many as one million people were converted to Christ. Pastor James W. Alexander of New York City reported in 1858 that the "publisher of Spurgeon's sermons, says he has sold a hundred thousand." Charles Haddon Spurgeon (1834–92), a young Baptist minister whose preaching attracted large crowds in London, was becoming well known across the Atlantic. A number of superb preachers graced pulpits during the Victorian era, yet Spurgeon garnered the title "the Prince of Preachers."

As a child Spurgeon had been taught Puritan writings by his parents and grandfather. On a snowy day in 1850, Spurgeon attended a Primitive Methodist chapel. The preacher addressed Spurgeon directly: "Young man, look to Jesus Christ. Look!" Spurgeon experienced a joyful conversion:

Charles Haddon Spurgeon.

> When the Lord first pardoned my sin, I was so joyous that I could scarcely refrain from dancing. On the road home from the house where I had been set free, I wanted to shout in the street the story of my deliverance. My soul was so happy that I wanted to tell every snowflake that was falling from heaven of the wondrous love of Jesus who had blotted out the sins of my most rebellious nature.

Even Spurgeon's earliest preaching drew large crowds. At age twenty-six he began a lengthy preaching ministry at the reconstructed Metropolitan Tabernacle in London, a building that could hold an audience of 5,000. In 1857 he spoke at the Crystal Palace to a crowd of 24,000; at least 100,000 copies of this message circulated. A contemporary described Spurgeon's preaching style: "thrilling description, touching anecdotes, sparkling wit, startling episodes, striking similes, all used to illustrate and enforce the deep, earnest home-truths of the Bible."

Spurgeon founded a Pastors' College, where young people could train for the ministry. He also published his sermons on a regular basis, edited the magazine *The Sword and the Trowel* (1865), and still had time to write more than seventy books. He did all these things while battling gout, dealing with family issues, and engaging in various theological discussions and sharp debates.

In the theological tradition of the scholar Dr. John Gill, Spurgeon was a Particular Baptist. As a Calvinist he affirmed a belief in election and predestination but not infant baptism. Spurgeon did come under sharp criticism from James Wells and other Particular Baptist colleagues for offering "Gospel invitations." The critics labeled his invitations for salvation "Arminian and unsound." For his part, Spurgeon viewed these Particular Baptists as "hyper-Calvinists." He countered that he was "as firm a believer in the doctrines of grace as any man living, and a true Calvinist after the order of John Calvin himself." However, he sought to maintain good relations with these Particular Baptists.

In an edition of *The Sword and the Trowel* in 1887, Spurgeon criticized those who he thought were undermining biblical authority. In the ensuing "Down-Grade Controversy" (1887–92), Spurgeon defended biblical inerrancy and eternal punishment against "post-mortem" salvation. In this he received little support from the members of the Baptist Union (founded in 1813 by Particular Baptists), some of whom were leaning toward the "New Theology." Spurgeon viewed this theology as a variant form of Protestant Liberalism. Spurgeon withdrew from the Baptist Union, as did his church, the Metropolitan Tabernacle.

Spurgeon continued to preach faithfully to packed audiences. He was one of the most popular evangelical writers of all times. His books went through multiple editions and were translated into many languages. Spurgeon was clear about his own goal in ministry: "He who searches all hearts knows that our aim and object is not to gather a band around self, but to unite a company around the Savior."

E. Christian Social Reformers in the Victorian Era

A number of Christians attempted to address the appalling social and economic needs of the poor in Victorian England. The Quaker Elizabeth Fry (1780–1845) ministered to women and children in England's overcrowded prisons and attempted to reform aspects of the prison system that she said "should never exist in a Christian and civilized country."

Shocked by horrific living conditions for women inmates at Newgate Prison, Fry in 1817 established an association "to provide for the clothing, instruction, and employment of women; to introduce them to a knowledge of Holy Scripture; and to form in them as much as possible those habits of sobriety, order and industry, which may render them docile and peaceable in prison and respectable when they leave it." She also created a training school for nurses, some of whom later worked for Florence Nightingale, the reformer of hospital nursing. Fry also urged other Christians to give of themselves in caring for the needy.

Thomas Barnardo (1845–1905), a philanthropist, also cared for the needy children of the streets by setting up shelters for them. His slogan: "No Destitute Child Ever Refused Admission."

George Mueller (1805–98) founded the Scriptural Knowledge Institution, established homes for thousands of orphaned children, and supported evangelistic missions. He prayed in faith that money would come in for his orphan homes, even if he did not specifically request funds from donors. The needed money always arrived on time (on occasion in the nick of time). Mueller hoped this demonstration of "God's faithfulness" would encourage other Christians to pray.

F. The Salvation Army

In 1855 William Booth (1829–1912), a Methodist, married Catherine Mumford (1829–90), whose father was an itinerant pastor. Both Booths appreciated Holiness teachings about sanctification and perfection and became preachers and evangelists. Catherine Booth indicated to her mother that the books of Mrs. Phoebe Palmer (*The Way of Holiness* [1843] and *Faith and Its Effects* [1849]) "have done me more good than anything else I have ever met with."

Palmer on occasion spoke to large crowds in her Holiness meetings. Nonetheless, she did not think women should be preachers. By contrast, Catherine Booth wrote a pamphlet, titled *Female Ministry: Or Women's Right to Preach the Gospel*, in which she defended the right of women to preach. In the Salvation Army, women could not only preach but also hold high offices in the organization.

In 1865 the Booths created the Christian Mission in the impoverished London East End. They focused on ministering to the "unwanted." In 1878 the Christian Mission was renamed the Salvation Army. William Booth served as its commanding general, and his directives were not to be disobeyed. The "Salvationists" included clergy members ("Officers") and laypeople ("Soldiers") who made a commitment to evangelistic outreach and the care of the weak and the poor: "For Christ's sake, to feed the poor, clothe the naked, love the unlovable and befriend the friendless." They worked with "fallen women," drunkards, "sluggards," and others who were in desperate physical and spiritual need. They provided "Soup, Soap, and Salvation."

The Salvationists used musical instruments, entertaining presentations, plain speech preaching, and distribution of tracts and Bibles as they tried to catch the attention of people in the streets.

In 1883 it was decided that Salvation Army members did not need to observe water baptism or the Lord's Supper. The Salvationists believed that church people sometimes counted on attendance on these ordinances as a means to salvation. By the 1880s, a number of Christians worried that large numbers of the working classes had no Christian affiliation at all. Sharing their concern, William Booth published *In Darkest England and the Way Out* (1890), an indicting book in which he compared the spiritual lostness of a tenth of the English citizenry with that of Africans who had never heard the gospel.

When Catherine Booth died in 1890, she was eulogized as "the most famous and influential Christian woman of the generation."

William received opposition from various sources, including the Anglican Church, alcohol-selling industries, and news media—the latter in part because he chose some of his children as key leaders in the movement. After Catherine's death, disputes arose between Booth and his children, and he also became blind. But he was honored as a Freeman of the City of London and was granted an honorary degree from the University of Oxford.

G. The Sunday School Movement and Public Education

Robert Raikes (1735–1811), editor of the English newspaper *Gloucester Journal*, was a principal founder of the Sunday school movement. Raikes noticed that children of the poor frequently haunted city streets on Sundays and got caught up in mischievous activities. During the weekdays many of these same children worked long hours in textile factories or in the mines. Whereas children from wealthy homes had schools they could attend or were taught by private tutors, no public education system was in place to serve the children of the poor. Moreover, charity schools were not especially numerous.

Between 1780 and 1783 Raikes opened up a series of Sunday schools. The children sang hymns, said prayers, and recited the catechism. Teachers—the majority of whom were women—tried to help the students learn about hygiene and discipline. Some taught reading and writing, others only reading. Eventually teachers, not all of whom were especially well educated, gave "lessons" to their children. In time, the attendees were called "scholars."

Proud of the effect attendance at Sunday shool sometimes had on the children, Raikes once wrote, "I have invited all my Sunday School children to dine with me on New Year's Day [1795] on beef and plum pudding. I wish you could step in and see what clean and joyous countenances we shall exhibit, and you would not be disappointed to hear how well they sing their Maker's praise."

During the nineteenth century many churches and chapels began Sunday schools. Some factory owners did so as well. In 1803 the Sunday School Union, largely led by Non-Conformists, was founded. Impoverished parents sent their children to Sunday schools as a way to provide them with at least "scraps" of education. The percentage of children from the working classes who attended Sunday schools grew dramatically, from 13.8 percent in 1801 to 49.6 percent in 1831 to 75.4 percent in 1851.

The Sunday school movement was an effective complement to what were known as "Ragged Schools" — that is, the formation of free public education for the down-and-out, a movement initiated in the late eighteenth century by Thomas Cranfield.

Yet, both of these school movements also attracted critics. Some claimed that factory owners began Sunday schools to promote a docile attitude among their child workers, that the quality of the education received at the Sunday schools was poor, and that the teachers attempted to inculcate either Anglican or Dissenters' doctrines into the children. Most parents who sent their children to Sunday schools or to Ragged Schools apparently ignored or were possibly unaware of these criticisms.

In 1870 the Elementary Education Act established public schools that offered free and compulsory education to children whatever their background. The act stipulated that "no catechism or formulary distinctive of any particular denomination would predominate the religious instruction." In fact, Non-Conformist members of Parliament, who had helped pass this act, complained that Anglicans and Catholics continued to exercise a disproportionate influence on English public education.

H. Victorian Morals and Domesticity

"Victorian religion," including its evangelical manifestations, undoubtedly influenced the social mores and religious practices of many British, especially the middle class. Historian Judith Flanders writes, "Evangelicals hoped to find a Christian path in all their actions, including the details of daily life: a true Christian must ensure that the family operated in a milieu that could promote relations among its members, between themselves and their servants, and between the family and the outside world."

In 1859 the author Charles Kingsley claimed that young English men were changing their ways: "One finds more and more, swearing banished from the universities, drunkenness and gambling from the barracks; one finds everywhere, whether at college, in camp, or by the coverside, more and more, young men desirous to learn their duty as Englishmen and if possible to do it." The Victorians placed an emphasis on the development of a person's moral character.

For many Victorians, the home was the cherished center of family life. The ideal Victorian mother assumed the respected role of running household affairs and caring for and nurturing the children, being—as John Angell James put it in a sermon in 1852—"the queen of the domestic circle."

By contrast, the husband worked outside the home in the rough-and-tumble, competitive world of industrial England. He sought to provide financial security for his family. Rather than spending an entire evening drinking at a pub after work, he would ideally return to his "castle"—a single family dwelling (even if attached to a row of other houses). There he ruled as the head of the household. He was responsible for leading his children and wife (and servants) in their Christian duties and family prayers. He was to caution members of his household about the perils of sin and encourage them to pursue godliness.

On Sundays the family attended church together and strictly observed the Lord's Day. Doing unnecessary "work" or pursuing "amusements" such as knitting, sketching, and cards, or reading frivolous literature, or playing sports was not permitted in many homes.

Critics accused the Victorians of prudishness, advocating old-fashioned religious beliefs, practicing hypocrisy in sexual morality ("slumming" in red-light, poor districts of certain cities), manifesting repressive attitudes toward women, and insensitivity to the economic and social plights of the lower classes. In their defense, historian William Heyck counters, "This hostility toward Victorian culture fails to give credit to the Victorians either for their achievements or for the sincerity of their efforts to deal with difficult problems."

I. Victorian Religion and a "Crisis of Faith"

"Victorian religion," whether embraced by Anglicans, Anglo-Catholics, or Dissenters, appeared secure as an enduring cultural force shaping British society. Paradoxically, however, a number of contemporaries acknowledged experiencing a "crisis of faith."

Mapping the contours of the impact of this crisis on the English public is a difficult task. In a society where Victorian religion could serve as a conventional belief, some English may have wrestled with doubts but hesitated to admit this for fear of public reproach. Moreover, a discrepancy could exist between those who were in fact "freethinkers," atheists, infidels, agnostics, humanists, and secularists versus those who were labeled as such. During acrid theological debates, disputants might resort to name-calling that did not necessarily identify accurately what their opponents believed. The "poor" as a class, for example, were sometimes unfairly portrayed as the "godless" poor. Finally, a number of people such as art critic John Ruskin (1819–1900) were apparently atheists for a time but then returned to the Christian faith. Dramatic reconversions were not unheard of.

Nonetheless, circumstantial evidence does suggest that a "crisis of faith" affected a considerable number of people. In 1850 Alfred Lord Tennyson published what became a classic poem, "In Memoriam A. H. H." (poet and essayist Arthur Hallam). Conversant with evolutionary theory (Robert Chambers's writings), Tennyson attempted to reconcile the Christian faith with an understanding of nature:

> Who trusted God was love indeed
> And Love Creation's final law—
> Tho' Nature, red in tooth and claw
> With ravine, shriek'd against his creed.

In 1851 William Hale White and two others were expelled from New College, London, because they would not profess an "orthodox" view of biblical inspiration. White later wrote "Mark Rutherford" novels that chronicled the difficulties of upholding the Christian faith in Non-Conformist Christian circles.

Elsewhere, in the Bampton Lectures at Oxford University (1860–61), vicar and professor J. W. Burgon complained vigorously that even the inspiration of Holy Scripture was under attack: "It is quite monstrous, in the first university of the most favored of Christian lands, that a man should be compelled thus to lift up his voice in defense of the very inspiration of God's Word."

In 1860, secularists G. J. Holyoake, Joseph Barker, J. B. Bebbington, and others spoke at a significant secularist gathering. In 1869 Henry Sidgwick specifically alluded to a religious "crisis": "I feel convinced that English religious society is going through a great crisis just now, and it will probably become impossible soon to conceal from anybody the extent to which rationalistic views are held, and the extent of their deviation from traditional opinion."

Matthew Arnold, an eminent literary critic, wrote in 1875, "In the present moment two things about the Christian religion must be clear to anybody with eyes in his head. One is, that men cannot do without it: the other, that they cannot do with it as it is." In 1888 Mrs. Humphry Ward published the novel *Robert Elsmere* that recounted a pastor's losing battle to retain his evangelical convictions. The novel scored a significant publishing success.

Some aristocratic notables and descendants of the evangelical "Clapham Sect" participated in the Bloomsbury Group, notorious as it was for embracing "amoral" anarchy.

J. The Christian Faith and "Modern" Scholarship

The flood of new information and findings of "modern" scholarship—as represented especially by Darwinism and "higher biblical criticism"—contributed to the significant unease about orthodox Christian doctrine. Responses to this modern scholarship took various forms. "Broad Church Anglicans" sought to accommodate Christian beliefs to the scholarship. They constituted a loosely organized movement consisting of clerics often associated with the 1860 book *Essays and Reviews* (a collection of articles written by eminent university professors and clerics—six out of seven of whom were Anglicans—as well as distinguished lay writers such as Arnold and Tennyson). As theological "liberals," they prided themselves on possessing a "breadth and freedom of view." They portrayed themselves not as "High" or "Low" but as "Broad" Churchmen—an expression that came into parlance in the late 1840s.

In 1889 the High Church Anglican Charles Gore published an edited volume *Lux Mundi, A Series of Studies in the Religion of the Incarnation*. Since 1875, at Oxford a number of the theological descendants of the Anglo-Catholic Tractarians had met to discuss privately how they could create a theology that was both "unchanging" (faithful to Scripture and the historic Anglican creeds) and "elastic" (responsive to the new scholarship). Under Gore's editorship, they published essays in *Lux Mundi*. It revealed publicly their general acceptance of "modern scholarship."

Gore penned a controversial article on biblical inspiration that countenanced higher criticism, especially in relation to the Old Testament. The popular book became one of the most influential theological volumes of the late nineteenth century. It went through at least ten editions in one year and provoked considerable alarm. Conservative commentators worried that its authors did not fully uphold the divinity of Christ. The authors claimed, for example, that in "emptying himself," Christ had allegedly given up divine omniscience. They also modified traditional understandings of biblical authority.

The response of agnostics such as Thomas Huxley (1825–95), Darwin's great defender, represented another kind of reaction to "modern scholarship." It will be recalled that Huxley had claimed that the emergence of "natural knowledge" as opposed to "revealed knowledge" constituted the most important intellectual trait of his day. He wanted to reform British education and make science its foundation.

Huxley was reluctant to say categorically that the Christian faith is either true or false: "When I reached intellectual maturity and began to ask myself whether I was an atheist, a theist, or a pantheist, a materialist or an idealist, a Christian or a freethinker, I found that the more I learned and reflected, the less ready was the answer." He proposed that Hume and Kant were "on his side" in this way of thinking.

In 1869 Huxley, discomforted by being labeled an "infidel," coined the word "agnosticism" to describe his position. The term caught on in the general public. Agnosticism gained a foothold among students in British universities and among members of the fashionable upper classes. Huxley also attempted to demonstrate that a "natural history" of the Bible would help solve the "synoptic problem" related to the Gospels.

A strain of more thoroughly "secular" thought also existed in England. It was reinforced by the new scholarship. By the early 1860s, at least four atheistic and infidel journals existed. John Stuart Mill (1806–73), the famous non-Christian author of *The System of Logic* (1843), *On Liberty* (1859), and other books, offered to the English people a version of utilitarianism, what some thought was a respectable non-Christian alternative to the Christian faith. He argued that happiness is the end-all of human existence. He optimistically suggested that with hard work and concern for neighbor, "most of the great positive evils of the world are in themselves removable, and will, if human affairs continue to improve, be in the end reduced within narrow limits."

Schooled initially by his father, Mill indicated he had never lost the Christian faith. Why? Because he had never been a Christian in the first place. Rather, John Stuart Mill the liberal gloried in "pagan self-assertion" and the exercise of the rights of the autonomous self. In 1869 Mill with Harriet Taylor published *The Subjection of Women*. They argued for women's rights to vote, to enjoy equal educational and employment opportunities, and to preserve property ownership rights for married women.

Mill paid special homage to the earlier "utilitarianism" of jurist Jeremy Bentham (1748–1832), who had announced his provocative desire to extirpate the very idea of religion. Bentham proposed a utilitarian, non-biblically based naturalistic ethic: human beings act in accordance with the motivations of pain and pleasure, even in the area of religion. The greatest good constitutes that which brings the greatest pleasure to the greatest number. "[N]ature has placed mankind under the governance of two sovereign masters, pain and pleasure. It is for them alone to point out what we ought to do, as well as to determine what we do."

In this secular form of utilitarianism, Bentham took aim at the "theological utilitarianism" of William Paley (1743–1805). In his *Principles of Moral and Political Philosophy* (1785), Paley had indicated that we are happy to the extent that we do God's will as discerned through Scripture and the light of nature. He wrote: "... private happiness is our motive, and the will of God our rule." By contrast, Bentham's secular utilitarianism tried to assuage the worry of divine retribution (God's judgment or blessing) for non-Christians. This view would suggest that Christ's atoning death for our sins as a necessary condition for our salvation and thus "happiness" is a meaningless concept, if not morally offensive.

In the second half of the nineteenth century, opponents of the Christian faith often criticized what they claimed were Christianity's ethical deficiencies. They excoriated among other doctrines the substitutionary atonement of Christ and the eternal damnation of those who do not follow Christ.

Critical of Mill's empiricism, Thomas Hill Green (1836–82) reinvigorated a movement of philosophical British idealism. As a monist interacting with the thought of both Kant and Hegel, he argued that a "spiritual principle" in nature created the unified world we experience. This principle reproduces itself in our world. Philosophers ranging from Green to Francis Bradley (1846–1924) made various expressions of British idealism a significant force in the intellectual life of England.

In the 1890s proponents of realism challenged idealism's validity. Realists proposed that the world is made up of unchanging facts not necessarily dependent on a knower or God. A person has an immediate intuition of these facts and does not need to resort to a concept of an "Absolute Principle" to account for them. Even beyond World War I, realists and idealists engaged in dogged criticisms of each other's views.

K. Attacks against the Doctrine of Biblical Infallibility

On one occasion Mill claimed that all thoughtful Englishmen of his day were by implication "either a Benthamite or a Coleridgean." Coleridge was likewise greatly appreciated by the Broad Churchmen.

In his posthumous *Letters of an Enquiring Spirit* (1841), Coleridge launched a direct attack on what he called the "popular belief" in the infallibility of Scripture. He acknowledged that representatives of all denominations—whether "Calvinist, Arminian, Quaker and Methodist, Dissenting Ministers and Clergymen, nay dignitaries of the Established Church"—agreed "that the Bible throughout was dictated by Omniscience, and therefore in all its parts infallibly true and obligatory." Coleridge argued that the doctrine of biblical infallibility stemmed from a misconceived dictation theory of biblical inspiration.

Coleridge had traveled to Germany and was steeped in German writers from Semler to Reimarus to Lessing and Schleiermacher. He introduced his English readers to elements of the higher criticism of the German Neologians. A Romantic, Coleridge also dismissed the apologetic value of "evidences" for God's existence, such as those championed by William Paley. He wrote, "Christianity is not a theory or a speculation ... but a life and a living process." The true evidence of Christianity would include "the actual *Trial* of the Faith in Christ...." If a person wanted a proof of Christianity, Coleridge urged, "Try it!"

In 1846 the novelist George Eliot (Mary Ann Evans, 1819–80), who had been raised as an evangelical, further abetted the entrance of German liberal theology into England by publishing an English translation of Strauss's *Das Leben Jesu* (*Life of Jesus*). She had accepted forms of higher criticism, largely due to her reading of Strauss's work and Charles Hennell's *Inquiry concerning the Origin of Christianity* (1838). Yet much of the British public did not become agitated by this literature. They were not privy to it. Some simply ignored a number of these writings due to their German origins.

Around 1859, however, a cluster of books appeared that did cause genuine consternation among conservative British Christians. Darwin's *Origins of Species* and John Stuart Mill's *On Liberty* were published that year. Many Christians perceived these books as directly challenging the validity of a biblically based worldview. (See chapter 15.) Their fears were not totally alarmist. An Anglican bishop, for example, later recalled that a reading of *Origin of Species* had led his father, a physician, to abandon his Christian beliefs:

> This [book] wrecked his faith, chiefly because it was not reconcilable with the biblical account of creation, and as the biblical revelation hung together and was all of one piece, if part of it fell out, the rest would fall out too. If Adam never existed, he did not sin; if he did not sin, man was not fallen; there was therefore no need for Christ to come. If the Bible was wrong in science, how could we be sure it was right in theology?

The publication of *Essays and Reviews* further alarmed many British Christians. The authors professed their desire to reconcile the Christian faith with the findings of contemporary scholarship. In his essay "On the Interpretation of Scripture," Benjamin Jowett wrote, "The Christian religion is in a false position when all the tendencies of knowledge are opposed to it." The authors discounted the Bible's infallibility and accepted aspects of German "higher criticism." Jowett added the controversial premise that Scripture should be evaluated just as any other book would be. Conservative Christians castigated the authors as "The

Seven Against Christ." Several of the authors were put on trial in ecclesiastical courts.

The heated controversy about *Essays and Reviews* lasted four years and unleashed a flood of tracts, sermons, magazine pieces, and books.

In 1862 the publication of J. W. Colenso's *The Pentateuch and the Book of Joshua Critically Examined* stirred up the caldron of religious controversy even further. Colenso, a missionary bishop in Natal, South Africa, argued that findings of geologists made it impossible for him to believe in a "universal Deluge" as described in Genesis. He denied that Moses had personally written the Pentateuch "as a whole." He also dismissed the Bible's infallibility.

In 1864 the poet Robert Browning (1812–89) attempted to capture in verse the impact of these writings on the English public:

> The candid incline to surmise of late
> That the Christian faith proves false, I find:
> For our Essays and Reviews debate
> Begins to tell on the public mind,
> And Colenso's words have weight.

Browning specifically linked attacks on the Bible's authority with a "crisis of faith" in the Victorian era.

In Scotland, as noted, the controversy over Professor William Robertson Smith's advocacy of higher criticism roiled the theological waters especially in the 1870s and 1880s. In 1870 Smith became the recipient of the chair of Hebrew and Old Testament Criticism at the University of Aberdeen. He disarmingly argued that "higher criticism does not mean negative criticism." In 1875 Smith, who had been trained at New College, Edinburgh, published a controversial article, "Bible," for the *Encyclopedia Britannica*. Smith proposed that Moses did not write the Pentateuch. He denied that prophets had predictive capabilities: "There is no reason to think that a prophet even received a revelation which was not spoken directly and pointedly of his own time."

Newspaper coverage of Smith's four-year trial (1877–81) by the General Assembly of the Free Church gave him a vehicle for popularizing his views on higher criticism within a large reading public.

For many Christians, the brilliant advances in biblical studies by the distinguished Cambridge University triumvirate B. F. Wescott (1825–1901), F. J. A. Hort (1828–92), and J. B. Lightfoot (1828–89) and others did much to answer the more severe attacks of critics on the Bible's authority. In 1881 Wescott and Hort published *The New Testament in the Original Greek*, a work seventeen years in the making. They also published the *Revised Version of the King James Bible*. Dean Burgon criticized sharply the presence of a Unitarian on the revision committee for the *Revised Version*. Lightfoot also masterfully edited *The Apostolic Fathers* and authored commentaries on such biblical books as the Pauline epistles.

An obituary for Lightfoot notably stated, "It was a characteristic of equal importance that Dr. Lightfoot, like Dr. Wescott, never discussed these subjects in the mere spirit of controversy."

Despite disturbing questions raised by "higher critics," scientists, and students of comparative religion, apparently the majority of Victorian Christians continued to evince respect for the Bible's authority, even if some limited the extent of its infallibility to matters of "faith and practice" and not history and science. Moreover, the fact that a number of Britain's leading secularists and "infidels" reconverted to Christianity (William Hone, J. B. Bebbington, and George Sexton among others) has led historian Timothy Larsen to suggest that a "crisis of doubt" was enmeshed with the "crisis of faith" during the Victorian era.

Standing aloof from these controversies as "separatists," the members of the dissenting Plymouth Brethren churches (whether "Exclusive," those who disallowed nonmembers to participate in Communion, or the "Open" Communion branch, those who permitted such) became especially well known for their commitment to the Bible's infallibility, including matters of history and science. Essentially a lay-led movement, the Brethren did not believe that the office of a pastor possessed biblical warrant. In their "assemblies" they "broke bread" together regularly and stressed Bible study and holy living.

The leader among the Exclusive Brethren was John Nelson Darby, who had a distinctly separatist bent and was an early advocate of "Dispensational theology" (see chapter 21).

VI. CONCLUSION

Only four years after the sixtieth-year celebration of Queen Victoria's long reign (1897), the Victorian era finally came to an end. On January 22, 1901, Victoria died. A newspaper article, dated January 23, described her death as the "greatest event in the memory of this generation, the most stupendous change in existing conditions that could possibly be imagined." It extolled Victoria as "the most respected of all women living or dead."

Between February 2 and 4 her body lay in state at the Albert Memorial Chapel. Then it was eventually escorted to the Frogmore Mausoleum and placed next to her beloved husband, Prince Albert. Behind the funeral cortège, Queen Victoria's son, the new King of England Edward VII, and her grandson, Kaiser Wilhelm II of Germany, solemnly walked side by side. Not many years later, their respective nations, England and Germany, would engage in the deadly battles of World War I (1914–18).

During the nineteenth century, the British had gained what looked like a position of unquestioned political and economic leadership in the world. Their empire stretched from sea to shining sea around the globe. Not only did they sing, "Rule, Britannia!" with gusto, but some now chimed in with rousing renditions of "Onward Christian Soldiers" (1865; 1871). Many Christians relished the "muscular Christianity" of contemporary missionaries such as C. T. Studd and rejoiced that hundreds of British were taking the gospel of Jesus Christ into far-off "heathen" lands. In 1896 a high point in missionary recruitment was reached.

Their Queen Victoria had enjoyed the longest reign of any English monarch. They had not experienced the waves of bloody revolutions that had severely lacerated France and Germany. Undoubtedly, some British were troubled by the increased economic competition from imperialistic European powers such as Germany and France, by steep downturns of the economy, by their own exploitation of colonial peoples, and by the spirit of revolt and the presence of grinding poverty in sectors of Irish society.

A number of evangelical reformers, theological liberals, Christian and non-Christian socialists, secular humanists (who emphasized "brotherhood"), and Marxists remained appalled that large numbers of the poor of both rural and urban England continued to live in deplorable conditions.

Moreover, deep-seated resentments against British rule festered among some native peoples in various corners of the British Empire. A firestorm of controversy erupted when a newspaper writer proposed that Africans living in areas where the Muslim faith dominated enjoyed better living conditions than those in areas colonized by British "Christians." Then again, England's victory in the Boer War (October 1899–May 1902) in South Africa had proved very costly in terms of soldiers and material.

At the close of the nineteenth century, many British still viewed themselves as self-reliant, optimistic individuals. Their military was apparently strong, their better businessmen were savvy capitalists, and their scholars were progressive and innovative. As with the Germans, they were witnessing stunning technological innovations (such as the automobile and movies), and some were wooed to join a "leisure revolution."

They were citizens of a "Christian country" (as they were prone to call England) that was both religiously tolerant and highly civilized. The observance of "Quiet Sundays" was still practiced, even if less rigorously so. In the 1880s both church and Sunday school attendance reached high-level marks. About 50 percent of youngsters between five and thirteen attended Sunday school. Parents still thought their children should be christened or baptized. Between the years 1902 and 1914, 66–70 percent of babies received an Anglican baptism, 5 percent a Roman Catholic baptism.

After the 1880s, Anglicans and Non-Conformists—especially from the upper middle class—attended church less regularly and engaged in less social service work among the poor. Agnosticism had emerged as a socially palatable belief among students and members of the upper classes. And after 1890, some British had an increased awareness that the culture at large was experiencing diverse kinds of religious crises.

Historian Hugh McLeod notes that in 1904 W. L. Courtney published selected letters addressed to *The Telegraph* newspaper for an article titled "Do We Believe?" After reading incoming letters, Courtney concluded that "the age is a skeptical one—a prey to skepticism due to a variety of causes, most of all perhaps, to the triumphant analysis of Science applied both to History and Biology." But Courtney added, "Dogmatic Christianity may indeed have decayed, but those instincts to which as a form of religion it appealed are as fresh and indomitable as ever."

Utopian political and socialist radicals and union organizers joined international parties and complained bitterly about indisputable inequities of the distribution of wealth in the society and the government's alleged callous attitude toward the poor and colonials. Various "secular forces" and the distractions of "modern" society were blamed for loosening the cultural grip of the Christian faith on the British people. Perhaps for this reason, the surprising religious power of the Welsh Revival (1904–5) caught many contemporaries off-guard. In addition, a number of articles appeared in American newspapers in 1905 suggesting that both Europe and the United States might soon be caught up in "continental" spiritual awakenings.

More generally, however, the British constituted a self-contented people, if the unrestrained way they celebrated Victoria's Golden Jubilee (1887) and Diamond Jubilee (1897) counts as evidence. An enthusiastic reporter for *The Times* described the Diamond Jubilee in exalted terms: "History may be searched, and searched in vain, to discover so wonderful an exhibition of allegiances and brotherhood among so many myriads of men."

With intoxicating sentiments of this kind drifting through the air and spinning heads, it is little wonder that numerous British continued to cultivate a long-standing sense of superiority toward peoples of other lands, even nearby Europeans living across the English Channel. It is to these continental Europeans we turn our attention once again.

FOR FURTHER STUDY

Bebbington, David. *Victorian Religious Revivals: Culture and Piety in Local and Global Contexts*. Oxford: Oxford University Press, 2012.

Foster, R. F. *Modern Ireland 1600–1972*. London: Penguin, 1989.

George, Timothy. *The Life and Mission of William Carey*. Worcester, PA: Christian History Institute, 1998.

Hempton, David. *Religion and Political Culture in Britain and Ireland: From the Glorious Revolution to the Decline of Empire*. Cambridge: Cambridge University Press, 1996.

Hemstadter, Richard, ed. *Victorian Faith in Crisis: Essays on Continuity and Change in Nineteenth-Century Religious Belief*. Stanford: Stanford University Press, 1990.

Larsen, Timothy. *Crisis of Doubt: Honest Faith in Nineteenth-Century England*. Oxford: Oxford University Press, 2006.

Moore, James. *The Post-Darwinian Controversies: A Study of the Protestant Struggle to Come to Terms with Darwin in Great Britain and America, 1870–1900*. Cambridge: Cambridge University Press, 1979.

Reardon, Bernard M. G. *Religion in the Age of Romanticism*. New York: Cambridge University Press, 1985.

Stead, W. T., and G. Campbell Morgan. *The Welsh Revival*. Boston: Pilgrim Press, 1905.

Tucker, Ruth A. *From Jerusalem to Irian Jaya: A Biographical History of Christian Missions*. Grand Rapids: Zondervan, 2004.

The Christian Churches on the European Continent

(1814–1914)

INTRODUCTION

In the 1830s nearly 50,000 English people crossed the English Channel to ports on the European continent. Many were tourists enthusiastic about the chance to explore foreign lands and cultures. On the eve of World War I, the annual wave of travelers had swollen to 660,000. In correspondence, diaries, and books, tourists sometimes left detailed descriptions of sites explored and people encountered. Not unexpectedly, travelers imbued with an ethnocentric sense of Protestant England's cultural and religious superiority often commented negatively about their perceptions of the restored strength of the Roman Catholic papacy's influence in countries such as France.

Queen Victoria publicly proclaimed that her subjects in India, regardless of their religion, should "enjoy the equal and impartial protection of the law." By contrast, in the middle years of her reign she privately was alarmed by the growing power of English Roman Catholics who had received the "protection of the law" (1829). Queen Victoria was especially disturbed by the bull of Pope Pius IX that reinstituted the Roman Catholic hierarchy in England (1850). She was likewise offended by John Henry Newman's claim that Pope Pius IX's bold initiative intimated that "the people of England are about of their own free will to be added to the Holy Church."

Two decades later, Queen Victoria, upon learning of Vatican I's declaration regarding the infallibility of the popes (1870), reportedly said to her prime minister, "The Queen will be pleased if you can find any legitimate opportunity of throwing dirt on the Council." Queen Victoria indicated that it was her duty and her family's "to maintain the true and real principles and spirit of our Protestant religion."

Members of the British public were not only separated from a predominantly Roman Catholic country such as France by the watery divide of the English Channel but more generally by a different mindset, an adherence to a different set of religious and cultural values. Historian James Moore writes, "Victorians themselves, who peered piously through the mists at republican France, fancied their isles a bastion of Christian civilization." Like their queen, many identified their homeland with Protestantism, a stable monarchy, treasured liberties, a spirit of toleration, and intellectual inquiry. They associated the French with unstable radical republicanism, Roman Catholicism, oppression, intolerance, and superstition.

The British had heard stock anti-Catholic stories recounted. Some were well acquainted with the horrors of the Saint Bartholomew's Day Massacre (1572), during which French Protestants had been slaughtered by Roman Catholics. Then again, had not French Protestants been the recent victims of the "White Terror" of 1815? Hundreds were killed, and their homes and churches destroyed, especially in the area around Nîmes in southern France. The British also retained negative memories about the bloody atrocities of the French Revolution and the costly warfare of the Napoleonic era.

By contrast, Victorian Catholics did sometimes evidence an appreciation for French Roman Catholicism. Nuns from French congregations in England, for example, meditated on devotional literature originating in France. Moreover, three-fourths of the Irish population was Roman Catholic, and large numbers of Irish immigrated to England.

British travelers to the Continent frequently described Roman Catholicism and Protestantism as if they were monolithic religions. This perspective was not especially helpful. Sharp divisions in fact existed between continental, "Ultramontane" Catholics (also present in Ireland and outside of Europe), who defended the papacy's authority sometimes without question, and "liberal Catholics," who often urged the papacy to accept democratic values including freedom of conscience.

In the last decades of the century, "liberal Catholics" (sometimes known after 1905 as "modernists") urged the papacy to evidence a greater openness to Darwinian science and higher biblical criticism. Moreover, certain regions of Europe were more "religiously devout" than others. In 1848 a report for the French Constituent Assembly proposed that Brittany, the Vendée, and the Pyrenees constituted areas of notable Roman Catholic religious observance, whereas Saintonge, Aunis, Périgord, the southwest, Provence, Burgundy, and the region around Paris were fairly "dechristianized."

In a similar fashion, Protestants were sometimes divided by denominational, theological, and regional loyalties. Theological "conservatives" and "liberals" could dispute with each other in the same denomination. Theological "moderates" sometimes sought to find common ground between various theological factions within their churches.

Christians on the Continent, whether Roman Catholic, Protestant, or Orthodox, on occasion shared with British believers a commitment to advance foreign missions. Some participated in religious renewal and "revivals." Continental Christians often faced similar questions: What stance should they assume regarding church and state relations? How should they interact with nationalistic aspirations and revolutions? What steps should they take to preserve or advance their own confessional or personal beliefs? What should they make of "modernity," the rise of anti-Christian "secularism," and the radical "anti-modernist" ferment in the arts and philosophy?

Many continental Christians belonged to religious institutions, religious orders, societies, church associations, and schools of theology that were supranational. The Roman Catholic Church represented one such prominent international institution. Its constituency numbered in the millions of the faithful dispersed throughout the European continent, the British Isles, and other regions of the world. Latin America had an especially large Roman Catholic population. The Roman Catholic faith likewise dominated the Caribbean Islands.

During the nineteenth century, the papacy reemerged as a vital force in European political, cultural, and religious life. Virulent anticlericalism episodically broke out in reaction to Roman Catholic advances. Some anti-Catholics were prepared to die as martyrs in the struggle to create national states such as "modern Italy." By contrast some anti-nationalists were ready to die as martyrs for the cause of the Roman Catholic Church and the papacy.

II. THE RESTORATION OF THE ROMAN PAPACY

Historian Christopher Clark aptly describes the complex dynamics of continental Roman Catholicism during the nineteenth century: "The history of Catholic societies in nineteenth-century Europe was marked by the paradoxical intertwining of two transformative processes: secularisation and religious revival." Even though the Roman Catholic Church suffered rounds of anticlerical hostility, the loss of papal lands, diminished temporal authority, and the curtailment of long-standing privileges, "a flowering of Catholic religious life across Europe" also occurred. A thriving "New Catholicism" on occasion appeared quite expansive.

The "religious revival" was characterized by an increased devotion to the Virgin Mary, a renewed commitment to missions, a certain "feminization" of devotional life, and the Catholic Church becoming more "romanized." Numerous new religious orders, whether male or female, were dedicated to the Sacred Heart of Mary. Between 1805 and 1854, twenty-three foundations devoted to the immaculate conception of the Virgin Mary were created. The faithful extolled not only Mary's immaculate conception, but also her purity and exemplary morality.

In France, many Roman Catholic women participated in Marian devotions. Apparitions of the Virgin Mary in places such as Lourdes, France, and Marpingen, Germany, fortified the Catholic faith of thousands. In *The Story of the Soul* (1895), Thérèse of Lisieux (canonized 1925) told a moving account of personal spirituality that became inspirational reading fare for many Roman Catholics worldwide.

The church's renewed commitment to missions and evangelism took various forms. In 1822 the Society for the Propagation of the Faith was established in Lyons, France. It gave financial aid to missionary initiatives. France emerged as the lead sending nation of Roman Catholic missionaries overseas. In 1881 Eucharistic Congresses began to meet regularly and attracted and inspired large numbers of the faithful.

The papacy exercised a greater role in European-wide Catholicism than it had in the eighteenth century, when Jansenist-influenced clergy and laity, Gallicans, and Josephists seriously contested Ultramontane claims.

A. The Papacy and the Birth of Modern Italy

During the nineteenth century the papacy confronted particularly serious challenges from revolutionaries such as the gifted organizer Guiseppe Mazzini, forced into exile in London and founder of Young Italy (a secret society); the anticlerical fighter Giuseppe Garibaldi; and the aristocratic Count Camillo Benso di Cavour, who sought the unification of Italy. They wanted to absorb the Papal States into that union.

The Papal States in 1859 consisted of 16,000 square miles and stretched across the center of the peninsula between the Adriatic and the Tyrrhenian Sea. To the north, the Austrians controlled both the republics of Lombardy and Venice. Also to the north were the states of Piedmont and the Kingdom of Sardinia, Parma, Modena, Romagna, and Tuscany. To the south was located the Kingdom of the Two Sicilies; it arched from the boot of Italy up toward Rome and belonged to the French Bourbons.

Nationalistic revolutionaries and politicians made repeated attempts to drive foreign powers such as the French and the Austrians out of Italy. Many assumed that the Papal States would have to be incorporated by force of arms if diplomatic accommodations with the papacy failed. The absence of the Papal States from any "unified Italy" would effectively split the new state into two geographically separated entities. Students, Freemasons, and Carbonari conspired in republican plots such as the Two Sicilies insurrection (1820–21) against local sovereigns. A number of revolutionaries trumpeted the virtues of liberty, democracy, the separation of church and state, freedom of conscience, and secular education—concepts that rankled the heightened sensitivities of the papacy.

During the French Revolution and the Napoleonic era the papacy's political power and influence had plummeted to a perilous low point. The troops of Napoleon had entered Rome and deposed Pope Pius VI in 1798 and incarcerated him in France, where he died.

In 1800 Pope Pius VII succeeded Pope Pius VI. In 1813, having likewise been subjected to physical and mental abuse by Napoleon, he agreed to the "Concordat of Fontainebleau." According to its terms, the pope ceded the temporal power of the Roman Catholic Church to the emperor. Napoleon even contemplated transferring the seat of the papacy to a French location. Troubled by this concession, Pius VII bravely renounced the concordat. In 1814 the defeat of Napoleon facilitated the pope's return to Rome. That same year, the pope reestablished the Society of Jesus; the order grew rapidly from approximately 800 members in 1814 to 2,000 in 1820 and 6,000 in 1850.

By the time Pius VII died in 1823, the restoration of papal power was noticeably under way. The conclave of 1823 elected Pope Leo XII (1823–29). The new pope proceeded to enforce rigorous standards of ethical conduct among Roman Catholics. He launched an attack on secret societies, targeting in particular ruthless antipapal rebels, the Carbonari ("Charcoal Burners"), who had perpetrated assassinations.

After Leo XII's death in 1829, the conclave of 1830 elected Pope Pius VIII. He died that same year. However, he did condemn the vernacular (Protestant) translations of the Bible that he said were "rarely without perverse little inserts to insure that the reader imbibes their lethal poison instead of the saving water of salvation." Also that same year, revolts broke out in France, Parma, and even in the Papal States. Revolutionary turmoil became widespread in Europe.

Pius VIII's successor, Pope Gregory XVI, who consecrated a bishop after his election as pope, faced daunting issues. Prior to this, state governments had been naming the vast majority of bishops. This egregious infraction of the pope's perceived apostolic authority to appoint bishops hindered his ability to shepherd the bishops in question.

Gregory XVI (1831–46), an Ultramontanist, also confronted revolutionaries intent on seizing the Papal States as they pursued the goal of Italian unification. He called on the Austrian government to provide troops to thwart the efforts of Guiseppie Mazzini's revolutionaries, who were members of "Young Italy" and touted the ideal of "God and People." This reliance on the Austrian troops precipitated alarm, especially among French and German diplomats.

Whereas Pope Gregory attempted to remove the "shame from all the Christian nations" by condemning the slave trade (1839), he stoked anger among theological liberals by ultimately disciplining radicals who had called for "a Free Church in a Free State." In the encyclical *Mirari Vos*, Gregory castigated political liberalism and "the poisonous spring of indifferentism that has flowed from that absurd and erroneous doctrine or rather delirium, that freedom of conscience is to be claimed and defended for all men."

Gregory XVI's policies reflected his deep-seated suspicions about liberal political and intellectual currents of the day. One of the pope's personal goals was to elevate the doctrine of the immaculate conception of Mary.

B. The Pontificate of Pius IX

The pontificate of Pius IX (1846–78) constituted one of the longest and most controversial in the history of the Roman Catholic Church. In 1848 he rejected the politically and religiously impractical proposal that he become the president of a federation of Italian states. He then attempted to impede the creation of a "new Italy." Revolutionaries such as Garibaldi and his soldiers ("Thousands of Redshirts") were constructing this new Italy through warfare and annexation.

Despite a falling out between Garibaldi and Cavour, the pieces of the national puzzle continued to fall into place. Between 1857 and 1866 such regions as Lombardy, Tuscany, the Kingdom of the Two Sicilies, and a portion of the Papal States became part of the new Italy. In early 1861 Victor Emmanuel II, King of Piedmont-Sardinia (1848–61), with Garibaldi's support, became the king of the new Italy in the making.

In 1864 Emperor Louis Napoleon III indicated he would remove French troops from Rome and did so by 1866. But in 1867 the papal army once again did receive some help from French forces. In 1870 the Franco-Prussian War erupted and prompted Louis Napoleon III to withdraw the remaining French military contingent in Rome. On September 20, 1870, Italian troops occupied Rome and the surrounding papal territory. In a controversial plebiscite that October, 153,681 voters to 1,507 overwhelmingly approved Rome's annexation to Italy. For the Italian nation builders, the last piece of the new Italy appeared in place.

In 1871 King Victor Emmanuel II presented a triumphal speech to the Italian Parliament: "The work to which we consecrated our life is accomplished. After long trials of expiation Italy is restored to herself and to Rome.... We have proclaimed the separation of Church and State. Having recognized the absolute independence of the spiritual authority, we are convinced that Rome, the capital of Italy, will continue to be the peaceful and respected seat of the Pontificate."

Pius IX categorically refused to accept the loss of his rights to temporal authority. In the encyclical *Ubi Nos* ("On Pontifical States") he promptly condemned the Italian state's "Law of Guaranties" (May 13, 1871). This law gave the papacy certain rights ("immunities and privileges") and a fixed sum of money per year, but reduced its actual landholdings essentially to Vatican City. For the rest of his pontificate Pius did not leave the confines of the Vatican, viewing himself as a virtual prisoner of the Kingdom of Italy and robbed of his "authority of making laws in regard to the religion and moral order."

Not until the Lateran Treaties of 1929 did the papacy "consider as finally and irrevocably settled the Roman Question which arose in 1870 by the annexation of Rome to the Kingdom of Italy."

Paradoxically enough, on the eve of the loss of the Papal States, Pius IX at Vatican I (1869–70) secured an epochal victory for an Ultramontane form of the papacy. The council delivered what appeared to be a knockout blow to long-standing Gallican and conciliarist theories of church governance that gave superior authority collectively to bishops. Yet, even though the pope condemned the "modern" theology of "liberals," he was not averse to using "modern" means in defending his traditional rights. He promoted his goals through loyal newspapers and also attempted to use political parties such as the pro-Catholic Center Party in Prussia to back his aims.

Pius had to reckon with severe challenges to his authority as pope. The challenges stemmed from multiple sources and came packaged in different formats.

III. THE PAPACY BUFFETED BY WINDS OF CULTURAL AND POLITICAL CHANGE

After 1848, especially strong winds of cultural and political change blew throughout parts of Europe, sometimes as storms with gale-force strength. They buffeted long-standing institutions from monarchies to prestigious universities to the Christian churches. Within and without the Roman Catholic Church, liberal voices could be heard calling on the papacy to embrace "modern civilization," to manifest a greater openness to science and biblical criticism, and to demonstrate appreciation for democratic ideals, including the separation of church and state and "freedom of conscience."

Moreover, many Italian nationalists became more than ever convinced that *Risorgimento* ("rising up," or resurgence), the unification of the Italian states, could only be achieved if the Papal States were integrated into a new national entity. Regional north-south loyalties were also hampering the movement toward national unification.

Pius IX struck some observers as a personable man, the epitome of charm. In a sermon, "The Pope and the Revolution" (October 7, 1866), John Henry Newman described Pius IX as most winsome in bearing: "He is one whom to see is to love, one who overcomes even strangers, even enemies, by his very look and voice." At the beginning of his pontificate, Pius was thought to be a "liberal" in spirit. He arranged for "modern" gas streetlights and railways in the Papal States. He appeared favorably disposed to the campaign for Italian unity.

The pope could also impress people as unbending. In the late 1840s his liberal reputation disappeared. He would not support efforts to drive the Austrians out of Italy. This signaled to revolutionaries and others that the pope did not fully back their nationalistic ambitions. After his prime minister was assassinated, a harassed Pius IX, disguised as a priest, fled the Papal States to Gaeta, in the Kingdom of the Two Sicilies. For a time, Mazzini's revolutionaries gained control of Rome, and a Constituent Assembly was instituted. Protestants and Jews were afforded religious liberties (1849). Only with the help of French troops did Pius IX, now noticeably wary of "liberal" causes, return to the Papal States (June 1850).

Thereafter Pius IX encountered additional serious challenges. They included the campaigns of Garibaldi's redshirt troops; the efforts of Cavour and Victor Immanuel II and others to bring about the unification of Italy; the government of Columbia in South America opting for a separation of church and state; the seizure of Roman Catholic properties; Chancellor Otto von Bismarck's *Kulturkampf* against the Roman Catholic Church in Prussia; and French Emperor Louis Napoleon III's unexpected support for Italian nationalism.

Pius believed that he had a God-given mission to affirm the doctrine of the immaculate conception of Mary. He promulgated this in the Apostolic Constitution *Ineffabilis Deus* in 1854. He also thought that it was his duty to warn the Catholic faithful regarding the dangers lurking in contemporary society. He was especially vexed by the teachings of Catholic "liberals." In 1863 Johann Joseph Ignaz von Dollinger, a distinguished theologian and church historian from Munich, Germany, criticized not only the Scholastic method of some Roman Catholic theologians but commended aspects of biblical criticism. Moreover, he declared, "The faults of science must be met with the arms of science; for the Church cannot exist without a progressive theology."

In the "Munich Brief" published in 1864, Pius IX condemned the right of the Catholic faithful to uphold any scholarship that contradicted the teachings of the Roman Catholic Church. Catholic liberals perceived this brief as a rude blow against academic freedom. In England, the Roman Catholic Lord Acton closed down the *Home and Foreign Review*, a journal that had advocated freedom of inquiry. For all practical purposes, the promotion of a "liberal Catholic" movement in England no longer appeared viable. A number of English Catholic liberals chose to remain silent about their beliefs.

A. Pius IX and the *Syllabus of Errors*

In 1864 Pope Pius IX also published the encyclical *Quanta Cura* ("Condemning Current Errors"), accompanied by the *Syllabus of Errors*. In *Quanta Cura* he indicated that Christian people were buffeted by a "truly awful storm excited by so many evil opinions." He was greatly alarmed about the status of Roman Catholicism in Europe and in Latin America.

Cardinal Luigi Bilio largely culled Pius IX's *Syllabus of Errors* from previous papal condemnations. The pope not only condemned eighty specific errors, but also targeted the "pests" of "socialism, communism, secret societies, biblical societies, clerico-liberal societies." In error 1 he condemned pantheism, naturalism, and absolute rationalism. In error 18 he stipulated that it was wrong to believe that "Protestantism is nothing more than another form of the same true Christian religion, in which form it is given to please God equally as in the Catholic Church." Likewise, he countered Catholic liberals by proposing that it was an error (80) to believe that the "Roman Pontiff can, and ought to, reconcile himself, and come to terms with progress, liberalism, and modern civilization."

Whereas many Ultramontane Catholics applauded the *Syllabus of Errors*, some Roman Catholics were aghast. They feared that Protestant scholars would gloat that this document revealed clearly the papacy's alleged hostility toward "modern" scholarship. In fact, one Protestant writer characterized the *Syllabus of Errors* as a "monumental declaration of war against the entirety of science, against the modern state, against contemporary education." The French Bishop Felix-Antoine-Philibert Dupanloup of Orléans attempted to counter negative perceptions of this kind by proposing that a proper understanding of the syllabus rendered it much less offensive. Dupanloup claimed that the pope was describing the principles (theses) for an ideal society, but that in the everyday world it was legitimate for Catholics to follow hypotheses that might vary somewhat from the ideal principles. Hundreds of Catholic bishops adopted Dupanloup's distinction between theses and hypotheses as the means to gain a proper sense of the document's teachings.

B. Vatican Council I: The Infallibility of the Pope

In 1864 Pius IX announced he planned to hold a general council. In 1869 the theologian-historian Dollinger published anonymous letters (*The Pope and the Council by Janus* in book form) against the *Syllabus of Errors* and papal infallibility. He also presumptiously warned that the council would be a "synod of flatterers."

Approximately 754 prelates attended Vatican I, a council designed to uproot "current errors." The clergy addressed issues such as rationalism, materialism, atheism, and Christian marriage. But their greatest debates focused on what emerged eventually as the council's teaching on papal infallibility:

> We teach and define as a revealed dogma that when the Roman pontiff speaks ex cathedra, that is, when 1. In the exercise of his office as shepherd and teacher of all Christians, 2. In virtue of his supreme apostolic authority, 3. He defines a doctrine concerning faith or morals to be held by the whole church, he possesses by the divine assistance promised to him in blessed Peter that infallibility which the divine Redeemer willed his church to enjoy in defining doctrine concerning faith and practice. Therefore, such definitions of the Roman pontiff are of themselves, and not by the consent of the church, irreformable.

The last phrase sounded clearly the death knell for the idea that a council could "reform" definitions of the pope when given ex cathedra ("from the chair").

On July 18, 1870, all but two of the 535 members of the council at the decisive session approved the doctrine as defined in *Pastor aeternus*, the "Dogmatic Constitution on the Church of Christ." Some 20 percent of the prelates—the anti-infallibilists and "inopportunists"—had exited the council earlier so that they would not have to vote. The "inopportunists" did not oppose the doctrine of papal infallibility but thought that it was inopportune to approve the teaching in the present circumstances.

Pius IX's Ultramontanism that concentrated church and doctrinal authority in the papacy had won a decisive victory over the conciliarist form of church governance that highlighted the superior authority of bishops. Ultimately, most of the prelates accepted the doctrine with only a few refusing to do so. The latter joined the Old Catholic Church, which included some of Dollinger's followers. In 1871 Dollinger was excommunicated.

The promulgation of papal infallibility represented a signature golden moment in Pius IX's pontificate. The moment, however, was in one sense quickly tarnished, because the next day the Franco-Prussian War broke out. The proceedings of Vatican I were interrupted.

A distraught Pope Pius IX entered a self-imposed imprisonment in the Vatican. His own bearing as a suffering pope and spiritual leader who passionately sought the recovery of the Papal States increased his stature among some of the Roman Catholic faithful.

Until his death in 1878, Pius IX resolutely opposed parliamentary democracies. He forbade the participation of Roman Catholics in the political life of the "usurper" Kingdom of Italy. He criticized strongly Bismarck's *Kulturkampf* against Roman Catholics in Germany. When Germany and Russia broke off diplomatic relations with the papacy, Pius's estrangement from European politics became even more painfully clear. News from South America was even less encouraging as President Federico Errázuriz of Chile, like a number of other South American leaders, disputed papal claims in his country.

Pius IX's adoption of a "siege mentality" hampered his capacity to interact in an accommodating and persuasive way with many academics, clerics, and political leaders who questioned Vatican I's definition of papal infallibility.

C. Pope Leo XIII: Accommodating "Modern" Culture?

Not all Roman Catholics shared Pius IX's rigid hostility toward the Kingdom of Italy and aspects of "modern" scholarship. A good number sought to accommodate their status as citizens of democratic states and their intellectual convictions with what they thought was a faithful acceptance of Roman Catholic doctrine.

The conclave of 1878 elected Leo XIII, age sixty-eight, who sought to make these kinds of rapprochement more feasible. Such was no simple task. He was aware of Catholic intellectuals, a number eventually known as "Catholic modernists," who wanted him to endorse forms of biblical higher criticism and evolutionary theory he deemed incompatible with Catholic doctrine. He faced hostile political movements in France, Germany, and elsewhere that propagated virulent anticlericalism. He was subject to pressures from Ultramontane conservatives who were suspicious of any form of accommodation with modern culture.

By and large, Leo XIII's pontificate enhanced the papacy's reputation for greater openness to modern scholarship and an appreciation of democratic and labor movements. This was quite an accomplishment, given the fact that the pope never forsook his desire to recover the Papal States and in various ways upheld many of the same doctrinal convictions and Marian devotions as his predecessor, Pius IX. Moreover, in the 1879 encyclical *Aeterni Patris* ("Of the Eternal Father"), Leo XIII urged the renewed teaching of Scholasticism (Thomistic) as the Christian philosophy capable of adequately addressing the "false conclusions concerning divine and human things" that originated from "schools of philosophy" that had "crept into all the Orders of the State" and had been "accepted by the common consent of the masses." In October 1879 the pope established the Roman Academy of St. Thomas.

Leo XIII often improved diplomatic efforts with European governments. He opened the Vatican archives for historians' research. He indicated that a democratic form of government is acceptable as long as it does not attempt to subvert the authority of the Roman Catholic Church. In his encyclical *Rerum Novarum* ("Of New Things," 1891), Leo, while rejecting Marxism, called for the working classes to be protected from exploitation by the owners of capital. He proposed that the Roman Catholic Church is not against progress or modern scholarship, but opposes "naturalism or rationalism, the essence of which is utterly to do away with Christian institutions and to install in society the supremacy of man to the exclusion of God."

In the encyclical *Testem Benevolentiae Nostrae* ("Concerning New Opinions, Virtue, Nature and Grace with regard to Americanism," 1899), Leo warned the bishops of the United States (through Cardinal James Gibbons) not to countenance "Americanism"—a cluster of beliefs including the freedom of the press and the separation of church and state—due to the risk that American Catholics might practice another form of their faith than that practiced by Roman Catholics worldwide.

D. Leo XIII's Encyclical *Providentissimus Deus*

The encyclical *Providentissimus Deus* (1893) of Pope Leo XIII served as one of the papacy's responses to issues evoked by biblical criticism and evolution. From the Flemish Jesuit Leonard Lessius to the English priest Henry Holden to the French priest Richard Simon to François Lenormant, certain Catholics had proposed theories of the Bible's authority that did not include verbal inspiration or inerrancy in history and science.

Leo XIII encouraged Catholic scholars to pursue rigorous scholarship and defend the authority of Holy Scripture and Catholic Tradition. He observed, "Now, we have to meet the Rationalists who deny that there is any such thing as revelation, or inspiration, or Holy Scripture at all." While affirming that the Vulgate was the authentic edition of Scripture, he urged Catholic scholars to engage in the "art of true criticism" by seeking to understand Holy Scripture as given in the original biblical languages and through the use of lower textual criticism. Moreover, he warned them about the dangers of higher criticism: "There has arisen, to the great detriment of religion, an inept method, dignified by the name of the 'higher criticism,' which pretends to judge of the origin, integrity, and authority of each Book from internal indications alone."

Pope Leo chided historians who were intent on finding errors within Scripture. He was also concerned about critics who were exploiting the physical sciences to throw disrepute on the Bible: "Attacks of this kind, bearing as they do on matters of sensible experience, are peculiarly dangerous to the masses."

The pope affirmed that "biblical inerrancy" had been the Roman Catholic Church's doctrine throughout its history: "But it is absolutely wrong and forbidden, either to narrow inspiration to certain parts only of Holy Scripture, or to admit that the sacred writer has erred." Scripture is true because God is its ultimate author: "... it is impossible that God Himself, the supreme Truth, can utter that which is not true. This is the ancient and unchanging faith of the Church, solemnly defined in the Councils of Florence and of Trent, and finally confirmed and more expressly formulated by the Council of the Vatican." He praised St. Augustine's adroitly crafted definition of the Bible's authority and inerrancy.

E. Catholic Modernism (1890–1910)

The Catholic scholars associated with "Catholic modernism," an international movement, included among others the Frenchmen Alfred F. Loisy, Maurice Blondel, and Edouard Le Roy; the Irish Jesuit George Tyrrel, and the German Friedrich von Hügel. The estimates of the number of "modernist" priests in France ranged widely, from 1,500 (Loisy) to 20,000 (Tyrrel). The papacy also believed that a Roman Catholic seminary in Milan, Italy, along with a number of other educational institutions constituted modernist hotbeds.

Catholic modernists often denied that they made up a movement. Whereas they generally appreciated each other, they did not share all beliefs in common or always work together in concert. For that matter, the term "modernism" was not coined until 1905.

In one sense the "Catholic modernist" movement was an extension of the earlier "Catholic liberalism" of Lammenais and "progressive" Catholic thought. Catholic modernists wanted the papacy to demonstrate a greater openness to modern scholarship. They called for the right to freedom of inquiry in their "scientific" theological, biblical, or historical research. They admired aspects of the scholarship of

Protestant liberals such as Adolph von Harnack and Auguste Sabatier, who appeared to enjoy a certain amount of intellectual freedom and supposedly were not fearful of ecclesiastical recriminations. "Liberal" Catholics often assumed that the adjustment of their religious beliefs to modern scholarship would help project a Catholicism attractive to well-educated members of the Roman Catholic Church who were aware of modern scholarship.

The Catholic modernists' rationales for their scholarly work did not satisfy the papacy. It accused them of serving "Protestant masters" and promoting rationalistic, historical biblical criticism.

Catholic modernists who denied biblical inerrancy and embraced higher criticism and doctrines of evolution ran the risk of condemnation as heretics. In 1893 Loisy, ordained a priest in 1879, was forced out of a teaching post at the Institut Catholique in Paris because he denied the inerrancy of Scripture. His expertise in the biblical languages, largely accrued as an autodidact, eventually won for him a professorial post at Hautes Etudes, the Sorbonne, Paris.

Loisy viewed himself as a biblical scholar, not a theologian. Nonetheless, he found John Henry Newman's perspective on the development of dogma helpful. He proposed that, whereas the truth of the Catholic faith remained constant, the expression of that truth might take different forms. Like the Protestant liberals Harnack and Sabatier, Loisy advocated free inquiry into the Scripture. However, in *The Gospel and the Church* (1902), Loisy took Harnack's popular work *The Essence of Christianity* (1900) to task as a deficient exposition of Christianity. He disputed the validity not only of Harnack's definition of the gospel but his teaching about the kingdom of God (see chapter 15). Loisy argued that Jesus as a man became convinced that he was God and died because he thought he was the Messiah.

In 1907 Pius X's *Lamentabili Sane* stipulated sixty-five condemnations of alleged errors found in the writings of Loisy and Tyrell, and his *Pascendi Dominici Gregis* delivered sharp criticisms of the Catholic modernists' "new Christianity," calling it in effect agnosticism. The Catholic modernists were suspected of embracing a Kantian immanentist perspective that denied reason could address issues beyond the world of phenomena. Both Loisy and Tyrell were excommunicated. Pius X may have attributed to the movement a larger bundle of common doctrinal and intellectual traits than it actually possessed.

So concerned was Pius X about Catholic modernism that in 1910 he required all "clergy, pastors, confessors, preachers, religious superiors, and professors in philosophical-theological seminaries" to henceforth swear an "Anti-Modernist Oath": "I . . . firmly embrace and accept each and every definition that has been set forth and declared by the unerring teaching authority of the Church, especially those principal truths which are directly opposed to the errors of this day."

IV. SPIRITUAL AWAKENING AND CONFESSIONAL RENEWAL IN NORTHERN EUROPE (1780–1850)

In 1798 King Frederick William III of Prussia envisioned the unification of the Reformed and Lutheran churches on the basis of a shared ritual (per the *Agenda*, the official Lutheran book of rites and ceremonies). In 1817 he approved the "Evangelical Church of the Union" comprising the two churches. He hoped this union would temper confessional struggles and animosities between Lutherans and Reformed Christians. It would also permit his wife and him to take Communion together.

The measure provoked both enthusiastic approval and stiff criticism. Pastor Clause Harms, an advocate of confessional Lutheranism, viewed the union as an outright capitulation to rationalism and Protestant liberalism. In 1817 he published Luther's *Ninety-five Theses* and ninety-five other theses (from 1517 to 1817). Among other charges, Harms claimed that reason had become "the pope of our time."

In 1829 the government attempted to enforce obedience to the *Agenda*. "Old Lutherans" and others refused. Some Lutheran pastors were incarcerated, and some Old Lutherans, seeking religious freedom, immigrated to Australia and the United States. A group of more than six hundred Saxon Lutherans also immigrated (1838–39) and eventually became part of the Lutheran Church—Missouri Synod. A significant division, then, existed among German Lutherans.

Deep into the nineteenth century, many lay members of the Lutheran and Reformed churches, especially in rural areas, rejected Protestant liberalism. They preferred old or traditional ways of worship that emphasized historical confessions, hymnbooks, catechisms, and prayer books. They revered Luther's translation of the Bible. Newly minted pastors who were partisans of Schleiermacher or other Protestant liberals sometimes found that their progressive theological ideas did not sit well with the laity in their parishes.

Large numbers of laypeople became caught up in a Pietist spiritual awakening that spread through Germany, Denmark, Sweden, Norway (ruled by Sweden from 1814 to 1905), and Finland (ruled by Russia). In time, some of those affected by the evangelical awakening began to view the Lutheran Confessions as pure expressions of the Christian faith. By the 1840s, a revitalized Lutheran movement had emerged. Its leaders—Pastors Clause Harms, Ludwig Adolph Petri, Johann Konrad Wilhelm Loehe, and Karl Grail—strongly opposed unionism and Protestant liberalism. They identified the Christian faith exclusively with the Lutheran Confessions. In 1841 Petri (1803–73), hailed as the "father of Lutheran missions," argued that "mission is nothing other than the church itself in its mission activity."

The Pietist awakening had disparate impulses. Influential pastoral theologies had earlier called on ministers to take greater spiritual care of their parishioners, preach the gospel, and urge faithful attendance upon the sacraments. Areas of southern Germany like Württemberg possessed significant Pietist and Moravian populations.

Restrictions on the practice of their faith along with poor economic conditions prompted about 1,600 "radical" or "Separatist" Pietists under the direction of Johann Georg Rapp to immigrate to the United States in 1803–4. Rapp formed the "New Harmony" colony in Pennsylvania and later other colonies. In 1819 another group of Pietists led by Pastor Gottlieb Wilhelm Hoffmann left Württemberg and formed a community in Korntal. By the 1830s, Pastor Christian Gottlob Barth helped Württemberg become a center for Pietist publishing with a focus on Bibles, tracts, and devotional and educational literature.

In the 1820s Reformed Pastors G. D. Krummacker and his son, F. W. Krummacker, witnessed large crowds attending church services in parishes of Westphalia and the Lower Rhine. Some of these parishioners passed out Bibles and tracts. In 1861 Heinrich Heppe, a distinguished Reformed theologian and church historian at the University of Marburg, published *Reformed Dogmatics*, a book that greatly influenced the thinking of Karl Barth.

Branches of the British and Foreign Bible Society in Germany and Scandinavia provided printed Bibles, books, and tracts that colporteurs and itinerant preachers distributed in the countryside and cities. On occasion, entire Scandinavian households of peasants and craftsmen in rural communities listened appreciatively to itinerant preaching. At the same time, some of the German nobility such as Princess Marianne Hessen-Homburg, who was married to Prince Wilhelm, supported the movement. She participated in a Pietist group in Berlin that included friends of Otto von Bismarck, the future chancellor and a Lutheran. Prayer meetings and Bible readings (1816–19) took place in their fashionable homes. These meetings attracted individuals from various social classes.

In Hamburg, Johann Hinrich Wichern began Inner Mission (1833), a charity whose members sought to care for the spiritual and material needs of impoverished men, orphans, and the infirm. A Danish Inner Mission (1853) was also founded that sought to evangelize Danes. In addition, between 1824 and 1842 a number of foreign mission societies were established.

Missionaries from Germany, Norway, Denmark, and Sweden set sail with the goal of preaching the gospel to the "heathen" in the far distant regions of the world. For example, the German Ludwig Ingwer Nommensen (1834–1918)—whom theologian Werner Raupp describes as one of the most "successful missionaries ever to preach the gospel"—ministered for fifty-six years in Dutch Sumatra to the Bataks, a Malayan tribe. Despite receiving harrowing death threats, Nommensen cared for the Bataks' physical and spiritual needs. By 1876, 2,000 Bataks had confessed Christ. By 1930, 180,000 belonged to the church Nommenson, the "Apostle to the Bataks," had founded.

The Norwegian Marie Monson (1872–1962) made a major contribution to evangelistic outreach in China. Swedish churches sent missionaries to Natal (1876), Lower Congo (1881), and other regions of Africa.

A heated, public clash between Danish theologian Henrik Nicolai Clausen, a partisan of Schleiermacher, and Nikolaj Grundtvig, curate of Copenhagen's Our Savior's Church (1822–26), put in bold relief thorny issues separating more liberal-oriented clergy and theological conservatives. Clausen, a professor at the University of Copenhagen, recommended, among other things, that Christians should use critical tools in interpreting Scripture. Grundtvig, a defender of the Apostles' Creed and the view that the living Christ is the head of the church, sharply criticized Clausen's theology. He asserted that Clausen "must either make the Christian Church a solemn apology for his unchristian and offensive doctrine, or resign his office and no longer call himself a Christian."

Clausen successfully sued Grundtvig for libel. An expert in Nordic literature, Grundtvig was forced out of a teaching post and resigned his pastoral position. A poet, popular preacher, and hymn writer (composer of 1,500 hymns such as "God's Word Is Our Great Heritage"), he called on the Danish people to repent and return to the Christian faith and their national roots. From his point of view, the nation had departed from its Christian Protestant heritage during the Napoleonic era.

The adoption of the Danish Constitution of 1849 afforded Danes the right to belong to a church other than the state Lutheran Church. Until its adoption, Danes had been obliged to belong to the Lutheran Church if they were to enjoy the rights of citizenship. For some Danes, attendance at church had become a civic duty and routinized. Worship services could appear devoid of spiritual vitality.

A. Søren Kierkegaard

Søren Kierkegaard (1813–55), a deeply sensitive and perceptive soul, a keen societal observer and anti-Hegelian, feared that the impact of the Christian faith on Danish culture had become perversely worldly or mundane. The writings of the German Johann Georg Hamann contributed significantly to the shaping of his thought. Kierkegaard, a loner prone to melancholia, became convinced that many contemporary Danes assumed they were Christians if they were good citizens and participated in the worship formalities of the Danish state church.

In 1854 Kierkegaard attacked what he thought was the hypocrisy of Christendom. He complained that his age was "devoid of passion." He wanted his contemporaries to abandon Christianity as a cultural religion in exchange for a life of following Christ through costly, personal discipleship.

Kierkegaard experienced the crucibles of depression, grief, and suffering. Despondency overtook him before and after he broke off an engagement with Regine Olsen, the love of his life. He was also deeply troubled by the death of a number of siblings. Several scholars suggest that after his father died, Kierkegaard determined to defend his father's more theologically conservative views against theological liberals and Hegelians. He believed that a person must die to self and follow Christ, even if "Christian" culture mocks costly discipleship.

In his discourses such as *Purity of Heart Is to Will One Thing*, *Works of Love*, and *The Sickness unto Death*, Kierkegaard indicated that our sin renders us incapable of winning God's favor. Rather, in the incarnation, Christ, the revealed Son of God in the flesh, died on the cross for our sins. Kierkegaard affirmed that Christ's incarnation and resurrection constitute paradoxes. Accepted by faith, these beliefs are not subject to rational demonstration (sin blinds us from understanding their truth). His other essential books included *Either/Or*, *Fear and Trembling*, and *Concluding Unscientific Postscript*.

The impact of Kierkegaard's "religious existentialism" and "religious subjectivity" ("Truth is subjectivity") would have significant effect on a wide range of thinkers in the twentieth century, including Karl Barth.

B. Norway, Sweden, and Finland

In 1814 Norway became independent of Denmark, only to be ceded to Sweden. Due to Norwegian resistance, Sweden invaded Norway. Norway retained its independence, but the Swedish crown ruled both countries until 1905. The Norwegian peasant Hans Nielsen Hauge, imprisoned for preaching to the laity (in violation of a 1741 law), had promoted the Pietist awakening among farmers and other workers in rural areas. The revival stimulated a greater interest in missions. Between the years 1842 and 1845, non-Lutherans in Norway began to receive the right to worship according to their own consciences.

The Dissenter Law of 1860 gave Swedes the right to take leave of the Swedish state church (the Evangelical Lutheran Church). Karl Olof Rosenius (1816–68), who stayed within the Lutheran Church, participated in a pietistically oriented spiritual awakening. Some of his followers separated from the state church and formed "Free Churches" such as the Swedish Mission Church. These churches consisted of "believers only" and adopted a congregational polity. They emphasized the importance of the Bible's supreme authority, the experience of a "new birth" through conversion, and the pursuit of godly living in anticipation of Christ's second coming.

Some "Free Church" Scandinavians immigrated to the United States, where they founded the Swedish Evangelical Free Mission (1884), the Swedish Evangelical Mission Church of America (1885), and Baptist churches. Women sometimes held leadership positions in these churches.

Following the Great Northern War (1700–1721), the province of Vyborg in Finland shifted from Swedish to Russian control. In the wake of the defeat of Sweden/Finland, a number of army officers were imprisoned in Russia. There they were ministered to by German Pietists. Upon their release, they returned to their respective homes and promoted Pietistic teaching.

In 1809 Finland was officially designated a Russian grand duchy. The tsar, the head of the Orthodox Church, also assumed the position of head of the Lutheran state church. Pietistically oriented revivalists such as Henrik Renqvist continued to preach in the countryside. Ministering outside the state church, they were on occasion harassed by state officials. In 1869 an official church act permitted the Finnish people (except for the Orthodox) to choose their own church. Russian Tsar Alexander II allowed Finland a certain measure of political autonomy and permitted its people the right to use the Finnish language (rather than Russian).

C. The Spiritual Awakening and "Awakened" German Academics

The German/Scandinavian awakening received backing from a number of notable academics. In Berlin, Johann August Neander (1789–1850), a convert from Judaism and an accomplished church historian with broad evangelical convictions, opposed the radical biblical criticism of D. F. Strauss and F. C. Baur. Neander introduced Friedrich August Tholuck (1799–1877), an expert in oriental languages, to members of the Pietistic circle of Baron Kottwitz in Berlin.

Tholuck strongly supported the Prussian Union. In 1826 he began a half century of a popular professorship in theology at the University of Halle. A proponent of a "mediating theology," he possessed warm-hearted Pietist tendencies and emphasized the importance of Christian conversion and discipleship. He persuaded many students who had embraced liberal Neologian theology to rethink their positions. Tholuck wrote well-respected books such as *Hours of Devotion, Commentary on the Gospel of John,* and *Light from the Cross.* He criticized what he thought were the excesses of Neologian rationalism and the speculative theology of Schleiermacher and Hegel. At the same time, he was wary of aspects of Protestant orthodoxy. He did not affirm the doctrine of the Bible's infallibility.

Contemporaries offered different responses to Tholuck's theology. The American James Marsh wrote to Tholuck and indicated approvingly that he thought the German's work meshed well with the (Romantic) theology of Samuel Coleridge. By contrast, Hegel accused Tholuck of advocating Unitarianism. The conservative Princetonian Charles Hodge, who met Tholuck in Halle, Germany, admired the German's deep piety and vast learning. The two theologians became close friends. After Hodge returned to Princeton, they entered into a lengthy trans-Atlantic correspondence.

Ernst Wilhelm Hengstenberg (1802–69) took a different theological path than Tholuck. He was likewise impacted by his interaction with the Pietistic circle in Berlin. An able Old Testament scholar and author of *The Christology of the Old Testament*, he defended the Bible as the infallible Word of God. As editor of the journal *Evangelische Kirchenzeitung*, he initially supported the Prussian Union. As time went on, however, he promoted more narrowly Lutheran confessional orthodoxy.

A fierce opponent of rationalism and radical biblical criticism, Hengstenberg had his enemies. The Swiss-born Philip Schaff, renowned author of the *History of the Christian Church* (eight volumes), observed that Hengstenberg "is one of the most unpopular and yet one of the most important and influential men in the kingdom of Prussia. He leads the extreme right wing of the orthodox party in the Established Church, and is the uncompromising opponent of all rationalists and semi-rationalists, all latitudinarians and liberals." Other Christians appreciated and accepted Hengstenberg's theology.

D. The Christian Churches and the Birth of "Modern Germany"

In 1814, at the fall of Napoleon, Germany—like Italy—did not exist as a modern nation. Rather, from 1815 to 1866, "Germany" consisted of a confederation of independent states (34), free cities (4), and kingdoms (Austria, Bavaria, Württemberg, Prussia). The idea of a national union enthused a number of political liberals. Nonetheless, the revolutions of 1830 and 1848 did not eventuate in the successful unification of Germany. Instead, it took Chancellor Otto von Bismarck of Prussia to forge the creation of modern Germany.

In 1866, in what has been called the "Seven Weeks War," Bismarck's well-trained and disciplined army defeated the Austrian military, thereby reducing Austria's influence in the confederation. Bismarck formed a North German Confederation to replace the German Confederation (1815–66), but a number of north German states did not join this body. Twenty-eight church federations, some Reformed and the others Lutheran, likewise existed.

Bismarck apparently provoked the French to declare war against Prussia (the Franco-Prussian War, 1870–71). He then persuaded three Roman Catholic German states in the south (Baden, Württemberg, and Bavaria) to join with Prussia in the war effort. Bismarck, a Prussian military leader from the Junker Prussian nobility, helped engineer a stunning German victory over the French.

On January 21, 1871, a second German Reich was born with Wilhelm I, the King of Prussia, its emperor or kaiser. The empire's population included more than 41 million people, of which 63 percent were Protestant, 36 percent Roman Catholic, and 1 percent Jewish.

In 1871 Bismarck became the "Iron Chancellor" of the new German Empire. A Protestant, he melded a form of liberal politics and conservative theology together. He was genuinely offended when he learned about Vatican I's definition of papal infallibility. He was concerned that the political loyalties of German Roman Catholics could be diverted and directed toward the papacy and not toward the new German state.

Bismarck launched a *Kulturkampf*, loosely defined as a "struggle of civilizations." With others, he extolled a triumphalist view of a German Protestant civilization and propagated a negative perception of a Roman Catholic civilization.

In the nineteenth century, anticlericalism could signify hostility toward a clergy's participation in politics, harassment or actual physical attacks on representatives of another church, and (in Prussia) the actions and rhetoric of political liberals like Bismarck against Roman Catholics. In Roman Catholic Bavaria, it could mean the state's seizure of church property and restrictions placed on the church's influence over education.

After 1850 a growing presence of Roman Catholics in Protestant Prussia became noticeable. The membership of Catholic monastic orders climbed rapidly: 713 monks and nuns in 1857, but 5,877 in 1867 and 8,795 in 1872. Jesuits and Redemptorists (Congregation of the Most Holy Redeemer) attempted to evangelize for the Catholic faith in public outdoor meetings. Alarmed by this palpable Roman Catholic advance, some Protestants in Berlin believed, quite uncritically, sensational printed stories and rumors about alleged deviant behavior of monks and nuns in monasteries and convents.

In 1869, attacks by Protestants against a Dominican/Franciscan orphanage in Berlin-Moabit signaled the inception of a larger anti-Catholic campaign. Protestants were often especially feared by Jesuits. In December 1870 the Roman Catholic politicians formed the Center Party (1870–1933) with the hope of protecting their interests and those of their coreligionists. The Protestant League and other such groups opposed the Center Party.

When Bismarck initiated the *Kulturkampf,* a significant segment of Prussian Protestant public opinion was ready to support him. Protestant liberals often seconded Bismarck, so worried were they about an alleged Roman Catholic subversive challenge to their vision of a modern German culture. The state drew up a series of laws directed against the Roman Catholic community, most notably the Falk Laws (May 1873), which allowed the state to determine which candidates for the priesthood were suitable and what kind of education they should receive. In 1872 (until 1917) Jesuits were banned from Prussia.

In 1875 "Old Catholics" who had dissented from the teaching on papal infallibility were granted privileges to use the church facilities of Roman Catholics. The Roman Catholic clergy in Prussia were thrown into disarray. By 1876 the Prussian bishops were imprisoned or had sought exile. A number of dioceses suffered badly from the loss of their priests.

Bismarck began to realize that the *Kulturkampf* could be counterproductive. It seriously complicated his task of nation building—that is, bringing about unity within the German Empire. It could only agitate Roman Catholics in the southern German areas. It reflected an illiberal spirit by fomenting religious persecution, something Bismarck had accused the papacy of doing. It energized the Roman Catholic Center Party. By 1878 the government evidenced a less severe approach toward Roman Catholics. The "Peace Laws" of 1886–87 brought about a formal end to the *Kulturkampf,* even though in some towns the Catholics continued to encounter opposition from some Protestants.

E. The Netherlands

In the nineteenth century the political, social, and religious landscape of the Netherlands, an essentially Protestant state, changed rapidly. From 1795 to 1806 the Netherlands was known as the Batavian

Republic; from 1806 to 1810, as the Kingdom of Holland functioning as a puppet state under Louis Napoleon Bonaparte; from 1810 to 1813, as a territory of Napoleon Bonaparte's French Empire; from 1813 to 1815, as the Netherlands; from 1815 to the present, as the United Kingdom of the Netherlands.

During the Revolution of 1830, Belgium, a largely Roman Catholic region in the south of the Netherlands, won its independence. In 1890 the grand duchy of Luxembourg did as well.

In 1816 the Netherlands Reformed Church, which had been disestablished in 1790, was reorganized and placed under the authority of the crown. But after 1848 the church gained a measure of independence from the state. Lutherans, Mennonites, and Remonstrants constituted the principal Protestant minorities. For their part, Jews gained more extensive rights and were incorporated more readily into Dutch society.

In 1853 the Roman Catholic Church (banned since the 1580s) reestablished its hierarchy in the Netherlands. Thereafter, a Roman Catholic parish system was established. Roman Catholic schools, press, and political parties came into existence.

In the wake of the French Revolution, conservative Calvinists were troubled by the widespread influence of liberal theology (especially in Christology) within the Reformed Church. In 1834 Pastor Hendrik de Cock, a proponent of the "Revival," led a group of Calvinists, many of whom were from the lower classes, to separate (*De Afscheiding*, "secession") from the state church. These Calvinists hoped to reestablish the church on the "Three Forms of Unity" (the Heidelberg Confession, the Belgic Confession, and the Canons of Dort). From this secession, two churches emerged: the Christian Seceded Church and Reformed Churches under the Cross. Some of those who separated decided to immigrate to Holland, Michigan.

F. Abraham Kuyper

Abraham Kuyper (1837–1920), a remarkably gifted theologian, politician, journalist, and educator, attended the University of Leiden Divinity School. Upon entering the pastorate, he espoused Protestant liberal theology. A reading of Charlotte Yonge's *The Heir of Redcliffe* and the warning of Pietronella Baltus, one of his early parishioners, to the effect that he was preaching false doctrine, prompted Kuyper to renew his study of Scripture and the writings of John Calvin and other Reformers. Kuyper became a confessional Calvinist. As a gifted orator, he committed himself to gospel preaching in ways the laity could understand.

Kuyper also dedicated himself to promoting a Reformed world-view:

> In spite of all worldly opposition, God's holy ordinances shall
> be established again in the home, in the school and in the State for
> the good of the people; to carve as it were into the conscience of the
> nation the ordinances of the Lord, to which the Bible and Creation
> bear witness, until the nation pays homage again to God.

Kuyper combated what he thought was the nefarious influence of the French Revolution's radical ideologies and non-Christian forms of "Enlightened" thought among his Dutch contemporaries.

In the late 1860s, Kuyper began ministering in Utrecht. He wrote for *The Herald* (*De Heraut*) and joined Groen Van Prinsterer's Anti-revolutionary Party. A critic of popular sovereignty, Kuyper believed that God is the ultimate Sovereign and lawgiver. He emphasized the value of Christian schools. In 1870 he assumed the post of a pastor at the prestigious Reformed Church in Amsterdam. There he urged pastors in the Reformed Church to uphold the Reformed Formula of Subscription.

Opponents successfully resisted Kuyper's effort to renew the state Reformed Church. Kuyper felt obliged to leave the church, and 200,000 congregants followed suit (1886). Their movement became known as the *De Doleantie*, or the "Grieving Ones." In 1892 they joined with those Calvinists who had earlier separated from the state church (1834), and they created the Reformed Churches in the Netherlands.

After his election to Parliament (1874), Kuyper left the pastorate. Despite his political duties, he wrote prolifically and edited two newspapers, *The Herald* and *The Standard*. He also founded and taught theology at the Free University of Amsterdam (1880) He intended that the disciplines—whether medicine, literature, science, or theology—be shaped by a "Reformed" worldview. In an inaugural address, "Sovereignty in the Distinct Spheres of Human Life," Kuyper famously declared that "there is not a square inch in the whole domain of our human existence over which Christ who is Sovereign over all, does not cry: 'Mine!'" Multiple spheres of life existed with their own rules.

Through their theological writings, Abraham Kuyper and Herman Bavinck (1854–1921), author of *Reformed Dogmatics* (1895–1901), provided theological guidance to Dutch conservative Calvinists.

In 1898 Kuyper gave the Stone Lectures on Calvinism at Princeton Theological Seminary in America. He indicated that in "Calvinism my heart has found rest." He once again characterized the French Revolution as "thoroughly anti-Christian" and lamented that its influence had "spread like a cancer."

Kuyper also argued that the experience of spiritual regeneration distinguishes sharply the way Christians think from the way non-Christians do. For instance, he claimed that our views of science are shaped by our religious beliefs. For him, there is no such thing as a "neutral" science. He assumed a largely "presuppositional" approach to doing theology.

In 1905 the Synod of Utrecht attempted to adjudicate a theological dispute between Kuyper and Bavinck. The synod in its "Conclusions" showed due respect for Kuyper's perspectives, but ruled in favor of Bavinck's views regarding supralapsarianism and infralapsarianism, justification from eternity, immediate regeneration, and assumed regeneration.

With the support of Roman Catholics, Kuyper's Anti-Revolutionary Party held political power briefly between the years 1888 and 1891. From 1901 to 1905 Kuyper, a notable advocate of a Reformed worldview perspective, served as the prime minister of the Netherlands.

V. THE FRENCH CHURCHES: PROTESTANT RESTORATION, REVIVAL, AND THEOLOGICAL DISPUTES

The trauma of the French Revolution's "movement of dechristianization" (1793–94) seriously weakened French Protestantism. Under the threats of revolutionary governments, the vast majority of the Reformed ministers abdicated their pastoral functions. In 1799 the French Reformed churches began the painful process of reconstituting their pastoral corps. Some ministers were excluded due to suspicions about their revolutionary activities. According to Napoleon's Concordat of 1802, Protestant pastors, whether Reformed or Lutheran, were—like the Roman Catholic clergy—to swear an oath of fidelity to the state and receive a salary in consequence.

By 1815 the French Reformed population numbered approximately 500,000 strong, the Lutheran population, some 200,000 principally in Alsace-Lorraine. Between October 1815 and January 1816, the "White Terror" broke out. After Napoleon's defeat (1814), Royalist troops returned to the area around Nîmes. Along with others, they targeted Reformed Protestants as potential republican rebels not loyal to Louis XVIII, the new king. More than 200 Protestants were killed, over 250 houses destroyed, and many women brutalized. Between the years 1818 and 1840 the French Protestant churches regained a relative sense of stability and respectability in the society at large.

In 1818 a spiritual revival (*Réveil*) began to spread within the Reformed (Calvinist) churches. Pietistic Swiss Christians in France played a key role in the revival, including Felix Neff and Ami Bost, who challenged the alleged rationalistic tendencies of the Protestant churches. Partisans of the revival often called for a return to the theology of the Reformers and taught the necessity of a spiritual "new birth." Both Charles Cook, an English Methodist who pursued an itinerant ministry in France (1818–34), and Robert Haldane, a Scottish layman evangelist, promoted the revival. Between the years 1817 and 1819 Haldane attempted to win divinity students and professors to embrace revival teaching at the Reformed seminary of Montauban. Also, in 1818 the Protestant Biblical Society was founded in France. Along with other societies, it supported the widespread revival movement with its publications.

Intense debates broke out within the Reformed churches between proponents and critics of the revival. By the late 1840s, orthodox Reformed Protestants engaged in disputes with Protestant liberals regarding whether the Reformed churches to which both parties belonged should have a mandatory confession of faith or, as the liberals urged, permit greater "freedom of examination" in doctrine.

In French-speaking Geneva, Switzerland, analogous conflicts between Protestant liberals and conservatives took place. In 1816 Robert Haldane led a Bible study on the book of Romans with a number of young men in Geneva. Robert L. Gaussen and Jean-Henri Merle d'Aubigné were greatly impacted by the Bible study.

The Genevan Venerable Company of Pastors in time disciplined Gaussen as a pastor for refusing to use a catechism he believed bore telltale signs of "rationalism." In 1832 Gaussen helped found the Oratoire, a theological school for the training of evangelical students. The Venerable Company of Pastors proceeded to remove his pastoral credentials. In 1834 Gaussen assumed the post of professor of dogmatic theology at the Oratoire. He was joined by d'Aubigné as a professor of church history. In 1840 Gaussen published *Théopneustie* (*The Plenary Inspiration of the Holy Scriptures*), a defense of the plenary inspiration and infallibility of Scripture. Charles Spurgeon, the famous English preacher, greatly esteemed this work.

In 1849 d'Aubigné, who wrote a popular thirteen-volume history of the Reformation, left the state Reformed Church. In 1849 he helped form the Evangelical Free Church in Geneva. Similarly, Frédéric Monod took the lead in establishing the Evangelical Free Churches of France (1849).

In 1850 Professor Edmond Schérer resigned his teaching position at the Oratoire in Geneva. Schérer indicated he could no longer uphold in good faith the school's doctrinal commitment to the infallibility and plenary inspiration of Scripture. This resignation stirred considerable controversy in Protestant Reformed circles in both France and Switzerland. Protestant liberals and orthodox Reformed Protestants such as the brothers Adolphe and Frédéric Monod, leaders of the French revival, debated the nature of the Bible's authority. Protestant liberals tended to esteem Schleiermacher's teaching. Some appreciated emerging forms of German biblical higher criticism.

At the end of the nineteenth century Auguste Sabatier, France's leading Protestant liberal theologian, retrospectively cited the Schérer controversy as a decisive turning point in the history of French/Genevan Protestant liberalism.

A. Roman Catholicism, the State, and Secularism

In 1814 Louis XVIII became king of a constitutional French monarchy. Numerous Roman Catholic missionaries fanned out through France determined to reinvigorate orthodox Roman Catholic teaching among the populace. It was feared that many French had forsaken their Roman Catholic faith during the revolution and the Napoleonic era. Catholic priests were sometimes dismayed by expressions of "popular religion" among peasants. Knowing little of elementary doctrine and enjoying festive celebration, the peasants sometimes embroidered into their Catholic practice a bewildering array of folktales, magic, and superstitions. At the same time, more acceptable practices such as acts of devotion to the Sacred Heart of Jesus flourished as well.

During the reign of King Charles X (1824–30) the Roman Catholic Church became once again the established church of France. Under the Villèle government, "Ultras" (royalist Catholics) took control of French education. Moreover, the government issued the Anti-Sacrilege Act (1825–30), which stipulated a range of punishments for sacrilege. It even mandated decapitation for the profanation of the eucharistic host or the holy utensils of worship (vases). No one was in fact decapitated for violating the law.

Following the July Revolution of 1830, the "liberal" regime of King Louis Philippe (1830–48) permitted greater religious liberties. François Guizot (1787–1874), on occasion one of Louis Philippe's principal ministers, was a Protestant. Felicité Lammenais's arguments for the compatibility of liberty and religion and the separation of church and state stirred considerable debate among Roman Catholics.

After the Revolution of 1848, Louis Napoleon Bonaparte was elected the president of the French Republic. In the wake of the coup of 1852, he assumed the title of Emperor Napoleon III, and the French Second Empire was born. By the mid-1850s, the emperor, an authoritarian leader, had emerged as a dominant political figure on the European scene. The French economy appeared prosperous. Prefect Haussmann's Paris was beginning to boast spacious new boulevards and an effective gaslighting system for streets.

Napoleon III apparently became overconfident regarding his successes on the home front. He initiated a disastrous foreign policy, which cost him dearly. He met with Cavour, the Sardinian nationalist leader, and backed efforts for the unification of Italy. This gambit, designed in part to reduce Austrian influence in Italy, naturally angered Pope Pius IX and stirred resentments among Ultramontane Roman Catholics in France. Moreover, Haussmann's reconstruction efforts were creating large monetary deficits. By the late 1860s, Napoleon III attempted to assuage the anger of radical critics and calm public unrest. He granted greater liberties to the press. The number of newspapers multiplied significantly.

The French became deeply worried about the possible candidacy of the German Leopold of Hohenzollern to become the king of Spain. As war fever against the Prussians intensified, Napoleon III suspected that France was ill-prepared for any conflict. He sent a forlorn telegram to his wife, the empress: "Nothing is ready. We do not have a sufficient number of troops. I consider us as lost in advance." Napoleon III pulled French troops out of Rome, where they had been defending the papacy of Pius IX.

During the Franco-Prussian War (1870–71), a string of disastrous defeats befell the French armies. At the Battle of Sedan near the Belgium border, Emperor Napoleon III surrendered. The Germans began a siege of Paris; they hoped to bomb and starve Parisians into submission. On February 28, 1871, after failed attempts to break the Prussian blockade of Paris, the defeated French government signed an armistice with the Germans. On March 1, Prussian troops entered Paris briefly but left after word arrived that the National Assembly located in Bordeaux had ratified the armistice. The newly elected national government of President Louis-Adolphe Thiers set up its headquarters in Versailles.

B. Radical Republicanism, the "Commune," and Anticlericalism

On March 28, 1871, the "Commune," an insurrection, erupted in Paris. Angered by various economic policies of the Thiers government, thousands of Parisians, especially workers, with radical republicans, anarchists, socialists, and communists in their midst, took over the city. They were incensed that the Thiers government had "betrayed" the French nation by suing for peace with the Prussians. The "Communards" held an election to give legitimacy to their actions. Archly anticlerical, their leaders sought to establish the separation of church and state and implement lay instruction in public schools. They coined their own money. With their red banners unfurled, the Communards controlled the city for about sixty days.

On May 21 the French troops of the Versailles government penetrated the walls of Paris. For a week, many Parisians, both men and women, fought the French army in a bloody, no-holds-barred civil war. Fire raged through portions of Paris, reducing some prominent buildings to rubble. Parts of the city became a huge, ghastly open-air morgue.

On the night of May 27/28, the last Communard holdouts fell. The overall carnage in the city was immense. Between 20,000 to 30,000 Parisians — men, women, and boys and girls — had perished in savage street-to-street fighting or were summarily executed. Thousands of Communards were deported to New Caledonia in the aftermath. Anticlericalism directed toward the Roman Catholic Church — including the execution of the archbishop of Paris — stood out as one hallmark of the Commune.

In preceding years, influential non-Christian writers had given anticlericalism a boost. In 1863 Ernest Renan, a former Roman Catholic priest, published *La Vie de Jesus* (*The Life of Jesus*), a rapid "bestseller." He claimed it was one of the first biographies of Christ written from "rational principles." Renan, a biblical critic, denied the divinity of Christ, even though he acknowledged that "among the sons of men, there is none born who is greater than Jesus." He discounted the gospel accounts of Christ's miracles as legends. He boldly denied Christ's resurrection. Renan acknowledged the influence of the radical German biblical critic Strauss on his thought.

For his part, Auguste Comte promoted "positivism" and a "religion of humanity." He defended the "perfectibility of the human race." Socialist writers such as Pierre Joseph Proudhon and Karl Marx provided a non-Christian analysis of the plight of workers in a capitalistic society. Emile Durkheim, author of *Rules of the Sociological Method* (1895), contributed to the acceptance of sociology as a recognized social science in the curricula of French universities. A proponent of a positivist and secular mind-set, Durkheim argued that religious experience and phenomena should be studied "scientifically" and not explained with any reference to potential divine origins.

VI. EXPANDING CHRISTIANITY TO THE FAR CORNERS OF THE EARTH

A. The Scramble for Colonies and Western Missionaries

Between the years 1870 and 1914 a new round of feverish European imperialism gripped politicians and businesspeople alike. Many European nations "scrambled" in ruthless competition. Vast swathes of Africa and Asia were colonized in the space of a few decades.

The U.S. government also engaged in expansionist activities.

President William McKinley (1897–1901) viewed the acquisition of colonies as potentially fulfilling a Christian "civilizing" mandate. He indicated that it was the United States' responsibility "to uplift and civilize and Christianize [the Filipinos], and by God's grace, do the very best we could by them as our fellow men for whom Christ also died." In the wake of the Spanish-American War (1898), the United States gained Cuba, the Philippine Islands, Guam, and Puerto Rico from a fading Spanish Empire.

The British government built the Suez Canal (opening in 1869) in Egypt. Egypt was run by a dynasty (1807–82) founded by Muhammed Ali, an Ottoman viceroy, who helped free the country from the domination of the Ottoman Empire. In 1882 Britain invaded the country and basically controlled it until 1914.

Governments often believed that acquisition of colonial possessions overseas was a key to retaining a balance of power in Europe and assuring continued economic growth at home. In 1884–85, diplomats at the Berlin Conference attempted to prevent armed conflicts in Africa by assigning "spheres of influence" in which European states might colonize without interference from other nations. Earlier, European powers had forced open Chinese ports through gunboat diplomacy and obliged the signing of advantageous treaties.

In the 1880s, needing more outlets for exports in view of the saturation of markets and emerging "protectionist" trade policies of Germany and the United States and also needing coal-fueling stations to keep her ships operational on far-off seas, France acquired a protectorate in Tunis, gained control of Madagascar, and had worked its way deep into the Congo and Niger.

By the last decades of the nineteenth century, French Catholic missionaries constituted two-thirds of Catholic missionaries worldwide. Some were intent on spreading the Roman Catholic faith while simultaneously promoting French colonialism. Such was the case in the region of Annam and Tonkin (Indochina). In 1867 Cardinal Charles Lavigerie, a distinguished academic and churchman, was transferred to Algeria. There he directed the missionary efforts of the "White Fathers" and "White Sisters," who evangelized, built hospitals and schools, and worked with Muslims in other ways. The tireless efforts of Lavigerie helped strengthen ties between various African colonies and France.

B. Missions to the Far East: Japan, China, and Korea

By the late 1540s, Portuguese traders and Jesuits had reached Kyushu, Japan. Daimyo Nobunaga, a prominent military leader in Japan, welcomed them and gave them properties in Kyoto. The Jesuits

Francis Xavier and Alessandro Valignano helped establish a successful missionary outreach in Japan. Thousands of Japanese converted to the Roman Catholic faith. But Daimyo Hideyoshi, another powerful figure, became convinced the Jesuits and their followers were conspiring to help Western powers subjugate Japan.

In 1597 an angry Hideyoshi unleashed the first of multiple rounds of persecution directed at the Jesuits and their converts. Within a few decades, the Roman Catholic presence in Japan was greatly reduced. Some Christians did apparently attempt to practice their faith in a covert fashion.

In China, the Jesuit Matteo Ricci (1552–1610) established a Roman Catholic mission in the late sixteenth century. After the papacy dissolved the Jesuit order in 1773, the Lazarists took their place at the Chinese court. Despite persecution, some 250,000 Roman Catholic laity, 31 missionaries, and about 90 native priests survived in China at the beginning of the nineteenth century. In 1811 Emperor Kia-Kin decreed that leaders of European religions in China should be executed. In 1815 Jean-Gabriel Dufresse, the Vicar Apostolic for Western China, was beheaded. A number of Chinese Roman Catholics were also martyred.

The Scot Robert Morrison (1782–1834), from the London Missionary Society, was the first Protestant missionary to reach China. Looking back on his arrival in Canton (1807), he wrote, "Twenty-five years have this day elapsed, since the first Protestant Missionary arrived in China, alone and in the midst of perfect strangers, with but few friends, and with many foes." He became a translator for the East India Company. This position allowed him to gain a far better knowledge of Chinese, and it sheltered him from persecution.

In 1814 Morrison baptized Tsae A-ko, the first Chinese Christian convert (Protestant). A year earlier, Morrison finished the translation of the New Testament in Chinese, and eventually he completed a Chinese dictionary. Morrison was joined in his translation efforts by Karl Gutzlaff, a Prussian missionary.

William Milne (1785–1822), another colleague, worked on the translation of the Old Testament into Chinese. To avoid interference from the Chinese government,

Francis Xavier.

Milne established a press (1815) and Christian school in Malacca, Malaysia. He wryly observed that those people who hoped to learn Chinese needed "bodies of iron, lungs of brass, heads of oak, hands of spring steel, eyes of eagles, hearts of apostles, memories of angels, and lives of Methuselah." Milne baptized the first Protestant Chinese pastor, Liang Fa.

In 1844 Emperor Daoguang gave permission to Roman Catholics to build churches and worship freely. He extended those rights to Protestants in 1845.

During the Taiping Rebellion (1850–64), the Qing Empire fought the forces of the "Taiping Heavenly Kingdom" led by Hong Xiuquan, who viewed himself as a messiah and a brother of Jesus Christ. At least 20 million people perished in this vicious conflict, one of the greatest human tragedies of the nineteenth century. Many Chinese came to resent Christianity, owing to the fact that Hong Xiuquan, a murderous tyrant, cloaked himself in Christian symbols.

In 1784 Yi Sung-hun, a Korean who had been baptized as a Roman Catholic in Beijing, China, returned to his native land, the "Hermit Kingdom." By the year 1801 there were 10,000 Roman Catholics in Korea. They were persecuted severely. In 1833 the Society for Foreign Missions of Paris (founded 1658–63) assumed the task of evangelizing Korea. French missionary priests were sometimes martyred. During the Great Persecution of 1866–71, thousands of Korean laity were killed. By 1900, 238 bishops and foreign missionaries ministered in Korea and Japan.

After 1882, Protestant missionaries began to enter Korea. Many were American confessional Presbyterians and Methodists. They upheld a high view of the Bible's authority and emphasized gospel preaching. A number belonged to the Student Volunteer Movement. Deeply affected by the Great Revival of 1907, 30,000 Koreans were baptized. An overly optimistic John R. Mott (1865–1955), the founder of the Student Volunteer Movement, claimed that "in the immediate future, Korea will be the first nation of the non-Christian world to become a Christian nation."

C. Western Missions and the Boxer Rebellion in China

The "Boxer Rebellion" (November 1899–September 1901) brought renewed bloodshed and agony to China. The ostensible cause of the rebellion was the heightened animosity of many Chinese toward "foreigners." Beginning in the 1840s, Western powers had used "gunboat diplomacy" to force the Chinese to open select ports to Western trade and accept a series of treaties deemed "unfair" by the Chinese.

Clauses of these treaties that ended the Opium War (1839–42) and Arrow War (1856–60) afforded both Roman Catholic and Protestant missionaries greater liberty to travel throughout China. Missionaries from Hudson Taylor's China Inland Mission and other mission societies donned Chinese clothes and trekked into the interior of China. At great personal sacrifice, they cared for orphans, the sick, and opium addicts. They distributed food to the hungry, preached the gospel, and set up churches, Christian schools, and hospitals.

Loyal adherents to ancestor worship, Buddhism, Taoism, and Confucianism included intellectuals, imperial governmental elites, peasants, and shopkeepers who sometimes fiercely opposed these missionary endeavors. They also took particular offense at the extensive property holdings and special privileges some missionaries possessed, such as living in comparatively luxurious housing compounds, in the summer retreating to mountain cottages to escape the sweltering heat of the plains, enrolling their children in superior European and American schools, and sometimes condescendingly speaking of the Chinese as "children."

Adding insult to injury, Japan's military humiliated China's forces (1894–95), and the Qing Dynasty (1649–1912) lost Korea and Taiwan in consequence. In 1897 the murder of two German missionaries afforded the kaiser an excuse to occupy the province of Shondong. Antiforeign sentiments and mob rule surged in certain regions and segments of Chinese society.

Chinese soldiers during the Boxer Rebellion.

Between 50,000 and 100,000 Boxers—members of a secret society, "the Righteous and Harmonious Fists"—and 70,000 imperial troops of the Qing Dynasty rebelled against people or institutions thought to be agents of foreign powers. Initially, the imperial government attempted to subdue the Boxers, but then the Empress Dowager Ci Xi backed them. Among other foreigners, the Boxers specifically targeted Western missionaries in their compounds and "stations." In marauding bands, the Boxers unleashed bloodcurdling shouts of "Death to the foreign devils!" and taunted Chinese believers as "secondary devils."

In the summer of 1900 the Boxers besieged Tianjin and Beijing. Foreigners in Beijing holed up in the diplomatic Legation Quarter of Beijing and desperately fought off attackers for two months.

On August 14, 1900, Western troops finally quashed the siege. The Boxers were ruthlessly hunted down by military expeditions from eight nations. Before their defeat, the Boxers had massacred 48 Catholic missionaries, 182 Protestant missionaries, some 18,000–30,000 Chinese Catholics, 500–2,000 Chinese Protestants, more than 200 Chinese Orthodox, and thousands of other civilians.

Fifty-eight missionaries and twenty-one children from the China Inland Mission perished in the bloodletting. Gruesome accounts of dismemberments and beheading multiplied. Other missionaries fled their "stations" and compounds, seeking safety in diplomatic quarters or with allied troops or attempting to make a perilous trip to the coast. They worried about the fate of the Chinese believers whom they had left behind and genuinely loved. Numerous Chinese believers were by no means "rice Christians"—people who had accepted Christianity only for material benefits their "conversions" might induce. Those Chinese Christians who refused to deny Christ were often executed.

In mastering the rebellion, the soldiers of the Allies looted and destroyed sacred Chinese temples and imperial palaces and killed and raped civilians. Moreover, in the "Boxer Protocol," the Allies imposed humiliating reparations on the Qing Dynasty. These measures stoked long-term resentments against the Western powers.

By contrast, Hudson Taylor, as a sign of the "meekness and gentleness of Christ," refused to accept any payments for the destruction of property or for the deaths of his fellow China Inland missionaries. Deeply saddened by their loss, Taylor could still write: "It is a wonderful honor ... to have among us so many counted worthy of a martyr's crown."

The massacre of Roman Catholic and Protestant missionaries and Chinese Christians of diverse confessions during the Boxer Rebellion dealt a severe blow to Western missionary efforts in China. It also stimulated greater interest in world missions among certain Christians.

D. French Secular Education and the Dreyfus Affair

Paradoxically enough, while the French republican governments generally benefitted from the work of Catholic missionaries in projecting and reinforcing French influence, the Republican prime minister Jules Ferry helped pass a law in 1882 that stipulated French students in the mother country should receive a free, secular education in primary public schools. The teachers should be laypeople, not Roman Catholic priests or nuns.

In an address to the Chamber of Deputies six years earlier, Ferry had claimed that the concept of secular education was not new. Christianity itself had allegedly promoted the separation of church and state in its first centuries. Moreover, the "key accomplishment" of the much revered French Revolution was to build a "secular state." In a letter to teachers, Ferry dismissed Catholic fears that a secular form of education might foster immorality. He urged teachers to promote "a common morality," that is, those beliefs of "human civilizations" traditionally reckoned as good. As for religious instruction, it "belongs to the home and church."

A Family Supper from Caran d'Ache in le Figaro, France, on February 14, 1898. The drawing depicts the divisions of French society during the Dreyfus Affair. At the top, someone says, "Above all, let us not discuss the Dreyfus Affair!" At the bottom, the whole family is fighting, and the caption says, "They have discussed it."

As the nineteenth century waned, the French people's enthusiasm for republicanism seemed to mount. Royalist pretenders to the French throne had little hope of overthrowing the French Republic. In 1882 Ernest Renan delivered an influential address titled, "What Is a Nation?" He claimed that whereas the German nation was based on race and language, the French nation was established on the free will of its people.

In 1884 and 1890, Pope Leo XIII encouraged French Catholics to embrace the republic. Festivities celebrating the French Republic flourished. Breaking accepted artistic conventions, Impressionist painters (such as Vincent van Gogh) and writers (such as Arthur Rimbaud) both shocked and tantalized the tastes of the French public.

UN DINER EN FAMILLE

(PARIS, CE 13 FÉVRIER 1898)

PAR CARAN D'ACHE

— Surtout! ne parlons pas de l'affaire Dreyfus!

... Ils en ont parlé...

The Dreyfus Affair (1894–1906), a cause célèbre of late nineteenth-century France, did, however, sharply divide French public opinion. Alfred Dreyfus, a high-ranking Jewish military officer, was falsely accused of treason, found guilty, and sentenced to Devil's Island. He had supposedly given the Germans secret intelligence. Anti-Dreyfusards included many Roman Catholics, lawyers, doctors, members of the press, and wealthy members of the bourgeoisie among others. Pro-Dreyfus partisans included republicans, socialists, members of the Collège de France, and intellectuals such as the sociologist Emile Durkheim and the writer Emile Zola, who signed *"J'accuse"* ("I accuse"), a provocative piece in Dreyfus's favor.

Eventually, it was established in many people's minds that Dreyfus had been framed. His name was cleared, and with honor he reentered French military service. Deep-seated anti-Semitism was not foreign to the Dreyfus Affair.

Republican opponents of anti-Dreyfusard Catholics worked with renewed vigor to bring about the separation of church and state in France. In 1905 the Chamber of Deputies passed a law that brought

Green Dancer by Impressionist painter Edgar Degas.

about this separation. It guaranteed "freedom of conscience." It also stipulated, "The Republic neither recognizes, nor salaries, nor subsidizes any religion." Henceforth all religious buildings were deemed the property of the state and local governmental entities. No longer would any member of the clergy be salaried by the state.

E. The Iberian Peninsula: Spain and Portugal

During the nineteenth century, anti-clerical forces in Spain and Portugal contested the premise that the Catholic Church should be the established church in their respective countries. In a display of non-friendly aggression, Napoleon Bonaparte annexed Spain, removed the Spanish Bourbon monarchy, and imposed his brother Joseph to sit on the Spanish throne.

In 1807 French troops likewise marched into Portugal. Britain, a longtime ally of Portugal, launched a naval rescue operation that aided the escape of Maria I and the Portuguese royal family to Brazil. In 1808 the Duke of Wellington landed in Portugal with British troops. He defeated the French troops, but then actually helped them return to France with their weapons and Portuguese loot in hand. Wellington's reputation suffered badly from this generous but ill-conceived decision. Two more French invasions followed. Both were repulsed with British help and at great cost to the Portuguese people.

During the Peninsular War (1808–14), Spanish fighters who favored the restoration of a Catholic monarchy waged a bitterly executed guerilla war for independence from France. Supported by Portuguese and English forces, they ultimately triumphed and ousted Joseph Bonaparte.

Retrospectively, Napoleon conceded that the defeat of his troops in the Iberian Peninsula was a "plague" and "the first cause of evils for France." Until losses in the Peninsular Wars, Napoleon had been generally successful in prosecuting voracious land conquests on the European continent. By contrast, the English, Portuguese, Russians, and others flaunted and violated Napoleon's "Continental System" that stipulated trade on the Continent should take place only between countries within the sphere of French authority. The French navy was not ultimately successful in enforcing the Continental System. It could not break a British naval blockade.

The Spanish victory over the French failed to usher in a much-hoped-for lasting peace on the Iberian Peninsula. Spain repeatedly seethed with religious-political turbulence and civil war. Traditionalist-minded Spaniards argued that adherence to the Roman Catholic Church should serve as *the* cornerstone of Spanish unity. Other Spaniards firmly rejected this premise. They were variously called "Moderates," "Liberals," "Republicans," and "Exaltados." Some were revolutionary, secular, and vehemently anticlerical; others remained Roman Catholic, moderates, and advocates of constitutional as opposed to absolute monarchy.

King Ferdinand VII (1808; 1814–33), a partisan of restoration, entertained close ties with the Roman Catholic Church. He rejected the Spanish Constitution of 1812 as politically liberal. In 1814 he sent troops to Latin America with the hope of holding onto Spain's colonies. Simon Bolivar, however, ultimately defeated Spanish armies and thereby won independence for Columbia (1819) and Venezuela (1821). Other Latin American countries gained independence as well. By contrast, Puerto Rico and Cuba remained in Spanish hands until 1898.

Ferdinand also had to contend with political "liberals" who between the years 1820 and 1823 gained control of the government. They closed down many monasteries and ended subsidies for the clergy. In 1823

French troops invaded Spain and helped Ferdinand drive the liberals from power. A return of the monasteries and financing took place.

The reign of Regent Maria Christina, Ferdinand VII's widow (1833–39), witnessed the government once again challenging the privileges of the Roman Catholic Church. Church properties were seized, monasteries closed, the Inquisition ended, and the clergy's control of education curtailed. The First Carlist War (1833–40) broke out.

The Count of Molina, Carlos V (often referred to as "Don Carlos"), a pretender to the throne, along with other counterrevolutionary traditionalists (including clerics), urged the return of a Catholic king as absolute monarch. Carlos V lamented that Catholic churches were being "profaned, vandalized, burned; priests degraded, publicly insulted, murdered with impunity."

Carlos V, with his Basque and Catalan supporters and other traditionalists—known as Carlists—advocated four essential themes: "God, fatherland, local autonomy, and King." The Carlists envisioned a Catholic Christian society in which the church worked with but remained independent from the state. The Carlists were defeated in the First Carlist War.

In 1844, during the reign of Queen Isabella II (1840–68), the moderates regained power. A Second Carlist War (1847–49) ensued. The Concordat of 1851 between the papacy and the Spanish government restored the Catholic Church to its former position as Spain's established church and to the exclusion of other religions. Jesuits and other Catholic clergy worked diligently to extend the church's influence. But in 1854 another revolution, one possessing an anticlerical thrust, rocked Spain. Thereafter, the secular (noninstitutional and nonmonastic) clergy lost even more of their properties.

With the "Glorious Revolution" of 1868, the reign of Queen Isabella II came to an end. Political and social unrest once again disrupted Spanish life. In 1869 the Cortes (Spanish Parliament) granted religious liberty for non-Catholics, including the small minority of Protestants. A radical republic was established in 1873. Not unsurprisingly, a Third Carlist War (1872–76) erupted.

A social and political respite of sorts emerged under the reigns of the kings Alfonso XII (1874–85) and Alfonso XIII (1888–1931). During the "Restoration" of 1875–1923, both conservative and liberal governments often demonstrated a willingness to recognize the legitimacy of the Catholic Church as playing an essential role in Spanish life.

Many clerics engaged in campaigns to reinvigorate the Catholic faith and counter radical, socialist movements. So-called "Levitical cities," located in the countryside, lent their steadfast support to these efforts to reinforce traditional Catholic values and practices. "Secular" cities resisted these same campaigns.

Cardinal Miguel Payá of Santiago de Compostela declared that on January 28, 1879, some 300 bone fragments of St. James had been uncovered behind the cathedral's altar. According to tradition, St. James had evangelized Spain. Quickly, the cult of St. James blossomed as pilgrims and tourists flocked to Santiago de Compostela. Church experts evaluated evidence concerning the bones' provenance. In 1884 Pope Leo XIII concluded in *Deus Omnipotens* that the bones were indeed those of James, thus official relics. Santiago de Compostela became a major pilgrim and tourist site. Many Spanish Roman Catholics were strengthened in their belief that Roman Catholicism constituted the national religion of Spain.

F. Brazil and Portugal

A number of Brazilians from the province of Minas Gerais studied in Europe and became enthusiastic about the writings of John Locke and Jean-Jacques Rousseau. They also admired the political writings of Thomas Jefferson and the democratic form of government of the United States.

In the last decades of the eighteenth century, small groups of Brazilians created clandestine networks whose purpose was to gain the independence of Brazil from Portugal. In 1798 Bahia rebels from the lower classes revolted against the monied classes that exploited them and showed little respect for their mixed blood and ethnic background. The rebels were defeated. The conspirators were executed, imprisoned, or exiled.

Other groups more specifically challenged Portuguese economic policies. Eventually, in 1822, Brazil declared its independence from Portugal.

In the nineteenth century Portugal constituted one of the most Catholic countries of western Europe. Its population grew from almost 3 million in 1801 to more than 5 million by 1900. The country witnessed repeated rounds of civil unrest and revolt, the confiscation of church properties, and disputes regarding what constituted the best form of government.

The Portuguese Constitution of 1822 was remarkably democratic and declared that "sovereignty resides essentially in the Nation." It eliminated the Inquisition and church courts. In 1834 a wave of anti-clericalism struck: male religious orders were shut down; colleges, convents, and monasteries were auctioned off; and church properties were seized. Nonetheless, even radical leaders regarded Portugal as a Catholic state. The Portuguese Catholic hierarchy worked with various governments and made concordats with the papacy.

In an 1851 coup, Duke João Carlos Saldanha, a hard-bitten soldier, took control of the Portuguese state and thereby ended the period of revolutionary turmoil (forty governments in thirty-one years). Royalists formed a democratic government with a two-party system. A "party of regeneration" led by Fontes Pereira de Melo, a statesman and engineer, tried to modernize the Portuguese economy.

Wealthy members of the upper middle classes in Lisbon enjoyed French, English, or Spanish modes of dress, culture, and the arts. The vast majority of the Portuguese, however, remained steeped in poverty and in overall backward conditions. Peasants engaged in subsistence farming. Rich landowners controlled large estates in rural regions.

Portugal had only limited success in the European scramble for empire. Its aspirations for imperial greatness were thwarted by the claim of Leopold II (1835–1909), the King of the Belgians, to the Congo Zaire (a region colonized for centuries by the Portuguese) and by the claim of the English financier and politician Cecil Rhodes (1853–1902) to the Zambezi basin. By 1900 Portugal retained only five colonies, including Indonesia, Mozambique, Angola, and two in China.

In 1910 an anticlerical republican government triumphed. Its leaders instituted the separation of church and state. Roman Catholicism lost its privileged status as the country's national religion.

VII. CENTRAL EUROPE

In the mid-nineteenth century the Hapsburg monarchy remained a dominant force in central Europe. Its history stretched back to 1526 when the Hapsburgs brought together into a union the Austrian, Slavonian, and Hungarian provinces. It consisted of multiple ethnic and religious groups (Roman Catholic, Protestant, Eastern Orthodox, and Muslim) joined in tenuous unity by the Hapsburg emperor, whose principal residence was in Vienna.

The Hapsburg Monarchy's lands included Austria, Bohemia, Moravia, a portion of Silesia, Galicia (located in southern Poland), Hungary (further subdivided into "Hungary," Transylvania, Croatia-Slavonia, and Vojvodina), and Bukovina. Austria and Galicia were overwhelmingly Roman Catholic, whereas Hungary had a large Protestant minority.

During the Hungarian Revolution (1848–49), the Magyar Lajos Kossuth, a skilled journalist and political reformer, called for Hungarian independence from Austria. In the summer of 1849, Russian armies helped the Hapsburg emperor Franz Joseph I suppress the revolution. Thereafter Franz Joseph I ruled with an iron hand. One of the emperor's primary goals was to keep the empire from disintegrating. In 1853 a Hungarian assassin nearly succeeded in killing the emperor.

In 1866 Bismarck's Prussian armies defeated the Austrians in the "Seven Weeks War." Franz Joseph I lost his capacity to influence the politics of German lands. Moreover, he became more amenable to making concessions to restless ethnic groups, especially Magyar Hungarians. Earlier, in 1861, the Austrian state had allowed Protestants the freedom to worship. Austrian conservative Catholics excoriated "liberal" concessions of this kind as serving Jewish interests.

During the 1860s and 1870s anti-Semitism sometimes poisoned Austrian political debate. Theodore Herzl, an Austro-Hungarian journalist and author, launched a political Zionist initiative to create a Jewish national state in Palestine, a safe haven for Jews. In 1897 the First Zionist Congress, chaired by Herzl, met in Basel, Switzerland. Twenty years later, on November 2, 1917, Arthur James Balfour, Foreign Secretary for the English government, wrote to Lord Walter Rothschild:

ETHNIC AND RELIGIOUS DIVERSITY IN THE AUSTRO-HUNGARIAN EMPIRE (circa AD 1900)

AUSTRIAN PROVINCES

1,225,000 Jews

607,000 Greek Eastern Orthodox

491,000 Protestants

1,000 Muslims

23,797,000 million Catholics (20,661,000 Latin Rite; 3,134,000 Greek Rite; 2,000 Armenian Rite)

HUNGARIAN PROVINCES

886,466 Jews

2,882,695 Greek Eastern Orthodox

3,823,061 Protestants

12,297,126 Catholics (10,299,190 Latin Rite; 1,907,936 Greek Rite)

BOSNIA AND HERZEGOVINA

8,000 Jews

673,000 Greek Eastern Orthodox

339,000 Catholics

549,000 Muslims

"His Majesty's Government view with favor the establishment in Palestine of a national home for the Jewish people."

The Compromise of 1867 (Ausgleich) transformed the Hapsburg Empire into a dual monarchy (Austria and Hungary) with the Emperor Franz Joseph also serving as the King of Hungary. The compromise put the Catholic Church of Hungary under the jurisdiction of the Ministry of Religion and Public Education. Magyar Protestant elites gained political and cultural autonomy. Some of them tried to impose their culture on minorities. They stipulated that Hungarian should be the language of the government and of the universities. Their efforts at establishing cultural hegemony engendered deep animosities among ethnic minorities such as Croats, Slovaks, Romanians, and Serbs.

By the turn of the twentieth century, seething ethnic and religious divisions had greatly weakened the Austro-Hungarian Empire.

A. The "Polish Question"

The dismemberment of Poland as a national entity continued in the nineteenth century. In 1863–64 the Russians crushed the Polish "January Insurrection." Polish revolutionaries had attempted to end the partition of Poland and gain independence from Russia. As retribution for the revolt, the Russians put to death thousands of Poles and sent other thousands to Siberia.

Poland-Lithuania no longer existed as a nation. Both the Germans under Bismarck and the Russians under Tsar Alexander II respectively consolidated their authority over the regions of partitioned Poland under their control. Some regions with large Polish populations became integral parts of Prussia with German laid down as the obligatory administrative language. In Russian Poland, the Polish language was forbidden in the schools and replaced by Russian.

Because some members of the Roman Catholic clergy had lent their support to the Polish insurrection, the Russians deposed suspect bishops and closed numerous monasteries. By contrast, Poles in Galicia (part of the Hapsburg Empire), after a state of siege, were given significant liberty to direct their own affairs. In 1873 Galicia became an autonomous province. Krakow flourished as a haven for the preservation of Polish culture and the Roman Catholic faith.

In the last decades of the nineteenth century, Polish nationalists attempted to keep the "Polish Question" before the "Christian" Western powers: Would the Polish nation ever be reconstituted and given the rights of self-determination? A good number of Polish revolutionaries fought for radical causes, some participating in the Commune in Paris.

B. The Decline of the Ottoman Empire

The defeat of the Ottoman Turks at the walls of Vienna in 1683 spelled the end of their much-feared advance into central Europe. In the wake of the Treaty of Karlowitz (1699) that marked the end of the Austro-Ottoman war (1683–97), the great powers began to carve up the Ottoman Empire, an operation that proceeded in fits and starts for more than two centuries, or until the Treaty of Lausanne (1923).

The Ottomans, despite efforts by reformers such as Sultan Abdul-hamid I (1725–89), often did not keep pace sufficiently well in economics or in weaponry and military strategies with the West. Nor did they do so in education. Only 3 percent of Ottomans could read in 1800, only 15 percent in 1900.

Ottoman Turks also faced the emergence of serious opposition from Wahhabi Suni Muslims. Muhammad Ibn Abd al-Wahhab (1703–92), a so-called "puritan" reformer of Muslim thought, believed that many Sufi and Shia Muslims had compromised the purity of the faith. These "heretics" made pilgrimages to the tombs of saints (the cult of saints) and worshiped material objects. By contrast, Wahhab argued that no intermediaries exist between God and man and God alone should be worshiped. He emphasized Tahwid (the oneness of God). He urged discipline on his followers and set standards for clothing and diet. Women were to enjoy few rights.

Wahhab expounded some of his views in the text *Kitab at Tawid*. He urged the Wahhabi "army of God" to pursue *jihad*—a holy war against unbelievers (highlighting one definition from the Qur'an over a more moderate Qur'an definition, a personal struggle for purity of motive and truthfulness in speech). The Sa'ud family—the ruling royal family of Arabia—adopted Wahhab's basic teachings.

The Wahhabi (sometimes known as the Salefis) came to believe that Turks were infidels and fought against them. In 1818 Ottoman and Egyptian armies destroyed the Wahhabi capital. Despite other defeats (as in 1889, for example), the Wahhabi regrouped. The Sa'ud king engaged in warfare with Britain against the Turks during World War I. After the war the Sa'ud Wahhabi king threatened war against European "occupiers" of Muslim lands in the Middle East. Western newspaper reporters warned their readers about the ferocity of the Wahhabi fighters: "As they believe they enter Paradise when killed in battle, they fight like demons."

In 1927 the British signed an agreement with the Sa'ud family that led to the creation of Saudi Arabia.

The Ottoman Empire faced other problems as well. It incurred huge debts to the Western powers and became increasingly vulnerable to territorial encroachments by both the Western powers and Russia.

Indeed, Western diplomats worried about the "Eastern Question": the apparent inability of the Ottomans to thwart the ambitions of Russia's tsars to gain trade-route access through the Dardanelles Straits to the Mediterranean, and to block the considerable influence of the Russians among peoples in the Balkans and Greece who sought independence.

The "Christian" Western powers such as England, France, and Germany not only competed with each other to acquire land and trade benefits from Turkey, the "Sick Man of Europe," but on occasion used or threatened military force in attempts to halt Russian westward expansion. In 1838 their forces (this time with the Russians as allies) intervened to save the Ottomans from Muhammad Ali Pasha, an Egyptian who sought to create an independent state. His armies had conquered sizeable portions of the Ottoman Empire. The Western allies defeated Muhammad Ali, but he continued to rule Egypt.

Earlier, in the eighteenth century, the Hapsburgs had taken Hungary from the Ottomans, and Russia added a segment of territory to the Ukraine (which in 1654 had been incorporated into Muscovy). The Treaty of Kuchuk Kainarji (1774) afforded the Russians lands north of the Black Sea and established them as the protectors of Orthodox Christians in Turkey, among other privileges. Some Russians hoped for the day when their troops might capture Constantinople, liberate the patriarch of Constantinople, and bring an end to Ottoman rule. They also propagated the idea that it was their responsibility to protect Christians living under Ottoman domination in the Balkans and in Greece.

VIII. THE RUSSIAN EMPIRE AND THE RUSSIAN ORTHODOX CHURCH

In 1723 Patriarch Jeremias of Constantinople recognized the founding of the Russian Holy Synod. The patriarch's approval masked sharp differences between the model of church governance Peter the Great had imposed on the Russian Orthodox Church and the form of governance sustaining the authority of the patriarchs in Constantinople and the Eastern Orthodox patriarchs.

Peter the Great eliminated the Russian patriarchate for twenty-one years (1700–1721). Emulating a German Lutheran ecclesiastical model, he then established a layperson (*Oberprokuror*) as the head of the Holy and Governing Synod. The procurator was a civil servant, not a cleric, and reported directly to Peter the Great. During the "Synodal" period of Russian Orthodox Church history (1700–1917), metropolitans replaced patriarchs as the principal clerical rulers of the church.

Between 1800 and 1880 the tsars added vast swathes of new territories to the Russian Empire's already huge geographical landmass.

Also, in 1809 Finland came under Russian jurisdiction. After 1815, Congress Poland (a kingdom in Poland) was forced to participate in a "union" with the Russians. From 1834 to 1859 the Chechens attempted to fend off Russian domination. The Russians repeatedly fought the Turks through most of the century.

A significant factor in this territorial expansion was the Pan-Slav movement that developed in the 1840s. Stimulated by similar earlier manifestations of the concept by various scholars, the movement sought to bring unity and shared identity (and freedom from tyranny) among the various Slavic peoples and other ethnic groups spread through parts of central Europe, the Balkan peninsula, and Russia.

The Western powers, despite their joint effort with the Russians to win Greek independence (1832) from the Turks, cast a wary eye at the Russian tsars' impressive sphere of influence in the Balkans and Greece. England, France, the Ottoman Empire, and Sardinia fought the Crimean War (1853–56) against Russia, in part to block Russian expansionary encroachments toward the west and southwest. During the Russian-Turkish War (1877–78), Russian troops reached the gates of Constantinople. Deeply concerned western European diplomats pushed through the Treaty of Berlin in an effort to stop the further advance of the Russians into Ottoman lands.

Some of the populace in the Balkans feared that they might be liberated from Ottoman rule only to fall under the heavy-handed governance of the Russians. The Russians also fixed their sights on gaining the principalities of Moldavia and Walachia (eventually known as Romania).

For a time the Russian Empire stretched across seemingly endless tracts of land from Congress Poland to Alaska in North America. Its peoples included Russians, Ukrainians, Belo-Russians, Poles, and various ethnic tribes.

In 1741 the Dane Vitus Bering, a member of the Russian navy, began a mission to discover if Asia was linked to North America. On July 26 Chirikov, one of his Russian crew members, reported that he and others had observed "some very high mountains, their summits covered in snow, their lower slopes, we thought covered in trees. This we thought must be America." The explorers celebrated the first Orthodox liturgy in America aboard a ship in Sitka Bay, Alaska. Monks from the monastery of Valaam, founded in 1794, spread the Orthodox faith among the natives of Alaska.

On March 30, 1867, however, the Russian government sold Alaska to the United States for $7,200,000. American critics lampooned the purchase of Alaska as "Seward's Folly"—a reference to Secretary of State William H. Seward, who had championed the purchase. Over time, the transaction turned out not to be foolish. The Americans bought Alaska for about 2.2 cents per acre. Subsequently, the first Orthodox Russian church in North America was built in California.

In the nineteenth century, powerful tsars ruled the vast Russian Empire. Tsar Nicholas I (1825–55) prosecuted ruthless policies to control his state. He viewed the Russian Orthodox Church as a pillar buttressing his authoritarian regime. In a *Letter to Gogol* (1847), the "Westernizer" Vissarion Belinsky intemperately excoriated the Russian Orthodox Church on just that point. He said the church served as "the bulwark of the whip and the handmaid of despotism." More "liberal" censors and moderate government officials did attempt to provide writers a modicum of freedom of expression.

The 1855 coronation of Tsar Alexander II unfolded with magnificent pomp and rich ceremonies followed by a Greek Orthodox mass. Count von Moltke, who witnessed the carefully staged celebration, was awed by the splendor of the event. He thought the tsar's authority was nearly boundless. The tsar did in fact rule over the largest contiguous empire of nineteenth-century Europe. Yet the striking defeat of Russian forces in the Crimean War by the combined armies of England, France, and Turkey revealed a worrisome military vulnerability.

Tsar Alexander II could act as both a cruel autocrat and a daring reformer. He oversaw the crushing defeat of the nationalistic aspirations of the Poles in the "January Insurrection." By contrast, he allowed greater political liberties to the Finnish and encouraged the use of Finnish as the national language. He also took certain dramatic steps to reform and modernize Russian life. In 1858 nineteen million peasants labored on state lands, whereas twenty-two million serfs worked on private lands. In 1861, two years before Abraham Lincoln delivered his famous Emancipation Proclamation that liberated slaves, the tsar promulgated the Edict of Emancipation that liberated serfs. The tsar even contemplated instituting a representative government with consultative powers.

The tsar eluded a series of assassination attempts. But in 1881 the "People's Will" set off two bombs, one of which badly wounded him. Tsar Alexander II died soon after, deprived of the chance to implement further reforms.

Tsar Alexander III proceeded to undo many of his father's reform measures. Anti-Semitism raised its ugly head during his reign. The rumors circulated that "the Jews" had been involved in planning the assassination of Alexander II. Rumors helped spark the tragic years of 1881–84, when many Jewish communities in Russian cities and towns became targets of violent anti-Jewish riots, or pogroms. Large numbers of Jews were killed and their properties seized or destroyed.

The government made the situation even worse by promulgating anti-Jewish legislation ("Temporary Regulations," 1882). In time, cities like Moscow were purged of Jews. The tsar justified his actions by blaming the Jews for Christ's crucifixion. Little wonder some Jews became more attracted to Zionism and the idea of emigration. From 1880 to 1920 as many as two million Jews sought havens of safety in more hospitable lands. They came in droves to the United States (about 1,750,000) — especially, New York City. A smaller contingent (45,000) immigrated to Palestine.

A. Reassessing Russian Church Life (1800–1917)

Russian Orthodox church life in the nineteenth and early twentieth centuries at one level was none too vibrant. After all, repressive tsarist regimes often did stifle personal religious and intellectual freedoms through censorship, forced exiles, the threat of imprisonment, the use of torture, and the meting out of death sentences.

The centralization of the Russian Orthodox Church's administration directed by its procurator could hamper initiatives by individual churches (which numbered 94,629 churches in 1914). More than 90 percent of Russian Orthodox bishops between 1721 and 1917 came from a privileged clerical class, and their autocratic control of the church governance and positions and their intrusive policies rankled those priests who felt blocked from advancement in the church's hierarchy.

In the 1850s a priest complained that "the relationship between priest and bishop is exactly like that between Negro and plantation owner." Many priests in the parish clergy (numbering 50,000 in 1914) were members of a hereditary class that possessed a sense of entitlement to their clerical positions. Laity were restricted in their rights such that they had little incentive to participate actively in parish life. Was there not at least some truth to Vissarion Belinsky's provocative claim that many of the peasants were atheists? The tsarist police so restricted the intellectual freedoms of philosophers in the period 1825–60 that it is properly called "the Philosophical Dark Age" in Russian philosophy.

A number of Orthodox historians such as Timothy Ware have countered that this grim picture of church life in nineteenth-century Russia is much too bleak. They do not deny the gravity of certain problems faced by the Russian Orthodox Church, but they contend that the nineteenth century also witnessed promising developments within the church. Education for the clergy improved. Philaret, the learned Metropolitan of Moscow, helped established seminaries for priests in sixty-seven dioceses. Four theological academies were founded — in Moscow, Saint Petersburg, Kiev, and Kazan — between 1769 and 1842.

The monastic movement also expanded significantly. In 1812 there were 452 monasteries; by 1914 there were 1,045 monasteries with 21,000 monks and 73,000 nuns. Earlier, in the eighteenth century, monks at Mount Athos such as Paisi Velichkovsky had launched a movement of spiritual renewal based on the ancient Hesychast tradition and the collected prayers found in the book *Philokalia*. In solitary stillness and great humility, monks devoted themselves to repeating the Jesus Prayer: "Lord Jesus Christ, Son of God, have mercy on me, a sinner." Influential *startsi* (elders or spiritual directors) in the Hesychast tradition provided examples of holy, ascetic, and joyful living. They gave wise, spiritual counsel to individual disciples as well as to large numbers of common people.

The Academy of Kazan helped prepare natives for missionary work. St. Innocent (1797–1879), as the Bishop of Alaska, displayed love and concern for native peoples. Other missionaries spread the Orthodox faith among tribes in Siberia and among Muslims. In the 1860s various attempts to reform church life took place. They included the distribution of monies in the poorer parishes. The respected, learned theologian and orator Metropolitan Philaret of Moscow and the Pan-Slav lay theologians Alexis Khomiakov and Ivan Kireyevsky engaged in efforts to renew Orthodox theology. During the reign of Tsar Nicholas I, F. Golubinsky helped create the Moscow School of Theistic Philosophy.

B. Dostoevsky and Tolstoy: Perceptive Analysts of the Human Condition

In the second half of the nineteenth century, two Russian writers began to gain a certain following in the European world of letters. They were Fyodor Dostoevsky (1821–81), author of works such as *Notes from Underground, Crime and Punishment,* and *The Brothers Karamazov,* and Leo Tolstoy (1828–1920), author of *War and Peace* and *Anna Karenina.* Painting with words, they created vast panoramic scenes from bloody battles to festive Russian dances as well as finely brushed psychological portraits of unforgettable characters. They presented polyphonic dialogues in which characters offered competing views of the same issue. Each personage had special mannerisms of speech.

As great writers are inclined to do, Dostoevsky and Tolstoy probed deeply, without shrinking back, some of the most profound if not painful problems we humans face: the origins of evil, disease and suffering, intense feelings of remorse and guilt, the inevitability of death, the pain of broken relationships, and much more.

Tolstoy, for example, was shaken by the horrors and havoc he personally witnessed as a combatant during the Crimean War. Given the savagery of warfare, how could Christian nations choose it as a means to settle their differences with each other? After 1869 Tolstoy was himself particularly haunted by fear of death and a recognition of his own mortality. In 1877 he made one of two trips to the Russian Orthodox Optina-Pustyn monastery in a quest to find spiritual solace. This did not occur. He thought about taking his own life.

During repeated waves of "discouragement and revival," Tolstoy wrote, "... I remembered that I had lived only when I believed in a God." In 1879 Tolstoy experienced a conversion to "the religion of Christ, but divested of faith and mysteries, a practical religion, not promising eternal bliss but providing bliss here on earth." He rejected the deity of Christ.

Upon reading the Gospels, Tolstoy developed what some deemed a radical, anarchic social ethic based on Jesus' teaching: "Resist not evil." He devoted a portion of his wealth and worked diligently to ameliorate the lives of the downtrodden. One of his characters explained how the quest for happiness is related to love of others and self-sacrifice: "Happiness consists in living for others. This also is clear. Man is endowed with a craving for happiness; therefore it must be legitimate." By the turn of the twentieth century, Tolstoy had become one of the most celebrated figures in the world. For example, the American William Jennings Bryan, a Progressive Democrat, admired him. In 1901 the Russian Orthodox Church excommunicated him.

The fact that Dostoevsky and Tolstoy (along with Alexander Pushkin, Ivan Turgenov, and Anton Chekkov) could emerge as world-class authors from tsarist Russia, a supposedly culturally backward and repressive society, surprised some western European observers. After all, the tsars' program of "autocracy, Orthodoxy, and nationality" did not offer especially auspicious conditions for the crafting of literary works of genius. Nor did some critics countenance the Pan-Slav premise that Russia, if she were to recover her purest, traditional Christian soul, should reject out of hand western European secular, "Enlightenment" values. Further, they viewed as a vain enterprise the Pan-Slav vision of reconstituting a pristine, rural Christian society in which tsars consulted with their people as existed before Peter the Great's reforms. Why? Quite simply, no such idealized society ever existed.

As a Pan-Slav, Dostoevsky did appreciate Russia's inward-looking cultural ambit. He had a deep love for Russia and the Russian Orthodox Church. He wrestled with the perplexing issue of how Russia could preserve the traditions of the Orthodox faith while adjusting to new challenges served up by rapid urbanization and industrialization, scientific positivism, radical unbelief, societal unrest, and subversive revolutionary ideologies, whether Western democratic or Marxist.

"What cravings can always be satisfied independently of external conditions? Love, self-denial" (Leo Tolstoy in his memoirs).

Dostoevsky's genuine concern for Russia's welfare was especially laudatory because the tsarist police had treated him very poorly. Falsely accused of being a socialist revolutionary, Dostoevsky—at the time a Utopian—was sentenced to death before a firing squad. His life was spared at the last minute due to a reprieve. He was obliged to do forced labor during a ten-year prison sentence at the Omsk Fortress, Siberia. He lived under horrendous conditions.

Animosity existed between serf and middle-class prisoners. Nonetheless, as Dostoevsky writes in *House of the Dead*, most of the convicts seemed to have a simple faith: "When, with the chalice in his hand, the priest came to the words '... receive me, O Lord, even as the robber,' nearly all the convicts fell kneeling to the ground with a jangling of fetters, apparently interpreting those words as a literal expression of their own thoughts." Dostoevsky drew upon his own autobiographical experiences in creating the characters that people his novels.

C. Religion in the Twilight of the Tsarist Romanov Dynasty

At the dawn of the twentieth century, many Russian people, despite economic distress, strikes by workers, and unrest among peasants, did not have a premonition that they were living in the twilight years of the Romanov Dynasty. They viewed suffering, poverty, and injustice as inescapable conditions of any age. They had just experienced a decade of severe famines. Would not the future be like the past?

This perception was not unreasonable. Moreover, Pan-Slavs such as Dostoevsky and Konstantin Leontiev warned their readers to reject the temptations of rebellion and social anarchy. They denounced as bogus and a devilish delusion the claims of revolutionaries that a Jacobin reenactment of the French Revolution would usher in a day of brotherhood and solve Russia's social and economic problems.

Could not the societal reform that many Russians favored come about without political upheaval and revolution? Were not efforts to create parish charities at least in part helping the needy? Had not a greater freedom to study philosophy emerged after Vladimir Solvyov defended a dissertation titled "The Crisis of Western Philosophy" (1874)? Between the years 1901–3, had not "religious-philosophical meetings" taken place in which intellectuals and clerics attempted to reinvigorate Russian Orthodox beliefs?

Certainly, a number of non–Russian Orthodox and unconventional religious groups existed, but most did not appear politically subversive. "God-seeking" intellectuals, writers, and artists searched for encounters with the divine through the paths of theosophy, spiritualism, kabbalistic studies, and Eastern mysticism. Nikolai Fedorov (1828–1903), a curious figure, even urged finding a way to raise the dead through the use of technology. Some members of Russia's educated classes participated in Masonic lodges and dabbled in occult practices (possibly even Satanism). Russian peasants evidenced a fascination for "supernatural" phenomena.

Protestant missionaries reported an openness for their evangelistic efforts among the Russian nobility. In the 1870s the Englishman Granville A. W. Waldegrave, Lord Radstock, was invited to lead Bible studies with prominent Russian military figures and nobles in Saint Petersburg. Colonel Vasilii A. Pashkov and Count Korff were converted to Christ and helped organize evangelical meetings.

The government's expulsion of Lord Radstock from Russia in 1878 did not thwart the evangelical advance. Sharing Radstock's Plymouth Brethren convictions, the German educator Frederick Baedeker (1823–1906) continued the work. Baedeker not only ministered in the palatial homes of Russian nobles such as Princess Nathalie Lieven, but gained permission to distribute Russian Bibles at prisons in Saint Petersburg and far-off Siberia.

In 1884 Colonel Pashkov organized a meeting attended by Shtundists, Baptists, Mennonites, and Pashkovites. ("Shtundists"—from the German *Stunde*, meaning "an hour"—were Orthodox believers influenced by revivalist German Pietists. They regularly studied the Bible for hours, as their name implied.) Police broke up the meeting and arrested the Russians present. Colonel Pashkov was ordered to leave Russia. As a result, John Kargel, a friend of Colonel Pashkov and a minister at the German Baptist congregation in Saint Petersburg, decided to leave Russia. In 1884 he founded a Baptist church in Ruse, Bulgaria, only to return to Russia to work with Pashkovites.

In 1894 specific anti-Shtundist laws were drawn up. The government suspected peasant Shtundists of involvement in the so-called "Chigirin populist conspiracy."

In 1914 an estimated 100,000 Mennonites lived in Russia (as well as Swiss Amish and Hutterites). During the reign of Catherine the Great, German Mennonites, who often originated from Anabaptist communities in the United Provinces, had immigrated to Russia from Prussia, Switzerland, and other countries. The Mennonites considered leaving Prussia because its government demanded they partake in military service. In 1789 and 1803, groups of Mennonites decided to take advantage of the Russian state's offer of free land, especially in southern Russia.

Various Mennonite groups in Russia such as the Mennonite Brethren, the *Kleine Gemeide*, the *Kirchliche Mennoniten*, and the Krimmer

"Unity in essentials, tolerance in non-essentials, moderation in all things" (Russian Mennonite principle).

Brethren formed autonomous, agrarian colonies. They maintained their own schools and churches with a congregational polity and governing administrations. They continued to speak German dialects, preserved traditional Mennonite beliefs and customs, and as pacifists remained exempt from military service. In the 1870s, however, fearing that the Russian government would soon take away their special exemptions, a number of Mennonites opted to immigrate to Canada (Manitoba) and to the United States (Kansas).

In 1882 disparate Russian Mennonite groups came together to form the General Conference of Mennonite Congregations. They adopted as their principle, "Unity in essentials, tolerance in non-essentials, moderation in all things."

D. The Russian Revolution of 1905–7

For many Russians, "Bloody Sunday"—January 22, 1905—shattered any illusions they had retained of living in a politically and socially stable society. The official government account of the massacre reads, "When a crowd of several thousand had assembled ... Father Gapon said prayers.... Despite pleas by local police officers and cavalry charges, the crowd did not disperse but continued to advance. Two companies opened fire, killing ten and wounding twenty.... The cavalry made a series of charges to disperse the crowd, but as this had no effect a number of volleys were fired into the crowd." In all likelihood, at least one thousand were killed, including women and children.

Across the empire, strikes broke out in Saint Petersburg, Kiev, Varsovie, Bakou, Lodz, Ivanovo-Voznesensk, Odessa, Riga, and elsewhere. Peasants torched chateaus in Georgia and the Volga area. "Soviets" (counsels) made their appearance in Moscow and Saint Petersburg.

Historians do not fully agree on what sparked the 1905 revolution. Certainly, Russia's disastrous defeat in the Japanese-Russian War (1904–5) had seriously deflated the tsarist regime's popularity and standing. In December 1904, 80,000 workers had gone on strike for better pay and working conditions in Saint Petersburg. Many peasants nursed long-standing grief toward upper-class landowners because they did not own enough land from which to make an adequate living.

Lenin (Vladimir Ilyich Oulianov).

LOC, LC-USZ62-101877

Nihilists, anarchists, and Marxists stirred hot fires of rebellion. In 1898 Vladimir Ilyich Oulianov (better known as Lenin), who in 1895 had been arrested, imprisoned, and exiled in Siberia, organized the Russian Social Democratic Labor Party. In 1899 he wrote that the final end of the class struggle was "the seizure of political power by the proletariat and the organization of a socialist society."

By contrast, Father George Gapon, the Russian Orthodox priest who organized the demonstration of January 22, 1905, was neither a revolutionary provocateur nor a hireling for the tsarist secret police (as some critics conjectured). Like a number of other priests, he wanted to improve the lot of oppressed workers in Saint Petersburg. He apparently never calculated that government troops would fire on his marchers. The government had been informed of the marchers' intention to present a petition of economic and political demands, thinking that the tsar, like a father, would hear them out. Members of the processions that converged on the tsar's Winter Palace (though he was not present) little expected that volleys of deadly bullets would cut them down.

Father Gapon had previously served as a missionary for the Society of Moral-Religious Enlightenment, a group that attempted to ameliorate the cultural life of workers. Then he organized the Assembly of Russian Factory and Mill Workers to function as a labor union. He hoped to negotiate better working conditions for its members, because he felt obliged to engage in social action.

The events of Bloody Sunday and the ensuing chaos and insurrections deeply troubled Tsar Nicholas II. He resorted to force to suppress dissenters, but in time, he did offer new rights to the Russian people. In a manifesto in October 1905 he acknowledged that the revolution threatened the stability of his regime, but also showcased the ways he sought "the improvement of order in the state." He permitted participation in the Duma (state government) for "those classes of the population which are at present deprived of voting powers" and granted "fundamental civil freedoms," including "real personal inviolability, freedom of conscience, speech, assembly and association."

The manifesto satisfied the demands of some revolutionaries, who desisted from any further rebellious activity, but the government arrested Father Gapon. The Russian Orthodox Church later defrocked him. In 1906 he was found hung.

After 1905, several Protestant groups benefitted from the new religious liberties. The number of Baptists and other evangelicals grew rapidly, to the discomfort of Russian Orthodox clergy. Most sadly, the Jews were once again targets of a devastating pogrom (1903–6).

Nicholas II did not sufficiently address the economic and social grievances that had helped precipitate the 1905 revolution, and resentments

"A servant of Christ must show the people, not by words, but by deeds, that he is their guide" (Russian Orthodox priest George Gapon).

against the tsarist Romanov family simmered. During the First World War, the Germans helped Lenin, who had been in exile, to return to Russia.

Lenin, a skilled organizer, knew how to exploit grievances and social injustices. During the Russian Revolution of 1917, he and his Bolshevik colleagues seized power. Nicholas II abdicated his throne, and members of the royal family were incarcerated. In the early morning of July 17, 1918, the tsar was told that he and his family were going to be moved to a place of safekeeping. They were led into a basement by twelve men, who then shot them to death: Nicholas II, Empress Alexandra (a granddaughter of Queen Victoria), their son, four daughters, and a number of servants and a physician. Some other family members were also stabbed. The victims' bodies were hauled away to a secluded woods, where they were soaked in benzine and sulpheric acid and burned—a vain effort to cover up the hideous crime. The twilight years of the Romanov Dynasty had come to a dramatic and tragic end.

The Russian Orthodox Church had backed "White Russian" (Belorussian) soldiers. These forces were defeated by Lenin and the Bolsheviks in a civil war. The Bolsheviks took over power in October 1917. As victors, Lenin and his colleagues proceeded to deal a severe blow to the church, stipulating that it would no longer be the official state church of Russia.

E. Eastern Orthodox Christian Churches and Ottoman Rule

Besides the Russian Orthodox Church, other members of the Orthodox family of churches included the Oriental Orthodox, whose long history stretched back into a distant, late patristic past. They belonged to the Assyrian, Nestorian, and Chaldean churches and to the non-Chalcedonian churches in Antioch and India, the Coptic Church in Egypt, the Armenian Church, and the Ethiopian Church.

Toward the mid-nineteenth century, Eastern Orthodox patriarchs, even if subjected to Ottoman rule, viewed themselves as members of the same "Orthodox Church." They were united in disputing the right of the pope in Rome to dictate their beliefs and practices. In 1848 the Eastern Orthodox patriarchs of Constantinople (the ecumenical patriarch), Alexandria (Egypt), Antioch (Anatolia), and Jerusalem (Palestine) issued a joint encyclical in which they thanked God for their "Apostolic Baptism," the "Orthodox Faith," and Christ's "One, Holy, Catholic, and Apostolic Church."

This encyclical rebuked the papacy of Pius IX for having not "ceased to annoy the peaceful Church of God," by sending "everywhere so-called missionaries, men of reprobate minds" to win the Orthodox to the Roman Catholic faith. They claimed that the pope had engaged in "despotism" by attempting to assert his authority over them. Moreover, they accused him of purveying the "new doctrine" that "the Holy Ghost proceeded from the Father and the Son" among other false doctrines. For the Orthodox, the Holy Spirit proceeds only from the Father.

Whereas officials of the Roman Catholic Church accused the Orthodox of destroying church unity, Eastern apologists riposted that it was the Catholic Church that had subverted church unity by attempting to force false doctrine on Eastern Christians.

Eastern Orthodox, Catholics, and Protestants under Ottoman rule lived in a world where they rubbed shoulders with peoples of mixed ethnic and religious backgrounds. They sometimes lived in the same neighborhoods as Muslims, filed lawsuits in Muslim court systems, and generally had friendly relations their Muslim neighbors. Historian Donald Quataert observes that "the Ottoman Empire for much of its history brought together multiple and different ethnic and religious groups. At times their interaction was co-operative and harmonious; but under the pressures of 'modern nationalism' those ethnic and religious relations deteriorated into hostilities and worse, massacres."

Europeans and Americans in Ottoman lands pursued varying goals and occupations. Some worked in business, trade, and diplomacy or for the military. Others served as educators, missionaries, and pastors or priests, or lived as members of monastic orders.

European Protestant missionaries held out the hope that the ancient Eastern Orthodox churches under Ottoman control might be "reformed." In 1899 Eugene Stock, a leading Protestant missionary wrote, "It is by bringing back these churches to the knowledge and love of the sacred scriptures that the blessing from on high may be expected to descend upon them."

A number of Western missionaries ministered directly to Muslims. They founded well-respected Christian schools that Muslim students attended.

Some Americans and Europeans were also enticed by exotic travel accounts to visit Ottoman lands as tourists. Their romantic reveries of the Middle East were sometimes dashed by what they actually saw during their touring junkets. For instance, Herman Melville, the famous American writer, who traveled to many parts of the world during his lifetime, was stunned by the ethnic diversity of the hordes of people he encountered while wending his way through the narrow streets of Istanbul: "Imagine an immense accumulation of the rags of all nations, and all colors rained down on a dense mob, all struggling for huge bales and bundles of rags, gesturing with all gestures and wrangling in all tongues."

Although impressed by the ancient monuments of Egypt, Melville was rudely disappointed by his visit to Palestine. He lamented, "No country will more quickly dissipate romantic expectations than Palestine." As for the possibility of Christianity challenging Islam's grip on Ottoman lands, the writer entertained little hope. From Melville's perspective, Middle Easterners had universally rejected "much of our morality, and all of religion." He thought that Christian missionaries might as well "attempt to convert bricks into bride-cake as the Orientals into Christians."

Whereas Melville's take on the Middle East was quite mixed, a number of American, French, British, and German scholars were fascinated by the region. After all, it included Palestine, the "Holy Land," brimming with biblical sites just waiting to be explored. In 1841 the American Edward Robinson, Professor of Bible at Union Theological Seminary, New York, published a seminal work in three volumes, *Biblical Researches in Palestine, the Sinai, Petraea and Adjacent Regions*. In 1842 Paul-Emile Botta began digs at the ancient Assyrian capitals of Ninevah and Khorsabad.

In 1858 Carl Keil defined the exciting new discipline of "biblical archaeology": "We call by the name of Biblical Archaeology ... the scientific, representation of the forms which life assumed among the people of Israel as that nation of antiquity which God had selected to be the bearer of the revelations in the Bible." The emerging discipline gave promise of helping Christians understand Holy Scripture better. In his book *The Land and the Book: Or Biblical Illustrations Drawn from the Manners and Customs, the Scenes and Scenery of the Holy Land* (1858), the author William Thomson wrote, "The Land and the Book constitute the all-perfect text of the Word of God, and can be best studied together. To read the one by the light of the other has been the privilege of the author for more than forty years, and the governing purpose in publishing is to furnish additional facilities for this delightful study to those who have not been thus exceptionally favored."

To fund archaeological explorations, respected societies were created: the Palestine Exploration Fund (1865), the Deutscher Palätina-Verein (1877), the École Biblique (1890), and the American School of Oriental Research (1900). The Egyptologist Flinders Petrie (1853–1943) developed stratigraphical guidelines (analysis of deposited layers) that permitted more accurate historical readings of excavations. In 1894 George Adam Smith published the influential *Historical Geography of the Holy Land*.

Some Ottomans on occasion did demonstrate unbounded hostility toward Christians residing in lands under their control. The Armenians, in particular, suffered profoundly due to horrific massacres and deportations: the Hamidian Massacre, 1894–96; the Adana Massacre, 1909; and—worst of all—the Armenian Genocide (a term the Republic of Turkey repudiates), 1915–17. Winston Churchill observed of the last, "There is no reason to doubt that this crime was planned and executed for political reasons. The opportunity presented itself for clearing Turkish soil of a Christian race opposed to all Turkish ambitions."

F. The Creation of Independent, Nationalistic Orthodox Churches

The Eastern Orthodox not only at times suffered persecution from Ottomans, but also experienced conflicts among themselves. Orthodox Christians often had differing views on what should be normative in their church governance. They wanted to hold onto their own languages, cultures, education, and forms of worship.

By contrast, highly educated Phanariot Greeks, whether members of the clergy or merchant classes, often insisted that the Greek language and Hellenic culture in general should prevail in Orthodox lands. The Phanariots, who served as agents of the sultans, worked closely with the patriarch of Constantinople. Sometimes they governed other Orthodox Christians in the millet system (see chapter 13).

The patriarch of Constantinople frequently chose Greek bishops with a Phanariot background to direct church life in Balkan states under Ottoman control. Orthodox Christians in these lands sometimes strongly resented what they perceived to be strong-armed attempts of the Phanariots to impose Hellenic culture on them. In the Danube Principalities, kings subservient to the Phanariots ruled from 1711 to 1821.

A deep-seated desire to preserve local languages, customs, beliefs, and practices could incite some Orthodox Christians to revolt against the Phanariots and the Ottomans. They sought to throw off the yoke of the Ottomans, establish autocephalous (self-governing) Orthodox churches, and if possible, reach some form of understanding with the patriarch of Constantinople. Sometimes they looked to the Russians for military assistance in their quest to gain liberation from the Ottomans.

In 1821 the Greek War for Independence broke out. Germanos, the Metropolitan of Old Patras, called for Greeks to revolt against the Turks. In the ensuing struggle, Greek revolutionaries massacred Turks, and Turks massacred Greeks. By 1832, with the help of European powers, the Greeks had won their independence from the Ottomans. In 1833 Greek bishops founded an autocephalous church. The power of the Phanariots was largely checked. In 1850 the patriarchate in Constantinople recognized the Orthodox Church in Greece.

In 1804 a Serbian revolution broke out. Eventually, in 1879, the Serbian kingdom won its independence from the Turks and established Serbian bishops as leaders of its church.

Under the leadership of Vassil Levski, hailed as an "Apostle of Freedom," a movement for Bulgarian independence from the Ottoman Turks gained momentum. In 1870 the Ottoman Turks recognized the independent status of the Bulgarian church. Then in May 1876 the Ottoman Turks harshly suppressed a Bulgarian insurrection, and many Bulgarians were massacred in cold blood. Detailed newspaper accounts of gruesome atrocities shocked the sensitivities of western Europeans.

In 1877–78 the Russians helped the Bulgarians win freedom from the Turks. In 1884 John Kargel founded a Baptist church in Ruse. Despite much opposition, a second Baptist church was formed in Lorn and later a third in Sofia. A 1900 census indicated there were 3,744,223 Bulgarians, of whom 80.6 percent (over 3 million) were Greek Orthodox; 17.4 percent were Muslims; 0.7 percent were Catholics of the Latin Rite and Uniate Greeks; and 0.12 percent (just over 4,500) were Protestants.

Romania was made up of Wallachia and Moldavia. (Transylvania and Bassarabia were added between the First and Second World Wars.) These states were ruled by the Ottoman Turks until the Turks were defeated in the Russian-Turkish War of 1828–29, after which they became essentially Russian protectorates. But then the Russians were defeated in the Crimean War, and the Congress of Paris placed the protectorates under Turkish control.

In 1872 the Orthodox churches came together and formed an autocephalous Romanian Orthodox Church. In 1883 the patriarchate of Constantinople recognized this church. In 1883 the Romanian Catholic Church of the Latin Rite was established with its center in Bucharest. In 1856 Germans founded the first Baptist church in Romania. By 1919 there were 600 Baptist churches in Romania with 19,000 in attendance.

The creation of nationalistic, independent Orthodox churches with their own ethnic identities dramatically reduced the number of faithful who accepted the ecclesiastical authority of the patriarchate of Constantinople.

IX. CONCLUSION

The fall of the Bastille in Paris on July 14, 1789, signaled the collapse of western Europe's "Old Order." The French Revolution and Napoleonic era contributed further to the dissembling of the *Ancien régime*. After 1814, some Europeans attempted to restore European institutions to a pre-1789 status. They had only limited success in their campaign. A number focused their efforts on strengthening the Christian churches in the face of countervailing, hostile secular forces. The papacy's influence on European culture increased. Revivals of the Christian faith in Europe and significant missionary expansion overseas did take place. At the end of the nineteenth century, many Europeans still believed they lived in "Christian" countries.

On June 28, 1914, the assassination of Archduke Ferdinand of Austria and his wife in Sarajevo, the capital of Bosnia and Herzegovina, helped precipitate the collapse of "liberal democratic Christian" Europe. This assassination served as a trip wire setting off what became known as World War I or "the Great War."

On August 1, 1914, Germany mobilized for war, the emperor sending a declaration of war to the Russian minister of foreign affairs. The Germans decided to make a preemptory military invasion of Belgium and France before facing the Russians. The Allies reeled before the ferocious German onslaught. They retreated in disarray. At the Battle of the Marne in September, the Allies counterattacked and staved off the Germans' military offensive.

Ominous war reports from Europe greatly distressed Woodrow Wilson, the President of the United States and a man of strong Christian convictions.

The horrific sounds of destruction and death generally rendered the western front in Europe anything but "quiet." Combatants settled

Trench warfare in World War I.

into the murderous savagery of trench warfare. Trenches were dug for hundreds of miles from Switzerland to the North Sea. A heavily barb-wired "no-man's-land" of scarred and scorched earth and deadly land mines separated the antagonists. The introduction of gas warfare made the fighting particularly lethal. (Some soldiers, including Adolf Hitler, were temporarily blinded by gas.) The fusillades of tanks and strafing planes added to the maiming and killing. The trenches were often flooded with water. The number of casualties on both sides escalated.

On Christmas Eve and Christmas Day 1914, at the beginning of the war, something surprising happened. An unofficial truce spread after the Germans and the English sang Christmas songs within hearing distance of each other's trenches. One soldier recounted his amazement that the Germans and the English enjoyed singing the same Christmas carols together: "They finished their carol and we thought that we ought to retaliate in some way, so we sang 'The First Noel,' and when we finished that they all began clapping; and then they struck up another favorite of theirs, 'O Tannenbaum.' And so it went on."

Sensing a Christmas spirit of goodwill, a number of the soldiers climbed out of their trenches and walked into no-man's-land without their weapons. There they exchanged pleasantries, cigarettes, and small items with enemy soldiers who had likewise climbed out of their trenches. There was even a pickup game of soccer between some of the Germans and the English.

Commanding officers later chided their soldiers for having fraternized with the enemy. The deadly trench warfare lasted for three years.

It is noteworthy that the Germans and the English were fighting for nations that had lingering "Christian" cultures. The soldiers had been raised with some kind of contact with the Christian faith, if only learning the lyrics of traditional Christmas carols. But now their "Christian nations" were at war. What effect World War I's epic struggle between "Christian nations" (and Ottoman allies) would have on the Christian churches' continuing ability to influence European culture was yet to be seen.

FOR FURTHER STUDY

Burrow, J. W. *The Crisis of Reason: European Thought, 1848–1914*. New Haven: Yale University Press, 2000.

Chadwick, Owen. *A History of the Popes, 1830–1914*. Oxford: Oxford University Press, 2003.

Clark, Christopher, and Wolfram Kaiser, eds. *Culture Wars: Catholic-Secular Conflict in Nineteenth-Century Europe*. Cambridge: Cambridge University Press, 2003.

Hope, Nicholas. *The Oxford History of Christianity: German and Scandinavian Protestants, 1700–1918*. Oxford: Oxford University Press, 1995.

Howard, Thomas. *Protestant Theology and the Making of the Modern German University*. Oxford: Oxford University Press, 2006.

Kselman, Thomas. *Miracles and Prophecies in Nineteenth-Century France*. New Brunswick, NJ: Rutgers University Press, 1983.

Latourette, Kenneth. *A History of Christianity, Vol. II: A.D. 1500 to A.D. 1975*. New York: Harper and Row, 1975.

Perrot, Michelle, ed. *A History of Private Life from the Fires of Revolution to the Great War. Volume IV*. Cambridge: Harvard University Press, 1990.

Taylor, Charles. *A Secular Age*. Cambridge: Harvard University Press, 2007.

Global Christianity

A Re-Centered Faith (20th and 21st Centuries)

I. INTRODUCTION

The last century has seen a rapid expansion of global economies that are highly interactive and interdependent. What happens on the New York Stock Exchange necessarily affects what happens on global stock markets in Shanghai, Hong Kong, Tokyo, and London.

During the twentieth century, globalization with its economic interdependence has accelerated more rapidly than anyone could have anticipated. The current wave of globalization emerged in the aftermath of the Second World War and has been driven by a worldwide shift to free-market economic systems, creating a myriad of new opportunities for international trade and investment. Since 1950, for example, the volume of world trade has increased by twenty times.

The astonishing advance of the Internet and communications technology have made the world smaller, or "flatter," as economist Thomas Friedman would say. Globalization has extended the reach of the individual by equalizing opportunity and allowing many more people to "connect, compete, and collaborate."

Of course, there is a sense in which globalization is not new. For thousands of years individuals and corporations have been buying and selling at great distances, such as with the famed Silk Road across central Asia that connected China and Europe during the Middle Ages.

While globalization is primarily regarded as an economic concept, one must also recognize that it is inevitably accompanied by environmental, cultural, and political implications. Even the Silk Road was not merely an avenue of economic trade, but also an avenue of cultural exchange.

Globalization has the potential to reshape religious ideas and realities in a way not seen before. For example, Pentecostal churches in

Africa, Asia, and Latin America have become avenues of economic renewal in impoverished societies. The emergence of global Pentecostalism in particular has played a decisive role in shifting the balance from what is called the "global North" to the "global South." In those nations most impacted by the expansion of Christianity in the Southern Hemisphere, religious identities have supplanted political loyalties. The twenty-first century has all the ingredients for a global transformation of unprecedented dimensions.

One of the seminal events of twentieth-century missions occurred in 1910 at the World Missionary Conference (WMC) held in Edinburgh, Scotland. Championed by the Student Volunteer Movement with its inspirational slogan, "The Evangelization of the World in This Generation," the conference was presided over by the American Methodist layman John R. Mott.

In contrast to earlier missionary assemblies, the Edinburgh conference had a more comprehensive vision, attracting the full spectrum of Protestants engaged in foreign missions. More than 1,200 delegates from various mission agencies attended to discuss such topics as Bible translation, mobilization of church support, and the training of indigenous leadership. Among other things, the conference launched a new journal, the *International Review of Missions*, to enhance scholarly discussion.

Another significant achievement was the establishment of an infrastructure to encourage internationally coordinated missionary efforts in the future. To that end the WMC created what would become the International Missionary Council (formally established in 1921), with Mott as the chairman. The IMC sought to establish international missionary networks as well as to encourage research into the key issues and practices in missionary outreach. Over the next years, Mott traveled widely and was able to stimulate the creation of some thirty national Christian councils around the globe. The purpose of these national councils was to highlight the ecclesiastical issues of that particular nation, encourage indigenous leadership, and promote unity and cooperation among the various Christian communities.

John Raleigh Mott.

The Edinburgh Missionary Conference set a trajectory that would shape the future of Protestant missions for much of the twentieth century. Mott's leadership also signaled a transition from British to American dominance in global missions.

Another notable achievement of the conference was laying the groundwork for the modern ecumenical movement. This bore fruit in 1961 when the International Missionary Council was renamed the Commission on World Mission and Evangelism and was incorporated into the World Council of Churches.

One of the historic hallmarks of Christianity has been the conjunction of Bible translation and missionary activity. As early as the second and third centuries, the New Testament was translated into Latin, Syriac, and Coptic. An astounding achievement in the Eastern Church was the work of the Greek brothers Cyril and Methodius, who invented the Glagothic alphabet (precursor to Cyrillic) in the ninth century in order to translate the Bible into Slavic, thus paving the way for the Christianization of the Slavs.

From Cornelius Ruyl to John Eliot, William Carey, and Robert Morrison, translation of the Bible into the language of the people has been a Christian commitment and especially identified with Protestant missions.

This Protestant propensity was taken to a new level by William Cameron Townsend with the founding of Wycliffe Bible Translators (WBT) in 1934. The WBT and its field organization, the Summer Institute of Linguistics, have made a significant contribution to the translations of the New Testament into nearly 1,200 language communities and the entire Bible in over 400 language communities. Portions of the New Testament have been translated into more than 2,300 languages.

Technological advances promise to accelerate Bible translation even more in the coming decades. New computer programs have made it feasible to translate Scriptures into some cognate languages in a relatively brief time. Significantly, certain cultural benefits accompany Bible translation. It not only speeds a church's growth, but often enhances literacy and enhances the cultural identity of a particular people group. It also ensures that Christian information becomes a permanent part of the native culture and literature.

II. NEW CENTERS OF GLOBAL CHRISTIANITY

By the mid-1980s one of the most significant developments of twentieth-century Christianity occurred—namely, the center of gravity in global Christianity had shifted from the Western to the non-Western world. It has been said, "The typical Christian is no longer an affluent, white, British, Anglican male about forty-five years old, but a poor, black, African Pentecostal woman about twenty-five years old."

Christianity is currently experiencing a precipitous decline in much of the West (especially Europe)—the global North (North America and

Europe)—and a majority of Christians now live outside the West in what is called the "global South" (Africa, Latin America, and Asia). At the beginning of the twenty-first century, Christians represented about one-third of the world population. Europe and North America have about 820 million Christian adherents. The global South has about a billion Christians: 480 million in Latin America, 360 million in Africa, and 313 million in Asia. By all estimates this pattern will only accelerate—with Christians in the global South numbering 1.7 billion by 2025.

A. Africa

It is sometimes forgotten that Africa figures significantly in the story of Jesus. Egypt was not only a refuge for the infant Jesus and his family during Herod's murderous rampage, but also a fulfillment of Hosea's prophecy: "Out of Egypt I called my son" (Hosea 11:1; see Matt. 2:13–15).

Although Christianity has often been portrayed as an alien intrusion from the West, it has a continuous history on the continent of Africa of nearly two thousand years. The Coptic tradition identifies Mark, the writer of one of the Synoptic Gospels, as the first Christian missionary in North Africa. Moreover, the continent was the scene of some of the greatest theological controversies in the history of the church: Arianism, Donatism, and Pelagianism. North African theologians such as Tertullian, Clement of Alexandria, Origen, Cyprian, Athanasius, and Augustine of Hippo decisively shaped the early development of Christianity.

Having entered North Africa through Egypt, Christianity then spread to ancient Nubia (largely modern Sudan and parts of southern Egypt) and Ethiopia. With the advance of Islam in the seventh century, Christianity began its long retreat in North Africa. Nubian Christianity eventually succumbed to Islam (in the fifteenth century), but Christianity did manage to survive as a minority religion in Egypt and Ethiopia.

Christianity made its first appearance in sub-Saharan Africa with the arrival of Portuguese missionaries in the fifteenth century. Catholicism gained a tenuous foothold in West Africa, but floundered over time. For the next several centuries the relationship between Europe and Africa centered on the slave trade, dominated at first by the Portuguese, then supplanted by the Dutch and then by the British and French.

With the Wesleyan revival in Britain at the end of the eighteenth century, there was a renewed Protestant interest in missions, but with a staunchly abolitionist stance. The missionary-explorer David Livingstone traveled extensively throughout East Africa, preaching the gospel, exploring virgin territory, and bewailing the suffering of Africans subjugated by slavery. In a letter to the editor of the *New York Herald*, Livingstone declared, "And if my disclosures regarding the terrible Ujijian slavery should lead to the suppression of the East Coast slave trade, I shall regard that as a greater matter by far than the discovery of all the Nile sources together."

One of the other farsighted missionary leaders, Henry Venn, famously advocated that the missionary task was to assist in the establishment of a self-governing, self-financing, and self-propagating church. Venn believed that each missionary endeavor had a terminus point at which the indigenous leadership took the reins of national churches.

At the beginning of the nineteenth century, Europeans were still largely oblivious to the continent of Africa. Europeans had confined themselves to trading mainly along the coast. Inland, the trading of slaves and commodities was handled by African and Arab merchants. By the end of the third quarter, France, Britain, Portugal, and Germany had established spheres of influence in different parts of Africa, largely in alliance with their commercial interests. Britain, in particular, and Germany were content with informal influence rather than the burden of formal annexation.

Things began to change as a result of political restlessness in Europe during the period 1876 to 1880. There was a sudden flurry of colonial activity by the Portuguese. From 1876 onward, Portugal dispatched a series of expeditions that by 1880 resulted in the annexation of Mozambique. Also, France revived its colonial initiatives in both Tunisia and Madagascar.

These actions on the part of France and Portugal were a clear indication that they were now committed to colonial expansion and establishment of formal control in Africa. This expansionist mood pressed both Britain and Germany into their own colonialism, leading to their annexations in southern, eastern, and western Africa. By the early 1880s, the scramble for territory was well under way, and with it came the inevitable threat of territorial disputes.

It was in the first frenzy of competing colonialism that the idea of an international conference emerged. In response to competing territorial claims in the Congo region, Portugal, fearful of losing its stake in Africa, initially suggested the need for a conference, and this was later taken up by the German Chancellor Bismarck.

The conference was held at Berlin between November 15, 1884, and November 26, 1885. Ostensibly, it was not the initial intention of the conference to attempt a general partition of Africa. Nevertheless, it ended up disposing of territory and establishing "the rules to be observed in future with regard to the occupation of territory on the coasts of Africa." In effect, the continent of Europe had arrogated to itself the right of occupying and partitioning the territory of another continent.

During the next two decades Africa was divided among the major European powers. In this scramble for Africa, tribal rulers were induced to sign treaties in which they surrendered sovereignty in return for protection. Between 1885 and 1914 much of Africa came under the control of European powers: Britain controlled nearly 30 percent of Africa's population, France 15 percent, Germany 9 percent, and Belgium 7 percent.

As the European powers carved up Africa among themselves, they inevitably had an impact on missionary endeavors there. Missionaries tended to be closely related to their sponsoring European nation and, whether they wanted it or not, became subject to and identified with the colonizing European powers. Missionaries all too often became a means by which the colonial rulers subdued and controlled their African colonies.

A second great watershed in the history of the modern African church came around 1960, when the churches, along with the nations that housed them, moved from colonialism to independence. Decolonization began soon after World War II and extended for half a century. The era of imperial collapse began when the British withdrew from India and Pakistan in 1947. In Africa, decolonization began with the independence of Ghana in 1957, which was followed in rapid succession over the next decade by Zaire and Nigeria in 1960, Algeria in 1962, and Zimbabwe in 1979. White rule survived in South Africa until 1994, with the overthrow of apartheid.

With the wholesale rejection of European colonialism and the rise of nationalism among colonized peoples, anti-Western sentiment often translated into anti-missionary rhetoric: missionaries were branded as a tool of imperialism. By the 1970s, Christian leaders in the Philippines, Kenya, and Argentina as well as the All Africa Conference of Churches even called for a "moratorium" on Western missionaries.

Just as African nations declared their independence from European colonialism, so also Africans began to chart their own course ecclesiologically. One of the most significant consequences of European decolonization was the emergence of African Indigenous Churches (AIC). Amid all the variety of Protestants (Anglicans to Pentecostals) and the different Catholic orders (Jesuits to Capuchins), the AIC typically developed from a Protestant mission context.

Born largely out of frustration with Western colonial exploitation, these indigenous churches have gone their own way and function without reference to overseas churches. They range from independent versions of Western Protestant churches to highly syncretistic Christian versions of traditional African religions. Some of the most important AICs emerged in Nigeria.

The largest of the AICs are the Aladura "Prayer People" churches, which grew out of the Anglican Church. In response to an epidemic in 1918, Joseph Sadare had a vivid dream about the need for constant prayer. Sparked by an affiliation with a Pentecostal group, the Aladura church was born in 1928, and it rapidly spread from Nigeria to Sierra Leone, Liberia, and Ghana. Today it is composed of a million adherents.

Various Christian movements sprang up in the first half of the twentieth century that had a decidedly anticolonial cast. One of the most significant was centered around Simon Kimbangu. Born near Kinshasa, in what was then the Belgian Congo (now the Democratic Republic of the Congo), he was converted and educated by British Baptist missionaries. In 1918 he reportedly had a religious vision in which the voice of Christ called him to a healing ministry and an Africanized Christianity.

Kimbangu initially ignored the vision, but eventually he heeded the call, returning to his home village. Almost immediately, he was reported to have healed a sick woman by the laying on of hands. Dozens of apparent miracles were attributed to Kimbangu, and he gained thousands of followers from surrounding villages and towns. Both Catholics and Protestants repudiated him. By June 1921 the Belgian authorities arrested him for inciting revolution. Four months later he was sentenced to death. Albert I of Belgium commuted his sentence to life in prison, where he remained until his death thirty years later, in 1951.

Colonial authorities assumed Kimbangu's movement would wither after his imprisonment and death, but the church flourished under the leadership of his son, Kuntima Diangienda, as it took up the cause against colonialism. Kimbanguism, characterized by faith healing and charismatic phenomena, spread rapidly throughout central Africa, making it the most popular indigenous form of Christianity in Africa. It is estimated to have nearly 5 million adherents.

African Indigenous Churches have continued to grow and proliferate, but tend to be less concerned with integrating Christianity into traditional African culture. In part this is because the African-led churches are more sensitive to the strengths of traditional African culture, and in part it is because African people are becoming less traditional, more urbanized, and more Western. AICs are increasingly coming to resemble Western Christian churches, particularly those of the more fervent Pentecostal variety.

With the dawn of the twenty-first century, Christianity is probably the main religion in most of sub-Saharan Africa, while in the northern part of the continent it is a minority religion existing alongside the Muslim majority. (Coptic Christians comprise a significant minority in Egypt.) There has been tremendous growth of Christians in Africa. As evidence, only 9 million Christians were in Africa in 1900, but by the year 2000, as stated earlier, there were an estimated 380 million Christians. According to a 2006 Pew Forum on Religion and Public Life study, 147 million African Christians were "renewalists" (a term that includes both Pentecostals and Charismatics).

Much of the Christian growth in Africa is now due to African evangelism rather than Western missionaries. In South Africa it is rare to find a person with no religious beliefs, which is almost always Christianity amongst the whites, but Christianity is also popular among the blacks, especially city dwellers. Christianity in Africa shows tremendous variety, from the ancient forms of Oriental Orthodox Christianity in Egypt, Ethiopia, and Eritrea to the newest African-Christian denominations of Nigeria, a country that has experienced massive conversions to Christianity in recent decades.

All indications are that by 2025 there will be 633 million Christians in Africa.

> "African Christianity might be the shape of things to come" (Gambia-born Professor Lamin Sanneh of Yale Divinity School).

B. China

According to tradition, the apostle Thomas brought the Christian gospel to China in the first century. While there is evidence that Christianity was firmly established in Persia by the early fourth century, there is no documentation that it had reached China. However, by the seventh century Christianity did make its way there. The Nestorian missionary Alopen followed the Silk Road to China, where he was warmly received by Emperor Taizong of the Tang dynasty in 635. The emperor permitted the first Christian church to be erected at Xi'an three years later and also permitted the first Chinese translation of a Christian book: *The Sutra of Jesus the Messiah*.

The discovery of the so-called "Nestorian Stele" in 1625 provides compelling evidence that Nestorian Christianity had indeed made its way to China in the seventh century. When the Tang dynasty was overthrown in 845, Christianity seems to have disappeared until the thirteenth century.

Over the centuries, Christianity had a mixed reception in China. It is estimated that some 200,000 Christians were in China in 1900 and more than 2,000 missionaries. Throughout the course of the nineteenth century, however, Christianity became increasingly associated with

Western colonialism. Growing xenophobia led to the Boxer Rebellion of 1900 and the deaths of thousands of Christians. Christianity received a much-needed reprieve with the rise of Chiang Kai-shek in the 1930s. After his marriage to the American-educated Methodist Song Meiling, Christianity gained ground in China.

After World War II, the Christian church grew significantly in Asian nations such as Korea, Taiwan, and Hong Kong. However, with the rise of communism in 1949, Chinese Christianity went underground, and foreign missionaries were expelled. The communist government allowed only state-sanctioned churches for Catholics (the Three-Self Movement in 1951) and for Protestants (the Three-Self Patriotic Movement in 1954). Both organizations were used by the state to eliminate foreign influence.

Christians underwent great suffering in the Great Leap Forward (1958–60) and the catastrophic Cultural Revolution (1966–69). Many feared that Christianity was doomed in China. However, with the demise of first-generation Communist Party leaders such as Mao Zedong and Zhou Enlai, the government began implementing a series of political and economic reforms advocated by Deng Xiaoping that eventually led to some relaxation of control over many areas of society.

Chairman Mao Zedong of China.

Mao Tse-tung, 1960s, Chinese Photographer (20th century)/Private Collection/Peter Newark Historical Pictures/The Bridgeman Art Library

By the late 1970s, underground churches, largely Protestant in orientation, began to proliferate.

As China modernized under Deng Xiaoping and embraced a market economy toward the end of the twentieth century, the restrictions on Christianity began to diminish. Then in 1989 the student-led pro-democracy movement reached a decisive moment in Beijing's Tiananmen Square. The repressive nature of the Communist Party resurfaced, and the student protests at Tiananmen Square were violently crushed by the Chinese military. This suppression had unintended consequences for the burgeoning "house church movement."

The harsh response of the Communist government and the killing of many hundreds of Chinese students had a dramatic impact on the collective psyche of the Chinese people. The people of China lost confidence in the Communist Party, and this in turn created a new openness to Christianity.

Especially since 1989, evangelical Christianity has exploded throughout China. The so-called "house church movement," led largely by laypeople—many of whom are women—spread like wildfire. Even the government-sponsored Three-Self Church has been impacted so that some have become evangelical. The best estimates for the first decades of the twenty-first century are that more than 100 million Christians are now active in China. There is little doubt that China has emerged as a global economic power but, with other Asian nations, is also poised to become a major force in world Christianity.

Still, Chinese Christian churches are bereft of theological leadership. With so many churches emerging, leadership is more happenstance. Many of the leaders are uneducated and subject to folk religion and superstition. In his book *The Corpse Walker: Real Life Stories, China from the Bottom Up*, Liao Yiwu tells the story of a man whose wife was burned alive because she was thought to be possessed by an evil dragon. He converted to Christianity, but still is fearful the evil dragon will return.

C. India

If tradition is to be given credence, then Christianity in India is as ancient as Christianity itself. According to tradition, the apostle Thomas in AD 52, following the ancient trade route between the Middle East and South India, is believed to have reached Kudungalur (modern Cranganore) on the southwest coast of the Indian state of Kerala. Local legend has it that Thomas converted the daughter of the Indo-Parthian King Gondophares. After establishing several churches in the region, he traveled to Mylapore (near modern-day Madras), where his preaching led to his martyrdom in AD 72.

From the fourth century, Christians in India (also called Thomas Christians) came under the influence of the Syrian (Nestorian) Church. Vasco da Gama, the Portuguese explorer, reached Calcutta in 1498 and established trade relations. This was the beginning of a long European presence in India. Franciscan, Dominican, Jesuit, and Augustinian missionaries soon arrived only to find that the Indian Christians were Nestorian in theology and Syrian in liturgy.

Backed by the *padroado* (papal treaties giving Spain and Portugal some ecclesiastical rights over colonies), European missionaries incessantly tried to impose their own liturgy and authority on the Thomas Christians. Eventually the Christian community in India split into the New Party, which retained Nestorianism and the Syrian liturgy, and the Old Party, which held to Latin theology and rites. In the 1600s the German Pietists Bartholomaeus Ziegenbalg and Heinrich Plütschau were among the first Protestant missionaries to work in India, but with sparse impact.

It was not until the nineteenth century that Protestant missions were able to make significant progress in India. The most important early Protestant missionary was the English Baptist William Carey (see chapter 16).

Carey was not the first foreign missionary, but he was the first one to be sent out by a missionary society. In June 1793 Carey, his family, and John Thomas, a medical doctor, set sail for India, arriving in Bengal in November. Having decided to be self-supporting, Carey took a job as the manager of an indigo plantation in Malda. He quickly learned the language and planted a church in 1795, set up a school, and successfully lobbied against the Indian custom of *sati*—the required death of a widow on her husband's funeral pyre—which was finally banned in 1829.

In 1799 Carey resettled in the Danish enclave of Serampore, where he was joined by the printer William Ward and the educator Joshua Marshman. The "Serampore Trio," as they became known, were energetically engaged in education, publishing, and translation work. Among their achievements were the publishing of the Bible in Bengali and other languages; creating grammars in Bengali, Sanskrit, and Marathi; establishing the first newspaper in India; founding Serampore College (1818); engaging in dialogue with Hindu intellectuals; and opening new mission stations in Bengal, Orissa, North India, and Ceylon. Carey also served as professor of Sanskrit, Bengali, and Marathi at the recently founded Fort William College in Calcutta, a post he held from 1801 to 1831.

Sometimes called the "Wycliffe of the East," Carey is well-remembered for his contributions to Bible translation. In addition to his early Bengali translation, Carey taught himself numerous other languages and dialects in order to make further Bible translations, including Sanskrit, Marathi, Hindi, and Oriva. He translated parts of the Bible, either directly or indirectly through supervising others, into thirty-four languages. It has been estimated that in the first three decades of the nineteenth century, 49 percent of all first translations of the Bible into new languages in the world were published at Serampore under Carey's direction.

Christians in North America followed Carey's work with great interest. American Congregationalists were the first to establish a missionary society in 1810: the American Board of Commissioners for Foreign Missions.

Among the first missionaries sent by the American Board were Adoniram and Ann Judson. They set sail for India in 1812, and during their journey they became convinced Baptists. After arriving in Calcutta, they resigned from the American Board and headed for Rangoon, Burma. Under the auspices of the General Missionary Convention of the Baptist Denomination in the USA for Foreign Missions, which was established in 1814, Judson engaged in a flurry of activity: establishing a church, preaching, and Bible translation. Judson spent twenty-four years translating the Bible into Burmese, completing it in 1834. He spent the remaining years of his life compiling a Burmese-English dictionary.

Judson made great personal sacrifices in losing two wives on the mission field: Ann in 1826, and Sarah in 1845.

Missionary activity in India took place amid British colonialism and economic expansion. At the dawn of the seventeenth century a group of British merchants formed the East India Company and were given monopoly privileges on all trade with the East Indies. Over the years, the company eclipsed Portuguese traders and saw a massive expansion of their trading operations in India. English communities developed around the key cities of Calcutta, Bombay, and Madras.

In the course of its economic expansion, the British East India Company found itself ruling an entire country. As the company's economic fortunes rose, it underwent a transformation from a trading venture to a ruling body.

The decisive point of this transformation was when one of its officials, Robert Clive, defeated the forces of the Nawab of Bengal, Siraj-ud-daulah, at the Battle of Plassey in 1757. The company in effect ruled over vast sections of India and even acquired the right to collect revenues from the people. When the economic and political burdens of rule began to overwhelm the company, the British state intervened. Lord North's India Bill (1773) provided for a governing alliance between the British East India Company and the British Parliament, which sent a governor-general to represent its interests. Even though the governing authority remained with the East India Company, it had to submit to increasingly close supervision by the British state and to periodical inquiries by Parliament.

In India, the governors of the company's commercial settlements became governors of provinces and administrators in the new British regime. Armies were created and used, not only to defend the company's economic interests, but also to coerce neighboring Indian states and crush any potential internal resistance.

Under this new arrangement British territorial expansion continued unabated. Regional wars against various Indian rulers led to British occupation over the entire Indian subcontinent. In some cases the British ruled indirectly by placing a British emissary at the court of the native ruler who was allowed sovereignty in domestic matters. One of the more notorious British policies was Lord Dalhousie's so-called "doctrine of lapse," whereby a native state became part of British India if there was no male heir at the death of the ruler.

In 1858 the East India Company was dissolved, and the administration of India became the exclusive responsibility of the British crown. Britain had become the largest colonial empire of the nineteenth century, and India was Britain's oldest, largest, and most lucrative colonial possession—the jewel in the crown. Native opposition to British rule coalesced after World War I under the leadership of the British-educated lawyer Mahatma Gandhi (1869–1948), who preached "nonviolent noncooperation." In response, British rulers gradually introduced political reforms and limited self-government.

In the aftermath of World War II, the call for Indian independence grew louder. The obstacle posed by the age-old conflict between Hindus and Muslims was resolved in 1947 when Muslim Pakistan and Hindu India were both granted independence.

Throughout the twentieth century, Christianity in India has been fraught with conflict and tensions between Catholics, Protestants, and Thomas Christians. But the overriding issue for all Christians in India centers on the caste system. Indeed, it is difficult to find any time in the history of Indian Christianity when this was not a burning issue. This has been and remains the enduring problem for all Christians in India. There are roughly 3,000 separate castes (*jatis*) in India, each ethnically distinct and forbidden from intermingling.

Mahatma Gandhi.

Thousands of years ago, Brahman elites devised a hierarchical social structure of four general categories (*varna*), each of which has hundreds of castes: Brahman, Kshatriya, Vaishiya, and Shudra. The top three *varna* make up about 15 percent of the population; the lowest *varna* (Shudra) represents about 50 percent.

There are two other groups of castes that are outside the established social structure. The first are the so-called "untouchables," or Dalits—which means "broken," "crushed," or "oppressed." The Dalits are considered subhuman and little better than animals. They have no opportunities for economic or social advancement and are confined to the most demeaning jobs in Indian culture, such as removing dung or cutting carcasses. They are permitted to dwell only outside the villages and are often subject to abuse.

Also beyond the pale are the Adivasis, aboriginal or tribal peoples of the northeast. The Adivasis are a fierce warrior people who refuse to submit to the Brahman social structure and thus remain out of mainstream society.

These social structures and taboos are so culturally ingrained that even Indian Christians tend to accept the caste system. Brahmans who become Christians are seen as Brahman-Christians, and Shudras who embrace Christianity usually are seen as Shudra-Christians. Churches all too often accept the same cultural boundaries and tend to be composed of members of the same caste. This culturally conditioned Christianity poses a serious challenge to the Indian church.

Christianity has begun to make inroads in all social communities of India, but especially among the disenfranchised Dalits and Adivasis. One of the principal vehicles of evangelization is the Pentecostal movement. Catholics remain the largest Christian community, although Protestant communities are on the rise. Scholars estimate that there are approximately 50 million Christians in India, making it the third-largest religion behind Hinduism and Islam.

Since the partition in 1947 and the emergence of Hindu India and Muslim Pakistan (as well as other autonomous neighboring nations—Bangladesh, Burma (Myanmar), Nepal, and Sri Lanka), the number of missionaries from abroad has declined. Hindu nationalists continue to view Indian Christians as a foreign intrusion, and hostility toward Christianity and its proselytizing activities has grown each decade. Much of this hostility has become institutionalized in various Indian political parties. This has resulted in the destruction of Christian churches and, in some cases, death.

Many mainline denominations such as the Anglicans, Methodists, and Congregationalists have merged to form the Church of South India. Other denominations such as the Thomas Christians have retained their

A group of untouchables near Bangalore, India.

separate identities. The Roman Catholic Church in India has undergone what some have called "Indianization"—that is, Christian in doctrine but culturally Indian. Vatican II encouraged such adaptation. The Jesuits in particular have provided significant academic leadership.

One of the ironies of the religious scene in India is that the Hindu elites of Indian aristocracy often send their children to Christian schools, which are generally considered the finest educational institutions in the country. The main regional concentrations of Christian population are the states of Kerala and Tamil Nadu in southern India, Goa in the southwest, and Manipur and Mizonran in the northeast. Northeast India accounts for 60 percent of the country's total Christian population, and in the southern states Christians make up a significant segment of the population.

D. Latin America

Although Latin America eventually achieved political independence from Spain, Iberian Catholicism had become imbedded in the warp and woof of its culture. The lands remained profoundly Catholic well into the twentieth century and were identified as such at the 1910 Edinburgh Missions Conference. Thus, this region of the world was regarded as off-limits to evangelization.

The first Protestant church in Latin America was established in Brazil in 1855, but it remained quite small and never had any significant impact until the arrival of Pentecostals. The earliest Pentecostals in Latin America were Methodist missionaries in Chile who were in contact with the Azusa Street Revival in 1907 and were subsequently energized by speaking in tongues.

Although Pentecostal Protestantism gained a foothold in Latin America soon after the turn of the century, still it was the Catholic Church that dominated religious and cultural experience until mid-century. In 1940 scholars estimate no more than a million Protestants were in all of Latin America. By the 1960s the *evangélicos* (Pentecostals/ Protestants) were rapidly gaining ground. From Chile, Pentecostalism spread to Argentina, Brazil, and Mexico and then to the whole of Latin America. By 2000 it is estimated there were more than 50 million *evangélicos* in Latin America.

For the better part of the twentieth century Latin America was a cauldron of political upheaval. The basic social issue confronting many nations on the continent was the profound discrepancy between the wealthy landowners (*hacendados*) and the poor peasants. In the eyes of many, the Catholic Church was an unspoken ally of the social status quo and this at a time when the gap between the rich and poor was at its greatest. But Vatican II (1962–65) marked an ecclesiastical sea change that had a special resonance in Latin America. With its emphasis on social justice, lay leadership, vernacular liturgy, and a special concern for the poor, Vatican II inspired new and sometimes radical thinking.

At the 1968 Conference of Latin American Bishops at Medellín, Columbia, the bishops began to reconceive the doctrine of sin in sociopolitical terms—that is, sin was identified especially with unjust and repressive social and political structures. This new thinking soon laid the groundwork for a theology of liberation (see chapter 19).

Closely linked with the emergence of "liberation theology" was the pastoral strategy of the *comunidades eclesiales de base* (base communities). Because of the critical shortage of priests, the Catholic Church established parish-type communities with lay leadership. This had the effect of shifting the religious focus from the mass to Bible study and social action.

As liberation theology and the lay-led base communities gained momentum in the 1970s and 1980s, steady resistance arose within the more conservative tiers of the church and the state. It made matters more complex when the United States, embroiled in the Cold War, intervened on the side of anticommunist Latin American dictators. Some Catholic priests joined the Sandinista socialist revolution in Nicaragua;

others opposed the U.S.-backed military dictatorships in Chile, Brazil, and Argentina.

As the confrontation between leftists and militarists spread across the continent, a significant number of priests were killed. The most notable was Archbishop Oscar Romero of San Salvador, who was murdered while celebrating mass in March 1980.

The collapse of communism in Russia and the conclusion of the Cold War undermined the anticommunist rationale for political involvement in Latin America, and so the United States began to reduce its presence south of its border.

The social and political upheavals plaguing Latin America provided an unprecedented opportunity for North American Protestantism to make inroads. By the 1960s North American evangelicals began to focus more attention on South and Central America. If not in collusion with American foreign policy aims, evangelical missionaries generally shared the same desire that communism should not gain a foothold in Latin America as it had in Cuba. North American Pentecostal television evangelists such as Jimmy Swaggart and Pat Robertson were well known for their anticommunist rhetoric as well as their aggressive evangelization throughout Latin America.

Population growth rates in the global South are astonishing. Africa and Latin America combined represented 13 percent of the world population in 1900. By 2050, Africa and Latin America will be home to 29 percent. Population projections suggest that between 2000 and 2050, the eight largest Latin American nations will increase from a total of 429 million to 600 million.

III. THE RISE OF PENTECOSTALISM

As we have seen, one of the most important religious developments to give shape and substance to twentieth-century global Christianity is the Pentecostal movement and its more contemporary and refined offspring, the "charismatic movement." Reputable scholars assert that in 2000, Pentecostal numbers worldwide were increasing at the rate of nearly 19 million a year. One scholar has concluded that the Pentecostal surge is the most significant religious movement since the birth of Islam or the Protestant Reformation and that Pentecostals may well by now "account for one of every three Christians in the world."

Pentecostalism has its roots in the American Wesleyan-Holiness movement of the late nineteenth century and takes its name from the Christian feast of Pentecost, which celebrates the coming of the Holy Spirit upon the disciples (Acts 2). Pentecostals believe in the continuing efficacy of the charismatic gifts and emphasize a post-conversion expe-

Pentecostals "account for one of every three Christians in the world."

rience that is signaled by ecstatic utterances in a language unknown to the speaker, called *glossolalia* or "speaking in tongues."

As a distinctive movement, Pentecostalism often traces its origins to Topeka, Kansas, and the teachings of a former Methodist preacher, Charles Fox Parham. At his Bethel Bible School, of which he was founder and the only teacher, Parham formulated the basic Pentecostal doctrine that after conversion and after sanctification (according to Holiness teaching), there is to be a third spiritual movement he called the "baptism of the Holy Ghost," and it is accompanied by "speaking in other tongues"—a replication of the day of Pentecost in Acts 2.

Parham's teaching first bore fruit in January 1901, when Agnes Ozman, a young student at the Bethel Bible School, spoke in tongues. Shortly thereafter Parham and other students had the same post-conversion experience, and the first seeds of the Pentecostal movement were planted.

It should be noted that speaking in tongues had appeared in the nineteenth century in both England and America, but it had never acquired the importance attributed to it by the later Pentecostals. In the 1830s *glossolalia* occurred under the ministry of the Scottish Presbyterian Edward Irving in London, but Irving's erratic theology led to his expulsion from the Church of Scotland, and his views never gained enough traction to lead to a significant movement.

Outbreaks of spiritual "gifts" appeared again in the 1830s in the worship at Shaker villages, as well as among Joseph Smith's Mormon followers in New York, Missouri, and Utah. The Pentecostals, however, were the first to give doctrinal primacy to the practice of speaking in tongues and the belief that the baptism of the Holy Spirit is a "second blessing" after conversion.

Although Parham was the first to articulate the distinctive doctrines of Pentecostalism (in particular, the experience of *glossolalia* as a sign of the baptism of the Holy Spirit), the emergence of Pentecostalism as a national and then worldwide movement came by way of his disciple, William J. Seymour, the son of a slave. Parham's distinctive ideas were parlayed into a full-orbed movement by a mild-mannered, one-eyed, black preacher from Louisiana. Believing he was living in the last days and that God was going to pour out his Spirit, Seymour made his way from Houston, Texas, to Los Angeles, California, in 1906, where he began holding revival meetings in an abandoned Methodist Church on Azusa Street, renamed the Apostolic Faith Gospel Mission.

The spark that burst into flame occurred on April 15, 1906, when Jenny Evans Moore spoke in tongues at the Azusa Street Mission. Within days, Los Angeles newspapers captivated readers with stories of "weird howlings" and the "gurgle of wordless talk." Shortly after the

"[Azusa Street Revival] turned a fairly localized and insignificant new Christian sect into an international movement that sent workers to more than twenty-five nations in only two years" (Allan Anders).

revival began, Seymour published his own broadsheet, the "Apostolic Faith," recounting conversions, miracle healings, and the outpouring of the Holy Spirit as evidenced by speaking in unknown tongues. Word spread quickly about the strange revival on Azusa Street.

Over the next three years the revival attracted thousands of people from all over the world—some merely curious, others seeking a genuine spiritual experience. The revival triggered new waves of evangelistic and missionary fervor around the world. Allan Anders noted that the Azusa Street Revival "turned a fairly localized and insignificant new Christian sect into an international movement that sent workers to more than twenty-five nations in only two years."

By the end of the twentieth century, what began as a few scattered local revivals had become a worldwide phenomenon of nearly a billion adherents. It also became very diverse and multilayered. With more than a billion adherents on every continent and populating literally thousands of denominations, the doctrinal perimeters of Pentecostalism has become broader. Certainly the most notable doctrinal characteristic is the affirmation of the continuing efficacy of the charismatic gifts, especially speaking in tongues.

Essentially, Pentecostalism is old-time revivalism that combines miraculous healings, tongues speaking, and a dispensational premillennialism with an expectation of the imminent rapture of the believers from a world rapidly spinning toward tribulation and final judgment. Pentecostal worship is characterized by lifting hands, dancing, shouting, clapping, exorcisms, and other forms of emotional expression.

As important as those distinctives are, the areas of doctrinal agreement place Pentecostals squarely within the boundaries of historic orthodoxy. In full accord with the Christian tradition, Pentecostals affirm the authority of the Scriptures, the centrality of the cross, and the resurrection of Christ, as well as an emphasis on repentance, conversion, and a godly life. Because Pentecostals believe we are living in the last days, they are emphatic about the need for world evangelism.

Perhaps it was inevitable that such a dynamic movement would engender controversy and division in its formative stages. The prime doctrinal deviation resulted in the emergence of the so-called "Oneness" or "Jesus Only" Pentecostals, who embrace a modern modalistic understanding of the Godhead, thus denying the traditional doctrine of the Trinity. In 1911 two Los Angeles Pentecostals, Glen Cook and Frank Ewart, began to teach that Jesus Christ was the one God who variously revealed himself under the name (or mode) of the Father, Son, and Holy Spirit.

Controversy erupted and resulted in a schism in 1916, which ultimately produced a new denominational branch of Oneness Pentecostals, the largest of which is the United Pentecostal Church. Through the years other controversies erupted over lesser doctrinal disputes and personality clashes. However, most Pentecostal denominations retained the orthodox doctrine of the Trinity.

Despite its origins in the Wesleyan Holiness movement, the majority of denominational leaders rejected Pentecostalism amid charges of demon possession and mental instability. These included the Church of the Nazarene, the Wesleyan Methodist Church, the Church of God (Anderson, Indiana), and the Salvation Army. However, other Holiness leaders investigated the revival on Azusa Street and quickly embraced the tenets of the new revival. Within a year after the revival, the Pentecostal message had spread around the nation.

Sharp denominational controversies led to the first Pentecostal denominations in America. This first wave of new Pentecostal churches to emerge included the Pentecostal Holiness Church, the Church of God in Christ, the Church of God (Cleveland, Tennessee), the Apostolic Faith (Portland, Oregon), and the United Holy Church. Most of these churches were located in the southern states and experienced rapid growth.

The Pentecostal movement also spread rapidly around the world after 1906. The leading pioneer was Thomas Ball Barratt, a Norwegian Methodist pastor who founded flourishing Pentecostal movements in Scandinavian nations and England. The movement soon spread to Latin America. The revival reached Chile in 1909 under the leadership of an American Methodist missionary, Willis C. Hoover. In 1910 two American Swedish immigrants, Daniel Berg and Gunnar Vingren, established Pentecostal churches in Brazil. Successful Pentecostal missions were also inaugurated by 1910 in China and Africa.

Pentecostalism has become the fastest-growing religious movement in Latin America and has been wielding increasing influence. It had a dramatic impact on Brazil, where Protestants/Pentecostals made up 15 percent of the population by 1990. Due largely to the efforts of Pentecostals, Protestantism at the turn to the twenty-first century represented as much as 20 percent of the population in such nations as Argentina, Mexico, Columbia, Chile, Nicaragua, Puerto Rico, El Salvador, Panama, and Venezuela. The country with the highest percentage of Protestants is Guatemala, accounting for nearly 35 percent.

Meanwhile, Pentecostalism was introduced to Russia and other Slavic nations through the efforts of Ivan Voronaev, a Russian-born immigrant. In 1919 Voronaev established the first Russian-speaking Pentecostal church in New York City, and the following year he began a ministry in Odessa, Russia, which in turn sponsored more than 350 congregations in the Soviet Union, Poland, and Bulgaria. His success caught the attention of the Soviet police, who arrested him in 1929 and sent him to a Siberian gulag, where he died in captivity.

Pentecostal churches enjoyed significant growth in North America after World War II. The emergence of faith-healing TV evangelists such as Oral Roberts in the 1950s exposed Pentecostalism to a broader range of American Christians. Pentecostals began to make inroads into the middle class, although it still could not shake off entirely the earlier perception of a movement largely born of rural communities and the economic margins of society.

By midcentury, Pentecostals began to take the first halting steps to emerge from their cultural isolation into acceptance within the mainstream of American evangelicalism. One of the early indications of this development occurred in 1943, when some of the largest Pentecostal denominations (Assemblies of God, the Church of God—Cleveland, Tennessee, the International Church of the Foursquare Gospel, and the Pentecostal Holiness Church) became charter members of the National Association of Evangelicals. The founding of the Full Gospel Businessmen's Fellowship by Demos Shakarian in 1951 challenged the working-class stereotype, showing that the Pentecostal message was being received among middle-class professionals and businessmen.

Pentecostalism entered a significant new phase (often called the "second wave") of cultural respectability when *glossolalia* first made its appearance in a mainline denomination. Father Dennis Bennett fired the verbal shot that was heard around the world on April 3, 1960, when he announced from his pulpit at St. Mark's Episcopal Church— a 2,600-member congregation in Van Nuys, California—that he had received the baptism of the Holy Spirit.

Bennett's announcement created something of a media sensation with featured articles in both *Newsweek* and *Time* magazines. Members of his vestry soon asked for his resignation, and, rather than subjecting his church to further turmoil, Bennett resigned his pastorate. However, it is important to note that he remained in the Episcopal denomination and was warmly welcomed to a new ministry at St. Luke's Episcopal Church in Seattle, Washington, where he remained until 1981. Under Bennett's leadership, St. Luke's experienced rapid growth with the introduction of Pentecostal-style worship, becoming a center of the charismatic movement.

The term "charismatic" entered the theological vocabulary in the early 1970s to designate this movement in the mainline churches and to distinguish it from the original or classical Pentecostals. The charismatic movement is similar to classical Pentecostalism in its emphasis on the exercise of certain gifts (particularly tongues and prophecy), but other important qualities of this movement make it distinctly different.

It differs from classical Pentecostalism in that it is trans-denominational in nature, it has no set theology of two-stage blessing, it incorporates a diversity of theological opinion, and it also provides a wealth of contemporary worship songs expressing personal and corporate devotion.

Unlike the rejection of the classical Pentecostals, the new wave of charismatic renewal was generally allowed to remain within the mainline churches. Favorable study reports by the Episcopalians (1963) and the Presbyterians (1970), while pointing out possible excesses, generally were tolerant and open to the existence of this kind of Pentecostal spirituality as a renewal movement within the traditional churches.

In 1967 the charismatic movement infiltrated the Roman Catholic Church during a weekend retreat at Duquesne University in Pittsburgh, Pennsylvania, led by theology professors Ralph Keiffer and Bill Story. Catholic charismatic prayer groups soon sprang up at Notre Dame University and the University of Michigan. By 1973 the movement had spread so rapidly that 30,000 Catholic Charismatics gathered at Notre Dame for a national conference. Official reports by Catholic theologians in 1969 and 1974 approved the renewal movement, but cautioned charismatic Catholics not to undermine the church's authority by the exercise of these spiritual gifts.

Within a decade of the first penetration, the movement spread to Catholic churches in over a hundred nations. The most prominent charismatic leader among Catholics was Joseph Leon Cardinal Suenens, who was named by Popes Paul VI and John Paul II as a special adviser to the renewal.

Scholars such as C. Peter Wagner of Fuller Theological Seminary in California have postulated a "third wave" of the Pentecostal-Charismatic movement. The central figure of this later manifestation was John Wimber, who—in the words of a 1998 editorial in *Christianity Today* magazine—was a "beer-guzzling, drug-abusing pop musician, who was converted at the age of 29 while chain-smoking his way through a Quaker-led Bible study."

Wimber had enjoyed some success as a backing musician with the popular singing duo The Righteous Brothers before his dramatic conversion in 1963. He soon began attending a Quaker church in Yorba Linda, California, where his evangelistic enthusiasm led to hundreds of converts. His ministry success came to the attention of Fuller Theological Seminary, and in 1974 he became the founding director of the Department of Church Growth at the Fuller Institute of Evangelism and Church Growth. By 1977 he had embraced some of the beliefs of the charismatic movement (although he did not like the "charismatic" label).

In 1982 Wimber joined the fledgling Vineyard movement, becoming its chief theologian and spokesperson. Both during his lifetime and

Global Christianity: A Re-Centered Faith

since his death in 1997, the Vineyard movement has established more than 1,500 churches across America and internationally with its particular version of the charismatic movement.

Wimber's approach to the charismatic gifts differed from classic Pentecostalism and the charismatic movement, particularly in their approach to speaking in tongues. Whereas the previous groups had emphasized the gift of tongues as the only evidence for the baptism of the Holy Spirit, Wimber emphasized that this was just one of the many spiritual gifts. This "third wave of the Holy Spirit," as Wagner termed it, does not disregard *glossolalia* or by any means rule it out, but neither does it make this the center of attention.

Drawing especially on chapters 12–14 of Paul's first letter to the Corinthians, Wimber viewed speaking in tongues as only one of several manifestations of the Holy Spirit. Wimber and the Vineyard churches focused more on the full range of spiritual gifts listed in First Corinthians than on the *glossolalia* in Acts. Fuller Professor George Eldon Ladd's theological writings on the kingdom of God convinced Wimber that all the gifts of the Holy Spirit are "signs and wonders" that the kingdom of God had come.

Wimber's association with a major evangelical seminary gave the Vineyard movement a kind of theological credibility, and his more moderate understanding of the charismatic gifts further removed theological stumbling blocks for some mainstream evangelicals.

Today the charismatic movement, in its many permutations, is so widely accepted that theological criticism rarely rises to the level of open debate. To be sure, there are those who formally reject such emotional experiences as speaking in tongues, but there is a growing acceptance of the charismatic experience in mainline and evangelical Protestantism as well as Roman Catholicism.

One striking example of the new tolerance may be observed in conservative Reformed circles, which until recently have been rather hostile to the Pentecostal-Charismatic movement. That began to change especially when third-wave charismatic theologian Wayne Grudem defied traditional theological categories by espousing a Reformed soteriology while at the same time embracing the charismatic gifts. His best-selling textbook *Systematic Theology*, with its advocacy of continuing charismatic gifts, is widely used in conservative evangelical and Reformed seminaries.

Grudem's distinctive conjunction of conservative Reformed theology with the charismatic gifts even has been implemented at the ecclesiastical level. Following in the wake of Grudem, the Reverend C. J. Mahaney established an energetic network of conservative Reformed and charismatic churches called Sovereign Grace Ministries. Furthermore, traditional non-charismatic Reformed theologians have joined in formal alliance with these new theological hybrids in conservative parachurch organizations such as the Gospel Coalition and the Council for Biblical Manhood and Womanhood. What was once theologically inconceivable has now become theologically acceptable.

Speaking more generally of the extent of charismatic influence on evangelicalism, the British Anglican writer Dave Tomlinson declares, "It is now clear that the whole centre ground of evangelicalism has become gradually charismaticized, adopting the style ... of the charismatic movement." The American historian Joel Carpenter goes so far as to conclude, "We are now entering a new chapter in evangelical history, in which the Pentecostal-charismatic movement is ... the most influential evangelical impulse at work today."

Evangelical churches are not generally charismatic in theology, but they have become increasingly tolerant, even welcoming to those who are. Many churches that have historically been non-charismatic have charismatic members who openly express their view. This theological difference is treated as a secondary matter and not an issue worth debating. Certainly, contemporary worship styles exhibit charismatic influences of music, lifting of arms, and various emotional expressions.

The growth of Pentecostalism is all the more remarkable in view of the fact that the movement as such has only been in existence since the beginning of the twentieth century and within that time frame has come to represent perhaps the most energetic missionary force in the history of the Christian church. Although one would never have thought it at the outset of the twentieth century, it may be legitimately argued that it is one of the most impactful religious movements of that century.

As the third millennium develops, the Pentecostal-Charismatic movement shows no sign of decline. In all three waves it still represents the most vibrant expression of Christianity in the world. The best estimates are that there are nearly a billion charismatic or charismatically influenced Christians spread throughout every nation of the world.

One concept that has emerged with particular force in the Pentecostal-charismatic world is known as the "Health and Wealth Gospel." (Other designations include "Faith Formula," "Prosperity," or "Word" movement.) This group combines traditional Pentecostalism with "positive thinking." Adherents not only embrace the charismatic gifts, but also portray God as both endlessly beneficent and perfectly predictable. One should distinguish this health-and-wealth movement from fundamentalism, evangelicalism, and even the Pentecostal-charismatic movement.

The exact place of this health-and-wealth movement in the broader spectrum of conservative Protestantism is disputed, since there

"We are now entering a new chapter in evangelical history, in which the Pentecostal-charismatic movement is ... the most influential evangelical impulse at work today" (Joel Carpenter).

are ambiguous and sometimes acrimonious relations among fellow Charismatics. Important leaders of the movement include Americans Kenneth Hagin, Oral Roberts, and Kenneth Copeland as well as internationals Reinhard Bonnke (Africa), Ulf Ekman (Sweden), and Paul Yonggi Cho (Korea).

IV. MISSIONS TO AMERICA

One of the notable developments at the dawn of the third millennium is that Christians from the global South are now sending missionaries to America and endeavoring to reclaim evangelical Christianity from what they perceive as the ruinous effects of post-Christian cultural decline. This reversal of roles has become especially evident in the Anglican Church—the third-largest Christian communion in the world, after the Roman Catholic Church and the Eastern Orthodox Churches.

The global Anglican Church is composed of thirty-eight provinces around the world, with the Church of England as the historic mother church. Although the archbishop of Canterbury is recognized as the symbolic head of the worldwide communion, he has no formal authority over the other provinces, which are free to act in accord with their own convictions. Increasingly, the Anglican provinces of the global South have exercised their independent authority in an effort to reassert historic Christian doctrine and traditional values. This newfound independence of Anglican primates from the global South is nowhere more evident than in North America.

In recent decades the American province of the Anglican Communion (also called the Episcopal Church in the United States of America—ECUSA) has been plagued with deep divisions. Amid growing concern that ECUSA had departed from the historic Christian gospel, evangelical Episcopalians began to explore ways to dissociate from the American province yet remain within the worldwide Anglican Communion.

In 1998 the evangelical St. Andrews Church of Little Rock, Arkansas, made the controversial decision to reject the authority of ECUSA and come under the oversight of the more conservative primate, Archbishop Emmanuel Kolini of Rwanda. The realignment continued in 2000 when archbishops Kolini and Moses Tay of Southeast Asia consecrated Chuck Murphy and John Rodgers as missionary bishops to America. Later that same year, an Anglican mission was officially established under the authority of the Rwandan archbishop, thus creating the Anglican Mission in the Americas (AMiA)—formerly the Anglican Mission in America. Four additional bishops were consecrated in 2001 by Archbishops Kolini and Yong Ping Chung (Archbishop Tay's successor).

AMiA is under the authority of the archbishop of Rwanda, and its bishops are full members of the Rwandan House of Bishops, which is responsible for overseeing Rwanda's missionary outreach to North America. The creation of AMiA provides a way for evangelical congregations and clergy to remain connected to the worldwide Anglican Communion through the leadership in Rwanda while being free of the American Episcopal Church.

Tensions escalated significantly in 2003, when ECUSA approved the consecration of Gene Robinson, an openly gay man, as the bishop of New Hampshire. Robinson was the first noncelibate homosexual to be ordained a bishop in a major Christian denomination. Robinson's consecration accelerated the crisis in the global Anglican Communion. While ECUSA supported Bishop Robinson, many of the Anglican provinces of the global South did not.

Growing disaffection with ECUSA led to yet another Anglican mission to North America. Largely because of the ordination of Robinson, Archbishop Peter Akinola, primate of the Anglican Church of Nigeria, in 2007 joined with conservative members of the Episcopal Diocese of Virginia to form the Convocation of Anglicans in North America (CANA). This is particularly notable because Archbishop Akinola represented the largest Anglican province in the world, with nearly 20 million people.

Resistance to the hierarchy of the Anglican Church found forceful expression in the Global Anglican Future Conference (GAFCON) held in Jerusalem only weeks before the opening of the 2008 Lambeth Conference called by the archbishop of Canterbury. The assembly of nearly 300 bishops and archbishops (as well as 1,100 lay leaders) issued the "Jerusalem Declaration," opposing the "false" gospel that had infiltrated the Anglican Communion, and declared they would no longer allow the archbishop of Canterbury to determine Anglican identity. That identity, they said, was to be demonstrated through adherence to fourteen tenets of historic orthodoxy, including "the unchangeable standard of Christian marriage between one man and one woman as the proper place for sexual intimacy and the basis of the family."

Anglican Bishop Gene Robinson.

What gave considerable weight to GAFCON was the fact that the leading participants included some of the most influential primates in the global Anglican Communion, such as Archbishops Peter Akinola of Nigeria, Benjamin Nzimbi of Kenya, Donald Mtetemela of Tanzania, Justice Akrofi of West Africa, Emmanuel Kolini of Rwanda, Henry Orombi of Uganda, Peter Jensen of Sydney, Australia, and Greg Venables of the Southern Cone (Argentina, Bolivia, Chile, Paraguay, Peru, and Uruguay), as well as prominent bishops from Canada and the United States. Together these leaders represented 30 million of the 55 million "active" Anglicans in the worldwide communion.

Finally, in 2008 conservative leaders of American Anglican organizations, in collaboration with leaders of the Anglican churches in Africa, Asia, Latin America, and Australia, made the groundbreaking decision to establish a new competing Anglican province: the Anglican Church in North America (ACNA).

With active support from Anglican churches from the global South, ACNA was established on December 4, 2008, in Wheaton, Illinois. At the first provincial assembly in June 2009, Robert Duncan was elected archbishop and primate. ACNA now comprises some 100,000 Anglicans in 700 parishes in 28 dioceses.

V. POST-CHRISTIAN EUROPE

After World War II, European Christianity underwent a precipitous decline. According to recent demographic studies, there are 560 million Christians in Europe, but that number is quite misleading. In Great Britain, for example, in a survey taken in 2000, 44 percent of the population claimed no religious affiliation. According to baptismal records, Great Britain has 25 million members of the Anglican Church, but that represents those baptized in the church, not those who attend church. The best estimates are that less than a million British attend church regularly. The decline of Christianity is especially acute among young people (ages 18–24), where two-thirds describe themselves as "nonreligious." In the same age group, nearly half do not believe Jesus really existed. Britain, like much of Europe, has become a secular society, or as some have labeled it, "post-Christian."

Post-Christian Europe reflects the rise of postmodernism. One of the characteristic features of postmodernism is rejection of ultimate religious truth. This relativist notion is not so much hostile to traditional Christianity, as it simply ignores the church as irrelevant. This picture is the same over much of Europe. In Germany, the official membership in Protestant churches is 28 million, but only about a million regularly attend church; and a quarter of the population claims no religious affiliation at all. The picture is much the same in France.

Even in Italy, a nation historically identified as the home of European Catholicism, there is widespread church absenteeism and dismissal of the teachings of the papacy. While most Italians are baptized as Catholics, with a resulting official membership of 55 million, the number of those who actively participate in church is significantly lower, perhaps as low as one-tenth of those baptized.

VI. CONCLUSION

If the contemporary portrait of a Christian in the twenty-first century is a "poor, black, African, Pentecostal woman about twenty-five years old," then there are necessary accompanying issues that will have to be addressed by Christians—especially evangelicals. The myriad of ancillary issues of youth, education, poverty, race, gender, non-Western cultural contextualization, and theological diversity must be carefully addressed, not just with orthodoxy but with orthopraxy.

The shift to the global South will bring some challenges to the enlightened Western world. For example, a July 2008 *Christianity Today* article told the story of a Nigerian Christian pastor, Benjamin Ojobu, who purchased the severed head of a recently deceased young woman from a cemetery to be used as a charm for fighting witchcraft and as a special offering for prosperity. When questioned, the pastor simply stated, "Yes, I am a man of God. But I do this outside Church hours." Many African Christians, especially in African Indigenous Churches, have a dual religious allegiance. Many under the influence of the "Health and Wealth Gospel" believe that Christ will bring prosperity, but just in case he does not, they also invoke occult practices. As Christianity expands in the global South, new challenges await.

FOR FURTHER STUDY

Cox, Harvey. *Fire from Heaven: The Rise of Pentecostal Spirituality and the Reshaping of Religion in the 21st Century*. Boston: Addison-Wesley, 1995.

Jenkins, Philip. *The Next Christendom: The Coming of Global Christianity*. Oxford: Oxford University Press, 2011.

Lewis, Donald M., ed. *Christianity Reborn: The Global Expansion of Evangelicalism in the Twentieth Century*. Grand Rapids: Eerdmans, 2005.

Miller, Donald E., and Tetsunao Yamamori. *Global Pentecostalism: The New Face of Christian Social Engagement*. Berkeley: University of California Press, 2007.

Modern Theological Trajectories

Spiraling into the Third Millennium (20th and 21st Centuries)

I. PROLOGUE: HISTORICAL CONTEXT

The twentieth and early twenty-first centuries have been witness to some of the greatest accomplishments in the history of humankind. Albert Einstein's theory of relativity and quantum physics set in motion a new scientific revolution. Humans explored outer space for the first time, even taking their first footsteps on the moon. Advances in medical science created new horizons with the development of genetic engineering, the mapping of the human genome, artificial hearts, and surgical procedures for transplanting organs. Antibiotics and vaccines have enabled millions to survive death-dealing infections and diseases of the past. In the last century, more technological advances have been made than in all prior history.

For all of its vaunted accomplishments, these two centuries also have been the deadliest in history. The most important historical fact of the last century is that it was an era saturated with brutality and war. One author notes that there have been some two hundred wars—and that is only since the end of World War II. Five major twentieth-century wars claimed more than six million military victims. If one takes into consideration all the collateral damage of wars (famine and disease), one estimate suggests that somewhere around 180 million people have died in the various atrocities—a far greater total than in any other century in human history.

Reflecting on the twentieth century, British Prime Minister Winston Churchill stated, "Little did we guess that what has been called the century of the common man would witness as its outstanding feature more common men killing each other with greater facilities than in any other five centuries together in the history of the world." Churchill was often prone to exaggeration, but in this case he exhibited the British proclivity for understatement.

World War II cast an ominous shadow over the second half of the twentieth century, and no aspect of civilization was unaffected by the specter of the bloodiest war in human history. In the wake of the Holocaust, the use of atomic weapons, and 60 million fatalities (20 million soldiers and 40 million civilians), any subsequent reflection about God could not possibly ignore the horror of human devastation and the apparent absence of God.

Perhaps no theologian's life and theology were more intertwined with the two world wars than Karl Barth. His entire understanding of theology was turned upside down by World War I, and then he was one of the most unrelenting opponents of Adolf Hitler during World War II. Barth's theology was shaped profoundly by his experience of war. The fact that Barth was the most influential theologian of the last century, when combined with his experience of war, makes him the theological referent for all modern theology. One may agree or disagree with him (as many do), but he is the theological force to reckon with in the last one hundred years and, if his theology is to be understood, the historical context of two world wars must be acknowledged.

In an effort to provide some measure of cogency to the theological diversities of the twentieth and twenty-first centuries, this chapter centers around that theologian. The framework for this chapter has two foci: (1) the birth of Neo-Orthodoxy arising from Barth's rejection of the dominant Protestant liberalism along with the main theological elaborations that drew inspiration from Barth; and (2) the theologies that have significantly gone beyond Barth and charted their own alternative trajectories. In some cases, even these theological alternatives owe some debt to Barth.

II. THE NEW THEOLOGICAL REFERENT: NEO-ORTHODOXY

During the second half of the nineteenth century, European nations had achieved unprecedented political, economic, and military power that stretched across the globe. The unification of Germany created a new rival to the established European powers in Britain, France, and Russia. It was only a matter of time before these rivalries erupted in war.

After the assassination of Austrian Archduke Ferdinand and his wife on June 28, 1914, the so-called Central Powers, Germany and the Austro-Hungarian Empire (with marginal support from Italy), squared off against the Triple Entente—Britain, Russia, and France. (The United

States joined the Entente in 1917.) When World War I finally ended in 1918, Europe's map would be redrawn. Austria-Hungary disintegrated into a half-dozen small states; Germany became a republic; and the Russian tsars were overthrown by the revolutionary Bolsheviks. The Treaty of Versailles (June 1919) restored peace in Europe, but left intact lingering resentments—which eventually erupted in a second world war in midcentury.

A. Karl Barth

War has always dramatically impacted the church and its doctrine. War was the beginning and the end of classical Protestant liberalism. In the aftermath of the Reformation, religious differences became religious wars culminating in the devastating Thirty Years War that left Europe looking like a desolate moonscape. The devastation of World War I dimmed the optimism of Protestant liberalism, and for the next half-century a new form of Protestantism, Neo-Orthodoxy, would hold sway.

In the wake of World War I, a young Karl Barth found he could no longer entertain the utopian aspirations of Protestant liberalism. He rejected the anthropocentric focus of his liberal teachers, declaring "one cannot speak of God simply by speaking of man in a loud voice." The much older Barth looked back at his early days and offered the following assessment:

> [Protestant] theology ... had become religionistic, anthropocentric, and in this sense humanistic. What I mean to say is that an external and internal disposition and emotion of man, namely his piety ... had become its object of study.... For this theology, to think about God meant to think in a scarcely veiled fashion about man.... There is no question about it: here man was made great at the cost of God.

Barth would become the prime architect of the demise of Protestant liberalism. In place of a man-centered Protestant liberalism, he crafted a God-centered theological outlook, which came to be known as Neo-Orthodoxy.

> "One cannot speak of God simply by speaking of man in a loud voice" (Karl Barth criticizing Protestant liberalism).

Karl Barth.

1. Beginnings

Born in Basel, Switzerland, Barth (1886–1968) spent his childhood years in Bern, where his father was a professor of theology at a Reformed seminary. Like his father, Barth went on to study theology under two of the most celebrated Protestant liberals of his day, Adolf von Harnack at Berlin and Wilhelm Herrmann at Marburg. After a short stint as a pastor in Geneva, he became a pastor of the Reformed Church in the small Swiss town of Safenwil on the border with Germany.

It was as a pastor that Barth first found that his training in liberal theology simply did not translate into meaningful ministry to the people of his small parish. His disillusionment with Protestant liberals was further exacerbated when his theological mentors publicly supported the German kaiser's decision to go to war in 1914. Barth was bitterly disappointed when he saw Harnack's signature on the so-called "Manifesto of the Ninety-Three German Intellectuals to the Civilized World." Barth was profoundly traumatized by what he called "a black day."

His disenchantment drove the young pastor to search St. Paul's epistle to the Romans for answers to his pastoral and theological frustrations. There he discovered a "strange new world"—one that was "very ancient, early oriental, indefinably sunny, wild, original." The result of this study led to the publication of *Der Römerbrief*, his commentary on Paul's epistle to the Romans, in 1919. But it was his revised version published in 1921 that "fell like a bomb on the playground of theologians."

Looking back at this decisive point in his life, Barth pictured it in his own inimitable manner: "As I look back upon my course, I seem to myself as one who, ascending the dark staircase of a church tower and trying to steady himself, reached for the banister, but got hold of the bell rope instead. To his horror, he had then to listen to what the great bell had sounded over him and not over him alone."

The success of this first publication led to a career transformation from pastor to university professor. In the decade following the First World War, Barth was linked with a number of other theologians—including Rudolf Bultmann, Eduard Thurneysen, Emil Brunner, and Friedrich Gogarten—who also had reacted against the prevailing liberalism. This movement was originally known as "Dialectical Theology" (*Dialektische Theologie*).

Barth was invited to become professor of theology at Göttingen (1921–25), Münster (1925–30), and Bonn (1930–35). While teaching at Bonn, he began working on what would be his crowning theological achievement: *Church Dogmatics*. The goal of this new theology was deceptively grand: to develop a "theology of the Word of God." This

Barth's revised edition of his *Commentary on Romans* (1922) "fell like a bomb on the playground of theologians."

project would remain unfinished at his death, but would rank with the great theological writings of Aquinas and Calvin.

2. Opposition to the Nazis

In Bonn, Barth suddenly found himself on the forefront of world politics. With the rise of the Third Reich, he felt he had to sound the alarm, so he became the primary author of the Barmen Declaration (*Barmer Erklärung*), which rejected the influence of Nazism on German Christianity: "We repudiate the false teaching that there are areas of our life in which we belong not to Jesus Christ but to another lord." He even sent this declaration to Hitler personally.

The declaration became one of the founding documents of the Confessing Church, and Barth was elected a member of its leadership council, the *Bruderrat*. Not surprisingly, he was forced to resign from the University of Bonn for refusing to swear an oath to Hitler, and he returned to his native Switzerland, where he assumed a chair in systematic theology at the University of Basel (1935–62). Writing to a friend in 1938, he described the Nazi regime as nothing other than a "revolution of nihilism" that must be resisted.

3. *Church Dogmatics*

Barth's reputation rests principally on his magum opus, *Church Dogmatics (Die Kirchliche Dogmatik)*. Beginning in 1932 and continuing to his death in 1968, Barth published thirteen massive volumes. He stressed that theology properly belongs within the context of the church: "If I am a theologian, I must try to work out broadly what I think I have perceived as God's revelation.... Yet not I as an individual, but as a member of the Christian Church. This is why I call my book *Church Dogmatics*."

He developed his theological perspective under five theological rubrics: revelation, God, creation, reconciliation, and redemption. Each volume is characterized by detailed biblical exegesis and constant interaction with the history of the church. Unfortunately, Barth did not live long enough to begin the fifth topic on redemption, nor was he able to put the finishing touches on the fourth rubric of reconciliation.

In reaction to his liberal teachers, Barth's work set forth a new christocentric theological method. On the one hand, he rejected unequivocally any knowledge of God by natural means. On the other hand, he was absolutely confident that God has overcome the epistemic chasm between heaven and earth by revealing himself uniquely in Jesus Christ. For Barth, Jesus is the supreme manifestation of the knowledge of God: "the eternal God is to be known in Jesus Christ and not elsewhere."

4. Revelation

One of the most contested concepts in modern theology centers on the meaning of divine revelation. Protestant liberalism tended to emphasize the general revelation of God in nature or human experience, thus turning Christianity into a kind of moral code. Conservative theologians, supposedly under rationalist influences, tended to identify revelation with propositional content of the Bible, resulting in a tendency to identify Christianity with a confessional doctrinal statement.

Barth rejected both liberal and conservative approaches of divine revelation and established his theological system on the basic principle that divine revelation is God communicating himself to us in human speech. *Deus dixit*—God speaks. This approach underscores the conviction that revelation is one-way—from God to humanity and not the other way around.

Barth specifically identified three forms of divine self-disclosure: Jesus himself, the witness of Scripture, and the proclamation of the gospel. Scripture and proclamation are properly understood to be instruments of divine revelation, but Jesus is the ultimate expression of God's Word. Barth was not referring to Jesus' teachings or example, but rather to the person of Jesus Christ. Jesus is God's perfect and complete self-disclosure, and all other vehicles of divine revelation depend on him.

The second form of divine disclosure is the Bible, but Barth was careful to stress that the Bible is not God's Word in the same sense that Jesus is God's Word. Jesus is the perfect and supreme revelation of God, and the Bible functions as the unique and divinely ordained "witness" to Jesus. "The Bible is God's Word to the extent that God causes it to be His Word, to the extent that He speaks through it."

Barth did not accept the notion of biblical inerrancy or infallibility. For Barth, there was only one inerrant revelation: Jesus. Regarding the Bible, he stated plainly, "The prophets and apostles as such ... were real, historical men as we are, and therefore sinful in the acting and capable and actually guilty of error in their spoken and written word." To him, the Bible was the unique vehicle of God, but it was nevertheless a human document. An inerrant Bible was not essential for Barth, because throughout history God employed fallible witnesses by which to reveal himself.

Although he did not accept inerrancy, Barth held the Bible in very high esteem. His denials of inerrancy were not intended to demean the authority of the Bible, but rather to exalt Jesus above all things.

Barth recognized a third form of divine revelation: the proclamation of the gospel. For him, it is in the power of preaching and teaching in the church that God speaks and draws people to himself. That is

The Word of God is "not how we find the way to him, but how he has sought and found the way to us" (Karl Barth).

not to suggest that every sermon is an encounter with Jesus, but only that the church provides the unique context in which God may reveal himself. The Scriptures maintain a special role in the church because they are the primary witness to Jesus. The church itself, insofar as it faithfully declares the gospel, is the special circumstance for the divine-human encounter.

5. Wholly Other

Søren Kierkegaard's concept of the "infinite qualitative distinction" was a mainstay of Barth's theology. The challenge, especially of his early theology, is how to bring the infinite qualitative distinction between God and humanity into proper relation.

For Barth, this Creator-creature distinction meant that God is the "Wholly Other" and must be distinguished from "everything human, and must never be identified with anything which we name, or experience or conceive or worship as God." Barth even defined faith with a distinctive Kierkegaardian flavor as "awe in the presence of the divine *incognito*; it is the love of God that is aware of the qualitative difference between God and man and God and the world."

Like Kierkegaard, Barth believed that finite beings cannot fully understand God, and therefore theologians must resort to the nomenclature of "paradox" in order to talk meaningfully about the infinite mysterious God. Some sense of this divine-human paradox is evident in a rather poignant comment on Romans 9:14:

> Who is this God.... Who is He who cannot be known and apprehended as God, except in the miracle of revelation and by the transformation from rejection to election? Who is He, who, whilst always making Himself accessible, yet, for that reason, always demands that men should search Him out;... Must we not, all of us, cry out instinctively that such a one cannot and must not be God?... There is no knowledge of God, no consolation, and no hope, apart from the catastrophe to which this possibility directs our attention. God would not be God, were He not liable to such accusations.

For Barth, if God is God, then finite minds cannot achieve a complete understanding of God. Human beings must simply embrace divine revelation and be satisfied that in Christ, seemingly opposed truths are yet true.

6. Double Predestination

Barth offered a new twist on the controversial doctrine of double predestination that forged a path beyond the traditional options, an approach that accounts for the reality of divine wrath as well as divine grace. He made the assertion that "the doctrine of election is the sum of the Gospel." As he interpreted it, predestination does not refer to the eternal destiny of humans but rather is bound up exclusively with Jesus. Predestination is a positive expression of divine love that finds its focal point in Jesus. But Barth also acknowledged a kind of soteriological symmetry where Jesus is at once both the object of God's election unto salvation and the object of divine reprobation unto damnation—that is, Jesus is both the "elect and reprobate man."

Barth put it this way: "The rejection which all men incurred, the wrath of God under which all men lie.... God in his love for men transfers from all eternity to Him in whom He loves and elects them." This is to say, in virtue of Christ's absolute identification with humanity, all humanity is chosen in the election of Christ, and at the same time, Christ suffers divine reprobation on behalf of all humanity. Jesus "is elected to make the rejection of man 'his own concern.' In the election of Jesus Christ, God has destined election, salvation and life for man and rejection, damnation and death for himself." On the cross Jesus manifested the full power of God's grace, which ultimately exhausts the wrath of God.

7. *Apokatastasis*

Does Barth's view of salvation imply *apokatastasis*—that is, universalism? The best interpreters of Barth disagree about this, but Barth himself always refused to embrace this descriptor. When asked whether he taught universalism, he responded, "Neither do I teach it nor do I not teach it."

The inner logic of Barth's doctrine of election would seem to imply universal salvation, as Hans Urs von Balthasar and many others assert. However, it must be remembered that Barth was a dialectical theologian and therefore cannot be pigeonholed. In the final analysis, the vastness of God's ways is unfathomable. Barth was thus content to speak of God's loving freedom and to defer further explanation to divine mystery.

B. Engaging Barth

Barth was not alone in his rejection of Protestant liberalism. Indeed, it was in conversation with a fellow Swiss pastor, Eduard Thurneysen, that Barth became convinced that it was necessary to abandon the theological outlook of his university mentors. Thurneysen and Barth were joined in this effort by Friedrich Gogarten (d. 1967), and the three of them founded in 1922 the theological journal *Zwischen den Zeiten* (*Between the Times*). Perhaps Barth's most significant collaborator in challenging liberalism during the early years was the Zürich theologian Emil Brunner. In the 1920s and 1930s these colleagues became the vanguard of a theological reformulation that signaled the death knell of nineteenth-century liberalism and reverberated throughout the rest of the century.

1. Emil Brunner

Although Barth was the primary advocate for Neo-Orthodoxy, he was ably seconded by his fellow Swiss theologian Emil Brunner (1889–1966). During his tenure at the University of Zürich (1924–53), Brunner came to be regarded as one of the preeminent theologians of the twentieth century. In North America he was initially the better-known proponent of the new theology, since he already had an established link with American theologians, having studied at Union Seminary in New York (1919–20) and served as a visiting professor at Princeton Theological Seminary (1937–38).

Drawing inspiration from the existentialism of Kierkegaard and the "I-Thou" approach of Martin Buber, Brunner developed a "theology of encounter," which he considered the most distinctive aspect of his thought. He describes this theology of encounter as follows:

> To know God in trustful obedience is not only to know the truth, but through God's self-communication to be in it.... The truth about man is founded in the divine humanity of Christ, which we apprehend in faith in Christ, the Word of God. This is truth as encounter.... Here truth happens, here we are in the truth, which is not in us but comes to us, which makes us free by restoring to us our true being.

"God does not reveal this and that—he reveals Himself by communicating Himself" (Emil Brunner).

Brunner believed that this notion of truth as encounter was a biblical alternative to the liberalism of Schleiermacher as well as the rationalism of traditional Roman Catholicism and orthodox Protestantism. Against the former he rejected the liberal portrait of Jesus as a noble human being, insisting that Jesus was God incarnate and central to salvation. Against the latter he pointed out that revelation is not primarily a doctrine but an act. He criticized conservative Protestants for what he called "*Bibelglaube*" (Bible faith), that is, having faith in the Bible rather than Christ. For Brunner, "God does not reveal this and that—he reveals Himself by communicating Himself." Accordingly, this personal encounter with God requires a decision—for or against.

It was quite a shock when these two Swiss comrades in the new dialectical theology famously had a falling out and hardly spoke to one another for decades. The flash point came in 1934 when Brunner published an article titled "Nature and Grace," in which he criticized Barth's rejection of natural theology. Although he fundamentally agreed that human reason can never reach God on its own, Brunner argued that the gospel provides a "point of contact" (*Anknüpfungspunkt*) for human nature.

Barth responded furiously with a terse essay titled *"Nein!"* Barth rejected all natural theology, all points of contact between the Christian and non-Christian, apologetics, and proofs for God's existence. For him, the gospel is its own proof. The best apologetic is proclamation. It is important to realize that Barth's response was written at a time of heightened political sensitivity, just after the Barmen Declaration and just when the Nazi regime was crushing resistance with the jackboot.

Brunner's article landed on Barth's desk amid intense political jostling that soon led to Barth's dismissal from the University of Bonn. On theological grounds, by allowing even a minimal natural theology, Barth felt Brunner had opened the door a crack for an implicit denial of salvation by grace through faith alone. The political implications were even worse. Barth callously accused Brunner of giving aid to that "theology of compromise" that was "leading to the subversion of the German church to Nazi theology."

Brunner was deeply wounded, and this war of words led to a breach in their friendship that lasted until the twilight of their lives. Barth likened his estrangement with Brunner to an elephant and a whale—"both are God's creatures, but they simply cannot meet."

Although Brunner continued to produce important theological works (especially his three-volume magnum opus *Dogmatics*), it was his misfortune to have lived at the same time as Barth, for he spent much of life overshadowed by his Basel neighbor. Despite his lack of recognition, most scholars agree that Brunner deserves greater acclaim as one of the giants of twentieth-century theology.

The estrangement in the relationship was finally reconciled not long before Brunner's death in April 1966. Barth sent his old friend this message: "[T]ell him, *Yes*, that the time that I had to say No to him is now long past, since we all live only by virtue of the fact that a great and merciful God says his gracious Yes to all of us." Barth's *Yes* was his last word to Brunner.

2. Rudolf Bultmann

In contrast to Brunner, Rudolf Bultmann (1884–1976) was a more peripheral participant in the early dialectical theology of Barth (who was never really persuaded that Bultmann had broken completely with liberalism). Bultmann did share with Barth a certain affinity for the existentialism of Kierkegaard as well as a mistrust of Protestant liberalism. But within a few years, it became clear that Bultmann was moving in a different direction. It did not enhance Barth's appreciation for

"... an historical fact which involves a resurrection from the dead is utterly inconceivable" (Rudolf Bultmann).

Bultmann to discover that his philosophical muse, Martin Heidegger, supported the Nazi regime.

As a biblical scholar, Bultmann believed the New Testament is not concerned primarily with the Jesus of history, but rather with the religious legacy of Jesus that arose from the faith of the early church— "the Christ of faith." He rejected the literal resurrection, asserting that "an historical fact which involves a resurrection from the dead is utterly inconceivable." Although he believed that Jesus really existed, what was important for moderns is the *kerygma*—the core message beneath the multiple perspectives of the gospel accounts.

Bultmann employed an approach he designated "demythologization" as the key to recovering the *kerygma*. By making use of Martin Heidegger's existentialist philosophy, he sought to *de*-mythologize the New Testament and thus capture the essential character of the kerygma. He was persuaded that very little could actually be known about the Jesus of history. However, to him, faith is not about one's ability to gain knowledge about the Jesus of history; it is about an existential encounter with Christ. True faith emerges in the moment when a human being, confronted with the kerygma of Christ, decides how to respond and then takes full responsibility for that decision. Most people avoid this existential decision, and thus they sink into "inauthentic existence." It is only by embracing the kerygma that one can enter into "authentic existence."

For Bultmann, the Christian gospel is that God has liberated humanity so that we can live authentically as human beings. In the final analysis, Bultmann went well beyond Barth, although he retained an appreciation.

3. Reinhold Niebuhr

Like Barth, Reinhold Niebuhr (1892–1971) was a refugee from Protestant liberalism. He was the son of German immigrants; his father, Gustav Niebuhr, was an evangelical pastor in the American branch of the Prussian Church Union (now part of the United Church of Christ).

Having imbibed Protestant liberalism at Yale, Niebuhr took his first pastorate at a small German-American church in Detroit, Michigan—Bethel Evangelical Church. Upon his arrival in Detroit, he began preaching the Social Gospel, which inevitably brought him into conflict with Ford Motor Company. Troubled by the demoralizing effects of industrialism on workers, he became an outspoken critic of Henry Ford.

His encounter with the auto industry brought the realization that the Social Gospel had a naïve understanding of sin and an unrealistic optimism. Niebuhr described his theological reorientation as follows:

"About midway in my ministry ... I underwent a fairly complete conversion of thought which involved rejection of almost all the liberal theological ideals and ideas with which I ventured forth in 1915." It was Barth's Neo-Orthodoxy with its robust concept of sin that caught Niebuhr's attention.

As Professor of Practical Theology (later Ethics and Theology) at Union Theological Seminary in New York (1928–60), Niebuhr had the opportunity to develop his ideas about sin and society, which established him as a leading member of the Neo-Orthodox movement. He worked out the social implications of the doctrine of original sin in one of his most influential books, *Moral Man and Immoral Society* (1932). Written during the Great Depression, it insists on the necessity of politics in the struggle for social justice because of the sinfulness of human nature. It argues that reason is not able to solve social injustice by moral means, "since reason is always the servant of interest in a social situation."

In his *Nature and Destiny of Man* (2 volumes, 1941, 1943), Niebuhr employed the term "Christian realism" to describe his approach to ethics. Niebuhr was concerned to recover the language of sin and to account seriously for the full impact of sin on the human moral condition. In a world devastated by the experience of Hitler, Stalin, and the Holocaust, Niebuhr could say that "the doctrine of original sin is the only empirically verifiable doctrine of the Christian faith." He argued for a realistic reevaluation of our ethical standards. While acknowledging that the selfless agape love of Jesus is the normative moral guide for Christians, there remains the need for justice in dealing with the inevitable and competing assertions of self-interest.

> "Man's capacity for justice makes democracy possible; but man's inclination to injustice makes democracy necessary" (Reinhold Niebuhr).

The task of the Christian realist is primarily one of crafting a way of living with the reality of sin and self-interest. According to Niebuhr, "A realist expects no final resolution to these conflicts, but a stable society must establish a working equilibrium between the claims of liberty and equality, freedom and order, or need and merit." A realist accepts that the ethical balancing of social and power disparities will necessarily entail coercion. "It is because men are sinners that justice can be achieved only by a certain degree of coercion on the one hand, and by resistance to coercion and tyranny on the other hand." A vital Christian faith must undertake a constant commerce with the culture of its day, borrowing and rejecting according to its best judgment. There is the promise of a new life in the gospel; but it is an eschatological hope.

4. Dietrich Bonhoeffer

Dietrich Bonhoeffer was born to a prominent family in Breslau, Germany, on February 4, 1906. His father, Karl Bonhoeffer, was a distinguished professor of psychiatry and neurology at Berlin University. His mother, Paula von Hase, was the daughter of Countess Klara von Hase. Despite the fact that his family was not particularly religious, he announced to his parents at the age of fourteen that he intended to become a pastor and theologian. Dietrich received his doctorate in theology from the University of Berlin in 1927. Although the prevailing influence at Berlin was one of the icons of Protestant liberalism, Adolf von Harnack, Bonhoeffer was more attracted to the writings of Karl Barth.

Bonhoeffer showed great promise for both an academic and ecclesiastical career, but that was cut short with the Nazi rise to power in January 1933. Like Barth, he was a determined opponent of the Nazis from the outset. Disheartened by the German churches' complicity with the Nazis, Bonhoeffer became actively involved in the Confessing Church. He served as head of the Confessing Church's seminary at Finkenwalde (1935–37), during which time he wrote two of his best-known books, *The Cost of Discipleship* and *Life Together*.

With the outbreak of World War II, in order to avoid conscription into the German army, Bonhoeffer became a lecturer in theology at Union Theological Seminary in New York in 1939. But almost as soon as he arrived, he became convinced that he had made the wrong decision and wrote to Reinhold Niebuhr, "I have come to the conclusion that I made a mistake in coming to America." Shortly thereafter he returned to Germany.

Soon after his return, he became active in the German resistance. Through his brother-in-law, Hans von Dohnanyi, he was recruited to a conspiracy to assassinate Hitler. In April 1943, the Gestapo arrested Bonhoeffer, not for his involvement in the conspiracy, but on suspicion of subverting Nazi policy toward Jews and evading military service. However, the failure of the July 1944 plot to assassinate Hitler (code-named Operation Valkyrie) led to the discovery of his connection to the conspirators.

Bonhoeffer was transferred to the concentration camp at Buchenwald and then to Flossenbürg. Even though the war was all but lost, Hitler ordered all the conspirators executed. As Bonhoeffer was led away, his last words to fellow prisoner Payne Best were "This is the end—for me the beginning of life." He was executed by hanging on April 9, 1945, just two weeks before American soldiers liberated the camp and a month before the end of the war. The German medical doctor at the Flossenbürg concentration camp wrote of Bonhoeffer's last moments on the gallows: "In the almost fifty years that I worked as a doctor, I have hardly seen a man die so entirely submissive to the will of God."

In assessing Bonhoeffer's theology, we must remember that his was an unfinished life, and we are left to put together the pieces of his thought, especially the writings of his final years. However, there are key themes that reveal the trajectory of his thought. Like Barth, Bonhoeffer had a distinctive Christological focus in his ethics as well as his theology in general. In *The Cost of Discipleship* he distinguishes between "cheap grace" and "costly grace." Cheap grace is a formalized Christianity by which one becomes a member merely by intellectual assent to certain doctrines, without any corresponding change in life. Costly grace is a rejection of mere theological assent, and a full-throttled call to self-sacrifice, obedience, and discipleship. To follow Christ is to boldly risk all for his sake.

According to Bonhoeffer, when assaulted by evil the Christian must oppose it directly. The failure to act is to condone evil. The ethical dilemma for such action is that in confronting evil, we have no prior justification for employing one response to evil over another. Nevertheless, the demand for action without any *a priori* justification is the moral reality Christians must face. Ultimately, all actions must be delivered up to God for judgment, and no one can escape reliance on God's mercy. Costly grace entails risk, even risking one's life.

Clearly, Bonhoeffer's ethics are directly related to the Nazi tyranny of his time and provide a general understanding for his willingness to participate in an assassination plot against Hitler.

Bonhoeffer is perhaps best known for his advocacy for what he called a "religionless Christianity." What did Bonhoeffer mean by that? In his judgment, the church now inhabited a world where God is no longer a working hypothesis. With the advances of science, the church retreated and sought to stake out the inner life of the individual as the realm of God. Bonhoeffer offered another vision, in which the gospel addresses the individual without them having to become "religious" in the conventional sense.

It must be stressed that "religionless" in no way meant "godless"; quite the contrary, the incarnate Christ was the vital center of his conception of a "religionless Christianity." While in prison, Bonhoeffer explained:

> It is only by living completely in this world that one learns to believe. One must abandon every attempt to make something of oneself, whether it be a saint, a converted sinner, a churchman, ... a righteous man or an unrighteous one, a sick man or a healthy one. This is what I mean by worldliness—taking life in one's stride.... It is such a life that we throw ourselves utterly into the arms of God and participate in his sufferings in the world.

With Bonhoeffer's untimely death, we are left with trying to determine the full implications and trajectory of his thought. Although he shows consistent development, it must remain incomplete—thanks to Adolf Hitler.

5. The Roman Catholic Response to Barth

In the second part of the first volume of his *Church Dogmatics*, Barth's rather critical remarks did nothing to endear him to Roman Catholics. He dismissively declares, "In the doctrine and worship of Mary there is disclosed the one heresy of the Roman Catholic Church which explains all the rest." Hans Urs von Balthasar was the first Catholic theologian to see theological merit in Barth, but it was not until the 1950s that Barth found his most enthusiastic disciple in the controversial Roman Catholic theologian Hans Küng. With a remarkable boldness, Küng's 1957 doctoral dissertation argued that Barth's doctrine of justification is in fundamental accord with the Council of Trent. Barth actually wrote a congratulatory letter to Küng, which Küng included in his preface to the dissertation:

> You can imagine my considerable amazement at this bit of news; and I suppose that many Roman Catholic readers will at first be no less amazed.... All I can say is this: If what you have presented in Part Two of this book is actually the teaching of the Roman Catholic Church, then I must certainly admit that my view of justification agrees with the Roman Catholic view; if only for the reason that the Roman Catholic teaching would then be most strikingly in accord with mine!

Although he warmly received Küng's work, Barth remained somewhat dubious, stating, "Of course, the problem is whether what you have presented here really represents the teaching of your Church. This you will have to take up and fight out with biblical, historical, and dogmatic experts among your coreligionists." In fact, Küng's hopes for a substantial reassessment of the justification doctrine were rejected.

6. The Evangelical Response to Barth

The initial American evangelical response to Karl Barth was quite negative. Among the first to read and assess Barth was Cornelius Van Til, Professor of Apologetics at Westminster Theological Seminary in Philadelphia, who declared Barth a "new modernist." Van Til thundered, "No heresy that appeared at any of [the councils of Nicea, Chalcedon, and Dort] was so deeply and ultimately destructive of the gospel as is the theology of Karl Barth."

In significant measure, Van Til's denunciation of Barth determined the rather cold reception among most American evangelicals. Although most American evangelicals remained suspicious of Barth, a few—

mainly academic voices—could be heard above the din, expressing appreciation of the Swiss theologian. Bernard Ramm of Fuller Seminary, initially an opponent, became an advocate. Others such as Donald Bloesch of the University of Dubuque Theological Seminary and G. W. Bromiley of Fuller Seminary found Barth congenial to evangelicalism.

It was not until the turn into the twenty-first century that a noticeable current of Barthian sympathizers began to emerge among American evangelicals. Some have even spoken of a "Barthian renaissance" in North America, Britain, and the Pacific Rim. More recently, Barth has received considerable interest from leaders of the emergent church, and among mainstream evangelical scholars, Barth is no longer *persona non grata*. The legacy of Neo-Orthodoxy is still being assessed, but in general, evangelicals remain critical yet appreciative of Barth.

III. NEW THEOLOGICAL ELABORATIONS

Barth's bold theology cast a long shadow over subsequent generations of theologians. Among the first generation of theologians to emerge in the wake of the Barthian revolution were two fellow Germans, Jürgen Moltmann and Wolfhart Pannenberg. Although both felt a theological debt to Barth, neither was afraid to criticize him or develop their own theological direction. Both Moltmann and Pannenberg illustrate the point that whether in agreement or opposition, any serious theologian had to engage the towering figure of Karl Barth.

A. Eschatological Theology

One of the most influential new theologies emerging from Germany in the wake of World War II era was "eschatological theology," closely associated with the writings of Moltmann and Pannenberg.

While their theologies are different in several ways, together they stimulated a new interest in an appreciation for eschatological realism in mainstream Christian theology. Protestant liberals talked about the kingdom of God, but they meant a human social order rather than the reign of God. On the other hand, fundamentalists tended to think of eschatology as a chronology of end-times events and often engaged in a wide variety of speculation about the return of Christ. Both Moltmann and Pannenberg sought to recover a realistic approach to eschatology completely apart from a social order or end-times chronology.

1. Jürgen Moltmann

As a young soldier in Hitler's army, Jürgen Moltmann (1926–) came to the dreadful realization that he had unwittingly served evil.

As the war came to an ignoble end, Moltmann became a prisoner of war in Great Britain from 1945 to 1948. While a POW, he was shown horrific photographs of the Auschwitz and Belsen concentration camps, and he fell into despair.

Amid his torment, he was given a Bible by an American chaplain, and in the Psalms especially he found renewed hope: "We were broken men, some of us fell sick during that time and died out of hopelessness. But I myself was gripped by a new hope which enabled me to survive. That hope was the hope of Christ."

As Moltmann tried to make sense of his painful experience in World War II, he found himself focused on the twin themes of suffering and hope, which in turn brought him to a theological consideration of the resurrection and the cross of Jesus Christ. It was while reading the second edition of Barth's *Der Römerbrief* that he came across an assertion that reoriented his thinking: "If Christianity be not altogether thoroughgoing eschatology, there remains in it no relationship whatever with Christ." This insight led Moltmann to explore a new theological method in which traditional theological categories were reconfigured in the light of eschatology.

Also influential was the publication of *The Principle of Hope* by the Marxist philosopher Ernst Bloch, which provided the immediate spark for Moltmann's "theology of hope."

Slave laborers in the Buchenwald concentration camp near Jena. Many had died from malnutrition by the time U.S. troops entered the camp in Germany on April 16, 1945.

Getty Images

In his first publication, aptly titled *The Theology of Hope* (1964), Moltmann concluded that genuine hope is necessarily bound up with the resurrection; and the resurrection is necessarily bound up with eschatology: "From first to last, and not merely in the epilogue, Christianity is eschatology, [it] is hope." His was not a "theology *about* hope," but a "theology *out of* hope."

When Moltmann speaks of eschatology, he does not mean the future as end-time events, but rather the announcement in temporal history of future possibilities. For him the future is not fixed, but open to possibilities. The theology of hope has a here-and-now focus, which not only gives hope to the believer in the present, but energizes the believer to actively work to bring about the promised future. This eschatological hope inspires a "passion for the possible."

Even with his theology of hope, Moltmann still had the painful memory of the Holocaust. He realized he still needed to deal with the fundamental problem of suffering and evil in the world. He turned his attention to the cross, which entailed two dimensions: Christ's solidarity with sinful humanity, and Christ's solidarity with the Trinity. In his famous work *The Crucified God*, the divine promise of the resurrection addresses the suffering of the "godless and the godforsaken" by identifying the suffering of Jesus on the cross with the suffering of humanity, which encompasses both the "oppressed and the oppressors."

Although Moltmann did not actively mistreat Jews or participate in the "final solution," he was nevertheless acutely aware that, however inadvertently, he stood on the side of the oppressor in World War II. His own spiritual devastation at having served the *Führer* led to the realization that oppressors also suffer in their own way. Such profound insight could only come to one who has suffered torment in the deep recesses of the soul. Thus for Moltmann, only a suffering God can rescue such suffering sinners.

Moltmann's concept of the cross as solidarity with the suffering entails a revisioned concept of God. He sees the cross not only as Christ's solidarity with suffering humanity, but also as the Son's solidarity with the Father. Moltmann grapples theologically with the Father's abandonment of the Son on the cross. If we are to engage in Christian theology, says Moltmann, we "must come to terms with Jesus' cry on the cross … 'Why has thou forsaken me?'"

Jesus' anguished cry leads Moltmann to conclude that not only did Jesus suffer on the cross, but so did the Father. In solidarity with the godforsaken world, the Son willingly surrenders himself in love for the world, and the Father willingly surrenders his Son in love for the world. At the deepest point of their separation, the Father and Son are

"From first to last, and not merely in the epilogue, Christianity is eschatology, [it] is hope" (Jürgen Moltmann).

united in their love for the world, and that becomes the very moment when the godforsakenness of the world is overcome.

This understanding of divine solidarity on the cross leads Moltmann to revolutionize the concept of God in two ways. First, he embraces the ancient idea *perichoresis*, that is, the mutual indwelling of the Trinity. If both the Father and the Son suffer on the cross, then there must be a deep mutual indwelling of the divine persons of the Trinity. Second, the divine suffering on the cross necessitates a doctrine of divine passibility—the notion that God experiences pain and suffering.

This runs counter to the traditional doctrine of God as impassible, which asserts that God does not express emotion since emotion necessarily connotes change and God cannot change. For Moltmann, such a reconceptualization of the being of God is required by God's love. Divine love is not merely the one-way relationship of active benevolence, but a genuinely two-way relationship in which God is so intimately engaged with his creation that he is affected by it. In Moltmann's words, "God in Auschwitz and Auschwitz in the crucified God—that is the basis for a real hope which both embraces and overcomes the world, and the ground for a love which is stronger than death." This is at the heart of divine love.

Moltmann's eschatological theology was a theology of *praxis* (oriented toward action). A right understanding of the resurrection and the cross necessarily leads to activism. The resurrection is "revolutionizing and transforming the present." That is to say, for Moltmann, the resurrection inspires a death-defying protest against all forms of death in all dimensions of life—religiously, socially, economically, or politically. The theology of hope in the crucified God is therefore an activist theology, resisting such forces of death as Hitler and believing the promises of God.

> The crucified God is ... the God of the poor, the oppressed and the humiliated. The rule of Christ who was crucified for political reasons can only be extended through liberation from forms of rule which make men servile and apathetic.... Christians will seek to anticipate the future of Christ according to the measure of the possibilities available to them, by breaking down lordship and building up the political liveliness of each individual.

Moltmann's work took on a decidedly political cast. Working in collaboration with the Roman Catholic theologian Johann Metz (1928–), he began to develop a political theology of liberation. It was not political in the sense of taking a particular stance, but it was political in that he insisted that the gospel requires activism. He was unafraid to ask, "What are the economic, social and political consequences of the gospel of the Son of Man who was crucified as a 'rebel'?" And he was unafraid to assert that the gospel "urges men on towards liberating actions, because it makes them painfully aware of suffering institutions of exploitation, oppression, alienation and captivity."

This stress on liberation found a strong reception among theologians working among the poor in Latin America and indeed provided some level of inspiration to the emergence of Liberation theology.

2. Wolfhart Pannenberg

Wolfhart Pannenberg (1928–) emerged onto the theological stage with the publication of his book *Jesus—God and Man* in 1964. In it he affirmed the rational verifiability of the historical event of the bodily resurrection of Jesus—something dismissed as impossible or mythological by most German theologians of the modern era. Along with Moltmann, Pannenberg understood the resurrection of Jesus as an eschatological event—the prolepsis and promise of the future divine kingdom when God will finally reveal his lordship.

In later writings such as *Theology and the Kingdom of God* (1969) and *The Idea of God and Human Freedom* (1973) Pannenberg made the startling claim that "God does not yet exist." This statement must not be misinterpreted. For Pannenberg, God exists in and of himself in all eternity, but he is "not yet" fully present as he will be in the future. In his eschatological theology, God, in an act of self-limitation, freely chooses to grant the world its awful freedom until the future kingdom finally and fully breaks into the present. Evils such as the Holocaust occur because God's kingdom has not yet come. However, God still exercises his lordship from his own futurity by sending Jesus and the Holy Spirit into the present world from the future to demonstrate his love and to release a spirit of anticipation into the stream of human history. In the end, God will come to his world and cancel out all sin and evil and make it his home.

B. Post-Liberal Theology

Barth's influence was also important for the emergence of what is called "post-liberal theology." Originally developed by Yale theologians Hans Frei (1922–88) and George Lindbeck (1923–), the term "post-liberal" was first coined by Lindbeck in his classic text, *The Nature of Doctrine* (1984). It refers to a loose constellation of theologians affiliated with Yale, and thus it is sometimes referred to as the "Yale School."

To call it a movement may be too much, since there are such varieties of emphasis and expression. Lindbeck may have coined the general term, but the true originator of the movement was Hans Frei, whose stress on the narrative structure of the Bible led to yet another designation: "narrative theology." The fact that there are multiple descriptors suggests that this is a theological perspective still in motion. Even so, there are enough shared concerns that warrant inclusion here.

1. Hans Frei

Nazi ferocity against the Jews forced many to flee Germany before Hitler could send them to the death camps. Like many other German Jews, the family of Hans Wilhelm Frei fled to the United States in 1938. Following the advice of H. Richard Niebuhr, Frei attended Yale, where he wrote his doctoral dissertation on Barth's doctrine of revelation. After returning to teach at Yale, he published his seminal work, *The Eclipse of Biblical Narrative* (1974), which gave birth to the new theological perspective.

Frei observed that there were two main hermeneutical strategies by which modern theologians deciphered scriptural meaning. On the one hand, liberal theologians looked for the real meaning of the Bible in the religious experience common to all humanity and otherwise deconstructed the biblical text into historical-critical fragments. On the other hand, conservatives pressed for the literal meaning of the Bible and, as a consequence, turned the text into source material for doctrinal propositions.

Frei was convinced that both modern conservative and liberal approaches to the Bible missed the point of Scripture by locating its meaning in something other than the scriptural story itself. He believed that the narrative of the biblical text had been obscured by both liberals and conservatives, since both were guilty of imposing an alien interpretive framework on the text. He feared that biblical interpretation had become "a matter of fitting the biblical story into another world with another story rather than incorporating that world into the biblical story."

He argued that the scriptural narrative should be allowed a normative function. He observed that early Christians made sense of their lives by viewing themselves as related to and participating within the story told in Scripture. What is important is not whether the gospel accounts are historically accurate. The key question is, how do the stories reveal the character of Jesus?

2. George Lindbeck

If Frei emphasized the primacy of scriptural narrative for theology, it was his Yale colleague, George Lindbeck, who insisted on the primacy of language over experience and added a theory about religion as a cultural-linguistic medium. Drawing on Austrian philosopher Ludwig

Wittgenstein's analysis of language and on the cultural anthropology of Princeton professor Clifford Geertz, Lindbeck's major work, *The Nature of Doctrine*, offered an account of contemporary theological options that reinforced and augmented Frei's argument.

Lindbeck identified three general theories of Christian doctrine. First, the "cognitive-propositionalist" theory lays stress on the cognitive aspects of religion, emphasizing that doctrine functions as truth claims. This approach is most often identified with conservative-evangelical theology. Such a view, as epitomized by Carl F. H. Henry, approaches the biblical text as "informational propositions or truth claims about objective realities." Lindbeck maintains that this perspective rests on the mistaken assumption that it is possible to state the objective truth about God definitively, exhaustively, and timelessly in propositional form.

The second approach, the "experiential-expressive" view, interprets doctrines as noncognitive symbols of inner human feelings, which Lindbeck identifies with theological liberalism. This view holds that there is a common universal "religious experience," which Christian theology attempts to express in words. The problem with this view for Lindbeck is that it is ultimately unverifiable.

In Lindbeck's analysis, both the "cognitive-propositional" and "experiential-expressive" approaches that have dominated theology during the modern age have failed. Thus, he argued for what he called the "cultural-linguistic" approach. It stresses that the heart of religion lies in living within a specific historical religious tradition and embracing its ideas and values. He contended that religious traditions are culturally and historically shaped and are governed by internal rules. In the case of Christianity, he, like Frei, asserts that it is scriptural narrative that shapes the cultural-linguistic world of the Christian community. Christian doctrines are not universalistic propositions or interpretations of a universal religious experience, but are more like the rules of grammar that govern the way we use language to describe the world.

Lindbeck argued that becoming a member of the Christian community entails learning a new language. Moreover, the meaning of Christian language can be found only within Scripture. Instead of trying to translate Scripture into *extrascriptural* categories (what he considered the mistake of both conservatives and liberals), Lindbeck proposed an *intratextual* approach. He wrote, "Religious communities are likely to be practically relevant in the long run to the degree that they do not first ask what is either practical or relevant, but instead concentrate on their own intra-textual outlooks and forms of life." In this approach, the story of the Bible becomes one's own story.

It followed for Lindbeck that Christian catechesis is a more appropriate emphasis for churches than the various modern strategies to make Christianity reasonable, attractive, or relevant. He pointed out that for the most part, early converts did not absorb Christian teaching cognitively and then decide to become Christians. They were attracted to what they saw of the faith and practices of early Christian communities, and only later did they come to intellectually apprehend the faith—usually after a prolonged period of catechetical instruction.

Post-liberalism positioned itself as a third way between liberal and conservative theology. With liberal theology, the post-liberal school assumes that the Bible is not infallible and that biblical higher criticism is fully legitimate and necessary. With conservative-evangelical theology, the post-liberal school emphasizes the primacy of biblical revelation, the unity of the biblical canon, and the saving uniqueness of Jesus Christ.

In recent years some evangelicals have shown considerable sympathy for the post-liberal school. At the same time, evangelicals such as Carl F. H. Henry have warned that post-liberal theology is nothing more than the latest manifestation of Barthian Neo-Orthodoxy. Henry argued that the narratives of Scripture carry meaning only insofar as they are restated in propositional form. Frei countered that the Bible conveys meaning primarily through stories and that doctrines are simply conceptual redescriptions of those biblical stories. Not long before his death, he appealed to both conservative and liberal factions for a "generous orthodoxy."

IV. NEW ALTERNATIVE THEOLOGICAL TRAJECTORIES

Barth continued to be a theological referent throughout the twentieth and twenty-first centuries, although new theological innovations emerged that went so far beyond him that he would not have recognized any resemblance. These alternative theologies continued to develop in a context of global military conflict. While Europe and Japan were digging out from the rubble of World War II, the United States and the Soviet Union engaged in political brinkmanship—christened the "Cold War"—and produced enough nuclear weapons to assure mutual destruction.

The Cold War between the superpowers produced a number of "hot wars" that were fought by proxy. The United States became embroiled in a decade-long war in Vietnam, and the Soviets became entangled in a war in Afghanistan—and both departed in defeat. By 1989 the Berlin Wall came down, and Russian satellite nations declared their independence. The United States had won the Cold War.

The 1960s was a period of profound cultural change. Galvanized by opposition to the Vietnam War, young people led a countercultural movement that significantly altered the social landscape of America. The Vietnam War was a significant stimulus to a cultural paradigm shift both in the United States and globally. Sexual mores were challenged, the drug culture emerged, youth movements and musical tastes shifted dramatically. As Bob Dylan sang, "The times, they are a-changing." Rebellion was in the air.

Each of the theological diversities included here claims to be Christian and attempts to translate the gospel into the present cultural context. Some of these theological movements have already fallen into obscurity, while others endure for the moment—and only time will tell if any of these movements have a lasting influence.

A. God as the Ground of Being

Widely acknowledged as a giant of twentieth-century theology, Paul Tillich had influence extending from the Weimar Republic in Germany to the countercultural sixties in America. Tillich (1886–1965) was an early voice of opposition to Hitler's Nazi Party and later to the turbulent 1960s in America. He was hailed as a "prophet of the death of God theology and bowdlerized by John A. T. Robinson's *Honest to God*" (1963). For a time he was the darling of the new radical theology, but as the revolutionary spirit of the 1960s waned, Tillich eventually fell out of fashion.

As with Barth, the thinking of Paul Tillich was shaped by the trauma of war. As a chaplain in World War I, close encounters with death led to two nervous breakdowns and a severe crisis of faith. During his tenure as professor of philosophy at the University of Frankfurt, he was one of the earliest voices of protest against the Nazis and soon came into open conflict with them. Under increasing harassment, he accepted Reinhold Niebuhr's invitation to Union Theological Seminary in New York.

A self-described "theologian of culture," Tillich redefined God as the "ground of being." Although controversial, Tillich insisted that God is not a "being" per se and therefore does not exist as beings exist. Rather, God is the power of being that is within every being, enabling it to exist and without which it would cease to exist. In Tillich's conception, the world is not something apart from God; it is the medium of his ongoing activity. In this view of God, there is an ineffable mystery and the only way humans can speak of him is through symbols.

For Tillich, Jesus was the ultimate answer to the existential quest for meaning as the unique man in complete unity with God who overcame all the existential trials of life. Jesus is not the Christ because of his own nature, but because God was present in him. Jesus is the "new being," and by following him, one finds the ultimate meaning of life.

Tillich's theology is vastly complex and substantially at odds with historic Christianity. His understanding of God is quite explicitly panentheistic—God is the power of being that suffuses the created order. The Bible is not the Word of God, but rather a medium recording the final revelation of Jesus the Christ. The Genesis story is not to be taken literally, but as a symbol of humanity's estrangement from God.

In addition, Tillich's view of the nature of Jesus has a distinctly adoptionistic flavor. Jesus was not a divine person but a real historical man who overcame the despair and alienation of humanity by his self-sacrifice. By his self-negation Jesus became the symbol by which the finite being overcomes the existential estrangement and establishes the possibility of the new being. The only thing that distinguishes Christianity from other religions is that it is based on the revelation of Jesus the Christ as the final revelation. In sum, Jesus is the answer to the existential dilemma, not because he was the Son of God, but because he exemplified self-sacrifice and thus points the way for others.

B. Death-of-God Theology

The countercultural outlook of the 1960s was nowhere more theologically relevant than in the emergence of a uniquely American movement, variously called "radical theology," "Christian atheism," or the "Death-of-God movement." Two young theologians took the lead: Thomas J. J. Altizer of Emory University and William Hamilton of Colgate Rochester Divinity School.

At a core level, Altizer and Hamilton reacted (some say overreacted) against Barth's absolute stress on the transcendence of God, to the diminution of his immanence. These theologians took divine immanence to the ultimate extreme. Borrowing from Nietzsche, they declared in no uncertain terms, "We do not know, do not adore, do not possess, do not believe in God.... God is dead. We are not talking about the absence of the experience of God, but about the experience of the absence of God."

To these two scholars, to say that God is dead was not just a symbolic statement, but an assertion of an actual fact of history. Altizer argued that God abandoned his divinity on the cross in order to become fully human in Christ. This was the ultimate act of *kenosis*, or self-emptying. In this act of self-annihilation, it is argued that God became identical with humanity, even to the point of death. For Altizer, "the God who acts in the world and history is a god who negates himself, gradually but decisively annihilating his own original Totality ... thus transcendence becomes immanence just as the Spirit becomes flesh."

From this perspective, God's death is viewed as a redemptive event.

"We do not know, do not adore, do not possess, do not believe in God.... God is dead. We are not talking about the absence of the experience of God, but about the experience of the absence of God" (Thomas J. J. Altizer and William Hamilton).

The death of Jesus was not final, but instead, like the phoenix rising from the ashes, the spirit of the suffering Jesus survives and inaugurates a new age in which Christians proclaim redemption by serving others. God is dead, but the spirit of Jesus continues in this world in the battle for justice and liberation.

Similarly, Hamilton argued that the death of God actually summons humanity to look to Jesus as a moral exemplar of how to live in our secular world. He defines Jesus not as a person but as "a place to be." Christianity is therefore not located "before an altar; it is in the world, in the city, with both the needy neighbor and the enemy."

Theological trajectories do not emerge in a vacuum. It is notable that Hamilton and Altizer dedicated their provocative 1966 book, *Radical Theology and the Death of God*, to Paul Tillich, whom Altizer described as "the Modern Father of Radical Theology." But the more direct influence on this movement was Dietrich Bonhoeffer, who had spoken of a "religionless" Christianity in a "world come of age." Most modern scholars judge that both Altizer and Hamilton greatly misunderstood Bonhoeffer's meaning, but his language did inspire them.

Within a few years of its birth, the Death-of-God movement had run its course and was widely rejected as too radical.

C. Secular Theology

Sometimes associated with the Death-of-God movement is so-called "secular theology." Although both movements share some common assumptions, they should not be lumped together. The two most prominent representatives of secular theology are J. A. T. Robinson, Anglican Bishop of Woolwich, and the Harvard theologian Harvey Cox.

Tillich's influence lingers in the background of secular theology, but even more important is the influence of Dietrich Bonhoeffer. Robinson's popular book *Honest to God* seeks to combine three apparently incompatible theological strands identified with Tillich, Bultmann, and Bonhoeffer. Robinson has been severely criticized, especially for his interpretation of Bonhoeffer's notion of a "religionless" Christianity. For Bonhoeffer this phrase referred to true Christianity in contrast to a false religion. But for Robinson, this idea was taken as the basis for abandoning traditional understandings of a transcendent God. He then turned to Tillich in defining God as the "ground of all being," adding his own twist in arguing that Jesus "discloses and lays bare the ground of man's being as Love."

Harvey Cox became widely known with the publication of *The Secular City* in 1965. It became immensely popular, selling more than one million copies. Although there was no direct connection with

Robinson, Cox too saw a world that was increasingly secularized. He distinguished "secularism" and "secularization"; the former he repudiates, the latter he embraces. Secularism is essentially an ordering of life without reference to God. Secularization is the inevitable historical process of liberation from a tribal village society and, with it, traditional conceptions of God and traditional ecclesiastical authority. In the modern world, humanity is now free to enter the secular realm of the city, which is indifferent to religion. However, according to Cox, "God is just as present in the secular as the religious realms of life."

This view contends that the church should not oppose this historical development, but embrace it. Far from being a protective religious community, the church should be in the forefront of secularization in society, celebrating the new ways religiosity is finding expression in the world. For Cox, churches should leave their palaces behind and "step into God's permanent revolution in history." By embracing secularization, the church is no longer focused on otherworldly metaphysics, but on the practical work of justice and reconciliation. This secularized vision is a clear marker of modern theological trajectories in which immanence trumps transcendence.

Like the Death-of-God theology, secular theology was also short-lived. In later years, Cox stepped back from his earlier assertions and concluded that secularization was "a myth." But Cox also felt that his work gave significant impetus to the liberations that soon followed.

V. LIBERATION THEOLOGIES

Liberation theologies are contextual theologies, arising as they do from specific situations of social injustice as well as political and economic oppression. Working and living in such oppressive contexts led theologians to rethink their conception of the church and its theology. They concluded that any theology that explicitly or implicitly sanctions the exploitation of the poor or socially marginalized is not the theology of Jesus. Liberation theologies acknowledge the sinfulness of humanity, but they especially link sin to social, economic, and political injustice. At its core, Liberation theology is an activist theology that self-consciously expresses itself in the social and political realm.

Fundamental to Liberation theology is the insistence that theological reflection follows praxis. That is to say, theology is a second act critically reflecting on the first act, which is commitment to and solidarity with the oppressed. This praxis is inspired by the guiding principle that God has a preferential love for the poor and oppressed. Theology is not conceived primarily as doctrinal principles logically derived from biblical texts.

Another significant tendency among liberation theologians is to think of "salvation" within a social construct rather than individualistically. In this they have much in common with the Social Gospel movement. However, they do look to the biblical message of the prophets and conclude that God sides with the oppressed and actively seeks to liberate them from all bondage, slavery, and inequality.

Liberation theologians believe the church is called by God to identify with the oppressed and marginalized people rather than with the rich, the powerful, and the privileged. Thus the Christian mission necessarily includes active participation by the Christian church in the liberation of oppressed people. In Latin America, liberation theologians are concerned to liberate the poor from structural poverty and political injustice. In North America, they are concerned to liberate from the oppression and injustice of racism and sexism.

In spite of the different particularities, all three major expressions of Liberation theology share a common outrage at injustice.

A. Latin American Liberation Theology

The term "liberation theology" was first coined in 1971 by the Peruvian Dominican priest Gustavo Gutiérrez (1928–) in his famous book *A Theology of Liberation*. This movement first emerged midcentury among Roman Catholic priests in Latin America. They were convinced that the overwhelming poverty they witnessed was caused by social and economic injustice. This realization gave rise to the *Consejo Episcopal Latinoamericano* (Latin American Episcopal Conference), also known as CELAM, established in 1955.

After the Second Vatican Council, CELAM held two conferences that were constitutive for Liberation theology: the first was held in Medellín, Colombia, in 1968, and the second in Puebla, Mexico, in January 1979. The Medellín conference especially was influenced by liberationist ideas when it issued the famous declaration concerning the "preferential option for the poor." This slogan represents what is considered the most significant innovation of Liberation theology, namely, conceiving of theology from the perspective of the poor and oppressed. Its proponents claim that Jesus was a revolutionary whose theology emerged from a class struggle against the religious and political oppressors of his day.

Liberation theology finds its primary source in Gutiérrez's own personal experience of poverty in the barrios of Lima, Peru. He was a *mestizo*—part Spanish and part Latin American native Indian—and suffered as a member of this oppressed ethnic group. Gutiérrez recognized that his experience was not unique but that more than half of his countrymen lived in similar circumstances of extreme poverty and social ostracism. He believed that poverty existed because of unjust and sinful cultural constructs.

It should be recalled that this was the period when Latin American dictators and military governments held sway, and right-wing death squads terrorized the populace. One of the most tragic examples of such brutality was the assassination of Archbishop Oscar Romero of El Salvador as he celebrated mass just one day after he publically called on Salvadoran soldiers to refuse orders to kill fellow citizens. It was in this context that Gutiérrez averred, "Poverty is not fate, it is a condition; it is not a misfortune, it is an injustice. It is the result of social structures and ... cultural categories."

In a sense, Gutiérrez's theology is a plea to the Roman Catholic Church to recover its mission to the poor and disenfranchised. He criticizes the church for having too often identified with the wealthy and the militaristic governments that oppressed their citizens. He makes an explicit appeal to the Bible, asserting that "the entire Bible, beginning with the story of Cain and Abel, mirrors God's predilection for the weak and abused of human history." Preference for the poor does not imply that God does not love the wealthy; it just means that the poor have a priority in terms of urgency. "Preference implies the universality of God's love, which excludes no one. It is only within the framework of this universality that we can understand the preference, that is, what comes first."

Gutiérrez can say, "To know God is to work for justice. There is no other path to reach God." There is for him an identification of "liberation" with the more traditional notion of "salvation." In making this identification, he does not exclude the traditional meaning of the individual spiritual experience of God's grace and forgiveness for sins; however, he does stress that there is more to salvation. "If we understand salvation as something with merely 'religious' or 'spiritual' value for the soul, then it would not have much to contribute to concrete human life."

When he implicated the Catholic Church as one of the social structures that implicitly supported the forces of oppression, Gutiérrez found himself in trouble with the Catholic hierarchy. Under the auspices of Cardinal Joseph Ratzinger (later Pope Benedict XVI), the Vatican's office for doctrinal orthodoxy, the Congregation for the Doctrine of the Faith (CDF), issued condemnations of Liberation theology.

The CDF denounced the tendency to politicize the Bible, but the most significant criticism was reserved for the use of Marxist analysis as an interpretative tool for understanding the causes of poverty in Latin America. Marxist categories of social analysis, the church argued, cannot be detached from its non-Christian (even atheistic) view of history and humanity. Liberation theologians responded that their use of Marx is no different than the use of pagan philosophers in the early church or Thomas Aquinas's use of Aristotle.

Critics of Latin American Liberation theology warn that it has been an incubator for violence, and they cite the example of the Catholic priest turned guerrilla, Camilo Torres Restrepo (1929–66). A committed socialist, Torres came to believe that armed struggle was justified in order to secure justice for the poor. He joined a guerilla organization (National Liberation Army) and was killed in combat with the Colombian military. He infamously stated that "If Jesus were alive today, He would be a *guerrillero*."

Gutiérrez never condoned violence, but he did acknowledge that violence may be justified in certain oppressive circumstances. "We cannot say that violence is all right when the oppressor uses it to maintain ... 'order,' but wrong when the oppressed use it to overthrow this same order."

Like most contemporary theological movements, Latin American Liberation theology has a variety of voices. Beside Gutiérrez, other leading voices include Catholic theologians Leonardo Boff of Brazil, Juan Luis Segundo of Uruguay, and Jon Sobrino of El Salvador. Although liberation theology is closely identified with Catholicism, some of its leading theologians were Protestant, such as José Miguez Bonino of Argentina and Emilio Castro of Uruguay.

Whatever the validity of the criticism, these theologians have reminded Christians of the injustice and oppression that most often accompanies poverty.

B. Black Liberation Theology

Black liberation theology was born out of the social struggles of African Americans for freedom and equality in America. The emergence of the Black Power movement in the mid-1960s signaled the growing frustration among younger African Americans with the nonviolent approach of Dr. Martin Luther King Jr. in the civil rights movement.

In July 1966 the National Committee of Negro Churchmen (fifty-one black pastors) published a "Black Power" statement in *The New York Times*. The black churchmen made it clear that their message of Black Power was derived from their commitment to the Christian gospel. As Christians, they were morally bound to address the "gross imbalance of power and conscience between Negroes and white Americans.... This is more important than who gets to the moon or the war in Vietnam."

As bold as the Black Power statement was, it seemed tame in comparison to the "Black Manifesto" published in April 1969. This manifesto, coming exactly one year after the assassination of Dr. King (and four years after the murder of Malcolm X in 1965), marked a new militancy. It warned: "No oppressed people ever gained their liberation until they were ready to fight, to use whatever means necessary, including the use of force and the power of the gun...." The essence of the manifesto was its demand for reparations from white America.

> ... white America has exploited our resources, our minds, our bodies, our labor. For centuries we have been forced to live as colonized people inside the United States, victimized by the most vicious, racist system in the world.... We are therefore demanding of the white Christian churches and Jewish synagogues ... that they begin to pay reparations to black people in this country. We are demanding $500,000,000.... This total comes to 15 dollars per nigger....

One of the authors of the manifesto, James Foreman, interrupted Sunday services at the historic (and white Protestant) Riverside Church in New York, demanding reparations. The Black Manifesto linked reparations to the Christian notion of repentance. This linkage to repentance had the dual benefit of identifying with a fundamental Christian doctrine and at the same time insinuating a threat.

A third historic document on "black theology" from the National Committee of Black Churchmen in June 1969 specifically links black liberation with the gospel of Jesus.

> Black Theology is a theology of black liberation. It seeks to plumb the black condition in the light of God's revelation in Jesus Christ.... It affirms the humanity of white people in that it says No to the encroachment of white oppression. The message of liberation is the revelation of God as revealed in the incarnation of Jesus Christ. Freedom IS the gospel. Jesus is the Liberator!

It is noteworthy that these statements of increasing militancy arose primarily from the African-American church. It was not until the efforts of James H. Cone that the academic world began to formalize the Black Liberation theology first expressed in the black church.

As the Charles Briggs Professor of Systematic Theology at Union Theological Seminary in New York, Cone used his academic platform to address the pressing issues facing African Americans. But even more importantly, it was his personal experience as a young black man raised in the South that especially qualified him to speak to these issues.

Cone grew up in Bearden, Arkansas, with its population of 400 blacks and 800 whites. The whites in Bearden, as Cone explains, "tried to make us believe that God created black people to be white people's servants." White racism permeated Southern culture with its segregated schools and restaurants as well as political and economic inequality. Cone's experiences led him to a very different approach to combating racism than Dr. King. Cone preferred to ally himself with the more radical Black Power movements.

Reviewing the course of the historical development of black liberation theology, Cone distinguished three stages. In the early period from 1966 to 1970 the movement was concentrated in the black churches. The second stage ranged from 1970 to 1977, and the movement shifted to academic institutions and theological reflection. Since 1977, black liberation theology has begun to engage with global liberation movements. In particular, Cone and others became affiliated with the Ecumenical Association of Third World Theologians (EATWOT), an association of Third World theologians committed to the liberation of oppressed peoples.

It was the publication of two groundbreaking and highly controversial volumes justifying black activism that brought Cone to prominence: *Black Theology and Black Power* (1969) and *A Black Theology of Liberation* (1970). He found that the theologians he studied in graduate school did not provide meaningful answers for African Americans. He asked, "What could Karl Barth possibly mean for black students who had come from the cotton fields of Arkansas, Louisiana, and Mississippi, seeking to change the structure of their lives in a society that had defined black as non-being?" Thus Cone developed a more radical theology, whose organizing principle was black liberation from white racism.

Black theology is defined specifically in terms of liberation. "It is a rational study of the being of God in the world in light of the existential situation of an oppressed community ... liberation is not only consistent with the gospel, but is the gospel of Jesus Christ." Blackness is the overarching theological metaphor that informs all theological rubrics. Therefore Cone makes the provocative statement that God is black. This is his way of asserting that God identifies with the marginalized of society. Divine revelation "is a black event."

For Cone, revelation is more than divine self-disclosure; it is the promise of liberation. The "essence of biblical revelation" is that it is God's declaration of "emancipation from death-dealing political, economic and social structures of society." Hence, Cone draws on the biblical narratives of God's deliverance of Israel from Egypt and gospel accounts of Jesus declaring that he has come "to set the oppressed free" (Luke 4:18). Furthermore, Jesus is the black Messiah. Cone writes that the

"What could Karl Barth possibly mean for black students who had come from the cotton fields ..., seeking to change the structure of their lives in a society that had defined black as non-being?" (James Cone).

importance of Jesus must be found in his blackness. If he is not black as we are, then the resurrection has little significance for our times.... In a society that defines blackness as evil and whiteness as good, the theological significance of Jesus is found in the possibility of human liberation through blackness. Jesus is the black Christ!

Salvation is reconceived in terms of liberation from racial injustice and is thus directed toward the social and political sphere more than the spiritual. To focus on the future reward of heaven is seen as an attempt to dissuade blacks from the goal of real liberation in the present. Cone's liberation theology carries an ominous warning that black patience has run out, and if white America does not respond, "then a bloody, protracted civil war is inevitable." Thus for Cone, theology is not mere abstraction, but anchored in the experience of black anger.

C. Feminist Liberation Theology

Feminist theology, like its counterparts in Latin America and the African-American community, is a contextual theology with strong political overtones. That is to say, it arises from a deep sense of ongoing injustice and oppression in the North American cultural and ecclesiastical context.

North American culture is seen by feminists as another manifestation of a much longer history of patriarchy in the Christian church. Although there have been isolated movements and individual women who have resisted the patriarchy of the culture and the church, none was successful in overturning the prevailing tendencies until the twentieth-century suffragette movement in North America. Historically, feminist liberation theology is generally distinguished in terms of three "waves," the first of which began in the mid-nineteenth century.

It was not until the 1960s that a more powerful women's movement emerged in which women's experience is the controlling presupposition to theology. Although feminist thought is multilayered, one can distinguish four broad categories of feminist theology: Post-Christian, Revisionist, Ethnic, and Evangelical.

1. Waves of Feminism

Led by Elizabeth Cady Stanton, the Seneca Falls Convention in New York in July 1848 marked the first wave of the women's movement, which culminated in the Nineteenth Amendment to the U.S. Constitution, passed by Congress in 1918 and ratified in 1920, granting women the right to vote. Although it was the law of the land, five southern states did not formally ratify the amendment until 1969 to

1971: Florida, South Carolina, Georgia, Louisiana, and North Carolina. Mississippi did not ratify it until 1984.

If the first wave of the women's movement centered on the right for women to vote, the second wave addressed a range of legal issues such as gender discrimination in the workplace and, perhaps most controversially, reproductive rights. The second wave, variously labeled the "Feminist Movement" or the "Women's Liberation Movement," was inaugurated by Betty Friedan's 1963 best-selling book *The Feminine Mystique*. Drawing from her own research as well as the earlier work of Simone de Beauvoir's *Le Deuxiéme Sexe* (*The Second Sex*, 1949), Friedan sparked a full-fledged movement in the United States.

In 1966 Friedan founded the National Organization for Women, with the aim of bringing women "into the mainstream of American society [in] fully equal partnership with men." The development of the birth control pill granted women, for the first time in history, nearly complete control over their reproductive capacity. A growing number of mainline Protestant denominations admitted women to ordination. Friedan was politically active and led efforts to secure landmark legislation and, most notably, the U.S. Supreme Court decision *Roe v. Wade* of 1973, which granted women the legal right to an abortion.

Third-wave feminism emerged in the early 1990s, but is especially resistant to easy categorization. While first- and second-wave feminism had defined goals, third-wave feminism is more diffuse. The third wave was in part a reaction to the perceived inadequacies of second-wave feminism, especially the failure to include women of different ethnicities and cultural backgrounds; it sought to challenge what it deemed the second wave's "essentialist" definitions of feminity, which often assumed a universal female identity and overemphasized the experiences of upper-middle-class white women.

There was also an affinity to punk-rock culture. "Riot grrrl" is an underground feminist punk movement (begun in the 1990s) that stresses female identity. Its music addresses distinctively feminist issues such as rape, domestic abuse, sexuality, and female empowerment.

2. Post-Christian Feminism

One of the most radical Christian feminists was the Boston College professor Mary Daly (1928–2010). She described herself alternatively as a "radical lesbian feminist" and "post-Christian feminist," which was her way of declaring that Christianity is a primary cause of women's oppression and the teachings of the Bible are the means by which women are subjected to male control and patriarchy.

Early in her career, although critical of ecclesiastical patriarchy, Daly believed that the Catholic Church was not beyond reform. By the

"If God is male, then male is God" (Mary Daly).

early 1970s, her thought turned more radical with the publication of her second book, *Beyond God the Father* (1973), in which she criticized Christianity itself and rejected the ultimate authority of the Bible as misogynist. It was in this volume that she coined the famous quote, "If God is male, then male is God." In the process of writing this book Daly abandoned Christianity altogether and issued a "call for the castration of sexist religion."

In subsequent writings Daly became increasingly radical. In *Gyn/Ecology: The Metaethics of Radical Feminism* (1978) she moved beyond the history of patriarchy and argued for a reversal of power between the genders—that women should rule over men. In a magazine interview she declared, "If life is to survive on this planet, there must be a decontamination of the Earth. I think this will be accompanied by an evolutionary process that will result in a drastic reduction of the population of males."

3. Revisionist Feminism

From the very beginning, feminist theologians have struggled with traditional Christianity. Many came to the conclusion that what was said to be normative human experience was in fact male experience. Feminists felt powerless and ignored in a religious world that is socially, sexually, ecclesiastically constructed by males. Although traditional theology acknowledges that God is neither male nor female, the Christian story largely has been told through the male voice from a male perspective.

In response, some feminist theologians like Daly have repudiated Christianity, while others have sought to revise it. Two of the leading revisionist feminist theologians, Rosemary Radford Ruether and Elisabeth Schüssler Fiorenza, although critical of traditional versions of Christianity, have retained their Christian identification.

Ruether (1936–), like all feminists, is concerned about patriarchy within Christianity. Her book *Sexism and God-Talk: Toward a Feminist Theology* (1993) is one of the first feminist systematic theologies. Provocatively, she asks, "Can a male savior save women?" Her answer is no—maleness is not essential to his role as savior. She argues that traditional theology has been constructed based on male experience, and as such, it reflects a patriarchal outlook. She writes, "Whatever denies, diminishes, or distorts the full humanity of women is, therefore, appraised as non-redemptive.... What does promote the full humanity of women is of the Holy."

Some early feminists affirmed the normative authority of the Bible and placed the blame for patriarchy on male interpreters and translators. Some revisionist feminists such as Ruether argue that the biblical text is so thoroughly patriarchal that women must move beyond it in order to construct a meaningful theology. For example, Phyllis Trible identifies what she calls "texts of terror," which reflect a deep-seated and violent patriarchy in the Bible. The story of Lot offering his daughters for gang rape in order to protect his houseguests (Gen. 19:4–8) is seen as both patriarchy and misogyny.

In response to the perceived patriarchy, revisionist feminists created a "canon within a canon," composed of biblical texts that have positive images of women and other texts from non-Christian sources. The Bible remains a theological resource, albeit not an exclusive one.

Fiorenza (1938–) is perhaps the most prolific feminist theologian at this time. A native German, she received her theological training at the University of Münster and became a professor at Harvard Divinity School. In her best-known book, *In Memory of Her: A Feminist Theological Reconstruction of Christian Origins* (1994), Fiorenza argues for the retrieval of the overlooked contributions of women in the early Christian church and challenges the inevitability of patriarchy in the formative period of early Christianity.

Inspired by various liberation theologians, she portrays Jesus as a liberator who challenges the dominant male structures that oppress the poor and women. Sin is reconceived in terms of social structures that alienate and exploit the disenfranchised. The image of God the Father is exchanged for the image of God as Spirit or as the Ground of Being.

Ruether, while critical of the intrinsic patriarchy in the Bible, nevertheless accepts that it does contain some liberating texts that are therefore authentic words from God. Fiorenza on the other hand, does not believe that the biblical text contains any divine revelation. Instead, she locates the revelatory role in the women-church community, which is "the hermeneutical center of feminist theology." In this way, the worshiping community of women functions as the magisterium for theological truth.

4. Ethnic Feminism

The growing presence of minority women was the single most important development in feminist theologies at the end of the twentieth century. While agreeing that the experiences of women are a vital theological resource, Latina and African-American women felt there was a world of difference between their experiences and those of white middle-class women who had been constructing feminist theology. These minority voices argued that the dominance of white women in the feminist movement mirrors the dominance of white culture. Speaking from their own ethnic context, African-American and Latina feminists developed their own distinctive kind of feminism.

African-American women used black theology and feminist theology as stepping-stones, but have embraced the more distinctive term "womanist," first coined by novelist Alice Walker. Womanist theology refers to a theological stance whose point of departure is the experience of African-American women. Such theology focuses not only on liberation but also on survival. Hagar in the Old Testament is seen as a model for all women who go into the world to make a living for themselves and their children. Believing that white feminist theology focuses on women alone, the womanist theology is shaped also by a concern for family and community.

According to Jacquelyn Grant, African-American women locate authority in the history of black women and their faith. The Bible remains an important source for theological reflection along with the experience of African-American women. For black women, Jesus was seen as the divine co-sufferer and thus a source of encouragement during the civil rights movement. Womanist theologians do not reject the Bible and its authority, for they find that it has been a source of comfort and strength for African-American women throughout their history. However, the communal experience of black women serves as an authoritative source for theology, alongside the Bible.

Inspired by the Spanish word for woman (*mujer*) and the womanist community of African-American women, Ada María Isasi-Díaz, a Cuban-American theologian, coined the term *mujerista* to stress Latina experiences as a source for feminist theology. Latina women have developed a theological outlook that centers on their particular experiences. In contrast to the white-dominated feminist theology that tends to place emphasis on the individual, *Mujerista* theology, like womanist theology, gives greater weight to the family and community.

Isasi-Díaz has gone on the offensive against the patriarchal machismo so often characteristic of Hispanic culture. For Latina women, the suffering Jesus is a viable source of encouragement to those who have been oppressed. They are less concerned with elaborate intellectual systems of theology and more focused on the practical matter of everyday justice. They view sin as resignation in the face of oppression and unwillingness to envision a better future.

5. Evangelical Feminism

As it developed in the twentieth century, evangelical theology has been known for its distinctive commitment to the authority of Scripture. Evangelical feminists, in keeping with that commitment, argue that when rightly interpreted, the Bible teaches the full equality of men and women and that all ministry roles are equally available to men and women. This view, termed "egalitarianism," is grounded in the

Christian conviction that all humanity was created in the image of God and therefore all have equal responsibility in the home and church to exercise their gifts in service to God.

Historically, however, the Christian church has not been egalitarian but hierarchical. In the traditional view, women were excluded from leadership roles in the home and the church. Based on their reading of Scripture, it is argued that God has ordained the different roles for men and women. The traditional view gained new impetus in reaction to the rise of twentieth-century feminism.

In 1987 the Council on Biblical Manhood and Womanhood was established to counter a perceived threat to the traditional structures of the church and family. In opposition to all forms of egalitarianism, they articulated what is now known as the "complementarian" view, which affirms that God has designed complementary roles for men and women.

In this view, both men and women are made in God's image, but have different roles and functions. Men are viewed as the spiritual leaders in the home, and wives are to submit to the husband's authority. In the church, women's gifts are acknowledged, but must be exercised under male authority and are generally encouraged in women's and children's ministries. The formal governing and teaching roles are restricted to men.

Complementarians insist that male leadership and female submission in the home and church are to be implemented in the context of Christian love. This complementarian view is reflected, for example, in article XVIII of the Southern Baptist Convention's *Baptist Faith and Mission* (2000).

As evangelicals, both complementarians and egalitarians are committed to the binding authority of the Bible, yet each view stresses different biblical texts in support of their position. The complementarians give prominence to texts such as 1 Timothy 2:12 ("I do not permit a woman to teach or to assume authority over a man"), while egalitarians put emphasis on Galatians 3:28 ("There is neither Jew nor Gentile, neither slave nor free, nor is there male and female, for you are all one in Christ Jesus"). A high view of Scripture does not resolve these differences of interpretation.

Evangelical feminists have gained considerable ground in the North American evangelical world. Many evangelical denominations now affirm the ordination of women, and even most complementarian seminaries now admit women to their ministerial programs (MDiv), even if women are excluded from certain classes such as preaching. On the other hand, it is worth noting that even within those denominations (both evangelical and nonevangelical) that ordain women, obstacles remain. Ordained women still find it difficult to secure positions as senior pastors of larger churches. Statistics demonstrate that ordained women most often are relegated to positions as assistants, associates, or pastors of small congregations or in interim positions.

Despite its achievements, the evangelical feminist movement has had its own challenges. With the emergence of the women's movement in the 1960s (second-wave feminism), evangelicals began to reconsider the traditional views of women. Leading the way was Letha Dawson Scanzoni and Nancy A. Hardesty with their 1974 book, *All We're Meant to Be*, which was one of the primary inspirations for the evangelical feminist movement. That same year, the Evangelical Women's Caucus International (EWCI) came into being. This group advocated what they called "biblical feminism," which affirmed both the authority of the Bible and the availability of all ministry positions to women, including ordination.

By 1986, divergences began to emerge. At the seventh conference of EWCI in Fresno, California, a resolution was passed that favored "civil-rights protection for homosexual persons." Opponents of the resolution feared that the real purpose was to approve a lesbian lifestyle as being congruent with Scripture. Many of the evangelical feminists believed that the Bible does not sanction homosexuality and therefore concluded they could not remain within the EWCI.

Led by Catherine Kroeger (1925–2011) of Gordon-Conwell Theological Seminary, a new organization was formed in 1988, Christians for Biblical Equality (CBE). The CBE mission was straightforward: The Bible is the final authority on matters of faith and practice, and based on their understanding of the Bible, all offices of the church are open to women. Furthermore, they affirmed that heterosexual marriage is the biblical teaching.

The breach among evangelical feminists underscores the conflicting interpretations of Scripture. By 1978 Scanzoni and Virginia Mollenkott produced a book, *Is the Homosexual My Neighbor?* (1978), which contends that the Bible does not condemn homosexuality but is silent. In the face of this silence, Scanzoni and Mollenkott argue that the experience of homosexual Christians becomes the most valid source for determining the church's position on homosexuality. Despite their agreement on the binding authority of Scripture, significant differences remain among evangelicals.

VI. PROCESS THEOLOGY

Throughout church history, philosophy and theology have been in constant conversation, the one influencing the other. In the early church, Christian thinkers used Hellenistic categories to communicate the biblical message to educated pagans of the Roman Empire. Augustine borrowed heavily from Neoplatonism in his doctrinal formulations. In medieval theology, Aquinas viewed Aristotelian philosophy as the "handmaid" of theology. Liberal theologians embraced this notion of utilizing philosophy in the service of the theological enterprise. One contemporary expression of a philosophically informed theology is "process theology."

A. Alfred North Whitehead

Process theologians have drawn their philosophical inspiration from the British mathematician-turned-philosopher Alfred North Whitehead (1861–1947). He did not take a traditional view of God as the creator, but rather as the great unifying presence. God is so closely identified with the world that Whitehead can assert, "... it is as true to say the world created God as that God created the world." The world is viewed as the divine "body" while God is the world's "soul" or "mind," and the two are always inseparable and interdependent. For Whitehead, God is neither omnipotent nor timeless. God is always evolving—that is, in every given moment God is becoming superior to himself.

> "... it is as true to say the world created God as that God created the world" (Alfred North Whitehead).

B. John Cobb

By the 1970s process theology was felt in various mainline Protestant seminaries and divinity schools. Claremont Graduate School of Theology (California) in particular became the center of process theology because of the most ardent advocate, John Cobb Jr. As with all process theologians, Cobb wanted to move Christian theology away from classical theism as it was developed in the early and medieval church.

Cobb's theological orientation reveals some of the more distinctive aspects of process theology. First, God in his essence is relational and dynamic rather than static and immutable. This dynamic relational understanding of God necessarily means that God is constantly changing as he interacts with the world. God does indeed have purposes and goals for the world, but is constantly revising them in light of his interactions.

Second, there is an emphasis on God's immanence. Cobb stresses God's personal nature, divine love, vulnerability, and suffering rather than divine power and sovereignty. In this regard, Cobb emphasizes the mutual relationship of interdependence between God and the world.

Third, Cobb rejects monergism and any description of God's work in the world as coercive. Rather, God always works through persuasion. God calls the world to its own fulfillment, but free creatures decide whether and how to respond.

Fourth, Cobb's process theology is naturalistic in that it rejects the whole idea of supernatural intervention by divine power in the natural order. While that does not rule out special persuasive acts of God, it does rule out the miraculous. God provides humanity with his vision for what they should become and seeks to lure them toward this vision, but God never interrupts the natural order of events or forces anything to happen against nature or free will.

Finally, Cobb's God cannot know the future with absolute certainty. Because the future is ultimately determined by the response of individuals to God's persuasion, it cannot be known. Accordingly, there is no guarantee that God will finally overcome human intransigence to his vision of good.

Cobb's view of God falls outside the traditional understanding of Christianity. It has been argued that process theology gained credibility because it seemed an antidote to the horrors of the twentieth century—the Holocaust, nuclear weapons, unrelenting wars, and genocide. To contemporary liberal theologians, these tragedies inclined them to seek a radical revision of traditional Augustinian notions of God's power and sovereignty. They believed that the Christian God would have stopped the mass killings of innocent people if he could. Therefore they concluded it must be the case that he could not stop them.

Process theologians found solace in Whitehead's concept of the God who suffers himself because of such tragedies, even if he cannot prevent them.

Because process theology differs considerably from historic Christian theology, many deny that process theology can be considered "Christian" in any legitimate sense. However, it is a mainstay in many liberal Protestant seminaries.

VII. CONTEXTUAL THEOLOGIES

When the twentieth century dawned, Christianity essentially had become a Western cultural movement. With 90 percent of all Protestants residing in the West, the perception was that Christianity was a Western religion. With the midcentury demise of colonialism, Christianity grew exponentially in the Third World. By the 1970s, the center of Christianity had shifted dramatically from the West to the global South, so much so that the nomenclature has changed from "Third World" to "Majority World."

This geographical and political shift has had significant theological implications. New African, Asian, and Latin American nations emerged, and with a new sense of national identity came a desire to define themselves theologically.

This geographical shift inevitably led to theological reconsiderations. The East African theologian John Mibiti rather poignantly posed the question to the Western church:

> We have eaten theology with you; we have drunk theology with you; we have dreamed theology with you. But it has all been one-sided; it has been, in a sense, your theology.... We know you theologically. The question is, "Do you know us theologically? Would you like to know us theologically?"

While each nation in Asia or Africa has its own distinct historical heritage, it remains the case that theological developments have several cultural realities that generally characterize these nations and impact their conception of Christian theology. First, it must be recognized that abject poverty is one of the basic realities of life. Second, Christianity inhabits a religiously pluralistic culture—in some cases, a culture long dominated by another religious tradition. Third, lingering suspicion remains about Western attitudes of superiority. Fourth, the spirit world is taken much more seriously. Fifth, Asian and African cultures actually think differently. If Christian theology is to be appropriately contextualized in the various cultures, these are some of the key issues that must be engaged.

A. Africa

The growth of Christianity in Africa in the twentieth century was nothing short of spectacular. The African continent has the highest numerical Christian growth rate in the world. As one looks at the theological developments of Christian Africa, one must bear in mind three historical facts: the slave trade, European colonization, and conflict with Islam.

For more than three centuries (c. 1550–1870), the primary contact between Europe and Africa was the slave trade. As many as 15 million Africans were taken from Africa to the Americas before Christian abolitionists successfully won the public battle, arguing that slavery is inconsistent with Christian theological principles.

With regard to colonization, economic opportunity led to political exploitation by Britain, France, Germany, Portugal, and Belgium. Between the Congress of Berlin in 1885 and the early twentieth century, most of Africa was divided among these European powers. By the turn of the century, Africa effectively had been partitioned into regional fiefdoms governed by powerful European competitors.

The third and perhaps most significant historical factor is the growing tension between Christians and Muslims. In sub-Saharan Africa the two monotheistic religions have generally peacefully coexisted for centuries. However, with the advent of Islamic militancy, tensions have dramatically increased, especially in nations such as Sudan and Nigeria.

Even before the decolonization of Africa (1950s to 1980s), European-trained Africans called for reclamation of the African heritage for Christian theology. The great challenge for African Christians was to define the relationship between historic Western theology and African Traditional Religions (ATR) — that is, those indigenous religious beliefs and practices that predated the arrival of Christianity: Are there aspects of ATR that can be utilized legitimately as a cultural and linguistic vehicle for the gospel?

Many African theologians remind Westerners that there are New Testament precedents for precisely this sort of thing. The apostle John used the Greek philosophical term *logos* to describe Jesus himself (John 1:1), although in the Hellenistic world *logos* referred to the abstract capacity for rational thought. Some African theologians draw a parallel to warrant the use of African concepts as vehicles to communicate the gospel. African theologians such as Bolaji Idowu argue that a "diffused monotheism" tends to characterize most ATRs.

In general, the indigenous African religious worldview envisions a three-tiered reality. The highest realm is occupied by a single Supreme Being. The second spiritual realm includes a wide variety of spiritual divinities, including dead ancestors. The third — earthly — dimension has a wide range of human intermediaries between the spirit world, such as witch doctors and shamans. African theologians argue that a biblically orthodox theology can appropriate these cultural forms in the service of Christian theology without becoming syncretistic.

South Africa faced a distinctive theological challenge. The struggle against apartheid gave shape to a more militant liberation theology rather than a theology of inculturation. South African theologians tended toward a more political protest theology that in part drew inspiration from the black theology of North America.

Steven Biko, one of the leading voices of this "protest theology," described South Africa as a country "teeming with injustice and fanatically committed to the practice of oppression, intolerance and blatant cruelty because of racial bigotry." He therefore advocated a "black theology," which "seeks to relate the present-day black man to God within the given context of the black man's suffering." Biko was murdered by the South African police in 1977, but remained a powerful symbol for those advocating a liberating theology.

B. Asia

The notion of Asian Christian theology is not a recent phenomenon. Efforts to present the Christian gospel in a way intelligible to the Asian context can be traced back to Mateo Ricci in China and Roberto de Nobili in India in the seventeenth century. In the latter part of the nineteenth and early twentieth centuries, the issue again surfaced in India, where some Christian missionaries presented Christ as the fulfillment of the aspirations of Hinduism. Some portrayed Jesus as "*Guru*" in order to make him more meaningful to Hindus.

After World War II, however, many Asian theologies moved beyond indigenization to a more fully developed contextualized Asian theology. Stephen Bevens maintains that theologians in non-Western societies "are becoming increasingly convinced that traditional approaches to theology do not really make sense within their own cultural patterns and thought forms." These theologians argue that just as God employed Jewish and then Greco-Roman cultures to reveal himself, so the gospel must be translated into the particular forms of Asian cultures.

Any consideration of Asian theologies needs to be fully aware of two primary contextual facts. First, Asian theologies often take place in the context of crushing poverty and economic despair. Second, such theologizing takes place in the context of multiple cultures and deep religiousness. Although there are many smaller local cultures, Confucianism is the sociopolitical framework that underlies Chinese culture, and Buddhism underlies the culture of India.

1. Water Buffalo Theology

After receiving his PhD from Princeton Theological Seminary in 1959, a young Japanese scholar, Kosuke Koyama, served as a Protestant missionary in Thailand from 1960 to 1968. While in Thailand, he decided to read his Bible as if he were standing alongside a water buffalo in a rice paddy—which led him to conceptualize Asian theology from the perspective of life at the elemental level of a water buffalo. He argued that real theology occurs while people "squat on the dirt ground, and not while sipping tea with missionary friends in the teak-floored shiny living room."

Koyama stressed what he called "neighborology"—that is, sharing the gospel not as a formal theological exercise, but as a dialogue within actual relationships with real people. The gospel, he said, "is something more than an idea. It is life, history, hope and love.... The God who says 'your problem is my problem' cannot be made real through 'communication-logy' but only through the life of the communicator."

"[The gospel] is something more than an idea. It is life, history, hope and love" (Water Buffalo theology of Kosuke Koyama).

Koyama's "Water Buffalo theology" sought to express culturally the meaning of the gospel message while rooted in the Asian cultural context, but without succumbing to syncretism. He defines contextualization in two respects: "First, to articulate Jesus Christ in culturally appropriate, communicatively apt words; and second, to criticize, reform, dethrone or oppose culture if it is found to be against what the name of Jesus Christ stands for."

2. *Minjung* Theology

Other Asian theologies draw significantly from Latin American liberation theologies. Latin American theologians focused on the structural causes of poverty, Western colonialism, economic exploitation by multinational corporations, institutional violence, and right-wing military dictatorships. In the 1970s Ahn Byung Mu, drawing lessons from the Latin American context, developed what he called *"Minjung* theology" ("theology of the people") as a Korean response to the oppressive military rule of Park Chung Hee in South Korea.

In *Minjung* theology, Jesus is portrayed as the liberator of the oppressed from social injustice, economic exploitation, political oppression, and racial discrimination.

3. Dalit Theology

An Indian version of liberation theology is the so-called "Dalit theology" of Arvind P. Nirmal (1936–95). Highly critical of the Brahmanic dominance of Christian theology in India, he believed that true, contextualized Christianity in India should reflect the struggle of Dalits, who make up about 70 percent of India's Christian population. Nirmal drew primarily on the concept of the "suffering servant" from Isaiah 53 to identify Jesus as a Dalit.

This movement emerged in the 1980s and embraced liberation themes of Jesus' preference for the poor and liberating the oppressed.

4. Third-Eye Theology

One of the more intriguing Asian liberation theologies is the "Third-Eye theology" of Choan Seng Song. Borrowing from Japanese Buddhism, Song employs the language of the "third eye" to mean viewing Christ through one's own cultural and spiritual context. With this goal in mind, he uses both traditional Asian stories and biblical stories, interpreting each in the light of the other. Jesus is understood as the God who suffers with his people, and as such, his story is the Asian story. "The cross" he states, "is the supreme symbol of God's suffering love." This same suffering Jesus is also the Resurrected One who liberates his people.

For Song, liberation entails both a political and spiritual dimension with Christians as the vanguard in the struggle for liberation. The Christian mission is not evangelization, but rather political liberation and the intersection of Christian and Asian spiritualities. The mission of the church is to engage other religions by "growing with them in the knowledge and experience of God's saving work in the world." Echoing German Catholic theologian Karl Rahner's concept of the "anonymous Christian," Song suggests that throughout human history "there are men and women who have gone about doing the king's business without being aware that they are in the King's service."

5. Pain of God Theology

Kazoh Kitamoiri's "Pain of God theology" derives from the distinctive situation of Japan. In the devastating aftermath of Japan's defeat in World War II, Katamoiri sought to develop a theology that would address the suffering of his countrymen. He drew the theological conclusion that the God of the Bible is the God of suffering and pain and can therefore empathize with the suffering and pain of the Japanese people. He appeals directly to Jeremiah 31:20, where God declares to Jeremiah, "Is not Ephraim my dear son, the child in whom I delight? Though I often speak against him, I still remember him." And then the operative phrase follows: "Therefore *my heart is pained*; I have great compassion for him." Martin Luther's own translation of this passage seemed to be confirmation: "Therefore my heart is broken" ("*Darum bricht mir mein Herz*"). Katamoiri's God is the God of compassion and hope, a theme that later inspired Jürgen Moltmann.

C. Implications of Non-Western Approaches to Theology

One of the striking implications of the interaction of African and Asian cultures with Western theologies is that they do not follow the conventions of Western logic. Timothy Tennent observes:

> We cannot therefore assume that the way systematic theology has been traditionally structured and presented throughout the history of Western civilization is the most logical, the most effective, or the only way in which theology can be systematically structured for the larger, global context.

Western theology tends to function on the supposition of the law of noncontradiction—that is, two contrary affirmations cannot be true at the same time. But Asians especially do not necessarily think in terms of "either-or" categories of thought. Rather, they tend toward "both-and" thinking, where two different affirmations are held simultaneously with each retaining its distinct identity. The one assertion is not necessarily viewed as a contradiction of the other.

Asian theologians such as Michael Amaladoss see potential dangers in the Western approach to theology. He has observed, "In a world governed by non-contradiction, if one is not for, then one must be against. It is a world of fundamentalists."

In non-Western cultures, rational argument is integrated with intuition, emotion, and experience. Stories play an integral part in religious discourse. The telling and transmission of stories attend to the whole person—not only rationality but also imagination and emotions. Thus, the parables of Jesus are more natural to them than creeds and catechisms. For Africans and Asians, theology tends to be as much about spiritual insight as it is about knowledge.

VIII. POST-VATICAN II THEOLOGICAL TRAJECTORIES

Among the constellation of innovative Catholic theologians such as Yves Congar, Hans Küng, and Hans Urs von Balthasar, none was more influential in the post-Vatican II period than Karl Rahner (1904–84). At the time of his death, the magnitude of his published works in Catholic theology was surpassed only by Thomas Aquinas. His collected works, *Theological Investigations*, fill twenty volumes. He is often portrayed as the Catholic counterpart to Karl Barth in terms of influence and impact in the twentieth century.

Although he deeply identified with the Thomistic tradition, he was not its slavish devotee. Rahner said of himself, "I consider myself a sincere and profound friend of St. Thomas. I do not, however, agree with those Thomists who are so locked into traditionalism that they can't imagine that any progress can be made independently of traditional Thomism."

If Thomas Aquinas was Rahner's inspiration, Martin Heidegger was his "teacher." Unfortunately, Rahner's philosophically flavored theological reflections are extremely difficult to understand. What is abundantly clear is that his main objective was to demonstrate that atheism is ultimately impossible and that all human thought finds its ultimate source in God as revealed in Jesus Christ.

Rahner is best known for two controversial theological concepts: the "supernatural existential" and "anonymous Christianity." Regarding the first concept, he posited that all human beings are gifted by God with a capacity to receive grace and thereby are by nature open to God's self-revelation in Jesus. In Rahner's own words, "God's self-communication as offer is also the necessary condition which makes its acceptance possible." This constitutive element of grace within all humans he calls the "supernatural existential" (a phrase borrowed from Heidegger), and it constitutes the possibility of salvation for all.

But it is the second concept, which builds on the first, that has generated the most dispute. Rahner argued that those who receive and respond to the "supernatural existential" are "anonymous Christians." That is, those individuals who embrace this inward grace (supernatural existential) will find full salvation whether or not they hear the explicit gospel message of Christ. Rahner does not overtly reject divine condemnation, but stresses that in order to be eternally damned to hell a person must explicitly reject God's offer of saving grace. And even then, those who reject this divine offer could yet be saved if their rejection is based on a false understanding of the gospel and they live a morally upright life pleasing to God.

Although controversial, Rahner's notion of the "anonymous Christian" was not so far from the teaching of Vatican II. Indeed, he was one of seven theologians who worked on the Second Vatican Council's *Lumen Gentium* ("Light of the Nations"), which teaches that those "who through no fault of their own, do not know the Gospel of Christ or His Church, but who nevertheless seek God with a sincere heart, and moved by grace, try in their actions to do His will as they know it through the dictates of their conscience—those too may achieve eternal salvation." Even though his theology was judged to be within the bounds of the Catholic Tradition, he was severely criticized by traditionalists and was even censored (1962) by the Catholic Church.

The combined influences of Vatican II and Karl Rahner's theological reflections caused the boundaries between Catholic theology, modern philosophy, and Protestant theology to become more porous. The Catholic priests and theologians influenced or trained by Rahner tend to be much more open to modern thought generally and to critical revision of Catholic Tradition specifically. They often affirm the whole church as the people of God so that Protestants are included in the true Christian church.

IX. THE NEW ATHEISM

A. Conventional Atheism

This survey of modern theologies would be less than complete if it did not give some consideration to atheism. Although the term "atheism" originated in sixteenth-century France, it can be traced back to pre-Socratic Greek philosophy. Cicero identifies the Greek philosopher Diagoras of the fifth century BC as the first atheist.

In the strict sense, atheism (from the Greek *atheos*, meaning "god-less") asserts that there are no deities. Some take a broader view that atheism is not so much an assertion but simply the absence of belief in deities. There is also a practical atheism (known as *apatheism)*, in which one lives as if there are no gods. This is not so much a rejection as it is a lack of interest in the question.

In his famous book *The Essence of Christianity* (1841), Ludwig Feuerbach (1804–72) argued that God is nothing more than a chimera—a human projection of human aspirations. Feuerbach's view exercised considerable influence on Karl Marx and through him on twentieth-century communism in the Soviet Union, Albania, China, North Korea, and Cuba. Influential philosophers such as Bertrand Russell and A. J. Ayer also were public advocates of atheism.

Although the demographics of atheism are difficult to quantify, it is estimated that atheists make up about 2–4 percent of the world population, while only 1.6 percent of Americans explicitly describe themselves as atheist or agnostic. Atheism is relatively common in Europe, Canada, Australia, New Zealand, and in former and current communist states. Because of the complexity of definition, it is difficult to determine whether or not atheism is growing.

B. The New Atheism

The twenty-first century was greeted with an aggressive advocacy of atheism through a series of best-selling books from the so-called "Four Horsemen of New Atheism." They are the American neuroscientist Sam Harris, Oxford evolutionary biologist Richard Dawkins, Tufts University philosopher Daniel Dennett, and the late British journalist Christopher Hitchens. They argue that it is time to take a far less accommodating attitude toward religion, superstition, and religion-based fanaticism than had been extended by traditional atheists. While they do not agree on all things, they are unified in a shared belief that religion should not be tolerated but exposed by rational analysis.

There is little that is *new* about the New Atheism. However, its proponents have managed more than previous atheists to capture popular attention. One may identify four notable reasons for their success. First, the New Atheists have taken arguments against religion that were long familiar to scholars and have repackaged them for a popular audience, thus exposing them to millions who would never otherwise pick up an atheist book.

Second, the New Atheists are unusually aggressive in public forums. They have been willing to debate opponents all over the world. Oxford theologian Alister McGrath (author of *The Dawkins Delusion?)*

has publically debated Dawkins before large audiences and has carried on a lively debate on the pages of the United Kingdom's *Sunday Times*.

As a measure of their commitment to their position, both Hitchens and Dennett faced life-threatening illnesses (leading to Hitchens's death in 2011), and both publically declared that the prospect of death would not produce a deathbed conversion. Dawkins, who has been dubbed "the U.K.'s Chief Atheist," has been equally militant in his own way. He actively participated in a 2008 publicity campaign in the U.K. with the slogan, "There's probably no God. Now stop worrying and enjoy your life."

Third, the New Atheists are convinced that advances in science have rendered religion unnecessary. Unlike earlier atheists who tended to think that science had nothing to say about God, the New Atheists argue that the "God Hypothesis" can be tested, and they have concluded that the hypothesis fails any such tests. They also aver that naturalism is sufficient to explain the universe, from the most distant galaxies to the origin of life. The New Atheists conclude that the universe does not imply a creator, but rather it appears as they would expect it to look if it were not designed at all. They coined the maxim "absence of evidence is evidence of absence."

Fourth, what is perhaps the most significant reason for the emergence of the New Atheists was the terrorist attacks of September 11, 2001, which demonstrated the danger of religious conviction. Dawkins notes:

> Many of us saw religion as harmless nonsense. Beliefs might lack all supporting evidence but, we thought, if people needed a crutch for consolation, where's the harm? September 11th changed all that. Revealed faith is not harmless nonsense, it can be lethally dangerous nonsense.... Dangerous because it gives them false courage to kill themselves, which automatically removes normal barriers to killing others.... And dangerous because we have all bought into a weird respect, which uniquely protects religion from normal criticism. Let's now stop being so damned respectful!

While stopping short of advocating religious persecution, Sam Harris goes so far as to advocate a benign, noncoercive, corrective form of religious intolerance. This would apply to all religions, but especially Islam, whose doctrines he believes are uniquely dangerous to civilization. "It is time we admitted that we are not at war with terrorism. We are at war with Islam." Hitchens echoed Harris, asserting that "the real axis of evil is Christianity, Judaism, and Islam."

Many people, including other atheists, have felt Harris goes too far in suggesting that "some propositions are so dangerous that it may

"There's probably no God. Now stop worrying and enjoy your life" (Richard Dawkins).

even be ethical to kill people for believing them." Critics have argued that such intolerance is as dangerous as the religious fanaticism Harris repudiates.

X. CONCLUSION

As Christianity moves through the third millennium, it faces an uncertain future. If all the demographic studies are accurate, Christianity will be around for another millennium. But what form will it take? Will it become largely Pentecostal? Will it be further fragmented between the global South and the West? With the extraordinary growth of Christianity in China, will Christianity eventually become a Sino-centric religion? Will Western theology still have a voice? Will the orchestral cacophony of Christian theologies ever be able to make sweet music in this pitiful fallen world?

These are important questions that cannot fully be answered at this point. There is, however, one question that looms especially large for Christians in the third millennium: Can the two largest and fastest-growing religions in the world tolerate the other? Put more succinctly: Can Christianity coexist with Islam? (See chapter 22.)

FOR FURTHER STUDY

Berlinski, David. *The Devil's Delusion: Atheism and Scientific Pretention.* New York: Basic Books, 2009.

Ford, David F., ed. *The Modern Theologians: An Introduction to Christian Theology in the Twentieth Century.* 3rd ed. Hoboken, NJ: Wiley-Blackwell, 2005.

Gibson, David, and Daniel Strange, eds. *Engaging with Barth: Contemporary Evangelical Critiques.* Edinburgh: T. and T. Clark.

Greenman, Jeffrey P., and Gene L. Green, eds. *Global Theology in Evangelical Perspective: Exploring the Contextual Nature of Theology and Mission.* Downers Grove, IL: InterVarsity Press, 2012.

Hunsinger, George. *How to Read Karl Barth: The Shape of His Theology.* Oxford: Oxford University Press, 1993.

McCormack, Bruce L., and Kelly M. Kapic, eds. *Mapping Modern Theology: A Thematic and Historical Introduction.* Grand Rapids: Baker, 2012.

Tennent, Timothy C. *Theology in the Context of World Christianity: How the Global Church Is Influencing the Way We Think and Discuss Theology.* Grand Rapids: Zondervan, 2007.

Catholicism and Orthodoxy

Collision to Collegiality
(20th and 21st Centuries)

I. EASTERN ORTHODOXY

The Great Schism between Rome and Constantinople left global Christianity divided between East and West. The rise of Islam and its conquest of the Byzantine Empire further drove a wedge between the two worlds. The once unified world of Christianity was no more.

Constantinople had been the bastion of Christianity in the East for more than a millennium (330–1453), but with the fall of the city, the Russian Orthodox Church assumed leadership in the Orthodox world and came to be known as the "third Rome." Philotheus, the "hegumen" (the ecclesiastical equivalent of an abbot) of the monastery in the city of Pskov, captured the spirit of this transference of authority in his sixteenth-century boast that "the Apostolic Church ... stands no longer in Rome or Constantinople, but in the blessed city of Moscow.... Two Rome's have fallen, but the third stands."

Formal recognition did not come until 1589, when the leader of the Russian Orthodox Church was granted the title of "Patriarch of Moscow" with the same honor and status as the ancient Eastern patriarchates of Constantinople, Alexandria, Antioch, and Jerusalem.

With the ascendancy of Tsar Peter the Great, the Russian Church found itself under the strong arm of a new master, no less brutal than the Muslim domination of the various patriarchates. In 1700, after the death of Patriarch Adrian of Moscow, Peter refused to name a successor. Twenty-one years later, Peter formally abolished the Russian patriarchy. In its place he created the Holy and Supreme Synod, presided over by the "metropolitan" (the ecclesiastical equivalent of an archbishop) of Saint Petersburg, but ultimately subject to the tsar. The Russian Church was constituted this way for the next two hundred years.

"... the Apostolic church ... stands no longer in Rome or Constantinople, but in the blessed city of Moscow.... Two Rome's have fallen, but the third stands" (Philotheus).

A. The Russian Revolution

On June 28, 1914, Gavrilo Princip, a Bosnian Serb student, fired the shot heard around the world. He killed Archduke Franz Ferdinand, heir to the Austro-Hungarian throne, and his wife, Sophie, in Sarajevo. Princip was a member of a shadowy Serb nationalist association known as the Black Hand, a group that sought independence from Austria-Hungary. The assassination in Sarajevo set into motion a series of fast-moving events that eventually escalated into a full-scale world war.

Within weeks of the assassination, military alliances were activated, and much of Europe was marching to war. The "Entente Powers" of France, the United Kingdom, and Russia squared off against the "Central Powers" of Germany and Austria-Hungary. Japan aligned with the Entente Powers in August 1914, as did Italy in April 1915 and the United States in April 1917. The Ottoman Empire joined the Central Powers in October 1914, followed a year later by Bulgaria.

Russia was not at all prepared for war and by 1917 was on the verge of total collapse. The Bolsheviks, led by Vladimir Lenin, seized the moment and launched a revolt in October. A bloody civil war engulfed Russia—during which an estimated 20 million Russians lost their lives, including Tsar Nicholas II and his family. In the early morning hours of July 16, 1918, Nicholas, Alexandra, and their children were executed. According to the diary of Leon Trotsky, another Bolshevik leader, the execution order came directly from Lenin in Moscow. By 1922 the civil war had run its course, and the Bolsheviks now held the reins of power.

In the chaos of the tribulations of the Russian Revolution, the Russian Orthodox Church restored the patriarchate. On August 15, 1917, Metropolitan Tikhon of Moscow (Basil Ivanovich Bellavin) became the church's first patriarch since it had been abolished by Peter the Great in 1700. Patriarch Tikhon took a bold stance against the Bolsheviks, anathematizing them in January 1918 and in July condemning the killing of the tsar. The Bolsheviks retaliated by imprisoning the patriarch. Although Tikhon was released in June 1923, his health had been severely impaired, and he died in April 1925.

As the first state to have an ideological objective to eliminate religion, the Communist regime of the Soviet Union confiscated church property, ridiculed religion, harassed believers, and propagated atheism in the schools. Orthodox priests and believers were variously tortured and sent to prison camps, labor camps, or mental hospitals. Many were executed. Between 1917 and 1935 an estimated 95,000 Orthodox priests were put to death, and the number of Orthodox churches in Russia fell from 29,584 to less than 500.

When Tikhon died, the Soviet authorities forbade patriarchal elections. The Metropolitan of Nizhny Novgorod, Sergius I (Ivan Stragorodsky), served as an acting patriarch. In an effort to stop the Soviet campaign of terror against the church, Sergius pursued reconciliation. On July 19, 1927, he issued his infamous Declaration, whereby he accepted the Soviet authority over the church and condemned political dissent within the church. However, persecution continued unabated, and by the outset of World War II only four bishops remained.

Only after the German invasion of the Soviet Union in 1941 did Soviet leader Joseph Stalin scale back the campaign of persecution. In exchange for its support of the new world war, Stalin allowed the church to elect a new patriarch. On September 8, 1943, Sergius was elected as the thirteenth patriarch of Moscow. With a newly restored patriarch, tensions between Communist officials and the Orthodox Church eased for a time. But in 1959 the new Communist leader, Nikita Khrushchev, initiated his own persecution of the church, which continued under his successor, Leonid Brezhnev. By 1985 fewer than 7,000 churches remained active.

B. *Glasnost* and Gorbachev

A pivotal point in the history of the Russian Orthodox Church came in 1988 with the millennial anniversary of the baptism of Grand Prince Vladimir of Kiev. Many older churches and some monasteries were reopened. Coinciding with these historic celebrations was the introduction of a new policy of *Glasnost* ("openness") by Soviet leader Mikhail Gorbachev.

Under Gorbachev, *Glasnost* brought greater openness and transparency in government activities as well as more religious freedom for citizens. For the first time in the history of the Soviet Union, people could see live transmissions of church services on television. The progressive leadership of Gorbachev eventually unleashed democratic forces, which led to the dismantling of the old Soviet Union in 1991. The new political climate in Russia saw the Russian Orthodox Church regain much of its lost prominence in the nation's society.

C. Global Orthodoxy

The Orthodox Church is a worldwide communion of independent, or "autocephalous," churches, sharing the same theological tradition but retaining their own authority, including the right to elect their own patriarch. Traditionally the ecumenical patriarch of Constantinople is recognized as *primus inter pares* (first among equals) of Orthodox bishops. He possesses privileges of chairmanship and initiative, but no direct doctrinal or administrative authority. The other ancient patriarchates have an established order of precedence: the patriarch of Alexandria, Egypt (with jurisdiction over Africa); the patriarch of Antioch, who actually resides in Damascus, Syria (with jurisdiction over the Arab-speaking Orthodox Christians in Syria, Lebanon, and Iraq); and the patriarch of Jerusalem (with jurisdiction over Palestine).

Even though four ancient patriarchates have ecclesial precedence, it is the Russian Orthodox Church that dominates Eastern Orthodoxy, representing the vast majority of the Orthodox Christians. The ancient patriarchates have been reduced to a small constituency of followers.

The autocephalous Orthodox churches exist in Georgia, Serbia, Romania, Bulgaria, Cyprus, Greece, Albania, Poland, Czech Republic/Slovakia, and the province of North America (although the latter is not universally recognized).

Beyond these autocephalous churches the Eastern Orthodox communion also includes a number of "autonomous" (semi-independent) churches, of which only two have universal recognition—the churches of Sinai and Finland. These autonomous churches enjoy a significant measure of independence, though the election of their primate is subject to nominal approval by a mother church.

By the turn of the twenty-first century, the complex of Orthodox churches numbered about 210 million adherents worldwide. Roughly two-thirds of all Orthodox followers belong to the Russian and Romanian Orthodox churches. Among the ancient patriarchates of Alexandria, Antioch, Constantinople, and Jerusalem, there are fewer than 10 million adherents.

D. Orthodox Diaspora

One of the most striking developments in modern Orthodoxy is the dispersion of Orthodox Christians to the West. Emigration from Greece and the Near East in the past hundred years has created a sizable Orthodox diaspora in western Europe, North and South America, and Australia. In addition, the Bolshevik Revolution forced thousands of Russian exiles westward. As a result, Orthodoxy's traditional eastern boundaries were altered. Millions of the Orthodox were no longer geographically "eastern," since they resided in their newly adopted countries in the West. Nonetheless, they remained Eastern Orthodox in their faith and practice.

Orthodoxy had its first appearance in North America in the middle of the eighteenth century, when Russian fur traders made their way to the Yukon. Although Alaska as the first port of entry brought many Russian Orthodox people into America, the main venue came through an influx of immigrants from a variety of other Orthodox countries.

The years 1890 through 1910 saw the greatest wave of Orthodox immigration into North America, and by 1916 there were approximately 100,000 Orthodox adherents. Immigrants from Greece, Russia, Lebanon, Romania, Syria, Bulgaria, Egypt, and Serbia formed ethnic enclaves in the industrial centers of America.

Initially, almost all Orthodox communities, regardless of ethnic background, were united under the Russian Orthodox Church. That church had established the first diocese in the United States, and the Russian churches were numerous and well-organized. But Russian Orthodoxy in America underwent dramatic change with the Bolshevik Revolution.

The Russian Orthodox Church in America has a complicated history of rivalry and sometimes outright hostility. There are two competing jurisdictions: the Russian Orthodox Church Outside Russia (ROCOR) and the *Metropolia*, later renamed the Orthodox Church in America (OCA). Both emerged in the wake of the Russian Revolution. Fearing the Bolsheviks, Patriarch Tikhon of Moscow issued a decree (*Ukaz*) in November 1920, calling on dioceses outside the borders of Russia to organize themselves autonomously until such time as normal communications and relations with the church in Russia could resume.

ROCOR came into being when a group of Russian bishops fled the country and organized themselves in Constantinople and Serbia. In America, the bishops took Tikhon's *Ukaz* as the basis for their own self-administration, organizing themselves in 1920. Meanwhile, the American branch of the mother Orthodox Church in Russia (*Metropolia*) also took Tikhon's *Ukaz* as a cue to declare in 1924 a state of "temporary self-government." Although these two jurisdictions cooperated initially, relations eventually turned sour.

Both ROCOR and the *Metropolia* opposed the Moscow patriarchate because they believed it was subservient to what ROCOR called the "Soviet atheistic regime." But in 1970, during a brief period of Soviet-American detente, the *Metropolia* reconciled with the Moscow patriarchate. Soon thereafter, the *Metropolia* (OCA) was officially granted the status of autocephalous. ROCOR repudiated the reconciliation as a capitulation to the Communist-dominated mother church.

With the breakup of the Soviet Empire, relations between ROCOR and the Moscow patriarchate gradually began to thaw. In May 2007 the Act of Canonical Communion was signed, and communion with the Moscow patriarchate was restored. Along with the restoration of canonical links with the Moscow patriarchate, ROCOR and the OCA also resumed full communion. While Orthodox churches in North America share the same faith and doctrine, separate jurisdictions remain.

It should be noted that the patriarchates of the four ancient seats of Orthodoxy (Jerusalem, Antioch, Constantinople, and Alexandria) refuse to recognize the OCA as canonical, averring that only the Ecumenical Patriarch of Constantinople in conjunction with the other three patriarchs can bestow autocephaly. This jurisdictional controversy is primarily political, however, and in practice, members of the OCA are in full communion with other Orthodox dioceses.

At present there are eleven primary Orthodox jurisdictions in the United States, representing different mother churches based in eastern Europe and the Middle East. These Orthodox churches, although separate, cooperate in the Standing Conference of Canonical Orthodox Bishops in the Americas (SCOBA). Founded in 1960, the purpose of SCOBA is to foster unity among the Orthodox churches for a more visible witness to the Orthodox faith. The Orthodox leaders meet semi-annually for dialogue on inter-Orthodox and ecumenical matters and cooperative ventures.

The Orthodox churches in SCOBA include the following: Greek Orthodox, Serbian Orthodox, Romanian Orthodox, Orthodox Church in America (OCA), Russian Orthodox, Russian Orthodox Church Outside Russia (ROCOR), Carpatho-Russian Orthodox, Antiochian Orthodox, Bulgarian Orthodox, Ukranian Orthodox, and Albanian Orthodox.

E. Evangelicals and Orthodoxy

One of the more intriguing developments in the short history of Orthodoxy in North America was the migration of evangelicals to the Orthodox faith. Perhaps most surprising was the journey of disgruntled leaders in the evangelical parachurch ministry, Campus Crusade for Christ (now known as Cru). In l968 Peter Gillquist and a handful of other top leaders left the organization in a quest for the "authentic" Christian church, whose historical roots could be traced to the first-century church of Jesus.

By 1975, Gillquist and his former Campus Crusaders banded together in a loosely organized religious group, the New Covenant Apostolic Order. The quest for the true New Testament church eventually led Gillquist and colleagues to Orthodoxy. Perhaps the most critical decision was the theological judgment that the Roman Catholic Church had veered away from the apostolic path, while the Eastern Orthodox Church remained truth to the faith of the apostles. Thus, in February 1979 the group formally established itself as the Evangelical Orthodox Church (EOC), with Gillquist as the presiding bishop.

The leaders of this independent Orthodox church still sought a formal connection to the historic Orthodox Church. EOC representatives began to meet with various Russian Orthodox theologians and decided to approach the Ecumenical Patriarch of Constantinople to come under his jurisdiction, but were rebuffed. However, the Metropolitan of the Antiochian Orthodox Church was more receptive, and in the spring of 1987 the EOC was officially accepted into the Orthodox communion through the AOC's jurisdiction. Virtually the entire EOC denomination of two thousand former evangelical Protestants and seventeen parishes was welcomed into the Antiochian Orthodox Church. The EOC was renamed the Evangelical Antiochian Orthodox Mission, a title it retained until 1995, when it was completely absorbed into the main diocesan framework of the Antiochian Church.

The entrance of the EOC into the Orthodox Church inspired other individuals and congregations to enter the church. Perhaps the most prominent evangelical leader to convert to Orthodoxy was Frank Schaeffer, son of the evangelical apologist Francis Schaeffer. In 1990 Frank Schaeffer joined the Greek Orthodox Church and became a noted critic of American evangelicalism. There were defections from the mainline churches as well. Jaroslav Pelikan, a prominent Yale University historian and lifelong member of the Evangelical Lutheran Church, joined the Orthodox Church in America in 1998.

One of the monumental ecclesiastical triumphs in nearly a millennium occurred in 1964, when Pope Paul VI and the Patriarchal Bishop of Constantinople, Athenagoras I, rescinded the mutual excommunications of 1054 that had given rise to the Great Schism between the Eastern and Western churches. Pope John Paul II furthered the ecumenical efforts in 2004 when he extended a formal apology for the sack of Constantinople eight hundred years earlier (1204) during the Fourth Crusade.

That it took eight hundred years only underscores the depth of the historic resentments. All grievances between East and West were not resolved, and the declaration did not result in unification, although it did herald new possibilities of improved church relations between the Eastern Orthodox Church and the Roman Catholic Church. When John Paul II visited Romania in 1999, the Romanian Patriarch Teoctist declared, "The second millennium of Christian history began with a painful wounding of the unity of the Church; the end of this millennium has seen a real commitment to restoring Christian unity."

II. ROMAN CATHOLICISM

A. Historical Arc

Throughout its long history the Roman Catholic Church enjoyed a privileged status among European sovereigns. As the vicar of God on earth, the pope believed the church had spiritual authority over the state, but increasingly that spiritual authority mutated into political power. Especially in the Middle Ages, the pope not only claimed authority over the Catholic kings of western Europe, but actually exercised that authority—sometimes successfully, as in the humiliation of King John of England, and sometimes not, as in the case of Philip the Fair of France, whose minions kidnapped and physically abused the captive pope.

Despite the ebb and flow of papal power, for more than a millennium the papacy proved to be a powerful political force with which every monarch had to reckon.

The Enlightenment presented a challenge to the historic privileges of the Catholic Church. Instead of its traditional position of cultural power and political influence in Western society, the church came under assault. The French Revolution added insult to injury with the *Fête de la Raison* ("Festival of Reason"), when Notre Dame Cathedral in Paris was declared a Temple of Reason and a young woman was placed in the pulpit and hailed as the Goddess of Reason (on November 10, 1793). A cultural paradigm shift was under way in which reason was exalted at the expense of faith.

Napoleon Bonaparte exploited the weakening political power of the papacy by invading Italy and imprisoning Pope Pius VI, who eventually died in captivity. In the Concordat of 1801, Napoleon later reached an agreement with the papacy (Pius VII) that acknowledged the Roman Catholic Church as the majority church in France, but French clergy were required to swear an oath of allegiance to the state. For all practical purposes, the French church became a dependent of the French state.

Pope Pius IX.

Italian nationalism had been enflamed during the Napoleonic period in 1848, when revolutions began to break out across Europe. In 1860, after prolonged civil unrest, Victor Emmanuel II seized nearly all of the Papal States, including a broad swath of territory across central Italy, leaving only Rome under papal control. Then in 1870, Victor Emmanuel captured Rome itself and declared it the new capital of a unified Italy, ending papal claims to temporal power.

The traditionally Catholic monarchs failed to come to the pope's rescue, and Pius IX (1846–78) withdrew in protest into the Vatican, where he lived as a self-proclaimed "prisoner" (as did his successors) and forbade Catholics on pain of excommunication to participate in elections in the new Italian state. It was not until 1929 that a treaty was signed with the Fascist dictator Benito Mussolini, recognizing the independence and sovereignty of the Holy See and thus creating the State of the Vatican City.

The loss of the Papal States meant that Pius IX was the last pope who was also a secular ruler of the Papal States. This setback, however, did not stop Pius IX from exercising considerable influence. He centralized the ecclesial administration and, more than his predecessors, used the papal pulpit to address the bishops of the world. Although one of the most conservative popes, Pius IX is paradoxically considered the first "modern" pope because the spiritual influence of the papacy grew in importance after the 1870 fall of the Papal States. The loss of secular power actually enhanced the spiritual authority of the papacy.

Under Pius IX, the Roman Church maintained its conservative stance. In addition to his issuing the infamous *Syllabus of Errors*, his antimodern stance was clearly manifested in the First Vatican Council, which convened in 1869.

B. The First Vatican Council

The First Vatican Council (1869–70) was the first ecumenical council of the Roman Catholic Church since the Council of Trent in the mid-sixteenth century. Like Trent, Vatican I was a reactionary council that repudiated modernist ideas and tightened ecclesiastical control of Tradition and biblical scholarship. The modernist spirit, with its tendency toward anti-supernaturalism, had begun to make inroads into Catholic institutions. The modernist challenge was met with staunch resistance in the rise of Ultramontanism, which euphemistically ascribed final ecclesiastical authority "beyond the mountain"—that is, in Rome.

Ultramontanism found its fullest expression at the First Vatican Council in the affirmation of papal infallibility. To counter the advance of modernism, it was asserted that whenever the pope spoke ex cathedra as the universal pastor and teacher of the church, his teachings on faith and ethics were infallible. Pius's authority was greatly enhanced by having the longest reign in the history of the papacy, more than thirty-one and a half years.

The Ultramontanist spirit of Vatican I was underscored by a revival of Thomism. In 1878 Pope Leo XIII issued the encyclical *Aeterni Patris* ("Of the Eternal Father"), declaring Thomas Aquinas as the eternal teacher of the church. This encyclical provided a charter for Thomism as the official philosophical and theological system of the Roman Catholic Church, and it was to be normative, not only in the training of priests at seminaries, but also in the education of the laity at universities.

The twentieth-century legacy of Vatican I was one of intense opposition to modernist trends. Indeed, for much of the first half of the twentieth century, a series of popes sought to root out all vestiges of modernism, which they judged to be theological and ecclesiological heresy. On September 8, 1907, Pope Pius X issued the papal encyclical *Pascendi Dominici Gregis* ("Feeding the Lord's Flock"), which was directed specifically against modernism. For Pius, modernism was the "synthesis of all heresies." That same year he published the papal decree *Lamentabili sane exitu* ("A Lamentable Departure Indeed") directed against the French Catholic exegete Alfred Loisy, whose views were thought to endanger some of the most cherished teachings of the Catholic faith such as the inspiration and authority of Scripture, the sacraments, the nature of the church, biblical exegesis, and the divinity of Christ. Such modernist ideas were not to be tolerated by the Catholic Church.

Pius was determined to protect the traditional authority of the church. To that end, he ordered all clerics to take an oath against modernism (*Sacrorum antistitum*). The Catholic philosopher Jacques Maritain (1882–1973) was a prominent advocate of the Thomistic renaissance, which provided intellectual aid and support for the antimodern stance of the church. Pius also encouraged the formation of the *Sodalitium Pianum* ("League of Pius V"), an antimodernist network of informants. His aggressive stance against modernism forced advocates to go underground or remain silent. Any theologian who wished to pursue such lines of inquiry would face conflict with the papacy, and even excommunication.

Marian devotion has always been sacred in the Catholic Tradition, but as the nineteenth turned into the twentieth century, popes began to promote the importance of Mary with even more determination as a time-honored bulwark against modernism. Pope Pius IX decisively acted on the centuries-old debate between Dominicans and Franciscans regarding the immaculate conception of Mary, deciding in favor of the Franciscan view.

Shortly after Pius promulgated the doctrine of Immaculate Conception in 1854, new apparitions of Mary began to occur. In 1858 a fourteen-year-old peasant girl, Bernadette Soubirous, believed that at Lourdes, France, she saw and conversed with the Virgin Mary eighteen times. Then, in 1917 Mary was reported to have appeared to three shepherd children in Fátima, Portugal, over a period of several months. Both Lourdes and Fátima became holy sites for pilgrims seeking miraculous healing. For many laity especially, the Blessed Virgin Mary proved to be a safeguard against the antisupernaturalism of the modernists.

C. Persecution of Catholics

For all of its spiritual sway, the Catholic Church also became the object of significant repression in the twentieth century. In Central and South America, a succession of anti-Catholic regimes came to power. The strident atheist Plutarco Elías Calles became president of Mexico in 1924, and during his decade of rule he enacted and enforced strict anti-Catholic legislation. The so-called "Calles Laws" prohibited religious orders, denied property rights to the church, and deprived clergy of civil liberties, including their right to trial by jury and the right to vote.

Catholic opposition to Calles led to the infamous "Cristero War" from 1926 to 1929, in which 90,000 Mexicans lost their lives. The Calles persecution resulted in the death or expulsion of more than 4,000 Catholic priests. By the end of Calles's presidency, the number of Mexican priests had declined from 4,500 to only 334.

Persecution took place in other Latin American contexts. In 1954, under the regime of General Juan Perón, Argentina saw extensive destruction of churches, denunciations of clergy, and confiscation of Catholic schools as Perón attempted to extend state control over national institutions. After Fidel Castro became premier of Cuba in 1959, he reduced the church's ability to function effectively through deportations of priests, governmental recriminations against Catholics in public life, and discrimination against Catholic education. The subsequent flight of 300,000 people from the island further diminished the influence of the Catholic Church in Cuba.

Harsh persecutions of the Catholic Church also took place in Spain and the Soviet Union. In Russia, persecution of the clergy began in the Bolshevik Revolution and continued until World War II. The civil war in Spain began in 1936, during which thousands of churches were destroyed and thirteen bishops and nearly 7,000 priests were assassinated.

After the massive persecutions in Mexico, Spain, and the Soviet Union, communism emerged as a prime adversary of the Catholic Church, which is reflected in the encyclical *Divini Redemptoris* ("Divine Redeemer") issued in March 1937. In this encyclical Pope Pius XI described communism as "a system full of errors and sophisms" that subverts the social order and destroys the foundation of faith.

"[Communism is] ... a system full of errors and sophisms" (Pope Pius XI).

D. World War I

When Pius X died in August 1914, Archduke Ferdinand had already been assassinated and Austro-Hungarian armies had already invaded Serbia. Every Catholic knew that war would be the dominant issue of the new pontificate. With Europe plunging headlong into war, the College of Cardinals chose Cardinal Giacomo della Chiesa, an experienced diplomat, on September 3, 1914, to wear the papal tiara. Despite having been a cardinal only three months, della Chiesa took the name of Benedict XV amid the gunfire of Europe. His diplomatic instincts led him to remain neutral throughout the war even as the nations of the world were taking sides.

For Benedict XV, World War I was not the "Great War," but "the suicide of Europe." His first encyclical, *Ad Beatissimi Apostolorum* (known as "Appealing for Peace"), extended a sincere if futile plea to end hostilities, insisting that there are other ways to resolve political tensions. He had hoped the neutrality of the Holy See would allow him to mediate peace, but all parties rejected his initiatives. National antagonisms between the warring factions were accentuated by religious differences. German Protestants renounced papal peace initiatives as veiled support for the Allied powers, and even French Catholics were wary of Vatican motives.

Having failed with diplomatic initiatives, Pope Benedict concentrated on humanitarian efforts, such as attending to prisoners of war, exchanging wounded prisoners, and providing food to war-torn refugee populations in Europe. When the war was over and the Treaty of Versailles was in place, Benedict warned that the harsh economic conditions imposed on Germany could prompt yet another war as soon as Germany regained its military prowess. Benedict's warning proved to be prophetic.

Official portrait of Adolf Hitler on his birthday, 1938.

E. World War II

Through political acuity, deceptiveness, and cunning, Adolf Hitler and the National Socialists—the Nazis—came to power in the fragile Weimar Republic of 1933. (Nazi is a short form of the official name *Nationalsozialist*.) In January 1933 an ailing and increasingly senile President Paul von Hindenburg was manipulated into appointing Hitler chancellor of Germany.

By 1937 Pope Pius XI had learned enough about Hitler to issue, in his encyclical *Mit Brennender Sorge* ("With Burning Anxiety"), a warning to German Catholics that anti-Semitism is incompatible with Christianity. Smuggled into Germany and read from Catholic pulpits, the encyclical was the first official denunciation of Nazism made by any institutional authority. By the time Pius XI died in February 10, 1939, it was clear that war clouds were again on the

European horizon. Given the gravity of the political circumstances, the conclave quickly chose Eugenio Pacelli, who as Cardinal Secretary of State had actually drafted *Mit brennender Sorge*. By the time he took the name Pius XII, he knew his pontificate would be defined by his dealings with Hitler.

The Nazis retaliated against the encyclical with even more severe measures. In Germany they staged a series of prosecutions of Catholic clergy accused of debauchery and homosexuality. The Nazis murdered more than 2,500 monks and priests in Poland and sent another 2,500 to concentration camps such as Dachau. Although Pius maintained a policy of public neutrality during the war, mirroring the tactics of Pope Benedict XV during World War I, he nevertheless condemned the partition of Poland under the Molotov-Ribbentrop Pact in his encyclical *Summi Pontificatus* (known as "On the Unity of Human Society"), issued in October 1939.

The papal policy of neutrality garnered considerable criticism toward Pius for not condemning Nazi atrocities against the Jews. Although he received considerable political pressure from the governments of the United States and Britain as well as reports from Catholic clergy of the massacres of Jews, Pius refrained from a public reproof. Neither did he publically condemn Nazi and Soviet massacres of Catholic clergy and civilians. His diplomatic instincts persuaded him that a neutral stance was a wiser course of action in a war where the outcome was far from clear.

Critics of Pius have argued that a long tradition of anti-Semitism dominated Vatican circles, which disinclined the papacy to view the plight of the Jews with a sense of urgency and moral outrage. But others have suggested that Pius XII had very little room to maneuver while Rome was under the boot of Mussolini and then later under Nazi occupation.

Covertly, Pius did endeavor to protect Jews. Following the German occupation of northern Italy (September 1943), when deportations of Jews from Italy were imminent, nearly 500 Jews were hidden in the Vatican itself and another 4,000 were protected in Italian monasteries and convents. Similarly, in March 1944 the pope secretly instructed papal legates in Hungary to shelter Jews. Some Israeli scholars estimate that as many as 860,000 European Jews were preserved from death camps through concealment in church facilities and the issuance of counterfeit baptismal certificates. Later on, many prominent Jewish leaders, including Prime Minister of Israel Golda Meir (1969–74), praised Pope Pius for his relief efforts and opposition to racial persecution.

In addition to the Nazis, Pius had to deal with the rise of communism and its brutal repression of Christianity. The Bolshevik Revolution of 1917 dramatically undermined the Orthodox Church, but it also virtually eliminated Catholic churches in the Soviet Union during the Stalinist era. Communist regimes virtually eradicated the Roman Catholic Church in Albania, Bulgaria, and Romania. The communist takeover of China also led to persecution and near eradication of the Catholic Church in the early 1950s.

The legacy of Pius is largely bound up with World War II, but he will also be remembered for invoking ex cathedra papal infallibility to declare the Assumption of Mary as dogma of the Roman Catholic Church in his Apostolic Constitution *Munificentissimus Deus* ("The Most Bountiful God") in1950. The assumption of Mary into heaven without dying became an established teaching across the Eastern and Western churches from at least the seventh century and perhaps as early as the fourth century. But it was Pius who made it an infallible dogma of the Catholic Church.

F. The Second Vatican Council

No one could have anticipated the sea change that was about to overtake the Catholic Church when it elected the seventy-four-year-old Angelo Giuseppe Roncalli as pope on October 28, 1958. After the long pontificate of Pope Pius XII, the College of Cardinals chose a man who, it was presumed because of his advanced age, would be a short-term pope. Even Roncalli was caught off-guard by his election. He had arrived in the Vatican with a return train ticket to Venice.

As it turned out, Roncalli, who took the name Pope John XXIII, was more than his fellow cardinals bargained for. Less than three months after his papal election, he called for the twenty-first ecumenical council to meet at the Vatican in Rome—the largest church council in history.

Vatican II opened under Pope John XIII on October 11, 1962, and closed under Pope Paul VI on November 21, 1965. At least four future pontiffs took part: Cardinal Giovanni Battista Montini, later Paul VI; Bishop Albino Luciani, the future Pope John Paul I; Bishop Karol Wojtyla, who became Pope John Paul II; and Father Joseph Ratzinger, who served as a *peritus* (theological advisor to the bishops), then became Pope Benedict XVI. Notable *periti* included Hans Küng, Henri De Lubac, Yves Congar, M. C. Chenu, Jean Daniélou, Teilhard de Chardin, and Karl Rahner.

Vatican II met in four sessions from 1962 to 1965 and revolutionized the Roman Catholic Church. While it did not propagate any new dogmas or radically alter doctrine, the council "threw open the windows of the church to let the fresh breezes blow through it." Pope John

The opening of the Second Vatican Council at St. Peter's Basilica in October 1962. The council was summoned by Pope John XXIII.

described his goal as *Aggiornamento* ("bringing up to date"), which came to define a spirit of change and open-mindedness. *Aggiornamento* signified that the Roman Catholic Church had emerged from its reactionary antimodernist isolation.

When Pope John died in June 1963, Vatican II was automatically suspended according to the dictates of canon law. But his successor, Paul VI, immediately declared his intention to reconvene Vatican II and see it to completion. Paul VI expressly adopted Pope John's maxim for himself:

> We cannot forget Pope John XXIII's word *aggiornamento* which we have adopted as expressing the aim and object of our own pontificate. Besides ratifying it and confirming it as the guiding principle of the Ecumenical Council, we want to bring it to the notice of the whole Church. It should prove a stimulus to the Church to increase its ever growing vitality and its ability to take stock of itself and give careful consideration to the signs of the times.

One of the most dramatic events occurred in the final days of Vatican II. On December 7, 1965, Pope Paul and the Orthodox Patriarch of Constantinople Athenagoras issued simultaneously in Rome and Istanbul a joint declaration of regret for past actions that led up to the Great Schism between the Eastern and Western churches. The declaration did not end the schism, but it laid the groundwork for further dialogue between the two churches.

From the Second Vatican Council came other changes that reshaped the face of Catholicism: a new openness to biblical scholarship, an expansive revision of the traditional liturgy, a stronger emphasis on ecumenism, and a more engaging view of the modern world. The laity were given greater voice; the role of the bishops was given renewed prominence; lists of banned books were abolished; Catholic scholars were given freedom to publish exploratory works without prior permission from the Catholic hierarchy; and the mass could be said in the vernacular. The council did not actually abolish Latin as the liturgical language of the Roman Rite, but it did grant permission to celebrate the mass in the vernacular—a permission that was accepted worldwide.

III. ECUMENISM

One of the distinguishing features of Vatican II was its new ecumenical outlook. Before Vatican II, Roman Catholics defined ecumenism primarily in terms of persuading estranged Christians to return to the mother church and thus restore the unity they had broken. In contrast, the new ecumenism of the Second Vatican Council stressed first the need for renewal from within the Roman Church itself. Such renewal would then serve as a basis for earnest dialogue, not only to explain the church's teaching, but also to understand other viewpoints. This new perspective on ecumenism is illustrated from the decree *Unitatis Redintegratio* ("Restoration of Unity"), issued on November 21, 1964:

> There can be no ecumenism worthy of the name without a change of heart. It is from renewal of the inner life of our minds, from self-denial, and from an unstinted love that desires of unity take their rise and develop in a mature way. We should therefore pray to the Holy Spirit for the grace to be genuinely self-denying, humble, and gentle in the service of others and have an attitude of brotherly generosity towards them.... The words of St. John hold good about sins against unity: "If we say we have not sinned, we make him a liar, and his word is not in us." So we humbly beg pardon of God and of our separated brethren, just as we forgive them that trespass against us.

The *Aggiornamento* of Vatican II denoted a significant shift in outlook toward Jews, the Eastern Orthodox, and Protestants. No longer seen as heretics, they were now "separated brethren" (*fratres seiuncti*).

With World War II still a vivid memory, the council issued *Nostra Aetate* ("In Our Age"), which averred that Jews were no more responsible for the death of Christ than Christians and therefore Jews should not be regarded as accursed by God. Moreover, Hindus, Buddhists, and other such faiths are to be regarded with "sincere reverence." Although differences remain, the Catholic Church affirmed that these religions "often reflect a ray of truth." Muslims are to be regarded with esteem, since they share the Christian belief in the one Creator God and regard Jesus and Abraham as prophets. *Nostra Aetate* concluded by asserting that all are created in God's image and that it is contrary to the teaching of the church to discriminate against any person or ethnic group on the basis of color, race, or religion.

In *Lumen Gentium* ("Light of the Nations"), the true church is specifically identified with "the successor of Peter" but immediately adds, "Nevertheless, many elements of sanctification and of truth are found outside its visible confines."

A. Theological Dialogues

After the council, ecumenical efforts between leading Catholic, Protestant, and Orthodox theologians led to meaningful discussions. Emblematic of how historic differences could be resolved was the "Common Christological Declaration between the Catholic Church and the Assyrian Church of the East," signed by Pope John Paul II and Patriarch Mar Dinkha IV in November 1994.

The division between the two churches goes back to the Council of Ephesus in 431 and the dispute over whether the Virgin Mary should be referred to as the "Mother of God" or the "Mother of Christ." Although using different expressions, the Common Declaration asserts, "We both recognize the legitimacy and rightness of these expressions of the same faith and we both respect the preference of each Church in her liturgical life and piety."

Pope Paul VI set the stage for ecumenical dialogue with the Anglican Church when he referred to it as "our beloved sister Church." In 1966 Archbishop of Canterbury Michael Ramsey made an official visit to Pope Paul, who welcomed him with these words: "By entering into our house, you are entering your own house, we are happy to open our door and heart to you."

The following year, the Anglican – Roman Catholic International Commission (ARCIC) was established. Significant agreements were achieved with Anglican theologians on baptism, ministry, and the Eucharist. Despite the progress of these discussions, dialogue was strained by the developments in some provinces of the Anglican Communion concerning such matters as the ordination of women, permissive teaching on abortion, and the ordination of noncelibate gay priests. In 2003 Pope John Paul II temporarily halted the ecumenical talks when the American Episcopal Church consecrated Gene Robinson, an openly gay man, as bishop in New Hampshire.

In a controversial move in November 2009, Pope Benedict XVI announced his intention, in his letter *Anglicanorum coetibus* ("Anglican assemblies"), to create a new ecclesiastical structure called the Personal Ordinariate, designed for Anglicans who return to the Catholic Church. The plan would create quasi-diocesan structures for former Anglicans, which would allow them to retain elements of Anglican liturgy, spirituality, and religious practice, including married priests (but not married bishops).

In a dialogue lasting more than thirty years, Lutherans and Roman Catholics produced a joint declaration on the critical theological issue at the root of the Protestant Reformation. The "Joint Declaration on the Doctrine of Justification" was issued in 1999 by the Pontifical Council for Promoting Christian Unity and the Lutheran World Federation. All agreed to the fundamental notion that because justification is "by grace alone, in faith in Christ's saving work and not because of any merit on our part, we are accepted by God and receive the Holy Spirit, who renews our hearts while equipping and calling us to good works."

Admittedly, the declaration does not cover all aspects of Lutheran and Catholic teaching, nor does it solve every difficulty, but it does assert that "the remaining differences in language, theological elaboration and emphasis in the understanding of justification … are acceptable." Furthermore, the remaining differences are no longer the object of mutual condemnation.

The declaration took the unprecedented step of disavowing prior excommunications relating to the doctrine of justification as set forth by the Council of Trent and proclaimed in the Lutheran Confessions. In July 2006 the World Methodist Council, meeting in Seoul, South Korea, voted unanimously to adopt this document as well.

> Because justification is "by grace alone, in faith in Christ's saving work and not because of any merit on our part, we are accepted by God and receive the Holy Spirit, who renews our hearts equipping and call us to good works" (Joint Declaration on the Doctrine of Justification).

B. Social Thought

The Industrial Revolution of the nineteenth century raised serious concerns about the poor working and living conditions of the new urban workforce. In May 1931, Pope Pius XI issued the encyclical *Quadragesimo Anno* ("Forty Years"), which heralded a new era of Catholic social teaching.

Already in 1891, Pope Leo XIII had published the encyclical *Rerum Novarum* ("Of New Things"), which affirmed the dignity and rights of industrial workers and argued for the establishment of a living wage and the right of workers to form trade unions. But *Quadragesimo Anno* went a step further and cautioned against unrestrained capitalism and totalitarian communism as major dangers to human freedom and dignity. Pope Paul's 1967 encyclical *Populorum Progressio* ("The Development of Peoples") affirmed that the economies of the world should serve to benefit all humankind and not just the wealthy. The encyclical added that world peace is contingent on justice for all.

For all of the progress made at Vatican II, some traditional values remained unchanged. Pope Paul VI published his encyclical *Sacerdotalis Caelibatus* ("Of the Celibate Priesthood") in June 1967, which reaffirmed priestly celibacy as an ideal state that continues to be mandatory for Roman Catholic priests. In 1968 he issued the encyclical *Humanae Vitae* ("Of Human Life"), which reiterated the traditional teaching of the Catholic Church prohibiting abortion and contraception. On basic church teachings, the papacy was unwavering.

The sexual revolution of the 1960s brought challenges to the post-Vatican II church. Efforts to persuade the church hierarchy to consider the ordination of women led Pope John Paul II to respond with two documents confirming traditional church teaching. In his 1988 apostolic letter *Mulieris Dignitatem* ("On the Dignity of Women"), John Paul advocated complementarianism, stressing the equal importance and complementary role of women in the work of the church. Then in 1994, he produced another apostolic letter, *Ordinatio Sacerdotalis* ("On Ordination to the Priesthood"), reserving "priestly ordination to men alone." The letter concludes with the words, "Wherefore, in order that all doubt may be removed regarding a matter of great importance ... We declare that the Church has no authority whatsoever to confer priestly ordination on women and that this judgment is to be definitively held by all the Church's faithful."

Ordinatio Sacerdotalis was not issued as an ex cathedra statement. However, it is considered infallible under the ordinary magisterium as a doctrine that has been held consistently by the church.

C. Pope John Paul II

When Pope John Paul II died in 2005, he was probably the most widely acclaimed pope of the twentieth century—adored by a billion Catholics and deeply admired by many Protestants. He was the longest-serving pope of the century, and his almost twenty-seven years

(1978–2005) was the second-longest pontificate in the history of the church.

John Paul shattered the conventional image of the austere bureaucrat who directed the affairs of the church from his lofty perch in the Vatican. He was the first non-Italian pope since 1522 and the only Polish pope in the history of the Catholic Church. During his reign he traveled extensively, visiting over a hundred countries, more than any of his predecessors. His fluency in multiple languages endeared him to millions of Catholics all over the world.

Pope John Paul II was born Karol Jozef Wojtyla on May 18, 1920, to a devout Catholic family in the industrial town of Wadowice, Poland, near Krakow. During the German occupation he began studying for the priesthood in an underground Krakow seminary. Ordained a priest in 1946, he was sent to Rome, where he earned doctorates in theology and philosophy. His meteoric rise in the church began in 1958, when Pope Pius XII appointed the thirty-eight-year-old professor of ethics as auxiliary bishop of Krakow. Six years later he was named archbishop of Krakow and then made a cardinal in 1967 at age forty-seven.

When Pope John Paul I died after only twenty-five days in office, the College of Cardinals elected Wojtyla on its eighth ballot (October 1978) as the 263rd successor to St. Peter. He was the youngest pope in more than a century. The conclave had been divided between two particularly strong candidates: Giuseppe Siri, the Archbishop of Genoa; and Giovanni Benelli, the Archbishop of Florence. With the conclave deadlocked, they finally settled on a compromise candidate, the fifty-eight-year-old Karol Jozef Wojtyla.

As pope, John Paul II was more than willing to leverage his influence to achieve political reform. During the first year of his papacy he strategically visited Poland and energized millions of the faithful, much to the dismay of Communist Party officials. It has been widely acknowledged that his elevation to the St. Peter's chair was catalytic for the Solidarity Movement in Poland and was instrumental in bringing about the collapse of Soviet communism.

John Paul's reign was almost cut short in May 1981 when he was critically wounded by Mehmet Ali Ağca, a Turkish terrorist. The assassination attempt in St. Peter's Square failed, and John Paul's life was spared. In one of the most poignant moments of his papacy, he forgave Ali Ağca and embraced him during a prison visit in 1983. In March 2006 an Italian parliamentary commission concluded that the Soviet Union was behind the attempted assassination in retaliation for John Paul II's support of the pro-democratic Solidarity Movement in Poland.

Ecumenical engagement was a hallmark of John Paul's papacy. In 1983 he became the first pope to visit a Lutheran church, and as noted earlier, in 1999 the churches reached consensus on the doctrine of justification, the key stumbling block between Catholics and Protestants since the sixteenth-century Reformation. He also reached out to Jews with unprecedented initiatives. He called Jews "elder brothers in faith," and in 1986 he became the first pope in nearly two thousand years to enter a synagogue.

Although John Paul was a staunch opponent of militant Islam, on a trip to Damascus, Syria, in 2001 he became the first pope to visit a mosque. (Umayyad Mosque was once a Christian church dedicated to John the Baptist, who is believed to be interred there.)

John Paul not only granted forgiveness, but asked forgiveness for past wrongs committed by the Catholic Church. He made public apologies for the trial against Galileo in 1633; for the church's involvement with the African slave trade; for the silence of Catholics during the Holocaust; for the execution of Jan Hus in 1415; and for the Crusader attack on Constantinople in 1204. The pope took the unusual but highly popular decision in 2000 to join forces with Irish rock stars Bob Geldof and Bono (Paul David Hewson) in their campaign for wealthy nations to forgive the debt of poor African nations.

Despite his global popularity, John Paul's relationship with America was sometimes strained. He was a prominent critic of the U.S.-led invasion of Iraq in 2003. The pope declared his opposition by stating, "No to war! War is not always inevitable. It is always a defeat for humanity." He condemned American cultural mores such as uninhibited capitalism as well as what he saw as "the culture of death" marked by abortion, the death penalty, and euthanasia.

Moreover, John Paul was often at odds with the more progressive American Catholic Church. He consistently resisted calls to open the priesthood to women or married men, strenuously opposed homosexuality, and insisted that divorced Catholics who had remarried should be barred from the Eucharist. Although John Paul saw his pontificate as fully in accord with the *Aggiornamento* spirit of Vatican II, he retained some of the more traditional values of the Catholic Church.

The Polish-born activist pope who redefined the relationship of Catholicism to the world died April 2, 2005, at the age of eighty-four, as one of the most popular popes in history. Since his death, a number of clergy at the Vatican and Catholics all over the world have referred to the late pontiff as "John Paul the Great"—only the fourth pope in history to be so acclaimed, and the first in more than a millennium. There is no official process for declaring a pope "Great"; the title simply establishes itself through popular and continued usage. It did not go without notice that his successor, Pope Benedict XVI, referred to him

"For all the times that Muslims and Christians have offended one another, we need to seek forgiveness from the Almighty and to offer each other forgiveness" (John Paul II at the Umayyad Mosque).

as "the great Pope John Paul II" in his first address from the loggia of St. Peter's Church.

D. Roman Catholicism in America

The American Catholic Church is not governed by a single primate, but by the U.S. Conference of Catholic Bishops, each member of which is answerable directly to the pope. The Catholic Church in America has more than 70 million adherents and is the largest single religious denomination in the United States—four times the size of the largest Protestant denomination, the Southern Baptist Convention. American Catholics represent about 24 percent of the American population, which is the fourth-largest Catholic population in the world (after Brazil, Mexico, and the Philippines).

Catholicism has a long history in North America, having originated with Spanish explorers in the late fifteenth century. In the colonial period, only a small fraction of the population was Catholic, primarily in Maryland. However, in the nineteenth century the number of Catholics began to grow through immigration, and by 1850 Catholics represented the largest single religious denomination in the United States. American Catholicism continues to expand in the twenty-first century, due to the dramatic increase of the Hispanic/Latino population, which represents nearly 30 percent of all American Catholics.

In the course of the twentieth century, the face of Roman Catholicism in America changed dramatically. This was largely socioeconomic, as the children and grandchildren of Catholic immigrants began to make their own way in American culture. These immigrants generally were of two minds about becoming Americans. The Irish were among the earliest Catholic immigrants, and they sought to assimilate into mainstream America. But for the late-coming Italians, it was much more important to preserve their natal identity. Italian neighborhoods tended to maintain Old World traditions, such as parades and carnivals for saints' days.

Twentieth-century America was not always hospitable to Catholics. Anti-Catholic prejudice was present in the Ku Klux Klan's resurgence in 1915, which included Catholics along with blacks and Jews as targets of hostility. Some Protestant fundamentalists also echoed anti-Catholic sentiments. But after World War II, animosity toward Catholics began to wane somewhat. Catholics had, after all, shed their blood fighting in two world wars. Their patriotism could no longer be called into question.

By the end of the 1950s, most Catholics saw little conflict between being Catholic and American, and most Protestants had stopped thinking that way also. The most visible forms of discrimination against Catholics had all but disappeared. Grant Wacker, a historian of American religion, described this wholesale change in Catholic-Protestant relations as the single biggest social transformation in twentieth-century America.

Widespread acceptance of Catholics into mainstream America was largely accomplished in the postwar era, but two major events of the 1960s brought the trend to completion. First, in 1960 John F. Kennedy was elected president of the United States. It had been the conventional wisdom that a Catholic could not win the presidency (ever since Al Smith lost his bid for the presidency in 1928). Yet Kennedy, a youthful, vigorous, and charismatic figure, not only won the presidency but became an icon for the nation and embodied a new optimism. When Kennedy was assassinated in 1963, Protestants and Catholics joined together in their grief.

The other event of the 1960s that brought Catholics more completely into the American mainstream was the Second Vatican Council. This "updating" of the church had a decisive impact on the American Catholic Church. Not only was the mass now in English, but there was also a new attitude toward Protestants. Before Vatican II, the Catholic Church cautioned against associating too freely with non-Catholics; now the bishops called on Catholics to "build bridges" with Protestants toward common goals.

E. Evangelicals and Catholics

Evangelicals and conservative Catholics discovered each other outside abortion clinics where they were protesting. They found a shared vision of restoring traditional values lost in the turbulent 1960s. In 1994, stimulated by the evangelical leader Charles Colson and the Roman Catholic editor Richard John Neuhaus, they formed a group of theologians to explore how they might provide a common witness to the modern world on the eve of the third millennium. They called themselves Evangelicals and Catholics Together (ECT) and produced a 1994 ecumenical document signed by leading evangelical and Roman Catholic scholars in the United States. Although the signatories did not view themselves as official spokespersons for their ecclesial communities, it was part of a larger ecumenical rapprochement that had begun in the 1980s with Catholic and evangelical collaboration in parachurch organizations.

The original ECT statement was born out of the common alliance between Roman Catholics and Protestants as cobelligerents against abortion, pornography, and the general decline in moral values in

"We understand
that what we
here affirm is
in agreement
with what the
Reformation
traditions have
meant by jus-
tification by
faith alone (*sola
fide*)" (The Gift
of Salvation/
Evangelicals
and Catholics
Together).

American culture. The signatories were also mindful that Protestants and Catholics were killing each other in Northern Ireland and Latin America, and they hoped to set an ecumenical example for others to emulate. The document acknowledged that this convergence is "in large part, a result of common effort to protect human life, especially the lives of the most vulnerable among us."

Perhaps the most important aspect of ECT was the recognition that "Evangelicals and Catholics are brothers and sisters in Christ." At its core, ECT affirmed the common theological heritage of the Nicene Creed and the theology of the New Testament. The signers of the document recognized that while significant theological differences remained, that did not prevent the two communities from joining together in addressing the important issues of the day.

The signatories to the document represented some of the leading evangelicals as well as prominent conservative Catholics. The evangelicals included such luminaries as Bill Bright, Os Guinness, Richard Mouw, Mark Noll, J. I. Packer, and Pat Robertson. Roman Catholic signatories included Cardinal John O'Connor, Archbishop Francis Stafford (elevated to cardinal in 1998), and Bishops Carlos A. Sevilla and Francis George (elevated to cardinal in 1998) in addition to prominent scholars such as George Weigel, Michael Novak, Avery Dulles (elevated to cardinal in 2001), and Peter Kreeft.

The first document provoked considerable debate in the evangelical community. The controversial statement on the doctrine of justification, "The Gift of Salvation," did so as well. In this ECT statement, both evangelicals and Catholics agreed on the historic doctrine of justification. Remarkably, this agreement between evangelicals and Roman Catholics was reached (between Lutherans and Catholics) a few years before the 1999 "Joint Declaration on the Doctrine of Justification."

ECT continues to meet, even after the death of some of the signatories, to explore areas of common moral concern as well as seek to clarify theological convergences.

IV. ROMAN CATHOLIC CHALLENGES TODAY AND TOMORROW

A. Pope Benedict XVI

The successor to John Paul II was his close friend and ally Joseph Alois Ratzinger, who took the name Pope Benedict XVI. Elected at the age of seventy-eight, he became the oldest person to occupy the papal throne in 275 years and the first German in 383 years. Among his first decisions as pope was to begin the beatification process for John Paul II. Normally, five years must pass after a person's death before the beatification process can begin. However, Pope Benedict cited "exceptional circumstances" allowing that the waiting period could be waived.

Born in 1927 in Bavaria, Germany, Ratzinger had the misfortune of being drafted into Hitler's German army and was briefly a prisoner of war. After the war, he enjoyed a distinguished career as a university theologian. He taught at the universities of Bonn and Münster and in 1966 was appointed to a chair in dogmatic theology at the University of Tübingen, where he was a colleague of Hans Küng. In 1969 he returned to Bavaria and the University of Regensburg, where he founded the theological journal *Communio* with Hans Urs von Balthasar and Henri de Lubac.

During his academic career, Ratzinger was an active participant in the Second Vatican Council. He served as a *peritus* (theological consultant) to Cardinal Frings of Cologne and was viewed as a progressive reformer aligned with other theologians such as Küng and Edward Schillebeeckx.

In 1977 Ratzinger's academic career took a backseat to his role as a churchman. That year he was appointed archbishop of Munich and Freising and then cardinal shortly afterward. In 1981 he settled in Rome as the Prefect of the Congregation for the Doctrine of the Faith, one of the most important offices of the Roman Curia. At the time of his election as pope, he was also Dean of the College of Cardinals. When he was elected pope, he had served longer as a cardinal than any pope since 1724.

Like his predecessor, Benedict XVI was theologically conservative, and he consistently defended traditional Catholic doctrine and values. He maintained such traditional views as the primacy of Peter, the celibacy of the priesthood, and opposition to same-sex marriage and abortion. He argued that the "central problem of our faith today" is the "dictatorship of relativism," which must be resisted by recovering the conviction that Christianity is the religion of reason.

> From the beginning, Christianity has understood itself as the religion of the Logos, as the religion according to reason.... In this connection, the Enlightenment is of Christian origin and it is no accident that it was born precisely and exclusively in the realm of the Christian faith.... We Christians must be very careful to remain faithful to this fundamental line: to live a faith that comes from the Logos, from creative reason.

Pope Benedict sought to continue the ecumenical efforts of his predecessor, but exhibited a proclivity to create offense rather than reconciliation. When he lifted the excommunication of Bishop Richard

Williamson, who openly denied the Holocaust, it generated charges of insensitivity toward Judaism and even of anti-Semitism.

His relations with Muslims did not fare any better. In September 2006 the pope delivered a lecture at the University of Regensburg in which he quoted from a fourteenth-century Byzantine emperor (Manuel II Paleologus), saying, "Show me just what Muhammad brought that was new and there you will find things only evil and inhuman, such as his command to spread by the sword the faith he preached." Islamic politicians and religious leaders registered their protest against what they felt was a mischaracterization of Islam.

Then, during a 2007 visit to Brazil, the pope sparked controversy by stating that the early Catholic explorers in South America proclaimed the gospel to the native population and that this "did not at any point involve an alienation of the pre-Columbus cultures, nor was it the imposition of a foreign culture." Latin American leaders found Benedict's words deeply troubling.

Pope Benedict took principled stands against consumerism, terrorism, and sexual tourism and strongly defended the rights of migrants and refugees as well as advocated for nuclear disarmament. But of all the controversies, the one that threatened to leave its mark on Benedict's papacy was the global scandal of priestly sexual abuse of minors.

B. Catholicism and Sexual Abuse

Since the 1980s the Catholic Church has been plagued by a series of scandals in which priests and members of religious orders have been charged with sexually abusing minors under their care. The scandal emerged initially in the United States and Ireland, but investigations have revealed the scandal extends to various other nations. It has been described as a "global crisis."

In 2004 the U.S. Conference of Catholic Bishops commissioned the John Jay College of Criminal Justice to conduct a study of the nature and scope of the problem of child sexual abuse in the Catholic Church in the United States. The John Jay Report identified 10,667 allegations of sexual abuse of a minor against 4,392 priests between 1950 and 2002. This represented 4 percent of the total number of priests in active ministry during that time. Of the nearly 11,000 allegations, 6,700 were substantiated, 1,000 were unsubstantiated, and the remaining 3,300 allegations were not investigated because the priests involved had died by the time the allegations were made.

Accusations led to criminal charges being brought against 384 priests, of whom 252 were convicted. Victims were overwhelmingly young males: 22 percent were age 10 or younger, 51 percent were aged

11 to 14, and 27 percent were aged 15 to 17. The Irish government also commissioned a study, and in May 2009 the commission released its 2,600-page Murphy Report that found 370 allegations of sexual abuse of children by clerics. The report characterized sexual molestation as "endemic" in some church-run schools and orphanages for boys.

Although nationwide enquiries have only been conducted in the United States and Ireland, cases of clerical sexual abuse of minors have been reported and prosecuted in many countries, including Australia, New Zealand, Canada, and countries in Europe, Latin America, and Asia. A college president, an archbishop (who remained a cardinal), and some bishops were among prominent clerics who resigned because of sexual abuse revelations.

Archbishop Silvano Maria Tomasi issued a statement on behalf of the Vatican in September 2009, acknowledging the extent of the problem: "We know now that in the last 50 years somewhere between 1.5% and 5% of the Catholic clergy has been involved in sexual abuse cases."

1. *Crimen sollicitationis*

In view of the global crisis of the sexual abuse of minors by priests, it was often alleged that the church hierarchy had created a culture of secrecy and obfuscation that led bishops to place the interests of the Catholic Church ahead of the safety of children. Bernard Law's resignation as archbishop of Boston is cited as evidence. He resigned in 2002 after investigations revealed he had covered up sexual abuse committed by priests in his archdiocese. Many interpreted his continuing as a cardinal and his reassignment as archpriest of the Basilica di Santa Maria Maggiore in Rome as a reward for protecting the church.

Similarly, the Murphy Report (2009), a three-year public inquiry conducted by the Irish government into the sexual abuse scandal in Dublin, concluded that there is "no doubt that clerical child sexual abuse was covered up by the Archdiocese of Dublin and other church authorities." It further asserted that the Dublin archdiocese was preoccupied with "the maintenance of secrecy, the avoidance of scandal, the protection of the reputation of the Church, and the preservation of its assets. All other considerations, including the welfare of children and justice for victims, were subordinated to these priorities." These reports led many to believe the Catholic hierarchy has a secret code that includes protecting the reputation of the church at all costs.

Some traced this code of silence to the *Crimen sollicitationis* ("The Crime of Soliciting"), a 1962 document from the Holy Office codifying procedures to follow in cases of clerics accused of making sexual advances to penitents. The document (which had its origins in 1922) was addressed to "all Patriarchs, Archbishops, Bishops and other Local Ordinaries" and gave specific instructions on how to deal with accusations of homosexual, pedophile, or zoophile behavior by clerics. The document imposed absolute confidentiality on the internal ecclesiastical proceedings. It prescribed an oath of secrecy for all members of the tribunal. Any violation incurred a penalty of automatic excommunication.

In 2006 canon lawyer Thomas Doyle described the tight secrecy demanded for the procedure as "an explicit written policy to cover up cases of child sexual abuse by the clergy [and] to punish those who would call attention to these crimes by churchmen." The Vatican repeatedly denied that this document sanctions a conspiracy to hide sexually abusive priests or to prevent the disclosure of sexual crimes committed by clerics to secular authorities.

2. The Pope and the Scandals

Pope Benedict's early years as pope were troubled by repeated accusations that the Catholic Church covered up the sexual abuse of children by priests. Benedict himself, at that time Cardinal Ratzinger, was deemed culpable as the head of the Congregation for the Doctrine of the Faith (CDF) from 1981 to 2005, which was responsible for handling all investigations and policies surrounding sexual abuse in the Catholic Church. The scandal took a personal turn when a sexual abuse inquiry in Europe landed at the doorstep of Pope Benedict. Allegations were made that in 1980, while he was archbishop of Munich and Freising, Ratzinger permitted a priest accused of molesting boys to resume pastoral duties after receiving therapy. The same priest later committed further abuses.

Later claims alleged that while he served as the head of the CDF, Cardinal Ratzinger protected a Wisconsin priest accused of molesting two hundred deaf boys. Court documents show that in 1996 the Wisconsin archbishop alerted Cardinal Ratzinger twice in writing of accusations against the priest. The priest personally wrote to Cardinal Ratzinger, pleading that he should not be put on trial because he had already repented and now was in poor health. Although there is no evidence that Ratzinger responded, the ecclesiastical trial was discretely canceled, and instead of being disciplined, the priest was quietly moved to another diocese in northern Wisconsin, where he spent his last twenty-four years working freely with children in parishes, schools, and a juvenile detention center. He died in 1998, still a priest.

Defenders of Benedict have pointed to the case of Father Marcial Maciel Degollado, a Mexican priest and founder of the Legion of Christ, who was repeatedly accused of sexual abuse. Some suggested Cardinal Ratzinger wanted to take action against Degollado, but John Paul II and other high-ranking officials prevented him. However, after becoming pope, Benedict began proceedings against Maciel, who was found guilty of raping underage males. The pope removed Maciel from active ministry, ordering him to spend the rest of his days in prayer and penance. In 2010 the Vatican issued a statement denouncing Maciel's "immoral acts," which represent "true crimes and manifest a life without scruples or authentic religious sentiment."

In March 2010 the pope sent a pastoral letter to the Catholic Church in Ireland addressing cases of sexual abuse of minors by Catholic priests, expressing sorrow and promising changes in the way allegations of abuse are handled. The pope then promised to introduce measures that would "safeguard young people in the future" and "bring to justice" priests responsible for abuse. In April the Vatican issued guidelines on how existing church law should be implemented. The guideline dictates that "Civil law concerning reporting of crimes . . . should always be followed."

By 2009, U.S. dioceses had paid more than 2.6 billion dollars in abuse-related costs since 1950. In many instances, dioceses were forced to declare bankruptcy as a result of the settlements. Many parishioners left the church as a consequence of the scandal. Others called for an end to priestly celibacy and for the ordination of women priests. The global crisis engendered by the sex scandal has indeed impacted the Roman Catholic Church, but it remains the world's largest Christian church, with more than a billion members. The full cost of the scandal will take years to measure.

C. Pope Francis

In one of the most startling developments in the history of the papacy, eighty-five-year-old Pope Benedict XVI announced unexpectedly in February 2013 that after eight years (2005 – 13) he was retiring as pontiff because he no longer had the strength to lead the church. Benedict was the first pope to resign since Gregory XII in 1415, who was forced to resign to end the Western Schism.

On March 13 the Cardinal Protodeacon declared, *"Habemus Papam Franciscum"* ("We have a Pope who takes the name Francis"), from the central balcony of St. Peter's Basilica at the Vatican as seventy-six-year-old Jorge Mario Bergoglio of Argentina was proclaimed as Benedict's successor and the 266th pope. Bergoglio chose the papal name "Francis" in homage to St. Francis of Assisi. Francis is referred to as the "pontiff of firsts" because he is the first Jesuit pope; the first from South America, the Americas, and the Southern Hemisphere; the first to take the name of "Francis"; and most significantly, he is the first pope from outside of Europe in more than 1,200 years. (Gregory III was born in Syria.)

The election of an Argentinean pope suggests full recognition of the new Christendom, namely, that the center of Christianity has now shifted to the global South. Latin America has more Catholics than any other continent, namely, 42 percent of the world's 1.2 billion Catholics. All indications are that Latin America will retain this demographic superiority throughout the twenty-first century.

1. The Jesuit

Born in Buenos Aires, Francis was one of five children born to the Italian immigrants Mario José Bergoglio, a railway worker, and his wife, Regina María Sívori. Initially Francis prepared for a career as a chemist, but later decided on the priesthood and was ordained a Jesuit in 1969 at the age of thirty-two. Despite his late start, he enjoyed a rapid rise. By 1973 he was appointed the provincial of the Argentine Jesuits (the highest Jesuit official in Argentina, who serves directly under the superior general), a position he held for six years (1973–79). Over the course of the next decade he held several academic posts and pursued further theological study in Germany. He was appointed auxiliary bishop of Buenos Aires in 1992 and archbishop in 1998. Pope John Paul II elevated him to the College of Cardinals in 2001.

2. The Dirty War

Bergoglio's early ecclesial career coincided with the so-called "Dirty War" in Argentina, which terrorized citizens from 1976 until 1983. It is estimated that as many as 30,000 people were killed or disappeared during the country's military dictatorship. Many Argentines remain angry over the church's acknowledged failure to confront openly a regime that was kidnaping and killing thousands of people in an effort to eliminate "subversive elements." Even today, more than two-thirds of Argentines are Catholic, but fewer than 10 percent regularly attend mass.

As the provincial of Argentina's Jesuit order during the Dirty War, Bergoglio was severely criticized for not doing more to oppose the military dictatorship. Although critical of human rights violations during the dictatorship, he was accused of complicity in the 1976 torture and kidnaping of two leftist Jesuit priests: Orlando Yorio and Francisco Jalics. The two priests had taken up residence in the *favela* (slums) to advocate for the poor.

Bergoglio had initially endorsed Yorio and Jalics's work among the poor, but under pressure from the military junta he allegedly ordered them to cease their ministry. Yorio and Jaliacs refused to leave the *favela*, and shortly thereafter they were arrested on suspicion of affiliating with the leftist guerrillas. After five months of brutal torture, they were found alive, drugged, and seminaked. Yorio accused Bergoglio of in effect handing them over to the death squads by failing to support them. It was later discovered that both men were freed after Bergoglio had taken extraordinary, behind-the-scenes action and appealed directly to dictator Jorge Videl to show mercy. More than two decades later, Yorio and Jalics reconciled with Bergoglio.

3. The Theological Conservative

Bergoglio is admired for his personal humility and austerity. Even after he became Argentina's top church official in 2001, he never lived in the ornate church mansion, preferring a simple bed in a downtown building, heated by a small stove. For years, he took public transportation around the city and cooked his own meals. He is well-known for his concern for the poor and for being a theological conservative, not unlike Pope John Paul II.

Bergoglio has taken a strong stance on social issues. In 2007, as Cardinal Archbishop of Buenos Aires, he presented the *Aparecida Document*, a joint statement of the bishops of Latin America and the Caribbean, which linked participation in the mass to acceptance of church teaching against "abominable crimes" such as abortion and euthanasia:

> We should commit ourselves to "eucharistic coherence," that is, we should be conscious that people cannot receive Holy Communion and at the same time act or speak against the commandments, in particular when abortion, euthanasia, and other serious crimes against life and family are facilitated.

Bergoglio's views on these issues led to public conflict with Argentine President Cristina Fernández de Kirchner, who said the church's tone was reminiscent of "medieval times and the Inquisition."

Social and moral issues remain a central focus of Bergoglio's ministry. He publically denounced homosexuality, same-sex marriage, and gay adoption. His outspoken criticism did not prevent Argentina from becoming the first Latin American country to legalize gay marriage or stop President Fernandez from promoting free contraception and artificial insemination. On other social issues Bergoglio was more progressive. He condemned child abuse as well as the calloused disregard of the elderly. Responding to parish priests who refused to baptize infants born out of wedlock, he called them hypocrites "who separate the people of God from salvation." Although a surprise to many, the *New York Times* reported that in a 2010 address to bishops, Bergoglio recommended that the church should support civil unions for gay couples, but not gay marriage or gay adoption. Pope Francis may not be as predictable as expected.

D. The Illusive Future of Catholicism

When it comes to the papacy, one's personal history is not always a definitive predictor of future actions. No one would have predicted that Pope Benedict XVI would voluntarily retire or that Pope John XXIII would surprise everyone by calling the historic Second Vatican Council. Only time will tell if the new pontiff has any surprises in store for the faithful.

As Catholicism continues to grow, it will face new challenges. Catholicism represents more than 17 percent of the world's population and is growing, especially in the global South. Even though 43 percent of the world's Catholics now live in Latin America, there are just 21 Latin American cardinals among the 117 eligible to elect the next pope. How the church responds to this shift to the global South will be a major factor in determining the future of the Catholic Church.

FOR FURTHER STUDY

Davis, Nathaniel A. *Long Walk to Church: A Contemporary History of Russian Orthodoxy*. 2nd ed. Boulder, CO: Westview Press, 2003.

Kerr, Fergus. *Twentieth-Century Catholic Theologians*. Hoboken, NJ: Wiley-Blackwell, 2006.

McBrien, Richard P. *Catholicism*. Revised ed. New York: HarperOne, 1994.

Rausch, Thomas P., and Catherine E. Clifford. *Catholicism in the Third Millennium*. New York: Michael Glazier, 2003.

Ware, Timothy. *The Orthodox Church*. 2nd ed. New York: Penguin, 1993.

21

Contemporary American Evangelicalism

*Permutations and Progressions
(20th and 21st Centuries)*

I. PROLOGUE

American evangelicalism proved to be one of the most significant and impactful religious movements in the twentieth century. Its moniker derives from the Greek *euangelium*, which is the New Testament word for the "good news" of the Christian message of eternal salvation offered through Jesus Christ. Because the gospel message lies at the heart of the movement, it has been christened "evangelicalism."

In the broadest sense, evangelicalism has been a vital pulse in Christianity from its first-century origins. It also was deeply influenced by the theological eruptions from the sixteenth-century Protestant Reformation. The followers of Martin Luther and other Protestant Reformers identified themselves as evangelicals, even before such labels as "Lutheran" or "Reformed" came into use.

(As noted earlier, in the sixteenth century "evangelical" was simply another word for "Protestant." The first Protestants appropriated the term because they believed they had recovered the *euangelium*, which they felt had been long obscured by the medieval church.)

As a historically defined phenomenon, American evangelicalism emerges from the twin tributaries of seventeenth-century German Pietism and the eighteenth-century Methodist revivals in England. These tributaries converged in the American colonies, giving birth to the "First Great Awakening" of the 1730s and 1740s. The principal revivalists of the American awakening included the Anglican George Whitefield, the Presbyterian Gilbert Tennent, the Dutch Reformed pastor Theodore Freylinghuysen, and the Congregationalist Jonathan Edwards.

One of the distinctive emphases of all revivalists was the stress on the "new birth," that is, an identifiable conversion experience. The

"[The Second Great Awakening was] the most influential revival of Christianity in the history of the United States" (Mark Noll).

American revival was often characterized by sudden and highly emotional conversions. Hence, one of the enduring attributes of American evangelicalism has been the conversion experience.

Closely related to the eighteenth-century "Great Awakening" was the nineteenth-century revival known as the "Second Great Awakening." In the wake of the Revolutionary War, church attendance suffered a precipitous decline. According to some estimates, less than 10 percent attended church in colonial New England in the immediate aftermath of the war. But by the time the nineteenth century arrived, a new wave of religious enthusiasm engulfed the young nation from the former English colonies on the east coast to the western frontier. To underscore the significance of this second awakening, Mark Noll contends it was "the most influential revival of Christianity in the history of the United States."

In a remarkable historical parallel, the grandson of Jonathan Edwards, Timothy Dwight (1752–1817), had become the president of Yale College in 1795 and, like his grandfather, was an avid supporter of revival. By 1802 a third of all the students at Yale had undergone dramatic conversions and upon graduation took the revival call to the corners of the new nation. Lyman Beecher (1775–1863), one of Dwight's students, became particularly active in transferring the revival impulse into permanent institutions such as the American Board for Foreign Missions (1810), the American Bible Society (1816), the American Tract Society (1825), and the American Society for the Promotion of Temperance (1826). These organizations ensured that revivalist evangelicalism would endure.

In the newly settled regions on the western frontier, the revival was transmitted through highly emotional weeklong camp meetings with an assortment of preachers. In sparsely populated areas, settlers came from miles around for fellowship and worship and then returned to their villages to establish new frontier churches. One of the largest camp meetings took place in Cane Ridge, Kentucky, in August 1801, where as many as 20,000 settlers gathered in rapturous excitement to hear Presbyterian, Baptist, and Methodist preachers passionately declaring the gospel. Baptist farmer-preachers spread the revival wherever they settled.

Under the incomparable leadership of Francis Asbury (1745–1816), the Methodists grew rapidly through the efforts of itinerant circuit-riding preachers, who furthered the revival in the remote areas of the frontier. Baptists and Methodists were also active in converting large numbers of the black population, although continued racism led to the establishment of their own churches. Richard Allen (1760–1831) broke away from the Methodist Church and founded the African Methodist

Episcopal Church in 1815, the first independent black denomination in the United States. Many slaves became Christians. Soon Baptists and Methodists surpassed the Episcopalians, Congregationalists, and Presbyterians as the largest denominations.

The western revival was also instrumental in fostering what came to be known as the Restorationist movement, which was led by the disaffected Presbyterians Barton Stone (1772–1844) and Thomas Campbell (1788–1866), who sought to restore the worship of the early New Testament church. Denominations such as the Church of Christ and the Christian Church (Disciples of Christ) have their roots in this movement.

Charles Grandison Finney (1792–1875) transported the populist atmosphere of the rural camp meeting revivals to the growing urban populations of the Northeast. He employed new methods such as public testimonies and the "anxious bench," a specially designated area near the podium where Finney called people forward for prayer and encouraged them to make a decision for Christ. Such revivalism became deeply entrenched in American religious culture.

By the time of the American Civil War (1860), evangelicalism constituted the prevailing religious orientation in North America. In his 1873 address to the Evangelical Alliance, Rev. Theodore Woolsey, former president of Yale, declared "that the vast majority of the people believe in Christ and the Gospel; that Christian influences are universal; that our civilization and intellectual culture are built on that foundation."

The evangelical prevalence continued to be a major force throughout the twentieth- and twenty-first-century religious landscape, but it was often accompanied by bitter controversy. Over the last century evangelicalism has undergone a number of permutations, largely determined by historical circumstances.

Drawing from its long heritage and refined by controversy, evangelicalism acquired definitive beliefs. David Bebbington developed a "quadrilateral" for defining the doctrinal nucleus of evangelicalism, despite a great many diversities. In modern theological parlance, an "evangelical" is one who affirms several core beliefs: the authority and sufficiency of Scripture (biblicism), the uniqueness of salvation through the cross of Jesus Christ (cruci-centricism), personal conversion (conversionism), and the urgency of evangelism (activism).

These evangelical core convictions, however, have never by themselves yielded theological or ecclesiological uniformity. Yet, by the beginning of the twenty-first century, American evangelicals rivaled Roman Catholics in numbers. Perhaps even more significantly, they are by far the most religiously active of Christians. Despite different ecclesiological structures and varying theological emphases, evangelicals find a commonality on these four commitments.

While all four evangelical distinctives are vital, it is the first principle that provides the foundation for all the others. As such, the authority of Scripture has been at the center of vigorous debate. American evangelicals have tended to identify the authority of Scripture with the doctrine of the inerrancy of Scripture—the notion that the Bible contains no errors in the original writings. Because of its foundational significance, this doctrine has been at the forefront of many of the key debates of the twentieth-century evangelical movement.

American evangelicalism is a complicated and nuanced historical phenomenon, and for our purposes, we will focus attention on four primary expressions of evangelicalism in the twentieth and twenty-first centuries: Fundamentalism, Neo-Evangelicalism, Postmodern Evangelicalism, and what we have described as Post-Evangelical Evangelicalism. One might well have included a section on Pentecostalism, but this particular development is dealt with more appropriately in the chapter on global Christianity.

We now turn to the rather beguiling phenomenon called American evangelicalism.

II. FUNDAMENTALISM

The Bible has always been the authoritative sourcebook for Christians. Drawing from their Reformational heritage, evangelicals stress the authority and sufficiency of the Bible so as to distinguish themselves from Roman Catholics, who recognize a twin source of authority—Scripture and church Tradition. This deep-seated conviction, as expressed in the Latin phrase *sola scriptura* (Scripture alone), was one of the rallying cries of the sixteenth-century Reformers, who insisted the Bible alone was the only authoritative source for Christians.

A. Higher Criticism

At the twilight of the nineteenth century, evangelicals were in cultural ascendancy in America and thus generally unconcerned about higher critical developments in Europe. But as the century moved toward the dawn of the twentieth century, storm clouds appeared on the horizon.

In Germany, Friedrich Schleiermacher had inspired a dramatic theological shift within historic Christianity. The Enlightenment had rejected the ultimate authority of the Bible and the church in favor of human reason, but in the nineteenth century Schleiermacher took a subjective turn, replacing the authority of reason with the conscious self (*Gefühl*). The emphasis in biblical studies shifted from the objective biblical text to the subjective individual. "Protestant liberalism," as Schleiermacher's movement came to be called, thus laid the foundation for the emergence of higher critical views of the Bible (see chapter 15).

Other German scholars—including David Friedrich Strauss, Julius Wellhausen, and Ferdinand Christian Baur—followed in Schleiermacher's footsteps (see chaper 15 for all). Strauss denied the miracles of Jesus in his *The Life of Jesus, Critically Examined*. Wellhausen developed his famous "documentary hypothesis," arguing that the five books of the Torah are a redaction of four originally independent texts, dating from several centuries after the time of Moses, their traditional author. Based on his studies of the New Testament, Baur concluded that only the epistles to the Galatians, Corinthians, and Romans were genuinely Pauline and that the book of Acts was the creation of the second-century church.

These scholars tended to view the Bible, not as divine revelation to be approached with the eyes of faith, but as an ancient composition open to precisely the same method of critical analysis and interpretation as any other ancient literature. The effect of these developments was to call into question the abiding validity of the foundational documents of the Christian faith.

B. Infallibility and Princeton

In the face of these intellectual challenges at the turn of the twentieth century, Princeton Theological Seminary took the lead in defending the Bible as the authoritative foundation for Christianity. One of Princeton's theological luminaries, Charles Hodge, boasted, "I am not afraid to say that a new idea never originated in this Seminary." At first sight, this sounds rather like an intellectual faux pas, but it was a statement made in the throes of theological controversy and was intended to assert that Princeton remained true to its Reformation heritage, with the Bible as the theological centerpiece.

Princeton had long been a staunch upholder of the authority of the Bible. From the first professor of the seminary, Archibald Alexander (1772–1851), through Charles Hodge (1797–1878) and his son, Archibald Alexander (A. A.) Hodge (1823–86),

"I am not afraid to say that a new idea never originated in this Seminary" (Charles Hodge).

Charles Hodge.

to Benjamin Breckinridge (B. B.) Warfield (1851–1921), Princeton unequivocally affirmed the authority of the Bible. In the seminal essay on "inspiration" in the *Princeton Review* (1881), A. A. Hodge and B. B. Warfield defined inspiration as the "absolute infallibility" of Scripture. This meant that the original writings of the Bible (autographs) are free from error in all their assertions, whether touching on matters of science and history or theology and ethics.

Warfield acknowledged that the biblical writings reflected the human personalities of their human authors and their varying educational levels and writing styles, but he insisted that God protected the original authors from error. While Hodge and Warfield allowed for human creativity in the writing process, the truthfulness of the original writings was guaranteed by the Holy Spirit, whose supernatural supervision precluded any errors. Hodge and Warfield acknowledged that infallibility did not apply to the subsequent copies made down through the centuries, only to the original autographs. Warfield argued that the authors of the Westminster Confession, while not using the same terminology, held the same conviction. In subsequent refinements, "inerrancy" became the preferred term to express what Hodge and Warfield asserted.

Benjamin Breckinridge Warfield.

C. Common Sense Realism

It has been argued that the seedbed for the flowering of the doctrine of inerrancy lay with the philosophy of Scottish Common Sense Realism (CSR) and Baconian inductivism. CSR was developed by Thomas Reid (1710–96), a Scottish moral philosopher and Presbyterian minister, in order to refute the skepticism of philosopher and historian David Hume.

By "common sense" Reid meant those truths known by universal human experience — common to all humanity. The human mind is trustworthy, he argued, because God designed it to work reliably in the world he created. According to Reid, average people, responsibly using the information gathered by their senses, actually grasp the world as it really is. The self-evident truths of human experience thus provide the firm foundation upon which to build the edifice of knowledge. For many nineteenth-century Americans, the common sense truths included the basic teachings of Christianity, such as God's existence and creation of the world.

Common Sense Realism is seen by some modern interpreters as having a natural affinity with the inductive methodology of Francis Bacon. With insights from Baconian inductivism, statements in Scripture were treated as analogous to the self-evident facts in nature and knowable in exactly the same way. Thus, Charles Hodge could claim, "The Bible is to the theologian what nature is to the man of science. It is a store-house of facts."

The combination of Scottish CSR with Baconianism would have provided the Princetonians with a useful philosophical and methodological framework to defend the long-held conviction of the absolute authority of the Bible. With this framework, one could be reassured that the Bible is exactly what it purports to be—the revelation of God. Any person with common sense can see this.

Modern critics have claimed that Hodge and Warfield advocated the inerrancy of the original autographs as a theological dodge to escape mounting attacks on Scripture. By defending only the original texts of the Bible, it was argued that Hodge and Warfield had shifted the debate to the realm of the unprovable, since the original autographs no longer exist. Ernest Sandeen argued that the Princetonian stress on the autographs was an innovation that "did not exist in either Europe or America prior to its formulation in the last half of the nineteenth century."

Others have challenged both the role of Common Sense Realism in shaping their view of inerrancy as well as Sandeen's assertion that inerrancy was a Princetonian innovation. Paul Helseth, while not denying the influence of Scottish philosophy, argues that such influences were subservient to "right reason"—that is, a "biblically informed ... theological aesthetic" that presupposes the twofold role of the Holy Spirit—initially as the ultimate author of Scripture and subsequently as the interior witness persuading believers of the divine authority of Scripture.

There can be little doubt that the Princetonians were theological heirs of the Reformation, and as such they inherited a robust understanding of the authority of Scripture. Even if the terminology did not exist previously, the essential idea of inerrancy (trustworthiness and authority of Scripture) was not new to nineteenth-century Princeton. Common Sense Realism and Baconian inductive methodology were part of the intellectual context, but one cannot simply conclude that they produced Princetonian inerrancy. An authoritative and accurate Bible was a Reformational inheritance, although the Princetonians would not have been adverse to a philosophical framework that reinforced their deeply held convictions.

"The Bible is to the theologian what nature is to the man of science. It is a store-house of facts" (Charles Hodge).

D. The Modernist-Fundamentalist Controversy

At the dawn of the twentieth century, the new learning emanating from Europe had a mixed reception in America. Initially, most churches were generally conservative and generally unaffected. However, as the twentieth century unfolded, these new ideas began to take root in America's elite academic institutions. Battle lines were drawn between the new theological impulses and traditional Protestantism, between modernists and fundamentalists.

"Modernism" is a notoriously vague and loose designation for a broad variety of Protestant Christian thought that initially emerged in the mid-seventeenth-century Enlightenment and found its fullest expression at the end of the nineteenth century. Rather than a set of specific doctrines, modernism was an intellectual mind-set with a predilection for incorporating into their Christianity the new advances of philosophy, biblical scholarship, and science. Modernism reflected a new *Zeitgeist*—a new spirit of the age.

Although there were many different theological applications of this new intellectual mood, modernists shared two overarching presuppositions. First, Christianity had to be reconstituted in the light of modern insights. The new insights of higher criticism, for example, should inform the understanding of biblical authority. Second, Christianity had to be debugged of supposed cultural accoutrements that had obscured the true teaching of the Bible. The new task was to strip away the cultural husks and find the essential kernel that lay beneath the encrustations of traditional religion. Modernists, for the most part, remained in their denominations, determined to reinterpret and redefine historic Christianity in the new light of modern thought.

American fundamentalism is also difficult to define precisely. The movement is often identified with a 1910 publication called *The Fundamentals* (although the term "fundamentalism" was not coined until 1920 by the Baptist Curtis Lee Laws). In a general sense, American fundamentalism was a reactionary fusion of varying conservative, traditional Protestants who banned together for the purpose of battling the perceived evils of modernism. As time would show, these alliances were fragile and temporary. Real theological differences existed, but the various groups were able to overlook those differences initially in order to mount a united assault on modernist liberals. At the most basic level, what bound them together was a devotion to the authority of a supernaturally inspired Bible. For the vast majority, that meant affirming biblical inerrancy.

The Princeton view of inerrancy was widely adopted by fundamentalists, but not all. James Orr (1844–1913), a Scottish theologian (and one of the contributing authors to *The Fundamentals*), was unwilling to draw the circle so tightly even though he shared a deep commitment to the supernatural inspiration of the Bible, which as such requires our sincere obedience. He argued that strict inerrancy is "a most suicidal position" that had the potential for destroying the "whole edifice of belief in revealed religion."

Orr's broadside foreshadowed one of the key distinctions between British and American evangelicals well into the twenty-first century. There were other fundamentalists who shared Orr's concerns, including A. H. Strong, Curtis Lee Laws, and Robert Stuart MacArthur.

As conservatives became more aware of the impact of Protestant liberals in their denominations and the bastions of higher learning, they banded together to launch a counteroffensive. There were two main varieties of fundamentalism: (1) an intellectual fundamentalism epitomized by J. Gresham Machen and the Calvinist orthodoxy of Princeton Seminary, and (2) a populist fundamentalism represented by the dispensationalist Cyrus Ingerson Scofield and his best-selling *Scofield Reference Bible*.

There were other subcurrents that flowed into the fundamentalist stream, including the revivalism of D. L. Moody and the Holiness Movement. Billy Sunday in his own inimitable style mocked German liberal thought, proclaiming, "Turn hell upside down and on the bottom it will say 'Made in Germany.'" These were popular subcurrents that often overlapped with the dispensationalist outlook. In some cases the popular subcurrents manifested themselves among conservative Presbyterians and Baptists.

Intellectual and populist fundamentalists forged a coalition that was theologically mismatched from the outset except for certain core doctrines and their sense of alarm. Machen, for example, captured the militant tenor of this fundamentalist coalition: "Despite the liberal use of traditional phraseology, modern liberalism is not only a different religion from Christianity, but belongs to a totally different class of religions."

The Scofield
Reference Bible.

THE SCOFIELD REFERENCE BIBLE

THE

HOLY BIBLE

CONTAINING THE

OLD AND NEW TESTAMENTS

AUTHORIZED VERSION

WITH A NEW SYSTEM OF CONNECTED TOPICAL REFERENCES TO ALL THE
GREATER THEMES OF SCRIPTURE, WITH ANNOTATIONS,
REVISED MARGINAL RENDERINGS, SUMMARIES,
DEFINITIONS, AND INDEX

TO WHICH ARE ADDED

HELPS AT HARD PLACES, EXPLANATIONS OF SEEMING DISCREPANCIES,
AND A NEW SYSTEM OF PARAGRAPHS.

EDITED BY

REV. C. I. SCOFIELD, D.D.

CONSULTING EDITORS:

REV. HENRY G. WESTON, D.D., LL.D.,
President Crozer Theological Seminary.
REV. JAMES M. GRAY, D.D.,
Dean of Moody Bible Institute.
REV. WILLIAM J. ERDMAN, D.D.,
Author "The Gospel of John," etc., etc.

REV. PROF. W. G. MOOREHEAD, D.D.,
Prof. in Xenia (U. P.) Theological Seminary.
REV. ELMORE G. HARRIS, D.D.,
President Toronto Bible Institute.
ARNO C. GAEBELEIN,
Author "Harmony of Prophetic Word," etc., etc.
REV. ARTHUR T. PIERSON, D.D.,
Author, Editor, Teacher.

OXFORD UNIVERSITY PRESS
AMERICAN BRANCH
NEW YORK: 35 WEST 32D STREET
HENRY FROWDE
LONDON, TORONTO AND MELBOURNE

"We are constantly told in our day that we ought not to attack error, but simply to teach the truth. This is the method of the coward and trimmer; it was not the method of Christ" (Reuben A. Torrey).

When the enemy posed such a great threat, the more willing the conservative factions were to join forces.

Reuben A. Torrey (1856–1928) reflects the feistiness of the fundamentalists: "Christ and His immediate disciples immediately attacked and exposed and denounced error. We are constantly told in our day that we ought not to attack error but simply teach the truth. This is the method of the coward and trimmer; it was not the method of Christ."

In many respects, the modernists determined the main issues of the debate with fundamentalists. Liberal doubts about the supernatural events of the Bible dictated the basic contours of the controversy. For the fundamentalists, the Bible is a divine book and describes supernatural events surrounding the life and ministry of Jesus, who, as the incarnate God-man, is the Bible's focal point.

In 1910 a group of conservative Presbyterians, in reaction to modernist assertions, responded with a declaration of five cardinal convictions that derive first and foremost from an inerrant Bible and that generally epitomized the parameters of fundamentalist coalition. The five points were (1) the inerrancy of the autographs; (2) the virgin birth of Jesus; (3) his substitutionary atonement; (4) his bodily resurrection; and (5) the miracles of Jesus. These five convictions managed to hold together a fractious coalition of fundamentalists in their battle against the modernists.

The fundamentalists were first galvanized into a broader and more cohesive movement by a set of booklets called *The Fundamentals: A Testimony to the Truth*, published from 1910 to 1915. Two wealthy Californians, Lyman and Milton Stewart, were determined opponents of liberalism and, to that end, not only funded the publication of *The Fundamentals*, but also the wide distribution of these volumes to religious leaders all over America. A. C. Dixon, pastor of Moody Church in Chicago, served as the first editor, and he assembled a formidable array of conservative American and British scholars as well as a number of popular writers.

The Fundamentals represents the movement at its initial stages, which provided strategic momentum for coalescence into a more cohesive movement. An estimated three million copies circulated before the outbreak of World War I to combat the threat of burgeoning modernism.

E. Dispensational Premillennialism

The primary impetus for *The Fundamentals* came from advocates of dispensational premillennialism, an eschatology embraced by many of the nineteenth-century revivalists. This particular variety of premillennialism, however, is relatively recent. Its theological progenitor was

John Nelson Darby (1800–1882), who was originally a lawyer, served as a priest and curate in the Anglican Church of Ireland, and then became one of the early founders of the Plymouth Brethren.

Darby was fascinated with biblical prophecy, to which he applied a rigidly "literal" reading of the texts of Scripture, resulting in a novel form of premillennial eschatology called "Dispensational theology." As with historic premillennialism, he expected the literal return of Christ would establish a literal thousand-year kingdom on earth. Jesus himself would rule the world from Jerusalem.

The term "dispensationalism" is derived from Darby's division of Bible history into eras, or dispensations, in which God dealt with his people in distinctive ways. Such divisions were not in themselves unusual, but his distinctive division of Israel and the church into two peoples of God was unknown in the history of Christianity. The dispensation from the time of Christ to the second coming was designated the "church age," which was seen to be a "parenthesis" in the prophetic unfolding of God's plan in history.

Darby's most notable innovation to premillennialism was his concept of the "rapture" of the church. He postulated that the second coming of Christ would be in two stages. In the first stage, Christ would momentarily return to earth and rescue (or "rapture") the church before the "great tribulation"—a literal seven-year period of intense persecution. The second stage was the final return of Christ to establish his millennial kingdom, from which he would rule over the earth and dispense final judgment.

In the 1850s Darby began to make frequent trips to America, the United Kingdom, and Europe, that spread his views in conservative Christian circles. This sparked a renewed interest in biblical prophecy and emphasized the doctrine of a "secret rapture." Through the Niagara Prophetic Bible conferences, Bible schools and seminaries, and the publication of the *Scofield Reference Bible* (1909), large numbers of American Protestants, including Dwight L. Moody, became proponents of Dispensational theology.

Although deriving in significant measure from the same conservative heritage, the fundamentalist coalition of dispensationalists and Princetonians remained tentative. There is a certain irony that Machen would be known as one of the chief spokespersons for the "fundamentalist" movement, since he actually despised the designation and much of its cultural and theological outlook. "Do you suppose that I do not regret my being called by a term that I greatly dislike, a 'Fundamentalist'? Most certainly I do."

However, the modernist threat drove Princetonians into the arms of the fundamentalists even though they embraced different theological convictions. Princetonians did not accept Darby's novel eschatology, which Machen once described as "a very serious heresy," but they shared a devotion to the authority of the Bible. Reluctantly, Machen reached the conclusion that "in the presence of a great common foe, I have little time to be attacking my brethren who stand with me in defense of the Word of God. I must continue to support an unpopular cause."

As the grand publishing project of the Stewart brothers took shape, the dispensationalists exercised considerable restraint in promoting their distinctive premillennial views. Although many of the participating authors were dispensational, they played down the differences for the sake of the alliance and the greater cause. Contributors included some of the leading theological conservatives at the turn of the century: the Princeton theologian Warfield, Anglican scholar H. C. G. Moule, and the dispensationalist Scofield. If the center was to hold, the differences would have to be held in abeyance for the time being.

Modernists were wary of the new fundamentalist coalition. The Baptist minister Harry Emerson Fosdick (1878–1969) threw down the gauntlet in New York City on May 22, 1922, when he preached his famous sermon titled "Shall the Fundamentalists Win?" His message highlighted the specter of fundamentalist intolerance: "The Fundamentalists propose to drive out from the Christian churches all the consecrated souls who do not agree with their theory of inspiration. What immeasurable folly." What American Christianity needed, he proclaimed, was toleration and freedom to employ the best insights of the modern world to better understand the Bible.

Fosdick's sermon ignited an explosion of fundamentalist attacks. It was distributed to 130,000 Protestant pastors across the nation, sparking a controversy that forced pastors to take sides. Machen's book *Christianity and Liberalism*, published the following year, was seen as a rejoinder to Fosdick's warning about the threat of fundamentalism. Fosdick and Machen thus emerged as the primary symbols of the modernist-fundamentalist controversy.

Fosdick's famous sermon brought long-simmering antagonism among Protestant leaders into open conflict. Although his salvo was a sermon and not an academic address, it reflected a dispute that had taken shape in the intellectual arena a half century before. Considering the gravity of the issues raised in the sermon—the nature of authority, knowledge, religion, and the moral order—one understands why the disputes galvanized both intellectual elites and ordinary citizens into religious factions that significantly convulsed American society for a century and altered the American religious terrain.

"The Fundamentalists propose to drive out from the Christian churches all the consecrated souls who do not agree with their theory of inspiration. What immeasurable folly" (Harry Emerson Fosdick).

F. Darwinian Evolution

On the scientific front, Darwin's theory of evolution posed yet another challenge to fundamentalist Christians. Charles Darwin (1809–82) set out on the HMS *Beagle* in 1831 for what proved to be a voyage of historic significance. His observations of the varied animal life in the remote Galapagos Islands, coupled with the insight of Thomas Malthus that humans reproduce more rapidly than their food supply, led Darwin to his famous theory of evolution. First published in his *Origin of Species* (1859), Darwin put forth the theory that organic life evolved from earlier forms through a process of natural selection.

To fundamentalists, Darwinian evolution appeared to strike at the heart of the Christian faith. Traditional Christian theology taught that the human species was created by a personal God, not by an impersonal process of natural selection. For many traditional Christians, evolution meant that the supernatural was superseded by the natural. Darwin seemed to leave no place for God's redemptive purposes through Jesus Christ. God was no longer necessary to explain the world. Darwin himself died an agnostic in 1882.

Princetonians landed on both sides of the Darwinian divide. The venerable Charles Hodge characterized Darwinianism as "a blind process of unintelligible, unconscious force, which knows no end." On the other side was one of the principle advocates for biblical inerrancy, B. B. Warfield. He concluded, "I do not think that there is any general statement in the Bible or any part of the account of creation, either as given in Gen. I & II, or elsewhere alluded to, that need be opposed to evolution." Machen, who was somewhat sympathetic to theistic evolution, declined to take part in the Scopes trial.

To many traditional Christians, the new science and the new biblical criticism seemed natural allies. The modernists seemed to be saying that the teachings of the Bible, like human beings, evolved from a primitive polytheism to the more highly complex ethical monotheism of Jesus. Such evolutionary ideas must be opposed and the truth defended. If orthodox Christianity was to survive, theological bulwarks must be established and defended. This was a battle the fundamentalists lost in a Dayton, Tennessee, courtroom in 1925.

Over time, the impact of the famous "Monkey Trial" in Dayton on public opinion was significant. In 1925 Tennessee, as had other Southern states, passed legislation prohibiting the teaching of evolution in public schools. This new law was immediately challenged by a young Dayton school teacher, John Scopes, who was brought to trial in July. The American Civil Liberties Union took up Scopes's cause and provided legal counsel in the person of Clarence Darrow, one of the

"I do not think there is any general statement in the Bible or any part of the account of creation, either as given in Gen. I & II, or elsewhere alluded to, that need be opposed to evolution" (B. B. Warfield).

foremost defense lawyers of the day. On behalf of the state, William Jennings Bryan took up the prosecution.

Bryan was a devout conservative Christian and well-known public person. He ran three times unsuccessfully as the Democratic candidate for president and served as Secretary of State under President Woodrow Wilson. He had taken stances against evolution and supported Prohibition. Perhaps more than any other politician of his day, Bryan wore his Christianity on his sleeve. In 1924 he declared openly, "If my party has given me the basis of my political beliefs, my Bible has given me the foundations of [my] faith."

The Scopes trial had less to do with John Scopes than with the broader cultural clash between secularists, modernists, and fundamentalists. Bryan attempted to uphold the authority of Scripture. He also sought to protect the rights of citizens to control the subject matter of what was taught in their schools. By contrast, the Left believed the individual liberties of teachers and students needed to be preserved against state interference.

Bryan has often been portrayed as the backward "loser" in the trial, but such was apparently not the perception in 1925. Historian Edward Larson observes, "At the time, in sharp contrast with later legends about the Scopes trial, no one saw the episode as a decisive triumph for the defense [Darrow]." Bryan was a great orator, but grossly overconfident in his theological abilities. He foolishly agreed to be cross-examined by Darrow on the accuracy of the Bible. Bryan declared, "I am not afraid to get on the stand in front of him and let him do his worst." Darrow, perhaps the best trial lawyer of his day, attempted to make him look foolish and ignorant.

William Jennings Bryan.

The trial made national news in significant measure due to the syndicated columnist for the *Baltimore Sun*, H. L. Mencken (1880–1956). A self-described freethinker, Mencken relished Bryan's feeble responses to Darrow. In his newspaper accounts Mencken heaped scorn not only on Bryan, but on the whole fundamentalist movement. Mencken mockingly wrote at the time of the Scopes trial, "You can't throw an egg out of a Pullman car without hitting a fundamentalist."

Even when Bryan suddenly died immediately after the trial, Mencken was unrelenting, linking fundamentalists with the Ku Klux Klan. Bryan's brand of Christianity was made to look like backwater superstition that, if permitted to flourish, would lead to a new dark age. Mencken's overwrought caricature of

© Everett Collection Inc/Alamy

The Scopes Trial,
July 10–21, 1925, in
Dayton, Tennessee,
with John Scopes's
attorney John R. Neal
(standing center)
and the prosecuting
attorney Clarence
Darrow (seated front
right).

fundamentalism undoubtedly affected public opinion. But some others, as Larson points out, were unaffected by the "Monkey Trial."

G. Fundamentalist Fragmentation

Fosdick was forced out of his pulpit at the First Presbyterian Church in New York City in 1927, but soon emerged as a leading voice for the modernists. With money and support from John D. Rockefeller Jr., Fosdick became an even more prominent exponent from his new pulpit at Riverside Church in New York City.

Machen, on the other hand, fell out of favor with his own institution. The president of Princeton Seminary, J. Ross Stephenson, considered Machen a troublemaker, which led to a reorganization of the seminary in 1929 to ensure a broader theological perspective. Machen resigned from Princeton Seminary that same year. Having failed to preserve the conservative theological legacy of Alexander, the Hodges, and B. B. Warfield, Machen led a dissident group of faculty and students from Princeton to Philadelphia, where he founded a rival seminary— Westminster Theological Seminary. Machen took with him several Princeton faculty: Cornelius Van Til, Oswald T. Allis, and Robert Dick Wilson—as well as several students: Harold J. Ockenga, Ned Stonehouse, and Carl McIntire. Eventually, in 1936 Machen was suspended from the ministry of the Presbyterian Church in the U.S.A.

Machen countered by founding a new denomination, which later became known as the Orthodox Presbyterian Church (1936). He died in 1937, but inclement decline was already in the forecast. One sign of declining influence was the fact that fundamentalists began to turn their fury, previously reserved for the liberals, toward one another. Within a year of its founding, Machen's new denomination suffered an acrimonious split, leading to yet another new denomination (Bible Presbyterian Church) and another seminary (Faith Theological Seminary in Philadelphia).

Carl McIntire (1906–2002) had been a student at Princeton and quite devoted to Machen. But when Machen refused to embrace fundamentalist distinctives such as premillennialism and abstinence from the use of tobacco and alcohol, McIntire demurred and went his own way. Other fundamentalist divisions occurred. In 1956 disaffected faculty left Faith Seminary and became founding members of Covenant Theological Seminary in Saint Louis. In 1971 still another rancorous fracture occurred when the president of Faith Theological Seminary, Allen A. MacRae (1902–97), resigned over McIntire's alleged suppression of academic freedom and went on to establish Biblical Theological Seminary in Hatfield, Pennsylvania. The fundamentalists were nothing if not fractious—something they proved again and again over the years.

The modernist-fundamentalist controversy continued, albeit in an attenuated form. A cultural divide existed between the elite fundamentalists of Westminster Seminary and the populist/revivalist fundamentalists. The fundamentalist coalition between dispensationalists and Calvinists unraveled into subgroups, thus undermining their national influence. The tide of popular opinion had turned, and thus the theological center could not hold, with the inevitable result that the fundamentalist coalition fractured.

Fundamentalists turned inward and circled the wagons. The populist/dispensationalist fundamentalists took a distinctive Pietistic turn. Their network of fundamentalist institutions especially were intended to promote evangelism and to fend off the corrupting influences of the world—alcohol, smoking, gambling, dancing, and movies. This hardened separatism, along with its dispensationalist and anti-Darwinian stance, was elevated to an article of faith and in certain circles fostered the perception of fundamentalists as backward, reactionary, and anti-intellectual. In Niebuhr's parlance, the populist/dispensationalist fundamentalists ostensibly pitted Christ *against* culture.

A few denominations with a confessional heritage remained largely free of the modernist impulse, such as the Missouri Synod Lutherans, the Christian Reformed Church, and the Reformed Episcopal Church. Among the nonconfessional denominations, Southern Baptists retained a significant contingent of fundamentalists, as did various churches from the Anabaptist and Holiness traditions. Declarations of the death of fundamentalism, as it turned out, were premature. Like the phoenix rising out of the ashes of defeat, a new, more progressive, and culturally relevant (and eventually more powerful) version of fundamentalism emerged onto the American scene.

III. NEO-EVANGELICALISM

By midcentury a new faction within fundamentalism had grown weary of its cultural isolation. Many from the older generation of fundamentalists had passed from the scene, and younger more progressive minds emerged. This new way of thinking (or rethinking) emerged among the offspring of the elite fundamentalists, and they sought to carve out new space in the American religious landscape between fundamentalism and modernist liberalism.

The Neo-Evangelicals or "New Evangelicals," as they called themselves, retained their belief in biblical inerrancy, but were more willing to engage the culture. This new approach proved attractive not only to conservative Baptists and Presbyterians, but also to groups that had not been part of their natural constituency—Holiness Wesleyans, Dutch Calvinists, Mennonites, and Scandinavian Lutherans who began to identify with the new evangelical movement in some measure. Although there were many who played key roles, three leaders especially stand out in the new evangelical movement: a pastor, an evangelist, and a theologian—Harold J. Ockenga, Billy Graham, and Carl F. H. Henry.

A. Harold John Ockenga

Harold John Ockenga (1905–85) was the main spark for the new evangelicalism. Although raised a Methodist, he had been an early protégé of Machen's at Princeton Theological Seminary. When Machen left Princeton and established Westminster Seminary in 1929, Ockenga followed and was in the first class of graduates. But Ockenga's admiration for Machen was tempered after the latter defied the Northern Presbyterian Church and organized a competing mission board, the Independent Board Board for Presbyterian Foreign Missions (1933). Ockenga came to distrust the increasingly separatist spirit of Machen's movement.

Ockenga wanted to create a more irenic, socially engaged movement that would avoid the infighting and harsh rhetoric of the earlier modernist-fundamentalist controversy. In the 1940s Ockenga, the young pastor of the historic Park Street Church in Boston, began heralding neo-evangelicalism, a designation that was simplified later to "evangelicalism." By commandeering the evangelical label, the neo-evangelicals were asserting that they were the legitimate heirs of two centuries of evangelical movements as well as staking a claim to Reformation evangelicals. With the appropriation of this term, the new progressives were laying claim to a long historical heritage.

The new evangelicals began as a protest by several of the younger fundamentalists against the internal divisiveness, anti-intellectualism, and disregard for the social implications of Christianity that had come to characterize the older movement. The new evangelicals sought, in Ockenga's words, to manifest "a spirit of cooperation, of mutual faith, of progressive action and of ethical responsibility." The architects of neo-evangelicalism took a stand against both hardened fundamentalism and modernist liberalism. They affirmed the same cardinal doctrines of historic orthodox Christianity, but they wanted to engage their culture rather than withdraw from it. The new evangelicals focused attention on a new social responsibility, setting forth an intellectually credible apologetic, presenting bold public evangelism, establishing educational institutions promoting scholarship, and having trans-denominational cooperation with other progressives of like mind.

To that end, Ockenga, along with other new evangelicals, established the National Association of Evangelicals (NAE) to revitalize conservative Christianity, but also to provide a credible alternative to both the more liberal National Council of Churches and the separatist-fundamentalist American Council of Christian Churches.

On April 7, 1942, Ockenga addressed 150 delegates assembled at the Hotel Coronado in Saint Louis, Missouri, and thus launched the NAE: "I believe we must first of all seek unity.... A terrible indictment may be laid against fundamentalism because of its failures, division and controversies. This must be admitted by those of us who believe in the fundamentals and who also seek a new outlook." The NAE incorporated into its membership a wide variety of evangelicals, including Baptists, Methodists, Lutherans, Christian Reformed, the Salvation Army, and Pentecostals.

Ockenga seemed to have a hand in all of the early initiatives of the neo-evangelicals. He was not only the founder of the NAE, but also the first president of Fuller Theological Seminary in Pasadena, California. The idea of a new seminary first occurred to Charles Fuller, a well-known radio evangelist and host of the *Old Fashioned Revival Hour*, in 1939, but it did not come to fruition until 1947, when Fuller and Ockenga joined forces. Ockenga was named the first president (although he remained in Boston as pastor of Park Street Church).

Within a few years of its founding, Billy Graham became a member of the board. Since Graham and Fuller were the two leading evangelists of the day, their joint association with Fuller Seminary gave powerful credibility and stature to the new evangelicalism.

One of the most important achievements of the new evangelicalism was the establishment of a national magazine called *Christianity Today*. This magazine was intended to become a beacon for the new evangelicalism and indeed became the chief organ of the growing movement. It was founded in 1955 by Billy Graham, Sun Oil founder J. Howard Pew, and Graham's father-in-law, Nelson Bell, with Ockenga as chairman of the board. Carl Henry was persuaded to leave Fuller Seminary to become the first editor.

Christianity Today sought to reach a broad audience and provide an evangelical alternative to the more liberal magazine *Christian Century*. Some of the old fractiousness of fundamentalism surfaced from time to time. Still, the magazine continued to have enormous influence over the evangelical world.

B. Carl F. H. Henry

The Baptist theologian Carl F. H. Henry (1913–2003), warned in 1967 that American evangelicalism was in danger of becoming a "wilderness cult in a secular society." Neo-evangelicalism, he argued, must distance itself from the older fundamentalism if it was to survive into the future. In the aftermath of the modernist-fundamentalist controversy, the intellectual fundamentalists—who did not have the same moral qualms about smoking, alcohol, movies, and dancing, and who in their heart of hearts viewed dispensationalism as a marginal sect—turned away from the more rigid fundamentalism and gradually emerged from their cultural isolation.

Although the neo-evangelicals fervently maintained the inerrancy of the Bible, they were not cultural separatists. These neo-evangelicals were governed by a different principle. Instead of Christ *against* the culture, they embraced the notion that Christ *transforms* culture. Thus, they decided to enter the secular realm instead of retreat from it. In significant measure, this meant that the neo-evangelicals would strive for intellectual credibility. If they were to transform culture, they had to participate in it.

Carl F. H. Henry.

If Ockenga was the chief organizer of the new evangelicalism, Carl F. H. Henry was its principal theologian. As the first president of Fuller Seminary, Ockenga was instrumental in building the first faculty: Everett Harrison in New Testament, Wilbur Smith in apologetics, Harold Lindsell in missions, and Carl Henry in theology and philosophy.

There is little doubt that Ockenga especially pinned his hopes for a new evangelicalism on the shoulders of Henry, who was lured away from his teaching post at Northern Baptist Theological Seminary to become the first dean of Fuller Seminary. Shortly after Fuller opened its doors in 1947, Henry's manifesto for a new evangelicalism was published: *The Uneasy Conscience of Modern Fundamentalism.* Henry depicted American fundamentalism as having retreated from the full gospel mission. He chastised fundamentalists for failing to preach against "such social evils as aggressive warfare, racial hatred, [and] intolerance." Ockenga penned the foreword because he felt that Henry had struck exactly the right trajectory for the seminary and the new evangelicalism.

Henry's theological formation was indebted to the Reformed philosopher Gordon H. Clark, whose own brand of Calvinism placed a high value on rationality. Following the direction of his mentor, Henry concluded that "faith without reason is not worth much, and that reason is not an enemy but an ally of genuine faith." Henry's rationalistic tendency, it has been argued, somewhat undermined his Calvinism. He seemed to suggest that the rational faculties were not so affected by the Adamic fall and therefore the truths of Christianity were as open to the average non-Christian as were the truths of natural science. For Henry, intellectual respectability was best achieved through a rationally cogent Calvinism.

Fuller Seminary's intellectual orientation soon laid the groundwork for reconsideration of some of the most cherished theological commitments of evangelicalism. When Ockenga decided he could not finally leave his Boston church, the distinguished evangelical theologian Edward J. Carnell was appointed president.

Carnell was a committed neo-evangelical, but he was amenable to rethinking the cardinal doctrine of both fundamentalists and neo-evangelicals: inerrancy. He explored the earlier ideas of James Orr and James Denny, two Scottish evangelicals who concluded that the Princeton view of inerrancy was indefensible. On a personal level, Carnell never abandoned the doctrine of inerrancy, but he did seek to broaden its range of meaning, which laid the groundwork for other Fuller faculty to press the matter in future years.

The neo-evangelicals were determined not to fall back into a rigid fundamentalism. Carl Henry resisted the more militant claim that inerrancy must be the litmus test for qualification as an evangelical. When

> "Faith without reason is not worth much, and that reason is not an enemy but an ally of genuine faith" (Carl F. H. Henry).

the Evangelical Theological Society (ETS) was established in 1949 as a trans-denominational forum of evangelical scholarship, it had only one theological requirement for membership—a commitment to inerrancy: "the Bible alone and the Bible in its entirety, is the Word of God written and is therefore inerrant in the autographs."

Henry supported the inerrancy requirement for ETS membership, but he fiercely resisted the notion that denial of inerrancy necessarily disqualified one as an evangelical. He denounced what he called the "somewhat reactionary elevation of inerrancy as the superbadge of evangelical orthodoxy." He added, "I think it highly unfortunate that the primary thing that should be said about men like F. F. Bruce and G. C. Berkouwer, men who have made significant contributions to the conservative position, ... is that they are not evangelicals because of their positions at this one point." This outlook echoed the sentiments of Machen, who earlier had written in his famous work, *Christianity and Liberalism:* "There are many who believe that the Bible is right at the central point, in its account of the redeeming work of Christ, and yet believe that it contains errors. Such men are not really liberals, but Christians."

As editor of *Christianity Today*, Henry was editorially committed to inerrancy, but he refused to make it the sole determinant of evangelical authenticity.

Some of Henry's fellow neo-evangelicals took a very different tack. Harold Lindsell, Henry's former colleague at Fuller and then at *Christianity Today*, flatly denied that one could rightfully "claim the evangelical badge once he has abandoned inerrancy." A war of words ensued. Lindsell accused Henry of opening the door to liberalism. Henry criticized Lindsell for effectively elevating inerrancy above the more foundational concepts of authority and inspiration.

Although Henry held firmly to inerrancy, he frankly acknowledged that inerrancy is not explicitly taught in Scripture but is a theological deduction from the doctrine of biblical inspiration. Therefore, colleagues such as Berkouwer and Bruce, who remained unconvinced that inerrancy is a necessary implication from biblical inspiration, should not be disqualified as orthodox evangelicals. This interevangelical debate reached a fever pitch with the publication of Lindsell's book *The Battle for the Bible* (1976). Evangelicalism was again divided.

Generally, there were three neo-evangelical responses to the debate. The first was the Lindsell view requiring inerrancy as a necessary affirmation of evangelicalism. The second was the Carnell-Henry view in which one personally holds to inerrancy, but does not make it an evangelical requirement. The third was to reject the term "inerrancy" as an inadequate expression of biblical inspiration while still holding to the authority of the Bible.

"There are many who believe that the Bible is right at the central point, in its account of the redeeming work of Christ, and yet believe that it contains errors. Such men are not really liberals, but Christians" (J. Gresham Machen).

Contemporary American Evangelicalism: Permutations and Progressions

Fuller Seminary carved out this third view when it dropped its inerrancy statement in 1962. Lindsell took Fuller Seminary and other moderates to task, arguing that to abandon inerrancy was to abandon the authority of Scripture. Others took up the inerrancy torch and issued the Chicago Statement on inerrancy in 1978, but evangelicalism remains divided on this matter to the present day.

European evangelicals never really embraced the notion of inerrancy. Leading British and Continental evangelicals such as I. Howard Marshall and Herman Ridderbos fully endorse the trustworthiness and supreme authority of Scripture, but express little anxiety over the factual accuracy of the biblical text. Most European evangelicals fall into the third evangelical category, rejecting the term "inerrancy" while still holding to the supreme authority of the Bible.

Thus, inerrancy has remained principally a topic of debate for American evangelicals.

C. Billy Graham

William Franklin "Billy" Graham Jr.

LOC_LC-DIG-ppmsc-02261

The most famous face of neo-evangelicalism is the Southern evangelist William Franklin "Billy" Graham Jr. (1918–). Born on a dairy farm near Charlotte, North Carolina, Graham was raised as a Presbyterian (Associate Reformed Presbyterian Church), but after his conversion experience in 1934, he was ordained a Southern Baptist (1939). Graham was shaped by rather diverse influences. He attended Bob Jones University in Tennessee before transferring to Wheaton College, from which he graduated in 1943. Torrey Johnson, the founder of the worldwide movement Youth for Christ, and Henrietta Mears of the First Presbyterian Church of Hollywood were especially instrumental in his spiritual development.

Graham had a meteoric career. With the energy of a new convert, Graham and Charles Templeton traveled the United States and Europe as evangelists for Youth for Christ. When Templeton began to question the authority of the Bible, he and Graham parted ways. At age thirty, Graham became the youngest person ever to serve as a sitting college president, when in 1948 he was appointed to the position at Northwestern College in Minnesota (where he served until 1952).

During a series of evangelistic meetings in Los Angles in 1949, Graham was catapulted into national notoriety by journalism moguls William Randolph Hearst and Henry Luce. Both believed Graham would be helpful in promoting their conservative anticommunist views. Hearst famously sent a telegram to his newspaper editors instructing them to "puff Graham" during his 1949 Los Angeles crusade. The result of the increased media exposure caused the crusade event to run for four weeks longer than planned. Luce later also put him on the cover of *Time* magazine. With the newfound popularity, the Billy Graham Evangelistic Association was established in 1950, and Graham began holding evangelistic crusades all over the world.

Early on, Graham identified with the neo-evangelicals. Soon after the establishment of the NAE, Billy joined with Ockenga and Henry as a leader in the NAE and neo-evangelicalism. Self-consciously they disavowed fundamentalist anti-intellectualism, vitriol, and separatism from culture while still sharing many of the moral proscriptions and doctrinal essentials with their fundamentalist cousins. Although not an intellectual or a scholar, Graham played a large role in promoting the intellectual enlightenment of evangelicalism. He did nursemaid *Christianity Today* into existence out of a desire to have a serious evangelical counterpart to mainline Protestant and Catholic journals of opinion.

Graham also lent his name and influence to several of the seminaries and colleges that hoped to reestablish evangelical academic respectability. Graham was notable for his willingness to cooperate with a wide variety of non-evangelical Christians in all parts of the world. But his willingness to associate with mainline Christians and his avoidance of invective toward liberals predictably earned him the anathemas of many fundamentalists.

The New York City Crusade of 1957 stoked existing tensions, if not a sharp division between Billy Graham and many fundamentalists such as John R. Rice, Jack Wyrtzen, and Bob Jones II. Alarms sounded when Graham allowed non-evangelicals to participate in the crusade. Some brands of fundamentalism required "second-degree separation," that is to say, a Christian should separate from any Christian who is not practicing "biblical separation" from liberals and those who are sliding down the slippery slope toward liberalism. Consequently, many fundamentalists separated not only from Billy Graham, but from anyone who did not separate from the evangelist. For many fundamentalists, the principle of separation had become a new doctrinal litmus test.

Like his fellow neo-evangelicals Henry and Ockenga, Graham publicly addressed some of the pressing social issues of his day—especially racial injustice. During the apartheid era, he consistently refused to visit South Africa until the government permitted his audiences to be desegregated. Then, at his first crusade in South Africa in 1973, he openly denounced apartheid. He also opposed segregation in the southern United States during the 1960s. At one point, Graham quietly put up bail money to secure the release from jail for Dr. Martin Luther King Jr. during the height of the civil rights movement.

Graham had much the same message and beliefs as the fundamentalists, but unlike his fundamentalist forebears, he was not a separatist and refused to condemn non-evangelicals. Indeed, in a famous interview with *McCall's* magazine (January 1978) Graham was quoted as saying,

> I am far more tolerant of other kinds of Christians than I once was. My contact with Catholic, Lutheran and other leaders ... has helped me, hopefully, to move in the right direction. I've found that my beliefs are essentially the same as those of orthodox Roman Catholics, for instance. They believe in the virgin birth, and so do I. They believe in the resurrection of Jesus and the coming judgment of God, and so do I. We only differ on some matters of later church tradition.

Billy Graham has been the most visible evangelical in history, largely because of his forty-plus crusades since 1948. Over the course of his ministry, he preached to live audiences of nearly 215 million people in more than 185 countries and reached hundreds of millions more through various media. One of Graham's most notable achievements was the Lausanne Congress (1974), which produced the *Lausanne Covenant*, an ecumenical doctrinal statement considered one of the most influential documents in modern Christianity. The Lausanne movement continued with international congresses in Manila, Philippines (1989), and in Cape Town, South Africa (2010).

Because of his global ministry, Graham overshadowed Ockenga and Henry to become the public visage of American evangelicalism. In the view of Mark Noll: "Through his cooperation with Ockenga, Henry and like-minded leaders, Graham provided the evangelical equivalent of an imprimatur for serious intellectual labor. More than any other public figure, Graham protected evangelical scholars from the anti-intellectualism endemic to the movement."

IV. POSTMODERN EVANGELICALISM

A. A Cultural Paradigm Shift

As the third millennium dawned, there was a broad consensus that the Western world was in the throes of a cultural paradigm shift from the modern to the postmodern era. The first notable hints of this cultural shift surfaced in the wake of the Vietnam War and the emergence of social and political discontent with traditional values. Although the term "postmodern" was first employed to describe a new style of architecture, it soon found currency in intellectual circles as the descriptor for a broader cultural phenomenon.

Amid much scholarly disagreement on its definition, there is a consensus on one point: this cultural phenomenon is marked by a rejection of a universal worldview. At its core, the postmodern mind-set is dubious of a unified, all-encompassing, and rationally valid explanation for truth. This is what philosopher Jean-François Lyotard (1924–98) meant when he spoke of "incredulity toward metanarrative." Leading theorists Jacques Derrida (1930–2004), Michel Foucault (1926–84), and Richard Rorty (1931–2007) reflect what has come to be the central dictum of postmodern philosophy: abandonment of the quest for a unified worldview (metanarrative). The postmodern world has no center, only differing perspectives.

Postmodern Christians have been willing, unlike many traditional evangelicals, to engage postmodernity to determine if they might legitimately appropriate some insights. There has been a particular interest in the work of post-liberal thinkers such as Hans Frei, George Lindbeck, and Stanley Hauerwas. The contributions of Lesslie Newbigin and Alasdair MacIntyre have also been of considerable importance.

The more controversial work of the leading secular postmodernists, while studied, hold little allure for postmodern evangelicals, because they cannot follow the secular postmodernists in denying ultimate truth. Most of these Christians affirm the central tenets of the faith, yet they are rather dubious of the accepted interpretations of truth handed down by the traditional church. For example, the historical fact that many eighteenth-century American evangelicals believed that the Bible sanctioned the owning of African slaves has created a deep-seated realization of the impossibility of fully getting outside one's own cultural milieu.

The postmodern Christians are cautious of socially constructed statements about God and faith. They deny neither ultimate truth nor the identification of truth with Jesus, nor even that the Bible is truth. However, they are wary of the assumption that divine truth can be captured in finite propositional systems. With this "chastened epistemology" they stress that the gospel is not just to be intellectually affirmed, but embodied. Broadly, these postmodern Christians believe that secular postmodernists have rightly identified the questions, even if they have not provided the right answers.

The new cultural paradigm of postmodernism means that many of these evangelicals no longer are willing to think in terms of the modernist-fundamentalist controversy or give it a controlling function in their theological outlook. They reject both modernism and fundamentalism, arguing that both derive from the same rationalist assumptions. They are cautious but willing to brave the new world of postmodernism—which they see as an unplowed field that needs to be cultivated by evangelicals. Postmodern evangelicals thus display quite different attitudes toward what were unassailable values of traditional American evangelicals.

B. Post-Conservative Politics

The term "post-conservative evangelical" was first coined by Baptist theologian Roger E. Olson in 1995 to describe what he saw as a new mood emerging among some evangelical theologians. Olson was careful not to describe it as a formal movement with a unified message. Rather, it was a loose affiliation of disaffected evangelicals who were alarmed at perceiving a shift back toward the fundamentalism of the early twentieth century.

Most of these post-conservatives view themselves as evangelical both sociologically and theologically, and they have no intention of discarding that moniker. They self-consciously embrace the four standard hallmarks of evangelicalism of the Bebbington quadrilateral: biblicism, conversionism, cruci-centricism, and evangelism. At a core level, post-conservative evangelicals believe that modern American evangelicalism has been conscripted by leaders who are really fundamentalists in evangelical garb, offering oversimplified answers to complex questions and exhibiting a proclivity to defend the political status quo.

Post-conservative evangelicals became increasingly disenchanted with the social and political direction of mainstream evangelicalism. Since the 1970s, American evangelicalism was often aligned with right-wing politics. One of the original sponsors of this political resurgence was the fundamentalist Baptist preacher Jerry Falwell, who garnered media attention when he formed the Moral Majority in 1979 to galvanize conservative Christians in support of Ronald Reagan's 1980 bid for the U.S. presidency.

Equally important was the conservative religious broadcaster Pat Robertson, who actually made a run for the presidency in 1988 and then used his campaign machinery to create a voter mobilization effort called the Christian Coalition. Robertson and his colleague Ralph Reed wielded sizable political influence among Christians by distributing voter guides and urging support for right-wing political candidates. Having entered the public sphere, conservative Christians came to be closely identified with certain political issues: pro-business economic policies, advocacy for a strong military, small central government, but especially opposition to social issues such as abortion and homosexuality.

As the twentieth century became the twenty-first century, growing doubts about right-wing politics began to erode the confidence of many younger evangelicals. In the wake of these developments, a new, more politically progressive evangelicalism began to emerge that was skeptical of the television preachers as well as the political right wing. The older evangelical alliance that coalesced around the single issue of abortion was no longer intact. When Pat Robertson endorsed a presidential candidate (Mayor Rudy Giuliani) in 2007, a longtime supporter of abortion rights, it was clear the old rules no longer were in play. Conservative evangelicals remain, but single issues no longer automatically command the evangelical vote. By 2008 a surprising number of evangelicals voted for the successful Democratic candidate Barack Obama.

C. Social Justice and the Gospel

The twenty-first century is also witnessing a growing concern among younger evangelicals for social justice. One of the most interesting developments is the influence of Irish rock star Bono (Paul David Hewson), who led a successful global effort to reduce Third World debt and to provide large-scale economic solutions for the poorer African nations. Somewhat surprising is the fact that Bono's humanitarian efforts are grounded in his Christian faith. There have long been progressive evangelical leaders, such as Jim Wallis and Ron Sider, who advocate on social issues such as care for the poor, women's rights, sex trafficking, immigration, HIV/AIDS, and opposition to the death penalty, but none has had a higher profile or influence than Bono.

Christian postmoderns have taken a particular interest in human rights abuse. For example, the International Justice Mission (IJM) is a faith-based organization that operates in countries all over the world to combat sexual exploitation of children, slavery, illegal detention, police brutality, and illegal land-seizure. Many other Christian organizations and individual churches have taken up advocacy for the poor and marginalized all over the globe, and they do so without regard to religious affiliation.

Critics fear that the concern for social justice is a revival of the early twentieth-century Social Gospel Movement of Walter Rauschenbusch, but for the most part such criticism has fallen on deaf ears. Far from embracing the Protestant liberalism of Rauschenbusch, postmodern evangelicals see themselves as actively living out the gospel, perhaps with more consistency than their forebears. Abandoning the left-right dichotomy, they believe Jesus exemplifies a generous orthodoxy joined with a generous orthopraxis.

D. Evolving Ecclesiology

Postmodern evangelicals do not see themselves as a conventional church movement or even a theological tradition in the strict sense, but instead prefer to view themselves as a loose network of conversation partners who want to explore afresh the nature and meaning of the Christian faith in the postmodern world. A central commitment is to engage in these dynamic conversations with complete freedom and honesty. While not necessarily antichurch, emerging evangelicals are prepared and perhaps even predisposed to reimagine the nature of the church.

The common descriptor of this loose affiliation of evangelicals is the emerging church movement. "Emerging churches" refers to the broader movement within evangelicalism. In their book *Emerging Churches: Creating Christian Community in Postmodern Cultures*, Eddie Gibbs and Ryan Bolger define emerging churches simply as "communities that practice the way of Jesus within postmodern cultures."

One of the distinctive expressions of the emerging church movement is the Emergent Village, which is an online clearinghouse dedicated to fostering communities and facilitating conversations about what it means to be a Christian in a postmodern world. The Emergent Village consists of cohorts from all over the world who are connected via the Internet. Annual events, blogs, podcasts, and publishing ventures comprise its main activities. At its core, the Emergent Village conceives itself as a social network that is characterized as a "growing, generative friendship." While there is no official spokesperson for the emerging church or the Emergent Village, leaders such as Tony Jones and Brian McLaren are viewed as representative voices.

These emerging communities are often independent house churches without any denominational affiliation and no doctrinal statement beyond the early Christian creedal statements such as the Apostles' Creed. They tend to look to the early church as a model and stress such fundamental Christian notions as ministry to others, imitation of Christ, and fellowship. There are no definitive indicators as to how large this movement is, but pollster George Barna estimated there may be as many as five million people who fall into this category.

There are many diverse motivations, but in general one may observe that most are frustrated with the traditional church and its guiding presuppositions; most manifest a heightened awareness of social justice; most display a more tolerant attitude toward non-Christians; and most embrace a missional perspective.

E. The Church as Mission

In the past half century there has been a subtle but nevertheless decisive shift in the understanding of Christian missions. In prior centuries "mission" was understood primarily in soteriological terms: as saving individuals from eternal damnation. However, much of contemporary missiology now understands missions as being derived from the very nature of God and thus is grounded in the doctrine of the Trinity rather than soteriology.

The classical doctrine of the *missio Dei* (mission of God) viewed God the Father as sending the Son, and God the Father together with the Son sending the Spirit. The new insight understood a third movement, in which the Father, Son, and Holy Spirit send the church into the world. Mission is therefore seen as a movement from God to the world, and the church is viewed as the instrument for that mission.

Younger postmodern Christians have closely identified with the new missional outlook and have worked out a different way of doing missions. Instead of viewing this as something missionaries do in underdeveloped countries around the world (although they do not preclude this), they stress that the church is "missional" by its very nature and every follower of Christ is a missionary. The missional church does not exist merely for its own members and is not seen as an institution to which outsiders must come in order to receive the gospel. Rather, the missional church shifts responsibility to the individual to participate in God's ongoing mission to the world.

In a postmodern culture, emergents tend to replace traditional propositional evangelism and proclamation with an embodied gospel and a more conversational approach to evangelism. Emergents do mission by faithfully living out the gospel in their postmodern cultural context.

For the postmodern evangelicals, the church does not *do* mission, but rather, the church *is* the mission. Indeed, mission is conceived as the true and authentic organizing principle of the church. Thus, one is missional by participating with God in the redemptive work God is doing in this world. Although there are varying nuances and connotations, there is a basic agreement among postmodern evangelicals about a missional view of the church. Because this missional outlook has rapidly entered the lexicon of the emerging church movement, it has enabled adherents to recognize each other across denominational lines.

Postmodern evangelicals have a special affection for the British missionary Lesslie Newbigin (1909–98). He served as a missionary in India, where he contextualized worship, discipleship, community, and service in order to engage effectively with the non-Christian society surrounding him. Returning to England after thirty years in India, he realized that the Western church was itself existing in a post-Christian society, but had failed to adapt to its new circumstance. So Newbigin became an advocate for the missional principle that the non-Christian, if he is to be reached, must be reached within his own culture.

This missional principle finds its origin, according to Newbigin, in the incarnation of Christ, who took on the form of a human being. As missionaries sent by Jesus, every Christian must incarnate themselves into their particular culture and thereby learn to exegete their surrounding culture, understanding the language, values, and ideas of the culture. With these insights, they may then take steps to reach people with the gospel message in the context of the surrounding culture.

F. The Role of Women in the Church

For all of the changes that have occurred in the postmodern evangelical church, there remain significant pockets of cultural traditionalism. This is nowhere more evident than in gender relations. One of the defining cultural features of twentieth-century America was the enhanced status of women in society. By the 1960s, the women's movement was changing the cultural dynamic of America. At the turn of the twenty-first century, women make up a majority of students in law schools, MBA programs, and medical schools. Women are heads of corporations and universities, and a woman was a serious candidate for president in 2008.

However, the advances of women in American society did not necessarily carry over into the church. Although mainline denominations have female clergy, they tend not to become senior ministers. In many evangelical churches and denominations it is a matter of theological conviction that women should be limited to traditional roles—women's ministries, hospitality, and the children's ministries.

The 1974 landmark book *All We're Meant to Be* by Letha Scanzoni and Nancy Hardesty sparked a gender debate among evangelicals that continues to this day. A group of evangelical leaders met together in 1987 and established Christians for Biblical Equality (CBE, which officially began in January 1988) in advocacy of Christian egalitarianism in the home and church. In direct reaction to Christian egalitarianism, theology professor Wayne Grudem and Baptist pastor John Piper established the Council for Biblical Manhood and Womanhood (CBMW) in 1987. Thus, by the late 1980s two ideologically opposed organizations were vying for the right to define the role of women in American evangelicalism.

The dispute was often openly hostile. For the complementarians (CBMW), the differences were seen as a battle for orthodoxy, arguing that egalitarianism is a wolf in sheep's clothing that ultimately undermines the authority of the Bible. Evangelical egalitarians did not remain passive; they mounted a vigorous challenge to the exegesis and theology of the complementarians. More recently, egalitarians even have charged the complementarians with verging toward heresy by advocating the eternal subordination of the Son in the Trinity.

As gender debates raged in the evangelical world, economic realities intruded into traditional household structures. The conventional paradigm of husband as breadwinner and wife has homemaker has been replaced by dual-income households. Inevitably, this cultural shift has impacted the evangelical subculture. The mere fact that the majority of evangelical women are now employed (approximately 56 percent), has led to what sociologist Sally Gallager calls "pragmatic egalitarianism." Dual-income families require that the husband and wife function more as partners in the household.

Although most evangelicals still affirm some version of male headship, it has been reconstituted as "servant leadership." Most evangelicals still are more likely to believe that the husband should in some sense be the spiritual leader in the home, but there is a growing consensus that marriage is a partnership of equals. A growing body of research suggests that the actual practice of most evangelical families is generally egalitarian—in parenting, decision making, and valuing family over career. This blending of the ideals of mutuality and hierarchy within marriage has become the evangelical norm by economic necessity.

Younger postmodern evangelicals have grown up with pragmatic egalitarianism in the home while living in a broader egalitarian culture. The contradictions have led to a measure of confusion for some, but many younger evangelicals incline toward egalitarianism in principle even if somewhat ill-defined.

G. The Decline of Denominationalism

America remains a generally religious nation, yet recent indicators suggest that the Christian church is eroding in numbers and influence. There has been significant loss of its capacity to shape culture the way it did just a few decades ago. Religion continues to be a powerful presence, but it is not the presence that once was. In the heyday of Rev. Jerry Falwell's Moral Majority (1980s), evangelicals were thought to constitute a third or more of the population, but recent research finds that evangelicals now account for just 7 perecent of Americans.

As a consequence, some scholars are now speaking of the "crisis" in the evangelical church while others are anticipating the "end of evangelicalism." The *Christian Science Monitor* published a controversial essay on "The Coming Evangelical Collapse." Even the most stalwart of conservative culture watchers, such as Al Mohler, president of Southern Baptist Seminary, have concluded:

> The most basic contours of American culture have been radically altered. The so-called Judeo-Christian consensus of the last millennium has given way to a post-modern, post-Christian, post-Western cultural crisis which threatens the very heart of our culture.

There is a new reality in the American church. Most notable is the widespread decline in church attendance. More accurate research methods reveal that regular church attendance actually hovers at around 20 percent, much less than previously thought. Sociologists refer to the "halo effect" that has led to exaggerated church attendance and a distorted perception of religious involvement.

This new reality has two obvious corollaries. First, Protestant denominations themselves are in decline. It has been well documented that mainline denominations (such as American Baptist Church USA, Christian Church/Disciples of Christ, Episcopal Church, Evangelical Lutheran Church, Presbyterian Church USA, Reformed Church in America, United Church of Christ, and United Methodist Church) have experienced a significant and sustained decline over the last fifty years.

During the same period, evangelical denominations (such as Southern Baptist, Assemblies of God, Lutheran Church–Missouri Synod) often enjoyed dramatic growth. However, that trend has reversed, and now evangelical denominations are beginning to show signs of decline. While the American population grows by roughly two million a year, attendance in evangelical churches has gradually declined, according to surveys of more than 200,000 congregations by the American Church Research Project.

Denominational loyalties are also fading. The Pew Religious Landscape survey concludes that 44 percent of adults have changed their religious affiliation (including transferring to another denomination, moving from "unaffiliated" to a church affiliation, or severing all church connection). In the culture of twenty-first-century America, Presbyterians and Methodists can easily move from one denomination to the other as though the theological tensions between Arminianism and Calvinism are of no consequence.

As loyalties dissipate, there is a corresponding lessening of the Christian denominational identity. Even in denominational churches, denominational affiliation is often downplayed. There is little to indicate that one of the flagship evangelical churches in America, Rick Warren's Saddleback Church, belongs to the Southern Baptist Convention.

Why the decline in evangelical churches in America? The answer to this question is multilayered and complex. Certainly, the scandals of fallen evangelical leaders, the worship wars, and theological fistfights among insiders (over such matters as justification, open theism, homosexuality, and the role of women in the church) have contributed to the growing disaffection with traditional expressions of evangelicalism, especially among the younger generation.

In his book *unChristian: What a New Generation Thinks about Christianity ... and Why It Matters*, David Kinnaman, president of the evangelical Barna Group, concludes that "Modern-day Christianity no longer seems Christian." His research found that the prevailing perception of Christians by outsiders is that they are hypocritical, too focused on getting converts, antihomosexual, out of touch, too political, and overly judgmental. The most startling conclusion in Kinnaman's research was that many of the under-thirty Christians actually share the same perception of American Christianity as the outsiders: 80 percent of churchgoers perceived the Christian church as antihomosexual; 52 percent judgmental; 50 percent too involved in politics; and 47 percent hypocritical. Even Al Mohler has decried what he called the "worst fault of evangelicals," namely, that they "invested far too much hope in a political solution to what are transpolitical issues and problems."

Such perceptions, by both insiders and outsiders, have contributed to noticeable decline in evangelical churches, especially among younger Christians. As a consequence, a growing number of younger evangelicals are abandoning local churches and instead are gathering informally in alternative faith communities for fellowship in places like Starbucks.

There is also a cultural factor at play in the decline of evangelical churches. Postmodernism has engendered a spirit of mistrust toward traditional ecclesial authorities and theological certainties. Mark Chaves has collated the trends of two ongoing national surveys (General Social Survey and the Gallup Poll) and identified "an unambiguous decline since the 1970s in belief in an inerrant Bible."

Postmodernism is itself a complex phenomenon that is difficult to define, but there is a general consensus that it entails, at the very least, a heightened sense of uncertainty, even about the Bible itself. This postmodern epistemic shift—joined with the public scandals, infighting, and suspicion of social justice—has loosened affinity and affection with traditional denominations.

> "[The] worst fault of evangelicals [is that they] invested far too much hope in a political solution to what were transpolitical issues and problems" (Al Moehler).

H. Ethnic Minorities

The global South has come to North America. Immigrant churches from Latin American, Africa, and Asia are making significant inroads into American evangelicalism. One of the postmodern realities is the growth of ethnic minorities.

1. African Americans

Most African Americans are the direct descendants of captive Africans from sub-Saharan Africa, although some are descendents of immigrants from African, Caribbean, Central American, or South American countries. African Americans make up the second largest racial minority in the United States, with 13.5 percent of the total population. Demographic analysis projects only a slight increase to 15 percent of the population by 2050.

Currently, more than half of the African-American population is part of historically black Protestant denominations, the largest of which is Baptist (the largest being the National Baptist Convention and the National Baptist Convention of America). The second-largest African-American denomination is Methodist (the largest being the African Methodist Episcopal Church and the African Methodist Episcopal Zion Church). Approximately 16 percent of African-American Christians attend predominantly white Protestant churches. A small percentage of African Americans (5 percent) attend Roman Catholic churches.

One notable development during the course of the twentieth century is the number of African Americans attracted to Islam. Historically, perhaps as many as a quarter of the African slaves brought to the Americas were Muslims, but most were converted to Christianity. A new distinctively American form of Islam emerged in 1930 when Wallace Fard Muhammad founded the Nation of Islam and asserted that blacks are a superior race and that whites are "devils." It was his successor, Elijah Muhammad, who attracted significant numbers of African Americans to this distinct version of Islam, largely through the influence of converts such as black nationalist Malcolm X (born Malcolm Little, also known as El-Hajj Malik El-Shabazz) and world boxing champion Muhammad Ali (born Cassius Marcellus Clay).

Due to a falling out with Elijah Muhammad, Malcolm X made a pilgrimage to Mecca and returned to establish the first mainstream (Sunni) Islamic movement among African Americans. He was murdered in 1965 by members of the Nation of Islam.

After the death of Elijah Muhammad in 1975, his son and successor, Warith Deen Muhammad, abandoned the black separatist views of his father and forged ties with Sunni Muslims. However, among those who resisted these changes was Louis Farrakhan, who revived the Nation of Islam in 1978 and returned it to its original teachings. African-American Muslims constitute 20 percent of the total U.S. Muslim population, the majority of whom are Sunni Muslims.

Dr. Martin Luther King Jr. remains a towering figure from the civil rights movement and perhaps the most influential African American in history. His tragic assassination in April 1968 in Memphis, Tennessee, sparked race riots in 125 cities. Although the civil rights movement continued to make significant cultural and legal advances, racial tensions have persisted.

For the most part, American evangelicals have been indifferent or even hostile toward Dr. King and the civil rights movement, thus creating an uneasy relationship between black and white American Christians, despite many of the same theological convictions and social values. The late Spencer Perkins, son of the civil rights leader John Perkins, has observed that many African-American leaders have grown weary of the reconciliation rhetoric of white evangelicals that focuses on personal piety without any biblical conception of racial justice.

Dr. King's famous statement that Sunday is "the most segregated day of the week" remains true for millions of African Americans, Hispanics, Asians, and other ethnic minorities. For all of its vaunted stress on evangelism, ethnic segregation remains the norm in American evangelical churches. Many evangelicals have called for racial reconciliation, and indeed, there have been successful efforts to establish multicultural congregations, but more often than not, ethnic minorities remain segregated from white evangelicals. One of the pressing challenges facing the contemporary evangelical church is that among Christian ethnic minorities there is a heightened concern that "racial reconciliation" amounts to assimilation to the dominant white culture and thus loss of cultural identity.

2. Latinos

Of the three main ethnic minorities, Hispanics/Latinos are the largest and fastest-growing ethnic minority in the United States and constitute 15.4 percent of the total population. By 2050, Hispanics are projected to be 30 percent of the total U.S. population. Historically, the large majority of Hispanics (68 percent according to Pew Research Center) has identified with Catholicism, but that has changed significantly in recent decades with the growing influence of Pentecostalism. Approximately 15 percent of Hispanics have left the Catholic Church for evangelical/Pentecostal churches. Catholics call these Hispanic evangelicals *hermanos separados* — separated brothers. Moreover, Pentecostalism is not only bringing Hispanics to evangelical Protestantism but is making inroads within Catholicism itself. Among Roman Catholics, about 20 percent are Pentecostal/Charismatic.

The terms *Hispanic* and *Latino* tend to be used interchangeably in the United States for people with origins in Spanish-speaking countries and include persons of Mexican, Puerto Rican, Cuban, Dominican, Central American, or South American origin. As Hispanic/Latino Americans have reminded us, they have been in North America for centuries, long before the English-speaking culture became dominant. Hispanic peoples have lived in the regions of California, Texas, Colorado, New Mexico, Arizona, Nevada, and Florida since the sixteenth century. In parts of Texas, Arizona, and New Mexico there are Hispanic communities (*Hispanidad*) that have continuously been the majority population since they were settled in the sixteenth and seventeenth centuries.

Many Hispanic evangelicals find common cause with white evangelicals because of shared social views. Like most white evangelicals, Hispanics tend to oppose gay marriage and believe abortion should be illegal. However, the matter of immigration threatens this coalition. According to a 2006 study by the Pew Research Center, nearly two-thirds of white evangelicals thought immigrants posed a threat to traditional American society and are a burden on the economy. However, nearly 60 percent of Hispanic evangelicals believe immigrants strengthen American society. Many white evangelicals see immigration as a law-and-order issue, but for Hispanics, immigration is a family values issue.

One of the most high-profile evangelical Hispanic leaders working on the immigration issue is Rev. Samuel Rodriguez, founder and leader of the National Hispanic Christian Leadership Conference (NHCLC). Rodriguez states bluntly that "Immigration puts us at odds with our white evangelical brothers." Because immigration has become a major political issue dividing the growing Hispanic evangelical community and the white mainstream evangelicals, future alliances are difficult to assess.

"Immigration puts us [Hispanics] at odds with our white evangelical brothers" (Samuel Rodriguez).

3. Asians

Asian Americans make up the third-largest minority group in the United States and are often considered the "model minority" because their culture encourages a strong work ethic, a respect for elders, professional and academic success, and a high valuation of family, education, and religion. Research indicates that Asian Americans have the lowest poverty rate and the highest educational attainment levels of any racial demographic in the United States.

Current estimates indicate that about 14.9 million people report themselves as having Asian heritage, which is around 5 percent of the U.S. population. The largest Asian subgroups are Chinese (3.53 million), Filipinos (3.05 million), Indians (2.77 million), Vietnamese (1.64 million), Koreans (1.56 million), and Japanese (1.22 million). The Asian-American population is heavily urbanized, with nearly three-quarters of Asian Americans living in large metropolitan areas.

Asian Americans are often portrayed as an elite group of successful, well-educated, intelligent, and prosperous people. However, postmodern Asian evangelicals resist the stereotype and challenge some of the core values of American evangelicalism.

Soong-Chan Rah, a Korean-American professor at North Park Seminary in Chicago, contends that ethnic churches and their leaders are often invisible to the white evangelical community. According to Rah, ethnic minorities, many of them immigrants from majority world countries, are often overlooked in the count of congregations and in leadership conferences. He protests that "while the demographics of Christianity are changing both globally and locally, the leadership of American evangelicalism continues to be dominated by white Americans." Indeed, Rah contends that there is a "western, white cultural captivity of the church" in the United States, a captivity he argues must change.

V. POST-EVANGELICAL EVANGELICALS

As the twenty-first century gains momentum, a growing segment of postmodern evangelicals have become deeply disenchanted with their own heritage. Repeated moral failures of prominent evangelical leaders, partisan political views, consumerism, restrictive interpretations of the Bible, misogyny, cultural insensitivity, and antihomosexual rhetoric have led some disheartened evangelicals to abandon the label entirely. The designation "post-evangelical" does not refer to any particular entity; it is more of a sensibility or mood. Many of the disenchanted believe American evangelicalism has in fact departed from the teachings of Jesus, so they have withdrawn, either formally or in spirit, from the evangelical mainstream.

Post-evangelicals resonate with historian Mark Noll's observation that "... much of what is *distinctive* about American Evangelicalism is not *essential* to Christianity." It is this recognition that has led many postmoderns to abandon American evangelicalism but not Jesus.

Post-evangelical Christians retain their evangelical convictions when it comes to speaking of their conversion to Christ, but they are post-evangelical when it comes to what they judge are the culturally defined dictums of American evangelicalism. They are suspicious of biblical proof-texting in general and especially the use of proof-texting as a weapon against social or political views with which evangelicals might disagree. To quote Bible verses against abortion and same-sex marriages, or in support of military action abroad or right-wing political stances, seems to post-evangelicals an abuse of Scripture and a gross disdain for the complexity of the Bible, as well as a disregard for the ethics of the Sermon on the Mount.

"... much of what is *distinctive* about American Evangelicalism is not *essential* to Christianity" (Mark Noll).

Reflecting something of their postmodern culture, post-evangelicals tend to avoid claims of theological certainty on matters not central to the gospel, and they disparage the evangelical tendency to dismiss those with whom they have theological differences as unbelievers. They are confident that Jesus is their personal Savior, but they are not convinced that one can have apodictic certainty on all matters. They are painfully aware of a long history of Christians who were sure they were right on a particular matter, only to discover in hindsight that they were wrong. They argue that Christians were wrong in the Crusades; they were wrong about slavery; maybe they are wrong about contemporary issues such as homosexuality.

As a result, this post-evangelical sensibility is somewhat suspicious of systematic theology because of the dizzying array of competing theological certainties. They do not necessarily reject theology, but prefer to view theology as an open-ended conversation about God.

Particularly troubling to post-evangelicals is the perceived evangelical tendency to conclude that those with whom they disagree are beyond the pale of salvation or at least must be excluded from their particular community. They see this tendency as a separatist hangover from fundamentalism, in which Roman Catholics and Orthodox Christians were shunned as unbelievers at worst or viewed with suspicion at best.

Post-evangelical concerns about the separatist mentality are perhaps most acute in relation to homosexuality. In 1994 homosexuality surfaced in the highest echelons of the evangelical community with the revelation that Reverend Mel White was gay. During the heyday of neo-evangelicalism from the 1960s to the 1980s, Mel White was a colleague and ghostwriter for such leaders as Jerry Falwell, Pat Robertson, and Billy Graham. White's autobiography, *Stranger at the Gate: To Be Gay and Christian in America* (1994), describes his unsuccessful efforts to cure his homosexuality, including psychotherapy, electro-convulsive treatment, and exorcism. After a failed suicide attempt he concluded that he was homosexual by God's design.

Such anguished stories, coupled with a growing cultural acceptance of homosexuality, have inclined post-evangelicals to a more tolerant attitude. Recent indications suggest that for the most part, their tolerance derives less from theological conviction than from general compassion and the personal experience of having gay friends. Tolerance for postmoderns is not quite the same as endorsement, but it signals that separatism is fading and signals a decided preference for dialogue rather than disengagement.

What does the future hold for American evangelicals and the post-evangelical evangelicals? It is not ours to predict. Yet there are intriguing cultural concurrences. The postmodern suspicion of the overprecision of systematic theology and the certainty of metanarrative—with its preference for dialogue, the *missio dei*, and engagement with pressing social issues—is paralleled by a resurgence of young, conservative, and broadly Reformed pastors and church planters who also embrace the church as missional and accept the urgency of social justice. Is it too much to hope that instead of another schism within American evangelicalism, each side will embrace the best of what the other side has to offer and go forward arm in arm?

FOR FURTHER STUDY

Gibbs, Eddie, and Ryan K. Bolger. *Emerging Churches*. Grand Rapids: Baker, 2005.

Gruder, Darrell L. *Missional Church: A Vision for the Sending of the Church in North America*. Grand Rapids: Eerdmans, 1998.

Marsden, George M. *Understanding Fundamentalism and Evangelicalism*. Grand Rapids: Eerdmans, 1990.

Noll, Mark A. *American Evangelical Christianity: An Introduction*. Hoboken, NJ: Wiley-Blackwell, 2000.

Olson, Roger E. *Reformed and Always Reforming: The Postconservative Approach to Evangelical Theology*. Grand Rapids: Baker, 2007.

Soong-Chan Rah. *The Next Evangelicalism: Freeing the Church from Western Cultural Captivity*. Downers Grove, IL: InterVarsity Press, 2009.

Christianity and Islam

The Challenge of the Future (21st Century)

I. CHRISTIANITY ON THE HORIZON

As this volume has been focused on history-past, we conclude with a brief inquiry into history-future—that is, a historically informed glimpse into what might be. The guiding question is, What might the future of Christianity be?

As the third millennium gains momentum, the Christian church finds itself weighed down by many of the same burdens it faced in the twentieth century: suffocating poverty, rampant sexual abuse especially against women and children, moral decline, hypocritical leaders, institutionalization, youthful rejection of traditional values and teachings, harsh internecine battles over increasingly fine points of theology, bounded versus centered ecclesial visions, racial and ethnic tensions, and clueless church hierarchies. The enduring challenge for all thoughtful Christians has always centered on how to live out their Christian faith in a fallen world.

If history-past reminds us that we are still wrestling with endemic challenges, what new trials might emerge on the horizon of history-future? We have addressed some of these issues in this volume, such as globalization, pluralism, shifting of the center of Christianity from the West to the global South, sexual identity, hermeneutical debates, cultural infiltration, authority, epistemology, the politics of religion, and postmodernism. From this cauldron of tribulations that await us in the future, there is yet one challenge that is more immediate than any other: the rise of militant Islam.

Putting a fine point on the precariousness of the future is Philip Jenkins, Professor of History at Baylor University, who made the following prognosis in his best-selling book *The Next Christendom*:

> If there is one thing we can reliably predict about the 21st century, it is that an increasing share of the world's people is going to

identify with one of two religions, either Christianity or Islam, and the two have a long and disastrous record of conflict and mutual incomprehension.

As this volume comes to a close, we would be wise to heed the words of our modern-day prophets, so we conclude with a brief if tentative excursion into this uncertain future.

II. 2001: A RELIGIOUS ODYSSEY

For as long as humans have roamed the earth, religion has been a vital life force within the human experience. Academic soothsayers of the twentieth century lost sight of this fundamental reality and predicted that religion would be absorbed by the secular. Reports of God's death, however, proved to be greatly exaggerated. Friedrich Nietzsche's boast that "God is dead" was empty. Contrary to expectations, religion is thriving and at the same time threatening to engulf the secular realm in an apocalypse of Abraham's offspring. If anyone wondered whether religion was still a potent force in the new millennium, all doubt was removed on a clear September day in 2001.

Smoke billowing from the World Trade Center in New York City before both buildings collapsed on September 11, 2001.

The worst fears were realized on what has become etched in the collective memories of Americans by the Arabic numerals 9 and 11. On that bloody Tuesday, a series of coordinated suicide attacks was launched against American symbols of economic and military power. The shadowy Islamic terrorist group al-Qaeda, headed by the Saudi militant Osama bin Laden, struck a deadly blow against American invincibility.

On that autumn morning, terrorists intentionally crashed two hijacked airliners into the Twin Towers of the World Trade Center in New York City, as millions gasped at their television screens. Both buildings collapsed within two hours, leaving a terrible scar on the New York cityscape. A second group of hijackers crashed a third airliner into the Pentagon. A fourth plane, headed for Washington, DC, crashed into a field near Shanksville in rural Pennsylvania after passengers courageously rushed the militants in an attempt to retake control of the plane.

Nineteen terrorists managed to take the lives of 2,999 people in the three attacks, including 358 Muslims.

Amid the flood of condolences from Muslim leaders around the world, other Muslims were celebrating the attack. Thousands of Palestinians poured into the streets of Nablus on the West Bank, chanting *"Allāhu Akbar"* ("God is the greatest"), blaring car horns, and holding up the "V sign" for victory.

A war on terrorism was declared, and American soldiers soon were locked into two simultaneous wars in two Muslim countries — Afghanistan and Iraq. Under the auspices of the radical Taliban regime, Afghanistan had provided the base of operations for the al-Qaeda terrorists and was therefore viewed as a legitimate target for U.S. retaliation. The Taliban were expelled from power, but the fighting lingered on. The war in Afghanistan now has the dubious distinction as the longest war in American history.

Fortified by a determination to exact punishment on all parties even remotely connected to what is now known as "9/11," and bolstered by unreliable reports of weapons of mass destruction, the United States invaded Iraq without the support of the United Nations. No weapons of mass destruction were found, but more than 4,400 American soldiers lost their lives trying to find them. After eight years in Iraq (2003–11), American troops withdrew in late 2011, having succeeded in bringing down the brutal dictator Saddam Hussein and orchestrating free elections.

Since 2001, many of the leaders of al-Qaeda have been killed in combat or by radar-guided bombs launched from high-tech military drones. The coup de grâce occurred in 2011 when American elite Special Forces killed Osama bin Laden in Pakistan. In spite of U.S. declarations to the contrary, many in the Arab world viewed the death of bin Laden and the wars in Afghanistan and Iraq, not as a war on terrorism, but as a war on Islam.

Some pundits in the West, such as the late Harvard professor Samuel Huntington, have agreed that the conflict between radical Muslims and the West is more than a war on terrorism; it is a clash of civilizations:

> The underlying problem for the West is not Islamic fundamentalism. It is Islam, a different civilization whose people are convinced of the superiority of their culture and are obsessed with the inferiority of their power.... It is the West, a different civilization whose people are convinced of the universality of their culture and believe that their superior, if declining power imposes on them the obligation to extend that culture throughout the world. These are the basic ingredients that fuel conflict between Islam and the West.

Whether or not Huntington's analysis is entirely plausible, it did offer a cogent explanation for why young militants would be willing to martyr themselves by detonating explosives strapped around their waists or flying planes into tall buildings to kill as many victims as possible (including fellow Muslims). The events of September 11, 2001, demonstrated that religion may be the most explosive force on the earth.

Osama bin Laden.

The religious dimension of the conflict between Islam and the West entails more than theology and dogmatics. It is a clash of cultures and values. America (and the West in general) is portrayed as an evil empire intent on proliferating its evil ways. In short, American values are judged both corrupt and corrupting. It is not simply that the West is inherently evil, but that it is an evil with a rapacious appetite. Islamic fundamentalists therefore view the very existence of the evil empire of the West as a clear and present danger that must be resisted by all means necessary. This begs the question: Can two billion Christians and more than one billion Muslims peacefully coexist?

The past is not always an accurate predictor of the future. However, reconnoitering the past can provide some sense of understanding and perhaps even suggest possible pathways for lowering the threat level between the two global religions. One immediate insight gained from the past is that for most of the last 1,400 years, Muslims have engaged the Christian West from a position of military power and the Christian East from the position of political power.

III. RELIGIONS IN CONFLICT

A. The First 1,400 Years

Christianity's first encounter with Islam was violent. In 638 Muslims took both Jerusalem and Antioch by military force. By 642, Muslims had taken Alexandria. Of the five ancient patriarchates, in which resided ultimate authority over the church, three were conquered by Muslims in the span of five years. Although the western European nations were ultimately repelled, the bloody Crusades of the Middle

Christianity and Islam: The Challenge of the Future

Muslim expansion into southeastern Europe.

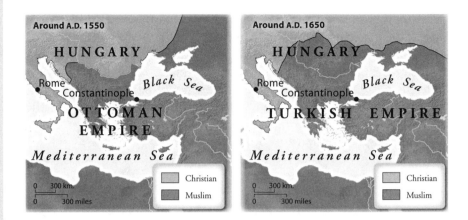

Ages left a bitterness that continues today. In light of this bitterness, it is not surprising that Osama bin Laden constantly referred to the West as "crusaders."

When Constantinople, the capital of Eastern Christianity, fell to Islam in 1453, the city was renamed Istanbul, and the largest Christian cathedral in the world for nearly a thousand years, the Hagia Sophia, became a Muslim mosque. At the height of its power in the sixteenth century, the Ottoman Empire spanned three continents, controlling much of southeastern Europe, the Middle East, and North Africa.

The Muslims remained a major threat to the West until the Battle of Vienna in 1683, which marked the end of Ottoman expansion into Europe. The failure to take Vienna set in motion a gradual decline in Muslim power over the next two centuries. However, for most of their history, Muslims were largely victorious in their confrontations with Western Christian nations. That changed at the turn of the twentieth century.

The fateful decision to side with Germany in World War I led to the final dissolution of the Ottoman Empire, which shared in Germany's defeat. The consequence was dismemberment of the empire, with the spoils going to the victors. The French took Lebanon and Syria. The British took Palestine, Jordan, Iraq, and part of the Arabian Peninsula. By the early decades of the twentieth century, more than 90 percent of Muslims lived under Western rule—a disgrace virtually unparalleled in their history.

In the aftermath of World War I, only four Muslim countries remained independent: Turkey, Iran, Afghanistan, and Saudi Arabia. Of these, Turkey and Iran became secular states with a Muslim population. Afghanistan remained poor and politically insignificant. Saudi Arabia remained the Islamic epicenter—the land of Mecca and Medina, the birthplace of Muhammad, the destination of the Hajj, and the geographical focal point of Muslim prayer.

It was during this period of Western domination that the Saudi royal family discovered the writings of the eighteenth-century radical Muhammad ibn al Wahhab (1703–92) and embraced his austere form of Sunni Islam.

Wahhab advocated an especially militant and punitive form of Islam. *Sharia* law was made the governing rule of the Arabian Peninsula. All other forms of Islam were rejected, and all opponents denounced as apostates and infidels. Wahhab even went so far as to assert that other Muslims who did not embrace Wahhabism should be killed and their property confiscated. Wahhabism might have remained a small obscure sect were it not for the discovery of oil beneath the sands of the Arabian Peninsula.

B. Petro-Islam

A turning point in the history of the Middle East came with the discovery of oil, first in Persia in 1908 and later in Saudi Arabia and then in other Persian Gulf states. The Middle East, it turned out, possesses the world's largest accessible reserves of crude oil. Rulers of the oil states became immensely rich, enabling them to consolidate their hold on power and giving them enormous political clout.

No Muslim nation benefitted more from the "black gold" than Saudi Arabia. Abdul Aziz Ibn Saud managed to consolidate the various political factions on the Arabian Peninsula under the house of Saud and to create the modern nation of Saudi Arabia in 1932. The discovery of oil in March 1938 eventually transformed Saudi Arabia from a regional kingdom to a global power broker by the 1970s. As tensions increased in the Middle East, Saudi Arabia began openly to use its oil wealth to fund Wahhabist proselytizing efforts all over the Islamic world—mosques, madrassas (schools or universities that are often part of a mosque), and journalism.

What had been a fringe sect of Islam became a force with which to reckon by both the moderate Muslims and the Western world.

C. Arab-Israeli Conflict

Perhaps the major pivot point in the twentieth-century Middle East was the establishment of the modern state of Israel in 1948. The birth of the nation of Israel and the consequent displacement of the Palestinian people led to more than half a century of bad blood and bloodshed between Jews and Muslims. Israelis were viewed by Muslims as invaders who had taken from the Palestinians what had been

Israel's Defense Minister Moshe Dayan (center), Army Chief of Staff Yitzhak Rabin (right), and Jerusalem Commander Uzi Narkis walking through the Lion's Gate into Jerusalem's Old City in June 1967 during the Middle East War, also known as the Six Day War.

Islamic territory for over a millennium. Religious solidarity compelled other Muslims to take up the Palestinian cause.

This inevitably led to a series of regional wars over the last half of the twentieth century and into the third millennium: the Arab-Israeli War (1948), the Suez Canal Crisis (1956), the Six Day War (1967), the Yom Kippur War (1973), the First Intifada (1987–93), the Second Intifada (2000–2005), the Lebanon War (2006), and too many military skirmishes to count. Each humiliating defeat at the hands of Israel deepened Muslim resentment and ensured that the Middle East would remain a powder keg for the foreseeable future. The Israeli military success was attributed in significant measure to the support of the United States. Consequently, militant Muslims have turned their sights on what some have called "the Great Satan."

D. The "Great Satan"

The Iranian Revolution of 1979 was one of the signal events in the late twentieth-century resurgence of Islamic militancy. The architect of the Islamic revolt was the Shiite cleric Ayatollah Ruhollah Khomeini, who made Iran the first modern Islamist state. Not only was the Iranian Revolution successful in ousting the Shah of Iran (Mohammad Reza Pahlavi); it also was seen as an act of defiance against the perceived imperialism of America, which Khomeini designated "the Great Satan." The Iranian Revolution not only overthrew the westernized secular monarchy of the shah, but also cut the strings of the puppet masters in America.

Khomeini viewed Western powers and westernizing Muslims as complicit in a global conspiracy against Islam. When Iranian students seized control of the U.S. embassy in November 1979 in violation of international law and held fifty-two Americans hostage for 444 days, Khomeini supported the students. No indignity was too great for the Great Satan.

The hostage crisis was a political humiliation for the American government, but for Khomeini it was Allah's vindication against the Great Satan as well as retaliation for Western interference in Iranian affairs. Many still recalled the coup d'état inspired by the U.S. Central Intelligence Agency (and Britain's MI6) to oust Iran's defiant prime minister, Mohammad Mosaddeqh, in 1953. Glorying in his triumph, Khomeini denounced the United States in religious terminology as the enemy of Islam.

This brief survey of some of the principal confrontations with a resurgent Islam is a reminder of the explosive tensions that continue to plague relations between Muslims and the West. While there have been periods of tolerance and goodwill between the Christian West and Muslims, that has not been the case in recent decades. Recent demographical studies reveal that tensions will almost certainly remain high for the foreseeable future.

Ayatollah Khomeini of Iran.

IV. THE DEVIL IN THE DEMOGRAPHICS

As is well known, the two largest religions in the world are Christianity and Islam. Demographic research indicates this will remain the case for centuries to come. At the

Ten of the largest nations "in 2050 could be profoundly divided between Islam and Christianity, and judging by present trends, any or all of them could be the scene of serious interfaith conflict" (Philip Jenkins).

turn of the twentieth century, these two religions collectively represented less than 50 percent of the world's population, but by 2050 they are projected to represent more than 60 percent. Currently, there are about 2.3 billion Christians in the world, or about 33 percent of the world population. Muslims number about 1.5 billion adherents and make up 22 percent.

Both religions are experiencing significant growth, especially Islam, which will have doubled its share of world population in 140 years (from 13 percent in 1910 to 27 percent in 2050). That 2050 projection sees 2.4 billion Muslims compared with 3.2 billion Christians (35 percent of the world population). Demographics in themselves are benign, but the devil is in the details.

One of the most ominous demographic projections is that "ten of the world's twenty-five largest states in 2050 could be profoundly divided between Islam and Christianity, and judging by present trends, any or all of them could be the scene of serious interfaith conflict." This nightmare scenario might unfold in a nation like Nigeria.

Nigeria is one of the more prominent nations in Africa—having the largest population on the African continent and being the seventh most populous country in the world. By the end of this century the United Nations estimates that the Nigerian population could approach one billion people. It is the world's eighth-largest oil exporter and has the tenth-largest proven oil reserves.

The disruption to the global Christian mission caused by the rise of Islam (as shown in the twenty-first century).

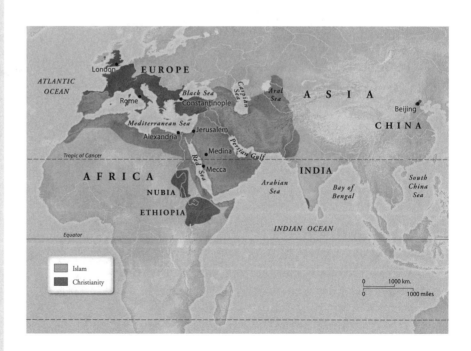

Precisely because Nigeria is such an important African nation, if religious violence breaks out there, the potential for a much larger conflagration is probable. Even more ominous is the fact that it is a nation evenly divided between Christians in the south and Muslims in the north. (A recent Pew Forum study reports that Christians in Nigeria hold a slight majority with 50.8 percent of the population.)

Tensions are in fact on the rise. In the 1990s Muslims in the north began demanding that *Sharia* law be implemented, and currently twelve of Nigeria's thirty-six states have instituted it. This is a legal code that prohibits any kind of Christian evangelism and prescribes the death penalty for any Muslim who dares to embrace Christianity. Of course, this development not only strikes fear in the hearts of Nigerian Christians, but severely constricts economic, social, and political interactions between north and south. Further entangling an already complicated situation, Nigeria has been and continues to be ruled by a Christian president.

The situation in Nigeria is not merely hypothetical. A more recent explosive development is the emergence of Boko Haram, a violent Islamic terrorist group committed to the eradication of the secular government and the establishment of *Sharia* law in the country. In August 2011 they bombed the United Nations building in Abuja. In 2011 its members killed at least 510 people and destroyed more than 350 churches. In the month of January 2012 alone, Boko Haram was responsible for fifty-four murders.

Religious violence could easily spread to some or all of the countries that border Nigeria. All have majority Muslim populations or possess significant minorities, such as Niger, which is 98 percent. Arab Wahhabists have turned up in Niger more recently, and for the first time, religious violence has erupted. Other countries bordering Nigeria are Chad (54 percent Muslim, 34 percent Christian), Benin (27 percent Christian, 24 percent Muslim), and Cameroon (70 percent Christian, 21 percent Muslim).

The Muslim population of these surrounding nations could become very significant if religious violence breaks out in Nigeria. To underscore the seriousness of the situation, Professor Philip Jenkins of Pennsylvania State University considers a worst-case scenario of Christian crusades and Muslim jihads "armed with nuclear warheads and anthrax."

A. 10/40 Christian Provocation

Christian missionaries often speak of the "10/40 window"—a term coined by missiologist Luis Bush in 1990 to identify that region of the planet where the spiritual and physical needs are greatest. It refers to geographic coordinates located between the latitudes of 10 and 40 degrees north of the equator and generally comprises the Middle East, North Africa, and Asia. This region is important to missiologists because it is the hub of the world's major non-Christian religions: 865 million Muslims, 550 million Hindus, and 275 million Buddhists. The 10/40 window also encompasses 82 percent of the world's poorest populations and has the least exposure to the Christian message.

The 10/40 window is one of the primary target areas of evangelical missionaries in the twenty-first century and also has the greatest potential for religious violence between Christians and Muslims. The Christian aim of converting Muslims is itself a crime in most Muslim-dominant countries and thus inevitably is perceived as a provocation by the West. To many Muslims the mere presence of Christian missionaries is not only a religious menace, but since Islam conjoins religious and political convictions, is perceived as a political threat as well.

There is also a supposed cultural challenge to Muslim identity and way of life. Western liberal social values are unacceptable to many Muslims, who see feminism, alcohol, open sexuality, and immodest dress as profoundly immoral and a sinister influence on young Muslims. For a Muslim to abandon his or her faith is not only apostasy; it is political and cultural treason—a violation punishable by death under Islamic law.

B. The Conflict within Islam

Divisions, oppositions, and violence have been a constitutive part of the Islamic tradition ever since the death of the prophet Muhammad. Islam has three main branches: Sunni, Shiite, and Sufi. Sunni is by far the largest branch of Islam, representing 86 percent, while the Shiites make up 13 percent. (Sufis are found in all traditions, much like Charismatics among Christians).

Tensions, especially between Sunni and Shiites, have portrayed a long and bloody history that continues into the present. Further, moderates and militants interpret the *Sharia* law in vastly different ways. The moderates interpret *Sharia* law much more loosely, while the militants take a rigid literal stance. Militants believe the Qur'an justifies *jihad* ("holy war"), while moderates assiduously declare that terrorism is a blatant violation of the Qur'an and historic Islamic teaching. The Islamic scholar Reza Aslan sums up this tension within modern Islam:

> What is taking place now in the Muslim world is an internal conflict between Muslims, not an external battle between Islam and the West. The West is ... an unwary yet complicit casualty of a rivalry that is raging in Islam over who will write the next chapter in its story.

V. A CONCLUDING CODA

Only time will tell if Christians and Muslims can peacefully coexist and share space on this small planet. From our human vantage point, we see the future only through a glass darkly. But it may be helpful to be reminded that Christianity was born amid a plurality of competing religious alternatives. In a culturally diverse matrix of Judaism, pagan mystery cults, philosophical Hellenism, and Roman domination, a message emerged that would survive them all. As one dares peer into the future, we may be reminded that the Christian gospel changed the world once before. Recall the rather eloquent words of Everett Ferguson as he began the first volume of this church history:

> Could anything be more improbable than that a religion following a man born of an unwed mother among a widely despised people in an out-of-the-way part of the world—a man then crucified by the ruling authorities on a charge of treason—should become the official religion of the Roman world, the formative influence on Western civilization, and a significant influence in other parts of the world? This is the story to be told in the following pages.

If it happened before, can it happen again?

The ultimate value of history lies not in its predictive ability or even its capacity for elucidation, but in its aptitude to teach humility. Church history, in particular, is an opportunity for self-reflection and, indeed, for self-correction. If the story of the Christian church can bestow on us a measure of this humility, then we will enter the uncertain future with a sure compass.

FOR FURTHER STUDY

Aslan, Reza. *No God But God: The Origins, Evolution and Future of Islam*. New York: Random House, 2011.

Esposito, John L. *What Everyone Needs to Know about Islam*. 2nd ed. Oxford: Oxford University Press, 2011.

Renard, John. *Islam and Christianity: Theological Themes in Comparative Perspective*. Berkeley: University of California Press, 2011.

Riddell, Peter, and Peter Cotterell. *Islam in Context: Past, Present, and Future*. Baker, 2003.

Volf, Miroslav. *Allah: A Christian Response*. New York: HarperOne, 2011.

General Bibliography

REFERENCE WORKS

Cambridge Modern History. 2nd ed. 14 vols. Cambridge: Cambridge University Press, 1957–1979.

Christian Tradition: A History of the Development of Doctrine. Jaroslav Pelikan. 5 vols. Chicago: University of Chicago Press, 1971.

Encyclopedia of Eastern Orthodoxy. John Anthony McGuckin. Hoboken, NJ: Wiley-Blackwell, 2011.

Handbook of European History (1400–1600): Late Middle Ages, Renaissance and Reformation. Edited by T. A. Brady, H. A. Oberman, and J. D. Tracy. 2 vols. Grand Rapids: Eerdmans, 1996.

History of Christian Doctrine. H. Cunliffe-Jones. Edinburgh: T & T. Clark, 1978.

History of Christianity. Kenneth S. Latourette. 2 vols. San Francisco: HarperOne, 1975.

History of Christianity in the United States and Canada. Mark Noll. Grand Rapids: Eerdmans, 1992.

History of Doctrines. R. Seeberg. Reprint. Grand Rapids: Baker, 1977.

History of the Christian Church. Philip Schaff. 7 vols. Reprint. Grand Rapids: Eerdmans, 1976.

Modern American Religion. Martin E. Marty. 2 vols. Chicago: University of Chicago Press, 1991.

New Catholic Encyclopedia. Edited by Thomas Carson. 2nd ed. 15 vols. Farmington Hills, MI: Gale, 2002.

Oxford Companion to Christian Thought. Edited by Adrian Hastings, Alistair Mason, and Hugh Pyper. Oxford: Oxford University Press, 2000.

Oxford Encyclopedia of Protestantism. Edited by Hans J. Hillerbrand. 4 vols. London: Routledge, 2004.

Oxford Encyclopedia of the Reformation. Edited by Hans J. Hillerbrand. 4 vols. Oxford: Oxford University Press, 1996.

Pelican History of the Church. 6 vols. London: Penguin, 1967–.

Religious History of the American People. S. E. Ahlstrom. New Haven: Yale University Press, 1972.

World History of Christianity. Edited by Adrian Hastings. Grand Rapids: Eerdmans, 1999.

RECOMMENDED READING FOR ENTHUSIASTS

Berger, Stefan, ed. *A Companion to Nineteenth Century Europe: 1789–1914*. Hoboken, NJ: Wiley-Blackwell, 2006.

Butler, Jon, and Harry Stout, eds. *Religion in American History*. New York: Oxford University Press, 1998.

Carpenter, Joel. *Revive Us Again: The Reawakening of American Fundamentalism*. New York: Oxford University Press, 1999.

Dorrien, Gary. *The Making of American Liberal Theology: Imagining Progressive Religion, 1805–1900*. Louisville: Westminster John Knox, 2001.

Hastings, Adrian. *The Church in Africa*. New York: Oxford University Press, 1994.

Hazard, Paul. *The European Mind: The Critical Years, 1680–1715*. 1935; reprint, New York: Fordham University Press, 1990.

Helseth, Paul. *"Right Reason" and the Princeton Mind: An Unorthodox Proposal*. Phillipsburg, NJ: P & R, 2010.

History of Women in the West. 5 vols. Cambridge: Harvard University Press, 1994–1998.

Holt, Mack P. *The French Wars of Religion, 1562–1629*. Cambridge: Cambridge University Press, 2005.

Howard, Michael, and William Louis, eds. *The Oxford History of the Twentieth Century*. Oxford: Oxford University Press, 2006.

Hyland, Paul, Olga Gomez, and Francesca Greensides, eds. *The Enlightenment Reader: A Sourcebook and Reader*. New York: Routledge, 2003.

Janz, Dennis R., and Shirley Jordan, eds. *Reformation Reader: Primary Texts with Introductions*. Minneapolis: Fortress, 2002.

Jenkins, Philip. *The Coming of Global Christianity*. Oxford: Oxford University Press, 2011.

Jenkins, Philip. *The New Faces of Christianity: Believing the Bible in the Global South*. New York: Oxford University Press, 2008.

Kelly, J. N. D. *The Oxford Dictionary of Popes*. New York: Oxford University Press, 1989.

Longfield, Bradley J. *The Presbyterian Controversy: Fundamentalists, Modernists and Moderates*. New York: Oxford University Press, 1993.

MacCuloch, Diarmaid. *The Reformation: A History*. New York: Viking, 2003.

Marsden, George. *Fundamentalism and American Culture: The Shaping of Twentieth-Century Evangelicalism, 1870–1925*. New York: Oxford University Press, 1982.

Marty, Martin E. *Modern American Religion*. 2 vols. Chicago: Chicago University Press, 1991.

McGuckin, John Anthony. *The Orthodox Church: An Introduction to its History, Doctrine, and Spiritual Culture*. Hoboken, NJ: Wiley-Blackwell, 2012.

McLeod, Hugh. *Religion and the People of Western Europe, 1789–1989*. 2nd ed. New York: Oxford University Press, 1998.

Moffet, Samuel. *A History of Christianity in Asia*. Vol. 2. Maryknoll, NY: Orbis, 1998.

Neil, S. *History of Christianity in India*. 2 vols. Cambridge: Cambridge University Press, 1984–1985.

Pelikan, Jaroslav. *The Christian Tradition: A History of the Development of Doctrine*. 5 vols. Chicago: Chicago University Press, 1971.

Rausch, Thomas P., ed. *Catholics and Evangelicals: Do They Share a Common Future?* Mahwah, NJ: Paulist, 2001.

Ross, James, and Mary McLaughlin, eds. *The Portable Renaissance Reader*. Reprint, New York: Penguin, 1977.

Schaff, Philip. *History of the Christian Church*. 7 vols. Reprint, Grand Rapids: Eerdmans, 1976.

Sweeney, Douglas. *The American Evangelical Story: A History of the Movement*. Grand Rapids: Baker, 2005.

Tucker, Ruth, and Walt Liefeld. *Daughters of the Church*. Grand Rapids: Zondervan, 1987.

Walls, Andrew. *The Missionary Movement in Christian History: Studies in the Transmission of Faith*. Maryknoll, NY: Orbis, 1996.

Zaspel, Fred. *The Theology of B. B. Warfield*. Wheaton, IL: Crossway, 2010.

Index

CHURCH HISTORY

CHURCH HISTORY

CHURCH HISTORY

S

CHURCH HISTORY